Dante in English literature

From Chaucer to Cary

(c. 1380-1844)

Paget Toynbee

Alpha Editions

This edition published in 2019

ISBN : 9789353704766

Design and Setting By
Alpha Editions
email - alphaedis@gmail.com

DANTE
IN
ENGLISH LITERATURE
FROM CHAUCER TO CARY

(C. 1380-1844)

BY

PAGET TOYNBEE

M.A., D.LITT. OXON.

WITH INTRODUCTION, NOTES, BIOGRAPHICAL NOTICES
CHRONOLOGICAL LIST, AND GENERAL INDEX

IN TWO VOLUMES

VOL. II.

Novisti forsan et ipse
Traxerit ut DANTEM Phoebus per celsa nivosi
Cyrrheos, mediosque sinus tacitosque recessus
Naturae, coelique vias terraeque marisque,
Aonios fontes, Parnasi culmen, et antra
Julia, Pariseos dudum, serusque BRITANNOS
(*Joan. Boccatius ad F. Petrarcham*)

METHUEN & CO.
36 ESSEX STREET W.C.
LONDON

CONTENTS OF VOLUME II

DANTE IN ENGLISH LITERATURE

WILLIAM WORDSWORTH

(1770-1850)

[William Wordsworth was the son of an attorney of Cockermouth, Cumberland, where he was born in 1770. He was educated at Hawkshead Grammar School and St. John's College, Cambridge, where he entered in 1787 and graduated in 1791. While at Cambridge he studied Italian under Agostino Isola, the teacher appointed by Gray (see vol. i. pp. 358-9). In 1790 he made a tour through France and Switzerland into Italy, which he revisited in 1820 and in 1837. In 1791 he again visited France and remained there for more than a year. Shortly after his return he published his first poems, the *Evening Walk* and *Descriptive Sketches* (1793). In or about 1795 he made the acquaintance of Coleridge, and in 1798 they published jointly *Lyrical Ballads*, to which Coleridge contributed the *Ancient Mariner*. In 1799 Wordsworth settled with his sister Dorothy at Grasmere, where he resided for the rest of his life. In 1807 he published two volumes containing some of his finest poems, including the *Ode to Duty* and *Ode on the Intimations of Immortality*. About 1813 Lord Lonsdale obtained for him the office of distributor of stamps for the county of Westmoreland, which he held until 1842, when Sir Robert Peel at the instance of Gladstone gave him a pension of £300 a year from the civil list. On Southey's death in 1843 Wordsworth was appointed Poet Laureate. He died at Grasmere in 1850. Of his longer poems, the *Excursion* was published in 1814, the *White Doe of Rylstone* in 1815, *Peter Bell* in 1819, and the *Prelude* (posthumously) in 1850.

Wordsworth possessed a copy of the *Divina Commedia*,[1] which he read, but he seems to have preferred Ariosto and Tasso to Dante, whom he admired apparently more as a patriot than as a poet. He expressed his appreciation, however, for Cary's translation, which in conversation with Alexander Dyce he described as 'a great national work.'[2]]

1805. Oct. 17. LETTER TO SIR GEORGE BEAUMONT (from Grasmere).

[The poetry of Dante and Michael Angelo]

THERE is a mistake in the world concerning the Italian language; the poetry of Dante and Michael Angelo proves that if there be little majesty and strength in Italian verse, the fault is in the authors, and not in the tongue.

(*Life of W. Wordsworth*, by W. Knight, vol. ii. p. 67.)

[1] [This book does not figure in the catalogue of the sale of Wordsworth's library, which took place in 1859.]

[2] [See vol. i. p. 466, note.]

1807-8. THE WHITE DOE OF RYLSTONE.[1]

Why comes not Francis?—From the doleful City[2]
He fled,—and, in his flight, could hear
The death-sounds of the Minster-bell:
That sullen stroke pronounced farewell
To Marmaduke, cut off from pity!
To Ambrose that! and then a knell
For him, the sweet half-opened Flower!
For all—all dying in one hour!
—Why comes not Francis?

(*Canto*, vi. ll. 1-9.)

1817. May 13. LETTER TO SAMUEL ROGERS (from Rydal Mount).

[Rogers and Dante]

Do you and Dante continue as intimate as heretofore? He used to avenge himself upon his enemies by placing them in H-ll, a thing Bards seem very fond of attempting in this day, witness the Laureate's[3] mode of treating Mr. W. Smith.[4] You keep out of these scrapes I suppose; why don't you hire somebody to abuse you? and the higher the place selected for the purpose the better. For myself, I begin to fear that I should soon be forgotten if it were not for my enemies.

(*Rogers and his Contemporaries*, ed. Clayden, vol. i. p. 241.)

1821. Sept. 3. LETTER TO WALTER SAVAGE LANDOR (from Rydal Mount).

[Latin translation of Dante]

I differ from you in opinion as to the propriety of the Latin language being employed by moderns for works of taste and imagination. Miserable would have been the lot of Dante, Ariosto, and Petrarch if they had preferred the Latin to their mother tongue (there is, by the by, a Latin translation[5] of Dante which you do not seem to know), and what could Milton, who was surely no

[1] [First published in 1815.]

[2] [York—a reminiscence of *Inf.* iii. 1, 'la città dolente' (cf. the poem headed 'Greenock,' below, p. 4).]

[3] [Southey.]

[4] [William Smith (1756-1835), M.P. for Norwich; 'in 1817 he expressed some indignation at the difference between the views of Robert Southey, as laureate and writer in the *Quarterly Review*, and as author of *Wat Tyler*, an early effort, which had just been printed without Southey's permission. Southey retorted in *A Letter to William Smith, Esq. M.P.*' (D.N.B.).]

[5] [Doubtless that by Carlo d' Aquino, in three volumes, published in 1728 with the imprint of Naples, but actually printed at Rome.]

mean master of the Latin tongue, have made of his *Paradise Lost*, had that vehicle been employed instead of the language of the Thames and Severn!

(*Life of Wordsworth*, by Knight, vol. iii. p. 92.)

1824. Jan. LETTER TO WALTER SAVAGE LANDOR.

[Dante 'grotesque' and 'tedious']

It has become lately, owing a good deal, I believe, to the example of Schlegel, the fashion to extol Dante above measure. I have not read him for many years. His style I used to think admirable for conciseness and vigour without abruptness; but I own that his fictions often struck me as offensively grotesque and fantastic, and I felt the poem tedious from various causes.

(*Works and Life of W. S. Landor*, vol. i. p. 240.)

1824. Jan. 21. LETTER TO WALTER SAVAGE LANDOR (from Rydal Mount).

[Copy of the *Divina Commedia* possessed by Wordsworth]

You promise me a beautiful copy of Dante, but I ought to mention that I possess the Parma folio of 1795[1]—much the *grandest* book on my shelves—presented to me by our common friend, Mr. Kenyon.[2]

(*Life of Wordsworth*, by Knight, vol. iii. p. 95.)

1827. REMINISCENCES.

[Dante, Ariosto and Tasso]

Ariosto and Tasso are very absurdly depressed in order to elevate Dante.

(*Ibid.* vol. ii. p. 324.)

1827. SONNET ON THE SONNET.

[Use of the sonnet by Shakespeare, Dante, Milton, and other great poets]

Scorn not the Sonnet; Critic, you have frowned,
Mindless of its just honours; with this key
Shakespeare unlocked his heart; the melody
Of this small lute gave ease to Petrarch's wound;

[1] [An edition of the *Divina Commedia* of 130 copies, edited by Dionisi, and printed by Bodoni.]
[2] [John Kenyon (1784-1856), the friend of Mr. and Mrs. Browning.]

A thousand times this pipe did Tasso sound;
With it Camöens soothed an exile's grief;
The Sonnet glittered a gay myrtle leaf
Amid the cypress with which Dante crowned
His visionary brow; a glow-worm lamp,
It cheered mild Spenser, called from Faery-land
To struggle through dark ways; and, when a damp
Fell round the path of Milton, in his hand
The Thing became a trumpet; whence he blew
Soul-animating strains—alas, too few![1]

1833. POEMS OF THE IMAGINATION COMPOSED DURING A TOUR IN THE SUMMER OF 1833.

Greenock.

Per me si va nella Città dolente.[2]

We have not passed into a doleful City,
We who were led to-day down a grim dell,
By some too boldly named 'the Jaws of Hell':
Where be the wretched ones, the sights for pity?
These crowded streets resound no plaintive ditty:—
As from the hive where bees in summer dwell,
Sorrow seems here excluded; and that knell,
It neither damps the gay, nor checks the witty.
Alas! too busy Rival of old Tyre,
Whose merchants Princes were, whose decks were thrones;
Soon may the punctual sea in vain respire
To serve thy need, in union with that Clyde
Whose nurseling current brawls o'er mossy stones,
The poor, the lonely, herdsman's joy and pride.

1837. AT FLORENCE.[3]

['Il Sasso di Dante']

Under the shadow of a stately Pile,
The dome of Florence, pensive and alone,
Nor giving heed to aught that passed the while,
I stood, and gazed upon a marble stone,
The laurell'd Dante's favourite seat.[4] A throne,
In just esteem, it rivals; though no style
Be there of decoration to beguile

[1] [Published in *Poetical Works*, 1827.] [2] [*Inf.* iii. 1.]

[3] [First published, among *Memorials of a Tour in Italy* in 1837, in *Poems, Chiefly of Early and Late Years*, 1842.]

[4] [The so-called *Sasso di Dante*, which is built into the wall of a house close to the Duomo.]

The mind, depressed by thought of greatness flown.
As a true man, who long had served the lyre,
I gazed with earnestness, and dared no more.
But in his breast the mighty Poet bore
A Patriot's heart, warm with undying fire.
Bold with the thought, in reverence I sate down,
And, for a moment, filled that empty Throne.

Note by Wordsworth on the foregoing Sonnet:—

Upon what evidence the belief rests that this stone was a favourite seat of Dante, I do not know; but a man would little consult his own interest as a traveller, if he should busy himself with doubts as to the fact. The readiness with which traditions of this character are received, and the fidelity with which they are preserved from generation to generation, are an evidence of feelings honourable to our nature. I remember how, during one of my rambles in the course of a college vacation, I was pleased on being shown a seat near a kind of rocky cell at the source of the river, on which it was said that Congreve wrote his "Old Bachelor." One can scarcely hit on any performance less in harmony with the scene; but it was a local tribute paid to intellect by those who had not troubled themselves to estimate the moral worth of that author's comedies; and why should they? He was a man distinguished in his day; and the sequestered neighbourhood in which he often resided was perhaps as proud of him as Florence of her Dante: it is the same feeling, though proceeding from persons one cannot bring together in this way, without offering some apology to the Shade of the great Visionary.

CHARLES SYMMONS

(1749-1826)

[Charles Symmons, born at Pembroke in 1749, was educated at Westminster School, Glasgow University, and Clare College, Cambridge, where he graduated B.D. in 1786. He took his D.D. degree at Oxford in 1794. Symmons, who died at Bath in 1826, was Rector of Narbert in Pembrokeshire (1778), Prebendary of St. David's (1789), and Rector of Lampeter (1794). He was the author of sundry poems, of a *Life of Milton* (1805), which contains some appreciative remarks upon Dante, a *Life of Shakespeare* (1826), and of a metrical translation of the *Aeneid* (1817).]

1806. LIFE OF JOHN MILTON.

[The sonnets of Dante and Petrarch]

LIKE every short poem, the sonnet requires strict unity of subject; but it solicits ornament from variety of thought, on the indispensable condition of a perfect subordination. The sentence may overflow the verse, but must not transgress the stanza. This little poem is impressible with various characters; and, while with Petrarch it is tender and pathetic, with Dante, in equal consistency with its nature, it is elevated and forcible.

(p. 223.)

[*Paradise Lost* ranked above the *Divina Commedia*]

With respect to grandeur of conception, the Paradise Lost must be regarded as the first, or to the general exhibition of intellectual power, as, unquestionably, the second among all the productions of human genius; while, in the subordinate excellencies of composition, it will be found to yield the precedency only to the wonderful Iliad, or to the august and polished Aeneid. When I make this assertion I am not ignorant of the great and daring imagination of Dante; of the sportive and affluent fancy of Ariosto; of the powerful yet regulated and classic genius of Tasso.

(p. 470.)

RICHARD DUPPA

(1770-1831)

[Richard Duppa, a native of Shropshire, was born in 1770. In his youth he studied art at Rome. In 1807, at the age of 37, he matriculated at Trinity College, Oxford. He entered at the Middle Temple in 1810, and graduated LL.B. at Trinity Hall, Cambridge, in 1814. He died in Lincoln's Inn in 1831. Duppa, who was a skilful draughtsman, was the author of numerous works on artistic, botanical, and political subjects. His best known publications are his *Life of Michael Angelo* (1806), which reached a third edition in his lifetime, and his *Life of Raffaelle* (1816). Sundry references to Dante occur in the former, which contains translations by Southey of Michael Angelo's two sonnets on Dante. Duppa also published anonymously in 1825 *Miscellaneous Observations and Opinions on the Continent*, in which he gives an account of Dante's death at Ravenna, with a drawing of his tomb.]

1806. THE LIFE OF MICHAEL ANGELO BUONARROTI.

[Michael Angelo and Dante]

DURING Michael Angelo's stay in Bologna, his evenings were spent in reading Dantè, Petrarch, and Boccaccio, to his friend M. Gianfrancesco Aldovrandi; to whom those authors were particularly interesting.

(Ed. 1816, p. 27.)

[Michael Angelo's proposed monument to Dante]

Leo X. not only kept Michael Angelo at the quarries of Pietra Santa, doing nothing which could be of any service to himself or the State, but refused him permission to make a monument to honour the poet Dantè, which he voluntarily offered to execute free of expense, to be placed in S. Maria Nuova, in Florence.

(p. 96 note.)

[Michael Angelo's sonnets on Dante—Dante's influence on him as an artist]

Among the authors Michael Angelo studied and delighted in most, were Dantè and Petrarch; of these it is said he could nearly repeat by memory all their poems: but Dantè appears to have held the highest place in his esteem; and as a poet, and a man, these two sonnets bear sufficient testimony of his admiration of him.

I

He from the world into the blind abyss
Descended and beheld the realms of woe;
Then to the seat of everlasting bliss,
And God's own throne, led by his thought sublime,
Alive he soar'd, and to our nether clime
Bringing a steady light, to us below
Revealed the secrets of eternity.
Ill did his thankless countrymen repay
The fine desire; that which the good and great
So often from the insensate many meet,
That evil guerdon did our Dantè find.
But gladly would I, to be such as he,
For his hard exile and calamity,
Forego the happiest fortunes of mankind.

II

How shall we speak of him, for our blind eyes
Are all unequal to his dazzling rays?
Easier it is to blame his enemies
Than for the tongue to tell his lightest praise.
For us did he explore the realms of woe;
And at his coming did high Heaven expand
Her lofty gates, to whom his native land
Refus'd to open hers. Yet shalt thou know,
Ungrateful city, in thine own despite,
That thou hast fostered best thy Dantè's fame;
For virtue when oppressed appears more bright,
And brighter therefore shall his glory be,
Suffering of all mankind most wrongfully,
Since in the world there lives no greater name?

Southey.[1]

[1] [In a paragraph at the end of the volume Duppa remarks—'to my friends Southey and Wordsworth I am indebted for the poetical translations which enrich my work' (p. 330).]

Michael Angelo in his own poetical compositions imitated Petrarch rather than Dantè; yet it is sufficiently obvious throughout his works in painting, that the poetical mind of Dantè influenced his feelings. The Demons in the Last Judgment,[1] with all their mixed and various passions, may find a prototype in *La Divina Commedia.* The figures rising from the grave, mark his study of *L' Inferno* and *Il Purgatorio;* and the subject of the Brazen Serpent, in the Sistine Chapel, must remind every reader of *Canto* XXV *dell' Inferno*, where the flying serpents, the writhing and contortions of the human body from envenomed wounds, are described with pathos and horror; and the execution of Haman, in the opposite angle of the same ceiling, is doubtless designed from these lines:—

Poi piovve dentro all' alta fantasia, etc.[2]

The edition of Dantè he used, was a large folio with Landino's commentary: and upon the broad margin of the leaves he designed, with a pen and ink, all the interesting subjects in the poem.[3]

(pp. 228-33.)

[Hints from Dante in Michael Angelo's 'Last Judgment']

The most serious exception made to the general composition of Michael Angelo's Last Judgment by his contemporaries, was that of violating decorum, in representing so many figures without drapery. The first person who made this objection was the Pope's Master of the Ceremonies, who, on seeing the picture when three parts finished, and being asked his opinion, told his Holiness that it was more fit for a brothel than the Pope's chapel. This circumstance caused Michael Angelo to introduce his portrait into the picture with ass's ears: and not overlooking the duties of his temporal office, he represented him as Master of the Ceremonies in the lower world, ordering, and directing the disposal of the damned; and, to heighten the character, he is entwined with a serpent, Dantè's attribute of Minos.[4] . . . It is recorded, that the Monsignore petitioned the Pope to have this portrait taken out of the

[1] [In the Sistine Chapel at the Vatican.]

[2] [Duppa here prints *Purg.* xvii. 25-30, with Boyd's version in a footnote.]

[3] This book was possessed by Antonio Montauti, a sculptor and architect in Florence, who, being appointed architect to St. Peter's, removed to Rome, and shipped his marbles, bronzes, studies, and other effects, at Leghorn, for Cività Vecchia, among which was this edition of Dantè; in the voyage the vessel foundered at sea, and was lost. [In a previous note Duppa gives a brief account of Dante, and translates Boccaccio's description of his person. He adds—'Michael Angelo, with the Florentine Academicians and others petitioned Leo X. to remove the remains of Dantè from Ravenna, where he was buried, to deposit them in his native city, and erect a monument to honour his memory. . . . This petition was dated October the 20th, 1519; but was not granted' (p. 232).]

[4] [Cary's rendering of *Inf.* v. 4-12 is here quoted, with the original in a footnote.]

picture, and that of the painter put in its stead; to which the Pope is said to have replied, 'Had you been placed in Purgatory, there might have been some remedy, but from Hell *nulla est redemptio.*' . . . Another objection made to the general design, by critics less prejudiced, is the introduction of a boat to convey the condemned souls to their place of torment; the idea being manifestly borrowed from pagan theology.[1] The objection would seem to be well founded; but . . . while the Centaurs and Sphingi of Tasso, and the Gorgons and Hydras of Milton, are tolerated in the greatest epic poems of the Christian world, I shall offer no apology for the Charon of Dantè and Michael Angelo.

(pp. 281-4.)

1825. MISCELLANEOUS OBSERVATIONS AND OPINIONS ON THE CONTINENT.

[Dantè at Ravenna—His tomb]

Ravenna.—Under the kind protection of Guido Novello da Polenta, here Dante found an asylum from the malevolence of his enemies, and here he ended a life embittered with many sorrows, as he has pathetically told to posterity, 'after having gone about like a mendicant: wandering over almost every part to which our language extends, shewing against my will the wound with which fortune has smitten me, and which is so often imputed to his ill-deserving on whom it is inflicted.'[2] The precise time of his death is not accurately ascertained; but it was either in July or September[3] of the year 1321. His friend in adversity, Guido da Polenta, mourned his loss, and testified his sorrow and respect by a sumptuous funeral, and, it is said, intended to have erected a monument to his memory; but the following year contending factions deprived him of the sovereignty which he had held for more than half a century; and he in his turn like the great poet whom he protected, died in exile. I believe, however, that the tomb, with an inscription purporting to have been written by Dante himself,[4] was erected at the time of his decease, and, that his portrait in bas-relief was afterwards added by Bernardo Bembo, in the year 1483, who, at that time, was a Senator and Podestà of the Venetian Republic.

The bas-relief was probably copied from a portrait of Dante by Giotto, but whether any such picture now exists I am ignorant;[5]

[1] The boatman in this part of the composition is designed from the *Inferno* of Dantè. [*Inf.* iii. 109-11.]

[2] [*Conv.* i. 3 (Cary's translation).]

[3] [It was on Sept. 14.]

[4] [Duppa here gives a sketch of the tomb, with the inscription.]

[5] [The Giotto portrait in the Bargello at Florence was not discovered until 1840.]

but this bas-relief and all the bad portraits which I have ever seen of Dante, seem to have had one common origin.

(pp. 147-8.)

ROBERT FELLOWES

(1771-1847)

[Robert Fellowes of Shottesham Hall, Norfolk, was born in 1771. He was educated at St. Mary Hall, Oxford (B.A. 1796). He was editor of the *Critical Review* from 1804 to 1811, and was the author of various miscellaneous works, political and theological. In 1806 he published a translation from the Latin of *Milton's Familiar Epistles*, among which is included the letter to Buonmattai containing Milton's avowal of his delight in reading Dante and Petrarch. Fellowes, who was a liberal benefactor of Edinburgh University, and of the London University, of which he was one of the promoters, died in London in 1847.]

1806. FAMILIAR EPISTLES OF JOHN MILTON, TRANSLATED.—LETTER TO BENEDETTO BUONMATTAI, FROM FLORENCE, Sept. 10, 1638.

[Dante and Petrarch among the authors eagerly read by Milton]

I WILL now mention the favourable opportunity which you have, if you wish to embrace it, of obliging foreigners, among whom there is no one at all conspicuous for genius or for elegance who does not make the Tuscan language his delight, and indeed consider it as an essential part of education, particularly if he be only slightly tinctured with the literature of Greece or of Rome. I, who certainly have not merely wetted the tip of my lips in the stream of those languages, but, in proportion to my years, have swallowed the most copious drafts, can yet sometimes retire with avidity and delight to feast on Dante, Petrarch, and many others; nor has Athens itself been able to confine me to the transparent wave of Ilissus, nor ancient Rome to the banks of its Tiber, so as to prevent my visiting with delight the stream of the Arno, and the hills of Faesolae.[1]

(*Milton's Prose Works*, ed. Bohn, 1848, vol. iii. p. 497.)

ROBERT BLAND

(c. 1779-1825)

[Robert Bland, who was born about 1779, was educated at Harrow (where he was afterwards for some years assistant master) and at Pembroke College, Cambridge (B.A. 1802). After holding for a time the appointment of minister to the English Church at Amsterdam, he accepted, in 1813, the curacy of Prittlewell in

[1] [For the original, see vol. i. p. 124.]

Essex, which he exchanged in 1816 for that of Kenilworth. He died at Leamington in 1825. Bland had a considerable reputation as a classical scholar. His best known work, *Translations, chiefly from the Greek Anthology; with Tales and Miscellaneous Poems*, was published in collaboration with John Herman Merivale in 1806, and received a complimentary notice from Byron in *English Bards and Scotch Reviewers* (see below, p. 190); a second and enlarged edition was published in 1813, under the title of *Collections from the Greek Anthology, and from the Pastoral, Elegiac and Dramatic Poets of Greece*; and a third edition appeared in 1833. Several references to Dante are introduced into this work. Bland contributed to the *Quarterly Review* in 1814 an article on the literary histories of Italy by Ginguenè and Sismondi, which contains an interesting criticism of the *Divina Commedia*, together with translations of sundry passages in *terza rima*.]

1806. TRANSLATIONS CHIEFLY FROM THE GREEK ANTHOLOGY, WITH TALES AND MISCELLANEOUS POEMS.

From Bianor the Bithynian.

[Parallels to the savagery of Dante's Ugolino]

IN Thebes the sons of Oedipus are laid;
But not the tomb's all desolating shade,
The deep forgetfulness of Pluto's gate,
Nor Acheron can quench their deathless hate.
E'en hostile madness shakes the funeral pyres;
Against each other blaze the pointed fires;
Unhappy boys! for whom high Jove ordains
Eternal Hatred's never sleeping pains.

This shocking instance of posthumous hatred is not unexampled in the superstitious annals of our own country. I remember to have somewhere seen an account of a Danish and a Saxon warrior who fell by mutual wounds, and by some accident were interred in the same tomb. A century afterwards their bodies were found grappling together as if in desperate fight, and covered with the blood that flowed from a thousand wounds but newly given and received. This bears some analogy to that most horrible description in Dante, where Hugolino is seen enjoying his savage repast on the head of his yet living enemy.

(pp. 50, 139-40.)

1813. COLLECTIONS FROM THE GREEK ANTHOLOGY, AND FROM THE PASTORAL, ELEGIAC, AND DRAMATIC POETS OF GREECE.

[The inscription over the gate of Dante's Hell]

True taste refuses all accommodation with fashion, every attempt at a composition or compromise, and sooner than yield in her pretensions, contents herself with obscurity, until the times themselves shall come round and bow to her jurisdiction. The author who aspires to after ages, should take leave of the age in which he lives.

To be drawn into the vortex of fashionable writing, is to pass that gate on which is inscribed

'Voi che intrate, lasciate ogni speranza.'[1]

(*Preface*,[2] pp. lvii-viii, ed. 1833.)

[Sappho and Dante contrasted]

The fire and enthusiasm, which so strongly mark the writings and pourtray the character of Sappho, appear in none of her works more unequivocally than in this little fragment.[3] It has the appearance of a burst of indignation at some homespun, mighty good sort of woman, who had neither a soul susceptible of poetry herself, nor the sense to admire, nor the candour to allow of it in others. This is a description of persons which has always been severely handled by poets; and the stigma of contempt with which they are branded by Sappho, is a luxury to what they are sentenced to undergo by Dante—

'Questi sciaurati, che mai non fur vivi,' &c.[4]

Those miserables, who never truly lived.

* * * *

No record of their names is left on high;
Mercy and Justice spurn them, and refuse.
Take we no note of them—Look, and pass by.[5]

(*Notes on Sappho*, p. 258, ed. 1833.)

1814. April. QUARTERLY REVIEW. ART. I. GINGUENÉ AND SISMONDI'S LITERARY HISTORY OF ITALY.[6]

[Criticism of the *Divina Commedia*]

If ever a poet, in any age or country, has elevated himself by his natural genius to a height which disdains the application of all the ordinary rules of measurement, it is assuredly Dante. His poem, that amazing monument of unrivalled powers, can be judged by itself alone; and while the critic laboriously traces a few faint marks of imitation in the spirit of the age, in the works of worthless and forgotten contemporaries, or lastly in the more splendid and durable models of antiquity, he must confess with some surprise, at the close of his examination, how little he has been able to

[1] [*Inf.* iii. 9, loosely quoted.]

[2] [This passage does not appear in the original edition (1806); it was added in the second edition (1813).]

[3] [That beginning κατθανοῖσα δὲ κεῖσ'.]

[4] [*Inf.* iii. 64 ff.]

[5] [The lines translated are *Inf.* iii. 64, 49-51.]

[6] [Review of Ginguené's *Histoire Littéraire d'Italie*, and Sismondi's *Histoire de la Littérature du Midi de l'Europe*.]

meet with that is not exclusively ascribable to the creative genius of the author. It is true that the popular superstition of the age naturally led the imagination to dwell on the self-embodied visions of an indistinct futurity. . . . But it is in the style and sentiments of the poet that his true originality consists; and where, in the works of preceding and contemporary versifiers, could Dante have discovered any specimens of that severe, yet energetic tone, the voice of nature herself, by which the reader is irresistibly struck even on approaching the vestibule of his immortal fabric?

It is in language like this, (of which we should be happy to persuade ourselves that we have been able to retain even a feeble impression,) that he apostrophizes his 'mighty master'.

'Or sei tu quel Virgilio, e quella fonte,' etc. (Inf. c. i.).

Art thou that Virgil then? the fountain head
Whence roll the streams of eloquence along?
—Thus, with a bashful front, I humbly said—
Oh light and glory of the sons of song!
So favour me, as I thy page have sought
With unremitting love, and study long!
Thou art the guide and master of my thought;
Sole author thou, from whom the inspired strain
That crowns my name with deathless praise I brought[1]—

The terrible inscription on the portal of hell,

'Per me si va nella città dolente,' etc.[2]

is another passage which arrests the reader forcibly by the austere sublimity of its style. . . . We next turn to a passage, singularly illustrative of the stern spirit of republican faction, which was exalted in the character of Dante by the keen sense of wrongs inflicted by a beloved and ungrateful country. The entrance to hell is thronged by myriads of spirits, of those who, in life, performed their appointed tasks equally without disgrace and without glory, and who are therefore classed as the fit companions of the neutral angels, who were neither rebellious nor faithful to their maker. In his strong and energetic language, he calls them

Those miserables, who never truly lived—[3]

The genius of Dante is in no respect less capable of being duly appreciated through the medium of translation than in the art which he so eminently possessed, 'of painting in words; of representing objects which are the pure creations of fancy, beings or actions out of all nature and out of all possibility, with so much truth and force, that the reader thinks he sees them before him,

[1] [*Inf.* i. 79-87.] [2] [*Inf.* iii. 1 ff.]
[3] [*Inf.* iii. 64. Bland here gives the rendering of ll. 49-51 printed above.]

and, after having read the description once, believes, all his life after, that he has actually beheld them.' Still less credit, we fear, is given to the poet for beauties of a very different sort, and generally considered as the peculiar growth of an age of excessive sensibility—the delineation of the calm and peaceful scenes of inanimate nature, of picturesque objects, and pastoral images. The very nature of the poem seems to exclude ornaments of this description, and, from expecting only the supernaturally terrible and sublime, we are, perhaps, too hastily led to conclude, that nothing else can, by any possibility, have found admission into such a composition. The fact is, however, quite the contrary, and the reader, thus prejudiced, will be astonished to find the frequent opportunities embraced by the poet of introducing into passages, seemingly the most inauspicious for his purpose, such exquisite representations of natural objects, and of the feelings which they are calculated to inspire, as can hardly be equalled by those of any poets in the most advanced period of mental luxury and refinement.

The cloud of anger and indignation that for a moment obscures the philosophical serenity of his immortal guide, is thus illustrated by a comparison with the vicissitudes incident to the face of nature in early spring, which conveys, in a few words, to our senses all the freshness, together with all the uncertainty of the season. The miser,[1] who is tormented with the thirst of Tantalus, is thus made perpetually to behold, without tasting, not water only, but

Rivulets, that from the verdant hills
  Of Casentin into the Arno flow,
Freshening its current with their cooler rills.[2]

So the flames, which illuminate the eighth circle of his infernal regions, are

Lights, numberless as by some fountain side
  The silly swain, reposing, at the hour
When beams the day-star with diminish'd pride,
  When the sunn'd bee deserts each rifled flower
And leaves to humming gnats the populous void,
  Beholds in grassy lawn, or leafy bower,
Or orchard-plot, of glow worms emerald bright—[3]

So the evening hour is attended with all the circumstances of soothing melancholy, with which it is wont to inspire a poetical imagination, in a passage of which the last line probably suggested to Gray the opening of his elegy.[4]

[1] [Not a miser, but the coiner, Maestro Adamo.]
[2] [*Inf.* xxx. 64-6.]
[3] [*Inf.* xxvi. 25-31.]
[4] [Not probably, but certainly—see vol. i. p. 234.]

'Twas now the hour when fond desire renews
To him who wanders o'er the pathless main,
Raising unbidden tears, the last adieus
Of tender friends, whom fancy shapes again;
When the late parted pilgrim thrills with thought
Of his lov'd home, if o'er the distant plain
Perchance, his ears the village chimes have caught,
Seeming to mourn the close of dying day.[1]

. . . . Among the most beautiful of the episodes in this admirable part of the poem [the Purgatorio] are the meeting of Dante with his friend, the musician Casella, which Milton has consecrated to the imagination of the English reader,[2] and that with the painter Oderisi da Gubbio, who is condemned to purgatory for having indulged the over-weening pride of art. It is into his mouth that the poet puts those celebrated reflections on the vanity of human endowments, in which he is suspected of having intended to introduce a boast of his own poetical excellence, somewhat at variance with the moral of humility which it is his object to impress.

Oh empty pride of human power and skill!
How soon the verdure on thy summit dies,
If no dark following years sustain it still!
Thus Cimabue the painter's honour'd prize
To Giotto yields; a happier rival's fame
Hath veil'd his glory from all mortal eyes.—
Who now repeats that elder Guido's name?
Another wears the poet's envied crown—
Perhaps this fleeting present hour may claim
One who shall bear from both their vain renown.
The world's applause is but a passing wind,
An idle blast, now this, now that way blown,
And changing name with every point assign'd, etc.

Our mortal fame is like the grass of hue,
That comes and goes, by the same sun decay'd,
From which it life, and health, and freshness drew,
When from crude earth burst forth the tender blade.[3]

Whatever may be the sense of this allusion, Dante has not left us to conjecture what was his own opinion of his poetical merits in comparison with those of his contemporaries. 'Do I behold in thee,' exclaims Bonaggiunta, (one of those early bards who sang of love according to the fashion of the times), 'do I behold in thee the author who has written poems of a new style, beginning

'Donne ch' avete intelletto d' amore?'—[4]

[1] 'Che paia 'l giorno pianger che si muore.' [*Purg.* viii. 1-6.]
[2] [See vol. i. p. 126.] [3] [*Purg.* xi. 91-102, 115-17.]
[4] This is the first line of one of Dante's most admired *Canzoni*.

'I am,' replies Dante, 'one who writes when love inspires, and give utterance to the thoughts which he imprints within me.' 'Alas, my brother!' returns the elder bard, 'I now see what it is that has withheld from myself and the poets of my own time, that new style, that style so sweet and soothing, to which I have listened this day. Your pen only set down the words which Love dictates. It was far otherwise with us; and the more we admitted of ornament from the mere study to please, the further were we removed from that mode of expression which we so admire in you.'[1]

Few, even among the warmest admirers of Dante, have had the enthusiasm to follow him, step by step, through the last division of his stupendous edifice. In the Inferno, the imagination is constantly kept on the stretch by that terrible machinery which the poet sets in motion and supports with unequalled powers. In the Purgatorio, hope is everything and everywhere about us. In both alike, the number of interesting episodes, the pictures of human character, and of objects both real and fantastic, 'but which we fancy real because they invest ideal beauties with the qualities perceptible to sense,' employ by turns the feeling, the judgment, and the fancy. . . . Nevertheless, it must not be believed that even the ineffable and fatiguing splendours, or the mystical theology of the Paradiso do not occasionally admit the introduction of such natural pictures and such moral reflections as we have already shewn to constitute some of the highest claims of the poet. Nor must we forget either the exquisitely graceful and simple delineation of the ancient manners of Florence,[2] which is intended by him as a vehicle of censure upon those of the age then present, or the melancholy and affecting colours in which he has displayed the miseries of exile, in the poetical prediction of his own banishment.[3] . . .

The want of a principal action, of a leading point of interest, the continual conflict of images, sacred and profane, ancient and modern, and the frequent admission of such as are either low and vulgar or even indecent and disgusting, are faults from which the warmest admirers among his own countrymen do not affect to exempt him. . . .

(Vol. xi. pp. 10-16.)

THOMAS MOORE

(1779-1852)

[Thomas Moore was the son of a grocer and wine merchant of Dublin, where he was born in 1779. He was educated at Trinity College, Dublin, and in 1799 entered at the Middle Temple with the intention of being called to the bar. In 1803 he was

[1] [*Purg.* xxiv. 49-62.] [2] [*Par.* xv. 97 ff.] [3] [*Par.* xvii. 46 ff.]

appointed Admiralty Registrar at Bermuda. Finding the office a sinecure he put in a deputy and returned to England by way of the United States and Canada. In 1807 commenced the publication of his *Irish Melodies*, which continued to appear until 1834; by these songs, which brought in a handsome income, Moore's reputation was established as the national lyrist of Ireland. In 1817 he published *Lalla Rookh*, his most famous poem, and shortly afterwards, having been rendered liable for a debt of £6000 by the defalcations of his deputy at Bermuda, he took refuge abroad and proceeded on a tour through Italy with Lord John Russell, not returning to England until 1822. After the death of Byron (1824) Moore undertook to write his life, which appeared in 1830 under the title of *Life, Letters, and Journals of Lord Byron*. In 1835 he received a pension. The first collected edition of his *Poetical Works* was published in 10 volumes in 1840-1. He died in 1852. His *Memoirs, Journals, and Correspondence*, edited by Lord John Russell, appeared in 1853-6 in 8 volumes. Moore appears to have been fairly well acquainted with the *Divina Commedia*. References to it are frequent in his poems and *Diary*; his *Dream of Two Sisters* is avowedly a close imitation of a passage from the twenty-seventh canto of the *Purgatorio*; while another poem is a parody of part of the fifth canto of the *Inferno*.]

1806. LINES WRITTEN AT THE FALLS OF THE MOHAWK RIVER.

[Motto from Dante]

GIÀ era in loco ove s' udia 'l ribombo
Dell' acqua—[1]

Dante.

(*Poetical Works*, ed. 1840-1, vol. ii. p. 306.)

1806. TO THE LADY CHARLOTTE RAWDON. FROM THE BANKS OF THE ST. LAWRENCE.

[Reminiscence of Dante]

Once more, embark'd upon the glittering streams,
Our boat flies light along the leafy shore,
Shooting the falls, without a dip of oar
Or breath of Zephyr, like the mystic bark
The poet saw, in dreams divinely dark,
Borne, without sails, along the dusky flood,
While on its deck a pilot angel stood,
And, with his wings of living light unfurl'd,
Coasted the dim shores of another world![2]

(*Ibid.* vol. ii. p. 333.)

[1] [*Inf.* xvi. 1.]

[2] 'Vedi che sdegna gli argomenti umani;
Sì che remo non vuol, ne altro velo,
Che l' ale sue tra liti sì lontani.
Vedi come l' ha dritte verso l' cielo
Trattando l' aere con l' eterne penne;
Che non si mutan, come mortal pelo.'
Dante, *Purgator.* cant. ii. [31-6].

1808. INTOLERANCE, A SATIRE.

[Dante's treatment of Pagans]

Yes,—rather plunge me back in Pagan night,
And take my chance with Socrates for bliss,[1]
Than be the Christian of a faith like this,
Which builds on heavenly cant its earthly sway,
And in a convert mourns to lose a prey.

(*Poetical Works*, ed. 1840-1, vol. iii. pp. 46-7.)

1814. Sept. EDINBURGH REVIEW. ART. VIII. LORD THURLOW'S POEMS.[2]

[Lord Thurlow and Dante]

'Moonlight' is dedicated to Lord Eldon. We shall try the patience and ingenuity of our readers with but one enigmatical extract from this poem. . . .

No soul has flown unto the gate of woe,
Or to the blissful soil, or brush'd the shore
Of Limbo with its wings; or flown and lived:
But yet intelligence from these has come,
By angels, and pale ghosts, and vexed fools,
That, straying as they wont, were blown athwart
The nether world, from the oblivious pool
Scarce 'scaping, on our scornful marge to land:
Thence to be blown by every idle wind,
Their tale half told, with a new flight of fools,
Eclectic, to the planetary void.

On this extraordinary passage,—its blown-about ghosts and eclectic flight of fools—we would willing pass no severer sentence than that which a Mufti pronounced upon some verses of the Turkish poet Misri:—'Le sens de ces vers ne peut être connu et entendu de personne que de Dieu et de Misri.' The noble author had evidently been reading Dante; and the same process appears to have taken place, which from his Lordship's peculiar affinities, must always occur upon his immersion into any such writers,—he comes out encrusted with a rich deposit of their faults. Not all the authority of Dante[3] can reconcile us to hearing the dog Cerberus called 'a worm' with 'an iron throat.'

(*Prose and Verse by Thomas Moore*, ed. R. H. Shepherd, pp. 44-5.)

[1] The poet Dante compromises the matter with the Pagans, and gives them a neutral territory or limbo of their own, where their employment, it must be owned, is not very enviable—'Senza speme vivemo in desio.'—Cant. iv. [*Inf.* iv. 42].

[2] [See below, pp. 148-9.]

[3] 'Quando ci scorse Cerbero il gran vermo.' *Inferno*, canto 6. The 'iron throat' is a tasteful supplement of his lordship's.

1819. DIARY.

[Dante's portrait at Florence]

Oct. 17. Florence. In the cathedral is the portrait of Dante,[1] but I could not judge of it; outside, by the *battisterio*, is what is called the Sasso di Dante, where it is supposed he used to sit.

(*Memoirs, Journal, and Correspondence of Thomas Moore*, ed. Lord John Russell, vol. iii. p. 38.)

[Michael Angelo and Dante]

Oct. 30. Rome. Michael Angelo a better architect, in Chantrey's opinion, than sculptor: a great affinity between him and Dante.

(*Ibid.* vol. iii. p. 54.)

1820. DIARY.

[Canning and Dante]

Oct. 27. Paris. Wordsworth spoke of the very little real knowledge of poetry that existed now; so few men had time to study. For instance, Mr. Canning; one would hardly select a cleverer man; and yet, what did Mr. Canning know of poetry? What time had he, in the busy political life he had led, to study Dante, Homer, &c. as they ought to be studied, in order to arrive at the true principles of taste in works of genius.

(*Ibid.* vol. iii. p. 162.)

1821. DIARY.

[Byron, Dante, and Milton]

July 3. Paris. I said that Lord Byron could not describe anything which he had not had actually under his eyes, and that he did it either on the spot or immediately afterwards. This, Lord Holland remarked, was the sign of a true poet, to write only from *impressions*; but where then do all the imaginary scenes of Dante, Milton, &c. go, if it is necessary to *see* what we describe in order to be a true poet?

(*Ibid.* vol. iii. p. 248.)

1822. DIARY.

['Dante Cary']

June 3. Paris. It appears that Dante Cary is the author of those pretty translations from the old French poets in the London Magazine.

(*Ibid.* vol. iii. p. 356.)

[1] [The picture by Domenico di Michelino over the north door.]

1823. DIARY.

['The translator of Dante' and 'Christabel']

April 1. London. Rogers asked me to dine with him, which I did; company, Wordsworth and his wife and sister-in-law, Cary (the translator of Dante), Hallam and Sharpe. . . . Wordsworth's excessive praise of 'Christabel,' joined in by Cary, far beyond my comprehension.

(*Memoirs, Journal, and Correspondence of Thomas Moore*, ed. Lord John Russell, vol. iv. p. 48.)

1823. DIARY.

[Lord Grenville and Dante]

Oct. 13. Bowood. Rogers produced some English verses of Lord Grenville's, to the surprise of all the party, who seemed to agree that he was one of the least poetical men they could point out. The verses were a paraphrastic translation of the lines at the beginning of the *Inferno*, 'O degli altri poeti onore e lume,'[1] and very spiritedly done.

(*Ibid.* vol. iv. p. 139.)

1826. DIARY.

[Gabriele Rossetti's commentary on Dante]

Sept. 6. London. At Mrs. Montgomerie's in the evening, M. Rosetti,[2] who has just published a commentary on Dante (proving it. I think, to be a satire), give us recitations from Tasso, and some Neapolitan songs.

(*Ibid.* vol. v. p. 102.)

1827. Oct. EDINBURGH REVIEW. ART. IV. PRIVATE THEATRICALS.

[Dante's idea of 'comedy' not dramatic]

On the arrival of dramatic poesy among the Italians, it was in private theatres—and, for a long period, in private theatres only—that any advances in the cultivation of the art were made. The slow growth, indeed, of this branch of literature in that country, and the few fruits of any excellence which it has even yet put forth, would seem to warrant the conclusion to which the French critics have long since come, that the Italians are not, any more than their great ancestors, a dramatic people. It is certain that

[1] [*Inf.* i. 82 ff. The translation was preserved by Rogers, and is printed in Clayden's *Rogers and his Contemporaries* (see below, p. 302).]

[2] [Gabriele Rossetti, the first volume of whose *Comento analitico della Divina Commedia* was published by Murray in 1826 (see below, p. 446).]

their literature had produced its brightest and most desirable wonders before even the ordinary scenery and decorations of a theatre were introduced among them; and the poetry of Dante and Petrarca, and the prose of Boccaccio, had carried their beautiful language to its highest pitch of perfection, near a century and a half before a single play in this language was attempted. Nothing can, indeed, more strongly prove how little dramatic ideas or associations were afloat in the time of Dante, than that he should have ventured to call his shadowy and awful panorama of Hell, Heaven, and Purgatory—a 'Comedy.'

(*Prose and Verse by Thomas Moore,* ed. R. H. Shepherd, p. 148.)

1828. IMITATION OF THE INFERNO OF DANTE.

[Parody of Dante]

Così quel fiato gli spiriti mali
Di quà, di là, di giù, di su gli mena.
Inferno, canto 5.

I turn'd my steps, and lo, a shadowy throng
Of ghosts came fluttering tow'rds me—blown along,
Like cockchafers in high autumnal storms,
By many a fitful gust that through their forms
Whistled, as on they came, with wheezy puff,
And puff'd as—though they'd never puff enough.
'Whence and what are ye?' pitying I inquir'd
Of these poor ghosts, who, tatter'd, tost, and tir'd
With such eternal puffing, scarce could stand
On their lean legs while answering my demand.
'We once were authors'—thus the Sprite, who led
This tag-rag regiment of spectres, said—
'Authors of every sex, male, female, neuter,
Who, early smit with love of praise and—*pewter*,[1]
On C-lb-n's shelves first saw the light of day,
In ——'s [2] puffs exhal'd our lives away—
Like summer windmills, doom'd to dusty peace,
When the brisk gales, that lent them motion, cease.
Ah, little knew we then what ills await
Much-lauded scribblers in their after-state;
Be puff'd on earth—how loudly Str—t can tell—
And, dire reward, now doubly puff'd in hell!'

[1] The *classical* term for money.
[2] The reader may fill this gap with any one of the *dissyllabic* publishers of London that occurs to him.

Touch'd with compassion for this ghastly crew,
Whose ribs, even now, the hollow wind sung through
In mournful prose,—such prose as Rosa's [1] ghost
Still at the accustom'd hour of eggs and toast,
Sighs through the columns of the M-rn-g P-t,—
Pensive I turn'd to weep, when he, who stood
Foremost of all that flatulential brood,
Singling a *she*-ghost from the party, said,
'Allow me to present Miss X.Y.Z.,[2]
One of our *lettr'd* nymphs—excuse the pun—
Who gain'd a name on earth by—having none;
And whose initials would immortal be,
Had she but learn'd those plain ones, A.B.C.
Yon smirking ghost, like mummy dry and neat
Wrapp'd in his own dead rhymes—fit winding-sheet—
Still marvels much that not a soul should care
One single pin to know who wrote "May Fair";—
While this young gentleman,' (here forth he drew
A dandy spectre, puff'd quite through and through,
As though his ribs were an Aeolian lyre
For the whole Row's soft *trade*-winds to inspire,)
'This modest genius breath'd one wish alone,
To have his volume read, himself unknown;
But different far the course his glory took,
All knew the author, and—none read the book.
Behold, in yonder ancient figure of fun,
Who rides the blast, Sir J-n-h B-rr-t-n;—
In tricks to raise the wind his life was spent,
And now the wind returns the complement.
This lady here, the Earl of ——'s sister,
Is a dead novelist; and this is Mister—
Beg pardon—*Honourable* Mister L-st-r,
A gentleman who, some weeks since, came over
In a smart puff (wind S.S.E.) to Dover.
Yonder behind us limps young Vivian Grey,
Whose life, poor youth, was long since blown away—
Like a torn paper-kite, on which the wind
No further purchase for a puff can find.'
'And thou, thyself'—here, anxious, I exclaim'd—
'Tell us, good ghost, how thou, thyself, art nam'd.'
'Me, Sir!' he blushing cried—'Ah, there's the rub—

[1] Rosa Matilda, who was for many years the writer of the political articles in the journal alluded to.

[2] *Not* the charming L. E. L. [Letitia E. Landon], and still less, Mrs. F. H. [Felicia Hemans], whose poetry is among the most beautiful of the present day.

Know, then—a waiter once at Brooks's Club,
A waiter still I might have long remain'd,
And long the club-room's jokes and glasses drain'd;
But, ah, in luckless hour, this last December,
I wrote a book, and Colburn dubb'd me "Member"—
"Member of Brooks's!"—oh Promethean puff,
To what wilt thou exalt even kitchen-stuff!
With crumbs of gossip, caught from dining wits,
And half-heard jokes, bequeath'd, like half-chew'd bits,
To be, each night, the waiter's perquisites;—
With such ingredients, serv'd up oft before,
But with fresh fudge and fiction garnish'd o'er,
I manag'd, for some weeks, to dose the town,
Till fresh reserves of nonsense ran me down;
And, ready still even waiter's souls to damn,
The Devil but rang his bell, and—here I am;—
Yes—"Coming *up*, Sir," once my favourite cry,
Exchang'd for "Coming *down*, Sir," here am I!'
  Scarce had the Spectre's lips these words let drop,
When, lo, a breeze—such as from ——'s shop
Blows in the vernal hour, when puffs prevail,
And speeds the *sheets* and swells the lagging *sale*—
Took the poor waiter rudely in the poop,
And, whirling him and all his grisly group
Of literary ghosts—Miss X.Y.Z.—
The nameless author, better known than read—
Sir Jo ——, the Honourable Mr. L-st-r,
And, last, not least, Lord Nobody's twin-sister—
Blew them, ye gods, with all their prose and rhymes
And sins about them, far into those climes
'Where Peter pitch'd his waistcoat'[1] in old times,
Leaving me much in doubt, as on I prest,
With my great master, through this realm unblest,
Whether Old Nick or C-lb-n puffs the best.

(*Poetical Works*, ed. 1841, vol. viii. pp. 281-6.)

1829. DIARY.

['Dante Carey']

Sept. 21. London. Went to Rogers's: Carey (Dante), and Danby the painter, with him.

(*Memoirs*, etc, vol. vi. p. 15.)

[1] A *Dantesque* allusion to the old saying, 'Nine miles beyond H-ll, where Peter pitched his waistcoat.'

1830. LIFE, LETTERS, AND JOURNALS OF LORD BYRON. WITH NOTES.

[Precocious love—Byron, Dante, Alfieri]

It was about this period [1796], when Byron was not quite eight years old, that a feeling partaking more of the nature of love than it is easy to believe possible in so young a child, took, according to his own account, entire possession of his thoughts, and showed how early in this passion, as in most others, the sensibilities of his nature were awakened. . . . Dante, we know, was but nine years old when, at a May-day festival, he saw and fell in love with Beatrice; and Alfieri, who was himself a precocious lover, considers such early sensibility to be an unerring sign of a soul formed for the fine arts.

(Ed. 1838, p. 9.)

[Dante a swordsman and a falconer]

In war, the most turbulent of exercises, Aeschylus, Dante, Camoens, and a long list of other poets, distinguished themselves; and, though it may be granted that Horace was a bad rider, and Virgil no tennis-player, yet, on the other hand, Dante was, we know, a falconer as well as swordsman; Tasso, expert both as swordsman and dancer; Alfieri, a great rider; Klopstock, a skaiter; Cowper, famous, in his youth, at cricket and football; and Lord Byron, pre-eminent in all sorts of exercises.

(*Ibid.* p. 21 note.)

[Dante's Rachel]

The poet Dante, a wanderer away from wife and children, passed the whole of a restless and detached life in nursing his immortal dream of Beatrice; while Petrarch, who would not suffer his only daughter to reside beneath his roof, expended thirty-two years of poetry and passion on an idealised love.

It is, indeed, in the very nature and essence of genius to be for ever occupied intensely with self, as the great centre and source of its strength. Like the sister Rachel, in Dante, sitting all day before her mirror,

'mai non si smaga
Del suo ammiraglio, e siede tutto giorno.'[1]

(*Ibid.* p. 268.)

[Unhappy marriages of great poets—Dante, Milton, Shakespeare, Dryden, Byron]

From whatever causes it may have arisen, the coincidence is no less striking than saddening, that, on the list of married poets who have been unhappy in their homes, there should already be found four such illustrious names as Dante, Milton, Shakspeare, and

[1] [*Purg.* xxvii. 104-5.]

Dryden; and that we should now have to add, as a partner of their destiny, a name worthy of being placed beside the greatest of them —Lord Byron.

Note.—By whatever austerity of temper or habits the poets Dante and Milton may have drawn upon themselves such a fate, it might be expected that, at least, the 'gentle Shakspeare' would have stood exempt from the common calamity of his brethren. . . .

It is by posterity only that full justice is rendered to those who have paid such hard penalties to reach it. The dross that had once hung about the ore drops away, and the infirmities, and even miseries, of genius are forgotten in its greatness. Who now asks whether Dante was right or wrong in his matrimonial differences? or by how many of those whose fancies dwell fondly on his Beatrice is even the name of his Gemma Donati remembered?

(Ed. 1838, pp. 271, 298.)

[Dante at Ravenna]

'On my departure from Venice,' writes Madame Guiccioli, 'Byron had promised to come and see me at Ravenna. Dante's tomb, the classical pine wood,[1] the relics of antiquity which are to be found in that place, afforded a sufficient pretext for me to invite him to come, and for him to accept my invitation.'

(*Ibid.* p. 399.)

[Dante and Giotto]

Though it may be conceded that Dante was an admirer of the Arts, his recommendation of the Apocalypse to Giotto, as a source of subjects for his pencil, shows, at least, what indifferent judges poets are, in general, of the sort of fancies fittest to be embodied by the painter.

(*Ibid.* p. 412 note.)

[Byron 'warm from the pages of Petrarch and Dante']

We have seen from Lord Byron's Journal in 1814, what intense interest he took in the last struggles of Revolutionary France under Napoleon. . . . Since then, he had but rarely turned his thoughts to politics; the tame, ordinary vicissitude of public affairs having but little in it to stimulate a mind like his, whose sympathies

[1] *Note by Moore*:—

'Tal qual di ramo in ramo si raccoglie
Per la pineta in sul lito di Chiassi,
Quando Eolo Scirocco fuor discioglie.'

Dante: *Purg.* canto xxviii.

Dante himself (says Mr. Cary, in one of the notes on his admirable translation of the poet) 'perhaps wandered in this wood during his abode with Guido Novello da Polenta.'

nothing short of a crisis seemed worthy to interest. This the present state of Italy gave every promise of affording him; and, in addition to the great national cause itself, in which there was everything that a lover of liberty, warm from the pages of Petrarch and Dante, could desire, he had also private ties and regards to enlist him socially in the contest.

(Ed. 1838, p. 467.)

[Byron compared with Dante and Petrarch]

So various and contradictory, were Lord Byron's attributes, both moral and intellectual, that he may be pronounced to have been not one, but many. . . . It was this multiform aspect exhibited by him that led the world, during his short wondrous career, to compare him with that medley host of personages, almost all differing from each other, which he thus playfully enumerates in one of his Journals:—

'I have seen myself compared . . . within these nine years, to Rousseau, Goethe, Young, Aretine, Timon of Athens, Dante, Petrarch. . . .'

We have seen that wrongs and sufferings were, through life, the main sources of Byron's inspiration. Where the hoof of the critic struck, the fountain was first disclosed; and all the tramplings of the world afterwards but forced out the stream stronger and brighter. The same obligations to misfortune, the same debt of the 'oppressor's wrong,' for having wrung out from bitter thoughts the pure essence of his genius, was due no less deeply by Dante!—'quum illam sub amarâ cogitatione excitatam, occulti divinique ingenii vim exacuerit et inflammarit.'[1]

In that contempt for the world's opinion, which led Dante to exclaim, 'Lascia dir le genti,'[2] Lord Byron also bore a strong resemblance to that poet,—though far more, it must be confessed, in profession than in reality. For, while scorn for the public voice was on his lips, the keenest sensitiveness to its every breath was in his heart; and, as if every feeling of his nature was to have some painful mixture in it, together with the pride of Dante which led him to disdain public opinion, he combined the susceptibility of Petrarch which placed him shrinkingly at its mercy.

His agreement, in some other features of character, with Petrarch, I have already had occasion to remark; and if it be true, as is often surmised, that Byron's want of a due reverence for Shakspeare arose from some latent and hardly conscious jealousy of that poet's

[1] Paulus Jovius.—Bayle, too, says of him, 'Il fit entrer plus de feu et plus de force dans ses livres, qu'il n'y en eût mis s' il avoit joui d'une condition plus tranquille.'

[2] [*Purg.* v. 13.]

fame, a similar feeling is known to have existed in Petrarch towards Dante; and the same reason assigned for it,—that from the living he had nothing to fear, while before the shade of Dante he might have reason to feel humbled,—is also not a little applicable in the case of Lord Byron.

(Ed. 1838, pp. 643-4.)

c. 1830. THE CHAPTER OF THE BLANKET: A FRAGMENT.

[Dante's 'piè fermo']

Dante says that in going up a hill the hinder foot should always be the firmer,[1] and assuredly in the uphill work of beginning a narrative, the hind foot of the story cannot be too firmly planted.

(*Chap. i.*—in *Prose and Verse by Thomas Moore*, ed. R. H. Shepherd, p. 347.)

1834. A CHARACTER.

[Simile from Dante]

* * * *

By Mother Church, high-fed and haughty dame,
The boy was dandled, in his dawn of fame;
List'ning, she smil'd, and bless'd the flippant tongue
On which the fate of unborn tithe-pigs hung.
Ah, who shall paint the grandam's grim dismay,
When loose Reform entic'd her boy away;
When shock'd she heard him ape the rabble's tone,
And, in Old Sarum's fate, foredoom her own!
Groaning she cried, while tears roll'd down her cheeks,
'Poor, glib-tongued youth, he means not what he speaks.
Like oil at top, these whig professions flow,
But, pure as lymph, runs Toryism below.
Alas, that tongue should start thus, in the race,
Ere mind can reach and regulate its pace!—
For, once outstripp'd by tongue, poor, lagging mind,
At every step, still further limps behind.
But, bless the boy!—whate'er his wandering be,
Still turns his heart to Toryism and me.
Like those odd shapes, portray'd in Dante's lay,[2]
With heads fix'd on, the wrong and backward way,
His feet and eyes pursue a diverse track,
While *those* march onward, *these* look fondly back.'

Poetical Works, ed. 1841, vol. ix. pp. 207-8.)

[1] 'Il piè dietro il più fermo.' [Misquoted, Dante says 'il piè fermo sempre era il più basso' (*Inf.* i. 30).]

[2] Che dalle reni era tornato 'l volto,
E indietro venir li convenia,
Perchè 'l veder dinanzi era lor tolto.
[*Inf.* xx. 13-15.]

1835. DIARY.

[Cary's and Wright's translations of Dante]

Dec. 9. London. Company at Crawford's: Mr. Ellis and his son, and one or two others whom I did not know. In talking of Carey's translation of Dante, I happened to say that I had once thought it impossible such *a tour de force* could ever be performed better than it had been done by Carey; but that, since then, there had appeared a translation in rhyme, by some one whose name I had now forgot, and which, as far as I could judge from the little I had seen of it, far exceeded even Carey's. On my saying this, a gentleman who sat next to me observed, 'My son has attempted to translate some parts of Dante, but how far he has succeeded I do not know.' 'May I ask his name?' said I. 'Wright,' he answered. 'The very man,' I exclaimed, to the no small pleasure of the modest father, and the amusement of the company.

(*Memoirs, Journal, and Correspondence*, ed. Lord John Russell, vol. vii. pp. 136-7.)

1841. THE POETICAL WORKS OF THOMAS MOORE. COLLECTED BY HIMSELF.

[The satire of Dante]

Even that sternest of all satirists, Dante, who, not content with the penal fire of the pen, kept an Inferno ever ready to receive the victims of his wrath,—even Dante, on becoming acquainted with some of the persons whom he had thus doomed, not only revoked their awful sentence, but even honoured them with warm praise;[1] and, probably, on a little further acquaintance, would have admitted them into his Paradiso. When thus loosely and shallowly even the sublime satire of Dante could strike its roots in his own heart and memory, it is easy to conceive how light and passing may be the feeling of hostility with which a partisan in the field of satire plies his laughing warfare; and how often it may happen that even the pride of hitting his mark hardly outlives the flight of the shaft.

(*Preface*, vol. ix. pp. viii-ix.

1841. THE DREAM OF THE TWO SISTERS.

From Dante

Nella ora, credo, che dell' oriente
Prima raggiò nel monte Citerea, etc.[2]
Dante, *Purg.* xxvii.

[1] In his *Convito* he praises very warmly some persons whom he had before abused. —See Foscolo, *Discorso sul Testo di Dante.* [As a matter of fact the reverse is the case, the *Convivio* having been written before the *Commedia.*]

[2] [Moore here prints *Purg.* xxvii. 94-108.]

'Twas eve's soft hour, and bright, above,
  The star of Beauty beam'd,
While lull'd by light so full of love,
  In slumber thus I dream'd—
Methought, at that sweet hour,
  A nymph came o'er the lea,
Who, gath'ring many a flow'r,
  Thus said and sung to me:—
'Should any ask what Leila loves,
  Say thou, to wreathe her hair
With flow'rets cull'd from glens and groves,
  Is Leila's only care.

'While thus in quest of flow'rets rare,
  O'er hill and dale I roam,
My sister, Rachel, far more fair,
  Sits lone and mute at home.
Before her glass untiring,
  With thoughts that never stray,
Her own bright eyes admiring,
  She sits the live-long day;
While I!—oh, seldom ev'n a look
  Of self salutes my eye;—
My only glass, the limpid brook,
  That shines and passes by.'

(*Poetical Works*, ed. 1841, vol. ix. pp. 411-12.)

1841. NEW HOSPITAL FOR SICK LITERATI.

[Dante's Ghosts]

* * * *

Falls, fractures, dangerous epic *fits*
(By some call'd *Cantos*), stabs from wits;
And, of all wounds for which they're nurst,
Dead cuts from publishers, the worst;—
All these, and other such fatalities,
That happen to frail immortalities,
By Tegg are so expertly treated,
That oft-times, when the cure's completed,
The patient's made robust enough
To stand a few more rounds of *puff*,
Till, like the ghosts of Dante's lay,
He's puff'd into thin air away!

(*Ibid.* vol. ix. p. 248.)

1842. DIARY.

[Moore's fame compared with that of Dante]

May 11. London. The best thing of the evening[1] (as far as *I* was concerned), occurred after the whole grand show was over. Irving and I came away together, and we had hardly got into the street, when a most pelting shower came on, and cabs and umbrellas were in requisition in all directions. As we were provided with neither, our plight was becoming serious, when a common cad ran up to me and said, 'Shall I get you a cab, Mr. Moore? Sure ain't *I* the man that patronizes your Melodies?' He then ran off in search of a vehicle, while Irving and I stood close up, like a pair of male caryatides, under the very narrow projection of a hall-door ledge, and thought at last that we were quite forgotten by my patron. But he came faithfully back, and, while putting me into the cab (without minding at all the trifle I gave him for his trouble) he said confidentially in my ear, 'Now, mind, whenever you want a cab, Misthur Moore, just call for Tim Flaherty, and I'm your man.' Now, this I call *fame*, and of a somewhat more agreeable kind than that of Dante, when the women in the street found him out by the marks of hell-fire on his beard (see Ginguené).

(*Memoirs*, etc. vol. vii. p. 321.)

ANONYMOUS

1806. May 25. BELL'S WEEKLY MESSENGER. CRITICISM UPON THE ROYAL ACADEMY EXHIBITION.

[Fuseli's picture of *Ugolino*[2]]

No. 19. COUNT UGOLINO, Chief of the Guelphs, at Pisa, locked up in the Torre della Fame, and starved to death. H. Fuseli, R.A.

Before we enter upon our examination of this Picture it will be necessary to ask a question—What are the requisites which the Critic would expect to find in a composition of this sort? What would he exact from the Artist; what would his taste approve; what would satisfy his judgment? He would expect, in the conception of the story, that which should distinguish it from all other subjects, and give it that peculiarity of character without which no work of the pencil can ever be rendered sufficiently decided to be original or lasting.—When we examine the above Picture by this

[1] [A dinner of the Literary Fund, at which Washington Irving was entertained.]
[2] [See vol. i. p. 427.]

rule, we cannot admit that the story is so told as to place it among those permanent compositions which preclude from success every effort upon a similar subject. In the character of Ugolino, under the peculiar misfortune of his imprisonment and overthrow, surrounded by his famished family, and in a situation which admitted no hope, we naturally expect to find the children looking to the father for assistance and consolation, who, incapable of affording them relief, but still expressing tenderness and compassion for them, has nothing left in his power but paternal affection and emotion. But in the present groupe, Ugolino has the appearance of a man who, having in a fit of phrenzy destroyed the young female who lies across his knees, has just returned to a sense of reason and remorse at the act which he has perpetrated. He has nothing of the character, either in action or passion, of a father who has lost a favourite child by famine. By this material error, that of the professed story, as it were, being not only imperfectly narrated, but absolutely untold, the artist has entirely lost the passion he must have intended to enforce; he has substituted horror for pathos, and depictured ferocity instead of sympathy.

The figure of the daughter, as thrown across the knees of the father, from the perpendicular hanging of the limbs in right angles with the position of the body, conveys more the idea of a drowned figure, just taken from the waters, than that of a female emaciated and contracted by famine. The sudden dropping of the limbs, likewise takes off from the length which the just proportions of the body require, and renders the drawing essentially imperfect. The body is too short; in fact there is scarcely any body at all; the whole figure is arms and legs. The scene of this Picture being cast in a dungeon, we of course expected to see a gloom pervading every part, but it should be remembered that there is a distinction always to be supported between the transparency of tints, though gloomy, and tints that are black and heavy; and we could have wished that this Picture did not partake so much of the last quality in point of the colour.[1]

(p. 167.)

LORD BYRON

(1788-1824)

[George Gordon Noel Byron, sixth Lord Byron, was born in London in 1788. On the death of his grand-uncle, the fifth Lord Byron, in 1798, he succeeded to the title, and was placed under the guardianship of his relative, the fifth Earl of Carlisle.[2]

[1] [For a protest by Blake against this criticism, see vol. i. p. 456.]
[2] [See vol. i. pp. 333 ff.]

He was educated at Harrow (1801-5), and Trinity College, Cambridge (1805-6, 1807-8, M.A. 1808). In 1807 he published *Hours of Idleness*, which was severely handled in the *Edinburgh Review* for Jan. 1808; in reply he issued *English Bards and Scotch Reviewers* (1809). In 1812 he published the first two cantos of *Childe Harold*, the immediate success of which was such that 'he woke one morning and found himself famous.' In 1815 he married Miss Milbanke, who left him a year later, upon which Byron, after signing a deed of separation, quitted England never to return. In 1819 he made the acquaintance of the Countess Guiccioli at Venice, with whom he lived at Venice, Pisa, and Genoa, until 1823, in the summer of which year he joined the Greek insurgents. He died of fever at Missolonghi in the following April.

Byron's knowledge of Dante dates from his Harrow days, but it was not till after he took up his residence in Italy (1817) that he became in any real sense acquainted with Dante's works. Besides frequent mentions in his letters and journals, there are references to Dante in many of his poems, viz. in the *Corsair* (1814); *Childe Harold*, Canto iv. (1818); *Don Juan*, Cantos i. and ii. (1819), Cantos iii. and iv. (1821), Cantos vi., vii., and x. (1823), and Canto xvi. (1824); and in the *Age of Bronze* (1823). In 1820 he translated the episode of Paolo and Francesca in *terza rima*, and in the following year he published the *Prophecy of Dante* in the same metre.[1] It has been suggested that Byron was indebted to Dante's account of Ugolino's imprisonment (*Inf.* xxxiii.) in the *Prisoner of Chillon* (1816).[2] Shelley remarked to Medwin[3] that Byron had evidently deeply studied Dante's description, and perhaps but for it would never have written the *Prisoner of Chillon;* while Sir Walter Scott in the *Quarterly Review*[4] institutes a comparison between the two; but the resemblances such as they are, are too slight to justify the inference. On the other hand Byron seems to have been consciously or unconsciously indebted to Chaucer's rendering of the Ugolino episode, for one of his lines, 'To see such bird in such a nest,' sounds like an echo of Chaucer's 'Swiche birddes for to putte in swich a cage.'[5]]

1806. Aug. 9. LETTER TO JOHN M. B. PIGOT (from Piccadilly).

[Byron invokes 'the shade of Dante']

YOU, with the rest of your family, merit my warmest thanks for your kind connivance at my escape from 'Mrs. Byron *furiosa*.'[6] Oh! for the pen of Ariosto to rehearse, in epic, the scolding of that momentous eve,—or rather, let me invoke the shade of Dante to inspire me, for none but the author of the Inferno could properly preside over such an attempt.

(*Letters and Journals of Lord Byron*, ed. Prothero, 1898, vol. i. p. 101.[7])

1813. Nov. 25. JOURNAL.

[Dante among those excepted from the 'idle brood' of writers]

Who would write, who had anything better to do? 'Action—action—action'—said Demosthenes: 'Actions—actions,' I say,

[1] [See *Introduction*, pp. xlii.-iii.]

[2] [The influence of Dante on Byron has been greatly exaggerated by some writers—see, for instance, A. Dobelli: *Dante e Byron* (in *Giornale Dantesco*, vi. 145-63.]

[3] [See below, p. 388.]

[4] [See vol. i. p. 444.]

[5] [See also Giulio Monti, *Studi Critici*, pp. 129-55.]

[6] [This letter was written after a quarrel of Byron with his mother, from whom, with the connivance of the Pigots, he had escaped to London.]

[7] [Copyright matter included in this edition is reproduced by kind permission of Mr. John Murray.]

and not writing,—least of all, rhyme. Look at the querulous and monotonous lives of the 'genus';—except Cervantes, Tasso, Dante, Ariosto, Kleist (who were brave and active citizens), Aeschylus, Sophocles, and some other of the antiques also—what a worthless, idle brood it is!

(*Letters and Journals of Lord Byron*, ed. Prothero, 1898, vol. ii. p. 345.)

1814. THE CORSAIR:—MOTTOES FROM DANTE.

[*Inf.* v. 121-3]

'—nessun maggior dolore
Che ricordarsi del tempo felice
Nella miseria,—'

(*Canto* i.)

[*Inf.* v. 120]

'Conosceste i dubbiosi desiri?'

(*Canto* ii.)

[*Inf.* v. 105]

'Come vedi—ancor non m' abbandona.'

(*Canto* iii.)

1818. CHILDE HAROLD'S PILGRIMAGE—CANTO THE FOURTH.

[The Poet's wreath worn by Dante]

Ferrara! in thy wide and grass-grown streets,
Whose symmetry was not for solitude,
There seems as 't were a curse upon the seats
Of former sovereigns, and the antique brood
Of Este, which for many an age made good
Its strength within thy walls, and was of yore
Patron or tyrant, as the changing mood
Of petty power impell'd, of those who wore
The wreath which Dante's brow alone had worn before.

(*Stanza* xxxv.)

[Dante, 'the Bard of Hell']

Great as thou[1] art, yet parallel'd by those,
Thy countrymen, before thee born to shine,
The Bards of Hell and Chivalry: first rose
The Tuscan father's comedy divine;
Then, not unequal to the Florentine,

[1] [He is addressing Tasso.]

The Southern Scott, the minstrel who call'd forth
A new creation with his magic line,
And, like the Ariosto of the North,
Sang ladye-love and war, romance and knightly worth.

(*Stanza* xl.)

[Dante, Petrarch, Boccaccio—'the all Etruscan three']

In Santa Croce's holy precincts lie
Ashes which make it holier, dust which is
Even itself an immortality,
Though there were nothing save the past, and this,
The particle of those sublimities,
Which have relapsed to chaos: here repose
Angelo's, Alfieri's bones, and his,
The starry Galileo, with his woes;
Here Machiavelli's earth return'd to whence it rose.

These are four minds, which, like the elements,
Might furnish forth creation:—Italy!
Time, which hath wrong'd thee with ten thousand rents
Of thine imperial garment, shall deny,
And hath denied, to every other sky,
Spirits which soar from ruin: thy decay
Is still impregnate with divinity,
Which gilds it with revivifying ray;
Such as the great of yore, Canova is to-day.

But where repose the all Etruscan three—
Dante, and Petrarch, and, scarce less than they,
The Bard of Prose, creative spirit! he
Of the Hundred Tales of love—where did they lay
Their bones, distinguish'd from our common clay
In death as life? Are they resolved to dust,
And have their country's marbles nought to say?
Could not her quarries furnish forth one bust?
Did they not to her breast their filial earth entrust?

Ungrateful Florence! Dante sleeps afar,
Like Scipio, buried by the upbraiding shore:
Thy factions, in their worse than civil war,
Proscribed the bard whose name for evermore
Their children's children would in vain adore
With the remorse of ages; and the crown
Which Petrarch's laureate brow supremely wore,
Upon a far and foreign soil had grown,
His life, his fame, his grave, though rifled—not thine own.

Boccaccio to his parent earth bequeath'd
His dust,—and lies it not her great among,
With many a sweet and solemn requiem breathed
O'er him who form'd the Tuscan's siren tongue?
That music in itself, whose sounds are song,
The poetry of speech? No;—even his tomb
Uptorn, must bear the hyaena bigot's wrong,
No more amidst the meaner dead find room,
Nor claim a passing sigh, because it told for *whom!*

And Santa Croce wants their mighty dust;
Yet for this want more noted, as of yore
The Caesar's pageant, shorn of Brutus' bust,
Did but of Rome's best Son remind her more:
Happier Ravenna! on thy hoary shore,
Fortress of falling empire! honour'd sleeps
The immortal exile;—Arqua, too, her store
Of tuneful relics proudly claims and keeps,
While Florence vainly begs her banish'd dead and weeps.

(*Stanzas* liv-lix.)

1819. DON JUAN. CANTO THE FIRST.

[Reminiscence of Dante]

. . . well fenced
In mail of proof—her purity of soul,[1]
She, for the future of her strength convinced,
And that her honour was a rock, or mole,
Exceeding sagely from that hour dispensed
With any kind of troublesome control. . . .

(*Stanza* lxxxii.)

1819. DON JUAN. CANTO THE SECOND.

[Pedrillo and Ugolino contrasted]

Of poor Pedrillo something still remain'd,
But was used sparingly,—some were afraid,
And others still their appetites constrain'd,
Or but at times a little supper made . . .

* * * *

[1] 'Coscienza l' assicura,
La buona compagna che l' uom francheggia
Sotto l' usbergo dell' esser puro.'—Dante.
[*Inf.* xxviii. 115-17—misquoted.]

And if Pedrillo's fate should shocking be,
  Remember Ugolino[1] condescends
To eat the head of his arch-enemy
  The moment after he politely ends
His tale: if foes be food in hell, at sea
  'Tis surely fair to dine upon our friends,
When shipwreck's short allowance grows too scanty,
Without being much more horrible than Dante.

(*Stanzas* lxxxii-lxxxiii.)

1819. Oct. 29. LETTER TO JOHN MURRAY (from Venice).

['The Prophecy of Dante']

I had written about a hundred stanzas of a *third* Canto to *Don Juan*, but the reception of the two first is no encouragement to you nor me to proceed.

I had also written about 600 lines of a poem, the *Vision* (or *Prophecy*) *of Dante*, the subject a view of Italy in the ages down to the present—supposing Dante to speak in his own person, previous to his death, and embracing all topics in the way of prophecy, like Lycophron's *Cassandra*.[2] But this and the other are both at a standstill for the present.

(*Letters and Journals*, vol. iv. p. 368.)

1820. Feb. 19. LETTER TO WILLIAM BANKES (from Ravenna).

[Dante's tomb at Ravenna]

I have room for you in the house here, as I had in Venice, if you think fit to make use of it. . . . I forget whether you admire or tolerate red hair, so that I rather dread showing you all that I have about me and around me in this city. Come, nevertheless,—you can pay Dante[3] a morning visit, and I will undertake that Theodore and Honoria[4] will be most happy to see you in the forest hard by.

(*Ibid.* vol. iv. pp. 403-4.)

[1] Quando ebbe detto ciò, con gli occhi torti
Riprese il teschio misero co' denti
Che furo all' osso, come d' un can forti.
[*Inf.* xxxiii. 76-8.]

[2] [The *Cassandra* of Lycophron (grammarian and poet of Alexandria, in the third century B.C.) consists of prophecies of events in Greek history.]

[3] [Dante's tomb at Ravenna.]

[4] [A reference to Dryden's poem *Theodore and Honoria*, which is based on one of the stories in the *Decameron* (Giorn. v. Nov. 8).]

1820. Feb. 21. LETTER TO JOHN MURRAY (from Ravenna).

['The Prophecy of Dante']

You enquire after 'Dante's prophecy': I have not done more than six hundred lines, but will vaticinate at leisure.

(*Letters and Journals*, vol. iv. p. 409.)

1820. Feb. 26. LETTER TO WILLIAM BANKES (from Ravenna).

[Commentaries on Dante at Ravenna]

There are some curious commentaries on Dante preserved here, which you should see.[1]

(*Ibid.* vol. iv. p. 412.)

1820. March 14. LETTER TO JOHN MURRAY (from Ravenna).

['The Prophecy of Dante']

Enclosed is *Dante's Prophecy—Vision*—or what not . . . the preface will explain all that is explicable. These are but the four first cantos: if approved, I will go on like Isaiah. Pray mind in printing; and let some good Italian scholar correct the Italian quotations.

(*Ibid.* vol. iv. p. 418.)

1820. March 15. SOME OBSERVATIONS UPON AN ARTICLE IN BLACKWOOD'S MAGAZINE.[2]

[The contemporary fame of Dante, Petrarch, and Ariosto]

I will not go so far as Wordsworth, . . . who pretends that *no* great poet ever had immediate fame; which being interpreted, means that William Wordsworth is not quite so much read by his contemporaries as might be desirable. This assertion is as false as it is foolish. . . . Dante, Petrarch, Ariosto, and Tasso, were all the darlings of the contemporary reader. Dante's Poem was celebrated long before his death: and, not long after it, States negotiated for his ashes, and disputed for the sites of the composition of the *Divina Commedia*. Petrarch was crowned in the Capitol. Ariosto was permitted to pass free by the public robber who had read the *Orlando Furioso*. I would not recommend Mr. Wordsworth to try the same experiment with his *Smugglers*. Tasso, notwithstanding the criticisms of the Cruscanti, would have been crowned

[1] [Colomb de Batines registers two MSS. of the *Divina Commedia* in the Biblioteca Classense at Ravenna, and a copy of the Latin commentary of Benvenuto da Imola (*Bibliografia Dantesca*, ii. 218-19, 309).]

[2] [No. xxix. August, 1819: addressed to I. D'Israeli, Esq. from Ravenna.]

in the Capitol, but for his death. . . . I am aware that Johnson has said, after some hesitation, that he could not 'prevail upon himself to wish that Milton had been a rhymer.' The opinions of that truly great man, whom it is also the present fashion to decry, will ever be received by me with that deference which time will restore to him from all; but, with all humility, I am not persuaded that the *Paradise Lost* would not have been more nobly conveyed to posterity, not perhaps in heroic couplets, although even *they* could sustain the subject if well balanced, but in the stanza of Spenser or of Tasso, or in the terza rima of Dante, which the powers of Milton could easily have grafted on our language.

(*Letters and Journals*, vol. iv. pp. 487, 490-1.)

1820. March 20. LETTER TO JOHN MURRAY (from Ravenna).

[Byron's translation of 'Fanny of Rimini']

Last post I sent you *The Vision of Dante*,[1]—four first cantos. Enclosed you will find, *line for line*, in *third rhyme* (*terza rima*), of which your British Blackguard reader as yet understands nothing, Fanny of Rimini. You know that she was born here, and married, and slain, from Cary, Boyd, and such people already. I have done it into *cramp* English, line for line, and rhyme for rhyme, to try the possibility. You had best append it to the poems already sent by last three posts. . . . If this is published,[2] publish it *with the original*, and *together* with the *Pulci* translation, *or* the *Dante Imitation*.

Francesca of Rimini

Translation from the Inferno of Dante, Canto 5th

'The Land where I was born sits by the Seas,
  Upon that shore to which the Po descends,
  With all his followers, in search of peace.
Love, which the gentle heart soon apprehends,
  Seized him for the fair person which was ta'en
  From me, and me even yet the mode offends.
Love, who to none beloved to love again
  Remits, seized me with wish to please, so strong,
  That, as thou see'st, yet, yet it doth remain.
Love to one death conducted us along,
  But Caina waits for him our life who ended:'
These were the accents utter'd by her tongue.—

[1] [Published, under the title of the *Prophecy of Dante*, in 1821.]
[2] [It was not published till 1830.]

Since I first listened to these Souls offended,
 I bow'd my visage and so kept it till—
 'What think'st thou?' said the bard; when I unbended,[1]
And recommenced: 'Alas! unto such ill
 How many sweet thoughts, what strong extacies
 Led these their evil fortune to fulfill!'
And then I turned unto their side my eyes,
 And said, 'Francesca, thy sad destinies
 Have made me sorrow till the tears arise.
But tell me, in the Season of sweet sighs,
 By what and how thy Love to Passion rose,
 So as his dim desires to recognise?'
Then she to me: 'The greatest of all woes
 Is to remind us of[2] our happy days
 In misery, and that[3] thy teacher knows.
But if to learn our passion's first root preys
 Upon thy spirit with such Sympathy,
 I will do even[4] as he who weeps and says.—
We read one day for pastime, seated nigh,
 Of Lancilot, how love enchained him too.
 We were alone, quite unsuspiciously,
But oft our eyes met, and our Cheeks in hue
 All o'er discolour'd by that reading were;
 But one point only wholly us o'erthrew;[5]
When we read the long-sighed-for[6] smile of her,
 To be thus kist by such devoted[7] lover,
 He, who from me can be divided ne'er,
Kissed my mouth, trembling in the act all over.
 Accursed was the book and he who wrote!
 That day no further leaf we did uncover.—
While thus one Spirit told us of their lot,
 The other wept so, that with pity's thralls
 I swoon'd as if by death I had been smote,
And fell down even as a dead body falls.[8]

(*Letters and Journals*, vol. iv. pp. 419-21.)

1820. March 23. LETTER TO JOHN MURRAY (from Ravenna).

[The 'Prophecy of Dante' and 'Francesca da Rimini']

Besides the four packets you have already received, I have sent . . . the four first Cantos of Dante's prophecy (the best thing I ever

[1] Alternative reading: *then I unbended.*
[2] Or, *recall to mind.*
[3] Or, *and this.*
[4] Or, *relate.* In a note Byron says: 'In some editions it is *diro*, in others *faro* —an essential difference between 'saying' and 'doing,' which I know not how to decide. Ask Foscolo. The d—d editions drive me mad.'
[5] Or, *wholly overthrew.*
[6] Or, *desired.*
[7] Or, *such a fervent.*
[8] [*Inf.* v. 97-142.]

wrote, if it be not *unintelligible*), and by last post a *literal* translation, word for word (versed like the original), of the episode of Francesca of Rimini.

(*Letters and Journals*, vol. iv. pp. 421-2.)

1820. April 3. LETTER TO LADY BYRON (from Ravenna).

[Byron's application of Dante's 'fiera moglie']

I received yesterday your answer dated March 10. My offer[1] was an honest one, and surely could be only construed as such even by the most malignant casuistry. . . . To the mysterious menace of the last sentence[2]—whatever its import may be—and I really cannot pretend to unriddle it,—I could hardly be very sensible, even if I understood it, as, before it could take place, I shall be where 'nothing can touch him farther.'[3] I advise you, however, to anticipate the period of your intention; for be assured no power of figures can avail beyond the present; and, if it could, I would answer with the Florentine—[4]

'Ed io, che posto son con loro in croce,
e certo
La *fiera moglie*, più ch' altro, mi nuoce.'

(*Ibid.* vol. v. pp. 1-2.)

1820. April 9. LETTER TO JOHN MURRAY (from Ravenna).

[Byron's 'Danticles']

In the name of all the devils in—the printing office, why don't you write to acknowledge the receipt of the second, third, and fourth packets, viz. the Pulci—translation and original, the *Danticles*, etc.? . . . Have you gotten the cream of translations, Francesca of Rimini, from the *Inferno?* Why, I have sent you a warehouse of trash within the last month, and you have no sort of feeling about you: a pastry-cook would have had twice the gratitude, and thanked me at least for the quantity.

(*Ibid.* vol. v. pp. 5-6.)

1820. May 24. LETTER TO THOMAS MOORE (from Ravenna).

['The Prophecy of Dante' and 'Francesca da Rimini]

Murray has four or five things of mine in hand—the new *Don Juan*, which his back-shop synod don't admire:—a translation of

[1] [Of a perusal of a memoir of his life.]

[2] 'For my own sake, I have no reason to shrink from publication; but, notwithstanding the injuries which I have suffered, I should lament some of the *consequences*.'

[3] *Macbeth*, Act III. Sc. 2.

[4] [These words are placed by Dante (*Inf.* xvi. 43-5) in the mouth of Jacopo Rusticucci, who owed his place in Hell to the savage temper of his wife.]

the first canto of Pulci's *Morgante Maggiore*, excellent; a short ditto from Dante, not so much approved; the *Prophecy of Dante*, very grand and worthy, etc., etc., etc.

(*Letters and Journals*, vol. v. p. 32-3.)

1820. Aug. 17. LETTER TO JOHN MURRAY (from Ravenna).

[The time ripe for the publication of his Dante poems]

The time for the *Dante* would be good now (did not her Majesty[1] occupy all nonsense), as Italy is on the eve of great things.

(*Ibid.* vol. v. p. 65.)

1820. Aug 31. LETTER TO THOMAS MOORE (from Ravenna).

[Byrons 'mezzo cammin']

D—n your *mezzo cammin*—[2] you shall say 'the prime of life,' a much more consolatory phrase. Besides it is not correct. I was born in 1788, and consequently am but thirty-two.

(*Ibid.* vol. v. p. 70.)

1820. Dec. 22. LETTER TO FRANCIS HODGSON (from Ravenna).

[Dante's tomb at Ravenna]

We have here the sepulchre of Dante and the forest of Dryden and Boccaccio,[3] all in very poetical preservation.

(*Ibid.* vol. v. p. 140.)

1821. DON JUAN. CANTO THE THIRD.

[Dante and Milton on marriage]

The only two that in my recollection
Have sung of heaven and hell, or marriage, are
Dante[4] and Milton, and of both the affection
Was hapless in their nuptials, for some bar
Of fault or temper ruin'd the connexion
(Such things, in fact, it don't ask much to mar);
But Dante's Beatrice and Milton's Eve
Were not drawn from their spouses, you conceive.

[1] [Queen Caroline.]

[2] 'I had congratulated him upon arriving at what Dante calls the *mezzo cammin* of life, the age of thirty-three' (Moore). [The age indicated by Dante is not thirty-three, but thirty-five, the half of three-score and ten.]

[3] [See note to letter of Feb. 19, 1820.]

[4] Dante calls his wife, in the *Inferno*, 'la fiera moglie.' [This is an error: the term is used by Dante (*Inf.* xvi. 45) not of his own wife, but of the wife of Jacopo Rusticucci.]

Some persons say that Dante meant theology
  By Beatrice, and not a mistress—I,
Although my opinion may require apology,
  Deem this a commentator's phantasy,
Unless indeed it was from his own knowledge he
  Decided thus, and show'd good reason why;
I think that Dante's more abstruse ecstatics
Meant to personify the mathematics.

(*Stanzas* x-xi.)

[*Purgatorio* viii. 1-6]

Soft hour! which wakes the wish and melts the heart
  Of those who sail the seas, on the first day
When they from their sweet friends are torn apart;
  Or fills with love the pilgrim on his way
As the far bell of vesper makes him start,
  Seeming to weep the dying day's decay;[1]
Is this a fancy which our reason scorns?
Ah! surely nothing dies but something mourns!

(*Stanza* cviii.)

1821. DON JUAN. CANTO THE FOURTH.

[Dante's tomb at Ravenna]

I canter by the spot each afternoon
  Where perish'd in his fame the hero-boy,
Who liv'd too long for men, but died too soon
  For human vanity, the young De Foix!
A broken pillar, not uncouthly hewn,
  But which neglect is hastening to destroy,
Records Ravenna's carnage on its face,
While weeds and ordure rankle round the base.

I pass each day, where Dante's bones are laid:
  A little cupola, more neat than solemn,
Protects his dust, but reverence here is paid
  To the bard's tomb, and not the warrior's column:

[1] 'Era già l' ora che volge 'l disio,
  A' naviganti, e 'ntenerisce il cuore,
Lo dì ch' han detto a' dolci amici a dio;
  E che lo nuovo peregrin d' amore
Punge, se ode squilla di lontano,
  Che paia 'l giorno pianger che si muore.'
Dante's *Purgatory*, canto viii.

This last line is the first of Gray's Elegy, taken by him without acknowledgment. [Not 'without acknowledgment,' Gray admitted that he had borrowed the line from Dante; see vol. i., p. 234.]

The time must come, when both alike decay'd,
  The chieftain's trophy, and the poet's volume,
Will sink where lie the songs and wars of earth,
Before Pelides' death, or Homer's birth.

With human blood that column was cemented,
  With human filth that column is defiled,
As if the peasant's coarse contempt were vented
  To show his loathing of the spot he soil'd:
Thus is the trophy used, and thus lamented
  Should ever be those blood-hounds, from whose wild
Instinct of gore and glory earth has known
Those sufferings Dante saw in hell alone.

(*Stanzas* ciii-v.)

1821. THE PROPHECY OF DANTE.[1]

Dedication[2]

Lady! if for the cold and cloudy clime,
  Where I was born, but where I would not die,
  Of the great Poet-Sire of Italy
I dare to build the imitative rhyme,[3]
Harsh Runic copy of the South's sublime,
  Thou art the cause; and howsoever I
  Fall short of his immortal harmony,
Thy gentle heart will pardon me the crime. . . .

Preface

In the course of a visit to the city of Ravenna in the summer of 1819, it was suggested to the author that having composed something on the subject of Tasso's confinement, he should do the same on Dante's exile,—the tomb of the poet forming one of the principal objects of interest in that city, both to the native and to the stranger.

'On this hint I spake,' and the result has been the following four cantos, in terza rima, now offered to the reader. . . . The reader is requested to suppose that Dante addresses him in the interval between the conclusion of the Divina Commedia and his death, and shortly before the latter event, foretelling the fortunes of Italy in general in the ensuing centuries. . . . The measure adopted is the

[1] [Written in 1819, but not published until 1821.]
[2] [To the Countess Guiccioli.]
[3] [The poem is in *terza rima*.]

terza rima of Dante, which I am not aware to have seen hitherto tried in our language, except it may be by Mr. Hayley,[1] of whose translation I never saw but one extract, quoted in the notes to Caliph Vathek;[2] so that—if I do not err—this poem may be considered as a metrical experiment. The cantos are short, and about the same length as those of the poet, whose name I have borrowed, and most probably taken in vain. . . . I would request the Italian reader to remember that where I have failed in the imitation of his great 'Padre Alighier,' I have failed in imitating that which all study and few understand, since to this very day it is not yet settled what was the meaning of the allegory in the first canto of the Inferno. . . .

Canto the First

Oh Beatrice! . . . without thy light
My paradise had still been incomplete.[3]

(ll. 26-7.)

I would have had my Florence great and free;[4]
Oh Florence! Florence! unto me thou wast
Like that Jerusalem which the Almighty He
Wept over. . . .

(ll. 59-62.)

Against the breast that cherish'd thee was stirr'd
Thy venom, and my state thou didst amerce,
And doom this body forfeit to the fire.[5]

(ll. 66-8.)

[1] [See vol. i., pp. 359 ff.]

[2] [See vol. i., p. 439.]

[3] 'Che sol per le belle opre
Che fanno in Cielo il sole e l' altre stelle
Dentro di lui *si crede il Paradiso,*
Così se guardi fiso
Pensar ben dèi ch' ogni terren' piacere
[Si trova in lei.]'

Canzone, in which Dante describes the person of Beatrice, Strophe third.

[This canzone, which begins 'Io miro i crespi e gli biondi capegli,' was formerly attributed to Dante.]

[4] 'L' Esilio che m' è dato onor mi tegno
* * * *
Cader tra' buoni è pur di lode degno.'

Sonnet of Dante,

in which he represents Right, Generosity, and Temperance as banished from among men, and seeking refuge from Love, who inhabits his bosom. [This sonnet, like the canzone quoted above, is not by Dante.]

[5] 'Ut si quis predictorum ullo tempore in fortiam dicti communis pervenerit, *talis perveniens igne comburatur, sic quod moriatur.*' Second sentence of Florence against Dante, and the fourteen accused with him. The Latin is worthy of the sentence.

Canto the Fourth

The stream of his[1] great thoughts shall spring from me,[2]
The Ghibelline, who traversed the three realms
Which form the empire of eternity.

(ll. 67-9.)

Florence! when this lone spirit shall return
To kindred spirits, thou wilt feel my worth,
And seek to honour with an empty urn
The ashes thou shalt ne'er obtain—Alas!
'What have I done to thee, my people?'[3]

(ll. 134-8.)

1821. Jan. 8. JOURNAL (at Ravenna).

[Print of the Ugolino]

Mem.—received to-day a print, or etching, of the story of Ugolino, by an Italian painter—different, of course, from Sir Joshua Reynolds's,[4] and I think (as far as recollection goes) *no worse*, for Reynolds is not good in history.

(*Letters and Journals*, vol. v. p. 160.)

1821. Jan. 29. JOURNAL (at Ravenna).

[Schlegel on Dante—the 'gentleness' of Dante]

Read Schlegel.[5] Of Dante he says, 'that at no time has the greatest and most national of all Italian poets ever been much the favourite of his countrymen.' 'Tis false! There have been more editors and commentators (and imitators, ultimately) of Dante than of all their poets put together. *Not* a favourite! Why, they talk Dante—write Dante—and think and dream Dante at this moment (1821) to an excess, which would be ridiculous, but that he deserves it. In the same style this German talks of gondolas on the Arno—a precious fellow to dare to speak of Italy! He says also that Dante's chief defect is a want, in a

[1] [Michael Angelo.]

[2] I have read somewhere (if I do not err, for I cannot recollect where), that Dante was so great a favourite of Michael Angelo's, that he had designed the whole of the Divina Commedia: but that the volume containing these studies was lost by sea. [No doubt Byron read this in Duppa's life of Michael Angelo (published in 1806), in which the incident is related (see above, p. 8).]

[3] "E scrisse più volte non solamente a particolari cittadini del reggimento, ma ancora al popolo, e intra l' altre una Epistola assai lunga che comincia: '*Popule mi, quid feci tibi?*'"—Vita di Dante scritta da Lionardo Aretino.

[4] [See vol. i., p. 343.]

[5] [Frederick Schlegel's *Lectures on the History of Literature*, translated by Lockhart in 1818 (see below, pp. 276-8).]

word, of gentle feelings. Of gentle feelings!—and Francesca of Rimini—and the father's feelings in Ugolino—and Beatrice—and 'La Pia'! Why, there is gentleness in Dante beyond all gentleness, when he is tender. It is true that, treating of the Christian Hades, or Hell, there is not much scope or site for gentleness—but who *but* Dante could have introduced any 'gentleness' at all into *Hell?* Is there any in Milton's? No—and Dante's Heaven is all love, and glory and majesty.

(*Letters and Journals,* vol. v. pp. 193-4.)

1821. Feb. 7. LETTER TO [JOHN MURRAY] ESQ. ON THE REV. W. L. BOWLES'S STRICTURES ON THE LIFE AND WRITINGS OF POPE (from Ravenna).

[Dante, Petrarch, Ariosto, Tasso, and Alfieri, the five great poets of Italy]

The Italians, with the most poetical language, and the most fastidious taste in Europe, possess now five *great* poets, they say, Dante, Petrarch, Ariosto, Tasso, and, lastly, Alfieri;[1] and whom do they esteem one of the highest of these, and some of them the very highest? Petrarch the *sonneteer*. . . . Were Petrarch to be ranked according to the 'order' of his compositions, where would the best of sonnets place him? with Dante and the other? no. . . . Religion does not make a part of my subject; it is something beyond human powers, and has failed in all human hands except Milton's and Dante's, and even Dante's powers are involved in his delineation of human passions, though in supernatural circumstances.

(*Ibid.* vol. v. pp. 553-4.)

1821. Feb. 20. JOURNAL (at Ravenna).

[Dante and Guido Cavalcanti]

The *Americani* (a patriotic society here, an under branch of the *Carbonari*) give a dinner in *the Forest* in a few days, and

[1] Of these there is one ranked with the others for his Sonnets, and *two* for compositions which belong to *no class* at all. Where is Dante? His poem is not an *epic;* then what is it? He himself calls it a 'divine comedy'; and why? This is more than all his thousand commentators have been able to explain. . . . Poets are classed by the power of their performance, and not according to its rank in a gradus. In the contrary case, the forgotten epic poets of all countries would rank above Petrarch, Dante, Ariosto, Burns, Gray, Dryden, and the highest names of various countries. . . . So far are the principles of poetry from being '*invariable,*' that they never were nor ever will be settled. These 'principles' mean nothing more than the predilections of a particular age; and every age has its own, and a different from its predecessor. It is now Homer, and now Virgil: once Dryden, and since Walter Scott; now Corneille, and now Racine; now Crebillon, now Voltaire. The Homerists and Virgilians in France disputed for half a century. Not fifty years ago the Italians neglected Dante—Bettinelli reproved Monti for reading 'that barbarian'; at present they adore him.

have invited me, as one of the C[i]. It is to be in *the Forest* of Boccacio's and Dryden's 'Hunstman's Ghost'; and, even if I had not the same political feelings (to say nothing of my old convivial turn, which every now and then revives), I would go as a poet, or, at least, as a lover of poetry. I shall expect to see the spectre of 'Ostasio degli Onesti'[1] (Dryden has turned him into Guido Cavalcanti—an essentially different person, as may be found in Dante) come 'thundering for his prey in the midst of the festival.' At any rate, whether he does or no, I will get as tipsy and patriotic as possible.

(*Letters and Journals*, vol. v. pp. 206-7.)

1821. March 25. A SECOND LETTER TO JOHN MURRAY, ESQ., ON THE REV. W. L. BOWLES'S STRICTURES ON THE LIFE AND WRITINGS OF POPE (from Ravenna).

[Shakespeare, Pope, Burns, Dante and Alfieri]

Far be it from me to presume that there ever was, or can be, such a thing as an *aristocracy* of *poets*; but there *is* a nobility of thought and of style, open to all stations, and derived partly from talent, and partly from education,—which is to be found in Shakespeare, and Pope, and Burns, no less than in Dante and Alfieri.

(*Ibid.* vol. v. p. 591.)

1821. May 31. LETTER TO RICHARD BELGRAVE HOPPNER (from Ravenna).

['The Prophecy of Dante']

What you say of the *Dante*[2] is the first I have heard of it— . . . Continue it!—Alas! what could Dante himself *now* prophesy about Italy? I am glad you like it, however, but doubt that you will be singular in your opinion.

(*Ibid.* vol. v. p. 302.)

1821. Nov. 16. LETTER TO THOMAS MOORE (from Pisa).

[Taaffe's commentary on Dante]

There is here Mr. Taaffe, an Irish genius, with whom we are acquainted. He hath written a really *excellent* Commentary on Dante, full of new and true information, and much ingenuity. But his verse is such as it hath pleased God to endue him withal.

[1] [Not Ostasio degli Onesti, but Guido degli Anastagi. The story is told in Boccaccio's *Decameron* (Giorn. v. Nov. 8) and in Dryden's *Theodore and Honoria.*]

[2] [His poem, the *Prophecy of Dante*, published in the previous month.]

Nevertheless, he is so firmly persuaded of its equal excellence, that he won't divorce the Commentary from the traduction, as I ventured delicately to hint. . . . But he is eager to publish all, and must be gratified, though the reviewers will make him suffer more tortures than there are in his original. Indeed, the *Notes* are well worth publication; but he insists upon the translation for company. . . . He is really a good fellow, apparently, and I daresay that his verse is very good Irish. Now, what shall we do for him? He says that he will risk part of the expense with the publisher. He will never rest till he is published and abused—for he has a high opinion of himself—and I see nothing left but to gratify him, so as to have him abused as little as possible; for I think it would kill him. You must write, then, to Jeffrey to beg him *not* to review him, and I will do the same to Gifford, through Murray. Perhaps they might notice the Comment without touching the text. But I doubt the dogs—the text is too tempting.[1]

(*Letters and Journals*, vol. v. pp. 475-6.)

1821. Dec. 4. LETTER TO JOHN MURRAY (from Pisa).

[Ugolino and the Lanfranchi]

I have got here into a famous old feudal palazzo, on the Arno, large enough for a garrison, with dungeons below and cells in the walls. . . . The house belonged to the Lanfranchi family (the same mentioned by Ugolino in his dream,[2] as his persecutor with Sismondi), and has had a fierce owner or two in its time.

(*Ibid.* vol. v. pp. 486-7.)

1821-22. CONVERSATIONS OF BYRON WITH MEDWIN AT PISA.[3]

[Ugolino and the Lanfranchi]

1821. 20th November. 'This is the Lung Arno: he [Byron] has hired the Lanfranchi palace for a year. It is one of those marble piles that seem built for eternity, whilst the family whose name it bears no longer exists,' said Shelley, as we entered a hall

[1] [Volume I (and no more) of Taaffe's *Comment on the Divine Comedy of Dante*, printed in Italy from the types of Didot, was published in London by Murray, without the author's name, in 1822. Shelley also interested himself in the work, and wrote to Ollier recommending it to him for publication (see Shelley's letter to Ollier below, pp. 223-4). For extracts from Taaffe's preface, and specimens of his translation, see below, pp. 341-4. For further remarks of Byron on the subject, see the extracts from Medwin's *Conversations of Lord Byron*, below, pp. 51-2.]

[2] [*Inf.* xxxiii. 32. For Shelley's account of the Lanfranchi palazzo, see below.]

[3] [From Medwin's *Journal of the Conversations of Lord Byron: Noted during a residence with his Lordship at Pisa, in the years* 1821 *and* 1822 (published in 1824). Other remarks of Byron on Dante are recorded by Medwin in his *Life of Shelley* (see below, pp. 385-90).]

that seemed built for giants. 'I remember the lines in the Inferno,' said I: 'a Lanfranchi was one of the persecutors of Ugolino.' 'The same,' answered Shelley; 'you will see a picture of Ugolino and his sons in his room. Fletcher, his valet, is as superstitious as his master, and says the house is haunted, so that he cannot sleep for rumbling noises overhead, which he compares to the rolling of bowls. No wonder; old Lanfranchi's ghost is unquiet, and walks at night.'

(*Medwin*, pp. 10-11.)

[Francesca da Rimini and Dante at Ravenna]

'The climate of Ravenna is delightful. I was unbroken in upon by society. It lies out of the way of travellers. I was never tired of my rides in the pine-forest: it breathes of the Decameron; it is poetical ground. Francesca lived, and Dante was exiled and died at Ravenna. There is something inspiring in such an air.'

(pp. 30-1.)

[Quotation from Dante in his letter to Lady Byron]

'A very full account of my marriage and separation is contained in my Memoirs. After they were completed, I wrote to Lady Byron, proposing to send them for her inspection, in order that any mistatements or inaccuracy . . . might be pointed out and corrected. In her answer she declined the offer, without assigning any reason; but desiring, if not on her account, for the sake of her daughter, that they might never appear, and finishing with a threat. My reply was the severest thing I ever wrote, and contained two quotations, one from Shakspeare, and another from Dante.'[1]

(pp. 35-6.)

[Dante and Beatrice]

'I never wrote anything worth mentioning till I was in love. Dante dates his passion for Beatrice at twelve.[2] I was almost as young when I fell over head and ears in love.'

(pp. 57-8.)

[Byron compares himself with Petrarch and Dante]

'For a man to become a poet (witness Petrarch and Dante) he must be in love, or miserable. I was both when I wrote the *Hours of Idleness*.'

(p. 63.)

[1] Medwin notes: 'I could not retain them.' [See extract from Byron's letter to Lady Byron, of April 3, 1820, above, p. 40.]

[2] [On the contrary, he was only nine.]

[Taaffe and Dante]

'You are a Protestant—you protest against all religions. There is T——[1] will traduce Dante till he becomes a Dantist.'

(p. 79.)

[Byron and Dante's hell]

'The Laureate[2] . . . exults over the anticipated death-bed repentance of the objects of his hatred. Finding that his denunciations or panegyrics are of little or no avail here, he indulges himself in a pleasant *vision* as to what will be their fate hereafter. The third Heaven is hardly good enough for a king, and Dante's worst berth in the "Inferno" hardly bad enough for me.'

(pp. 146-7.)

['The Prophecy of Dante']

'I wrote *The Prophecy of Dante* at the suggestion of the Countess. I was at that time paying my court to the Guiccioli, and addressed the dedicatory sonnet to her. She had heard of my having written something about Tasso, and thought Dante's exile and death would furnish as fine a subject. I can never write but on the spot. . . . The place of Dante's fifteen years' exile, where he so pathetically prayed for his country, and deprecated the thought of being buried out of it; and the sight of his tomb, which I passed in my almost daily rides,—inspired me. Besides, there was somewhat of resemblance in our destinies—he had a wife, and I have the same feelings about leaving my bones in a strange land. I had, however, a much more extensive view in writing that poem than to describe either his banishment or his grave. Poets are sometimes shrewd in their conjectures. . . . This poem was intended for the Italians and the Guiccioli, and therefore I wished to have it translated. . . . *Terza Rima* does not seem to suit the genius of English poetry—it is certainly uncalculated for a work of any length. In our language, however, it may do for a short ode. The public at least thought my attempt a failure, and the public is in the main right. . . . But if I had wanted a sufficient reason for giving up the Prophecy—the Prophecy failed me.'

(pp. 158-60.)

[The Italians and Dante]

'I don't wonder at the enthusiasm of the Italians about Dante. He is the poet of liberty. Persecution, exile, the dread of a foreign grave, could not shake his principles. There is no Italian gentleman, scarcely any well-educated girl, that has not all the finer passages of Dante at the fingers' ends—particularly the Ravennese.

[1] [No doubt Taaffe, see below, pp. 51-2.]

[2] [Southey.]

The Guiccioli, for instance, could almost repeat any part of the *Divine Comedy*; and, I daresay, is well read in the *Vita Nuova*, that prayer-book of love.'

(p. 160.)

[Shelley, and Taaffe, and Dante]

'Shelley always says that reading Dante is unfavourable to writing, from its superiority to all possible compositions. Whether he be the first poet or not, he is certainly the most untranslatable of all poets. You may give the meaning; but the charm, the simplicity—the classical simplicity—is lost. You might as well clothe a statue, as attempt to translate Dante. He is better, as an Italian said, *nudo che vestito*.

'There's Taaffe is not satisfied with what Carey has done, but he must be *traducing* him too. What think you of that fine line in the *Inferno* being rendered, as Taaffe has done it?

"I Mantuan, capering, squalid, squalling."

There's alliteration and inversion enough, surely! I have advised him to frontispiece his book with his own head, *Capo di Traditore*, the head of a *traitor*; then will come the title-page comment—Hell!'

(p. 161.)

[Dante and his commentators]

'I'll leave you to be my commentator, and hope you will make better work with me than Taaffe is doing with Dante, who perhaps could not himself explain half that volumes are written about, if his ghost were to rise again from the dead. I am sure I wonder he and Shakspeare have not been raised by their commentators long ago.'

(p. 163.)

[Shelley and Dante]

'Shelley's acquirements were great. He was, perhaps, the first classic in Europe. The books he considered the models of style for prose and poetry were Plato and the Greek dramatists. He had made himself equally master of the modern languages. Calderon in Spanish, Petrarch and Dante in Italian, and Goethe and Schiller in German, were his favourite authors. French he never read, and said he never could understand the beauty of Racine.'

(p. 254.)

1822. Jan. 22. LETTER TO JOHN MURRAY (from Pisa).

[Taaffe's commentary on the *Commedia*]

The enclosed letter, with the annexed packet, will explain its object. I can only say that the work[1] appears a desideratum in

[1] [Taaffe's *Comment on the Divine Comedy of Dante* (see above, p. 48, note to letter to Moore of 16 Nov. 1821).]

literature (especially in English literature), and with a lift in the *Quarterly* would be likely to go off well. Foscolo can tell you this better than I. Taaffe is a very good man, with a great desire to see himself in print, and will be made very happy by such a vision. He was persuaded to add his translation, which is *not* good; but the Comment is really valuable. If *you* will engage in the work, you will serve him, and oblige me: if not, at least recommend it to some of the other publishers, as I should feel sorry to disappoint a very good-natured man, who is publishing an useful work.

(*Letters and Journals*, vol. vi. p. 7.)

1822. March 6. LETTER TO JOHN MURRAY (from Pisa).

[Taaffe's commentary on the *Commedia*]

What is to be done about Taaffe and his Commentary?[1] He will die if he is *not* published: he will be damned, if he *is*; but that *he* don't mind. You must publish him.

(*Ibid.* vol. vi. p. 37.)

1822. March 8. LETTER TO THOMAS MOORE (from Pisa).

[Taaffe's commentary on the *Commedia*]

Do tell Murray that one of the conditions of peace is, that he publisheth (or obtaineth a publisher for) Taaffe's *Commentary on Dante*, against which there appears in the trade an unaccountable repugnance. It will make the man so exuberantly happy. . . . I have not the heart to tell him how the bibliopolar would shrink from his Commentary;—and yet it is full of the most orthodox religion and morality. In short, I make it a point that he shall be in print. . . . He naturally thirsts to be an author, and has been the happiest of men for these two months, printing, correcting, collating, dating, anticipating, and adding to his treasures of learning.

(*Ibid.* vol. vi. pp. 39-40.)

1822. May 4. LETTER TO JOHN MURRAY (from Pisa).

[The translation of Francesca da Rimini]

The *Mystery* and *Werner* I mean to print in one volume, with the lines to the 'Po,' and the translation of 'Francesca' from 'Dante.'[2]

(*Ibid.* vol. vi. p. 60.)

[1] [On Dante—see previous note. In a subsequent letter (March 15) Byron says: 'You must really get something done for Mr. Taaffe's Commentary. What can I say to him?']

[2] [The translation was not published till six years after Byron's death.]

1823. CONVERSATIONS OF BYRON WITH LADY BLESSINGTON AT GENOA.[1]

[Byron on fame—quotations from Dante and Petrarch]

There was a time when fame appeared the most desirable of all acquisitions to me; it was my 'being's end and aim,' but now—how worthless does it appear! Alas! how true are the lines—

La Nominanza è color d' erba,
Che viene e va; e quei la discolora
Per cui vien fuori della terra acerba.[2]

And dearly is fame bought, as all have found who have acquired even a small portion of it,—

Che seggendo in piuma
In Fama non si vien, nè sotto coltre.[3]

No! with sleepless nights, excited nerves, and morbid feelings, is fame purchased, and envy, hatred, and jealousy follow the luckless possessor.

O ciechi, il tanto affaticar che giova?
Tutti tornate alla gran madre antica,
E il vostro nome appena si ritrova.[4]

Nay, how often has a tomb been denied to those whose names have immortalized their country, or else granted when shame compelled the tardy justice! Yet, after all, fame is but like all other pursuits, ending in disappointment—its worthlessness only discovered when attained, and

Senza la qual chi sua vita consuma
Cotal vestigio in terra di sè lascia
Qual fummo in aere, ed in acqua la schiuma.[5]

(*Conversations of Byron with Countess of Blessington*, ed. 1850, pp. 279-80.)

[Byron and Dante on the memory of past happiness]

Memory precludes happiness, whatever Rogers may say to the contrary, for it borrows from the past, to imbitter the present, bringing back to us all the grief that has most wounded, or the happiness that has most charmed us; the first leaving its sting, and of the second,—

Nessun maggior dolore,
Che ricordarsi del tempo felice,
Nella miseria.[6]

(*Ibid.* vol. vi. pp. 281-2.)

[1] [From *Journal of the Conversations of Lord Byron with the Countess of Blessington*, published in 1834.]
[2] [*Purg.* xi. 115-17.]
[3] [*Inf.* xxiv. 47-8.]
[4] [Petrarch, *Trionfo della Morte*, i. 106-8.]
[5] [*Inf.* xxiv. 49-51.]
[6] [*Inf.* v. 121-3.]

1823. THE AGE OF BRONZE.

[Dante and the Scaligers of Verona]

Thrice blest Verona! since the holy three
With their imperial presence shine on thee!
Honour'd by them, thy treacherous site forgets
The vaunted tomb of 'all the Capulets';
The Scaligers—for what was 'Dog the Great,'
'Can Grande,' (which I venture to translate),
To these sublimer pugs? Thy poet too,
Catullus, whose old laurels yield to new;
Thine amphitheatre, where Romans sate;
And Dante's exile shelter'd by thy gate. . . .

(*Stanza* ix. ll. 1-10.)

1823. DON JUAN—CANTO THE SIXTH.

[Dante's 'wood obscure']

At length she [1] said, that in a slumber sound
  She dream'd a dream, of walking in a wood—
A 'wood obscure,' [2] like that where Dante found
  Himself in at an age when all grow good;
Life's half-way house, where dames with virtue crown'd
  Run much less risk of lovers turning rude. . . .

(*Stanza* lxxxv.)

1823. DON JUAN—CANTO THE SEVENTH.

[Dante, Solomon, and Cervantes]

They accuse me—*Me*—the present writer of
  The present poem—of—I know not what—
A tendency to under-rate and scoff
  At human power and virtue, and all that;
And this they say in language rather rough.
  Good God! I wonder what they would be at!
I say no more than has been said in Dante's
Verse, and by Solomon and by Cervantes. . . .

(*Stanza* iii.)

[1] [The odalisque Dudù.]

[2] 'Nel mezzo del cammin di nosta vita,
Mi ritrovai per una selva oscura,' etc.

Inferno.

1823. DON JUAN—CANTO THE TENTH.

['Grim Dante's obscure wood']

And this same state[1] we won't describe: we would
  Perhaps from hearsay, or from recollection;
But getting nigh grim Dante's 'obscure wood,'[2]
  That horrid equinox, that hateful section
Of human years, that half-way house, that rude
  Hut, whence wise travellers drive with circumspection
Life's sad post-horses o'er the dreary frontier
Of age, and looking back to youth, give *one* tear;—

I won't describe,—that is, if I can help
Description. . . .

(*Stanzas* xxvii-viii.)

1824. DAN JUAN—CANTO THE SIXTEENTH.

[The Gate of Dante's Hell]

What open'd next?—the door.

It open'd with a most infernal creak,
  Like that of hell. 'Lasciate ogni speranza
Voi ch' entrate!' the hinge seemed to speak,
  Dreadful as Dante's rhima,[3] or this stanza;

(*Stanzas* cxv-xvi.)

ANONYMOUS

1806. ANNUAL REVIEW AND HISTORY OF LITERATURE. BIOGRAPHY. ART. XVII. THE LIFE AND LITERARY WORKS OF MICHEL ANGELO BUONARROTI. BY R. DUPPA.[4]

[Dante's profile]

MR. DUPPA, in his former magnificent work,[5] had given the bust of Michel Angelo, and we noticed at the time its Homeric character. This is a side face; there is much propriety in giving both: the side and front face are often so different, as to express almost a different character each from the other;—nor can the true effect of a countenance be under-

[1] [The court of 'Russia's royal harlot,' the Empress Catherine.]
[2] 'Mi ritrovai per una selva oscura.'—*Inferno*, *Canto* i.
[3] [*Inf.* iii. 9.]
[4] [See above, pp. 6 ff.]
[5] [*A selection of twelve heads from the Last Judgment of Michel Angelo*, 1801.]

stood, unless it be seen in both directions. This is remarkably the case with Dante, whose profile is almost as supernatural as his poem. It is to be wished that Mr. Cary would give it in one of the remaining parts of his most faithful and praiseworthy translation.[1]

(Vol. v. p. 411.)

ANONYMOUS

1806. TRAVELS THROUGH ITALY, IN THE YEARS 1804 AND 1805. BY AUGUSTUS VON KOTZEBUE.[2]

[Dante's mention of the leaning tower at Bologna]

BOLOGNA.—Two towers which lean extremely are well worth seeing. Before you are accustomed to the sight, you imagine every moment that they will fall upon your head. . . . That two opulent nobles, who lived 700 years ago, could find no other way to distinguish themselves than to build these towers, is scarcely credible. The simpletons have, however, attained the end they proposed, that of perpetuating their names: for the towers are still called by their names, Asinelli and Gariscadi[3]; nay, what is still more, Dante has done them the honour to mention the circumstance in one of his poems.[4]

(Vol. iv. pp. 217-18.)

JOHN FLAXMAN

(1755-1826)

[John Flaxman, whose father was a maker of plaster casts, was born in York in 1755. His precocity was remarkable—at the age of twelve he gained the first prize of the Society of Arts for a medal, and at fifteen he carried off the silver medal at the Royal Academy Schools, and in the same year (1770) he first exhibited at the Academy. In 1787 he left England for Italy where he resided, chiefly at Rome, until 1794. He made a great reputation in Italy by his designs from the *Iliad* and *Odyssey*, which led to his receiving a commission from Thomas Hope of Amsterdam (who settled in England about 1796) for a similar series from the *Divina Commedia*. The compositions from Dante were engraved by Piroli and published at Rome in 1793.[5] The first English edition was published in London in 1807. Flaxman returned to England in 1794, and resided in London 'as an artist of acknowledged fame and standing' until his death in 1826. He was elected A.R.A. in 1797, R.A.

[1] [Cary's *Inferno* had just been published—he did not avail himself of the suggestion made in the text.]

[2] [The dramatist (1761-1819)—his translator's name is not recorded.]

[3] [*Sic*, for Garisenda.]

[4] [Dante mentions the Garisenda tower, *Inf.* xxxi. 136-8.]

[5] [See vol. i. p. 517.]

in 1800, and was appointed to the newly created post of Professor of Sculpture at the Academy in 1810. Among Flaxman's friends was the diarist, Henry Crabb Robinson, who has recorded some interesting remarks concerning the Dante designs in his *Diary* under Jan. 17, 1811 (see vol. i. p. 632).]

1807. COMPOSITIONS FROM THE DIVINE POEM OF DANTE ALIGHIERI, CONTAINING HELL, PURGATORY, AND PARADISE. WITH QUOTATIONS FROM THE ITALIAN, AND TRANSLATIONS FROM THE VERSION OF THE REVEREND HENRY BOYD TO EACH PLATE. ENGRAVED BY THOMAS PIROLI, FROM THE DRAWINGS IN POSSESSION OF THOMAS HOPE, ESQ. 1793.[1]

[These compositions, which were originally published at Rome in 1793, are 111 in number, viz. Frontispiece portrait of Dante; thirty-eight plates from the *Inferno* (one each for Cantos i-iv, vi-xx, xxii-xxxii, and two each for cantos v, xxi, xxxiii, xxxiv); thirty-nine from the *Purgatorio* (one each for cantos iii-viii, x-xxx, xxxii-xxxiii, two each for cantos i, ix xxxi, three for canto ii, and one entitled 'Faith, Hope, and Charity'); and thirty-three from the *Paradiso* (one for each canto).]

ANONYMOUS

1807. HISTORIC GALLERY OF PORTRAITS AND PAINTINGS; OR, BIOGRAPHICAL REVIEW: CONTAINING A BRIEF ACCOUNT OF THE LIVES OF THE MOST CELEBRATED MEN, IN EVERY AGE AND COUNTRY.

[Biographical notice of Dante]

DANTE ALLIGHIERI was the first poet of any celebrity that appeared in modern Italy, after the æra of ignorance and barbarism. If we reflect on the epoch in which he wrote, and on the dissensions that distracted his country, in which he took uncommon interest, we shall not be surprised at the incongruities observable in his poem, or, as he himself entitled it, his *Comedia;* a name which it should seem he applied to this wonderful performance, from being incapable of characterizing it with propriety. . . .

Of all poetical conception, the *Divina Comedia* of Dante is that of which it is the least possible to convey an idea to those who are unacquainted with it: At once ingenious and original, this unequal composition excites at times the most lively interest, occasionally disgust, and frequently a species of fatigue. Hell, purgatory, and paradise are successively visited by the poet. In the infernal regions Virgil is his guide; there crimes of every description are punished by torments, that in number and variety astonish the imagination. In this part of the poem Dante rises to the true sublime; no language presents anything superior to

[1] [London, May 1, 1807. The title is engraved. An alternative (engraved) title is 'Compositions from the Hell, Purgatory, and Paradise, of Dante Alighieri.']

the terrific episodes of Ugolino, Françoise d' Arimini, and some other passages of the *Inferno*.—When Dante quits this abode of grief, Virgil disappears, and Beatrice, the mistress of the poet, conducts him into purgatory and paradise. . . .

The episode of Ugolino, in common with the choicest pieces of the best poets, has been appropriated by neighbouring nations, with the utmost zeal. By the arts it has been equally appreciated. The picture of Ugolino, by Sir Joshua Reynolds,[1] is known by its engraving throughout Europe.

(Vol. i. pp. 26 ff.)

LANSDOWNE MSS. AT THE BRITISH MUSEUM

1807. In this year the MSS. collected by William Petty (Lord Shelburne), first Marquis of Lansdowne (1737-1805), were purchased by vote of Parliament for the British Museum for £4925. Among them was a fifteenth century MS. of the *Divina Commedia* (Lansd. 839).[2]

NATHANIEL HOWARD

(fl. 1800)

[Nathaniel Howard, as appears from a remark of his friend James Northcote in his *Memoirs of Sir Joshua Reynolds*, was a native of Plymouth, and 'an ornament to his country.' Besides a blank verse translation of the *Inferno*, a specimen of which is given below, and from which Northcote quotes the Ugolino episode (see below, p. 136), Howard was the author of *Bickleigh Vale and Other Poems*, descriptive of the scenery in the neighbourhood of Plymouth, which was published in 1804; and a *Vocabulary of English and Greek, for the use of Young Persons*, published in 1808. His *Inferno* was favourably reviewed in the *Monthly Review* for October, 1807, and in the *British Critic* for April, 1808 (see below, pp. 60-1, 66-7).]

1807. THE INFERNO OF DANTE ALIGHIERI, TRANSLATED INTO ENGLISH BLANK-VERSE. WITH NOTES, HISTORICAL, CLASSICAL, AND EXPLANATORY, AND A LIFE OF THE AUTHOR.

[The Translator's apology]

THE translator offers the following work to the candid judgment of the public. He intends not to enter into a formal defence of himself for adopting blank-verse, but rather regrets that national custom obliged Dante to confine his great genius to the shackles of rhyme. Blank-verse seems more

[1] [See above, vol. i. p. 343. It was engraved by John Dixon in 1774.]

[2] [This MS. was purchased at the Askew sale in 1775 for £7 7s.—See description in the catalogue published in 1819 (below, p. 288).]

analogous to his sublime manner, and therefore it is preferred in this translation. . . . That the poet, like our immortal Shakspeare, hurried away by the effervescence of imagination, has been guilty of many extravagances, and ludicrous images, is readily admitted; but these defects in both should be rather attributed, perhaps, to the vicious taste of the age in which they lived, than to the authors themselves. But bold extravagance is the peculiar fault of genius. A vindication of the irregularities of Dante is not intended, and high panegyric on his merits is unnecessary, since five centuries have elapsed, and left him still the subject of admiration for sublimity and originality. . . . It is universally allowed that the Inferno is the grandest production of Dante: for the Purgatorio and Paradiso, though affording numerous passages of singular strength and beauty, are certainly too much tinctured with the philosophy and scholastic theology of the age, to be understood and relished by modern readers: a version, therefore, of the Inferno alone is now submitted to the public.

(*Preface*, pp. v, vi, viii.)

Ulysses relates the Adventures of his Voyage
Inferno xxvi. 90-142

'What time I broke from Circè whose strong charms
Thro' twelve full months enthrall'd me on that shore
Caïeta, ere Aeneas gave it name,
Nor sweet affection for an infant son,
Nor reverence for an aged sire, nor love
That should have blest Penelopè with joy,
Could quench the ardour, raging in my breast,
To coast around the various world, and learn
The vice and virtue of the human race.
Full on the rough abyss of shoreless sea
I ventur'd, in a solitary bark,
Steer'd by a faithful few; each shore I saw
From Celtiberia to Marocco's land,
Sardinia, and full many a nameless isle,
Bath'd by the circling ocean. Ere we touch'd
The straits, beyond whose bound Alcides meant
Mortals should never dare, slow, withering age
Crept on us; on the right by Seville's realm,
And Ceuta on the left, we sail'd along.
O band of brothers! who have past, I cried,
Through countless perils, coasting now the west,
Our senses have but little more to watch,
Small share of life remains; be resolute,
Follow the sun, and new, unpeopled worlds

Explore. Cherish in mind your noble birth:
Ye were not, heroes! form'd to live like brutes,
But dare where Virtue and fair Science lead.
 Forth at this brief harangue, my fellow crew
Leapt for the voyage with electric joy,
Scarce could I bridle them from running wild.
Our stern we pointed to the rising morn,
Our oars were pinioned for the giddy flight;
Leftward we glided . . . soon th' Antartic pole
Blaz'd with the fires of night, while lowly sank
Our starry watch beneath the marble sea.
Her disk, five times, the moon kindled with light,
Five times, the lustre from her visage fled,
Since down the deep we voyag'd, when afar
His vastness a dun mountain full upheav'd,
Immeasurably high! such height before
Was never seen. Our bosoms throbb'd with joy;
But joy soon turn'd to sadness. For uprear'd
A whirlwind from the new-discover'd shore,
Full-smiting on our bark. The demon storm,
Thrice with the deafening billows, whirl'd us round,
Then rais'd our shatter'd poop, and whelm'd us deep.
Such was the dread decree of fate,—we sank,
And o'er our heads the foamy surges clos'd.'

(pp. 158-60.)

ANONYMOUS

1807. October. MONTHLY REVIEW. ART. 17. THE INFERNO OF DANTE ALIGHIERI, TRANSLATED INTO ENGLISH BLANK-VERSE, WITH NOTES . . . AND A LIFE OF THE AUTHOR. BY NATHANIEL HOWARD.[1]

[Howard's translation compared with that of Boyd]

WE had lately occasion to offer our remarks on a translation of Dante's Inferno, by Mr Boyd; and without entering into any minute comparison of the merits or defects of the rival versions, we may be permitted to assert that, in the present instance, the solemnity of blank-verse is better suited than rhyme to the grave and gloomy cast of the original; and that a freedom from the constraint of recurring sounds enables the translator to perform his task with greater ease and fidelity. Mr. Howard has, in most instances, rendered the meaning with sufficient accuracy; and if his lines are not always highly poetical, they are seldom

[1] [See above, pp. 58 ff.]

harsh, or carelessly constructed. . . . To the principal events recorded in the life of Dante, we have formerly adverted. Mr. Howard has sketched them with brevity and neatness. His notes are chiefly valuable as they point to parallel passages, or imitations, in the writings of other celebrated poets.

(Vol. liv. pp. 206-9.)

WILLIAM BELOE

(1756-1817)

[William Beloe was the son of a tradesman of Norwich, where he was born in 1756. He was educated under Dr. Samuel Parr at Stanmore, and at Bene't College, Cambridge. For three years he was assistant master under Parr at Norwich Grammar School. In 1796 he became rector of All Hallows, London Wall, and in 1803 he was appointed Keeper of Printed Books at the British Museum. He was dismissed from his post in the Museum in 1806 owing to the discovery that a protégé of his had committed extensive thefts of prints which were under Beloe's charge. He died in 1817. Besides translations from the classics, and various miscellaneous works Beloe was the author of *Anecdotes of Literature and Scarce Books* (6 vols., 1807-12), and of the *Sexagenarian, or Recollections of a Literary Life* (2 vols.) published in 1817 after his death. In the former he gives details of two rare editions of the *Divina Commedia*.]

1807-12. ANECDOTES OF LITERATURE AND SCARCE BOOKS.[1]

[The 1568 Venice edition of the *Divina Commedia*]

DANTE *Con l' espositione de M. Bernardino Daniello da Lucca. In Venetia appresso Pietro da Fino.* M.D. LXVIII.

There is a great singularity observable in this edition. In the sixth Canto, del Purgatorio, twelve verses are omitted,[2] which are found in every other edition. The circumstance is thus mentioned by Fontanini in his Biblioteca della Eloquenza Italiana,[3] and seems worth the attention of the curious.

'Se a questa edizione si aggiungono a penna *dodici versi* che per isbaglio le mancano nel Canto VI del Purgatorio ella si puo dir la migliore, che abbia le spiegazioni, e queste son di Trifon Gabriello.'

(Vol. i. pp. 4-5.)

[The 1481 Florence edition of the *Divina Commedia*]

DANTE. *Il medesimo Dante Alighieri cioè: l' Inferno, il Purgatorio, et il Paradiso; col Commento di Christophoro*

[1] [In six volumes; a second edition, with the addenda and corrigenda inserted in their places, was published in 1814.]

[2] [Ll. 106-17; the commentary on these lines is included.]

[3] [Published at Rome in 1726.]

Landino Fiorentino. In Firenze per Nicolo di Lorenzo della Magna, Anno 1481, *in fol. forma Majori.*

This is a most beautiful edition, and the first of Dante, with Landino's commentary. There is a fine copy on vellum in the Magliabechi Library at Florence, but the following remarks are suggested from the superb impression in the Cracherode Collection.[1]

This is said to be the first book, in which the Art of Engraving en taille-douce was introduced,[2] but this however is not true. In the Cracherode copy the first plate is at the bottom of the first page, it might have been placed at the bottom of the opposite side where there is sufficient space for it. . . .

It is most likely that Baldini or Botticelli engraved plates for all the Cantos; as he seems, by Vasari's account of him, to have been whimsical, it is very likely that he did not work fast enough for the printer, who not choosing to stay longer, worked off the two first which were finished, and left room for the rest, which probably were afterwards printed separately; and no one has ever thought it worth while to collect the whole together, and in all probability they may never be compleated in one copy.

This copy in the Cracherode Collection has nine plates, but one is a duplicate. But the two first plates only of this edition of 1481, are worked off with the Letter Press. All the others by the same hand will be found to be pasted on the paper.

M. Heineken in the third volume of the Dictionnaire des Artistes,[3] under the article Botticelli, gives an account of nineteen vignettes.

M. De Brienne had a copy of this edition with nineteen vignettes, and sixteen pen drawings in the same style. It was sold at Paris in 1792, and is now in the Bibliotheque Nationale.

There is a fine copy of this book in the King's Library, but it has only one Plate. It was purchased at Smith's sale,[4] who was English Consul at Venice. The plate was removed for the insertion of Smith's arms in the first page.

Mr. R. Wilbraham has a copy with nineteen vignettes. Lord Spencer,[5] in 1792, purchased a copy of this edition, which has also nineteen vignettes, of which, two are pen drawings. Mr. Fountaine,

[1] [Clayton Mordaunt Cracherode (1730-1799), left the whole of his valuable collection of books and prints to the British Museum, where Beloe was for a short time Keeper of Printed Books.]

[2] [For a detailed description of these plates, see W. Y. Ottley's *History of Engraving* (1816), vol. i. pp. 415-25.]

[3] [Leipzig, 1788-90; only four volumes (as far as *Diz.*) were printed.]

[4] [Joseph Smith (1682-1770), Consul at Venice, 1740-1760. His library was purchased by George III. in 1765, and now forms part of the King's Library at the British Museum.]

[5] [George John, second Earl Spencer (1758-1834), who made the great collection described by Dibdin in the *Bibliotheca Spenceriana* (see below, p. 79).]

of Narford Hall, in Norfolk, has also another copy with nineteen vignettes.[1] . . .

An imperfect copy of this scarce book sold at Dr. Monro's[2] sale for six guineas and a half. It had eight plates, and appears to have been the property of our Charles the First. The Pinelli copy sold for eighteen guineas, and was bought by Mr. Tighe.

Mr. Johnes,[3] the elegant translator of Froissart, &c. has a copy of this edition of Dante, with an additional large plate, representing Il Gran Diabolo swallowing his victims, and voiding them again by a most extraordinary process.[4] . . . In 1805, Messrs Payne and Mackinlay had a superb copy of this edition, with nineteen vignettes, for which they demanded fifty guineas. Earl Spencer gave 100 guineas for his copy.[5]

(Vol. i. pp. 4-9.)

FRANCIS DOUCE

(1757-1834)

[Francis Douce, the antiquary, was born in London in 1757. In early life he studied law, but abandoned it for literary and antiquarian pursuits. For a time he was Keeper of Manuscripts at the British Museum, where he catalogued the Lansdowne MSS. In 1807 he published his best-known work, *Illustrations of Shakespeare*, in which some apt illustrations from Dante are introduced. In 1823 he inherited a handsome fortune from Nollekens, the sculptor, which enabled him to indulge his tastes as a collector. He died in 1834, and left his magnificent collection of books, MSS., prints, and coins to the Bodleian Library at Oxford, in acknowledgment of the courtesy he received from Dr. Bandinel, Bodley's Librarian, when he visited Oxford in 1830 in company with Isaac D'Israeli. A catalogue of the books (among which are several editions of Dante) and MSS. was published in 1840.]

1807. ILLUSTRATIONS OF SHAKSPEARE, AND OF ANCIENT MANNERS.

[Dante and the 'Man in the Moon']

Ste. I was the *man in the moon.*

Tempest, Act II. Scene 2.

THIS is a very old superstition, founded, as Mr. Ritson has observed, on *Numbers* xv. 32. So far the tradition is still preserved among nurses and schoolboys; but how the culprit came to be imprisoned in the moon, has not yet

[1] [In the collection made by Sir Andrew Fountaine (1676-1753), since dispersed.]

[2] [John Monro, M.D. (1715-1791); he had a fine collection of engravings, and assisted Strutt in his *History of Engravers*.]

[3] [Thomas Johnes (1748-1816).]

[4] [This paragraph occurs in the *Addenda* to vol. vi. (1812) of the first edition.]

[5] [A copy of this edition, with nineteen plates, was sold at the Carmichael sale at Sotheby's (No. 270) on March 24, 1903, for £1000.]

been accounted for. . . . With the Italians Cain appears to have been the offender, and he is alluded to in a very extraordinary manner by Dante in the twentieth canto of the *Inferno*, where the moon is described as *Caino e le spine*.[1] One of the commentators on that poet says, that this alludes to the popular opinion of Cain loaded with the bundle of faggots, but how he procured them we are not informed.[2]

(Ed. 1839, pp. 9-10.)

[Dante's reference to the word *fico* as a term of contempt]

Pist. Die and be damn'd: and *figo* for thy friendship.
Henry V. Act. III. Scene 6.

The practice of thrusting out the thumb between the first and second fingers to express the feelings of insult and contempt has prevailed very generally among the nations of Europe, and for many ages been denominated *making the fig*, or described at least by some equivalent expression. . . . The earliest Italian authority for the use of this phrase is the *Inferno* of Dante. In the twenty-fifth canto are the following lines:—

Al fine delle sue parole, il ladro
Le mani alzò, con ambeduo *le fiche*
Gridando: togli Dio, ch' a te le squadro.

The miscreant who utters the blasphemy, refines on the gesticulation, and doubles the measure of it. . . . In the present play, ancient Pistol, after spurting out his '*figo* for thy friendship,' as if he were not satisfied with the *measure* of the contempt expressed, more emphatically adds, 'the fig of Spain' . . . the *Spanish fig*, as a term of contempt, must have been very familiar in England in Shakspeare's time, otherwise the translator of Della Casa's *Galateo* would not have used such an expression, when it was neither in his original nor in Dante.[3]

(*Ibid.* pp. 302, 305, 307.)

1840. CATALOGUE OF THE PRINTED BOOKS AND MSS. BEQUEATHED BY FRANCIS DOUCE, ESQ. TO THE BODLEIAN LIBRARY.

[Among the books bequeathed by Douce to the Bodleian were 16 Dante items, including five editions of the *Divina Commedia*, viz. Bressa (Boninus de Boninis), 1487; Venice (Aldus), 1515; Venice (Giunta), 1529; Venice (Marcolini), 1544; Florence (Manzani), 1595; three French translations, viz. Grangier, 1596; Clairfons, 1776; Artaud, 1812; Rogers' *Inferno*, 1782; Taaffe's *Comment*, 1822; and the third edition of the *Convivio*, Venice, 1529.]

[1] [*Inf.* xx. 126; cf. *Par.* ii. 49-51.]
[2] [See Toynbee's *Dante Dictionary*, s.v. *Caino*.]
[3] [See Robert Peterson's translation of the *Galateo* (1576), quoted above, vol. i. p. 61.]

HARLEIAN MSS. AT THE BRITISH MUSEUM

1808. CATALOGUE OF THE HARLEIAN MSS. IN THE BRITISH MUSEUM.[1]

[MSS. of Dante in the Harleian Collection]

No. 3459. THE Commedia of Dante complete: with a Commentary subjoined to each Canto. . . . Chazona di Dante. 'Guai a chi nel tormento.' XV. . . .

No. 3460. Another copy of the same work, more clear in Writing, and more modern in Orthography. XV . . . written in a kind of print hand. (Dated 1469.)

No. 3478. A Paper book, containing Canzoni, ballate, and other poems of Dante. . . . XV.

No. 3488. Part of the Commedia of Dante; namely the Inferno, with a part of the Purgatorio, as far as Canto xx. ver. 135, with a copious commentary. Written on vellum in the Gothic Letter. XV.

No. 3513. The Commedia of Dante, elegantly written on vellum. XV. . . . The Life of Dante by Leonardo Aretino.

No. 3581. Dante Alighieri, Comedia dell' Inferno, del Purgatorio, et del Paradiso: dated 1464 . . . in Paper. XV.

No. 4082. La Vita di Dante Alighieri, per Messere Giovanni Bocchacci. XV.

(Vol. iii. pp. 28, 31, 33-5, 44, 113.)

ANONYMOUS

1808. April. MONTHLY REVIEW. CARY'S INFERNO.

[Excellence of Cary's version of the *Inferno*]

IN the first grand requisite of a translator, *fidelity*, Mr. Cary seems to have outstripped his predecessors; for it is seldom indeed that we have been able to detect him in the too common operations of adding to or subtracting from his original. When we add that his versification is generally poetical and harmonious, and that his biographical sketch and notes are expressed with brevity and neatness, we conceive that we have duly appreciated the character of his labours. The introduction to the 24th Canto combines the rare merit of closeness and beauty.[2]

(Vol. lv. p. 438.)

[1] [Compiled by R. Nares, Sir H. Ellis, and T. H. Horne. A summary catalogue of these MSS., which were purchased in 1753 (see vol. i. p. 255), was printed in 1759 (see vol. i. p. 320).]

[2] [The reviewer here quotes the first sixteen lines of Cary's translation of Canto xxiv.]

ANONYMOUS

1808. April. BRITISH CRITIC. ART. 16. THE INFERNO OF DANTE ALIGHIERI; TRANSLATED INTO ENGLISH BLANK VERSE, WITH NOTES . . . AND A LIFE OF THE AUTHOR. BY NATHANIEL HOWARD.[1] 1807.

[Comparison between Howard and Cary as translators of the *Inferno*]

ANOTHER English Dante, after Mr. Boyd's[2] in rhyme, and Mr. Cary's[3] in blank verse, is rather more than we expected. This is also in blank verse; and Mr. Howard does not even mention the name of either of his predecessors. Of these the translator with whom he comes most immediately into competition, is Mr. Cary; and in making the comparison between them, we find the present author standing on respectable ground. Sometimes he is more poetical than his predecessor, sometimes less so; always less literal, and therefore less fit to serve as an interpreter to the student who aspires to read the original. Mr. H. seems to confine his design to the *Inferno*. Mr. C., if we mistake not, means to go on to the *Purgatorio* and *Paradiso*, which complete this famous poem. The obvious matters of comparison between the two blank-verse translators, are the Versions and the Notes; on each of which we shall very briefly remark. Mr. H. thus renders the opening of the 2nd Canto:

> 'Low sank the day: the dusky air enwrapt
> All weary *beasts* in night, and from their toils
> Released them. *I alone sustain'd* the war
> Of woes, and mazy perils of the way,
> *Which now my mind unerring shall retrace.*
> O Muses! O *bright* Genius! raise my thoughts. . . .'

The whole of this opening is much inferior to that of Mr. Cary, though it departs further from the original. Instead of *beasts*, it should be *animals*; *I alone sustain'd*, should be, I alone 'prepared to sustain,' as in Cary, 'M' apparecchiava a sostener.' The fifth is so similar, that, were it not in translating the same thing, imitation would be suspected. Mr. Cary's is, 'which my unerring memory shall retrace.' The transition from the invocation to the speech, wants the distinctness which the original gives it, and Mr. Cary equally: and 'bright genius' is neither so literal nor so good, as 'high genius.' We are not quite satisfied with either translator in the opening of Canto iii., where is the famous,

> 'Per me si va nella città dolente.'

But we rather prefer Cary. We could point out passages, in which we prefer Howard. Mr. Cary has printed the original with the

[1] [See above, pp. 58 ff.] [2] [See vol. i. pp. 410 ff.]
[3] [See vol. i. pp. 469 ff.]

translation, Mr. Howard has not; yet, oddly enough, the latter, at the head of each note, cites the original only, which his reader may not happen to possess or understand; nor has the English always any thing literally answering to it. . . . But for this inconvenience, the notes of Mr. H. seem to be well compiled and sufficiently explanatory. We should not indeed, on the whole, find any material fault with Mr. Howard's translation, except that, the other having been published before, it appears to be rather superfluous.

(Vol. xxxi. pp. 436-8.)

ANONYMOUS

1808. Nov. MONTHLY MAGAZINE.

[Alleged mistake of Dante]

DANTE in the nineteenth canto of his Inferno uses these words:

> Ahi, Constantin, di quanto mal fu matre,
> Non la tua conversion, ma quella dote,
> Che da te prese il primo ricco patre,

which Milton has thus translated,

> Ah Constantine, of how much ill was cause
> Not thy conversion, but those rich domains,
> That the first wealthy Pope received of thee.

Two distinct Constantines are in this passage confounded. The first emperor of that name was indeed a convert to Christianity; but he did not bestow on the church those temporal dominions, which are called the Patrimony of St. Peter.

Constantine, the fourth Byzantine emperor of that name, was he who bestowed the sacred territory on Pope Zechariah. This *ricco patre*, as the poet fitly calls him, subsidized Pepin of France, with the wealth of the church, to reconquer from Astolfo, king of the Lombards, the exarchate of Ravenna, the March of Ancona, and other provinces, which had been usurped from the Greek emperor. For thus rescuing the heart of Italy out of the hands of the barbarians, Constantine IV ceded to the popes of Rome the expedient jurisdiction and independence, and allowed them to nominate *the patrician*, or civil governor, of Rome. But this Constantine was no convert to Christianity. He was born a Christian. His nick-name Copronymus (which it is not more easy to translate delicately than the name of a color once called among our neighbours *caca du dauphin*) originated in his sullying, when an infant, the baptismal font during the initiatory rite, an accident, which put out of fashion the hitherto Catholic practice of baptism by immersion.

Petrarch and Ariosto both repeat Dante's story, but it is surprising that Milton, instead of correcting them by his learning, should have lent circulation to their error.[1]

(Vol. xxvi, pp. 353-4.)

ENGLISH EDITIONS OF THE *DIVINA COMMEDIA*

1808. LA DIVINA COMMEDIA DI DANTE. PASSO PASSO RISCONTRATA, CON LUNGA E SCRUPOLOSA DILIGENZA, SU I TESTI DELLE PIÙ APPROVATE EDIZIONI, ANTICHE E MODERNE, E DA OGNI TIPOGRAFICO NEO TERSA ED EMENDATA. DA G. B. BOSCHINI. LONDRA. 3 VOLS. 16MO.

[This (or the following, published in the same year) is the first edition of the complete text of the *Commedia* printed and published in England.[2] It was issued 'da' torchi di P. da Ponte, 15 Poland Street,' and dedicated to the Ladies Elizabeth and Emily Percy, daughters of the second Duke of Northumberland. It contains the text only, without notes. A brief life of Dante is prefixed to the first volume.]

1808. LA DIVINA COMMEDIA DI DANTE ALIGHIERI, ILLUSTRATA DI NOTE DA VARJ COMENTATORI SCELTE ED ABBREVIATE DA ROMUALDO ZOTTI. LONDRA. 3 VOLS. 12MO.

[This is the second (or possibly the first—see above) edition of the *Divina Commedia* printed and published in England. It was issued 'dai torchi di R. Zotti,' from whom it was to be had at '16 Broad Street, Golden Square.' The three volumes are dedicated respectively to the Countess of Lonsdale, the Countess of Dartmouth, and Mrs. Pilkington. It contains the text, accompanied by notes in Italian. A life of Dante, and other preliminary matter, is prefixed to the first volume. The third volume contains an index of proper names. A fourth volume, containing Dante's lyrical poems, was issued in the following year (see below).]

ENGLISH EDITION OF THE *CANZONIERE* OF DANTE

1809. CANZONI E SONETTI DI DANTE ALIGHIERI, PER LA PRIMA VOLTA DI NOTE ILLUSTRATI DA ROMUALDO ZOTTI. LONDRA. 12MO.

[This was issued as a fourth volume of Zotti's edition of the *Divina Commedia*, published in the previous year (see above). This is the first collection of Dante's lyrical poems printed and published in England. A few of the poems had been previously printed by T. J. Mathias in his six volumes of *Componimenti Lirici*, published in 1802 and 1808, (see vol. i. p. 560). Zotti's collection, which is based on that published by Cristoforo Zane at Venice in 1731, and on the collections of Giusto de' Conti, Allacci, and others, includes ninety-one poems, many of which are certainly not by Dante, while several of Dante's genuine poems, on the other hand, are omitted. This volume also contains Merian's dissertation on the *Divina Commedia*. A list of English subscribers to the four volumes of Zotti's edition is printed at the end of the fourth volume.]

[1] [From 'Extracts from the Portfolio of a Man of Letters.']

[2] [An edition of the *Divina Commedia* with the imprint *Londra* appeared in 1778, but this was actually printed not in London, but at Leghorn.]

ANONYMOUS

1809. Jan. EDINBURGH REVIEW. ART. XI. JOHNES'S TRANSLATION OF JOINVILLE.

[No 'authentic' MS. of Dante]

THOUGH Joinville has long been known, it is not long that his features have been undisguised. After the invention of printing, a custom long prevailed, excusable enough in popular works, however repugnant to strict notions of accuracy, of reforming the language of early writers according to that of the age in which the editor gave them to the world. Thus Dante, if we are not mistaken, has never yet been printed from any authentic manuscript:[1] the orthography, at least of his time, had grown obsolete before the close of the fifteenth century. But the change of French during the corresponding period, was much greater than that of Italian; though Joinville wrote in the *Langue d' Oil*, which most resembled the modern dialect.

(Vol. xiii. p. 472.)

ANONYMOUS

1809. May. QUARTERLY REVIEW. ART. III. PORTUGUEZE LITERATURE.

[Dante, Chaucer, Shakespeare, and Milton]

IF these writers, who are considered as the fathers of Portugueze poetry, are utterly unworthy to be compared with Dante and Chaucer, let it be remembered that Dante still remains unrivalled and unapproached among the Italians, and that except Shakespeare and Milton (who are above all other men, the ancients as well as the moderns) England has produced no poet of greater powers than Chaucer.

(Vol. i. p. 273.)

JOHN WALKER

(1770-1831)

[John Walker, antiquary, born in London in 1770, was educated at Winchester (1783-8), and Brasenose College, Oxford (B.C.L. 1797). He was Fellow of New College from 1797 to 1820, and in 1819 accepted the College living of Hornchurch in Essex, where he died in 1831. Walker published various miscellaneous collections, the most valuable of which were *Oxoniana* (4 vols. 1809), consisting of selections from books and MSS. in the Bodleian Library relating to University matters; and *Letters written by Eminent Persons, from the Originals in the Bodleian Library and Ashmolean Museum* (2 vols. 1813).]

[1] [No 'authentic' MS. of the *Commedia* (if by that is meant one derived from Dante himself) is known to exist. The earliest belongs to 1335 or 1336, fourteen or fifteen years after Dante's death.]

[1809.] OXONIANA.[1]

[Dante's use of the term 'comedy']

NOTE on the word 'comedy':—The nature and subject of Dante's Comedies, as they are styled, is well known.

(Vol. i. p. 47.)

LORD WOODHOUSELEE

(1747-1813)

[Alexander Fraser Tytler was born in Edinburgh in 1747. He was educated at the High School, and University of Edinburgh, and in 1770 was called to the Scottish bar. In 1780 he was appointed Professor of Universal History in Edinburgh University, in which capacity he published numerous historical works. In 1790 he became Judge-Advocate of Scotland; in 1802 he was raised to the bench with the title of Lord Woodhouselee, and in 1812 he was made a Lord of Justiciary. He died in Edinburgh in 1813. In addition to his legal and historical works he published anonymously in 1810 *An Historical and Critical Essay on the Life and Character of Petrarch*, in which are sundry references to Dante.]

1810. AN HISTORICAL AND CRITICAL ESSAY ON THE LIFE AND CHARACTER OF PETRARCH.[2]

[Boccaccio's reference to Dante in his sonnet on the death of Petrarch]

THAT beautiful sonnet, which Boccacio, recently after the death of Petrarch, composed in memory of his departed friend, is formed on that favourite thought, which is most natural to the soul on the near prospect of death:

Or se' salito, caro Signor mio, etc.

Friend of my soul! thou leav'st this guilty world,
To share the bliss that waits the faithful few,
God's own elect! To reach those mansions pure,
Where Laura, gone before thee ever dwells,
And draws thee to herself—and where with her,
My lov'd, my lost Fiammetta, meet compeer,
Sits in the sight of Heaven's eternal King.
Now, long escap'd the dull confines of earth,
Senuccio, Cino, Dante, erst belov'd,
All-joyful hail thy coming—sure of rest
And bliss for ever. . . .

(pp. 200-2.)

[Portraits of Dante and Petrarch mentioned by Vasari]

Vasari, in his life of Raphael, describing the celebrated painting in the Vatican of Mount Parnassus, observes that this great painter

[1] [Published anonymously and without date.] [2] [Published anonymously.]

has introduced Petrarch in that picture, among the poets, who are ranged on either side of the groupe of Apollo and the muses: *Sono vi ritratti di naturale tutti i più famosi, e antichi, e moderni Poeti. . . . Vi è il divinissimo Dante, il leggiadro Petrarcha, e l' amoroso Boccaccio. . . .*

Andrea del Castagno, a painter of considerable eminence, who flourished about a century after Petrarch, painted a portrait of him, among the other poets of Italy; as we learn from Vasari, in his life of that artist: *Dipinse in casa di Carducci, hoggi di Pandolphini, alcuni huomini famosi—fra questi è Dante, Petrarca, il Boccaccio, e altri.*

Vasari, who was himself a very able artist, informs us in his own life, that, among the pictures he painted at Florence, was a portrait of Petrarch: *Fui forzato a tornarmene a Fiorenza, dove feci alcuni quadri, fra gli altri, uno, in cui era Dante, Petrarca, Guido Cavalcanti, il Boccaccio, Cino da Pistoia, e Guittone d' Arezzo. . . .*

(pp. 233 ff.)

SAMUEL ROGERS*

(1763-1855)

[Samuel Rogers, poet and banker, was born at Stoke Newington in 1763. He was educated at private schools, and in obedience to his father's wishes entered the bank in which his father was a partner. On his father's death in 1793 he inherited considerable means, which enabled him to indulge his taste for travel and for society. In 1815 he visited Italy and again in 1822, on which occasion he became intimate with Byron and Shelley at Pisa. In 1850, on the death of Wordsworth, he was offered the laureateship, which he declined. He died in 1855 at the age of 92. Rogers's best known poems are the *Pleasures of Memory*, published anonymously in 1792, and *Italy*, originally published anonymously in 1822, and reissued in a revised form in 1830. Rogers was familiar with the *Divina Commedia*, and his interest in Dante displayed itself in his exertions on behalf of Cary, whose translation he introduced to the notice of Wordsworth, by whom, according to one version of the story, it was shown to Coleridge (see vol. i. p. 466 and note 3). Rogers claimed to have had a hand in the favourable article on Cary's Dante which appeared in the *Edinburgh Review* in Feb. 1818 (see below, pp. 161 ff.).]

1810. THE VOYAGE OF COLUMBUS.

[Motto on title-page]

CHI se' tu, che vieni—?
Da me stesso non vegno.
Dante.[1]

(*Poems*, 1839, p. 231.)

[Dante's 'tragic rhyme']

Round, at Primero, sat a whiskered band;
So Fortune smiled, careless of sea or land!
Leon, Montalvan (serving side by side;

[1] [*Inf.* viii. 33 and x. 61.]

* [Before Rogers should come FRANCIS HARDY, accidently omitted (see *Appendix*, below, pp. 699-700).]

Two with one soul—and, as they lived, they died)
Vasco the brave, thrice found among the slain . . .
Albert of Florence, who, at twilight-time,
In my rapt ear poured Dante's tragic rhyme,
Screened by the sail as near the mast we lay,
Our nights illumined by the ocean spray.

(*Canto* iv. *Poems*, 1839, pp. 258-9.)

[Dante and the Southern Cross]

And now in opener skies
Stars yet unnamed of purer radiance rise!
Stars, milder suns, that love a shade to cast,
And on the bright wave fling the trembling mast!
Another firmament! the orbs that roll,
Singly or clustering, round the Southern pole!
Not yet the four that glorify the Night—
Ah, how forget when to my ravished sight
The Cross shone forth in everlasting light![1]

(*Canto* vi. *ibid.* p. 265.)

[Reminiscences of Dante]

All melt in tears! but what can tears avail?
These climb the mast, and shift the swelling sail.
These snatch the helm; and round me now I hear
Smiting of hands, out-cries of grief and fear.[2]

(*Canto* vii. *ibid.* p. 270.)

Twice the Moon filled her silver urn with light.
Then from the Throne an Angel winged his flight . . .
As he descended thro' the upper air,
Day broke on day[3] as God Himself were there!
Before the great Discoverer, laid to rest,
He stood, and thus his secret soul addressed.[4] . . .

(*Canto* xii. *ibid.* p. 291.)

[1] The Cross of the South; 'una Croce maravigliosa, e di tanta bellezza,' says Andrea Corsali, a Florentine, writing to Giuliano of Medicis in 1515, 'che non mi pare ad alcuno segno celeste doverla comparare. E s' io non mi inganno, credo che sia questo il crusero di che Dante parlò nel principio del Purgatorio *con spirito profetico*, dicendo,

I' mi volsi a man destra, e posi mente
All' altro polo, e vidi quattro stelle,' &c.

[*Purg.* i. 22-7.]

[2] Voci alte e fioche, e suon di man con elle.—Dante [*Inf.* iii. 27].

[3] E di subito parve giorno a giorno
Essere aggiunto, come quei, che puote,
Avesse 'l Ciel d' un' altro Sole adorno.

Paradiso i. 61.

[4] Saprai di tua vita il viaggio.—Dante [*Inf.* x. 132].

1829. April. LETTER TO CHARLES LAMB.

[Daniel Rogers and Dante]

The verses are beautiful.[1] I need not say with what feelings they were read. Pray accept the grateful acknowledgments of us all, and believe me when I say that nothing could have been a greater cordial to us in our affliction than such a testimony from such a quarter. . . . He was an admirable scholar. His Dante and his Homer were as familiar to him as his Alphabets.

(*Works of Charles and Mary Lamb*, ed. Lucas, vol. vii. p. 812.)

1830. ITALY: A POEM.

[Dante and the Scaligers]

The gate that bore so long, sculptured in stone,
An eagle on a ladder . . .[2]

(Ed. 1839, p. 45. 'Bergamo.')

[Ezzelino da Romano]

The top of an old dungeon-tower,
Whence blood ran once, the tower of Ezzelin.[3]

(*Ibid.* p. 55. 'Venice.')

[Ugolino]

Like the Pisan[4] gnaw the hairy scalp
Of him who had offended.

(*Ibid.* p. 101. 'Foscari.')

[Paolo and Francesca]

Discovering many a glimpse
Of knights and dames, such as in old romance,
And lovers, such as in heroic song,
Perhaps the two, for groves were their delight,
That in the spring-time, as alone they sat,
Venturing together on a tale of love,
Read only part that day.[5]

(*Ibid.* p. 111. 'Ginevra.')

[1] [Lamb had sent Rogers a sonnet on the death of Daniel Rogers, the banker-poet's elder brother (see *Works*, ed. Lucas, vol. vii. p. 804).]

[2] The house of Mastino de la Scala, the Lord of Verona, which had always been open to the unfortunate. In the days of Can Grande all were welcome; Poets, Philosophers, Artists, Warriors. . . . Dante, as we learn from himself, found an asylum there:

Lo primo tuo rifugio, e 'l primo ostello
Sarà la cortesia del gran Lombardo,
Che 'n su la scala porta il santo uccello.

[*Par.* xvii. 70-2.]

[3] Ezzelino is seen by Dante in the river of blood. [*Inf.* xii. 110.]

[4] Count Ugolino.—*Inferno*, 32.

[5] *Inferno*, v.

[Byron and Dante]

He[1] had just left that Place
Of old renown, once in the Adrian sea,
Ravenna! where, from Dante's sacred tomb
He had so oft, as many a verse declares,[2]
Drawn inspiration.

(Ed. 1839, p. 118. 'Bologna.')

['Il Sasso di Dante']

On that ancient seat,
The seat of stone that runs along the wall,[3]
South of the Church, east of the belfry-tower,
(Thou canst not miss it) in the sultry time
Would Dante sit conversing, and with those
Who little thought that in his hand he held
The balance, and assigned at his good pleasure
To each his place in the invisible world,
To some an upper region, some a lower;
Many a transgressor sent to his account,[4]
Long ere in Florence numbered with the dead;
The body still as full of life and stir
At home, abroad; still and as oft inclined
To eat, drink, sleep; still clad as others were,
And at noon-day, where men were wont to meet,
Met as continually; when the soul went,
Relinquished to a demon, and by him
(So says the Bard, and who can read and doubt?)
Dwelt in and governed.—Sit thee down awhile;
Then, by the gates so marvellously wrought,
That they might serve to be the gates of Heaven,
Enter the Baptistery. That place he loved,
Loved as his own;[5] and in his visits there
Well might he take delight! For when a child
Playing, as many are wont, with venturous feet
Near and yet nearer to the sacred font,

[1] [Byron.]

[2] See the *Prophecy of Dante*.

[3] Il Sasso di Dante. It exists, I believe, no longer, the wall having been taken down; but enough of him remains elsewhere. Boccaccio delivered his lectures on the Divina Commedia in the church of S. Stefano.

[4] *Inferno*, 33. A more dreadful vehicle for satire cannot well be conceived. Dante, according to Boccaccio, was passing by a door in Verona, at which some women were sitting, when he overheard one of them say in a low voice to the rest, Do you see that man? He it is, who visits Hell, whenever he pleases; and who returns to give an account of those he finds there.—I can believe it, replied another. Don't you observe his brown skin, and his frizzled beard?

[5] 'Mio bel Giovanni.'—*Inferno*, 19.

Slipped and fell in, he flew and rescued him,
Flew with an energy, a violence,
That broke the marble—a mishap ascribed
To evil motives; his, alas, to lead
A life of trouble, and ere long to leave
All things most dear to him, ere long to know
How salt another's bread is, and the toil
Of going up and down another's stairs.[1]

(Ed. 1839, pp. 122-4. 'Florence.')

[The Tower of Famine at Pisa]

Sullen was the splash,
Heavy and swift the plunge, when they[2] received
The key that just had grated on the ear
Of Ugolino,[3] ever-closing up
That dismal dungeon thenceforth to be named
The Tower of Famine.[4]

(*Ibid*. p. 141. 'The Campagna of Florence.')

[Buondelmonte]

Fatal was the day
To Florence, when, at morn, at the ninth hour,
A noble Dame, in weeds of widowhood,
Weeds by so many to be worn so soon,
Stood at her door; and like a sorceress, flung
Her dazzling spell. Subtle she was, and rich,
Rich in a hidden pearl of heavenly light,
Her daughter's beauty; and too well she knew
Its virtue! Patiently she stood and watched;
Nor stood alone—but spoke not—In her breast
Her purpose lay; and, as a Youth passed by,
Clad for the nuptial rite, she smiled and said,
Lifting a corner of the maiden's veil,
'This had I treasured up in secret for thee.
This hast thou lost!' He gazed and was undone!
Forgetting—not forgot—he broke the bond,
And paid the penalty, losing his life
At the bridge-foot;[5] and hence a world of woe!

(*Ibid*. pp. 143-4. 'The Campagna of Florence.')

[1] *Paradiso*, 17. [2] [The waters of Arno.]
[3] [*Inf*. xxxiii. 46-7.] [4] [*Inf*. xxxiii. 23.]
[5] Giovanni Buondelmonte was on the point of marrying an Amidei, when a widow of the Donati family made him break his engagement in the manner here described. The Amidei washed away the affront with his blood, attacking him, says G. Villani, at the foot of the Ponte Vecchio, as he was coming leisurely along in his white mantle on his white palfrey; and hence many years of slaughter.

'O Buondelmonte, quanto mal fuggisti
Le nozze sue, per gli altrui conforti.'—Dante.
[*Par*. xvi. 140-1.]

[Dante's description of evening]

The hour is come,
When they that sail along the distant seas,
Languish for home; and they that in the morn
Said to sweet friends 'farewell,' melt as at parting;
When, just gone forth, the pilgrim, if he hears,
As now we hear it—echoing round the hill,
The bell that seems to mourn the dying day,
Slackens his pace and sighs, and those he loved
Loves more than ever.[1]

(Ed. 1839, p. 150. 'The Campagna of Florence.')

[Reminiscence of Dante]

On he wheels,
Blazing by fits as from excess of joy,[2]
Each gush of light a gush of ecstasy.

(*Ibid.* p. 200. 'The Fire-Fly.')

[The Maremma]

From that low,
That level region, where no Echo dwells,
Or, if she comes, comes in her saddest plight,
Hoarse, inarticulate—on to where the path
Is lost in rank luxuriance, and to breathe
Is to inhale distemper, if not death.[3]

(*Ibid.* p. 281. 'A Farewell.')

[Verona]

When we enter Verona, we forget ourselves, and are almost inclined to say with Dante,

'Vieni a veder Montecchi, e Cappelletti.'

[*Purg.* vi. 106.]

(*Ibid.* p. 292. *Additional Notes.*)

[1] The conclusion is borrowed from that celebrated passage in Dante, 'Era già l' ora,' etc. [*Purg.* viii. 1 ff.]

[2] 'For, in that upper clime, effulgence comes
Of gladness.'—*Cary's Dante.*

[3] It was somewhere in the Maremma, a region so fatal to so many, that the unhappy Pia, a Siennese lady of the family of Tolommei, fell a sacrifice to the jealousy of her husband. Thither he conveyed her in the sultry time,

'tra 'l Luglio e 'l Settembre' [*Inf.* xxix. 47];

having resolved in his heart that she should perish there, even though he perished there with her. . . .

Siena mi fe; disfecemi Maremma.
Salsi colui, che 'nnanellata pria,
Disposando, m' avea con la sua gemma.' [*Purg.* v. 134-6.]

The Maremma is continually in the mind of Dante; now as swarming with serpents, and now as employed in its great work of destruction.

[Homer, Dante, Milton, Virgil]

It is remarkable that the noblest works of human genius have been produced in times of tumult; when every man was his own master, and all things were open to all. Homer, Dante, and Milton appeared in such times; and we may add Virgil.

(Ed. 1839, p. 308. *Additional Notes.*)

1838. Aug. 15. LETTER TO LORD MELBOURNE.

[Appeal on behalf of Cary]

You have received a representation from the Trustees of the British Museum (Lord Aberdeen has just written to inform me of it) in favour of Mr. Cary, and I am sure you mean to do something.[1] But at his age every month is a loss, and the time will come, for, I know enough of you to know it—when you will be sorry to have overlooked him. With his translation of Dante you cannot be unacquainted, and perhaps you have looked into his translation of Pindar. Of his genius and learning there can be no doubt.

(*Rogers and his Contemporaries*, ed. Clayden, vol. ii. p. 172.)

18—. RECOLLECTIONS OF THE TABLE-TALK OF SAMUEL ROGERS.[2]

[Hayley's translation from Dante]

If Hayley was formerly over-rated, he is now undervalued. He was a most accomplished person. . . . His translation of the First Canto of the *Inferno*[3] is on the whole good; but he has omitted some of the striking circumstances in the original.

(p. 57.)

[Fox and Sir Joshua Reynolds' 'Ugolino']

Fox did not much admire Sir Joshua's pictures in the grand style; he greatly preferred those of a playful character: he did not like much even the Ugolino;[4] but he thought the boys in the Nativity were charming.

(p. 86.)

[1] [Clayden remarks: 'Rogers was at this time attempting to get a pension for Cary. He had called the attention of Wordsworth to the translation of Dante. Wordsworth admired it greatly, as Rogers did, and considered it a great national work. Wordsworth showed it to Coleridge, and Coleridge at once spoke of it in high terms in one of his lectures. But it was little known till attention was called to it by an article in the *Edinburgh Review*, which was written by Foscolo with some assistance from Rogers and Mackintosh.' Lord Melbourne eventually, in 1841. conferred a pension of £200 on Cary, which he only lived three years to enjoy. (See further, note to notice of Cary, vol. i. p. 466).]

[2] [Edited by A. Dyce, 1856.]

[3] [Hayley translated the first three cantos of the *Inferno*—see vol. i. pp. 365 ff.]

[4] [See vol. i. p. 343.]

[Flaxman's designs from Dante]

The neglect which Flaxman, the greatest sculptor of his day, experienced is something inconceivable. Canova, who was well acquainted with his exquisite illustrations of Dante,[1] &c., could hardly believe that a man of such genius was not an object of admiration among his countrymen.

(p. 156.)

ANONYMOUS

1810. Nov. QUARTERLY REVIEW. ART. XI. SOUTHEY'S HISTORY OF BRAZIL.

[Dante's account of Ulysses]

TO the voyage of St. Brandan and his monks, and that of Mr. Southey's Cambrian Hero,[2] may be added the extraordinary expedition of Dante's Ulysses, whom the poet conducts in a second ramble, far more adventurous than the first, and, by the same track with Columbus, to suffer shipwreck on the dusky and mountainous shore of the Terrestrial Paradise (Inferno, Canto 26).[3]

(Vol. iv. p. 456.)

JOHN BERNARD TROTTER

(1775-1818)

[John Bernard Trotter, born in co. Down in 1775, was educated at the Grammar School at Downpatrick, and at Trinity College, Dublin, where he graduated B.A. in 1795. He went to London in 1798, and entered as a student at the Temple. In this year he made the acquaintance of Charles James Fox, whom in 1802, after the conclusion of the Peace of Amiens, he accompanied to Paris, and when Fox was appointed Foreign Secretary in Feb. 1806 he became his private secretary. In 1811 he published *Memoirs of the Latter Years of Charles James Fox*, of which a third edition was called for in the same year. He died in destitution at Cork in 1818. In the *Memoirs* are included some letters of Fox to Trotter, in which classical and Italian literature are discussed. Two of them contain interesting remarks of Fox upon Dante (see vol. i. pp. 610-11).]

1811. MEMOIRS OF THE LATTER YEARS OF THE RIGHT HONOURABLE CHARLES JAMES FOX.

[Motto on Title-Page]

DI cui la fama ancor nel mondo dura
E durerà quanto 'l moto, lontana.[4]

Dante.

[1] [See above, pp. 56-7.]
[2] [Southey's *Madoc* was published in 1805.]
[3] [*Inf.* xxvi. 90-142.]
[4] [*Inf.* ii. 59-60.]

THOMAS FROGNALL DIBDIN

(1776-1847)

[Thomas Frognall Dibdin, the bibliographer, whose father was a captain in the navy, and whose uncle was Charles Dibdin, the song-writer, was born in India in 1776. He was educated at St. John's College, Oxford (B.A. 1801; D.D. 1825). After studying for the bar for a time, he decided to take holy orders, and was ordained in 1804. In 1802 he published his earliest bibliographical work, the *Introduction to the Knowledge of Rare and Valuable Editions of the Greek and Latin Classics*, which brought him to the notice of the second Earl Spencer, who was already known as the possessor of one of the most valuable private libraries in England. 'Lord Spencer proved Dibdin's patron through life, made him at one time his librarian, obtained church patronage for him, and made the Althorp library the wonderful collection it since became, very much under his direction.' Between 1802 and 1838 Dibdin published numerous bibliographical works, among the most important being his catalogue of Lord Spencer's library, which was published under the title of *Bibliotheca Spenceriana* in 1814-15, supplements being issued in 1822 and 1823. In 1811 he printed privately an account of *Book Rarities in Lord Spencer's Library*, consisting chiefly of a description of the editions of Dante and Petrarch at Spencer House. Dibdin, who was appointed rector of St. Mary's, Bryanston Square, in 1824, died in 1847.]

1811. BOOK RARITIES IN LORD SPENCER'S LIBRARY.

[In this account, which was printed privately, Dibdin registers, among the books at Spencer House, the three first editions of the *Divina Commedia*, viz. Foligno, 1472; Mantua, 1472; and Jesi, 1472.—The last is an exceedingly rare edition; only six copies are known, three of which are in England (see *Athenæum*, June 23, and July 14, 1900).]

1815. BIBLIOTHECA SPENCERIANA; A DESCRIPTIVE CATALOGUE OF THE BOOKS PRINTED IN THE FIFTEENTH CENTURY, IN THE LIBRARY OF GEORGE JOHN EARL SPENCER. VOLUME. IV.

[In this work Dibdin registers the following fifteenth-century editions of the *Commedia*, viz. Foligno, 1472 (*editio princeps*); Mantua, 1472; Jesi, 1472; Venice, 1477; Florence, 1481; and the *editio princeps* of the *Convivio* (Florence, 1490).—In the *Supplement*, printed in 1822, he registers three more fifteenth-century editions of the *Commedia*, viz. Venice, 1478; Venice, 1491 (Petro Cremonese); and Venice, 1493.—In the *Descriptive Catalogue of the Books Printed in the Fifteenth Century, lately forming part of the Library of the Duke di Cassano Serra, and now the property of George John Earl Spencer*, printed in 1823, Dibdin registers two more early editions of the *Commedia*, viz. Naples, 1477; and Venice, 1484.—The whole of these, with the rest of the Althorp library, are now in the John Rylands Library at Manchester.]

1824. THE LIBRARY COMPANION: OR, THE YOUNG MAN'S GUIDE, AND OLD MAN'S COMFORT, IN THE CHOICE OF A LIBRARY.

[In this work, under *Italian Poetry*, Dibdin mentions the most 'desirable' editions of the *Divina Commedia*, viz. the three of 1472 (mentioned under *Book Rarities in Lord Spencer's Library*—see above); the very rare undated edition published at Naples (probably in 1474) by Francisco del Tuppo; the first Florentine edition (1481); the first Aldine (1502); the Venetian editions of 1512 and 1586; the editions, with

Lombardi's commentary, of 1791 and 1815; and the edition of the *Opere di Dante* published in five volumes at Venice in 1757-8. At the beginning of the section he draws attention to the 'masterly' article on Dante by Foscolo in the *Edinburgh Review* in 1818 (see below, pp. 161 ff.).]

JOSEPH HUME

(1777-1855)

[Joseph Hume, 'the Radical,' was the son of a shipmaster of Montrose, Forfarshire, where he was born in 1777. After studying medicine in Aberdeen, Edinburgh, and London, in 1796 he became a member of the Edinburgh College of Surgeons. In 1797 he was appointed an assistant-surgeon in the service of the East India Company. He rendered important services in India, medical and political, and returned home in 1808 with a fortune of £40,000. After spending two or three years in travel at home and in the South of Europe, in 1812 he entered Parliament as member for Weymouth. In the same year he published a 'blank verse' translation of the *Inferno*, which is probably the worst translation of any portion of Dante's works ever published; while the blank verse is worthy of the translation, lines ending with *the*, *and*, *of*, *to*, etc. being of frequent occurrence. Hume, who 'for thirty years was a leader of the radical party,' and did good service in exposing abuses, especially in the matter of public expenditure, died in 1855. He was a Fellow of the Royal Society, and of the Royal Asiatic Society, and was twice Lord Rector of Aberdeen University.]

1812. INFERNO: A TRANSLATION FROM DANTE ALIGHIERI, INTO ENGLISH BLANK VERSE.

[Lucifer in the Pit of Hell]

BANNERS were in the distance waving high.
'Look forward (said MY GUIDE) th' Infernal King
Approaches.' Like a huge mill on ev'ning
Seen obscurely, or in black storm, onward
He strode. Behind MY FRIEND I ran to screen
Myself, for the wind blew, tempestuously,
Most piercing frost. The wretched SHADES were swath'd
In ice, who reeds resembled cas'd in glass.
In ev'ry posture they :—recumbent and
Erect, upon their head or feet, crouching,
With their head downward, or backward thrown
The face upward. Near to that BEING once
Beauteous, majestic, me MY GUARDIAN led,
Saying—'Now gaze on DIS!' O, reader, what
Of cold unprecedented here I felt,
Can be imagin'd but when felt the pain
Ere grows the sense benumb'd; or when again
By agony acute the sense returns.

This EMPEROR OF WOE, tho' from the chest
Above the ice but visible, expos'd
A form stupendous! His arm surpass'd the
Bulkiest giant's, as bulkiest giant's mine!
Comeliest of BEINGS this, before he rear'd
With haughty daring vengeful, his great soul
To war against his MAKER! How odious,
To a scaring monster chang'd! For his head,
(Terrific sight!) express'd three visages!
The front blaz'd with a deep vermillion: that
Whose widen'd chin on the left shoulder press'd,
Was sallow: that on the right, dingy as
The soil, foul refuse of subsiding Nile.
Two wings he had unfeather'd, like the bat's,
Filmy; that when open'd, extended far
Their sheets;—no largest vessel's sails so large!
Thrice should he flap them, thence would rise a wind
Transmuting COCYTUS, tho' fluent then,
To one vast mass of ice. From his six eyes
Tears ever stream'd, and bloody mucus from
His mouths. He ev'ry SINNER seiz'd: and at
One cranch of his huge teeth, his bones were to
The least, like flax beneath an engine, mash'd!

THREE by this triple-headed FIEND I saw
At once tortur'd. 'He (said MY GUARDIAN then)
Whose head is grip'd within the foremost jaws;
And, flay'd at ev'ry gnaw, the greatest pangs
Endures—JUDAS ISCARIOT is. He from
The dingy muzzle hanging by the legs
Downwards; and who, tho' tortur'd, utters not—
Is BRUTUS. The third, like his fellow hung
Down revers'd, tense all his muscles—CASSIUS.
But night returneth: we must now depart,
For all is shewn thee bearing int'rests dire!'

Complying; I, tight round MY GUARDIAN's neck
Clung instantly. He, fit moment chusing,
And a spot, when mov'd the monster's wing, grasp'd
Hard his shaggy cov'ring: thence down his side,
Clotted with ice, he slowly, the labor
Great, descended. On his projected hip
Breathless resting awhile—'This (remarked he)
A dangerous toil: the sole escape from Hell!'

(*Canto* xxxiv. 1-78, pp. 267-70.)

ROXBURGHE LIBRARY

1812. CATALOGUE OF THE LIBRARY OF THE LATE JOHN DUKE OF ROXBURGHE.

[The library of John Ker, third Duke of Roxburghe (1740-1804), was sold by Evans in May-July, 1812. The sale, which lasted 45 days, consisted of 10,120 items, and realised upwards of £23,000. The sensation of the sale was the contest between the Marquis of Blandford and Earl Spencer for the Valdarfer *Decameron* (1471), which was secured by the former for £2260. The collection contained seven editions of the *Divina Commedia*, all of the sixteenth century, of which only one (Venice, 1564; sold for 28s.) fetched more than £1.]

ANONYMOUS

1812. June. QUARTERLY REVIEW. ART. X. SISMONDI'S HISTOIRE DES REPUBLIQUES ITALIENNES.

[Dante and the *Divina Commedia*]

BUT, to view the scenes of nature with the eye of a painter is a gift exclusively appropriated to more civilized times and people. This gift the Italians of the thirteenth century had already attained. Dante in several parts of his extraordinary poem, employs it with great poetical advantage.

* * * *

The famous battle of the Arbia, which took place on the 4th of September, 1260, and, for a time replaced the Gibelin exiles in the government of which they had been dispossessed, was not less important in its consequences to the republic, than it is interesting, even to our own age, from the associations which will forever accompany it. . . . We forbear to quote the animated paraphrase which our author gives of the celebrated passage from Dante, and only refer the reader to the original, (Inferno, c. x, v. xxii) 'O Tosco, chi per la città del fuoco, etc.) as strikingly illustrative of the state of Florence, of the character of its principal inhabitants, and of the factions which disturbed it. Even in this cold and phlegmatic climate we have frequent reason to deplore the mournful effects of party-spirit; yet we have no idea of political attachment and hatred, such as inflamed the ardent souls of the Italian republicans.

The shade of Farinata (who, when living, was distinguished by his moderation in the cause with which he was engaged, and for a spirit of patriotism which sometimes placed him in opposition to the violent and baneful designs of his own party) is supposed, by the poet, to taunt him with the defeat of the Guelphs. 'If they were beaten,' returns Dante, 'they knew how to recover what they lost; an art which your friends have not yet acquired.' 'This reflection,' replies the unhappy ghost, 'torments me even more than the pains of hell which I endure.'

'Ciò mi tormenta più, che questo letto.'

'However,' he adds, with malignant satisfaction, 'before the mistress of these regions (the moon) shall have fifty times rekindled her face, you also will have learned how difficult is that art.'

In this the poet alludes to the factions of the Neri and Bianchi, which broke out in Tuscany within a few years after the second expulsion of the Gibelines from Florence, and, in the beginning of the 14th century, divided the Guelphs in every city where they possessed the ascendancy. Two parties could not long subsist together under the same government with such a spirit as animated the factions of Italy. The Bianchi, to whom Dante was attached, were expelled by their rivals from Florence, and many among them threw themselves into the arms of their hitherto implacable enemies the Gibelines. Dante himself does not appear to have engaged in any political affairs subsequently to his expulsion. He acted a more patriotic part by submitting to his fate, and composed, in his exile, that extraordinary and magnificent poem which has exalted his reputation very high above that of the age in which he lived, even (in the opinion of many competent judges) to a superiority over all the Italian poets who have succeeded him.

(Vol. vii. pp. 361, 370-1.)

ANONYMOUS

1812. Dec. QUARTERLY REVIEW. ART. X. ULTIME LETTERE DI JACOPO ORTIS.

[Homer, Dante, Shakespeare, Metastasio, and Alfieri]

THE same language which is a lyre in the hands of Metastasio, becomes a trumpet in those of Dante and Alfieri.

* * * *

The author treats with great contempt that affectation of general literature, which, as it should seem, is a folly not confined to ourselves, many passages prove the extent of his reading, and he appears to have no common acquaintance with the English writers. A mind like his was calculated to receive the impressions of our sovereign poet.

"Omero, Dante e Shakespeare," he exclaims, "i tre maestri di tutti gl' ingegni sovrumani hanno investito la mia immaginazione ed infiammato il mio cuore: ho bagnato di caldissime lagrime i loro versi, ed ho adorato le loro ombre divine come se le vedessi assise su le volte eccelse che sovrastano l' universo, a dominare l' eternita."

(Vol. viii. pp. 438, 444.)

WALTER SAVAGE LANDOR

(1775-1864)

[Walter Savage Landor, born in 1775, was educated at Rugby (where he was a contemporary of Cary, the translator of Dante), and at Trinity College, Oxford, whence he was rusticated in 1794, after a year's residence. He showed no inclination to follow a profession, but devoted himself to literature, and in 1798 published his *Gebir*, which was praised by Southey, Coleridge, and others, and brought him into notice as a writer. In 1815 he went to Italy, where he resided for the next twenty years (at Como, 1815-18; Pisa, 1818-21; Florence, 1821-35). In 1824 he published the first two volumes of his *Imaginary Conversations*, which were followed by a third in 1828, and a fourth and fifth in 1829. In 1835 he returned to England, and in 1838 settled at Bath, which was his home until 1858. In that year he went back to Florence, where he died at the age of ninety in 1864. In 1836 Landor published the *Pentameron*, which consists for the most part of a prolonged dialogue between Petrarch and Boccaccio as to the merits and demerits of Dante. In this work he puts into the mouth of Petrarch some exceedingly severe, not to say abusive, criticisms of the *Divina Commedia*, tempered, however, by occasional expressions of admiration.[1] In later years he became more appreciative, and numbered Dante with Homer, Shakespeare, and Milton, as one of 'the four giants' of the poetical world. In *Last Fruit off an Old Tree*, published in 1853, he couples Dante repeatedly with these three, as well as with Aeschylus and Pindar. In August, 1840, Landor sent an interesting account to the *Examiner* of the discovery in the previous month in the Bargello at Florence, of the famous fresco by Giotto containing the portrait of Dante as a young man (see below, pp. 112-13).]

1812. CHARLES JAMES FOX: A COMMENTARY ON HIS LIFE AND CHARACTER.[2]

[Of the irresistible fascination of Dante]

I HARDLY know any book so pleasant to read in, or so tiresome to read through, as *Orlando Furioso*—of course, I except the *Faery Queene*. I will never believe that any man has overcome twelve or fifteen thousand lines of allegory, without long intervals of respite and repose. I was seventeen years in doing it, and I never did anything which I would not rather do again. In the gloomy deserts of Dante, some scenes are stupendous both from their grandeur and their solitude, and lose nothing of

[1] [See *Introduction*, pp. xlvi.-vii.; see also E. N. S. Thompson, *Dante and Landor*, in *Modern Language Notes*, April, 1905.]

[2] [Written in 1811, printed anonymously in 1812, and first published in 1907. The work is a commentary on *Memoirs of the Latter Years of Charles James Fox*, by J. B. Trotter, published in 1811 (see above, p. 78).]

their distinctness by their elevation; in Ariosto, if there are a few misshapen ornaments, yet everything around them is smiling in sunshine and fertility. No man ever lays his poem down without a determination to resume it, but he lays it down often and negligently. Let him once be under the guidance of Dante, and—

> Revocare gradum superasque evadere ad auras,
> Hic labor, hoc opus est.[1]

He is determined not to desist; he may find another passage as striking as the last; he goes on and reads through.

(Ed. 1907, pp. 154-5.)

1820. DE CULTU ATQUE USU LATINI SERMONIS ET QUAMOBREM POETAE LATINI RECENTIORES MINUS LEGANTUR.[2]

[Dante and other Italian Poets lived in troubled times]

Mirari licet in Italiâ universâ quoties viguerint ac paene extinctae fuerint elegantiores literae. Neque enim bellis ego intestinis causam ejus rei, quod multi faciunt, possum attribuere, ista namque non modò non obtundere verùm etiam acuere solent ingenia, ita ut aliis nullis temporibus tot boni scriptores vel olim vel recentiùs extiterint. Harum videlicet eruptionum cineres maximam secum afferunt fertilitatem. Petrarcha, Dantes, Ariostus, Tassus, in mediis patriae calamitatibus floruerunt: Alfierius in vastas circumcirca solitudines, ut Pyramis, prospectabat.

(*Poemata et Inscriptiones*, ed. 1847, p. 264.)

[As to Latin translations of Dante, Ariosto, and Boccaccio]

Quantum campi adimeres humanae menti si adimeres Latinitatem! Permulta sunt quae sermonibus nostri saeculi minime convenirent, ut contra quae veteribus. Quis Ariosti vel Dantis carmina[3] vel Boccacii suavissimas narrationes in latinum convertat?

(*Ibid.* p. 267.)

[The surpassing excellence of Dante's Ugolino and Alfieri's Brutus]

Musae Latinae in carmine heroico quiddam firmius postulant quàm quod Ariostus ipse suppeditet, cujus poema, ut fructus aquosiores succum coloremque contrectatione perdit, et speciem certam quandam marcoris exhibet. Primus est sui generis, sed generis non primi; quod minime a nomine operis pendet, sed totum ab opere, sit illud duntaxat grave. Pindarus et Sophocles in summis et habiti et habendi sunt: Tryphiodorus et Statius et

[1] [*Aen.* vi. 128-9—misquoted.]
[2] [Originally published at Pisa in 1820.]
[3] [The *Divina Commedia* was translated into Latin prose by Giovanni da Serravalle at the beginning of the fifteenth century, and into Latin hexameters by Carlo d' Aquino in 1728.]

Silius et V. Flaccus nec in primâ classe nec in secundâ nec, si quatuor sint, in tertiâ sedebunt. Primi non tantùm animos jucunde movent sed et vehementer, ut Dantes in Ugolino, Alfierius in Bruto, ubi pater nomina filiorum legit inter conjuratos, quum legere collega non sustineat. Hos duos locos memoro, quia nihil in Europae (ut loquuntur) continente simile aut secundum inventum est post literas resuscitatas, nihil praestantius antea.

(*Poemata et Inscriptiones*, ed. 1847, p. 263.)

[Bettinelli's criticisms of Dante—Lack of critical faculty among the Italians]

Aves quae lusciniam imitantur sua voce naturali parum canorae sunt. Ars autem critica, quam omnes se scire profitentur, non tam citò doceri potest: in hac Metastasius et Gravina laudandi sunt, ut qui suo sermone primi apud Italos aliquid profecerint. Futilis Bettinellii [1] subtilitas sub magno Dante jacet, ut sub Tasso frivola ista disceptatio Academiae cujusdam Tuscae. Miror equidem apud Etruscos adeò parum floruisse et vigere criticam, quam gens optimos habuerit historicos; ars autem critica his praecipue necessaria est.

(*Ibid.* p. 281.)

[Of the modernisation of spelling—Chaucer, Milton, Shakespeare, Dante and others]

Nonnulli sunt veteribus adeò infensi, ut quum novam editionem faciant Lucretii, Catulli, Virgilii, sibi mirificè gratulentur se maculas vetustatis eluisse. Apud nostrates Chaucerus integrâ cute, et vestitu neque mutato neque resarcito, evasit; Miltonus propemodum; sed medius Shakspeare totam imaginem, a calce ad caput, scriptionibus novis exaratam erigit. Veruntamen est aliquid historicum, quod plerique non vident, in orthographiâ, et ii ipsi qui eundem scribendi modum Lucano ac Lucretio, Catullo atque Claudiano, attribuerent, inter Dantem et Metastasium discriminis aliquid permitterent. . . . Velim videre numquid, et quanto, comptior et urbanior in sermone tum recens agresti Dantes fuerit, quàm obscuriores isti qui antecesserant, quem verò postea progressum fecerint Boccacius et Petrarcha, et quatenus ab iis Machiavellus et Bembus discrepent.

(*Ibid.* pp. 294-5.)

[The green oases in the parched desert of Dante]

Miltonum, uti venerationem probent, vincunt compedibus tinnulis suis, et primis humani generis parentibus crines miramur

'Vibratos calido ferro myrrhâque madentes.'

His decorationibus occupati, nondum invenerunt in Dantes arenâ vastâ et saevâ siccitate sacras quasdem et viridissimas oases, nec in Homero vident quidquam nisi rixas et somnia et compotationes.

(*Ibid.* p. 344.)

[1] [See vol. i. pp. 210-11.]

c. 1822. HENDECASYLLABI.

Poetas Florentia semper exulasse

Oro, per teneram deam Quiritum
Cujus nomine nuncuparis, oro
Ne, Florentia, me voces poetam:
Nam collem peragrare Faesulanum
Jucundum est mihi, nec lubenter hortos
Fontesque, aut nemorum algidos recessus,
Primo invisere mane vesperique
Exul desinerem; exulatque quisquis
O Florentia, dixeris poetam.[1]

(*Poemata et Inscriptiones*, ed. 1847, p. 134.)

Dantes Caenotaphium Ligneum

Danten saecula quina transiêrunt
Cum Florentia funebres honores
Solvit manibus optimi poetae.
En pauper locupletibus supremo
Certat munere, prodigis avarus.
Sed magni exulis ossa denegantur
Ingratae patriae: locum abnuistis
Cives! nunc dare non licere fletis.
Nequicquam sinit introire fanum
Nec senos cubitos negat sepulchro
Laurenti solio potitus hospes.

(*Ibid.* p. 143.)

c. 1822. MINORA VARIA.

Florentiae scriptum ad sepulchrum Alfierii

Alfieri, aeternùm posito victure cothurno,
O senis Eridani maxime vates, ave!
Respice quem parilem jactaret Etruria Dantem!
Respice quo fato dispare condit humus!
Distulit hinc vacuum per saecula ponere marmor[2]
Externoque jacent exulis ossa solo.

(*Ibid.* p. 231).

[1] [With especial allusion, of course, to the exile of Dante.]
[2] [In a later version of this poem Landor altered *Distulit* in this line to *Destitit* and *ponere* to *tollere*.]

1823. IMAGINARY CONVERSATIONS: SOUTHEY AND PORSON.

[Many lines without beauty in Dante, Homer, Shakespeare, and Milton]

Porson. I must bring you to a confession that in your friend Wordsworth there is occasionally a little trash.

Southey. A haunch of venison would be trash to a Brahmin, a bottle of Burgundy to the Xerif of Mecca.

Porson. I will not be anticipated by you. Trash, I confess, is, no proof that nothing good can lie above it and about it. The roughest and least manageable soil surrounds gold and diamonds. Homer and Dante and Shakspeare and Milton have each many hundred lines worth little; lines without force, without feeling, without fancy; in short, without beauty of any kind. . . .

Southey. No ideas are so trivial, so incorrect, so incoherent, but they may have entered the idle fancy, and have taken a higher place than they ought in the warm imagination of the best poets. We find in Dante, as you just now remarked, a prodigious quantity of them; and indeed not a few in Virgil, grave as he is and stately.

(*Works*, ed. 1846, vol. i. pp. 13, 14.)

1824. IMAGINARY CONVERSATIONS: THE ABBÉ DELILLE AND WALTER LANDOR.

[Voltaire and Dante]

Landor. M. de Voltaire, like M. Boileau, spoke flippantly and foolishly of Ariosto: he afterwards gave his reasons for having done it.

Delille. I do not remember them at present. Were they at all satisfactory, or at least ingenious?

Landor. They were very good ones indeed, and exactly such as might have been expected from a critic of his spirit and quickness.

Delille. Do you remember the sum of them?

Landor. He had never read him! To make amends, he took him kindly by the hand, and preferred him to Dante.

Delille. He might have held back there. But where we have dirted one shoe we may dirt the other: it does not cost a farthing more to clean a pair than an odd one.

(*Ibid.* vol. i. p. 100.)

1824. IMAGINARY CONVERSATIONS: ALFIERI AND SALOMON THE FLORENTINE JEW.

[The defects and beauties of Dante]

Salomon. Certainly no race of men upon earth ever was so unwarlike, so indifferent to national dignity and to personal honour, as the Florentines are now: yet in former days a certain pride, arising from a resemblance in their government to that of Athens, excited a vivifying desire of approximation, where no danger or loss accompanied it; and genius was no less confident of his security than of his power. Look from the window. That cottage on the declivity was Dante's: that square and large mansion, with a circular garden before it elevated artificially, was the first scene of Boccaccio's *Decameron*. A boy might stand at an equal distance between them, and break the windows of each with his sling. . . . A town so little that the voice of a cabbage-girl in the midst of it may be heard at the extremities, reared within three centuries a greater number of citizens illustrious for their genius, than all the remainder of the Continent (excepting her sister Athens) in six thousand years. My ignorance of the Greek forbids me to compare our Dante with Homer. . . . Dante had not only to compose a poem, but in great part a language. Fantastical as the plan of his poem is, and, I will add, uninteresting and uninviting; unimportant, mean, contemptible, as are nine-tenths of his characters and his details, and wearisome as is the scheme of his versification; there are more thoughts highly poetical, there is more reflection, and the nobler properties of mind and intellect are brought into more intense action, not only than in the whole course of French poetry, but also in the whole of Continental: nor do I think (I must here also speak with hesitation) that any one drama of Shakspeare contains so many. Smile as you will, signor Conte: what must I think of a city where Michel-Angelo, Frate Bartolomeo, Ghiberti (who formed them), Guicciardini, and Machiavelli, were secondary men? And certainly such were they, if we compare them with Galileo and Boccacio and Dante.

(*Works*, ed. 1846, vol. i. pp. 191-2.)

c. 1826. TO CAREY,[1] ON HIS APPOINTMENT TO A LOW OFFICE IN THE BRITISH MUSEUM.[2]

Carey,[1] I fear the fruits are scanty
Thou gatherest from the fields of Dante,
But thou hast found at least a shed
Wherin to cram thy truckle-bed;
The porter's lodge of the Museum
May daily hear thee sing *Te Deum*.
  Peaches and grapes are mostly found
Richest the nearest to the ground:
Our gardeners take especial care
To keep down low all boughs that bear.

[1] [*Sic.*]

[2] [Cary was appointed Assistant-Keeper of Printed Books at the British Museum in 1826.]

Dante's long labyrinthine line
Is straiten'd and drawn tight by thine:
Hell, devil, dog, in force remain,
And Paradise blooms fresh again.

(Printed in *Heroic Idylls*, ed. 1863, p. 122.)

1828. IMAGINARY CONVERSATIONS: LANDOR, ENGLISH VISITER, AND FLORENTINE VISITER.

[Dante and the Florentines]

English Visiter. Scarcely anything is more interesting than the history of this central hive of honeyed and stinging little creatures, your Florentines. Although they have now lost their original figure and nature for the most-part, and possess not even their own lily to alight on, yet they hum, and show wonderful instinct. They were not created for the gloom of Dante, but they are alive and alert in the daylight of Petrarca and Boccaccio.

(*Works*, ed. 1846, vol. i. p. 330.)

1834. LETTER TO HENRY FRANCIS CARY (from Fiesole).

[Cary's translations of Dante and Pindar]

Among the unaccountable things in me, and many are so even to myself, is this, that I admired Pindar somewhat more in youth than in what ought to be a graver age. However, his wisdom, his high-mindedness, and his excellent selection of topics, in which no writer of prose or verse ever equalled him, render him worthy to spend the evening with one who has passed the earlier part of the day with Dante.[1]

(*Works and Life of W. S. Landor*, vol. i. p. 363.)

1836. THE PENTAMERON; OR, INTERVIEWS OF MESSER GIOVANNI BOCCACCIO AND MESSER FRANCESCO PETRARCA . . . SHOWING HOW THEY DISCOURSED UPON THAT FAMOUS THEOLOGIAN MESSER DANTE ALIGHIERI, AND SUNDRY OTHER MATTERS.

[Petrarch and Boccaccio on the merits and demerits of Dante]

Petrarca. You told me that, if it pleased God to restore you to your health again, you are ready to acknowledge his mercy by

[1][Cary, whose translation of the *Divina Commedia* was published in 1814, had published in 1833 a translation of Pindar. Landor had a high opinion of Cary's translation of Dante. Writing in 1860 (four years before his death) to R. Lytton (afterwards Lord Lytton) he said: 'Do not despise Cary's Dante. It is wonderful how he could have turned the rhymes of Dante into unrhymed verse with any harmony: he has done it.' Cary had been a school-fellow of Landor at Rugby.]

the holocaust of your *Decameron*. What proof have you that God would exact it? If you could destroy the *Inferno* of Dante, would you?

Boccaccio. Not I, upon my life! I would not promise to burn a copy of it on the condition of a recovery for twenty years.

Petrarca. You are the only author who would not rather demolish another's work than his own; especially if he thought it better: a thought which seldom goes beyond suspicion.

Boccaccio. I am not jealous of any one: I think admiration pleasanter. Moreover, Dante and I did not come forward at the same time, nor take the same walks. His flames are too fierce for you and me: we had trouble enough with milder. I never felt any high gratification in hearing of people being damned; and much less would I toss them into the fire myself. . . .

* * * *

Petrarca. Let it be recorded of me that my exhortations and intreaties have been successful, in preserving the works of the most imaginative and creative genius that our Italy, or indeed our world, hath in any age beheld.

Boccaccio. I would not destroy his poems, as I told you. . . . Even the worst of the Florentines, who in general keep only one of God's commandments, keep it rigidly in regard to Dante:

'Love them that curse you.'

He called them all scoundrels, with somewhat less courtesy than cordiality, and less afraid of censure for veracity than adulation: he sent their fathers to hell, with no inclination to separate the child and parent: and now they are hugging him for it in his shroud! . . . The idea of destroying a single copy of Dante! And what effect would that produce? There must be fifty, or near it, in various parts of Italy. . . .

* * * *

Petrarca. Little more than a tenth of the *Decameron* is bad: less than a twentieth of the *Divina Commedia* is good.

Boccaccio. So little?

Petrarca. Let me never seem irreverent to our master.

Boccaccio. Speak plainly and fearlessly, Francesco! Malice and detraction are strangers to you.

Petrarca. Well then: at least sixteen parts in twenty of the *Inferno* and *Purgatorio* are detestable, both in poetry and principle: the higher parts are excellent indeed.

Boccaccio. I have been reading the *Paradiso* more recently. . . . Preparation for my lectures made me remember a great deal of the poem. I did not request my auditors to admire the beauty of the metrical version;

Osanna sanctus deus Sabbaoth,
Super-illustrans charitate tuâ
Felices ignes horum Malahoth,[1]

nor these, with a slip of Italian between two pales of latin;

Modicum,[2] et non videbitis me,
Et iterum, sorelle mie dilette.
Modicum et vos videbitis me.[3]

I dare not repeat all I recollect of

Pepe Satan, Pepe Satan, aleppe,[4]

as there is no holy-water-sprinkler in the room: and you are aware that other dangers awaited me, had I been so imprudent as to show the Florentines the allusion of our poet. His *gergo* is perpetually in play, and sometimes plays very roughly.

Petrarca. We will talk of him again presently. I must now rejoice with you over the recovery and safety of your prodigal son, the *Decameron*.

Boccaccio. So then, you would preserve at any rate my favourite volume from the threatened conflagration.

Petrarca. Had I lived at the time of Dante, I would have given him the same advice in the same circumstances. Yet how different is the tendency of the two productions! . . . .

Boccaccio. I dare not defend myself under the bad example of any: and the bad example of a great man is the worst defence of all. Since however you have mentioned Messer Dante Alighieri, to whose genius I never thought of approaching, I may perhaps have been formerly the less cautious of offending by my levity, after seeing him display as much or more of it in hell itself.

Petrarca. The best apology for Dante, in his poetical character, is presented by the indulgence of criticism, in considering the *Inferno* and *Purgatorio* as a string of *Satires*, part in narrative and part in action; which renders the title of *Commedia* more applicable. The filthiness of some passages would disgrace the drunkenest horse-dealer; and the names of such criminals are recorded by the poet as would be forgotten by the hangman in six months. I wish I could expatiate rather on his injudiciousness than on his ferocity, in devising punishments for various crimes; or rather, than on his malignity in composing catalogues of criminals to inflict them on. Among the rest we find a gang of coiners. He calls by name all the rogues and vagabonds of every

[1] [*Par.* vii. 1-3.]

[2] It may puzzle an Englishman to read the lines beginning with *Modicum*, so as to give the metre. The secret is, to draw out *et* into a dissyllable, *et-te*, as the Italians do, who pronounce latin verse, if possible worse than we, adding a syllable to such as end with a consonant.

[3] [*Purg.* xxxiii. 10-12.]

[4] [*Inf.* vii. 1.]

city in Tuscany, and curses every city for not sending him more of them. You would fancy that Pisa might have contented him; no such thing. He hoots,

'Ah Pisa! scandal to the people in whose fine country *sì* means *yes*, why are thy neighbours slack to punish thee? May Capraia and Gorgona stop up the mouth of the Arno, and drown every soul within thee!'[1]

Boccaccio. None but a prophet is privileged to swear and curse at this rate, and several of those got broken heads for it.

Petrarca. It did not happen to Dante, though he once was very near it, in the expedition of the exiles to recover the city. Scarcely had he taken breath after this imprecation against the Pisans, than he asks the Genoese why such a parcel of knaves as themselves were not scattered over the face of the earth.[2]

Boccaccio. Here he is equitable. I wonder he did not incline to one or other of these rival republics.

Petrarca. In fact, the Genoese fare a trifle better under him than his neighbours the Pisans do.

Boccaccio. Because they have no Gorgona and Capraia to block them up. He can not do all he wishes, but he does all he can, considering the means at his disposal. . . .

Petrarca. Our great fellow citizen, if indeed we may denominate him a citizen who would have left no city standing in Italy, and less willingly his native one, places in the mouth of the devil, together with Judas Iscariot, the defenders of their country, and the best men in it, Brutus and Cassius. Certainly his feeling of patriotism was different from theirs. I should be sorry to imagine that it subjected him to any harder mouth or worse company than his own, although in a spirit so contrary to that of the two Romans, he threatened us Florentines with the sword of Germans. The two Romans, now in the mouth of the devil, chose rather to lose their lives than to see their country, not under the government of invaders, but of magistrates from their own city placed irregularly over them; and the laws, not subverted, but administered unconstitutionally. That Frenchmen and Austrians should argue and think in this manner, is no wonder, no inconsistency: that a Florentine, the wisest and greatest of Florentines, should have done it, is portentous. . . . What an argument is here! how much stronger and more convincing than philosophers could devise or than poets could utter, unless from inspiration, against the placing of power in the hands of one man only, when the highest genius at that time in the world, or perhaps at any time, betrays a disposition to employ it with such a licentiousness of inhumanity.

[1] [*Inf.* xxxiii. 79-81.] [2] [*Ibid.* 151-3.]

Boccaccio. He treats Nero with greater civility. . . . Messer Dante Alighieri does not indeed make the most gentle use of the company he has about him in hell and purgatory. Since however he had such a selection of them, I wish he could have been contented, and could have left our fair Florentines to their own fancies in their dressing-rooms.

'The time,' he cries, 'is not far distant, when there will be an indictment on parchment,[1] forbidding the impudent young Florentines to show their breast and nipples.'[2]

Now, Francesco, I have been subject all my life to a strange distemper in the eyes, which no oculist can cure, and which, while it allows me to peruse the smallest character in the very worst female hand, would never let me read an indictment on parchment where female names are implicated, although the letters were a finger in length. I do believe the same distemper was very prevalent in the time of Messer Dante; and those Florentine maids and matrons who were not afflicted by it, were too modest to look at letters and signatures stuck against the walls.

He goes on, 'Was there ever girl among the Moors or Saracens, on whom it was requisite to inflict spiritual or *other* discipline to make her go covered?' . . . 'If the shameless creatures,' he continues, 'were aware of the speedy chastisement which Heaven is preparing for them, they would at this instant have their mouths wide open to roar withal.'[3]

Petrarca. This is not very exquisite satire, nor much better manners.

* * * *

Petrarca. Nothing is easier in the world than to find and accumulate its sufferings. Yet this very profusion and luxuriance of misery is the reason why few have excelled in describing it. . . . Here again we return to the *Inferno* of Dante, who overcame the difficulty. In this vast desert are its greater its less oasis: Ugolino and Francesca di Rimini. The peopled region is peopled chiefly with monsters and moschitoes: the rest for the most part is sand and suffocation.

Boccaccio. Ah! had Dante remained through life the pure solitary lover of Bice, his soul had been gentler, tranquiller, and more generous. He scarcely hath described half the curses he went through, nor the roads he took on the journey: theology, politics, and that barbican of the *Inferno*, marriage, surrounded with its 'Selva selvaggia ed aspra e forte.'[4]

[1] [A curious slip—Dante says *in pergamo*, 'from the pulpit,' not *in pergamena*.]
[2] [*Purg.* xxiii. 99-102.]
[3] [*Ibid.* 103-8.]
[4] [*Inf.* i. 5.]

Admirable is indeed the description of Ugolino, to whoever can endure the sight of an old soldier gnawing at the scalp of an old archbishop.

Petrarca. The thirty lines from 'Ed io sentii,'[1] are unequalled by any other continuous thirty in the whole dominions of poetry.

Boccaccio. Give me rather the six on Francesca: for if in the former I find the simple, vigorous, clear narration, I find also what I would not wish, the features of Ugolino reflected full in Dante. The two characters are similar in themselves; hard, cruel, inflexible, malignant, but, whenever moved, moved powerfully. In Francesca, with the faculty of divine spirits, he leaves his own nature (not indeed the exact representative of theirs) and converts all his strength into tenderness. . . .

Quando legemmo il disiato viso
  Esser baciato di cotanto amante,
Questi, chi mai da me non sia diviso![2]
  La bocca mi baciò tutto tremante. . . .
Galeotto fu il libro, e chi lo scrisse. . . .
  Quel giorno più non vi legemmo avante.[3]

In the midst of her punishment, Francesca, when she comes to the tenderest part of her story, tells it with complacency and delight; and, instead of naming Paolo, which indeed she never has done from the beginning, she now designates him as

'Questi chi mai da me non sia diviso!'

Are we not impelled to join in her prayer, wishing them happier in their union?

Petrarca. If there be no sin in it.

Boccaccio. Ay, and even if there be. . . . God help us! What a sweet aspiration in each cesura of the verse! three love-sighs fixed and incorporate! Then, when she hath said,

'La bocca mi baciò, tutto tremante,'

she stops: she would avert the eyes of Dante from her: he looks for the sequel: she thinks he looks severely: she says, '*Galeotto* is the name of the book,' fancying by this timorous little flight she has drawn him far enough from the nest of her young loves. No, the eagle beak of Dante and his piercing eyes are yet over her. '*Galeotto* is the name of the book.'—'What matters that?'—'And of the writer.'—'Or that either.' At last she disarms him: but how? '*That* day we read no more.' Such a depth of intuitive judgment, such a delicacy of perception, exists not in any other work of human genius; and from an author, who on almost all occasions, in this part of the work, betrays a deplorable want of it.

Petrarca. Perfection of poetry! The greater is my wonder at

[1] [*Inf.* xxxiii. 46-75.] [2] [Read 'non fia diviso.'] [3] [*Inf.* v. 133-8.]

discovering nothing else of the same order or cast in this whole section of the poem. He who fainted at the recital of Francesca,

'And he who fell as a dead body falls,'

would exterminate all the inhabitants of every town in Italy! What execrations against Florence, Pistoia, Siena, Pisa, Genoa! what hatred against the whole human race! what exultation and merriment at eternal and immitigable sufferings! Seeing this, I can not but consider the *Inferno* as the most immoral and impious book that ever was written. Yet, hopeless that our country shall ever see again such poetry, and certain that without it future poets would be more feebly urged forward to excellence, I would have dissuaded Dante from cancelling it, if this had been his intention. Much however as I admire his vigour and severity of style in the description of Ugolino, I acknowledge with you that I do not discover so much imagination, so much creative power, as in the Francesca. I find indeed a minute detail of probable events: but this is not all I want most in a poet: it is not even all I want most in a scene of horror. Tribunals of justice, dens of murderers, wards of hospitals, schools of anatomy, will afford us nearly the same sensations, if we hear them from an accurate observer, a clear reporter, a skilful surgeon, or an attentive nurse. There is nothing of sublimity in the horrific of Dante, which there always is in Aeschylus and Homer. If you, Giovanni, had described so nakedly the reception of Guiscardo's heart by Gismonda, or Lorenzo's head by Lisabetta, we could hardly have endured it.

Boccaccio. Prythee, dear Francesco, do not place me over Dante: I stagger at the idea of approaching him.

Petrarca. Never think I am placing you blindly or indiscriminately. . . .

* * * *

Boccaccio. What is terror in poetry is horror in prose. We may be brought too close to an object to leave any room for pleasure. Ugolino affects us like a skeleton, by dry bony verity.

* * * *

Petrarca. In the novel . . . the very warmth and geniality of the season shed their kindly influence on us; and we are renovated and ourselves again by virtue of the clear fountain where we rest. Nothing of this poetical providence comes to our relief in Dante, though we want it oftener. It would be difficult to form an idea of a poem, into which so many personages are introduced, containing so few delineations of character, so few touches that excite our sympathy, so few elementary signs for our instruction, so few topics for our delight, so few excursions for our recreation. Nevertheless, his powers of language are prodigious; and, in the solitary places where he exerts his force rightly, the stroke is irresistible. But how greatly to be pitied must he be, who can find nothing in paradise better than sterile theology! and what an object of sadness and of consternation, he who rises up from hell like a giant refreshed! . . . Tragedy has no bye-paths, no resting-places; there is everywhere action and passion. What do we find of this nature, or what of the epic, in the Orpheus and Judith, the Charon and Can della Scala, the Sinon and Maestro Adamo?

Boccaccio. Personages strangely confounded! In this category it required a strong hand to make Pluto and Pepe Satan keep the peace, both having the same pretensions, and neither the sweetest temper.

Petrarca. Then the description of Mahomet is indecent and filthy. Yet Dante is scarcely more disgusting in this place, than he is insipid and spiritless in his allegory of the marriages, between Saint Francesco and Poverty, Saint Dominico and Faith. I speak freely and plainly to you, Giovanni, and the rather, as you have informed me that I have been thought invidious to the reputation of our great poet; for such he is transcendently, in the midst of his imperfections. Such likewise were Ennius and Lucilius in the same period of Roman literature. They were equalled, and perhaps excelled: will Dante ever be, in his native tongue? The past generations of his countrymen, the glories of old Rome, fade before him the instant he springs upward, but they impart a more constant and a more genial delight.

* * * *

Boccaccio. None who are acquainted with your character, can believe that your strictures on Dante are invidious or uncandid.

Petrarca. I am borne toward him by many strong impulses. Our families were banished by the same faction: he himself and my father left Florence on the same day, and both left it for ever. This recollection would rather make me cling to him than cast him down. Ill fortune has many and tenacious ties: good fortune has few and fragile ones. I saw our illustrious fellow citizen once only, and when I was a child. Even the sight of such a poet, in early days, is dear to him who aspires to become one, and the memory is always in his favour. The worst I can recollect to have said against his poem to others, is, that the architectural fabric of the *Inferno* is unintelligible without a long study, and only to be understood after distracting our attention from its inhabitants. Its locality and dimensions are at last uninteresting, and would better have been left in their obscurity. The zealots of Dante compare it, for invention, with the infernal regions of Homer and Virgil. I am ignorant how much the Grecian poet invented, how much existed in the religion, how much in the songs and traditions of the people. But surely our Alighieri has taken the same idea, and even made his descent in the same part of Italy, as Aeneas had done before. In the *Odyssea* . . . we have a man, although a shade, in his own features, in his own dimensions . . . vigorous and elastic, he is such as poetry saw him first; he is such as poetry would ever see him. In Dante, the greater part of those who are not degraded, are debilitated and distorted. . . .

Boccaccio. I must confess there are nowhere two whole cantos in Dante which will bear a sustained and close comparison with the very worst book of the *Odyssea* or the *Aeneid*. . . . The *Inferno*, the *Purgatorio*, the *Paradiso*, are pictures from the walls of our churches and chapels and monasteries, some painted by Giotto and Cimabue, some earlier. In several of these we detect not only the cruelty, but likewise the satire and indecency of Dante. Sometimes there is also his vigour and simplicity, but oftener his harshness and meagreness and disproportion. I am afraid the good Alighieri, like his friends the painters, was inclined to think the angels were created only to flagellate and burn us; and Paradise only for us to be driven out of it. . . . The opening of the third canto of the *Inferno* has always been much admired. There is indeed a great solemnity in the words of the inscription on the portal of hell:[1] nevertheless, I do not see the necessity for three verses out of six. After

'Per me si va nell' eterno dolore,'

it surely is superfluous to subjoin

'Per me si va fra la perduta gente';

for, beside the *perduta gente*, who else can suffer the eternal woe? And when the portal has told us that 'Justice moved the high Maker to make it,' surely it might have omitted the notification that his 'divine power' did it:

'Fecemi la divina potestate.'

The next piece of information I wish had been conveyed even in darker characters, so that they never could have been decyphered. The following line is,

'La somma Sapienza e 'l primo Amore.'

If God's first love was hell-making, we might almost wish his affections were as mutable as ours are. . . .

Petrarca. Very justly do you remark that our churches and chapels and monasteries, and even our shrines and tabernacles on the road-side, contain in painting the same punishments as Alighieri hath registered in his poem: and several of these were painted before his birth. Nor surely can you have forgotten that his master, Brunetto Latini, composed one on the same plan. The Virtues and Vices, and persons under their influence, appear to him likewise in

[1] [*Inf.* iii. 1 ff.]

a wood, wherein he, like Dante, is bewildered. Old walls are the tablets both copy: the arrangement is the devise of Brunetto.

* * * *

Second Day

Petrarca. At present we fly to princes as we fly to caves and arches, and other things of mere earth, for shelter and protection. . . . What Dante saw in his day, we see in ours. . . .

* * * *

Petrarca. In high situations like Certaldo and this Villetta, there is no danger from fogs or damps of any kind. The skylark yonder seems to have made it her first station in the air.

Boccaccio. To welcome thee, Francesco!

Petrarca. Rather say, to remind us both of our Dante. All the verses that ever were written on the nightingale are scarcely worth the beautiful triad of this divine poet on the lark.

'La lodoletta che in aere si spazia,
Prima cantando, e poi tace contenta
Dell' ultima dolcezza che la sazia.'[1]

In the first of them do not you see the twinkling of her wings against the sky? As often as I repeat them my ear is satisfied, my heart (like her's) contented.

Boccaccio. I agree with you in the perfect and unrivalled beauty of the first; but in the third there is a redundance. Is not *contenta* quite enough, without *che la sazia?* The picture is before us, the sentiment within us, and behold! we kick when we are full of manna.

Petrarca. I acknowledge the correctness and propriety of your remark; and yet beauties in poetry must be examined as carefully as blemishes, and even more; for we are more easily led away by them, although we do not dwell on them so long. We two should never be accused, in these days, of malevolence to Dante, if the whole world heard us. Being here alone, we may hazard our opinions even less guardedly, and set each other right as we see occasion.

Boccaccio. Come on then; I will venture. I will go back to find fault; I will seek it even in Francesca. To hesitate, and waver, and turn away from the subject, was proper and befitting in her. The verse, however, in no respect satisfies me. Any one would imagine from it that Galeotto was really both the title of the book, and the name of the author; neither of which is true. Galeotto, in the Tavola Ritonda, is the person who interchanges the correspondence between Lancilotto and Ginevra. The appellation is now become the generic of all men whose business it is to

[1] [*Par.* xx. 73-5.]

promote the success of others in illicit love. Dante was stimulated in his satirical vein, when he attributed to Francesca a ludicrous expression, which she was very unlikely in her own nature, and greatly more so in her state of suffering, to employ or think of, whirled round as she was incessantly with her lover. Neither was it requisite to say, 'the book was a Galeotto, and so was the author,' when she had said already that a passage in it had seduced her. Omitting this unnecessary and ungraceful line, her confusion and her delicacy are the more evident, and the following comes forth with fresh beauty. In the commencement of her speech I wish these had likewise been omitted,

> 'E ciò sa il tuo dottore';

since he knew no more about it than anybody else. As we proceed, there are passages in which I cannot find my way, and where I suspect the poet could not show it me. For instance, is it not strange that Briareus should be punished in the same way as Nimrod, when Nimrod sinned against the living God, and when Briareus attempted to overthrow one of the living God's worst antagonists, Jupiter? an action which our blessed Lord, and the doctors of the holy church, not only attempted, but (to their glory and praise for evermore) accomplished.

Petrarca. Equally strange that Brutus and Cassius (a remark which escaped us in our mention of them yesterday) should be placed in the hottest pit of hell for slaying Caesar, and that Cato, who would have done the same thing with less compunction, should be appointed sole guardian and governor of purgatory. . . . Alighieri not only throws together the most opposite and distant characters, but even makes Jupiter and our Saviour the same person.

> E se lecito m' è, o sommo *Giove!*
> Che fosti in terra per noi *crocifisso.*[1]

Boccaccio. Jesus Christ ought no more to be called Jupiter than Jupiter ought to be called Jesus Christ.

Petrarca. In the whole of the *Inferno* I find only the descriptions of Francesca and Ugolino at all admirable. Vigorous expressions there are many, but lost in their application to base objects; and insulated thoughts in high relief, but with everything crumbling round them. Proportionally to the extent, there is a scantiness of poetry, if delight is the purpose or indication of it. Intensity shows everywhere the powerful master: and yet intensity is not invitation. A great poet may do everything but repel us. Established laws are pliant before him: nevertheless his office hath both its duties and its limits.

[1] [*Purg.* vi. 118-9.]

Boccaccio. The simile in the third canto, the satire at the close of the fourth, and the description at the commencement of the eighth, if not highly admirable, are what no ordinary poet could have produced.

Petrarca. They are streaks of light in a thundercloud. You might have added the beginning of the twenty-seventh, in which the poetry of itself is good, although not excellent, and the subject of it assuages the weariness left on us, after passing through so many holes and furnaces, and undergoing the dialogue between Sinon and master Adam.

Boccaccio. I am sorry to be reminded of this. It is like the brawl of the two fellows in Horace's *Journey to Brundusium*. They are the straitest parallels of bad wit and bad poetry that ancient and modern times exhibit. Ought I to speak so sharply of poets who elsewhere have given me so great delight?

* * * *

Petrarca. When a language grows up all into stalk, and its flowers begin to lose somewhat of their character, we must go forth into the open fields, through the dingles, and among the mountains, for fresh seed. Our ancestors did this, no very long time ago. Foremost in zeal, in vigour and authority, Alighieri took on himself the same patronage and guardianship of our adolescent dialect, as Homer of the Greek. . . .

* * * *

Petrarca. Impatience and intolerance are sure to be excited at any check to admiration in the narratives of Ugolino and of Francesca: nothing is to be abated: they are not only to be admirable, but entirely faultless. . . .

Boccaccio. Vague and indefinite criticism suits only slight merit, and presupposes it. Lineaments irregular and profound as Dante's are worthy of being traced with patience and fidelity. . . . I would not detract one atom from the worth of Dante; which cannot be done by summing it up exactly, but may be by negligence in the computation.

Petrarca. Your business, in the lectures, is not to show his merits, but his meaning; and to give only so much information as may be given without offence to the factions.

* * * *

Boccaccio. We will carry this volume with us, and show Dante what we have been doing. . . .

Petrarca. Come, as you proposed, let us now continue with our Dante. Ugolino relates to him his terrible dream, in which he fancied he had seen Gualando, Sismondi, and Lanfranco, killing his children: and he says that, when he awakened, he heard them moan in their sleep. In such circumstances, his awakening ought rather to have removed the impression he laboured under; since it showed him the vanity of the dream, and afforded him the consolation that the children were alive. Yet he adds immediately, what, if he were to speak it at all, he should have deferred, 'You are very cruel if you do not begin to grieve, considering what my heart presaged to me; and, if you do not weep at it, what is it you are wont to weep at?'[1]

Boccaccio. Certainly this is ill-timed; and the conference would indeed be better without it anywhere.

Petrarca. Further on, in whatever way we interpret

'Poscia più che 'l dolor potè 'l digiuno,'[2]

the poet falls sadly from his sublimity.

Boccaccio. If the fact were as he mentions, he should have suppressed it, since we had already seen the most pathetic in the features, and the most horrible in the stride, of Famine. Gnawing, not in hunger, but in rage and revenge, the archbishop's scull, is, in the opinion of many, rather ludicrous than tremendous.

Petrarca. In mine, rather disgusting than ludicrous: but Dante (we must whisper it) is the great master of the disgusting. . . .

* * * *

Boccaccio. Now do tell me, before we say more of the *Paradiso* what can I offer in defence of the Latin scraps from litanies and lauds, to the number of fifty or thereabouts?

Petrarca. Say nothing at all, unless you can obtain some Indulgences for repeating them.

Boccaccio. And then such verses as these, and several score of no better:

'I' credo ch' ei credette ch' io credesse.'[3]

'O Jacomo, dicea, di sant' Andrea.'[4]

'Come Livio scrisse, che non erra.'[5]

'Nel quale un cinque cento dieci e cinque.'[6]

'Mille ducento con sessanta sei.'[7]

'Pepe Satan, Pepe Satan, Pepè.'[8]

'Raffael mai *amec, sabe, almi.*'[9]

'Non avria pur dell' orlo fatto *crich.*[10]

* * * *

[1] [*Inf.* xxiii. 40-2.]
[2] [*Inf.* xxxiii. 75.]
[3] [*Inf.* xiii. 25.]
[4] [*Inf.* xiii. 133.]
[5] [*Inf.* xxviii. 12.]
[6] [*Purg.* xxxiii. 43.]
[7] [*Inf.* xxi. 113.]
[8] [*Inf.* vii. 1.]
[9] [*Inf.* xxxi. 67.]
[10] [*Inf.* xxxii. 30.]

Petrarca. We must do for our poet that which other men do for themselves; we must defend him by advancing the best authority for something as bad or worse. . . . It will gratify the national pride of our Florentines, if you show them how greatly the nobler parts of their fellow-citizen excel the loftiest of his Mantuan guide.

Boccaccio. Of Virgil?

Petrarca. Even so.

Boccaccio. He had no suspicion of his equality with this prince of Roman poets, whose footsteps he follows with reverential and submissive obsequiousness.

Petrarca. Have you never observed that persons of high rank universally treat their equals with deference; and that ill-bred ones are often smart and captious? . . . Small critics and small poets take all this courage when they licentiously shut out the master; but Dante really felt the veneration he would impress. Suspicion of his superiority he had none whatever. . . .

Boccaccio. But surely if there are some very high places in our Alighieri, the inequalities are perpetual and vast; whereas the regularity, the continuity, the purity of Virgil, are proverbial.

Petrarca. It is only in literature that what is proverbial is suspicious; and mostly in poetry. Do we find in Dante, do we find in Ovid, such tautologies and flatnessess as these,

'Quam si dura silex . . . *aut stet Marpessia cautes.*'

'Majus adorta nefas . . . *majoremque orta furorem.*'
&c. &c.

. . . In your comparison of poet with poet, the defects as well as the merits of each ought to be placed side by side. This is the rather to be expected, as Dante professes to be Virgil's disciple. You may easily show that his humility no more became him than his fierceness. . . . We will now return again to Virgil, and consider in what relation he stands to Dante. Our Tuscan and Homer are never inflated. . . .

Boccaccio. Virgil and Dante are altogether so different, that, unless you will lend me your whole store of ingenuity, I shall never bring them to bear one upon the other. . . . I shall never dare to employ half your suggestions in our irritable city, for fear of raising up two new factions, the Virgilians and the Dantists.

* * * *

Third Day

Boccaccio. How happens it, O Francesco! that nearly at the close of our lives, after all our efforts and exhortations, we are standing quite alone in the extensive fields of literature? We are only like to *scoriae* struck from the anvil of the gigantic

Dante. . . . I cannot but think again and again, how fruitlessly the bravest have striven to perpetuate the ascendency or to establish the basis of empire, when Alighieri hath fixed a language for thousands of years, and for myriads of men; a language far richer and more beautiful than our glorious Italy ever knew before, in any of her regions, since the Attic and the Dorian contended for the prize of eloquence on her southern shores. Eternal honour, eternal veneration, to him who raised up our country from the barbarism that surrounded her! Remember how short a time before him, his master Brunetto Latini wrote in French; prose indeed. . . .

Petrarca. Brunetto! Brunetto! it was not well done in thee. An Italian, a poet, write in French! . . . Several things in Dante himself you will find more easy to explain than to excuse. You have already given me a specimen of them, which I need not assist you in rendering more copious.

Boccaccio. There are certainly some that require no little circumspection. Difficult as they are to excuse, the difficulty lies more on the side of the clergy than the laity.

Petrarca. I understand you. The *gergo*[1] of your author has always a reference to the court of the Vatican. Here he speaks in the dark: against his private enemies he always is clear and explicit. Unless you are irresistibly pressed into it, give no more than two, or at most three lectures, on the verse which, I predict, will appear to our Florentines the cleverest in the poem:

'Chi nel viso degli uomini legge OMO.'[2]

* * * *

Boccaccio. With all its flatnesses and swamps, many have preferred the *Paradiso* to the other two sections of the poem.

Petrarca. There is as little in it of very bad poetry, or we may rather say, as little of what is no poetry at all, as in either, which are uninviting from an absolute lack of interest and allusion, from the confusedness of the ground-work, the indistinctness of the scene, and the paltriness (in great measure) of the agents. If we are amazed at the number of Latin verses in the *Inferno* and *Purgatorio*, what must we be at their fertility in the *Paradiso*, where they drop on us in ripe clusters through every glen and avenue! We reach the conclusion of the sixteenth canto before we come in sight of poetry, or more than a glade with a gleam upon it. Here we find a description of Florence in her age of innocence: but the scourge of satire sounds in our ears before we fix the attention.

Boccaccio. I like the old Ghibelline best in the seventeenth, where he dismisses the doctors, corks up the Latin, ceases from

[1] [Gabriele Rossetti's *Spirito Antipapale*, in which this theory of the *gergo* was developed, had been published four years before.]

[2] [*Purg.* xxiii. 32.]

psalmody, looses the arms of Calfucci and Arigucci, sets down Caponsacco in the market, and gives us a stave of six verses which repays us amply for our heaviest toils and sufferings.

'Tu lascerai ogni cosa diletta, &c.'

But he soon grows weary of tenderness and sick of sorrow, and returns to his habitual exercise of throwing stones and calling names. Again we are refreshed in the twentieth. Here we come to the simile: here we look up and see his lark, and are happy and lively as herself. Too soon the hard fingers of the master are round our wrists again: we are dragged into the school, and are obliged to attend the divinity-examination, which the poet undergoes from Saint Simon-Peter. He acquits himself pretty well, and receives a handsome compliment from the questioner, who, *inflamed with love*, acknowledges he has given *a good account of the coinage, both in regard to weight and alloy.*[1]

'Tell me,' continues he, 'have you any of it in your pocket?' 'Yea,' replies the scholar, 'and so shining and round that I doubt not what mint it comes from.'[2] Saint Simon-Peter does not take him at his word for it, but tries to puzzle and pose him with several hard queries. He answers both warily and wittily, and grows so contented with his examining master, that, instead of calling him *a sergeant of infantry*,[3] as he did before, he now entitles him *the baron*.[4] I must consult our bishop ere I venture to comment on these two verses,

Credo una essenza, sì una e sì trina
Che soffera congiunto *sunt et este*,[5]

as, whatever may peradventure lie within them, they are hardly worth the ceremony of being burnt alive for, although it should be at the expense of the Church. . . . With how true and entire a pleasure shall I point out to my fellow-citizens such a glorious tract of splendour as there is in the single line,

'Ciò ch' io vedevo mi sembrava un riso
Dell' universo!'[6]

With what exultation shall I toss up my gauntlet into the balcony of proud Antiquity, and cry *Descend! Contend!* I have frequently heard your admiration of this passage, and therefore I dwell on it the more delighted. Beside, we seldom find anything in our progress that is not apter to excite a very different sensation. School-divinity can never be made attractive to the Muses; nor will Virgil and Thomas Aquinas ever cordially shake hands. The unrelenting rancour against the popes is more tedious than unmerited: in a poem I doubt whether we would not rather find it

[1] [*Par.* xxiv. 82-4.]
[2] [*Par.* xxiv. 85-7.]
[3] [' Primipilo,' *Par.* xxiv. 59.]
[4] [*Par.* xxiv. 115.]
[5] [*Par.* xxiv. 140-1.]
[6] [*Par.* xxvii. 4-5.]

unmerited than tedious. For of all the sins against the spirit of poetry, this is the most unpardonable. . . .

Petrarca. I do not wonder they make Saint Peter *redden*, as we hear they do, but I regret that they make him stammer,

'Quegli che usurpa in terra il luogo mio,
Il luogo mio, il luogo mio, &c.'[1]

Alighieri was not the first catholic who taught us that papacy is usurpation, nor will he be (let us earnestly hope) the last to inculcate so evident a doctrine. . . . Beatrice, in the place before us, changes colour too, as deeply as ever she did on earth; for Saint Peter, in his passion, picks up and flourishes some very filthy words. He does not recover the use of his reason on a sudden; but, after a long and bitter complaint that faith and innocence are only to be found in little children; and that the child moreover who loves and listens to its mother while it lisps, wishes to see her buried when it can speak plainly; he informs us that this corruption ought to excite no wonder, since the human race must of necessity go astray, not having any one upon earth to govern it.[2] . . .

Boccaccio. Well is it for me that my engagement is to comment on Alighieri's *Divina Commedia* instead of his treatise *De Monarchiâ*. He says bold things there, and sets apostles and popes together by the ears. That is not the worst. He would destroy what is and should be, and would establish what never can or ought to be.

Petrarca. If a universal monarch could make children good universally, and keep them as innocent when they grow up as they were in the cradle, we might wish him upon his throne to-morrow. But Alighieri, and those others who have conceived such a prodigy, seem to be unaware that what they would establish for the sake of unity, is the very thing by which this unity must be demolished. . . .

* * * *

Boccaccio. We cannot help the Florentines: we have made the most of them, like the good tailor who, as Dante says, cuts his coat according to his cloth.[3]

Petrarca. Do you intend, if they should call upon you again, to give them occasionally some of your strictures on his prose writings?

Boccaccio. It would not be expedient. Enough of his political sentiments is exhibited, in various places of his poem, to render him unacceptable to one party; and enough of his theological, or rather his ecclesiastical, to frighten both. . . . Because the popes took away our christianity, he was so angry he would throw Italy's freedom after it. Any thorn in the way is fit enough to toss the battered rag on. A German king will do; Austrian or Bavarian,

[1] [*Par.* xxvii. 22-3.] [2] [*Par.* xxvii. 127 ff.] [3] [*Par.* xxxii. 140-1.]

Swabian or Switzer. And, to humiliate us more and more, and render us the laughing stock of our household, he would invest the intruder with the title of Roman emperor. . . . Let us endure a French pope, or any other, as well as we can; there is no novelty in his being a stranger. . . . Dante is wrong, I suspect, in imagining the popes to be infidels; and, no doubt, they would pay for indulgences as honestly as they sell them, if there were anybody at hand to receive the money.

* * * *

Fourth Day

Petrarca. Do not throw aside your *Paradiso* for me. Have you been reading it again so early?

Boccaccio. Looking into it here and there. I had spare time before me.

Petrarca. You have coasted the whole poem, and your boat's bottom now touches ground. But tell me what you think of Beatrice.

Boccaccio. I think her in general more of the seraphic doctor than of the seraph. It is well she retained her beauty where she was, or she would scarcely be tolerable now and then. And yet, in other parts, we forget the captiousness in which Theology takes delight, and feel our bosoms refreshed by the perfect presence of the youthful and innocent Bice. . . . Above all, I have been admiring the melody of the cadence in this portion of the *Divina Commedia.* Some of the stanzas leave us nothing to desire in facility and elegance. Alighieri grows harmonious as he grows humane, and does not, like Orpheus, play the better with the beasts about him.

Petrarca. It is in Paradise that we might expect his tones to be tried and modulated.

Boccaccio. None of the imitative arts should repose on writhings and distortions. Tragedy herself, unless she lead from Terror to Pity, has lost her way.

Petrarca. What then must be thought of a long and crowded work, whence Pity is violently excluded, and where Hatred is the first personage we meet, and almost the last we part from?

Boccaccio. Happily the poet has given us here a few breezes of the morning, a few glimpses of the stars, a few similes of objects to which we have been accustomed among the amusements or occupations of the country. Some of them would be less admired in a meaner author, and are welcome here chiefly as a variety and relief to the mind, after a long continuance in a painful posture.

* * * *

Petrarca. If our countrymen presented any flagrant instances of ingratitude, Alighieri would have set apart a *bolgia* for their reception.

Boccaccio. When I correct and republish my *Commentary*, I must be as careful to gratify, as my author was to affront them. I know, from the nature of the Florentines and of the Italians in general, that in calling on me to produce one, they would rather I should praise indiscriminately than parsimoniously. And respect is due to them for repairing, by all the means in their power, the injustice their fathers committed; for enduring in humility his resentment; and for investing him with public honours, as they would some deity who had smitten them. . . .

Petrarca. In the precincts of those lofty monuments, those towers and temples, which have sprung up amid her factions, the name of Dante is heard at last, and heard with such reverence as only the angels or the saints inspire.

Boccaccio. There are towns so barbarous, that they must be informed by strangers of their own great man, when they happen to have produced one. . . . There are such; but not in Italy. I have seen youths standing and looking with seriousness, and indeed with somewhat of veneration, on the broad and low stone bench,[1] to the south of the cathedral, where Dante sat to enjoy the fresh air in summer evenings; and where Giotto, in conversation with him, watched the scaffolding rise higher and higher up his gracefullest of towers. It was truly a bold action, when a youngster pushed another down on the poet's seat.

* * * *

Petrarca. Aware you must be that there are many more defects in our author than we have touched or glanced at: principally, the loose and shallow foundation of so vast a structure; its unconnectedness: its want of manners, of passion, of action, consistently and uninterruptedly at work toward a distinct and worthy purpose; and lastly (although least importantly as regards the poetical character) that splenetic temper, which seems to grudge brightness to the flames of hell, to delight in deepening its gloom, in multiplying its miseries, in accumulating weight upon depression, and building labyrinths about perplexity.

Boccaccio. Yet, O Francesco! when I remember what Dante had suffered and was suffering from the malice and obduracy of his enemies; when I feel (and how I do feel it!) that you also have been following up his glory through the same paths of exile; I can rest only on what is great in him, and the exposure of a fault appears to me almost an inhumanity. . . .

Petrarca. With such feelings, which are ours in common, there is little danger that we should be unjust toward him; and, if ever our opinions come before the public, we may disregard the petu-

[1] [The so called 'sasso di Dante']

lance and aspersions of those whom nature never constituted our judges, as she did us of Dante. . . .

Boccaccio. Every family in Florence is a portion of the government or has been lately. Every one preserves the annals of the republic; the facts being nearly the same, the inferences widely diverging, the motives utterly dissimilar. A strict examination of Dante would involve the bravest and most intelligent. . . .

Petrarca. Posterity will regret that many of those allusions to persons and events, which we now possess in the pages of Dante, have not reached her.

* * * *

Petrarca. Some scholars will assert that everything I have written in my sonnets is allegory or allusion; others will deny that anything is; and similarly of Dante. It was known throughout Italy that he was the lover of *Beatrice* Portinari. He has celebrated her in many compositions; in prose and poetry, in Latin and Italian. Hence it became the safer for him afterwards to introduce her as an allegorical personage, in opposition to the *Meretrice;* under which appellation he (and I subsequently) signified the Papacy. Our great poet wandered among the marvels of the Apocalypse, and fixed his eyes the most attentively on the words,

'Veni, et ostendam tibi sponsam, uxorem Agni.'

He, as you know, wrote a commentary on his *Commedia* at the close of his treatise *De Monarchiâ.* But he chiefly aims at showing the duties of pope and emperor, and explaining such parts of the poem as manifestly relate to them. The Patarini accused the pope of despoiling and defiling the church; the Ghibellines accused him of defrauding and rebelling against the emperor; Dante enlists both under his flaming banner, and exhibits the *Meretrice* stealing from *Beatrice* both the *divine* and *august* chariot; the church and empire.

* * * *

Petrarca. We have loved; and so fondly as we believe none other ever did; and yet, although it was in youth, Giovanni, it was not in the earliest white dawn, when we almost shrink from its freshness, when everything is pure and quiet, when little of earth is seen, and much of heaven. It was not so with us; it was with Dante. The little virgin Beatrice Portinari breathed all her purity into his boyish heart, and inhaled it back again. . . . If Dante enthroned his Beatrice in the highest heaven, it was Beatrice who conducted him thither.

* * * *

Boccaccio. The best poets are the most impressive, because their steps are regular; for without regularity there is neither strength nor state. Look at Sophocles, look at Aeschylus, look at Homer.

Petrarca. I agree with you entirely to the whole extent of your observations; and, if you will continue, I am ready to lay aside my Dante for the present.

Boccaccio. No, no; we must have him again between us: there is no danger that he will sour our tempers. . . . I will express my doubt whether Dante felt all the indignation he threw into his poetry. . . . Our Alighieri had slipped into the habit of vituperation; and he thought it fitted him; so he never left it off. . . .

Petrarca. The chief desire in every man of genius is to be thought one; and no fear or apprehension lessens it. Alighieri, who had certainly studied the gospel, must have been conscious that he not only was inhumane, but that he betrayed a more vindictive spirit than any pope who is enshrined within the fretwork of his golden grating.

Boccaccio. Unhappily, his strong talon had grown into him, and it would have pained him to suffer its amputation.

* * * *

Petrarca. Be more serious, Giovanni . . . hardly Dante himself could make you grave.

Boccaccio. I do not remember how it happened that we slipped away from his side. One of us must have found him tedious.

Petrarca. If you were really and substantially at his side, he would have no mercy on you.

Boccaccio. In sooth, our good Alighieri seems to have had the appetite of a dogfish or shark, and to have bitten the harder the warmer he was. I would not voluntarily be under his manifold rows of dentals. He has an incisor to every saint in the calendar. I should fare, methinks, like Brutus and the Archbishop. He is forced to stretch himself, out of sheer listlessness, in so idle a place as Purgatory: he loses half his strength in Paradise: Hell alone makes him alert and lively: there he moves about and threatens as tremendously as the serpent that opposed the legions on their march in Africa. He would not have been contented in Tuscany itself, even had his enemies left him unmolested.

* * * *

Petrarca. Ghibellines and Guelphs will have been contested for only by the worms, long before the *Decameron* has ceased to be recited on our banks of blue lilies and under our arching vines. Another plague may come amidst us; and something of a solace in so terrible a visitation would be found in your pages. . . .

Boccaccio. I do indeed think my little bevy from Santa Maria Novella would be better company on such an occasion, than a devil with three heads, who diverts the pain his claws inflicted, by sticking his fangs in another place.

Petrarca. This is atrocious, not terrific nor grand. Alighieri is grand by his lights, not by his shadows; by his human affection, not by his infernal. As the minutest sands are the labours of some profound sea, or the spoils of some vast mountain, in like manner his horrid wastes and wearying minutenesses are the chafings of a turbulent spirit, grasping the loftiest things and penetrating the deepest, and moving and moaning on the earth in loneliness and sadness.

* * * *

Boccaccio. Let our prose show what we are, and our poetry what we have been.

Petrarca. You would never have given this advice to Alighieri.

Boccaccio. I would never plough porphyry; there is ground fitter for grain. Alighieri is the parent of his system, like the sun, about whom all the worlds are but particles thrown forth from him. We may write little things well, and accumulate one upon another; but never will any be justly called a great poet unless he has treated a great subject worthily. . . . A throne is not built of birds'-nests, nor do a thousand reeds make a trumpet.

Petrarca. I wish Alighieri had blown his on nobler occasions.

Boccaccio. We may rightly wish it: but, in regretting what he wanted, let us acknowledge what he had: and never forget (which we omitted to mention) that he borrowed less from his predecessors than any of the Roman poets from theirs. . . .

Petrarca. Imitation, as we call it, is often weakness, but it likewise is often sympathy.

Boccaccio. Our poet was seldom accessible in this quarter. Invective picks up the first stone on the wayside, and wants leisure to consult a forerunner.

Petrarca. Dante (original enough everywhere) is coarse and clumsy in this career. Vengeance has nothing to do with comedy, nor properly with satire. . . . Lucretius, in his vituperation, is graver and more dignified than Alighieri. Painful: to see how tolerant is the atheist, how intolerant the Catholic: how anxiously the one removes from among the sufferings of Mortality, her last and heaviest, the fear of a vindictive Fury pursuing her shadow across rivers of fire and tears; how laboriously the other brings down Anguish and Despair, even when Death has done his work. How grateful the one is to that beneficent philosopher who made him at peace with himself, and tolerant and kindly toward his fellow-creatures! how importunate the other that God should forego his divine mercy, and hurl everlasting torments both upon the dead and the living!

Boccaccio. I have always heard that Ser Dante was a very good man and sound Catholic: but Christ forgive me if my heart is oftener on the side of Lucretius!

* * * *

Fifth Day

Boccaccio. We have had enough of Dante: I believe few of his beauties have escaped us: and small faults, which we readily pass by, are fitter or small folks, as grubs are the proper bait for gudgeons.

* * * *

Remarks on the alleged jealousy of Boccaccio and Petrarca

Such was Boccaccio's reverential modesty, that, to the very close of his life, he called Petrarca his master. Immeasurable as was his own superiority, he no more thought himself the equal of Petrarca, than Dante (in whom the superiority was almost as great) thought himself Virgil's. . . . Our country has produced four men so pre-eminently great, that no name, modern or ancient, excepting Homer, can stand very near the lowest: these are, Shakspeare, Bacon, Milton, and Newton. Beneath the least of these (if any one can tell which is least) are Dante and Aristoteles; who are unquestionably the next. Out of Greece and England, Dante is the only man of the first order; such he is, with all his imperfections. Less ardent and energetic, but having no less at command the depths of thought and treasures of fancy, beyond him in variety, animation, and interest, beyond him in touches of nature and truth of character, is Boccaccio. Yet he believed his genius was immeasurably inferior to Alighieri's. . . . Milton and Homer may be placed together; on the continent Homer will be seen at the right hand; in England, Milton. Supreme, above all, immeasurably supreme, stands Shakspeare. I do not think Dante is any more the equal of Homer than Hercules is the equal of Apollo. Though Hercules may display more muscles, yet Apollo is the powerfuller without any display of them at all. Both together are just equivalent to Milton, shorn of his *Sonnets*, and of his *Allegro* and *Penseroso;* the most delightful of what (wanting a better name) we call *lyrical* poems.

(*Works*, ed. 1846, vol. ii. pp. 301 ff.)

1840. August 16. THE EXAMINER.

[Landor's account of the discovery of the Giotto portrait of Dante in the Bargello at Florence]

A grand discovery has been made at Florence of some Frescoes by Giotto. They exist in a lumber-room, formerly the chapel of the *Palazzo del Podestà*, which became the residence of the Duke of Athens when he took possession of the republic. It was afterwards converted into a prison, and called the *Bargello*. In the year preceding the exile of Dante, the portrait of that poet was painted on the walls of this chapel, together with Brunetto Latini, Corso Donati, and other illustrious citizens of the Florentine commonwealth. Several coats of whitewash had covered them over, so that not a vestige was perceptible. The first who proposed to bring them into light again was the Canonico Moreni, a very distinguished antiquarian, now advanced in years. Cioni, professor of chemistry, discovered a mode of removing the lime and plaster, without injuring in the slightest degree the solid *intonaco* underneath. But, as the modern artists of Italy, and particularly the Florentines, entertain small reverence for their ancient predecessors, not even the majesty of Giotto was recognised by them; and Moreni found very few voices to second him in his application to the authorities. At last, after twenty more years, Mr. Aubrey Bezzi, a gentleman no less intelligent than zealous in everything that relates either to the arts or to letters, presented, in the month of May, 1839, his first petition to resuscitate the most illustrious of the Italians, their earliest great painter and their greatest poet. Several months elapsed; at last an answer, an evasive one, was given. It stated that 'the Grand Duke would not be advised to undertake the restoration of the fresco, without ascertaining beforehand the *exact* cost; and that his dignity prevented him from profiting by Mr. Aubrey Bezzi's offer *of incurring the whole expense*.'

To overcome this difficulty, Mr. Aubrey Bezzi sent in another memorial, offering to accomplish the undertaking for two hundred and fifty *francesconi*, or dollars, which the Grand Duke might reimburse when the operation was completed. After a delay of many additional months, he obtained a decree, appointing him a commissioner, with two others, and limiting the expense to two hundred and fifty dollars; which moderate sum has actually sufficed. The figures are unimpaired. In one compartment is a Holy Family, with an angel, which those who have seen it, and are capable of estimating it, represent as of great beauty. It was offered by the Authorities to Mr. Aubrey Bezzi, who declined to mar the unity of the work by removing any part of it.

There are artists to whom the recovery of a painting by Giotto will be uninteresting: there are others, and some persons not artists, who will receive the intelligence of it with the same enthusiasm as of a hymn by Homer. To such, and such only, is this discovery announced. We now possess, what was wanting until now, a sure original portrait of Dante: and we, and our descendants all over the world, must own ourselves indebted for it to the indefatigable zeal of Mr. Aubrey Bezzi.

(p. 518.)

1840. LETTER TO JOHN FORSTER (from Bath).

[Dante's story of Francesca da Rimini]

I have written now the last drama[1] of the trilogy; imperfect no doubt, as you will discover, but better, I promise you, both as poetry and drama, than the two first. You will like what one of my characters says on reading Dante's story of Francesca da Rimini:

Piteous, most piteous, for most guilty passion,
Two lovers are condemned to one unrest
For ages. I now first knew poetry,
I had known song and sonnet long before:
I sail'd no more amid the barren isles,
Each one small self; the mighty continent
Rose and expanded; I was on its shores.

(*Works and Life of W. S. Landor,* vol. i. p. 397.)

1842. IMAGINARY CONVERSATIONS: SOUTHEY AND PORSON (Second Conversation).

[Homer, Dante, Milton and Shakespeare]

Southey. I think you are wrong in your supposition that the poet and the man are usually dissimilar.

Porson. There is a race of poets; not however the race of Homer and Dante, Milton and Shakespeare; but a race of poets there is, which nature has condemned to a Siamese twinship. Wherever the poet is, there also must the man obtrude obliquely his ill-favoured visage. From a drunken connection with Vanity this surplus offspring may always be expected. In no two poets that ever lived do we find the fact so remarkably exemplified as in Byron and Wordsworth.

(*Works,* ed. 1846, vol. i. p. 68.)

1843. LETTER TO JOHN FORSTER (from Bath).

['The four giants,' Homer, Shakespeare, Milton and Dante]

Gray's Elegy will be read as long as any work of Shakespeare, despite of its moping owl and the tin-kettle of an epitaph tied to its tail. It is the first poem that ever touched my heart, and it

[1] [*Fra Rupert,* published in 1841; which had been preceded in 1839 by *Andrea of Hungary* and *Giovanna of Naples.*]

strikes it now just in the same place. Homer, Shakespeare, Milton, Dante, the four giants who lived before our last Deluge of poetry, have left the ivy growing on the churchyard wall.

(*Works*, ed. 1846, vol. i. p. 426.)

1843. FRANCESCO PETRARCA.[1]

[Dante and the poet's crown]

I will not discuss the question, how great or how little was the glory of this coronation of Petrarch; a glory which Homer and Dante, which Shakespeare and Milton, never sought,[2] and never would have attained.

(*Ibid.* vol. viii. p. 434.)

[The *Decameron* and the *Divina Commedia*]

In January (1348) Petrarch left Parma for Vienna, where on the 25th he felt the shock of an earthquake. In the preceding month a column of fire was observed above the pontifical palace. After these harbingers of calamity came that memorable plague, to which we owe the immortal work of Boccaccio; a work occupying the next station, in continental literature, to the *Divina Commedia*, and displaying a greater variety of powers. . . .

There are stories in the *Decameron* which require more genius to conceive and execute than all the poetry of Petrarca, and indeed there is in Boccaccio more variety of the mental powers than in any of his countrymen, greatly more deep feeling, greatly more mastery over the human heart, than in any other but Dante.

(*Ibid.* pp. 439, 441.)

[Petrarch and the *Divina Commedia*]

On his return to Florence, Boccaccio sent his friend the *Divina Commedia*, written out likewise by himself, and accompanied with profuse commendations. Incredible as it may appear, this noble poem, the glory of Italy, and admitting at that time but one other in the world to a proximity with it, was wanting to the library of Petrarca. His reply was cold and cautious: the more popular man, it might be thought, took umbrage at the loftier. He was jealous even of the genius which had gone by, and which bore no resemblance to his own, excepting in the purity and intensity of love: for this was a portion of the genius in both.

(*Ibid.* p. 445.)

[1] [Originally published in the *Foreign Quarterly Review* for July, 1843.]

[2] [So far as Dante is concerned this is certainly not true: in the *Divina Commedia* he openly expresses his desire for the poet's crown (see *Par.* xxv. 7-9; and also *Ecl.* i. 42-4).]

[Petrarch excelled in beauty by Dante only]

Petrarca's 'Triumph of Death' is truly admirable. . . . In the second part Laura comes to the poet in a dream, holds out her hand, and invites him to sit by her on the bank of a rivulet, under the shade of a beech and a laurel. Nothing, in this most beautiful of languages, is so beautiful, excepting the lines of Dante on Francesca, as these:—

> E quella man già tanto desiata,
> A me, parlando e sospirando, porse.

(*Works*, ed. 1846, vol. i. p. 458.)

JAMES HENRY LEIGH HUNT

(1784-1859)

[Leigh Hunt, whose father was a popular preacher, was born at Southgate in Middlesex in 1784. In 1792 he went to Christ's Hospital, where among his friends was Thomas Barnes (afterwards editor of the *Times*), with whom he learnt Italian. At an early date he occupied himself with writing poetry, and in 1801 a collection of his poems, written between the ages of twelve and sixteen, was published under the title of *Juvenilia*. In 1808 he became editor of the *Examiner*, in which in 1812 he published an article reflecting on the Prince Regent, for which he was sentenced to a fine of £500 and two years' imprisonment. In 1816 Hunt published his best-known poem, *The Story of Rimini*, based on the episode of Paolo and Francesca in the fifth canto of the *Inferno*. In 1822 he joined Shelley and Byron at Pisa in the establishment of a quarterly magazine, called the *Liberal*, which only lived through four numbers.[1] After Shelley's death in July of that year, he went to Genoa, and afterwards to Florence, where he resided for two years. From the time of his return to England in 1825 till his death at Putney in 1859, he was actively engaged in producing poems and essays on literary subjects, many of which he himself collected and reprinted in *Men, Women, and Books*, in 1847. Leigh Hunt had a good knowledge of Italian, and was familiar with the *Divina Commedia*,[2] references to which abound in his prose writings, and which he summarised in prose, with occasional verse renderings, in his *Stories from the Italian Poets* (1846).[3]]

1812. Sept. 27. LETTER TO HENRY BROUGHAM.[4]

[Dante's bitterness against Florence]

ACCEPT my best thanks for your packets about Ravenna. . . . Dante's strange epitaph[5] I remember well; but I should rather look upon its conclusion as corroborative of his being the author than otherwise. He was very bitter, you know,

[1] [See below, pp. 359 ff.] [2] [See *Introduction*, p. xlvi.]

[3] [This book, being subsequent to 1844, does not come within the scope of the present work. A list of the passages translated from Dante is given in Report xxiv. of the Cambridge (U.S.A.) Dante Society (*Chronological List of English Translations from Dante*), 1906.]

[4] [Afterwards Lord Brougham.] [5] [See vol. i. p. 91.]

against Florence, and particularly so against the vice he imputes to his countrymen.[1] In his *Inferno* he devotes a whole canto to it, and does not scruple, among his criminals, to place his old master, Brunetto Latini, whom, nevertheless, he treats with the greatest respect, both in that and other passages of his works. He was an unaccountable sort of fellow, and, I take it, must have been *bilious.*

(*Correspondence of Leigh Hunt*, vol. i. p. 61.)

1816. THE STORY OF RIMINI, A POEM.

[The episode of Paolo and Francesca in the *Divina Commedia*]

The following story is founded on a passage in Dante, the substance of which is contained in the concluding paragraph of the third canto. . . . The passage in question—the episode of Paulo and Francesca—has long been admired by the readers of Italian poetry, and is indeed the most cordial and refreshing one in the whole of that singular poem the Inferno, which some call a satire, and some an epic, and which, I confess, has always appeared to me a kind of sublime night-mare. We even lose sight of the place, in which the saturnine poet, according to his summary way of disposing both of friends and enemies, has thought proper to put the sufferers; and see the whole melancholy absurdity of his theology, in spite of itself, falling to nothing before one genuine impulse of the affections.

The interest of the passage is greatly increased by its being founded on acknowledged matter of fact. Even the particular circumstance which Dante describes as having hastened the fall of the lovers,—the perusal of Launcelot of the Lake,—is most likely a true anecdote; for he himself, not long after the event, was living at the court of Guido Novello da Polenta, the heroine's father; and indeed the very circumstance of his having related it at all, considering its nature, is a warrant of its authenticity. . . .

The Italians have been very fond of this little piece of private history, and I used to wonder that I could meet with it in none of the books of novels, for which they have been so famous; till I reflected that it was perhaps owing to the nature of the books themselves, which such a story might have been no means of recommending. The historians of Ravenna, however, have taken care to record it; and besides Dante's episode, it is alluded to by Petrarch and by Tassoni.

(*Preface*,[2] ed. 1817, pp. vii-x.)

[1] [Hunt evidently accepted *pravi* (instead of *parvi*) *amoris* as the correct reading in the last line.]

[2] [Compare Leigh Hunt's reference to this poem in the preface to his *Poetical Works* (1832); and the *Argument* prefixed in that edition (see below, pp. 127-8).]

[Imitation of *Inf.* v. 127 ff.]

There's apt to be, at conscious times like these,
An affectation of a bright-eyed ease,
An air of something quite serene and sure,
As if to seem so, were to be, secure:
With this the lovers met, with this they spoke,
With this they sat down to the self-same book,
And Paulo, by degrees, gently embraced
With one permitted arm her lovely waist;
And both their cheeks, like peaches on a tree,
Leaned with a touch together, thrillingly;
And o'er the book they hung, and nothing said,
And every lingering page grew longer as they read.
  As thus they sat, and felt with leaps of heart,
Their colour change, they came upon the part
Where fond Geneura, with her flame long nurst,
Smiled upon Launcelot when he kissed her first:—
That touch, at last, through every fibre slid;
And Paulo turned, scarce knowing what he did,
Only he felt he could no more dissemble,
And kissed her, mouth to mouth, all in a tremble.
Sad were those hearts, and sweet was that long kiss:
Sacred be love from sight, whate'er it is.
The world was all forgot, the struggle o'er,
Desperate the joy.—That day they read no more.

(From *Canto iii.* ed. 1817, pp. 77-8.)

1818. Aug. 4. LETTER TO MARY WOLLSTONECRAFT SHELLEY.

[Dante 'the night of the Italian day']

I think you would like Ariosto's minor poems and satires. But Petrarch, Boccaccio, and Dante, are the morning, noon, and night of the great Italian day; or, rather, Dante, Petrarch, and Boccaccio, are the night, morning, and noon. 'And the evening and the morning were the first day.'

(*Correspondence,* vol. i. p. 123.)

1818. Nov. 12. LETTER TO PERCY BYSSHE AND MARY WOLLSTONECRAFT SHELLEY.

[Specimens of Italian Poets from Dante to Metastasio]

I am now resuming my drama; and am going to propose to Constable, that when I have done it I will undertake specimens of the Italian poets from Dante to Metastasio.

(*Correspondence,* vol. i. p. 126.)

1819-21. THE INDICATOR.

[Dante's description of mist]

No. XV. Mists and Fogs.—We must mention another instance of the poetical use of a mist, if it is only to indulge ourselves in one of those masterly passages of Dante, in which he contrives to unite minuteness of detail with the most grand and sovereign effect. It is in a lofty comparison of the planet Mars looking through morning vapours; the reader will see with what (*Purgatorio*, c. ii. v. 10). Dante and his guide Virgil have just left the infernal regions, and are lingering on a solitary sea-shore in purgatory; which reminds us of that still and far-thoughted verse:—

Lone sitting by the shores of old romance.

But to our English-like Italian.

Noi eravam lungh' esso 'l mare ancora, &c.

That solitary shore we still kept on,
  Like men, who musing on their journey, stay
  At rest in body, yet in heart are gone;
When lo! as at the early dawn of day,
  Red Mars looks deepening through the foggy heat,
  Down in the west, far o'er the watery way;
So did mine eyes behold (so may they yet)
  A light, which came so swiftly o'er the sea,
  That never wing with such a fervour beat.
I did but turn to ask what it might be
  Of my sage leader, when its orb had got
  More large meanwhile, and came more gloriously:
And by degrees, I saw I knew not what
  Of white about it; and beneath the white
  Another. My great master uttered not
One word, till those first issuing candours bright
  Fanned into wings; but soon as he had found
  Who was the mighty voyager now in sight,
He cried aloud, 'Down, down, upon the ground;
  It is God's Angel.'[1]

(Ed. 1834,[2] vol. i. pp. 76-7.)

[Dante's account of the death of Ulysses]

No. XVII. More News of Ulysses.—Talking the other day with a friend[3] about Dante, he observed, that whenever so great a poet

[1] [*Purg.* ii. 10-29.]

[2] [The reprint is entitled *The Indicator and the Companion; a Miscellany for the Field and the Fire-side.*]

[3] The late Mr. Keats.

told us anything in addition or continuation of an ancient story, he had a right to be regarded as classical authority. For instance, said he, when he tells us of that characteristic death of Ulysses in one of the books of his *Inferno*, we ought to receive the information as authentic, and be glad that we have more news of Ulysses than we looked for. We thought this a happy remark, and instantly turned with him to the passage in question. The last account of Ulysses in the ancient poets, is his sudden re-appearance before the suitors at Ithaca. There is something more told of him, it is true, before the Odyssey concludes; but with the exception of his visit to his aged father, our memory scarcely wishes to retain it; nor does it controvert the general impression left upon us, that the wandering hero is victorious over his domestic enemies; and reposes at last, and for life, in the bosom of his family. . . . It is impossible to say, whether Dante would have left Ulysses quietly with Penelope after all his sufferings, had he known them as described in Homer. The old Florentine, though wilful enough when he wanted to dispose of a modern's fate, had great veneration for his predecessors. At all events, he was not acquainted with Homer's works. They did not make their way back into Italy till a little later. But there were Latin writers extant, who might have informed him of the other stories relative to Ulysses; and he saw nothing in them, to hinder him from giving the great wanderer a death of his own.

He has, accordingly, with great attention to nature, made him impatient of staying at home, after a life of such adventure and excitement. But we will relate the story in his own order. He begins it with one of his most romantic pieces of wildness. The poet and his guide Virgil are making the best of their difficult path along a ridge of the craggy rock that overhangs the eighth gulph of hell; when Dante, looking down, sees the abyss before him full of flickering lights, as numerous, he says, as the fire-flies which a peasant, reposing on a hill, sees filling the valley, of a hot evening. Every flame shot about separately; and he knew that some terrible mystery or other accompanied it. As he leaned down from the rock, grasping one of the crags, in order to look closer, his guide, who perceived his earnestness, said, 'within those fires are spirits; every one swathed in what is burning him.' Dante told him, that he had already guessed as much; and pointing to one of them in particular, asked who was in that fire which was divided at top, as though it had ascended from the funeral-pile of the hating Theban brothers. 'Within that,' answered Virgil, 'are Diomed and Ulysses, who speed together now to their own misery, as they used to do to that of others.' They were suffering the penalty of the various frauds they had perpetrated in concert;

such as the contrivance of the Trojan horse, and the *theft* of the Palladium. Dante entreats, that if those who are within the sparkling horror can speak, it may be made to come near. Virgil says it shall; but begs the Florentine not to question it himself, as the spirits, being Greek, might be shy of holding discourse with him. When the flame has come near enough to be spoken to, Virgil addresses the 'two within one fire'; and requests them, if he ever deserved anything of them as a poet, great or little, that they would not go away, till one of them had told him how he came into that extremity.

At this, says Dante, the greater horn of the old fire began to lap hither and thither, murmuring; like a flame struggling with the wind. The top then, yearning to and fro, like a tongue trying to speak, threw out a voice, and said: 'When I departed from Circe, who withdrew me to her for more than a year in the neighbourhood of Gaieta, before Aeneas had so named it, neither the sweet company of my son, nor pious affection of my old father, nor the long-owed love with which I ought to have gladdened Penelope, could conquer the ardour that was in me to become wise in knowledge of the world, of man's vices and his virtue. I put forth into the great open deep with only one bark, and the small remaining crew by whom I had not been left. I saw the two shores on either side, as far as Spain and Morocco; and the island of Sardinia, and the other isles which the sea there bathes round about. Slowly we went, my companions and I, for we were old; till at last we came to that narrow outlet, where Hercules set up his pillars, that no man might go further. I left Seville on the right hand: on the other I had left Ceuta. O brothers, said I, who through a hundred thousand perils are at length arrived at the west, deny not to the short waking day that yet remains to our senses, an insight into the unpeopled world, setting your backs upon the sun. Consider the stock from which ye sprang: ye were not made to live like the brute beasts, but to follow virtue and knowledge. I so sharpened my companions with this little speech on our way, that it would have been difficult for me to have withheld them, if I would. We left the morning right in our stern, and made wings of our oars for the idle flight, always gaining upon the left. The night now beheld all the stars of the other pole; while our own was so low, that it arose not out of the ocean-floor. Five times the light had risen underneath the moon, and five times fallen, since we put forth upon the great deep; when we descried a dim mountain in the distance, which appeared higher to me than ever I had seen any before. We rejoiced, and as soon mourned: for there sprung a whirlwind from the new land, and struck the foremost frame of our vessel. Three times, with all the waters, it whirled us round; at the fourth it dashed the stern up in air, and the prow downward; till, as seemed fit to others, the ocean closed above our heads.'[1]

> Tre volte il fè girar con tutte l' acque:
> A la quarta levar la poppa in suso,
> E la prora ire in giù, come altrui piacque,
> Infin ch 'l mar fu sopra noi richiuso.

Why poor Ulysses should find himself in hell after his immersion, and be condemned to a swathing of eternal fire, while St. Dominic, who deluged Christianity with fire and blood, is called a Cherubic Light,[2] the Papist, not the poet, must explain. He puts all the Pagans in hell. because, however good some of them may have been, they lived before Christ, and could not worship God properly —(*debitamente*). But he laments their state, and represents them as suffering a mitigated punishment: they *only* live in a state of perpetual desire without hope (*sol di tanto offesi*)![3] A sufficing misery, it must be allowed; but compared with the horrors he fancies for heretics and others, undoubtedly a great relief. Dante, throughout his extraordinary work, gives many evidences of great natural sensibility; and his countenance, as handed down to us, as well as the shade-struck gravity of his poetry, shews the cuts and disquietudes of heart he must have endured. But unless the occasional hell of his own troubles, and his consciousness of the mutability of all things, helped him to discover the brevity of individual suffering as a particular, and the lastingness of nature's benevolence as an universal, and thus gave his poem an intention beyond what appears upon the surface, we must conclude, that a bigoted education, and the fierce party politics in which he was a leader and sufferer, obscured the greatness of his spirit.

(Ed. 1834, vol. i. pp. 84-91.)

[Dante and Quevedo]

No. XX. Thieves, Ancient and Modern.—Quevedo, no ordinary person, is very amusing. His *Visions of Hell* in particular, though of a very different kind from Dante's, are more edifying.

(*Ibid.* vol. i. p. 141.)

[Dante and Virgil]

No. XXIII. Spirit of the Ancient Mythology.—Virgil, in a well-known passage of the Georgics: 'Felix qui potuit,' etc.. exalts either Epicurus or Lucretius as a blessed being, who put hell and terror under his feet. A sickly temperament appears to have made him wish, rather than be able, to carry his own scepticism so

[1] [*Inf.* xxvi. 91-142.] [2] [*Par.* xi. 39.] [3] [*Inf.* iv. 37-42.]

far; yet he insinuates his disbelief in Tartarus, in the sixth book of his epic poem, where Aeneas and the Sybil, after the description of the lower world, go out through the ivory gate, which was the passage of false visions.*

* Did Dante forget this, when he took Virgil for his guide through the Inferno?

(Ed. 1834, vol. i. p. 177.)

[Dante's description of dolphins]

No. XXVII. Dolphins.—Dante, with his tendency to see things in a dreary point of view, has given an illustration of the agonies of some of the damned in his *Inferno*, at once, new, fine, and horrible. It is in the 22nd book, 'Come i delfini' &c.[1] He says that some wretches swimming in one of the gulphs of hell, shot out their backs occasionally, like Dolphins, above the pitchy liquid, in order to snatch a respite from torment; but darted them back again like lightning. The devils would prong them as they rose. Strange fancies these for maintaining the character of religion!

(*Ibid.* vol. i. p. 197.)

[Dante's head-dress]

No. XXIX. A Chapter on Hats.—The Romans copied the Greeks in their dress, as in every thing else; but the poorer orders wore a cap like their boasted Phrygian ancestors, resembling the one which the reader may see about the streets upon the bust of Canova's Paris. The others would put their robes about their heads upon occasion,—after the fashion of the hoods of the middle ages, and of the cloth head-dresses which we see in the portraits of Dante and Petrarch. Of a similar mode are the draperies on the heads of our old Plantagenet kings and of Chaucer.

(*Ibid.* vol. i. p. 219.)

[Dante and the Southern Cross]

No. XXXI. The Realities of Imagination.—America began to be richer for us the other day, when Humboldt came back and told us of its luxuriant and gigantic vegetation: of the myriads of shooting lights, which revel at evening in the southern sky; and of that grand constellation,[2] at which Dante seems to have made so remarkable a guess. (*Purgatorio*, cant. i. v. 22).

(*Ibid.* vol. i. p. 244)

[Dante, Milton, and Homer]

No. L. Remarks upon Andrea di Basso's Ode to a Dead Body.—When Dante and Milton shall cease to have any effect as religious

[1] [*Inf.* xxii. 19 ff.]

[2] [The Southern Cross.]

dogmatizers, they will still be the mythological poets of one system of belief, as Homer is of another. So immortal is pleasure, and so surely does it escape out of the throng of its contradictions.

(Ed. 1834, vol. ii. p. 76.)

[Dante's notice of his contemporaries and predecessors]

No. LIV. On Commendatory Verses.—Varius and Gallus, two eminent Roman poets, scarcely survive but in the panegyrics of their contemporaries. Dante notices his, and his predecessors. Petrarch and Boccaccio publicly honoured, as they privately loved, one another.

(*Ibid.* vol. ii. p. 155.)

[Pickles suggestive of Dante]

No. LVII. Of Dreams.—It is probable that a trivial degree of indigestion will give rise to very fantastic dreams in a fanciful mind; while on the other hand, a good oxthodox repletion is necessary towards a fanciful creation in a dull one. It shall make an epicure, of any vivacity, act as many parts in his sleep as a tragedian, 'for that night only.' The inspirations of veal, in particular, are accounted extremely Delphic; Italian pickles partake of the spirit of Dante; and a butterboat shall contain as many ghosts as Charon's.

(*Ibid.* vol. ii. pp. 126-7.)

[Dante, Petrarch, and Homer]

No. LXIII. My Books.—Dante puts Homer, the great ancient, in his *Elysium*, upon trust; but a few years afterwards, *Homer*, the book, made its appearance in Italy, and Petrarch, in a transport, put it upon his book-shelves, where he adored it, like 'the unknown God.'

(*Ibid.* vol. ii. p. 194.)

1825. CRITICISM ON FEMALE BEAUTY.[1]

[Dante on female beauty]

It is agreed on all hands that a female eyebrow ought to be delicate, and nicely pencilled. Dante says of his mistress's, that it looked as if it was painted.

'Il ciglio
Pulito, e brun, talchè pinto pare.'[2]
Rime, Lib. V.

'The eyebrow,
Polished and dark, as though the brush had drawn it.'

* * * *

[1] [Originally published in *New Monthly Magazine*, July-August, 1825.]

[2] [This and the following quotations are from the canzone 'Io miro i crespi e gli biondi capegli' (*Canzoniere*, ed. Fraticelli, pp. 236-9), formerly attributed to Dante.]

The nose in general has the least character of any of the features. . . . The poets have been puzzled to know what to do with it. They are generally contented with describing it as straight, and in good proportion. The straight nose, quoth Dante,—'il dritto naso.' 'Her nose directed streight,' said Chaucer.

* * * *

The most graceful and modest of the women of Italy have a certain want of retirement. Their movements do not play inwards, but outwards: do not wind and retreat upon themselves, but are developed as a matter of course. If thought of, they are equally suffered to go on, with an unaffected and crowning satisfaction, conquering and to conquer. This is the walk that Dante admired:—

'Soave a guisa va di un bel pavone;
Diritta sopra sè, come una grua.'

'Sweetly she goes, like the bright peacock; straight
Above herself, like to the lady crane.'

(*Men, Women, and Books*, ed. 1847, pp. 252, 255, 282.)

1828. LORD BYRON AND SOME OF HIS CONTEMPORARIES; WITH RECOLLECTIONS OF THE AUTHOR'S LIFE, AND OF HIS VISIT TO ITALY.

[The Countess Guiccioli and Dante]

'There is no man, nor well educated woman in Italy, that cannot quote all the finer passages of the favourite author (Dante).'—(A great mistake.)—'The Guiccioli could repeat almost all the Divine Comedy.'—*Byron.*—Three volumes of stern writing about Hell, Purgatory, and Paradise! *Credat Medwin!* I remember very well, that his Lordship's fair friend was quite horrified at the poem of Andrea di Basso, a writer of a Dantesque order of mind. It was addressed to the corpse of a proud beauty. Lord Byron showed it her to enjoy her impatience. She was quite vexed and mortified.

(Vol. i. p. 222.)

[Dante, Spenser, Milton, and the sea]

All this corner of the Peninsula is rich in ancient and modern interest. There is Cape St. Vincent; Trafalgar, more illustrious; Cadiz, the city of Geryon; Gibraltar, and the other pillar of Hercules; Atlantis, Plato's Island, which he puts hereabouts; and the Fortunate Islands, . . . which lay in this part of the Atlantic, according to Pliny. Here, also, if we are to take Dante's word[1] for it, Ulysses found a grave, not unworthy of his life in the

[1] [*Inf.* xxvi. 91-142.]

'Odyssey.' . . . It is observable, that Milton does not deal much in descriptions of the ocean, a very epic part of poetry . . . the best describer of the sea, among our English poets, is Spenser, who was conversant with the Irish Channel. Shakspeare, for an inland poet, is wonderful. . . . Milton and Dante speak of the ocean as a great plain. Shakspeare talks as if he had ridden upon it, and felt its unceasing motion. . . . As to Spenser, see his comparisons of 'billows in the Irish sounds'; his 'World of waters wide and deep,' in the first book,—much better than 'the ocean floor' (*suol marino*)[1] of Dante.

(Vol. ii. pp. 336-8.)

[Influence of climate on poetry]

Poetry is the internal part, or sentiment, of what is material; and therefore, our thoughts being driven inwards, and rendered imaginative by these very defects of climate which discolour to us the external world, we have had among us some of the greatest poets that ever existed. It is observable, that the greatest poets of Italy came from Tuscany, where there is a great deal of inclemency in the seasons. The painters were from Venice, Rome, and other quarters; some of which, though more northern, are more genially situated. The hills about Florence made Petrarch and Dante well acquainted with winter; and they were travellers, and unfortunate. These are mighty helps to reflection. Titian and Raphael had nothing to do but paint under a blue sky for half the day, and play with their mistress's locks all the rest of it. Let a painter in cloudy and bill-broking England do this if he can.

(Vol. ii. p. 355.)

[Dante and Petrarch compared with the Augustan poets]

Augustus is nobody, or ought to be nobody, to a traveller in modern Italy. He, and twenty like him, never gave me one sensation, all the time I was there; and even the better part of the Romans it is difficult to think about. There is something formal and cold about their history, in spite of Virgil and Horace. . . . And their poets, even the best of them, were copiers of the Greek poets, not originals like Dante and Petrarch.

(Vol. ii. pp. 400-1.)

1828. THE COMPANION.

[Dante and St. Paul on Heaven]

No. I. An Earth upon Heaven.—It is a pity that none of the great geniuses, to whose lot it has fallen to describe a future state,

[1] [*Inf.* xxvi. 129.]

has given us his own notions of heaven. Their accounts are all modified by the national theology; whereas the Apostle himself has told us, that we can have no conception of the blessings intended for us. 'Eye hath not seen, nor ear heard,' &c. After this Dante's shining lights are poor.

(Ed. 1834, vol. ii. p. 230.)

1832. THE WORLD OF BOOKS.[1]

[Dante and Italy]

The globe we inhabit is divisible into two worlds; one hardly less tangible, and far more known than the other,—the common geographical world, and the world of books; and the latter may be as geographically set forth. A man of letters, conversant with poetry and romance, might draw out a very curious map, in which this world of books should be delineated and filled up. . . . Italy would be covered with ancient and modern romance; with Homer, Virgil, Ovid, Dante, Boccaccio, &c.; with classical villas, and scenes Elysian and infernal. . . .

Chaucer (with Spenser, Shakespeare, and Milton) is one of the Four Great English Poets; and it is with double justice that he is called the Father of English Poetry, for, as Dante did with Italian, he helped to form its very language.

(*Men, Women, and Books*, ed. 1847, vol. i. pp. 132 ff.)

1832. THE POETICAL WORKS OF LEIGH HUNT.

[The Episode of Paolo and Francesca in the *Divina Commedia*]

I took up the subject of the *Story of Rimini* at one of the happiest periods of my life: otherwise I confess I should have chosen a less melancholy one. . . . I remember I was never more astonished than when some of the critics of the poem in question (not altogether impartial, however, on the political score), found out, that the hero and heroine had not suffered enough for the cause of good morals. . . . This I know, that I thought the catastrophe a very dreadful one when I wrote it, and the previous misery worse; and that although I certainly intended no moral lesson, or thought about it, when I was led by the perusal of the story in Dante to attempt making a book of it, the subject gradually forced upon me the consideration of those first causes of error, of which I have been speaking. I thought of putting for a motto to the second edition, a passage out of the *Orlando Innamorato*:

'Bisogna ben guardare
Al primo errore, ed inconveniente'

'Guard well against the first, unfit mistake.'

[1][Originally published in *Tait's Edinburgh Magazine*, May, 1832.]

But so little did I suspect that any one could remain unimpressed with the catastrophe, that I doubted whether the motto itself would not be mixed up too exclusively with the principal sufferers. I am glad to think it is now likely to be otherwise, and that to those who choose to reflect on the tragedy of Dante's story, no link in the chain of moral causes need be lost sight of.

(*Preface*, pp. xxxix-xli.)

The Story of Rimini—This poem is founded on the beautiful episode of Paulo and Francesca in the fifth book of the *Inferno*, where it stands like a lily in the mouth of Tartarus. The substance of what Dante tells us of the history of the two lovers is to be found at the end of the third Canto. The rest has been gathered from the commentators.

(*Argument*,[1] p. lxiii.)

1837. OF DECEASED STATESMEN WHO HAVE WRITTEN VERSES.[2]

[Sackville and Dante]

Sackville's Induction to the *Mirror of Magistrates* is a *look in* at the infernal regions, or is like a portal to the allegorical part of the *Fairy Queen*, or rather to the sadder portion of that part. . . . Perhaps a better comparison would be that of the quaint figures of the earliest Italian painters, compared with those of Raphael. Or it is a bit of a minor Dante.

(*Men, Women, and Books*, ed. 1847, vol. i. p. 293.)

1839. SOCIAL MORALITY: SUCKLING AND BEN JONSON.[3]

[Dante's 'disagreeable muse']

Ben is an anomaly in the list of great poets; and we can only account for him, as for a greater (Dante,—who has contrived to make his muse more grandly disagreeable), by supposing that his nature included the contradictions of some ill-matched progenitors, and that, while he had a grace for one parent or ancestor, he had a slut and a fury for another.

(*Ibid.* vol. ii. p. 4.)

[1] [Added in the present edition; for the original *Preface* (of 1816) see above, p. 117.]

[2] [Originally published in the *Monthly Repository*, 1837, vol. i. pp. 279-83, 410-16.]

[3] [Originally published in the *Monthly Chronicle*, Feb. 1839.]

1841. June 25. LETTER TO MACVEY NAPIER.[1]

[Petrarch and Dante]

Petrarch was not so great as Dante; but there has been a tendency of late, in consequence of the discovery of that truth, to undervalue his nightingale muse, with the lesson which it taught of faith in love.

(*Correspondence*, vol. ii. p. 18.)

1843. ONE HUNDRED ROMANCES OF REAL LIFE.

[The second on the list is the *Story of Madonna Pia* (referred to by Dante in the fifth canto of the *Purgatorio*), as told by Hazlitt in his *Notes of a Journey through France and Italy* (see below, pp. 185-6).]

1844. IMAGINATION AND FANCY; OR SELECTIONS FROM THE ENGLISH POETS, ILLUSTRATIVE OF THOSE FIRST REQUISITES OF THEIR ART.

[Imagination and fancy in Dante, and other great poets]

An Answer to the Question, What is Poetry?—Of imaginary creatures, none out of the pale of mythology and the East, are equal, perhaps, in point of invention, to Shakspeare's Ariel and Caliban; though poetry may grudge to prose the discovery of a Winged Woman, especially such as she has been described by her inventor in the story of Peter Wilkins; and in point of treatment, the Mammon and Jealousy of Spenser, some of the monsters of Dante, particularly his Nimrod,[2] his interchangements of creatures into one another,[3] and (if I am not presumptuous in anticipating what I think will be the verdict of posterity) the Witch in Coleridge's Christabel, may rank even with the creations of Shakspeare. It may be doubted, indeed, whether Shakspeare had bile and nightmare enough in him to have thought of such detestable horrors as those of the interchanging adversaries (now serpent, now man), or even of the huge, half-blockish enormity of Nimrod,—in Scripture, the 'mighty hunter' and builder of the tower of Babel,—in Dante, a tower of a man in his own person, standing with some of his brother giants up to the middle in a pit in hell, blowing a horn to which a thunder-clap is a whisper, and hallooing after Dante and his guide in the jargon of a lost tongue! The transformations are too odious to quote: but of the towering giant we cannot refuse ourselves the 'fearful joy' of a specimen. It was twilight, Dante tells us, and he and his guide Virgil were silently pacing through one of the dreariest regions of hell, when the sound of a tremendous

[1] [Editor of the *Edinburgh Review*.]

[2] [*Inf.* xxxi. 46 ff.]

[3] [*Inf.* xxv. 97 ff.]

horn made him turn all his attention to the spot from which it came. He there discovered through the dusk, what seemed to be the towers of a city. Those are no towers, said his guide; they are giants, standing up to the middle in one of these circular pits.

Come quando la nebbia si dissipa, &c.[1]

I look'd again; and as the eye makes out,
By little and little, what the mist conceal'd
In which, till clearing up, the sky was steep'd;
So, looming through the gross and darksome air,
As we drew nigh, those mighty bulks grew plain,
And error quitted me, and terror join'd:
For in like manner as all round its height
Montereggione crowns itself with towers,
So tower'd above the circuit of that pit,
Though but half out of it, and half within,
The horrible giants that fought Jove, and still
Are threaten'd when he thunders. As we near'd
The foremost, I discern'd his mighty face,
His shoulders, breast, and more than half his trunk,
With both the arms down hanging by the sides.
His face appear'd to me, in length and breadth,
Huge as St. Peter's pinnacle at Rome,
And of a like proportion all his bones.
He open'd, as we went, his dreadful mouth,
Fit no sweeter psalmody; and shouted
After us, in the words of some strange tongue,
Ràfel ma-eè amech zabeè almee!—
"Dull wretch!" my leader cried, "keep to thine horn,
And so vent better whatsoever rage
Or other passion stuff thee. Feel thy throat
And find the chain upon thee, thou confusion!
Lo! what a hoop is clench'd about thy gorge."
Then turning to myself, he said, "His howl
Is its own mockery. This is Nimrod, he
Through whose ill thought it was that humankind
Were tongue-confounded. Pass him, and say nought:
For as he speaketh language known of none,
So none can speak save jargon to himself."

Assuredly it could not have been easy to find a fiction so uncouthly terrible as this in the hypochondria of Hamlet. Even his father had evidently seen no such ghost in the other world. All his phantoms were in the world he had left. Timon, Lear, Richard, Brutus, Prospero, Macbeth himself, none of Shakspeare's men had,

[1] [Leigh Hunt here quotes *Inf.* xxxi. 34-48, 58-60, 67-81, in the original.]

in fact, any thought but of the earth they lived on, whatever supernatural fancy crossed them. The thing fancied was still a thing of this world, "in its habit as it lived," or no remoter acquaintance than a witch or a fairy. Its lowest depths (unless Dante suggested them) were the cellars under the stage. Caliban himself is a cross-breed between a witch and a clown. No offence to Shakspeare; who was not bound to be the greatest of healthy poets, and to have every morbid inspiration besides. What he might have done, had he set his wits to compete with Dante, I know not: all I know is, that in the infernal line he did nothing like him; and it is not to be wished he had. It is far better that, as a higher, more universal, and more beneficent variety of the genus Poet, he should have been the happier man he was, and left us the plump cheeks on his monument, instead of the carking visage of the great, but over-serious, and comparatively one-sided Florentine. Even the imagination of Spenser, whom we take to have been a "nervous gentleman" compared with Shakspeare, was visited with no such dreams as Dante. Or, if it was, he did not choose to make himself thinner (as Dante says *he* did)[1] with dwelling upon them. He had twenty visions of nymphs and bowers, to one of the mud of Tartarus. Chaucer, for all he was "a man of this world" as well as the poet's world, and as great, perhaps a greater enemy of oppression than Dante, besides being one of the profoundest masters of pathos that ever lived, had not the heart to conclude the story of the famished father and his children, as finished by the inexorable anti-Pisan. But enough of Dante in this place. . . .

Imagination belongs to Tragedy, or the serious muse; Fancy to the comic. Macbeth, Lear, Paradise Lost, the poem of Dante, are full of imagination: the Midsummer Night's Dream and the Rape of the Lock, of fancy: Romeo and Juliet, the Tempest, the Fairy Queen, and the Orlando Furioso, of both. . . .

Spenser has great imagination and fancy too, but more of the latter; Milton both also, the very greatest, but with imagination predominant; Chaucer, the strongest imagination of real life, beyond any writers but Homer, Dante, and Shakspeare, and in comic painting inferior to none; Pope has hardly any imagination, but he has a great deal of fancy; Coleridge little fancy, but imagination exquisite. Shakspeare alone, of all poets that ever lived, enjoyed the regard of both in equal perfection. . . .

It is to be doubted whether even Shakspeare could have told a story like Homer, owing to that incessant activity and superfœtation of thought, a little less of which might be occasionally desired even in his plays;—if it were possible, once possessing anything of

[1] [*Par.* xxv. 3.]

his, to wish it away. Next to Homer and Shakspeare come such narrators as the less universal, but still intenser Dante; Milton, with his dignified imagination; the universal, profoundly simple Chaucer; and luxuriant, remote Spenser. . . .

Truth, of any great kind whatsoever, makes great writing. This is the reason why such poets as Ariosto, though not writing with a constant detail of thought and feeling like Dante, are justly considered great as well as delightful. . . . Ariosto occasionally says as fine things as Dante, and Spenser as Shakspeare; but the business of both is to enjoy; and in order to partake their enjoyment to its full extent, you must feel what poetry is in the general as well as the particular, must be aware that there are different songs of the spheres, some fuller of notes, and others of sustained delight; and as the former keep you perpetually alive to thought or passion, so from the latter you receive a constant harmonious sense of truth and beauty, more agreeable perhaps on the whole, though less exciting. Ariosto, for instance, does not *tell a story* with the brevity and concentrated passion of Dante; every sentence is not so full of matter, nor the style so removed from the indifference of prose; yet you are charmed with a truth of another sort, equally characteristic of the writer, equally drawn from nature and substituting a healthy sense of enjoyment for intenser emotion.

(Ed. 1845, pp. 11-16, 31, 32-3, 62, 64-6.)

[Spenser and Dante]

Selections from Spenser.—Spenser, in some respects, is more southern than the south itself. Dante, but for the covered heat which occasionally concentrates the utmost sweetness as well as venom, would be quite northern compared with him. . . . His wholesale poetical belief, mixing up all creeds and mythologies, but with less violence, resembles that of Dante and Boccaccio. . . . Spenser is not so great a poet as Shakspeare or Dante;—he has less imagination, though more fancy, than Milton. He does not see things so purely in their elements as Dante; neither can he combine their elements like Shakspeare. . . .

Upton thinks it not unlikely that Spenser imagined the direful, deadly and black fruits which his infernal garden of Proserpine bears, from a like garden which Dante describes, *Inferno*, Canto 13, v. 4.

Non frondi verdi, ma di color fosco, &c.
No leaves of green were theirs, but dusky sad;
No fair straight boughs, but gnarl'd and tangled all;
No rounded fruits, but poison-bearing thorns.

Dante's garden, however, has no flowers. It is a *human grove*; that is to say, made of trees that were once human beings. . . .

Virgil appears to have been the first who ventured to find sublimity in a loathsome odour. . . . A greater genius, Dante, followed him in this, as in other respects; and, probably, would have set the example had it not been given him. Sackville followed both. . . .

Spenser's Tantalus, and his Pontius Pilate, and indeed the whole of the latter part of his hell, strike us with but a poor sort of cruelty compared with any like number of pages out of the tremendous volume of Dante. But the sooty golden cave of Mammon, and the mortal beauty of the garden of Proserpine, with its golden fruit hanging in the twilight; all, in short, in which Spenser combines his usual luxury with grandeur, are as fine as anything of the kind which Dante or any one else ever conceived.

(Ed. 1845, pp. 74, 96-7, 100, 101.)

[Shakespeare, Chaucer, and Dante]

Selections from Shakspeare.—Shakspeare is equal to the greatest poets in grandeur of imagination; to all in diversity of it; to all in fancy; to all in everything else, except in a certain primæval intensity, such as Dante's and Chaucer's; and in narrative poetry, which he certainly does not appear to have had a call to write.

(*Ibid.* p. 149.)

[Excess of theology in Dante and Milton]

Selections from Middleton, Decker and Webster.—Either from self-love, or necessity, or both, too much writing is the fault of all ages and of every author. Even Homer, says Horace, sometimes nods. How many odes might not Horace himself have spared us! How many of his latter books, Virgil! What theology, Dante and Milton! What romances, Cervantes! What comedies, Ariosto! What tragedies, Dryden! What heaps of words, Chaucer and Spenser! What *Iliads*, Pope!

(*Ibid.* p. 218.)

[Milton, Homer, Dante, and Shakespeare]

Selections from Milton.—Milton was a very great poet, second only (if second) to the very greatest, such as Dante and Shakspeare; and, like all great poets, equal to them in particular instances. He had no pretensions to Shakspeare's universality; his wit is dreary; and (in general) he had not the faith in things that Homer and Dante had, apart from the intervention of words. He could not let them speak for themselves without helping them with his learning.

(*Ibid.* p. 237.)

[Keats and Dante]

Selections from Keats.—

The sculptur'd dead on each side seem'd to freeze,
Imprison'd in black, purgatorial rails:
Knights, ladies, praying in dumb orat'ries,
He passeth by; and his weak spirit fails
To think how they may ache in icy hoods and mails.

(*The Eve of Saint Agnes*, ii. 5-9.)

'To think how they may ache'—the germ of this thought, or something like it, is in Dante, where he speaks of the figures that perform the part of sustaining columns in architecture.[1] Keats had read Dante in Mr. Cary's translation, for which he had a great respect. He began to read him afterwards in Italian, which language he was mastering with surprising quickness.

(*Ibid.* p. 331.)

JAMES NORTHCOTE

(1746-1831)

[James Northcote was the son of a watchmaker of Plymouth, where he was born in 1746. After serving for a time as apprentice in his father's trade he went to London in 1771, where he worked as an assistant in Sir Joshua Reynolds's studio, and studied in the Royal Academy Schools. He occasionally sat as a model to Reynolds, in whose famous 'Ugolino' he figures as one of the young men. In 1776 Northcote set up as a portrait-painter on his own account, and in the next year he went to Rome where he studied for about two years. After he had exhibited portraits at the Royal Academy for some fourteen years he was elected R.A. in 1787. He was an enthusiastic admirer of Sir Joshua, and published in 1813 *Memoirs of Sir Joshua Reynolds*, in which he gives an interesting account of the origin of the 'Ugolino' picture. Northcote died in London in 1831. Among his acquaintances in his old age was William Hazlitt, who in 1830 published a volume of *Conversations with James Northcote*, portions of which had already appeared in the *New Monthly Magazine* in 1826 (see below, pp. 186-7).]

1813. MEMOIRS OF SIR JOSHUA REYNOLDS, KNT. LATE PRESIDENT OF THE ROYAL ACADEMY.

[The origin of Sir Joshua's 'Ugolino']

TO Goldsmith, in particular, Sir Joshua was always attentive; . . . Mr. Cumberland,[2] in his own Memoirs, says that 'from Goldsmith he caught the subject of his famous Ugolino. . . .' Mr. Cumberland, however, is, perhaps, rather inaccurate in his assertion respecting the painting of 'Ugolino,' which

[1] [*Purg.* x. 130-4.]
[2] [Richard Cumberland (1732-1811); his *Memoirs* were published in 1806.]

was finished in this year, (1773,) and begun, not long before, as an historical subject.

The fact is, that this painting may be said to have been produced as an historical picture by an accident: for the head [1] of the Count had been painted previous to the year 1771, and finished on what we painters call 'a half length canvas,' and was, in point of expression, exactly as it now stands, but without any intention, on the part of Sir Joshua, of making it the subject of an historical composition, or having the story of Count Ugolino in his thoughts. Being exposed in the picture gallery, along with his other works, it was seen, either by Mr. Edmund Burke, or Dr. Goldsmith, I am not certain which, who immediately exclaimed, that it struck him as being the precise person, countenance, and expression of the Count Ugolino, as described by Dante in his 'Inferno.'

This affecting description is given in the thirty-third Canto of the first part of his Comedia, where, in his supposed passage through hell, he introduces Ugolino gnawing the head of his treacherous and cruel enemy, the Archbishop Ruggiero, and then telling his own sad story on the appearance of the poet.

The historical facts are simply these, that in the latter end of the thirteenth century there were great intestine divisions, in the city and state of Pisa in Italy, for the sovereignty; divisions which gave rise to the well known contests of the Guelphs and Ghibellines. The former of these consisted of two parties, at the head of which were Visconti and Ugolino: whilst the Archbishop Ruggiero led the third.

Between this latter and Ugolino a compromise took place, by which means Visconti and his partizans were driven out; when Ruggiero, finding the Guelph faction considerably weakened, immediately plotted against his quondam friend, already elected sovereign. The mob being excited by the crafty priest against their new prince, the unfortunate Ugolino was overpowered, and he and his two sons, together with two grandsons, were then conveyed to the city prison, where they remained some months, until the Pisans being excommunicated by the Pope, they became so enraged, that they determined to revenge themselves on the unhappy prisoners; and having accordingly strongly secured and barricaded the doors of the dungeon, they threw the keys of the prison into the river Arno, so that Ugolino and his unhappy offspring perished.

Thus far the historian—when the imagination of the poet undertook to fill up the awful hiatus between the sealing of their doom and the last moments of expiring nature: and of the poet's powers I am happy to be able to give an illustration, in the following

[1] [See vol. i. p. 343.]

beautiful translation by my friend Mr. Nathaniel Howard,[1] of Plymouth, Devon, who is an ornament to his country:

> La bocca sollevò dal fiero pasto
> Quel peccator, &c.
>
> The sinner pausing from his grim repast,
> Wip'd in the miscreant's hair his gory jaws,[2] etc.

After this exquisite detail by the poet, the subject was taken up by the sculptor, and Richardson[3] in his 'Science of a Connoisseur,' relates that Michael Angelo Buonarotti composed a bas-relief of the Count sitting with his four children, one of which lay dead at his feet: over their heads were a figure to represent Famine, and beneath them another personifying the river Arno, on whose banks the tragedy was acted.

The whole subject is well handled by Richardson, and may be read with pleasure, as relative to the picture, although written long before the idea started by Burke was adopted by Sir Joshua, who immediately had his canvas enlarged in order that he might be enabled to add the other figures, and to complete his painting of the impressive description of the Italian poet.

The picture when finished was bought by the late Duke of Dorset[4] for four hundred guineas; and it has since been noticed by Dr. Joseph Warton,[5] who in his 'Essay on the Genius and Writings of Pope,' introduces the story in exemplification of some pathetic passages in that writer.

(pp. 174-9.)

BIBLIOTHECA STANLEIANA

1813. BIBLIOTHECA STANLEIANA: A SPLENDID SELECTION OF RARE AND FINE BOOKS FROM THE DISTINGUISHED LIBRARY OF COLONEL STANLEY.

[Thomas Stanley (1749-1818), of Cross Hall, co. Lancaster, whose family belonged to a collateral branch of the house of Derby, was Colonel of the 1st Regiment of the Royal Lancashire Militia, and M.P. (1780-1812) for the county of Lancaster. He was the owner of a famous collection of books, 'bound by our choicest binders,' says Dibdin, and containing 'whatever is splendid and precious in the Belles Lettres, Voyages, and Travels.' A selection from Colonel Stanley's library was sold by Evans in April-May, 1813. The sale, which lasted for six days, consisted of 1136 lots, among which were three editions of the *Divina Commedia* in fine bindings, viz.

[1] [Howard's version of the *Inferno* was published in 1807 (see above, pp. 58 ff.).]
[2] [Northcote here prints Howard's translation of the Ugolino episode (*Inf.* xxxiii. 1-78).]
[3] [See vol. i. pp. 199 ff.]
[4] [John Frederick Sackville, third duke, died 1799.]
[5] [See vol. i. pp. 302-3.]

Venice (Marcolini), 1544 (sold for £2 15s.); Lyon (Rovillio), 1571 (sold for £1 15s.); and Venice (Zatta), 1757, 5 vols. large paper, 'with 212 plates in different coloured inks' (sold for £37 16s.); also a copy of Grangier's French translation, 3 vols. Paris, 1597 (sold to Heber for £3 3s.); and of Carlo d' Aquino's Latin translation, 3 vols. Naples, 1728 (sold for £4 5s.).]

THOMAS DUNHAM WHITAKER

(1759-1821)

[Thomas Dunham Whitaker, topographer, was born in 1759 at Rainham, Norfolk, of which place his father was curate. He was educated at St. John's College, Cambridge (LL.B. 1781, LL.D. 1801), and was ordained in 1785. He was perpetual curate of Holme, Lancashire, 1797; and vicar of Whalley, 1809, and of Blackburn, 1818, till his death in 1821. Whitaker, who was the author of several topographical works relating to Lancashire and Yorkshire, in 1813 published a sumptuous edition of the *Vision of William concerning Piers Plouhman.*]

1813. VISIO WILLI' DE PETRO PLOUHMAN, ITEM VISIONES EJUSDEM DE DOWEL, DOBET, ET DOBEST. OR THE VISION OF WILLIAM CONCERNING PIERS PLOUHMAN, AND THE VISIONS OF THE SAME CONCERNING THE ORIGIN, PROGRESS, AND PERFECTION OF THE CHRISTIAN LIFE. ASCRIBED TO ROBERT LANGLAND.

[Whether Langland imitated Dante]

THE writer of these Visions had a smattering of French, but no Italian. I have endeavoured in vain to discover in them any imitations of Dante, whose Inferno and Purgatorio, in some respects, resemble them. But the boldness of those works, which the familiarity of the Italians with the vices of their Popes rendered tolerable, and even popular, beyond the Alps, would have appalled the courage of a tramontane satirist, and shocked the feelings of his readers, in the fourteenth century.

(*Introductory Discourse*, p. xxxvii.)

ALEXANDER CHALMERS

(1759-1834)

[Alexander Chalmers was the son of a printer of Aberdeen, where he was born in 1759. In 1777 he left Aberdeen with the intention of taking up an appointment as surgeon in the West Indies, but changing his mind went to London, where he soon established a connection with the periodical press. After spending nearly sixty years in literary work in London, he died in 1834. His most important publication was a new edition of the *General Biographical Dictionary*, which was issued in 32 volumes between 1812 and 1817. A notice of Dante, with a criticism of the *Divina Commedia*, was contributed by Chalmers to the eleventh volume, published in 1813.]

1813. THE GENERAL BIOGRAPHICAL DICTIONARY:[1] CONTAINING AN HISTORICAL AND CRITICAL ACCOUNT OF THE LIVES AND WRITINGS OF THE MOST EMINENT PERSONS IN EVERY NATION. . . .

[Criticism of the *Divina Commedia*]

THE 'Commedia' of Dante is a species of satiric epic, in which the reader is conducted through the three stages, the "Inferno," the "Purgatorio," and "Paradiso," the whole consisting of a monstrous assemblage of characters, pagan heroes and philosophers, Christian fathers, kings, popes, monks, ladies, apostles, saints, and hierarchies; yet frequently embellished with passages of great sublimity and pathos (of the latter, what is comparable to the tale of Ugolino?) and imagery and sentiments truly Homeric. The highest praise, however, must be given to his "Inferno," a subject which seems to have suited the gloomy wildness of his imagination, which appears tamed and softened even in the most interesting pictures in the "Purgatorio" and "Paradiso." Whether, says an excellent living critic, Dante was stimulated to his singular work by the success of his immediate predecessors, the Provençal poets, or by the example of the ancient Roman authors, has been doubted. The latter opinion Mr. Roscoe thinks the more probable. In his "Inferno" he had apparently the descent of Aeneas in view, but in the rest of his poem there is little resemblance to any antecedent production. Compared with the Aeneid, adds Mr. Roscoe, "it is a piece of grand Gothic architecture at the side of a beautiful Roman temple," on which an anonymous writer[2] remarks that this Gothic grandeur miserably degenerates in the adjoining edifices, the "Purgatorio" and "Paradiso".

(Vol. xi. p. 274.)

JOSEPH FORSYTH

(1763-1815)

[Joseph Forsyth, the son of a merchant of Elgin, where he was born in 1763, was educated at King's College, Aberdeen (M.A. 1779). He was intended for the Church, but preferred the scholastic profession. After serving for a time as assistant master at a school in Newington Butts, he purchased the school, and carried it on for thirteen years. In 1801, after the Peace of Amiens, Forsyth set out for Italy, to visit which had been the great desire of his life. He spent eighteen months in the more famous cities of Italy, and was at Turin on his way home in May, 1803, when, the war having been renewed, he was taken prisoner. He was kept in captivity in France until 1814, and died at Elgin in the following year. During his detention Forsyth composed his *Remarks on Antiquities, Arts, and Letters, during*

[1] [A new edition, revised and enlarged by A. Chalmers.]
[2] [In *Critical Review* (March, 1803) (see vol. i. p. 657).]

an Excursion in Italy, in the years 1802 *and* 1803, which was published in London in 1813, in the vain hope that Napoleon as a patron of literature and art might consent to his release. In this work Forsyth displays an intimate acquaintance with the *Divina Commedia*, numerous quotations from which are effectively introduced in the narrative. A selection from these is given below.]

1813. REMARKS ON ANTIQUITIES, ARTS, AND LETTERS, DURING AN EXCURSION IN ITALY, IN THE YEARS 1802 AND 1803.

[Alfieri and Dante]

FLORENCE.—Libraries. In the older illuminations I saw nothing to admire but the brilliancy of their colours, which were used in their virgin state. . . . Some of those illuminations came from the pencil of Oderisi, whom Dante extols as 'the honour of the art.'[1]—The Theatre. Alfieri is, next to Dante, the Italian poet most difficult to Italians themselves. . . . His very strength and compression, being new to the language and foreign to its genius, have rendered his style inverted, broken, and obscure; full of ellipses, and elisions; speckled even to affectation with *Dantesque*[2] terms.

(pp. 45, 59-60.)

[Portraits and tomb of Dante—Dante and Shakespeare]

Florence.—Architecture. This cathedral contains very few pictures, and none of any value. I remarked a portrait of the English condottiero John Hawkwood. . . . Next to our honest countryman, stands an antique picture of Dante, painted by Orcagna[3] several years after his death, and placed here by the same republic which had condemned him to the stake. Such was the poor *palinodia* of Florence to the man who made her language the standard of Italy: while three foreigners, in three different ages, raised to him in a foreign state his sarcophagus and tomb and funeral chamber.[4] Well might he call his countrymen

Quello 'ngrato popolo maligno
Che discese di Fiesole ab antico,
E tien' ancor del monte e del macigno.[5]

I have been assured that not only this, but all the portraits now existing of Dante are, like those of '*our* divine poet,' posthumous:[6]

[1] [*Purg.* xi. 79-80.]
[2] [This is the earliest recorded example of the use of this word in English.]
[3] [Not by Orcagna, but by Domenico di Michelino, a pupil of Fra Angelico.]
[4] [Dante's tomb at Ravenna, originally projected by Guido da Polenta, was restored in 1483 by Bernardo Bembo; again in 1692 by Cardinal Domenico Maria Corsi; and a third time, in 1780, by Cardinal Gonzaga, who erected the existing mausoleum.]
[5] [*Inf.* xv. 61-3.]
[6] [The portrait in the Bargello, ascribed to Giotto, was not discovered until 1840.]

yet as all resemble this venerable work of Orcagna, uniformity has given a sanction to the common effigy of the bard. Not so Shakspeare's. Most of the portraits that pass for his, are dissimilar. Dante and Shakspeare form a striking parallel—as the master-bards of Italy and England—oppressed with praise and annotation at home, and ridiculed as barbarians by foreign critics—Dante rose before the dawn of letters in Italy: and Shakspeare soon after they had spread in England.—Finding their native tongues without system or limit, each formed another language within his own; a language peculiar as their creators, and entering only like authorities into common Italian and English: to add nerve, and spirit, and dignity, and beauty. Both have stood the obliterating waste of ages, have seen younger styles grow old and disappear; have survived all the short-lived fopperies of literature, and flourish now in unabated fashion, inviting and resisting ten thousand imitations.

(pp. 64-5.)

[Dante's references to Camaldoli, Romena, and Fonte Branda]

Camaldoli.—From Vallombrosa, the region of the fir and larch, we rode through a forest of oak and beech, and returned to the country of the olive and fig-tree. . . . We were obliged to put up at a solitary inn called Uomo Morto, an object as woful in aspect as in name. Its name it derives from the execution of a coiner[1] whom Dante has packed among the damned, as an accomplice to the three counts of Romena.

Ivi è Romena, là dove io falsai
La lega suggellata del Battista;
Perch' io il corpo suso lasciai:
Ma s' i' vedessi qui l' anima trista
Di Guido, o d' Alessandro, o di lor frate,
Per fonte Branda non darei la vista.[2]

The castle of Romena, mentioned in these verses, now stands in ruins on a precipice about a mile from our inn, and not far off is a spring which the peasants call Fonte Branda. Might I presume to differ from his commentators, Dante, in my opinion, does not mean the great fountain of Siena, but rather this obscure spring; which, though less known to the world, was an object more familiar to the poet himself who took refuge here from proscription, and an image more natural to the coiner who was burnt on the spot. . . . We passed the night at the monastery of Camaldoli, and next morning rode up by steep traverses to the Santo Eremo, where Saint Romualdo lived. . . . I was surprised to find, among hermits immured on the mountains and restricted to books of devotion, a

[1] [Maestro Adamo, of Brescia.] [2] [*Inf.* xxx. 73-8.]

library so rich in the earliest classics, and in works approaching the very *incunabula* of printing. Among these were Cennini's Virgil, the first Greek Homer, the first edition of Dante and of Lascari's Grammar. . . .

(pp. 85-9.)

[Dante and the Casentino]

Excursion to Cortona.—On returning down to the Casentine we could trace along the Arno the mischief which followed a late attempt to clear some Apennines of their woods. Most of the soil, which was then loosened from the roots and washed down by the torrents, lodged in this plain; and left immense beds of sand and large rolling stones, on the very spot where Dante describes

Li ruscelletti che de' verdi colli
Del Casentin discendon giuso in Arno,
Facendo i lor canali e freddi e molli.[1]

. . . The Casentines were no favourites with Dante, who confounds the men with their hogs.[2] Yet, following the *divine poet* down the Arno, we came to a race still more forbidding. The Aretine peasants seem to inherit the coarse, surly visages of their ancestors, whom he styles *Bottoli*. Meeting one girl who appeared more cheerful than her neighbours, we asked her, how far it was from Arezzo, and received for answer—*Quanto c' è*.[3]

The valley widened as we advanced, and when Arezzo appeared, the river left us abruptly, wheeling off from its environs at a sharp angle, which Dante converts into a snout, and points disdainfully against the currish race:—

Bottoli trova poi venendo giuso
Ringhiosi più che non chiede lor possa:
E a lor disdegnoso torce 'l muso.[4]

(pp. 93, 94-95.)

[Dante and Siena]

Siena.—The pavement of this cathedral is the work of a succession of artists, from Duccio down to Meccarino, who have produced the effect of the richest mosaic, merely by inserting grey marble into white, and hatching both with black mastic. . . . Dante, who was almost contemporary with Duccio, had perhaps seen some work of this kind when he wrote these verses—

Mostrava ancor lo duro pavimento . . .
Qual di pennel fu maestro, o di stile,
Che ritraesse l' *ombre e' tratti*, ch' ivi
Mirar farieno uno 'ngegno sottile![5]

(pp. 102-3.)

[1] [*Inf.* xxx. 64-6.] [2] [*Purg.* xiv. 43.] [3] [' As far as it is.']
[4] [*Purg.* xiv. 46-8.] [5] [*Purg.* xii. 49, 64-6.]

[Dante's references to Bologna]

Journey to Venice. Bologna.—Bologna excelled only in painting. In no age has its architecture been pure. Dante's Garisenda [1] (for whatever the Divine Poet once names becomes Dante's) is a coarse brick tower which, if really built with its present inclination, was but deformed for the sake of difficulty. . . . The university is the oldest in Europe, at least the first where academical degrees were invented and conferred: but, like other old establishments, it is now fallen into decrepitude. Yet with all this learning in its bosom, Bologna has suffered its dialect, that dialect which Dante admired as the purest of Italy,[2] to degenerate into a coarse, thick, truncated jargon, full of apocope, and unintelligible to strangers.

(pp. 330, 333.)

[The Florentines and French influence]

Manners of Florence.—

Poi Firenze rinnuova genti e modi.

Dante.[3]

Such is the influence of power over national taste, that the French have produced a very general change in the exterior manners of the Tuscans, though they remain the object of their secret abhorrence. . . . They have cropped the hair of the powdered fop, have hedged his cheeks with the whiskers of a sapeur, and stuck a cigar into his mouth. They have restored

Alle sfacciate donne Fiorentine
L' andar mostrando colle poppe il petto.[4]

. . . After this came a ghost from purgatory, and haunted the wood of Villamagna near Florence. . . . It appeared and spoke only to a little shepherdess. A crucifix was raised in the haunted spot. Myriads of seraphim ('cun nugolo di bambini,' said the child) fluttered round it, and the multitude fell down in devotion,

Cantando miserere a verso a verso.[5]

. . . For more than three ages did the Tuscan nobility surpass all Europe in literature and science, as poets, as physicians, as professors. They were the exclusive historians of their own country, and very generally employed as the ambassadors of foreign courts. Dante, Petrarch, Cimabue, Michelangelo, Galilei, Macchiavel, the six greatest Tuscans that perhaps ever existed, were all noble.

(pp. 365-6, 373-4, 378-9.)

[Pasquin and Dante]

Genoa.—Monti had been secretary and pimp to the Pope's niece. Hence when his Galiotti Manfredi first appeared at the theatre,

[1] [*Inf.* xxxi. 136.] [2] [*V.E.* i. 15, ll. 3 ff.] [3] [*Inf.* xxiv. 144.]
[4] [*Purg.* xxiii. 101-2.] [5] [*Purg.* v. 24.]

some child of Pasquin wrote on the doors that memorable verse of Dante,

Galeotto fu il libro e chi lo scrisse.[1]

(p. 425.)

[Dante and Lucca]

Lucca.—I was not long enough among the Lucchese to enter much into their character. Dante swept all the men into his hell at one fell swoop,[2] with the broom of a true Florentine. Their wives, perhaps, are more correct than their neighbours; for the Santa Zitta swarms with prostitutes, a profession which is hardly necessary at Pisa.

(p. 430.)

[Dante's mention of the Arsenal at Venice]

Venice.—I found the arsenal scrupulously guarded and difficult of access, though no longer, as in Dante's days,

Nell' Arzanà de' Venitiani
Bolle l' inverno la tenace pece,
A rimpalmar li legni lor non sani.[3]

With her marine, Venice has lost her commercial ascendant in the Adriatic, and lost that hope, which alone could repair all other losses.

(p. 441.)

JOHN CHETWODE EUSTACE

(c. 1762-1815)

[John Chetwode Eustace, the classical antiquary, was born in Ireland about 1762. He was educated at Douay, and was ordained priest at the Maynooth College. He resided both at Oxford and Cambridge at various periods as tutor to relatives of Lord Petre. In 1802 he made a tour through Italy, with three companions, to one of whom (John Cust, afterwards Lord Brownlow) Eustace dedicated the account of his travels, the famous *Classical Tour through Italy*, which was first published in 1813; in the third edition (1815) the title by which the work is now generally known was substituted for the cumbrous title of the original. Eustace visited Italy again in 1815, in which year he died at Naples while collecting materials for a new volume of his *Tour*. The work contains sundry references to Dante, the most interesting of which is the account of the 'Slavini di Marco' near Trent, which he identifies with the locality described in *Inferno* xii. 4-6.]

[1] [*Inf.* v. 137.] Galeotto, who catered like Monti for the amours of his mistress Ginevra, passes among the Italians as an appellative for ruffiano or pimp.
[2] [*Inf.* xxi. 38-42.]
[3] [*Inf.* xxi. 7-9.]

1813. A TOUR THROUGH ITALY, EXHIBITING A VIEW OF ITS SCENERY, ANTIQUITIES, AND MONUMENTS, PARTICULARLY AS THEY ARE OBJECTS OF CLASSICAL INTEREST, WITH AN ACCOUNT OF THE PRESENT STATE OF ITS CITIES AND TOWNS, AND OCCASIONAL OBSERVATIONS ON THE RECENT SPOLIATIONS OF THE FRENCH.

[Dante and the Slavini di Marco]

THE descent becomes more rapid between *Roveredo* and *Ala*; the river which glided gently through the valley of Trent, assumes the roughness of a torrent; the defiles become narrower; and the mountains break into rocks and precipices, which occasionally approach the road, sometimes rise perpendicular from it, and now and then hang over it in terrible majesty. Amid these wilds the traveller cannot fail to notice a vast tract called the *Slavini di Marco*, covered with fragments of rock torn from the sides of the neighboring mountains by an earthquake, or perhaps by their own unsupported weight, and hurled down into the plains below. They spread over the whole valley, and in some places contract the road to a very narrow space. A few firs and cypresses scattered in the intervals, or sometimes rising out of the crevices of the rocks, cast a partial and melancholy shade amid the surrounding nakedness and desolation. This scene of ruin seems to have made a deep impression upon the wild imagination of Dante, as he has introduced it into the twelfth canto of the Inferno, in order to give the reader an adequate idea of one of his infernal ramparts.

Era lo loco ove a scender la riva &c.[1]

(Ed. 1821, vol. i. pp. 108-9.)

[Dante's reference to Pietola]

We may venture to infer, in opposition to great authority, the impropriety of fixing Virgil's farm at *Pietole*:—

E quell' ombra gentil per cui si noma
Pietola, più che villa Mantovana.

Purgatorio, xviii.

From these verses we may infer that it was not only the opinion of Dante, but the tradition of his times, that *Pietole* occupied the site of Andes.

(Ed. 1821, vol. i. p. 222.)

[Some of the details of the 'infernal regions' of Milton and Dante suggested by volcanic phenomena]

Milton seems to have taken some features of his infernal regions from this repository of fire and sulphur.[2] . . . All the great poets,

[1] [Eustace here quotes *Inferno* xii. 1-9.]

[2] [The Solfatara near Pozzuolo.]

from the days of Virgil down to the present period, have borrowed some of their imagery from the scenery which now surrounds us, and have graced their poems with its beauties, or raised them with its sublimity. . . . *Dante* has borrowed some of the horrors of his *Inferno* from their fires and agitations; and *Tasso* has spread their freshness, their verdure, and their serenity over the enchanted gardens of his *Armida*.

(Vol. ii. pp. 425-6.)

[Portrait and tomb of Dante]

To the historical embellishments we may add the additional awfulness which the cathedral of *Florence* derives from the illustrious persons who repose under its pavement. Among these are the well-known names of *Brunellesco*, *Giotto*, and *Marsilius Ficinus*. A picture only[1] records the memory of *Dante*, whose remains, notwithstanding the lustre which his genius reflects upon his country, slumber in exile at *Ravenna*, in a tomb erected and inscribed by *Bernardo*, father of the Cardinal *Bembo*. Another epitaph, supposed to have been penned by the poet himself,[2] ends with a gentle complaint:

Hic claudor Dantes patriis extorris ab oris,
Quem genuit parvi Florentia mater amoris.

Here Dante, whom the lovely Florence bore
Lies buried, exil'd from his native shore.

The Florentines have indeed at various times endeavored to recover the relics of their illustrious citizen and particularly during the reign of Leo X. when Michael Angelo himself is said to have exerted his influence to obtain them;[3] but in vain: the people of *Ravenna*, who had the honor of affording the exiled poet an asylum when living, conceive that they had the best title to the honor of preserving his ashes when dead—'Exulem a Florentia excepit Ravenna,' says the epitaph, 'vivo furens, mortuum colens . . . tumulum pretiosum musis S. P. Q. Rav. jure ac aere suo tamquam thesaurum suum munivit, instauravit, ornavit.' In fine, the Florentine republic voted a magnificent cenotaph to be erected in this cathedral; but even this vote has proved ineffectual, and the picture alluded to above continues still to occupy the place allotted to the monument.

(Vol. iii. pp. 344-5.)

[1] [The picture over the north door, painted by Domenico di Michelino in 1466.]

[2] [This epitaph was not written by Dante, but by one Bernardo Canaccio, who composed it in 1357, more than 30 years after Dante's death.]

[3] [See Toynbee's *Life of Dante*, pp. 137 ff.]

[The so-called darkness of the middle ages in Italy enlightened by the genius of Dante and other great men]

Our ideas of the middle ages are in many respects the mere prejudices of childhood. Europe, or at least Italy, was never involved in such utter darkness as some of our modern oracles endeavor to make their unthinking readers imagine. . . . Surely, the century and the country that produced *Cimabue* and *Giotto*, *Arnolfo* and *Ugolini*, *Dante* and *Petrarca*, could not have been deficient in genius or criticism, in painting or sculpture, in design or in architecture.

(Vol. iii. pp. 346-7.)

[The Tower of Famine at Pisa]

Among the towers which rise in different parts of Pisa, one is still shown as the scene of the horrid catastrophe of Count *Ugolino* and his sons, described in so affecting a manner by *Dante*, *Inferno*, *Canto* xxxiii.

(Vol. iii. p. 450.)

[The language of Dante, Ariosto, and Tasso]

As for the want of energy in the Italian language, it is a reproach which he may make who has never read *Dante*, *Ariosto*, or *Tasso*; he who has perused them knows that in energy both of language and of sentiment, they yield only to their illustrious masters, Virgil and Homer.

(Vol. iv. p. 165.)

[Dante, Petrarch, and Boccaccio creators of the Italian language]

To infuse as much of the genius and spirit of Latin into the new language as the nature of the latter would permit, seems to have been the grand object of these first masters of modern Italian. Among them *Brunetto Latini*, a Florentine, seems to have been the principal; and to him his countrymen are supposed to be indebted for the pre-eminence which they then acquired, and have ever since enjoyed in the new dialect, which from them assumed the name of *Tuscan*. *Dante*, *Petrarca*, and *Boccacio* completed the work which *Brunetto* and his associates had commenced; and under their direction the Italian language assumed the graces and the embellishments that raise it above all known languages, and distinguish it alike in prose or verse, in composition or conversation.

(Vol. iv. pp. 184-5.)

[The 'originality and grandeur' of Dante]

If the Greek language can boast the first, and Latin the second, epic poem, Italian may glory in the third; and *Tasso*, in the opinion of all candid critics has an undoubted right to sit next in honor and in fame to his countryman Virgil. *Dante* and *Ariosto* have claims of a different, perhaps not an inferior, nature, and in originality and grandeur the former, in variety and imagery the latter, stands unrivalled.

(Vol. iv. p. 188.)

ANONYMOUS

1813. July. QUARTERLY REVIEW. ART. XII. VILLANI'S ISTORIE FIORENTINE.

[Villani and Dante]

IT appears that in the year 1301, Villani was present at the grand public entry of Charles de Valois into Florence to attempt the restoration of tranquillity, in which from his general spirit, it may be believed that he cordially assisted; but in vain; since the year after witnessed the banishment of the chiefs of the *parte bianca*, and among others of the illustrious poet Dante, from Florence. . . .

In Book X is a pretty fair specimen of our author's credulity in matters of astrology, in which science various passages of his work evince him to have been a firm believer. It must be remembered however, that it was a science so fully established in those days in the judgments of the learned and of the unlearned, that to disbelieve, would have been regarded as a proof of incredulity deserving of punishment in that circle of Dante's Inferno to which the poet has doomed Farinata and Cavalcante, the Emperor Frederic, and the Cardinal Ubaldini.[1] . . .

The latter half of the thirteenth century, and the beginning of the fourteenth, have been aptly called the heroic age of Florentine history; . . . Dante,[2] the first and greatest of Italian poets, Guido Cavalcanti, one of the earliest among those who dared to judge for themselves on the great questions of philosophy and religion, Cimabue and Giotto, Arnolfi and Brunnelleschi, were all contemporaries and fellow-citizens of the Herodotus of Florence.

(Vol. ix. pp. 458, 460-1, 463-4.)

[1] [*Inf.* x. 22 ff.]

[2] The high reputation which this poet enjoyed, even among his contemporaries, is plainly shown, not only by the passages in which Villani expressly dwells on the circumstances of his banishment and death, but by the frequent references which he makes to the historical allusions with which his poem abounds.

LORD THURLOW

(1781-1829)

[Edward Thurlow, afterwards Hovell-Thurlow, second Baron Thurlow, was born in London in 1781. He was the eldest son of Thomas Thurlow, successively Dean of Rochester (1775), Bishop of Lincoln (1779), Dean of St. Paul's (1782), and Bishop of Durham (1787-91). He was educated at the Charterhouse, and at Magdalen College, Oxford (M.A. 1801), and on the death of his uncle, Lord Chancellor Thurlow, he succeeded to the Barony of Thurlow, 1806. In 1785 he was appointed one of the principal registrars in the diocese of Lincoln, and he held in addition several sinecure offices, which he retained until his death at Brighton in 1829. Lord Thurlow was the author of several volumes of verse, which contain sundry allusions to Dante, from one of which it appears that in his old age Lord Chancellor Thurlow was a reader of Dante.]

1813. AN APPENDIX TO POEMS ON SEVERAL OCCASIONS; BEING A CONTINUATION OF THE SYLVA.

[Dante, Shakespeare, and Ariosto]

IF those great wits, that but in story live,
In this time-lessen'd age could live again,
Their boundless labours no delight would give,
Nor they themselves could the neglect sustain.

If Dante, who could ope the gates of Hell,
And with the sacred Morning speed his flight,
Should now survive, that spirit he must quell,
Which would be for a fallen World too bright.

O Shakspeare! let thy restless spirit pine,
O Ariosto! mix thy tears with me;
The soul, that is inflam'd with light divine,
Must perish in most dark obscurity!

(*Althea*, St. 87-9, p. 23.)

1814. MOONLIGHT: THE DOGE'S DAUGHTER: ARIADNE: CARMEN BRITANNICUM, OR THE SONG OF BRITAIN: ANGELICA, OR THE RAPE OF PROTEUS.

[Homer, Dante, and Euripides]

I question then, O Muse, in love divine,
Where that immortal Spirit[1] may abide,
That in his just vocation of this world,
With favour of the King, maintain'd the sway
Of jurisprudence in this triple realm?
Well known to thee: that, in his aged thought,

[1] Edward Lord Thurlow, Lord High Chancellor of Great Britain.

With Homer and great Danté did converse,
And sweet Euripides, whose mournful song
Flows in his numbers, like the silver Po,
In weeping tribute to the Adrian sea.
(*Moonlight*, ll. 213-22, pp. 11-12.)

[Homer, Virgil, Ariosto, Dante, Petrarch, and Tasso]

Where now is Homer? or great Virgil where?
Or in what shades does Ariosto walk,
That with Orlando's madness charm'd the world?
Where now is Danté? in what region pure
Of that unbounded World he sung so well?
Or Petrarch, that to love was sworn to death?
Or Tasso, in whose stately verse we see
Whatever the great Roman was before?
(*Ibid.* ll. 268-75, p. 14.)

c. 1820. SONNET.

[On seeing the Head of Dante, engraved by Mr. Cardon,[1] from a picture of Raphael, crowned with Laurel.]

Thy mournful face, expressive of keen thought,
Like pale and melancholy Winter drawn
Before my eyes, by Raphael's pencil brought,
Declares a soul, that was to misery pawn:
Wither'd with woe, yet darting kingly fire
And the lean cheek laid out in sallow scorn,
Methinks thou hast seen Hell, thy sad desire,
And pass'd between the amber gates of Morn!
Yet Hate and Envy wander'd by thy side
Beyond the shallow bound'ry of the World:
And Banishment was thy ungrateful bride:
Thence is thy lip with bitter action curl'd,
And ev'ry look, altho' thy crown be there,
Is full of grief, oblivion and despair.[2]

THOMAS MITCHELL

(1783-1845)

[Thomas Mitchell, classical scholar, son of a London riding-master, was born in 1783. He was educated at Christ's Hospital, and Pembroke College, Cambridge (B.A. 1806). In 1809 he was elected Fellow of Sidney Sussex College. In 1813 he

1 [Anthony Cardon (1772-1813), a Flemish painter and engraver, who settled in England and died in London.]
2 [From MS. copy inserted in Charles Rogers Cotton's copy of Charles Rogers' *Translation of the Inferno*.]

commenced a series of articles in the *Quarterly Review* on Aristophanes, several of whose plays he subsequently translated into English verse (1820-2). His editions of Aristophanes (1834-8), and Sophocles (1842-3), with English notes, are well known. He died near Woodstock in 1845. Mitchell was a school-fellow of Leigh Hunt, who in June, 1813, invited him to dinner, with Byron and Moore, in Horsemonger Lane Gaol. In a letter written to Leigh Hunt during his imprisonment he introduces an apt quotation from the *Inferno*.]

1813. Feb. 9. LETTER TO LEIGH HUNT.

[Lines from Dante applied to Leigh Hunt]

YOUR *Examiner* of this day has given me the highest pleasure: it does equal honour to your head and your heart. I think your situation,[1] untoward as it is at present, an enviable one. It depends upon yourself now to be among those—

'Spiriti magni,
Che di vederli in me stesso n' esalto';[2]

which I think is the highest compliment a man can either wish or deserve.

(*Correspondence of Leigh Hunt*, vol. i. p. 71.)

CAPELL LOFFT

(1751-1824)

[Capell Lofft, miscellaneous writer (the similarity of whose initials with those of Charles Lamb caused the latter some annoyance), was born in London in 1751. He was educated at Eton, and Peterhouse, Cambridge, and was called to the bar in 1775. He settled at Turin in 1822, and died at Moncalieri in 1824. Lofft was the author of various legal and political works, besides poems and translations. His latest publication, entitled *Laura: or An Anthology of Sonnets* (1813-14), contains versions (made seven or eight years before) of several of the sonnets of Dante.]

1813-14. LAURA: OR AN ANTHOLOGY OF SONNETS (ON THE PETRARCHAN MODEL) AND ELEGIAC QUATUORZAINS: ENGLISH, ITALIAN, SPANISH, PORTUGUESE, FRENCH, AND GERMAN; ORIGINAL AND TRANSLATED.

[The Sonnets of Dante]

THE great Dante was born at *Florence* 1262,[3] and died 1321. His extended Poems, with much of Imagination and of Sublimity, and even of occasional Sweetness, have much harshness and obscurity both of Style and Sentiment, amid a peculiar Splendor of Genius. If his Excellences are less striking,

[1] [Leigh Hunt was in prison, on account of an attack on the Prince Regent in his newspaper the *Examiner*.]

[2] [*Inferno* iv. 118-19.]

[3] [Not 1262, but 1265.]

his Defects and Faults are also less in Sonnets. These have Simplicity, Perspicuity, and even Pathos.

(Vol. i. p. lxii.)

[Michael Angelo and Dante]

In the house of *Lorenzo de' Medici*, *Michel-Angelo* liv'd on as easy Terms as if he had been a belov'd and respected Brother. And this probably was one cause which inspir'd him with that affectionate veneration for *Dante* and *Petrarca*, and that Love for the *Sonnet;* which, alike in his severest and most continued troubles and the plenitude of Success and Honors, never forsook him. . . . He is said to have had great part of the poems of *Dante* and of *Petrarca* by heart. His Soul was in unison with the Greatness of the one and the tender Gracefulness of the other; true though it be that Sublimity is his predominant Character.

(Vol. i. pp. lxxxvi-viii.)

[Sonnet of Boccaccio on Dante]

Dante Aligieri son ; Minerva oscura, &c.

Dante I am ;—the Oracle obscure
Of Genius and of Art: and as I sung
The wondrous Graces of my native Tongue
Rose to Perfection ever to endure.
My Fancy prompt and daringly secure,
Pass'd unrestrain'd infernal Worlds among,
From *Tartarus* to Beauty ever young
Which glows through *Heaven*—thus knew I to allure
To Truths most aweful and sublime.—I own
Florence my Parent; though unkind to me:
An Error due to slanderous Tongues alone.
Ravenna sooth'd my exil'd Destiny,
And guards my Ashes. *Heaven* my Spirit keeps:
And Envy pines below, and her vain Triumph weeps.

(Vol. iii. Son. 353.)

[Sonnet of Dante]

Io maledico il dì ch' io vidi inprima[1] &c.

I execrate the Day which first disclos'd
Of those seductive eyes the baneful light,
The moment when those Beauties caught my sight
Which the recesses of my Soul expos'd;

[1] [*Son.* xxxiii. in Oxford Dante.]

I execrate the skill with which I gloz'd
  Those Charms, in Truth less than in Fancy bright
  And thee, a dazzling Image of Delight,
To the vain World's Idolatry propos'd.
I execrate my stubbornness of Mind
  Which makes me cling perversely to my Bane
That Form, those Looks, to snare Men's Hearts design'd,
In all Love's Frauds and Perjuries refin'd:
  While general Mockery is all my Gain
  Who Fortune's wheel would fix, and master thy Disdain.

(Vol. iii. Son. 435.) [1]

[Second Translation of the Same [2]]

I execrate the Day when first I saw
  Of those seductive eyes the baneful Light;
Those Charms, of force the ravisht Soul to draw
  Forth from its hold, slave to the eager Sight:
I execrate my Verse, which without flaw
  Presented thee, an Idol of Delight;
Made thee to the admiring World give Law
  With Charms, in Truth less than in Fancy bright.
I execrate my stubborn Mind, which clings
  Perverse, to thee, the Cause of all my Woe;
While all thy guilty Charms Remembrance brings;
And Oaths, forswearing thee, are fragile things;
  Though all the giddy World derides me so,
For seeking thee to fix, and Fortune's changeful Wings.

(Vol. iii. Son. 436.) [3]

[Sonnet of Dante]

Io son sì vago della bella Luce &c. [4]

So charm'd am I with the too lovely Beam
  Of those perfidious eyes, which me have slain,
  That still Desire conducts my steps again
To Her, to whom my pangs and sorrows seem
A Tale for mockery and an idle Dream.
  And, if my captive Fancy can retain
  A sense of aught, I wander;—taught in vain
By Reason and by Virtue to redeem

[1] [Dated, 28 Aug. 1806.]

[2] In this the order of the Rhimes in the original is preserved. And one may say as to the Perspicuity of the Sonnet of this great Poet in the original,

Quam Critici Gladium potuisset temnere, si sic
Omnia dixisset!

[3] [Dated, 28 Aug. 1806.]

[4] [*Son.* xxxv. in Oxford Dante.]

My wasted moments.—Thus she hurries me
Through sweet illusions to my wretched Fate;
Known, by severest Proof, alas, too late!
And haply I lament my hopeless State:—
But more lament my Shame, that others see
Pure Love with me betray'd for Gain to Misery.

(Vol. iii. Son. 445.)[1]

[Sonnet of Dante]

What is Love

Molti volendo dir che foss' Amore &c.[2]

Many to utter what Love is have sought:
But what he truely is have not explain'd;
Nor e'en to semblance of the Truth attain'd;
Nor to Description his just Value brought.
Some that he is an Extasy of Thought
By contemplation of the Fancy gain'd;
And some a strong Desire, whose Power hath reign'd
By sense of Pleasure in the Bosom wrought.
This I affirm:—that Love no substance is;
Nor in corporeal state or figure dwells:
But is a Passion of Desire; whose Bliss,
Plac'd in the Will, all other joy excells,
And, while the sentiment remains, can own
No Pleasure, no Support, but from itself alone.

(Vol. iii. Son. 491.)[3]

[Sonnet of Dante]

Deh, Pellegrini, che pensosi andate, &c.[4]

Pilgrims, who pensive bend your mournful way,
Full, as it seems, of some remoter thought,
Come ye then from so far, not to be fraught
(Since no such sympathy your looks pourtray,)
With that Affliction which should deeply prey
On those who of our City knowing aught
Feel to what height its Sorrows now are brought;
Sorrows which no expression would convey.
If ye but stopt to hear what caus'd our Sighs,
My Heart informs me ye would weep indeed,
And make the anguish we endure your own.
This City mourns the Loss of Beatrice!
The Praises from her Virtues which proceed,
And the Regrets, would teach Mankind to moan.

(Vol. iv. Son. 573.)[5]

[1] [Dated, 30 Aug. 1806.] [2] [*Son.* xxxviii. in Oxford Dante.]
[3] [Dated, 18 Sept. 1806.] [4] [*Son.* xxiv. *V.N.* § 41.] [5] [Dated, 7 June, 1807.]

[Sonnet]

Here end, my Muse, thy long, thy lov'd Career;
Here bound thy flight, who from the Italian Plains
Hast brought those gentle, pure, and polish'd Chains,
To the Phoebean Choir for ever dear.
Those who for Freedom rais'd the generous Spear,
In whose blest Verse divine Parnassus reigns
With heavenly Beauty who inspir'd their strains;
Whom every Virtue loves, all Arts revere,
Cherisht the Sonnet of harmonious flow.
Here *Guidi*, *Cino*, *Dante*, *Angelo*,
And the *Petrarchan* sweetest graces shine;
The *Medicean*, *Sannazarian* Name,
The Wreath of *Tasso*, the *Vittorian* Fame;
Here the *Miltonian* Palm, and *British* Harp divine.

(Vol. v. *La Corona*, Son. 15.) [1]

JOSEPH BERINGTON

(1746-1827)

[Joseph Berington, who was born in Shropshire in 1746, was educated at St. Omer, and after being ordained, exercised his priestly functions in France for several years. On his return to England he took an active part in the controversies of the day, and as a catholic divine was regarded as of doubtful orthodoxy by his co-religionists. In 1786 he appears to have been the priest at Oscott, in Staffordshire, and in 1814 he was appointed priest at Buckland, in Berkshire, where he died in 1827. Berington was the author of numerous philosophical, historical, and theological works, of which the latest, published in 1814, was a *Literary History of the Middle Ages*. This work, which has been twice reprinted (1846 and 1883), and has been translated into French, contains a brief account of Dante, with a notice of the *Divina Commedia*.]

1814. A LITERARY HISTORY OF THE MIDDLE AGES; COMPREHENDING AN ACCOUNT OF THE STATE OF LEARNING, FROM THE CLOSE OF THE REIGN OF AUGUSTUS, TO ITS REVIVAL IN THE FIFTEENTH CENTURY.

[Dante and the *Divina Commedia*]

DANTE DEGLI ALIGHIERI was born at Florence in the year 1265; where he studied, as well as in other cities of Italy, collecting from all quarters, and even, it is said, from the universities of Paris and Oxford, whatever was deemed most excellent in philosophy, theology, and the liberal arts. On his return to his own city, he was employed in many honourable offices. The cultivation of the Italian tongue, which was yet rude

[1] [Dated, 1807.]

and inharmonious—but which the muses were now about to adopt as their own—had deeply engaged his attention. Thus was Dante occupied; when in 1302, in one of those civil commotions, to which the free cities of Italy were, at this time, daily exposed, the party, which he had espoused, was vanquished by its antagonists, and he was himself forced into exile. To Florence he never returned; but the cities of Italy continued to afford him an asylum; the regrets of banishment which he felt with the keenest severity, did not however suspend his literary ardour. He died at Ravenna in 1321.

The works of Dante, on various subjects, in prose and verse, some of which were composed in Italian, and others in Latin, may be considered as almost absorbed in the renown of that to which his admiring countrymen have affixed the lofty title of the *Divina Commedia.* They, indeed, can be the only judges of its merit. . . . The Italians allow, that this work of Dante is not a regular composition; that it abounds with wild and extravagant passages; that his images are often unnatural; that he makes Virgil utter the most absurd remarks; that some whole cantoes cannot be read with patience; that his verses are frequently unsufferably harsh, and his rhymes devoid of euphony; and, in one word, that his defects, which no man of common judgment will pretend to justify, are not few nor trifling. But, whatever may be the sum of his imperfections or the number of his faults, they are amply compensated, by the highest beauties:—by an imagination of the richest kind; a style sublime, pathetic, animated; by delineations the most powerfully impressive; a tone of invective withering, irresistible, and indignant; and by passages of the most exquisite tenderness. The story of Count Ugolino and his children, than which the genius of man never produced a more pathetic picture, would alone prove, that the Muses were returned to the soil of Latium. When it is, besides, considered, that the Italian poetry had hitherto been—merely an assemblage of rhymed phrases, on love or some moral topic, without being animated by a single spark of genius—our admiration of Dante must be proportionally increased. Inspired, as it were, by him whose volume, he says, he had sought, and whom he calls his master,[1] he rose to the heights of real poesy; spoke of things not within the reach of common minds; poured life into inanimate nature; and all this in a strain of language to which as yet no ear had listened.

Among the various attractions which I have enumerated, and to which may be added the rich colouring with which the poet had the skill to invest all the arts and literature of the age, as they make their appearance in his work, I ought to state that the many

[1] [Virgil, *Inf.* i. 82-7.]

living, or at that time well-known characters, whom he brought forward, and whose good and bad deeds he tells without reserve, greatly augmented the interest of his work, and rendered it a feast for the censorious or malevolent.

Scarcely had this poem seen the light, when the public mind was seized as if by a charm. Copies were multiplied, and comments written, within the course of a few years. Even chairs, with honourable stipends, were founded in Florence, Bologna, Pisa, Venice, and Piacenza: whence able professors delivered lectures on the *divina commedia* to an admiring audience.

(*Book* vi. pp. 413-6.)

HELEN MARIA WILLIAMS

(1762-1827)

[Helen Maria Williams, daughter of an officer in the army, was born in London in 1762. In 1782 she published a tale in verse, *Edwin and Eltruda*, the success of which determined her to adopt a literary career. In 1788 she went over to France to visit a married sister, and thenceforth she almost continuously resided in that country. She was an ardent supporter of the principles of the Revolution, of which she wrote 'with a fervour that amounted almost to frenzy.' In 1793 she was imprisoned by Robespierre and narrowly escaped execution. In 1817 she became a naturalised Frenchwoman, and she died in Paris in 1827. She published several political works relating to France, besides poems, and translations, among the last being Humboldt's *Travels*, in which occurs an interesting reference to Dante's supposed mention of the Southern Cross.]

1814. PERSONAL NARRATIVE OF TRAVELS TO THE EQUINOCTIAL REGIONS OF THE NEW CONTINENT, DURING THE YEARS 1799-1804. WRITTEN IN FRENCH BY A. DE HUMBOLDT AND TRANSLATED INTO ENGLISH BY HELEN MARIA WILLIAMS.

[Dante and the Southern Cross]

IMPATIENT to rove in the equinoctial regions, I could not raise my eyes towards the starry vault without thinking of the Cross of the South, and without recalling the sublime passage of Dante, which the most celebrated commentators have applied to this constellation:

'Io mi volsi a man destra, e posi mente
All' altro polo, e vidi quattro stelle
Non viste mai fuor che alla prima gente.
Goder pareva il ciel di lor fiammelle.
O settentrional vedovo sito,
Poichè privato sei di mirar quelle!'[1]

(Vol. ii. p. 21.)

[1] [*Purg.* i. 22-7.]

ANONYMOUS

1814. CRITICAL REVIEW, OR, ANNALS OF LITERATURE. ART. 22. 'THE VISION; OR HELL, PURGATORY, AND PARADISE, OF DANTE ALLEGHIERI, TRANSLATED BY THE REV. A. F. CAREY.'[1]

[Cary's Dante]

THE study of the Italian language ranks, so essentially among the accomplishments of the present day, that we apprehend those possessing the advantage of reading *Dante* in the original language, would never barter his chaste beauties, for the fanciful portrait of an English artist. The subject is sublime—not so the prevailing language of this translator.

(IVth Series, vol. v. p. 647.)

ANONYMOUS: CRITO

1814. March. GENTLEMAN'S MAGAZINE—CRITICAL REMARKS FROM CARY'S DANTE.

['Cerbero il gran vermo']

MR. URBAN, some time since, a gentleman of Oxford published a book, in which he showed the Reviewers, how they would have tutored Milton, if he had been so happy as to have lived in the days wherein they flourish. The best illustration of this, that I have seen, is the review of Lord Thurlow's[2] Moonlight, in the last British Critic: and, in particular, there is one passage so excellent, that I cannot help quoting it:
Thus the Poet—

'What soul that lives, from off this upper stage
Has down descended to the gate of woe,
Where Cerberus, the cruel worm of Death,
Keeps watchful guard, and with his iron throat
Affrights the spirits in their pale sojourn?'

Thus the Critic—

'The idea of descending to the infernal regions through a trapdoor, at the sound of the Prompter's bell, is happily conceived, and would form an appropriate conclusion to Shakspeare's seven ages of life. But the most extraordinary discovery in Mythology remains to be discussed, that Cerberus is a worm, not a dog. This will hereafter puzzle many a dull commentator on the beauties of English literature. Till a better comment be produced, we shall venture an elucidation of his Lordship's meaning, and shall suggest,

[1] [*Sic.*]   [2] [See above, pp. 148-9.]

that he has, after all, only used the well-known figure of *pars pro toto*, the worm to be found under the puppy's tongue, for the entire animal; we defy Professor Heyne himself to have invented a more ingenious or probable explanation.'

Has this man ever read Dante? In the Inferno, Canto vi, are these lines:

> 'Quando ci scorse Cerbero il gran vermo,
> Le bocche aperse, e mostrocci le sanne:
> Non avea membro, che tenesse fermo.'

The sense of which is thus given in the noble and worthy translation of Mr. Cary:

> 'When that great worm
> Descried us, savage Cerberus, he op'd
> His jaws, and the fangs show'd us; not a limb
> Of him but trembled.'

For the more edification of the Critic, I will transcribe the note of Mr. Cary on this passage. . . .

CRITO.

(Vol. lxxxiv. Part i. p. 237.)

ANONYMOUS: A. R.

1814. April. GENTLEMAN'S MAGAZINE.

Dante's 'Worm'.

Crito informs us that Lord Thurlow follows Dante in giving the appellation of *Worm* to Cerberus; but he would do well to consider the great licences which that eminent Poet allowed himself. . . . Although greater liberties ought to be allowed to those who find a language in an unformed state, Dante himself has not escaped reprehension. One of his Commentators says, 'Ha recato meraviglia a molti l' apellazion di verme usata da Dante.'

A. R.

(Vol. lxxxiv. Part i. p. 320.)

ANONYMOUS

1814. Oct. QUARTERLY REVIEW. ART. III. CHALMERS' ENGLISH POETS.

[Dante's style]

THE Spaniards have not yet discovered the high value of their metrical history of the Cid . . . of all the poems which have been written since the Iliad, this is the most Homeric in its spirit: but the language of the peninsula was at that time crude and unformed, and the author seems to have lived too near Catalonia. He built with rubbish and unhewn stones; Dante and Petrarca with marble. . . .

Chaucer drew much from the French and Italian poets, but more from observation and the stores of his own wealthy and prolific mind. . . . Dante holds a higher place in literature because he wrought with materials which were capable of displaying and preserving his exquisite skill. Dante may be classed above all other poets for strength and severity of style: Nothing can be worse than the plan of the Divina Comedia; the matter is sometimes puerile, sometimes shocking, frequently dull, but the style is uniformly perfect. . . .

'Italian, Aaron Hill[1] says, is the language wherein love would chuse to sigh, or laughter to be light and wanton. It supplies with fulness and delight the uses of intrigue and conversation, but wants weight and spring for passion, and bends under the demand of comprehensiveness. 'Tis like the flowing of soft sand in hour glasses; seeming liquid while confined to its close currency, but flies dispersed, and opens its loose quality as soon as shaken out, and trusted to hard weather.' This is well said in the manner of Owen Feltham, but Aaron Hill would not have said it if he had remembered Dante and Filicaia.

(Vol. xii. pp. 64, 65, 83.)

UGO FOSCOLO

(1778-1827)

[Ugo Foscolo, who was of Venetian descent, was born in Zante in 1778. After a stormy career in Italy he came to England in 1816 and settled in London, where he accomplished much valuable literary work on Dante, Petrarch, Boccaccio, and Tasso. In 1814 an English version was published of his *Ultime Lettere di Jacopo Ortis*, an autobiographical work, which contains sundry references to Dante. In 1818 he contributed two essays on Dante to the *Edinburgh Review*, in one of which he reviewed very appreciatively Cary's translation of the *Divina Commedia*. He himself projected a commentary on the *Commedia*, of which one volume only (containing the *Discorso sul Testo*) was published in his lifetime (London: Pickering, 1825). The complete work was issued some years after his death in four volumes under the editorship of G. Mazzini (London: Rolandi, 1842-3). In 1823 he published his *Essays on Petrarch*, which include an interesting *Parallel between Dante and Petrarch*, and a translation of the recently discovered Letter of Dante to a Florentine friend on the occasion of the proposed amnesty of the Florentine exiles. Foscolo died at Turnham Green in 1827, and was buried at Chiswick, whence his remains were transferred in 1871 to the Church of Santa Croce at Florence.]

[1] [Aaron Hill, dramatist (1685-1750).]

1814. THE LETTERS OF ORTIS TO LORENZO.

[Reminiscences of Dante]

I WANDERED here and there, and up and down, in the interim, like the souls of the slothful, driven by Dante to the gates of hell; not being by him, accounted worthy of a place among the completely damned.

(p. 42.)

The unfortunate alone, can redress the wrongs of fate, by reciprocally comforting each other; but he who has obtained a seat at the rich man's table, soon, although too late, discovers

How bitter tastes
The bread of others.[1]

(p. 61.)

I have passed over the whole of Tuscany. All the mountains and fields are famed for the *fraternal* battles of four centuries back. The corpses, meanwhile, of innumerable Italians, have lain as foundations for the thrones of Emperors and Popes. I went up to Monteaperto, where the memory of the overthrow of the Guelfi[2] is, still, held infamous.

(p. 138.)

Rocky roads, craggy piles of mountains, all the rigour of the weather, all the fatigue and lassitudes attendant on travelling, and then? . . .

Nuovi tormenti e nuovi tormentati.[3]

I write from a little spot, at the foot of the Maritime Alps.[4]

(p. 161.)

Death alone, to whom the awful change of all things is committed, offers me peace. . . . Upon thy urn, oh! Father Dante![5] . . . While embracing it, I became still more fixed in my resolution. Didst thou see me? Didst thou, oh Father! inspire me with so much strength of mind and heart, whilst, upon my knees, with my head leaning against thy sculptured marbles, I meditated on thy greatness of mind, thy love, thy ungrateful country, thy exile, thy poverty, and thy heavenly genius? For I parted from thy shade, both more resolved, and more resigned.

(pp. 189-90.)

[1] 'Come sa di sale Lo pane altrui.' Dante. [*Par.* xvii. 58-9.]

[2] Dante touches, admirably, on this battle in the Tenth Canto of the Inferno; and those lines, perhaps, suggested to Ortis to visit Monteaperto. [*Inf.* x. 85 ff.]

[3] 'New torments, still, and new tormented beings.' Dante. [*Inf.* vi. 4.]

[4] From La Pietra, February 15th.

[5] [Ortis was then at Ravenna.]

1818. Feb. EDINBURGH REVIEW. BIAGIOLI'S EDITION OF THE DIVINA COMMEDIA.—CARY'S VISION OF DANTE.[1]

[Dante and his translators]

The poem of Dante is like an immense forest, venerable for its antiquity, and astonishing by the growth of trees which seem to have sprung up at once to their gigantic height by the force of nature, aided *by some unknown art*. It is a forest, curious from the extensive regions which it hides, but frightful from its darkness and its labyrinths. The first travellers who attempted to cross it have opened a road. Those who followed have enlarged and enlightened it: but the road is still the same; and the greater part of this immense forest remains, after the labour of five centuries, involved in its primitive darkness. . . .

All the other great poems in the world, taken together, have, perhaps, not so many allusions as the single work of Dante. He comprehends the whole history of his age—all that was then known of art, literature, and science—the usages and morals of his time, and their origin in preceding ages—together with theological opinions, and the great influence which they then exercised over the mind and actions of men. His allusions are rapid, various, multiplied—succeeding each other with the rapidity of flashes of lightning, which leaves short intervals of darkness between them. . . .

Shakespeare unfolds the character of his persons, and presents them under all the variety of forms which they can naturally assume. He surrounds them with all the splendour of his imagination, and bestows on them that full and minute reality which his creative genius could alone confer. Of all tragic poets, he most amply develops character. On the other hand, Dante, if compared not only to Virgil, the most sober of poets, but even to Tacitus, will be found never to employ more than a stroke or two of his pencil, which he aims at imprinting almost insensibly on the hearts of his readers. Virgil has related the story of Eurydice in two hundred verses; Dante, in sixty verses, has finished his masterpiece—the Tale of Francesca da Rimini. . . .

Of all the translators of Dante with whom we are acquainted, Mr. Cary is the most successful; and we cannot but consider his work as a great acquisition to the English reader. It is executed with a fidelity almost without example; and, though the measure he has adopted conveys no idea of the original stanza, it is perhaps the best for his purpose, and what Dante himself would have chosen, if he had written in English and in a later day. The

[1] [Mackintosh and Rogers were partly responsible for the review of Cary. Foscolo afterwards utilized parts of this article in his *Essays on Petrarch* (see below, pp. 167 ff.).]

reasons which influenced the mind of our own Milton would most probably have determined the author of the Inferno.

Some years ago,[1] Mr. Hayley published a translation of the three first Cantos of that Poem, in which he endeavoured to give an idea of Dante's peculiar manner, by introducing his triple rhyme. It was written with a considerable degree of spirit and elegance; but we cannot much regret that he proceeded no further. The difficulties which he had to encounter were almost insurmountable; at least he has led us to think so, by his many deviations from the text. Of these there is a remarkable instance in the third Canto. When the poet enters in at the gate, his ears are instantly assailed by a multitude of dismal sounds, among which he distinguishes

'Voci alte e fioche, e suon di man con elle.'

'Voices deep and hoarse,
With hands together smote.'

The last circumstance, the most striking of them all, is entirely passed over by Mr. Hayley. . . . Of such offences we cannot accuse Mr. Cary. Throughout he discovers the will and the power to do justice to his author. He has omitted nothing, he has added nothing; and though here and there his inversions are ungraceful, and his phrases a little obsolete, he walks not unfrequently by the side of his master, and sometimes perhaps goes beyond him. We may say in the language of that venerable Father of Italian Poetry,

Hor ti riman, lettor, sopra 'l tuo banco,
Dietro pensando a ciò che si preliba, &c.
Paradiso x [ll. 22 ff.]

'Now rest thee, reader! on thy bench, and muse
Anticipative of the feast to come;
So shall delight make thee not feel the toil.'

. . . Mr. Cary reminds us sometimes of Shakespeare,—oftener of Milton; but, in his anxiety to imitate them, he becomes more antiquated than either; and we hope, that, when he republishes his translation, which, we trust, he soon will, in a larger and more legible character,[2] he will think proper to modernize the language a little, and give more simplicity and sweetness to many parts of it.

(Vol. xxix. pp. 454 ff.)

1818. Sept. EDINBURGH REVIEW. CANCELLIERI'S OBSERVATIONS CONCERNING THE QUESTION OF THE ORIGINALITY OF THE POEM OF DANTE.

[Alleged indebtedness of Dante to the Vision of Alberic]

An extract, or rather a short abstract of an old Vision, written in Latin, appeared in a pamphlet published at Rome in 1801, with

[1] [In 1782—see vol. i. pp. 359 ff.]

[2] [Cary's *Vision of Dante* was first issued in 1814 in three diminutive vols. in very small type (see vol. i. pp. 466 ff.)]

an insinuation, that the primitive model of Dante's poem had at length been discovered. . . . Mr. Cancellieri, a professed black-letter scholar, and animated, no doubt, with a laudable zeal for religion as well as literature, published the Vision entire in 1814, on the return of his Holiness to Rome. He accompanied it with an Italian translation, the whole comprising some sixty pages, preceded by twice that number of pages of his own remarks. . . . Alberic was born about the year 1100. When in his ninth year, he fell sick, and remained in a lethargy for nine days. Whilst in this state, a dove appeared to him, and catching him by the hair lifted him up to the presence of Saint Peter, who, with two angels, conducted the child across Purgatory, and, mounting thence from planet to planet, transported him into Paradise, there to contemplate the glory of the blessed. His vision restored him to perfect health;—the miraculous cure was published to the world; —the monks received the child at Monte-Cassino;—and . . . took care to have the vision of Alberic reduced to writing, first by one of their own lettered brethren, and, some years after, by Alberic himself. . . .

If there existed but this one vision before the time of Dante, there might be some ground for presuming, that it suggested to him the idea of his poem. But the truth is, that such visions abounded from the very earliest ages of Christianity. . . . About the tenth century, the great object was to establish the doctrine of Purgatory, in which the period of expiation was shortened in favour of souls, in proportion to the alms given by their heirs to the Church. The monk Alberic describes Purgatory with minuteness, and sees Hell only at a distance. All these visions having the same object, resembled each other; and whoever will take the trouble to examine the legends of the saints, and archives of the monasteries, will find hundreds, of the same epoch, and the same tenor. It may be said, that Dante either profited by all, or by none. . . . It is possible that he may have taken some ideas here and there from the Visions which abounded in his age. There are involuntary plagiarisms, which no writer can wholly avoid;—for much of what we think and express is but a new combination of what we have read and heard. But reminiscences in great geniuses are sparks that produce a mighty flame; and if Dante, like the monks, employed the machinery of visions, the result only proves, that much of a great writer's originality may consist in attaining his sublime objects by the same means which others had employed for mere trifling. He conceived and executed the project of creating the Language and the Poetry of a nation—of exposing all the political wounds of his country—of teaching the Church and the States of Italy, that the imprudence of the Popes, and the civil wars of the cities, and the consequent introduction of foreign arms, must lead to the eternal slavery and disgrace of the Italians. He raised himself to a place among the reformers of morals, the avengers of crimes, and the asserters of orthodoxy in religion; and he called to his aid Heaven itself, with all its terrors and all its hopes, in what was denominated by himself

Il poema sacro
Al qual ha posto mano e Cielo e Terra (Parad. Cant. 25).

(Vol. xxx. pp. 317 ff.)[1]

[Dante's conciseness]

Dante condenses all his thoughts and feelings in the facts he relates—and expresses himself invariably by images, and those images often what the Italian painters call *in iscorcio*. Even his largest groups are composed of a very few strokes of the pencil and in none does he ever stop to fill up the design with minute or successive touches, but passes hastily on through the boundless variety of his subject, without once pausing to heighten the effect, or even to allow its full development to the emotion he has excited. A single word flung in apparently without design, often gives its whole light and character to the picture.

(p. 339.)

[Dante's lyrical poems]

But few literary men are acquainted with Dante's lyric compositions; and his prose is scarcely ever mentioned. The elegant treatise[2] written by him, to prove that in a nation, divided by so many dialects as Italy, it must be impossible to adapt the dialect of Florence exclusively, was the principal cause of the little value set by the academy of La Crusca and its adherents upon the prose of our poet. For La Crusca always maintained that the language should not be called Italian, or even Tuscan, but Florentine. Nevertheless, the literary language of Italy, though founded upon the Tuscan, is a distinct language, created by the commonwealth of authors, never spoken, but alway written: as Dante had seen and foreseen. His own prose is a fine model of forcible and simple style, harmonious without studied cadences, and elegant without the affected graces of Boccaccio and his imitators. . . .

The lyric poetry of Italy was not indeed invented or perfected, though greatly improved, by Dante. It is mentioned by himself in his prose works, that 'lyric composition had been introduced above a century before, by Sicilian poets, into Italy';[3] from which time it was gradually cultivated, down to Guido Cavalcanti, who pro-

[1] [In this article Foscolo finds fault with some of Cary's renderings—a fact to which Cary refers in a letter to T. Price (vol. i. p. 484).]

[2] [The *De Vulgari Eloquentia*.]

[3] [*V.E.* i. 12.]

duced some very fine essays—the finest until those of Dante, who in that kind was, in his turn, surpassed by Petrarca. But still the germs of all that is most enchanting in the strains of Laura's lover, may be found in the verses which had previously celebrated Beatrice. . . .

(pp. 346-7, 348.)

1821. Jan. QUARTERLY REVIEW. ART. XI. MADAME DE GENLIS' PETRARQUE ET LAURE.[1]

[Petrarch and Dante]

The poets who preceded Petrarch adorned their works with the philosophy of love ; but they sought rather to be admired than to be understood. Guido Cavalcanti, the intimate friend of Dante, professes that he does not expect to be read, except by elevated minds

'Perch' io non spero ch' uom di basso core
A tal ragione porti conoscenza.'

This canzone, which begins 'Donna mi prega,' has had some celebrated commentators, among others, Pico della Mirandola, but it has not been made more intelligible. Dante has himself commented on his own love-verses, an example which Lorenzo de' Medici followed two centuries afterwards. . . .

Although this kind of poetry had been in use with the Sicilians and the Provençals for more than two centuries, and Dante had brought almost to perfection the Canzone, a sort of majestic ode, the character and form of which belong exclusively to the Italians, Petrarch subsequently managed it in a way, that no other person has been able to approach. . . . All the love-poetry of his predecessors, except that of Dante and Cino, wants both sweetness of language and of rhythm ; but the sweetness of Petrarch's verses is accompanied with a variety, a warmth, and a glow, which even Dante and Cino never knew. In order to form a style which should be quite his own, he assures us that he would never possess a copy of Dante's great poem, whose style he affected to despise. . . .

Tiraboschi, who writes in the character of a Jesuit, had his own reasons for dissembling the boldness of the language which Petrarch used towards the church and the great, and for exaggerating the same boldness in Dante. Amorous poetry, which alone, of all the works of Petrarch, is generally read, is admirably adapted to the purpose of a Jesuit's College, since it inspires mysticism and flatters those passions which emasculate the minds of young persons : that of Dante produces quite the contrary effect, and it was

[1] [Foscolo afterwards utilised parts of this article in his *Essays on Petrarch* (see below, pp. 167 ff.).]

banished the schools. From the anecdote that Dante was expelled from Verona for a single expression which he dared to use concerning the passion of Can della Scala for buffoons, Tiraboschi concludes that, if he continued to live a pauper and a vagrant, it must be imputed to the little respect which he showed to princes. This anecdote has been preserved by Petrarch,[1] who, whilst he gave his fortune and his studies to render his contemporaries illustrious, records rather the errors than the virtues of Dante, and affects to mingle his name without distinction with those whom his own works had occasioned to be forgotten:—

> 'Ma ben ti prego, che in la terza spera
> Guitton saluti, e Messer Cino, e Dante,
> Franceschin nostro, e tutta quella schiera.'
>
> P. ii. Son. 19.

> 'Ecco Dante e Beatrice, ecco Selvaggia,
> Ecco Cin da Pistoja, Guitton d' Arezzo,
> Ecco i due Guidi.'
>
> Trionf. c. 4.

Boccaccio, deterred by the merit and celebrity of the poetry of Dante and Petrarch, determined to burn his own; but Petrarch diverted him from this purpose. . . . Boccaccio sent Dante's poem to Petrarch, and entreated, that 'he would not disdain to read the work of a great man from whom exile and death, while he was still in the vigour of life, had snatched the laurel.'—'Read it, I conjure you; your genius reaches to the heavens, and your glory extends beyond the earth: but reflect that Dante is our fellow-citizen; that he has shown all the force of our language; that his life was unfortunate; that he undertook and suffered everything for glory; and that he is still pursued by calumny and envy in the grave. If you praise him you will do honour to him—you will do honour to yourself—you will do honour to Italy, of which you are the greatest glory and the only hope.' Petrarch, in his answer, is angry, 'that he can be considered jealous of the celebrity of a poet, whose language is coarse, though his conceptions are lofty.'—'You must hold him in veneration and gratitude, as the first light of your education, whilst I saw him only once and afar off in my childhood. He was exiled on the same day with my father, who submitted himself to his fortunes and devoted himself solely to the care of his children. The other, on the contrary, thought only of glory, and neglected everything else. If he were still alive, and if his character were as congenial with mine as his genius is, he would not have a better friend than me.' . . .

Petrarch is incessantly endeavouring to dazzle our imagination

[1] Rerum Memor. lib. iii. c. 4.

by the ornaments of his style, and he borrows his metaphors from the highest phenomena of the creation; whilst the metaphors of Dante oblige us to reflect deeply, because they spring less from the actual appearance than from the most inward, and till then unnoticed, qualities of each object he describes. Instead of selecting, as Petrarch does, the most elegant and melodious phrases, Dante often invents new words, and compels his language to furnish him with every combination to represent not only the images of his creation, but the loftiest conceptions, the most familiar accidents of human nature, the vices of the wicked, the virtues of heroes, the most abstract ideas of philosophy, and the most abstruse mysteries of religion. Such was the taste of Petrarch, that he hardly has employed a word that is not even now written without affectation by the Italians. On the other side, though many of the words of Dante have become obsolete, his elocution is constantly wonderful: no one dares to imitate it, because it is felt that the style of a bold creative genius belongs exclusively to him. He often sacrifices dignity and elegance, and sometimes clearness and perspicuity; but it is always to give more fidelity and energy to his pictures, or greater depth to his reflections.

(Vol. xxiv. pp. 546 ff.)

1823. ESSAYS ON PETRARCH.

[Dante's opinion of professional rhymesters]

Professional lovers addressed rhymes to their mistresses, which singers and wandering troubadours repeated at the banquets of their patrons. According to Dante's opinion and that of his friend Guido Cavalcanti, they were rather *dicitori per rima*, than deserving of the name of poets.[1]

(p. 88.)

[The perfection of Dante's love-verses]

Dante has himself commented on his own love-verses; an example which was followed two centuries afterwards by Lorenzo de' Medici. . . . By a comparison of some verses, in which Guido, Dante, Petrarch, and Giusto de Conti, describe the supernatural beauty of their mistresses, it is easy to trace the progress of this sort of poetry, and to perceive that its perfection had been nearly attained by Dante.

(pp. 89-90.)

[Petrarch's style inferior to that of Dante]

In order to form a style which should be quite his own, Petrarch assures us that he never possessed a copy of Dante's great poem,

[1] [*V. N.* § 25.]

whose diction he affects to despise. . . . Petrarch's letters, far from possessing the elegance and grammatical correctness of Dante and Boccaccio, or indeed of their minor contemporaries, are remarkable only for the warmth of feeling and perspicuity of thought peculiar to his style.

(pp. 93-4.)

[A parallel between Dante and Petrarch]

These two founders of Italian literature, were gifted with a very different genius, pursued different plans, established two different languages and schools of poetry, and have exercised till the present time a very different influence. Instead of selecting, as Petrarch does, the most elegant and melodious words and phrases, Dante often creates a new language, and summons all the various dialects of Italy to furnish him with combinations that might represent, not only the sublime and beautiful, but even the commonest scenes of nature; all the wild conceptions of his fancy; the most abstract theories of philosophy, and the most abstruse mysteries of religion. A simple idea, a vulgar idiom, takes a different colour and a different spirit from their pen. The conflict of opposite purposes *thrills in the heart* of Petrarch, and *battles in the brain* of Dante—

Nè sì nè no nel cor dentro mi suona.—*Petr.*
Che sì e no nel capo mi tenzona.[1]—*Dante.*

(p. 167.)

[The versification of Petrarch and Dante compared]

As to their versification, Petrarch attained the main object of erotic poetry; which is, to produce a constant musical flow in strains inspired by the sweetest of human passions. Dante's harmony is less melodious, but is frequently the result of more powerful art—

S' i' avessi le rime e aspre e chiocce,
Come si converebbe al tristo buco
Sovra 'l qual pontan tutte l' altre rocce,
I' premerei di mio concetto il suco
Più pienamente: ma perch' i' non l' abbo
Non senza tema a dicer mi conduco:
Che non è impresa da pigliare a gabbo,
Descriver fondo a tutto l' universo,
Nè da lingua, che chiami mamma o babbo.
Ma quelle donne ajutino 'l mio verso,
Ch' ajutaro Anfione a chiuder Tebe,
Sì che dal fatto il dir non sia diverso.[2]

[1] [*Inf.* viii. 111.]

[2] [*Inf.* xxxii. 1-12.]

Here the poet evidently hints that to give colour and strength to ideas by the sound of words, is one of the necessary requisites of the art. The six first lines are made rough by a succession of consonants. But when he describes a quite different subject, the words are more flowing with vowels—

O anime affannate,
Venite a noi parlar, s' altri nol niega.
Quali colombe dal disio chiamate,
Con l' ali aperte e ferme al dolce nido,
Volan per l' aer dal voler portate.[1]

The plan of Dante's poem required that he should pass from picture to picture, from passion to passion. He varies the tone in the different scenes of his journey as rapidly as the crowd of spectres flitted before his eyes; and he adapts the syllables and the cadences of each line, in such an artful manner as to give energy, by the change of his numbers, to those images which he intended to represent.

(pp. 169-71.)

[The imagery of Petrarch and Dante compared]

Petrarch's images seem to be exquisitely finished by a very delicate pencil: they delight the eye rather by their colouring than by their forms. Those of Dante are the bold and prominent figures of an *alto rilievo*, which, it seems, we might almost touch, and of which the imagination readily supplies those parts that are hidden from the view. The common-place thought of the vanity of human renown is thus expressed by Petrarch—

O ciechi, il tanto affaticar che giova?
Tutti tornate alla gran madre antica,
E il vostro nome appena si ritrova.[2]

and by Dante,

La vostra nominanza è color d' erba,
Che viene e va; e quei la discolora
Per cui vien fuori della terra acerba.[3]

The three lines of Petrarch have the great merit of being more spirited, and of conveying more readily the image of the earth swallowing up the bodies and names of all men; but those of Dante, in spite of their stern profundity, have the still greater merit of leading us on to ideas to which we should not ourselves have reached. Whilst he reminds us, that time, which is necessary for the consummation of all human glory, ultimately destroys it, the changing colour of grass presents the revolutions of ages, as the natural occurrence of a few moments. . . . Again, instead of the agency

[1] [*Inf.* v. 80-4.]
[2] [*Trionfo della Morte*, i. 106-8.]
[3] [*Purg.* xi. 115-7.]

of time, Dante employs the agency of the sun; because, conveying to us a less metaphysical idea, and being an object more palpable to the senses, it abounds with more glorious and evident images, and fills us with greater wonder and admiration. Its application is more logical also, since every notion which we have of time, consists in the measure of it, which is afforded by the periodical revolutions of the sun.

(pp. 174-6.)

[Petrarch appeals to the heart, Dante to the imagination]

To judge fairly between these two poets, it appears, that Petrarch excels in awakening the heart to a deep feeling of its existence; and Dante, in leading the imagination to add to the interest and novelty of nature. Probably a genius never existed, that enjoyed these two powers at once in a pre-eminent degree. Having both worked upon plans suited to their respective talents, the result has been two kinds of poetry, productive of opposite moral effects. Petrarch makes us see every thing through the medium of one predominant passion, habituates us to indulge in those propensities which by keeping the heart in perpetual disquietude, paralize intellectual exertion—entice us into a morbid indulgence of our feelings, and withdraw us from active life. Dante, like all primitive poets, is the historian of the manners of his age, the prophet of his country, and the painter of mankind; and calls into action all the faculties of our soul to reflect on all the vicissitudes of the world. He describes all passions, all actions—the charm and the horror of the most different scenes. He places men in the despair of Hell, in the hope of Purgatory, and in the blessedness of Paradise. He observes them in youth, in manhood, and in old age. He has brought together those of both sexes, of all religions, of all occupations, of different nations, and ages; yet he never takes them in masses—he always presents them as individuals; speaks to every one of them, studies their words, and watches their countenances.—'I found,' says he, in a letter to Can della Scala, 'the original of my Hell, in the earth we inhabit.'

(pp. 183-4.)

[The natures of Dante and Petrarch essentially different]

The endeavours of Dante and Petrarch to bring their country under the government of one sovereign, and to abolish the Pope's temporal power, forms the only point of resemblance between these two characters. Fortune seemed to have conspired with nature, in order to separate them by an irreconcilable diversity. Dante went through a more regular course of studies, and at a time when Aristotle and Thomas Aquinas reigned alone in universities. Their stern methods and maxims taught him to write only after long meditation—to keep in view 'a great practical end, which is that of human life'[1]—and to pursue it steadily with a predetermined plan. Poetical ornaments seem constantly employed by Dante, only to throw a light upon his subjects; and he never allows his fancy to violate the laws which he had previously imposed upon his own genius—

L' ingegno affreno,
Perchè non corra che virtù nol guidi.—Inferno.[2]
Più non mi lascia gire il fren dell' arte.—Purg.[3]

(pp. 193-4.)

[Dante's character]

Pride was the prominent characteristic of Dante. He was pleased with his sufferings, as the means of exerting his fortitude, —and with his imperfections, as the necessary attendants of extraordinary qualities,—and with the consciousness of his internal worth, because it enabled him to look down with scorn upon other men and their opinions—

Che ti fa ciò che quivi si pispiglia?—
Lascia dir le genti;
Sta come torre ferma che non crolla
Giammai la cima per soffiar de' venti.[4]

The power of despising, which many boast, which very few really possess, and with which Dante was uncommonly gifted by nature, afforded him the highest delight of which a lofty mind is susceptible. . . .

Dante was one of those rare individuals who are above the reach of ridicule, and whose natural dignity is enhanced, even by the blows of malignity. In his friends he inspired less commiseration than awe; in his enemies, fear and hatred—but never contempt. His wrath was inexorable; with him vengeance was not only a natural impulse but a duty:[5] and he enjoyed the certainty of that slow but everlasting revenge, which 'his wrath brooded over in secret silence'—

Fa dolce l' ira sua nel suo secreto.[6]

(pp. 197 ff.)

[Dante a great example]

Being convinced 'that Man is then truly happy when he freely exercises all his energies,'[7] Dante walked through the world with an assured step 'keeping his vigils'—

[1] Dante, Convito [iv. 6, ll. 64-5].

[2] [*Inf.* xxvi. 21-2.]

[3] [*Purg.* xxxiii. 141.]

[4] [*Purg.* v. 12-15.]

[5] *Che bell' onor s' acquista in far vendetta.* Dante, Canzon.—See also, Inferno, cant. xxix. vers. 31-36.

[6] [*Purg.* xx. 96.]

[7] *Humanum genus, potissimè liberum, optimè se habet.*—Dante, de Monarchia [i. 12, ll. 1-2.]

So that, nor night nor slumber with close stealth
Convey'd from him a single step in all
The goings on of time.[1]

Cary's Transl.

He collected the opinions, the follies, the vicissitudes, the miseries and the passions that agitate mankind, and left behind him a monument, which while it humbles us by the representation of our own wretchedness, should make us glory that we partake of the same nature with such a man; and encourage us to make the best use of our fleeting existence.

(p. 207.)

[Dante's letter to a Florentine friend]

From a letter of Dante lately discovered, it appears that about the year 1316, his friends succeeded in obtaining his restoration to his country and his possessions, on condition that he compounded with his calumniators, avowed himself guilty, and asked pardon of the commonwealth. The following was his answer on the occasion, to one of his kinsmen. . . .

'From your letter, which I received with due respect and affection, I observe how much you have at heart my restoration to my country. I am bound to you the more gratefully, since an exile rarely finds a friend. But, after mature consideration, I must, by my answer, disappoint the wishes of some little minds; and I confide in the judgment to which your impartiality and prudence will lead you. Your nephew and mine has written to me, what indeed had been mentioned by many other friends, that, by a decree concerning the exiles, I am allowed to return to Florence, provided I pay a certain sum of money, and submit to the humiliation of asking and receiving absolution; wherein, father, I see two propositions that are ridiculous and impertinent. I speak of the impertinence of those who mention such conditions to me: for, in your letter, dictated by judgment and discretion, there is no such thing. Is such an invitation to return to his country glorious for Dante, after suffering in banishment almost fifteen years? Is it thus, then, they would recompense innocence which all the world knows, and the labour and fatigue of unremitting study? Far from the man who is familiar with philosophy, be the senseless baseness of a heart of earth, that could act like a little sciolist, and imitate the infamy of some others, by offering himself up as it were in chains. Far from the man who cries aloud for justice, be this compromise, for money, with his persecutors. No, father, this is not the way that shall lead me back to my country. But I shall return with hasty steps, if you or any other can open me a way that shall not derogate

[1] [*Purg*. xxx. 103-5.]

from the fame and honour of Dante; but if by no such way Florence can be entered, then Florence I will never enter: What! shall I not everywhere enjoy the sight of the sun and stars? and may I not seek and contemplate, in every corner of the earth under the canopy of heaven, consoling and delightful truth, without first rendering myself inglorious, nay infamous, to the people and republic of Florence? Bread, I hope, will not fail me.

(pp. 202-4.) [1]

[Literal translation of Dante's Sonnet 'Negli occhi porta la mia Donna Amore' [2]]

'In the eyes of my mistress, Love is seated, for they ennoble everything she looks upon. Where she passes, men turn and gaze; and whomsoever she salutes, his heart trembles; the colour forsakes his downcast face, and he sighs for all his unworthiness. Pride and anger fly before her. Assist me, ladies, to do her honour! All gentleness, all thoughts of love and kindness, spring in the hearts of those who hear her speak, so that it is very blessedness first to behold her. But when she faintly smiles, it passes both utterance and conception; so wondrous is the miracle, and so gracious!

(*Comparative Descriptions of Female Beauty . . . by the early Italian Poets*, p. 265.)

1825. DISCORSO SUL TESTO E SU LE OPINIONI DIVERSE PREVALENTI INTORNO ALLA STORIA E ALLA EMENDAZIONE CRITICA DELLA COMMEDIA DI DANTE.

[Published in London by Pickering. Dedicated to Hudson Gurney. This is the first volume of a projected commentary on the *Divina Commedia*, of which no more was issued in Foscolo's lifetime. The complete work, edited by Mazzini, was published in 1842-3 (see under).]

1842-3. LA COMMEDIA DI DANTE ALLIGHIERI ILLUSTRATA DA UGO FOSCOLO.

[Published in London, in four volumes, by Rolandi, who is said by the editor (G. Mazzini) to have purchased the MS. (apparently from Pickering, the publisher of the *Discorso*) for £400. The first volume contains the *Discorso;* the second the *Inferno;* the third the *Purgatorio* and *Paradiso;* the fourth a Chronology of the Life of Dante, an account of the MSS. and printed editions of the *Commedia*, and a Vocabulary of the poem.] [3]

WILLIAM HAZLITT

(1778-1830)

[William Hazlitt, the son of a Unitarian preacher, was born in 1778; he was educated for the Unitarian ministry, but at the age of twenty abandoned his projected

[1] [The Latin text of this letter, printed for the first time in England, is given on pp. 276-7 of Foscolo's volume.]

[2] [Sonnet xi. in the *Vita Nuova*.]

[3] [See notice in *Athenæum*, below, p. 682.]

career, and turned his attention to reading and to painting. Among the portraits painted by him was that of Charles Lamb as a Venetian Senator, now in the National Portrait Gallery, which was his last attempt (1805). Hazlitt now devoted himself to literature, which was his chief occupation until his death in London in 1830. His numerous Essays and Lectures, contributed to various periodicals, and recently reprinted in his Collected Works, contain frequent allusions to Dante, with occasional translations.]

1814. THE ROUND TABLE.[1]—ON POSTHUMOUS FAME.

[Dante and fame]

CHAUCER seems to have derived his notions of fame more immediately from the reputation acquired by the Italian poets, his contemporaries, which had at that time spread itself over Europe; while the latter, who were the first to unlock the springs of ancient learning, and who slaked their thirst of knowledge at that pure fountain-head, would naturally imbibe the same feeling from its highest source. Thus, Dante has conveyed the finest image that can perhaps be conceived of the power of this principle over the human mind when he describes the heroes and celebrated men of antiquity as 'serene and smiling,' though in the shades of death,

—'Because on earth their names
In Fame's eternal volume shine for aye.'[2]

(*Collected Works,* vol. i. p. 23.)

1814. THE ROUND TABLE—WHY THE ARTS ARE NOT PROGRESSIVE?

[Homer, Shakespeare, Dante, and other great artists]

The greatest poets, the ablest orators, the best painters, and the finest sculptors that the world ever saw, appeared soon after the birth of these arts, and lived in a state of society which was, in other respects, comparatively barbarous. Those arts, which depend on individual genius and incommunicable power, have always leaped at once from infancy to manhood, from the first rude dawn of invention to their meridian height and dazzling lustre, and have in general declined ever after. This is the peculiar distinction and privilege of each, of science and of art; of the one, never to attain its utmost summit of perfection, and of the other, to arrive at it almost at once. Homer, Chaucer, Spenser, Shakspeare, Dante, and Ariosto (Milton alone was of a later age, and not the worse for it), Raphael, Titian, Michael Angelo, Correggio, Cervantes, and Boccaccio—all lived near the beginning of their arts—perfected, and all but

[1] [Originally contributed to the *Examiner;* published in book form in 1817.]

[2] [Apparently meant for a free rendering of *Inf.* iv. 76-8—the same quotation occurs again in the essay on Sismondi (see below, p. 177).]

created them. These giant sons of genius stand, indeed, upon the earth, but they tower above their fellows, and the long line of their successors does not interpose anything to obstruct their view, or lessen their brightness. In strength and stature they are unrivalled, in grace and beauty they have never been surpassed.[1]

(*Collected Works*, vol. i. pp. 161-2.)

1814. WILSON'S LANDSCAPES, AT THE BRITISH INSTITUTION.[2]

[Michael Angelo and Dante]

There is a fine apostrophe in a sonnet of Michael Angelo's to the earliest Poet of Italy:

Fain would I, to be what our Dante was,
Forego the happiest fortunes of mankind.

What landscape-painter does not feel this of Claude!

(*Ibid.* vol. xi. p. 202.)

1814. L. BUONAPARTE'S 'CHARLEMAGNE.'[3]

[The 'severe grandeur' of Dante]

There is no one who has borrowed his materials more than Milton, or who has made them more completely his own: there is hardly a line which does not breathe the same lofty spirit, hardly a thought or image which he has not clothed with the majesty of his genius. It is the same in reading other great poets. The informing mind is everywhere present to us. Who is there that does not know and feel sensibly the majestic copiousness of Homer, the polished elegance of Virgil, enamoured of his own workmanship,—the severe grandeur of Dante, the tender pathos of Tasso, the endless voluptuousness of Spenser, and the unnumbered graces of Ariosto?

(*Ibid.* vol. xi. p. 235.)

1815. THE ROUND TABLE.—ON MILTON'S VERSIFICATION.

[Milton and Dante]

There is a decided tone in Milton's descriptions, an eloquent dogmatism, as if the poet spoke from thorough conviction, which he probably derived from his spirit of partisanship, or else his spirit of partisanship from the natural firmness and vehemence of his mind.

[1] [Part of the above was afterwards repeated in *Lectures on the English Poets* (Lecture iii.).]

[2] [Originally published in the *Champion*, July 17, 1814. This passage was afterwards repeated in the *Essay on the Fine Arts* (1824).]

[3] [Originally published in the *Champion*, Dec. 25, 1814.]

In this Milton resembles Dante (the only one of the moderns with whom he has anything in common), and it is remarkable that Dante, as well as Milton, was a political partisan.[1]

(*Collected Works*, vol. i. p. 37.)

1815. ON SISMONDI'S LITERATURE OF THE SOUTH.[2]

[Dante and the *Divina Commedia*]

M. Sismondi is right in saying that the Mystery of the Passions, and the moralities performed by the French company of players, laid the foundations of the drama in various parts of Europe, and also suggested the first probable hint of the plan of the *Divine Comedy* of Dante; but it is not right to say that the merit of this last work consists at all in the design. The design is clumsy, mechanical, and monotonous; the invention is in the style. . . . It is from the work of Dante, the first lasting monument of modern genius, that we should strictly date the origin of modern literature. . . . M. Sismondi seems to have understood the great poet of Italy little better than his other commentators: and indeed the *Divine Comedy* must completely baffle the common rules of French criticism, which always seeks for excellence in the external image, and never in the internal power and feeling. But Dante is nothing but power, passion, self-will. In all that relates to the imitative part of poetry, he bears no comparison with many other poets; but there is a gloomy abstraction in his conceptions, which lies like a dead-weight upon the mind; a benumbing stupor from the intensity of the impression; a terrible obscurity like that which oppresses us in dreams; an identity of interest which moulds every object to its own purposes, and clothes all things with the passions and imaginations of the human soul, that make amends for all other deficiencies. Dante is a striking instance of the essential excellences and defects of modern genius. The immediate objects he presents to the mind, are not much in themselves;—they generally want grandeur, beauty and order; but they become everything by the force of the character which he impresses on them. His mind lends its own power to the objects which it contemplates, instead of borrowing it from them. He takes advantage even of the nakedness and dreary vacuity of his subject. His imagination peoples the shades of death, and broods over the barren vastnesses of illimitable space. In point of diction and style, he is the severest of all

[1] [This passage was afterwards repeated in *Lectures on the English Poets* (Lecture iii.).]

[2] [Contributed to the *Edinburgh Review*, June, 1815. The greater part of this article was afterwards embodied by Hazlitt in the first of his *Lectures on the English Poets*, delivered in 1818 (see below, pp. 180 ff.).]

writers, the most opposite to the flowery and glittering—who relies most on his own power, and the sense of power in the reader —who leaves most to the imagination.[1] Dante's only object is to interest; and he interests only by exciting our sympathy with the emotion by which he is himself possessed. He does not place before us the objects by which that emotion has been excited; but he seizes on the attention, by showing us the effect they produce on his feelings; and his poetry accordingly frequently gives us the thrilling and overwhelming sensation which is caught by gazing on the face of a person who has seen some object of horror. The improbability of the events, the abruptness and monotony in the Inferno, are excessive; but the interest never flags, from the intense earnestness of the author's mind. Dante, as well as Milton, appears to have been indebted to the writers of the Old Testament for the gloomy tone of his mind, for the prophetic fury which exalts and kindles his poetry. But there is more deep-working passion in Dante, and more imagination in Milton. Milton, more perhaps than any other poet, elevated his subject, by combining image with image in lofty gradation. Dante's great power is in combining internal feelings with familiar objects. Thus the gate of Hell, on which that withering inscription is written, seems to be endowed with speech and consciousness, and to utter its dread warning, not without a sense of mortal woes. The beauty to be found in Dante is of the same severe character, mixed with deep sentiment. The story of Genevra,[2] to which we have just alluded, is of this class. So is the affecting apostrophe, addressed to Dante by one of his countrymen, whom he meets in the other world.

'Sweet is the dialect of Arno's vale!
Though half consumed, I gladly turn to hear.'[3]

And another example, even still finer, if anything could be finer, is his description of the poets and great men of antiquity, whom he represents 'serene and smiling,' though in the shades of death,—

'because on earth their names
In fame's eternal records shine for aye.'[4]

This is the finest idea ever given of the love of fame. Dante habitually unites the absolutely local and individual with the greatest wildness and mysticism. In the midst of the obscure and shadowy regions of the lower world, a tomb suddenly rises up, with this inscription, 'I am the tomb of Pope Anastasius the Sixth':[5] —and half the personages whom he has crowded into the Inferno

[1] See, among a thousand instances, the conclusion of the story of Genevra.—'And all that day we read no more!' [*Inf.* v. 138.]

[2] [Apparently Francesca is meant.]

[3] [From Boyd's translation of *Inf.* xxvii. 19-24.]

[4] [*Inf.* iv. 76-8 ?]

[5] [*Inf.* xi. 8—Pope Anastasius II.]

are his own acquaintance. All this tends to heighten the effect by the bold intermixture of realities, and the appeal, as it were, to the individual knowledge and experience of the reader. There are occasional striking images in Dante—but these are exceptions; and besides, they are striking only from the weight of consequences attached to them. The imagination of the poet retains and associates the objects of nature, not according to their external forms, but their inward qualities or powers; as when Satan is compared to a cormorant.[1] It is not true, then, that Dante's excellence consists in a natural description or dramatic invention. His characters are indeed 'instinct with life' and sentiment; but it is with the life and sentiment of the poet. In themselves they have little or no dramatic variety, except what arises immediately from the historical facts mentioned; and they afford, in our opinion, very few subjects for picture. There is indeed one gigantic one, that of Count Ugolino, of which Michael Angelo made a bas-relief, and which Sir Joshua Reynolds ought not to have painted. Michael Angelo was naturally an admirer of Dante, and has left a sonnet to his memory.

The Purgatory and Paradise are justly characterised by M. Sismondi as 'a falling off' from the Inferno. He however points out a number of beautiful passages in both these divisions of the poem. That in which the poet describes his ascent into heaven, completely marks the character of his mind. He employs no machinery, or supernatural agency, for this purpose; but mounts aloft 'by the sole strength of his desires—fixing an intense regard on the orbit of the sun!'[2]

This great poet was born at Florence in 1265, of the noble family of the Alighieri—and died at Ravenna, September 14th, 1321. Like Milton, he was unfortunate in his political connexions, and, what is worse, in those of his private life. He had a few imitators after his death, but none of any eminence.

(*Edinburgh Review*, vol. xxv. pp. 45-9.)

1816. ON SCHLEGEL'S LECTURES ON DRAMATIC LITERATURE.[3]

[Dante and Virgil]

The constant reference to a former state of manners and literature, is a marked feature in modern poetry. We are always talking of the Greeks and Romans;—*they* never said anything of us. This circumstance has tended to give a certain abstract elevation, and ethereal refinement to the mind, without strengthening it. We are lost in wonder at what has been done, and dare not think of

[1] [*Paradise Lost*, iv. 196.] [2] [*Par.* i. 53 ff.]
[3] [Contributed to the *Edinburgh Review*, Feb. 1816.]

emulating it. The earliest modern poets, accordingly, may be conceived to hail the glories of the antique world, dawning through the dark abyss of time; while revelation, on the other hand, opened its path to the skies: As Dante represents himself as conducted by Virgil to the shades below; while Beatrice welcomes him to the abodes of the blest.

(*Edinburgh Review*, vol. xxvi. pp. 75-6.)

[Shakespeare and Dante]

The universality of Shakespeare's genius has, perhaps, been a disadvantage to his single works: the variety of his resources has prevented him from giving that intense concentration of interest to some of them which they might have had. He is in earnest only in Lear and Timon. He combined the powers of Aeschylus and Aristophanes, of Dante and Rabelais, in his own mind. If he had been only half what he was, he might have seemed greater.[1]

(*Ibid.* p. 100.)

1816. ON LEIGH HUNT'S STORY OF RIMINI.[2]

[The style of Dante]

In the subject he has selected, Mr. Hunt has ventured indeed upon sacred ground; but he has not profaned it. The passage in Dante, on which the story of Rimini is founded, remains unimpaired by the English version, and has even received a new interest from it. The undertaking must be allowed to have been one of great nicety. An imitation of the manner of Dante was an impossibility. That extraordinary author collects all his force into a single blow: His sentiments derive an obscure grandeur from their being only half expressed; and therefore, a detailed narrative of this kind, a description of particular circumstances done upon this ponderous principle, on enumeration of incidents leading to a catastrophe, with all the pith and conclusiveness of the catastrophe itself, would be intolerable. Mr. Hunt has arrived at his end by varying his means; and the effect of his poem coincides with that of the original passage, mainly, because the spirit in which it is written is quite different. With the personages in Dante, all is over before the reader is introduced to them; their doom is fixed;—and his style is as peremptory and irrevocable as their fate. But the lovers, whose memory the muse of the Italian poet had conse-

[1][Part of the above was afterwards repeated in *Lectures on the English Poets* (Lecture iii.).]

[2][Contributed to the *Edinburgh Review*, June, 1816. The authorship of this review has been disputed. Lord Cockburn ascribes it to Jeffrey. See Hazlitt's *Collected Works*, vol. x. p. 407.]

crated in the other world, are here restored to earth, with the graces and the sentiments that became them in their lifetime.

(*Edinburgh Review*, vol. xxvi. p. 477.)

1816. THE LIFE OF THOMAS HOLCROFT.

[The Germans and Dante]

The admiration of the Germans for English literature, and their contempt for the French, are well known. Molière is the only man among the latter, to whom they allow much genius. Their notions of excellence are indeed rather hypercritical than common-place. They seem in general to assign the highest stations to the greatest men, but their list of great men is short. There are only four whom they consider as *poets*, that is to say, inventors of a new style, namely, Homer, Dante, Shakspeare, and Goethe. Why the last should have this high rank assigned to him, I do not know.

(Book iv. Chap. 8, *Complete Works*, vol. ii. p. 229.)

1818. LECTURES ON THE ENGLISH POETS. DELIVERED AT THE SURREY INSTITUTION.

[Dante 'the father of modern poetry']

Lecture I. On Poetry in General.—I shall conclude this general account with some remarks on four of the principal works of poetry in the world, at different periods of history—Homer, the Bible, Dante, and let me add Ossian. In Homer, the principle of action or life is predominant; in the Bible, the principle of faith and the idea of Providence; Dante is a personification of blind will; and in Ossian we see the decay of life, and the lag end of the world. . . . Dante was the father of modern poetry, and he may therefore claim a place in this connection. His poem is the first great step from Gothic darkness and barbarism; and the struggle of thought in it to burst the thraldom in which the human mind had been so long held, is felt in every page. He stood bewildered, not appalled, on that dark shore which separates the ancient and the modern world; and saw the glories of antiquity dawning through the abyss of time, which revelation opened its passage to the other world. He was lost in wonder at what had been done before him, and he dared to imitate it. Dante seems to have been indebted to the Bible for the gloomy tone of his mind, as well as for the prophetic fury which exalts and kindles his poetry; but he is utterly unlike Homer. His genius is not a sparkling flame, but the sullen heat of a furnace. . . .[1]

(*Collected Works*, vol. v. pp. 15 ff.)

[1] [The remainder of this Lecture, in so far as it relates to Dante, is a repetition of Hazlitt's article on Sismondi's *Literature of the South*, in the *Edinburgh Review*, June, 1815 (see above, pp. 176 ff.).]

[Chaucer and Dante]

Lecture II. On Chaucer and Spenser.—Chaucer received a learned education at one, or at both of the universities, and travelled early into Italy, where he became thoroughly imbued with the spirit and excellences of the great Italian poets and prose-writers, Dante, Petrarch, and Boccace.

(*Collected Works*, vol. v. p. 19.)

[Milton, Tasso, and Dante]

Lecture III. On Shakespeare and Milton.—Milton was too magnanimous and open an antagonist to support his argument by the bye-tricks of a hump and cloven foot; to bring into the fair field of controversy the good old catholic prejudices of which Tasso and Dante have availed themselves, and which the mystic German critics would restore. He relied on the justice of his cause, and did not scruple to give the devil his due. . . .[1]

(*Ibid.* p. 45.)

1820. LECTURES ON THE LITERATURE OF THE AGE OF ELIZABETH. DELIVERED AT THE SURREY INSTITUTION.

[The Elizabethans and Italian literature]

Lecture I.—In the age of Elizabeth there were translations of Tasso by Fairfax, and of Ariosto by Harrington. . . . Boccaccio, the divine Boccaccio, Petrarch, Dante, the satirist Aretine, Machiavel, Castiglione, and others were familiar to our writers.

(*Ibid.* vol. v. p. 186.)

['Divine Comedy' a misnomer]

Lecture VII.—Sir Thomas Brown tells us that he often composed a comedy in his sleep. It would be curious to know the subject or the texture of the plot. It must have been something like Nabbes's *Mask of Microcosmus*; or else a misnomer, like Dante's *Divine Comedy of Heaven, Hell, and Purgatory*.

(*Ibid.* vol. v. p. 334.)

1822. THE FIGHT.[2]

[A prize fighter likened to a figure in Dante's *Inferno*]

Hickman generally stood with his back to me; but in the scuffle, he had changed positions, and Neate just then made a tremendous lunge at him, and hit him full in the face. It was doubtful whether

[1] [The remainder of this Lecture, so far as it relates to Dante, is a repetition of matter previously printed in the *Round Table* (1814) and *Edinburgh Review* (1816).]

[2] [Originally published in the *New Monthly Magazine*, Feb. 1822.]

he would fall backwards or forwards; he hung suspended for a second or two, and then fell back, throwing his hands in the air, and with his face lifted up to the sky. I never saw anything more terrific than his aspect just before he fell. All traces of life, of natural expression were gone from him. His face was like a human skull, a death's head, spouting blood. The eyes were filled with blood, the nose streamed with blood, the mouth gaped blood. He was not like an actual man, but like a preternatural, spectral appearance, or like one of the figures in Dante's *Inferno*. Yet he fought on after this for several rounds.

(*Collected Works*, vol. xii. p. 12.)

1824. ON THE FINE ARTS.[1]

[Reynolds's picture of Ugolino]

The highest subject which Sir Joshua has attempted was the *Count Ugolino*, and it was, as might be expected from the circumstances, a total failure. He had, it seems, painted a study of an old beggar-man's head; and some person,[2] who must have known as little of painting as of poetry, persuaded the unsuspecting artist that it was the exact expression of Dante's Count Ugolino, one of the most grand, terrific and appalling characters in modern fiction. Reynolds, who knew nothing of the matter but what he was told, took his good fortune for granted, and only extended his canvass to admit the rest of the figures, who look very much like apprentices hired to sit for the occasion from some neighbouring workshop. There is one pleasing and natural figure of a little boy kneeling at his father's feet, but it has no relation to the supposed story. The attitude and expression of Count Ugolino himself are what the artist intended them to be, till they were pampered into something else by the officious vanity of friends,—those of a common mendicant at the corner of a street, waiting patiently for some charitable donation. There is all the difference between what the picture is and what it ought to be, that there is between Crabbe and Dante. The imagination of the painter took refuge in a parish workhouse, instead of ascending the steps of the Tower of Famine. The hero of Dante is a lofty, high-minded, and unprincipled Italian nobleman, who had betrayed his country to the enemy, and who, as a punishment for his crime, is shut up with his four sons in the dungeon of the citadel, where he shortly finds the doors barred upon him, and food withheld. He in vain watches with eager feverish eye the opening of the door at the accustomed hour, and

[1] [Originally contributed to the *Encyclopædia Britannica*.]
[2] [Said by Northcote (see above, pp. 134 ff.) to have been Burke or Goldsmith.]

his looks turn to stone; his children one by one drop down dead at his feet; he is seized with blindness and, in the agony of despair, he gropes on his knees after them,

'Calling each by name
For three days after they were dead.'

Even in the other world he is represented with the same fierce, dauntless unrelenting character, 'gnawing the skull of his adversary, his fell repast.' The subject of the *Laocoon* is scarcely equal to that described by Dante. The horror *there* is physical and momentary; in the other, the imagination fills up the long, obscure, dreary void of despair, and joins its unutterable pangs to the loud cries of nature. What is there in the picture to convey the ghastly horrors of the scene, or the mighty energy of soul with which they are born?

(*Literary Remains*, pp. 400-1.)[1]

1825. THE SPIRIT OF THE AGE—LORD BYRON.

[Byron and Dante]

Lord Byron has strength and elevation enough to fill up the moulds of our classical and time-hallowed recollections, and to rekindle the earliest aspirations of the mind after greatness and true glory with a pen of fire. The names of Tasso, of Ariosto, of Dante, of Cincinnatus, of Caesar, of Scipio, lose nothing of their pomp or their lustre in his hands, and when he begins and continues a strain of panegyric on such subjects, we indeed sit down with him to a banquet of rich praise, brooding over imperishable glories.

'Till Contemplation has her fill.'

(*Collected Works*, vol. iv. p. 257.)

1825. THE SPIRIT OF THE AGE—MR. WORDSWORTH.

[Wordsworth and Dante]

Milton is Mr. Wordsworth's great idol, and he sometimes dares to compare himself with him. His sonnets, indeed, have something of the same high-raised tone and prophetic spirit. Chaucer is another prime favourite of his, and he has been at the pains to modernize some of the Canterbury Tales. Those persons who look upon Mr. Wordsworth as a merely puerile writer, must be rather at a loss to account for his strong predilection for such geniuses as Dante and Michael Angelo.

(*Ibid*. vol. iv. p. 276.)

[1] [With the addition of omitted passages printed as notes on pp. 473-4.]

1826. OF PERSONS ONE WOULD WISH TO HAVE SEEN.[1]

[Hazlitt's desire to see Dante]

Dante is as interesting a person as his own Ugolino, one whose lineaments curiosity would as eagerly devour in order to penetrate his spirit, and the only one of the Italian poets I should care much to see.

(*Collected Works*, vol. xii. p. 30.)

1826. THE PLAIN SPEAKER: OPINIONS ON BOOKS, MEN, AND THINGS.

[Michael Angelo and Dante]

Essay VI. On Application to Study—Michael Angelo was a prodigy of versatility of talent—a writer of Sonnets (which Wordsworth has thought worth translating) and the admirer of Dante.

(*Ibid.* vol. vii. p. 61.)

[Fuseli and Dante]

Essay IX. On the Old Age of Artists—Fuseli is undoubtedly a man of genius, and capable of the most wild and grotesque combinations of fancy. It is a pity that he ever applied himself to painting, which must always be reduced to the test of the senses. He is a little like Dante or Ariosto, perhaps; but no more like Michael Angelo, Raphael or Correggio, than I am.

(*Ibid.* vol. vii. p. 94.)

[The new *Political Millenium* likened to Dante's *Inferno*]

Essay XVII. The New School of Reform.—You cannot take the measure of human nature with a pair of compasses or a slip of parchment: nor do I think it an auspicious opening to the new *Political Millenium* to begin with setting our faces against all that has hitherto kindled the enthusiasm, or shutting the door against all that may in future give pleasure to the world. Your Elysium resembles Dante's *Inferno*—"who enters there must leave all hope behind!"[2]

(*Ibid.* vol. vii. p. 194.)

1826. NOTES OF A JOURNEY THROUGH FRANCE AND ITALY.[3]

[Delacroix and Dante]

Chapter VII. The Luxembourg Gallery.—A small picture, by Delacroix,[4] taken from the Inferno, *Virgil and Dante in the boat*.[5]

[1] [Originally published in the *New Monthly Magazine*, Jan. 1826.]
[2] [Adapted from *Inf.* iii. 9.]
[3] [Originally contributed to the *Morning Chronicle*, 1824-5.]
[4] [Eugène Delacroix (1799-1863); he exhibited the picture in question in the Paris Salon in 1822.]
[5] [*Inf.* viii. 25 ff.]

is truly picturesque in the composition and the effect, and shows a real eye for Rubens and for nature. The forms project, the colours are thrown into masses.

(*Collected Works*, vol. ix. p. 137.)

[Dante and the Tuscan dialect]

Chapter XVI.—Now, every one who is not a Frenchman, or who does not gabble French, is no better than a stammerer or a changeling out of his own country. I do not complain of this as a very great grievance; but it certainly prevents those far-famed meetings between learned men of different nations, which are recorded in history, as of Sir Thomas More with Erasmus, and of Milton with the philosophers and poets of Italy.

"Sweet is the dialect of Arno's vale:
Though half consumed, I gladly turn to hear."[1]

So Dante makes one of his heroes exclaim. It is pleasant to hear or speak one's native tongue when abroad; but possibly the language of that higher and adopted country, which was familiar to the scholar of former times, sounded even sweeter to the ear of friendship or of genius.

(*Ibid.* vol. ix. pp. 218-19.)

[Dante's story of Pia]

Chapter XX.—The following story . . .[2] is related by Mr. Beyle,[3] in his charming little work, entitled *De l' Amour*, as a companion to the famous one in Dante; and I shall give the whole passage in his words, as placing the Italian character (in former as well as latter times) in a striking point of view.

"I allude," he says, "to those touching lines of Dante:

Deh! quando tu sarai tornato al mondo
Ricordati di me, che son la Pia;
Sienna mi fê: disfecemi Maremma:
Salsi colui, che inannellata pria,
Disposando, m' avea con la sua gemma."

(*Purgatorio*, c. 5.)[4]

The woman who speaks with so much reserve, had in secret undergone the fate of Desdemona, and had it in her power, by a single word, to have revealed her husband's crime to the friends whom she had left upon earth.

Nello della Pietra obtained in marriage the hand of Madonna Pia, sole heiress of the Ptolomei, the richest and most noble family

[1] [*Inf.* xxvii. 19-24 (Boyd).]

[2] [This story was reproduced by Leigh Hunt in his *Hundred Romances of Real Life*, published in 1843.]

[3] [Marie Henri Beyle (1783-1842), better known as Stendhal; the work alluded to was published in 1822.]

[4] [*Purg.* v. 130-6.]

of Sienna. Her beauty, which was the admiration of all Tuscany, gave rise to a jealousy in the breast of her husband, that envenomed by false reports and by suspicions continually reviving, led to a frightful catastrophe. It is not easy to determine at this day if his wife was altogether innocent; but Dante has represented her as such. Her husband carried her with him into the marshes of Volterra, celebrated then, as now, for the pestiferous effects of the air. Never would he tell his unhappy wife the reason of her banishment into so dangerous a place. His pride did not deign to pronounce either complaint or accusation. He lived with her alone, in a deserted tower, of which I have been to see the ruins on the sea-shore; here he never broke his disdainful silence, never replied to the questions of his youthful bride, never listened to her entreaties. He waited unmoved by her for the air to produce its fatal effects. The vapours of this unwholesome swamp were not long in tarnishing features the most beautiful, they say, that in that age had appeared upon earth. In a few months she died. Some chroniclers of these remote times report, that Nello employed the dagger to hasten her end: she died in the marshes in some horrible manner; but the mode of her death remained a mystery, even to her contemporaries. Nello della Pietra survived to pass the remainder of his days in a silence which was never broken.

Nothing can be conceived more noble or more delicate than the manner in which the ill-fated Pia addresses herself to Dante. She desires to be recalled to the memory of the friends whom she had quitted so young: at the same time, in telling her name and alluding to her husband, she does not allow herself the smallest complaint against a cruelty unexampled, but thenceforth irreparable; and merely intimates that he knows the history of her death.

. . . This story is interesting and well told. One such incident, or one page in Dante or Spenser is worth all the route between this and Paris, and all the sights and all the post-roads in Europe. O Sienna! if I felt charmed with thy narrow, tenantless streets, or looked delighted through thy arched gateway over the subjected plain, it was that some recollections of Madonna Pia hung upon the beatings of my spirit, and converted a barren waste into the regions of romance!

(*Collected Works*, vol. ix. pp. 250-2.)

1830. CONVERSATIONS OF JAMES NORTHCOTE.[1]

[Northcote, Hazlitt, and Dante]

Conversation the Third.—*Hazlitt.* I inquired if he remembered much of Johnson, Burke, and that set of persons? He said, Yes,

[1] [Originally published in the *New Monthly Magazine* in 1826 and 1827, under the title 'Boswell Redivivus;' they were issued in volume form, with revisions and additions, in 1830.]

a good deal, as he had often seen them. Burke came into Sir Joshua's painting-room one day, when Northcote, who was then a young man, was sitting for one of the children in Count Ugolino.[1] (It is the one in profile with the hand to the face.)

(*Collected Works*, vol. vi. p. 348.)

Conversation the Sixteenth.—*Hazlitt.* What! shall a man have read Dante and Ariosto, and be none the better for it?

(*Ibid.* vol. vi. p. 425.)

Conversation the Twentieth.—*Northcote.* In the *Revolutionist's Jolly-boat*, after the Opposition were defeated, Gilray has placed Fox, and Sheridan, and the rest, escaping from the wreck: Dante could not have described them as looking more sullen and gloomy.

(*Ibid.* vol. vi. p. 455.)

1830. FOOTMEN.[2]

[The lady's maid in Florence]

Of all situations of this kind, the most enviable is that of a lady's maid in a family travelling abroad. . . . See our Abigail, setting out on the grand tour as fast as four horses can carry her,—crossing the Alps and Apennines in breathless terror and wonder,—seeing everything, and understanding nothing, in a full tide of health, fresh air, and animal spirits, and without one qualm of taste or sentiment, and arriving at Florence, the city of palaces, with its amphitheatre of hills and olives, without suspecting that such a person as Boccaccio, Dante, or Galileo, had ever lived there. . . .

(*Ibid.* vol. xii. p. 134.)

JOHN COLIN DUNLOP

(c. 1790-1842)

[John Colin Dunlop was born in Glasgow about 1790. He was admitted an advocate in 1807, but did not practice at the bar. In 1814 he published his best-known work, *The History of Fiction*, of which a second edition appeared in 1816, and a third (after the author's death) in 1845. He also published a *History of Roman Literature* (1823-8), and *Memoirs of Spain* (1834). Dunlop died in Edinburgh in 1842. He was well read in the Greek and Latin classics, and in French, German, Spanish, and Italian literature; and appears to have been well acquainted with the *Divina Commedia*, sundry references to which are introduced in his *History of Fiction*.]

[1] [See above, pp. 134 ff.]
[2] [Originally contributed to the *New Monthly Magazine*, Sept. 1830.]

1814. THE HISTORY OF FICTION: BEING A CRITICAL ACCOUNT OF THE MOST CELEBRATED PROSE WORKS OF FICTION FROM THE EARLIEST GREEK ROMANCES TO THE NOVELS OF THE PRESENT AGE.

[Dante and the Arthurian Romances]

ORIGIN of Italian Tales—It seems not a little remarkable that Italy, which produced the earliest and finest specimens of romantic poetry, should scarcely have furnished a single prose romance of chivalry. This is the more remarkable, as the Italians seem to have been soon and intimately acquainted with the works of the latter description produced among the neighbouring nations. . . . Dante represents the perusal of the story of Lancelot, as conducting Paolo and Francesca *al doloroso passo* (Inf. c. 5), and elsewhere shows his acquaintance with the fabulous stories of Arthur and Charlemagne (Inf. c. 31 and 32, Parad. c. 16 and 18) . . . At the time when France and England were principally engaged with compositions of chivalry . . . the three most distinguished and earliest geniuses of Italy were employed in giving stability to modes of composition at total variance with the romantic. Those who were accustomed to regard the writings of Dante and Petrarch as standards of excellence, would not readily have bestowed their approbation on Tristan, or the Sons of Aymon. . . .

(*History of Fiction,* Chap. vii. pp. 186-7, ed. 1845.)

[Dante and the Troubadours]

The Provençal poets, or Troubadours, have been acknowledged as the masters of the early Italian poets, and have been raised to perhaps unmerited celebrity by the imposing panegyrics of Dante and Petrarch. . . .

(*Ibid.* pp. 195-6)

[Dante one of the supposed authors of the *Cento Novelle Antiche*]

The *Cento Novelle Antiche*, commonly called in Italy *Il Novellino*, was the first regular work of the class with which we are now engaged that appeared in Europe; its composition being unquestionably prior to that of the *Decameron* of Boccaccio. . . . That the stories were compiled by different authors, is apparent from the great variety of style; but who these authors were is still a problem in the literary annals of Italy. A number of them were long supposed to have been the work of Dante and Brunetto Latini, but this belief seems to rest on no very solid foundation.

(*Ibid.* p. 203.)

[The *Decameron* and Dante]

The *Decameron* of Boccaccio succeeds, in chronological order, to the *Cento Novelle*, and is by far the most renowned production in this species of composition. It is styled *Decameron*, from ten days having been occupied in the relation of the tales, and is also entitled *Principe Galeotto*—an appellation which the deputies appointed for correction of the *Decameron* consider as derived from the 5th canto of Dante's *Inferno*, Galeotto being the name of that seductive book, which was read by Paulo and Francesca:—

'Galeotto fu il libro e chi lo scrisse,' &c.

. . . The story of Giannotto (Day 1, Nov. 2) is related as having really happened, by Benvenuto da Imola, in his commentary on Dante, which was written in 1376. . . . The eighth story of Day 2 does not possess much merit or originality of invention. The revenge taken by a queen of France for a slighted passion, is as old as the story of Bellerophon, though it has been directly imitated by Boccaccio from that of Pier della Broccia and the Lady of Brabant in Dante.[1] . . . The characters in the tale of Lizio da Valbona (Day 5, Nov. 4) are mentioned by Dante in his Purgatory. A Spirit, complaining of the degeneracy of the Italians, exclaims:—

Ov' è 'l buon Lizio, e Arrigo Manardi.—c. 14.

(Chap. vii. pp. 206, 212, 215, 225.)

[Sacchetti's anecdote of Dante]

Italian Imitators of Boccaccio—The following is a specimen of the manner of Sacchetti, in the style of composition which he has chiefly adopted.

One day while a blacksmith was singing, or rather bawling out the verses of Dante, that poet happened to pass at the time, and in a sudden emotion of anger, threw down all the workman's utensils. On the blacksmith complaining of this treatment, Dante replied, 'I am only doing to your tools what you do to my verses: I will leave you unmolested, if you cease to spoil my productions.' . . .

(Chap. viii. p. 245.)

[Anecdote of Dante in Cinthio's *Ecatommithi*]

The whole of the seventh decade of Cinthio's *Ecatommithi* consists of jests and repartees; for example—the poet Dante dining at the table of Cane Della Scala, lord of Verona, that prince ingeniously contrived to throw all the bones which had been picked at table at the feet of Dante, and on the table being removed affected the utmost amazement at the appetite of a poet who had left such remains. 'My lord,' replied Dante, 'had I been a *dog* (cane) you would not have found so many bones at my feet.' Even this indifferent story is not original, being copied from the *Dantis Faceta Responsio* of Poggi,[2] which again is merely an application to an Italian prince and poet of the Fabliau *Les Deux Parasites*.

(*Ibid.* p. 266.)

[1] [*Purg.* vi. 22-3.]

[2] [For Poggio's anecdote, see vol. i. pp. 611-12.]

[Ford and Dante]

Origin of Spiritual Romance—The notion of future punishments, appropriate to the darling sins of the guilty, has been common with poets. It occurs in Dante, and we are told in one of Ford's dramas, that

> There are gluttons fed
> With toads and adders: there is burning oil
> Poured down the drunkard's throat; the usurer
> Is forced to sup whole draughts of molten gold;
> There is the murderer for ever stabb'd,
> Yet can he never die.

After Guerin Meschino had witnessed the pains of purgatory, he had a display of hell itself, which in this work,[1] is divided into circles, precisely on the plan laid out in Dante's *Inferno*. Indeed, the whole of this part of the romance must have been suggested by the unearthly excursions in the *Divina Commedia*.

(Chap. ix. p. 296.)

[Bunyan and Dante]

The *Pilgrim's Progress* was written while the author was in prison, where he lay from 1660 to 1672: so that the date of its composition must be fixed between those two periods. This celebrated allegory is introduced in a manner which, in its mysterious solemnity, bears a striking resemblance to the commencement of the Vision of Dante:[2]—"As I walked through the wilderness of this world, I lighted on a certain place where was a den, and laid me down in that place to sleep; and as I slept I dreamed a dream," &c.

(Chap. ix. p. 301.)

JOHN HERMAN MERIVALE

(1779-1844)

[John Herman Merivale was born at Exeter in 1779. He was educated at St. John's College, Cambridge, but did not take a degree. In 1804 he was called to the bar at Lincoln's Inn; he was appointed a Chancery Commissioner in 1824, and Commissioner in Bankruptcy in 1831. He died in 1844. Merivale, who was an accomplished classical and Italian scholar, published in 1806, in collaboration with Robert Bland,[3] and others, a volume of *Translations from the Greek Anthology, with Tales and Miscellaneous Poems*. These were highly praised by Byron, and earned the two authors a mention in *English Bards and Scotch Reviewers* (ll. 881-90), where they are addressed as 'associate bards,' and adjured 'to resign Achaia's lyre and strike your

[1] [The History of Guerino Meschino.]

[2] [This similarity had already been remarked upon by Dr. Johnson (see vol. i. pp. 342, 463).]

[3] [See above, pp. 10 ff.]

own.' In 1814 Merivale published *Orlando in Roncesvalles*, in *ottava rima*, of which Byron wrote to him, 'You have written a very noble poem. . . . Your measure is uncommonly well chosen and wielded.' Into this poem he introduced a passage translated from Dante, which was afterwards, in a somewhat different form, included, with other translations from Dante (in *terza rima*), in his *Poems, Original and Translated*, published in 1838 (second edition, with translations revised, 1844). The following is a list of the translations from the *Divina Commedia*, specimens of which are given below:—The Entrance of Hell (*Inf.* iii. 1-136); Paul and Francesca (*Inf.* v. 25-141); Ciacco, the Glutton (*Inf.* vi. 34-100); Filippo Argenti (*Inf.* viii. 31-64); Dante and Farinata (*Inf.* x. 1-136); Peter de Vineis (*Inf.* xiii. 1-108); Lano and Sant' Andrea (*Inf.* xiii. 109-151); Dante and Casella (*Purg.* ii. 67-133); Manfred (*Purg.* iii. 103-145); Sordello (*Purg.* vi. 59-151); Conrad Malaspina (*Purg.* viii. 1-18, 109-139); Provenzano Salvani (*Purg.* xi. 91-142); the Praises of Ancient Florence (*Par.* xv. 97-148); Dante and Cacciaguida (*Par.* xvii. 13-142). Several of Merivale's versions from Dante were communicated by him to Ugo Foscolo, by whom they were printed in his 'Parallel between Dante and Petrarch' (in *Essays on Petrarch*, published in 1823).]

1814. ORLANDO IN RONCESVALLES. A POEM IN FIVE CANTOS.

[Illustrations from Dante]

DARKLY indeed and doubtfully we trace
Shadows that flit behind the eternal veil.
Sometimes we view them imaged in the face
Of outer heaven in colours dim and pale,
But nothing certain.

(Canto ii. St. 13.)

Speaking of the power of spirits to penetrate futurity, Dante makes Farinata degli Uberti declare,

Noi veggiam, come quei che a mala luce
Le cose, disse, che ne son lontano.

(Inferno, c. 10 [ll. 100-1].

(pp. 31, 48.)

Can human tears for happy angels flow?
Ah! how much rather, if but rightly deem'd,
Those tears should fall for human vice and woe,
The retchlessness of life, the fear to die,
Hopeless desire, heart-sinking infamy!

(Canto iii. St. 28.)

Dante makes the punishment of souls in limbo consist in desire without hope.

Sol di tanto offesi,
Che senza speme vivemo in desìo.

Inferno, c. 4. [ll. 41-2].

(pp. 64, 74.)

'Twas now the hour when fond Desire renews
To those who wander o'er the pathless main,
Raising unbidden tears, the last adieus
Of tender friends whom fancy shapes again;
When the late parted pilgrim who pursues
His lonely walk o'er some unbounded plain,
If sound of distant bells fall on his ear,
Seems the sad knell of his departed joys to hear.[1]
(Canto iv. St. 16.)

Era già l' hora che volge 'l disio &c.[2]
Dante Purg. c. 8.
(pp. 82, 96.)

Lights, numberless as by some fountain's side
The silly swain reposing (at the hour
When beams the day star with diminisht pride,
When the sunn'd bee deserts each rifled flower,
And yields to humming gnats the populous void),
Beholds in grassy lawn, or leafy bower,
Or orchard plot, of glow-worms emerald bright,
Flamed in the front of that ambrosial night.
(Canto iv. St. 17.)

Quante il villan, ch' al poggio si riposa, &c.
Dante Inf. c. 26 [ll. 25 ff.].
(pp. 83, 96.)

Orlando sped
To gain a hillock that adjoining lay:
And there "he blew a blast so loud and dread,"
The Paynim host all trembled with dismay.
Another, and another yet, he blew:
With the third blast, that horn was burst in two.
(Canto v. St. 10.)

I must not forget the sublime passage in which Dante compares the sound of the horn, at the entrance into the ninth circle of his Inferno, to that [of Orlando] which forms the subject of this note.

Ma io senti sonare un' alto corno, &c.[3]
Inf. c. 31.
(pp. 106, 125.)

[1] [For another rendering by Merivale of these lines, see p. 196.]
[2] [Merivale here quotes *Purg.* viii. 1-6.]
[3] [Merivale here quotes *Inf.* xxxi. 12-18.]

1838. POEMS ORIGINAL AND TRANSLATED. NOW FIRST COLLECTED.

[Criticism of recent translations of Dante]

As the translations from Dante are among the latest of the author's poetical productions, he deems it necessary to preface them with the disavowal of any design on his part to place them on a footing of comparison with either of the very excellent versions of the entire poem, which have been recently presented to the English reader. The object with which they were put together was that of a long contemplated essay in illustration of the Life and Times of the Poet; a work which, when viewed more nearly, it becomes very improbable that, considering the advancing age and public avocations [1] of the author, he will ever have the industry or hardihood to accomplish. The reason of his having preferred the experiment of a new translation rather than the appropriation of either of the previous ones, for the foundation of his labours, was his persuasion that both are in fault as to the method that ought to be pursued in rendering the sense and spirit of Dante, and not his hope of doing more himself than merely indicate a style worthier of future adoption. He is indeed convinced that the true character of the 'Divine Comedy' is essentially at variance with the Miltonic style, according to which it was Mr. Cary's endeavour to render it; and that, although Mr. Wright has improved on the preceding translator, not only in the superior closeness of his version to the literal sense of the original, but also by his adoption of rhyme, the distinguishing vehicle of Gothic and mediaeval poetry; yet the division into measured stanzas is equally fatal to the design of transfusing the spirit of that original into the translation. The author of these specimens now offered to the public is, at the same time, so fully sensible of the extreme difficulty of rendering the *Terza Rima* of Dante by a corresponding measure in English, as greatly to doubt the possibility of its ever being satisfactorily accomplished by an entire translation. Hayley [2] has indeed wielded this perplexing metre with some dexterity; Byron,[3] with much of his native power; Mr. Roscoe,[4] in his translation of the work of Sismondi on the Literature of the South of Europe, more successfully, perhaps, than either. But their experiments only show that it is possible to employ it in rendering detached passages, not that the task is easy even on a scale so limited.

(*Preface*, vol. i. pp. xi-xiii.)

[1] [Merivale, at this time in his fifty-ninth year, held a Commissionership in Bankruptcy, to which he had been appointed in 1831.]

[2] [See vol. i. pp. 359 ff.]

[3] [See above, pp. 38-9.]

[4] [See below, pp. 351 ff.]

The Entrance of Hell

[*Inferno* iii. 1-21.]

'Through me ye pass into the realm of woe;
  Through me ye pass, eternal pain to prove;
  Through me amidst the ruin'd race ye go:
Justice my heavenly builder first did move;
  My mighty fabric Power Divine did rear,
  Supremest Wisdom, and Primaeval Love.
None but eternal things created were
  Before me; and, eternal, I endure.
  All hope abandon, ye who enter here!'
These lines inscribed in dark entablature
  Over a gateway arch I saw, and said,
  'Master, to me their sense is most obscure.'
Then he, like one in mystic lore deep read;
  'Here all suspicion must be cast aside,
  Here every base ignoble thought be dead.
We've reach'd the place, where, late I signified,
  Thine eyes the dolorous people should survey
  Who have made shipwreck of their reason's pride.'
Therewith, his hand on mine he soft did lay
  With cheering smile, whence I some comfort took,
  While to those secret things he led the way.

(Vol. ii. p. 207.)

Paul and Francesca

[*Inferno* v. 97-142. Francesca speaks :—]

'My place of birth is seated by the main,
  On that sea-shore to which descendeth Po,
  In quest of peace, with all his vassal train.
Love, whom the gentle heart soon learns to know,
  Him bound a slave to that fair form, which I
  Was doom'd—(ah how reluctant!—) to forego.
Love, that no loved one suffers to deny
  Return, entwined us both with cords so strong
  That, as thou seest, he still is ever nigh.
Love to one fate conducted us along,
  While Caina 'waits him who our lives did spill.'
  Such was the burthen of that mournful song,
Which, with their tale, did so my bosom thrill,
  As made me droop my head, and bend full low;
  When thus the bard; 'Thy mind what evils fill?'

Thereon I recommenced, 'Alas for wo!
  How many sweet thoughts, what intense desire,
  Has brought them to this dolorous pass below?'
I then turn'd back to them, and thus to' inquire
  Began—'Francesca! thy sad destinies
  With grief and pity' at once my breast inspire.
But tell me,—in the season of sweet sighs—
  How, and by what degrees thy passion rose,
  So as to read his love's dim phantasies.'
Then she to me, 'Among severest woes
  Is to remember days of dear delight
  In misery—and this thy teacher knows.
But if thou hast so fond an appetite
  From its first source our love's sad maze to thread,
  Though tears may flow, I will the tale recite.
One day, for pastime, we together read
  Of Lancelot—how love his heart enchain'd.
  We were alone, and knew no cause for dread.
But oft as met our eyes, our cheeks were stain'd
  With blushes by the glowing tale inspired;
  Till one sole point the fatal victory gain'd.
For when we read the smile, so long desired,
  Which to the lover's kiss her answer bore,
  He who shall ne'er from me be parted—fired
With passion—kiss'd my lips, all trembling o'er
  Like his. The book was pandar to our thought,
  And he that wrote. That day we read no more.'
Thus, while one spake, that other spirit was wrought
  To such a flood of tears, that with the swell
  Of pity all my sense was quite o'erfraught;
And, as a lifeless body falls, I fell.

(Vol. ii. pp. 213-6.)

Manfred

[*Purgatorio* iii. 103-32.]

Then one of them began—'Whoe'er thou be,
  Thus moving onward, this way bend thine eye,
  And tell if e'er on earth thou didst me see.'
Tow'rds him I turn'd, and view'd him steadfastly.
  Light skinn'd, well favour'd, and of noble air—
  But a deep gash had scarr'd his forehead high.
Him humbly I disclaim'd, as one I ne'er
  Before had seen; whereat he said, 'Behold!'
  And show'd a wound that on his breast he bare.

Then, smiling, thus his name and lineage told.
'Manfred am I—of the Empress Constance heir;
And therefore pray thee, when thou tread'st on mould,
Thou to my royal daughter do repair,
(Whom Spain and Sicily hold in reverence due,)
And give her of my fate the truth to hear—
That when two mortal strokes had traversed thro'
My earthly frame, I render'd up my sprite,
In tears, to Him who pardons them that sue.
Huge were my sins; but goodness infinite
Hath arms so wide, that in their vast embrace
All things that seek its sheltering shade unite.
And, if Cosenza's shepherd, whom in chase
Of me that unrelenting pontiff sent,
Had in God's holy word survey'd his face,
My bones had still, in hallow'd burial pent,
At the bridge-head, by Benevento, lain
Safe guarded by their rude-piled monument.
Now are they stirr'd with wind, and drench'd with rain,
Where, driven by him beyond the kingdom's bound,
On Verdè's brink they unanneal'd remain.'

(Vol. ii. pp. 233-4.)

Conrad Malaspina

[*Purgatorio* viii. 1-18]

'Twas now the hour that wakes desire anew,
Melting the heart, in men at sea, the day
They to sweet friends have bidden long adieu—
That thrills with love the pilgrim on his way,
(Late parted,) if some distant chime he hear
Seeming to mourn the sun's expiring ray;[1]
When I began to close my vacant ear
On speech; and saw a spirit above the rest,
As if it audience claim'd, itself uprear.
Both palms it join'd and raised, and tow'rds the east
Earnestly gazed, as if to God above,
All else despised, that gesture were address'd.
'Te lucis ante,' with such ardent love,
And such sweet cadence, from its lips then fell,
That my whole self out of myself it drove.
The others after, with like dulcet swell,
And eyes still watching the supernal wheels,
Pursued to the close that solemn canticle.

(Vol. ii. pp. 238-9.)

[1] [For another rendering of these first six lines by Merivale, see above, p. 192.]

The Praises of Ancient Florence

[*Paradiso* xv. 97-129]

Florence, inclosed within that ancient round,
  That calls her still to morn and even prayer,
  Sober and chaste, in pristine peace was found.
Her dames nor carkanet nor crown did wear,
  Nor 'broider'd shoon; nor did the fair one's zone
  Attract the gazer, than herself more fair.
Nor yet a daughter's birth made fathers groan
  With thinking of the marriage and the dower,
  Earlier in years, and more in measure grown.
No houses then, in faction's vengeful hour,
  Were desert made; no soft Assyrian wight
  Yet taught lascivious arts in lady's bower:
Nor yet the traveller saw a statelier sight
  In Arno's vale, than Tiber's: soon to be
  Lower in fall, as loftier in our height.
Then might you Bellincione Berti see
  In bone-clasp'd leathern belt; and, from her glass,
  His dame, with face unvarnish'd, follow free;
The lords of Nerli and of Vecchio pass
  In plain buff jerkin for their only wear,
  And arm'd with distaff every high-born lass.
Thrice happy!—sure sepulchral rites to share
  In native soil, and none yet left to press
  A lonely couch, exchanged for Gallic air.
Her cradled charge with matron watchfulness
  One lull'd asleep to the selfsame strains that, troll'd
  From infant lips, are wont the sire to bless—
Another at her wheel grave legends told,
  To entertain her circling family,
  Of Rome, or Fiesole, or Ilium old.
It had been then far greater prodigy
  A shameless quean, or ermined knave, to meet,
  Than Cato or Cornelia now to see.

(Vol. ii. pp. 242-3.)

1843. Feb. 13. LETTER TO LEONARD HORNER (from London).

[Francis Horner and Dante]

I am much obliged for the opportunity which you have given me of looking over the records of Mr. Horner's[1] first impressions while studying the great poem of Dante, and enjoying the pleasure of

[1] [Francis Horner (1778-1817), brother of Leonard Horner.]

travelling again over that favourite ground in the company of a critic of so much taste and acuteness.

I had understood from you that Mr. Horner only took up this pursuit during leisure hours in his visit to Italy, and under the pressure of his last fatal illness.[1] Of course, therefore, I did not expect to find him conversant with the *Commedia* after the fashion of Italian scholars, who make it a study of years, and seem often to become so exclusively Dantesque in their mode of regarding the poet, that they never judge him at all by ordinary rules, and illustrate him, as Scripture is illustrated, only on a system of concordances. I do not know from what source he derived the conjecture as to the allegorical meaning of the Wolf in the first canto: if original, it was a curious anticipation on his part of the doctrine which Professor Rossetti has since set forth with such abundance of ingenuity. But, with this exception, I do not perceive that he troubled himself with the inner meaning or meanings of the poem, more than a casual reader for the first time may be expected to do. And it is plain enough that he noted down his observations as he read, and did not revise them. For example, I do not think that he would have expressed himself as he has done in a note on Canto X respecting Dante's want of philosophical sentiment on general human affairs, if he had then read the *Purgatorio* and the *Paradiso*, and am very certain that he would not have accused him, a little farther on, of deficiency in love of country, in the modern or classical sense of the phrase, when he had got as far as the fifteenth Canto of the latter Cantica. It was not, however, as an exercise on Dante that these remarks have chiefly interested me; but from the illustrations they afford of the taste and genius of the writer himself,—of the manner in which the principal characteristics of the Italian poet struck him on the first reading, coming to the task with little or no especial preparation, but with a mind full of literary wealth, a strong sense of beauty of style, and an acute and practised critical discernment. Nothing can be happier than his appreciation of some of the peculiar beauties of Dante's style. I have an hundred times read the remark, that he is the most picturesque of poets; but I do not know when I have seen the meaning of the phrase so well explained, or the *trick* of Dante's pictures, if I may use the phrase, so neatly described, as in the following passage:—

'This is an instance(I have passed by many finer) of the talent which this poet possessed of placing before the very eye of the reader the object he represents. In point of execution, the success of such passages greatly depends on a well-ordered conciseness;

[1] [He died at Pisa in Feb. 1817—see below, pp. 239 ff.]

for a difference in the relative position of two words, and the use or omission of some very ordinary phrase, may make the whole obscure or bright as a picture. All great writers, indeed, must possess this graphical power, or they fail in an essential part of writing; but their manner varies: some erring by having aimed at brevity, and forcing the parts of their description too close upon one another; others, by aiming at a prolongation of the effect by a succession of pictures running into one another, like the circle of a panorama. Both fail to give their reader, if I may say so, a point of sight: the former seems confused and obscure; the latter becomes weak, lax, and obscure too. A selection of instances, not only perfect ones, but of some that are defective both ways, taken from the best classics of different languages, and accompanied with a criticism in search of what this defect or excellence turns on, would be a useful exercise for the student who made it. . . . One cause of the vividness of Dante's pictures is, I think, *that he generally chooses one moment of time*, and rarely attempts to represent successive actions.'

Another instance (to my mind) of the same intuitive correctness of judgment occurs in the comparison of Dante with Tacitus, the only ancient writer of whom Mr. Horner found himself in the least degree reminded by the subject of his new studies. It is plain that the rhetorical excellences of the poet are those which impressed him most; and I think Lord Brougham says, that the study of Dante formed an important part of his own discipline as an orator.[1] I am struck, too, with the evident preference with which, he, fresh from the political excitement of English state commotions, fixes on the magnificent episode of Farinata degli Uberti: for in Dante, as in Shakspeare, every man selects by instinct that which assimilates with the course of his own previous occupation and interests. As to Mr. Horner's criticisms on the defects of taste and style which pervade the *Commedia*, I believe that in these days, when it is the fashion to view the poet through a medium of transcendentalism, such criticisms are considered a kind of leze-majesty, as much as in the case of Shakspeare aforesaid: but I am not ashamed to confess that all my affection for him does not save me from feeling often oppressed under the

'In eterno faticoso manto'[2]

of far-fetched extravagance, in which so much of his nobler thought is enveloped.

One thing only I was sorry to meet with: I mean the depreciation of the *Purgatorio*. I fancy it is not uncommon on a first reading to regard it as much less interesting than the first division;

[1] [See below, p. 432.]

[2] [*Inf.* xxiii. 67.]

but not, I should have imagined, with one of Mr. Horner's taste and feeling. But am I wrong in suspecting that the gradual depression of long illness acted in this instance on his judgment, rendering him averse from that steady and minute attention, that labour of love, by which alone the deep-seated beauties of this part of the poem are to be reached? Certainly, of all undertakings, I should have thought the first perusal of Dante least calculated for the relaxation of a sick chamber, and that of a man in the full tide of life, whose heart must have been wrapt up in interests of a far more stirring character. I never knew the Florentine heartily studied, except when taken up in youth, while there are yet time and energy to spare, and with no call on the mind to husband its resources; but, when once mastered, what a mine of wealth to resort to in after days! The more reason (though of all men I ought least to say so to yourself [1]) for regretting a little the *rabbia Tedesca*, which seems to have invaded our education of late years to such an extent as to have thrown the great Italian masters somewhat in the background.

(*Memoirs and Correspondence of Francis Horner*, 1843, vol. ii. pp. 445-8.)

1844. POEMS ORIGINAL AND TRANSLATED. A NEW AND CORRECTED EDITION.

[Further criticism of recent translations of Dante]

It has been asked me in some quarters to which I owe all respect in point of judgment, why I have not . . . devoted my leisure hours during this last five years' interval to the completion of a translation of the immortal work of Dante, upon the model of the specimens which appear in the second volume of these collections. But, while I am by no means insensible to the praise implied in this question, I cannot but feel it a sufficient answer that the ground is already occupied—if not fully, to the extent of all that I conceive to be possible in the shape of translation—yet enough to render any renewal of the attempt, at least for some time to come, unnecessary, and perhaps invidious. Mr. Wright's [2] version in many parts excellent, is throughout remarkable above all preceding ones for fidelity to the sense of the original, such as to render it a work safely to be referred to by those who, not being themselves Italian scholars, are desirous of being acquainted with the great poet's thoughts and sentiments. The translator has, in my judgment indeed unnecessarily, departed from the metre of the original, and in so doing, sacrificed much of the *spirit* which

[1] [Leonard Horner resided for some time in Germany, at Bonn.]
[2] [See below, pp. 568 ff.]

might, I think, be preserved by a stricter adherence to the *form*. But this abandonment of the Dantesque manner, much as I think it to be regretted, seems scarcely to afford a sufficient ground in itself for hoping the success of a new translation in competition with two others of such just celebrity as both Wright's and Carey's,[1] the authors of which are still living—and, if there were room to entertain any such expectation, there is already another competitor for the laurel in the person of Mr. Shannon,[2] who has published ten cantos, and tells us he has completed many more in the *Terza Rima*, and in a style of versification which, though occasionally disfigured by the application of a theoretical principle, in the art of rhyming unsupported either by any but obsolete English usage, or by the example of the original, is yet sufficiently free and animated greatly to increase the discouragement to which any new attempt must be liable.

(*Advertisement*, vol. i. pp. xviii-xix.)

ANONYMOUS

1814. THE EUROPEAN MAGAZINE, AND LONDON REVIEW.

[Review of the *Divina Commedia*]

HOWEVER the facilities and improvements of modern education may render the attainment of mediocrity both in poetry and the arts more easy, and, therefore, more frequent, we are still to look for the finest examples of sublimity and grandeur in the works of those masters who flourished in the more rugged and less enlightened ages. And whose talents, as it were from an inaccessible height, exhibit a sublimity and grandeur which are not to be attained by the more cultivated plains below. Among the poets to be ranked in this class, one of the most eminent is Dante Alighieri, to whose Divina Comedia so many poets have been indebted, and whom our Milton himself did not disdain frequently to imitate. . . .

In Dante's descriptions, we always see the object which he wishes to represent painted as it were before us. The originality of his expressions surprises and enchants us. His comparisons, like those of Homer, sometimes elevated and sublime, sometimes common and taken from the meanest objects, present an infinite number of striking yet natural images.

This father of Italian poetry excels in every style of composition. In the graceful, he is not surpassed by Petrarch himself. In

[1] [*Sic*, for Cary.]

[2] [See below, pp. 606 ff.]

melody and harmony, not even by Ariosto or Marino. In the terrible and pathetic, he rises above them all. No one can read his History of Count Ugolino without feeling mingled emotions of pity and horror. . . .

Having said much of the beauties of this poem, justice requires that I should notice its defects: the greatest of these has been thought by some to be the want of a regular and continued action. If it had been the object of Dante to compose an epic poem, this objection might have weight: but he professes no such thing: his poem is peculiar in its kind, but that does not detract from its merit. . . . A more just objection to the Divina Comedia applies to that mixture, or accozzamento, as the Italians call it, of ancient history with modern, and of the sacred with the fabulous. He is frequently obscure; but this must be in a great degree rather attributed to the remote period in which he wrote. M. G. di Cesare,[1] one of Dante's commentators, accuses him of misconception, unmeaning phrases, and vulgar proverbs; of introducing puns and images low, and sometimes indecent; and an injudicious affectation of Latinity. But, notwithstanding these heavy accusations, there will be found in the Divina Comedia, a simplicity of design, a beauty of expression, and a sublimity of effect, which will ever justify its being regarded as one of the sublimest efforts of human genius.

(Vol. lxvi. pp. 104, 197, 315-16.)

ANONYMOUS

1815. THE EUROPEAN MAGAZINE, AND LONDON REVIEW.

[Review of the *Divina Commedia*, continued]

I SHALL now lay before your readers a few of the most beautiful passages of this poem. . . . Among the many descriptive passages that might be selected, how fine are the following:—

1. The flowers opened by the sun.

Quale i fioretti, &c.

Inferno, c. 2, v. 27.

2. The sounds which the poet hears at his entrance into the infernal regions.

Quivi sospiri, &c.

Inferno, c. 3, v. 25.

3. The doves.

Quali colombe, &c.

Inferno, c. 5, v. 82.

[1] [*Esame della D.C.*, s.l. 1807.]

4. The signs which precede the coming of an angel.

E già venia, &c.

Inferno, c. 9, v. 64.

5. Virgil's admonition to Dante, which has often been quoted.

Fama di loro, il mondo esser non lassa.
Misericordia e giustizia gli sdegna:
Non ragioniam di lor, ma guarda e passa.

Inferno, c. 3, v. 49.

6. A more noble passage than the following is not to be found among the classic writers of antiquity.

Omai convien, che tu così ti spoltre,
Disse 'l maestro; che seggendo in piuma
In fama non si vien, ne sotto coltre,
Senza la qual, chi sua vita consuma
Cotal vestigio in terra di sè lascia
Qual fumo in aere od in acqua la schiuma.

Inferno, c. 24, v. 46.

7. The metamorphose of the robbers into serpents. Here Lucan and Ovid must yield to Dante. He surpasses them both.

Se tu se' or, Lettore, a creder lento, &c.

Inferno, c. 25, v. 46.

8. The comparison of Sordello to a lion.

Ma vedi là un' anima, &c.

Purgatorio, c. 6, v. 58.

9. The sick man.

E se ben ti ricordi, &c.

Purgatorio, c. 148, v. 6.

10. The approach of evening.

Era già l' ora, &c.

Purgatorio, c. 8, v. 1.

11. The wonder of the rustic when entering a city for the first time.

Non altrimenti stupido, &c.

Purgatorio, c. 26, v. 67.

12. The entrance of the three poets, Virgil, Dante, and Statius, into the terrestrial paradise.

Vago già di cercar, &c.

Purgatorio, c. 28, v. 1.

13. Matilda gathering flowers.

Come si volge con le piante strette, &c.

Purgatorio, c. 28, v. 55.

14. The appearance of the morning.
Io vidi già nel cominciar del giorno, &c.
Purgatorio, c. 30, v. 22.

15. The parent bird and her young.
Come l' augello intra l' amate fronde, &c.
Paradiso, c. 23, v. 1.

The finest instance of the satyrical style in which Dante so much excels, is the story of Count Montrefeltro in the Inferno, from which I shall only transcribe the syllogistic dispute between Saint Benedict [1] and Satan, when contending for the possession of the Count's soul.

Francesco venne poi, &c.
Inferno, c. 27, v. 111.

(Vol. lxvii. pp. 12-13.)

ANONYMOUS

1815. March. MONTHLY REVIEW. CARY'S DANTE.

[Merits and defects of Cary's version]

THE chronological view and the notes are in one respect far from *modish*; since instead of being unduly extended, or drawn into prolixity, they are eminently characterized by conciseness and brevity, and in almost every instance, they throw some light on the multifarious and local topics of the poem. As to the translation itself, it is evidently the work of no ordinary pains and diligence, and may safely, we think, aspire to the praise of fidelity; at least, it is not often that we would venture to dissent from Mr. Cary's interpretations. The uniform gravity, too, the occasional harshness, and the antiquated quaintish air of many of his lines, singularly harmonize with the kindred qualities of his celebrated exemplar. If, in short, we overlook the absence of rhyme, the present version appears to be a close approximation to the original, and to breathe much of its peculiar and singular spirit. . . . Some blemishes have occurred to our notice. Chiefly of a trivial description; yet such as we cannot very patiently tolerate in any performance of classical pretensions. . . . Those of our readers who value their eyes more than their purse, will scarcely thank Mr. Cary for the microscopical typography with which he has been pleased to afflict them: [2] and it is a melancholy fact that we, aged

[1] [Not St. Benedict, but St. Francis.]

[2] [The first edition of Cary's *Dante* was printed at his own expense, in three diminutive volumes (18mo, containing 223, 212, and 216 pp. respectively) which measured about 4½ in. × 3 in.]

and conscientious reviewers, who have painfully explored his volumes by the help of our spectacles and midnight oil, never fancied ourselves completely emancipated from *Hell* and *Purgatory* till *Paradise* closed on our sight.

(Vol. lxxvi. pp. 322 ff.)

ANONYMOUS

1815. April. QUARTERLY REVIEW. ART. I. MIOT'S MÉMOIRES DE L'ÉXPEDITION EN ÉGYPTE.

[Napoleon in a Dantesque situation]

LARREY accompanied Buonaparte across the desert. The whole way, he says, was tracked with the bones and bodies of men and animals who had perished in those dreadful wastes: if the eagles and vultures had arrived in time, bones only were left to bleach upon the burning sands; otherwise the carcass was presently dried up till it resembled a mummy. There was but one single tree to be seen along the whole journey; and to warm themselves at night . . . they gathered these dry bones and bodies of the dead; and it was by a fire composed of this fuel that Buonaparte lay down to sleep in the desert! The imagination of Dante could not have conceived a more emblematic situation for this incarnate Moloch.

(Vol. xiii. p. 23.)

GEORGE FREDERICK NOTT

(1767-1841)

[George Frederick Nott, whose father was a prebendary of Winchester, was born in 1767. He was educated at Christ Church, Oxford (B.A. 1788), and was elected to a fellowship at All Souls. His sermons as Bampton lecturer in 1802, brought him to the notice of the King, who appointed him sub-preceptor to Princess Charlotte of Wales. Preferment rapidly followed, and he received prebends successively at Chichester (1802), Winchester (1810), and Salisbury (1814). He died at Winchester in 1841. Nott, who spent much time in Italy, was an accomplished Italian scholar, and in 1831 published an Italian translation of the English 'Book of Common Prayer.' His best-known work is an exhaustive edition, published in 1815, of *The works of Henry Howard, Earl of Surrey, and of Sir Thomas Wyatt, the Elder*, in which he displays a wide knowledge of the early Italian poets, including Dante. Nott seems to have had a special interest in Dante, for he commissioned the Viennese artist, Josef Anton Koch (1768-1839), to make a series of drawings from the *Divina Commedia*, forty of which, in sepia, illustrating the *Inferno* and part of the *Purgatorio*, eventually came into the possession of King John of Saxony (the translator of the *Commedia*, under the pseudonym of 'Philalethes'), and are now preserved at Dresden. Nott's library, which was sold at Winchester in 1842, contained a large number of Dante books. Among these were three MSS. of the *Divina Commedia*, a MS. of Boccaccio's *Vita di Dante*, and upwards of eighty editions of the *Commedia*, including the following, all of which are more or less rare:—Foligno, 1472 (*editio princeps*); Mantua, 1472; Naples, 1477; Venice, 1477; Milan, 1478; Florence, 1481; Venice, 1497; Aldus, 1515; Lyon, 1551; and Vicenza, 1613. There were also several editions of the *Vita Nuova* (including the *editio princeps*, 1576), and *Convivio* and one of the 25 copies of the *Epistolae* printed by Witte at Padua in 1827.]

1815. THE WORKS OF HENRY HOWARD, EARL OF SURREY, AND OF SIR THOMAS WYATT, THE ELDER.

[Attitude of the Italians towards the works of Dante, Petrarch, and Boccaccio]

THE principal object proposed in this republication of Surrey's Poems was to mark out the improvements he had made in the English language, and to shew at what precise period it began to be moulded into that form which it now wears. But how could this have been accomplished had the old orthography been retained? The generality of readers could not be expected . . . to devote their attention to the ungrateful task of tracing the real features of our language through the Cimmerian darkness of an orthography which was never settled upon any certain laws; was always accommodated to the mode of pronunciation familiar to the person who wrote; and was constantly varying under the hands of careless and illiterate printers. In this respect the Italians have given us a lesson of practical wisdom which we should do well to observe. They were sensible that all the beauties of their language were to be found in Dante, Petrarch, and Boccaccio. They determined therefore on giving those authors as wide a circulation as possible, that persons of either sex, and of every age and description, might study them for the formation both of their taste and style.

(*Preface*, vol. i. pp. 11-12.)

[Ten-syllable lines in the *Divina Commedia*]

Mr. Tyrwhitt supposes our versification to have been completely metrical in Chaucer's time; each Heroic verse consisting of eleven syllables. He admits that verses sometimes occur which have only ten syllables; but he contends that these verses do not affect Chaucer's general system, any more than the Troncated Hendecasyllabic verse of the Italian poets does theirs. Thus in the following passage, the first and third lines have only ten syllables, notwithstanding which they are used mixed with verses that have eleven.

Qual è colui che cosa innanzi a sè
Subita vede, ond'ei si maraviglia,
Che crede e no, dicendo, 'Ell' è, non è;'
Tal parve quegli; e poi chinò le ciglia.

Purgat. Can. vii. *l.* 10.

(*A Dissertation on the State of English Poetry before the Sixteenth Century*, vol. i. p. cxxxix.)

[Verses of more than eleven syllables used by Dante and Boccaccio]

If Chaucer formed himself on any foreign model, it must have been on that of the Italian poets. But it is by no means certain that the Italian versification was at that time altogether metrical as it is at present. The specimen preserved by Crescimbeni from Ciullo d' Alcamo, proves it to have been originally rhythmical; and it may be easily shewn that Dante, Boccaccio, and the poets of that period used verses of more than eleven syllables.

(*A Dissertation on the State of English Poetry before the Sixteenth Century*, vol. i. p. cxlvi.)

[Chaucer's 'prosaical' version of Dante's story of Ugolino]

A striking proof of Chaucer's want of taste in translation occurs in his Canterbury Tales, where he attempts a version of Dante's famous story of Ugolino. A few lines may serve as a specimen. With what prosaical tameness and meanness of circumstance does he paraphrase the following lines, in which Ugolino describes how his suspicion was excited as to the fate which awaited his unfortunate family and himself.

Gia' eran desti; e l' ora s' appressava
Che 'l cibo ne soleva essere addotto,[1] &c.

The translation bears no more resemblance to the original than did the shade of Hector to Hector's self when he appeared to Aeneas in the troubled visions of the night!

Hei mihi! qualis erat; quantum mutatus ab illo!

(*Ibid.* vol. i. pp. cexliv-vi.)

[Dante, Petrarch, and Boccaccio frequenters of Courts]

The great reformers of all the languages of modern Europe lived in Courts, and were accustomed to move in them on terms of no common favour with their sovereigns. In France Marot, if the reformation and refinement of the French language is to be dated from him; and in Italy, Dante, Petrarch, and Boccacio, all lived in Courts the most elegant and polished of their times, and were the friends and companions of Princes. In Spain Garcilaso de la Vega, the great improver of Castilian poetry, enjoyed all the advantages which high birth and a distinguished situation in life could bestow.

(*Ibid.* vol. i. p. cclxv.)

[Simplicity and majesty of Dante's style]

In Dante we contemplate a stern sublimity of mind which makes him stand alone almost a species of himself. The excellence he most admired and studied most was simplicity. To this he must

[1] [Nott here prints *Inf.* xxxiii. 43-8, 55-63, with Chaucer's rendering in the *Monk's Tale* (see vol. i. pp. 11-12).]

be allowed the praise of having attained in an eminent degree. But it was a simplicity peculiar to himself, resulting not so much from his mode of expressing his subject as from his manner of conceiving it. His style too is his own. It carries an imposing character of majesty with it, and a sort of authority of command, to which no writer but himself did ever as fully attain. Every picture he draws presents itself to the mind with the distinctness of living objects. The passions he pourtrays are all those simple passions which exist as first principles in the human mind; such as fear, hope, love, hatred, and the like, and not those accidental feelings which result from casual modifications of manners. Dante, strictly speaking, was a satiric poet: but his satire never applied to foibles; therefore it is not limited to any particular time or place. He instances the guilt of individuals; but his scope is universal. He operates not so much by shame, as by conscience, and makes us see that vice is deformity; sin, degradation. His language is of the same cast with his ideas. It is manly, daring, and original. He frequently succeeds in expressing happily thoughts which few writers would have attempted; and by a bold combination of words says in one short sentence, what many would have diffused over several periods.

(*A Dissertation on the State of English Poetry before the Sixteenth Century*, vol. i. pp. cclxxi-ii.)

[Dante's use of the word *spogliare*]

The word 'despoiled' ('once have the winds the trees despoiled clean') is used frequently by our early poets. It corresponds with the word 'spogliato' in Italian: 'stripped of its covering.' Thus Ugolino's children, when they saw him bite his hands from agony of mind, thinking that he did it from hunger, exclaimed

Padre! assai ci fia men doglia
Se tu mangi di noi; tu ne vestisti
Queste misere carni, e tu le spoglia!

'Thou gavest us this covering of flesh, do thou *despoil* us of it.'
Dante, *Inferno* Canto xxxiii. l. 61.

(*Ibid.* vol. i. p. 234.)

[Use of the word *governo* by Dante and Petrarch]

This use of the word 'govern' ('So doth this cornet govern me') is not usual in our language. Surrey adopted it from the Italian, where it means *conciar male*, 'to evil entreat,' as the old phrase expresses it.

E chi de' nostri duci, che 'n duro astro
Passar l' Eufrate, fece 'l mal governo.
Petrarcha, Trionfo della Fama, cap. 2, l. 127.

In like manner Dante!

Tu te ne porti di costui l' eterno,
Per una lagrimetta, che 'l mi toglie;
Ma i' farò dell' altro altro governo.

Purgat. Canto v. *ver.* 106.

'Do thou,' says the Angel of Darkness, contending with a good Angel for the body of Jacobo del Cassero,[1] 'Do thou take his eternal part; that is, his soul, which the tear of penitence he shed deprives me of; his other part, his body, shall receive from me a different sort of treatment.'

(*A Dissertation on the State of English Poetry before the Sixteenth Century*, vol. i. p. 273.)

[Wyatt's Paraphrase of the Penitential Psalms perhaps suggested by Dante.]

Wyatt's Paraphrase of the Penitential Psalms seems to have been suggested by Dante's prior Paraphrase, or by that of Alamanni. . . . Dante's Seven Penitential Psalms appear to have been first published by Spira[2] at the end of the Comedia, in folio, at Venice in 1477. They were afterwards printed in 1478 at Milan, in folio likewise.[3] Quadrio republished them in 8vo at Milan in 1752, with notes. Which edition has been incorporated by Zatta into his complete edition of Dante's works in 4to at Venice in 1758. . . . Both Dante and Alamanni used the Terza Rima. Dante aims at being literal. Alamanni is paraphrastic. Wyatt's paraphrase bears no marks of having been imitated from either. . . . Dante opens his Paraphrase of the 36th Psalm thus.

Signor! non mi riprender con furore
E non voler correggermi con ira,
Ma con dolcezza e con perfetto amore.
Io son ben certo che ragion ti tira
Ad esser giusto contro a' peccatori;
Ma pur benigno sei a chi sospira.
Aggi pietate de' miei gravi errori,
Però ch' io sono debile ed infermo,
Ed ho perduto tutti i miei vigori.
Difendimi, O Signor, dallo gran vermo
E sanami, imperò ch' io non ho osso
Che conturbato possa omai star fermo.

(*Essay on Wyatt's Poems*, vol. ii. pp. cxvi-xvii.)

[1] [Not Jacobo del Cassero, who was the previous speaker in the canto in question, but Buonconte da Montefeltro.]

[2] [That is, Vendelin da Spira. It was Dante's *Credo*, not the *Salmi Penitenziali*, which was printed at the end of the editions of 1477 and 1478.]

[3] [See previous note.]

[Dante's use of the word *grame*]

Grame means sorrow: it is derived from the Saxon, but it occurs with precisely the same meaning in the Italian. As in this passage from Dante:

Ed una lupa, che di tutte brame
Sembrava carca, con la sua magrezza,
E molte genti fè già viver grame.

Inferno Can. i. *v.* 49.

(*Essay on Wyatt's Poems*, vol. ii. p. cxxiii.)

[Dante's Paraphrase of the Penitential Psalms]

Wyatt sometimes in his Paraphrase of the Penitential Psalms gives a new and ingenious turn to the original. . . . As in the following passage.

For like as smoke my days been pass'd away;
My bones dried up as furnace in the fire;
My heart, my mind, is wither'd up like hay,
Because I have forgot to take my bread,
My bread of life, the word of Truth.

The common translation is simply, 'my heart is smitten and withered like grass, so that I forget to eat my bread.' . . . Dante is as usual literal:

Percosso io sono, come il fien ne' prati,
Ed è già secco tutto lo mio core,
Perchè li cibi miei non ho mangiati.

(*Ibid.* vol. ii. p. cxxxiii.)

[Petrarch's jealousy of Dante]

Petrarch was preceded in his own country by many writers of great genius and learning, who had gone a considerable way towards perfecting the Italian language before he began to write, and had left specimens in every branch of composition which he is found to have attempted. Not to mention Guido d' Arezzo, and Guido Cavalcanti, and Dante himself, of whose fame Petrarch was said to have been jealous (though he so studiously imitated him in his Triumphs that he has been styled in consequence 'il Dante ingentilito'), if we consider the works of Cino da Pistoja, those alone will be sufficient to prove that Petrarch was greatly indebted to the poets who preceded him. . . . Quadrio thus describes the several poets that have been mentioned above. 'Dante è ne' suoi pensamenti, nerboruto, fantastico, e forte: . . . Cino è naturale, tenero e soave; Petrarca è maravigliosamente affettuoso, gentile e pulito.' *Storia d' ogni Poesia*, vol. iii. p. 62.

(*Ibid*, vol. ii. pp. clxv-vi.)

[A passage in Wyatt illustrated from Dante]

'Nought but the case' is an inelegant expression. . . . The thought is to be found originally in Dante. See Paradiso, *Can.* i. *v.* 21:

> Entra nel petto mio, e spira tue;
> Sì come quando Marsia traesti
> Della vagina delle membre sue.

(*Notes*, vol. ii. p. 553.)

[Wyatt's expression 'to deep' possibly borrowed from Dante]

'Deep yourself in travail more and more.' The word 'to deep,' in the sense used here by Wyatt occurs in Chaucer. It might have been originally taken from Dante.

> Nostro intelletto si profonda tanto
> Che retro la memoria non può ire.
>
> *Paradiso, c.* i. *v.* 8.

(*Ibid.* vol. ii. p. 562.)

[The corruptions of Papal Rome condemned by Dante and Petrarch]

It is a circumstance much to the honor of polite literature, that at the revival of letters, poets should be among the first to point out and inveigh against the corruptions of Papal Rome. In Italy, Dante and Petrarch were the first to note them. They have been ranked in consequence by some among the earliest reformers.

(*Ibid.* vol. ii. p. 564.)

SHARON TURNER

(1768-1847)

[Sharon Turner, born in 1768 at Pentonville, where he was educated, practised as an attorney, but devoted much of his time to historical research, the outcome of which was his well-known *History of England*, the first instalment of which was published in 1799, and the last, forty years after, in 1839. He retired from practice in 1829, and died in London in 1847. Turner several times mentions Dante in his *History of England*, in connection with the influence of the early Italian poets on Chaucer and his contemporaries.]

1815. HISTORY OF ENGLAND.

[Influence of Dante, Petrarch, and Boccaccio on Gower and Chaucer]

A GENERAL activity and improvement of mind seem to have actuated Europe during the thirteenth century; and the effects were peculiarly visible in Italy, and in her literature as much as in her civil transactions. The Provençal troubadours, who first nurtured the fancy of her people, gave way to a new race of native Italian poets, apparently beginning in Sicily, but soon prevading and animating all the peninsula. At the end of the thirteenth, and during the progress of the fourteenth century, Dante, Petrarch, and Boccacio, suddenly appeared with superior genius, with cultivated taste, and classical compositions. These men not only illuminated the countries where they were born or lived, but operated, by the diffusion of their works, to increase the intellectual light of nations more remote. . . . Our Gower,[1] Chaucer,[2] and Lydgate, discover in several passages of their works that they were benefited from this source.

(Vol. ii. Part v. Chap. iii. pp. 479-81.)

[Gower and Dante]

Gower was so anxious to keep his work from the machinery of the cloister, that he builds his fable on Venus, Cupid, and Genius, as Dante, apparently aiming at the same thing as far as he dared, made Virgil his guide even through the Inferno and the Purgatorio. These apparent anomalies of invention may be referred to a desire of escaping from the trammels of the legend, and of instructing mankind without too much offending the prejudices of the age.

(*Ibid.* Chap. iii. p. 494.)

[Chaucer and Dante]

Chaucer's quotations from Seneca and Juvenal, and his translation of Boethius, announce his attention to the classics. Of Dante and Petrarch, he speaks repeatedly in terms of high commendation, as if their works had been his favourities.[3]

(*Ibid.* Chap. iv. p. 507.)

JOHN BLACK

(1783-1855)

[John Black, the son of a Berwickshire farm-labourer and quondam pedlar, was born near Dunse in 1783. He was for a time in an accountant's office in Edinburgh, where he studied in the University. In 1810 he went to London and found employment as translator of foreign correspondence and reporter to the *Morning Chronicle*, of which he became editor in 1817, an appointment he held till 1843. In this capacity he was able to lend a helping hand to Charles Dickens, who began his literary career as reporter for the *Chronicle*. He died at Maidstone in 1855. For the first few years of his residence in London Black was engaged in making translations of various German works, among which was the *Lectures on Dramatic Art and Literature* of August Wilhelm von Schlegel (1767-1845), which were originally

[1] Gower mentions an anecdote of Dante in his 7th book, p. 222. [See vol. i. p. 17.]

[2] Chaucer tells the famous story of Ugolino from Dante, and calls him 'the grete poete of Itaille.' Monkes Tale, p. 126. Chal. ed. [See vol. i. pp. 11-12.]

[3] "He calls Dante 'The wise poet of Florence,' Cant. Tales, p. 52, and often mentions him, at pp. 55, 127." [See vol. i. pp. 1 ff.]

delivered in Vienna in 1808. This translation was first published in 1815, and reissued in 1840. Black reproduces some interesting remarks of Schlegel's on Dante as compared with Aeschylus, Shakespeare, and Milton.]

1815. LECTURES ON DRAMATIC ART AND LITERATURE, BY AUGUSTUS WILLIAM SCHLEGEL.

[Dante, 'the father of modern poetry']

IT is well known that three centuries and a half ago, the learned maintained that nothing could be hoped for the human mind but in the imitation of the ancients; and they only esteemed in the works of the moderns whatever resembled, or seemed to bear a resemblance to those of antiquity. Everything else was rejected by them as barbarous and unnatural. It was quite otherwise with the great poets and artists. However strong their enthusiasm for the ancients, and however determined their purpose of entering into competition with them, they were compelled by the characteristic peculiarity of their minds, to proceed in a track of their own, and to impress upon their productions the stamp of their own genius. Such was the case with Dante among the Italians, the father of modern poetry; he acknowledged Virgil for his instructor, but he produced a work which, of all others, differs the most from the Aeneid, and far excels it in our opinion, in strength, truth, depth, and comprehension.

(Ed. 1840, Lect. i. vol. i. pp. 5-6.)

[Aeschylus, Dante, and Shakespeare]

Aeschylus endeavours to swell out his language to a gigantic sublimity, corresponding with the standard of his characters. Hence he abounds in harsh combinations and overstrained epithets, and the lyrical parts of his pieces are obscure in the extreme, from the involved nature of the construction. He resembles Dante and Shakspeare in the very singular casts of his images and expressions. These images are nowise deficient in the terrible graces, which almost all the writers of antiquity celebrate in Aeschylus.

(*Ibid.* Lect. iv. vol. i. p. 95.)

[Shakespeare, Homer, and Dante]

To me Shakspeare appears a profound artist, and not a blind and wildly luxuriant genius. . . . Even in such poets, as are usually given out for careless pupils of nature, without any art or school discipline, I have always found, on a nearer consideration, when they have really produced works of excellence, a distinguished cultivation of the mental powers, practice in art, and views worthy in themselves and maturely considered. This applies to Homer as well as Dante.

(*Ibid.* Lect. xii. vol. ii. p. 127.)

[Milton's 'daemons' compared with those of Dante and Tasso]

Since *The Furies* of Aeschylus, nothing so grand and terrible as *Macbeth* has ever been composed. The Witches are not, it is true, divine Eumenides, and are not intended to be so: they are ignoble and vulgar instruments of hell. A German poet therefore very ill understood their meaning, when he transformed them into mongrel beings, a mixture of fates, furies, and enchantresses, and clothed them with tragical dignity. Let no man lay hands on Shakspeare's works to change anything essential in them: he will be sure to punish himself. The bad is radically odious, and to endeavour in any manner to ennoble it is to violate the laws of propriety. Hence, in my opinion, Dante, and even Tasso, have been much more successful in their portraiture of daemons than Milton.

(Ed. 1840, Lect. xii. vol. ii. p. 204.)

PERCY BYSSHE SHELLEY

(1792-1822)

[Shelley was born at Field Place, near Horsham, in Sussex, on 4 Aug. 1792. At the age of twelve he went to Eton; and in October, 1810, he entered University College, Oxford, whence he was expelled in the following March, in consequence of his having circulated a pamphlet on *The Necessity of Atheism*. In the spring of 1818 Shelley (who two years before had married, as his second wife, Mary Godwin) went to Italy, where he remained until his death in July, 1822, when he was lost in a storm in the Bay of Spezzia. From the period of Shelley's permanent residence in Italy dates the intimate acquaintance with Dante's works which is such a marked feature of many of his later writings, both poetry and prose.[1] As will be seen from the passages printed below, he was familiar with all three divisions of the *Divina Commedia*—a rare accomplishment in those days, as he himself observes[2]—as well as with the *Vita Nuova*, and portions of the *Canzoniere*. The poems, perhaps, in which the influence of Dante is the most perceptible are *Prometheus Unbound* (1820), *Epipsychidion* (1821), and the *Triumph of Life* (1822), but in the two former[3] the resemblances are rather in tone than in actual phraseology. From Dante, too, Shelley borrowed the *terza rima*, which he employed in several of his shorter poems (*e.g.*, the *Woodman and the Nightingale*, the *Tower of Famine*, suggested by Dante's story of Ugolino, and the *Triumph of Life*, on which he was engaged at the time of his death), as well as in his translation from the *Purgatorio* (xxviii. 1-51). According to Medwin (*Life of Shelley*, vol. ii. pp. 18-22), Shelley had no small share in the *terza rima* rendering of the Ugolino episode which Medwin made at Shelley's request (see below, pp. 385 ff.). He also translated one of Dante's sonnets, and one of the Canzoni of the *Convivio*.]

[1] [See *Introduction*, pp. xliii.-v.]

[2] [See his remarks in the essay *On the Devil, and Devils* (below, p. 228). For other remarks of Shelley on Dante besides those here recorded see under Medwin, below, pp. 380 ff.]

[3] [On Shelley's indebtedness to Dante in these two poems, see O. Kuhns, *Dante and the English Poets*, pp. 181 ff. (see also below, pp. 222-3, 224-5).]

1815. ON THE REVIVAL OF LITERATURE.[1]

[Dante and Petrarch forerunners of the revival of letters]

IN the fifteenth century of the Christian era, a new and extraordinary event roused Europe from her lethargic state, and paved the way to her present greatness. The writings of Dante in the thirteenth, and of Petrarch in the fourteenth, were the bright luminaries which had afforded glimmerings of literary knowledge to the almost benighted traveller toiling up the hill of Fame. But on the taking of Constantinople, a new and sudden light appeared: the dark clouds of ignorance rolled into distance, and Europe was inundated by learned monks, and still more by the quantity of learned manuscripts which they brought with them from the scene of devastation.

(*Prose Works*, ed. Forman, 1880, vol. ii. p. 333.)

1815. SPECULATIONS ON MORALS.[2]

[Dante among the masters of expression]

An essay on the progressive excellence perceptible in the expressions—of Solomon, Homer, Bion and the Seven Sages, Socrates, Plato, Theodorus, Zeno, Carneades, Aristotle, Epicurus, Pythagoras, Cicero, Tacitus, Jesus Christ, Virgil, Lucan, Seneca, Epictetus, Antoninus[3] . . . Sulpicius, Severus, Mahomet, Manes, the Fathers—Ariosto, Tasso, Petrarch, Dante, Abeillard, Thomas Aquinas—the Schoolmen. . . .

(*Ibid.* vol. ii. pp. 303-4.)

1816. SONNET FROM THE ITALIAN OF DANTE.

[Dante Alighieri to Guido Cavalcanti[4]]

Guido, I would that Lapo, thou, and I,
Led by some strong enchantment, might ascend
A magic ship, whose charmèd sails should fly
With winds at will where'er our thoughts might wend,
And that no change, nor any evil chance
Should mar our joyous voyage; but it might be,
That even satiety should still enhance
Between our hearts their strict community:
And that the bounteous wizard then would place

[1] [First published by Medwin in the *Athenæum* (Nov. 24, 1832), and reprinted by him in the *Shelley Papers* (pp. 170-4); the date (1815) is conjecturally assigned to the piece by Rossetti.]

[2] [The date (1815) is conjectural.]

[3] [The gap is in the original.]

[4] ['Guido, vorrei che tu e Lapo ed io' (*Son.* xxxii. in Oxford Dante).]

Vanna and Bice and my gentle love,
Companions of our wandering, and would grace
With passionate talk, wherever we might rove,
Our time, and each were as content and free
As I believe that thou and I should be.

(*Poetical Works*, ed. Hutchinson, 1904, pp. 814-15.)

1816. SONNET TRANSLATED FROM THE ITALIAN OF CAVALCANTI.

[Guido Cavalcanti to Dante Alighieri[1]]

Returning from its daily quest, my Spirit
Changed thoughts and vile in thee doth weep to find:
It grieves me that thy mild and gentle mind
Those ample virtues which it did inherit
Has lost. Once thou didst loath the multitude
Of blind and madding men—I then loved thee—
I loved thy lofty songs and that sweet word
When thou wert faithful to thyself and me.
I dare not now through thy degraded state
Own the delight thy strains inspire—in vain
I seek what once thou wert—we cannot meet
As we were wont. Again and yet again
Ponder my words: so the false Spirit shall fly
And leave to thee thy true integrity.

(*Ibid.* p. 820.)

1816. FRAGMENT, ADAPTED FROM THE LAST THREE LINES OF SONNET XI IN THE VITA NUOVA.[2]

What Mary is when she a little smiles
I cannot even tell or call to mind,
It is a miracle so new, so rare.

(*Ibid.* p. 818.)

1818. April 20. LETTER TO THOMAS LOVE PEACOCK (from Milan).

[Dante read by Shelley in Milan Cathedral]

This cathedral is a most astonishing work of art. It is built of white marble, and cut into pinnacles of immense height, and the utmost delicacy of workmanship, and loaded with sculpture. The effect of it, piercing the solid blue with those groups of dazzling

[1] [' Io vegno 'l giorno a te infinite volte.'—The date assigned is conjectural.]

[2] [These lines (from the sonnet ' Negli occhi porta la mia donna Amore') 'are said to have been scratched by Shelley on a window-pane at a house wherein he lodged while staying in London.' (*Forman.*) The date (1816) is conjectural.]

spires, relieved by the serene depth of this Italian heaven, or by moonlight when the stars seem gathered among those clustered shapes, is beyond any thing I had imagined architecture capable of producing. The interior, though very sublime, is of a more earthly character, and with its stained glass and massy granite columns over-loaded with antique figures, and the silver lamps, that burn for ever under the canopy of black cloth beside the brazen altar and the marble fretwork of the dome, give it the aspect of some gorgeous sepulchre. There is one solitary spot among those aisles, behind the altar, where the light of day is dim and yellow under the storied window, which I have chosen to visit, and read Dante there.

(*Prose Works,* ed. Forman, vol. iv. pp. 11-12.)

1818. Nov. 10. LETTER TO THOMAS LOVE PEACOCK (from Bologna).

[The evanescence of painting as compared to literature]

Books are perhaps the only productions of man coeval with the human races. Sophocles and Shakespeare can be produced and reproduced for ever. But how evanescent are paintings, and must necessarily be. Those of Zeuxis and Apelles, are no more, and perhaps they bore the same relation to Homer and Aeschylus, that those of Guido and Raffael bear to Dante and Petrarch.

(*Ibid.* vol. iv. p. 55.)

1818. A DISCOURSE ON THE MANNERS OF THE ANCIENTS RELATIVE TO THE SUBJECT OF LOVE.

[Shakespeare, Dante, Petrarch, and Homer]

Perhaps Shakspeare, from the variety and comprehension of his genius, is to be considered, on the whole, as the greatest individual mind, of which we have specimens remaining. Perhaps Dante created imaginations of greater loveliness and energy than any that are to be found in the ancient literature of Greece. Perhaps nothing has been discovered in the fragments of the Greek lyric poets equivalent to the sublime and chivalric sensibility of Petrarch. But, as a poet, Homer must be acknowledged to excel Shakespeare in the truth, the harmony, the sustained grandeur, the satisfying completeness of his images, their exact fitness to the illustration, and to that to which they belong. Nor could Dante, deficient in conduct, plan, nature, variety, and temperance, have been brought into comparison with these men, but for those fortunate isles, laden with golden fruit, which alone could tempt any one to embark in the misty ocean of his dark and extravagant fiction.

(*Ibid.* vol. iii. p. 241.)

1819. Feb. 25. LETTER TO THOMAS LOVE PEACOCK (from Naples).

[Michael Angelo and Dante]

The royal collection of paintings in this city is sufficiently miserable. Perhaps the most remarkable is the original studio by Michael Angelo, of the 'Day of Judgment,' which is painted in fresco on the Sixtine chapel of the Vatican. It is there so defaced as to be wholly indistinguishable. I cannot but think the genius of this artist highly overrated. He has not only no temperance, no modesty, no feeling for the just boundaries of art (and in these respects an admirable genius may err), but he has no sense of beauty, and to want this is to want the sense of creative power of mind. What is terror without a contrast with, and a connexion with, loveliness? How well Dante understood this secret—Dante, with whom this artist has been so presumptuously compared!

(*Prose Works*, ed. Forman, vol. iv. pp. 86-7.)

1819. August. LETTER TO THOMAS LOVE PEACOCK (from Livorno).

[Shelley reads Dante with Mrs. Shelley]

My employments are these: I awaken usually at seven; read half an hour; then get up; breakfast; after breakfast ascend *my tower*, and read or write until two. Then we dine. After dinner I read Dante with Mary,[1] gossip a little, eat grapes and figs, sometimes walk. . . .

(Dowden's *Life of Shelley*, vol. ii. pp. 274-5.)

1819. Sept. 3. LETTER TO LEIGH HUNT (from Livorno).

[Michael Angelo and Dante]

With respect to Michael Angelo, I dissent, and think with astonishment and indignation on the common notion that he equals, and in some respects exceeds Raphael. He seems to me to have no sense of moral dignity and loveliness; and the energy for which he has been so much praised, appears to me to be a certain rude, external, mechanical quality, in comparison with anything possessed by Raphael; or even much inferior artists. . . . He has been called the Dante of painting; but if we find some of the gross and strong outlines, which are employed in the few most distasteful passages of the *Inferno*, where shall we find *your* Francesca,[2]—where, the

[1] [Dowden says: 'It was the *Purgatorio* of which Shelley now read two cantos daily with Mary.']

[2] [*Inf.* v.—a reference to Leigh Hunt's *Story of Rimini*.]

spirit coming over the sea in a boat, like Mars rising from the vapours of the horizon,[1]—where, Matilda gathering flowers,[2] and all the exquisite tenderness, and sensibility, and ideal beauty, in which Dante excelled all poets except Shakespeare?

(*Prose Works*, ed, Forman. vol. iv. pp. 121-2.)

1819. Sept. 27. LETTER TO LEIGH HUNT (from Livorno).

[Dante, Petrarch, and Boccaccio]

I have been lately reading this most divine writer [Boccaccio.] He is, in a high sense of the word, a poet, and his language has the rhythm and harmony of verse. I think him not equal certainly to Dante or Petrarch, but far superior to Tasso and Ariosto, the children of a later and of a colder day. I consider the three first as the productions of the vigour of the infancy of a new nation—as rivulets from the same spring as that which fed the greatness of the republics of Florence and Pisa, and which checked the influence of the German emperors; and from which, through obscurer channels, Raffaelle and Michael Angelo drew the light and the harmony of their inspiration. When the second-rate poets of Italy wrote, the corrupting blight of tyranny was already hanging on every bud of genius, Energy, and simplicity, and unity of idea, were no more. In vain do we seek, in the finest passages of Ariosto and Tasso, any expression which at all approaches in this respect to those of Dante and Petrarch.

(*Ibid.* vol. iv. p. 127.)

1820. THE FIRST CANZONE OF THE CONVITO.[3] TRANSLATED FROM THE ITALIAN OF DANTE.

I

Ye who intelligent the Third Heaven move,
Hear the discourse which is within my heart,
  Which cannot be declared, it seems so new.
The Heaven whose course follows your power and art,
  O gentle creatures that ye are! me drew,
  And therefore may I dare to speak to you,
Even of the life which now I live—and yet
  I pray that ye will hear me when I cry,
  And tell of mine own heart this novelty;
How the lamenting Spirit moans in it,
And how a voice there murmurs against her
Who came on the refulgence of your sphere.

[1] [*Purg.* ii. 13-8.]
[2] [*Purg.* xxviii. 40-2—this episode was translated by Shelley; see below, pp. 221 ff.]
[3] ['Voi che intendendo il terzo ciel movete.']

II

A sweet Thought, which was once the life within
  This heavy heart, many a time and oft
    Went up before our Father's feet, and there
  It saw a glorious Lady throned aloft;
And its sweet talk of her my soul did win,
  So that I said, 'Thither I too will fare.'
  That Thought is fled, and one doth now appear
Which tyrannizes me with such fierce stress,
  That my heart trembles—ye may see it leap—
  And on another Lady bids me keep
Mine eyes, and says—Who would have blessedness
Let him but look upon that Lady's eyes,
Let him not fear the agony of sighs.

III

This lowly Thought, which once would talk with me
Of a bright seraph sitting crowned on high,
  Found such a cruel foe it died, and so
  My Spirit wept, the grief is hot even now—
And said, Alas for me! how swift could flee
That piteous Thought which did my life console!
  And the afflicted one   questioning
    Mine eyes, if such a Lady saw they never,
  And why they would . . .
    I said: 'Beneath those eyes might stand forever
He whom   regards must kill with . . .
To have known their power stood me in little stead,
Those eyes have looked on me, and I am dead.'

IV

'Thou art not dead, but thou hast wanderèd,
  Thou Soul of ours, who thyself dost fret,'
A spirit of gentle Love beside me said;
  For that fair Lady, whom thou dost regret,
That so transformed the life which thou hast led,
Thou scornest it, so worthless art thou made.
And see how meek, how pitiful, how staid,
Yet courteous, in her majesty she is.
  And still call thou her Woman in thy thought;
  Her whom, if thou thyself deceivest not,
Thou wilt behold decked with such loveliness,
That thou wilt cry [Love] only Lord, lo! here
Thy handmaiden, do what thou wilt with her.

V

My song, I fear that thou wilt find but few
  Who fitly shall conceive thy reasoning
    Of such hard matter dost thou entertain.
  Whence, if by misadventure chance should bring
Thee to base company, as chance may do,
    Quite unaware of what thou dost contain,
    I prithee comfort thy sweet self again,
My last delight; tell them that they are dull,
And bid them own that thou art beautiful.[1]

(*Poetical Works*, ed. Hutchinson, 1904, pp. 815-16.)

1820. MATILDA GATHERING FLOWERS.[2] (FROM THE PURGATORIO OF DANTE, CANTO, XXVIII. 1-51.)

And earnest to explore within—around—
The divine wood, whose thick green living woof
Tempered the young day to the sight—I wound

Up the green slope, beneath the forest's roof,
With slow, soft steps leaving the mountain's steep,
And sought those inmost labyrinths, motion-proof

Against the air, that in that stillness deep
And solemn, struck upon my forehead bare,
The slow, soft stroke of a continuous . . .

In which the   leaves tremblingly were
All bent towards that part where earliest
The sacred hill obscures the morning air.

Yet were they not so shaken from the [3] rest,
But that the birds, perched on the utmost spray,
Incessantly renewing their blithe quest,

With perfect joy received the early day,
Singing within the glancing leaves, whose sound
Kept a low burden to their roundelay,

Such as from bough to bough gathers around
The pine forest on bleak Chiassi's shore,
When Aeolus Sirocco has unbound.

[1] [This last stanza was subsequently published as an *envoi* to *Epipsychidion*; see below, p. 225.]

[2] [Medwin published a version of this fragment in the *Angler in Wales* (vol. i. pp. 218-29), and afterwards in his *Life of Shelley*, which differs materially from the above; see below, pp. 383 ff.]

[3] [Rossetti conjectures *their*.]

My slow steps had already borne me o'er
Such space within the antique wood, that I
Perceived not where I entered any more,—

When, lo! a stream whose little waves went by,
Bending towards the left through grass that grew
Upon its bank, impeded suddenly

My going on. Water of purest hue
On earth, would appear turbid and impure
Compared with this, whose unconcealing dew,

Dark, dark, yet clear, moved under the obscure
Eternal shades, whose interwoven looms
The rays of moon or sunlight ne'er endure.

I moved not with my feet, but 'mid the glooms
Pierced with my charmèd eye, contemplating
The mighty multitude of fresh May blooms

Which starred that night, when, even as a thing
That suddenly, for blank astonishment,
Charms every sense, and makes all thought take wing,—

A solitary woman! and she went
Singing and gathering flower after flower,
With which her way was painted and besprent.

'Bright lady, who, if looks had ever power
To bear true witness of the heart within,
Dost bask under the beams of love, come lower

Towards this bank. I prithee let me win
This much of thee, to come, that I may hear
Thy song: like Proserpine, in Enna's glen,

Thou seemest to my fancy, singing here
And gathering flowers, as that fair maiden when
She lost the Spring, and Ceres her, more dear.'

(*Poetical Works*, ed. Hutchinson, 1904, pp. 816-18.)

1820. PROMETHEUS UNBOUND—PREFACE.

[Dante and Shakespeare]

The imagery which I have employed will be found, in many instances, to have been drawn from the operations of the human mind, or from those external actions by which they are expressed. This is unusual in modern poetry, although Dante and Shakespeare are full of instances of the same kind: Dante indeed more than any other poet, and with greater success. . . . Poets, not otherwise than philosophers, painters, sculptors, and musicians, are in one sense, the creators, and, in another, the creations, of their age. From this subjection the loftiest do not escape. There is a similarity between Homer and Hesiod, between Aeschylus and Euripides, between Virgil and Horace, between Dante and Petrarch, between Shakespeare and Fletcher, between Dryden and Pope; each has a generic resemblance under which their specific distinctions are arranged.

(*Poetical Works*, ed. Hutchinson, 1904, pp. 222, 223-4.)

[Reminiscences of Dante]

Behold'st thou not two shapes from the east and west
Come, as two doves to one belovèd nest,
Twin nurslings of the all-sustaining air
On swift still wings glide down the atmosphere?[1]

(I. 752-5.)

I looked,
And behold, thrones were kingless, and men walked
One with the other even as spirits do,
None fawned, none trampled; hate, disdain, or fear,
Self-love or self-contempt, on human brows
No more inscribed, as o'er the gate of hell,
'All hope abandon ye who enter here.'[2]

(III. iv. 130-6.)

1821. June 16. LETTER TO CHARLES OLLIER (from Pisa).

[Taaffe's 'Comment on the Divine Comedy']

['In June, 1821,' says Dowden,[3] 'Shelley wrote to Ollier, sending a specimen of Taaffe's translation of Dante and commentary, which had been printed at Pisa from the types of Didot, and begging that he would arrange with the author for its publication in England.' Shelley continues:—]

The more considerable portion of this work will consist of the *Comment*. I have read with much attention this portion, as well as the verses up to the end of the eight canto; and I do not hesitate to assure you that the lights which the annotator's labours have thrown on the obscurer parts of the text are such as all foreigners and most Italians would derive an immense additional knowledge

[1] [Obviously suggested by *Inf*. v. 74, 82-4.]
[2] [*Inf*. iii. 9.]
[3] [*Life of Shelley*, vol. ii. p. 364.]

of Dante from. They elucidate a great number of the most interesting facts connected with Dante's history and the history of his times, and everywhere bear the mark of a most elegant and accomplished mind. I know that you will not take my opinion on poetry, because I thought my own verses very good, and *you* find that the public declare them to be unreadable. Show them to Mr. Procter, who is far better qualified to judge than I am; there are certainly passages of great strength and conciseness; indeed, the author has sacrificed everything to represent his original truly in this latter point. Pray observe the great beauty of the typography; they are the same types as my 'Elegy on Keats' is printed from.[1]

(Dowden's *Life of Shelley*, vol. ii. pp. 364-5.)

1821. Sep. 25. LETTER TO CHARLES OLLIER (from Pisa).

[National character of the Italians much the same as in the time of Dante]

It will give me great pleasure if I can arrange the affair of Mrs. Shelley's novel with you. . . . The romance is called *Castruccio, Prince of Lucca*. . . . The author visited the scenery which she describes in person; and one or two of the inferior characters are drawn from her own observation of the Italians, for the national character shows itself still in certain instances under the same forms as it wore in the time of Dante.

(*Life and Letters of Mary Wollstonecraft Shelley*, vol. i. p. 313.)

1821. ADVERTISEMENT TO EPIPSYCHIDION.

[*Epipsychidion* compared to the *Vita Nuova*]

The present poem, like the *Vita Nuova* of Dante, is sufficiently intelligible to a certain class of readers without a matter-of-fact history of the circumstances to which it relates; and to a certain other class it must ever remain incomprehensible, from a defect of a common organ of perception for the ideas of which it treats. Not but that, *gran vergogna sarebbe a colui, che rimasse cosa sotto veste di figura, o di colore rettorico: e domandato non sapesse denudare le sue parole da cotal veste, in guisa che avessero verace intendimento.*[2]

The present poem appears to have been intended by the Writer as the dedication to some longer one. The stanza on the opposite page is almost a literal translation from Dante's famous Canzone

Voi, ch' intendendo, il terzo ciel movete, &c.[3]

[1] [The first volume of Taaffe's *Comment on the Divine Comedy* was published in England by Murray in 1822; no second volume appeared. See below, p. 341.]

[2] [*Vita Nuova*, § 25, ll. 106-11.]

[3] [The first canzone in the *Convivio*—for Shelley's translation of the whole poem, see above, pp. 219-21.]

The presumptuous application of the concluding lines to his own composition will raise a smile at the expense of my unfortunate friend: be it a smile not of contempt, but pity.

My Song, I fear that thou wilt find but few
Who fitly shall conceive thy reasoning,
Of such hard matter dost thou entertain;
Whence, if by misadventure, chance should bring
Thee to base company, (as chance may do)
Quite unaware of what thou dost contain,
I prithee, comfort thy sweet self again,
My last delight! tell them that they are dull,
And bid them own that thou art beautiful.[1]

(*Poetical Works*, ed. Hutchinson, 1904, pp. 453-4.)

1821. A DEFENCE OF POETRY.

[Appreciation of Dante, among the great poets of the world]

A poet participates in the eternal, the infinite, and the one; as far as relates to his conceptions, time and place and number are not. The grammatical forms which express the moods of time, and the difference of persons, and the distinctions of place, are convertible with respect to the highest poetry, without injuring it as poetry; and the choruses of Aeschylus, and the book of Job, and Dante's Paradise, would afford, more than any other writings, examples of this fact, if the limits of this essay did not forbid citation.

* * * *

All the authors of revolutions in opinion are not only necessarily poets as they are inventors, nor even as their words unveil the permanent analogy of things by images which participate in the life of truth; but as their periods are harmonious and rhythmical, and contain in themselves the elements of verse; being the echo of the eternal music. Nor are those supreme poets, who have employed traditional forms of rhythm on account of the form and action of their subjects, less capable of perceiving and teaching the truth of things, than those who have omitted that form. Shakespeare, Dante, and Milton (to confine ourselves to modern writers) are philosophers of the very loftiest power.

* * * *

The abolition of personal slavery is the basis of the highest political hope that it can enter into the mind of man to conceive.

[1] [In the first two drafts of this *Advertisement* (printed in *Poetical Works*, ed. Hutchinson, 1904, pp. 467-8) the quotations from, and references to, Dante do not appear. There are sundry reminiscences of Dante in this poem; *e.g.* cf. ll. 160-1 and *Purg.* xv. 60-75; l. 249 and *Inf.* i. 1 ff.; l. 321 and *Inf.* i. 2; ll. 410-11 and *Purg.* i. 131.]

The freedom of women produced the poetry of sexual love. Love became a religion, the idols of whose worship were ever present. It was as if the statues of Apollo and the Muses had been endowed with life and motion, and had walked forth among their worshippers; so that earth became peopled by the inhabitants of a diviner world. The familiar appearances and proceedings of life became wonderful and heavenly, and a paradise was created as out of the wrecks of Eden. And as this creation itself is poetry, so its creators were poets; and language was the instrument of their art: 'Galeotto fu il libro, e chi lo scrisse.'[1] The Provençal Trouveurs, or inventors, preceded Petrarch, whose verses are as spells, which unseal the inmost inchanted fountains of the delight which is in the grief of love. It is impossible to feel them without becoming a portion of that beauty which we contemplate: it were superfluous to explain how the gentleness and elevation of mind connected with these sacred emotions can render men more amiable, more generous and wise, and lift them out of the dull vapours of the little world of self. Dante understood the secret things of love even more than Petrarch. His *Vita Nuova* is an inexhaustible fountain of purity of sentiment and language: it is the idealised history of that period, and those intervals of his life which were dedicated to love. His apotheosis of Beatrice in Paradise, and the gradations of his own love and her loveliness, by which as by steps he feigns himself to have ascended to the throne of the Supreme Cause, is the most glorious imagination of modern poetry. The acutest critics have justly reversed the judgment of the vulgar, and the order of the great arts of the *Divina Commedia*, in the admiration which they accord to the Hell, Purgatory, and Paradise. The latter is a perpetual hymn of everlasting love.

* * * *

The poetry of Dante may be considered as the bridge thrown over the stream of time, which unites the modern and ancient world. The distorted notions of invisible things which Dante and his rival Milton have idealized, are merely the mask and the mantle in which these great poets walk through eternity enveloped and disguised. It is a difficult question to determine how far they were conscious of the distinction which must have subsisted in their minds between their own creeds and that of the people. Dante at least appears to wish to mark the full extent of it by placing Riphaeus, whom Virgil calls *justissimus unus*, in Paradise,[2] and observing a most heretical[3] caprice in his distribution of rewards and punishments. And Milton's poem contains within itself a philosophical refutation of that system of which, by a strange and natural

[1] [*Inf.* v. 137.] [2] [*Par.* xx. 68.] [3] [Originally, *poetical.*]

antithesis, it has been a chief popular support. . . . The *Divina Commedia* and *Paradise Lost* have conferred upon modern mythology a systematic form; and when change and time shall have added one more superstition to the mass of those which have arisen and decayed upon the earth, commentators will be learnedly employed in elucidating the religion of ancestral Europe, only not utterly forgotten because it will have been stamped with the eternity of genius.

Homer was the first and Dante the second epic poet: that is, the second poet, the series of whose creations bore a defined and intelligible relation to the knowledge and sentiment and religion of the age in which he lived, and of the ages which followed it: developing itself in correspondence with their development. For Lucretius had limed the wings of his swift spirit in the dregs of the sensible world; and Virgil, with a modesty that ill became his genius, had affected the fame of an imitator, even whilst he created anew all that he copied; and none among the flock of mock-birds, though their notes are sweet, Apollonius Rhodius, Quintus Calaber, Smyrnaeus, Nonnus, Lucan, Statius, or Claudian, have sought even to fulfil a single condition of epic truth. Milton was the third epic poet. For if the title of epicin its highest sense be refused to the *Aeneid*, still less can it be conceded to the *Orlando Furioso*. the *Gerusalemme Liberata*, the *Lusiad*, or the *Fairy Queen*.

Dante and Milton were both deeply penetrated with the ancient religion of the civilised world; and its spirit exists in their poetry probably in the same proportion as its forms survived in the unreformed worship of modern Europe. The one preceded and the other followed the Reformation at almost equal intervals. Dante was the first religious reformer, and Luther surpassed him rather in the rudeness and acrimony, than in the boldness of his censures, of papal usurpation. Dante was the first awakener of entranced Europe; he created a language, in itself music and persuasion, out of a chaos of inharmonious barbarisms. He was the congregator of those great spirits who presided over the resurrection of learning; the Lucifer of that starry flock which in the thirteenth century shone forth from republican Italy, as from a heaven, into the darkness of the benighted world. His very words are instinct with spirit; each is as a spark, a burning atom of inextinguishable thought; and many yet lie covered in the ashes of their birth, and pregnant with a lightning which has yet found no conductor.

* * * *

The age immediately succeeding to that of Dante, Petrarch, and Boccaccio, was characterized by a revival of painting, sculpture, and architecture. Chaucer caught the sacred inspiration, and the superstructure of English literature is based upon the materials of Italian invention.

* * * *

The exertions of Locke, Hume, Gibbon, Voltaire, Rousseau, and their disciples, in favour of oppressed and deluded humanity, are entitled to the gratitude of mankind. Yet it is easy to calculate the degree of moral and intellectual improvement which the world would have exhibited, had they never lived. A little more nonsense would have been talked for a century or two; and perhaps a few more men, women, and children burnt as heretics. We might not at this moment have been congratulating each other on the abolition of the Inquisition in Spain. But it exceeds all imagination to conceive what would have been the moral condition of the world if neither Dante, Petrarch, Boccaccio, Chaucer, Shakespeare, Calderon, Lord Bacon, nor Milton, had ever existed; if Raphael and Michael Angelo had never been born; if the Hebrew poetry had never been translated; if a revival of the study of Greek literature had never taken place; if no monuments of ancient sculpture had been handed down to us; and if the poetry of the religion of the ancient world had been extinguished together with its belief.

(*Prose Works*, ed. Forman, 1880, vol. iii. pp. 99 ff.)

1821. ON THE DEVIL, AND DEVILS.[1]

[The Devil of Milton, Dante, and Tasso]

The Devil owes everything to Milton. Dante and Tasso presents us with a very gross idea of him. Milton divested him of a sting, hoof, and horns, and clothed him with the sublime grandeur of a graceful but tremendous spirit.

* * * *

[The *Purgatorio* a finer poem than the *Inferno*]

There are fewer Raphaels than Michael Angelos; better verses have been written on Hell than Paradise. How few read the *Purgatorio* or the *Paradiso* of Dante, in the comparison of those who know the *Inferno* well. And yet the *Purgatorio*, with the exception of two famous passages, is a finer poem than the *Inferno*.

(*Ibid.* vol. ii. pp. 390, 402.)

1821. July. THE BOAT ON THE SERCHIO.

[Monte San Giuliano—an echo of Dante]

All rose to do the task He set to each,
  Who shaped us to his ends and not our own;
The million rose to learn, and one to teach
  What none yet ever knew or can be known.

[1] [The date (1821) is conjectural.]

And many rose
Whose woe was such that fear became desire;—
Melchior and Lionel were not among those;
They from the throng of men had stepped aside,
And made their home under the green hill side.
It was that hill, whose intervening brow
Screens Lucca from the Pisan's envious eye,[1]
Which the circumfluous plain waving below,
Like a wide lake of green fertility,
With streams and fields and marshes bare,
Divides from the far Apennines—which lie
Islanded in the immeasurable air.

(*Stanza* iv.)

1821. Aug. 15. LETTER TO MRS. SHELLEY (from Ravenna).

[Dante's tomb at Ravenna]

I have seen Dante's tomb, and worshipped the sacred spot. The building and its accessories are comparatively modern, but the urn itself, and the tablet of marble, with his portrait in relief, are evidently of equal antiquity with his death.[2] The countenance has all the marks of being taken from his own; the lines are strongly marked, far more than the portraits, which, however, it resembles except, indeed, the eye, which is half closed, and reminded me of Pacchiani. It was probably taken after death.

(*Prose Works*, ed. Forman, vol. iv. p. 228.)

1821. June 18. LETTER TO JOHN GISBORNE (from Lerici).

[The beauties of the *Purgatorio* and *Paradiso*]

I do not think much of——not admiring Metastasio; the *nil admirari*, however justly applied, seems to me a bad sign in a young person. I had rather a pupil of mine had conceived a frantic passion for Marini himself, than that she had found out the critical defects of the most deficient author. When she becomes of her own accord full of genuine admiration for the finest scene in the *Purgatorio*, or the opening of the *Paradiso*, or some other neglected piece of excellence, hope great things.

(*Ibid.* vol. iv. p. 282.)

[1] [Monte San Giuliano is described by Ugolino as 'il monte Per che i Pisan veder Lucca non ponno' (*Inf.* xxxii. 29-30).]

[2] [As a matter of fact the marble relief of Dante dates only from the end of the fifteenth century, it having been erected by Bernardo Bembo in 1483.]

1822. THE TRIUMPH OF LIFE.[1]

[Dante and the *Divina Commedia*]

Behold a wonder worthy of the rhyme

Of him[2] who from the lowest depths of hell,
Through every paradise and through all glory,
Love led serene, and who returned to tell

The words of hate and awe; the wondrous story
How all things are transfigured except Love;
For deaf as is a sea, which wrath makes hoary,

The world can hear not the sweet notes that move
The sphere whose light is melody to lovers—
A wonder worthy of his rhyme.[3]

(ll. 471-80.)

ANONYMOUS

1816. Jan. QUARTERLY REVIEW. ART. II. ALFIERI'S LIFE AND WRITINGS.

[Alfieri's admiration of Dante]

ALFIERI was a passionate admirer of the Italian tongue; and he knew not why that language, which displays itself with such strength and energy in Dante, should become effeminate and feeble in the Drama.

* * * *

Alfieri regarded Metastasio with bitter and intolerant contempt; —he had gone to the well-head of Italian poetry, and drunk at Dante's living spring;—the milk and honey of Metastasio sickened him.

(Vol. xiv. pp. 349, 356.)

BRITISH MUSEUM CATALOGUE

1816. LIBRORUM IMPRESSORUM, QUI IN MUSEO BRITANNICO ADSERVANTUR, CATALOGUS.

[The list of printed editions of Dante's works in the British Museum at this date is chiefly remarkable for its poverty, there being no separate edition of the *Convivio*,

[1] [Not published until 1824.] [2] [Dante.]

[3] [There are many reminiscences of Dante in this poem; e.g. cf. ll. 7-8 with *Purg.* xxviii. 14-17; ll. 182 ff. with *Inf.* xiii. 25 ff.; ll. 315-16 with *Purg.* xxviii. 25-27; ll. 375-6 with *Purg.* xxviii. 14-18; l. 416 with *Purg.* i. 19; ll. 448-9 with *Purg.* xxviii. 41-42; ll. 528-9 with *Inf.* iii. 112-14.]

nor of the *De Monarchia*, and only one of the many fifteenth-century editions of the *Commedia*. The Dante items are 24, in which are included two editions of the *Opere di Dante*, viz. Venice, 1741; and Venice, 1760;—fourteen editions of the *Commedia*, viz. Florence, 1481 (with nine plates); Aldus, 1502, and 1515; one of the Paganini (undated) editions; Venice, 1544; Lyon, 1547, and 1552; Venice, 1555; the three editions with the commentaries of Landino and Vellutello, Venice. 1564, 1578, and 1596; Daniello's edition, Venice, 1568; Padua, 1726-7; Venice, 1739;—also the *editio princeps* of the *De Vulgari Eloquentia* in Trissino's translation, Vicenza, 1529; and the *editio princeps* of the *Vita Nuova*, Florence, 1576;—besides Villegas' Castilian translation of the *Inferno* (Burgos, 1515); and the English translations of Rogers (Hell), 1782; Boyd (Hell), 1785; and Cary (The Vision), 1814.]

WILLIAM YOUNG OTTLEY

(1771-1836)

[William Young Ottley, writer on art, was born near Thatcham in Berkshire in 1771. After studying in the Royal Academy schools, he went to Italy in 1791, where he stayed for ten years studying art, and collecting drawings and engravings. His first publication was *The Italian School of Design*, in three parts (1805-13-23), which was followed by numerous others, among them *An Inquiry into the Origin and Early History of Engraving upon Copper and in Wood* (1816), which contains an account (after Vasari) of Botticelli's work upon the *Divina Commedia*, together with a detailed description of the nineteen engravings made for the 1481 Florence edition of the *Commedia*. In 1833 Ottley was appointed Keeper of Prints at the British Museum, which post he held until his death in 1836.]

1816. AN INQUIRY INTO THE ORIGIN AND EARLY HISTORY OF ENGRAVING UPON COPPER AND IN WOOD.

[Botticelli and the *Divina Commedia*]

AS many doubts have been suggested by recent writers relative to the engravings of Sandro Botticelli[1]—especially to his prints for the Dante of 1481—and as the account given us by Vasari[2] has been frequently misinterpreted, I have judged it the safest method to introduce the old Florentine artist to my readers in a careful translation of Vasari's life of him. . . .

'. . . At Florence, being a person fond of novel pursuits, Botticelli commented upon a part of Dante; and designed and engraved the Inferno; about which work he consumed a great deal of time. . . .' Vasari proceeds to relate a couple of anecdotes of Sandro's pleasantry, not worth translating; and a third, which, as it contains a second mention of his Commentary on Dante, is not wholly uninteresting.

'It is recounted of Sandro,' says Vasari, 'that, for a joke, he accused one of his acquaintance, to the vicar, of heresy; and that the person having appeared, and demanded the name of his accuser,

[1] [1447-1510.]

[2] [Giorgio Vasari, 1511-1574; his *Vite de' più eccellenti pittori, scultori ed architettori*, was first published at Florence in 1550.]

and the nature of the alleged offence, was informed that it was Sandro; and that he had asserted him to hold the opinion of the Epicureans, who say, that the soul dies with the body. The accused person, therefore, desired that he might be brought, face to face with his accuser, before the judge; when, Sandro having appeared, he thus addressed the tribunal:—It is indeed true that I entertain this opinion of the soul of that fellow, because he is a beast. Besides which, do you not perceive that he is a heretic—seeing that, although he is so destitute of learning, that he can scarcely read, he has the assurance to write a commentary on Dante,[1] and takes his revered name in vain.'

(Vol. i. pp. 404, 409, 410-1.)[2]

STEFANO EGIDIO PETRONJ

(fl. 1810)

[Petronj, who describes himself on the title-page of his books as 'Membro della Grande Accademia Italiana e di altre Accademie di Europa,' published in London in 1816 an analysis (in Italian) of the poems of Dante, Ariosto, and Tasso, of which a second edition appeared in 1822. In 1819 he published, also in London, an edition of the *Divina Commedia*, in three small volumes (Schulze e Dean presso Bain), which is practically a reprint of Boschini's London edition of 1808.]

1816. DANTE, ARIOSTO E TASSO. EPITOME DELLA LOR VITA, ED ANALISI DEI LORO PRINCIPALI POEMI. OPERA SCRITTA AD USO DEGLI STUDIOSI DELL' ITALICA LINGUA DA STEFANO EGIDIO PETRONJ.[3]

THE contents of *Parte Prima*, in which Dante is treated of, are as follows:—

Capo I. Notizie sulla vita di Dante specialmente civile.

Capo II. Notizie sulla sua vita specialmente letteraria.

Capo III. D' onde debba ripetersi l' origine della Divina Commedia; ed estratto completo d' un' opera nuova interessantissima su tale argomento.

Capo IV. Riflessioni sul piano generale e sull' invenzione di questo poema.

Capo V. Analisi dell' Inferno.

Capo VI. Analisi del Purgatorio.

Capo VII. Analisi del Paradiso.

(pp. 1-221.)

[1] [Nothing is known of any 'commentary on Dante' by Botticelli.]

[2] [Ottley subsequently discusses the question as to whether the 19 plates in the 1481 edition of the *Commedia*, of which he gives a detailed description, were the work of Botticelli or of Baldini (pp. 413-24).]

[3] [London: Treuttel e Würtz.]

THOMAS BARNES

(1785-1841)

[Thomas Barnes, editor of 'The Times,' was born about 1785, and was educated at Christ's Hospital, and Pembroke College, Cambridge. On leaving the University he settled in London as a journalist, and in 1817 was appointed editor of 'The Times,' which position he held until his death in 1841. Barnes was a friend of Leigh Hunt, Hazlitt, and Charles Lamb. A conversation with the last on the subject of Dante and Shakespeare is recorded by Talfourd in his *Memorials of Charles Lamb*, from which it appears that Barnes was a student and admirer of Dante.]

1816. T. N. TALFOURD gives the following reminiscence of a conversation between Thomas Barnes and Charles Lamb on the subject of Dante, in this year:—

I well remember Barnes, late one evening, in the year 1816, when only two or three friends remained with Lamb and his sister, long after 'we had heard the chimes at midnight,' holding inveterate but delighted controversy with Lamb, respecting the tragic power of Dante as compared with that of Shakspeare. Dante was scarcely known to Lamb; for he was unable to read the original, and Cary's noble translation was not then known to him; and Barnes aspired to the glory of affording him a glimpse of a kindred greatness in the mighty Italian with that which he had conceived incapable of human rivalry. The face of the advocate of Dante, heavy when in repose, grew bright with earnest admiration as he quoted images, sentiments, dialogues, against Lamb, who had taken his own immortal stand on Lear, and urged the supremacy of the child-changed father against all the possible Ugolinos of the world.

(*Memorials of Charles Lamb*, ed. 1892, p. 199.)

THOMAS LOVE PEACOCK

(1785-1866)

[Thomas Love Peacock, the novelist, was born at Weymouth in 1785. He was intended for a mercantile career, but devoted himself to literature, and became a good classical scholar and proficient in French and Italian. In 1812 he made the acquaintance of Shelley, from whom he for a time received a pension. In 1819 he entered the East India Company's service in London, and in 1837 succeeded James Mill in the chief-examinership, which he held until 1856. He died in 1866. Peacock's career as a novelist began with the publication of *Headlong Hall* in 1816, which was followed by *Nightmare Abbey* and *Melincourt* in 1818, *The Misfortunes of Elphin* in 1829, and *Crotchet Castle* in 1831. Peacock was evidently well read in Dante—A song from Dante, based on the opening lines of Canto viii. of the *Purgatorio*, is introduced in *Headlong Hall*, and 'a volume of Dante' plays an important part in an amusing scene in *Nightmare Abbey* in which Shelley figures as Scythrop. Quotations from the *Commedia* occur in several of the other novels.]

1816. HEADLONG HALL.[1]

[A song from Dante]

FROM Chapter XIII:—'Now, when they had eaten and were satisfied,' Squire Headlong called on Mr. Chromatic for a song; who, with the assistance of his two accomplished daughters, regaled the ears of the company with the following

TERZETTO[2]

Grey Twilight, from her shadowy hill,
  Discolours Nature's vernal bloom,
And sheds on grove, and field, and rill,
  One placid tint of deepening gloom.

The sailor sighs 'mid shoreless seas,
  Touched by the thought of friends afar,
As, fanned by ocean's flowing breeze,
  He gazes on the western star.

The wanderer hears, in pensive dream,
  The accents of the last farewell,
As, pausing by the mountain stream,
  He listens to the evening bell.

(Ed. Garnett, 1891, p. 155.)

1818. NIGHTMARE ABBEY.[3]

[Dante 'growing fashionable']

From Chapter VI:—In the evening, the whole party met, as usual, in the library. Marionetta sat at the harp; the Honourable Mr. Listless sat by her and turned over her music, though the exertion was almost too much for him. The Reverend Mr. Larynx relieved him occasionally in this delightful labour. Scythrop,[4] tormented by the demon Jealousy, sat in the corner biting his lips and fingers. Marionetta looked at him every now and then with a smile of most provoking good humour, which he pretended not to see, and which only the more exasperated his troubled spirit. He took down a volume of Dante, and pretended to be deeply interested in the *Purgatorio*, though he knew not a word he was reading, as Marionetta was well aware; who, tripping across the room, peeped into his book, and said to him, 'I see you

[1] [Written in 1815.]
[2] Imitated from a passage in the *Purgatorio* of Dante. [Canto viii. 1-6.]
[3] [Written in 1817.]
[4] [Usually supposed to represent Shelley.]

are in the middle of Purgatory.'—'I am in the middle of hell,' said Scythrop furiously. 'Are you?' said she; 'then come across the room, and I will sing you the finale of Don Giovanni.'

'Let me alone,' said Scythrop. Marionetta looked at him with a deprecating smile, and said, 'You unjust, cross creature, you.'—'Let me alone,' said Scythrop, but much less emphatically than at first, and by no means wishing to be taken at his word. Marionetta left him immediately, and returning to the harp, said, just loud enough for Scythrop to hear—'Did you ever read Dante, Mr. Listless? Scythrop is reading Dante, and is just now in Purgatory.'—'And I,' said the Honourable Mr. Listless, 'am not reading Dante, and am just now in Paradise,' bowing to Marionetta.

Marionetta.—You are very gallant, Mr. Listless; and I dare say you are very fond of reading Dante.

The Honourable Mr. Listless.—I don't know how it is, but Dante never came in my way till lately. I never had him in my collection, and if I had had him I should not have read him. But I find he is growing fashionable, and I am afraid I must read him some wet morning.

Marionetta.—No, read him some evening, by all means. Were you ever in love, Mr. Listless?

The Honourable Mr. Listless.—I assure you, Miss O'Carroll, never—till I came to Nightmare Abbey. I dare say it is very pleasant; but it seems to give so much trouble that I fear the exertion would be too much for me.

Marionetta.—Shall I teach you a compendious method of courtship, that will give you no trouble whatever?

The Honourable Mr. Listless.—You will confer on me an inexpressible obligation. I am all impatience to learn it.

Marionetta.—Sit with your back to the lady and read Dante; only be sure to begin in the middle, and turn over three or four pages at once—backwards as well as forwards, and she will immediately perceive that you are desperately in love with her—desperately.

(*The Honourable Mr. Listless sitting between Scythrop and Marionetta, and fixing all his attention on the beautiful speaker, did not observe Scythrop, who was doing as she described.*) . . .

Mr. Flosky (*joining them from another part of the room*).—Did I not hear Mr. Listless observe that Dante is becoming fashionable?

The Honourable Mr. Listless.—I did hazard a remark to that effect, Mr. Flosky, though I speak on such subjects with a consciousness of my own nothingness, in the presence of so great a man as Mr. Flosky. I know not what is the colour of Dante's devils, but as he is certainly becoming fashionable, I conclude they are blue; for the blue devils, as it seems to me, Mr. Flosky, constitute the fundamental feature of fashionable literature.

Mr. Flosky.—The blue are, indeed, the staple commodity; but as they will not always be commanded, the black, red, and grey may be admitted as substitutes. Tea, late dinners, and the French Revolution, have played the devil, Mr. Listless, and brought the devil into play.

Mr. Toobad (starting up).—Having great wrath.

Mr. Flosky.—This is no play upon words, but the sober sadness of veritable fact. . . .

The Honourable Mr. Listless.—And what has all that to do with Dante, and the blue devils?

Mr. Hilary.—Not much, I should think, with Dante, but a great deal with the blue devils.

* * * *

All were silent, and Marionetta sung:—

Why are thy looks so blank, grey friar?
&c. &c. &c.

Scythrop immediately replaced Dante on the shelf, and joined the circle round the beautiful singer. Marionetta gave him a smile of approbation that fully restored his complacency, and they continued on the best possible terms during the remainder of the evening.

(Ed. Garnett, 1891, pp. 52 ff.)

1818. MELINCOURT, OR SIR ORAN HAUT-TON.[1]

[Quotation from Dante]

From Chapter XX:—The first meadow in which we gather cowslips, the first stream on which we sail, the first home in which we awake to the sense of human sympathy, have all a peculiar and exclusive charm, which we shall never find again in richer meadows, mightier rivers, and more magnificent dwellings; nor even in themselves, when we revisit them after the lapse of years, and the sad realities of noon have dissipated the illusions of sunrise. It is the same, too, with first love, whatever be the causes that render it unsuccessful: the second choice may have just preponderance in the balance of moral estimation: but the object of first affection, of all the perceptions of our being, will be most divested of the attributes of mortality. The magical associations of infancy are revived with double power in the feelings of first love; but when they too have departed, then, indeed, the light of the morning is gone.

Pensa che questo dì mai non raggiorna![2]

(Ed. Garnett, 1891, vol. i. pp. 197-8.)

[1] [Written in 1817.]

[2] [*Purg.* xii. 84.]

1822. MAID MARIAN.[1]

[Parody of Dante]

From Chapter X:—Matilda received intimation of Prince John's design by the usual friendly channel of a blunt arrow, which must either have been sent from some secret friend in the prince's camp, or from some vigorous archer beyond it: the latter will not appear improbable, when we consider that Robin Hood and Little John could shoot two English miles and an inch point-blank.

Come scrive Turpino, che non erra.[2]

(Ed. Garnett, 1889, pp. 93-4.)

1829. THE MISFORTUNES OF ELPHIN.

[Motto from Dante to Chapter XI]

L' ombra sua torna ch' era dipartita—Dante.[3]

(Ed. Garnett, 1891, p. 96.)

1831. CROTCHET CASTLE.[4]

[Miss Touchandgo a reader of Dante]

From Chapter XIV:—Miss Susannah Touchandgo had read the four great poets of Italy, and many of the best writers of France.

(Ed. Garnett, 1891, p. 138.)

CLARA MARY JANE CLAIRMONT

(1798-1879)

[Clara Clairmont (or Claire, as she preferred to call herself) is known to fame in connection with Byron and Shelley. When she was three years old (in 1801) her mother married William Godwin, as his second wife. In 1814 Clara accompanied Shelley and Mary Godwin in their elopement, and remained with them during their travels on the continent. Two years later she introduced herself to Byron, and became by him the mother of a daughter, Allegra, who was born 12 Jan. 1817 at Bath. After the death of the child in 1822, she went to Vienna, and thence as a governess to Russia. She subsequently returned to Italy, and after residing for a time in Paris, finally settled at Florence, where she died in 1879, at the age of eighty-one.]

1816. (After March.) LETTER TO LORD BYRON (from Arabella Row, Pimlico).

[Shelley's Dante translations—Dante's inscription over the Gate of Hell applied to marriage]

SHELLEY is now turned three and twenty, and interested as I am in all he does, it is with the greatest pleasure I receive your approbation. *Alastor* is a most evident proof of improvement; but I think his merit lies in translation. The sonnets

[1] [Written in 1818.] [2] [*Inf.* xxviii. 12: 'Come Livio scrive, che non erra.']
[3] [*Inf.* iv. 81.] [4] [Written in 1830.]

from the Greek of Moschus and from Dante are the best. If you think ill of his compositions, I hope you will speak; he may improve by your remarks. . . . I transcribe the Italian Sonnet of Dante's, as few editions contain it,[1] that you may see how nearly exactly it is translated[2]:—

From Dante Alighieri to Guido Cavalcanti

Guido, vorrei, che tu ed Lapo ed io
Fossimo presi per incantamento
E messi ad un vassel, che ad ogni vento
Per mare andasse a voler vostro e mio.
Sicché Fortuna, ad[3] altro tempo rio
Non ci potesse dare impedimento
Anzi, vivendo in noi sempre talento[4]
Di stare insieme crescesse il disio.
E Monna Vanna, e monna Bice poi,
Con quella in il numer delle trenta,[5]
Con noi ponesse il buono incantatore;
E quivi ragionar sempre d' amore.
E ciascuna di lor fosse contenta,
Siccome io credo che sariamo noi.

I believe this is quite correct, but as I transcribe it from memory I am not certain. 'Anzi, vivendo in noi sempre talento, di stare insieme crescesse il disio'—is a blessing which I think the goodness of God ought to have bestowed upon married people, since he has imposed such an evil on the world. I wonder how Dante, with such a peculiarly unpleasant countenance, could have thought of such a pleasant way of passing life. Do you remember his inscription over the gate of Hell—

'Lasciate ogni speranza voi ch' entrate.'

I think it a most admirable description of marriage. The subject makes me prolix. I can never resist the temptation of throwing a pebble at it as I pass by.

(*Letters and Journals of Lord Byron*, ed. Prothero, 1898, vol. iii. pp. 431-3.)

1821. April 12. JOURNAL.

[Her yearning for the absent Allegra likened to that of Dante for the last cantos of the *Divina Commedia*]

When the *Divina Commedia*, after being lost in the troubles of the civil war, was found and brought to Dante, he pressed it to

[1] [This sonnet is not included in Zotti's edition (1809) of Dante's lyrical poems. It is *Son.* xxxii. in the Oxford Dante.]

[2] [For Shelley's translation, see above, pp. 215-16.]

[3] [Read *od.*] [4] [Read *vivendo sempre in un talento.*]

[5] [Read *Con quella ch' è sul numero del trenta.*]

his heart and exclaimed, 'It appears to me as if I had recovered my lost immortality.' So it would be to me if I recovered my lost Allegra[1] as if I had come back to the warmth of life after the stiffness of the grave.

(Dowden's *Life of Shelley*, vol. ii. p. 482.)

ANONYMOUS

1816. July. MONTHLY MAGAZINE. SELECT NOTICES OF ITALIAN LITERATURE.—DANTE.

[Dante and the 'Vision of Tantalus']

AT the conclusion of the fifth volume of the Lives of the Holy Fathers, is a long vision of Tantalus, a rich and dissolute young man, whose soul having, by divine judgment, been, for a limited time, separated from his body, was accompanied by his angel to hell, to purgatory, and to paradise. This vision is divided into seventeen chapters, and is different from, and more ancient than that of the monk Alberico, from whom this celebrated poet has been heretofore supposed to have taken the first idea of his "Divine Comedy." It is probable that he could not have had access to the latter, the only manuscript copy of which was locked up in the library of a convent. Between the vision of Tantalus here spoken of, and the poem of Dante, there is this remarkable difference, that in the former the sins of the guilty are expurgated in hell by suitable punishments, whereas in the latter the purification is with greater propriety accomplished in purgatory.

(Vol. xli. p. 491.)

FRANCIS HORNER

(1778-1817)

[Francis Horner, politician, best known in connection with his 'bullion report' (1810), recommending the resumption of cash payments, was born at Edinburgh in 1778. He was educated at the High School and University of Edinburgh (1786-1795), and was called to the Scotch bar in 1800; a few years later he joined the English bar, and settled in London. Horner, together with Jeffrey and Sydney Smith, was one of the original founders of the *Edinburgh Review*, to the first number of which (November, 1802) he contributed no less than four articles. He entered Parliament in 1806 and sat successively for St. Ives (1806-7), Wendover (1807-12), and St. Mawes (1813-17). In October, 1816, he left England on account of failing health, and took up his residence at Pisa, where he died in the following February. While at Pisa Horner began the study of the *Divina Commedia*, a copy of

[1] [Her daughter by Lord Byron.]

which (edited by Poggiali, 4 vols. 8vo, Livorno, 1807) he had bought at Leghorn on his way out. In the course of his few weeks' reading he made 'somewhat copious notes on the *Inferno*,' a few of which have been preserved.[1]]

1816. Dec. 6. LETTER TO JOHN ARCHIBALD MURRAY (from Pisa).

[Study of Dante]

I HAVE cast myself headlong into Italian literature, meaning, however, to confine myself to their first-rate authors among the historians and poets. . . . At present I am engaged with Dante and Machiavel.

(*Memoirs and Correspondence*, ed. 1843, vol. ii. p. 373.)

1816. Dec. 13. LETTER TO LADY HOLLAND (from Pisa).

I am making a study of Dante, which is rather too big a word for any reading of mine now; but I do not find it a task, and he will make all other writers more easy to me.

(*Ibid.* vol. ii. p. 375.)

1816. NOTES ON THE INFERNO OF DANTE.

[Dante's account of the voyage of Ulysses]

The account which Ulysses gives of his expedition and death in the Atlantic ocean, is a more extended piece of narrative than is anywhere else to be found in this poem. It is clear, interesting, and expressed throughout with a noble propriety of diction. No extract from Dante taken by itself would be more pleasing, though it would not afford a specimen of his characteristic. It has some of his excellences in a high degree; a perspicuous conciseness, and in some parts great force of expression. It begins beautifully:

'Nè dolcezza di figlio, nè la pieta
Del vecchio padre' &c. &c.[2]

In the progress of the introductory narrative he introduces with great judgment a circumstance of which he is afterwards to make use:—

'Io e i compagni eravam *vecchi* e *tardi*.'[3]

The terms in which he mentions the pillars of Hercules are original and grand:—

'Quando venimmo a quella foce stretta
Ov' Ercole segnò li suoi *riguardi*,
Acciocchè l' uom più oltre non si metta.'[4]

The generality of the other expression, *l' uom*, 'in order that *man* might not think of going farther,' while it sets out the pride of

[1] [See below, pp. 240-1; and also a letter of Herman Merivale to Leonard Horner (above, pp. 197-200).]
[2] [*Inf.* xxvi. 94 ff.] [3] [*Inf.* xxvi. 106.] [4] [*Inf.* xxvi. 107-9.]

Hercules, seems to magnify the exploit on which Ulysses was about to venture. There is shortly after this a poetical image, of eminent beauty, which I do not know how to translate into English, the change in our customs having left us no word to express that on which the metaphor turns. By a very pleasing figure, we say 'the evening of our days,' for the last calm remnant of life. Ulysses, rousing his old worn-out companions to a last effort of adventure, calls their remnant of life, 'this short vigil of our senses':—

'A questa tanto picciola vigilia
De' vostri sensi, ch' è del remanente
Non vogliate negar,' &c.[1]

The *vigilia*, in the Romish church, is the service which is performed the night before interment, the corpse being laid out; 'the vigil of the senses,' therefore is, in this poetical use of the phrase, the interval of old age, after the senses may be said to be dead, before the final extinction of breath.

(Printed in C. Lyell's *Poems of the Vita Nuova and Convito*, 1842, pp. ccxvii-viii.)[2]

1817. Feb. 2. NOTES OF A PLAN OF STUDY AT PISA.[3]

Poets to be habitually studied, the principles of their works to be thoroughly examined:—

Iliad and Odyssey; tragedies of Euripides; Virgil, both works; Ovid, the Metamorphoses; Dante, Inferno; Ariosto, Orlando Furioso; Racine, Molière, Shakspeare, Milton.

(*Memoirs and Correspondence*, vol. ii. p. 454.)

ANONYMOUS

1817. July. QUARTERLY REVIEW. ART. III. HISTORY OF HOFER—TRANSACTIONS IN THE TYROL.

[*Inferno* xii. 4-9]

DANTE'S description of the scenery near Trent is well known; and spots of equal sublimity and grandeur are to be met with in every direction in this picturesque region.

(Vol. xvii. p. 352.)

[1] [*Inf.* xxvi. 114-16.]

[2] [Lyell notes: 'In the autumn of 1816 Mr. F. Horner, then in his thirty-eighth year, and attacked by a fatal disease, had fled from professional and parliamentary labours to pass the winter in Italy. In December he took up Dante for the first time, at Pisa, as a recreation in sickness, congenial to his powerful and undebilitated mind. In the February following he expired: so that the last of these notes were written literally in the short remaining remnant of his life, *nella vigilia de' sensi*, "in the vigil of the senses," as he has well interpreted the phrase' (pp. ccxvi-vii).]

[3] [Written within a week of his death.]

CANONICI MSS. AT OXFORD

1817. ANNALS OF THE BODLEIAN LIBRARY.

[MSS. of Dante in the Bodleian]

IN this year the large Canonici collection of MSS. was purchased from Venice. The collection was formed by Matheo Luigi Canonici, a Venetian Jesuit, who was born in 1727, and died in 1805 or 1806. Fifteen MSS. of Dante came in the Canonici collection;[1] with the exception of one (a late fifteenth-century copy) which came with the D'Orville[2] MSS. in 1805, they were the first the library possessed. This fact is worth mentioning, on account of an extraordinary story told by Girolamo Gigli, in his *Vocabolario Cateriniano*, p. cciii (a book the printing of which was commenced at Rome in 1717, but which was suppressed, by bull, before completion), that in the Bodleian Library at 'Osfolk,' there was a MS. of the *Divina Commedia*, which from being employed in enveloping a consignment of cheese (and so imported into England by a mode of conveyance said to have been usually adopted by Florentine merchants, with a view of spreading at once a knowledge of their luxuries and their literature), had become so saturated with a caseous savour as to require the constant guardianship of two traps to protect it from the voracity of mice. Hence, according to this marvellous traveller's story, the MS. went by the name of the *Book of the Mousetrap*![3]

(W. D. Macray, *Annals of the Bodleian Library*, ed. 1890, pp. 299, 301 n.)

GEORGE CRABBE

(1754-1832)

[Crabbe was born at Aldeburgh in Suffolk in 1754. After practising surgery for a time in his native place, in 1780 he went to London, where he was befriended by Edmund Burke, who persuaded Dodsley to publish Crabbe's poem the *Library* (1781). The success of this poem gave Crabbe a literary position, and shortly after, having by Burke's advice taken orders, he was appointed curate at Aldeburgh (1781), and chaplain to the Duke of Rutland (1782-5). In 1789 he was given the livings of Muston in Leicestershire and Allington in Lincolnshire, and in 1814 he was presented to the rectory of Trowbridge in Wiltshire, which he held until his death in 1832. Crabbe's earliest poem, *Inebriety*, was published (anonymously) in 1775; his latest volume, *Tales of the Hall*, appeared in 1819. In 1817 he paid a visit to London, where his poetical fame procured him a welcome at Holland House, and

[1] [These were all MSS. of the *Divina Commedia*; descriptions of them are given by Colomb de Batines in his *Bibliografia Dantesca*, ii. 264-5, and by Dr. Moore in his *Textual Criticism of the D.C.*, pp. 511-38.]

[2] [See vol. i. p. 677.]

[3] See *Notes and Queries*, I. Ser. i. 154.

attentions from Rogers, Moore, and others. On this occasion, as is recorded in his *Journal*, he made the acquaintance of Ugo Foscolo, and discoursed with him on Dante. On a subsequent visit to London in 1822 he met Scott, with whom he afterwards stayed in Edinburgh during the reception of George IV. Crabbe, says his son, 'taught himself both French and Italian, so as to read and enjoy the best authors in either language,' and he evidently had some slight acquaintance with Dante, as appears from a reference to the inscription over the Gate of Hell in Book xii of *Tales of the Hall*.]

1817. June 24. JOURNAL IN LONDON.

MR. ROGERS; his brother, and family. Mr. and Mrs. Moore, very agreeable and pleasant people. Foscolo, the Italian gentleman. Dante,[1] &c.

(*Life of Crabbe*, by his Son, ed. 1834, p. 239.)

1819. TALES OF THE HALL.

[The inscription over the gate of Hell]

How! words offend you? I have borne for years
Unheeded anguish, shed derided tears,
Felt scorn in every look, endured the stare
Of wondering fools, who never felt a care;
On me all eyes were fix'd, and I the while
Sustain'd the insult of a rival's smile.
And shall I now—entangled thus my foe,
My honest vengeance for a boy forego?
A boy forewarn'd, forarm'd! shall this be borne,
And I be cheated, Charles, and thou forsworn?
Hope not, I say, for thou mayst change as well
The sentence graven on the gates of hell—
'Here bid adieu to hope,—here hopeless beings dwell.'[2]

(Book xii. *Sir Owen Dale*, ll. 463-75, ed. 1834, vol. vii. pp. 22-3.)

JOHN BELL

(1763-1820)

[John Bell, surgeon, was born in Edinburgh in 1763. He was educated at the Edinburgh High School, and in 1786 became a Fellow of the Royal College of Surgeons, of Edinburgh, where for twenty years he was the leading operating surgeon. In 1817, his health having broken down, he went to Italy, and occupied himself with the study of Italian art. The fruits of his studies were published after his death (which took place at Rome in 1820) under the title of *Observations in Italy*.]

[1] [Presumably as a subject of conversation with Foscolo.]
[2] [*Inf.* iii. 9.]

1817-19. OBSERVATIONS IN ITALY.[1]

[Statues of Dante, Boccaccio, and Petrarch, at the gates of Florence]

THE Gallery of Florence is situated in the upper part of a vast edifice, supported in front by Doric pillars, which were formerly adorned with statues. Perhaps the Florentines more than any moderns have sought to honour and perpetuate the memories of their celebrated men. We have a list from an author, who wrote in the first year of the fifteenth century, recording the names of distinguished poets and artists, whose statues were placed at each gate in the entrance of the city, among whom Dante, Boccaccio, and Petrarch are mentioned. Time and chance have caused the destruction or removal of these honourable testimonies of departed work.

(Ed. 1825, p. 265.)

JOHN KEATS

(1795-1821)

[John Keats, whose father was a livery stableman, was born in London in October, 1795. He was educated at Enfield by John Clarke, with whose son, Charles Cowden Clarke, he formed a lifelong friendship. At school he acquired a fair knowledge of Latin, with some French, which language, as well as Italian, he studied in later life. In 1810 he was withdrawn from school and apprenticed to a surgeon; and in 1816 he was appointed a dresser at Guy's Hospital, but he shortly after abandoned the profession and devoted himself to poetry. In March, 1817, he published his first volume of poems, which was coldly received; *Endymion* was published in May, 1818, and was savagely reviewed both in *Blackwood's Magazine* and in the *Quarterly Review*; in July, 1820, he published his last volume, containing *Lamia*, *Isabella*, and other poems. In the summer of 1818 Keats went on a tour with Charles Armitage Brown through the Lakes, and up the west coast of Scotland into the Highlands as far as Inverness, whence he returned to London by sea. The fatigue and exposure of this tour, which included the ascent of Ben Nevis, severely tried Keats' strength, and aggravated a constitutional weakness, which before long developed into consumption. Being advised to try the effect of a winter in Italy, he left England in Sept. 1820 with his friend Joseph Severn for Rome, where he died a few months later (23 Feb. 1821).

Keats was indebted for such knowledge as he possessed of Dante to Cary's translation, a copy of which, in the diminutive three volume edition of 1814, he carried in the corner of his knapsack on his tour in the north in 1818.[2] Mr. H. Buxton Forman, in whose possession these little volumes now (1908) are, states[3] that the *Inferno*, besides containing the rough draft of the sonnet entitled *A Dream*, 'is marked throughout both by underlining and lines drawn in the margin, all with pen and ink,' showing that it was carefully read and studied by Keats. Neither of the other two volumes is marked, nor do any of the three contain any annotations. Lord Houghton, in his *Life and Letters of Keats*, states[4] that 'the family of George

[1] [Published posthumously in 1825, under the editorship of Bishop Sandford, of Edinburgh.]

[2] [See *Introduction*, p. xlvi.]

[3] [In a private letter to the editor of this work.]

[4] [Ed. 1867, p. 235.]

Keats in America possess a Dante covered with his brother's marginal notes and observations.' These unfortunately do not appear to have been printed. An interesting estimate of Dante by Keats is contained in a letter to Haydon, written in 1817. The influence of Dante upon Keats' poetry as a whole was but slight. It has been suggested that the attempted reconstruction of *Hyperion* in the form of a vision (as *The Fall of Hyperion*) was due to Keats' study of the *Commedia*, but this seems very doubtful.[1]]

1817. Nov. 20. LETTER TO BENJAMIN ROBERT HAYDON (from Leatherhead).

[Dante compared with Goethe]

YOU are right.[2] Dante ranks among us in somewhat of the same predicament with Goethe. Both seem vapid and uninspired to those who cannot drink of their fountains at the rocky source. But the Florentine has this advantage over the bard of Weimar: that time, which alone forms the enduring crystal, has tested by upwards of half a thousand ages the hardness of his reputation, and proved that it is not glass. The opinion of what we call the world—the contemporary world—is fallacious; but the judgment of the real world, the world of generations, must be accepted; the one is the seeming horizon, that extends a little way only; the other is the true one, which embraces the hemisphere. In this universal verdict, how few are the names, from the great flood, which may justly be catalogued with Dante? And even of these how few are not indebted to that which no genius can compass—the luck of precedency of date? He has not, indeed, left one of those universal works which exact tribute from all sympathies. There is an individuality in his imagination which makes those whose fancies run wholly in another vein, sensible only of his difficulty or his dullness. He is less to be commended than loved, and they who truly feel his charm will need no argument for their passionate fondness. With them he has attained that highest favour of an author—exemptions from those canons to which the little herd must bow. Dante, whether he has been glorified by the Germans, or derided by the French, it matters little. Consider too, how far his fame has travelled. It is true, mere wideness of reputation is nothing now-a-days, except as it is concomitant with durability. But as Horace, amid the groves of Tibur already pinfeathered in imagination, could plume himself on the prospect of being one day read beside the Rhone; let it also be remembered what a stretch it is from Arno to the Thames.

(Houghton's *Life and Letters of John Keats*, ed. 1867, pp. 49-51.)

[1] [See De Sélincourt's edition, p. 516.]

[2] [Haydon's letter to Keats, to which this is an answer, does not seem to have been preserved.]

1817. Dec. 21. ON EDMUND KEAN AS A SHAKESPEARIAN ACTOR.[1]

[Kean compared to Dante's Saladin]

Other actors are continually thinking of their sum-total effect throughout a play. Kean delivers himself up to the instant feeling, without a shadow of a thought about anything else. He feels his being as deeply as Wordsworth, or any other of our intellectual monopolists. From all his comrades he stands alone, reminding us of him, whom Dante has so finely described in his Hell:

'And sole apart retir'd, the Soldan fierce.'[2]

(*Complete Works*, ed. Forman, 1901, vol. iii. pp. 231-2.)

1818. Jan. 4. ON 'RETRIBUTION, OR THE CHIEFTAIN'S DAUGHTER,' A TRAGEDY[3] ACTED AT COVENT GARDEN THEATRE.[4]

[The names of old plays]

What exquisite names did our old dramatists christen their plays withal! The title of an old play gives us a direct taste and surmise of its inwards, as the first lines of the Paradise Lost smack of the great Poem. The names of old plays are Dantean[5] inscriptions over the gates of hell, heaven, or purgatory. Some of such enduring pathos that in these days we may not for decency utter them, 'honor dishonorable'—in these days we may but think of passion's seventh heaven, and but just mention how crystalline the third is.

(*Ibid.* vol. iii. p. 240.)

1818. April. ENDYMION: A POETIC ROMANCE.

Muse of my native land! loftiest Muse!
O first-born on the mountains! by the hues
Of heaven on the spiritual air begot:
Long didst thou sit alone in northern grot,
While yet our England was a wolfish den;
Before our forests heard the talk of men;
Before the first of Druids was a child;—
Long didst thou sit amid our regions wild
Rapt in deep prophetic solitude.
Then came an eastern voice of solemn mood:—

1 [Contributed to the *Champion.*]
2 [From Cary's translation, *Hell*, iv. 126.]
3 [By John Dillon.]
4 [Contributed to the *Champion.*]
5 [The earliest instance of this word in the *New English Dictionary* is dated 1850.]

Yet wast thou patient. Then sang forth the Nine,
Apollo's garland :—yet didst thou divine
Such home-bred glory, that they cry'd in vain,
'Come hither, Sister of the Island!' Plain
Spake fair Ausonia ; and once more she spake [1]
A higher summons :—still didst thou betake
Thee to thy native hopes. O thou hast won
A full accomplishment!

(Bk. iv. 1-18.)

1818. June 10. LETTER TO BENJAMIN BAILEY [2] (from London).

[Cary's Dante]

I am not at home, and your letter being there I cannot look it over to answer any particular—only I must say I feel that passage of Dante. If I take any book with me [3] it shall be those minute volumes of Carey,[4] for they will go into the aptest corner.

(*Works*, ed. Forman, 1901, vol. iv. p. 115.)

1818. July 22. LETTER TO BENJAMIN BAILEY (from the Isle of Mull).

You say I must study Dante—well, the only books I have with me are those 3 little volumes.[3] I read that fine passage you mention a few days ago.

(*Ibid.* vol. iv. p. 145.)

1819. April 18. LETTER TO GEORGE AND GEORGIANA KEATS (from Wentworth Place, Hampstead).

[Paolo and Francesca]

The fifth canto of Dante pleases me more and more—it is that one in which he meets with Paulo and Francesca. I had passed many days in rather a low state of mind, and in the midst of them I dreamt of being in that region of Hell. The dream was one of the most delightful enjoyments I ever had in my life. I floated about the whirling atmosphere as it is described with a beautiful figure, to whose lips mine were joined, as it seemed for an age—and in the midst of all this cold and darkness I was warm—even flowery tree-tops sprung up, and we rested on them, sometimes with the

[1] [A reference perhaps to Dante—see De Sélincourt's edition, p. 445.]
[2] [Undergraduate of Magdalen Hall, Oxford ; afterwards Archdeacon of Colombo.]
[3] [To Scotland, for which he set out at the end of the month.]
[4] [The first complete edition of Cary's Dante, published in 3 vols. 32mo ($4\frac{1}{2}$ in. × $2\frac{3}{4}$ in.) in 1814.]

lightness of a cloud, till the wind blew us away again. I tried a sonnet upon it—there are fourteen lines but nothing of what I felt in it—O that I could dream it every night—

As Hermes once took to his feathers light,
  When lulled Argus, baffled, swoon'd and slept,
So on a Delphic reed, my idle spright
  So play'd, so charm'd, so conquer'd, so bereft
The dragon-world of all its hundred eyes;
  And seeing it asleep, so fled away—
Not to pure Ida with its snow-cold skies,
  Nor unto Tempe where Jove griev'd a day;
But to that second circle of sad hell,
  Where 'mid the gust, the whirlwind, and the flaw
Of rain and hail-stones, lovers need not tell
  Their sorrows. Pale were the sweet lips I saw,
Pale were the lips I kiss'd, and fair the form
I floated with, about that melancholy storm.[1]

(*Works*, ed. Forman, 1901, vol. v. pp. 45-6.)

1819. Sept. 21. LETTER TO GEORGE KEATS (from Winchester).

[Ariosto and Dante read by Keats]

In the course of a few months I shall be as good an Italian scholar as I am a French one. I am reading Ariosto at present, not managing more than six or eight stanzas at a time. When I have done this language, so as to be able to read it tolerably well, I shall set myself to get complete in Latin, and there my learning must stop. I do not think of venturing upon Greek. I would

[1] [The sonnet is here given in its final form, as printed by Forman in vol. iii. pp. 16-18, who there supplies the following note: 'The beautiful Sonnet on a Dream seems to have been written originally in the first volume of the miniature Cary's Dante which Keats carried through Scotland in his knapsack; and it is copied with scarcely any variation in the journal-letter begun on the 14th of February. The composition should doubtless be assigned to the early part of April 1819. . . . There is a fair transcript written on one of the blank leaves at the end of the copy of *Endymion* in Sir Charles Dilke's possession. The sonnet was published over the signature "Caviare" in the *Indicator* for the 28th of June 1820. Inside the recto cover of the little *Inferno* Keats began by writing the words "Amid a thousand"; and he then seems to have turned the book round for a fresh start; for inside the verso cover he has written—

Full in the midst of bloomless hours my spright / soul
Seeing one night the dragon world asleep
Arose like Hermes. . . .

The sonnet is finally written in a cramped manner on the last end-paper, and is almost identical with the fair copy; but it shows the cancelled seventh line

But not olympus-ward to serene skies . . .

though finally agreeing with the other copy in reading "Not to pure Ida," instead of "Not unto Ida," as the *Indicator* reads. Both manuscripts read "that day" instead of "a day" in line 8.']

not go even so far if I were not persuaded of the power the knowledge of any language gives one. The fact is I like to be acquainted with foreign languages. It is, besides, a nice way of filling up intervals, &c. Also the reading of Dante is well worth the while; and in Latin there is a fund of curious literature of the Middle Ages, the works of many great men—Aretino and Sannazaro and Machiavelli.

(*Works,* ed. Forman, 1901, vol. v. pp. 120-1.)

1819. THE EVE OF ST. AGNES.

His prayer he saith, this patient, holy man;
Then takes his lamp, and riseth from his knees,
And back returneth, meagre, barefoot, wan,
Along the chapel aisle by slow degrees:
The sculptur'd dead, on each side, seem to freeze,
Emprison'd in black, purgatorial rails:
Knights, ladies, praying in dumb orat'ries,
He passeth by; and his weak spirit fails
To think how they may ache in icy hoods and mails.

(Stanza ii.)

Leigh Hunt, who printed this poem in his *London Journal* for Jan. 21, 1835, with a running commentary between the stanzas, has the following note on the above stanza: 'The germ of the thought, or something like it, is in Dante, where he speaks of the figures that perform the part of sustaining columns in architecture.[1] Keats had read Dante in Mr. Cary's translation, for which he had a great respect. He began to read him afterwards in Italian, which language he was mastering with surprising quickness. A friend of ours has a copy of Ariosto, containing admiring marks of his pen.'

(*Ibid.* vol. ii. p. 64.)

NOTES WRITTEN BY KEATS IN HIS COPY OF MILTON'S PARADISE LOST.[2]

[The opening of the *Divina Commedia*]

On the Opening.—There is always a great charm in the openings of great Poems, more particularly where the action begins—that of Dante's Hell. Of Hamlet, the first step must be heroic and full of power; and nothing can be more impressive and shaded than the commencement of the action here—

'round he throws his baleful eyes.'

(*Ibid.* vol. iii. p. 257.)

[1] [*Purg.* x. ll. 119-24, in Cary's translation.]

[2] [These notes were written by Keats in a pocket edition of *Paradise Lost* in two volumes, published in 1807, by W. and J. Deas, of High Street, Edinburgh, and now in the possession of Sir Charles Dilke (*Forman*).]

[The pathos of Dante]

On Book IV, lines 268-72.—There are two specimens of a very extraordinary beauty in the Paradise Lost; they are of a nature as far as I have read, unexampled elsewhere—they are entirely distinct from the brief pathos of Dante—and they are not to be found even in Shakespeare—these are according to the great prerogative of poetry better described in themselves than by a volume. The one is in the following—'which cost Ceres all that pain'[1]—the other is that ending 'Nor could the Muse defend her son'[2]—they appear exclusively Miltonic without the shadow of another mind ancient or modern.

(*Works*, ed. Forman, 1901, vol. iii. p. 264.)

WILLIAM SOTHEBY

(1757-1833)

[William Sotheby, poet and translator, was born in London in 1757. He was educated at Harrow, and entered the army, from which he retired on his marriage in 1780. He thereupon devoted himself to literature, which was his main pursuit for the rest of his life. In 1791 he went to reside in London, where he soon became a prominent figure in literary society, among his intimate associates being Scott, Wordsworth, Coleridge, Rogers, Byron, Moore, Southey, Hallam, Mrs. Siddons, Joanna Baillie, and Maria Edgeworth. In 1794 he was elected F.R.S. and F.S.A. In 1798 he published a translation of Wieland's 'Oberon,' which was followed in 1800 by a version of the 'Georgics.' Between 1800 and 1814 Sotheby wrote six blank verse tragedies, one of which was acted at Drury Lane, with Mrs. Siddons and Kemble in the principal parts. In 1816 he went to Italy, where he remained for nearly two years. On his return he published *Farewell to Italy*, with other poems (1818), which were recast and reissued, with additions, in 1825, and again in 1828. In the poems on Italy in these collections occur several references to Dante. In the last years of his life Sotheby completed a verse translation of the 'Iliad' (1831) and 'Odyssey' (published posthumously in 1834). He died in London in 1833.]

1818. FAREWELL TO ITALY, AND OCCASIONAL POEMS.

[Florence and Dante]

Athens of Italy! fair Arno's vale!
  Fair Arno! and the windings of her stream,
  Delightful vision of poetic dream;
Birth-place, and throne of Genius, Florence hail!

* * * *

What though the rage of mad dissension clos'd
  Thy gates against the Bard, whose chord of fire
Flam'd when the hand of Terror struck his lyre:
Yet there the laurell'd Bard of Love repos'd,
And Beauty passing o'er her brow a veil
Bow'd down her roseate cheek o'er gay Boccacio's tale.

(From *Florence*, pp. 33, 35.)

[1] [*P. L.* iv. 271.] [2] [*P. L.* vii. 32-8.]

1825. ITALY AND OTHER POEMS.

[Sculpture inspired by Dante]

I leave awhile unsought
Each statue breathing of the olden time:
Wrecks of the wonderous works that Phidias wrought,
By Homer's song inspir'd—
Here Sculpture, in his own Italian clime,
By Ariosto charm'd or Dante fired,
Fashions the shapeless marble, and beholds
Beneath him, at his touch creative, start
Life from the rock. . . .

(From *Rome*, ed. 1828, p. 53.)

[Florence and Dante]

I fondly sought, where, in what hallow'd ground
Eternally renown'd,
Where, in what tow'ring pyramid enclos'd,
Or brazen monument by Florence plac'd;
And Bonarotti grac'd,
The relics of the Tuscan Bard repos'd;
Or were it but an unadorned stone
By Dante's memory known:
Or were it but a grassy-mantled sod
O'er which a laurel grew,
And morn and eve refresh'd with drops of heav'nly dew.

In vain I sought around:
Tomb, nor funeral mound
On Florence rose, the hallow'd spot revealing:
No monumental rhyme
Beneath his native clime,
Grav'd on the votive stone a nation's feeling.
Athens of Italy! where's Dante urn?
Was thine the gate that on the Exile clos'd?
The gate that never witness'd his return?
Not on thy lap his brow in age repos'd:
Not, where his cradle rock'd, Death seal'd his eyes;
Beneath Ravenna's soil Hetruria's glory lies.

Yet—when o'er stranger earth the Exile stray'd,
His thoughts alone had rest
In the lov'd spot that first his foot had prest.
His spirit linger'd where the boy had play'd,

And join'd the counsels where the man bore part.
And could his lofty soul have stoop'd to shame,
There had the Eld in peace his breath resign'd.
But—to harsh exile with unbending mind
Went Dante, went the muse, went deathless fame,
And his pure soul, where'er the wanderer trod,
Dwelt communing with God.

What recks it that thy sons, in after age,
When centuries had seen his stranger tomb,
Revers'd the Exile's doom?
That Florence tore the record from her page,
And woo'd the remnant of his ancient race
To greet their native place?—
They may return, and in their birth-place die,
Shrouded in still obscurity.
But sooner shall the Appennine
On Arno's vale recline
And Arno's crystal current cease to flow,
Ere that again in man a Dante's genius glow.

Guard then as thy palladium, Florence! guard,
Guard as the Muse's shrine
This sacred stone,[1] sole relic of the Bard.
There, on his youthful dream, the form divine
Dawn'd, ere the beacon of relentless hate
Flam'd o'er th' unclosing gate;
And there, in after-time,
An eagle soaring in the might of youth,
Yet not unknown of fame,
From distant Thames, and the bleak northern clime,
Britannia's Milton came:
Led by the Tuscan Muse, whose wide career
Now reach'd heav'n's highest sphere,
Now fathom'd the Tartarean depth below:
Or when to earth devote,
As Love and Terror smote,
Swell'd the deep chord that ic'd the blood with fear
At Ugolino's feast, or sad and slow
Drew from the heart the tear that wept Francesca's woe.

(From *Florence*, ed. 1828, pp. 109-11.)

[1] [The so-called 'sasso di Dante.']

HENRY HALLAM

(1777-1859)

[Henry Hallam, the historian, was born in 1777 at Windsor, where his father (afterwards Dean of Bristol) was Canon. He was educated at Eton, and Christ Church, Oxford (B.A. 1799). On leaving the University he was called to the bar, and practised for some years on the Oxford circuit; but becoming possessed of independent means he abandoned the law and devoted himself to the study of history. In 1818 he published *A View of the State of Europe during the Middle Ages*, which immediately established his reputation as a historian. This was followed in 1827 by his *Constitutional History of England*, and in 1837-9 by the *Introduction to the Literature of Europe in the 15th, 16th, and 17th Centuries*. Hallam died in London in 1859. In his works on the Middle Ages and on the literature of Europe, Hallam displays a fairly close acquaintance with Dante, not only with the *Divina Commedia* and *Vita Nuova*, but also with the comparatively little known *De Vulgari Eloquentia*. His earliest work contains an interesting appreciation of Dante and of the *Commedia*.]

1818. VIEW OF THE STATE OF EUROPE DURING THE MIDDLE AGES.

[The *Divina Commedia* written in exile]

AN outrage committed at Pistoja in 1300 split the inhabitants into the parties of Bianchi and Neri; and these, spreading to Florence, created one of the most virulent divisions which annoyed that republic. In one of the changes which attended this little ramification of faction, Florence expelled a young citizen who had borne offices of magistracy, and espoused the cause of the Bianchi. Dante Alighieri retired to the courts of some Ghibelin princes, where his sublime and inventive mind, in the gloom of exile, completed that original combination of vast and extravagant conceptions with keen political satire, which has given immortality to his name, and even lustre to the petty contests of his time.

(Ed. 1855, vol. i. pp. 402-3.)

[Dante's comparison of Florence to a sick woman]

The changes of internal government and vicissitudes of success among factions were so frequent at Florence for many years after this time that she is compared by her great banished poet to one in sickness, who, unable to rest, gives herself momentary ease by continual change of posture in her bed. They did not become much less numerous after the age of Dante.

E se ben ti ricordi, e vedi il lume,
  Vedrai te somigliante a quella inferma,
  Che non può trovar posa in sù le piume,
Ma con dar volta suo dolore scherma.

Purgatorio, cant. vi.

(*Ibid.* vol. i. p. 420.)

[Dante's contrast between Florence of the olden time and that of his day]

Italy, though the better days of freedom had passed away in most of her republics, made a rapid transition from simplicity to refinement. 'In those times,' says a writer about the year 1300, speaking of the age of Frederic II., 'the manners of the Italians were rude. A man and his wife ate off the same plate. . . . The clothes of men were of leather unlined: scarcely any gold or silver was seen on their dress. . . . The portions of women were small; their dress, even after marriage, was simple. . . . But now frugality has been changed for sumptuousness; every thing exquisite is sought after in dress; gold, silver, pearls, silk, and rich furs. . . .'[1] Dante speaks of the change of manners at Florence from simplicity and virtue to refinement and dissoluteness, in terms very nearly similar to those quoted above.

Bellincion Berti vid' io andar cinto &c.[2]
Paradis. canto. xv.

See too the rest of this canto. But this is put in the mouth of Cacciaguida, the poet's ancestor, who lived in the former half of the twelfth century.

(Ed. 1855, vol. iii. pp. 342-3.)

[Dante's application of the Apocalyptic denunciations to the corruptions of Rome]

The application of the visions of the Apocalypse to the corruptions of Rome has commonly been said to have been first made by the Franciscan seceders. But it may be traced higher, and is remarkably pointed out by Dante.

Di voi pastor s' accorse 'l Vangelista
Quando colei, chi siede sovra l' acque,
Puttaneggiar co' regi a lui fu vista.
Inferno, cant. xix.

(*Ibid.* vol. iii. p. 388 note.)

[Dante's panegyrics of the Troubadours]

The great reputation acquired by the troubadours, and the panegyrics lavished on some of them by Dante and Petrarch, excited a curiosity among literary men, which has been a good deal disappointed by further acquaintance.

(*Ibid.* vol. iii. p. 435.)

[Dante's reference to the *Lingua Oil* in the *De Vulgari Eloquentia*]

The French language was employed in prose as well as in metre. Indeed it seems to have had almost an exclusive privilege in this respect. 'The language of Oil,' says Dante, in his treatise on

[1] Ricobaldus Ferrarensis.

[2] [Hallam here quotes *Par.* xv. 112-17.]

vulgar speech, 'prefers its claim to be ranked above those of Oc and Si (Provencal and Italian), on the ground that all translations or compositions in prose have been written therein, from its greater facility and grace, such as the books compiled from the Trojan and Roman stories, the delightful fables about Arthur, and many other works of history and science.' Prose e Rime di Dante, Venez. 1758, t. iv. p. 261. Dante's words, 'biblia cum Trojanorum Romanorumque gestibus compilata,' seem to bear no other meaning than what I have given. But there may be a doubt whether *biblia* is ever used except for the Scriptures; and the Italian translator renders it, 'cioè la bibbia, i fatti de i Trojani, e de i Romani.' In this case something is wrong in the original Latin, and Dante will have alluded to the translations of parts of Scripture made into French.[1]

(Ed. 1855, vol. iii. p. 441.)

[Dante's account of the dialects of Italy]

After the middle of the thirteenth century the Tuscan poets awoke to a sense of the beauties which their native language, refined from the impurities of vulgar speech could display. Dante, in his treatise De vulgari Eloquentia, reckons fourteen or fifteen dialects, spoken in different parts of Italy, all of which were debased by impure modes of expression. But the 'noble, principal, and courtly Italian idiom,' was that which belonged to every city, and seemed to belong to none, and which, if Italy had a court, would be the language of that court, p. 274, 277. Allowing for the metaphysical obscurity in which Dante chooses to envelop the subject, this might perhaps be said at present. The Florentine dialect has its peculiarities, which distinguish it from the general Italian language, though these are seldom discerned by foreigners, nor always by natives, with whom Tuscan is the proper denomination of their national tongue.

(*Ibid.* vol. iii. p. 444.)

[Dante's *Vita Nuova*]

The style of the Vita Nuova of Dante, written soon after the death of his Beatrice, which happened in 1290, is hardly distinguishable, by a foreigner, from that of Machiavel or Castiglione. Yet so recent was the adoption of this language, that the celebrated master of Dante, Brunetto Latini, had written his *Tesoro* in French; and gives as a reason for it, that it was a more agreeable and useful language than his own.

(*Ibid.* vol. iii. p. 445 note.)

[1] [Hallam's first interpretation is the correct one; there is no question of Scripture in the passage.]

[Dante and the *Divina Commedia*]

At the beginning of the next age arose a much greater genius, the true father of Italian poetry, and the first name in the literature of the middle ages. This was Dante, or Durante Alighieri, born in 1265, of a respectable family at Florence. Attached to the Guelf party, which had then obtained a final ascendency over its rival, he might justly promise himself the natural reward of talents under a free government, public trust and the esteem of his compatriots. But the Guelfs unhappily split into two factions, the Bianchi and the Neri, with the former of whom, and, as it proved, the unsuccessful side, Dante was connected. In 1300 he filled the office of one of the Priori, or chief magistrates at Florence; and having manifested in this, as was alleged, some partiality towards the Bianchi, a sentence of proscription was passed against him about two years afterwards, when it became the turn of the opposite faction to triumph. Banished from his country, and baffled in several efforts of his friends to restore their fortunes, he had no resource but at the courts of the Scalas at Verona, and other Italian princes, attaching himself in adversity to the Imperial interests, and tasting, in his own language, the bitterness of another's bread.

Tu proverai si (says Cacciaguida to him)
come sà di sale
Il pane alturi, e come è duro calle
Il scendere e 'l salir per altrui scale.
Paradiso. cant. 16.

In this state of exile he finished, if he did not commence, his great poem, the Divine Comedy; a representation of the three kingdoms of futurity, Hell, Purgatory, and Paradise, divided into one hundred cantos, and containing about 14,000 lines. He died at Ravenna in 1321.

Dante is among the very few who have created the national poetry of their country. For notwithstanding the polished elegance of some earlier Italian verse, it had been confined to amorous sentiments; and it was yet to be seen that the language could sustain, for a greater length than any existing poem except the Iliad, the varied style of narration, reasoning, and ornament. Of all writers he is the most unquestionably original. Virgil was indeed his inspiring genius, as he declares himself, and as may sometimes be perceived in his diction; but his tone is so peculiar and characteristic, that few readers would be willing at first to acknowledge any resemblance. He possessed, in an extraordinary degree, a command of language, the abuse of which led to his obscurity and licentious innovations. No poet ever excelled him in conciseness, and in the rare talent of finishing his pictures by a few bold touches; the merit of Pindar in his better hours. How prolix would the stories of Francesca or of Ugolino have become in the hands of Ariosto, or of Tasso, or of Ovid, or of Spenser! This excellence indeed is most striking in the first part of his poem. Having formed his plan so as to give an equal length to the three regions of his spiritual world, he found himself unable to vary the images of hope or beatitude, and the Paradise is a continual accumulation of descriptions, separately beautiful, but uniform and tedious. Though images derived from light and music are the most pleasing, and can be borne longer in poetry than any others, their sweetness palls upon the sense by frequent repetition, and we require the intermixture of sharper flavours. Yet there are detached passages of great excellence in this third part of Dante's poem; and even in the long theological discussions which occupy the greater proportion of its thirty-three cantos, it is impossible not to admire the enunciation of abstract positions with remarkable energy, conciseness, and sometimes perspicuity. The first twelve cantos of the Purgatory are an almost continual flow of soft and brilliant poetry. The last seven are also very splendid; but there is some heaviness in the intermediate parts. Fame has justly given the preference to the Inferno, which displays throughout a more vigorous and masterly conception; but the mind of Dante cannot be thoroughly appreciated without a perusal of his entire poem.

The most forced and unnatural turns, the most barbarous licences of idiom, are found in this poet, whose power of expression is at other times so peculiarly happy. His style is indeed generally free from those conceits of thought which discredited the other poets of his country; but no sense is too remote for a word which he finds convenient for his measure or his rhyme. It seems indeed as if he never altered a line on account of the necessity of rhyme, but forced another, or perhaps a third, into company with it. For many of his faults no sufficient excuse can be made. But it is candid to remember, that Dante, writing almost in the infancy of a language which he contributed to create, was not to anticipate that words which he borrowed from the Latin, and from the provincial dialects, would by accident, or through the timidity of later writers, lose their place in the classical idiom of Italy. If Petrarch, Bembo, and a few more, had not aimed rather at purity than copiousness, the phrases which now appear barbarous, and are at least obsolete, might have been fixed by use in poetical language.

The great characteristic excellence of Dante is elevation of sentiment, to which his compressed diction and the emphatic cadences of his measure admirably correspond. We read him, not as an amusing poet, but as a master of moral wisdom, with reverence and awe. Fresh from the deep and serious, though somewhat barren studies of philosophy, and schooled in the severer discipline of experience, he has made of his poem a mirror of his mind and life, the register of his solicitudes and sorrows, and of the speculations in which he sought to escape their recollection. The banished magistrate of Florence, the disciple of Brunetto Latini, the statesman accustomed to trace the varying fluctuations of Italian faction, is for ever before our eyes. For this reason, even the prodigal display of erudition, which in an epic poem would be entirely misplaced, increases the respect we feel for the poet, though it does not tend to the reader's gratification. Except Milton, he is much the most learned of all the great poets, and, relatively to his age, far more learned than Milton. In one so highly endowed by nature, and so consummate by instruction, we may well sympathise with a resentment which exile and poverty rendered perpetually fresh. The heart of Dante was naturally sensible, and even tender; his poetry is full of simple comparisons from rural life; and the sincerity of his early passion for Beatrice pierces through the veil of allegory which surrounds her. But the memory of his injuries pursues him into the immensity of eternal light; and, in the company of saints and angels, his unforgiving spirit darkens at the name of Florence (Paradiso, cant. 16).

This great poem was received in Italy with that enthusiastic admiration which attaches itself to works of genius only in ages too rude to listen to the envy of competitors, or the fastidiousness of critics. Almost every library in that country contains manuscript copies of the Divine Comedy, and an account of those who have abridged or commented upon it would swell to a volume. It was thrice printed in the year 1472, and at least nine times within the fifteenth century. The city of Florence in 1373, with a magnanimity which almost redeems her original injustice, appointed a public professor to read lectures upon Dante; and it was hardly less honourable to the poet's memory that the first person selected for this office was Boccaccio. The universities of Pisa and Piacenza imitated this example; but it is probable that Dante's abstruse philosophy was often more regarded in their chairs than his higher excellencies. Italy indeed, and all Europe, had reason to be proud of such a master. Since Claudian, there had been seen for nine hundred years no considerable body of poetry, except the Spanish poem of the Cid, of which no one had heard beyond the peninsula, that could be said to pass mediocrity: and we must go much further back than Claudian to find any one capable of being compared with Dante. His appearance made an epoch in the intellectual history of modern nations, and banished the discouraging suspicion which long ages of lethargy tended to excite, that nature had exhausted her fertility in the great poets of Greece and Rome. It was as if, at some of the ancient games, a stranger had appeared upon the plain, and thrown his quoit among the marks of former casts which tradition had ascribed to the demigods. But the admiration of Dante, though it gave a general impulse to the human mind, did not produce imitators. I am unaware at least of any writer, in whatever language, who can be said to have followed the steps of Dante: I mean not so much in his subject as in the character of his genius and style. His orbit is still all his own, and the track of his wheels can never be confounded with that of a rival.[1]

(Ed. 1855, vol. iii. pp. 445-9.)

1837-39. INTRODUCTION TO THE LITERATURE OF EUROPE, IN THE FIFTEENTH, SIXTEENTH, AND SEVENTEENTH CENTURIES.

[Dante and Petrarch]

No industry has hitherto retrieved so much as a few lines of real Italian till near the end of the twelfth century; and there is not much before the middle of the next. Several poets, however, whose versification is not wholly rude, appeared soon afterwards. The Divine Comedy of Dante seems to have been commenced before his exile from Florence in 1304.[2] The Italian language was much used in prose during the times of Dante and Petrarch, though very little before. Dante and Petrarch are, as it were, the morning stars of our modern literature. . . . Dante does not stand in such close connexion as Petrarch with the fifteenth century, nor had he such influence over the taste of his age. In this respect Petrarch has as much the advantage over Dante, as he was his inferior in depth of thought and creative power.

(Ed. 1864, vol. i. pp. 43-4.)

[The episode of Francesca da Rimini]

I will not dwell on the story of Francesca da Rimini, because no one perhaps is likely to dispute that a Romagnol lady in the age of Dante would be able to read the tale of Lancelot. But that romance had long been written; and other ladies doubtless had read it, and possibly had left off reading it in similar circumstances, and as little to their advantage.

(*Ibid.* vol. i. p. 54.)

[1] The source from which Dante derived the scheme and general idea of his poem has been a subject of enquiry in Italy. To his original mind one might have thought the sixth Aeneid would have sufficed. But besides several legendary visions of the 12th and 13th centuries, it seems probable that he derived hints from the Tesoretto of his master in philosophical studies, Brunetto Latini.

[2] [The correct date is 1302.]

[Dante and Petrarch pre-eminent by force of genius]

Ginguéné remarks that patronage was more indispensable in the fifteenth century than it had been in the last. Dante and Petrarch shone out by a paramount force of genius ; but the men of learning required the encouragement of power in order to excite and sustain their industry.

(Ed. 1864, vol. i. p. 104.)

[Dante and Giotto]

A style of painting appeared in the works of Giotto and his followers, rude and imperfect, according to the skilfulness of later times, but in itself pure, noble, and expressive, and well adapted to reclaim the taste from the extravagance of romance to classic simplicity. Those were ready for the love of Virgil, who had formed their sense of beauty by the figures of Giotto and the language of Dante. The subject of Dante is truly mediæval ; but his style, the clothing of poetry, bears the strongest marks of his acquaintance with antiquity.

(*Ibid.* vol. i. pp. 107-8.)

[Landino's commentary on the *Divina Commedia*]

Leonard Aretin wrote lives of Dante and Petrarch in Italian, which, according to Corniani,[1] are neither valuable for their information nor for their style. . . . Filelfo, among his voluminous productions, has an Italian commentary on Petrarch, of which Corniani speaks very slightingly. The commentary of Landino on Dante is much better esteemed, but it was not published till 1481.

(*Ibid.* vol. i. pp. 164-5.)

[Warton's analysis of the *Divina Commedia*]

A copious account of the Mirrour for Magistrates occupies the forty-eighth and three following sections of Warton's History of Poetry. In this Warton has introduced rather a long analysis of the Inferno of Dante, which he seems to have thought little known to the English public, as in that age, I believe, was the case.

(*Ibid.* vol. ii. p. 219 note.)

[Spenser surpassed by Dante alone among foreign poets]

We must not fear to assert, with the best judges of this and of former ages, that Spenser is still the third name in the poetical literature of our country, and that he has not been surpassed, except by Dante, in any other.

(*Ibid.* vol. ii. pp. 240-1.)

[1] [Giambattista Corniani, author of *I secoli della letteratura italiana dopo il suo risorgimento.* Brescia, 1804-13 ; second ed., 1818 ; third ed., 1833-4.]

[Comparison between the *Numancia* of Cervantes and the *Ugolino* of Dante]

Few, probably, would desire to read the Numancia of Cervantes a second time. But it ought to be remembered that the historical truth of this tragedy, though, as in the Ugolino of Dante, it augments the painfulness of the impression, is the legitimate apology of the author. Scenes of agony, and images of unspeakable sorrow, when idly accumulated by an inventor at his ease, as in many of our own older tragedies, and in much of modern fiction, give offenceto a reader of just taste, from their needlessly trespassing upon his sensibility. But in that which excites an abhorrence of cruelty and oppression, or which, as the Numancia, commemorates ancestral fortitude, there is a moral power, for the sake of which the sufferings of sympathy must not be flinched from.

(Ed. 1864, vol. ii. p. 261.)

[Controversy in Italy as to the merits of Dante]

Varchi, in a passage of the Ercolano, having extolled Dante even in preference to Homer, gave rise to a controversy wherein some Italian critics did not hesitate to point out the blemishes of their countryman. Bulgarini [1] was one of these. Mazzoni [2] undertook the defence of Dante in a work of considerable length, and seems to have poured out, still more abundantly than his contemporaries, a torrent of philosophical disquisition. Bulgarini replied again to him.

(*Ibid.* vol. ii. p. 306.)

[The Satan of Dante contrasted with that of Milton]

The conception of Satan is doubtless the first effort of Milton's genius. Dante could not have ventured to spare so much lustre for a ruined archangel, in an age when nothing less than horns and a tail were the orthodox creed.

(*Ibid.* vol. iv. p. 236.)

[Milton and Dante]

Milton has taken less in direct imitation from Homer than from several other poets. His favourites had rather been Sophocles and Euripides; to them he owes the structure of his blank verse, his swell and dignity of style, his grave enunciation of moral and abstract sentiment, his tone of description, neither condensed like that of Dante, nor spread out with the diffuseness of the other Italians and of Homer himself. . . .

Though Milton was abundantly conversant with Ariosto, Tasso, and Marini, we cannot say that they influenced his manner, which,

[1] [Belisario Bulgarini, *Alcune Considerazioni sopra 'l discorso di G. Mazzoni fatto in difesa della Comedia di Dante*, Siena, 1583.]

[2] [Giacopo Mazzoni, *Della Difesa della Comedia di Dante*, Cesena, 1573.]

unlike theirs, is severe and stately, never light, nor, in the sense we should apply the words to them, rapid and animated.

To Dante, however, he bears a much greater likeness. He has in common with that poet an uniform seriousness, for the brighter colouring of both is but the smile of a pensive mind, a fondness for argumentative speech, and for the same strain of argument. This indeed proceeds in part from the general similarity, the religious and even theological cast of their subjects; I advert particularly to the last part of Dante's poem. We may almost say, when we look to the resemblance of their prose writings, in the proud sense of being born for some great achievement, which breathes through the Vita Nuova, as it does through Milton's earlier treatises, that they were twin spirits, and that each might have animated the other's body, that each would, as it were, have been the other, if he had lived in the other's age. As it is, I incline to prefer Milton, that is, the Paradise Lost, both because the subject is more extensive, and because the resources of his genius are more multifarious. Dante sins more against good taste, but only perhaps because there was no good taste in his time; for Milton has also too much a disposition to make the grotesque accessory to the terrible. Could Milton have written the lines on Ugolino? Perhaps he could. Those on Francesca? Not, I think, every line. Could Dante have planned such a poem as Paradise Lost? Not certainly, being Dante in 1300; but living when Milton did, perhaps he could. It is, however, useless to go on with questions that no one can fully answer. To compare the two poets, read two or three cantos of the Purgatory or Paradise, and then two or three hundred lines of Paradise Lost. Then take Homer, or even Virgil, the difference will be striking. Yet notwithstanding this analogy of their minds, I have not perceived that Milton imitates Dante very often, probably from having committed less to memory while young (and Dante was not the favourite poet of Italy when Milton was there), than of Ariosto and Tasso.

Each of these great men chose the subject that suited his natural temper and genius. . . . Yet even as religious poets, there are several remarkable distinctions between Milton and Dante. It has been justly observed that, in the Paradise of Dante, he makes use of but three leading ideas, light, music, and motion, and that Milton has drawn heaven in less pure and spiritual colours.[1] The philosophical imagination of the former, in this third part of his poem, almost defecated from all sublunary things by long and solitary musing spiritualises all that it touches. The genius of Milton, though itself subjective, was less so than that of Dante; and he has to recount, to describe, to bring deeds and passions before the eye.

[1] *Quarterly Review*, June, 1825. [This article was by Keble; see below, p. 436.]

And two peculiar causes may be assigned for this difference in the treatment of celestial things between the Divine Comedy and the Paradise Lost; the dramatic form which Milton had originally designed to adopt, and his own theological bias towards anthropomorphism, which his posthumous treatise on religion has brought to light.

(Ed. 1864, vol. iv. pp. 237-9.)

[Milton a less exact observer than Spenser or Dante]

Milton describes visible things, and often with great powers of rendering them manifest, what the Greeks called ἐνάργεια, though seldom with so much circumstantial exactness of observation as Spenser or Dante.

(*Ibid.* vol. iv. p. 241.)

ANONYMOUS

1818. Feb. MONTHLY MAGAZINE. L'APE ITALIANA. NO. IV.—DANTE.

[The *Divina Commedia*]

THERE are certain periods in the history of every country that has arrived at a high degree of civilization, at which literature and the arts have flourished with peculiar vigour, which genius has adorned with her brightest splendours, and rendered illustrious to all succeeding ages. Such to Italy were the fourteenth and sixteenth centuries. In the first of these distinguished æras, Dante, Petrarch, and Boccaccio, rise like three mighty columns, the earliest and noblest monuments of reviving taste and learning. . . .

The brief outline of Dante's history [1] will account for, and excuse the gloomy and sarcastic spirit apparent in his poetry, which, though softened occasionally, by a tender and affecting melancholy, never brightens into the radiance of cheerfulness and joy. The scenes of the invisible world, divided, according to the Catholic faith, into the three regions of hell, purgatory, and paradise, are the subject of his great work, the Divina Commedia; and the theme was congenial to his Muse. In the awful exhibition of Divine vengeance, all the power of his genius is displayed; but, with Milton, he has failed in the attempt to give interest to the scenes of penitence and of celestial bliss, and the Purgatorio and Paradiso, like the Paradise Regained, though containing passages of great beauty, cannot be read with interest or pleasure.

The general plan of this extraordinary production is as follows:—

[1] [In the preceding paragraph a brief biographical sketch of Dante had been given.]

The poet supposes, that, at the close of the century, in Easter-week, of the year 1300, he was lost in a desert near Jerusalem, infested by beasts of strange and ferocious aspect. As he is flying from one of these, he is met by the shade of Virgil, who informs him, that the only passage out of the wilderness, lies through the shades below, whither he has a divine commission to conduct him; thus, allegorically intimating, that the contemplation of the invisible world is the only means of escaping from the fury of the passions. Encouraged by the assurance of celestial protection, Dante proceeds with his friendly guide on the awful expedition, and arrives at the portal of hell, over which he reads, in the dark characters, this appaling inscription;

'Through me the entrance lies to realms of woe!
Through me the entrance lies to endless pain!
Through me the entrance lies to gulphs below,
Where, lost to hope and heaven, the guilty weep in vain![1]
Almighty justice, wisdom, power, and love,
Ere Time began, my firm foundations laid;
Nor shall they fail when Time shall cease to move,
And all but things eternal pass away and fade.
O ye who enter here no longer hope retain!'

Confiding, however, in their divine warrant, the two poets pass the tremendous barrier, and enter the infernal shade. 'But here, says Dante, such a dismal sound of sighs and groans, and loud lamentations, met my ear, that the tears started into my eyes. Strange voices, horrid dialects, exclamations of grief, and bursts of rage, dull moans and piercing shrieks with wringing of hands, mingled in dire confusion, circulated in dismal murmurs through the starless air, like sand whirled by the wind.'[2] These mournful sounds arose from an ignoble multitude, who had lived in the world, at once without guilt and without virtue. Their punishment was of the same negative kind as their lives had been, and they suffered no other torments than those inflicted by conscience. 'Heaven, (says Virgil.) hath rejected them, lest its beauty should be tarnished by them; and hell is forbidden to receive them, lest the guilty should receive some glory from them. Disdained alike by justice and by mercy, the earth retains no memorial of them. Let us not waste our attention upon them, but behold, and pass on.'[3] . . .

Dante and his conductor first arrive at the abodes of the sages and philosophers of the heathen world, whom the Roman Church condemns to eternal punishment, because they died without baptism. Their tears and lamentations were not occasioned by any positive suffering, but by their everlasting regret of the blessed-

[1] The words are thus repeated in the original, *Inferno*, canto 3, *v.* 1 *et seq.*
[2] [*Inf.* iii. 22-30,] [3] [*Inf.* iii. 40-51.]

ness they had lost. . . . After the heroes of antiquity, the next they meet with in their descent, are those whom love has rendered criminal. 'This region is deprived of all light; it roars like the troubled sea, vexed by contending winds. An infernal hurricane incessantly whirls round the spirits, as flights of small birds are driven before the tempest.'[1] Among the number of these unfortunates, Dante finds Francesca, the daughter of his patron Guido di Polenta, who, married to Lancelot Malatesti, was detected in criminal intercourse with her brother-in-law, and killed by her husband. . . . To those who wish to know more of this affecting story, we recommend the perusal of Mr. Leigh Hunt's 'Tale of Rimini,' of which it is the subject.[2]

In the third circle, they witness the chastisement of the gluttonous and intemperate; who, stretched on putrid mire, are eternally exposed to a freezing shower. One of Dante's fellow-countrymen,[3] who is among them, is permitted for a few moments to rise and converse with him on the state of Florence. But the interval of grace soon expires, and he falls again into his former state of fetid rigidity. The epiphonema which the poet pronounces over him is, in the original, truly striking,

'Then said my guide,—He falls, to rise no more,
Till the archangel's trumpet loud shall sound;
When each shall wear his mortal dress once more,
To hear what in his ears forever shall resound.'[4]

In the fourth circle are placed the avaricious and the prodigal, who are punished together, and mutually reproach and torment each other. To these succeed the choleric, immersed in a horrible quagmire; in which miserable situation, Dante finds Filippo Argenti, another Florentine,—for the poet has not neglected the opportunity for satire, which his expedition affords him. Proceeding onwards, they arrive at the infernal metropolis surrounded by the black marshes of the Styx, and guarded by demons and furies. These grim monsters refuse them admittance, and Virgil is obliged to invoke celestial aid. The approach of the angel who is sent to enforce the divine mandate is thus described:

'Sudden there rushed across the turbid wave,
An awful sound, which made the dark shores quake,
As when some storm in Summer's heats doth rave,
And through the echoing woods its furious course doth take.
The shepherds fly, the beasts are struck with fear,
The branches crash, the leaves are scattered round,
Th' impetuous blast holds on its proud career,
And, wrapt in dusty clouds, sweeps o'er the smoking ground.'[5]

[1] [*Inf.* v. 28 ff.] [2] [See above, pp. 117-18.] [3] [Ciacco, *Inf.* vi.]

[4] 'E'l duca disse a me: Più non si desta,' &c. *Inferno, Canto* 6. *v.* 94 *et seq.*

[5] 'E già venia su per le torbid 'onde,' &c. *Inferno, Canto* 9. *v.* 64.

The gloomy portals fly open at the resistless touch of the seraph's wand; who, after a severe and haughty rebuke to his fallen brethren, again takes wing, without deigning to notice Dante or his companion: 'like one, says the poet, whose thoughts are intent on other subjects.'[1]

They now enter the dread enclosure, and find themselves in a horrible cemetery of fiery sepulchres—the mansions appointed for the sowers of heresy and discord. 'They glowed (says the narrator,) like iron just taken from the furnace; they were partly open: dismal cries proceeded from them; and, as I passed near one of them, I was thus accosted: O Tuscan, who art permitted living to traverse this city of fire, stay thy steps a moment; thy graceful accents declare the to be a native of that noble country, to which I have perhaps occasioned too many troubles.'[2] The man who thus speaks from amidst the flames is Farinata degli Uberti, the leader of the Gibeline party in Florence, the conqueror of the Guelphs at the battle of the Arbia, and the saviour of his country, which the Gibelines would have sacrificed to their own security. Farinata is one of those great characters, to which we can find a parallel only in antiquity, or in the middle ages. Master of events and of men, he appears superior even to destiny, and the torments of hell are unable to disturb his haughty indifference. He is admirably painted in the discourse which Dante has attributed to him: his whole interest is still concentrated in his country, and in his party; and the exile of the Gibelines gives him more pain than the fiery bed on which he is stretched. . . .

On a plain of burning sand, incessantly exposed to a shower of fire, Dante meets with men, who notwithstanding the degrading vices of which they are suffering the penalty; were, in other respects, worthy of his affection or esteem:—Brunetto Latino, who had been his preceptor in poetry and eloquence; Guido Guerra, Jacopo Rusticucci, and Tegghiaio Aldobrandini, the most virtuous and disinterested of the Florentine republicans of the preceding generation. 'Could I have preserved myself from the fire, (says Dante,) I would have cast myself at their feet, and Virgil would doubtless have permitted me to do so. I was born in the same country with you, cried I, your revered names are familiar to my ear, and engraven on my heart.'[3] . . .

We shall not any longer follow the poet from circle to circle, and from abyss to abyss. To render supportable the exhibition of such hideous objects, requires all the magic of his style and versification; it requires that power of description, which places the new world he has created, before the eyes of his readers. . . .

[1] [*Inf.* ix. 101-2.] [2] [*Inf.* ix. 118 ff.; x. 22 ff.] [3] [*Inf.* xvi. 46 ff.]

The general conception of the unknown world, which Dante has unveiled, is in itself grand and sublime. The empire of the dead, as described by the ancient poets, is confused, and almost incomprehensible; that of Dante presents itself with an order, a grandeur, a regularity, which strike the imagination and render it impossible to conceive of it otherwise. . . .

The *Purgatory* is in many respects, a fainter image of hell, since the same crimes are punished there by chastisement of the same nature, but which are only temporary, because the death of the sinner has been preceded by repentance. . . . The scene, therefore, is more confined, the actions slower; and, as Dante has made the Purgatorio of equal length with the other two parts of his poem, it drags on heavily. Uninteresting discourses, dreams, and visions, fill the cantos, and render the reader impatient to arrive at the end of the mysterious expedition.

After traversing the seven galleries of purgatory, Dante reaches the terrestrial Paradise, situated on the top of the mountain. He gives a description of it full of gracefulness, but which is too frequently interlarded with scholastic dissertations: here Beatrice, the woman whom he had loved, descends from heaven to meet him; and, at her approach while he is trembling in her presence, through the power of his former attachment, Virgil, who had been his companion hitherto, quits him. The poem of the Paradiso contains but few descriptions; the painter who has given such terrible pictures of hell, has not attempted to delineate heaven. After ascending from one sphere to another, which the reader quits in the same ignorance as he enters them, the poem terminates in the contemplation of the mysterious union of the persons in the godhead.

(Vol. xlv. pp. 20 ff.)

ANONYMOUS

1818. April. QUARTERLY REVIEW. ART. IX. CHILDE HAROLD'S PILGRIMAGE.

[Dante, 'the bard of Hell']

THROUGH the delightful regions of Italy the Pilgrim wanders. . . . Arqua, 'the mountain where he died,' suggests the name of Petrarch; the deserted Ferrara the name and fate of Tasso, fitly classed with Dante and Ariosto, the bards of Hell [1] and Chivalry.

(Vol. xix. p. 224.)

[1] [Byron's view of Dante as the 'bard of Hell' (*Childe Harold*, iv. 40) was characteristic of the period, when the *Inferno* was the only portion of the *Divina Commedia* which was known to English readers.]

CHARLES ARMITAGE BROWN

(1786-1842)

[Charles Armitage Brown, the friend of Keats, after spending five years (1805-10) in business in St. Petersburg, settled in London and devoted himself to literature. He made the acquaintance of Keats in 1817, and in the following year accompanied him on his tour in the north of Scotland. On their return he persuaded Keats to live with him at Wentworth Place, Hampstead, where he introduced Keats to Fanny Brawne. In 1822, shortly after the death of Keats, Brown went to Italy, where he remained until 1835. While in Italy he read widely in Italian literature, his knowledge of which is displayed in his volume on Shakespeare's Sonnets, published in 1838. An allusion to Dante occurs in one of his letters to C. W. Dilke, written during his Scotch tour with Keats in 1818. Brown went to New Zealand in 1841, and died there in the following year.]

1818. August. LETTER TO CHARLES WENTWORTH DILKE[1] (from Scotland).

['Dante's inhabitants of the Sulphur Kingdom']

WHAT shall I write about? I am resolved to send you a letter; but where is the subject? I have already stumped away on my ten toes 642 miles, and seen many fine sights, but I am puzzled to know what to make choice of. Suppose I begin with myself,—there must be a pleasure in that,—and, by way of variety, I must bring in Mr. Keats. Then, be it known, in the first place, we are in as continued a bustle as an old dowager at home—always moving—moving from one place to another, like Dante's inhabitants of the Sulphur Kingdom in search of cold ground—prosing over the map—calculating distances—packing up knapsacks, and paying bills.

(*The Papers of a Critic: selected from the writings of the late C. W. Dilke*, vol. i. p. 3.)

ANONYMOUS

1818. Dec. QUARTERLY REVIEW. ART. IX. HAZLITT'S LECTURES ON THE ENGLISH POETS.

[Dante 'the personification of blind will']

MR. HAZLITT is fond of running parallels between great poets; and his parallels have only two faults—the first, that it is generally impossible to comprehend them—the second that they are in no degree characteristic of the poets to whom they are applied. In Homer the principle of action or life is predomi-

[1] [Grandfather of Sir Charles W. Dilke.]

nant; in the Bible, the principle of faith and the idea of providence; Dante is a personification of blind will; and in Ossian we see the decay of life and the lag end of the world.

(Vol. xix. p. 430.)

JOHN CAM HOBHOUSE

(1786-1869)

[John Cam Hobhouse, son of Benjamin Hobhouse,[1] was born near Bristol in 1786. He was educated at Westminster School and Trinity College, Cambridge (B.A. 1808). On leaving Cambridge he travelled with Byron in Spain, Portugal, Greece, and Turkey. In 1815 he acted as 'best man' at Byron's wedding, and in the next year he visited Rome and Venice with Byron, and wrote the notes for Canto IV. of *Childe Harold*, which were afterwards published with the poem. In 1820 Hobhouse entered Parliament as member for Westminster. He was Secretary at War, 1832-3, and Chief Secretary for Ireland, March-April, 1833. In 1834 he was Commissioner of Woods and Forests, and President of the Board of Control, 1835-41, and 1846-52. He was created a peer as Baron Broughton de Gyfford in 1851, and died in London in 1869. Besides the notes already mentioned, Hobhouse published in 1818 *Historical Illustrations of the Fourth Canto of Childe Harold*, which, like the notes, contain sundry references to Dante.]

1818. NOTES TO THE FOURTH CANTO OF CHILDE HAROLD.[2]

[Dante and the *Divina Commedia*]

DANTE was born in Florence, in the year 1261.[3] He fought in two battles, was fourteen times ambassador, and once prior of the republic. When the party of Charles of Anjou triumphed over the Bianchi, he was absent on an embassy to Pope Boniface VIII., and was condemned to two years' banishment, and to a fine of 8000 lire; on the non-payment of which he was further punished by the sequestration of all his property. The republic, however, was not content with this satisfaction, for in 1772 was discovered in the archives at Florence a sentence in which Dante is the eleventh of a list of fifteen condemned in 1302 to be burnt alive: *Talis perveniens igne comburatur sic quod moriatur.* The pretext for this judgment was a proof of unfair barter, extortions, and illicit gains: *Baracteriarum iniquarum, extorsionum, et illicitorum lucrorum*, and with such an accusation it is not strange that Dante should have always protested his innocence, and the injustice of his fellow-citizens. His appeal to Florence was accompanied by another to the Emperor Henry; and the death of that sovereign in 1313 was the signal for a sentence

[1] [See vol. i. p. 537.]

[2] [Published with the first edition of the Fourth Canto—see Byron's dedication of this Canto to Hobhouse.]

[3] [Not 1261, but 1265.]

of irrevocable banishment. He had before lingered near Tuscany with hopes of recall; then travelled into the north of Italy, where Verona had to boast of his longest residence; and he finally settled at Ravenna, which was his ordinary but not constant abode until his death. The refusal of the Venetians to grant him a public audience, on the part of Guido Novello da Polenta, his protector, is said to have been the principal cause of this event, which happened in 1321. He was buried ('in sacra minorum aede') at Ravenna, in a handsome tomb, which was erected by Guido, restored by Bernardo Bembo in 1483, praetor for that republic which had refused to hear him, again restored by Cardinal Corsi, in 1692, and replaced by a more magnificent sepulchre, constructed in 1780 at the expense of the Cardinal Luigi Valenti Gonzaga. The offence or misfortune of Dante was an attachment to a defeated party, and, as his least favourable biographers allege against him, too great freedom of speech and haughtiness of manner. But the next age paid honours almost divine to the exile. The Florentines, having in vain and frequently attempted to recover his body, crowned his image in a church, and his picture is still one of the idols of their cathedral. They struck medals, they raised statues to him. The cities of Italy, not being able to dispute about his own birth, contended for that of his great poem, and the Florentines thought it for their honour to prove that he had finished the seventh Canto before they drove him from his native city. Fifty-one years after his death, they endowed a professorial chair for the expounding of his verses, and Boccaccio was appointed to this patriotic employment. The example was imitated by Bologna and Pisa, and the commentators, if they performed but little service to literature, augmented the veneration which beheld a sacred or moral allegory in all the images of his mystic muse. His birth and his infancy were discovered to have been distinguished above those of ordinary men: the author of the Decameron, his earliest biographer, relates that his mother was warned in a dream of the importance of her pregnancy: and it was found, by others, that at ten years of age he had manifested his precocious passion for that wisdom or theology, which, under the name of Beatrice, had been mistaken for a substantial mistress. When the Divine Comedy had been recognised as a mere mortal production, and at the distance of two centuries, when criticism and competition had sobered the judgment of the Italians, Dante was seriously declared superior to Homer;[1] and through the preference appeared to some casuists 'an heretical blasphemy worthy of the flames,' the contest was vigorously maintained for nearly fifty years. In later times

[1] By Varchi in his Ercolano. The controversy continued from 1570 to 1616.

it was made a question which of the lords of Verona could boast of having patronised him, and the jealous scepticism of one writer would not allow Ravenna the undoubted possession of his bones. Even the critical Tiraboschi was inclined to believe that the poet had foreseen and foretold one of the discoveries of Galileo.—Like the great originals of other nations, his popularity has not always maintained the same level. The last age seemed inclined to undervalue him as a model and a study: and Bettinelli one day rebuked his pupil Monti, for poring over the harsh and obsolete extravagances of the Commedia. The present generation having recovered from the Gallic idolatries of Cesarotti, has returned to the ancient worship, and the *Danteggiare* of the northern Italians is thought even indiscreet by the more moderate Tuscans. There is still much curious information relative to the life and writings of this great poet, which has not as yet been collected even by the Italians; but the celebrated Ugo Foscolo meditates to supply this defect, and it is not to be regretted that this national work has been reserved for one so devoted to his country and the cause of truth.

(*Note to Stanza* lvii. 1.)

[Dante, Petrarch, and Boccaccio]

It is satisfactory to find that all the priesthood do not resemble those of Certaldo, and that one of them who did not possess the bones of Boccaccio, would not lose the opportunity of raising a cenotaph to his memory. Bevius, canon of Padua, at the beginning of the sixteenth century, erected at Arquà, opposite to the tomb of the Laureate, a tablet, in which he associated Boccaccio to the equal honours of Dante and of Petrarch.

(*Note to Stanza* lviii. 1.)

1818. HISTORICAL ILLUSTRATIONS OF THE FOURTH CANTO OF CHILDE HAROLD: CONTAINING DISSERTATIONS ON THE RUINS OF ROME; AND AN ESSAY ON ITALIAN LITERATURE.

[' The compressed style of Dante ']

Angelo Mazza's first essay was made in the year 1764, when he translated the *Pleasures of the Imagination*,[1] and convinced the Italians that the compressed style of Dante was capable of being applied to their blank verse, which as yet was little more than a string of sonorous syllables.

(p. 362.)

[1] [By Akenside; published in 1744.]

[Parini and Dante]

Parini was not remarkable for his erudition, and knew but very little Greek. . . . His favourite Italian studies were Dante, Ariosto, and the *Aminta* of Tasso; yet he imitated none of these great writers. . . . Parini employed his whole life in carrying into practice the maxim that *poetry should be painting*; for, with the exception of Dante, the other Italian poets have only occasional pictures: all the rest is but description. Parini effected by dint of meditation that which was the natural production of the wonderful genius of Dante.

(pp. 384, 386.)

[Monti and Dante]

The beginning of one of the cantos of Monti's *Cantica in morte di Ugo Basville* reminds us of that of Dante's Ugolino:

'La bocca sollevò dal fero pasto
Quel peccator.' . . .

The difficulty of handling a cotemporary topic, was not too great for the capacity of Monti, and had he continued his Basville to the victory of Waterloo, he might have occupied, next to Dante, that place which Virgil possesses in the vicinity of Homer. The voyage of the angel with the shade of Basville is taken from that of Dante with the spirit of Virgil. The *terze rime*, a metre perfected by the father of Italian poetry, was, in the true sense of the word, ennobled ('ingentilito') by Monti. It is true that he has not the same harmonious variety, nor the same boldness of expression, nor the same loftiness of thought as are found in his model. But he is more equal, more clear, more finished in every part. . . . Dante had before called upon the islands of Capraja and Gorgona to block up the mouth of the Arno, and drown the inhabitants of Pisa, for their cruelty to the children of Ugolino; and Monti now invoked Sardinia, and told it to fly away, that the 'last of monsters' might not find even a tomb to shelter him. . . . Monti's poem, *Il Bardo della Selva Nera*, is in different metres; in blank verse, in heroical and in lyrical stanzas; a mixture which has had great success with us, but is far from agreeable to the Italians, who have been taught by Dante to run into any embarrassments rather than facilitate the art of poetry. . . . Monti, in this poem, has with his usual taste profited by the Ossian of Cesarotti and the French prose translation of Gray's Odes, and of Shakespeare. He does not read English, but he is as ardent an admirer of our great dramatist as he is of Dante. The writer has heard him pronounce his decided judgment, that the world has produced but three *poets*, properly so called: and Homer, with the two just mentioned, form his triumvirate.

(pp. 429 ff.)

CHARLES MILLS

(1788-1826)

[Charles Mills, born at Greenwich in 1788, was educated for the law, which after a few years he abandoned for literature. He was the author of a *History of Muhammedanism* (1817), *History of the Crusades* (1818), *Travels of Theodore Ducas—Italy* (1822), and *History of Chivalry* (1825). In several of these works (from which a few representative passages are given below) he displays a considerable knowledge of Dante. In the *Travels of Theodore Ducas* is inserted (vol. i. pp. 200 ff.) a lengthy analysis of the *Divina Commedia*, with extracts from the original text, accompanied sometimes by Cary's translation, sometimes by prose versions by Mills himself. Mills, who died at Southampton in 1826, was a few months before his death elected a Knight of Malta, in recognition of his tribute to the Knights in his *History of the Crusades*.]

1818. THE HISTORY OF THE CRUSADES FOR THE RECOVERY AND POSSESSION OF THE HOLY LAND.

[Dante's reference to the Crusades]

BY the negligence of the Greeks, the sepulchre of Jesus Christ had fallen into the hands of the Turks.—This was the general opinion of the world; but when the Popes became unpopular, all the odium was cast on them. Dante makes a Crusader, in the second holy war, say,

Poi seguitai lo 'mperador Currado,
Ed ei mi cinse della sua milizia;
Tanto per bene oprar gli venni in grado.
Dietro gli andai incontro alla nequizia
Di quella legge, il cui popolo usurpa
Per colpa del pastor vostra giustizia.

Del Paradiso, canto 15 [ll. 139-44].[1]

(Ed. 1822, vol. i. Chap. ix. pp. 379-80.)

1822. THE TRAVELS OF THEODORE DUCAS IN VARIOUS COUNTRIES IN EUROPE, AT THE REVIVAL OF LETTERS AND ART. PART THE FIRST. ITALY.[2]

[Beauties and defects of the *Divina Commedia*]

The Divina Commedia abounds with passages of unrivalled beauty on every subject. What can be more classical than the description of the pagan deity, Fortune, in the seventh canto of the Inferno; or the personification of Fraud in the sixteenth canto of the same book? With what truth and dignified severity he

[1] [Cary's translation is appended.]

[2] [No more was published, this first part having proved unsuccessful. The work purports to be the travels of T. Ducas of Candia, who arrived in Rome in 1514, at the age of 14, and passed 40 years in visiting the countries and cities of Europe.]

paints the avarice of the popes in the nineteenth canto. How brilliant is his opening of the second part of his poem; and how soothing and picturesque is the description of evening, in the eighth canto of that part.[1]

. . . Poetical comparisons with rural scenery abound in every description. The views of external nature which Dante has given, are particularly observable; for no Italian or Sicilian poets before his time had painted the fine scenery they lived in. There are some passages as beautiful and sublime as those I have mentioned: and, perhaps, our admiration of the Divina Commedia proceeds rather from the excellence of particular parts than from the strength of the whole. Dante's rich and energetic sentiments impress themselves on the mind. His pregnant brevity is convenient for solitary meditation and conversational quotation. The misfortune is, that we feel no interest in the story. . . . The reader feels no interest for Beatrice. She is too visionary, mystical, and allegorical to excite any sentiment in our minds. Although we are told that she grows more bright and beautiful the higher she ascends into heaven, still we affix no ideas to such seraphic charms, and cannot sympathize with a metaphysical abstraction. For the innumerable flitting shadows in the drama, our interest is equally faint. The mixture of profane and sacred characters is offensive to good taste. The legend is as much borrowed from as real history. With all Dante's endeavour to vary the punishments of hell, still there is left upon the mind only one general impression of horror and disgust. There is nothing that can raise or soften the feelings in a description of liquid pitch, boiling blood, gales of fire and snow, the mixing of the bodies of men and serpents, and the cries and shrieks of the damned. A picture of corporeal sufferings must be repulsive whether it be drawn in a sermon or a poem, by a minor friar or by Dante. Would that the author of the Inferno had described the character, the councils and the actions of the Prince of Darkness! But his description of Lucifer, his making him a beast rather than a being of intellectual energy, checks the wish. Nor do I greatly admire his account of the demons, in the twenty-first canto of the Inferno. What can be more offensive to delicacy than the conclusion of that canto?

The Purgatory is only an adumbration of the Inferno; for sinners of the same description are in both worlds. . . . The Paradise is not, I believe, often read, even by Italians themselves. The want of passion is more felt in this part of the poem than in the preceding cantos. In resolving to make, at all hazards, the third book as long as each of the others, Dante did not consider the dangers of

[1] [Mills quotes *Purg.* viii. 1-6.]

prolixity. Metaphysical and scholastic subtleties appear occasionally in the Purgatory, but they abound to satiety in the Paradise. Poetry, the language of passion, is ill calculated for discussions on the nature of angels, free will, original sin, and the mysteries of redemption. . . .

If the character of his times had led him to a happier theme, and had his learning been that of the sixteenth instead of the thirteenth century, our admiration of Dante's genius would be greater than what it is. We read the Divina Commedia as a task, and feeling that the invisible world is a subject, which even the genius of the great Florentine cannot describe, we wish that he had treated of matters purely of terrestrial interest. His religion is not the pure Gospel, his philosophy is not divine, and the awfulness of his subject should have forbidden him from making his book a political satire. But so beautiful are his rural images, so fine are his occasional paintings of the workings of passion; he is so energetic and so pathetic; his moral strain is so sublime, (except when he inculcates revenge as a sacred duty) and his satire is so keen, as to impress upon his poem a character of merit so far transcending all former attempts at rhyme in the Italian language, that we hail him as the father of his country's poetry, and apply to him his praise of Virgil,—that his fame will be co-existent with the world's duration:—

O anima cortese—
Di cui la fama ancor nel mondo dura,
E durerà quanto 'l moto lontano.[1]

(Vol. i. pp. 231-5, 237-40.)

1825. THE HISTORY OF CHIVALRY, OR KNIGHTHOOD AND ITS TIMES.

[Dante's mention of the tournament]

A chivalric taste was diffused over the manners of public and private life in Italy. The amusement of hawking, which the fathers of chivalric Italy had introduced, was indulged in at every court; and the Ferrarese princes were generally attended in the field by a hundred falconers, so proud and magnificent was their display. Every great event was celebrated by a tournament or a triumphal show. Dante speaks of the tournament as the familiar amusement of the fourteenth century.

—'e vidi gir gualdane,
Ferir torniamenti, e correr giostra.'
Inferno, c. 22.[2]

(Vol. ii. Chap. vi. p. 338.)

[1] [*Inf.* ii. 58-60.]

[2] [*Inf.* xxii. 5-6.]

JOHN GIBSON LOCKHART

(1794-1854)

[John Gibson Lockhart, best known as the son-in-law and biographer of Sir Walter Scott, was born in 1794. He was educated at Glasgow University and Balliol College, Oxford, where he took a first class in classics in 1813. After leaving Oxford he studied law in Edinburgh and became an advocate in 1816. He devoted himself, however, chiefly to literature, and was a frequent contributor to *Blackwood's Magazine*. In 1818 he made the acquaintance of Scott, whose eldest daughter he married in 1820. In 1825 he was appointed to the editorship of the *Quarterly Review*, which he held until the year before his death, which took place at Abbotsford in 1854. Lockhart was an accomplished scholar, and well read in Spanish, Italian, French, and German. Besides a *Life of Burns* (1828), and his well-known *Ancient Spanish Ballads* (1823), and *Life of Scott* (1837-8), he published anonymously in 1818 a translation of Schlegel's *Lectures on the History of Literature*, which contains interesting remarks upon Dante.[1] Lockhart's own references to Dante are few. It is recorded of him that in the last year of his life, while at Rome, he wrote a warm appreciation of the poetry of Dante, his acquaintance with whom he had been deepening under the guidance of an Italian scholar.[2]]

1818. REMARKS ON THE PERIODICAL CRITICISM OF ENGLAND.

[Goethe entitled to stand in the same class as Dante and Shakespeare]

WHEN the good and venerable Goethe told the stories of his youth to a people who all look upon him with the affectionate admiration of children, this foreigner,[3] who cannot read our language, amused his countrymen, equally ignorant as himself, with an absurd and heartless caricature of the only poet, in modern times, who is entitled to stand in the same class with Dante, Calderon, and Shakespeare.

(*Blackwood's Magazine*, March, 1818, p. 676.)

1818. LECTURES ON THE HISTORY OF LITERATURE, ANCIENT AND MODERN. FROM THE GERMAN OF FREDERICK SCHLEGEL.

[The unique character of the *Divina Commedia*]

The most rich, dignified, and inventive of all the three great old Italian poets was unquestionably Dante; whose work, comprehending within itself the whole science and knowledge of the time, the whole life of the later middle age, the whole personages and events in which the poet personally had interest; and not only all this, but also a complete description of heaven, hell, and purgatory, such as these were then conceived to be, is a production entirely

[1] [Some of Schlegel's criticisms of Dante aroused the wrath of Byron; see above, pp. 45-6.]

[2] [See Lang's *Life of Lockhart*, vol. ii. p. 403.]

[3] [The reference is to Jeffrey, editor of the *Edinburgh Review*; Lockhart was writing as a German, under the name of Baron von Lauerwinkel.]

unique, and can be ranked under no class of compositions. It is true, indeed, that many such allegorical poems were composed during the middle age, more particularly in the language of the Provencials; but these have all perished or been forgotten. Dante has towered so high above all his predecessors in this sort of writing, that both they and their works have been completely overshadowed.

(Vol. ii. pp. 4-5.)

[Estimate of Dante as a Christian poet]

As soon as the poet attempts to reveal directly the mysteries of our religion, we perceive that he has made election of a subject which is above the standard of his powers. . . . We remark the defect in Dante, the first and oldest of all great Christian poets, and it is no less frequently to be observed in the works of his later followers, Tasso, Milton, and Klopstock. By Dante himself, there is no doubt that heavenly appearances, and holy ecstasies are described in far more vivid colours, and with more true power of imagination than by any other Christian poet. But his most zealous admirers must admit, that even in him the poetry and the Christianity are not always perfectly in harmony with each other, and that his work, if it aspire to the name of a manual of doctrine and theology, must found its pretensions not upon its general scope, but upon some particular passages with which it is enriched. Although his genius was thoroughly poetical, and indulged itself with the greatest partiality in the boldest visions of imagination, it is evident that the prevailing scholastics of the day had exerted a very great power over this remarkable spirit. His singular poem is rich beyond all other example in its representations of human life. By his plan of describing the three great regions of darkness, of purification, and of light, he has found an opportunity of introducing every variety of human character, incident, and fortune; he has depicted, with equally strong and masterly touches of horror, tenderness, and enthusiasm, every situation in which the human spirit can be placed, beginning with the deepest gloom and hell and despair, and then shading away this blackness into softer sorrows, and illuminating these again with gradually brightening tints of hope, till on the summit of his picture he pours the warmest radiance of serenity and joy. Those who are able thoroughly to comprehend his spirit, and to enter into all his views and purposes, cannot fail to discover in his apparently most miscellaneous poem, the strongest unity and connection of design. It is difficult to know which are most worthy of admiration, the daring imagination which could first venture to form such a plan, or that phalanx of unparalleled powers which could accompany him steadily through its execution.

(Vol. ii. pp. 12-14.)

[Dante not a favourite with his countrymen]

He that comes properly prepared to the study of Dante, must bring with him stores of science and knowledge of the most various kinds, far beyond what is required from the reader of any other poet. To his own contemporaries, and the immediately following generation, his geography and astronomy must have been far less foreign than they are to us; his perpetual allusions to the Florentine history must also have been far less obscure, and even the philosophy of the poet was that of the age in which he lived. Yet even then it appears that his work stood in great need of a commentary; and the truth is, that at no time has the greatest and the most national of all Italian poets ever been much the favourite of his countrymen.[1]

(Vol. ii. p. 14.)

[The Ghibellinism of Dante]

There are among the poets of his own nation none who can sustain the most remote comparison with Dante either in boldness and sublimity of imagination, or in the delineation of character: none have penetrated so deeply into the Italian spirit, or depicted its mysterious workings with so forcible a pencil. The only reproach which we can find against him in regard to these things, is his perpetual Ghibellinism. This term may appear unintelligible, but not to those who are well acquainted with the age of Dante. In those later periods of the middle age, the Ghibelline party were animated by designs which aimed at nothing but the establishment of merely worldly dominion, and conducted every enterprise in which they were engaged with a spirit of pride, haughtiness, and harshness, of which if we would form an idea we must study the histories and monuments of the time. . . . The Ghibelline harshness appears in Dante in a form noble and dignified; but although it may perhaps do no injury to the outward beauty, it certainly mars in a very considerable degree the internal charm of his poetry. His chief defect is, in a word, a want of gentle feelings.[2]

(Vol. ii. pp. 15-16.)

1837. MEMOIRS OF THE LIFE OF SIR WALTER SCOTT.

[Scott introduced to Cary's Dante by Miss Seward]

In the first week of May [1807] we find Scott at Lichfield, having diverged from the great road to Scotland for the purpose of visiting Miss Seward. Her account of her old correspondent, whom

[1] [For Byron's remarks on this passage, see above, p. 45.]
[2] [For Byron's indignation on reading this statement, see above, pp. 45-6.]

till now she had never seen, was addressed to Mr. Cary, the translator of Dante.[1] . . . She relates, that she showed Scott the passage in Cary's Dante where Michael Scott occurs, and that though he admired the spirit and skill of the version, he confessed his inability to find pleasure in the Divina Commedia. 'The plan,' he said, 'appeared to him unhappy; the personal malignity and strange mode of revenge presumptuous and uninteresting.'

(Vol. ii. pp. 121-2.)

[Scott past the 'mezzo cammin' of life]

The really able lawyers of Scott's own or nearly similar standing had ere that time [1818] attained stations of judicial dignity, or were in the springtide of practice. . . . Their tables were elegantly, some of them sumptuously spread; and they lived in a pretty constant interchange of entertainments upon a large scale. . . . Among such prosperous gentlemen, like himself past the *mezzo cammin*,[2] Scott's picturesque anecdotes, rich easy humour, and gay involuntary glances of mother-wit, were, it is not difficult to suppose, appreciated above contributions of a more ambitious stamp.

(Vol. iv. p. 156.)

1843. THEODORE HOOK.

[Hook, according to Coleridge, 'as true a genius as Dante']

The first time I ever witnessed Hook's talents as an *improvisatore* was at a gay young bachelor's villa near Highgate, when the other lion was one of a very different breed, Mr. Coleridge. Much claret had been shed before the 'Ancient Mariner' proclaimed that he could swallow no more of anything, unless it were punch. The materials were forthwith produced—the bowl was planted before the poet, and as he proceeded in his concoction, Hook, unbidden, took his place at the piano. He burst into a bacchanal of egregious luxury, every line of which had reference to the author of the 'Lay Sermons' and the 'Aids to Reflection.' The room was becoming excessively hot,—the first specimen of the new compound was handed to Hook, who paused to quaff it, and then exclaiming that he was stifled, flung his glass through the window. Coleridge rose with the aspect of a benignant patriarch, and demolished another pane—the example was followed generally—the window was a sieve in an instant—the kind host was furthest from the mark, and his goblet made havoc of the chandelier. The roar of laughter was drowned in Theodore's resumption of the song—and window and chandelier and the peculiar shot of each individual destroyer had

[1] [For this letter, see vol. i. pp. 408-9.]

[2] [*Inf.* i. 1.]

apt, in many cases exquisitely witty, commemoration. In walking home with Mr. Coleridge, he entertained * * * and me with a most excellent lecture on the distinction between talent and genius, and declared that Hook was as true a genius as Dante—*that* was his example.

(*Quarterly Review*, May, 1843, pp. 65-6.)

MARY WOLLSTONECRAFT SHELLEY

(1797-1851)

[Mary Wollstonecraft, only daughter of William Godwin, was born in London in 1797. Her mother died a few days after her birth, and she was brought up by a step-mother, formerly Mrs. Clairmont. In July, 1814, she accompanied Shelley (whom she had first seen in 1812) and Jane Clairmont to Italy, and in Dec. 1816, on the death of Shelley's first wife, she was married to the poet. Soon after Shelley's death in 1822 she returned to England, but she visited Italy again in 1840-3, and wrote an account of her travels, which was published in 1844, under the title of *Rambles in Germany and Italy*. She died in London in 1851. Mrs. Shelley, as appears from her *Journal*, was a constant student of Dante during her brief married life—she records that Shelley read the *Vita Nuova* aloud to her at Pisa not long before his death; and she read and re-read the *Divina Commedia* in after days, as may be gathered from her *Rambles in Germany and Italy*, in which she frequently quotes and discusses Dante. Mrs. Shelley was the authoress of several novels, of which the best known is *Frankenstein* written in 1816 and published in 1818.]

1818. FRANKENSTEIN; OR THE MODERN PROMETHEUS.

[The monster more hideous than any conception of Dante's]

I BEHELD the wretch—the miserable monster whom I had created. . . . Oh! no mortal could support the horror of that countenance. A mummy again endued with animation could not be so hideous as that wretch. I had gazed on him while unfinished; he was ugly then; but when those muscles and joints were rendered capable of motion, it became a thing such as even Dante could not have conceived.

(Ed. 1839, Chap. v. p. 44.)

1818. April 11. JOURNAL.

[Shelley's reading of Dante]

We arrive at Como about five. Shelley has finished the 'Life of Tasso' and reads Dante.[1]

(Dowden's *Life of Shelley*, vol. ii. pp. 195-6.)

[1] [Dowden states that previous entries record that Shelley during March this year finished the *Purgatorio* and began the *Paradiso*. (*Life of Shelley*, vol. ii. p. 198.)]

1818. Sept. 5. JOURNAL.

Arrive at Este. . . . Shelley writes his drama of *Prometheus*. Read seven cantos of Dante.

(*Life and Letters of Mary Wollstonecraft Shelley*, vol. i. p. 225.)

1819. August 4. JOURNAL.

Leghorn. Since I left home I have read several books of Livy, Antenor, Clarissa Harlowe, the *Spectator*, a few novels, and am now reading the Bible, and Lucan's *Pharsalia*, and Dante. . . . Shelley reads *Paradise Lost* to me. Read two cantos of *Purgatorio*.

(Dowden's *Life of Shelley*, vol. ii. pp. 271-2.)

1819. Aug. 28. LETTER TO MRS. LEIGH HUNT (from Leghorn).

I write in the morning, read Latin till two, when we dine; then I read some English book, and two cantos of Dante with Shelley.

(*Correspondence of Leigh Hunt*, vol. i. p. 144.)

1821. January. LETTER TO CLAIRE CLAIRMONT (from Pisa).

[Medwin as a translator of Dante]

You have no idea how earnestly we desire the transfer of Medwin to Florence. In plain Italian, he is a *seccatura*.[1] He sits with us, and be one reading or writing, he insists on interrupting one every moment to read all the fine things he either writes or reads. Besides writing poetry, he translates. He intends, he says, to translate all the fine passages of Dante, and has already the canto concerning Ugolino. Now, not to say that he fills his verses with all possible commonplaces, he understands his author very imperfectly, and when he cannot make sense of the words that are he puts in words of his own, and calls it a misprint; so sometimes falsifying the historical fact, always the sense, he produces something as like Dante as a rotten crab-apple is like a fine nonpareil. For instance, those lines of Dante—but I have not time or paper for examples.

(Dowden's *Life of Shelley*, vol. ii. pp. 365-6.)

[1] [That is, a bore. Dowden quotes Medwin's own explanation—'a drying-up of all our faculties, mental and bodily.']

1821. Jan. 31. JOURNAL.

[Shelley reading the *Vita Nuova*]

Pisa.—Shelley reads the *Vita Nuova* aloud to me in the evening. Feb. 12. Finish the *Vita Nuova*.

(*Life and Letters of M. W. Shelley*, vol. i. pp. 285-6.)

1825. Jan. 2. LETTER TO MISS CURRAN.

[Taaffe's translation of Dante]

You have in Rome a Mr. Taaffe,[1] a countryman of yours, who translates Dante, and rides fine horses that perpetually throw him.

(*Ibid.* vol. ii. p. 131.)

1835. Feb. LETTER TO MRS. GISBORNE.

[Montgomery's Life of Dante]

The volume of Lardner's *Cyclopaedia*, with my *Lives*, was published on the first of this month ; it is called *Lives of Eminent Literary Men*, vol. i. The lives of Dante and Ariosto are by Mr. Montgomery,[2] the rest are mine.

(*Ibid.* vol. ii. p. 264.)

1844. RAMBLES IN GERMANY AND ITALY, IN 1840, 1842, AND 1843.

[Italy still the country of Dante, Michael Angelo, and Raphael]

Cadenabbia, Aug. 10, 1840.—The Italians are a noble race of men—a beautiful race of women ; the time must come when again they will take a high place among nations. Their habits, fostered by their governments, alone are degraded and degrading ; alter these, and the country of Dante and Michael Angelo and Raphael still exists.

(Vol. i. p. 87.)

[The calm of the *Paradiso*]

Cadenabbia, Aug. 30, 1840.—I sat long on my favourite seat. . . . My heart was elevated, purified, subdued. I prayed for peace to all ; and still the supreme Beauty brooded over me, and promised peace ; at least there where change is not, and love and enjoyment unite and are one. From such rapt moods the soul returns to earth, bearing with it the calm of Paradise :—

Quale è colui, che sognando vede, &c.[3]

(Vol. i. p. 93.)

[1] [See below, pp. 340 ff.] [2] [See below, pp. 596 ff.]
[3] [Mrs. Shelley quotes *Par.* xxxiii. 58-66.]

[The *Purgatorio* and *Paradiso* more attractive than the *Inferno*]

Cadenabbia, Sept. 7, 1840.—I have been chiefly occupied by Dante, who, so to speak, is an elemental poet; one who clothes in the magic of poetry the passions of the heart, enlightened and ennobled by piety, and who regards the objects of the visible creation with a sympathy, a veneration, otherwise only to be found in the old Greek poets. I have read the *Purgatorio* and *Paradiso*, with ever new delight. There are finer passages in the *Inferno* than can be found in the two subsequent parts; but the subject is so painful and odious, that I always feel obliged to shut the book after a page or two. The pathetic tenderness of the *Purgatorio*, on the contrary, wins its way to the heart; and again the soul is elevated and rapt by the sublime hymns to heavenly love, contained in the *Paradiso*. Nothing can be more beautiful than the closing lines, which I quoted in a late letter, which speaks of his return to earth, his mind still penetrated by the ecstacy he had lately felt.

(Vol. i. p. 96.)

[Dante's description of the Lago di Garda]

Sept. 13, 1842.—The valley of the Adige is very grand. . . . Several valleys branch off here; and there is another route to Venice. We were sorry not to see the famous Slovino di San Marco, or avalanche of stone, near Serravalle, celebrated by Dante,[1] who was for some time a guest at the Castello Lizzana; where, exiled from Florence, he was entertained by the lord of Castelbarco. . . . We got to Riva safe. It stands exactly at the head of the Lago di Garda:—

Suso in Italia bella giace un laco, &c.[2]

(Vol. ii. pp. 66-8.)

[The language of the *Divina Commedia*]

Venice, Oct. 1842.—It has been averred that the first colonists from Padua brought this dialect of the Latin with them, and that it is a remnant of the vernacular of Roman Italy. Nine centuries later, the *lingua Toscana* could scarcely be said to exist; the language of Brunetto Latini, Dante's master, being very scant and inefficient. I am told that Dante himself hesitated whether to write his *Divina Commedia* in Latin or Venetian, till fortunately he became aware that the talk of the common people of Tuscany possessed all the elements of expression; and he, collecting them with that life-giving power proper to genius, 'created a language, in itself heroic and persuasive, out of a chaos of inharmonious barbarisms.'[3]

(Vol. ii. pp. 124-5.)

[1] [*Inf.* xii. 4-9.]
[2] [Mrs. Shelley quotes *Inf.* xx. 61-6.]
[3] Shelley's *Defence of Poetry*.

[Dante's description of the Po]

Florence, Nov. 1842.—If I could, I would visit every spot mentioned in Florentine history—visit its towns of old renown; and ramble amid scenes familiar to Dante, Boccaccio, Petrarch, and Machiavelli. . . . Sometimes the Arno rises so high that it threatens a flood: on these occasions, it is watched and guarded like a wild beast, and every inch, as it rises, is proclaimed. I like to hear it, roaring and rushing in its course—

'Per aver pace co' seguaci sui,'

as Dante says of the Po[1]; and any one witnessing the turbulence of these tideless Italian rivers when swollen by rains; who views their precipitate speed, and listens to their thunder, as the mountain torrents, named by the poet their pursuers, come dashing after, to augment their fury, whoso sees this, is conscious that in this passage Dante displays his peculiar and high power of putting a sentient soul into nature, and representing it to our mind by images suggested by a quick and poetic feeling of her vitality.

(Vol. ii. pp. 134, 135.)

[Vividness of Dante's descriptions of scenery]

Vallombrosa, Nov. 1842.—Vallombrosa is situated on the verge of the mountainous region of the Casentino. . . . The rain made the scene dreary; but it ceased at last, and we mounted our ponies. The sun broke out as we descended; and the sparkling torrent murmured softly as it danced along. I hailed it with delight, as one of

'Li ruscelletti, che de' verdi colli
Del Casentin discendon giuso in Arno,
Facendo i lor canali e freddi e molli'—[2]

Verses are these that might refresh a thirsty wanderer in a hot sandy desert. There is scarcely a spot in Tuscany, and those parts of the North of Italy, which he visited, that Dante has not described in poetry that brings the very spot before your eyes, adorned with graces missed by the prosaic eye, and yet which are exact and in perfect harmony with the scene.

(Vol. ii. pp. 138, 139.)

[Discovery of Giotto's portrait of Dante—The 'restoration' of the picture approved of by Mrs. Shelley]

Florence, Jan. 1843.—One of the most interesting paintings in the world has been lately[3] discovered at Florence; the portrait of Dante, by his friend Giotto. Vasari mentions that Giotto was employed to paint the walls of the chapel of the Palace of the Podestà

[1] [*Inf.* v. 99.] [2] [*Inf.* xxx. 64-6.] [3] [July 21, 1840.]

at Florence, and that he introduced into his picture a portrait of his contemporary and dear friend, Dante Alighieri, in addition to other renowned citizens of the time. This palace has been turned to the unworthy use of a public prison, and the desecrated chapel was whitewashed, and divided into cells. These have now been demolished, and the whitewash is in process of being removed. Almost at the first the portrait of Dante was discovered: he makes one in a solemn procession, and holds a flower in his hand. Before it vanishes all the preconceived notions of the crabbed severity of his physiognomy, which have originated in portraits taken later in his life. We see here the lover of Beatrice. His lip is proud—for proud, every contemporary asserts that he was—and he himself confesses it in the *Purgatorio*; but there is sensibility, gentleness and love; the countenance breathes the spirit of the *Vita Nuova*. The common prints taken from this picture are very unworthy of it; they seem to substitute sensuality for sensibility, in the lines of the countenance. Mr. Kirkup's drawing, made for Lord Vernon, is excellent. Unfortunately, in removing the whitewash or plaster, a slight injury was done to the eye in the picture. The painter employed by the Grand Duke has restored this; but Mr. Kirkup is indignant with the restoration; and the print, taken from his drawing, exhibits the blemish. I confess, that to me the restoration seems judicious. The ball of the eye alone was injured; and as the colour of Dante's eyes was known from other pictures, the portrait has gained in expression, and not lost in authenticity by its being repainted.

(Vol. ii. pp. 158-9.)

[Dante, Petrarch, and Ariosto, untrammelled by Aristotelian rules]

Feb. 1843.—The first Italian poets never obeyed, but on the contrary resisted, Aristotelian rules. Dante, the greatest of all—Petrarch and Ariosto, abandoned themselves to the genuine impulse of their minds, and were great; great, because free.

(Vol. ii. p. 191.)

[Raphael's portrait of Dante in the 'Disputa']

Rome, April 5, 1843.—In Raffaelle's picture named the Dispute of the Sacrament . . . there is an assemblage of all the doctors of the church, and among them Raffaelle boldly placed Dante, with his laurel crown, and, still more boldly, Savonarola, who ten years before had been publicly burned at Florence as a heretic.

(Vol. ii. p. 220.)

[Dante's description of Paradise]

Rome, April 20, 1843.—It is one of the mysteries of our nature, that the feelings which most torture and subdue, yet, if idealized—

elevated by the imagination—married harmoniously to sound or colour—turn those pains to happiness; inspiring adoration; and a tremulous but ardent aspiration for immortality. Such seems the sentient link between our heavenly and terrestrial nature; and thus, in Paradise, as Dante tells, glory beatifies the sight, and seraphic harmony wraps the saints in bliss.

(Vol. ii. pp. 231-2.)

[Dante's denunciation of the temporal power of the Church]

Rome, May 3, 1843.—The papal government is considered the worst in Italy; and the temporal rule of the Church is looked upon as the chief source of the nation's misfortunes. This is no novel assertion. You may remember Dante's apostrophe:—

'Ahi, Costantin, di quanto mal fu matre,
Non la tua conversion, ma quella dote,
Che da te prese il primo ricco patre.'[1]

(Vol. ii. p. 244.)

[The poetry of Dante the offspring of northern, not southern, Italy]

Sorrento, June 1, 1843.—It seems to me as if I had never before visited Italy—as it now, for the first time, the charm of the country was revealed to me. At every moment the senses, lapped in delight, whisper—this is Paradise. Here I find the secret of Italian poetry: not of Dante; he belonged to Etruria and Cisalpine Gaul: Tuscany and Lombardy are beautiful—they are an improved France, an abundant, sunshiny England—but here only do we find another earth and sky.

(Vol. ii. p. 262.)

ABRAHAM REES

(1743-1825)

[Abraham Rees, a native of Montgomeryshire, son of a well-known Nonconformist minister, was born in 1743, and was educated for the ministry. He was resident tutor at Hoxton Academy, 1762-85, tutor in Hebrew and mathematics at Hackney College, 1786-96, and pastor to the Old Jewry Congregation in London from 1783 till his death in 1825. After re-editing Chambers' *Cyclopaedia* (1778-86), on the completion of which he was elected a Fellow of the Royal Society, Rees projected a similar work on a larger scale, which was published in 45 volumes, between 1802 and 1820, under the title of the *Cyclopaedia; or, Universal Dictionary of Arts, Sciences, and Literature*. Among the biographies in this work is a brief notice of Dante.]

[1] [*Inf.* xix. 115-17.]

1819. THE CYCLOPAEDIA; OR, UNIVERSAL DICTIONARY OF ARTS, SCIENCES, AND LITERATURE.

[Dante Alighieri]

THE fame of Dante did not depend on marble or brass: his 'Divina Commedia' has given him an unfading and immortal reputation. The subject of this work is the description of a vision in which the author is led through hell, purgatory, and paradise; it is full of extravagances, but it contains a variety of passages of singular strength and sincerity. The admirers of this poem contend that no work of Italian poetry bears such a stamp of original and sublime genius; and that in grandeur of conception, warmth of feeling, and energy of expression, no composition of modern times can compare with it. . . . Dante was a considerable writer in the Latin as well as in his own language; but his 'Commedia' is the only work to which he is indebted for celebrity.

(Vol. xi. p. 3 ff.)

SIR RICHARD COLT HOARE

(1758-1838)

[Sir Richard Colt Hoare, historian of Wiltshire, was born at Stourhead in Wiltshire in 1758. After spending some time in the family banking-house, he retired from business, and in 1785 left England for a prolonged tour on the Continent. Returning in 1787, in which year he succeeded to his father's baronetcy, he left England again in 1788 and spent three years abroad, chiefly in Italy. The fruit of his travels appeared in 1819 in the shape of *A Classical Tour through Italy and Sicily*, which was designed as a supplement to the well-known *Classical Tour* of Eustace. Besides the accounts of his foreign travels, Hoare produced the well-known *Ancient History of North and South Wiltshire* (1812-21), which was followed by the *History of Modern Wiltshire*, left incomplete at his death (1838). A reference to Dante occurs in the description of the ascent of Mt. Aetna in the *Classical Tour*.]

1819. A CLASSICAL TOUR THROUGH ITALY AND SICILY.[1]

[The crater of Aetna compared to Dante's Hell]

JOURNEY to Mount Aetna.—After observing the sun rise, and contemplating its ascent, I mounted to the *ne plus ultra*. However disappointed in my first expectation, with regard to the majestic prospect, so emphatically described by every traveller, I was most amply repaid by the spectacle now displayed

[1] [Undertaken in 1790-91; the account was written in 1815, for in a note on Elba (vol. i. p. 40) the author observes: 'This note had not been written one hour, when the escape of Buonaparte from Elba was announced to me by the London newspapers, 10th March, 1815.']

before me. It would be an impracticable task either to express my feelings, or to paint its horrors. Even the glowing colours, in which a Dante and a Milton have depicted the infernal regions of fire and tempest, would convey a very inadequate idea of the crater of Aetna. One vast unfathomable abyss, breathing forth volumes of thick smoke, was so close beneath me, that I stood within a few paces of its dreadful verge. Beyond was another infinitely greater, throwing out so dense a vapour, that its circumference, and precipitous border were seen only as through a thick fog. From hence issued a continued roar, like that of a tempestuous sea. These two gulfs are separated by a narrow ridge of rock; and above the last, towers a lofty pinnacle, the highest point of the mountain, incessantly vomiting forth a thick volume of smoke, mixed with flames.

(Vol. ii. pp. 323-4.[1])

LANSDOWNE MSS. AT THE BRITISH MUSEUM

1819. CATALOGUE OF THE LANSDOWNE MANUSCRIPTS IN THE BRITISH MUSEUM.[2]

[MS. of Dante in the Lansdowne Collection]

IN poetry, . . . two beautiful MSS. of the fifteenth century, on vellum, one containing the sonnets of Petrarch, the other the Comedia of Dante.

(p. xi.)

No. 839. folio. An Italian Volume, very neatly written on vellum towards the end of the fifteenth century, containing the three parts of Dante's Comedia, complete.[3] . . . This MS. was purchased at Dr. Askew's sale for seven guineas.

(p. 199.)

ANONYMOUS

1819. April. QUARTERLY REVIEW. ART. I. SCHLEGEL'S LECTURES ON THE HISTORY OF LITERATURE.

[Aristophanes and Dante]

IT has been remarked by W. Schlegel as one of the peculiarities of Aristophanes, that he is fond of adopting a metaphor literally, and exhibiting it in this way before the eyes of the spectators. All early literature, in fact, is fond of these associa-

[1] [Two editions of this work were issued in the same year; the first in one volume 4to, the second in two volumes 8vo.]

[2] [See under 1807 (above, p. 58.). This catalogue was compiled by Francis Douce, the antiquary, while Keeper of MSS. at the British Museum.]

[3] [See E. Moore, *Textual Criticism of the Divina Commedia*, p. 592.]

tions. We may turn to every page almost of the *Inferno* of Dante for examples. The schismatics, in the 28th Canto, who walk 'Fessi nel volto dal mento al ciuffetto,'[1] and the headless trunk,[2] which bears its head in its hand, 'Perch' i' parti' così giunte persone' occur to us at the moment.

(Vol. xxi. pp. 300-1.)

ANONYMOUS

1819. April. QUARTERLY REVIEW. ART. IV. CEMETERIES AND CATACOMBS OF PARIS.

[Unbelievers in Dante's Hell]

M. DE THURY at first named the spring which rises here the 'Spring of Oblivion,' and inscribed over it these lines of Virgil:—

'Animae quibus altera fato
Corpora debentur, Lethaei ad fluminis undam
Securos latices et longa oblivia potant.'

This inscription has very properly been changed for the most apposite text which could have been found in Scripture:—'Whosoever drinketh of this water shall thirst again: &c.' A few exceptionable inscriptions still remain; such perhaps is the mutilated verse of Dante, so fine in its proper place:—

'Lasciate ogni speranza voi chi entrate.'[3]

* * * *

. . . Some daring spirits have chosen to testify their contempt for the national church by rejecting the last of its fine services, testifying also that they rejected the Mediator and Redeemer, and died without hope like the beasts that perish. For souls like these, who would be contented with utter death, (a miserable faith, which proceeds far more frequently from the corruption of the heart than the aberration of intellect) Dante has imagined a tremendous destination—sepulchres in hell, wherein they shall be enclosed alive.[4]

(Vol. xxi. pp. 388, 396.)

[1] [*Inf.* xxviii. 33.]
[2] [Of Bertran de Born, *Inf.* xxviii. 139.]
[3] [*Inf.* iii. 9.]
[4] [*Inf.* x. 10 ff.]

ANONYMOUS

1819. April. QUARTERLY REVIEW. ART. IX. NARRATIVE AND ROMANTIC POEMS OF THE ITALIANS.

[Dante's reference to Roland]

IT has been justly observed by Mr. Merivale,[1] that there is only one authentic document of the middle ages in which we find any mention of Orlando, the Roland of the French, and in this he appears as Ruitlandus, Governor of the Marches of Brittany; yet this obscure chieftain is the Achilles of romantic poetry. Dante himself, in spite of his historical accuracy has adopted some fabulous traditions relating to this hero, and to the battle of Roncesvalles.

'Dopo la dolorosa rotta, quando
Carlomagno perdè la santa gesta,
Non sonò sì terribilmente Orlando.'[2]

* * * *

[Dante ignorant of Homer]

It is a mistake to suppose that Dante was acquainted with Homer: before his time the Italians often quoted a Latin translation of the Iliad ascribed to one Pindar, a poet of Thebes. Forty years after the death of Dante, and not till then, Homer was really translated from the original by Leontius, a learned Calabrese, who made his translation at the suggestion of Boccaccio; and Petrarca, who did not understand the Greek language himself, induced the novelist to urge the accomplishment of the task.[3] It is an error to suppose that Dante alludes to Homer in the following verses:—

'Di quel Signor de l' altissimo canto
Che sovra gli altri come aquila vola.'[4]

If these lines are read attentively, and compared with the context, and if, at the same time, the reader takes care not to look at the commentators, it will be clear that the praises of Dante are to be applied only to Virgil.[5] Dante employed a few words of Greek origin, which he found in the Latin poets. When his commentators adduce these vocables as proofs of his knowledge of Greek, they do their best to deceive the world; the contrary appears most plainly from his own confession: in quoting a passage from

[1] [In the preface to his *Orlando in Roncesvalles*—see above, pp. 190 ff.]

[2] [*Inf.* xxxi. 16-18.]

[3] [For the history of this translation, see Toynbee's *Dante Studies and Researches*, pp. 206 ff.]

[4] [*Inf.* iv. 95-6.]

[5] [Nevertheless, it is commonly held that the reference is to Homer.]

Aristotle in his Convito he acknowledges his difficulties; 'because,' as he says, 'the two Latin translations, which I use, contradict each other.'[1] And in one of his songs he states in the plainest terms that he was wholly ignorant of the Greek language.[2] The allusions which Dante makes to the Trojan war refer to events which are not related in the Iliad; and the history of the voyage of Ulysses in the twenty-sixth canto of the Inferno is wholly different from that contained in the Odyssey. Dante made use of the matter which he found in Virgil; he also consulted the apocryphal traditions of Guido delle Colonne, which served also as a text-book to Chaucer and Shakspeare.

(Vol. xxi. pp. 511, 512.)

ANONYMOUS

1819. July. QUARTERLY REVIEW. ART. VIII. HAZLITT'S SKETCHES OF PUBLIC CHARACTERS.

[Parallel between Franklin and Dante]

FRANKLIN said that he met persons in the world whom he conceived to be already placed in a state of damnation. Dante mingled with the infernal crew the spirits of some whose bodies still walked the earth;[3] and there is a convulsive agony in the view which Mr. Hazlitt takes of the peaceful security of those whom he would pull down, and of the dissolute abandonment of those from whom alone he can hope for alliance, which might induce a belief that the fiction of the poet, and the fancy of the philosopher have some foundation in reality.

(Vol. xxii. p. 159.)

GEORGE ENSOR

(1769-1843)

[George Ensor, born in Dublin in 1769, died at Ardress, co. Armagh in 1843, was educated at Trinity College, Dublin (B.A. 1790). He was the author of numerous 'advanced' political works dealing with poor-relief, reform, the English government of Ireland, &c. In his *Radical Reform* (1819) he has a reference to Dante.]

[1] [*Conv.* ii. 15, ll 59 ff.]

[2] [The poem here referred to is not now accepted as genuine. As to Dante's knowledge of Greek, see Toynbee's *Dante Studies and Researches*, pp. 102, 114.]

[3] [The reference is to *Inf.* xxxiii. 122 ff.]

1819. RADICAL REFORM, RESTORATION OF USURPED RIGHTS.

[Moderate reformers no better than Dante's neutrals]

MODERATE reform is a mere subterfuge, it is a cant of slaves and tyrants. . . . Moderation and mediocrity are twins of the same ignoble parentage. Moderate men are the neuters whom Solon punished by his laws, and whom Dante placed among unmeaning sights in the last sad receptacle of fantastic mortality.[1]

(pp. 234-5.)

WILLIAM STEWART ROSE

(1775-1843)

[William Stewart Rose, second son of George Rose, the statesman (1744-1818) was born in 1775, and was educated at Eton. Shortly after leaving school he was, together with his father, returned to Parliament for Christchurch (1796). In 1800, he resigned his seat, on being nominated by his father reading clerk of the House of Lords and clerk of private committees, which appointments he held until 1824. In 1814 Rose went abroad and settled for a time in Italy, where he devoted himself to the study of Italian literature. Subsequently he published an account of his travels in the shape of *Letters from the North of Italy*, addressed to Henry Hallam (1819), which was issued anonymously. In 1823 was published the first volume of his metrical translation of Ariosto (undertaken at the instigation of Scott, whose acquaintance he had made in London in 1803), the final volume of which appeared in 1831. He died in 1843. Rose was well read in Italian authors, and was familiar with the works of Dante, as appears from his *Letters* above mentioned, and from the notes to his Ariosto, both of which contain metrical translations of passages from the *Commedia*.]

1819. LETTERS FROM THE NORTH OF ITALY. ADDRESSED TO HENRY HALLAM, ESQ.

[Dante's taunt against Florence applied to the Emperor]

VICENZA, October 1817.—The Austrians, on recovering possession of Venice, dismissed the judges of all the principal tribunals. They then composed them of a sort of wine and water mixture of half Germans and half Venetians. They next remodelled them afresh, and cast them all German. How happily does Dante's accusation of Florence apply to this government, and how justly might one object to the Emperor,

'Ch' a mezzo Novembre
Non giunge quel che tu d' Ottobre fili.'

'The thread you spin
Scarce reaches from October to November.'[2]

(*Letter* xiv. vol. i. p. 172.)

[1] [*Inf.* iii. 34 ff.]

[2] [*Purg.* vi. 143-4.]

[Dante's guide his own imagination]

Vicenza. October 1817.—Dante chooses Virgil for a leader; but what guidance did he follow but that of his own marvellous imagination? His lights are his own, and his darkness like that of his own Purgatory is a shadow projected by himself.[1]

(*Letter* xviii. vol. i. p. 205.)

[The opening line of *Orlando Furioso* borrowed from Dante]

Vicenza. October 1817.—Instead of the opening line, as it stands at present, a folio edition of the *Orlando* (I believe the first) has the following:

'*I* donne e cavalier, l' armi, gli amori'

Now though such a construction may possibly be justifiable on the principles of philosophical grammar, it is not necessary to observe to you, that it is at least foreign to the genius of the Italian. What renders the thing more extraordinary is, that this line was clearly suggested by one in Dante; according to an after and more accurate recollection of which he appears to have refashioned it. The verse to which I allude, to be found in the 14th Canto of the *Purgatorio*, is

'Le donne e i cavalieri, gli affanni e gli agi'[2]

(*Letter* xxi. vol. i. pp. 232-3.)

[Dante's description of the sun seen through mist]

Venice. November 1817.—Whilst you in this melancholy month see

'la faccia del sol nascere ombrata,
Sì, che per temperanza di vapori,
L' occhio lo sostiene lunga fiata.'[3]

Dante.

'Whilst you behold the sun in northern sky
Rise with a washy disc so dimm'd by vapour,
That you may fix him with a fearless eye,'

we have lately had a long continuance of weather, that, according to Paley's notions, might make the happiness of an oyster, aye, even of an oyster of the bay of Naples.

(*Letter* xxvi. vol. i. p. 266.)

[Dante's use of the word *co*—His praise of the Bolognese dialect]

Venice, November 1817.—Words leave letters as we leave luggage behind us in our travels. Thus the Tuscan word *capo*, has

[1] [Canto iii. del Purgatorio [ll. 16 ff.].
[2] [*Purg.* xiv. 109.]
[3] [*Purg.* xxx. 25-7.]

lost its *p* by the time it arrives at Venice, and becomes *cao*. In its further progress to Milan, it drops its *a* and becomes *co;* in which state it may be found in the *Inferno* of *Dante* who uses the expression *in co del ponte*. . . After stating the Venetian to be the best of the dialects, I will (though I cannot venture to discriminate intermediate shades) state what I conceive to be decidedly the worst. These are the vernacular of Bologna, Genoa, and Milan. . . . It is very difficult to understand what *Dante* has said respecting the Bolognese dialect. The only supposition which can explain his encomium is, either, that it has totally changed its character, a thing which appears impossible, or that *Dante*, in his inveterate hatred to Florence, sought to exalt another city at its expense. The latter is my own belief.

(*Letter* xxxii. vol. ii. p. 13.)

[The speech of the lower orders in Italy more like Dante's language than that of the upper classes]

Venice, November 1817—Of all living inartificial tongues, the Tuscan, or (to take hold of something more palpable) the Florentine, is the most poetical and picturesque. But it is rarely that foreigners fish deep enough to find its pearls, for these are only to be collected amongst the lowest orders of the people. . . . Thus, while the gentleman drones out his common place modes of speech, the journeyman distiller talks almost in the tone of Dante, of a *silent spirit* (meaning a tasteless one,) the barber, of a razor's *cutting sweet*, and the labourer of its being *cruel cold*.

(*Letter* xxxiii. vol. ii. pp. 35, 37.)

[Voltaire, Dante, and the Southern Cross]

Venice, January 1818.—*Voltaire*, with his usual flippancy, dismisses, you will recollect, the famous passage of *Dante*, as a mere accidental coincidence with truths afterwards established; and says the poet talked metaphorically, signifying the cardinal virtues by the four stars; and spoke of purgatory, and not of a real land.[1] As to the first; *he* must have read Dante with very little attention who does not observe how often he speaks of things in a double sense; that is to say, in one real and figurative; and how accurate he was in applying his astronomical lights, according to the site in which he lays his scene. Nor was it extraordinary, that any one should at that period consider the islands in question as the actual purgatory. *Voltaire*, I believe, might have learned from the Fathers, with whom he affects so intimate an acquaintance, that Paradise occupied a certain defined situation; which is even as-

[1] [See vol. i. pp. 206-7.]

signed to it in the *mappamondo* of *Frà Mauro*. And why then should not one of the Western Islands have passed as well for the site of Purgatory, according to the notions at that time entertained? But a document indeed exists, which may throw more light on the probability of that for which I contend. *Pietro d' Abano*, a physician of celebrity, mentions in a letter, *Marco Polo's* having delineated for him what was apparently one of the four stars of *Dante*. Now this man was contemporary with the poet, who you know, made a long residence at Venice.

(*Letter* l. vol. ii. pp. 178-9.)

[A passage from Dante applied to Petrarch]

Paris, September 1818.—If we allow . . . weight to the position of *Alfieri*, who asserts that, in lyric poetry, expression is everything, *Parini* has accomplished no ordinary enterprize. But of all styles of diction, that in which this author excells is perhaps the least likely to take with foreigners. Its character is elegant simplicity. Now if it requires no common sense of the beautiful to enjoy the "numbers which Petrarch flowed in," respecting whom I might perhaps say that

"Io non soffersi molto, nè sì poco
Ch' io nol vedessi sfavillar d' intorno
Qual ferro che bollente esce del fuoco."[1]

Il Paradiso.

I gaz'd not yet so dazzled or so darkling,
But what I saw him flame and flash like steel
Snatch'd freshly from the forge, red-hot and sparkling;

it asks a yet steadier sight to distinguish the lights of *Parini*.

(*Letter* liv. vol. ii. p. 205.)

1823. ORLANDO INNAMORATO TRANSLATED INTO PROSE FROM THE ITALIAN OF FRANCESCO BERNI AND INTERSPERSED WITH EXTRACTS IN THE SAME STANZA AS THE ORIGINAL.

[Imitation of Dante]

The next extract commences with Berni's favourite figure of the barque. . . . It forms the opening of the second book. The two first lines the reader will trace to *Dante*.[2] . . .

Launched on a deeper sea, my pinnace, rear
Thy sail, prepared to plough the billows dark;
And you, ye lucid stars, by whom I steer
My feeble vessel to its destined mark,

[1] [*Par.* i. 58-60.] [2] [*Purg.* i. 1-2.]

Shine forth upon her course benign and clear,
And beam propitious on the daring barque
About to stem an ocean so profound:
While I your praises and your works resound.

(pp. xxxvi-vii.)

1823-31. THE ORLANDO FURIOSO TRANSLATED INTO ENGLISH VERSE: WITH NOTES.

[Indebtedness of Ariosto to Dante]

'Than half-clothed churl to win the cloth of red.'

Canto i. Stanza xi. line 4.

In the foot-race. Dante uses the same comparison in his Inferno, canto xv [ll. 121-4].

Poi si rivolse e parve di coloro
 Che corrono a Verona 'l drappo verde
 Per la campagna; e parve di costoro
Quegli che vince e non colui che perde.

With that he turned, and seemed as one of those
 Who race upon Verona's spacious plain
 For the green cloth; nor seemed of them who lose,
But he who the disputed prize will gain.

(Vol. i. p. 32—1823.)

'Like a lifeless body lies.'

Canto ii. Stanza lv. line 7.

Ariosto, who, like most successful poets, was a free borrower, is indebted to Dante for the original line, of which this is a translation:

E caddi come un corpo morto cade.

L'Inferno, canto v. [l. 142]

The first line, indeed, of his first stanza, so often altered, is a close parody of a verse in the Purgatorio:

Le donne e i cavalier, gli affanni e gli agi.

Il Purgatorio, canto xiv. [l. 109].

(Vol. i. p. 67—1823.)

For the beginning of stanza xxvii of canto vi the author is indebted to Dante. I cannot here agree with one of his commentators in the opinion that he has improved the image of his original by expanding it: I think, on the contrary, though Ariosto's stanza is a very pretty one, that the idea has suffered from dilation. Dante says (applying the simile also to a limb torn from a man, transformed into a tree)

Come d' un stizzo verde ch'arso sia
  Da l' un de' lati,[1] che da l' altro geme,
  E cigola per vento, che va via.
L'Inferno, canto xiii. [ll. 40-2].[2]

Where Rogero also offers, if in his power, to compensate the myrtle for the injury he had inflicted, Ariosto has followed Dante, describing the same prodigy, in his xiiith canto.

(Vol. i. pp. 210-11—1823.)

'I thought, and think, and still shall think, &c.'
Canto ix. Stanza xxiii. line 7.

The want of inflection in our tenses precluded a nearer approach to the original, of which I have sought to imitate the tone.

Io credea, e credo, e creder credo il vero;

which again is an imitation of Dante's

Io credo ch' ei credette ch' io credessi.
Inf. Canto xiii. [l. 25].

(Vol. ii. p. 120—1824.)

'When unavailing is the feeble note,
She weeps and clasps her hands in agony.'
Canto x. Stanza xxv. lines 1 and 2.

Defoe, the true observer of nature, remarks, that every nation has its peculiar sound indicative of pain and grief, and, it may be added, that different ages have also different signs for expressing their emotions, which symbols appear to be purely conventional. Thus clapping of the hands, now a sign of pleasure and approbation, has been used as expressive of pain; and we read in Dante,

Diverse lingue, orribili favelle,
  Parole di dolore, accenti d' ira
  Voci alte e fioche e suon di man con elle.
Infern. 3, ver. 25-28.

(Vol. ii. pp. 173-4—1824.)

[Dante's reference to the Donation of Constantine]

It is hardly necessary to observe, that when Constantine transferred the seat of empire to Constantinople, the riches left by him formed the endowment of the Latin Church. Ariosto is here (Canto xvii. Stanza lxxviii) evidently indulging in one of his quiet sneers; for, though a catholic, he was no more a papist than Dante, who has recorded his sentiments in the famous

[1] [Read *capi.*]

[2] [Cary's translation is appended.]

Ahi! Costantin, di quanto mal fu madre
  Non tua conversion, ma quella dote,
  Che da te prese il primo ricco padre![1]

Ah! Constantine, how bitterly we rue,
  Not thy conversion, but that evil dower,
Which erst from thee the first rich father drew!

(Vol. iii. p. 239—1825.)

[The use of allegory by Virgil, Dante, Ariosto, &c.]

It is curious to observe the different means by which great poets work in a successful experiment. Virgil calling up a phantom, purely allegorical, as Fame, only shows her for an instant, lest we should detect her visionary character. Ariosto dresses up his fantastic personages with care, surrounds them with circumstance, and ventures to detain them on the stage, till by dint of gazing on them we almost believe them to be real. In this he imitated Boiardo, and Boiardo Dante, who has so *embodied* his allegorical phantoms as often to deceive his commentators. Dante again imitated Alphonso of Castile and Brunetto Latini, in their respective poems of the *Tesoro* and *Tesoretto*. Such was the descent of Italian allegory.

(Vol. iii. p. 310—1825.)

[Ariosto's imitations of Dante]

He hurries with such speed, that not with more
  The lizard darts at noon across the way.
    Canto xviii. Stanza xxxvi. lines 5 and 6.

So Dante in canto xxv of the Inferno:

Come il ramarro sotto la gran fersa
  Dei dì canicular, cangiando siepe
  Folgore par, se la via attraversa.[2]

The lizard so, beneath the burning ray
  Of the fierce dog-star, changing hedge for hedge,
Seems lightning, if he dart across the way.

(Vol. iii. p. 311—1825.)

'Him humbly underneath the hips embraced.'
    Canto xviii. Stanza lxix. line 4.

In the original,

E sotto l' anche ed umile abbracciollo.

So in Dante,

E umilmente ritornò ver lui,
E abbracciollo, ove il minor s' appiglia.[3]

[1] [*Inf.* xix. 115-17.] [2] [*Inf.* xxv. 79-81.] [3] [*Purg.* vii. 14-15.]

This servile sort of salutation is said to have originated in the Greek empire. It certainly exists at present in the country which was its seat; and I well remember that, riding in the neighbourhood of Constantinople, I had my thigh embraced by a Greek beggar, on whom I had bestowed three or four paras.

(Vol. iii. p. 312.)

[The allegory of the wolf in the *Inferno*]

One simple explanation of the figure will no more satisfactorily illustrate this typical monster [the 'Cruel Beast' in Canto xxvi. Stanza xxxi], than one simple explanation would unriddle the Beast in the Revelations, or those in the *Inferno*, whose significations the Signor Rossetti has so ingeniously interpreted. (Of which Dante says:—

E una lupa, che di tutte brame
Sembiava carca con la sua magrezza,
E molte genti fè già viver grame.
Inferno, Canto i.)[1]

(Vol. v. pp. 94-5—1827.)

[Strictness of Dante and Petrarch in the matter of rhyme]

An injustice committed by English critics is, that while in criticising foreign poetry, they take false views of its licences, they seem to have no notion whatever of its rigors. Thus an English versifier does not scruple to employ the same word, used in the same sense, as a rhyme, often within two lines of its first occurrence. On the other hand, so little latitude is permitted to the Italian, except in long poems, that I doubt whether there is any instance of the same word being repeated as a rhyme in any canto of Dante,[2] or canzone of Petrarch.

(Vol. v. p. 153—1827.)

[Conceit borrowed by Ariosto from Dante]

'Dating from the incarnate word, the year
Shall marked by men with M and D appear.'
Canto xxxv. Stanza iv. lines 7 and 8.

In the original:

Che col M e col D fosse notato
L' anno corrente dal verbo incarnato.

Mr. Hoole supposes these lines to have been taken from the Paradiso, canto xix. verse 129, and so they probably were. If so,

[1] [*Inf.* i. 49-51. Hayley's rendering is appended.]

[2] [Rose, of course, intended to exclude such instances as the repetition in rhyme of *Cristo* (*Par.* xiv. 104, 106, 108; xix. 104, 106, 108), *ammenda* (*Purg.* xx. 65, 67, 69), &c.]

however, we must admit that Ariosto has given us the husk without the kernel of Dante. The lines are,

> Vedrassi al ciotto di Gerusalemme
> Segnata con un *I* la sua bontate,
> Quando il contrario segnerà un *Emme*;

and are thus spiritedly given by Mr. Carey[1]:

> The lame one[2] of Jerusalem shall see
> A unit for his virtue, for his vices
> No less a mark than millions.

(Vol. vi. p. 219—1828.)

WILLIAM CLARKE

(fl. 1810)

1819. REPERTORIUM BIBLIOGRAPHICUM; OR, SOME ACCOUNT OF THE MOST CELEBRATED BRITISH LIBRARIES.

[In this work Clarke registers the following Dante items, which include four MSS.; and nineteen fifteenth century copies of the *Divina Commedia*, viz. five of the Foligno edition, 1472 (*editio princeps*); two of Venice, 1477; two of Milan, 1478; and ten of Florence, 1481; which are distributed as follows:—

British Museum: Florence, 1481 (with nine plates).
Bodleian Library: Venice, 1477; Florence, 1481 (with three plates).
Hunterian Museum at Glasgow: Venice, 1477.
King's Library: Foligno, 1472; Milan, 1478 (on vellum); Florence, 1481.
Duke of Devonshire: Foligno, 1472.
Marquis of Douglas and Clydesdale: Florence, 1481.
Thomas Grenville: Florence, 1481.
George Hibbert: Florence, 1481 (with seventeen plates).
Duke of Marlborough at Blenheim: Foligno, 1472.
Earl of Pembroke at Wilton: Foligno, 1472.
Sir Mark Masterman Sykes[3] at Sledmere: Foligno, 1472; Florence, 1481.
Roger Wilbraham: Milan, 1478.
James Edwards:[4] Florence, 1481 (with plate of Hell from the Campo Santo at Pisa).
William Roscoe: Florence, 1481 (with two plates, and a drawing by Botticelli).[5]

Other items are:—

William Beckford at Fonthill:[6] MS., with illuminations, of a French translation of the *Paradiso*.
Marquis of Douglas and Clydesdale: MS., with miniatures, of the *Divina Commedia* (Saec. xiv); MS. (incomplete), of the *Commedia*, with 88 original designs attributed to Botticelli.
Earl Spencer at Althorp: *Commedia*, Aldus, 1502 (on vellum).
Thomas Allen: MS., with miniatures, of a French translation of the *Paradiso*.
William Roscoe: *Commedia*, Venice, 1564 (with the woodcuts illuminated).
John Duke of Roxburghe: *Convivio*, Florence, 1490 (*editio princeps*).[7]]

[1] [*Sic.*]
[2] [Cary wrote 'The halter.']
[3] [Third Baronet (1771-1823); his library was sold in 1824 for nearly £10,000.]
[4] [Bookseller and bibliographer (1757-1816).]
[5] [Sold in 1816; see vol. i. p. 532.]
[6] [The account of Beckford's library was written by himself.]
[7] [Sold in 1812, for £7 12s.]

FRANCES BUNSEN

(1791-1876)

[Frances Bunsen, wife of Baron Christian Bunsen, was the eldest daughter of Benjamin Waddington. She was born in 1791, and in 1816 accompanied her parents to Rome, where, in the following year she was married to Bunsen, then Secretary of the Prussian Legation at Rome. She lived abroad for more than twenty years, until 1841, when Bunsen was appointed Ambassador to England, which post he held until 1854. After his death in 1860, Baroness Bunsen went to reside at Carlsruhe, where she died in 1876. In a letter to her mother, published in her *Life and Letters*, she records an interesting remark of Thirlwall's on the subject of the *Divina Commedia*.]

1819. March 16. LETTER TO MRS. WADDINGTON[1] (from Rome).

[Thirlwall's preference of the *Paradiso* to the *Inferno* and *Purgatorio*]

MR. THIRLWALL[2] speaks of Dante in a manner that would seem to prove a thorough taste for his poetry, as well as that he has really and truly studied it; for he said to me that he thought no person who had taken the trouble to understand the whole of the *Divina Commedia* would doubt about preferring the *Paradiso* to the two preceding parts,[3] an opinion in which I thoroughly agree.

(*Life and Letters of Baroness Bunsen*, ed. A. J. C. Hare, vol. i. p. 138.)

ENGLISH EDITIONS OF THE *DIVINA COMMEDIA*

1819. LA DIVINA COMMEDIA DI DANTE. NUOVA EDIZIONE CORRETTA DA S. E. PETRONJ. LONDRA. 3 VOLS. 16MO.

[Printed by Schulze and Dean; published by James Bain. Prefixed to the first volume is a brief historical notice of Dante. This is the third edition of the *Commedia* printed and published in England (the two previous editions were issued in 1808).]

1819-20. LA DIVINA COMMEDIA DI DANTE ALIGHIERI, ILLUSTRATA DI NOTE DA ROMUALDO ZOTTI. SECONDA EDIZIONE DI NUOVE OSSERVAZIONI ACCRESCIUTA E MIGLIORATA. LONDRA. 3 VOLS. 12MO.

['Presso di R. Zotti, 16 Broad Street, Golden Square.' The first volume is dated 1819, the second and third, 1820. This, which is a new issue, with the notes recast, of Zotti's edition of 1808 (see above, p. 68), is the fourth edition of the *Commedia* printed and published in England (previous editions were issued in 1808 and 1819).]

[1] [Her mother.]

[2] [Connop Thirlwall (afterwards Bishop of St. David's); he had come to Rome with an introduction to Me. Bunsen, whose husband was Secretary of the Prussian Legation there. (See below, pp. 654, 655).]

[3] [In a note in *Old Friends at Cambridge* (p. 97), J. Willis Clark observes: 'An old friend of Bishop Thirlwall informs us that he retained his preference for the *Paradiso* in after years.']

LORD GRENVILLE

(1759-1834)

[William Wyndham Grenville, youngest son of George Grenville, born in 1759, was educated at Eton, and Christ Chruch, Oxford (B.A. 1780), when he gained the Chancellor's prize for Latin verse in 1779. After filling various public offices, including the Speakership of the House of Commons (Jan.-June, 1789), in 1790 he was created Baron Grenville. He was Prime Minister in the administration of 'All the Talents' (1806-7), and in 1823 retired from public life to Dropmore, where he died in 1834. Grenville was a reader of Dante. A rendering by him of *Inferno* i. 79-84, was preserved by Samuel Rogers in his *Commonplace Book*. Rogers produced the lines at a party at Bowood in 1823, to the surprise of those present, writes Moore in his *Diary*,[1] 'who seemed to agree that Grenville was one of the least poetical men they could point out. The verses were a paraphrastic translation of the lines at the beginning of the *Inferno*, "O degli altri poeti onore e lume," and very spiritedly done'. In his *Nugae Metricae*, issued privately in 1824, Grenville printed a version of *Paradiso* xvii. 55-60 in Latin Elegiacs.]

c. 1820. FROM DANTE.[2]

THOU art that Virgil, thou that fountain head
Whence the rich stream of eloquence has spread
From age to age its pure and ample tide;
And by the zeal and love I ever bore
For thee, thy volumes, and thy sacred lore
Glory and light of those famed bards of yore,
Through all my studious course be Thou my guide.

(Printed in Clayden's *Rogers and his Contemporaries*, vol. i. p. 364.)

1824. NUGAE METRICAE.[3]

Dante

Tu lascerai ogni cosa diletta
Piu caramente, e questo e quello strale
Che l' arco del esilio pria saetta;
Tu proverai come si sa di sale
Il pane altrui, e come e duro calle
Lo scendere e' l salir per altrui scale.[4]

Hinc ego cuncta, mihi fuerant quae cara, reliqui;
Hoc primo exilium vulnere corda ferit;
Hinc didici, quam sunt [5] tardi ingratique saporis,
Quas dat supplicibus mensa aliena dapes,
Quique Larem alterius miser et peregrina fatigat
Limina, quam tristes itque reditque vias.[6]

(No. xvii. *Exul Gallicus*, p. 47.)

[1] [See above, p. 20.] [2] [*Inf.* i. 79-80, 81-4—see prefatory note, above.]
[3] [Privately printed.]
[4] [*Par.* xvii. 55-60. The text is reproduced as printed by Grenville.]
[5] [In the presentation copy from Lord Grenville to Thomas Dyke Acland (1831) this is altered in MS. to *sint*.]
[6] [In T. D. Acland's copy altered in MS. to 'Quique Larem alterius peregrinaque limina quaerit Quam tristes redeat semper, eatque vias.']

WILLIAM ARCHIBALD CADELL

(1775-1855)

[William Archibald Cadell, traveller and mathematician, son of an ironmaster, was born at Carron Park, near Falkirk, in 1775. He was educated at Edinburgh University, and joined the Scottish bar, but did not practise, his taste being for scientific and antiquarian research, which he pursued at home and abroad. He was elected a Fellow of the Royal Society, at the instance of Sir Joseph Banks, in 1810. While travelling on the Continent during the war with France he was taken prisoner, and was detained for several years. In 1820 he published an account of his *Journey in Carniola, Italy, and France, in the years* 1817, 1818, in which he makes several references to Dante, and quotes the *De Vulgari Eloquentia*. He died in Edinburgh in 1855.]

1820. A JOURNEY IN CARNIOLA, ITALY, AND FRANCE, IN THE YEARS 1817, 1818.

[Dante and Giotto]

FLORENCE.—An old picture by Orcagna,[1] representing Dante in a Garden, serves as a memorial of that great poet in the cathedral of this his native city. His body lies at Ravenna, where a monument is erected over his grave. Near the entrance, and within the church, is a monument in memory of Giotto, the most distinguished of the early Florentine painters, and architect of the Campanile, adjacent to the cathedral. He was the friend of Dante, and is spoken of as a great painter by his contemporaries and countrymen, Petrarch and Boccaccio.

(Vol. i. Chap. iv. pp. 152-3.)

[Dante and the Italian language]

The Italian used by good writers, and in the conversation of the better classes, is called by Dante *Volgare Illustre*.[2] This book and conversation language was founded upon the Tuscan dialect, because the principal authors, at the revival of letters, Dante, Petrarch, and Bocaccio, were natives of Florence. After Dante's time, therefore, it was called Tuscan, lingua Toscana or Fiorentina. The great reputation of the writings of these three authors occasioned their language to be generally adopted, and in particular the extensive circulation of the Decameron, or Tales of Bocaccio.

(*Ibid.* pp. 232-3.)

[1] [Not by Orcagna, but by Domenico di Michelino.]

[2] See Dante de Vulgari Eloquio, Paris, 1572 [1577] a work in which the author enumerates fourteen different dialects of Italian, which are very much altered by political changes and other causes since his time. Some of them have become less coarse. The Neapolitan is the least changed.

[Dante's tomb]

Ravenna.—*Tomb and Monument of Dante.*—On the outside wall of a church, and facing the street, is the monument in memory of Dante, adorned by Bembo the Venetian praetor or governor of Ravenna in 1483. The inscription on the monument is as follows:—

Jura monarchiae, superos, phlegetonta lacusque,[1] &c.

* * * *

The Florentines several times requested leave to remove the remains of Dante from Ravenna to Florence, but without success; and they had the intention of erecting a monument at his memory. The only public monument that exists of Dante at this day in Florence is the picture by Orcagna,[2] in the cathedral of Santa Maria del Fiore, in which the portrait of Dante is at full length, and surrounded by a landscape.

(Vol. ii. Chap. vii. pp. 40-1.)

PETER BAYLEY

(c. 1778-1823)

[Peter Bayley, son of a solicitor at Nantwich, was born about 1778. He was educated at Rugby and Merton College, Oxford, and was called to the bar, but neglected his profession for music and literature, and at last found himself in prison for debt. He died in 1823. Besides a volume of poems (1803), Bayley published in 1820 and 1821 under the pseudonym of 'Giorgione di Castel Chiuso,' two series of *Sketches from St. George's Fields* in verse, in which he introduced sundry quotations from the *Inferno*.]

1820. SKETCHES FROM ST. GEORGE'S FIELDS. BY GIORGIONE DI CASTEL CHIUSO.

[Motto on Title-Page]

ALL hope abandon ye who enter here.—Cary's Dante.

[Simile from *Inferno* ii. 130 ff.]

Now down those steps, as easy of descent
As was the Avernian entrance, Belcour went,
As easy of descent, as hard to scale
As was the way from that dark world of bale.
Those scoffing fiends were still about the door,
And still their mirth indignantly he bore;

[1] [For this epitaph (which Cadell prints in full), see under Fynes Moryson, vol. i. p. 91.]
[2] [See note on previous page.]

But soon advancing, Ranger met his way
His leader and adviser for the day.
Not with more grateful gladness by his side
Great Alighieri saw his Mantuan guide,
When through the regions of eternal woe
His round of terror he prepared to go,[1]
Than Belcour felt, as eagerly he flew
To meet his friend, to him and breakfast true.

(*Part* ii. ll. 54-69, pp. 40-1.)

[Reminiscence of *Inferno* iii. 25-8]

The tumult swells, and rage, and hate
And blows are mingled in the fierce debate,
The clangor[2] of resounding hands, and cries.
And words obscene, and frightful blasphemies,
Threats and revilings, execrations dire
And all the coarseness of the lowest ire;
In divers tongues the clamorous shouts rebound,
And spacious galleries tremble to the sound.

(*Ibid.* ll. 144-53, p. 46.)

1821. SKETCHES FROM ST. GEORGE'S FIELDS. SECOND SERIES. BY GIORGIONE DI CASTEL CHIUSO.

[Motto on Title-Page]

Lassat' ogni speranza, voi che 'ntrate. *Dante.*

[Paraphrase of *Inferno* iii. 109-12]

And I have bowed me to the power divine
And forceful spells of the great Florentine;
And seen with him the fierce-eyed demon's oar[3]
Brandished on that discomfortable shore,
Where wailing ghosts the fated bark receives,
That shivering crowd the brink, countless as autumn's leaves.

(*Introduction*, ll. 50-5, p. 4.)

[1] [*Inf.* ii. 130 ff.]

[2] Diverse lingue; horribili favelle,
Parole di dolore; accenti d' ira;
Voci alte e fioche, e suon di man con elle
Facevan un tumulto.
Dante. Inf. iii. [ll. 25-8].

[3] Charon dimonio con occhi di bragia
Lor accennando tutte le raccoglie:
Batte col remo qualunque s' adagia.
Come d' autunno se levan le foglie
L' un' appresso de l' altra, infin che 'l ramo
Vede à la terra tutte le sue spoglie;
Similimente il mal seme d' Adamo
Gittasi di quel lito, &c.
Dante. Inferno, cap. 3 [ll. 109-16].

[Translation of *Inferno* iii. 1-9]

Now are we in the outer court; and lo
The door that closes on the world of woe;
On which, with slightest change, would read full well
The legend seen upon the gates of Hell,
In that dread vision, fitly styled divine,
Imagined by the mighty Florentine:
'Thro' me you pass to mourning's drear domain,[1]
Thro' me you pass to ever-during pain,
Thro' me among the ruin'd men you pass;
Eternal Justice for this mighty mass
The deep and durable foundations laid;
The fabric highest Power and Wisdom made;
Such thrall shall last while lasts the human kind.
Ye who come in! leave every hope behind.'

(*Part* i. *La Visita*, ll. 105-18, p. 24.)

[Reminiscence of *Inferno* i. 99]

The Leech drops off when saturate of blood;
The Vampire flies, gorged with the crimson flood;
But these when feasted more in hunger rave,[2]
And their foul food with fiercer fury crave.

(*Part* vi. *I Procuratori*, ll. 210-13, p. 236.)

T. B. DEFFERRARI

(fl. 1810)

1820. SELECTIONS OF CLASSIC ITALIAN POETRY FROM THE MOST CELEBRATED WORKS OF TASSO, ARIOSTO, DANTE, AND PETRARCH, FOR THE USE OF STUDENTS IN THE ITALIAN LANGUAGE; EXHIBITING THE GRAMMATICAL ORDER OF THE WORDS IN THE ORIGINAL, AND ILLUSTRATED WITH ENGLISH NOTES.

[In this work Defferrari prints (vol. ii. pp. 1-201) the following extracts from the *Divina Commedia*, viz. *Inferno* i-x, xiii. xxvi. 76-142 ('the narrative of Ulysses'), xxxiii. 1-88 ('the episode of Ugolino'); and *Paradiso* iii, xvii. 19-142 ('Prediction of misfortunes to Dante from M. Cacciaguida, his grandfather'), xxiv. 34-154 ('Dante's Profession of Faith'); with notes almost entirely grammatical.]

[1] Per me si và ne la citta dolente:
Per me si và nell' eterno dolore:
Per me si và tra la perduta gente.
Giustitia mosse il mio alto fattore,
Fecemi la divina potestate,
La somma sapienza, e 'l prim' amore.
Dinanz' à me non fur cose create,
Se non eterne; et io eterno duro.
Lassat' ogni speranza, voi che' 'ntrate.
Dante. Inf. c. 3 [ll. 1-9].

[2] E dopo 'l pasto ha piu fame che pria.
Dante [*Inf.* i. 99].

ANONYMOUS

1820. July. MONTHLY MAGAZINE. L' APE ITALIANA. NO. XVI.—SACCHETTI.

[Sacchetti's anecdotes of Dante]

AS that excellent poet, Dante Allighieri, whose fame shall never fade, was going by St. Peter's Gate, in Florence, he heard a blacksmith singing his verses, as he worked at the anvil, and miserably transforming and mangling them. Dante walked into the shop; and without saying anything, began to throw the man's tools into the street. The blacksmith, starting up with a menacing gesture, asked him if he were mad, or what the devil he was about. "I may rather ask what are you about," rejoined the poet. "I am minding my business," said the man, "and I wish you would do the same, and not spoil my tools in the way you are doing." "Well," said Dante, "if you will not spoil my things, I will not spoil yours." "What things of yours have I spoiled," said the blacksmith. "My verses," replied the poet: "you were singing out of my book, and did not sing as I wrote it." The man, astonished, made no reply, but picking up his tools, resumed his work, and the time to come confined himself to Tristrem and Lancelot, and left off Dante.

At another time, he met a dustman singing his poetry as he drove his asses, and at every two or three lines he stopped to beat his cattle, crying out *Ge-up!* Dante, hearing this, gave him a stroke across the shoulders, saying: *That is not in the text.* The man, not knowing who he was, nor why he struck him, cracked his whip, and called *Ge-up* again, and when he had got to a little distance, lolled out his tongue, and made grimaces at him. The poet, instead of losing his temper, as many would have done, merely observed, *I would not give you one of mine for a hundred of yours*—a calm and gentle reply which confounded his opponent and drew upon him the applauses of all who were present.[1]

(Vol. xlix. p. 511.)

ANONYMOUS

1820. July. QUARTERLY REVIEW. ART. V. SPENCE'S ANECDOTES OF BOOKS AND MEN.

[Pope, Milton, and Dante]

IN the contrast of human tempers and habits, in the changes of circumstances in society, and the consequent mutations of taste, the objects of poetry may be different in different periods; pre-eminent genius obtains its purpose by its adaptation

[1] [From *Novella* 114.]

to this eternal variety; and on this principle, if we would justly appreciate the creative faculty, we cannot see why Pope should not class, at least in file, with Dante, or Milton. It is probable that Pope could not have produced an 'Inferno,' or a 'Paradise Lost,' for his invention was elsewhere: but it is equally probable that Dante and Milton, with their cast of mind, could not have so exquisitely touched the refined gaiety of 'the Rape of the Lock.'

(Vol. xxiii. p.410.)

ANONYMOUS

1820. October. QUARTERLY REVIEW. ART. III. ITALIAN TRAGEDY.

[Alfieri, Foscolo, and Dante]

AT length Alfieri arose, and at a fortunate period; for the peculiar talents of Metastasio, the exquisite purity of his language, the occasional felicity of his plots, the elegant faultlessness of his manner, and the music of his verse, were rapidly confirming the prejudice, that effeminacy was the distinguishing character of Italian literature; and that the language of Dante and Machiavelli could not aspire to a higher flight than an amorous madrigal or a pastoral dialogue.

* * * *

We consider that this single beautiful example [from Silvio Pellico's *Francesca da Rimini*] would be sufficient to justify our opinion, that the Italians should look at home for their tragic subjects. Why should not Dante be to them what Homer was to the Greek tragedians? . . . To Signor Foscolo, whose mastery over his own language, the language of Dante, Petrarch, and Tasso, is only so great as to lead him to a somewhat wanton and capricious display of power in inventing it, and condensing it into epigrammatic conciseness, we would say that the name of Foscolo should be known to posterity as something greater than that of the author of Ortis's Letters, or even of Ricciarda.

(Vol. xxiv. pp. 82, 100-1.)

BRYAN WALLER PROCTER

(1787-1874)

[Bryan Waller Procter, best known as a writer by his pseudonym Barry Cornwall, was born at Leeds in 1787. He was educated at Finchley and Harrow, where he was a contemporary of Peel and Byron. On leaving school he was articled to a solicitor and he ultimately gained a considerable practice as a conveyancer. In 1815 he began to contribute to the *Literary Gazette*, and thenceforth for many years he devoted much of his time to literature, among his literary friends being Leigh Hunt, Lamb, and Dickens. His first volume of poems appeared in 1819, and in the next year he published *Marcian Colonna*, in which he makes mention of Dante. Between this date and 1832, when he was made a commissioner in lunacy, he published numerous volumes of poems and songs. His last important work, his biography of Lamb, appeared in 1866. He died in 1874.]

1820. MARCIAN COLONNA. AN ITALIAN TALE, WITH THREE DRAMATIC SCENES AND OTHER TALES.

[Eternity of the fame of Dante, Petrarch, and Boccaccio]

O THOU romantic land of Italy! . . .
First of all thy sons were they who wove
Thy silken language into tales of love,
And fairest far the gentle forms that shine
In thy own poets' faery songs divine. . . .
Long as the stars, like ladies' looks, by night
Shall shine,—more constant and almost as bright:
So long, tho' hidden in a foreign shroud,
Shall Dante's mighty spirit speak aloud;
So long the lamp of fame on Petrarch's urn
Shall, like the light of learning, duly burn;
And he be loved—he with his hundred tales,
As varying as the shadowy cloud that sails
Upon the bosom of the April sky,
And musical as when the waters run
Lapsing through sylvan haunts deliciously.

(pp. 3, 4, 5.)

HENRY MATTHEWS

(1789-1828)

[Henry Matthews, son of John Matthews of Belmont, Herefordshire, born in 1789, was educated at Eton and at King's College, Cambridge, of which he became a Fellow. After travelling for several years on the Continent for the sake of his health, he was in 1821 appointed Advocate-Fiscal of Ceylon, which office he held until 1827, when he was made a judge. He died in Ceylon in the following year. His *Diary of an Invalid*, the journal of his tour on the Continent, published in 1820 (fifth edition, 1835), contains occasional references to Dante in the part relating to Italy.]

1820. THE DIARY OF AN INVALID: BEING THE JOURNAL OF A TOUR IN PURSUIT OF HEALTH, IN PORTUGAL, ITALY, SWITZERLAND, AND FRANCE, IN THE YEARS 1817, 1818, AND 1819.

[The relation between painting and poetry]

FLORENCE, Nov. 1817—The liberal lover of the arts looks for those higher excellencies, which have placed painting in the same rank with poetry. For what, in fact, are the works of Michael Angelo—Raphael—Murillo—Salvator Rosa—

Claude—Nicholas Poussin—and Sir Joshua Reynolds, but the sublime and enchanting—the terrific and heart-rending conceptions of a Homer—a Virgil—a Shakspeare—a Dante—a Byron—or a Scott, "turned into shapes"!—They are the kindred productions of a congenial inspiration.

(Chap. ii. p. 50, ed. 1835.)

[Dante's portrait in the Duomo at Florence]

The most interesting church here is the *S. Croce*—the Westminster Abbey of Florence—for here are the bones and the tombs of Galileo, Machiavelli, Michael Angelo, and Alfieri. . . . The Florentines would gladly have recovered the bones of Dante, whom they exiled, to die at Ravenna; and they point with pride to an original picture of him in fresco on the wall of the cathedral.[1]

(*Ibid.* pp. 54-5.)

[Michael Angelo and Dante]

Rome, Jan. 1818—Michael Angelo's *Last Judgment* has been so much injured by time and cleaning, that, as the light now falls on it, the figure of the Saviour appears to be standing up. Everybody has noticed the solecism of introducing into this picture a personage from the Heathen Mythology;—*Charon* is employed in ferrying over the bodies. Michael Angelo probably followed Dante, without thinking much about the matter:—

'Caron, dimonio, con occhi di bragia,
Loro accennando, tutte le raccoglie.
Batte col remo qualunque s' adagia.'[2]

(Chap. v. p. 108.)

JOHN PAYNE COLLIER

(1789-1883)

[John Payne Collier, the Shakespearean critic, was born in London in 1789. In 1809 he succeeded his father as reporter to 'The Times,' on the staff of which he remained until 1821, when he joined the 'Morning Chronicle,' for which he acted as parliamentary reporter, and literary and dramatic critic, until 1847. He was called to the bar in 1829, but soon abandoned the legal profession for more congenial literary pursuits, with which he occupied himself for the greater part of his long life. In 1820 he had published the *Poetical Decameron*, dealing with the less-known English poets; in 1831 appeared his *History of English Dramatic Poetry*, which brought him to the notice of the Duke of Devonshire, who appointed him his librarian. In 1835-6-9 he published 'New Facts' and 'New Particulars' concerning Shakespeare and his works, which were subsequently, like many other of his alleged Shakespeare 'discoveries,' proved to be based on his own forgeries and

[1] [No doubt the picture (not in fresco) by Domenico di Michelino is meant.]
[2] [*Inf.* iii. 109-11.]

falsifications. Besides numerous papers on English ballad and dramatic literature, published for various societies, Collier issued several annotated editions of Shakespeare (1842-4, 1858, 1875-8), and a valuable edition of Spenser (1862). He died at Maidenhead in 1883, at the age of 94.]

1820. THE POETICAL DECAMERON, OR TEN CONVERSATIONS ON ENGLISH POETS AND POETRY.

[Dante's use of the term *tragedia*]

ELLIOT. You mentioned just now 'the *Tragedy* of Shore's Wife' by Churchyard. Did it come upon the stage, or has Rowe availed himself of it in his 'Jane Shore'?

Bourne. You mistake; the word *tragedy* there does not mean a dramatic composition: it refers to his Legend of Jane Shore, in the Mirror for Magistrates; many poems of a tragical nature, but not at all in the form of plays, were at that time called Tragedies: Dante (*Inf.* xx. 113), in the same way, makes Virgil speak of his Aeneid as,

L' alta mia Tragedia in alcun loco, &c.

and he further explains the application of the word in his work *Della volgare Eloquenza—Per tragœdiam superiorem stilum induimus, per comœdiam inferiorem, per elegiam stilum intelligimus miserorum.*[1]

(*Seventh Conversation*, vol. ii. pp. 90-1.)

ANONYMOUS

1820. ITALIAN SCENERY. FROM DRAWINGS MADE IN 1817, BY MISS BATTY.

[The descriptions in this work were written by 'a friend of the publisher.' Under Pisa (p. 41) is a reference to the story of Ugolino, 'one of the finest episodes in Dante.']

JAMES AUGUSTIN GALIFFE[2]

(fl. 1810)

1820. ITALY AND ITS INHABITANTS; AN ACCOUNT OF A TOUR IN THAT COUNTRY IN 1816 AND 1817.

[An eruption of Vesuvius beyond the descriptive powers of Dante]

WHAT we had seen was a splendid fire-work, such as supernatural beings might have prepared for some heavenly celebration; what remained behind was a terrific revelation of the mysteries of hell; and Dante himself

[1] [*V. E.* ii. 4, ll. 39-41.]

[2] [A native of Geneva.]

would have blenched at the idea of describing it. Scenes of such tremendous sublimity are only debased and disfigured, by the efforts of poetical description; and simplicity of language affords the only escape from affectation and bombast.

(Vol. ii. p. 279.)

THOMAS GRIFFITHS WAINEWRIGHT

(1794-1852)

[Wainewright, who was born at Chiswick in 1794, was an artist and art-critic of some reputation, and exhibited for several years at the Royal Academy (1821-5). He was one of the earliest contributors to the *London Magazine*, his connexion with which brought him into contact with Hood, Allan Cunningham, Hazlitt, De Quincey, Charles Lamb, and many other literary men of the day. In the well-known *Letter of Elia to Robert Southey*, Lamb speaks of him as 'the light, and warm-as-light hearted Janus of the London': and after Wainewright had severed his connexion with the Magazine in 1823, Lamb writes to Bernard Barton deploring the loss of 'their best stay, kind light-hearted Wainewright, their Janus.' Within three years from this date Wainewright committed a forgery on the Bank of England, for which eleven years afterwards (in 1837) he was tried and transported to Van Diemen's Land, where he died a convict in 1852. He had previously been suspected of poisoning his uncle, his wife's mother, and her half sister, for the sake of their property and of various insurances he had effected on the life of the last. The crimes were never brought home to him, but the insurance companies refused payment, and he was obliged to take refuge on the Continent, where he passed a considerable time in prison (in Paris). Wainewright's contributions to the *London Magazine* (from 1820 to 1823), which contain sundry references to Dante, were mostly under the pseudonyms of 'Egomet Bonmot,' and 'Janus Weathercock.' He had no knowledge of Dante in the original, as he himself confesses in one of his articles, but like many of his contemporaries was indebted to the translation of Cary. A collection of his 'Essays and Criticisms' was published in 1880 under the editorship of W. C. Hazlitt. An account of Wainewright is given by Talfourd, who was personally acquainted with him, in his *Memoirs of Charles Lamb*. Charles Dickens, who saw him in Newgate in 1837, published an account of his last years in *All the Year Round* (Jan. 1867), and introduced certain details of his career into his story *Hunted Down*. He figures as Varney in Bulwer Lytton's *Lucretia*.]

1820. Jan. LONDON MAGAZINE.

[The poet of the *Inferno*]

MODEST Offer of Service from Mr. Bonmot to the Editor —I know how to apply sententious opinions in the mode of modern infallibility. As, for instance, in noticing the poet of the Inferno, I should say—there's Dante mingling the bitterness of satire with the gloomy grandeur of his sublime genius;—if I would be ringing changes upon other great ones of the olden time, who blazed the comets of their season, I should talk of the elegant licentiousness of Boccaccio; the delightful varieties of Ariosto; the tender querulence of laureate Petrarch's erotic conceits. . . .

(Vol. i. p. 22.)

1820. April. LONDON MAGAZINE.

[Rembrandt and Dante]

Sentimentalities on the Fine Arts.[1] No. III—The longer we look at Rembrandt's *Crucifixion*, the deeper its terrors grow. There is nothing in it of Rembrandt's usual concentrated flash: but, watery lights stream down, like the waning moon seen dimly behind clouds when chilling rains fall strait through the air.—Another atmosphere, clammy, and putrefying, has been created for the actors in this bloody tragedy, through which they move like phantoms, 'doing unearthly deeds'! Another firmament hangs low, over their sacrilegious heads—gross—palpable—murky—like a fixed ceiling.—

Hell's dunnest gloom, or night unlustrous, dark,
Of every planet reft, and pall'd in clouds,
Did never spread before the sight a veil
In thickness like that fog—[2]

Dante.

(Vol. i. p. 407.)

1821. July. LONDON MAGAZINE.

[Flaxman 'the illustrator of Dante']

Exhibition of the Royal Academy.[3]—For one person who talks of the juicy Hilton,[4] we have ten who rave about Edwin Landseer,[5] and Captain Jones.[6] The elegant Westall[7] and the classical Howard[8] are not much better off; and the spirited illustrator[9] of Homer, Hesiod, Aeschylus, and Dante, is forgotten before the bust of Turnerelli,[10] or the ineffable fopperies of the effeminate Canova.[11]

(Vol. iv. p. 71.)

1822. July. LONDON MAGAZINE.

[Quotation from Dante]

The Delicate Intricacies.—My good curious people who stand outside the garden-gate and wish you could get in—tell me if you have ever studied the Parma Correggios? Ah! miserable, who

[1] [By 'Janus Weathercock.']
[2] [*Purg.* xvi. 1-5, Cary's translation.]
[3] [Signed 'Cornelius van Vinkbooms,' another of Wainewright's pseudonyms.]
[4] [William Hilton, historical painter (1786-1839).]
[5] [The celebrated animal-painter (1802-1873).]
[6] [George Jones, historical painter, at one time in the army (1786-1869).]
[7] [Richard Westall, historical painter (1765-1836).]
[8] [Henry Howard, portrait and historical painter (1769-1847).]
[9] [John Flaxman (1755-1826).]
[10] [Peter Turnerelli, sculptor (1774-1839).]
[11] [Antonio Canova, the famous Italian sculptor (1757-1822).]

never truly lived,[1] your countenances are negative! Where do you expect to go?

(Vol. vi. p. 74.)

ALFRED TENNYSON

(1809-1892)

[Alfred Tennyson was born at Somersby, in Lincolnshire, of which his father was rector, in 1809. He was educated partly by his father at home, and partly at the Grammar School at Louth (1817-20). In 1828 he matriculated at Trinity College, Cambridge, when he first made the acquaintance of Arthur Hallam, son of the historian, who became his dearest friend, and was afterwards commemorated in *In Memoriam*. In 1827 Tennyson had published with his elder brother Charles a volume of *Poems by Two Brothers*, and in 1829 he won the Chancellor's medal for English verse at Cambridge with a poem on the subject of 'Timbuctoo,' his friend, Arthur Hallam, being among the competitors. In 1830 he published *Poems chiefly Lyrical*, which was reviewed by Arthur Hallam in the *Englishman's Magazine* (see below, pp. 421 ff.). In 1831 Tennyson left Cambridge without taking a degree, and in the next year he published a new volume which, though severely handled in the *Quarterly Review* (April, 1833), contained what were afterwards recognised as some of his finest poems, among them being *Oenone* and the *Lotos-Eaters*. The publication ten years later (1842) of his *Poems* established Tennyson's fame as the foremost living poet, and in 1850, the year which saw the publication of *In Memoriam*, on the death of Wordsworth, he was appointed to the poet-laureateship, which he held until his death, 42 years later, in 1892. He was buried in Westminster Abbey. In 1884, on the recommendation of Gladstone, Tennyson was created a peer. His publications before 1844 were as follows:—*Poems chiefly Lyrical*, 1830; *Poems*, 1832; *Poems*, 1842.

Tennyson's first mention of Dante occurs in a letter written when he was eleven years old. His real knowledge of Dante dates probably from the days of his friendship at Cambridge with Arthur Hallam, who 'admired Dante with idolatry' (see below, p. 417). It is recorded by Coventry Patmore that 'he learned Italian so as to be able to read Dante, in one fortnight's study.' The latest reference to Dante in Tennyson's works which falls within the scope of this book, is the reminiscence in *Locksley Hall* of the same lines which he had quoted in the letter mentioned above. Published at the same time as *Locksley Hall* (1842) was the poem on *Ulysses*, 'the germ, the spirit and sentiment' of which are from *Inferno* xxvi. 90-142, where Ulysses relates how he came by his death. Tennyson himself said of the poem—'there's an echo of Dante in it.'[2]

In 1865, at the time of the celebration of the sixth centenary of Dante's birth, Tennyson, in response to a request from the Florentines for some lines in honour of the occasion, sent the following:—

To Dante

King, that hast reign'd six hundred years, and grown
In power, and ever growest, since thine own
Fair Florence honouring thy nativity,
Thy Florence now the crown of Italy,
Hath sought the tribute of a verse from me,
I, wearing but the garland of a day,
Cast at thy feet one flower that fades away.

[1] [*Inf.* iii. 64: 'Sciaurati, che mai non fur vivi'.] See remarks on this numerous class in the second [third] canto of the Inferno. 'But I am guiltless of Italian'! I know it. But the noble Ghibelline recites his verses in eloquent and classic English undefiled, through the lips of his most favoured pupil, the Rev. H. F. Cary.

[2] [See an interesting article on *Tennyson and Dante*, by T. H. Warren, in the *Monthly Review*, Jan. 1904.]

Several of Tennyson's criticisms of Dante are recorded in the *Life* by his son. 'Ugolino, and Paolo and Francesca, in Dante, equal anything anywhere.' He held that 'as the English language is much finer than the Italian for variety of sound, so Milton, for sound, is often finer than Dante.' He added, in illustration, 'what can be more monotonous than the first lines of the *Inferno*, with their *a*'s?'

Edward Fitzgerald records that 'once looking with Alfred Tennyson at two busts of Dante and Goethe in a shop window in Regent Street, I said: "What is there wanting in Goethe which the other has?" Alfred Tennyson replied: "The Divine."' On another occasion he observed: 'We must distinguish Keats, Shelley, and Byron from the great sage poets of all, who are both great thinkers and great artists, like Aeschylus, Shakespeare, Dante, and Goethe. Goethe lacked the divine intensity of Dante.' He recognised too the 'grimness' and 'humour,' of Dante, as well as his divine qualities (see below, p. 316).]

1820. LETTER TO HIS AUNT, MARIANNE FYTCHE (from Somersby).[1]

[Milton, Byron, and Dante]

WHEN I was at Louth you used to tell me that you should be obliged to me if I would write to you and give you my remarks on works and authors. I shall now fulfil the promise which I made at that time. Going into the library this morning, I picked up *Sampson*[2] *Agonistes*, on which, (as I think it is a play you like) I shall send you my remarks. The first scene is the lamentation of Sampson,[2] which possesses much pathos and sublimity. This passage,

Restless thoughts, that like a deadly swarm
Of hornets arm'd, no sooner found alone,
But rush upon me thronging, and present
Times past, what once I was, and what am now,

puts me in mind of that in Dante, which Lord Byron has prefixed to his *Corsair*—'Nessun maggior dolore, Che ricordarsi del tempo felice, Nella miseria.'[3]

(*Memoir of Lord Tennyson*, by his Son, vol. i. pp. 7-8.)

1830. THE POET.

The poet[4] in a golden clime was born,
With golden stars above;
Dower'd with the hate of hate, the scorn of scorn,
The love of love.

He saw thro' life and death, thro' good and ill,
He saw thro' his own soul.
The marvel of the everlasting will,
An open scroll,

Before him lay.

[1] [Written at the age of eleven.]
[2] [*Sic.*]
[3] [*Inf.* v. 121-3.]
[4] [Supposed to be meant for Dante.]

1832. THE PALACE OF ART.[1]

['Grim Dante']

Then in the towers I placed great bells that swung,
Moved of themselves, with silver sound;
And with choice paintings of wise men I hung
The royal dais round.

There deep-haired Milton like an angel tall
Stood limnèd, Shakespeare bland and mild,
Grim Dante pressed his lips, and from the wall
The bald blind Homer smiled.

* * * *

And in the sun-pierced Oriels' coloured flame
Immortal Michael Angelo
Looked down, bold Luther, large-browed Verulam,
The King of those who know.[2]

1833. March 10. LETTER TO HIS AUNT, MRS. RUSSELL (from Somersby).

[Quotation from Dante]

I would have forwarded this portrait to you long ago, and likewise visited you by the proxy of a letter, but to me as to Dante, 'La diritta via era smarrita,'[3] for I knew not where you were. What astrologer can point out the place of any star that moves perpetually under a cloud?

(*Memoir,* vol. i. p. 100.)

1838. LETTER TO EMILY SELLWOOD.[4]

[The humour of Dante]

I dare not tell how high I rate humour, which is generally most fruitful in the highest and most solemn human spirits. Dante is full of it, Shakespeare, Cervantes, and almost all the greatest have been pregnant with this glorious power.

(*Memoir,* vol. i. p. 167.)

1842. THE PALACE OF ART.[5]

['World-worn Dante']

Then in the towers I placed great bells that swung,
Moved of themselves, with silver sound;
And with choice paintings of wise men I hung
The royal dais round.

[1] [For another version of the two last stanzas, see under 1842.]
[2] ['Il maestro di color che sanno.' *Inf.* iv. 131 (of Aristotle).]
[3] [*Inf.* i. 3.]
[4] [Whom he married in 1850.]
[5] [For another version of the two last stanzas, see under 1832.]

For there was Milton like a seraph strong,
  Beside him Shakespeare bland and mild;
And there the world-worn Dante grasp'd his song
  And somewhat grimly smiled.

* * * *

And thro' the topmost Oriels' coloured flame
  Two god-like faces gazed below;
Plato the wise, and large-browed Verulam,
  The first of those who know.[1]

1842. ULYSSES.[2]

['Echo of Dante']

It little profits that an idle king,
By this still hearth, among these barren crags,
Match'd with an aged wife, I mete and dole
Unequal laws unto a savage race,
That hoard, and sleep, and feed, and know not me.
I cannot rest from travel: I will drink
Life to the lees: all times I have enjoy'd
Greatly, have suffer'd greatly, both with those
That loved me, and alone; on shore, and when
Thro' scudding drifts the rainy Hyades
Vext the dim sea: I am become a name;
For always roaming with a hungry heart
Much have I seen and known; cities of men
And manners, climates, councils, governments,
Myself not least, but honour'd of them all;
And drunk delight of battle with my peers,
Far on the ringing plains of windy Troy.
I am a part of all that I have met;
Yet all experience is an arch where thro'
Gleams that untravell'd world, whose margin fades
For ever and for ever when I move.
How dull it is to pause, to make an end,
To rust unburnish'd, not to shine in use!
As tho' to breathe were life. Life piled on life
Were all too little, and of one to me
Little remains: but every hour is saved

[1] [*Inf.* iv. 131.]

[2] [*Ulysses*, which was written soon after Arthur Hallam's death (1833), though not published till 1842, was suggested by *Inferno* xxvi. 90-142. Tennyson himself said, 'There's an echo of Dante in it.']

From that eternal silence, something more,
A bringer of new things; and vile it were
For some three suns to store and hoard myself,
And this gray spirit yearning in desire
To follow knowledge like a sinking star,
Beyond the utmost bound of human thought.
This is my son, mine own Telemachus,
To whom I leave the sceptre and the isle—
Well-loved of me, discerning to fulfil
This labour, by slow prudence to make mild
A rugged people, and thro' soft degrees
Subdue them to the useful and the good.
Most blameless is he, centred in the sphere
Of common duties, decent not to fail
In offices of tenderness, and pay
Meet adoration to my household gods,
When I am gone. He works his work, I mine.
There lies the port; the vessel puffs her sail:
There gloom the dark broad seas. My mariners,
Souls that have toil'd, and wrought, and thought with me—
That ever with a frolic welcome took
The thunder and the sunshine, and opposed
Free hearts, free foreheads—you and I are old;
Old age hath yet his honour and his toil;
Death closes all: but something ere the end,
Some work of noble note, may yet be done,
Not unbecoming men that strove with Gods.
The lights begin to twinkle from the rocks:
The long day wanes: the slow moon climbs: the deep
Moans round with many voices. Come, my friends,
'Tis not too late to seek a newer world.
Push off, and sitting well in order smite
The sounding furrows; for my purpose holds
To sail beyond the sunset, and the baths
Of all the western stars, until I die.
It may be that the gulfs will wash us down:
It may be we shall touch the Happy Isles,
And see the great Achilles, whom we knew.
Tho' much is taken, much abides; and tho'
We are not now that strength which in old days
Moved earth and heaven; that which we are, we are;
One equal temper of heroic hearts,
Made weak by time and fate, but strong in will
To strive, to seek, to find, and not to yield.

1842. LOCKSLEY HALL.

[Reminiscence of Dante]

This is truth the poet sings,
That a sorrow's crown of sorrow is remembering happier things.

ANONYMOUS

1820. Feb. LONDON MAGAZINE. POETRY AND PROSE, BY A MEMBER OF PARLIAMENT.

[Byron's tribute to Dante and other Italian poets]

THE great value of the influence of Lord Byron's poetry on the public mind, is to be found in the sympathy which it is well calculated to excite with the honours of ancient and famous places, and of illustrious names. . . . What has he left unsaid, that enthusiasm the most fervent could suggest, in behalf of Dante, of Ariosto, and of him whose tomb is in Arqua!

(Vol. i. p. 125.)

ANONYMOUS

1820. Feb. LONDON MAGAZINE. THE SPIRIT OF FRENCH CRITICISM, AND VOLTAIRE'S NOTICES OF SHAKSPEARE.

[La Harpe on Dante and Milton]

LA HARPE,[2] who was lecturer to the ladies and gentlemen of Paris, thus defines the portion of fame fairly due to Dante and to Milton—'They knew the ancient writers, and, if we still remember their names, in connection with some monstrous works, it is because one finds in these monsters some fine parts, executed according to the rules.'

(Vol. i. p. 130.)

W. CORNELIUS

(fl. 1820)

1820. May. LONDON MAGAZINE. SONNET TO ITALY.

[Dante and Raphael, sons of Italy]

MOTHER of Dante and Raffaelle—Italy,
Poets will ever love thy skies of calm,
And voice of music, and warm breath of balm,
And glorious forms of grace and majesty.

[1] [A recollection of 'Nessun maggior dolore Che ricordarsi del tempo felice Nella miseria' (*Inf.* v. 121-3)—a passage which was quoted by Tennyson in a letter written at the age of eleven (see above, p. 315).]

[2] [Jean François de la Harpe (1739-1803).]

Old Chaucer loved thee for Boccaccio's stories,
Spenser for Tasso's; and Milton trod
Thy viney fields—Milton, minstrel of God—
And loved idolatrously thy olden glories.

(Vol. i. p. 531.)

ANONYMOUS

1820. June. LONDON MAGAZINE. THE ENEID OF VIRGIL, TRANSLATED INTO ITALIAN, BY ANNIBALE CARO. WITH PLATES.

[Reminiscence of Dante]

MR. MONTGOMERY, an English traveller, has adorned the fifth book with a view of Mount Eryx. . . . The same artist gives us the Shore of Cuma, with a sunny sky, a woody country, and distant mountains; as Dante would say, 'quanto può mietere un occhio.'

(Vol. i. p. 705.)

ANONYMOUS

1820. RETROSPECTIVE REVIEW. VOL. II. PART I. ART. I. SIR PHILIP SIDNEY'S ARCADIA.

[Sir Philip Sidney contrasted with Dante]

SIR PHILIP SIDNEY'S fairy pencil was principally formed to delineate the pensive and milder workings of feeling. His transparent mirror reflected the emotions of the human mind; but it was not the mind awakened by crime and exasperated by scorn; it was not the mind preyed upon by remorse or tormentors generated within itself. His province was not to pourtray the dark and horrible in nature, or the dark and horrible in man. His was not the gloomy colouring of Dante or Salvator Rosa.

(Vol. ii. p. 39.)

ANONYMOUS

1821. RETROSPECTIVE REVIEW. VOL. III. PART I. ART. III. CAREY'S GODFREY OF BULLOIGNE.

[Tasso compared with Dante and Ariosto]

AMONGST so many causes of just pride, perhaps, the highest boast of Italy is, that she has been the birthplace of such men as Dante, and Petrarcha, and Tasso; and it is in our opinion one of the surest tests of the correctness and truth of public taste at the present day, that these old poets of Italy, and the worthy imitators of them in our own country, have regained that place in the estimation of our scholars and poets, which they seemed to be in danger of losing for ever. Notwithstanding the occasional *concetti* in which even the earliest of the Italian poets indulged, they uniformly addressed themselves to the heart; to rouse its sympathies and its passions was their great object. . . .

The style of thinking observable in Tasso's works is much more simple and natural than in many others of the great Italian authors—Certainly as a pastoral poet he displays much fewer involutions of sentiment and expression than many of his celebrated countrymen, and his Epic, when compared with the works of Dante and Ariosto, possesses very little of what may be called the extravagance of poetry.

(Vol. iii. p. 49.)

ANONYMOUS

1821. RETROSPECTIVE REVIEW. VOL. III. PART II. ART. VI. THE WARS OF CHARLEMAGNE IN SPAIN.

[Pulci's imitations of Dante]

WE now arrive at the treachery of Ganelon of Pontiers, that famous piece of infamy, which led to the calamitous event, referred to by Dante, in the thirty-first Canto of his *Inferno*, in terms that seem dictated by an immediate contemplation of the bloody field, on which were strewed the bodies of the twelve Paladins, and the flower of France. His words are:

Dopo la dolorosa rotta, quando
Carlo magno perdè la santa gesta,
Non sonò sì terribilmente Orlando.[1]

We know that it was proverbial in England, in the days of Chaucer, who had himself travelled in France and Italy, and has translated much from Dante. He alludes to the treachery of Gan, (as he is often contemptuously called) in his *Monk's Tale*. . . . It is in this tale that Chaucer translates the story of Ugolino, under the title of 'Hugeline of Pise'. . . . It is remarkable, that Pulci, in the opening of his *Morgante*, speaking of the dreadful overthrow of the Christians at Roncesvalles, uses precisely the words of Dante. . . . The first view Oliver obtains of the approaching enemy, is thus related.

[1] [*Inf.* xxx. 16-18.]

'When o'er the brighten'd world the sun 'gan rise,
Oliver cast an anxious look t'ward Spain,
As an old tailor at his needle pries:
He saw a host come marching on amain,
But o'er one fourth he could not cast his eyes,
So num'rous were they upon hill and plain. . . .'

This stanza is remarkable, not only for the striking and picturesque manner in which the advance of 'numbers numberless' is described, but for the introduction of a simile, in the line printed in italic, copied from Dante (*Inf.* xv)

Come 'l vecchio sartor fa ne la cruna.[1]

(Vol. iii. pp. 307 ff.)

ANONYMOUS

1821. RETROSPECTIVE REVIEW. VOL. IV. PART I. ART. II. POETICAL LITERATURE OF SPAIN.

[Dante's knowledge of Provençal]

OF late, the priority of Sant Jordi to Petrarch has been much contested; but we happen to possess a MS. copy of the whole poem, in which the lines copied by Petrarch are to be found. They clearly form an original part of the whole, and have not the slightest appearance of having been dovetailed into the compositions. The imitation is so close and obvious, that one must necessarily have been copied by the other, and in Petrarch they are brought in with some artifice. . . . Dante, and the early Italian poets, decidedly studied the Provençal, and have, in fact, introduced Provençal verses in their original form, while there is no proof at this period, as far as we recollect, that the language of Italy was studied in Spain so early as the thirteenth century. In cases of doubt, therefore, as to priority of claim to any passage, the more probable originality of the Trobador must be recognised.

(Vol. iv. p. 46.)

ANONYMOUS

1821. July. QUARTERLY REVIEW. ART. VI. HUNT'S TASSO'S JERUSALEM DELIVERED.

[Ariosto compared with Dante and Tasso]

IT was on the Italian School that the original English school of poetry was formed. Whatever other lessons it has since derived from France or Germany have been, at best, of doubtful advantage, and the scions thus transplanted have never readily

[1] [*Inf.* xv. 21.]

taken root in our soil. It is by a return to our original models that our ancient vigour and correctness is most likely to be restored: and we are, therefore, grateful to the labours of Mr. Carey and Mr. Hunt, of whom the first opened to us the wild and romantic recesses of Dante's Vision,[1] and the second [2] has brought forward Tasso in a costume at once accurate and graceful. Ariosto yet remains, inferior to Dante in severe sublimity, inferior to Tasso in taste and correctness, but superior to both in the richness and various delight of his enchanted and enchanting wilderness. What bard will undertake the adventure? [3]

(Vol. xxv. p. 436.)

THOMAS CAMPBELL

(1777-1844)

[Thomas Campbell, the poet, was born in 1777 in Glasgow, where his father had been in business. He was educated at the Grammar School and University of Glasgow (1791-6); after acting for a time as a tutor, he settled in Edinburgh with the intention of studying law. In 1799 he published his *Pleasures of Hope*, which at once attained popularity, and established his reputation as a poet. After travelling in Germany and Denmark (1800-1), and spending some time in England, he eventually settled near London, where he spent the last forty years of his life as a man of letters (1804-44). In 1819 he published *Specimens of the British Poets* in seven volumes. From 1820 to 1830 he was editor of the *New Monthly Magazine*, to which he contributed *Lectures on Poetry*, delivered at the Royal Institution in 1819. He was Lord Rector of Glasgow University from 1826 to 1829. He died at Boulogne in 1844, and was buried in Westminster Abbey. Towards the close of his life Campbell published various prose works, among which was a *Life of Petrarch* in two volumes (1841, second edition, 1843). In this work he claims that he 'can relish Dante to his highest value,' but he does not display more than a superficial acquaintance with Dante's works.]

1821. LECTURES ON POETRY, DELIVERED AT THE ROYAL INSTITUTION.

[Dante's influence on Italian language and literature]

SHAKSPEARE is said to have never blotted a line. . . . Were we to follow the inference that is sometimes drawn from mere tradition respecting Shakspeare, we might imagine that negligence is the parent of felicity in poetry. But Tasso, Ariosto, Dante, Virgil, Euripides, and Milton, did not think so. And who shall despise that solicitous cultivation of diction, which they avowed and fervidly practised? . . . Chaucer, for want of style, left the English language unfixed and barbarous for an hundred and

[1] [Cary's Dante was published in 1814.]

[2] [J. H. Hunt (1780-1859), editor of the *Critical Review*—his Tasso was published in 1818.]

[3] [W. S. Rose published his translation of Ariosto in 1823-31 (see above, pp. 296 ff.).]

fifty years after his death. Had the diction of Dante been no better, the history of Italian literature would have also been postponed. But the *Divina Commedia* is popular in Italy, whilst Chaucer's works are scarcely intelligible in England; for Dante's poetry gave a bulwark to his native speech against the ravages of time.

(Lecture I. Part 2.—*New Monthly Magazine*, vol. i. pp. 134-5.)

[Homer and Dante]

Whilst the *Odyssey* resembles the *Iliad* in its diction and descriptive manner, it opens an interesting variety in epic poetry. . . . Had the poet been equally disposed to have sported with the marvellous in the *Iliad*, the vicinity of the Troade to Greece would have been a check upon his fancy. But the scene of fiction was now to be shifted, and expanded over scenes that might be peopled at will with giants, enchanters, and semideities, or extended even to the shadowy empire of the dead. Homer has ventured into that darkest realm of fancy, the intrepid and long-distant precursor of Virgil and Dante. It would be unfair to compare a mere episode of the Odyssey with an entire fabric of poetry, which the last of those geniuses has devoted to the same subject. But Homer's world of death has its sublimity, though more simple than that of the Florentine poet. He gives expressiveness to human character even in delineating its spectral shade.

(Lecture IV.—*Ibid.* vol. ii. pp. 226-7.)

1841. LIFE AND TIMES OF PETRARCH. WITH NOTICES OF BOCCACCIO AND HIS ILLUSTRIOUS CONTEMPORARIES.

[Petrarch and Dante]

I do not believe the surmise that Petrarch envied Dante's fame. I am aware that Boccaccio, in sending a copy of the *Divina Commedia* to our poet, seems to hint a suspicion that the latter judged harshly of Dante, and Ugo Foscolo says that Petrarch was angry at being considered jealous of a poet 'whose language is coarse, though his conceptions are lofty.' But the circumstance of a man being angry at an accusation is not a proof that he is guilty. Boccaccio might hint that Petrarch judged harshly of his great precursor, because his poems were not in the library of Vaucluse; but Petrarch has satisfactorily accounted for that circumstance, as having been merely accidental. Besides, supposing our poet to have judged harshly of Dante in the opinion of Boccaccio, it does not imply that Boccaccio charged him with envy. If Petrarch thought that 'Dante's language is coarse, though his thoughts are lofty,' he had a right to express an opinion, which should rather be called candid than invidious.

* * * *

A reader will take the critics' word, with slender proving, for any fault alleged against a poet; but, in order to be penetrated with a sense of his super-prevailing merits, he must have evidence in some adequate translation of the works of that foreign poet, if the reader be an Englishman little or not at all imbued with the foreign language. Now, where shall we apply for the means of rendering such justice to Petrarch? We have Homer and Dante transferred, as it were, soul and body into English; but who has succeeded in fully transferring Petrarch's graces into our tongue? . . . I have studied the Italian language with assiduity, though perhaps at a later period of my life than enables the ear to be *perfectly* sensitive to its harmony, for it is in youth, nay, almost in childhood alone, that the melody and felicitous expressions of any tongue can touch our deepest sensibility; but still I have studied it with pains—I can relish Dante, I think, to his highest value; I can perceive much in Petrarch that is elevated and tender. . . . I have certainly felt, in the perusal of Petrarch's amatory sonnets, sensations exceedingly different in the degree of respect for him which they inspire. . . . Laura ever and anon presents herself, a minute picture, to the mind's eye—her very veil and mantle, her features, her smile, her step—and we are in love with Laura. I must say, however, that we are rather smitten by her outward beauty than rapt into interest with her mind. Dante contrives, one scarcely can tell by what insensible traits, to make us the fond friends of his Beatrice, as well as to admire her; but what do we know of the secrets of Laura's heart? . . . I demur to calling Petrarch the first of modern poets who refined and dignified the language of love. Dante had certainly set him the example.

(Vol. ii. pp. 324-5, 346-9.)

['Petrarchists' and 'Danteists']

In modern Italian criticism there are two schools of taste, whose respective partizans may be called the Petrarchists and the Danteists. The latter allege that Petrarch's amatory poetry, from its platonic and mystic character, was best suited to the age of cloisters, of dreaming voluptuaries, and of men living under tyrannical governments, whose thoughts and feelings were oppressed and disguised. The genius of Dante, on the other hand, they say, appeals to all that is bold and natural in the human breast, and they trace the grand revival of his popularity in our own times to the re-awakened spirit of liberty. On this side of the question the most eminent Italian scholars and poets have certainly ranged. The most gifted man of that country with whom I was ever personally acquainted, Ugo Foscolo, was a vehement Danteist. Yet his copious memory was well stored with many a sonnet of Petrarch's, which he could repeat by heart; and, with all his Danteism, he infused the deepest tones of admiration into his recitation of the Petrarchan sonnets.

(Vol. ii. pp. 356-7.)

[Translations of Petrarch and of Dante]

I despair of ever seeing in English verse a translation of Petrarch's Italian poetry that shall be adequate and popular. The term adequate, of course, always applies to the translation of genuine poetry in a subdued sense. It means the best that can be expected, after making allowance for that escape of etherial spirit which is inevitable in the transfer of poetic thoughts from one language to another. The word popular is also to be taken in a limited meaning regarding all translations. Cowper's ballad of John Gilpin is twenty times more popular than his Homer; yet the latter work is deservedly popular in comparison with the bulk of translations from antiquity. The same thing may be said of Carey's Dante; it is like Cowper's Homer, as adequate and popular as translated poetry can be expected to be. Yet I doubt if either of those poets could have succeeded so well with Petrarch. Lady Dacre[1] has shewn much grace and ingenuity in the passages of our poet, which she has versified; but she could not transfer into English those graces of Petrarchan diction, which are mostly intransferable. She could not bring the Italian language along with her. Is not this, it may be asked, a proof that Petrarch is not so genuine a poet as Homer and Dante, since his charm depends upon the delicacies of diction that evaporate in the transfer from tongue to tongue, more than on hardy thoughts that will take root in any language to which they are transplanted?

(Vol. ii. pp. 360-1.)

LADY MORGAN*

(c. 1783-1859)

[Sydney Owenson, a native of Dublin, afterwards (1812) the wife of the surgeon Sir Thomas Charles Morgan, made her reputation as a novelist. In 1818, on the strength of the success of a book of hers on France, Colburn the publisher offered her £2000 for a similar work on Italy. After a residence of more than a year in Italy (1819-20) Lady Morgan published the book in 1821. It was praised by Byron as

[1] [Barbarina, wife of Thomas Brand, twenty-first Lord Dacre; her translations from Petrarch were privately printed in 1836, but many of them had already been printed by Ugo Foscolo in his *Essays on Petrarch* published in 1823.]

* [Before Lady Morgan should come A. Pozzesi, accidently omitted (see *Appendix*, below, pp. 700-1).]

'fearless and excellent,' and was proscribed by the King of Sardinia, the Emperor of Austria, and the Pope (to whom Lady Morgan had been presented in Rome). In spite of severe attacks upon it in the English press, a sêcond edition was called for within six months, and it was reprinted in France and Belgium. In the course of this work, from which a few representative extracts are printed below, Lady Morgan frequently quotes, and occasionally translates, passages from the *Divina Commedia*. Lady Morgan died in London in 1859.]

1821. ITALY.

[Dante's political opinions]

DANTE, at the time of his banishment from Florence, was, like all his family, a Guelph or *liberale*. His exile was at first the result of faction; and he continued true to liberty, and to his own 'Carità del natío loco,'[1] up to the writing of the tenth book of his *Inferno*, where he places the Emperor Frederick II. and Cardinal Ubaldino in hell. It was not until his impatience and resentment at his long exile getting the better of all discretion and patriotism, that he changed his party, and attacked the Florentines, 'quello ingrato popolo maligno.'[2] Of this temporary desertion from his party, through pique, he is accused by one of his most ancient and partial biographers. When it was known that he openly invoked the Italians to

'Lasciar seder Cesare nella sella,'[3]

then he was accused of treason, and his exile was for life.

(Vol. i. pp. 179-80.)

[Political weathercocks stigmatized by Dante]

These are the nobles whose names echoed in the circle of Marie Antoinette, whose persons lined the anti-rooms of Napoleon, and whose eye sued for notice from Louis *le Désiré*. . . . These are the true weathercocks, which, as Dante described,

'Non furon rebelli,
Nè fur fedeli a Dio, ma per sè stessi.'[4]

Although no rebels to the heav'nly throne
Still were they false, and served—themselves alone.

(Vol. i. p. 289.)

[The name of Dante odious to the Papal Court]

The police at Florence is in perpetual activity of espionage, and the press has not even a shadow of liberty; for even to praise Dante with too much ardour, is to incur the suspicion of hostility to that Papal influence, which he was the first so boldly and so nobly to attack. When an improvisatore recently arrived in

[1] [*Inf.* xiv. 1.] [2] [*Inf.* xv. 61.] [3] [*Purg.* vi. 92.]
[4] [*Inf.* iii. 38-9: read 'per sè foro.']

Florence, and advertised as his theme the raising of a monument to the memory of Dante, he was silenced by the police;—that subject being too ticklish for the Florentine authorities.

(Vol. ii. p. 222.)

[The claim that Dante founded the Italian language]

'When Dante,' says Perticari, 'wrote his poem in a noble dialect, taken from those of all Italy, then, we say, he founded the Italian language.' This proposition is supported upon the authority of Dante himself, in his treatise *De vulgari eloquentia;* but upon an extension of the meaning of his words which places them in contradiction with physical possibility. . . . As the dialects of Italy all sprang from a common origin, it was doubtless possible for Dante, in struggling against the difficulty of writing in an uncultivated, and as it were nascent language, to adopt, from time to time, a single expression from any of the surrounding dialects, which struck him as more sounding, significant, appropriate, or elegant, than that of the spoken dialect of his own country. . . . But there must have been a grammatical substructure of conjugations and declensions known and intelligible to the people whom Dante addressed, upon which he raised his new edifice; or he must have written a jargon which could not have been understood without a grammar and dictionary composed expressly for a key. If, therefore, the general construction of the language adopted by Dante, and the other fathers of the written Italian, was that in use amongst the people of Florence, and among none other of the population of Italy, that is sufficient to justify the claims of the Florentines. . . . If it be admitted that there was a court and poetic language common to all the polished and educated classes of Italy (a proposition that appears untenable, from the broken up condition of the Continent), how came this to be the language of the common people of Florence? If Dante, as it is pretended, had imported it, his book, unintelligible to the common people, would never have become popular:—but the contrary is the known fact; and however much Dante might have refined his native tongue, it demonstrably subsisted as a popular dialect before he was born.[1]

(Vol. ii. pp. 471-4.)

[The episode of Francesca da Rimini]

Rimini, rich in historical and poetical recollections, from Dante to Pellico, the seat of the feudal sway of those brave bold *Condottieri*, the Malatestas, bears every symptom of its great antiquity and former military importance. . . . The fine old Castle of Rim-

[1] [From an appendix by Sir T. C. Morgan.]

ini, romantic as it looks, (even though now a Papal barrack), was not that dwelling, where the *Francesca* of Dante passed the 'tempo de' dolci sospiri'[1] (the season of sweet sighs). It was not the site of that refined frailty, which leaves even the eloquent pages of Goethe and Rousseau, with all their sentimental sorcery, far behind. The voluptuous delicacy which Dante, in his short episode, has thrown over the loves of Francesca da Rimini and Paolo dei Malatesti, has often been imitated, but never equalled, and still less surpassed.

(Vol. iii. pp. 321-3.)

ANONYMOUS

1821. NEW MONTHLY MAGAZINE. REMARKS ON THE LIFE AND WRITINGS OF UGO FOSCOLO.

[Foscolo's opinion of Dante]

THOUGH the genius of Ugo Foscolo is highly national, it is also, like Alfieri's, a good deal in unison with some of our old English writers, who were understood also to have imitated the poets of Italy. We thus find him extremely well read in English literature, and in the old English poets, as well as in the best authors of antiquity. 'Homer, Dante, and Shakspeare,' he exclaimed, 'are the only three great masters of the human soul—they are indelibly impressed upon my imagination and my heart—I have bathed their verses with my tears—and I seem to hold converse with their divine shades, as if I really beheld them throned upon the clouds of heaven, holding dominion over time and eternity.'

(Vol. i. p. 83.)

1821. NEW MONTHLY MAGAZINE. ON THE LESS CELEBRATED PRODUCTIONS OF THE AUTHOR OF DON QUIXOTE.

[The study of Dante in England]

The cessation of the long war which closed the Continent upon English travellers, admitting a vast influx into the provinces of Italy, has tended to facilitate to our youth of the male sex the pronunciation of the delicate language 'dove il sì suona';[2] and to teach them the conversational idiom, which their former method of study, commencing with the reading of Tasso and concluding with Dante or Petrarch, as little enabled them to attain, as a

[1] [*Inf.* v. 118.] [2] [*Inf.* xxxiii. 80.]

draught from the 'pure wells of English undefiled,' that bubbled in the Elizabethan age, would render a foreigner *au fait* to the compliments of a London levee.

(Vol. i. p. 113.)

1821. NEW MONTHLY MAGAZINE. WINTER.

[The scenery of Dante's Hell and of Milton's Paradise]

Some sapient critic, in noticing Hunt's story of Rimini, remarks tauntingly that we may guess at the fidelity of the Italian descriptions of scenery, when the author had never wandered beyond the confines of Highgate and Hampstead Heath. . . . Such matter-of-fact critics might quarrel with Dante for never having been in Hell, and with Milton for not having visited Paradise before he presumed to describe it.

(Vol. i. p. 161.)

1821. NEW MONTHLY MAGAZINE. THE POETRY OF THE TROUBADOURS.

[Dante, Petrarch, and the Provençal Poets]

'The Provençal Poets, or Troubadours,' says Dunlop in his *History of Fiction*,[1] 'have been acknowledged as the masters of the early Italian poets, and have been raised to, perhaps, unmerited celebrity by the imposing panegyrics of Dante and Petrarch. Their compositions contain violent satires against the clergy, absurd didactic poems, moral songs versified from the works of Boethius, and insipid pastorals.' The poets, to whom Dante and Petrarch confessed their obligations, will not suffer from censures like these,—so *roundly* bestowed.

(Vol. i. p. 279.)

1821. NEW MONTHLY MAGAZINE. REVIEW OF THE PROPHECY OF DANTE. BY LORD BYRON.

[Byron and Dante]

If ever poet deserved to be a prophet, it was Dante. Had he lived in ancient Jerusalem, instead of Florence, it is likely that Providence would have commissioned his intrepid and public-spirited genius to have stood pre-eminent among the masters of sacred oracle. Indeed, by the strength of his political sagacity he predicted future events in the history of Italy; and if he failed to communicate a portion of his own magnanimity to his country, he left writings calculated after the lapse of ages to revive a masculine tone of taste and sentiments in the breasts of posterity. Ever

[1] [Ed. 1845, pp. 195-6.]

since a dawn of patriotism has shone during this and the last century upon Italy, the admirers of Dante have increased in number, whilst those of Petrarch have diminished. Dante applied his poetry to the vicissitudes of his own time, when liberty was making her dying struggle, and he descended to the tomb with the last heroes of the middle ages; whilst Petrarch lived among those who prepared the inglorious heritage of servitude for the next fifteen generations. . . .

Lord Byron's poem is divided into four cantos, and is written in Dante's own *terza rima.* His lordship's attempt to engraft this measure on our language does not seem to us felicitous. Dante's triplets, generally including a full and succinct portion of sense, remind us of the three-forked thunderbolt; whilst the rhyme in the poem before us is scattered in the midst of sentences, and rather breaks than strengthens the harmony of versification. The poem has great intrinsic beauty, but the style of its egotism is too diffuse to be a just imitation of Dante, whether we suppose him to act the part of a prophet or a poet.

(Vol. i. pp. 725-6.)

1821. NEW MONTHLY MAGAZINE.

Ugolino [1]

Then paused the sinner from his foul repast,
And from his mouth the gory remnants cast;
Till, cleansed his lips from clotted blood and hair,
The gloomy tale his accents thus declare:
'Thou ask'st a thing, whose thought to desperate pain
The past recalling, harrows up my brain;
And, ere my tongue the direful scene unroll,
Remember'd anguish loads my wretched soul.
But should these words, these tears, with guilt and shame
Blast in the realms of day the traitor's name,
Whose hateful scull with ravening tooth I bare—
Nor words this mouth, nor tears these eyes shall spare.
Who thou may'st be, and through the realms of pain
How thou hast wander'd here, to guess were vain;
But the sweet accent of my native land
Bespeaks thee born on Arno's flowery strand.
Count Ugolino was my name;—my prey
This felon's scull once did a mitre sway;
Ruggiero was he call'd;—now learn the cause
Of this our doom by Hell's unerring laws.

[1] See Dante, Inferno, Canto 33 [ll. 1-78].

My faith by him abus'd—my hapless fate
Consign'd to chains, 'twere needless to relate:
But the dark secrets of that prison drear
Thou hast not heard—and now thou art to hear.
    Full many a moon had shot a silvery dew
Through the small chink that air'd our narrow mew[1]—
The Tower of Famine, named from me (now I
The only wretch there doom'd immured to die),
When, as I slept, a dream of awful power
Rent the dark veil that shrouds the future hour.
Me thought to those fair hills with olives green
Which Pisa's haughty walls from Lucca screen,
Ruggiero, proud in hot and arduous chace
Held a dark wolf and all his brindled race;
Gualandi, Sismond, Lanfranc led the way,
And fierce and meagre hounds pursued the prey.
Short space the weary brutes have strength to fly;
They faint—they sink—the hunters yell—they die.
Breathless I wake, and hear a feeble scream,—
Oh God! it is my little ones that dream;
I hear them moan, as wrapt in sleep they lie,
And, "Father, give us bread," they faintly cry.
Think, mortal, then what flash'd upon my brain;
And in that thought if thou from tears refrain
Stern, stern indeed art thou, and pitiless of pain.
And now, our slumbers past, the hour draws nigh
That brings of daily food the scant supply.
Silent we sit, and lost in thoughtful gloom,
In the dark dream each scans the coming doom;
When the drear tower shook with a horrid jar—
It was the clang of bolts and creaking of the bar.
Then all was silent;—for I did not moan—
Despair and horror froze my soul to stone.
I gazed upon the innocents—and they
Wept sorely—and I heard one falt'ring say
(My little Anselm) "Father, look not so—
What ails thee, father?"—in that day of woe
I spake not, wept not;—nor in the long night
That follow'd—nor till broke the morning light;
When, as my image in the wretched four,
Paternity's sweet pledge, I saw once more,
In bitterness of grief my very hands I tore;
And they, believing that for want of bread
I gnaw'd my flesh, quick started up and said,

[1] 'Muda.'—Dante.

"Feed on *us*, father! less will be the pain,—
Thou gav'st these wretched limbs, and take them back again."
I then was silent, that I might not wring
Their tender souls with added suffering.
That day in silence, and the next were pass'd—
Oh God! Oh God! why were they not the last!
The fourth morn, at my feet, in agony
My Gaddo fell; and "Help me, father, why
Dost thou not help me!" was the dying cry
Of that dear child; and thus the other three,
Ere the sixth morn arrived, had ceased to be.
Famine and tears then quench'd the visual light,
And, staggering sightless in the grave of night,
I sought my children—and these fingers stray'd
O'er their cold limbs, and with their features play'd.
Three days I call'd their names—but they were dead;
The fourth in ling'ring pangs the father's spirit fled.'
  Thus spake the Fiend; and as he spake, his eyes
Shot forth askaunt the wrath that never dies.
With grin malign he clench'd the traitor's head,
And to their vengeful task his teeth indurate sped.

(Vol. ii. pp. 327-8.)

1821. NEW MONTHLY MAGAZINE. BOTANY.

[Quotation from Dante applied to Linnæus]

Linnæus, to whom every botanist must say, as Dante said to Virgil, 'Tu duca, tu Signor, e tu Maestro,'[1] is intelligible in his original garb to but few ladies; but there are many excellent works in our own language which will lead them farther than the generality will choose to follow.

(Vol. ii. p. 369.)

1822. NEW MONTHLY MAGAZINE. MODERN PILGRIMAGES.

[The experience of genius like that of Dante]

Genius must undergo a purgatory of neglect, and must pay its visit, like Dante, to the infernal regions of oblivion, ere it can reach the paradise of lasting fame.

(Vol. iv. p. 220.)

1822. NEW MONTHLY MAGAZINE. ITALIAN POETS. NO. I. MICHEL ANGELO.

[Michael Angelo and Dante]

Never did Michel Angelo foresee that the verses which he composed as a relaxation and outpouring of his feelings, would one day

[1] [*Inf.* ii. 140.]

be compared with those to which Dante and Petrarch had consecrated their toil, their life, and all the rare faculties of their intellect. Michel Angelo was evidently endowed with a disposition to poetry; and in his youth his evenings were spent in reading Dante and Petrarch to his friends; and his attempts to catch their spirit shew that he had profited by the study. Yet these same attempts are sufficient to convince us, that had he even devoted to poetry the whole power of his talent, he would nevertheless have remained inferior to his great models; and that, at all events, he would have approached nearer Petrarch than Dante. . . . As Phidias acknowledged having found the original of his Jupiter Olympius in the first book of the *Iliad*, so Michel Angelo professed to have designed his figures, arranged his groups, given the attitude to their limbs, and the expression to their physiognomy, out of the poem of Dante. He translated (if we may use the term) this poem in a series of designs, forming a large volume, which he unfortunately lost by a shipwreck. His admiration for Dante was accompanied with a sympathy which almost amounted to filial respect; and he spoke of him as though he had been the companion of his misfortunes, and had passed with him a portion of his life. . . . But the more successful Michel Angelo was in adopting, and even improving on the conceptions of Dante, as an artist, the less did he succeed—nor, in truth, did he attempt it—in equalling him as a poet. The poetry of Dante consists chiefly in images; that of Michel Angelo, like Petrarch's, is a compound of thought and sentiment, which always excites to meditation, and sometimes touches the heart; but neither describes, nor paints, nor works powerfully on the imagination.

(Vol. iv. pp. 343-5.)

1822. NEW MONTHLY MAGAZINE. THE CONFESSIONAL. NO. I. LOVE.

[Francesca da Rimini's story of her love]

It is a vulgar error, to suppose that we necessarily take delight in recalling to the memory events which gave us delight as they were passing, but which are actually passed, and can never be renewed. The certainty that they *are* passed, and cannot return, more than neutralizes the pleasure the remembrance of them might otherwise bring to us: it changes the phantom of joy into a mockery of it. This was well known to one who looked more deeply into the dungeons of the human heart than any other modern has done. . . .

'Nessun maggior dolore
Che ricordarsi del tempo felice
Nella miseria.'[1]

Infer. c. 5. Quoted in Corsair.

What greater pain
Than thinking upon happiness gone by
In the midst of grief?

Such are the words the mighty poet of the *Inferno* puts into the mouth of his gentle Francesca, when she is called upon to relate the story of her love—to tell the brief tale of her past happiness, while she is pining and withering away in penal fires. Mark, too, the effect even on the poet himself, mere spectator as he is, and 'one, albeit, unused to the melting mood':—

'Mentre che l' uno spirto questo disse,
L' altro piangeva sì, che di pietade
I' venni men così, com' io morisse:
E caddi, come corpo morto cade.'[2]

While one of these sad spirits thus discoursed,
The other wept so, that from very pity,
A death-like faintness seized me, and I fell
Prone to the earth, as a dead body falls.

A less deep insight into the secret places of the human heart, would have induced the poet to invest the lips of his lovers with a momentary smile, at the imaginary renewal of their loves.

(Vol. iv. p. 351.)

1822. NEW MONTHLY MAGAZINE. ITALIAN POETS. NO. II. FREDERICK THE SECOND AND PIETRO DELLE VIGNE.

[Episodes from the *Divina Commedia*]

Among the productions of the minor poets of Italy we meet with many which were composed fifty, eighty, and even more than a hundred years earlier than the great work of Dante. . . . The enterprize, almost superhuman, of creating a new literary language, which Dante achieved, will be less astonishing, when we consider that it was encouraged and facilitated by such predecessors as Pietro delle Vigne. . . . A beautiful passage of Dante, admirably translated by Mr. Cary, will, in some measure, compensate for the scanty relics of Pietro delle Vigne's poetry; and will, at the same time, instruct our readers in all which is certainly known as to the tragic death of this uncommon man. . . . Dante, in his circuit of Hell, enters upon a forest—

[1] [*Inf.* v. 121-3.]

[2] [*Inf.* v. 139-42.]

'Where no track
Of steps had worn away. Not verdant there
The foliage, but of dusky hue; not light
The boughs and tapering, but with knares deform'd
And matted thick: fruits there were none, but thorns
Instead, with venom fill'd.'

Hell, *Canto* xiii. *v*. 3.

From the trees of this forest wailings and deep groans issue forth; and Dante, stretching out his hand, gathers a branch from a great wilding:—when a voice from the trunk exclaims—

'"Why pluck'st thou me?"—
Then, as the dark blood trickled down its side,
These words it added: "Wherefore tear'st me thus?
Is there no touch of mercy in thy breast?
Men once were we, that now are rooted here. . . ."
I, letting fall the bough, remained as one
Assail'd by terror.'

* * * *

To make the unhappy soul some amends for the wrong he had done it in wrenching off the branch from the tree in which it was confined, Dante demands the name it bore in the world above, in order that he, on his return, may revive its fame:—it answers—

"I it was who held
Both keys to Frederick's heart, and turn'd the wards
Opening and shutting, with a skill so sweet,
That besides me into his inmost breast
Scarce any other could admittance find.
The faith I bore to my high charge was such,
It cost me the life-blood that warm'd my veins.
The harlot,[1] who ne'er turn'd her gloating eyes
From Caesar's household, common vice and pest
Of courts, 'gainst me inflamed the minds of all;
And to Augustus they so spread the flame,
That my glad honours changed to bitter woes.
My soul, disdainful and disgusted, sought
Refuge in death from scorn, and I became,
Just as I was, unjust toward myself.
By the new roots, which fix this stem, I swear
That never faith I broke to my liege lord,
Who merited such honour: and if you,
If any to the world indeed return,
Clear he from wrong my memory, that lies
Yet prostrate under envy's cruel blow."

Hell, *Canto* xiii. *v*. 60.

(Vol. iv. pp. 455, 461-2.)

[1] Envy.

1822. NEW MONTHLY MAGAZINE. ITALIAN POETS. NO. III. GUIDO CAVALCANTI.

[Guido Cavalcanti and Dante]

'Thus hath one Guido from the other snatch'd
The letter'd prize,—and he perhaps is born
Who shall drive either from their nest.'[1]
Dante, *Purg.* c. xi.

Such is the modest pride with which Dante anticipates the superiority of his own renown; adding, however,

'The noise
Of worldly fame is but a blast of wind
That blows from divers points, and shifts its name
Shifting the point it blows from. Your renown
Is like the herb, whose hue doth come and go.'[1]

And yet he endured every suffering to acquire that celebrity which he thus pronounced to be fluctuating and perishable. . . . The eldest of the three Guidos was born at Bologna, of the noble family of Guinicelli, and died in 1276. It is of him that Dante says—'He was father to me, and to those my betters, who have ever used the sweet and pleasant rhymes of love—

His dulcet lays, as long
As of our tongue the beauty does not fade,
Shall make us love the very ink that traced them.'

Dante was not a critic to lavish his praises; he never flattered the living, and why should he flatter the dead? Still we doubt whether his praises would be justified by any of the known pieces of Guido Guinicelli. . . . Pathos belongs to all time, and may be expressed in every language; yet we find nothing but coldness in the verses of Guinicelli. In this perhaps we are wrong, since Mr. Carey[3] has thought them worthy, precisely for their pathos, to be inserted among those extracts of early poetry with which he has enriched his translation of Dante. . . . The character of Guido Cavalcanti was so strongly marked, that his fellow-citizens and the historians of his times all agreed in their manner of pourtraying it. 'He was,' says Villani, 'for a philosopher, skilful in many pursuits; but somewhat too irritable and harsh.' Dino, another eye-witness, speaks of him as 'courteous and ardent, though scornful, solitary, and immersed in study'; and Dante himself, who possessed, in an uncommon degree, the same good and bad qualities, called him 'his first friend,'—yielded with deference to his literary opinions, and stood in awe of his remonstrances. During an access of idle

[1] [From Cary's translation.]
[2] [From Cary's translation—*Purg.* xxvi. 112-4.]
[3] [*Sic.*]

melancholy, to which in his youth he was often liable from his too strong feelings, he was severely reproached by Guido. . . .

Philip Villani, the son and nephew of the two Florentine historians, in giving the earliest example of literary history and criticism, confirmed the decision of the learned of his age, who pronounced the lyric pieces of Guido equal to those of Dante. Indeed the energy and originality which form the two characteristics of Dante's genius appear still more strongly in the lyrics of Guido, but always deformed by a primitive rudeness, which Dante, who was born twenty years later, more successfully avoided. Guido found the art in its infancy, and in raising it to adolescence, displayed greater force than skill; but in the productions of Dante strength and address marched with an equal step, and in tempering the harshness incident to all early poetry, he had the sagacity to choose the style of Virgil as his model. Besides Dante made poetry his study and his chief glory: Guido, aspiring to a higher reputation, considered the single merit of fine poetry as insufficient to entitle any man, even Virgil himself, to rank with a philosopher.

(Vol. v. pp. 1 ff.)

1822. NEW MONTHLY MAGAZINE. THE POETRY OF LIFE.

[Quotation from Dante]

'Whip me under the gallows' the cold philosopher that would banish the Muses from his republic; but the wretch that would wish the Poetry of life and feeling to be extinct, let him for ever dwell *In caldo, e 'n gielo*,[1] as Dante has it—

'In flame, in frost, in ever-during night.'

(Vol. v. pp. 163-4.)

1822. March. NEW MONTHLY MAGAZINE. FOREIGN VARIETIES. ITALY.

[Commemoration of the five-hundredth anniversary of the death of Dante]

Dante. A society of literary men and distinguished artists met together on the 14th of September last, to keep the anniversary of the death of Dante, in remembrance of that illustrious poet. The meeting took place in a country-house beyond the bridge of Milvio. Every thing was arranged to imitate the ancient funeral rites called *Parentalia*. A banqueting table was placed in the middle of the house, and at the head a pedestal, which contained a bust of the poet, with the following inscription:

[1] [*Inf.* iii. 87.]

Danti . Aligherio
Italicae . poeseos . parenti
Qua . die . fato . obiit
Quingentos . post . annos
Carmina . et . epulum . funebre.

The ceremony of the day was intermingled with libations, and literary discourses relative to the occasion, in the manner of the Saturnales of Macrobius.

(Vol. vi. pp. 117-18.)

1822. October. NEW MONTHLY MAGAZINE. FOREIGN VARIETIES. ITALY.

[The *Vision of Alberico* and the *Divina Commedia*]

A manuscript, entitled 'The Story of the Vision of Alberico,' was discovered some two or three months ago in the library of the ancient monastery of Monte Casino. This story was written in the monastery in the beginning of the 12th century; it narrates the vision of Alberico, who was a native of Settefrati, a little town in the district of Atina, and when at the age of nine years suddenly fell into a swoon that continued nine days, during which he was (in vision) conducted by the Prince of Apostles through Hell, Purgatory, and Paradise; and observed the punishments and enjoyments of the three regions. It is known that Dante visited Naples twice at the end of the 13th century; and as his curiosity would have probably led him to so renowned a place as Monte Casino, it is thought that he might have there seen the Vision of Alberico, and taken the idea of his Divina Commedia from it. This Vision is preparing for publication.[1]

(Vol. vi. p. 454.)

ANONYMOUS

1822. April. QUARTERLY REVIEW. ART. II. HISTORY OF THE AEOLIC DIGAMMA.

[Dante's fondness for 'hiatus']

DANTE, from the very third line

'Che la diritta via era smarrita,'

to the end of his long poem, seems to delight in hiatus, which none of his successors would have ventured to admit, yet which, in his verse, could not be altered without changing altogether

[1] [As a matter of fact the Vision of Alberico was published in 1814, and was utilized by Cary in the notes to his second (1819) and subsequent editions.]

the original character of a poetic language created by him; and destroying at the same time a species of melody, which seems the music of nature herself. The second of the following lines offers an instance both of the melting of the vowels, and of the hiatus, equally shocking to a modern ear—

'Queste parole di colore oscuro,
Vidi io scritte al sommo d' una porta.'

—The *vidi io*, of which no versifier from Petrarch downwards, would have made more than two syllables, *vid' io*, must be pronounced, in Dante, either *vi-dii-o*, or *vi-di-io*, in both ways making three syllables, otherwise the accent does not fall in its proper place, and the measure is incomplete.[1]

(Vol. xxvii. p. 62.)

ANONYMOUS

1822. July. QUARTERLY REVIEW. ART. VI. PANEGYRICAL ORATORY OF GREECE.

[Dante on the love of fame]

As compared with the funeral speeches of his competitors, we more particularly recognise in Lysias that intense love of glory, which belonged equally to the Greek and Italian republics; which in Athens made statesmen strangers to their beds; and which in Dante renders the very damned less thoughtful of their punishments below, than of the state of their fame in the world above.

(Vol. xxvii. p. 402.)

JOHN TAAFFE

(fl. 1820)

[John Taaffe, an Irishman resident in Italy, was an acquaintance of Byron and Shelley, to both of whom he appealed for help in getting a publisher for a work of his on Dante, consisting of a translation of the *Divina Commedia*, with a commentary. Both Byron and Shelley thought well of the commentary, but the translation was a very sorry performance. Byron wrote to Murray (see letters of Jan. 22, and March 6, 1822)[2] and Shelley to Ollier (see letter of June 16, 1821)[3] on Taaffe's behalf, and eventually the first volume of the commentary, with a few incidental specimens of the translation (in octosyllabic *terza rima*), printed in Italy from the types of Didot, was published in London by Murray. The work was severely

[1] [Modern editors, as a matter of fact, print *vid' io* in this passage (*Inf.* iii. 11).]

[2] [See above, pp. 51-2; see also letters to Moore of Nov. 16, 1821, and March 8, 1822 (above, pp. 47-8, 52); and Medwin's Conversations with Byron (above, p. 51).]

[3] [See above, pp. 223-4.]

handled by Cary (whose translation Taaffe attacks in his preface) in the *London Magazine* for March and April, 1823.[1] Whatever his qualifications as a translator of the *Commedia*, Taaffe was a serious student of Dante, and his commentary, which contains sundry translations from the *Vita Nuova* and *Convivio*, is by no means without value.]

1822. A COMMENT ON THE DIVINE COMEDY OF DANTE ALIGHIERI. BY * * * *

[Of the metre of the *Divina Commedia* and of certain English translations of the poem]

OF the Divina Commedia there are many translations in prose and verse. The one which least dissatisfies me, is the Latin version of Carlo d'Aquino.[2] In English I am acquainted with two: although I did not know anything of the existence of either, until very lately. With regard to one of them, it it unnecessary to notice it; for ramblingly paraphrastic, as it is, I believe if the title page were cut out and the book handed to me, I should not be aware it was intended for a translation of Dante.[3] The other is indeed a very different production, I mean that of Mr. Cary. Its fidelity is exemplary; and though somewhat of a paraphrase, it is far from loose. But whatever be its *literal* merits, it does not give, nor pretend to give any of the melody of its Original. Dante writes in rhyme and in a metre whose chief characteristics are pliancy and concision. Mr. Cary in blank verse imitative of the stateliness and occasional prolixity of Milton. Be it observed, that before Dante neither *terza rima* nor blank verse (versi sciolti) existed in Italian, though both now do; and Cesarotti, Alfieri, Parini, Bettinelli, etc. prove, that the latter is no less adapted to the genius of the language, than the former. Dante then might just as easily have invented *blank verse*, as terza rima; if there was not something in rhyme which pleased his ear more. He had begun his poem in Latin heroics, but soon changed both tongue and metre. Who knows how many metres he might have tried, before he decided for terza rima? His smaller poems display a variety of metres. Any of these, or blank verse were as easy an invention as terza rima. But in choosing this last, he, in my opinion, chose well; for no other seems capable of such variety—being alike proper for the highest and the lowest themes, and susceptible of every gradation of sound, to accompany each colour of eloquence, from rapid argument to playful imagery, from expanding tenderness to sarcasm and vehemence, from the sublimest simplicity to magnificence of description. Concision however is the

[1] [See vol. i. pp. 487-8.]
[2] [In hexameters—published at Naples in 1728.]
[3] [No doubt the translation here referred to is that by Boyd, published in 1802 (see vol. i. pp. 410 ff.).]

chief peculiarity of Dante's style; even where he enters into descriptive details (which is rarely), his expressions are conciser, than those of any other writer would have been on a similar occasion: no rhythm then is more unlike his than the Miltonic. Why then imagine that he would have selected it, had he written in English? He might have changed language, yet not ear. If we are to argue from analogy, it will not follow that because he prefer'd rhyme in his native tongue, he would blank verse in ours; and that he would choose in English, the metre most entirely dissimilar to the one he liked best in Italian. Before Lord Byron employed terza rima, it might have been objected that there was something in that fine metre not agreeing with the form of our language: but that doubt is now vanished. Perhaps Mr. Haley[1] removed it before; but I cannot speak of his verses, having never seen them. But there is a far more ancient and higher authority for English terza rima than Mr. Haley—authority of which I was not aware till this very morning, the authority of the partial translator, and frequent imitator of Dante—Milton. His version of the second Psalm is in regular terza rima. But Prior and Pope are not more different in their manner, than Milton in his Paradise Lost and Dante in his Divine Comedy. I use the first names that occur, and not certainly intending to institute a comparison between Prior and Dante. But there is nothing in our literature which conveys a specimen of the style of the Divina Commedia (for neither Mr. Haley's fragment, nor Milton's short Psalm is of extent enough to merit an exception)—at least there was none, until the *Prophecy of Dante*; and even this is restricted to one feature of the Italian, its melancholy grandeur and force. In Dante's long poem there are vast varieties of scenes, speculations, personages, sentiments, etc. with which our noble countryman had nothing to do; yet with all these the Italian terza rima takes corresponding modulations, with wondrous flexibility.

Long before seeing Mr. Cary's translation, I had begun to attempt one conformably to the principles just disclosed. That translation of mine I have since suppressed: yet not until two Cantos were printed, as well as the comments on them.

(*Preface*, pp. xix-xxii.)

[Of *terza rima* in English]

About six years since, I turned five Cantos of Dante into precisely the same measure which is in the *Prophecy of Dante*: but afterwards found it so heavy that I renounced it. The fault was possibly intirely my own; but also I could not remedy it. With-

[1] [*Sic*, for Hayley (see vol. i. pp. 359 ff.).]

out troubling others, I meditated on the matter; and the consequence was, that I at last determined to allow myself the liberty of varying my lines from eight to ten syllables, instead of giving them all the fine heroic complement; as well as of using double rhymes at pleasure. Even his Lordship uses these. Dryden introduces a somewhat similar variety into his heroics by the free use of triplets and Alexandrines; which give a rich variety to his versification, that, at least to my ear, is more grateful than the regularity of Mr. Pope's couplets. With me, a full heroic line answers to the Alexandrine—this being a length which I never permit myself. Nor do I think the liberty I have thus assumed is equal to that which the Italian furnished to Dante—so superior is it to English in copiousness of rhyme and phrase and freedom of syntax. Yet were it otherwise, neither my Author's nor his Lordship's genius is a rule for others. They might have been able to modulate a continuous English terza rima of ten syllables with all the varieties of the Divine Comedy. I certainly could not: and the same reasons which made me leave off attempting it before I saw the *Prophecy of Dante*, still subsist in full vigour.

(*Preface*, pp. xxiii-iv.)

[Criticism of Cary's translation]

Now I must refer more particularly to the version which my readers, who are not sufficiently masters of Italian, will probably employ—that of Mr. Cary. He is, I believe, a fair antagonist; and I will meet him fairly. After protesting (as I hereby most solemnly do) against his metre, its want of harmony, his paraphrases, and, in fine, all that appertains to style, as totally inadequate to convey the remotest resemblance to the poetry of his original—after doing this justice to my author once for all, I circumscribe my future observations on Mr. Cary to his *literal* pretensions; and here, it must be allowed, he is entitled to much encomium. Not that he is always so: or that there is a Canto in which there are not some inaccuracies. . . . Having enumerated what I conceive to be his defects (*considered merely literally*) and repeated, for the last time, my entire disapproval of his style throughout the whole poem, I do not hesitate to avow again that Mr. Cary's verbal fidelity is in general laudable. Had he written in prose, he might perhaps have been faithfuller to Dante's characteristic concision, and as much so to his various melody as blank verse can well be.

(*Ibid.* pp. xxv-vi, xxx.)

[Flaxman's designs from Dante]

The designs of Mr. Flaxman are of the noblest productions of art, and frequently display a sublime simplicity which is worthy of his great original. Indeed he, who is so able to transfer such creations from one fine art to another, seems of a mind but little inferior to his who could first conceive them. To borrow the words of an excellent Italian sculptor: 'Mr. Flaxman has translated Dante best; for he has translated him into the universal language of nature.'

(p. xxxi.)

[Translations from the *Divina Commedia* in octosyllabic *terza rima*]

Oh! loathing breeds
Your lust of lucre, Pastors! Knaves!
Whom did the scribe of Patmos view
In her, the harlot throned on waves
And whoring with the kings of earth, but you?
Hell, Canto xix. [ll. 106-8].

(p. 33.)

I see my Jesus mocked again
And drench'd again with vinegar and gall
And amid living robbers slain.
Purg. Canto xx. [ll. 88-90].

(p. 74.)

What once was sword-work now is done
By a denial of that bread
The Sire of Mercy keeps from none:
O thou, who writest but to cancel, dread
The planters of the vine thou seek'st to cut!
Nor Paul nor martyr'd Peter's dead.
But answer bold:—my hopes are put
In the great Eremite alone,
Who bled in Jewry for a slut;
To me your Paul and fisherman's unknown.
Parad. Canto. xviii. [ll. 127-36].

(p. 76.)

Came Cephas, and came poor and bare
The Vessel elect in lowliest gait,
Unshod, content with any fare;
Not such our modern Pastors' state
With squires and toilets and to saddle-bow
Raised with labour—Oh! men of weight!
Whose mantles down their palfreys flow,
A single hide upon a pair of brutes!—
How far thy patience, Heaven, can go!
Parad. Canto. xxi. [ll. 127-35].

(p. 77.)

[Dante's *Vita Nuova*]

Dante wrote prose for Beatrice as well as rhyme; and the history, he has left us of his strangely pure and exalted courtship and of her decease, is (with the exception of verses interspersed here and there) in prose burning with the very essence of love, and, at last, melting with the tenderest sorrow. It is indeed an enchanting volume, and discovers that intense glow of refined passion, which Rousseau alone has sometimes equalled, when it may be with fullest justice said of him that

with ethereal flame
Kindled he was.

Child Harold, Canto iii.

But alas! the Genevese experienced only the lightning of a disordered brain that blasted him; his heart remained unvisited by any holy warmth; and even his most spiritual creations are such, as morality cannot avoid censuring. Not so Dante: whose affections were at first engaged naturally by a fellow-creature; and, when death rendered the object of them ideal, it only gave a loftier elevation to both his heart and genius; nor did his pen transgress his own precept, that, 'a gentleman should never use an expression improper for a female to hear'—il pudico e nobile uomo mai non parla sicchè a una donna non fossero oneste le sue parole (Convito, p. 199). In the composition alluded to above (the Vita Nuova) he, more than once, enters into details both as to the person and dress of Beatrice—'she was of a sanguine complexion, and wore a girdle and such other ornaments as became a girl of her tender age' (Cinta, ed ornata, alla guisa che alla sua giovanissima età si convenia, p. 1): and he tells us they were both in their ninth year, she just commencing hers and he closing his, when first they met—dal principio del suo nono anno apparve a me, ed io la vidi quasi al fine del mio. . . .—'After that' (continues the young author of the Vita Nuova) 'I had several casual glimpses of the juvenile angel, but at a distance; so that I had never yet been blessed with the music of her voice: when, one evening (it was the very last of my ninth year) I observed the glorious creature, who indeed, as Homer represents Helen, seemed, not so much the offspring of any mortal, as of a God, come out to take a walk in company with two elderly ladies. Her dress I remember was white. Passing along the street, her eyes happened to fall upon me in the corner where I stood gazing and trembling violently; when, with that ineffable courtesy which has already obtained its unfading recompense in Paradise, she condescended to make me a curtsy, and to address me in a few words of so much virtue and kindness, that they transported me, as it were, to the extreme of rapture.

Nothing can efface that moment from my memory: it was precisely nine o'clock. That, as I have said, being the first time I caught her dulcet accents, there came over me such a sensation of sweetness, that, inebriated with pleasure, I retired from the crowd into my little, lonely room; and shut myself up in order to muse at my leisure upon one so courteous and beautiful. Ere long, I experienced a slight slumber attended by a strange dream. Methought there entered the chamber a flame-tinged cloud, and, within it, stood a personage on whom, albeit his aspect was terrible, I could not avoid gazing steadfastly. It was a marvel how dazzling he seemed with joy: and several words did he utter in latin, of which I only comprehended these, *Behold thy Lord!* In his arms appeared a form sleeping, and naked, with the exception of a light crimson drapery, in which it was wrapt up: and looking on it with attention, I at length recognised the lady of my soul, her who had deigned to salute me that evening. Then he who bore her seemed, in one hand, to hold something all on fire; and turning to me pronounced again in latin—*see thy heart!* After some pause he apparently awoke her who slept; and endeavoured with much art to persuade her to eat of that which burned in his hand; so at last she began the eating of it, though as if doubtingly. But it was not long before the lordly figure, who had been so brilliant and festive, dissolved in a flood of tears, and, weeping bitterly, folded up that lady again in his arms, and appeared to fly away again aloft with her to heaven; leaving me in such a fit of anguish that I awoke.'—Upon this he composed a sonnet, which is really very pretty, and, considering that it was the production of a mere child, astonishingly so: its last lines are these:—

Allegro mi sembrava Amor, tenendo
   Mio core in mano, e nelle braccia avea
   Madonna, involta in un drappo dormendo.
Poi la svegliava, e d' este core ardendo
   Lei paventosa umilmente pascea;
   Appresso gir lo ne vedea piangendo.

It was (as I have said) immediately published, though without a name; so that, it is certain, we have it in its original state free of any subsequent correction. The author's own account of the affair is:—'many replied to my anonymous verses in various ways, and amongst them, he whom I always designate as my *first* friend. His reply was also a sonnet beginning, Vedesti al mio parere ec., and it was indeed upon this occasion that the friendship between us originated; for he came and sought my acquaintance, as soon as he knew it was with me he corresponded.'

(pp. 93-8.)

[Translations from the *Vita Nuova*]

She's gone! our Beatrice is gone
  To heaven amid the angel-kind;
She lives in that high realm of bliss
  And leaves you, ladies, all behind!

The Lord enamoured of her charms
  Has called her for his own delight;
And deemed this lowly world of ours
  Unworthy of a thing so bright.[1]

(p. 110.)

How oft my weeping and my sighs
  My ever-flowing, bitter brine
Brought pity's dew to other eyes,
  You saw yourselves, O eyes of mine![2]

(p. 111.)

[Translations from the *Divina Commedia*]

Not wild Charibdis, when the wildest masses
  Of breakers combat in its pool renown'd,
  Chafes like the innumerous troop that waltzes.
Hell, Canto vii. [ll. 22-4].
(p. 425.)

Spinning their weights around, around,
  While breasts strike breasts with pangs condign,
  Ho! charge, hurra, jolt, bound, rebound!
Ho! foe to foe, and line to line!
  Each cursing each, and madly crying
  "Why closed thy palm?" "why open thine?"
Then thwart the sooty cavern flying
  Still, as they bandy railing, raging,
  That savage taunt that fierce replying;
And face about and form—engaging
  For ever in that rude, unvaried tilt.
Hell, Canto vii. [ll. 27-35].
(p. 430.)

The wisdom beyond wisdom beaming,
  Who made the heavens, made each a guide
  To minister the radiant streaming
And circles of creation wide;
  And also placed a Queen o'er chance
  Of mundane splendors with their tide
Of phantasms. . . .

[1] Ita n' è Beatrice in l' alto cielo etc. [*V.N.* § 32, *Canz.* iv. ll. 16-28].
[2] [*V.N.* § 38, *Son.* xxi. ll. 1-4.]

Matter no whit your plots on plot;
  She orders, sees, foresees the whole.
  Guardian and Goddess of her lot,
Her orb that never finds a gaol
  She keeps—and must—still fleetly tost;
  While human fates as fleetly roll.
Yea! this is she whom slanders long have crost:
  Pure, holy Fair so crucified!
  And most by those who owe her most.
But such she hears not—wheeling wide.
  Her sphere the primal race divine among;
  Conscious, like them, of bliss and naught beside.
Hell, Canto vii. [ll. 73-7, 85-93].

(pp. 445-6.)

ANONYMOUS

1822. Jan. LONDON MAGAZINE. SKETCHES ON THE ROAD (No. VI).

[Dante's reference to Monte San Giuliano]

THE regular coach road from Pisa to Lucca is about fourteen miles, but as we travelled by the *Cavalli di San Francisco*, we went by a short cut, not exceeding eight miles, across the mountain of San Giuliano, which, by the bye, is the one to which Dante refers in the following passage of his Conte Ugolino:—

Questi pareva a me maestro e donno,
Cacciando 'l lupo e i lupicini *al monte*,
Perchè i Pisan veder Lucca non ponno.[1]
Inferno, Canto xxxiii.

(Vol. v. pp. 62-3.)

1822. Feb. LONDON MAGAZINE. CONTINUATION OF DR. JOHNSON'S LIVES OF THE POETS. (No. IV. GOLDSMITH.)

[Statement of Goldsmith's about Dante]

In 1759 Goldsmith published his Inquiry into the Present State of Polite Learning. . . . There is, I doubt, in this little essay more display than reality of erudition. It would not be easy to say

[1] [The writer quotes in a footnote Cary's translation of the passage, and adds:]— On this passage a solemn commentator on Dante observes that such is really the fact that, if Mon S. Giuliano were removed, the inhabitants of either city might see the towers of the other. Such silly observations are not uncommon among commentators.

where he had discovered 'that Dante was persecuted by the critics as long as he lived.' [1]

(Vol. v. p. 107.)

1822. May. LONDON MAGAZINE. THE DRAMA—THE SCHOOL FOR SCANDAL.

[Lady Teazle 'the *Divina Commedia* of womanhood']

Lady Teazle, with her gallant powers of scandal; her virtue, wavering through thoughtlessness; her charming self-restoration, and her constant inimitable spirit, is an elegant comedy in herself! She is the *Divina Commedia*, not of Dante, but of womanhood!

(Vol. v. p. 481.)

1822. July. LONDON MAGAZINE. ON MAGAZINE WRITERS.

[Lines from Dante applied to ephemeral writers]

There is a large class, which, undaunted by difficulty, uninstructed by experience, and unabashed by ridicule, still bear up against every sort of obstacle, 'bating no jot of heart or hope.' These, with some pretensions to erudition, and some habit of reflection—assist to swell out the pages of reviews and magazines, those foundling hospitals for the bastard progeny of prurient imaginations. They buzz for a while about the fields of literature, loud, busy and importunate—till some chilling blast or rude hand sweeps them away for ever, leaving behind

—cotal vestigio
Qual fummo in aere ed in acqua la schiuma.[2]

(Vol. vi. p. 22.)

THOMAS ROSCOE

(1791-1871)

[Thomas Roscoe, fifth son of William Roscoe, the historian, was born in Liverpool in 1791. He was educated privately. Soon after his father's pecuniary embarrassments, in 1816, he began to write in local magazines and journals, and he continued to follow literature as a profession until a few years before his death in London in 1871. Roscoe was the author of various original works, including history, travels, and poems, besides numerous translations, among which were the *Memoirs of Benvenuto Cellini* (1822)—practically a 'conveyance' of Nugent's translation—; Sismondi's *Literature of the South of Europe* (1823); and Lanzi's *History of Painting in Italy* (1828). Roscoe acquired a good working knowledge of modern languages, including French, Italian, Spanish, and German. References to Dante (some of which are given below) are not infrequent in the works translated or edited by him. In his translation of Sismondi's *Literature of the South of Europe* he has inserted an interesting experimental rendering in *terza rima* of the Ugolino episode (*Inf.* xxxiii. 1-75.)]

[1] [See vol. i. p. 321.]

[2] [*Inf.* xxiv. 50-1.]

1822. MEMOIRS OF BENVENUTO CELLINI. . . . WRITTEN BY HIMSELF. . . . NOW FIRST TRANSLATED BY THOMAS ROSCOE.[1]

[Dante and Giotto in France—Giotto's portrait of Dante]

NOTE on Cellini's statement that 'Dante and Giotto the painter were together in France, and visited Paris.'[2]—Giovanni and Philippo Villani, Boccaccio, Gio. Mario Filelfo, and Benvenuto da Imola, all attest the fact of Dante's visit to Paris. Filelfo pretends that he went thither as orator of the Fiorentine Republic, previous to his exile, which was in 1302. Others, placing this journey some years afterwards, suppose that it was undertaken by him for the sole purpose of withdrawing his mind from his misfortunes by studying in the University of Paris, where, according to Boccaccio, he supported a public disputation upon various theological questions.

It is equally certain that Giotto (called Ambrogiotto) di Bondone visited France, being conducted thither by Pope Clement V. in 1308, and that he remained there till 1316. It is uncertain whether this celebrated restorer of the art of painting was at Paris, and particularly whether he was there along with Dante.

The journey of Dante and Giotto together to France is probably a mere supposition of Cellini, who was well aware of the intimate ties of esteem and friendship which united those great men. It is well known that Giotto, in one of his first public labours, that of the painting in fresco, in the Chapel del Podestà at Florence, introduced the portrait of Dante; and that the latter, in his compositions, never ceased to furnish subjects for the pencil of his friend, and to supply him with ideas to assist his invention. Dante went to reside with the family of Giotto in Padua, when the latter was employed in painting in that city.

(Vol. ii. pp. 99-101.)

1823. HISTORICAL VIEW OF THE LITERATURE OF THE SOUTH OF EUROPE. BY J. C. L. SIMONDE DE SISMONDI.

[Dante the father of Italian poetry]

On the Italian language—Dante: No poet had yet arisen, gifted with absolute power over the empire of the soul; no philosopher had yet pierced into the depths of feeling and of thought; when Dante, the greatest name of Italy, and the father of her poetry, appeared, and demonstrated the mightiness of his genius, by availing himself of the rude and imperfect materials within his reach, to con-

[1] [Roscoe's 'translation' of this work is in fact an almost word for word appropriation from the translation of Thomas Nugent, published in 1771 (see vol. i. p. 247).]

[2] [For the whole passage see Nugent's translation (vol. i. pp. 251-2), which is printed verbatim by Roscoe as his own.]

struct an edifice resembling, in magnificence, that universe whose image it reflects. Instead of amatory effusions, addressed to an imaginary beauty; instead of madrigals, full of sprightly insipidity, sonnets laboured into harmony, and strained or discordant allegories, the only models, in any modern language, which presented themselves to the notice of Dante; that great genius conceived, in his vast imagination, the mysteries of the invisible creation, and unveiled them to the eyes of the astonished world.

(Vol. i. Chap. ix. p. 366.)

[The Ugolino episode—*Inferno* xxxiii. 1-75—translation in *terza rima*]

Translator's note: Without detracting from the spirit and ingenuity with which M. Sismondi has executed his laborious task [of translating the Ugolino episode into French verse], it is not too much to say, that the admirer of the unequalled original will turn with pleasure, heightened by the contrast, to the excellent translation of this episode by Mr. Cary. Disclaiming any intention of entering into competition with either of these versions, the editor has ventured to attempt an original translation, in which he has preserved, in the English, the form of the Italian terza rima, and has adhered as literally as possible, and line for line, to the original. This species of verse is certainly difficult in our own language, to which, however, it is much more congenial than to the French. It has been employed with considerable success by Lord Byron, in his Prophecy of Dante, where the reader will be enabled fully to estimate all that it is capable of effecting in our language.—

In the last circle of the infernal world, Dante beholds those who have betrayed their native land, entombed in everlasting ice. Two heads, not far distant from each other, raise themselves above the frozen surface. One of these is that of Count Ugolino della Gherardesca, who, by a series of treasons, had made himself absolute master of Pisa. The other head is that of Ruggieri de' Ubaldini, archbishop of that state, who, by means not less criminal, had effected the ruin of the count, and having seized him, with his four children, or grandchildren, had left them to perish, by famine, in prison. Dante does not at first recognise them, and shudders when he sees Ugolino gnawing the skull of his murderer, which lies before him. He inquires into the motive of this savage enmity, and with the count's reply the thirty-third canto commences:

His mouth upraising from his hideous feast,
 And brushing, with his victim's locks, the spray
 Of gore from his foul lips, that sinner ceas'd:
Then thus: 'Will'st thou that I renew the sway
 Of hopeless grief, which weighs upon my heart
 In thought, ere yet my tongue that thought betray?

But, should my words prove seeds from which may start
 Ripe fruits of scorn for him, whose traitor head
 I gnaw, then words and tears, at once, shall part.
I know thee not; nor by what fortune led
 Thou wanderest here; but thou, if true the claim
 Of native speech, wert in fair Florence bred.
Know, then, Count Ugolino is my name,
 And this the Pisan prelate at my side,
 Ruggier.—Hear, now, my cause of grief, his shame.
That by his arts he won me to confide
 In his smooth words, that I was bound in chains,
 Small need is, now, to tell, nor that I died.
But what is yet untold, unheard, remains,
 And thou shalt hear it—by what fearful fate
 I perish'd. Judge, if he deserves his pains.
When, in those dungeon-walls emmew'd, whose gate
 Shall close on future victims, called the Tower
 Of Famine, from my pangs, the narrow grate
Had shewn me several moons, in evil hour
 I slept and dream'd, and our impending grief
 Was all unveil'd by that dread vision's power.
This wretch, methought, I saw, as lord and chief,
 Hunting the wolf and cubs, upon that hill
 Which makes the Pisan's view towards Lucca brief.
With high-bred hounds, and lean, and keen to kill,
 Gualandi, with Sismondi, in the race
 Of death, were foremost, with Lanfranchi, still.
Weary and spent appear'd, after short chase,
 The sire and sons, and soon, it seem'd, were rent
 With sharpest fangs, their sides. Before the trace
Of dawn, I woke, and heard my sons lament,
 (For they were with me), mourning in their sleep,
 And craving bread. Right cruel is thy bent,
If, hearing this, no horror o'er thee creep;
 If, guessing what I now began to dread,
 Thou weep'st not, wherefore art thou wont to weep?
Now were they all awake. The hour, when bread
 Was wont to be bestow'd, had now drawn near,
 And dismal doubts, in each, his dream had bred.
Then lock'd, below, the portals did we hear
 Of that most horrible Tower. I fix'd my eye,
 Without one word, upon my children dear:
Harden'd like rock within, I heav'd no sigh.
 They wept; and then I heard my Anselm say,
 'Thou look'st so, Sire! what ails thee?' No reply

I utter'd yet, nor wept I, all that day ;
  Nor the succeeding night, till on the gloom
  Another sun had issued. When his ray
Had scantily illum'd our prison-room,
  And in four haggard visages I saw
  My own shrunk aspect, and our common doom,
Both hands, for very anguish, did I gnaw.
  They, thinking that I tore them through desire
  Of food, rose sudden from their dungeon-straw,
And spoke : 'Less grief it were, of us, O Sire !
  If thou would'st eat—These limbs, thou, by our birth
  Didst clothe—Despoil them now, if need require.'
Not to increase their pangs of grief and dearth,
  I calm'd me. Two days more, all mute we stood :
  Wherefore did'st thou not open, pitiless Earth !
Now, when our fourth sad morning was renew'd,
  Gaddo fell at my feet, outstretch'd and cold,
  Crying, 'Wilt thou not, father ! give me food ?'
There did he die ; and as thine eyes behold
  Me now, so saw I three, fall one by one,
  On the fifth day and sixth : whence, in that hold,
I, now grown blind, over each lifeless son,
  Stretch'd forth mine arms. Three days, I call'd their names ;
  Then Fast achiev'd what Grief not yet had done.

(Vol. i. Chap. ix. pp. 399-404.)

[Estimate of the *Divina Commedia*]

The power of the human mind was never more forcibly demonstrated, in its most exquisite masterpieces, than in the poem of Dante. Without a prototype in any existing language, equally novel in its various parts, and in the combination of the whole, it stands alone, as the first monument of modern genius, the first great work which appeared in the reviving literature of Europe. In its composition, it is strictly conformable to the essential and invariable principles of the poetical art. It possesses unity of design and of execution ; and bears the visible impress of a mighty genius, capable of embracing, at once, the parts and the whole of its scheme ; of employing, with facility, the most stupendous materials, and of observing all the required niceties of proportion, without experiencing any difficulty from the constraint. In all other respects, the poem of Dante is not within the jurisdiction of established rules. It cannot with propriety be referred to any particular class of composition, and its author is only to be judged by those laws which he thought fit to impose upon himself.

(Vol. i. Chap. x. pp. 405-6.)

1825. THE ITALIAN NOVELISTS: SELECTED FROM THE MOST APPROVED AUTHORS IN THAT LANGUAGE. . . . TRANSLATED FROM THE ORIGINAL ITALIAN. ACCOMPANIED WITH NOTES, CRITICAL AND BIOGRAPHICAL.

[Dante's reference to the Lancelot Romance]

The series of novels, entitled 'Il Decamerone,' has also frequently appeared under the name of 'Il Principe Galeotto,' derived it is supposed, from a similar interesting production, thus entitled, whose attractions are celebrated by Dante, as having fostered the unhappy loves of Paulo and Francesca:

'Galeotto fu il libro e chi lo scrisse.'[1]

(Vol. i. p. 62.)[2]

1828. LANZI'S HISTORY OF PAINTING IN ITALY, FROM THE PERIOD OF THE REVIVAL OF THE FINE ARTS TO THE END OF THE EIGHTEENTH CENTURY.[3]

[Giotto's portrait of Dante]

The real art of portrait painting commenced with Giotto; to whom we are indebted for correct likenesses of Dante, of Brunetto Latini, and of Corso Donati.[4]

(Ed. 1847, vol. i. p. 47.)

[Orcagna and Dante]

In the Strozzi chapel in the church of S. Maria Novella, Andrea and Bernardo Orcagna painted Paradise, and over against it the Infernal Regions; and in the Campo Santo of Pisa, Death and the Judgment were executed by Andrea and Hell by Bernardo. The two brothers imitated Dante in the novel representations which they executed at those places; and that style was more happily repeated by Andrea in the church of Santa Croce, where he inserted portraits of his enemies among the damned, and of his friends among the blessed spirits. These pictures are the prototypes of similar pictures preserved in S. Petronio, at Bologna, in the cathedral of Tolentino, in the Badia del Sesto, at Friuli, and some other places, in which Hell is distinguished by abysses and a variety of torments, after the manner of Dante.

(*Ibid.* vol. i. pp. 63-4.)

[1] [*Inf.* v. 137. The book referred to by Dante was the romance of *Lancelot du Lac.*]

[2] [Roscoe makes sundry other references to Dante in the course of this work, chiefly in connection with persons mentioned in the *Cento Novelle Antiche.*]

[3] [The *Storia Pittorica d' Italia* of Luigi Lanzi (1732-1810) was first published in 1792-6; third edition, Bassano, 1809.]

[4] [This is doubtless given on the authority of Vasari, for the fresco (in the Bargello at Florence) containing these portraits was not rediscovered until 1840 (see above, pp. 112-14).]

[Michael Angelo compared to Dante]

During the four years that Michelangelo remained in the house of Lorenzo the Magnificent he laid the foundation of all his acquirements: he especially studied poetry, and thus was enabled to rival Vinci in his sonnets, and to relish Dante, a bard of a sublimity beyond the reach of vulgar souls.[1] Bonarruoti studied design in the chapel of Masaccio, he copied the antiques in the garden of Lorenzo, and attended to anatomy, a science to which he is said to have dedicated twelve years, with great injury to his health, and which determined his style, his practice, and his glory. To this study he owed that style from which he obtained the name of the Dante of the art. As this poet made choice of materials, difficult to be reduced to verse, and from an abstruse subject extracted the praise of sublimity and grandeur, in like manner Michelangelo explored the untrodden path of design, and in pursuing it, displayed powers of execution at once scientific and magnificent. . . . The poet and the painter have other points of resemblance; a display of knowledge, from which Dante appears sometimes a disclaimer[2] rather than a poet, Bonarruoti, an anatomist rather than a painter; a neglect of elegance, from which the first often, and if we subscribe to the opinions of Caracci and of Mengs, the second, sometimes, degenerated into harshness. On points like these, which depend wholly on taste, I shall content myself with warning the reader that such comparisons should not be pushed too far: for this poet, from his desire of surmounting difficulties in conception and versification, has sometimes so deviated from the usual path, that he cannot always be proposed as a model for imitation: but every design of Michelangelo, every sketch, as well as his more finished works, may be regarded as a model in art; if in Dante we trace marks of labour, in Michelangelo everything exhibits nature and facility.

(Ed. 1847, vol. i. pp. 134-5.)

1830. THE LANDSCAPE ANNUAL: THE TOURIST IN SWITZERLAND AND ITALY.[3]

[The leaning-towers at Bologna (*Inf.* xxxi)]

The most remarkable edifices in Bologna are the watch-towers. During the twelfth century, when the cities of Italy, 'tutte piene

[1] He was very partial to this poet, whose flights of fancy he embodied in pen-drawings in a book, which, unfortunately for the art, has perished, and to whose memory he wished to sculpture a magnificent monument, as appears from a petition to Leo X. In it the Medicean Academy requests the bones of the divine poet; and among the subscribers we read the name of Michelangelo, and also his offer.

[2] [*Sic.*]

[3] [This work contains numerous other references to Dante besides those here given.]

di tiranni,' [1] were rivals in arms as afterwards in arts, watch-towers of considerable elevation were frequently erected. In Venice, in Pisa, in Cremona, in Modena, and in Florence these singular structures yet remain; but none are more remarkable than the towers of the Asinelli and the Garisenda in Bologna. The former, according to one chronicler, was built in 1109, while other authorities assign it to the year 1119. The Garisenda tower, constructed a few years later, has been immortalised in the verse of Dante. When the poet and his guide are snatched up by the huge Antaeus, the bard compares the stooping stature of the giant to the tower of the Garisenda, which, as the spectator stands at its base while the clouds are sailing from the quarter to which it inclines, appears to be falling upon his head

> 'Qual pare a riguardar la Carisenda
>   Sotto 'l chinato, quand' un nuvol vada
>   Sovr' essa, sì ched ella incontro penda;
> Tal parve Anteo a me, che stava a bada
>   Di vederlo chinare'—[2]

(pp. 247-8.)

1832. THE LANDSCAPE ANNUAL: THE TOURIST IN ITALY.

[Dante and the Visconti]

The marriage of Galeazzo Visconti with Beatrice d' Este was considered by Dante a death-blow to the Ghibelline party, and he bitterly inveighed against it. Although Nino of Gallura, the first husband of Beatrice, was originally a Guelph, Dante spoke of him not only with respect, but with affection, on account of his misfortunes. Nino was son of a daughter of Ugolino della Gherardesca, and, together with his grandfather, commanded the Guelphs of Pisa. The Archbishop Ruggieri degli Ubaldini, with Lanfranchi, Gualandi, and Sismondi, were the chiefs of the Ghibellines. Ugolino, wishing to become master of Pisa, joined the Archbishop, and consented to sacrifice his grandson Nino, who was to be exiled or murdered if taken. . . . The Archbishop Ruggieri would not allow Ugolino to enjoy the fruit of his treachery. After Nino had fled from Pisa, Ugolino was proclaimed lord of the city: but the Archbishop accused him soon after of having entered into an understanding with his grandson, and delivered up to him some castles belonging to Pisa. The populace ran to his house, killed a natural son and a grandson of his, drove out of Pisa all his relations, and having taken him, two of his sons, and two (others

[1] [*Purg.* vi. 124-5.]
[2] [*Inf.* xxxi. 136-40. Cary's translation is appended.]

say three) of his grandsons, threw them into a dungeon, nailed the door, and starved them to death. It is on this fact that the splendid passage in the thirty-third canto of Dante's *Inferno* is founded: and it is because Ugolino had betrayed his grandson Nino that Dante places him in the sphere destined to traitors in the infernal regions.

The passage of Dante which alludes to the marriage of Galeazzo with Beatrice is full of beauty. It occurs in the eighth canto of the *Purgatorio*. The affection with which Dante speaks to Nino, whom he is glad to meet in Purgatory, when he was afraid lest he might have been lost for ever—the bitterness of his reproach to Beatrice, whom he detested as belonging to the house of Este, the object of Dante's unrelenting and deep abhorrence,—his silence against Visconti, whose conduct he could not approve, and yet, not to lower the character of a Ghibelline chief, he could not openly condemn,—all these are points which should never escape the readers' attention in perusing those noble lines where Dante, walking with Sordello through Purgatory, is represented as inviting him [1] to descend into the valley, and hold converse with the mighty shadows below.

(pp. 17-19.)

[Neglect of Dante by the Florentines]

The spectator will turn from the ornaments of sculpture and architecture, to gaze with veneration and delight on the sacred spots which contain the ashes of the most illustrious Florentines. Yet a painful feeling passes across the mind while indulging in these contemplations, as the eye fixes itself on the picture [2] which recals to memory that Dante was a citizen of Florence, but that his remains are committed to a foreign soil. This oldest and most magnificent of Italian poets was driven to seek an asylum from the fury of his political enemies in the states of neighbouring princes. Ravenna was the last place of his abode; and there, some time after his death, a monument was raised to his immortal memory by Bernardo Bembo. To the credit, however, of the later Florentines be it spoken that they sought for many ages to recover the ashes of their poet. The gifted Michael Angelo exercised his influence to effect this purpose, but nothing could induce the people of Ravenna to give up the sacred possession, and Florence was obliged to content itself with passing a vote for raising a splendid monument to the honor of her exiled son. Whether want of means, or the agitations to which the republic has been since exposed, or

[1] [On the contrary, Sordello invites Dante (*Purg.* viii. 43-4).]
[2] [By Domenico di Michelino, in the Duomo at Florence.]

both these causes, have prevented its being erected, is uncertain; but it has never been carried into effect; and a picture is all the monumental fame which the great Dante enjoys in his native city.[1]

(pp. 93-4.)

[Dante and Giotto]

The poet Dante, in exile at Ravenna, hearing that his distinguished fellow-citizen was then staying at Ferrara, sent to invite him to come and join him, and he painted for the lords of Polenta several frescoes in the church of San Francesco. It was here a friendship was formed between these extraordinary men which served to soothe the grief and bitter feelings of the poet's mind. From Giotto he is said to have acquired that knowledge and skill in matters of art in which he is known to have been no mean proficient, and which may perhaps have given to his poem that vivid and picturesque force which, while striking terror to the soul of the reader, brings the shadowy forms before the eye. While at Florence, in the year 1322, tidings were received by Giotto of the death of his friend—the celebrated poet—whose ashes have twice refused to rest in the bosom of his ungrateful country:—

'Even in his ashes live his wonted fires';

as if his spirit, speaking from the urn, spurned the futile offer of being reconciled to his hated persecutors. Though in the midst of his successful and splendid career, Giotto was much concerned at this event; and some of the next works he executed for the King of Naples—comprehending the Apocalypse and other histories, at Assisi—he is stated to have owed, from the conversations he had held with him, to the fine invention of Dante, who thus amply repaid him.

(p. 99.)

ENGLISH EDITION OF THE *DIVINA COMMEDIA*

1822-3. LA DIVINA COMMEDIA DI DANTE ALIGHIERI. LONDRA. 2 VOLS. 32MO.

[Printed by Corrall, published by Pickering. Dedicated to George John, Earl Spencer. The first volume is dated 1823, the second 1822. The two volumes are paged continuously. Vol. i. contains the *Inferno* and *Purgatorio* i-xviii; vol. ii., which has a separate title-page, contains *Purgatorio* xix-xxxiii, and the *Paradiso*. This is the fifth edition of the *Commedia* printed and published in England (previous editions having appeared in 1808, 1819, and 1819-20).]

[1] [This is no longer true—there is now a cenotaph to Dante in the church of Santa Croce, and a statue in the Piazza opposite the church.]

ANONYMOUS

[In 1821 a proposal was made to Leigh Hunt by Shelley and Byron, who were then in Italy, to join them in the establishment of a quarterly liberal magazine, the profits to be divided between Hunt and Byron. Hunt reached Leghorn, with his wife and family, in June, 1822, a few days before Shelley was drowned. Byron's interest in the projected magazine soon began to cool, and when it at length appeared under the name of the *Liberal* it only lived through four numbers (1822-3). Byron's contributions included the *Vision of Judgment*, *Letter to the Editor of my Grandmother's Review*, *Epigrams on Castlereagh* (in No. I.); *Heaven and Earth* (in No. II.); *The Blues* (in No. III.); and *Morgante Maggiore* (in No. IV.). The bulk of the remainder was written by Hunt, with the assistance of Hazlitt.]

1822-23. THE LIBERAL. VERSE AND PROSE FROM THE SOUTH.

[Dante and Milton among those to whom the editors pay homage]

ALTHOUGH we condemn by wholesale certain existing demands upon our submission and credulity, we are not going to discover every imaginative thing even in a religion to be nonsense, like a semi-liberalized Frenchman; nor, on the other hand, to denounce all levity and wit to be nonsense and want of feeling, like a semi-liberalized German. If we are great admirers of Voltaire, we are great admirers also of Goethe and Schiller. If we pay our homage to Dante and Milton, we have tribute also for the brilliant sovereignties of Ariosto and Boccaccio.

(*Preface*, vol. i. p. xii.)

[Pisa and Dante]

Letters from Abroad. No. I. From Pisa.—In entering the city, the impression is beautiful. What looked white in the distance remains as pure and fair on closer acquaintance. You cross a bridge, and cast your eye up the whole extent of the city one way, the river Arno (the river of Dante, Petrarch, and Boccaccio) winding through the middle of it under two more bridges; and fair elegant houses of good size bordering the wide pavement on either side. . . .

You soon find that Italy is the land, not of the venerable, but the beautiful; and cease to look for old age in the chosen country of the Apollo and the Venus. The only real antiquities are those in Dante and the oldest painters, who treat of the Bible in an ancient style. . . .

Among the mansions on the Lungarno is that still belonging to the family of the Lanfranchi, formerly one of the most powerful in Pisa. The Lanfranchi were among the nobles, who conspired to pull down the traitorous ascendancy of Count Ugolino, and wreaked that more infamous revenge on him and his young children. I need not remind the reader of the passage in Dante; but perhaps he is not aware, that Chaucer has worthily related the story after him, referring, with his usual modesty, for a more sufficing account, to 'the grete poete of Itaille.' See the Monk's Tale, part the last, entitled 'Hugelin of Pise.' . . .[1]

One evening, in August, I saw the whole inside of the cathedral lit up with wax in honour of the Assumption. . . . There was a gigantic picture of the Virgin displayed at the upper end, who was to be supposed sitting in heaven, surrounded with the celestial ardours; but she was 'dark with excess of bright.' It is impossible to see this profusion of lights, especially when one knows their symbolical meaning, without being struck with the source from which Dante took his idea of the beatified spirits. His heaven, filled with lights, and lights too arranged in figures, which glow with lustre in proportion to the beatitude of the souls within them, is clearly a sublimation of a Catholic church. . . . When Dante was asked where he found his hell, *he* answered 'upon earth.' He found his heaven in the same place; and no disparagement either to a future state. . . .

The crowning glory of Pisa is the Campo Santo. . . . I do not quarrel with the presence of things Pagan in a Christian edifice; not only because the Pagan and Catholic religions have much that is common externally, their draperies, altars, incense, music, winged genii, &c.; but because from a principle which the author of a new Comment on Dante has noticed, there is in fact an identity of interests and aspirations in all these struggles of mortal man after a knowledge of things supernatural.[2]

The paintings on the walls, the great glory of Pisa, are by Orgagna, Simon Memmi, Giotto, Buffalmacco, Benozzo, and others, —all more or less renowned by illustrious pens; all, with more or less gusto, the true and reverend harbingers of the greatest painters of Italy. Simon Memmi is the artist celebrated by Petrarch for his portrait of Laura; Buffalmacco is the mad wag (grave enough here) who cuts such a figure in the old Italian novels; and Giotto, the greatest of them all, is the friend of Dante, the hander down of his likeness to posterity, and himself the Dante of his art. . . . Even in the very rudest of his pictures, where the souls of the

[1] [See vol. i. pp. 11-12.]

[2] See a 'Comment on the Divine Comedy of Dante Alighieri,' just published. It is written in the style of one who has been accustomed to speak another language, and ventures upon some singularly gratuitous assumptions respecting the doctrine of eternal punishment: but the poetical reader will consider it a valuable addition to the stock of criticism on Dante, and wish that the author may continue it. It contains some happy local illustrations, a complete account of the real history of Paulo and Francesca, a settlement of the question respecting Beatrice, and a variety of metaphysico-theological remarks in as good and deep a taste as those abovementioned are idle. [The author of this commentary, which was published in 1822, was John Taaffe; see above, pp. 340 ff.]

dying are going out of their mouths in the shape of little children, there are passages not unworthy of Dante or Michael Angelo. . . . Since I have beheld the Campo Santo, I have enriched my day-dreams and my stock of the admirable, and am thankful that I have names by heart, to which I owe homage and gratitude. Tender and noble Orgagna, be thou blessed beyond the happiness of thine own heaven! Giotto, be thou a name to me hereafter, of a kindred brevity, solidity, and stateliness, with that of thy friend Dante! . . .

A look out upon the Lungarno at noon-day is curious. A blue sky is overhead—dazzling stone underneath—the yellow Arno gliding along, generally with nothing upon it, sometimes a lazy sail; the houses on the opposite side, sleeping with their green blinds down; and nobody passing but a few labourers, carmen, or country women in their veils and handkerchiefs, hastening with bare feet, but never too fast to forget a certain air of strut and stateliness. Dante, in one of his love poems, praises his mistress for walking like a peacock, nay even like a crane, *strait above herself*:—

Soave a guisa va di un bel pavone,
Dritta sopra sè, come una grua.[1]

Sweetly she goes, like the bright peacock; strait
Above herself, like to the lady crane.

This is the common walk of Italian women, rich and poor.

(Vol. i. No. i. pp. 99 ff.)

[Can Grande and Dante]

There was a prince in Italy, call'd Can Grande,
Which means Great Dog, the lord too of Verona,
A mighty petty sovereign, and a dandy,
Who in his wit once threw a bard [2] a bone a-
Cross his high board, which made 'em every man die.
The bard agreed 'twas princely. I have known a-
Nother, of whom the people used to say,
A greater puppy never had his day.[3]

('The Dogs'—Vol. i. No. ii. p. 255.)

[Dante's diet]

Letters from Abroad. No. III. Italy:—In all countries the devil (to speak after the received theory of good and ill) seems to pro-

[1] [These lines occur in a canzone, beginning 'Io miro i crespi e gli biondi capegli,' which is attributed to Dante, but is almost certainly not by him.]

[2] [The bard in question was Dante, according to the well-known story—see Toynbee's *Life of Dante*, p. 178.]

[3] [Stanza 27.]

vide for a due diminution of health and happiness by something in the shape of meat and drink. The northern nations exasperate their bile with beer, the southern with oil, and all with butter and meat. I would swear, that Dante was a great eater of minestra.[1]

(Vol. ii. No. iii. pp. 63-4.)

[The opening of the *Divina Commedia*]

Beginnings please us, some for the mere style,
Some for the sentiment, and some for both.

* * * *

Dante's first lines are simple, grave, sincere,
Too full of awe for show:—Milton's the same.[2]

I do not mean to say that both these exordiums are not very impressive, particularly Dante's. The following is the commencement of the great saturnine Italian, who, except in the bitterness of his intolerance, was more a northern genius than a southern. The strong apprehension of the literal imagery in unison with the metaphorical, announces at once the hand of a great poet. The trunks of his trees are tangible and gigantic: and every thing admirably expresses the fierce and gloomy doubts likely to fall upon a mind subject to violent passions, but capable of reflection.

Nel mezzo del cammin di nostra vita[3]
&c. &c.

('The Book of Beginnings'—Vol. ii. No. iii. pp. 102-3.)

[Dante's mention of fire-flies]

Letters from Abroad. No. IV.:—The earliest mention of fire-flies with which I am acquainted, is in Dante (Inferno, Canto 26) where he compares the spirits in the eighth circle of hell, who go about swathed in fire, to the *lucciole* in a rural valley of an evening. A truly saturnine perversion of a beautiful object!

(Vol. ii. No. iv. p. 258.)

[Dante's saying about the Genoese and the letter Z]

Dante says, in his treatise *De Vulgari Eloquentiâ*, that if the Genoese were deprived of the letter Z, they would be dumb.[4] But Dante's dislikes did not stand upon ceremony.

(*Ibid.*)

[1] [A kind of gruel.]
[2] [Stanzas 17, 20.]
[3] [The first seven lines of the *Inferno* are quoted, with Cary's translation.]
[4] [Bk. i. Ch. 13, ll. 48-52.]

[Villani and Dante]

Giovanni Villani—It may be conjectured why I like, and how I would excuse, the dear, rambling old fashioned pages of Giovanni Villani, the author of the Croniche Fiorentine; the writer who makes the persons of Dante's Spirits familiar to us. . . . Dante's commentators had made me familiar with the name of Villani, and I became desirous of obtaining what appeared to be the key of the mysterious allusions of the Divina Comedia. . . . The Italian is old and delightfully ill-spelt: I say delightfully, for it is spelt for Italian ears, and the mistakes let one into the secrets of the pronunciation of Dante and Petrarch better than the regular orthography of the present day. . . .

I will conclude my extracts and remarks by Villani's chapter upon the death, character, and writings of Dante.

Book ix. Of the Poet Dante, and how he died. (Cap. 135.)

'In this same year (1321) in the month of July,[1] Dante died at the city of Ravenna, in Romagna, having returned from an embassy to Venice in the service of the lords of Polenta, with whom he lived. He was buried with great honour, in the guise of poet and great philosopher, at Ravenna, before the gate of the principal church. He died, an exile from the commune of Florence, at the age of about fifty-six years. This Dante was an antient and honourable citizen of Florence, of the division of the gate of San Piero. His exile from Florence was thus occasioned. When Messer Carlo di Valois, of the house of France, came to Florence in the year 1301, and exiled the *Bianchi* (a party so called) as we have before related, this same Dante was the highest governor of our city, and of that party, though a Guelph.[2] And thus, free from guilt, he was driven out with the *Bianchi*, and exiled from Florence, whence he retired to study at Bologna, and afterwards to Paris, and other parts of the world. He was very learned in almost every science. though a layman; he was a great poet, a philosopher, and a perfect rhetorician, as well in writing, either prose or verse, as in speaking. He was the noblest maker of verses, with the finest style, that had ever been in our language until his own time and

[1] [An error for September.]

[2] Villani, who was townsman and contemporary of Dante, appears to have also been his friend, and to wish to reinstate him in the good graces of the Florentines, by saying that he was a Guelph. Dante, as a reasonable man, endeavoured to reconcile the absurd differences of all parties, but he was not a Guelph. His discrepancy of opinion from Villani may be gathered from the opposite judgments that they pass on the same persons. The poet prepares a choice place of torture for Boniface VIII in his dreary hell, while Villani exalts him as a saint. Dante rails at all the Popes; Villani respects them all. Dante sweetly and pathetically dwells on the wrongs and virtues of Manfred, and places him on the high road to heaven. Villani vituperates him, and consigns him as a *scomunicato* to the devil.

later. He wrote in his youth the beautiful book of the 'New Life of Love,' and afterwards, when in exile, he wrote twenty excellent moral and amatory *canzoni*. Among other things he wrote three noble epistle ; one of which he sent to the government of Florence, mourning his banishment as an innocent man; the other he sent to the Emperor Henry (of Luxembourg) when he was at the siege of Brescia, reprehending his abiding there, with almost the foreknowledge of a prophet; the third was to the Italian Cardinals during the vacancy after Pope Clement, advising them to accord in the election of an Italian Pope, all in Latin, in magnificent language, with excellent sentences and authorities, the which were much praised by the holy men who understood them. He wrote also the *Comedia*, where, in elegant verse, with great and subtle questions of morality, natural philosophy, astrology, philosophy and theology, and with beautiful and new metaphors and similes, he composed an hundred chapters or cantos, of having been in Hell, Purgatory, and Paradise, in as noble a manner as it is possible to have done. But in this discourse, whoever is of a penetrating understanding may well see and comprehend that he greatly loves in that drama to dispute and vituperate, after the manner of poets, perhaps in some places more than is decent. Probably his exile also made him write his Treatise on Monarchy,[1] where in excellent Latin he treats of the offices of Pope and Emperor. He began a comment upon fourteen of his before-mentioned moral *canzoni*, which, on account of his death, he did not finish; and only three were found, the which, from what we see, would have been a great, beautiful, subtle, and eminent work. He also wrote a book entitled, 'of Vulgar Eloquence'—which, he says, was to consist of four books, but only two are found, probably on account of his unexpected death, where, in strong and elegant Latin, he reprobates all vernacular Italian. This Dante, on account of his knowledge, was somewhat presumptuous, satirical, and contemptuous. He was uncourteous, as it were, after the manner of philosophers; nor did he well know how to converse with laymen. But on account of his other virtues, his science, and his merit as a citizen, it appeared just to give him perpetual memorial in this our Chronicle, although his great works left in writing bestow on him a true testimony, and an honourable fame on our city.'

(Vol. ii. No. iv. pp. 285-6, 295-7.)

[1] I must again remark, that Dante and Villani must have been personal friends, or that reverence for the poet's talent made the latter seek for every circumstance that might excuse the opinions of Dante to the Florentines, who were then all Guelphs, and to whom the Treatise on Monarchy was peculiarly obnoxious.

ANONYMOUS

1823. Feb. BLACKWOOD'S EDINBURGH MAGAZINE.—OF DANTE, AND HIS TIMES.

[Dante's imagination and power of expression—compared with Shakespeare]

GREAT stress has been laid by Dante's admirers upon his imagination, by which is generally meant, the original conception of the three kingdoms of the other world—Hell, Purgatory, and Heaven; the local arrangement and division of these realms, the distribution of pleasure and of pain, and, in fine, all the immense farrago of his creation. And great pains have been taken to prove, as well as to contradict, that the ideas originated in his own mind, and were not borrowed or suggested by any other person or work. Many critics have shown, as they think, the sources whence Dante took the idea of his *Commedia*. . . . His having borrowed the original idea or not, leaves his genius with us estimated at precisely the same value. . . . The vehicle of the poetry, the frame-work, is nothing; it is unworthy of Dante; and to say that he borrowed it from the account of St. Patrick's Purgatory in Guerin Meschino, which is most likely, is merely to exculpate his genius from having originated such nonsense. Lord Byron says, that imagination is a vulgar quality, and no great exertion of genius; his antagonists think much the same of his *Ethics;* and taking the terms in the particular significations in which they are applied, both sides are right. It is not for that faculty which supplied Dante with his stores of ice, and hail, and pitch, and torture, an imagination more worthy of a Dominican than a poet; for that which inspired him with the noble idea, that Hell was laid out like a corkscrew, nor yet for the Ethics or *Rettitudine*, which so absurdly perform the office of supreme judge—it is not for these, that we rank his genius in the first grade of excellence, but for that faculty by which he imagined so many beings, depicting them in person and situation with all the powers of a descriptive poet, and making them speak and act with all those of a dramatic one. The variety of his characters, as of those of Shakespeare, is the more natural and admirable for not being purposely arranged and contrasted, like that in the classic poets. The heroes of Homer, of Virgil, and, in imitation of them, the Angels of Milton, differ in shades, and present so many regular gradations of human excellence. But Dante had none of this poetic foresight; his personages start upon the canvass, undrilled and unprepared, depicted from life or familiar fame; they are not brought forward to represent any *ideal*, or produce any moral effect; they are simple nature, and no more. Of the same kind are Shakespeare's pictures, conveying certainly a moral, as nature in all modes must present, yet only that which nature would suggest of herself. Dante, though he raises a hundred characters, enters but into one. As a descriptive poet, he had command over all Europe; as a dramatic poet, he possessed the key but of one portal; though alive to all in depicting what was external to him, he could lose himself in no character that was not warmed by political resentment. But Shakespeare was the poet of all mind—no matter what personage his fertile imagination raised—no matter what character or figure, with what fantasy or passion endowed—Ariel or Imogen or Caliban or Richard, the proper spirit of the poet instantly informed it; he was like the demons of which we read in Scripture, which could not quit one body, without instantly entering another. Thus Shakespeare, lord of all the passions, and Dante, powerful over one, are like two eccentric circles that touch but in one point; and when they do touch, there are to be met many points of resemblance. . . .

Dante's powers of expression were immense, and indeed ought to have been so, considering that he had an infant language to mould as he pleased. But this rudeness of the tongue was of disadvantage as well as advantage; if it led to novelty, force, and denseness of expression, it also checked a continued flow of thought. The ear alone, as in perfected languages, did not instantaneously suggest the musical expression; and the poet was obliged to pause and search for unfamiliar terms—a process, that, however favourable to taste, completely checks the glow of inspiration. Thus the descriptions with which he opens his cantos seldom extend beyond six lines, and a round period of thought is often shrunk within the limits of half a line. The poet never seems elevated to a complete mastery over his verse, unless when giving vent to those political passions and resentments, in which he became absorbed. His descriptive poetry resembles etching, where all is told by the magic of a single stroke; and the genius of Flaxman proves the truth of the comparison. How beautiful is the picture of Beatrice addressing him,—

> 'Regalmente nell' atto ancor proterva,
> Continuò, come colui, che dice,
> E 'l più caldo parlar dietro riserva.'[1]

'Tis needless again to mention the pictures of Farinata, Ugolino, and Sordello,

> 'In guisa di leon, quando si posa';[2]

Nor the brief compressiveness of the few words of Francesca da Rimini,

[1] [*Purg*. xxx. 70-2.] [2] [*Purg*. vi. 66.]

'La bocca mi baciò tutto tremante;
Galeotto fu il libro, e chi lo scrisse;
Quel giorno più non vi leggemmo avante.'[1]

(Vol. xiii. pp. 155-7.)

ANONYMOUS

1823. NEW MONTHLY MAGAZINE. THE TROUBADOURS.

[Dante's mention of Thibaut of Champagne]

THE productions of Thibaut Count of Champagne and King of Navarre, who died about the middle of the thirteenth century, were the subject of general admiration in France and Italy. Dante has immortalized his muse.[2] . . .

Petrarch in his triumph mentions fifteen of the Troubadours, and places Arnaud Daniel at their head. . . . They were warriors as well as poets. . . . Dante had before extolled their works; Boccace borrowed freely from their thoughts and expressions; and it is candidly admitted by Cardinal Bembo, that the Tuscan was indebted to them for many of its noblest ornaments.

(Vol. vii. pp. 372-3.)

WILLIAM COXE

(1747-1828)

[William Coxe, historian, son of Dr. William Coxe, physician to the household of George II., was born in London in 1747. He was educated at Eton and King's College, Cambridge, of which he became Fellow in 1768. Shortly after being ordained he became tutor to the eldest son of the Duke of Marlborough, and he subsequently held several similar appointments. In 1788 he was presented by Lord Pembroke to the rectory of Bemerton, in Wiltshire, where he chiefly resided until his death in 1828. He was appointed Archdeacon of Wiltshire in 1804. Coxe was the author of numerous historical works, the best known of which is his *History of the House of Austria*, published in 1807. He also published anonymously in 1823, *Sketches of the Lives of Correggio, and Parmegiano*, in which he compares the 'Corrigesque smile' to that described by Dante in the episode of Paolo and Francesca.]

1823. SKETCHES OF THE LIVES OF CORREGGIO, AND PARMEGIANO.[3]

[Dante and the 'Corrigesque' smile]

WE cannot close our observations on Correggio's powers of expression, without adverting to a beauty which he possessed exclusively; or, at least, shared only with Leonardo da Vinci, namely, the lovely and exquisite smile, which

[1] [*Inf.* v. 136-8.]
[2] [In the *De Vulgari Eloquentia*, i. 9; ii. 5, 6.]
[3] [Published anonymously.]

plays on his female countenances, and which has been distinguished by the epithet of Corrigesque, or the grace of Correggio. This trait, as difficult to describe as to imitate, has been happily indicated by Dante, the father of Italian Poetry, in his

'Della bocca il disiato riso.'

Inferno.[1]

(pp. 160-1.)

ALLAN CUNNINGHAM

(1784-1842)

[Allan Cunningham, author of the well-known song, 'A wet sheet and a flowing sea,' was born at Keir, in Dumfriesshire, in 1784. He was apprenticed to a stonemason, and early began writing ballads, many of which were published in a volume in London in 1810, whither he had gone in that year. After being employed as a sculptor's assistant, and on journalism for several years, in 1814 he was appointed secretary to Chantrey, the famous sculptor, a post which he retained until Chantrey's death in 1841. He himself died in London in the following year. Cunningham was a fellow contributor with Cary, Charles Lamb, Hazlitt, De Quincey, Procter, Tom Hood, and Carlyle, to the *London Magazine*. The following letter, in which he expresses his admiration for Dante, with whom he became acquainted through Cary's translation, was written in answer to an invitation from Cary to one of the 'Magazine dinners' at which the contributors periodically met.]

1823. June 30. LETTER TO REV. H. F. CARY.

[Appreciation of Dante and of Cary's translation]

I ACCEPT your kind invitation with much pleasure, and shall be faithful to tryste.

I wished long ago to have told you how deep a hold your Dante had taken of my heart and mind, and what a bold and original picture you had placed before me. It is true I know nothing of the Italian Dante, but men tell me and, what is as good, I feel that the loss cannot be great; I can hardly conceive how a poem can be more touching and more terrible. When I descended to the shades with the Greek and the Roman, I hardly felt that I was in a place of punishment; but when I went down with Dante I beheld the words, 'Depart from me, ye cursed,' written on every brow. But he is too awful to be ever very popular—for the multitude will turn away from his severe and brief majesty. Yet he is too great ever to be forgotten, and a man must have an unreasonable wish for the endurance of fame to desire to live longer than Dante.

[1] [*Inf.* v. 133—misquoted.]

I know that I had no right to inflict my opinion on you, but I was too much moved to be able to suppress it.

(*Memoir of Rev. H. F. Cary, by his Son,* vol. ii. pp. 101-2.)

ANONYMOUS

1823. Jan. QUARTERLY REVIEW. ART. V. MILLS' TRAVELS OF THEODORE DUCAS.[1]

[Criticism of the *Divina Commedia*—'Dante will never be popular']

MR. MILLS' praise of Petrarch is, all through, too extravagant. . . . On the Divina Commedia he is more fortunate in his criticisms. The merits of Dante are at length pretty accurately settled. The strangeness, if not the richness, of his ideas, his energetic brevity of expression, the keenness of his satire, and the sublimity of his moral strain, are fully and freely acknowledged; but however striking may be the majestic beauties of the Inferno, or we should rather say of *passages* of the Inferno, such is the tediousness of the Purgatorio and the Paradiso, that we read the poem altogether as a task. In invention, Dante is far below many poets, particularly Milton, with whom it is most natural to compare him. Dante created no new worlds; the people in his Stygian shades talk and act perfectly like beings of common earthly mould—like monks in a subterranean cloister. In all his descriptions of the circles, rocks, and bridges of hell, and his journey with Virgil, there is much tediousness and some confusion, and nothing comparable for sublimity with the solitary flight of Satan from Pandemonium. Dante's Lucifer is far from being that great though fallen spirit whose hellish rancour and intellectual energy Milton has so powerfully drawn. The demons in the twenty-first canto of the Inferno more nearly resemble the devils in a modern pantomime, than the Molochs and Belials of the great council of the rebellious angels. Dante was brought into fashion in England by Sir Joshua Reynolds' Ugolino, and some other accidental circumstances, but he will never be popular; and notwithstanding Mr. Carey's translation—the best we ever read of any work—we believe that his success amongst us is rapidly declining.[2]

(Vol. xxviii. p. 370.)

[1] [See above, pp. 273-5.]

[2] [That this opinion was unfounded is amply proved by the subsequent pages of this work.]

ANONYMOUS

1823. October. QUARTERLY REVIEW. ART. II. ROSE'S ORLANDO FURIOSO.

[Dante and Homer]

GREEK was not understood by Petrarch, and Boccacio began to learn it late, and probably made in it no great progress. Dante, it is true, in a well-known passage, assigns to Homer the first place in poetry;[1] it is a compliment, however, that he might have paid him at second hand after all, without much acquaintance with the author; (for Petrarch is no less loud in his praises, though all that he knew of him was confessedly by Latin translations of detached passages:) and that such a compliment it was, seems the more probable, from the ill-assorted company with which he classes him,[2] and from the absence of all accurate Homeric allusions in the further progress of his noble work.

(Vol. xxx. p. 45.)

ANONYMOUS

1823. November. MONTHLY REVIEW. ART. I. A COMMENT ON THE DIVINE COMEDY OF DANTE ALIGHIERI. BY —— VOL. I.[3]

[Taaffe on the *Divina Commedia*]

WE are here invited to engage in a task of no common magnitude; the 'vista of years,'—of commentary on commentary,—seems to open to our view; and we do not believe that the voluminous annals of the period will afford an instance of greater ambition and intrepidity of mind than that which has here been evinced by Mr. Taaffe,[4] who is reported to be the projector of this new series of Herculean labors: which would occupy about *twelve* huge tomes, if we may judge by the portion that has been already achieved. . . . Mr. T.'s distinctions and differences from all preceding interpretations, more especially from those of Mr. Cary, in the minutest points, really sometimes do not in the least alter the meaning, and would be termed in parliamentary language both 'frivolous and vexatious;' while, as a singular contradiction to his own system, his version of some of the passages of the poem, with which he has favoured us, is less severe, chastened, and correct, than the corresponding translations by the writer

[1] [*Inf.* iv. 88, 95-6.] [2] [*Inf.* iv. 88-90.]
[3] [Printed in Italy from the Types of Didot, for Murray, London, 1822.]
[4] [See above, pp. 340 ff.]

whom he attacks. . . . It is chiefly as a *general* comment on the more obscure portions of the *Divina Commedia*, that Mr. T.'s book will be found valuable as a guide to English students, and as a sort of supplement to, and a review of, the previous labors and explanations of foreign critics. So far the work is new to our English literature: for, though we are in possession of notes and fragments on the same subject by various hands, we have nothing so full and complete, or on such an extensive scale, as the present undertaking: which, long and laborious as it promises to be, will not be deemed either too arduous or too protracted by those who have learnt, or by those who wish to learn, the extent of the great and inexhaustible treasures which belong only in common with Homer to the mighty Florentine. His genius embraces the age in which he lived; and, as it has been said of his only predecessor, the Grecian bard, there is no species of knowledge on which his poem does not flash the light of an instructive and a prophetic mind. He belongs to no school, because he could have no imitators. The great master-spirit of his times, he takes, like some mighty actor, full possession of the stage, and stands in solitary grandeur, not with Italy alone but the whole world for his spectators. Shakspeare, Spenser, Milton, the geniuses of all other periods and nations, have had 'their co-mates and brothers' in glory: but Dante, in 'his spirit's exile,' had none. They were at the head of schools, each filling up the portion of the ages assigned to them, and surrounded by their imitators and companions; while Homer and Dante held themselves aloof, and begged their way on foot from city to city. . . .

We must now take our leave of Mr. Taaffe and this first of his twelve Herculean labors, 'things unattempted yet in prose or rhime:' but we must wish him long life and health, if we are to indulge the hopes of receiving an annual importation of 'Comment' from Italy. Had *we* more time and space, we could farther remark on the various advantages which, we think, English literati and English literature might derive from such an accession to its strength in a department of criticism but little explored, and too long and unaccountably neglected. When we reflect how greatly we have been indebted to the transcendent genius of Italy, above that of all other countries, in supplying our early dramatic, epic, romantic, and pastoral writers of every description with models for their pen, and with sources of poetic imagery and feeling, we conceive it to be quite incumbent on us to direct a portion of our critical inquiries to the exact nature, character, and importance of the productions of Italy's 'master-spirits' of their age. Above all these, Dante towers like a giant: he deserves, and he will bear, all the tomes of commentary which Mr. T. can lay on him; and when an Italian opens the *Divina Commedia*, he ought to address him, as the poet addresses Virgil:

> 'O pregio eterno del luogo, ond' i' fui:
> Qual merito, O qual grazia mi ti mostra?'
> *Purgat.* c. vii. v. 18.

(Vol. cii. pp. 225 ff.)

HENRY HART MILMAN

(1791-1868)

[Henry Hart Milman, son of Sir Francis Milman, afterwards physician to George III., was born in London in 1791. He was educated at Eton, and Brasenose College, Oxford, of which he became Fellow in 1814. In 1812 he won the Newdigate prize with a poem on the Apollo Belvidere, and while still at Oxford he composed a drama, *Fazio*, which was subsequently acted with great success in London under the title of *The Italian Wife*. Milman, who had been ordained in 1816, was appointed to the Professorship of Poetry at Oxford in 1821, which he held until 1831. In 1835 he was made Canon of Westminster, and Rector of St. Margaret's, and in 1849 he was appointed to the Deanery of St. Paul's. He died in 1868. Besides numerous poems Milman published several important historical works, the best known of which are his *History of the Jews* (1830) and *History of Latin Christianity* (1855). For the purposes of the latter work he carefully studied the writings of Dante, of whom, as he declared in a letter to Longfellow, he had been a worshipper from his youth up. In 1823 Ugo Foscolo printed in his *Essays on Petrarch* sundry translations by Milman from Petrarch's poems, in which is included the passage in the third Canto of the *Triumph of Love*, where Dante and Beatrice are introduced.]

1823. TRANSLATIONS FROM PETRARCH.[1]

[Dante in the 'Triumph of Love']

SALUTE, I pray thee, in the sphere of love,
Guitton, my master Cino, Dante too,
Our Franceschin, all that blest band above.—

Thus while my gazing eyes around me rove,
I saw upon a slope of flowery green
Many that held their sweet discourse of love:
Here Dante and his Beatrice, there were seen
Selvaggia and Cino of Pistoia; there
Guitton the Aretine; and the high-priz'd pair,
The Guidi: and Onesto these among,
And all the masters of Sicilian song.

(*Triumph of Love*, Canto iii.)[2]

[1] [Printed in *Essays on Petrarch*, by Ugo Foscolo, 1823]
[2] [Foscolo, p. 164].

ANONYMOUS

1823. RETROSPECTIVE REVIEW. VOL. VII. PART II. ART. X. POEMS OF SHAKESPEARE.

[' The terrible strength of Dante ']

IT is the fashion to admire Shakespeare before every other writer of our country:—and the fashion is good. He was beyond doubt the rarest spirit that ever spoke, uninspired, to man. The scholar and the antiquarian,—the Greek, the Roman, and the Italian, may contend for the high excellence of others. They may laud the originality and majesty of Homer, the grace of Virgil, and the terrible strength of Dante. We admit them all. Those great authors may (or may not) be more original than our own poet. They certainly possessed the doubtful advantage of having lived (and died) before him. But that the one is more original where *he* claims originality, or that the others surpassed him in occasional grace, or could compete with him in general power, we utterly deny.

(Vol. vii. p. 379.)

1824. RETROSPECTIVE REVIEW. VOL. IX. PART II. ART. IV. ARIOSTO'S ORLANDO FURIOSO.

[Ariosto compared with Dante and Tasso]

IN all qualities of style Ariosto is the most chaste and correct of all the Italian poets. In pathos and intensity of feeling, Dante was his superior, and Tasso in judgment and original design. In execution, however, in the minuter graces and elegancies of diction, in accuracy of delineation, and felicity of expression, Ariosto ranked above both.

(Vol. ix. p. 289.)

1824. RETROSPECTIVE REVIEW. VOL. X. PART I. ART. VIII. HANS SACHS.

[Hans Sachs, Aristophanes, and Dante all used vigorous language in their denunciations]

IT must be confessed, that sometimes Sachs' colouring is a little high, and his words grate harshly upon the delicate ears of a modern audience; for such is the morbid sensibility at which we have arrived, that the most nefarious atrocities must have the demulceat of a pious phraseology. But Luther, Hutten, and Sachs, did not think in this canting manner; and with frank and round expressions, called things by their proper names. Aristophanes himself, who lived in the most polished city of the world, was by no means so delicate in his choice of terms; and Dante, in his *Inferno*, rebukes the vices of popes and kings, and Pisans and Florentines, in language of no studied sweetness.

(Vol. x. p. 121.)

1824. RETROSPECTIVE REVIEW. VOL. X. PART II. ART. VI. FILICAIA.

[Filicaja, Dante, and Petrarch]

Francesco Redi, in a letter dated Oct. 4th, 1687, says, 'From the days of Frà Guittone to the present time, I had found no poetry which pleased me more than that of Filicaja.' Fortunate Signor Redi! to find, at last, in the rhymes of Filicaja, that delicious repast, with which neither Dante nor Petrarch could regale his refined poetical palate.

The indifference of the modern Italians towards the works of a poet so lately celebrated as incomparable, deserves some consideration. It cannot be regarded as a mere caprice of fashion; for many of the Italians, whilst they neglect this poet, profess a more passionate study, a more profound veneration, a more lively enthusiasm than ever existed in former times, for two ancient illustrious poets of Italy, Dante and Petrarch.

In taking the political events of his time for the arguments of his poems, Filicaja discovered a correct and sublime notion of the genius of true poetry. . . . A spark of that patriotic enthusiasm which had kindled the thoughts of Dante and Petrarch, appeared to revive in him, and through him, to his readers.

(Vol. x. pp. 316 ff.)

THE 'KING'S LIBRARY'

1824. BIBLIOTHECAE REGIAE CATALOGUS.

[The 'King's Library' was the collection of tracts (15,000 volumes) and printed books (65,000) made by George III., at the cost of about £130,000. It was presented (on terms) by George IV., in 1823, to the British Museum, where it is preserved as a separate collection. The Catalogue, in five folio volumes (1820-9), was prepared by the Royal Librarian, Sir F. A. Barnard. The collection was fairly rich in editions of Dante, among them being *editiones principes* of the *Commedia* (Foligno, 1472), the *Convivio* (Firenze, 1490), the *De Vulgari Eloquentia* in Trissino's translation (Vicenza, 1529), and the *Vita Nuova* (Firenze, 1576). Besides the *editio princeps* the collection contained the following fifteenth-century editions of the *Commedia* viz. Venice, 1477; Milan, 1478; Florence, 1481; Venice, 1484; Bressa, 1487; and Venice, 1491 (Petro Cremonese), as well as a copy on vellum of the Aldine edition of 1502.]

ANONYMOUS

1824. HISTORICAL LIFE OF JOANNA OF SICILY, QUEEN OF NAPLES AND COUNTESS OF PROVENCE; WITH CORRELATIVE DETAILS OF THE LITERATURE AND MANNERS OF ITALY AND PROVENCE IN THE THIRTEENTH AND FOURTEENTH CENTURIES.[1]

[Petrarch and Dante]

KING ROBERT seems to have been wholly unacquainted with the poetry of his Florentine contemporary, the immortal Dante; but this is the less surprising when we learn that even Petrarch had no copy of the works of Dante in his valuable library, till Boccaccio, with his own hand, transcribed one for him. The writings of these three great men fixed the earliest-formed and the most harmonious of the languages of modern Europe. 'Dante and Petrarch, in the reign of Robert of Naples established the standard of Italian poetry; Bocacccio fixed that of Italian prose by a work written for his natural daughter, Maria of Sicily, during the reign of his successor Joanna.

(Vol. i. pp. 37-8.)

[Dante, like Milton, an erudite poet]

The title of Brunetto Latini to the name of *poet* is founded on his Tesoretto, which some have supposed to have suggested to Dante the idea of his Inferno; and his strongest claim on the gratitude of posterity is his able and zealous cultivation of his illustrious pupil's faculties from their earliest dawn. He happened to be at Florence at the period of the birth of the immortal Dante Alighieri, and being eminent as an astrologer, was employed by his parents to draw his horoscope, and foretold for the new-born babe a glorious career in literature and science. Dante early lost his father, but his mother Bella, as the astrologer's prediction was confirmed by the fond dreams of maternal love[2] previous to the birth

[1] [In this work, the authorship of which has not been ascertained, various illustrative passages are quoted from the *Commedia*, some in the original, but for the most part in the version of Cary.]

[2] Whenever Dante wishes to describe the celestial benignity of the beatified Beatrice, he draws some exquisite picture of maternal love. His filial piety was the most tender sentiment of his nature. The following lines must speak to every mother's heart—

> Astounded, to the guardian of my steps,
> I turn'd me, like the child who always runs
> Thither for succour where he trusteth most.
> And she was like the mother, who her son
> Beholding pale and breathless, with her voice
> Soothes him, and he is cheer'd.
>
> *Cary's Translation*, *Paradise*, Canto 22 [iv. 1-6].

In this passage the English poet is fully equal to the original.

of her child, took the utmost care of his education, and gave him Brunetto as a preceptor[1] who, by carefully imparting to him his own knowledge in grammar, philosophy, theology, and political science, contributed not a little to the fulfilment of his astrological prediction. Hence it happened that Dante, like our own Milton, to whom he has often been compared, was one of the most erudite of poets. He, however, cultivated not only the abstruser sciences, but the fine arts, in his youth, particularly music and painting, and was also remarkable for the beauty of his hand-writing. These various tastes led him to cultivate the friendship of the poets, painters, and musicians of Florence; he was equally intimate with the poet Guido Cavalcanti, the painter Giotto, and the musician Casella.

(Vol. i. pp. 79-81.)

[The minor works of Dante]

The *Divina Commedia*, which has given Dante the first rank amongst Italian poets, is too well known in this country through the medium of a late excellent translation,[2] to require or admit of comment here. This great work, destined to perpetuate the name of Beatrice, was preceded by a composition in prose entitled *Vita Nuova*, in which he relates all the circumstances of his passion, and introduces his early poetry as the circumstances arise which occasioned it. The canzonets of Dante, twenty in number, would constitute him the best poet of his day, if he had never produced anything superior. . . . He wrote also, in the vulgar tongue, the *Convito*, a commentary on his own canzonets, in which he displays his knowledge of the Platonic philosophy, and of the astronomy and other sciences of his times, according to the formula then adopted in school learning. This was the last of his works, and he had only arrived at the third of his poems, when he was arrested by the hand of death. In latin he wrote three celebrated Epistles, the first to his native city,[3] complaining of his unjust exile, the second to the Emperor Henry of Luxemburg,[4] and the third to the Sacred College,[5] after the death of Pope Clement V, exhorting the cardinals to elect an Italian pope; a treatise on the literature of the Italian language, entitled *De Vulgari Eloquentia*, and another on the universal monarchy claimed by the German Emperors as the successors of the Caesars. This latter work,[6] though forgotten in our days, was so much esteemed in the fourteenth

[1] [Brunetto Latini's active participation in the education of the young Dante is now generally discredited.]

[2] [The reference, of course, is to Cary's version.]

[3] [*Epist.* vi.] [4] [*Epist.* vii.] [5] [*Epist.* viii.]

[6] [The *De Monarchia*.]

century, that after the death of Dante the anti-pope, established by Louis of Bavaria, sustained from it the validity of his election, and the legate of pope John XXII demanded that the bones of its author should be dug up and burned.

(Vol. i. pp. 88-9.)[1]

RICHARD PRICE

(1790-1833)

[Richard Price, philologist and antiquary, born in 1790, was called to the bar in 1830, and practised on the Western Circuit. In 1824 he published a revised edition of Warton's *History of Poetry*, in which he incorporated the notes of preceding editions, and added some of his own. In one of these are interesting quotations from Dante's Latin works in illustration of his views on tragedy and comedy. In 1830 Price issued a new edition of Blackstone's *Commentaries*. He died in 1833.]

1824. THE HISTORY OF ENGLISH POETRY. BY THOMAS WARTON. NEW EDITION, CAREFULLY REVISED [BY RICHARD PRICE].

[Dante's definition of tragedy and comedy]

IN the dedication of his *Paradise* to Can della Scala, Dante thus explains his own views of Tragedy and Comedy:

'Est comoedia genus quoddam poeticae narrationis ab omnibus aliis differens. Differt ergo in materia a tragoedia per hoc, quod tragoedia in principio est admirabilis et quieta, in fine sive exitu, foetida et horribilis. . . . Comoedia vero inchoat asperitatem alicujus rei, sed ejus materiam[2] prospere terminatur.—Similiter differunt *in modo loquendi*.'[3]

He has also expatiated upon the distinctive styles peculiar to such compositions, in his treatise 'De Vulgari Eloquentia'; though his precepts when opposed to his practice have proved a sad stumbling-block to the critics:

'Per Tragoediam superiorem stylum induimus, per Comoediam inferiorem. . . . Si tragice canenda vicentur,[4] tum adsumendum est vulgare illustre. Si vero comice, tum quandoque mediocre, quandoque humile vulgare sumatur.' Lib. ii. c. iv. [ll. 38-40, 41-3, 44-6.]

(Vol. ii. p. 67 n.)

[1] [This work contains sundry other references to Dante.]
[2] [Read *materia*.]
[3] [*Epist*. x. 196-9, 203-5.]
[4] [Read *videntur*.]

SUSAN EDMONSTONE FERRIER

(1782-1854)

[Susan Edmonstone Ferrier, the novelist, was born in Edinburgh in 1782. Her father was a colleague of Sir Walter Scott as one of the principal clerks of session, and through him she became acquainted with the leaders of literary society in Edinburgh. Her three novels, *Marriage* (1818), *The Inheritance* (1824), and *Destiny* (1831), were published anonymously: her name appeared on the title-page for the first time in the edition of 1850. Miss Ferrier visited Scott at Ashestiel in 1811, and at Abbotsford in 1829 and 1831. He mentions her in his diary (May 12, 1831) as 'simple, full of humour, and exceedingly ready at repartee, and all this without the least affectation of the blue-stocking.' She died in Edinburgh in 1854. Miss Ferrier several times quotes from Cary's translation of the *Divina Commedia* in her *Inheritance* and *Destiny*. She seems to have had no acquaintance with the original.]

1824. THE INHERITANCE.

[Mottoes from Dante]

'WHAT silence hides, that knowest thou.'
Dante.[1]
(Vol. i. Chap. 20, ed. 1882.)

'Never in my breast
Did ignorance so struggle with desire
Of knowledge, . . .
As in that moment; nor—dar'd I
To question, nor myself could aught discern.'
Cary's Dante.[2]
(Vol. i. Chap. 22.)

[Dante and Tasso 'the noblest bards of Italy']

The blessing of God and the applause of posterity seem to have perpetuated the fame of genius devoted to religious subjects more than the fame of those men who abused their noble gifts by dedicating them solely to the service of their fellow-creatures. . . . Milton is undoubtedly the first poet of our country, and what was his theme? He sang in noble strain of Him

'Unspeakable, who sit'st above these heavens
To us invisible, or dimly seen
In these Thy lowest works.'

The greatest poet of Germany was Klopstock, and his subject the great Messiah; . . . the noblest bards of Italy were Dante and Tasso; Metastasio has had recourse to sacred subjects for his operas; Racine for his Athalie. . . .

(Vol. i. Chap. 45, p. 390, ed. 1882.)

[1] [*Inf.* xix. 39, from Cary's version.]

[2] [*Purg.* xx. 145-9.]

[Mottoes from Dante]

'Now rest thee, reader! on thy bench, and muse
Anticipative of the feast to come;
So shall delight not make thee[1] feel thy toil.
Lo! I have set before thee; for thyself
Feed now.'

Dante.[2]
(Vol. i. Chap. 48.)

'But that shall gall thee most,
Will be the worthless and vile company
With whom thou must be thrown into these straits.'

Dante.[3]
(Vol. ii. Chap. 40.)

1831. DESTINY.

[Dante's description of evening]

Now the evening was fair and sweet, and her father's pinnace had been stationed at the ferry to receive him; but Edith sighed as she saw its white sails, gilded by the setting sun, still flapping idly in the evening breeze.

'Now was the hour that wakens fond desire
In men at sea, and melts their thoughtful heart,
Who in the morn have bid sweet friends farewell;
And pilgrim newly on his road, with love
Thrills if he hear the vesper bell from far,
That seems to mourn for the expiring day.'[4]

But faint were such tender remembrances compared to the feelings which filled Edith's heart as she watched the coming of Reginald.

(Vol. ii. Chap. 2, pp. 133-4, ed. 1841.)

[Motto from Dante]

'For I have seen
The thorn frown rudely all the winter long,
And after bear the rose upon its top.'

Cary's *Dante.*[5]
(Vol. iii. Chap. 30.)

[1] [Read 'make thee not.']
[2] [*Par.* x. 22-5, from Cary's version.]
[3] [*Par.* xvii. 61-3, from Cary's version.]
[4] [From Cary's Dante, *Purg.* viii. 1-6.]
[5] [*Par.* xiii. 133-5.]

THOMAS MEDWIN

(1788-1869)

[Thomas Medwin was born at Horsham in 1788. He was a cousin of Shelley (his mother being a first cousin of the poet's mother), who was his school-fellow and friend. Medwin entered the army, and in 1813 became a lieutenant in the 24th dragoon guards, with which regiment he subsequently went to India. After about ten years' service he retired with the rank of captain. In 1821 he went to Italy, and at Pisa was introduced by Shelley to Byron with whom he lived for several months at the Palazzo Lanfranchi. After Byron's death in 1824, Medwin published an interesting *Journal of the Conversations of Lord Byron*. In 1833 he published a *Memoir of Shelley*, which was afterwards expanded into a *Life of Shelley* (1847). These works, as well as the *Angler in Wales* (1834), contain many very interesting records of the opinions of Byron and Shelley with regard to Dante, besides translations (by Shelley and by himself) of two well-known passages of the *Divina Commedia*, into *terza rima*. After a more or less unsettled life, some twenty years of which were spent in retirement at Heidelberg, Medwin died at Horsham in 1869.]

1824. JOURNAL OF THE CONVERSATIONS OF LORD BYRON: NOTED DURING A RESIDENCE WITH HIS LORDSHIP AT PISA, IN THE YEARS 1821 AND 1822.

[The entries in this Journal relating to Dante are given under Byron (see above, pp. 48-51).]

1833. THE SHELLEY PAPERS. MEMOIR OF PERCY BYSSHE SHELLEY. AND ORIGINAL POEMS AND PAPERS. NOW FIRST COLLECTED.

[Shelley's 'despair' when reading Dante]

WHAT Shelley's real opinion of Byron's genius was, may be collected from a sonnet he once showed me, and which the subject of it never saw. The sentiments accord well with that diffidence of his own powers—that innate modesty which always distinguished him. It began thus—

If I esteemed him less, envy would kill
Pleasure, and leave to wonder and despair
The ministration of the thoughts that fill
My soul, which, as a worm may haply share
A portion of the unapproachable,
Marks his creations rise as fast and fair
As perfect worlds at the Creator's will.

Shelley used to say, that reading Dante produced in him the same despair.[1]

(*Memoir of Shelley*, p. 37.)

[[1]Medwin repeated this statement in his *Life of Shelley*, published in 1847.]

[Shelley on liberty and Dante]

Until Florence was betrayed into the hands of those polished tyrants, the Medici, 'freedom had one citadel where it could find refuge from a world that was its foe.'

To this cause Shelley attributed the undisputed superiority of Italy, in literature and the arts, above all its cotemporaries—the union, and energy, and beauty, which distinguish from all other poets the writings of Dante—that restlessness of fervid power, which surpassed itself in painting and sculpture, and from which Raphael and Michael Angelo drew their inspiration.

(*Memoir of Shelley*, pp. 56-7.)

[Shelley's reading of Dante]

In the autumn of 1820 I accepted Shelley's invitation to winter with him at Pisa. He had been passing part of the summer among the chestnut forests of that delicious retreat—the baths of Lucca; and I found him at those of St. Julian, at the foot of the mountain, which Dante calls the Screen of Lucca.[1] . . .

Shelley's whole time was dedicated to study. He was then reading Calderon, and mad about the Autos; but he did not the more lay aside his favourite authors, the Greek dramatists: a volume of Sophocles he used to take with him in his rambles: he generally had a book even at dinner, if his abstemious meal could be called one; and told me he always took a book to bed with him. In the evenings he sometimes read aloud a canto of Dante or Tasso, or a canzone of Petrarch. Though his voice was somewhat broken in the sound, his recitation of poetry was wonderfully effective, and the tones of his voice of varied modulation. He entered into the soul of his author, and penetrated those of his listeners.

(*Ibid.* pp. 57-8, 60-1.)

1834. THE ANGLER IN WALES, OR DAYS AND NIGHTS OF SPORTSMEN.

[The 'mezzo del cammin']

Among other topics, our inquiries turned upon what each had been doing during this long span in our existence, this best part of the life of man; for, of all my acquaintances, I have never known one quite *sound* at five-and-thirty, and Julian and I had both passed that 'Mezzo del cammin di nostra vita.'[2]

(Vol. i. p. 3.)

[The *Bolge* of the *Inferno*]

At night every thing assumed a worse aspect, for the torch's glare gave horrible indistinctness to objects, and as we threaded

[1] [*Inf.* xxxiii. 29-30.]

[2] [*Inf.* i. 1.]

vast jungles, I expected a tiger to spring on us at every step; or when we emerged from some black forest, fancied myself about to plunge into one of the Bolgi [1] in the Inferno, escorted by demons, who kept up (like my black attendants) a continual concert of groans.

(Vol. i. p. 160.)

[Reynolds' picture of Ugolino]

We had found the road literally avenued with pilgrims from the remotest parts of India, emaciated, half-starved creatures, such as Dante describes Ugolino,[2] or Sir Joshua Reynolds [3] painted him.

(Vol. i. p. 256.)

[Dante's Purgatory]

Humphrey has a belief in the transmigration of souls into the bodies of animals, a sort of purgatory, by which men at last get absolution for all their sins; and so they ought, seeing it is not a very comfortable persuasion, nor half so agreeable as Dante's, some of whose 'circles' must be rather pleasant places.

(Vol. i. p. 281.)

[Dante's reproach of the Kings of France]

Ages of misgovernment under that 'mala stirpe,' as Dante calls the Kings of France,[4] (and Ferdinand was a Bourbon,) had reduced to destitution and misery half the population of Naples.

(Vol. ii. p. 37.)

[Sir Humphrey Davy and the forest of Ravenna]

When I was at Rome, an English squire, whose name I shall not mention, went there solely for snipe-shooting; and Sir Humphrey Davy travelled, as the Guiccioli told me, to the evergreen forest at Ravenna, consecrated by the memory of Dante,[5] and the divine lines of Byron,[6] expressly from London to kill woodcocks!

(Vol. ii. p. 97.)

[Shelley's reading of Dante]

Our days were passed on the lake,[7] in sauntering along its banks till the shades of evening set in; then Shelley would read to us his

[1] [A mistake for *bolge*—the eighth circle of Dante's Hell is called *Male-bolge* or Evil-pits (*Inf.* xviii. 1).]
[2] [*Inf.* xxxiii. 1 ff.] [3] [See vol. i. p. 343.]
[4] [Not 'mala stirpe,' but 'mala pianta' (*Purg.* xx. 43).]
[5] [*Purg.* xxviii. 20.]
[6] [In *Don Juan*, Canto iv.]
[7] [Of Geneva.]

favourite poets, Dante or Petrarch, or explain passages from that romantic and wild drama of Goethe, whence Byron drew the inspiration of Manfred, or *he* would charm away the night in recounting his adventures in those lands where he passed the first days of his travels.

(Vol. ii. p. 173.)

[Byron's life at Venice worthy of punishment in Dante's Hell]

The life Byron led at Venice surpassed Rochester's or Faublas's, and fitted him well for the Bolgi[1] of the 'Inferno,' into which Dante plunges those immersed in such degrading pursuits as he then indulged in.

(Vol. ii. p. 175.)

[Picture of Ugolino possessed by Byron]

I found Byron in his sanctum.[2] The walls of it were stained, and against them hung a picture of Ugolino, in the 'Torre della fame,'[3] the work of one of the Guiccioli's sisters.

(Vol. ii. p. 178.)

[Medwin's version of Shelley's translation of *Purg.* xxviii. 1-51]

Nothing can surpass the scenery of the Tivy; the character ever changing—now broad and placid, it walks with a *signorile passo* through meadows green as emerald—now almost stunning with its deafening torrent, and shouting "with a giddy and frantic gladness,"—sometimes confined to a channel of a few yards,—now eddying and boiling like a cauldron in a basin it has worn for itself among the rocks—now shadowed by woods of oak that overhang the whole stream, and make more dark the water, itself of a pitchy blackness, reminding me of Dante's lines, in the "Purgatorio," admirably translated by Shelley;[4] and as the version has never been published, it will serve to fill up my day's journal better than I can do. I have marked in double inverted commas the words most appropriate to this subject. In no language has inspiration gone beyond this divinest descriptive passage:—

And earnest to explore, within, around,
That divine wood, whose thick, green, living roof[5]
Tempered the young day to the sight, I wound

[1] [See note on previous page. The reference is to *Inf.* xviii. 22-99.]
[2] [In the Casa Lanfranchi, at Pisa.]
[3] [*Inf.* xxxiii. 22-3.]
[4] [In 1820. Medwin's version of this fragment, which he afterwards reprinted in his *Life of Shelley*, differs considerably from that printed by Dr. Garnett in *Relics of Shelley* (pp. 56-8), and reproduced by later editors of Shelley's poems (see above pp. 221 ff.). For further information about this translation, see below, p. 385.]
[5] [In other versions, "woof".]

Up a green slope, beneath the starry roof,
With slow slow steps, leaving the mountain's steep;
And sought those leafy labyrinths, motion-proof

Against the air, that in that stillness, deep
And solemn, struck upon my forehead bare,
Like the sweet breathing of a child in sleep:

Already had I lost myself so far
Amid that tangled wilderness, that I
Perceived not where I entered, but no fear

Of wandering from my way disturbed, when nigh
A little stream appeared; the grass that grew
Thick on its banks impeded suddenly

My going on; "Water, of purest dew
On earth, would appear turbid and impure
Compared with this, whose unconcealing hue,

Dark, dark, yet clear, moved under the obscure
Of the close boughs, whose interwoven looms
No rays of moon or sunshine would endure."

My feet were motionless, but mid the glooms
Darted my charmed eyes contemplating
The mighty multitude of fresh May-blooms

Which starred that night; when, even as a thing
That suddenly for blank astonishment
Charms every sense, and makes all thought take wing,

Appeared a solitary maid,—she went
Singing, and gathering flower after flower,
With which her way was painted and besprent;

"Bright lady! who, if looks had ever power
To bear true witness of the heart within,
Dost bask under the beams of love, come lower

Unto this bank,—I prithee,[1] let me win
This much of thee. Oh come! that I may hear
Thy song: like Proserpine, in Enna's glen,

[1] [In *Life of Shelley* "prithee O!"]

Thou seemest to my fancy, singing here,
And gathering flowers, as that fair maiden when
She lost the Spring, and Ceres *her* more dear."

(Vol. ii. pp. 218-20.)

[1847.] THE LIFE OF PERCY BYSSHE SHELLEY.[1]

[Shelley and the *terza rima*]

Shelley had originally, it would seem, after the Divine Comedy, intended to have written the Revolt of Islam in terza rima, of which he made an experiment in Prince Athanase; but soon after abandoned that metre as too monotonous and artificial, and adopted instead the stanza of Spencer.

(Vol. i. pp. 304-5.)

[Shelley's translation of *Purg.* xxviii. 1-51]

I had the advantage of reading Dante with Shelley; he lamented that no adequate translation existed of the Divina Commedia, and though he thought highly of Carey's work, with which he said he had for the first time studied the original, praising the fidelity of the version—it by no means satisfied him. What he meant by an adequate translation, was, one in terza rima; for in Shelley's own words, he held it an essential justice to an author, to render him in the same form. I asked him if he had never attempted this, and looking among his papers, he shewed, and gave me to copy, the following fragment from the Purgatorio, which leaves on the mind an inextinguishable regret, that he had not completed—nay, more, that he did not employ himself in rendering other of the finest passages. In no language has inspiration gone beyond this picture of exquisite beauty, which undoubtedly suggested to Tennyson his 'Vision of Fair Women.'

And earnest to explore within—around, &c.[2]

(Vol. ii. pp. 15 ff.)

[Medwin and Shelley's translation of the Ugolino episode]

Lord Byron has left a translation of the Rimini's story from the Inferno, which affords as poor an idea of the passage in Dante, as an easel copy does of an old fresco of Giotto's. It is a hard, cold, rough, cast-iron impress, dry and bald, and in many parts unfaithfully rendered; and at Shelley's request, and with his assistance, I attempted to give the Ugolino, which is valuable to the admirers

[1][The details here given about Shelley, though not published until 1847, were obviously written many years previously, consequently they are included in this place.]

[2][Here follows the version already printed by Medwin in the *Angler in Wales* (see above, pp. 383 ff.).]

of Shelley, on account of his numerous corrections, which almost indeed make it his own:

Now had the loophole of that dungeon, still
Which bears the name of Famine's Tower from me,
And where 'tis fit that many another will

Be doomed to linger in captivity,
Shown through its narrow opening in my cell,
Moon after moon slow waning, when a sleep,

That of the future burst the veil, in dream
Visited me—it was a slumber deep
And evil—for I saw, or I did seem

To see, *that* tyrant Lord his revels keep,
The leader of the cruel hunt to them
Chasing the wolf and wolf-cubs up the steep

Ascent, that from *the Pisan is the screen*
Of Lucca; with him Gualandi came,
Sismondi, and Lanfranchi, *bloodhounds lean*,

Trained to the sport and eager for the game,
Wide ranging in his front; but soon were seen,
Though by so short a course, with *spirits tame*,

The father and *his whelps* to flag at once,
And then the sharp fangs gored their bosoms deep.
Ere morn I roused myself, and heard my sons,

For they were with me, moaning in their sleep,
And begging bread. Ah for those darling ones!
Right cruel art thou, if thou dost not weep,

In thinking of my soul's sad augury;
And if thou weepest not now, weep never more!
They were already waked, as wont drew nigh

The allotted hour for food, and in that hour
Each drew a presage from his dream. When I
Heard locked beneath me, of that horrible tower

The outlet, then into their eyes alone
I looked to read myself, without a sign
Or word. I wept not—turned within to stone.

They wept aloud, and little Anselm mine,
Said,—'twas my youngest, dearest little one,—
'What ails thee, father! why look so at thine?'

In all that day, and all the following night,
I wept not, nor replied; but when to shine
Upon the world, not us, came forth the light

Of the new sun, and thwart my prison thrown,
Gleamed thro' its narrow chink—a doleful sight,—
Three faces, each the reflex of my own,

Were imaged by its faint and ghastly ray;
Then I, of either hand unto the bone,
Gnawed, in my agony; and thinking they

'Twas done from hunger pangs in their excess,
All of a sudden raise themselves, and say,
'Father! our woes so great, were not the less

Would you but eat of us,—'twas *you who clad*
Our bodies in these weeds of wretchedness,
Despoil them.' Not to make their hearts more sad,

I *hushed* myself. That day is at its close,—
Another—still we were all mute. Oh had
The obdurate earth opened to end our woes!

The fourth day dawned, and when the new sun shone,
Outstretched himself before me as it rose,
My Gaddo, saying, 'Help, father! hast thou none

For thine own child—is there no help from thee?'
He died—there at my feet—and one by one,
I saw them fall, plainly as you see.

Between the fifth and sixth day, ere 'twas dawn,
I found *myself blind-groping o'er the three.*
Three days I called them after they were gone.

Famine of grief can get the mastery.[1]

This translation I shewed afterwards to Byron, and remember his saying, that he interpreted the last words, Più che dolor potè

[1] [*Inf.* xxxiii. 22-75. This translation was apparently written about the year 1820.]

il digiunò[1] to mean (an interpretation in which Shelley by no means agreed with him) that Ugolino actually did feed on his children after their deaths, and which Lord Byron thought was clearly borne out by the nature of the retribution of his tormentor, as well as the offer of the children to make themselves a sacrifice for their father. 'The story,' observed Shelley, 'is horrible enough without such a comment,'—and he added, 'that Byron had deeply studied this death of Ugolino, and perhaps but for it, would never have written the Prisoner of Chillon.'

(Vol. ii. pp. 18-22.)

[Taaffe's translation of the *Divina Commedia*]

Speaking of Dante, among Shelley's acquaintances at Pisa, was a Mr. Taafe,[2] of whom Byron makes mention in his letters. . . .

Mr. Taafe had the monomania that he could translate the Divina Comedia, and we were much amused by his version, which he brought from time to time, of some of the cantos of the Inferno, which he had rendered in octosyllabics; one of the strangest metres to adopt for a serious drama, and a metre that did not admit even of fidelity, for though our own language is extremely monosyllabic, to squeeze three hexameter terza rimas into short ones, was an utter impossibility and despair. Mr. Taafe told Shelley that a brother of his in the Austrian service was occupied in a similar pursuit, and Shelley remarked that it was hard upon poor Dante, that his spirit, after a lapse of six centuries, could not be allowed to remain at rest, but must be disquieted by two Milesians.

Let not Mr. Taafe take ill these remarks—he was an amiable and clever man, and his commentary on Dante appeared to me excellent,—as well as to Byron, who recommended Murray to publish it.[3]

(Vol. ii. pp. 23-4.)

[Dante among the books in Shelley's library]

Shelley's library was a very limited one. He used to say that a good library consisted not of many books, but a few chosen ones; and asking him what he considered such, he said 'I'll give you my list—catalogue it can't be called:—The Greek Plays, Plato, Lord Bacon's Works, Shakspeare, The Old Dramatists, Milton, Göthe and Schiller, Dante, Petrarch and Boccacio, and Machiavelli and Guicciardini,—not forgetting Calderon; and last, yet first, the Bible.'

(Vol. ii. p. 31.)

[1] [Misprinted *diguinno.*] [2] [*Sic*, for Taaffe.] [3] [See above, pp. 51-2.]

This admirable piece of eloquence [the apostrophe to Love (entitled 'Il vero Amore') written by Emilia Viviani] was perhaps the source of the inspiration of the Epipyschidion, a poem that combines the pathos of the 'Vita Nuova' of Dante with the enthusiastic tenderness of Petrarch.

(Vol. ii. p. 72.)

[Effect on Shelley of reading Byron or Dante]

Shelley used to say, that the magnetism of Byron—'the Byronic Energy,' as he called Byron—was hostile to his powers; that like the reading of Dante, the outpouring of his works,

vast and fair
As perfect worlds at the Creator's will,

produced in him a despair.[1]

(Vol. ii. pp. 161-2.)

[Byron and Shelley on the *Divina Commedia*]

Byron's mystifications were not confined to his contemporaries. I have a note of a conversation which escaped me, with him and Shelley on Dante. When it suited Byron's purpose in defence of Prophecy of Dante, (see Moore's Life, p. 123), he could talk a very different language; though the expression of the opinions here orally detailed, correspond with the sentiments contained in a note to Don Juan.

'The Divine Comedy,' said he, 'is a scientific treatise of some theological student, one moment treating of angels, and the next demons, far the most interesting personages in his Drama; shewing that he had a better conception of Hell than Heaven; in fact, the Inferno is the only one of the trilogy that is read. It is true,' he added, 'it might have pleased his contemporaries, and been sung about the streets, as were the poems of Homer; but at the present day, either human nature is very much changed, or the poem is so obscure, tiresome, and insupportable, that no one can read it for half-an-hour together without yawning, and going to sleep over it . . .; and the hundred times I have made the attempt to read it, I have lost my labour. If we except the 'Pecorelle escon del chiuso,'[2]—the simile, 'Come d' autunno si levan le foglie'[3]—the Francesca di Rimini,[4] the words, 'Colore oscuro' &c. inscribed on the portal of Hell,[5]—the Death of Ugolino,[6]—the 'Si volge all' acqua,'[7] &c., and a dozen other passages, what is the rest of this

[1] [See a similar statement in the *Shelley Papers* (above, p. 380).]
[2] [*Purg.* iii. 79 ff.—Misprinted by Medwin 'Pecchie chi uscino. . . .']
[3] [*Inf.* iii. 112 ff.]
[4] [*Inf.* v. 73 ff.]
[5] [*Inf.* iii. 10 ff.]
[6] [*Inf.* xxxiii.]
[7] [*Inf.* i. 22 ff.]

very comic Divine Comedy? A great poem! you call it; a great poem indeed! *That* should have a uniformity of design, a combination of facts, all contributing to the development of the whole. The action should go on increasing in beauty and power and interest.

Has the Divina Comedia any of these characteristics? Who can read with patience, fourteen thousand lines, made up of prayers, dialogues, and questions, without sticking fast in the bogs and quicksands, and losing his way in the thousand turns and windings of the inextricable labyrinths of his three-times-nine circles? and of these fourteen thousand lines, more than two-thirds are, by the confession of Fregoni, Algarotti, and Bettinelli, defective and bad; and yet, despite of this, the Italians carry their pedantry and national pride to such a length, as to set up Dante as the standard of perfection, to consider Dante as made for all time; and think, as Leigh Hunt and the Cockneys do of Shakspeare, that the language came to a stand-still with the god of their idolatory, and want to go back to him.'

That Shelley did not agree with Lord Byron in this criticism, I need scarcely observe. He admitted, however, as already recorded, that the Divine Comedy was a misty and extravagant fiction, and redeemed only by its 'Fortunate Isles, laden with golden fruit.' 'But,' said he, 'remember the time in which he wrote. He was a giant.

> Quel signor dell' altissimo canto,
> Chi sovra gli altri come aquila vola.

Read the Paradiso, and parts of the Purgatorio, especially the meeting with Matilda.'

He afterwards told me that the more he read Dante, he the more admired him.

He says in his Letters, p. 225, that he excelled all poets, except Shakspeare, in tenderness, sublimity, and ideal beauty. In his Defence of Poetry, Shelley calls the Apotheosis of Beatrice in the Paradiso, and the gradations of his own love and her loveliness, by which, as by steps, he figures himself to have ascended to the throne of the Supreme Cause, as the most glowing images of modern poetry; calls the Paradiso a perfect hymn of everlasting love, and the poetry of Dante the bridge thrown over the stream of time, which unites the modern and ancient world. Nay, more, he admired Dante as the first reformer, and classes him with Luther, calling him the first awakener of Europe, and the creator of a language in itself music.[1]

(Vol. ii. pp. 251-5.)

[1] [See above, pp. 226-7.]

ANDRÉ VIEUSSEUX

(fl. 1820)

1824. ITALY AND THE ITALIANS IN THE NINETEENTH CENTURY.

[The country of Dante the true classical ground of Italy]

IT is in the Southern division that we find the true classical ground of Italy. . . . It is the country of Dante, of Macchiavelli, and of Tasso; it was the birthplace of Scipio, of Caesar, and of Cicero.

(Vol. i. pp. 3-4.)

[Alfieri and Monti disciples of Dante]

Dante, of whom Alfieri professed himself a disciple, had given him a model of that nervous, laconic, and sometimes harsh diction which Alfieri adopted, thinking it adapted to express violent passions. . . . Monti, like Alfieri, is a great partisan of Dante, and his *Basvilliana* is as close and as happy an imitation of the *Divina Commedia* as the difference of the subject and the originality of Monti's plan could allow.

(Vol. ii. pp. 268, 272.)

JOHN CHARLES TARVER

(1790-1851)

[Tarver was born of English parents, at Dieppe, in 1790, and was brought up in France, where he resided until his twenty-fifth year. On coming to England he obtained the post of French master at Macclesfield free school, and while there made the first beginnings of his great work, the French and English Dictionary, which was eventually published in 1845. Having been appointed French tutor to Prince George of Cambridge he went to reside at Windsor (1818); and in 1826 was appointed French master at Eton, a post which he held for twenty-five years, until his death in 1851. In 1824 he published a French prose translation (printed at Windsor, and dedicated to the Princess Augusta) of the *Inferno*.]

1824. L' ENFER DE DANTE ALIGHIERI, TRADUIT EN FRANÇAIS, ACCOMPAGNÉ DE NOTES EXPLICATIVES, RAISONNÉES, ET HISTORIQUES, SUIVIES DE REMARQUES GÉNÉRALES SUR LA VIE DE DANTE, ET SUR LES FACTIONS DES GUELFES ET DES GIBELINS.[1]

[Vol. i. contains the translation of the *Inferno*, accompanied by the Italian text, and an index of proper names. Vol. ii. contains the notes and 'remarques générales.' In his preface Tarver remarks on the study of Italian and of Dante in England, where, he says, 'les oeuvres de Dante sont encore, pour ainsi dire, une terre inconnue'; and he criticizes the translation of Cary as not always faithfully interpreting the meaning of the original.]

[1] ['A Londres: chez C. Knight; de l' Imprimerie de C. Knight, à Windsor.']

THOMAS BABINGTON MACAULAY

(1800-1859)

[Thomas Babington Macaulay, afterwards Lord Macaulay, was born at Rothley Temple, Leicestershire, in 1800. He was educated at private schools and at Trinity College, Cambridge, of which he was elected Fellow in 1824. In 1826 he was called to the bar, but never practised. He entered Parliament as member for Calne in 1830. In 1833 he was appointed member of the supreme council of India, and sailed in the following year, returning home in 1838. In India Macaulay accomplished the important work of composing a criminal code, which became law in 1860. In the autumn of 1838 he made a tour in Italy, and spent ten days in Florence. In 1839 he was elected M.P. for Edinburgh, and shortly after was made Secretary at War. In 1846 he was Paymaster of the Forces. Losing his seat in the next year, he was re-elected for Edinburgh in 1852, and resigned in 1856. In 1857 he was created Baron Macaulay of Rothley. He died in London in December, 1859, and was buried in Westminster Abbey.

Macaulay began his literary career in 1823 by contributing to *Knight's Quarterly Magazine*, in which he published in 1824 *Criticisms on the Principal Italian Writers*, the first article being on Dante. In August, 1825, he contributed an article (on Milton) to the *Edinburgh Review*, the first of a long series, which were eventually (in 1843) republished under the title of *Critical and Historical Essays*. In 1842 he published the *Lays of Ancient Rome*; and in 1848 appeared the first two volumes of his *History of England*, of which the third and fourth volumes were issued in 1855, and the fifth (after his death) in 1861.

Macaulay's intimate knowledge of the *Divina Commedia* is evidenced by the numerous quotations and references in his various essays.[1] His parallel between Dante and Milton in his essay on the latter in the *Edinburgh Review* is famous. With Dante's prose works he appears to have had little or no acquaintance. Trevelyan in his *Life of Macaulay* records of him (vol. i. p. 183, ed. 1877) that on a visit to his uncle at Rothley Park in the early thirties, 'he is remembered as sitting at the window in the hall, reading Dante to himself, or translating it aloud as long as any listener cared to remain within earshot'; and he quotes (vol. ii. p. 198) from Lord Carlisle's journal 'a list of six poets whom Macaulay places above all others, in the order of his preference: Shakespeare, Homer, Dante, Aeschylus, Milton, Sophocles.' Occasional renderings (in prose) of passages from the *Commedia* occur here and there in the essays. Macaulay had a very high opinion of Cary's translation, of which he says, 'it is difficult to determine whether the author deserves most praise for his intimacy with the language of Dante, or for his extraordinary mastery over his own.'[2]]

1824. CRITICISMS ON THE PRINCIPAL ITALIAN WRITERS. NO. I. DANTE.[3]

[Dante and his works]

'FAIREST of stars, last in the train of night,
If better thou belong not to the dawn,
Sure pledge of day, that crown'st the smiling morn
With thy bright circlet.'

Milton.

[1][Macaulay's application of three lines from the *Inferno* to the description of a dead man in one of Robert Montgomery's poems (see below, p. 410) is perhaps one of the happiest things of the kind in English literature.]

[2][See below, p. 403.]

[3][Originally published in *Knight's Quarterly Magazine*.]

In a review of Italian literature, Dante has a double claim to precedency. He was the earliest and the greatest writer of his country. He was the first man who fully described and exhibited the powers of his native dialect. The Latin tongue, which, under the most favourable circumstances, and in the hands of the greatest masters, had still been poor, feeble, and singularly unpoetical, and which had, in the age of Dante, been debased by the admixture of innumerable barbarous words and idioms, was still cultivated with superstitious veneration, and received, in the last stage of corruption, more honours than it had deserved in the period of its life and vigour. It was the language of the cabinet, of the university, of the church. It was employed by all who aspired to distinction in the higher walks of poetry. In compassion to the ignorance of his mistress, a cavalier might now and then proclaim his passion in Tuscan or Provençal rhymes. The vulgar might occasionally be edified by a pious allegory in the popular jargon. But no writer had conceived it possible that the dialect of peasants and market-women should possess sufficient energy and precision for a majestic and durable work. Dante adventured first. He detected the rich treasures of thought and diction which still lay latent in their ore. He refined them into purity. He burnished them into splendour. He fitted them for every purpose of use and maginficence. And he has thus acquired the glory, not only of producing the finest narrative poem of modern times, but also of creating a language, distinguished by unrivalled melody, and peculiarly capable of furnishing to lofty and passionate thoughts their appropriate garb of severe and concise expression.

To many this may appear a singular panegyric on the Italian tongue. Indeed the great majority of the young gentlemen and young ladies, who, when they are asked whether they read Italian, answer 'yes,' never go beyond the stories at the end of their grammar,—the Pastor Fido,—or an act of Artaserse. They could as soon read a Babylonian brick as a canto of Dante. Hence it is a general opinion, among those who know little or nothing of the subject, that this admirable language is adapted only to the effeminate cant of sonnetteers, musicians, and connoisseurs.

The fact is that Dante and Petrarch have been the Oromasdes and Arimanes of Italian literature. I wish not to detract from the merits of Petrarch. No one can doubt that his poems exhibit, amidst some imbecility and more affectation, much elegance, ingenuity, and tenderness. . . . The florid and luxurious charms of his style enticed the poets and the public from the contemplation of nobler and sterner models. In truth, though a rude state of society is that in which great original works are most frequently produced, it is also that in which they are worst appreciated. This may appear paradoxical; but it is proved by experience, and is consistent with reason. To be without any received canons of taste is good for the few who can create, but bad for the many who can only imitate and judge. Great and active minds cannot remain at rest. In a cultivated age they are too often contented to move on in the beaten path. But where no path exists they will make one. Thus the Iliad, the Odyssey, the Divine Comedy, appeared in dark and half barbarous times: and thus of the few original works which have been produced in more polished ages we owe a large proportion to men in low stations and of uninformed minds. . . .

But these circumstances, while they foster genius, are unfavourable to the science of criticism. Men judge by comparison. They are unable to estimate the grandeur of an object when there is no standard by which they can measure it. One of the French philosophers . . . , who accompanied Napoleon to Egypt, tells us that, when he first visited the great Pyramid, he was surprised to see it so diminutive. It stood alone in a boundless plain. There was nothing near it from which he could calculate its magnitude. But when the camp was pitched beside it, and the tents appeared like diminutive specks around its base, he then perceived the immensity of this mightiest work of man. In the same manner, it is not till a crowd of petty writers has sprung up that the merit of the great master-spirits of literature is understood.

We have indeed ample proof that Dante was highly admired in his own and the following age. I wish that we had equal proof that he was admired for his excellencies. But it is a remarkable corroboration of what has been said, that this great man seems to have been utterly unable to appreciate himself. In his treatise *De Vulgari Eloquentia* he talks with satisfaction of what he has done for Italian literature, of the purity and correctness of his style. '*Cependant*,' says a favourite writer of mine (Sismondi, Littérature du Midi de l' Europe), '*il n'est ni pur, ni correct, mais il est créateur.*' Considering the difficulties with which Dante had to struggle, we may perhaps be more inclined than the French critic to allow him this praise. Still it is by no means his highest or most peculiar title to applause. It is scarcely necessary to say that those qualities which escaped the notice of the poet himself were not likely to attract the attention of the commentators. The fact is, that, while the public homage was paid to some absurdities with which his works may be justly charged, and to many more which were falsely imputed to them,—while lecturers were paid to expound and eulogise his physics, his metaphysics, his theology, all bad of their kind,—while annotators laboured to detect allegorical meanings of which the author never dreamed, the great powers of his imagination, and the incomparable force of his style, were neither admired nor imitated. Arimanes had prevailed. The Divine Comedy was to that age what St. Paul's Cathedral was to Omai. The poor Otaheitean stared listlessly for a moment at the huge cupola, and ran into a toyshop to play with beads. Italy, too, was charmed with literary trinkets, and played with them for four centuries.

From the time of Petrarch to the appearance of Alfieri's tragedies, we may trace in almost every page of Italian literature the influence of those celebrated sonnets, which, from the nature both of their beauties and their faults, were peculiarly unfit to be models for general imitation. Almost all the poets of that period, however different in the degree and quality of their talents, are characterised by great exaggeration, and, as a necessary consequence, great coldness of sentiment; by a passion for frivolous and tawdry ornament; and, above all, by an extreme feebleness and diffuseness of style. . . .

It may be thought that I have gone too far in attributing these evils to the influence of the works and the fame of Petrarch. It cannot, however, be doubted that they have arisen, in a great measure, from a neglect of the style of Dante. This is not more proved by the decline of Italian poetry than by its resuscitation. After the lapse of four hundred and fifty years, there appeared a man capable of appreciating and imitating the father of Tuscan literature—Vittorio Alfieri. . . . In every line of the Philip and the Saul, the greatest poems, I think, of the eighteenth century, we may trace the influence of that mighty genius which has immortalised the ill-starred love of Francesca, and the paternal agonies of Ugolino. Alfieri bequeathed the sovereignty of Italian literature to the author of the Aristodemus[1]—a man of genius scarcely inferior to his own, and a still more devoted disciple of the great Florentine. It must be acknowledged that this eminent writer has sometimes pushed too far his idolatry of Dante. To borrow a sprightly illustration from Sir John Denham, he has not only imitated his garb, but borrowed his clothes. He often quotes his phrases; and he has, not very judiciously as it appears to me, imitated his versification. Nevertheless, he has displayed many of the higher excellencies of his master. . . .

The man to whom the literature of his country owes its origin and its revival was born in times singularly adapted to call forth his extraordinary powers. Religious zeal, chivalrous love and honour, democratic liberty, are the three most powerful principles that have ever influenced the character of large masses of men. Each of them singly has often excited the greatest enthusiasm, and produced the most important changes. In the time of Dante all the three, often in amalgamation, generally in conflict, agitated the public mind. The preceding generation had witnessed the wrongs and the revenge

[1] [Vincenzo Monti (1754-1828).]

of the brave, the accomplished, the unfortunate Emperor Frederic the Second,—a poet in an age of schoolmen,—a philosopher in an age of monks,—a statesman in an age of crusaders. During the whole life of the poet, Italy was experiencing the consequences of the memorable struggle which he had maintained against the Church. The finest works of imagination have always been produced in times of political convulsion, as the richest vineyards and the sweetest flowers always grow on the soil which has been fertilised by the fiery deluge of a volcano. To look no further than the literary history of our own country, can we doubt that Shakspeare was in a great measure produced by the Reformation, and Wordsworth by the French Revolution? Poets often avoid political transactions; they often affect to despise them. But, whether they perceive it or not, they must be influenced by them. . . . This will be the case even in large societies, where division of labour enables many speculative men to observe the face of nature, or to analyse their own minds, at a distance from the seat of political transactions. In the little republic of which Dante was a member the state of things was very different. These small communities are most unmercifully abused by most of our modern professors of the science of government. In such states, they tell us, factions are always most violent: where both parties are cooped up within a narrow space, political difference necessarily produces personal malignity. Every man must be a soldier; every moment may produce a war. No citizen can lie down secure that he shall not be aroused by the alarum-bell, to repel or avenge an injury. In such petty quarrels Greece squandered the blood which might have purchased for her the permanent empire of the world, and Italy wasted the energy and abilities which would have enabled her to defend her independence against the Pontiffs and the Caesars.

All this is true: yet there is still a compensation. Mankind has not derived so much benefit from the empire of Rome as from the city of Athens, nor from the kingdom of France as from the city of Florence. The violence of party feeling may be an evil; but it calls forth that activity of mind which in some states of society it is desirable to produce at any expense. Universal soldiership may be an evil; but where every man is a soldier there will be no standing army. . . . It was something that the citizen of Milan or Florence fought, not merely in the vague and rhetorical sense in which the words are often used, but in sober truth, for his parents, his children, his lands, his house, his altars. . . . Surely this state of things was not unmixedly bad: its evils were alleviated by enthusiasm and by tenderness; and it will at least be acknowledged that it was well fitted to nurse poetical genius in an imaginative and observant mind.

Nor did the religious spirit of the age tend less to this result than its political circumstances. Fanaticism is an evil, but it is not the greatest of evils. It is good that a people should be roused by any means from a state of utter torpor;—that their minds should be diverted from objects merely sensual, to meditations, however erroneous, on the mysteries of the moral and intellectual world; and from interests which are immediately selfish to those which relate to the past, the future, and the remote. . . .

In this point Dante was completely under the influence of his age. He was a man of a turbid and melancholy spirit. In early youth he had entertained a strong and unfortunate passion, which, long after the death of her whom he loved, continued to haunt him. Dissipation, ambition, misfortunes had not effaced it. He was not only a sincere, but a passionate believer. The crimes and abuses of the Church of Rome were indeed loathsome to him; but to all its doctrines and all its rites he adhered with enthusiastic fondness and veneration; and, at length, driven from his native country, reduced to a situation the most painful to a man of his disposition, condemned to learn by experience that no food is so bitter as the bread of dependence, and no ascent so painful as the staircase of a patron,—

> 'Tu proverai sì come sa di sale
> Lo pane altrui, e come è duro calle
> Lo scendere e 'l salir per l' altrui scale.'
>
> *Paradiso,* canto xvii—

his wounded spirit took refuge in visionary devotion. Beatrice, the unforgotten object of his early tenderness, was invested by his imagination with glorious and mysterious attributes; she was enthroned among the brighest of the celestial hierarchy: Almighty Wisdom had assigned to her the care of the sinful and unhappy wanderer who had loved her with such perfect love—

> 'L' amico mio, e non della ventura.'
>
> *Inferno,* canto ii.

By a confusion, like that which often takes place in dreams, he has sometimes lost sight of her human nature, and even of her personal existence, and seems to consider her as one of the attributes of the Deity.

But those religious hopes which had released the mind of the sublime enthusiast from the terrors of death had not rendered his speculations on human life more cheerful. This is an inconsistency which may often be observed in men of a similar temperament. He hoped for happiness beyond the grave: but he felt none on earth. It is from this cause, more than from any other, that his description of Heaven is so far inferior to the Hell or the Purgatory. With the passions and miseries of the suffering spirits he feels a strong sympathy. But among the beatified he appears as one who has nothing in common with them,—as one who is incapable of comprehending, not only the degree, but the nature of their enjoyment. We think that we see him standing amidst those smiling and radiant spirits with that scowl of unutterable misery on his brow, and that curl of bitter disdain on his lips, which all his portraits have preserved, and which might furnish Chantrey with hints for the head of his projected Satan.

There is no poet whose intellectual and moral character are so closely connected. The great source, as it appears to me, of the power of the Divine Comedy is the strong belief with which the story seems to be told. In this respect, the only books which approach to its excellence are Gulliver's Travels and Robinson Crusoe. The solemnity of his asseverations, the consistency and minuteness of his details, the earnestness with which he labours to make the reader understand the exact shape and size of everything that he describes, give an air of reality to his wildest fictions. I should only weaken this statement by quoting instances of a feeling which pervades the whole work, and to which it owes much of its fascination. This is the real justification of the many passages in his poem which bad critics have condemned as grotesque. I am concerned to see that Mr. Cary, to whom Dante owes more than ever poet owed to translator, has sanctioned an accusation utterly unworthy of his abilities. 'His solicitude,' says that gentleman,[1] 'to define all his images in such a manner as to bring them within the circle of our vision, and to subject them to the power of the pencil, renders him little better than grotesque, where Milton has since taught us to expect sublimity.' It is true that Dante has never shrunk from embodying his conceptions in determinate words, that he has even given measures and numbers, where Milton would have left his images to float undefined in a gorgeous haze of language. Both were right. Milton did not profess to have been in heaven or hell. He might therefore reasonably confine himself to magnificent generalities. Far different was the office of the lonely traveller, who had wandered through the nations of the dead. Had he described the abode of the rejected spirits in language resembling the splendid lines of the English Poet,—had he told us of—

'An universe of death, which God by curse
Created evil, for evil only good,
Where all life dies, death lives, and Nature breeds
Perverse all monstrous, all prodigious things,
Abominable, unutterable, and worse
Than fables yet have feigned, or fear conceived,
Gorgons, and hydras, and chimaeras dire'—[2]

[1] [In the *Life of Dante* prefixed to his translation (ed. 1819, vol. i. pp. xliii-xliv).]
[2] [*Paradise Lost*, ii. 622-8.]

this would doubtless have been noble writing. But where would have been that strong impression of reality, which, in accordance with his plan, it should have been his great object to produce? It was absolutely necessary for him to delineate accurately 'all monstrous, all prodigious things,'—to utter what might to others appear 'unutterable,'—to relate with the air of truth what fables had never feigned,—to embody what fear had never conceived. And I will frankly confess that the vague sublimity of Milton affects me less than these reviled details of Dante. We read Milton, and we know that we are reading a great poet; when we read Dante, the poet vanishes. We are listening to the man who has returned from 'the valley of the dolorous abyss'—'La valle d' abisso doloroso,' *Inferno*, canto iv;—we seem to see the dilated eye of horror, to hear the shuddering accents with which he tells his fearful tale. Considered in this light, the narratives are exactly what they should be,—definite in themselves, but suggesting to the mind ideas of awful and indefinite wonder. They are made up of the images of the earth,—they are told in the language of the earth.—Yet the whole effect is, beyond expression, wild and unearthly. The fact is, that supernatural beings, as long as they are considered merely with reference to their own nature, excite our feelings very feebly. . . . This difficult task of representing supernatural beings to our minds, in a manner which shall be neither unintelligible to our intellects nor wholly inconsistent with our ideas of their nature, has never been so well performed as by Dante. I will refer to three instances, which are, perhaps, the most striking: —the description of the transformations of the serpents and the robbers, in the twenty-fifth canto of the Inferno,—the passage concerning Nimrod, in the thirty-first canto of the same part,—and the magnificent procession in the twenty-ninth canto of the Purgatorio.

The metaphors and comparisons of Dante harmonise admirably with that air of strong reality of which I have spoken. They have a very peculiar character. He is perhaps the only poet whose writings would become much less intelligible if all illustrations of this sort were expunged. His similes are frequently rather those of a traveller than of a poet. He employs them not to display his ingenuity by fanciful analogies,—not to delight the reader by affording him a distant and passing glimpse of beautiful images remote from the part in which he is proceeding,—but to give an exact idea of the objects which he is describing, by comparing them with others generally known. The boiling pitch in Malebolge was like that in the Venetian arsenal:—the mound on which he travelled along the banks of Phlegethon was like that between Ghent[1] and

[1] [Not Ghent, but Wissant (*Inf.* xv. 4). Macaulay, however, is quoting not from the original, but from Cary.]

Bruges, but not so large:—the cavities where the Simoniacal prelates are confined resemble the fonts in the Church of John at Florence. Every reader of Dante will recall many other illustrations of this description, which add to the appearance of sincerity and earnestness from which the narrative derives so much of its interest.

Many of his comparisons, again, are intended to give an exact idea of his feelings under particular circumstances. The delicate shades of grief, of fear, of anger, are rarely discriminated with sufficient accuracy in the language of the most refined nations. A rude dialect never abounds in nice distinctions of this kind. Dante therefore employs the most accurate and infinitely the most poetical mode of marking the precise state of his mind. Every person who has experienced the bewildering effect of sudden bad tidings,—the stupefaction,—the vague doubt of the truth of our own perceptions which they produce,—will understand the following simile:—'I was as he is who dreameth his own harm,—who, dreaming, wishes that it may be all a dream, so that he desires that which is as though it were not.'[1] This is only one out of a hundred equally striking and expressive similitudes. The comparisons of Homer and Milton are magnificent digressions. It scarcely injures their effect to detach them from the work. Those of Dante are very different. They derive their beauty from the context, and reflect beauty upon it. His embroidery cannot be taken out without spoiling the whole web. I cannot dismiss this part of the subject without advising every person who can muster sufficient Italian to read the simile of the sheep, in the third canto of the Purgatorio. I think it the most perfect passage of the kind in the world, the most imaginative, the most picturesque, and the most sweetly expressed.

No person can have attended to the Divine Comedy without observing how little impression the forms of the external world appear to have made on the mind of Dante. His temper and his situation had led him to fix his observation almost exclusively on human nature. The exquisite opening of the eighth canto of the Purgatorio[2] affords a strong instance of this. He leaves to others the earth, the ocean, and the sky. His business is with man. To

[1] [*Inf.* xxx. 136-8.]

[2] I cannot help observing that Gray's imitation of that noble line

'Che paia 'l giorno pianger che si muore,'—

is one of the most striking instances of injudicious plagiarism with which I am acquainted. Dante did not put this strong personification at the beginning of his description. The imagination of the reader is so well prepared for it by the previous lines, that it appears perfectly natural and pathetic. Placed as Gray has placed it, neither preceded nor followed by anything that harmonises with it, it becomes a frigid conceit. Woe to the unskilful rider who ventures on the horses of Achilles! . . .

other writers, evening may be the season of dews and stars and radiant clouds. To Dante it is the hour of fond recollection and passionate devotion,—the hour which melts the heart of the mariner and kindles the love of the pilgrim,—the hour when the toll of the bell seems to mourn for another day which is gone and will return no more.

The feeling of the present age has taken a direction diametrically opposite. The magnificence of the physical world, and its influence upon the human mind, have been the favourite themes of our most eminent poets. The herd of blue-stocking ladies and sonnetteering gentlemen seem to consider a strong sensibility to the 'splendour of the grass, the glory of the flower,' as an ingredient absolutely indispensable in the formation of a poetical mind. . . . The orthodox poetical creed is more Catholic. The noblest earthly object of the contemplation of man is man himself. The universe, and all its fair and glorious forms, are indeed included in the wide empire of the imagination; but she has placed her home and her sanctuary amidst the inexhaustible varieties and the impenetrable mysteries of the mind.

> 'In tutte parti impera, e quivi regge;
> Quivi è la sua cittade, e l' alto seggio.'
>
> *Inferno*, canto i.[1]

. . . To those who think thus, the insensibility of the Florentine poet to the beauties of nature will not appear an unpardonable deficiency. On mankind no writer, with the exception of Shakspeare, has looked with a more penetrating eye. I have said that his poetical character had derived a tinge from his peculiar temper. It is on the sterner and darker passions that he delights to dwell. All love, excepting the half-mystic passion which he still felt for his buried Beatrice, had palled on the fierce and restless exile. The sad story of Rimini is almost a single exception. I know not whether it has been remarked, that, in one point, misanthropy seems to have affected his mind as it did that of Swift. Nauseous and revolting images seem to have had a fascination for his mind; and he repeatedly places before his readers, with all the energy of his incomparable style, the most loathsome objects of the sewer and the dissecting-room.

There is another peculiarity in the poem of Dante, which, I think, deserves attention. Ancient mythology has hardly ever been successfully interwoven with modern poetry. . . . Dante alone, among the poets of later times, has been, in this respect, neither an allegorist nor an imitator; and, consequently, he alone has introduced the ancient fictions with effect. His Minos, his Charon,

[1] [ll. 127-8.]

his Pluto, are absolutely terrific. Nothing can be more beautiful or original than the use which he has made of the River of Lethe. He has never assigned to his mythological characters any functions inconsistent with the creed of the Catholic Church. He has related nothing concerning them which a good Christian of that age might not believe possible. On this account, there is nothing in these passages that appears puerile or pedantic. On the contrary, this singular use of classical names suggests to the mind a vague and awful idea of some mysterious revelation, anterior to all recorded history, of which the dispersed fragments might have been retained amidst the impostures and superstitions of later religions. Indeed the mythology of the Divine Comedy is of the elder and more colossal mould. It breathes the spirit of Homer and Aeschylus, not of Ovid and Claudian.

This is the more extraordinary, since Dante seems to have been utterly ignorant of the Greek language; and his favourite Latin models could only have served to mislead him. Indeed, it is impossible not to remark his admiration of writers far inferior to himself; and, in particular, his idolatry of Virgil, who, elegant and splendid as he is, has no pretensions to the depth and originality of mind which characterise his Tuscan worshipper. . . .

The style of Dante is, if not his highest, perhaps his most peculiar excellence. I know nothing with which it can be compared. The noblest models of Greek composition must yield to it. His words are the fewest and the best which it is possible to use. The first expression in which he clothes his thoughts is always so energetic and comprehensive that amplification would only injure the effect. There is probably no writer in any language who has presented so many strong pictures to the mind. Yet there is probably no writer equally concise. This perfection of style is the principal merit of the Paradiso, which, as I have already remarked, is by no means equal in other respects to the two preceding parts of the poem. The force and felicity of the diction, however, irresistibly attract the reader through the theological lectures and the sketches of ecclesiastical biography, with which this division of the work too much abounds. It may seem almost absurd to quote particular specimens of an excellence which is diffused over all his hundred cantos. I will, however, instance the third canto of the Inferno, and the sixth of the Purgatorio, as passages incomparable in their kind. The merit of the latter is, perhaps, rather oratorical than poetical; nor can I recollect anything in the great Athenian speeches which equals it in force of invective and bitterness of sarcasm. I have heard the most eloquent statesman[1] of the age remark that, next to Demosthenes, Dante is the writer who ought

[1] [Brougham—see J. W. Thomas, introduction to his trans. of *Purgatorio*.]

to be most attentively studied by every man who desires to attain oratorical eminence. . . .

I cannot refrain from saying a few words upon the translations of the Divine Comedy. Boyd's is as tedious and languid as the original is rapid and forcible. The strange measure which he has chosen, and, for aught I know, invented, is most unfit for such a work. Translations ought never to be written in a verse which requires much command of rhyme. The stanza becomes a bed of Procrustes; and the thoughts of the unfortunate author are alternately racked and curtailed to fit their new receptacle. The abrupt and yet consecutive style of Dante suffers more than that of any other poet by a version diffuse in style, and divided into paragraphs, for they deserve no other name, of equal length.

Nothing can be said in favour of Hayley's attempt, but that it is better than Boyd's. His mind was a tolerable specimen of filigree work,—rather elegant, and very feeble. All that can be said for his best works is that they are neat. All that can be said against his worst is that they are stupid. He might have translated Metastasio tolerably. But he was utterly unable to do justice to the

'rime e aspre e chiocce,
Come si converrebbe al tristo buco.'
Inferno canto xxxiii.[1]

I turn with pleasure from these wretched performances to Mr. Cary's translation. It is a work which well deserves a separate discussion, and on which, if this article were not already too long, I could dwell with great pleasure. At present I will only say that there is no version in the world, as far as I know, so faithful, yet that there is no other version which so fully proves that the translator is himself a man of poetical genius. Those who are ignorant of the Italian language should read it to become acquainted with the Divine Comedy. Those who are most intimate with Italian literature should read it for its original merits: and I believe that they will find it difficult to determine whether the author deserves most praise for his intimacy with the language of Dante, or for his extraordinary mastery over his own.

(*Miscellaneous Writings*, ed. 1875, pp. 21-32.)

1824. CRITICISMS ON THE PRINCIPAL ITALIAN WRITERS. NO. II. PETRARCH.[2]

[Dante's reputation eclipsed by that of Petrarch and Cervantes]

His admirers will scarcely maintain that the unassisted merit of Petrarch could have raised him to that eminence which has not

[1] [ll. 1-3.] [2] [Originally published in *Knight's Quarterly Magazine*.]

yet been attained by Shakspeare, Milton, or Dante,—that eminence, of which perhaps no modern writer, excepting himself and Cervantes, has long retained possession,—an European reputation.

(*Miscellaneous Writings*, ed. 1875 p. 32.)

[Petrarch lacking in the power of description in which Dante excels]

Petrarch did not possess the art of strongly presenting sensible objects to the imagination;—and this is the more remarkable, because the talent of which I speak is that which peculiarly distinguishes the Italian poets. In the Divine Comedy it is displayed in its highest perfection. It characterises almost every celebrated poem in the language.

(*Ibid.* p. 35.)

[Impossible for the *Divina Commedia* ever to become hackneyed]

A line may be stolen; but the pervading spirit of a great poet is not to be surreptitiously obtained by a plagiarist. The continued imitation of twenty-five centuries has left Homer as it found him. If every simile and every turn of Dante had been copied ten thousand times, the Divine Comedy would have retained all its freshness.

(*Ibid.* p. 38.)

1825. ESSAY ON MILTON.[1]

[Parallel between Dante and Milton]

The only poem of modern times which can be compared with the Paradise Lost is the Divine Comedy.[2] The subject of Milton, in some points, resembled that of Dante; but he has treated it in a widely different manner. We cannot, we think, better illustrate our opinion respecting our own great poet, than by contrasting him with the father of Tuscan literature.

The poetry of Milton differs from that of Dante, as the hieroglyphics of Egypt differed from the picture-writing of Mexico. The images which Dante employs speak for themselves; they stand simply for what they are. Those of Milton have a signification which is often discernible only to the initiated. Their value depends less on what they directly represent than what they remotely suggest. However strange, however grotesque, may be the appearance which Dante undertakes to describe, he never shrinks

[1] [Originally published in the *Edinburgh Review* (August, 1825).]

[2] ['A warm admirer of Robert Hall, Macaulay heard with pride how the great preacher, then well-nigh worn out with that long disease, his life, was discovered lying on the floor, employed in learning by aid of grammar and dictionary enough Italian to enable him to verify the parallel between Milton and Dante' (Trevelyan: *Life of Macaulay*, vol. i. p. 119, ed. 1877). (See below, p. 428.)]

from describing it. He gives us the shape, the colour, the sound, the smell, the taste; he counts the numbers; he measures the size. His similes are the illustrations of a traveller. Unlike those of other poets, and especially of Milton, they are introduced in a plain, business-like manner; not for the sake of any beauty in the objects from which they are drawn; not for the sake of any ornament which they may impart to the poem; but simply in order to make the meaning of the writer as clear to the reader as it is to himself. The ruins of the precipice which led from the sixth to the seventh circle of hell were like those of the rock which fell into the Adige on the south of Trent. The cataract of Phlegethon was like that of Aqua Cheta at the monastery of St. Benedict. The place where the heretics were confined in burning tombs resembled the vast cemetery at Arles.

Now let us compare with the exact details of Dante the dim intimations of Milton. We will cite a few examples. The English poet has never thought of taking the measure of Satan. He gives us merely a vague idea of vast bulk. In one passage the fiend lies stretched out huge in length, floating many a rood, equal in size to the earth-born enemies of Jove, or to the sea-monster whom the mariner mistakes for an island. When he addresses himself to battle against the guardian angels, he stands like Teneriffe or Atlas: his stature reaches the sky. Contrast with these descriptions the lines in which Dante has described the gigantic spectre of Nimrod. 'His face seemed to me as long and as broad as the ball of St. Peter's at Rome; and his other limbs were in proportion; so that the bank, which concealed him from the waist downwards, nevertheless showed so much of him, that three tall Germans would in vain have attempted to reach his hair.' [1] We are sensible that we do no justice to the admirable style of the Florentine poet. But Mr. Cary's translation is not at hand; and our version, however rude, is sufficient to illustrate our meaning.

Once more, compare the lazar-house in the eleventh book of the Paradise Lost with the last ward of Malebolge in Dante. Milton avoids the loathsome details, and takes refuge in indistinct but solemn and tremendous imagery. Despair hurrying from couch to couch to mock the wretches with his attendance, Death shaking his dart over them, but, in spite of supplications, delaying to strike. What says Dante? 'There was such a moan there as there would be if all the sick who, between July and September, are in the hospitals of Valdichiana, and of the Tuscan swamps, and of Sardinia, were in one pit together; and such a stench was issuing forth as is wont to issue from decayed limbs.' [2]

[1] [*Inf.* xxxi. 58-64.]

[2] [*Inf.* xxix. 46-51.]

We will not take upon ourselves the invidious office of settling precedency between two such writers. Each in his own department is incomparable; and each, we may remark, has wisely, or fortunately, taken a subject adapted to exhibit his peculiar talent to the greatest advantage. The Divine Comedy is a personal narrative. Dante is the eye-witness and ear-witness of that which he relates. He is the very man who has heard the tormented spirits crying out for the second death, who has read the dusky characters on the portal within which there is no hope, who has hidden his face from the terrors of the Gorgon, who has fled from the hooks and the seething pitch of Barbariccia and Draghignazzo. His own hands have grasped the shaggy sides of Lucifer. His own feet have climbed the mountain of expiation. His own brow has been marked by the purifying angel. The reader would throw aside such a tale in incredulous disgust, unless it were told with the strongest air of veracity, with a sobriety even in its horrors, with the greatest precision and multiplicity in its details. The narrative of Milton in this respect differs from that of Dante, as the adventures of Amadis differ from those of Gulliver. The author of Amadis would have made his book ridiculous if he had introduced those minute particulars which give such a charm to the work of Swift. . . .

Of all the poets who have introduced into their works the agency of supernatural beings, Milton has succeeded best. Here Dante decidedly yields to him. . . . Poetry which relates to the beings of another world ought to be at once mysterious and picturesque. That of Milton is so. That of Dante is picturesque indeed beyond any that ever was written. Its effect approaches to that produced by the pencil or the chisel. But it is picturesque to the exclusion of all mystery. This is a fault on the right side, a fault inseparable from the plan of Dante's poem, which, as we have already observed, rendered the utmost accuracy of description necessary. Still it is a fault. The supernatural agents excite an interest; but it is not the interest proper to supernatural agents. We feel that we could talk to the ghosts and daemons, without any emotion of unearthly awe. We could, like Don Juan, ask them to supper, and eat heartily in their company. Dante's angels are good men with wings. His devils are spiteful ugly executioners. His dead men are merely living men in strange situations. The scene which passes between the poet and Farinata is justly celebrated. Still, Farinata in the burning tomb is exactly what Farinata would have been at an *auto da fe*. Nothing can be more touching than the first interview of Dante and Beatrice. Yet what is it, but a lovely woman chiding, with sweet austere composure, the lover for whose affection she is grateful, but whose vices she reprobates? The feelings which give the passage its charm would suit the streets of Florence as well as the summit of the Mount of Purgatory. . . .

To return to the parallel which we have been attempting to draw between Milton and Dante, we would add that the poetry of these great men has in a considerable degree taken its character from their moral qualities. They are not egoists. They rarely obtrude their idiosyncrasies on their readers. . . . Yet it would be difficult to name two writers whose works have been more completely, though undesignedly, coloured by their personal feelings.

The character of Milton was peculiarly distinguished by loftiness of spirit, that of Dante by intensity of feeling. In every line of the Divine Comedy we discern the asperity which is produced by pride struggling with misery. There is perhaps no work in the world so deeply and uniformly sorrowful. The melancholy of Dante was no fantastic caprice. It was not, as far as at this distance of time can be judged, the effect of external circumstances. It was from within. Neither love nor glory, neither the conflicts of earth nor the hope of heaven could dispel it. It turned every consolation and every pleasure into its own nature. It resembled that noxious Sardinian soil of which the intense bitterness is said to have been perceptible even in its honey. His mind was, in the noble language of the Hebrew poet, 'a land of darkness, as darkness itself, and where the light was as darkness.' The gloom of his character discolours all the passions of men, and all the face of nature, and tinges with its own livid hue the flowers of Paradise and the glories of the eternal throne. All the portraits of him are singularly characteristic. No person can look on the features, noble even to ruggedness, the dark furrows of the cheek, the haggard and woful stare of the eye, the sullen and contemptuous curve of the lip, and doubt that they belong to a man too proud and too sensitive to be happy.[1]

Milton was, like Dante, a statesman and a lover; and, like Dante, he had been unfortunate in ambition and in love.

(*Critical and Historical Essays*, ed. 1866, vol. i. pp. 9 ff.)

1827. ESSAY ON MACHIAVELLI.[2]

[The *Divina Commedia* second only to the *Iliad* and *Odyssey*]

A new language, characterised by simple sweetness and simple energy, had attained perfection. No tongue ever furnished more gorgeous and vivid tints to poetry; nor was it long before a poet

[1] [The Bargello portrait of Dante, as a young man, commonly attributed to Giotto, had not been discovered at the date when Macaulay wrote.]

[2] [Originally published in the *Edinburgh Review* (March, 1827).]

appeared who knew how to employ them. Early in the fourteenth century came forth the Divine Comedy, beyond comparison the greatest work of imagination which had appeared since the poems of Homer. The following generation produced indeed no second Dante: but it was eminently distinguished by general intellectual activity.

(*Critical and Historical Essays*, ed. 1866, vol. i. p. 33.)

[Quotation from Dante applied to Florence]

With peculiar pleasure, every cultivated mind must repose on the fair, the happy, the glorious Florence. . . . Alas for the beautiful city! Alas for the wit and the learning, the genius and the love!

'Le donne, e i cavalier, gli affanni, e gli agi,
Che ne 'nvogliava amore e cortesia
Là dove i cuor son fatti sì malvagi.'[1]

A time was at hand, when all the seven vials of the Apocalypse were to be poured forth and shaken out over those pleasant countries.

(*Ibid.* pp. 33-4.)

1828. ESSAY ON JOHN DRYDEN.[2]

[Dante as judged by his countrymen]

Every reader of the Divine Comedy must be struck by the veneration which Dante expresses for writers far inferior to himself. He will not lift up his eyes from the ground in the presence of Brunetto, all of whose works are not worth the worst of his own hundred cantos. He does not venture to walk in the same line with the bombastic Statius. His admiration of Virgil is absolute idolatry. If, indeed, it had been excited by the elegant, splendid, and harmonious diction of the Roman poet, it would not have been altogether unreasonable; but it is rather as an authority on all points of philosophy, than as a work of imagination, that he values the Aeneid. The most trivial passages he regards as oracles of the highest authority, and of the most recondite meaning. He describes his conductor as the sea of all wisdom—the sun which heals every disordered sight. As he judged of Virgil, the Italians of the fourteenth century judged of him; they were proud of him; they praised him; they struck medals bearing his head; they quarrelled for the honour of possessing his remains; they maintained professors to expound his writings. But what they admired was not that mighty imagination which called a new world into existence, and made all its sights and sounds familiar to the eye and ear of the

[1] [*Purg.* xiv. 109-11.]
[2] [Originally published in the *Edinburgh Review* (January, 1828).]

mind. They said little of those awful and lovely creations on which later critics delight to dwell—Farinata lifting his haughty and tranquil brow from his couch of everlasting fire—the lion-like repose of Sordello—or the light which shone from the celestial smile of Beatrice. They extolled their great poet for his smattering of ancient literature and history; for his logic and his divinity; for his absurd physics, and his more absurd metaphysics; for everything but that in which he pre-eminently excelled. Like the fool in the story, who ruined his dwelling by digging for gold, which, as he had dreamed, was concealed under its foundations, they laid waste one of the noblest works of human genius, by seeking in it for buried treasures of wisdom which existed only in their own wild reveries. The finest passages were little valued till they had been debased into some monstrous allegory. Louder applause was given to the lecture on fate and free-will, or to the ridiculous astronomical theories, than to those tremendous lines which disclose the secrets of the tower of hunger, or to that half-told tale of guilty love, so passionate and so full of tears. We do not mean to say that the contemporaries of Dante read with less emotion than their descendants of Ugolino groping among the wasted corpses of his children, or of Francesca starting at the tremulous kiss and dropping the fatal volume. Far from it. We believe that they admired these things less than ourselves, but that they felt them more. We should perhaps say that they felt them too much to admire them.

(*Miscellaneous Writings*, ed. 1875, pp. 86-7.)

[Monti and Dante]

In the present age, Monti has successfully imitated the style of Dante; and something of the Elizabethan inspiration has been caught by several eminent countrymen of our own. But never will Italy produce another Inferno, or England another Hamlet.

(*Ibid.* 91.)

[The imagination of Dryden as compared to that of Homer, Dante, and Milton]

Some indulgent critics have represented this failing [a tendency to bombast] as an indication of genius, as the profusion of unlimited wealth, the wantonness of exuberant vigour. . . . Dryden surely had not more imagination than Homer, Dante, or Milton, who never fall into this vice.

(*Ibid.* p. 100.)

1828. ESSAY ON HISTORY.[1]

[Reynolds' picture of Ugolino]

The history of Thucydides differs from that of Herodotus as a portrait differs from the representation of an imaginary scene; as

[1] [Originally published in the *Edinburgh Review* (May, 1828).]

the Burke or Fox of Reynolds differs from his Ugolino or his Beaufort.

(*Miscellaneous Writings*, ed. 1875, p. 110.)

1828. ESSAY ON HALLAM'S CONSTITUTIONAL HISTORY.[1]

[Quotation from Dante applied to Cranmer]

If the memory of archbishop Cranmer had been left to find its own place, he would have soon been lost among the crowd which is mingled

'A quel cattivo coro
Degli angeli, che non furon ribelli,
Nè fur fedeli a Dio, ma per sè foro.'[2]

And the only notice which it would have been necessary to take of his name would have been

'Non ragioniam di lui; ma guarda, e passa.'[3]

(*Critical and Historical Essays*, ed. 1866. vol. i. p. 57.)

1830. ESSAY ON ROBERT MONTGOMERY'S POEMS.[4]

[Quotation from Dante applied to a description of Montgomery's]

We ought not to pass unnoticed . . . the slain warrior who, while 'lying on his bleeding breast,' contrives to 'stare ghastly and grimly on the skies.' As to this last exploit, we can only say, as Dante did on a similar occasion,

Forse per forza già di parlasia
Si travolse così alcun del tutto:
Ma io nol vidi, nè credo che sia.[5]

(*Ibid.* vol. i. p. 129.)

[Montgomery's poems far more popular than Cary's Dante]

The circulation of this writer's poetry has been greater than that of Southey's Roderick, and beyond all comparison greater than that of Cary's Dante or of the best works of Coleridge.

(*Ibid.* p. 131.)

1831. ESSAY ON MOORE'S LIFE OF LORD BYRON.[6]

[Homer, Dante, Shakespeare, and Milton, the most correct of poets]

A writer who describes visible objects falsely and violates the propriety of character, . . . may be said, in the high and just

[1] [Originally published in the *Edinburgh Review* (September, 1828).]
[2] [*Inf.* iii. 37-9.] [3] [*Inf.* iii. 51.]
[4] [Originally published in the *Edinburgh Review* (April, 1830).]
[5] [*Inf.* xx. 16-18.]
[6] [Originally published in the *Edinburgh Review* (June, 1831).]

sense of the phrase, to write incorrectly. He violates the first great law of his art. His imitation is altogether unlike the thing imitated. The four poets who are most eminently free from incorrectness of this description are Homer, Dante, Shakspeare, and Milton. They are, therefore, in one sense, and that the best sense, the most correct of poets.

(*Critical and Historical Essays*, ed. 1866, vol. i. p. 153.)

[The descriptive powers of Homer and Dante inferior to those of a painter or sculptor]

The imitations of the painter, the sculptor, and the actor, are indeed, within certain limits, more perfect than those of the poet. The machinery which the poet employs consists merely of words; and words cannot, even when employed by such an artist as Homer or Dante, present to the mind images of visible objects quite so lively and exact as those which we carry away from looking on the works of the brush and the chisel.

(*Ibid.* p. 156.)

[Alfieri on the language of Dante]

Alfieri speaks with scorn of the tragedies of his predecessors. 'Mi cadevano dalle mani per la languidezza, trivialità e prolissità dei modi e del verso, senza parlare poi della snervatezza dei pensieri. Or perchè mai questa nostra divina lingua, sì maschia anco, ed energica, e feroce, in bocca di Dante, dovra ella farsi così sbiadata ed eunuca nel dialogo tragico?'

(*Ibid.* p. 159.)

1834. July 1. LETTER TO THOMAS FLOWER ELLIS (from Ootacamund).

[Dante's place among the poets of the world]

My power of finding amusement without companions was pretty well tried on my voyage. I read insatiably; the Iliad and Odyssey, Virgil, Horace, Caesar's Commentaries, Bacon de Augmentis, Dante, Petrarch, Ariosto, Tasso, Don Quixote. . . . I liked the Jerusalem better than I used to do. I was enraptured with Ariosto; and I still think of Dante, as I thought when I first read him, that he is a superior poet to Milton, that he runs neck and neck with Homer, and that none but Shakespeare has gone decidedly beyond him.

(Trevelyan's *Life of Macaulay*, vol. i. pp. 371-2.)

1834. Sept. LETTER TO MARGARET MACAULAY (from Calcutta).

[The *Divina Commedia* and *Don Quixote*, the only two foreign works which did not disappoint at a first reading]

I never read any famous foreign book, which did not, in the first perusal, fall short of my expectations; except Dante's poem, and

Don Quixote, which were prodigiously superior to what I had imagined. Yet in these cases I had not pitched my expectations low.

(Trevelyan's *Life of Macaulay*, vol. i. p. 385.)

1835. ESSAY ON SIR JAMES MACKINTOSH'S HISTORY OF THE REVOLUTION.[1]

[The relation of the historian to poets such as Homer, Shakespeare, Dante, and Milton]

It is not the business of the historian to create new worlds and to people them with new races of beings. He is to Homer and Shakspeare, to Dante and Milton, what Nollekens was to Canova, or Lawrence to Michael Angelo.

(*Critical and Historical Essays*, ed. 1866, vol. i. p. 314.)

1837. ESSAY ON LORD BACON.[2]

[Dante never tedious]

The silent converse which we hold with the highest of human intellects . . . is disturbed by no jealousies or resentments. These are the old friends who are never seen with new faces, who are the same in wealth and in poverty, in glory and in obscurity. With the dead there is no rivalry. In the dead there is no change. Plato is never sullen. Cervantes is never petulant. Demosthenes never comes unseasonably. Dante never stays too long. No difference of political opinions can alienate Cicero. No heresy can excite the horror of Bossuet.

(*Ibid.* vol. i. p 347.)

[Quotation from Dante applied to Bacon]

We are forced to say with Bacon that this celebrated philosophy ended in nothing but disputation, that it was neither a vineyard nor an olive-ground, but an intricate wood of briars and thistles, from which those who lost themselves in it brought back many scratches and no food. We readily acknowledge that some of the teachers of this unfruitful wisdom were among the greatest men that the world has ever seen. If we admit the justice of Bacon's censure, we admit it with regret, similar to that which Dante felt when he learned the fate of those illustrious heathens who were doomed to the first circle of Hell.

[1] [Originally published in the *Edinburgh Review* (July, 1835).]
[2] [*Ibid.* (July, 1837).]

Gran duol mi prese al cuor quando lo 'ntesi,
Perocchè gente di molto valore
Conobbi che 'n quel limbo eran sospesi.[1]
(*Critical and Historical Essays,* ed. 1866, vol. i. p. 391.)

1838. JOURNAL IN ITALY.

[Dante's monument in Santa Croce—San Giovanni]

Florence, November 3.—To the Church of Santa Croce: an ugly mean outside; and not much to admire in the architecture within, but consecrated by the dust of some of the greatest men that ever lived. It was to me what a first visit to Westminster Abbey would be to an American. The first tomb which caught my eye, as I entered, was that of Michael Angelo. I was much moved, and still more so when, going forward, I saw the stately monument[2] lately erected to Dante. The figure of the poet seemed to me fine and firmly placed; and the inscription very happy; his own words, the proclamation which resounds through the shades when Virgil returns,

Onorate l' altissimo poeta.[3]

The two allegorical figures were not much to my taste. It is particularly absurd to represent Poetry weeping for Dante. These weeping figures are all very well, when a tomb is erected to a person lately dead; but, when a group of sculpture is set up over a man who has been dead more than five hundred years, such lamentation is nonsensical. Who can help laughing at the thought of tears of regret shed because a man who was born in the time of our Henry the Third is not still alive? Yet I was very near shedding tears of a different kind as I looked at this magnificent monument, and thought of the sufferings of the great poet, and of his incomparable genius, and of all the pleasure which I have derived from him, and of his death in exile, and of the late justice of posterity. I believe that very few people have ever had their minds more thoroughly penetrated with the spirit of any great work than mine is with that of the Divine Comedy. His execution I take to be far beyond that of any other artist who has operated on the imagination by means of words.

O degli altri poeti onore e lume,
Vagliami il lungo studio e 'l grande amore
Che m' han fatto cercar lo tuo volume.[4]

I was proud to think that I had a right to apostrophise him thus.

November 9. Went to Dante's 'bel San Giovanni,'[5] and heard Mass there.

(Trevelyan's *Life of Macaulay*, vol. ii. pp. 22-3, 26.)

[1] [*Inf.* iv. 43-5.]
[2] [By Stefano Ricci, erected in 1829.]
[3] [*Inf.* iv. 80.]
[4] [*Inf.* i. 82-4.]
[5] [*Inf.* xix. 17.]

1838. ESSAY ON SIR WILLIAM TEMPLE.[1]

[Temple's place in Dante's *Inferno*]

Had Temple been brought before Dante's infernal tribunal, he would not have been condemned to the deeper recesses of the abyss. He would not have been boiled with Dundee in the crimson pool of Bulicame, or hurled with Danby into the seething pitch of Malebolge, or congealed with Churchill in the eternal ice of Giudecca; but he would perhaps have been placed in the dark vestibule next to the shade of that inglorious pontiff—

'Che fece per viltate il gran rifiuto.'[2]

(*Critical and Historical Essays*, ed. 1866, vol. ii. p. 3.)

[Dante among those omitted by Temple from his list of great authors]

Temple gives us a catalogue of those whom he regards as the greatest writers of later times. It is sufficient to say that, in his list of Italians, he has omitted Dante, Petrarch, Ariosto, and Tasso; in his list of Spaniards, Lope and Calderon; in his list of French, Pascal, Bossuet, Molière, Corneille, Racine, and Boileau; and in his list of English, Chaucer, Spenser, Shakspeare, and Milton.[3]

(*Ibid.* p. 46.)

1840. ESSAY ON RANKE'S HISTORY OF THE POPES.[4]

[Dante's reference to the outrage on Boniface VIII]

The fiercest and most highminded of the Roman Pontiffs,[5] while bestowing kingdoms and citing great princes to his judgment-seat. was seized in his palace by armed men, and so foully outraged that he died mad with rage and terror. 'Thus,' sang the great Florentine poet, 'was Christ, in the person of his vicar, a second time seized by ruffians, a second time mocked, a second time drenched with the vinegar and the gall.'[6]

(*Ibid.* vol. ii. p. 133.)

1843. Feb. 6. LETTER TO MACVEY NAPIER (from the Albany, London).

[Quotation from Dante applied to Addison]

There is in the press, I believe, a life of Addison by Miss Aikin, which contains some new and curious information. You must allow

[1] [Originally published in the *Edinburgh Review* (October, 1838).]

[2] [*Inf.* iii. 60.]

[3] [In his *Essay upon the Ancient and Modern Learning* (1692):—'The great wits among the moderns have been, in my opinion, and in their several kinds, of the Italian, Boccace, Machiavel, and Padre Paolo; among the Spaniards, Cervantes (who writ Don Quixote) and Guevara; among the French, Rabelais and Montaigne; among the English, Sir Philip Sidney, Bacon, and Selden.']

[4] [Originally published in the *Edinburgh Review* (October, 1840).]

[5] [Boniface VIII.]

[6] [*Purg.* xx. 87-9.]

me to bespeak that subject.[1] I look on it as peculiarly my own, for I know him almost by heart. As Dante says—

> Vagliami il lungo studio e il grande amore,
> Che m' han fatto cercar lo tuo volume.[2]

(*Correspondence of Macvey Napier*, p. 426.)

1843. ESSAY ON THE LIFE AND WRITINGS OF ADDISON.[3]

[Dante not named by Addison in his *Travels in Italy*—His indifference to modern Italian literature]

Addison's Narrative of his Travels in Italy contains little, or rather no information, respecting the history and literature of modern Italy. To the best of our remembrance, he does not mention Dante,[4] Petrarch, Boccaccio, Boiardo, Berni, Lorenzo de Medici, or Machiavelli. He coldly tells us, that at Ferrara he saw the tomb of Ariosto, and that at Venice he heard the gondoliers sing verses of Tasso. But for Tasso and Ariosto he cared far less than for Valerius Flaccus and Sidonius Apollinaris. The gentle flow of the Ticin brings a line of Silius to his mind. The sulphurous steam of Albula suggests to him several passages of Martial. But he has not a word to say of the illustrious dead of Santa Croce; he crosses the wood of Ravenna without recollecting the Spectre Hunstman, and wanders up and down Rimini without one thought of Francesca. . . . The truth is, that Addison knew little, and cared less, about the literature of modern Italy. His favourite models were Latin. His favourite critics were French. Half the Tuscan poetry that he had read seemed to him monstrous, and the other half tawdry.

(*Critical and Historical Essays*, ed. 1866, vol. ii. p. 334.)

1844. ESSAY ON THE EARL OF CHATHAM.[5]

[Simile from Dante applied to the state of English political parties under George I.]

Dante tells us that he saw, in Malebolge, a strange encounter between a human form and a serpent. The enemies, after cruel wounds inflicted, stood for a time glaring on each other. A great cloud surrounded them, and then a wonderful metamorphosis began. Each creature was transfigured into the likeness of its antagonist. The serpent's tail divided itself into two legs; the man's

[1] [Macaulay's article on Addison was published in the *Edinburgh Review* in the following July.]

[2] [*Inf.* i. 83-4.]

[3] [Originally published in the *Edinburgh Review* (July, 1843).]

[4] [Not only is Dante not mentioned in this work, but there is no reference to him in the *Spectator* nor in any other work of Addison's.]

[5] [Originally published in the *Edinburgh Review* (October, 1844).]

legs intertwined themselves into a tail. The body of the serpent put forth arms; the arms of the man shrank into his body. At length the serpent stood up a man, and spake; the man sank down a serpent, and glided hissing away.[1] Something like this was the transformation which, during the reign of George the First, befell the two English parties. Each gradually took the shape and colour of its foe, till at length the Tory rose up erect the zealot of freedom, and the Whig crawled and licked the dust at the feet of power.

(*Critical and Historical Essays*, ed. 1866, vol. ii. p. 362.)

18—. MARGINAL NOTES BY LORD MACAULAY.[2]

[Miss Seward's opinion of Dante criticised]

"The chief amusement," wrote Miss Seward,[3] "that the Inferno gives me is from tracing the plagiarisms which have been made from it by more interesting and pleasing bards than Dante; since there is little for the heart, or even for the curiosity as to story, in this poem. Then the plan is most clumsily arranged:—Virgil, and the three talking quadrupeds, as guides! An odd association!"

"What can she mean?" notes Macaulay; "she must allude to the panther, the lion, and the she-wolf in the First Canto. But they are not guides; and they do not talk."

(*Marginal Notes by Lord Macaulay*, selected and arranged by Sir G. O. Trevelyan, 1907, pp. 5-6.)

[Socrates' legend in the *Phaedo* compared to Dante's poem]

On the beautiful legend about the purification of souls in Acheron and Cocytus, with which Socrates concluded his final talk on earth, Macaulay remarks: "All this is merely a fine poem, like Dante's. Milton has borrowed largely from it; and, considered as an effort of the imagination, it is one from which no poet need be ashamed to borrow."

(*Ibid.* p. 63.)

ARTHUR HENRY HALLAM

(1811-1833)

[Arthur Hallam, son of Henry Hallam, the historian, was born in London in 1811. He was educated at Eton, and Trinity College, Cambridge, where he formed

[1] [*Inf.* xxv. 49-141.]
[2] [Printed by kind permission of Sir G. O. Trevelyan.]
[3] [In a letter to Miss Ponsonby dated 13 June, 1805 (see vol. i. p. 401).]

the intimacy with Tennyson, which is immortalized in *In Memoriam*. He graduated in 1832 and began studying for the bar, and about the same time he became engaged to Tennyson's sister. In 1833 he travelled with his father in Germany, and in September of that year he died suddenly at Vienna. He was buried at Clevedon, in Somersetshire.

Arthur Hallam at an early age displayed an interest in Dante. While at Eton, in 1824, when he was only thirteen, he translated the Ugolino episode into Greek iambics. This translation was printed in 1834, the year after his death, in the privately issued volume of his *Remains in Verse and Prose*; edited by his father, who in the preface says: 'It is remarkable that he should have selected the story of Ugolino, from a poet with whom, and with whose language he was then but very slightly acquainted, but who was afterwards to become, more perhaps than any other, the master mover of his spirit.' In 1827 and 1828, after spending eight months in Italy, he wrote several sonnets in Italian, of which Panizzi said: 'They are much superior not only to what foreigners have written, but to what I thought possible for them to write in Italian.' To one of these, addressed 'To an English Lady,' is prefixed a motto from Dante (*Purg.* xxiv. 12-13). 'His growing intimacy with Italian poetry,' writes his father, 'led him naturally to that of Dante. No poet was so congenial to the character of his own reflective mind; in none other could he so abundantly find that disdain of flowery redundance, that perpetual reference of the sensible to the ideal, that aspiration for somewhat better and less fleeting than earthly things, to which his inmost soul responded. Like all genuine worshippers of the great Florentine Poet, he rated the Inferno below the two later portions of the Divina Commedia; there was nothing even to revolt his taste, but rather much to attract it, in the scholastic theology and mystic visions of the Paradiso.' In a letter, written to his father by W. E. Gladstone, an intimate friend, shortly after his death, it is stated that 'Dante and Shakespeare were certainly the two poets whom he regarded as the highest and noblest of their class.' Gladstone continues: 'I have often heard him complain that Dante was not properly appreciated even by his admirers, who dwell only on his gloomy power and sublimity, without adverting to the peculiar sweetness and tenderness which characterise, as he thought, so much of his poetry. . . . Of Milton he always spoke with due reverence; but I do not believe that he recurred to him with so much delight or rated him quite so high as his favourite Dante.' His father records that about 1832 'he had a design to translate the Vita Nuova of his favourite Dante, a work which he justly prized as the development of that immense genius in a kind of autobiography which best prepares us for a real insight into the Divine Comedy.' He rendered into verse most of the sonnets in the *Vita Nuova*, but does not appear to have made any progress with the prose translation. The sonnets, as 'appearing rather too literal, and consequently harsh,' were not considered by his father worth printing.[1] In 1831, while at Cambridge, he delivered an oration on the influence of Italian upon English literature, and in 1832 he published 'Remarks upon Rossetti's *Disquisizioni sullo Spirito Antipapale*,' extracts from both of which are given below. Tennyson has left a record in *In Memoriam* of Hallam's devotion to Dante and Petrarch, whom he loved to read aloud to his intimates—

O bliss, when all in circle drawn
  About him, heart and ear were fed
  To hear him, as he lay and read
The Tuscan poets on the lawn—

It is interesting to note that Hallam selected *terza rima* for the metre of his poem *Timbuctoo*,[2] written in 1829 for the University Prize at Cambridge (which he failed to obtain, the prize being awarded to Tennyson).]

[1] [One of them, however, is introduced into the Remarks upon Rossetti's *Disquisizioni*, and is given below.]

[2] [Printed in *Remains*, ed. 1863, pp. 20-30.]

1824. TRANSLATION OF THE UGOLINO EPISODE FROM DANTE INTO GREEK IAMBICS.[1]

Ex Inferis Dantis Aligieri Graecè redditum.

ΟΥΓΟΛΙΝΟΣ ΛΕΓΕΙ

Αἰσχρὸν λέγειν με καὶ κακόν τι δυσφορον κ.τ.λ.

(59 lines, printed in *Remains*, ed. 1834, pp. 90-2.)

1828. ITALIAN SONNET TO AN ENGLISH LADY.

[Motto from Dante]

'Tra bella e buona non so qual fosse più.'[2]

(*Remains*, ed. 1863, p. 33.)

c. 1830. LETTER TO ALFRED TENNYSON.

[Proposed work on Dante]

I expect to glean a good deal of knowledge from you concerning metres, which may be serviceable, as well for my philosophy in the notes as for my actual handiwork in the text. I purpose to discuss considerably about poetry in general, and about the ethical character of Dante's poetry.[3]

(*Memoir of Lord Tennyson*, by his Son, vol. i. p. 45.)

1831. March 4. LETTER TO WILLIAM HENRY BROOKFIELD (from Somersby).

[Cedit Dantes amori]

I can find no sort of time as yet for anything the interest of which is not strictly confined within the walls of Somersby.[4] How I am to read Blackstone here is one of those mysteries which I consider insoluble by human reason: even Dante, even Alfred's poetry, is at a discount.

(*Some Letters from Arthur Hallam*, in *Fortnightly Review*, July, 1903, p. 173.)

[1] [This translation was written as an 'Eton exercise,' when Hallam was only thirteen. His father says of it: 'Great judgment and taste are perceptible in this translation, which is by no means a literal one; and in which the phraseology of Sophocles is not ill substituted, in some passages, for that of Dante' (*Preface to Remains*).]

[2] [*Purg.* xxiv. 13-14—said of Piccarda Donati by her brother Forese.]

[3] [Hallam was engaged about this time on a translation of the *Vita Nuova*, with notes and prefaces.]

[4] [Somersby Rectory, the residence of Tennyson's father. Hallam alludes to his attachment to the poet's sister, Emily, to whom he shortly after became engaged.]

1831. ORATION ON THE INFLUENCE OF ITALIAN WORKS OF IMAGINATION ON THE SAME CLASS OF COMPOSITIONS IN ENGLAND.

[The rhyme of Dante and Petrarch]

No poetry in the world was so founded on rhyme as the Arabian; and some of its most complicated were transferred without alteration to the Langue d' Oc, previous to their obtaining immortality in the hands of Dante and Petrarca.

(*Remains*, ed. 1863, p. 126.)

[Dante's 'sense of community']

Who can doubt that the minds of Italians would spring up to meet the utterance of Cicero, Livy, and Virgil, with a far deeper and stronger sense of community, than any other nation could have done! What a beautiful symbol of this truth is contained in that canto of the 'Purgatorio' which relates the meeting between Sordel and Virgil. Centuries, and the mutations of centuries lapse into nothing before that strong feeling of homogeneity which bursts forth in the 'O Mantovano!'[1]

(p. 128.)

[Dante a representative Italian mind]

The base of the love-poetry of the Italians is undoubtedly the Troubadour poetry, but upon this they have reared a splendid edifice of Platonism and surmounted it with the banner of the cross. In his treatise 'De Vulgari Eloquentia,' Dante asserts of the Lingua di Sì, that even before the date of his own writings 'qui dulcius, subtiliusque poetati sunt, ii familiares et domestici sui sunt.'[2] I think we cannot read the poems of Cino da Pistoja, or either Guido,[3] without perceiving this early superiority and more masculine turn of thought. But it was not in scattered sonnets that the whole magnificence of that idea could be manifested, which represents love as at once the base and pyramidal point of the entire universe, and teaches us to regard the earthly union of souls, not as a thing accidental, transitory, and dependent on the condition of human society, but with far higher import, as the best and the appointed symbol of our relations with God, and through them of his own ineffable essence. In the 'Divine Comedy,' this idea received its full completeness of form; that wonderful work of which, to speak adequately we must borrow the utterance of its conceiving mind—

'La gloria di colui, che tutto muove,
Per l' universo penetra, e risplende,
In una parte più, e meno altrove.'[4]

[1] [*Purg*. vi. 74.]
[2] [I. 10, ll. 28-30.]
[3] [Guido Cavalcanti and Guido Guinicelli.]
[4] D. C. Paradiso, c. i., v. 1.

This is not the occasion for entering into a criticism, or detailed encomium of Dante; I only wish to point him out as an entire and plenary representation of the Italian mind, a summary in his individual self of all the elements I have been describing, which never before had co-existed in unity of action, a signal point in the stream of time, showing at once how much power was at that exact season aggregated to the human intellect, and what direction was about to be impressed upon it by the 'rushing mighty wind,' the spirit of Christianity, under whose conditions alone a new literature was become possible. Petrarch appears to me a corollary from Dante; the same spirit in a different mould of individual character, and that a weaker mould; yet better adapted, by the circumstances of its position, to diffuse the great thought which possessed them both, and to call into existence so great a number of inferior recipients of it, as might affect insensibly, but surely, the course of general feeling. Petrarch was far from apprehending either his own situation, or that of mankind, with any thing like the clear vision of Dante whom he affected to undervalue, idly striving against that destiny which ordained their co-operation. His life was restless and perplexed; that continual craving for sympathy, taking in its lighter moods the form and name of vanity, which drove him, as he tells us himself, 'from town to town, from country to country,' would have rendered him incapable of assuming the decisive, initiatory position which was not difficult to be maintained by the proud Ghibelline spirit, who depended so little on others, so much on his own undaunted energies.

(pp. 130-1.)

[Milton's debt to Dante]

Well, indeed, did it befit the Christian poet, who was raised up to assert the great fundamental truth of modern civilisation, that manners and letters have a law of progression, parallel, though not coincident, with the expansion of spiritual religion,—to assert this, not indeed with the universality and depth with which the same truth had been asserted by Dante, yet with some relative advantages over him, which were necessarily obtained from a Protestant and English position; well, I say, did it befit our venerable Milton to draw weapons for his glorious war from the inexhaustible armoury of the Divina Commedia, and acknowledge his honourable robberies.[1]

(p. 140.)

[1] [Hallam here quotes Milton's Latin letter to B. Buonmattai, for which see vol. i. p. 124.]

['The quiet beauty' of Dante]

An English mind that has drunk deep at the sources of Southern inspiration, and especially that is imbued with the spirit of the mighty Florentine, will be conscious of a perpetual freshness and quiet beauty, resting on his imaginations and spreading gently over his affections, until by the blessing of heaven, it may be absorbed without loss, in the pure inner light, of which the voice has spoken, as no other can :

'Light intellectual, yet full of love,
Love of true beauty, therefore full of joy,
Joy, every other sweetness far above.'[1]

(p. 145.)

1831. SONNET.

Lady,[2] I bid thee to a sunny dome
Ringing with echoes of Italian song ;
Henceforth to thee these magic halls belong,
And all the pleasant place is like a home.
Hark, on the right with full piano tone,
Old Dante's voice encircles all the air ;
Hark yet again, like flute-tones mingling rare,
Comes the keen sweetness of Petrarca's moan.
Pass thou the lintel freely : without fear
Feast on the music : I do better know thee,
Than to suspect this pleasure thou dost owe me
Will wrong thy gentle spirit, or make less dear
That element whence thou must draw thy life ;—
An English maiden and an English wife.

(*Remains*, ed. 1863, p. 85.)

1831. ON SOME OF THE CHARACTERISTICS OF MODERN POETRY, AND ON THE LYRICAL POEMS OF ALFRED TENNYSON.[3]

[Shakespeare, Dante, Homer]

Love, friendship, ambition, religion, etc., are matters of daily experience, even amongst imaginative tempers. The forces of association, therefore, are ready to work in these directions, and little effort of will is necessary to follow the artist. For the same reason such subjects often excite a partial power of composition, which is no sign of a truly poetic organisation. We are very far

[1] 'Luce intellettual, piena d' amore,
Amor di vero ben, pien di letizia,
Letizia, che trascende ogni dolzore.'
D. C. Paradiso, c. 30 [ll. 40-2].

[2] [Tennyson's sister, Emily, to whom Hallam became engaged in this year.]

[3] [Originally published in the *Englishman's Magazine* for August, 1831.]

from wishing to depreciate this class of poems, whose influence is so extensive, and communicates so refined a pleasure. We contend only that the facility with which its impressions are communicated, is no proof of its elevation as a form of art, but rather the contrary. What then, some may be ready to exclaim, is the pleasure derived by most men from Shakespeare, or Dante, or Homer, entirely false and factitious? If these are really masters of their art, must not the energy required of the ordinary intelligences, that come in contact with their mighty genius, be the greatest possible? How comes it then that they are popular? Shall we not say, after all, that the difference is in the power of the author, not in the tenor of his meditations? Those eminent spirits find no difficulty in conveying to common apprehension their lofty sense, and profound observation of Nature. They keep no aristocratic state, apart from the sentiments of society at large; they speak to the hearts of all, and by the magnetic force of their conceptions elevate inferior intellects with a higher and purer atmosphere.

['The meditative tenderness' of Dante]

Beyond question, the class of poems, which, in point of harmonious combination, *Oriana* most resembles, is the Italian. Just thus the meditative tenderness of Dante and Petrarch is embodied in the clear, searching tones of Tuscan song. These mighty masters produce two-thirds of their effect by *sound*. Not that they sacrifice sense to sound, but that sound conveys their meaning, where words would not.

(*Remains*, ed. 1863, pp. 300 ff.)

1832. REMARKS ON PROFESSOR ROSSETTI'S 'DISQUISIZIONI SULLO SPIRITO ANTIPAPALE.'

[Beatrice and the *Vita Nuova*]

We should certainly feel grateful for any theory that should satisfactorily explain the Vita Nuova. No one can have read that singular work, without having found his progress perpetually checked, and his pleasure impaired, by the occurrence of passages apparently unintelligible, or presenting only an unimportant meaning, in phrases the most laborious and involved. These difficulties we have been in the habit of referring, partly to corruptions in the text, for of all the works of Dante there is none in which the editions are so at variance, and the right readings so uncertain; partly to the scholastic forms of language with which all writers at the revival of literature—but none so much as Dante, a student in many universities, and famous among his countrymen and foreigners for the depth of his scientific acquirements—delighted to overload the simplicity of their subject. Certainly, until Signor Rossetti suggested the idea, we never dreamed of looking for Ghibelline enigmas in a narrative apparently so remote from politics. Nor did it occur to us to seek even for moral meanings, that might throw a forced and doubtful light on these obscurities. Whatever uncertain shape might, for a few moments, be assumed by the Beatrice of the Comedia, imparadised in overpowering effluences of light and music, and enjoying the immediate vision of the Most High, here at least, in the mild humility and modest nobleness of the living and loving creature, to whom the sonnets and canzones are addressed, we did believe we were safe from allegory. Something indeed there was of vagueness and unreality in the picture we beheld: but it never disturbed our faith; for we believed it to arise from the reverential feeling which seemed to possess the poet's imagination, and led him to concentrate all his loftiest sentiments and pure ideas of perfection in the object of his youthful passion, consecrated long since and idealised to his heart, by the sanctities of the overshadowing tomb. It was a noble thing, we thought, to see the stern politician, the embittered exile, the man worn by the world's severest realities, who knew how sharp it was to mount another's stairs, and eat another's bread, in his old age; yet, amidst these sufferings and wounded feelings, recurring with undaunted memory to the days of his happy boyhood: not for purposes of vain regret; not for complaints of deceived expectation; not to colour the past time with the sombre tints of the present: but to honour human nature; to glorify disinterested affection; to celebrate that solemn, primeval, indissoluble alliance, between the imagination and the heart. It was this consideration, we confess, that imparted its principal charm to the character of Beatrice; both in the Vita Nuova, and the great poem, which seemed its natural prolongation. We liked to view these works in what appeared to be their obvious relation; nor could we ever read without emotion that passage in the conclusion of the former, in which the poet, feeling even then his lips touched by the inspiring cherubim, speaks loftily, but indistinctly, of that higher monument he was about to raise to her whom he had already celebrated with so ample a ritual of melodious eulogy.

(*Remains*, ed. 1863, pp. 240-2.)

[Sonnet from the *Vita Nuova*[1]]

I have no thought that does not speak of love;
  They have in them so great variety,
  That one bids me desire his sovranty,
  One with mad speech his folly would approve;

[1] [Son. vi. *V. N.* § 13: 'Tutti li miei pensier parlan d' amore.' Hallam prints the original.]

Another, bringing hope, brings pleasantness,
And yet another makes me often weep:
In one thing only do they concord keep,
Calling for Pity, in timorous distress.
So know I not which thought to choose for song;
Fain would I speak, but wild words come and go,
And in an amorous maze I wander long.
No way but this, if Concord must be made,
To call upon Madonna Pity's aid;
And yet Madonna Pity is my foe.

(p. 246.)

[Dante a religious poet]

We defy any man, of competent abilities, to read the poems of Dante, without a conviction that he is reading the works of a religious poet. The spirit of Catholic Christianity breathes in every line. The Ghibelline, indeed, hates the Papal party and Papal usurpations; he makes no secret of it! no words can express more plainly or more energetically than his, a just and courageous indignation against all ecclesiastical tyranny. But the man is a devout Catholic, and respects the chair of the Apostle, while he denounces those who sat upon it. The sword of Peter, not the keys of Peter, is the object of his aversion. The same voice, he would tell us, that said, 'Put up thy sword,' in the garden by the Mount of Olives, said also, 'Tu es Petrus, et super hanc petram fundabo Ecclesiam meam.' . . . If the Divina Comedia is the work of a heretic, whose Paradise was entirely limited to this world, so may also be the Confessions of Augustin or the Thoughts of Pascal. The former, indeed, has often struck us as bearing no little resemblance in spirit to the compositions of the Florentine bard. In both there is a freshness, an admiring earnestness, about their expression of Christian ideas, which shows the novelty of those ideas to the frame of European thought. This indeed is much more evident in Augustin, because he wrote six centuries earlier, and wrote in Latin, so that the discrepancy between the new wine and old bottles is perpetually betraying itself. The Ciceronian language is far too effete a frame to sustain the infused spark of heavenly fire. It heaves beneath those active stirrings with the throes of a convulsive weakness. In Dante, on the other hand, the form and spirit perfectly correspond, as if adapted to each other by preestablished harmony. But in earnestness and apparent sincerity, we know not any difference between the bishop of Hippo and the exile of Ravenna. If the one is an impostor, so may be the other.

(pp. 288-91.)

FRANCES ANNE KEMBLE (MRS. BUTLER)

(1809-1893)

[Frances Anne Kemble, commonly known as Fanny Kemble, the well-known actress, born in London in 1809, was the daughter of Charles Kemble. She made her first appearance on the stage in 1829 as Juliet at Covent Garden. In 1833 she visited America, where in the following year she married Pierce Butler, whom she divorced in 1848. She then began a series of Shakespeare readings, which she gave both in England and America. She returned to England for good in 1878, and died in London at the age of 84 in 1893. Fanny Kemble published several volumes of journals and reminiscences, among which was the *Record of a Girlhood* (3 vols. 1878). In this work she mentions her early study of Dante under Biagioli in Paris, and her life-long admiration of the *Divina Commedia*, from which she frequently quotes in her journals and correspondence.]

c. 1824. RECORD OF A GIRLHOOD.[1]

[Biagioli and the *Divina Commedia*]

MY Italian master, Biagioli, was a political exile, of about the same date as his remarkable contemporary, Ugo Foscolo; . . . He was at that time one of the latest of the long tribe of commentators on Dante's 'Divina Commedia.' . . .[2] Dante was his spiritual consolation, his intellectual delight, and indeed his daily bread; for out of that tremendous horn-book he taught me to stammer the divine Italian language, and illustrated every lesson, from the simplest rule of its syntax to its exceedingly complex and artificially constructed prosody, out of the pages of that sublime, grotesque, and altogether wonderful poem. . . . I have forgotten my Italian grammar, rules of syntax and rules of prosody alike, but I read and re-read the 'Divina Commedia' with ever increasing amazement and admiration. Setting aside all its weightier claims to the high place it holds among the finest achievements of human genius, I know of no poem in any language in which so many single lines and detached passages can be found of equal descriptive force, picturesque beauty, and delightful melody of sound; the latter virtue may lie, perhaps, as much in the instrument itself as in the master hand that touched it,—the Italian tongue, the resonance and vibrating power of which is quite as peculiar as its liquid softness.

(Vol. i. pp. 95-6, ed. 1878.)

1831. April 23. JOURNAL.

[Ladies have the 'intelletto d' amore']

After dinner there was a universal discussion as to the possibility and probability of Adorni's self-sacrifice in 'The Maid of Honour.'

[1] [Published in 1878.]

[2] [Giosafatte Biagioli's Italian commentary on the *Commedia* was published in 3 vols. in Paris in 1818-9.]

and as the female voices were unanimous in their verdict of its truth and likelihood, I hold it to be likely and true, for Dante says we have the 'intellect of love.'[1]

(*Remains*, ed. 1863, vol. iii. p. 2.)

1831. May 29. JOURNAL.

[Quotation from Dante]

An 'eternal, cursed, cold, and heavy rain,' as Dante sings.[2]

(*Ibid.* vol. iii. p. 30.)

1832. Sept. LETTER FROM NEW YORK.

['Mosconi e vespe']

We spend our lives in murdering hecatombs of creeping and jumping things, and vehemently slapping our own faces with intent to kill the flying ones that incessantly buzz about one. It is rather a deplorable existence, and reminds me of one of the most unpleasant circles in Dante's 'Hell,'[3] which I don't think could have been much worse.

(*Ibid.* vol. iii. p. 244.)

1832. JOURNAL.[4]

[Dante's 'sapphire-blue']

Aug. 16. On the voyage to America.—The day was light, and bitter cold,—the sea blue, and transparent as that loveliest line in Dante,

'Dolce color di oriental zaffiro,'[5]

with a lining of pearly foam, and glittering spray.

(Vol. i. p. 10.)

[Dante on fame]

Aug. 20.—Read a canto in Dante,[6] ending with a valuation of fame.[7] 'O spirito gentil!' how lived fair wisdom in your soul—how shines she in your lays!

(*Ibid.* p. 20.)

[Sir Walter Scott; and Dante on fame]

Aug. 22.—Began writing journal, and was interrupted by hearing a bustle in the dining-room. The gentlemen were all standing

[1] [Canz. i. in the *Vita Nuova*: 'Donne, ch' avete intelletto d' amore.']
[2] [*Inf.* vi. 7-8.]
[3] [*Inf.* iii. 65-6.]
[4] [Published in 1835.]
[5] [*Purg.* i. 13.]
[6] [This entry recurs repeatedly throughout the *Journal* (see vol. i. pp. 28, 78, 82, 191, 195, 198; vol. ii. pp. 23, 24, 29, 41.]
[7] [No doubt *Purg.* xi.]

up, and presently I heard Walter Scott's name passed round:—it made me lay down my pen. Oh! how pleasant it sounded—that unanimous blessing of strangers upon a great and good man. . . . Poor, poor Sir Walter! And yet no prayer that can be breathed to bless, no grateful and soul-felt invocation can snatch him from the common doom of earth-born flesh,[1] or buy away one hour's anguish and prostration of body and spirit, before the triumphant infirmities of our miserable nature. I thought of Dante's lines, that I read but a day ago;[2] and yet—and yet—fame is something. His fame is good—is great—is glorious.

(Vol. i. pp. 22-3.)

[Dante a 'philosopher-poet']

Oct. 15. Philadelphia.—After dinner, read a canto in Dante: he is my admiration!—great, great master!—a philosopher profound, as all poets should be; a glorious poet, as I wish all philosophers were.

(*Ibid.* p. 195.)

[Where are the Dantes of America?]

Nov. 10. On the Hudson River.—Where are the poets of this land? Why such a world should bring forth men with minds and souls larger and stronger than any that ever dwelt in mortal flesh. Where are the poets of this land? They should be giants, too; Homers and Miltons, and Goethes and Dantes, and Shakspeares.

(*Ibid.* p. 270.)

[On the fame of actors as compared with that of musicians, poets, and painters]

Dec. 29. Philadelphia.—Art must be to a certain degree enduring. It must not be a transient vision, which fades and leaves but a recollection of what it was, which will fade too. . . . And here it is that the miserable deficiency of acting is most apparent. . . . Whilst Dante, Boccaccio, that giant, Michael Angelo, yet live, and breathe, and have their being amongst us, through the rich legacy their genius has bequeathed to time; whilst the wild music of Salvator Rosa, solemn and sublime as his paintings, yet rings in our ears, and the souls of Shakspeare, Milton, Raphael, and Titian, are yet shedding into our souls divinest influences from the very fountains of inspiration;—where are the pageants that night after night, during the best era of dramatic excellence, riveted the gaze of thousands and drew forth their acclamations?—gone, like rosy sunset clouds.

(Vol. ii. pp. 84-5.)

[1] [Scott died, a month after this was written, on Sept. 21, 1832.]
[2] [On fame (*Purg.* xi.)—see previous entry.]

1843. April. LETTER TO CHARLES GREVILLE (from London).

[Dryden, compared with Spenser, Dante, and Milton]

The 'Leaf and the Flower' is very gorgeous, but it does not touch the heart like earnest praise of a virtue, loved, felt, and practised; and Dryden's 'Hymns to Chastity' would scarcely, I think, satisfy me, even had I not in memory sundry sublime things of Spenser, Dante, and Milton, on the same theme.[1]

(*Records of Later Life*, vol. ii. p. 292.)

ROBERT HALL

(1764-1831)

[Robert Hall, the well-known Baptist divine and preacher, was born in Leicestershire in 1764. He was minister successively at Bristol (1785-90), Cambridge (1791-1806), and Leicester (1807-25). He returned to Bristol in 1826, where he died in 1831. Hall was a great student of Milton, and was led to learn Italian for the sake of reading the *Divina Commedia*, after reading Macaulay's article on Milton in the *Edinburgh Review* for August, 1825. Trevelyan records that Macaulay learned 'with pride' that he had been instrumental in introducing the great preacher to the study of Dante (see above, p. 404, note).]

[1825.] MEMOIR OF ROBERT HALL, BY OLINTHUS GREGORY (1832).

SHORTLY before he quitted Leicester, a friend found him one morning, very early, lying on the carpet, with an Italian dictionary and a volume of Dante before him. Being about to quit the room, he said 'No, sir, don't go. I will tell you what I have been about for some weeks. A short time since, I was greatly delighted with a parallel between the Paradise Lost and the Divine Comedy of Dante, which I read in the *Edinburgh Review*.[2] But in matters of taste, as well as others, I always like to judge for myself; and so I have been studying Italian. I have caught the idiom, and am reading Dante with great relish, though I cannot yet say, with Milton:

> Now my task is smoothly done,
> I can fly as I can run.'[3]

(Ed. 1850, p. 132.)

[1] Mr. Greville had lent me Dryden's 'Fables,' which I had never before read.

[2] [In Macaulay's famous article on Milton, which appeared in August, 1825 (see above, pp. 404 ff.).]

[3] [*Comus*, ll. 1012-3.]

JANE BAILLIE WELSH (MRS. CARLYLE)

(1801-1866)

[Jane Baillie Welsh, the only child of John Welsh, a physician of Haddington, was born in 1801. She was of precocious powers, and wrote a tragedy at the age of fourteen. At Haddington she made the acquaintance of Edward Irving and hoped to marry him. In 1823 Irving married a lady to whom he had long been engaged; in the same year Thomas Carlyle proposed to Jane Welsh and was eventually accepted in 1825, the marriage taking place in the following year. They resided first at Edinburgh and Craigenputtock, and in 1834 removed to London, where Mrs. Carlyle died in 1866.]

1825. Jan. 13. LETTER TO THOMAS CARLYLE (from Haddington).

[Proverb from Dante]

I LITTLE thought that my joke about your farming Craigenputtock was to be made the basis of such a serious and extraordinary project. If you had seen the state of perplexity which your letter has throw me into, you would have practised any self-denial rather than have written it. But there is no use in talking of what is done. *Cosa fatta ha capo.*[1]

(Froude's *Life of Carlyle*, 1795-1835, vol. i. p. 276.)

1838. May 27. LETTER TO HELEN WELSH (from Chelsea).

[Reminiscence of Dante]

O Cousin, gracious and benign,[2]—Beautiful is it to see thy tender years bearing such blossoms of tolerance. . . .

(*Letters and Memorials of Jane Welsh Carlyle,* vol. i. p. 92.)

1842. Jan. 19. LETTER TO JOHN STERLING (from Chelsea).

[Mazzini and Dante]

To-day I have a letter from Forster, from which I extract the most important paragraph (most important for the business in hand that is, for it contains an invitation to dinner, with bright schemes for going to the play):—'Will you propose the article on Dante to Mazzini,[3] and I want you to write and ask John Sterling (indication of celebrity) to write an article for the next *Foreign Quarterly*.'

(*Letters and Memorials of Jane Welsh Carlyle,* vol. i. p. 136.)

[1] [*Inf.* xxviii. 107.]
[2] [Imitation of *Inf.* v. 88: 'O animal grazioso e benigno.']
[3] [John Forster (1812-1876) was at this time editor of the *Foreign Quarterly Review*. Mazzini's article appeared in April, 1844 (vol. xxxiii. pp. 1-30).]

ANONYMOUS

1825. March. QUARTERLY REVIEW. ART. I. HAYLEY'S LIFE AND WRITINGS.

[Hayley's translations from Dante]

THE specimens of the Araucana in Hayley's notes to his Essay on Epic Poetry were given in couplets, the worst form of verse for long narration, and one which Hayley wrote neither with skill nor vigour. His translations from Dante[1] were in the trinal rhyme of the original, and perhaps a better example could not be adduced to show how greatly the style of a poet is influenced by the metre wherein he composes. We have heard a living poet say of this measure, observing how admirably its solemn and continuous movement is suited to the tone and subject of the poem, that, 'you get into it and never get out of it;' there is no end of its linked solemnity, long drawn out. Of all Hayley's compositions these specimens are far the best; and it is evident that he is more indebted for their merit to the mould in which they were cast, than to the model that was before him. He had been trained in a school which unfitted him for comprehending or feeling the excellencies of Dante's severe and perfect style, and had he put the Inferno into couplets, it would have come from that operation as flat as if it had been put through a rolling press. But the barbarisms and common-place affectations, which had so long disfigured our rhymed heroic verse that they had become the received language of poetry, were not transferable to a new measure like a trinal rhyme: and in thus following his original Hayley was led into a sobriety and manliness of diction which, though now and then tainted by the prevailing vices of the popular style, approached in its general tone to the manner of a better age. Mr. Carey's version of Dante is executed with consummate and unparalleled fidelity; and yet we wish that Hayley had given a complete translation of this great poet, (or at least of the Inferno,) for, if the likeness to the original, feature by feature, is not so faithful, the general resemblance is greater, because the costume is preserved.

(Vol. xxxi. pp. 283-4.)

[1] [See vol. i. pp. 359 ff.]

ANONYMOUS

1825. April. EDINBURGH REVIEW. ART. II. ENGLISH POETRY.

[Milton and Dante]

COMPARISONS have been instituted between our great poet [Milton] and Dante; and there are certainly occasional resemblances in the speeches and similes; for instance—

As cranes
Chaunting their dolorous notes, traverse the sky
Stretched out in long array, so I beheld
Spirits who came loud wailing, hurried on, &c.

(*Inf.* c. v.)[1]

And again—

And now there came o'er the perturbed waves
Loud-crashing, terrible, a sound that made
Either shore tremble, as if of a wind
Impetuous, from conflicting vapours sprung
That 'gainst some forest driving all its might
Plucks off the branches, &c.

(*Inf.* c. xi.)[1]

But Dante oftener reminds us of Virgil than Milton, and as often of Spenser, we think, in the treatment of his subject. We recollect the latter, particulary when we read Dante's personifications of Pleasure, of Ambition and Avarice (in the first canto of the Inferno), and the punishment of Fucci for blasphemy (in the twenty-fifth canto), and other things similarly treated. Dante's genius seems to consist in a clear and striking detail of particulars, giving them the air of absolute fact. His strength was made up of units. Milton's, on the other hand, was massy and congregated. His original idea (of Satan) goes sweeping along, and colouring the subject from beginning to end. Dante shifts from place to place, from person to person, subduing his genius to the literal truths of history, which Milton overruled and made subservient. However excellent the Florentine may be (and he *is* excellent), he had not the grasp nor the soaring power of the English poet. The images of Dante pass by like the phantasms on a wall, clear, indeed, and picturesque; but although true, in a great measure, to fact, they are wanting in reality. They have complexion and shape, but not flesh or blood. Milton's earthly creatures have the flush of living beauty upon them, and show the changes of human infirmity.

(Vol. xlii. pp. 56-7.)

[1] [Cary's translation.]

ANONYMOUS

1825. RETROSPECTIVE REVIEW. VOL. XI. PART II. ART. I. THE HOLY BIBLE.

[The Bible compared with the poems of Homer, Virgil, Dante, and others]

WERE the Bible but the ruin of a history, it would be venerable; were it a fiction only, it would be a grand one. . . . There is nothing in Homer which can mate with the soaring spirit of its poetry; there is nothing in Virgil which can equal the gentle pathos of its strains: Dante is less awful, and Ariosto less wild. Even Milton who has topped the sublimity of all other writers, and Shakspeare, who has surpassed the united world in prodigality of imagery and variety of thought, must yield to the infinite grandeur and beauty which is impressed upon the prophetic oracles of the Hebrew writings, or scattered almost at random over its many stories.

(Vol. xi. pp. 204-5.)

HENRY PETER BROUGHAM (LORD BROUGHAM)

(1778-1868)

[Henry Peter Brougham was born in 1778 at Edinburgh, where he was educated at the High School and the University. After finishing his course he read law, and passed advocate in 1800. In 1802 he joined with Sydney Smith, Jeffrey, and others in starting the *Edinburgh Review*, to the first twenty numbers of which he contributed no less than eighty articles. In 1803 he was admitted a member of Lincoln's Inn, and in 1805 he settled in London, and was called to the English bar in 1808. He entered Parliament as member for Camelford in 1810. and afterwards (1815) sat for Winchelsea. When the Princess of Wales, whose adviser he had been for some years, became Queen she appointed Brougham her Attorney-General, and he defended her during her trial (1820). In 1825 he was elected Lord Rector of Glasgow University. In 1830 Brougham became Lord Chancellor in Lord Grey's administration, and was created Baron Brougham and Vaux. He lost office in 1834 on the dismissal of Lord Melbourne, and gradually withdrawing from politics busied himself in the cause of law reform, education, and the suppression of slavery. He died at Cannes, which place he practically created as a winter-resort, in 1868, in his ninetieth year. He was Chancellor of Edinburgh University (1859), honorary D.C.L. of Oxford, and Fellow of the Royal Society. Brougham throughout his life was a great admirer and student of Dante. Macaulay in his essay on Dante, published in *Knight's Quarterly Magazine* in 1824, says: 'I have heard the most eloquent statesman of the age remark that, next to Demosthenes, Dante is the writer who ought to be most attentively studied by every man who desires to attain oratorical eminence.'[1] In his inaugural address on being installed as Lord Rector of Glasgow University in 1825 Brougham dwells on the conciseness and concentrated force of Dante's style.[2] Wright's translation of the *Inferno*, published in 1833, is dedicated to him as 'one of the most ardent admirers of Dante;' and another translator of Dante, J. W. Thomas,

[1] [See above, pp. 402-3.] [2] [See below, p. 433.]

who visited Brougham in 1859, speaks of the familiarity with the *Divina Commedia* displayed by him, and 'his evident appreciation of its brilliant and striking passages—he seemed never tired of quoting the original, which he did with ease and fluency'[1] (at the age of 81). Brougham possessed a copy of the 1481 edition of the *Divina Commedia*, the first printed at Florence, which was presented to him by Queen Caroline. He says in his *Life and Times* (posthumously published in 1871): 'In consequence of the absurd reports spread in the county that a room at Brougham had been built by the Queen after the trial, I may say that I never receivd any present whatever from her, except a magnificent copy of Dante (the great Florentine edition)' (vol. ii. p. 34).]

1825. April 6. INAUGURAL DISCOURSE ON BEING INSTALLED LORD RECTOR OF THE UNIVERSITY OF GLASGOW.

[The conciseness of Dante's style]

IN nothing, not even in beauty of collocation and harmony of rhythm, is the vast superiority of the chaste, vigorous, manly style of the Greek orators and writers more conspicuous than in the abstinent use of their prodigious faculties of expression. A single phrase—sometimes a word—and the work is done—the desired impression is made, as it were, with one stroke, there being nothing superfluous interposed to weaken the blow, or break its fall. The commanding idea is singled out; it is made to stand forward; all auxiliaries are rejected. . . . The great poet of modern Italy, Dante,[2] approached nearest to the ancients in the quality of which I have been speaking. In his finest passages you rarely find an epithet; hardly ever more than one; and never two efforts to embody one idea. 'A guisa di leon quando si posa,'[3] is the single trait by which he compares the dignified air of a stern personage to the expression of the lion slowly laying him down. It is remarkable that Tasso copies the verse entire, but he destroys its whole effect by filling up the majestic idea, adding this line, 'Girando gli occhi

[1] [See *Essay on the style of Dante* in the translation of the *Purgatorio*, by J. W. Thomas (1862), pp. xxix-xxx.]

[2] This great poet abounds in such master strokes. To give only a few examples. The flight of doves:—

'Con l' ali aperte e ferme al dolce nido
Volan per l' aer, dal voler portate.'—(*Inf.* v.)

The gnawing of a skull by a mortal enemy:—

'Co' denti
Che furo all' osso, come d' un can, forti.'—(*Inf.* xxxiii.)

The venality and simoniacal practices of the Romish church:—

'Là dove Cristo tutto dì si merca.'—(*Parad.* xvii.)

The perfidy of a Bourbon:—

'Senz' arme n' esce, e solo con la lancia
Con la qual giostrò Giuda.'—(*Purg.* xx.)

The pains of dependence:—

'Tu proverai sì come sa di sale
Lo pane altrui, e com' è duro calle
Lo scendere e 'l salir per l' altrui scale.'—(*Parad.* xvii.)

[3] [*Purg.* vi. 66—of Sordello.]

e non movendo il passo.' A better illustration could not easily be found of the difference between the ancient and the modern style. Another is furnished by a later imitator of the same great master. I know no passage of the *Divina Commedia* more excursive than the description of evening in the *Purgatorio* ;[1] yet the poet is content with somewhat enlarging on a single thought—the tender recollections which that hour of meditation gives the traveller, at the fall of the first night he is to pass away from home, when he hears the distant knell of the expiring day. Gray adopts the idea of the knell in nearly the words of the original, and adds eight other circumstances to it, presenting a kind of ground-plan, or at least a catalogue, an accurate enumeration (like a natural historian's), of every one particular belonging to nightfall, so as wholly to exhaust the subject, and leave nothing to the imagination of the reader. Dante's six verses, too, have but one epithet, *dolci* applied to *amici*. Gray has thirteen or fourteen; some of them mere repetitions of the same idea which the verb or the substantive conveys—as *drowsy* tinklings *lull*,—the *moping* owl *complains*,—the ploughman *plods* his *weary* way. Surely when we contrast the simple and commanding majesty of the ancient writers with the superabundance and diffusion of the exhaustive method, we may be tempted to feel that there lurks some alloy of bitterness in the excess of sweets.

(*Works of Lord Brougham*, ed. 1856, vol. vii. pp. 129, 133-4.)

1843. HISTORICAL SKETCHES OF STATESMEN WHO FLOURISHED IN THE TIME OF GEORGE III. THIRD SERIES.

[Personalities in Milton and Dante]

The licence and the personalities in which the members of the Convention were wont to indulge with levity and coarse humour, formed a strange and even appalling contrast to the dreadful work in which they were engaged. Legendre was a butcher. . . . His calling was not infrequently brought up against him in the Convention.—"Tais-toi, massacreur de bœufs!" said one whom he was denouncing. "C'est que j'en ai assommé qui avoient plus d'esprit que toi!" was the butcher's immediate reply. Another being on his defence against a motion for a decree of accusation to put him on his trial, Legendre then presiding said, "Décrète qu'il soit mis"—'Décrète,' said the other, interrupting him, 'décrète que je suis bœuf, et tu m'assommeras toi-même.'—Such passages remind one of the grotesque humours of the fiends in 'Paradise Lost,' whose scoffing raillery in their "gamesome mood" Milton has so

[1] [*Purg.* viii. 1-6.]

admirably painted, to the extreme displeasure, no doubt, of his prudish critic, in whose estimation this is by "far the most exceptionable passage of the whole poem."—*Note.* See Addison, "Spectator," No. 279. The dialogue of mutual sarcasm between Adamo and Sinon in Dante's "Inferno,"[1] would have given the same offence to the critic; and the poet seems as if conscious of the offence he was offering to squeamish persons, when he makes Virgil chide his pupil for listening to such ribaldry.

(*Works of Lord Brougham,* ed. 1856, vol. v. pp. 81-2 (Camille Desmoulins—St. Just).)

GEORGE CRABB

(1788-1851)

[George Crabb, miscellaneous writer, was born at Palgrave, in Suffolk, in 1788. He was educated in Germany and at Magdalen Hall, Oxford (M.A. 1822). He died in 1851. In 1825 Crabb published a *Universal Historical Dictionary* (second edition, 1833), which contains a brief notice of Dante.]

1825. UNIVERSAL HISTORICAL DICTIONARY.

[The *Divina Commedia* 'a species of satiric epic']

DANTE ALIGHIERI, an Italian statesman and poet, descended from one of the first families in Florence, was born in 1265, and died in 1321, in exile at Ravenna, after having been embroiled, as governor of Florence, in all the tumults raised by the opposing factions of the Guelphs and Ghibelins. He is better known at present for his poetical works, the most important of which is his 'Divina Commedia,' a species of satiric epic, of which there have been numerous editions; the best is said to be that of Venice, 3 vols. 4to. 1757. It was first printed in 1472 at Foligno in a folio volume, without place; the second is in folio, and the third in 4to of the same date.

JOHN KEBLE

(1792-1866)

[John Keble was born at Fairford, in Gloucestershire, in 1792. He was educated at home by his father and gained a scholarship at Corpus Christi College, Oxford, in 1806. In 1811 he took a double-first and was elected Fellow of Oriel. In the following year he won the University prizes for the English and the Latin essays. Keble, who was ordained in 1815, resided in Oxford as examiner and tutor till 1823, when he retired to Fairford. In 1827 he published anonymously the *Christian Year*, which passed through 95 editions in his lifetime. In 1831 he was elected Professor of Poetry at Oxford. In 1836, in which year he published an edition of Hooker's

[1] [*Inf.* xxx. 100-48.]

works, he accepted the living of Hursley, near Winchester, which he held until his death (at Bournemouth) in 1866. In 1841, when his professorship terminated, he published his lectures (which were delivered in Latin) under the title of *De Poeticae Vi Medica*. Keble was a student of Dante, references to whom occur in several of his writings, including his lectures, which contain an interesting parallel between Dante and Lucretius.]

1825. June. QUARTERLY REVIEW. ART. IX. SACRED POETRY.

[Milton and Dante]

IT is a well-known complaint among many readers of Paradise Lost, that they can hardly keep themselves from sympathizing in some sort, with Satan, as the hero of the poem. The most probable account of which surely is, that the author himself partook largely of the haughty and vindictive republican spirit, which he has assigned to the character, and consequently, though perhaps unconsciously, drew the portrait with a peculiar zest. These blemishes are in part attributable to the times in which he lived: but there is another now to be mentioned, which cannot be so accounted for: we mean a want of purity and spirituality in his conceptions of Heaven and heavenly joys. His Paradise is a vision not to be surpassed; but his attempts to soar higher are embarrassed with too much of earth still clinging as it were to his wings. Remarks of this kind are in general best understood by comparison, and we invite our readers to compare Milton with Dante, in their descriptions of Heaven. The one as simple as possible in his imagery, producing intense effect by little more than various combinations of *three* leading ideas—light, motion, and music [1]—as if he feared to introduce anything more gross and earthly, and would rather be censured, as doubtless he often is, for coldness and poverty of invention. Whereas Milton, with very little selection or refinement, transfers to the immediate neighbourhood of God's throne, the imagery of Paradise and Earth.[2]

(Vol. xxxii. p. 229.)

1836. THE WORKS OF THAT LEARNED AND JUDICIOUS DIVINE, MR. RICHARD HOOKER. ARRANGED BY THE REV. JOHN KEBLE.

[Dante's references to the celestial hierarchies]

God's own eternity is the hand which leadeth Angels in the course of their perpetuity; their perpetuity the hand that draweth out celestial motion. (*Eccles. Pol.* Bk. V. Ch. 69 § 2). *Keble's note.* This favours an opinion not uncommon among the Fathers and

[1] [This passage is quoted by Henry Hallam in his *Introduction to the Literature of Europe*—see above, p. 262.]

[2] [Reprinted in *Occasional Papers and Reviews*, p. 104.]

schoolmen, of a correspondence between the intellectual and material heavens in such sort, that the nine spheres of which the latter, according to the Ptolemaic system, was composed, answered to, and were influenced respectively by, the nine orders of the celestial hierarchy, as expounded in the books ascribed to Dionysius the Areopagite. . . . Dante has several allusions to this opinion: see Parad. canto viii. terz. 12, 13; and xxix. 15; but especially xxviii. throughout.

(Ed. 1841, vol. ii. p. 381.)

[1841.] DE POETICAE VI MEDICA. PRAELECTIONES ACADEMICAE OXONII HABITAE, ANNIS MDCCCXXXII . . . MDCCCXLI.

[Dante among the poets who wrote sonnets]

Praelectio xxiv[1]:—Effloruit aevo recentiore, hodieque ut maxime viget, ea formula poeseos,[2] quae severissime omnium scribentis ingenium coercet intra suos fines, angustos illos quidem; eam intelligo quam nos hic ante memoravimus, quam primus, ut arbitror, excoluit apud Italos Petrarca. Quae cum spatiis utatur adeo exiguis, (nam ex lege quadam sacrosancta nunquam excurrit ultra quatuordecim versiculos); cumque praeterea in se receperit conditionem illam minime facilem, sonorum non modo parium verum etiam similium, certis recurrentium intervallis, atque inter se jungendarum obliquo ac difficili nexu: mirere sane, quid adeo fuerit in causa, cur tot animi rapidi ac ferventes ultro sibi imposuerint istos terminos. Praeter enim illum, quem modo nominavi, Petrarcam, dedit operam istiusmodi carminibus, quo nemo severius scripsit, nemo religiosius, Dantes Aligherus: dedit Michael Angelus ille Buonarotius . . . : dedit etiam Spenserus noster.

(Vol. ii. pp. 473-4.)

[Parallel between Dante and Lucretius]

Praelectio xxxiii[3]:—Jam ne dicat aliquis fuisse id Lucretio proprium, cum magnus esset in simplici illo genere, ut lubens tamen saltibus et sylvarum involucris frueretur; quid si docebo, tale aliquid evenisse apud alium quoque Poetam, qui proxime omnium tangere videatur Lucretium, quod ad ea attinet, quae obscura sunt et infinita? Intelligo Florentinum Illum, triplici carmine nobilem, de triplici mortuorum statu. Quanto ille vir splendidissimae Poeseos apparatu variaverit instrumentum satis per se exile, partim musicorum modorum, partim radiorum supernae lucis, partim nescio quo orbe mirifice saltantium, novit unusquisque, qui primis modo labris fontem ejus plane divinum hauserit. Atque

[1] [Delivered in 1837.] [2] [The sonnet.] [3] [Delivered in 1840.]

ut ea sola memorem, quae ad caelestem Lucem pertinent; quale illud, quod Virgo laudatissima, qua duce usurus erat Poeta per regionem beatorum, oculis modo in Solem fixis, et illum mutare potuit et in caelum ipsa eniti[1]! Quid, quod piae cujusque animae accessu rident quodammodo, si fides Poetae, novaque se luce vestiunt singulae tum stellae tum Sanctorum quoque umbrae?[2] Quid? commentum illud singulare de Choro beatorum Manium, qui velut sidera quaedam componuntur nunc in Aquilae nunc in Coronae formam,[3] nonne optime convenire videtur cum excelsa illa ac purissima caeli regione? Dies profecto me deficeret, narrantem omnia quae habet ejusmodi Comoedia illa vero Divina. Ex quibus effectum est, ut qua materia turpissime labi soleat vulgus scriptorum, in ea solus ferme recte se habuerit Dantes. Cum enim illis plerumque moris sit, crassa ac terrena transferre in Elysia sua ac Paradisos, hic ne hortorum quidem amoenitates, neque castissimam formarum pulchritudinem, ullo tempore admittit in suum aethera: tribus illis, ut dicebam, ferme contentus; Luce, Motu, Cantu.

Iam vero, cui suffecit ut plurimum suppellex adeo brevis et angusta idem alioqui significat se non modice delectari sylvarum flexibus, obscuroque ac dubio per nemora ac saltus itinere: velut ibi, sub ipso operis initio, narrat se via erravisse in valle nescio qua sylvestri et horrida: vel multo etiam magis in suavissimo carmine,[4] quo Terrestris adumbratur Paradisus.

Immo etiam, ut id quod sentio dicam, qui Dantem in deliciis habent, non alia, maximam partem, voluptate fruuntur, atque ii qui libere per nemora avia gradiuntur, incerti quid quoque tempore futurum sit obvium. Adeo non incredibile videtur id quod in Lucretio modo docebam: si quem commovere soleant amore quodam obscurae et infinitae res, eidem scriptori cordi fore non apertum modo aequora, ignesque sidereos, verum etiam nubium profunda et secretos sylvarum calles. Verum haec semel animadvertisse satis sit. Sibi quisque volo venetur exempla, modo hoc teneat, neque tempori nec labori parcendum, si quis se ex animo accingat ad ejus Poematis lectionem. Neque porro refugiendum putet ob duo quaedam vel tria, quae severius paullo sonare, ne dicam horridius, videantur.

(Vol. ii. pp. 678-9.)

[Dante's choice of Virgil as a guide]

From *Praelectio* xl[5]:—Siqui vel illo saeculo, quod proprio nomine appellatur *obscurum*, vel postea, literis viguerunt;—qui

[1] Dante, *Paradiso* ii. 22-30, et alibi.
[2] E.g. *ibid.* v. 106.
[3] *Ibid.* xviii. 100-8; x. 64.
[4] Dante, *Purgatorio*, xxviii.
[5] [Delivered in 1841.]

primo quidem pauciores fuerunt, post millesimum a Christo annum frequentiores;—apud illos certe omnes unice ferme dominatus est Virgilius. Illum admirantur: eximia quaeque ab illius scriptis recitare amant: illi prae choro universo Ethnicorum absque controversia primum tribuunt locum. Quid quod laudatissimus ille Dantes, primarius non solum Poeta verum etiam Theologus, Maronem potissimum elegit, quem ducem sibi adhiberet per arcana et infima loca? Num parum aperte profitetur, eum ex antiquis omnibus, quos quidem noverit illa aetas, optimam munire viam, veritatem indagantibus? Neque enim credibile est, Poeticam vim ac dulcedinem fuisse solam in causa tam gravi scriptori, cur in tali re subsidio ejus uteretur. Immo vero Platonica Virgilii, mihi credite, somnia, obscuraque di Diis Manibus et de statu mortuorum auguria, insederant altius in ipsis praecordiis magni ac praeclari viri; neque ullo modo sibi temperare potuit, quin Virgilium judicaret divinitus quodammodo dari hominibus, qui orditum pararet ingenuo cuique ad veram solidamque pietatem.

(Vol. ii. pp. 805-6.)

EDGAR TAYLOR

(1793-1839)

[Edgar Taylor (born at Banham in Norfolk in 1793, died in London in 1839), who was a lawyer by profession, was an accomplished linguist, being familiar with French, German, Spanish, and Italian. He is best known as an author by his translation of Grimm's Fairy Tales, which was originally published anonymously, under the title 'German Popular Stories,' with illustrations by George Cruikshank, in 1824-6. A second edition, entitled 'Gammer Grethel,' appeared in 1839, the year of his death. His earliest original work, also published anonymously, was on the 'Lays of the Minnesingers;' in this occur frequent references to Dante, a few of which are given below.]

1825. LAYS OF THE MINNESINGERS OR GERMAN TROUBADOURS OF THE TWELFTH AND THIRTEENTH CENTURIES: ILLUSTRATED BY SPECIMENS OF THE CONTEMPORARY LYRIC POETRY OF PROVENCE AND OTHER PARTS OF EUROPE: WITH HISTORICAL AND CRITICAL NOTICES.

[Dante and the alleged *Lancelot du Lac* of Arnaut Daniel]

ARNAUD DANIEL, a Troubadour poet, who, in the opinion of Dante,

'versi d' amore e prose di romanzi
Soverchiò tutti,'—[1]

published Lancelot du Lac in his own tongue;[2] for the German translator, in the 13th century, expressly names him as the author

[1] [*Purg.* xxvi. 118-9.]
[2] [The theory that Arnaut wrote a Provençal Lancelot is now exploded.]

whom he followed. Probably the Provençal was the language in which Francesca and Paulo perused this romance in the beautiful story told in the Inferno,[1] c. 5.

> 'Noi leggiavamo un giorno per diletto
> Di Lancilotto, come amor lo strinse:
> Soli eravamo, e senza alcun sospetto.' &c.

(pp. 23-4.)

[Dante and the Troubadours]

Considering the perfection in which the earliest known specimens exhibit the language of Italy,—the delight which it is clear its inhabitants felt in the poetry and romances of the North and South French,—and the free intercourse with other nations which existed during their connexion with the Norman princes of Sicily and with the German Empire,

> 'Sotto l' imperio del buon Barbarossa'[2]

and his successors.—it appears strange that Italian literature should have been so far behind that of almost every other country; —that its earliest poets should have preferred foreign tongues, without making any attempt to cultivate their own, though in many respects superior;—and yet that, after so much torpor, it should at length break forth all at once in such comparative splendour and perfection. The Provençal writers must have been perfectly familiar to the Italians; for their early writers, such as Guittone d' Arrezzo (in his Letters), Dante and Petrarch, are full of allusions to them, and of the warmest eulogiums on their works. Several of the Troubadours themselves, for example Sordel (who is introduced in the 6th and 9th cantos of the Purgatorio), Boniface Calvo, and Folquet, . . . were Italians.

(pp. 50-1.)

[Dante's tribute to the Swabian Emperors as patrons of literature]

The German emperors of the house of Swabia not only admired and patronized every where the popular French poetry, but stimulated their subjects to emulation in their native tongues. . . . Dante (de Vulg. Eloq. 1, 12), as quoted by Mr. Carey,[3] bears express testimony to the salutary influence of the Imperial patronage:—'Those illustrious worthies, Frederic the Emperor and his son Manfredi, manifested their nobility and uprightness of form as long as fortune remained, by following pursuits worthy of men,

[1] [Dante's references are to the Old French (Langue d'Oil) version of the Lancelot Romance.]
[2] [*Purg*. xviii. 119.]
[3] [*Sic*—the passage occurs in Cary's note on *Purg*. iii. 110.]

and disdaining those which are suited only to brutes. Such, therefore, as were of lofty spirit and graced with natural endowments, endeavoured to walk in the track which the majesty of such great princes had marked out for them; so that, whatever was in their time attempted by eminent Italians first made its appearance in the court of crowned sovereigns; and because Sicily was a royal throne, it came to pass that whatever was produced in the vernacular tongue by our predecessors was called Sicilian, which neither we nor our posterity shall be able to change.' . . .

Frederic II. himself was one of the earliest Italian rimers. . . . With him we must place his learned but unfortunate chancellor Petrus de Vineis, who uses a purer idiom; indeed, one that seems as classical as that of Dante.

(pp. 58 ff.)

GEORGE PROCTER

(fl. 1820)

1825. THE HISTORY OF ITALY, FROM THE FALL OF THE WESTERN EMPIRE TO THE COMMENCEMENT OF THE WARS OF THE FRENCH REVOLUTION.[1]

[Dante's denunciation of Pisa]

THE crimes of Ugolino might have demanded expiation on the scaffold; but the atrocity of his punishment has deservedly branded his enemies with eternal infamy; and the horror and pity of mankind may still echo the stern reproach with which the indignant numbers of Dante apostrophized 'the modern Thebes'—the murderess of his guiltless offspring:—

'Ahi Pisa, vituperio delle genti
Del bel paese là, dove 'l sì suona;' &c.[2]

(Vol. i. Chap. iv. Part. i. p. 272.)

[The exile of Dante]

One interesting circumstance in this revolution in Florence has deserved to survive the long oblivion of ages. Among the White Guelfs, who were included in the sentence of banishment and proscription, was Dante, or more properly, Durante Alighieri, who had held the office of prior while that party acquired ascendancy in the state. It was during a lingering and cruel exile, which

[1] [This first edition was published under the pseudonym of George Perceval; the author's real name was appended to the second edition (1844), on the title-page of which he is described as Colonel Procter, late of Sandhurst College.]

[2] [Procter quotes *Inf.* xxxiii. 79-90, with Cary's translation.]

lasted unto his death, that he composed or completed his vision of Hell, Purgatory, and Paradise,—the *Divina Commedia*,—one of the most sublime and original works of human genius. Seeking a refuge at the courts of the Della Scala, lords of Verona and other Ghibelin chieftains, he tasted all the bitterness of dependence and poverty;[1] and, pouring out in terrific invective and political satire the indignation of a lofty and imaginative spirit which had darkened in adversity, he filled the awful scenes of his great poem with the personages of contemporary history, and branded the crimes and dissensions of his age in numbers that will live for ever.

(Vol. i. Chap. iv. Part i. pp. 283-4.)

EMMA ELEONORA KENDRICK

(1788-1871)

[Emma Eleonora Kendrick, miniature-painter, daughter of Josephus Kendrick, sculptor, was born in 1788. She exhibited at the Royal Academy for the first time in 1811, and was from that date until 1840 a constant exhibitor there, as well as at the Society of British Artists, and at the Old Water-Colour Society. In 1831 she was appointed Miniature-Painter to the King. She died in 1871.]

1826. IN this year E. E. Kendrick exhibited at the Society of British Artists a picture with the following title :—

Captive Hugolino ; after Sir Joshua Reynolds.

(*Catalogue of the Society of British Artists*, 1826, No. 627.)

JOHN BROWNING

(fl. 1820)

1826. THE HISTORY OF TUSCANY ; FROM THE ITALIAN OF LORENZO PIGNOTTI.[2]

[Dante to be judged by comparison with his predecessors]

WHEN we read the rude, harsh, and insipid verses written in Italy, even after the middle of the thirteenth century, and at the close of it the greater part of the wonderful poem of Dante,—we cannot look upon the progress of the language

[1] That he should find 'how salt was the taste of another's bread, and how painful it was to climb and descend another's stairs,' is the prophecy which he makes the shade of his ancestor address to him in Paradise:

'Tu proverai sì come sa di sale
Lo pane altrui, e com'è duro calle
Lo scendere e 'l salir per l' altrui scale.'
Paradiso, Canto 17.

[2] [Pignotti's *Storia della Toscana* was published in 1813-16. The translator is described on the title-page as 'Deputy Purveyor of the Forces; several years Resident in Florence.']

without the greatest admiration, or rather the divine genius of that great bard. We cannot form a just idea of the merits of Dante, without reading the writings of his predecessors, in order to ascertain the poverty of the language. He has been, in fact, the creator, and particularly of the poetical. The greatest poets are even more rare than great philosophers; because the talents of the former are formed from two elements, rarely found united, and which appear, on the contrary, incompatible,—namely, a very lively imagination, and a cold and settled judgment. . . . The poems of great imagination arise in times in which that severe criticism is not yet formed, which often extinguishes the fine poetic fire with its cold circumspection. This very rare talent, composed of these two ingredients in their proper dose, was granted by nature to Dante as a singular gift; and he was enabled to create not only the poetic language, but many words and phrases with which prose was also enriched. Scarcely do we perceive how much we are indebted to this great writer; because the riches he has brought into our language have become common to succeeding authors. . . . he may be said to have done what Augustus did, who found Rome built of brick, and left it of marble.

(Vol. i. pp. 251-2.)

[The perennial freshness of Dante]

Everything yields to time, everything at least undergoes a progressive change, and particularly languages; our own, however, has resisted more than others, and where is there among the living languages one that has preserved its disposition, and its character, from its birth down to our time, so well as the Italian? What language can show writers, who, born in the first development of it, have maintained themselves fresh, to use the expression, and flourish in the same language for five ages, and are still relished, like Dante? The Italian owes this advantage to the great writers, who after a long infancy conducted it rapidly to the vigour of strength: Dante, Petrarch, and Boccaccio, having been always read, have preserved the language fresh and vigorous.

(Vol. i. p. 259.)

[The simile borrowed from Dante by Gray in the *Elegy*]

One of the poems, considered by the English among their most perfect, is the celebrated Elegy of Gray upon the Country Churchyard. He has begun it with an idea drawn from Dante, which he does not deny: on the contrary, whose verses he quotes: [1]

se ode squilla di lontano
Che paja il giorno pianger che muore.

[1] [See vol. i. p. 234.]

The idea is genteel: the bell that rings at the dusk of evening is adapted to awaken a noble melancholy. The English is thus literally expressed: *la campana batte il funerale del giorno che muore*,[1] but the funeral of the day will appear to many an expression a little bold, and of a colouring that *shoots*, to use a painter's phrase. Observe how judiciously Dante, in his original verses, has put the word *paja*, which softens the colouring, and reduces it to its real rank. I could observe, also, how much more true and touching the image of Dante becomes with that *di lontano*; as it cannot be denied, that the effect of waking a melancholy sentiment is not [2] greater when far around in the country we listen in the evening to that sound, rendered more melancholy and obtuse from the distance itself.

(Vol. i. pp. 263-4.)

[Parallel between Dante and Michael Angelo]

It has been said of Buonarroti,[3] that by the certain frankness of his hand he has expressed features, which no other man would have ventured to imitate, because he was not certain, like him, of the success of execution. The same may be said of Dante;—the horrid attitudes of those who are condemned to eternal punishment, the fierce complexion of Ugolino, that of Lucifer, and many other such pictures, if they had been executed with weakness, instead of a sublime horror, would excite our ridicule. Even the furies, lively expressed; the horrible skull of Medusa of Leonardo da Vinci; penetrate us with a delightful horror. If the song of Hell particularly resembles in design the Universal Judgment of Michael Angelo, we find the same conformity also in the colouring of the latter: which, being strong, and somewhat deep, is better adapted to express grand and sublime ideas than the softness and sweetness of the most genteel painters. Dante, however, is not without suavity of style; and this chord, which has afterwards done so much honour to Petrarch, was not wanting to his cittern, which, from time to time, appears still more acceptable from its variety. The pathetic images in the doleful history of the brothers-in-law in Hell,[4] are expressed with a sweetness, which forms a contrast to the strong and powerfully sublime style in which the atrocious history of Ugolino is recounted; but more frequent examples are found in the other two songs, which are better fitted to the subject. It is necessary, therefore, to seek the roses in the midst of the

[1] 'The curfew tolls the knell of parting day.'

[2] [*Sic.*]

[3] [That is, Michael Angelo.]

[4] [Paolo and Francesca are meant, who were brother and sister-in-law: the mistake in the text is due to the translator.]

thorns. There are readers, who, too hastily tired with the harshness of the verses, with the obscurity of expressions, and images which are sometimes a little vulgar . . . abandon the lecture and judge him too lightly for a poet, whose merit consists in the imagination of his adorers. 'It is easy,' says a great English poet, 'to perceive the defects of a writer; the straw, the froth, the filth of the sea, are borne swimming to us, but we must go deep into it in order to fish for the pearls.'

(Vol. ii. pp. 160-1.)

[Dante's minor works—the 'weak prose' and 'middling verse' of the *Vita Nuova*]

The other works of Dante, either in verse or in prose, are far from possessing the merit of the Divine Comedy. Among these the *Vita Nuova* is made to celebrate the beautiful Beatrice; but her timid, delicate and metaphysical love expressed in weak prose, mixed with middling verse, cannot much entertain our readers. His *Convivio*, so called as an instructive food to readers, is a comment upon three of his songs, in which we discover his extensive knowledge in the philosophy of Aristotle and Plato, and in astronomy; knowledge of great weight in those times, and useless in our own. More particular attention should be paid to his other two works, one of *Monarchy*, the other of *Vulgar Eloquence*. In the first, the primacy of the imperial authority is maintained over the pontifical: an opinion which placed all his writings in danger of undergoing ecclesiastical censures. . . . The work worthy of most consideration is that of *Vulgar Eloquence*, as it contains the sentiment of Dante upon the nature of the vulgar tongue, and what is the noblest in Italy that should be followed; he does not give the privilege to any city, not even to Florence; but says that this is a language, according to his expressions, *illustre, cardinale, aulica, cortigiana, che non è propria d' alcuna città d' Italia, ma può appartenere a tutte.* This opinion of Dante, perhaps, was just in his days; the noble Italian language was fluctuating, because not yet well formed; but after his divine work, after Petrarch and Boccaccio, who still more established that which Dante had begun, the prerogative of belonging to a particular country was decided in favour of Tuscany.

(Vol. ii. pp. 165-8.)

GABRIELE ROSSETTI

(1783-1854)

[Gabriele Pasquale Giuseppe Rossetti, to give him his full name, was born at Vasto in the Kingdom of Naples in 1783. In 1824 he came as a political refugee to England, and settled in London, where in 1831 he was appointed professor of

Italian in King's College. He published in England several remarkable works on Dante,[1] in which he attempts to establish the esoteric anti-papal significance of the *Divina Commedia*. The best known of these, *Sullo Spirito Anti-papale che produsse la Riforma* (published in 1832, translated into English by Caroline Ward in 1834) had the distinction of being placed on the pontifical index. The theory attracted and more or less convinced John Hookham Frere (whose acquaintance Rossetti made in the early days of his exile at Malta, 1822-24); and Charles Lyell, the translator of the *Canzoniere* of Dante, who printed a long essay on the subject[2] in 1842, an Italian translation of which, by Gaetano Polidori, was published in London in 1844. Unfavourable critics of the theory were Panizzi, in the *Foreign Review*[3] (1828), and Arthur Hallam, in *Remarks on Rossetti's Disquisizioni*[4] (London, 1832). Rossetti, who in 1826 married Francesca, second daughter of Gaetano Polidori (see below, p. 689), died in London in 1854, leaving four children, of whom three inherited his zeal for the study of Dante, viz. Maria Francesca (1827-1876), authoress of the *Shadow of Dante* (1871); Dante Gabriel (1828-1882), translator of the *Vita Nuova* (published in 1861 in *Early Italian Poets*, and reprinted in 1874 as *Dante and his Circle*); and William Michael, who translated the *Inferno* (1865).]

1826-27. LA DIVINA COMMEDIA DI DANTE ALIGHIERI, CON COMENTO ANALITICO, IN SEI VOLUMI.

[Published in London by Murray. Only two volumes out of the six announced on the title-page ever saw the light. The first volume was dedicated to John Hookham Frere, the second to Edward Davenport, M.P. for Shaftesbury. 'The intention was to publish the whole of the *Divina Commedia*: but, the expense proving too great, the *Inferno* alone came out. The great majority of the comment on the *Purgatorio* was written—not any of that on the *Paradiso*. . . . Rossetti regarded Dante as a member, both in politics and in religion, of an occult society, having a close relation to what we now call Freemasonry; and he opined that the *Commedia* and other writings of Dante, and also the books of many other famous authors in various languages and epochs, are of similar internal significance.'[5]]

1832. SULLO SPIRITO ANTIPAPALE CHE PRODUSSE LA RIFORMA, E SULLA SEGRETA INFLUENZA CH' ESERCITÒ NELLA LETTERATURA D' EUROPA, E SPECIALMENTE D' ITALIA, COME RISULTA DA MOLTI SUOI CLASSICI, MASSIME DA DANTE, PETRARCA, BOCCACCIO.

[Published in London for the author by Rolandi and others. It was dedicated to Charles Lyell. An English translation by Caroline Ward was published in 1834.[6] 'In this work the author develops and extends the ideas, which he had conceived during his study of Dante, as to a secret society to which that poet and many other writers belonged, and as to the essentially anti-christian as well as anti-papal opinions covertly expressed in their writings.'[7]]

1840. IL MISTERO DELL' AMOR PLATONICO DEL MEDIO EVO DERIVATO DAI MISTERI ANTICHI.

[Printed in London by Taylor, in five volumes. Dedicated to S. K. (i.e. Seymour Kirkup). 'This extensive and rather discursive work follows up the line of speculation and argument shown in the author's two previous works. Rossetti wrote it

[1] [See the list below.] [2] [See below, p. 593.]
[3] [See below, pp. 515 ff.]
[4] [See above, pp. 422-4. Rossetti was also reviewed in the *Literary Gazette* (1826), the *Foreign Quarterly Review* (1830) and the *Edinburgh Review* (1832)—see below, pp. 447-8, 537-9, 547-8.]
[5] [W. M. Rossetti, in *Gabriele Rossetti: A Versified Autobiography*, pp. 65-6.]
[6] [See below, pp. 590 ff.] [7] [W. M. Rossetti, *ubi supra*, p. 67.]

with a consciousness that the themes of religion or irreligion which it discusses were volcanic matter for readers to handle, as well as perilous to his own professional position in England. He therefore exhibited his subject with some amount of reticence, meandering through thickets of very audacious thought—the thought of great writers of the past as interpreted (but also to a great extent deprecated) by himself. As Mr. Frere, partially seconded by Mr. Charles Lyell, pronounced the book to be foolhardy, it was withheld from publication in England, and was only put on sale on the Continent with precaution and in small numbers.'[1] A presentation copy of this work from the author to John Hookham Frere, with many marginal notes by the latter, is preserved in the British Museum.]

1842. LA BEATRICE DI DANTE. RAGIONAMENTI CRITICI.

[Published in London by Rolandi. Dedicated to Charles Lyell, 'Esimio Traduttore del Canzoniere di Dante.' This work is 'an argument that Dante's Beatrice was not in any sense a real woman, but an embodiment of Philosophy. The reasoning extends a good deal beyond this limit, into regions explored in the three previous works. Rossetti completed the work in three disquisitions—or indeed, according to the final arrangement, in nine disquisitions. Only the first of these was published. The others were entrusted to a French writer, M. E. Aroux. He studied them, and published a book named *Dante Hérétique, Révolutionnaire, et Socialiste*—a book which Rossetti, on seeing it in print, did not acknowledge as by any means faithful to his own views.'[2]]

ANONYMOUS

1826. Jan. LITERARY GAZETTE, AND JOURNAL OF THE BELLES LETTRES. ROSSETTI'S DIVINA COMMEDIA DI DANTE ALIGHIERI, CON COMENTO ANALITICO.[3]

[Rossetti's 'important discovery' with regard to Dante]

IN this age of literary discovery, that which we have to announce, in giving a short account of Signor Rossetti's edition of Dante, is, perhaps, the most extraordinary, and will be considered, probably, by his countrymen and the admirers of Dante, as the most important. Extraordinary it must be considered, since a poem which has been the subject of commentary and research for nearly five complete centuries, is now, for the first time, demonstrated to contain, throughout its whole context, a hidden sense, which has either escaped the acuteness or been dissembled by the timidity of former commentators, and this demonstration is conveyed with such a clearness of proof, and such an abundance of testimony, as might be deemed superfluous and pedantic, if the object had been less arduous than that of removing a misapprehension so inveterate, and sanctioned by the silence or concurrence of so many learned men, during so very long a period. The important discovery to which Signor Rossetti has called the attention of the world, is, in fact, delivered by Dante himself, in words which,

[1] [W. M. Rossetti, *ubi supra*, pp. 67-8.]
[2] [*Ibid.*, pp. 68-9]
[3] [See above, p. 446.]

though hitherto most unaccountably overlooked, cannot admit of any other interpretation; and it is briefly this, that the Inferno is an allegorical picture of the then existing state of government and society. '*Poeta agit de Inferno isto in quo peregrinando ut viatores, mereri et demereri possumus.*' 'The Inferno in which we are wandering as strangers and pilgrims, and in which we are capable of guilt or merit, becoming obnoxious to punishment, or entitled to reward.'

This Inferno, thus described as it is by Dante himself,[1] in his dedicatory epistle, must be understood to signify this present world and its existing inhabitants;—if the poet had chosen to say in distinct words, 'My poem is a picture of this world such as it is,' he would only have expressed the same meaning without a periphrasis; but he would not have conveyed it in a manner more positive or unambiguous. . . .

We must not dwell too long upon a single point, or attempt even an abstract of the evidence which Signor Rossetti has accumulated. . . . The dead of the Inferno are typical of the living dead of his own times, whom Dante and other contemporary authors of the same principles and party describe as 'dead in vice and ignorance.' . . . The *città del fuoco*[2] into which Dante and Virgil are denied admittance, is the city of Florence, from which Dante had been before banished, and where he was now condemned to be *burnt alive*. . . . Lastly, the *Messo del Cielo*[3] who comes with the golden rod to open the gates of the city, and who appears to be conscious of no obstacle but that of the heavy atmosphere, *aer grasso*, is the emperor, who in his enterprise against Florence experienced no obstacle but from the unhealthiness of the season and climate, to which he fell a victim. These and an infinite variety of other allusions are proved with a degree of detail which may be necessary for establishing a new principle of interpretation, but which, when it is once established, will be capable of considerable abridgment.

(No. 468, p. 8.)

ANONYMOUS

1826. March. QUARTERLY REVIEW. ART. IX. NOVELS OF FASHIONABLE LIFE.

[Of the originality of Homer, Dante, and Ariosto]

WHAT poet—with the exception of Homer, about whose predecessors we know nothing—appears to be so original as Ariosto? Yet what poet has borrowed so much both of sentiment and incident? If there be a more original poet,

[1] [The words quoted are not Dante's.] [2] [*Inf.* ix. 36 ff.] [3] [*Inf.* ix. 64 ff.]

it is Dante; yet, imperfectly as we are acquainted with his Provençal and Italian models, do we not find enough to satisfy ourselves that he too had drawn most largely upon others? But these two men, and those who have trodden in their steps, have recast the coin, whose intrinsic value they had discovered, and have given it universal worth and currency, by stamping on it an image of themselves.

(Vol. xxxiii. p. 489.)

ANONYMOUS

1826. June. QUARTERLY REVIEW. ART. I. WIFFEN'S TRANSLATION OF TASSO.

[Cary's translation of Dante]

SOMEHOW or other, for reasons which it would be difficult to explain, the beautiful work of Fairfax, and that of Harrington,[1] fell into desuetude, and their matchless originals were taken up and *done into* English by that most contemptible of translators, Hoole. . . . In the meantime, some of the greatest geniuses of Italy had been entirely neglected, and Dante, Petrarch and Berni were without a translation. English literature, however, was destined to be refreshed with new streams from the fountain by which it had originally been fed. *Petrarch* had been pronounced to be untranslatable, and his rainbow-tints seemed to defy imitation; yet parts of him have been of late transferred into English verse with a care, delicacy, and success, which completely justify the boldness of the experiment.[2] . . . *Dante* was also most successfully undertaken by Mr. Carey,[3] and we have at last a complete version of the *Inferno*, *Purgatorio*, and *Paradiso;* a version which admirably preserves the austere character, the over-mastered feeling, the dignity and the majestic repose of the original. One drawback only there is from the admiration which we profess for this work—we cannot but regret that Mr. Carey should have chosen what Dr. Johnson has termed the most diffusive of all species of versification, as the representative of that which is among the most succinct. Every one acquainted with the *terza rima*, knows that in this metre, with the necessary exception of the conclusion, the sense as regularly closes with the triplet, as it does, in the elegiac measure of the Latins, with the pentameter. Nothing, therefore, can afford a stronger contrast to such a metre than blank verse,

[1] [Their respective translations of Tasso and Ariosto.]

[2] [The reference is to the privately printed translations of Barbarina, Lady Dacre (1768-1854).]

[3] [*Sic.*]

however judiciously it may be managed; and surely the dress of the original and that of the portrait should be similar, if they be not the same. . . . Now Mr. Carey's translation[1] is very good, but does not give so exact an idea of the original as it might. Dante marches over his ground with a sort of spectral pace; Mr. Carey moves vigorously and gravely, but he does not (as we would have him) tread in the exact steps of his predecessor, nor yet follow him quite fast enough. A phrase in the Italian poet should be the watchword of his translators—*Sie breve e arguto.*[2]

* * * *

The improvement of his native language is, next to giving a faithful version of his author, the best praise to which a translator can aspire. Nor does it require such poor qualifications to accomplish this, as is often vulgarly supposed. To do that well in which Spenser failed although Milton succeeded, is no ordinary achievement. But what are, it will be said, the rules for accomplishing this? We answer, a religious, but not superstitious, reverence, founded upon a thorough love and knowledge, of our own language; to which must be added such tact as shall prevent us from any involuntary violation of its character or spirit in our innovations. We will explain what we mean by citing a successful and unsuccessful attempt at the naturalization of a foreign word, which will moreover illustrate what we have said respecting Spenser and Milton. When the first introduced *spals* (spalle) into English, he imported what could never take root; but when the latter did the same by *imparadised,*[3] a word, by the bye, first coined by Dante,[4] he transplanted what promised to be a lasting ornament to our language.

(Vol. xxxiv. pp. 6-9, 14-5.)

ANONYMOUS

1826. Oct. WESTMINSTER REVIEW. NO. XII. ART. VIII. WIFFEN'S TASSO.

[Dante's simile of doves]

THE idea of doves is invariably connected with that of ardour, fidelity, and impatient desire of love. Propertius somewhere observes,

> Errat, qui finem vesani quaerit amoris,
> Verus amor nullum novit habere modum:
> Exemplo junctae tibi sint in amore columbae.

[1] [The reviewer quotes *Inf.* xx. 55-72, and Cary's version of the passage.]
[2] [*Purg.* xiii. 78.] [3] [*Par. Lost*, iv. 506.] [4] [*Par.* xxviii. 3.]

Francesca D'Arimino and her lover are wandering together amidst all the terrors of the infernal tempest,

Quali colombe dal desio chiamate.[1]

[Dante's self-restraint as an artist]

When the translator of Tasso, by following the path of long-continued experience, assisted by those talents which nature bountifully bestowed on him, shall have attained to more perfect knowledge of the same art, he will, perhaps, perceive that, in his case, it must exert itself in checking and regulating rather than in displaying the luxuries of poetical diction. The most free and enterprising genius[2] that ever encountered and surmounted obstacles, not only in his representations of human nature as it exists, but in creating and investing another and a higher with all the illusion of reality in his own ideal worlds, was endowed above all poets with the fortitude of sacrificing scattered beauties to the effect of the whole. On being allured by spectacles which filled his imagination with wonder, and burning to expand his description, he suddenly arrests his spirit in its wild career—'The bridle of my art bids me go no further'.
Piu non mi lascia ire il fren dell' arte'—Dante, *Purgat.* c. 33.[3]

(Vol. vi. pp. 440-1, 445.)

ANNA BROWNELL JAMESON

(1794-1860)

[Anna Brownell Jameson, daughter of Denis Brownell Murphy, a well-known miniature painter, was born in Dublin in 1794. Before her marriage (in 1825) to Robert Jameson (a barrister, who eventally became Speaker and Attorney-General of the Province of Toronto), she had been a governess, in which capacity she travelled in France and Italy. A journal kept during her Continental tour was published in 1826, under the title of the *Diary of an Ennuyée*. In 1829 she published the *Romance of Biography*, otherwise known as the *Loves of the Poets*. In this work, which contains numerous references to Dante, a chapter is devoted to Dante and Beatrice, from which extracts are given below. Mrs. Jameson displays considerable acquaintance with Dante's works, especially the *Vita Nuova*, from which she gives prose renderings of several of the poems. Besides the above, she published numerous other works, among which the best known are the charming *Characteristics of Women*, essays on Shakespeare's female characters (1832), and the valuable series of standard works on *Sacred and Legendary Art* (1848-52). She died at Ealing in 1860.]

[1] [*Inf.* v. 82.]
[2] [Dante.]
[3] [*Purg.* xxxiii. 141: 'Non mi lascia più ir lo fren dell' arte.']

1826. THE DIARY OF AN ENNUYÉE.

[Florence called by Dante the daughter of Rome]

FLORENCE, Nov. 8.—'La bellissima e famosissima figlia di Roma' as Dante calls Florence [1] in some relenting moment.

(Ed. 1838, p. 69.)

[Song from Dante in *Otello*]

Florence, Nov. 15.—Magnelli, the Grand Duke's Maestro di Cappella, the finest tenor in Italy, gave us last night the beautiful recitative which introduces Desdemona's song in Othello—

'Nessun maggior dolore,
Che ricordarsi del tempo felice
Nella miseria! [2]

(*Ibid.* pp. 81-2.)

1829. THE ROMANCE OF BIOGRAPHY; OR MEMOIRS OF WOMEN LOVED AND CELEBRATED BY POETS, FROM THE DAYS OF THE TROUBADOURS TO THE PRESENT AGE.

[Dante and Beatrice]

Had I taken chronology into due consideration, Dante ought to have preceded Petrarch, having been born some forty years before him,—but I forgot it. . . . Dante and his Beatrice are best exhibited in contrast to Petrarch and Laura. Petrarch was in his youth an amiable and accomplished courtier, whose ambition was to cultivate the arts, and please the fair. Dante early plunged into the factions which distracted his native city, was of a stern commanding temper, mingling study with action. Petrarch loved with all the vivacity of his temper; he took a pleasure in publishing, in exaggerating, in embellishing his passion in the eyes of the world. Dante, capable of strong and enthusiastic tenderness, and early concentrating all the affections of his heart on one object, sought no sympathy; and solemnly tells us of himself,—in contradistinction to those poets of his time who wrote of love from fashion or fancy, not from feeling,—that he wrote as love inspired, and as his heart dictated:

Io mi son un che, quando
Amore spira, noto, ed in quel modo
Ch' ei detta dentro, vo significando.

Purgatorio, c. 24.[3]

[1] [*Conv.* i. 3, ll. 21-2.] [2] [*Inf.* v. 121-3.] [3] [ll. 52-4.]

A coquette would have triumphed in such a captive as Petrarch; and in truth, Laura seems to have 'sounded him from the top to the bottom of his compass:'—a tender and impassioned woman would repose on such a heart as Dante's, even as his Beatrice did. Petrarch had a gay and captivating exterior; his complexion was fair, with sparkling blue eyes and a ready smile. . . . Dante, too, was in his youth eminently handsome, but in a style of beauty which was characteristic of his mind: his eyes, were large and intensely black, his nose aquiline, his complexion of a dark olive, his hair and beard very much curled, his step slow and measured, and the habitual expression of his countenance grave, with a tinge of melancholy abstraction. . . . When years of persecution and exile had added to the natural sternness of his countenance, the deep lines left by grief, and the brooding spirit of vengeance, he happened to be at Verona, where since the publication of the *Inferno*, he was well known. Passing one day by a portico, where several women were seated, one of them whispered, with a look of awe,—'Do you see that man? that is he who goes down to hell whenever he pleases, and brings us back tidings of the sinners below!'—'Ay, indeed!' replied her companion, 'very likely; see how his face is scarred with fire and brimstone, and blackened with smoke, and how his hair and beard have been singed and curled in the flames!'

Dante had not, however, this forbidding appearance when he won the young heart of Beatrice Portinari. They first met at a banquet given by her father, Folco de' Portinari, when Dante was only nine years old, and Beatrice a year younger. His childish attachment, as he tells us himself, commenced from that hour; it became a passion, which increased with his years, and did not perish even with its object. . . . In one of his canzoni, called 'il Ritratto' (the Portrait) Dante has left us a most minute and finished picture of his Beatrice, 'which,' says Mr. Carey, 'might well supply a painter with a far more exalted idea of female beauty, than he could form to himself from the celebrated Ode of Anacreon on a similar subject.' . . .

I will quote the following sonnet of Dante as a general picture of female loveliness, heightened by some tender touches of mental and moral beauty, such as never seem to have occurred to the debased imagination of the classic poets:

Negli occhi porta la mia Donna Amore, &c.[1]

Translation

'Love is throned in the eyes of my Beatrice! they ennoble every thing she looks upon! As she passes, men turn and gaze; and whomsoever she salutes, his heart trembles within him; he bows his head, the colour forsakes his cheek, and he sighs for his own un-

[1] [Mrs. Jameson here prints *Son.* xi from the *Vita Nuova*, § 21.]

worthiness. Pride and anger fly before her! Assist me, ladies, to do her honour! All sweet thoughts of humble love and good-will spring in the hearts of those who hear her speak, so that it is a blessedness first to behold her, and when she faintly and softly smiles—ah! then it passes all fancy, all expression, so wondrous is the miracle, and so gracious!'

The love of Dante for his Beatrice partook of the purity, tenderness, and elevated character of her who inspired it, and was also stamped with that stern and melancholy abstraction, that disposition to mysticism, which were such strong features in the character of her lover. . . . His love shakes his whole being like an earthquake; it beats in every pulse and artery; it has dwelt in his heart till it has become a part of his life, or rather his life itself. It borrows even the solemn language of Sacred Writ to express its intensity:

Nelle man vostre, o dolce donna mia!
Raccomando lo spirito che muore.

* * * *

Every tender emotion of Dante's feeling heart seems to have been called forth when Beatrice lost her excellent father. Folco Portinari died in 1289; and the description we have of the inconsolable grief of Beatrice and the sympathy of her young companions,—so poetically, so delicately touched by her lover,—impress us with a high idea both of her filial tenderness and the general amiability of her disposition, which rendered her thus beloved. In two of the poet's sonnets, we have, perhaps, one of the most beautiful groups ever presented in poetry. Dante meets a company of young Florentine ladies, who were returning from paying Beatrice a visit of condolence on the death of her father. Their altered and dejected looks, their downcast eyes, and cheeks 'colourless as marble,' make his heart tremble within him; he asks after Beatrice—'*our* gentle lady,' as he tenderly expresses it: the young girls raise their downcast eyes, and regard him with surprise. 'Art thou he,' they exclaim, 'who hast so often sung to us the praises of Beatrice? the voice, indeed, is his; but, oh! how changed the aspect! Thou weepest!—why shouldest *thou* weep?—thou hast not seen *her* tears;—leave *us* to weep and return to our home, refusing comfort; for we, indeed have heard her speak, and seen her dissolved in grief; so changed is her lovely face by sorrow, that to look upon her is enough to make one die at her feet for pity.'[1] . . .

In the *Vita Nuova* there is a fragment of a canzone, which breaks off at the end of the first strophe; and annexed to it is the following affecting note, originally in the handwriting of Dante:—

'I was engaged in the composition of this Canzone, and had completed only the above stanza, when it pleased the God of justice

[1] Sonnetto 13 (Poesie della Vita Nuova).

to call unto himself this gentlest of human beings; that she might be glorified under the auspices of that blessed Queen, the Virgin Maria, whose name was ever held in especial reverence by my sainted Beatrice.'[1] . . .

To the first Canzone, written after the death of Beatrice, Dante has prefixed a note, in which he tells us, that after he had long wept in silence the loss of her he loved, he thought to give utterance to his sorrow in words; and to compose a Canzone, in which he should write (weeping as he wrote), of the virtues of her who through much anguish had bowed his soul to the earth. . . One stanza of this Canzone is unequalled, I think, for a simplicity at once tender and sublime. The sentiment, or rather the meaning, in homely English phrase, would run thus:—

'Ascended is our Beatrice to the highest Heaven, to those realms where angels dwell in peace; and, you her fair companions, and Love and me, she has left, alas! behind. It was not the frost of winter chilled her, nor was it the heat of summer that withered her; it was the power of her virtue, her humility, and her truth, that ascending into Heaven, moved the Eternal Father to call her to Himself, seeing that this miserable life was not worthy of any so fair so excellent!'[2] . . .

Dante concludes the collection of his *Rime* (his miscellaneous poems on the subject of his love) with this remarkable note:—

'I beheld a marvellous vision, which has caused me to cease from writing in praise of my blessed Beatrice, until I can celebrate her more worthily; which that I may do, I devote my whole soul to study, as *she* knoweth well; in so much, that if it please the Great Disposer of all things to prolong my life for a few years upon this earth, I hope hereafter to sing of my Beatrice what never yet was said or sung of woman.'[3]

And in this transport of enthusiasm, Dante conceived the idea of his great poem, of which Beatrice was destined to be the heroine. . . .

* * * *

Now where, in the name of all truth and all feeling, were the heads, or rather the hearts, of those commentators, who could see nothing in the Beatrice thus beautifully pourtrayed, thus tenderly lamented, and thus sublimely commemorated, but a mere allegorical personage, the creation of a poet's fancy? Nothing can come of nothing; and it was no unreal or imaginary being who turned the course of Dante's ardent passions and active spirit, and burning enthusiasm, into one sweeping torrent of love and poetry, and gave to Italy and to the world the *Divina Commedia!*

(*The Love of Dante for Beatrice Portinari*, vol. i. pp. 105 ff.)

[1] [*Vita Nuova*, § 29, ll. 4-11.] [2] [*Canz.* iv. ll. 15-28.]
[3] [*Vita Nuova*, § 43, ll. 1-11.]

RICHARD RYAN

(1796-1849)

[Richard Ryan, born in 1796, was the son of a bookseller in Camden Town, whose business he seems to have followed. He was the author of various works of a miscellaneous character, including plays, songs, biography, etc. In 1826 he published, under the title of *Poetry and Poets*, a collection of anecdotes relating to poets, among which is one of the numerous stories about Dante. He died in 1849.]

1826. POETRY AND POETS: BEING A COLLECTION OF THE CHOICEST ANECDOTES RELATIVE TO THE POETS OF EVERY AGE AND NATION.

[Dante at the court of Can Grande]

DANTE.—This celebrated Italian poet being banished from his native city of Florence, obtained an asylum at Verona, and had for his patron, Can della Scalla, or the prince of that country. There were in the same Court several strolling players, gamesters, and other persons of that description, one of whom, distinguished for his ribaldry and buffoonery, was much caressed beyond the others. The Prince one day, when this man and Dante were both present, highly extolled the former, and, turning to the Poet, said, 'I wonder that this foolish fellow should have found out the secret of pleasing us all, and making himself admired, while you, who are a man of great sense, are in little esteem.' To which Dante freely replied, 'You would cease to wonder at this, if you knew how much conformity of character is the real source of friendship.' [1]

(Vol. ii. pp. 218-9.)

ANONYMOUS

1826. JANUS; OR, THE EDINBURGH LITERARY ALMANACK.[2]

[Dante and Milton]

THE mind of Dante was not formed for the muses only; it took share in the passions of the agitated times to which he belonged. . . . With fortunes confiscated, and long condemned to the exile in which he died, he looked to that Florence, from which he was estranged by persecuting hate, with the passionate

[1] [In vol. i. pp. 211-2, Ryan reprints from Spence's *Anecdotes* Dr. Cocchi's remarks upon Dante (see vol. i. pp. 219-20). In vol. iii. pp. 169-71, is given a slightly different version of the anecdote printed above, which was originally recorded by Michele Savonarola, grandfather of the famous Florentine preacher and reformer, Girolamo Savonarola—see Toynbee's *Life of Dante*, pp. 177-8 (ed. 1904).]

[2] [Only this one volume was published.]

feelings of an outcast son; and this temper, which should seem to have no part in the solemn incantations of the poet who sung of heaven, and purgatory, and hell, blends itself with the inspiration of his austere and lofty genius. He seems to have forsaken earth by the subject of his poem; but his terrestrial loves and hates accompany him whithersoever he aspires or descends, and that earth which he had left re-appears alike in Paradise and in the abysses of eternal punishment. It would not have been thought that one of the greatest works of poetical genius should be stamped throughout with the personal and perishing affections of a private man; in which the subject, the most vast and illimitable with which the powers of the human mind can contend, should be swallowed up in the expression of transitory and local passions: yet, by the extraordinary combination of powers in one mind, we find that the poetical ability which could produce a language almost out of darkness;—an imagination which could travel secure and unfaltering in the utmost heights and depths that can be opened to human thought;—a strong dark faith in the dreams of early superstition:—an intellect severe, sagacious, and searching;—and political and personal animosities, the most passionate, bitter, and unrelenting; and, on the other hand, affections the most warm, and gentle, and tender, may be all combined in one mind and in one work; imparting to it a character which nothing resembles, and which is at once august by its subject, and by the power of genius it displays, and fearful by the strong pictures of human passion and crime which he only could have drawn, who, with the same mind, could feed on the fears and wonders of imagination, and mix as an actor and sufferer in the stern and bitter realities of life.

The illustrious Poet of our own country, who has embraced in one poem the same vast subject, though with events which make it still vaster . . . shows how like passions may be divided, and similar (in some respects) elements of the mind held in separation. For he too took part in the political passions and troubles of his country; he too suffered, and the fierce animosities of personal life held strong possession of that mind, which, when following its genius, passed out from this world, and left the clouds and griefs of this 'dim spot,' to open up to itself and to us a world of feelings and beings remote in the greatest degree from all personal and transitory thoughts. . . . The work of Dante is over-run with personal feelings, and that of Milton is almost entirely pure from them. The result is, that the one is regarded as a production strange and anomalous, in which, though the extraordinary power of genius displayed by the author abashes and silences all censure, yet we feel that, in order to admire, we are obliged to forego all our ordinary principles of judgment; and that we look on the work in part only as a poem, and in part as the exhibition of a singular individual character, and as the historical record of the temper and even facts of the times. But that of Milton is the model of all that is great and awful in his art; a poem entirely sublime, into which we enter only to feel the utmost dilatation of all our faculties and powers; and are transported out of the narrowness and bonds of ordinary existence into worlds of pure power, glory, and beauty. In reading the poem of Dante there is often, almost always, a painful sense of the oppression which our strong human passions lay upon the great powers of our souls. In reading that of Milton, there is felt a sudden exemption from that bondage, an enlargement of the paths of the spirit, a wafting, a flight into the regions of its uncontrolled liberty and power.

(pp. 180-3.)

ANONYMOUS

[The anonymous author of this translation of the first canto of the *Inferno*, extracts from which are given below, has not been identified. The translation, which was issued in a pamphlet of 16 pages in 1832 (printed by Gilbert and Rivington),[1] is dated from Pisa, Dec. 29, 1826. With it are included a translation of Claudian's epigram on the old man who lived in the territory of Verona (dated, Hemstead, April 5, 1825), and of a strophe and antistrophe from the *Medea* of Euripides (dated, Cambridge, Sept. 1825).]

1826. AN ATTEMPT AT AN ENGLISH TRANSLATION, IN TERZA RIMA, OF THE FIRST CANTO OF DANTE'S INFERNO, &C. &C. BY A LATE SCHOLAR OF TRINITY COLLEGE, CAMBRIDGE.

IN the mid journey of my life I found
  My footsteps wandering midst a forest's shade,
  For the true path had vanished all around;
And all so thick the gloom that then arrayed
  The rugged wood, it baffles words to tell,
  E'en at the thought my memory stands dismayed.
Oh! 'twas a feel like bidding earth farewell!
  But other sights and scenes I must disclose,
  To sing the good that there my heart befell.
I cannot well say, how first on me rose
  The darksome forest; such the sleepy frost,
  That all my heart and soul and senses froze
Up to the hour when the right path I lost.

(vv. 1-12.)

[1] [A copy is in the British Museum.]

'Art thou that Virgil, from whose verse such deep,
Deep streams of poesy have flowed afar?'
I said, as modest shame began to creep
Across my downcast face—'Most gracious star
Of poetry's bright firmament below,
Oh! let the mighty love, the studious war
Of days, and nights, and years—the pallid brow
To win thy volume's treasures, to inhale
The breathings of thy soul, befriend me now!
If aught *my* verse, if aught *my* toil, avail,
And human hearts grow warm the while they read,
Thou art the guiding light (howe'er I fail),
The source, the author, and be thine the meed.
Behold the monster, from whose sight I fly;
Help me, I pray thee, in this hour of need,
For fainting dread comes o'er me, and I die!'

(vv. 79-90.)

ELIZABETH BARRETT BARRETT

(1809-1861)

[Elizabeth Barrett, eldest daughter of Edward Moulton, who afterwards took the name of Barrett, was born at Burn Hall, Durham, in 1809. She began to write poems at the age of eight, and published her first volume, the *Essay on Mind*, in 1826, when only seventeen, from which time she continued to write and publish prose and verse. At the age of fifteen she injured her spine by a fall, which obliged her to spend many years on her back. In 1845 she met Robert Browning, whom she married in the next year. Thenceforth the Brownings mainly resided in Italy, chiefly at Florence, until Mrs. Browning's death there in 1861. Her best-known poem, *Aurora Leigh*, was published in 1857. As an ardent lover of Italy Mrs. Browning was a devoted student of Dante, whose name is mentioned in her earliest published poem, and recurs frequently in her later works (but seldom before 1844). The most numerous and characteristic allusions occur in *Casa Guidi Windows*, published in 1851. Story, the American sculptor, records that 'Dante's grave profile' hung on the walls of the room in which Mrs. Browning usually sat in the Casa Guidi.]

1826. AN ESSAY ON MIND.

[Of intellectual poetry—'the sublime Dante']

I AM aware how often it has been asserted that poetry is not a proper vehicle for abstract ideas—how far the assertion may be correct, is with me a matter of doubt. We do not deem the imaginative incompatible with the philosophic, for the name of Bacon is on our lips; then why should we expel the argumentative from the limits of the poetic? If indeed we consider Poetry as Plato considered her, when he banished her from his republic; or as Newton, when he termed her 'a kind of ingenious nonsense;' or as Locke, when he pronounced that 'gaming and poetry went usually together;' or as Boileau, when he boasted of being acquainted with two arts equally useful to mankind—'writing verses and playing at skittles.'—we shall find no difficulty in assenting to this opinion. But while we behold in poetry, the inspiritings of political feeling, the 'monumentum aere perennius' of buried nations, we are loth to believe her unequal to the higher walks of intellect: when we behold the works of the great though erring Lucretius, the sublime Dante, the reasoning Pope,—when we hear Quintillian acknowledge the submission due from Philosophers to Poets, and Gibbon declare Homer to be 'the lawgiver, the theologian, the historian, and the philosopher of the ancients,' we are *unable* to believe it. Poetry is the enthusiasm of the understanding; and, as Milton finely expresses it, there is 'a high reason in her fancies.'

(*Preface*, v-vii.)

[Of the various dispositions of different minds—The themes of Dante and Petrarch exchanged]

Thou thing of light! that warm'st the breasts of men,
Breath'st from the lips, and tremblest from the pen!
Thou, form'd at once t' astonish, fire, beguile,—
With Bacon reason, and with Shakespeare smile!
The subtle cause, ethereal essence! say,
Why dust rules dust, and clay surpasses clay;
Why a like mass of atoms should combine
To form a Tully, and a Cataline?
Or why, with flesh perchance of equal weight,
One cheers a prize-fight, and one frees a state?
Why do not I the muse of Homer call,
Or why, indeed, did Homer sing at all?
Why wrote not Blackstone upon love's delusion,
Or Moore, a libel on the Constitution?
Why must the faithful page refuse to tell
That Dante, Laura sang, and Petrarch, Hell—
That Tom Paine argued in the throne's defence—
That Byron nonsense wrote, and Thurlow sense—
That Southey sigh'd with all a patriot's cares,
While Locke gave utterance to Hexameters!
Thou thing of light! instruct my pen to find
Th' unequal pow'rs, the various forms of Mind!

(*Book* i. ll. 19-40.)

1842. THE BOOK OF THE POETS.[1]

[Wordsworth's mention of the 'Sasso di Dante' at Florence]

Anxious to conclude our extracts . . . we have hesitated, as we turned the leaves of Mr. Wordsworth's volume, before many touching and beautiful poems, wise in their beauty—before the 'Grave of Burns,' for instance, and the 'Widow of Windermere,' and the 'Address to the Clouds,' and others beyond meaning—a certain sonnet[2] which discovers our poet sitting on the chair of Dante at Florence, tempting us for many reasons. . . .

(*Poetical Works of E. B. Browning*, ed. 1904, p. 657.)

1844. A VISION OF POETS.

['Dante stern and sweet']

Spenser drooped his dreaming head
(With languid sleep-smile you had said
From his own verse engenderèd)

On Ariosto's, till they ran
Their curls in one.—The Italian
Shot nimbler heat of bolder man

From his fine lids. And Dante stern
And sweet, whose spirit was an urn
For wine and milk poured out in turn.

(*Stanzas* cxvi-cxviii, *ibid.* p. 167.)

[Dante 'poor in mirth']

One dulled his eyeballs, as they ached
With Homer's forehead, though he lacked
An inch of any. And one racked

His lower lip with restless tooth,
As Pindar's rushing words forsooth
Were pent behind it. One, his smooth

Pink cheeks did rumple passionate,
Like Aeschylus—and tried to prate
On trolling tongue, of fate and fate.

[1] [Reprinted from *Athenæum*, Aug. 27, 1842—a review of Wordsworth's *Poems, Chiefly of Early and Late Years*, published in this year.]

[2] [For this sonnet, see above, pp. 4-5.]

One set her eyes like Sappho's—or
Any light woman's! one forbore
Like Dante, or any man as poor

In mirth, to let a smile undo
His hard-shut lips. And one that drew
Sour humours from his mother, blew

His sunken cheeks out to the size
Of most unnatural jollities,
Because Anacreon looked jest-wise.

(*Stanzas* ccviii-ccxiii, *ibid.* p. 170.)

KENELM HENRY DIGBY

(1800-1880)

[Kenelm Henry Digby, author of *The Broadstone of Honour*, born in 1800, was the youngest son of William Digby, Dean of Clonfert, a member of the Irish branch of the family of Lord Digby. He was educated at Trinity College, Cambridge, where he graduated in 1819. While at the University he made a special study of medieval antiquities and scholastic theology, with the result that at an early age he became a Roman Catholic. His subsequent life was spent chiefly in travel in Italy and other foreign countries, and in literary pursuits in London, where he died in 1880. Digby was a voluminous writer. His best-known works are 'that noble manual for gentlemen,' as Julius Hare called it, *The Broadstone of Honour* (first published anonymously in 1822, and afterwards, rewritten and greatly enlarged, in 4 vols. in 1826-7); and *Mores Catholici: or the Ages of Faith* (11 vols. 1831-42). In both of these works, and especially in the latter, Digby displays an intimate acquaintance with the *Divina Commedia*, which he read not in the original, but in Cary's translation. This translation, large portions of which he evidently knew almost by heart, is quoted two or three hundred times in *Mores Catholici*, in which work Digby acknowledges his great debt to Cary as the interpreter of Dante, 'the great poet of the ages of faith.' In his enumeration of the sources from which he drew his material, he names especially 'the verses of that great Christian poet of the middle ages, whose mind was so thoroughly imbued with the theology of the school, and with the sentiments that prevailed among all ranks of the people, and who is always so precise and accurate in his expressions of them, that wherever the peculiar prejudices of an unhappy political party do not break out, his sublime and wondrous creation may be received in one sense as a view of the intellectual condition of mankind during the period in which he lived; and here the genius of Cary had facilitated the task by supplying me with the thoughts already clothed in the English tongue as nearly as possible as they had been first conceived in the mind of the great master of mysterious song, who is assuredly not more admirable as a poet, than as a kind of divine instructor to repeat the eternal truths of revelation to the forgetful and thoughtless race of men.' (Bk. i. chap. 8, pp. 134-5, ed. 1841.) Digby was also acquainted with the *Vita Nuova*, a passage from which, translated (very inaccurately) by himself, he has inserted in the sixth book of the *Mores Catholici*.]

1826-7. THE BROAD STONE OF HONOUR: OR THE TRUE SENSE AND PRACTICE OF CHIVALRY.

[A matter-of-fact judgment of Dante]

THERE are men, and in some countries they form no small portion of society, who seem destitute of all spiritual elevation. . . . Speak to them of romance—they offer their vapid interpretations of a poetical story. . . . The account of Aeneas's descent into Hell should be omitted in a translation of the Aeneid 'as a tale manifestly forged, and not to be believed by any rational reader.' 'Dante's poem is in truth a satirical history of his own times.' King Arthur's round table is a symbol of the horrible mystery of iniquity. . . .

(*Godefridus*, § 7, pp. 29, 31, ed. 1829.)

[Dante's love for the old romances]

It is to be expected that some persons will ask upon what grounds the use of chivalrous romances can be reconciled with the introduction of history, philosophy, and religion, or, in other words, of reality and truth: and though the answering this enquiry fully might lead to an entire dissertation which, however interesting, would lead us too far beyond our prescribed limits, I cannot proceed without producing some apology. I pass over the mere literary objections of men like Landino, the commentator on Dante, who speaks of the 'fabulous and inelegant books of the round table.' . . . Nor need I seek to defend the chivalrous romances with the poems of Dante against the sweeping and immoral censures of Cornelius Agrippa,[1] whose professed object is to level all intellectual greatness. . . . We all have repeatedly heard that such reading has been condemned by holy persons as being at least injurious, if not absolutely opposed, to the interests of the spiritual life, a lesson awfully exemplified in the most sublime passage of the greatest Christian poet, where he sings of Francesca and the son of Rimini's proud lord, whose tale of surpassing woe, beginning with that day 'when for delight they read of Lancelot,' caused such bitter cries of sorrow, that heart-struck, he

> Through compassion fainting, seem'd not far
> From death, and like a corse fell to the ground.[2]

(*Ibid.* § 12, pp. 63-4.)

[Such poems as the vision of Dante intolerable to the school of Hume]

'The Crusades,' says David Hume, 'are a monument of human folly, and the whole religion of our ancestors was mistaken.' Be it so; with the Sophist of Glasgow I have no wish to argue. . . . but

[1] [See vol. i. p. 55.] [2] [*Inf.* v. 141-2 (Cary).]

thus much I will say even to these revilers, that if mankind had always been imbued with such a philosophy, we should never have possessed the paintings of Raphael, or the poetry of Tasso; we should have essays moral and metaphysical, not the visions of Dante and the Minstrel's Lay; our creed would be the maxims of selfishness, not the religion of chivalry and honour.

(*Tancredus*, § 4, pp. 43-4.)

[The threefold soul of man according to Dante]

The faithful on earth were joined in fellowship with the angels. Hence Dante says, 'As man is endowed with a triple soul, vegetable, animal, and rational, so he walks in a triple path. Inasmuch as he is vegetable, he seeks utility, in quo cum plantis communicat; inasmuch as he is animal, he seeks pleasure, in which he participates with brutes; inasmuch as he is rational, he seeks for honour, in which he is either alone, or is associated with the angels, vel angelicae naturae sociatur.' [1]

(*Ibid.* § 19, pp. 337-8.)

[Dante's avoidance of the name of Christ in the *Inferno*]

'Thou that abhorrest idols, dost thou commit sacrilege?' was the question often addressed to the leaders and supporters of the Revolution, and all who are conversant with the writings which gave rise to it, must be prepared to admit its propriety. What a contrast do they present to the spirit of men like Dante, who was afraid to write the blessed name of Jesus in that division of his poem where he describes the abyss of hell, lest the same page should contain words unsuitable to the infinite reverence which is due to it?

(*Morus*, p. 94.)

[Dante's alleged visit to Santa Croce di Fonte Avellana]

Dante is said to have composed many cantos of the Divine Vision in a monastery on the outskirts of Verona,[2] that of Santa Croce di fonte Avellana, where strangers are still shown his apartment. And what son of chivalry can enter a religious house, and not exult in a blessed institution which administered relief and peace to the gentle and heroic Tasso? In our time poets are pleased to represent monasteries as the abode of everything wicked and base and contemptible.

(*Ibid.* p. 235.)

[1] *De Vulg. Eloquent.* ii. 2 [from Cary's note on *Purg.* xxvi. 120].
[2] [Not near Verona, but near Gubbio in Umbria.]

[Dante's respect for the arbitrament of the duel]

Dante maintained the justice of the Romans' claim to empire, on the ground of its having been given to them in duel, when the Horatii and Curiatii fought, and afterwards in the wars with the Sabines and Samnites.[1] Hence he seems to have deemed high qualities necessary for those who engage in such combats: 'Scilicet, ut non odio, non amore, sed solo justitiae zelo, de communi assensu agonistae seu duelliones palaestram ingrediantur.'[2]

(*Orlandus*, ed. 1876, § 8, vol. i. p. 189.)

['The swan-like tones of Dante']

The night before Socrates received Plato among his disciples, he saw in a dream a swan, which flew towards him, and rested in his bosom, and the monastic schools of Paris and of Oxford might have caught amidst the responses of a theological student the swan-like tones of Dante.[3]

(*Ibid.* § 22, vol. ii. p. 225.)

[Dante's simile of the cranes]

Agesilaus had checked those who extolled the happiness of the King of Persia. 'Have patience,' he said, 'for even King Priam was not unfortunate at his age.' Such were the views of the philosophers respecting life, nor did the race of men pass before the poet's mind in less mournful semblance.

As cranes,
Chanting their dolorous notes, traverse the sky,
Stretched out in long array; so I beheld
Spirits, who came loud wailing, hurried on
By their dire doom.[4]

(*Ibid.* § 23, vol. ii. p. 363.)

1831-42. MORES CATHOLICI: OR AGES OF FAITH.

[The gloom of modern minds—Dante's exhortation]

What is it which renders the minds of many of the moderns, among whom assuredly is many a soul of mighty worth, so gloomy and apprehensive; why do they appear at times so lonely and disconsolate, amidst the wastes of their interminable speculations, afflicted like those spirits seen by Dante, who lived 'desiring without hope,'[5] . . . if it be not that the magnificent chain of Christian

[1] *De Monarchia*, lib. ii. [2] *Ibid.*

[3] He studied theology at both these places: 'dicebatur magnus theologus.'

[4] Dante, *Hell* v. [46-9 (Cary)—see Digby's reference to this passage in his *Mores Catholici* (below, p. 468)].

[5] [*Inf.* iv. 42 (Cary).]

history and ecclesiastical tradition has been broken to them. . . . Such men are taught to believe that faith was lost in the middle ages, and that they are the best judges of what should be the form and course of a Christian life. Whereas, other men, by merely turning to the old Christians, are filled with a desire to follow them.

And their most righteous customs make them scorn
All creeds besides.[1]

Then they hear themselves addressed as if by the poet of Christians:—

Why dost thou not turn
Unto the beautiful garden, blossoming
Beneath the rays of Christ? Here is the rose
Wherein the Word divine was made incarnate,
And here the lilies, by whose odour known
The way of life was followed.[2]

(Ed. 1841, vol. i. Bk. i. Chap. i. pp. 10-11.)

[Crowland Abbey—Dante's description of dawn]

Lo, yonder are the shattered arches of some abbey, on a river's bank, more lonesome than the roads that traverse desert wilds. It is Crowland, and at that calm and solemn hour

When near the dawn, the swallow her sad lay,
Rememb'ring haply ancient grief, renews;
When our minds, more wand'rers from the flesh,
And less by thought restrain'd, are, as 'twere, full
Of holy divination.[3]

You approach and kneel upon the spot, and the long deserted walls of the ruined sanctuary wonder at the pious stranger, who seems to bear alone, through a benighted world, the torch of faith. Where is now that devout assembly for the early sacrifice; where that rich and varied order, the gorgeous vestments, and the bright gems, and all

The beauteous garniture of altars on a festal time?[4]

. . . We may not be able to frequent the assemblies of the holy people who worship in vast cathedrals, and repeat with innumerable voices the solemn hymn which marks the yearly return of some most holy time, but we can walk alone in the woods and sing the *Stabat Mater*, while the nightingale will lend her long and plaintive note to deepen and prolong the tones of that sweet and melancholy strain, and then our tears will fall upon the wild flowers, and we shall feel in communion with the holy dead; with

[1] [*Purg.* xxii. 86-7 (Cary, adapted).]
[2] *Hell*, xxiii. [corr. *Par.* xxiii. 71-5 (Cary)].
[3] Dante. *Purg.* ix. [13-8 (Cary)].
[4] *Ibid.* [not Dante].

those who so oft had sung it, sad and sighing, like the Beatrice of Dante, in such a mood 'that Mary, as she stood beside the cross, was scarce more changed.' [1]

(Vol. i. Bk. i. Chap. i. pp. 13-15.)

['Mirth' in Dante]

Were examples to be produced of the gaiety of men in these ages of faith, so innocent and from the heart, there are formal pedants who would turn away in disdain; yet even the most refined taste need not prescribe silence on this head, for Virgil, in his heroic rhapsody, introduces the ludicrous misadventure of Menoetes and the laughter of the spectators, yet without loss of dignity and grace, and real piety would assuredly take no offence. When Dante, who well understood its spirit, enters into conversation with Cacciaguida, upon subjects which had no connection with what is sacred, he only intimates the change by saying, that Beatrice, who represented heavenly wisdom, stood at a little distance,—

And Beatrice, that a little space
Was sever'd, smiled.[2]

Our ancestors seem to have delighted in contrasts, in order to relieve. or, perhaps, rather to increase and deepen the solemnity of the august and awful objects with which they loved to be surrounded, . . . There was with them, as with the spirits which Dante saw in Paradise, 'mirth,' or as it is expressed in the XXth Canto, 'gamesome mirth,' [3] not for the fault, which on these occasions did not come to mind, 'but for the virtue, whose over-ruling sway and providence had wrought thus quaintly.' [4]

(Vol. i. Bk. i. Chap. 8, pp. 119-20.)

[The manners of Dante]

Dante evinces noble humility, when, on being questioned by Guido del Duca, he modestly declines giving his name:

To tell ye who I am were words mis-spent,
For yet my name scarce sounds on rumour's lips.[5]

To the manners of Dante, in this respect, Philip Villani bears a beautiful testimony, where he says, that 'if it had not been for the courtesy which he always evinced, his countenance would have worn a melancholy tone.' How admirable is that trait of a delicate and courteous heart when he beholds in purgatory the wretched souls of the envious, and, being himself invisible, scruples to advance.

[1] *Purg.* xxxiii. [5-6 (Cary)].
[2] *Paradise*, xvi. [13 (Cary)].
[3] [*Par.* xx. 117, according to Cary's rendering of *gioco.*]
[4] Canto ix. [103-5 (Cary)].
[5] *Purg.* xiv. [20-1 (Cary)].

It were a wrong, methought, to pass and look
On others, yet myself the while unseen.
To my sage counsel, therefore, did I turn.
He knew the meaning of the mute appeal,
Nor waited for my questioning, but said,
Speak, and be brief, be subtile in thy words.[1]

(Vol. i. Bk. ii. Chap. i. p. 152.)

[The Forest of Ravenna—Dante's and Dryden's references]

In Florence is the house of Michael Angelo, in which everything remains as if he had walked out but yesterday; and there you may gaze upon the seat[2] of the awful Dante hard by the dome which he so dearly loved. . . . Who has not heard of that sombre forest of pines which conceals Ravenna from the sea, like a funeral veil thrown by nature over the ruins of the fallen city; a forest celebrated in the annals of history; wonderful among the scenes of nature; dear to poets since it was sung by Dante and by Dryden![3] I first beheld it on a summer's evening. . . . I shall never forget the feeling with which I beheld it, and gazed upon its vast and solemn line, which was only broken at intervals by the broad top of some more elevated stem, which rose above the horizon. A pale moon had just risen over it in a blue heaven, but towards the west a deep range of clouds gave index of a storm. At the same moment a vast flight of cranes traversed the sky, coming from the Adriatic, and reminded me of a sublime passage, in which Dante describes their clamorous course,[4] which I repeated with an additional degree of interest, as I returned to the ancient city.

(Vol. i. Bk. iii. Chap. i. pp. 353-4.)

[The *Divina Commedia* and its commentators]

The applause with which the divine comedy of Dante was received at the time, is attested by the fact of pulpits having been erected in many cities, from which it was expounded. Boccaccio was employed for that purpose by the Florentine republic: to him succeeded in the same office Antonio Padovano and Philip Villani. In Bologna, Benvenuto of Imola, became a public lecturer upon it in the year 1375. In Pisa, Francesco of Bartolo da Buti gave a similar course in the year 1386. The celebrated Giovanbatista Gelli, from being a shoemaker in the streets of Florence, became one of the greatest writers of Tuscany, through the intense admira-

[1] *Purg.* xiii. [73-8 (Cary)].
[2] [The so-called 'Sasso di Dante.']
[3] [In *Theodore and Honoria.*]
[4] [*Inf.* v. 46-9. Digby quotes the passage, in Cary's translation, in the *Broadstone of Honour* (see above, p. 465).]

tion which he conceived for the Divine Comedy. He used to say, that after being born a Christian, he knew no greater happiness than to have been born in the country of Dante. Yet when that immortal poem first appeared, there was nothing new or singular in its design, which was but a development of the deepest and loftiest thoughts that had long moved indistinctly through the minds of men, perpetuated by the tradition of many visions.

(Vol. ii. Bk. iii. Chap. 4, p. 38.)

[Dante's simile of the clock]

To the night of the middle ages belonged many solemn and poetic things, of which the trace only remains, as in some towns of England, where, at particular seasons of the year, during the night, one hears a small bell tolled a certain number of times, and then, in a mournful tone, some rude verses chaunted, which had been substituted, no doubt, for the ancient invitation to pray for the dead at that hour, a devotion to which indulgences were attached. In Italy during the octave at All Souls, the bell for the dead tolls the whole night long, or at least for a considerable space about midnight. . . . On arriving in Italy the traveller is soon reminded of the beautiful similitude which Dante draws from the tones that sanctify a Catholic night:

As clock, that calleth up the spouse of God
To win her bridegroom's love at matin's hour,
Each part of other fitly drawn and urg'd,
Sends out a tinkling sound, of note so sweet,
Affection springs in well-disposed breast.[1]

(Vol. ii. Bk. v. Chap. 2, p. 361.)

[Dante's theory of government]

In the second age St. Irenaeus wrote against the Gnostics his book on the unity of the principle of the world—De Monarchia. Such is again the title of Dante's work, on the unity of the social world. A French historian[2] adds, 'that his book is extravagant, but that its formula is peace, as the condition of development, peace under one sovereign.' . . . Dante, like Vincent of Beauvais, would have attached the organisation of Christian Europe to the traditions of the ancient Roman Empire, in the establishment of which he traced the designs of Providence, providing for the good of men. Peace is the great object, in his theory of government; which indeed explains all those axioms of the middle ages respecting the monarch being the minister of all.[3] These ideas of the temporal

[1] *Parad.* x. [139-44 (Cary)].
[2] Michelet, Hist. de France, iii. 59.
[3] Dante, *de Monarchia*, ii.

society entered even into his mystic visions, as when he saw the command to love justice written in characters of fire, till the letter M alone remained in a crown of glory, as the initial of monarchy, which was then superseded by an eagle, as an emblem of the holy Roman Empire.[1]

(Ed. 1839, Bk. ix. Chap. 7, p. 225.)

[Farewell to the Reader—Dante's 'Banquet']

Thus, reader, have we surveyed the ages which were influenced by the belief and manners of that class of men of whom the ancient writers say, that they were in faith and action Catholic, 'fide et actu Catholicus,'—ages whose philosophy was sung by Dante, whose practices of life by Shakspeare, whose faith produced 'a world all sincere, a believing world.' . . . Reader, I will say with Dante,

Lo! I have set before thee; for thyself feed now.[2]

Feed, and reserve for the hungry some morsels from so high a table; for those you leave behind have vulgar, often bestial food; and you who know how wretchedly they fare, and who have tasted the sweets of this banquet, composed of such varied and such precious things, should learn pity.[3]

(Ed. 1842, Bk. xi. Chap. 13, pp. 452, 455.)

LORD HOLLAND

(1773-1840)

[Henry Richard Vassall Fox, third Lord Holland, only son of the second Baron and nephew of Charles James Fox, was born in 1773, and succeeded to the title in 1774. He was educated at Eton and Christ Church, Oxford. After spending several years on the Continent, during part of which time he resided at Florence, in 1796 he took his seat in the House of Lords, where he soon became the recognised spokesman of the Whigs. He was Lord Privy Seal in Lord Grenville's ministry of 'All the Talents,' 1806-7; and Chancellor of the Duchy of Lancaster under Lord Grey and Lord Melbourne (with brief intervals) from 1830 till his death in 1840. Lord Holland was a good classic, and an accomplished Spanish and Italian scholar. In addition to his political writings, he published (anonymously) an *Account of the Lives and Writings of Lope de Vega* (1806), and a metrical version of the seventh satire of Ariosto, which was printed in vol. v. of W. S. Rose's translation of *Orlando Furioso* (1827). He was a student of Dante as appears from a note appended to his translation from Ariosto, as well as from a letter written (c. 1836) to Edward Shannon, the author of an incomplete translation of the *Divina Commedia* (see below, p. 611).]

[1] [*Par.* xviii. 91-108.]
[2] *Parad.* x. [25 (Cary)].
[3] *Convito* i. [1, ll. 51 ff.].

1827. TRANSLATION OF THE SEVENTH SATIRE OF ARIOSTO.[1]

[Dante's 'triplet and alternate rhyme']

THE metre of the Satires of Ariosto adds to the embarrassment of the Englishman who engages in the translation of them. It is the triplet and alternate rhyme like that in which Dante composed his immortal work. Such a metre is not only unusual in English, but is singularly ill-adapted in our language to convey that apparent carelessness of style and real delicacy of thought which constitute the charm of the original. A casual remark to this effect led in fact to the present attempt. The translator had been asked his opinion as to the metre best suited to an English version of Ariosto's Satires. After acknowledging the impossibility of moulding English triplets with alternate rhymes to any such purpose . . . he ventured to pronounce judgment in favour of the ten syllable couplet.

Seventh Satire of Ariosto

Content, then, near my usual haunts to stay,
Who moves me tears me from myself away.
Not ease, not wealth, not all that Heav'n can give,
Could now persuade me far from thence to live.
E'en here, but that I sometimes fidget home,
And take a look at old Ferrara's dome,
And the bronze statues that our square adorn,
The distance would have killed me, or have worn
To skin and bone, a lean and famished wretch,
Like Dante's meagre ghosts,[2] that strive the fruit to catch.

(ll. 144-53.)

ANONYMOUS

1827. June. QUARTERLY REVIEW. ART. II. TODD'S EDITION OF MILTON.[3]

[Milton and Dante[4]]

WHEREVER the Reformation has extended, poetry in general, and sacred poetry in particular, has assumed a new character. It has become more sublime and less picturesque, more philosophical and less popular, more argumenta-

[1] [Printed by W. S. Rose in vol. v. pp. 303 ff. of his translation of Ariosto's *Orlando Furioso*.]

[2] An allusion to a passage in the twenty-fourth Canto of the *Purgatorio*, where the ghosts of gluttons are represented in a state of hunger, catching, like Tantalus, at the apples of a tree, which seems within their reach, but is removed beyond it whenever they stretch out their hands.

[3] [See vol. i. pp. 587 ff.]

[4] [The anonymous writer of this review gives an interesting rendering of two passages from the *Divina Commedia* into Spenserian stanzas—see below, pp. 474-6.]

tive and less descriptive. And here, we conceive, is to be found the true cause of the remarkable difference which subsists between two poems written on somewhat similar subjects, and by authors of a somewhat similar taste—the 'Divina Commedia' and the 'Paradise Lost.' Dante had in him much of Milton—more of him than a cursory perusal of his writings would discover, for the direct coincidences between them are not numerous. We believe that Milton might be more frequently traced to Tasso and Ariosto than to Dante, though, in spirit, he had not much in common with either of them—with the former scarcely anything. It is probable, indeed, that Dante was naturally more of an Epicurean than our great poet, yet it was by the influence of Divine Wisdom, (if Beatrice is to be considered in that light, which is questionable,) that he was preserved or rescued from the thraldom of the flesh, an influence to which the puritan ascribed the same practical and important consequences—(*Purg.* xxx.). Both had a strong taste for satire, and were not infrequently content to sacrifice poetry and propriety to the inordinate and unseasonable indulgence of it.—Both were remarkable for their love of political liberty, which drove them into active opposition to the governments under which they lived; nor was Dante less alive than Milton himself to the abuses of the church, or more temperate in the language with which he exposed them. . . . Dante does not confine himself to expressions of regret for the fatal gift of Constantine: he attacks the Pope as an unclean thing, chewing, indeed, the cud, but not having the cleft-hoof,[1] and reprobates the 'woman that sits upon the scarlet-coloured beast, and plays the wanton to the princes of the nations,' with the indignation of a soldier of Cromwell.[2] But for all this, the rites and ceremonies of his gorgeous church had taken fast hold of him, and in spite of his inclination for an ideal world—(which may often be traced both in the choice of his subject and in his treatment of it, and which, had he lived in Milton's age and country, would have made itself more manifest;) in spite of a fondness for mysticism and theological speculation such as the Schoolmen taught him—in spite of a rage for the metaphysics of his day, in which he buries (especially in his 'Paradise') both himself and his reader beyond redemption—in spite of all this, the dramatic character of his church has made itself felt on his susceptible imagination, and the disposition of that church to embody every religious conception in some corporeal form had nurtured in him (that which he had not by nature) a taste for poetical materialism. Accordingly, the 'Divina Commedia' is a Catholic poem, the 'Paradise Lost' a Protestant, almost a puritan poem throughout. . . . 'Paradise Lost' is a poem which a painter can scarcely touch: the 'Divina

[1] *Purg.* xvi. [2] *Purg.* xxxii.

Commedia' teems with subjects which challenge the bold brush and substantial colours of a mortal man: the one cannot be translated into bodily parts—much of the other may. There is that difference between them which subsists between the Tempest and Coriolanus, —both noble productions of the mind, but one losing in representation on the stage as much as the other gains. Milton's similes always exalt his subject, but do not illustrate: Dante's illustrate, but do not always exalt. When the spirits in council applaud, it is 'as the sound of waters deep'—when they rise, 'their rising is as thunder heard remote'—when they pursue their sports, it is 'as when armies rush to battle in the clouds.' On the other hand, when the robber is dissolved into ashes by the sting of a serpent, he revives astonished like a man from epilepsy (*Infern.* xxiv.). When Beatrice casts upon Dante a look of pity for his ignorance, it is as when a mother gazes upon her crazy offspring (*Par.* i.). When the halo of glory envelops the beatified spirits of the moon, it is like the ball which encloses the silk-worm (*Par.* viii.). When Dante and his companion shoot up into the second heaven, the immortal inhabitants congregate around them like fishes about a bait (*Par.* v.). Milton delights in abstract terms, far more than his illustrious forerunner in the paths of Hell and Paradise. It is not the round shield that hangs upon the shoulders of Satan, but 'its *broad circumference.*' The swan does not row her proud body but 'rows her *state* with oary feet.' . . . Milton's descriptions, again, are broad, general, in the mass—Dante's sharp, dramatic, and touched from the life. The covetous spirit in Paradise Lost admires—

> 'The riches of heaven's pavement, trodden gold.'[1]

In the Inferno, he lies with his face upon the earth, and exclaims—

> 'Adhesit pavimento anima mea.'[2]

Milton astonishes, but does not interest: we have too little in common with him or his. His subject does not allow him to be much conversant with human passions, for into Paradise human passions had not entered. We listen to the speeches of his mortal and immortal agents, as to the words of superior beings whom we may fear and reverence, but—not love. Dante, on the contrary, is perpetually striking a note, by which all our sympathies are awakened: it is one of his characteristic charms, that he contrives to introduce man, and the feelings of man, into all his scenes, animate or inanimate. How exquisite is his picture of evening!—we know not how to translate it—indeed Gray knew not how, for he tried the last lines.[3]

[1] [*Par. Lost*, i. 682.]

[2] [*Purg.* xix. 73.]

[3] [In the *Elegy*—see vol. i. p. 234.]

Era già l' ora che volge 'l disio
  A' naviganti, e 'ntenerisce 'l cuore
  Lo dì, ch' han detto a' dolci amici, A Dio:
E che lo nuovo peregrin d' amore
  Punge, se ode squilla di lontano,
  Che paja 'l giorno pianger, che si muore.

Purg. viii.

Who would exchange this touching thought, which must come home to the heart of every man, (especially if his steps have ever led him to a foreign land,) for the most faithful representation of twilight, Hesperus, and the nightingale?

We have said that Dante not unfrequently writes in Milton's vein, and, laying aside his materialism, assumes a lofty indistinctness, which gives abundant scope to the fancy of his readers. Thus, when Virgil inquires his way from the Souls of the Proud, an answer reaches him like that from the Spirit of Job: there comes a voice, but he can discern no form from which it comes. When the Spirits of the Envious fly rapidly past the two poets, they hear the rustle of their wings and their dolorous cry, till it dies in the distance; but the shades themselves are invisible. Of the same kind is his picture of the approach of an angel with a boat freighted with souls for Purgatory, a mountain-island, according to Dante, on the opposite hemisphere.

  Meanwhile we tarried near the rippling tide
  As men that muse upon their destined way,
  Who move in thought, though still their limbs abide—
  When lo! as sometimes Mars, with fiery ray,
  Gleams through the grosser air at dawn of day,
  From forth the western ocean—such the sight,
  (Strongly my memory can that hour portray,)
  As onward o'er the waters rushed a light
In speed surpassing far the eagle's nimblest flight.

  Thence, for a little space, I turn mine eye,
  Bent through my guide that mystery to explore,
  And look I once again, and now espy
  The object larger, brighter than before—
  Somewhat of white on either side it bore,
  But what I knew not—shapeless all it seemed,
  And issuing by degrees; and somewhat lower,
  A like appearance indistinctly gleamed,
Till plain, at length, confessed an angel's pinions streamed.

Purg. ii. [10-26].

We may be forgiven for citing one passage more of the same character; for we do not think that credit has been always given to Dante for possessing the faculty of filling the mind by one ample undetailed conception. Access to the city of Dis, where the heretics receive their reward, is denied to Dante and Virgil by the refractory gate-keepers: they pause awhile, well assured that the Almighty will soon despatch his swift angel to open for them a way. His advent is thus described.

And now came up along that turbid tide
A crashing uproar pregnant with dismay:
Trembled thereat the shores on either side,
No less than when the whirlwind tears his way,
Invited where the sultry vapours play,
To fill the void impetuous. At one swoop
It storms the wood—nor brooks it there delay;
Before its dusty vanguard proud trees stoop
Branchless and bloomless—flies each herd and shepherd troop.

My eyes unhooding—'Now,' quoth he, 'thy nerve
Of vision stretch along yon ancient lake
Mantling with yeasty foam—and well observe
Where chief the dusky vapour throngs opaque'—
As scud the frogs at sight of hostile snake,
And hie them all for safety to the shore,—
So did I mark those abject spirits quake,
And haste their flight by thousands: one before
Who crossed with foot unstained the Stygian torrent o'er—

And he, his left hand waving to and fro,
Cleaved from before his face that murky sky,
Unwearied but for this—and now I know
In him heaven's sovereign messenger was nigh.
Then turn I to my guide—his eloquent eye
Bade me be still, and lowly to the plain
Bow, as the spirit immortal passed me by—
He toward the gate, ah! in what huge disdain,
Advanced, and with his wand he smote and oped amain—

'Outcasts of heaven! O race accursed!' he cries,
While yet his steps on that dread threshold stand,
What hardihood is this? What bold emprize
Dares ye to kick against his high command
Whose word is steadfast—whose Almighty hand

Can vex your senses with a tenfold hell?
Have ye for this your mastiff's sufferings scanned,
Whose chain-worn throat and muzzle still may tell,
Whose fate ordains her law, 'tis bootless to rebel!'

He said—and back that noisome path pursued,
Nor word to us he spake—but seemed like one
Whose thoughts on other, deeper subjects brood,
Than care of ought his eyes might light upon.

Infern. ix. [64-103].

There are many other passages in this beautiful poet of a similar class, which justify us, we conceive, in our assertion, that the general *style* of his poetry was the result of the circumstances in which he was placed, rather than of the temper with which he was born. Though Milton had been both an Italian, and a Catholic, it may be doubted whether he would have been as graphic as Dante—but had Dante been an Englishman, and a Protestant, it is not improbable that he would have been as sublime as Milton.

In the foregoing passage will be seen some of that learning which Dante is so fond of producing, and so frequently misapplies. His gates of purgatory, on being opened, grate like the doors of the Roman treasury when Caesar entered and plundered it.[1] The indolent are punished, not only like the Israelites, who were cut off in the wilderness, and did not live to see the promised land; but, like the Trojans, who deserted Aeneas in Sicily, and thereby had no share in the glory of the foundation of Rome. Statius relates the primary cause of his conversion to have been the reading of Virgil's Pollio;[2] and, in the true spirit of those times, when Christianity and Paganism were almost confounded, we hear of *Jupiter* having been crucified for the children of men.[3] Often, indeed, he is more happy; but in general his mixture of the sacred and profane argues his participation in that depravity of taste, which has not been thoroughly corrected, even in our country, till very recent times; and the prodigality with which he illustrates his subject, by reference to Roman history, and occasionally to that of Greece, (which he obtained at second-hand,) savours, to us, of the crude learning of a school theme. In the management of his scholarship, as, indeed, in the measure of it, Milton far surpassed him.

(Vol. xxxvi. pp. 49-54.)

[1] [*Purg.* ix. 133-8.] [2] [*Purg.* xxii. 67 ff.]
[3] [*Purg.* vi. 118-9, where Dante speaks of God as 'Sommo Giove,' thinking more probably of Jehovah than of Jupiter.]

ANONYMOUS

1827. Oct. QUARTERLY REVIEW. ART. IV. SCROPE'S GEOLOGY OF CENTRAL FRANCE.

[The geologist likened to Dante on his journey through Hell]

THE geologist must become intimately acquainted with the wreck of matter treasured up in the ancient strata, and must study anew the living works of nature, interpreting the phenomena of former ages by rigidly examining and comparing with them the results of existing causes, before he can hope that his students will confide themselves to his guidance, as Dante in his sublime vision followed the footsteps of his master, and beheld, with mingled admiration and fear, in the subterranean circles environing the deep abyss, the shades of beings who once walked the surface in the light of day, and who still, changed as they were, and unconscious of the present, could draw the veil from the mysteries of the future, and recal from oblivion the secrets of the past.

(Vol. xxxvi. p. 473.)

CHARLES STRONG

(1784-1864)

[Charles Strong was born at Tiverton in 1784. In 1801 he was elected to a scholarship at Wadham College, Oxford, of which he became Fellow in 1810. In 1811 he was appointed to the Crown living of Broughton Gifford, Wilts, which he held until 1848. He died at Dawlish in 1864. In 1827 Strong published anonymously *Specimens of Sonnets from the most celebrated Italian Poets; with Translations*, in which is included a verse translation of one of the sonnets in the *Vita Nuova*. The volume is dedicated to the well-known Italian scholar, T. J. Mathias.[1]]

1827. SPECIMENS OF SONNETS FROM THE MOST CELEBRATED ITALIAN POETS; WITH TRANSLATIONS.

Dante Alighieri

"DEH, pellegrini, che pensosi andate. . . ."[2]

Say, pilgrims, ye that onward journey slow,
Musing, perchance, on things remote and dear,
From such far distant people come ye here,
As from your outward guise ye seem to show?

[1] [See vol. i. pp. 556 ff.]
[2] [Son. xxiv. from the *Vita Nuova*, § 41. The Italian is printed on the opposite page to the translation.]

Why through the mourning city straightway go,
Your cheeks unmoistened with a single tear;
All heedless of her sorrow ye appear,
Like those who never heard her tale of woe.
If ye but stay with wish to hear it told,
The sighs that rend my breast assure me this,
That ye would sorely weep ere ye withdrew;
She hath for ever lost her Beatrice—
And the discourse that one of her might hold,
Would even strangers' eyes with tears bedew.

(p. 3.)

AUGUSTUS WILLIAM HARE AND JULIUS CHARLES HARE

(1792-1834) (1795-1855)

[Augustus William and Julius Charles Hare, authors of *Guesses at Truth, by Two Brothers*, were the second and third sons of Francis Hare-Naylor, the intimate friend of Fox, and cousin by marriage of Georgiana, Duchess of Devonshire. Augustus, who was born at Rome in 1792, was educated at Winchester and New College, Oxford, where he became tutor in 1818. In 1825 he was ordained, and in 1829 he accepted the College living of Alton Barnes, Wilts, which he held until his death at Rome in 1834. Julius, born near Vicenza in 1795, was educated at Charterhouse, and Trinity College, Cambridge. He was elected Fellow of Trinity in 1818, and was appointed classical lecturer in 1822. He was ordained in 1826, and in 1832 took the family living of Hurstmonceaux, Sussex, where he died in 1855, having been Archdeacon of Lewes since 1840. The famous joint production of the two brothers, *Guesses at Truth*, was originally published in 1827. It contains sundry references to the *Divina Commedia*, with which the authors, both of them born in Italy, were doubtless well acquainted.]

1827. GUESSES AT TRUTH. BY TWO BROTHERS.

[Shakespeare and Dante intensifiers of mental vision]

BOOKS, as Dryden has aptly termed them, are spectacles to read Nature. Eschylus and Aristotle, Shakspeare and Bacon, are the priests who preach and expound the mysteries of man and the universe. They teach us to understand and feel what we see, to decipher and syllable the hieroglyphics of the senses. Do you not, since you have read Wordsworth, feel a fresh and more thoughtful delight, whenever you hear a cuckoo, whenever you see a daisy, whenever you play with a child? Have not Thucydides and Machiavel aided you in discovering the tides of feeling and the currents of passion by which events are borne along the ocean of Time? Can you not discern something more in man, now that you look at him with eyes purged and unscaled by gazing upon Shakspeare and Dante? From these terrestrial and celestial globes we learn the configuration of the earth and of the heavens.

(1st Series, ed. 1838, pp. 42-3.)

[Homer and Dante, the two fathers of poetry]

We from the first find a far greater body of reflective thought in modern poetry than in the ancient. Dante is not, what Homer was, the father of poetry springing in the freshness and simplicity of childhood out of the arms of mother earth: he is rather, like Noah, the father of a second poetical world, to whom he pours forth his prophetic song, fraught with the wisdom and the experience of the old world.

(1st Series, ed. 1838, p. 56.)

[Contrast between Homer and Dante]

While with the Greeks the unseen world was the world of shadows, in the great works of modern times there is a more or less conscious feeling that the outward world of the eye is the world of shadows, that the tangled web of life is to be swept away, and that the invisible world is the only abode of true living realities. How strongly is this illustrated by the contrast between the two great works which stand at the head of ancient and Christian literature, the Homeric poems and the *Divina Commedia!* While the former teem with life, like a morning in spring, and everything in them, as on such a morning, has its life raised to the highest pitch, Dante's wanderings are all through the regions beyond the grave. He begins with over-leaping death, and leaving it behind him: and to his imagination the secret things of the next world, and its inhabitants, seem to be more distinctly and vividly present than the persons and things around him.

(*Ibid.* pp. 88-9.)

[Virgil's influence on Dante]

The revival of letters, while it opened to men's eyes the ancient world, almost compelled them to acknowledge that in intellectual culture, they were mere barbarians in comparison with the Greeks and Romans: and for a long time men's judgements were spellbound, as Dante's was by Virgil, so that they vailed their heads, as before their masters, even when their genius was mounting above them.

(2nd Series, ed. 1848, p. 35.)

[Dante ignored in Dryden's famous epigram]

As to Dryden's epigram on Milton, it seems to me nearly impossible to pack a greater number of blundering thoughts into so small a space. . . . Milton's 'majesty' is not, like Virgil's, without 'loftiness of thought;' nor his 'loftiness of thought,' like Homer's, without 'majesty.' And the combination of these two elements, which are almost identical, exhausts the power of Nature! This is one of the blustering pieces of bombast thrown out by those who neither know nor think what they are talking of. Eschylus, and Sophocles, and Pindar, and Aristophanes, and Dante, and Cervantes, and Shakspeare had lived,—every one of them having more in common with Homer, than Milton had: yet a man dares say, that the power of God has been worn out by creating Homer and Virgil! and that he could do nothing after, except by strapping them together.

(2nd Series, ed. 1848, p. 78.)

[Sophocles and Dante sparing in the use of ornamental epithet]

Ornamental epithets are not essential to poetry: should you fancy they are, read Sophocles, and read Dante. Or if you would see how the purest and noblest poetry may be painted and rouged out of its grandeur by them, compare Pope's translations of Homer with the original, or Tate and Brady's of the Psalms with the prose version.

(*Ibid.* p. 99.)

[Dante's superiority to Tasso]

Who, that has made friends with Dante, has not had his intellect nerved and expanded by following the pilgrim through his triple world? and would Tasso have done as much for him?

(*Ibid.* p. 230.)

THOMAS CARLYLE

(1795-1881)

[Thomas Carlyle, whose father was a stone mason, was born at Ecclefechan, Dumfriesshire, in 1795. He was educated at the parish school, and at Annan grammar school, and entered Edinburgh University in 1809. His early years were spent in teaching, among his pupils being Charles Buller (1822-4). In 1826 he married Jane Baillie Welsh, and settled in Edinburgh. In the following year he began to write for the *Edinburgh Review*, to which he contributed eight articles between 1827 and 1832. In 1828 the Carlyles moved to Craigenputtock, Dumfriesshire, and thence in 1834 to London, where Mrs. Carlyle died in 1866, and Carlyle in 1881. In 1837 Carlyle published his *French Revolution*, which established his reputation; in 1837-40 he delivered four courses of lectures on literature, the last course being *On Heroes*, which was published in 1841. His other principal works were published as follows: *Chartism*, 1839; *Past and Present*, 1843; *Life and Letters of Oliver Cromwell*, 1845; *Life of Sterling*, 1851; *Frederick the Great*, 1858-65. Carlyle mentions Dante incidentally in several of his earlier articles, but he does not appear to have attempted a serious study of the *Commedia* until 1837, when (as Froude records) he read the *Inferno*, which he found 'uphill work.' In the following year (May, 1838) he gave a lecture on Dante, one of a course of twelve *On the History of Literature;* and in May, 1840 he chose Dante as the subject of his lecture on *The Hero as Poet*, in the series of lectures *On Heroes.* Characteristic references to Dante appear at intervals in his various essays. His acquaintance with Dante's life and writings, if not 'extensive' was at any rate 'peculiar.' He asserts, for instance, that Dante nowhere expressly announces his poem to be a vision, and that the form of a vision is soon lost as the poem proceeds[1]—an assertion to which no attentive reader of the *Commedia* could have committed himself. Again, he mistranslates, and misquotes,[2] and puts into Dante's mouth fictitious statements, such as that 'he says he knew Francesca's father,'[3] and that he mentions Beatrice's wedding.[4] These inaccuracies are more marked in the later lecture on Dante than in the earlier one, suggesting that Carlyle got up the subject on the first occasion and neglected to refresh his memory afterwards. It may be mentioned here that a scholarly edition of the *Inferno*, accompanied by notes and a prose translation, was published in 1849 by John Aitken Carlyle, a younger brother of Carlyle.]

1827. STATE OF GERMAN LITERATURE.[5]

['The lurid fire of Dante']

EVERY literature of the world has been cultivated by the Germans; and to every literature they have studied to give due honour. Shakspeare and Homer, no doubt, occupy alone the loftiest station in the poetical Olympus; but there is space in it for all true Singers out of every age and clime. Ferdusi and the primeval Mythologists of Hindostan live in motherly union with the Troubadours and ancient Storytellers of the West. The wayward mystic gloom of Calderon, the lurid fire of Dante, the auroral light of Tasso, the clear icy glitter of Racine, all are acknowledged and reverenced.

(*Critical and Miscellaneous Essays*, ed. 1872, vol. i. p. 46.)

1828. ESSAY ON BURNS.[6]

[Keats, Dante, Shakespeare]

Poetry, except in such cases as that of Keats, where the whole consists in a weak-eyed maudlin sensibility, and a certain vague random tunefulness of nature, is no separate faculty, no organ which can be superadded to the rest, or disjoined from them; but rather the result of their general harmony and completion. The feelings, the gifts that exist in the Poet are those that exist with more or less development, in every human soul: the imagination, which shudders at the Hell of Dante, is the same faculty, weaker in degree, which called that picture into being. How does the Poet speak to men, with power, but by being still more a man than they? Shakspeare, it has been well observed, in the planning and completing of his tragedies, has shown an Understanding, were it nothing more, which might have governed states, or indited a *Novum Organum*.

(*Ibid.* vol. ii. p. 18.)

[1] [See below, pp. 486-7.]
[2] [He speaks of the 'Hall of Dite,' and the 'Lake of Malebolge,' and ruins by misquotation one of the most beautiful lines in the *Commedia* (*Purg.* i. 117).]
[3] [See below, p. 490.]
[4] [See below, p. 499.]
[5] [Originally published in the *Edinburgh Review*, No. 92 (Oct. 1827).]
[6] [*Ibid.* No. 96 (Dec. 1828).]

1831. HISTORIC SURVEY OF GERMAN POETRY.[1]

[The Germans without a Dante]

At more than one era the grand Tendencies of Europe have first embodied themselves into action in Germany, the main between the New and the Old has been fought and gained there. We mention only the Swiss Revolt, and Luther's Reformation. The Germans have not indeed so many classical works to exhibit as some other nations; a Shakspeare, a Dante, has not yet been recognised among them; nevertheless, they too have had their Teachers and inspired Singers.

(*Critical and Miscellaneous Essays*, ed. 1872, vol. iii. p. 226.)

1831. EARLY GERMAN LITERATURE.[2]

['The mystic song of Dante']

The number of poets, or rather versifiers, henceforth greatly diminishes; their style also, and topics, are different and less poetical. Men wish to be practically instructed rather than poetically amused: Poetry itself must assume a preceptorial character, and teach wholesome saws and moral maxims, or it will not be listened to. Singing for the song's sake is now nowhere practised; but in its stead there is everywhere the jar and bustle of argument, investigation, continuous activity. Such throughout the fourteenth century is the general aspect of mind over Europe. In Italy alone is there a splendid exception; the mystic song of Dante, with its stern indignant moral, is followed by the light love-rhymes of Petrarch, the Troubadour of Italy, when this class was extinct elsewhere: the master minds of that country, peculiar in its social and moral condition, still more in its relations to classical Antiquity, pursue a course of their own. But only the master minds; for Italy too has its Dialecticians, and projectors, and reformers; nay, after Petrarch, these take the lead; and there as elsewhere, in their discords and loud assiduous toil, the voice of poetry dies away.

(*Ibid.* vol. iii. pp. 169-70.)

1837. ESSAY ON MIRABEAU.[3]

[The doom of 'trimmers' in Dante's Hell]

Still more interesting is it, not without a touch almost of pathos, to see how the rugged *Terrae Filius* Danton begins likewise to

[1] [A review of William Taylor's work with this title published in the previous year, contributed to the *Edinburgh Review*, No. 105 (March, 1831).]

[2] [Originally published in the *Foreign Quarterly Review*, No. 16 (Oct. 1831).]

[3] [Originally published in *London and Westminster Review*, No. 8. (Jan. 1837).]

emerge, from amid the blood-tinted obscurations and shadows of horrid cruelty, into calm light; and seems now not an Anthropophagus, but partly a man. On the whole, the Earth feels it to be something to have a 'Son of Earth;' *any* reality, rather than a hypocrisy and formula! With a man that went honestly to work with himself, and said and acted, in any sense, with the whole mind of him, there is always something to be done. Satan himself, according to Dante, was a praiseworthy object, compared with those *juste-milieu* angels (so over-numerous in times like ours) who 'were *neither* faithful nor rebellious,'[1] but were for their little selves only: trimmers, moderates, plausible persons, who, in the Dantean Hell, are found doomed to this frightful penalty, that 'they have not the hope to die (non han speranza di morte);'[2] but sunk in torpid death-life, in mud and the plague of flies, they are to doze and dree for ever,—'hateful to God and to the Enemies of God:'[3]

'*Non ragioniam di lor, ma guarda e passa!*'[4]

(Ed. 1872, p. 207.)

[Dante the boy and Dante the exile]

The Mirabeaus were Riquettis by surname, which is a slight corruption of the Italian *Arrighetti*. They came from Florence: cast out of it in some Guelph-Ghibelline quarrel, such as were common there and then, in the year 1267. Stormy times then as now! The chronologist can remark that Dante Alighieri was a little boy, of some two years, that morning the Arrighettis had to go, and men had to say, 'They are gone, these villains! They are gone these martyrs!' the little boy listening with interest. Let the boy become a man, and he too shall have to go: and prove *come è duro calle*,[5] and what a world this is; and have his poet-nature not killed, for it would not kill, but darkened into Old-Hebrew sternness, and sent onwards to Hades and Eternity for a home to itself. As Dame Quickly said in the Dream—'Those were rare times, Mr. Rigmarole!'—'Pretty much like our own,' answered he.

(*Ibid.* pp. 215-6.)

1837. JOURNAL.

[Reading the *Inferno* 'uphill work']

Froude records (apparently on the authority of Carlyle's *Journal*) that in this year Carlyle, while writing his essay on Scott, was

[1] [*Inf.* iii. 38-9.]
[2] [*Inf.* iii. 46.]
[3] [*Inf.* iii. 63.]
[4] [*Inf.* iii. 51.]
[5] [*Par.* xvii. 59.]

reading Dante's *Inferno*, which he found 'uphill work,' 'but a great and enduring thing.'

(*Carlyle's Life in London*, 1834-1881, vol. i. p. 121.)

1838. May 15. JOURNAL.

[Lecture on Dante]

Delivered yesterday, at the Lecture Rooms, 17 Edward Street, Portman Square, a lecture on Dante, the fifth there.[1] Seven more are yet to come. A curious audience; a curious business. It has been all mismanaged; yet it prospers better than I expected once. The conditions of the thing! Ah, the conditions! It is like a man singing through a fleece of wool. One must submit; one must struggle and sing even *so*, since not otherwise.

(*Ibid.* vol. i. p. 136.)

1838. ESSAY ON SIR WALTER SCOTT.[2]

[The *Divine Comedy* not written 'easily']

In the way of writing, no great thing was ever, or will ever be done with ease, but with difficulty! . . . Virgil and Tacitus, were they ready-writers? The whole *Prophecies of Isaiah* are not equal in extent to this cobweb of a Review Article. Shakspeare, we may fancy, wrote with rapidity; but not till he had thought with intensity: long and sore had this man thought, as the seeing eye may discern well, and had dwelt and wrestled amid dark pains and throes,—though his great soul is silent about all that. It was for him to write rapidly at fit intervals, being ready to do it. And herein lies truly the secret of the matter: such swiftness of mere writing, after due energy of preparation, is doubtless the right method; the hot furnace having long worked and simmered, let the pure gold flow out at one gush. It was Shakspeare's plan; no easy-writer he, or he had never been a Shakspeare. Neither was Milton one of the mob of gentlemen that write with ease; he did not attain Shakspeare's faculty, one perceived, of even writing fast *after* long preparation, but struggled while he wrote. Goethe also tells us he 'had nothing sent him in his sleep;' no page of his but he knew well how it came there. It is reckoned to be the best prose, accordingly, that has been written by any modern. Schiller, as an unfortunate and unhealthy man, '*konnte nie fertig werden*, never could get done;' the noble genius of him struggled not wisely but too well, and wore his life itself heroically out. Or did Petrarch write easily? Dante sees himself 'growing lean' over his

[1] [These are the *Lectures on the History of Literature*, from which extracts are printed below, pp. 485 ff.]

[2] [Originally published in *London and Westminster Review*, No. 12 (Jan. 1838).]

Divine Comedy;[1] in stern solitary death-wrestle with it, to prevail over it, if his uttermost faculty may: hence, too, it is done and prevailed over, and the fiery life of it endures for evermore among men. No: creation, one would think, cannot be easy; your Jove has severe pains, and fire-flames, in the head out of which an armed Pallas is struggling!

(*Critical and Miscellaneous Essays*, ed. 1872, vol. vi. pp. 73-4.)

1838. LECTURES ON THE HISTORY OF LITERATURE.[2]

[The *Niebelungen Lied* the finest medieval poem before Dante]

The probable date of the *Niebelungen Lied* is the twelfth century; it is by far the finest poem connected with the Middle Ages, down to Dante.

(Ed. R. P. Karkaria,[3] *Lecture* iv. p. 71.)

[Dante and the *Divina Commedia*]

Italy has produced a far greater number of great men than any other nation, men distinguished in art, thinking, conduct, and everywhere in the departments of intellect. Dante, Raphael, Michael Angelo, among others, are hardly to be paralleled, in the respective department of each of these. . . .

In our limits it is impossible to attempt the delineation of the Italian people; but in every people there is to be found some one great product of intellect, and when we shall have explained the significance of that one, we shall not fail to understand all the rest. In this instance we shall take Dante, one of the greatest men that ever lived; perhaps the very greatest of Italians, certainly one of the greatest. The *Divina Commedia* is Dante's work. He was from Florence, a town of all others fertile in great men; he was born in 1265. Florence had already come into note 200 years before that; it was first founded by Sylla. In the Middle Ages it played a great part, and it was there that Dante was born. His family was one of the greatest in Florence, that of Durante Alighieri (Durante since corrupted to Dante). He was well educated. We hear mention made of the schoolmaster who taught him grammar, and other great men of the day who had to do with him in different branches of education. He was much occupied in public employments in his native town. Twice he was engaged in battle, on one occasion with the Republic of Pisa, I believe; and he was employed in fourteen embassies.[4] It was in his twenty-fifth year that he first

[1] [*Par.* xxv. 3.]

[2] [Delivered at 17 Edward Street, Portman Square, in April, May, June, 1838.]

[3] [Collated with the edition of J. R. Greene.]

[4] [Carlyle repeats the statements as to Dante's embassies, etc., as they were current in his day. More recent criticism has discredited many of these stories.]

fought for Florence—in the battle of Arezzo,[1] I think; and finally he became Prior or chief magistrate of Florence. . . . We can make nothing out of the quarrels of the Guelphs (the people that favoured the Pope) and Ghibellines (those who favoured the Emperor), except that in every town of Italy party hatred raged violently, and each faction directed its utmost endeavours to supplant the other. Dante favoured the side of the Emperor. There being a very small number of families in Florence, the party hatred was proportionally more violent. Banishments of the highest personages were quite common there, and were employed as often as one party was trodden down by its enemies. Dante accordingly, being then absent upon some embassy, was banished by his enemies. He was then in his thirty-fifth year. He afterwards made some attempt, with others of his friends, to get back to Florence, and made an attack by arms upon the city, which, proving unsuccessful, so exasperated the citizens that nothing could appease them. Dante was then as good as confiscated;[2] he had been fined before that. There is still to be seen an act of that time in the archives of Florence, charging all magistrates to burn Dante alive when he should be taken, such violent hatred had they conceived against him! Dante was afterwards reduced to wander up and down Italy, a broken man! His way of life is difficult to conceive of, with so violent a mind, a deep feeling, sad and joyful. Thenceforth he had sorrow for his portion. It is very mournful to think of, but, at the same time, the work he had to do could not have been done so well had his lot been less unhappy. He was ever a serious man, always meditating on some religious or moral subject. After his misfortunes, besides, there was no hope extant for him; he tells us that he "had left everything he could love." This gave him double and treble earnestness of character. The world was now all over for him; he looked now only to the great kingdoms of eternity! It has been disputed whether he had begun the *Divina Commedia* before he left Florence. He had, at all events, not written much of it. He completed it in his exile, that he might secure to himself powerful friends, who could shelter him; and he therefore got it published, to be descanted on now 500 years after that, and to continue to be so for 1000 years and more to come!

There are few things that exist worth comparing to it. Aeschylus, Dante, Shakespeare—one really cannot add another greater name to these! Theirs were the utterances out of the great heart of nature, sincere outpourings of the mind of man! His *Divina Commedia* assumes at first the form of a vision, though it soon

[1] [Campaldino.]
[2] [So printed—perhaps for 'Dante had then his goods confiscated.']

loses it as he proceeds. Indeed, he nowhere expressly announces it at all, though he begins suddenly, as if it were a vision.[1] The three great kingdoms of eternity are the subject of the poem: Hell, the place of final expiation of guilt, where a stern, inexorable justice reigns without pity, charged to inflict punishments for infraction of the laws of the Most High; Purgatory, a place where the sin of man is, under certain conditions, cleansed away; and Paradise, where the soul enjoys felicity for ever! This was the greatest idea that we have ever yet had—the experience of entering into the soul of man, more full than any other of the elements of grandeur. And it fell to the lot of one who was singularly appropriated by his way of life for the task. He was a man "full of sorrows," "a man of woe;" by nature of a serious turn of mind, and rendered doubly and trebly so by his way of life. Accordingly, I think that when all records of Catholicism shall have passed away; when the Vatican shall have crumbled into dust, and St. Peter's and Strasburg Minster be no more; for thousands of years to come Catholicism will survive in this sublime relic of antiquity!

In seeking the character of Dante's poem, we shall admire first that grand, natural, moral depth, that nobleness of heart, that grandeur of soul, which distinguish him. Great in all directions, in his wrath, his scorn, his pity. Great above all in his sorrow! That is a fine thing which he says of those in a state of despair, 'They have not the Hope to die'—'*Non hanno speranza di morte!*'[2] What an idea that is in Dante's mind there of death. To most persons death is the dreaded being, the King of terrors, but to Dante to be imprisoned for ever in a miserable complexity, without hope of release, is the most terrible of things! Indeed, I believe, notwithstanding the horror of death, no human creature but would find it to be the most dreadful doom not to be suffered to die, though he should be decreed to enjoy all youth and bloom immortally! For there is a boundlessness, an endless longing, in the breast, which aspires to another world than this.

That, too, is a striking passage where he says of certain individuals that they are "hateful to God, and to the enemies of God!"[3] There was a deep feeling in Dante of the enormity of that moral baseness, such as had never before gone into the mind of any man. These of whom he speaks were a kind of moral trimmers; men that had not even the merit to join with the devil. He adds: '*Non ragioniam di lor, ma guarda e passa!*'[4]—"Let us say nothing of them, but look and pass!" The central quality of Dante was greatness of

[1] [These are characteristic specimens of Carlyle's inaccuracy of statement. Dante twice at least describes his poem as a vision (*Par.* xvii, 128; xxxiii. 62); and the fiction of the vision is strictly maintained from first to last.]

[2] [*Inf.* iii. 46.] [3] [*Inf.* iii. 63.] [4] [*Inf.* iii. 51.]

heart; from this all the others flowed as from a natural source. This must exist in every man that would be great; it is impossible for him to do anything good without it, and by his success we may trace, in every writer, his magnanimity and his pusillanimity. In Dante there was the greatness of simplicity, for one thing. All things are to be anticipated from the nobleness of his moral opinions. Logically speaking, again, Dante had one of the finest understandings, remarkable in all matters of reason; as, for instance, in his reflections on fortune, free-will, and the nature of sin. He was an original, quick, far-seeing man, possessing a deep insight into all matters, and this, combined with the other quality which we noticed, his greatness of heart, constitutes the principal charm in Dante. In the third place, his poem was so musical that it got up to the length of singing itself, his soul was in it; and when we read there is a tune which hums itself along. These qualities, a great heart, insight, and song, are the stamp of a genuine poem at all time. They will not be peculiar to any one age, but will be natural in all ages. For, as I observed, it is the utterance of the heart, of life itself, and all earnest men, of whatever age, will there behold, as in a mirror, the image of their own convexed beam, and will be grateful to the poet for the brotherhood to him in which they stand. Then as to simplicity, there is in the poem throughout that noble character, insomuch that one would almost suppose that there is nothing great there. For he remains intent upon the delineation of his subject, never guilty of bombastic inflation, and does not seem to think that he is doing anything very remarkable. Herein he is very different from Milton. Milton, with all his genius, was very inferior to Dante; he has made his angels large, huge, distorted beings. He has sketched vividly his scenes of heaven and hell, and his faculty is certainly great; but I say that Dante's task was the great thing to do. He has opened the deep, unfathomable oasis of woe that lay in the soul of man; he has opened the living fountains of hope, also of penitence! And this I say is far greater than towering as high as Teneriffe, or twice as high!

In his delineations he has a most beautiful sharp grace, the quickest and clearest intellect. It is just that honesty with which his mind was set upon his subject, that carries it out. Take, for instance, the scene of the monster Geryon, with Virgil and Dante, where he describes how he landed with them in the eighth circle. He says that Geryon was like a falcon in quest of prey, hovering without seeing either the lure or the game. When the falconer cries, '*Oimè tu cali*' ('Come down!')[1] he descends, wheeling

[1] [*Inf.* xvii. 129—not imperative, as Carlyle renders, but, 'Alack! thou stoopest (i.e. descendest).']

round and round, and sits at a distance disdainful and disobedient. Just so was Geryon. And then "he bolted up like an arrow out of the bow." There are not above a dozen words in this picture, but it is one that will last for ever!

So also his description of the city of Dis, to which Virgil carried him, possesses a beautiful simplicity and honesty. "The light was so dim that the people could hardly see, and they winked at him, just as people wink their eyes under the new moon, or as an old tailor winks threading his needle, when his eyes are not good."[1] There is a contrast between his subject and this quaint similitude that has a beautiful effect. It brings one home to the subject; there is much reality in this similitude. So his description of the place they were in. "Flakes of fire came down like snow,"[2] falling on the skin of the people, and burning them black! Among these he sees his old schoolmaster, who taught him grammar, he winks at him in the manner described, but he is so burnt that Dante can hardly recognise him.

There are many of his greatest qualities in the celebrated passage about Francesca, whom he finds in the circle of Inferno appropriated to those who had erred in love. I many times say I know nowhere a more striking passage; if any one would select a passage characteristic of a great man, let him study that. It is as tender as the voice of mothers, full of the gentlest pity, though there is much stern tragedy about it. It is very touching. In "a place without light, which groaned like a stormy sea,"[3] he sees two shadows which he wishes to speak to, and they come to him. He compares them to doves whose wings are open and not fluttering. Francesca, one of these, utters her complaint, which does not occupy twenty lines, though it is such an one that a man may write a thousand lines about it, and not do ill. It contains beautiful touches of human weakness. She feels that stern justice encircles her all around. 'Oh, living creature,' she says, 'who hast come so kindly to visit us, if the Creator of the World' (poor Francesca! she knew that she had sinned against His inexorable justice) 'were our friend, we would pray Him for thy peace!' 'Love, which soon teaches itself to a gentle heart,' inspired her Paolo (beautiful womanly feeling that). 'Love forbids that the person loved shall not love in return.' And so she loved Paolo. 'Caina awaits him who destroyed our life,' she adds with female vehemence. Then, in three lines, she tells the story how they fell in love. 'We read one day of Launcelot, how love possessed him, we were alone, we regarded one another: when we read of that laughing kiss, he trembling, kissed me! That day, she adds, 'we read no further!'[4]

[1] [*Inf.* xv. 18-21.]
[2] [*Inf.* xiv. 29-30.]
[3] [*Inf.* v. 28-9.]
[4] [*Inf.* v. 73 ff.]

The whole is beautiful, like a clear, piping voice heard in the middle of a whirlwind: it is so sweet, and gentle, and good!

Then the Hunger Tower of Ugolino. This, however, is a much more brutal thing than the punishment of Francesca. But the story of Francesca is all a truth. He says that he knew her father:[1] her history becomes a kind of concern in the mind of Dante, and when he hears her relate it "he falls as a dead body falls." This, too, is an answer to a criticism against Dante, and a paltry criticism it is. Some have regarded the poem as a kind of satire upon his enemies, on whom he revenged himself by putting them into Hell. Now, nothing is more unworthy of Dante than such a theory. If he had been of such an ignoble nature, he never could have written the *Divina Commedia*. It was written in the purest spirit of justice. Thus he pitied poor Francesca, and would not have willingly placed her in that torment; but it was the justice of God's law that doomed her there!

How beautiful is his description of the coming eve, the hour when sorrow awakens in the hearts of the sailors who have left their land ('*squilla di lontano*'), the dying day.[2] No one ever quitted home and loved ones whose heart does not respond to that!

We must not omit Farinata, the beautiful illustration of a character much found in Dante. He is confined in the black dome where the heretics dwell. In the same tomb is Cavalcante de' Cavalcanti, father of one of Dante's most loved friends. The description is striking of the sarcophaguses in which these people are enclosed, 'more or less heated' (there is nothing in Teneriffe like that); the lids are to be kept open till the last day, and are then to be sealed down for ever. He hears Dante speaking in the Tuscan dialect, and he accosts him. He is a man of great haughtiness (*gran dispitto, sdegnoso*).[3] This spirit of defiance of suffering, so remarkable in Aeschylus, occurs two or three times in Dante. Farinata asks him, what news of Florence? For in all his long exile Dante himself thinks continually of Florence, which he loves so well, and he makes even those in torment anxious after what is doing in Florence. Then Cavalcanti asks Dante why is he there, and not his son. Where is he? And Dante replies that perhaps he had disdain for Virgil. *Had?* Cavalcanti asks (*ebbe*): does he not live then? And, as Dante pauses a little without replying, he plunges down, and Dante sees him no more!

These sudden and abrupt notions are frequent in Dante. He is, indeed, full of what I can call military movements: many of his gestures are extremely significant. In another place three men

[1] [This is an invention of Carlyle's.]
[2] [*Purg.* viii. 1 ff.] [3] [*Inf.* x. 36, 41.]

'looked at one another, like men that believed.' In these words one sees it all, as it seemed to Dante! This is a feature I don't know how to name well, but it is very remarkable in Dante. Those passages are very striking where he alludes to his own sad fortunes. There is in them a wild sorrow, a savage tone of truth, a breaking heart; the hatred of Florence, and with it the love of Florence! In one place, 'Rejoice, O Florence, that thou art so famous in hell!'[1] In another place he calls her well-guided.[2] His old schoolmaster tells him: 'If thou follow thy star, thou canst not miss a happy harbour.'[3] That was just it. That star occasionally shone on him from the blue eternal depths, and he felt he was doing something good; but he soon lost it again as he fell back into the trough of the sea, and had to journey on as before. And when his ancestor predicts his banishment, there is the wild sincerity again. He must leave every delightful thing; he must learn to dwell on the stairs of another man.[4] Bitter! bitter! Poor exile, none but scoundrelly persons to associate with! There are traces here and there of a heart one would always wish to see in man. He is not altogether, therefore, an unconscious man like Shakespeare, but more morbid and narrower. Though he does not attempt to compute it, he seems to feel merely the conviction, the humble hope, that he shall get to heaven in the end!

A notable passage that on fame! No man, if he were Alexander the Great, if he were Dante, if he were all men put together, could get for himself eternal fame! He feels that, too. Fame is not of any particular moment to him. That contradiction between the greatness of his mind and his humble attachment to Florence, is difficult of utterance, and it seems as if the spirit of the man were hampered with the insufficient dialects this world imposes on him.

The 'Inferno' has become of late times mainly the favourite of the three divisions of Dante's great poem. It has harmonised well with the taste of the last thirty or forty years, in which Europe has seemed to covet more a violence of emotion and a strength of convulsion than almost any other quality. It is no doubt a great thing; but to my mind the 'Purgatorio' is excellent also, and I question even whether it is not a better and a greater thing on the whole. It is very beautiful to see them get up into that black, great mountain in the western ocean, where Columbus had not yet been. To trace *giro* after *giro*, the purification of souls is beautiful exceedingly; the sinner's repentance, the humble hope, the peace and joy that is in them.

There is no book so moral as this, the very essence of Christian morality! Men have, of course, ceased to believe these things—

[1] [*Inf.* xxvi. 1 ff.]

[2] ['la ben guidata' (*Purg.* xii. 102).]

[3] [*Inf.* xv. 55-6.]

[4] [*Par.* xvii. 55 ff.]

that mountain rising up in the ocean, or that Male-bolge, with its black gulfs. But still men of any knowledge at all must believe that there exists the inexorable justice of God, and that penitence is the great thing here for man. For life is but a series of errors, made good again by repentance; and the sacredness of that doctrine is asserted in Dante in a manner more moral than anywhere else. Any other doctrine is with him comparatively not worth affirming or denying. Very touching is that gentle patience, that unspeakable thankfulness with which the souls expect their release after thousands of years. Cato is keeping the gate. That is a beautiful dawn of morning. The dawn drove away the darkness westward with a quivering of the sea on the horizon:

'Sì che di lontano
Conobbi il tremolar della marina.'[1]

He seems to seize the word for it. Anybody who has seen the sun rise at sea will recognise it. The internal feeling of the 'Purgatorio' keeps pace with that. One man says: 'Tell my Giovanna that I think her mother does not love me now'—that she has laid aside her weeds![2] The parable with which he concludes his lament is as beautiful as it can be.

Then, too, the relation he stands in to Virgil and Beatrice; his loyalty, faith, and kindly feeling for Virgil's nobleness. Loyalty, we remarked, was the essence of the Middle Ages. Virgil was never angry with him but once, when Dante seems to pay too much attention to two falsifiers quarrelling. 'A little more,' he says, 'and I would quarrel with these.'[3] Dante owns himself in the wrong, and Virgil then tells him it is not proper to listen to such things. Beatrice was actually a beautiful little girl, whom he had seen in his boyhood at a ball. She was a young child, nine years old when he was ten. He had never heard her speak but once, when she was talking to someone at the corner of the street. She was cinctured with a garland of olive,[4] and appeared '*mirae pulchritutinis*.' Such was the mood of beauty, he says, in which her aspect placed him, that that night, when he fell asleep, he dreamed of her. This was at nine o'clock, for though it was many years after he remembered it quite well. They had met but little, but he seemed to know that she loved him, as he her. She married another afterwards, but not willingly. When all else is dark with misery for him, this is the only recollection that is beautiful, for nothing had occurred to render it disagreeable to him, and his whole soul flies to it. Providence sent an angel always to interfere

[1] [*Purg.* i. 116-7.]
[2] [Nino Visconti—*Purg.* viii. 71 ff.]
[3] [*Inf.* xxx. 132.]
[4] [This is a confusion of a passage in the *Vita Nuova* (§ 3) with *Purg.* xxx. 68.]

when the worst came. In Paradise,[1] when Virgil vanishes and he sees Beatrice, by this time purified from mortal stain, how deep is the expression of his joy! How heavily the love he bore her weighed upon his heart! The mother of Beatrice treated him with much seeming harshness (*barbarezza*), wasting his very life away with severity; but it was all through her apprehension that if she were to give vent to her love for him she should kill him; it would be too much for him. But he reads in her eye all the while her deep affection; in the flush of joy with which she regards him, his successes, and good actions.[2] One can well understand, in this point of view, what the Germans say of the three parts of the *Divina Commedia*. The first is the architectural, plastic part, as of statuary; the second is the pictorial, or picturesque; the third is the musical, the melting into song. But I can afford no more time to speak of Dante. . . . We must quit Italy and Dante altogether with these imperfect remarks.

(*Lecture* v. pp. 75-89.)

[Dante's 'way of thinking' of necessity soon became obsolete]

In our last lecture we saw the remarkable phenomenon of one great mind making of himself, as it were, the spokesman of his age, and speaking with such an earnestness and depth that he has become one of the voices of mankind itself, making his voice to be heard in all ages, for he was filled in every fibre of his mind with that principle, belief in the Catholic Church. . . . I may observe that Dante's way of thinking was one which from its very nature could not long continue; indeed it is not given to man that any of his works should long continue, of the works of mind, any more than the things which he makes with his hand. But there was something in the very nature of Dante's way of thinking which made it very natural that it should have become generally altered even in the next generation. Dante's son even must have lived in an increased horizon of knowledge, which the theory of Dante could no longer fit; as, for example, man had then sailed to the Western Ocean, and had found that the Mountain of Purgatory was not there at all. . . . In Italy the same Catholic Church, which was the mother of the mind of Dante, inspiring it with every feeling and thought was there, afterwards condemned Galileo to renounce what he knew to be true. . . . Any theory of Nature is, at most, temporary; but, on the other hand, all theories contain something within them which is perennial. In Dante that was belief, the communion which the heart of hearts can hold with

[1] [The Terrestrial Paradise.]

[2] [Carlyle seems to have been drawing on his imagination in these last two paragraphs.]

Nature. . . . All theories approximate more or less to the great Theory, which remains itself always unknown, and in that proportion contain something which must live. Therefore, whatever opinion we may form of his doctrines, we do not dissent from Dante's piety, that will always be admired.

(*Lecture* vi. pp. 91-2.)

[The tradition that Dante was at the Universities of Paris and Oxford]

Cervantes lived more than two centuries after Dante; though we select him as the most remarkable of his age there were, no doubt, before him many other people very valuable in influencing the human mind. All people, indeed, from Charlemagne's time. had already made rapid advances in all departments of culture. We may here remark one or two symptoms of that restless effort after advancement then in action everywhere in Europe. First there was the institution of universities, which was long before Dante. The University of Paris had come into decided note in the time of Dante. There is a tradition that Dante himself was at it, as there is a vague tradition that he was at Oxford too, but this last is very doubtful.

(*Ibid.* p. 93.)

[Dante's works mainly influenced by religion and loyalty]

The two great things which we have remarked in the Middle Ages—first, Christianity: the Catholic religion; and next, loyalty—had mainly the influence over Dante's works.

(*Ibid.* pp. 95-6.)

[Points of resemblance between *Don Quixote* and the *Divina Commedia*]

Don Quixote is the very reverse of the *Commedia* of Dante; but in one respect it is analogous to it. Like it, it is the free utterance of the heart of man and nature.

(*Ibid.* p. 103.)

[Milton and Dante]

Milton must not be ranked with Shakespeare. He stands relative to Shakespeare as Tasso or Ariosto does to Dante, as Virgil to Homer. . . . *Paradise Lost* is a very ambitious poem, a great picture painted on huge canvas; but it is not so great a thing as to concentrate our minds upon the deep things within ourselves as Dante does, to show what a beautiful thing the life of man is; it is to travel with paved streets beside us, rather than lakes of fire. This Dante has done, and Milton not.

(*Lecture* viii. p. 147.)

[David Hume contrasted with Dante]

It is very strange to look at scepticism in contrast with a thing that preceded it; to contrast, for example, David Hume with Dante, two characters distant by five centuries from one another, two of the greatest minds in their respective departments (the mind of both was to do the best that could be done in their existing circumstances); to contrast them, I say, and see what Dante made of it and what Hume made of it. Dante saw a solemn law in the universe, pointing out his destiny with an awful and beautiful certainty, and he held to it. Hume could see nothing in the universe but confusion, and he was certain of nothing but his own existence; yet he had instincts which were infinitely more true than the logical part of him, and so he kept himself quiet in the middle of it all, and did no harm to any one.

(*Lecture* xi. p. 165.)

[Dante and Homer]

All things are mortal in this world; everything that exists in time exists with the law of change and mortality imprinted upon it. . . . It is the law of all things. Paganism, for example, in its time produced many great things, brave and noble men, till at last it came to fall and crumble away into a mere disputatious philosophy. And so down to the Protestant system; for the Middle Ages in this respect answered to the Heroic Ages of all Greece, and as Homer had lived, so Dante lived.

(*Lecture* xii. p. 185.)

[Richter compared with Dante]

Richter's dreams are as deep as those of Dante: dreams of annihilation, not surpassed, perhaps, except by the prophetic books of the Bible.

(*Ibid.* p. 197.)

1838. Sept. 25. LETTER TO RALPH WALDO EMERSON (from Ecclefechan).

['A *Dante*, or undying thing']

My Wife says she received your American Bill of so many pounds sterling for the Revolution Book, with a 'pathetic feeling' which brought 'tears' to her eyes. From beyond the waters there is a hand held out; beyond the waters too live brothers. I would only the Book were an Epic, a *Dante*, or undying thing, that New England might boast in after times of this feat of hers; and put stupid, poundless, and penniless Old England to the blush about it!

(*Correspondence of Carlyle and Emerson*, vol. i. p. 177.)

1839. Feb. 8. LETTER TO RALPH WALDO EMERSON (from Chelsea).

[The 'Lake of Malebolge']

Ah me! I often swear I will be *buried* at least in free breezy Scotland, out of this insane hubbub, where Fate tethers me in life! If Fate always tethers me;—but if ever the smallest competence of worldly means be mine, I will fly this whirlpool as I would the Lake of *Malebolge*[1] and only visit it now and then.

(*Ibid.* vol. i. p. 214.)

1839. CHARTISM.

['Wretchedness like a Dantean Hell']

Be it with reason or with unreason, too surely working men do in verity find the time all out of joint; this world for them no home, but a dingy prison-house, of reckless unthrift, rebellion, rancour, indignation against themselves and against all men. Is it a green flowery world, with azure everlasting sky sketched over it, the work and government of a God; or a murky-simmering Tophet, of copperas-fumes, cotton-fuzz, gin-riot, wrath and toil, created by a Demon, governed by a Demon? The sun of their wretchedness merited and unmerited welters, huge, dark and baleful, like a Dantean Hell, visible there in the statistics of Gin: Gin justly named the most authentic incarnation of the Infernal Principle in our times, too indisputable an incarnation. . . . If from this black unluminous unheeded *Inferno*, and Prisonhouse of souls in pain, there do flash up from time to time, some dismal wide-spread glare of Chartism or the like, notable to all, claiming remedy from all,—are we to regard it as more baleful than the quiet state, or rather as not so baleful?

(*Critical and Miscellaneous Essays*, ed. 1872, vol. vi. Chap. iv. p. 132.)

[The *Divina Commedia* 'the mournfulest of books']

Dante's *Divina Commedia* is called the mournfulest of books: transcendent mistemper of the noblest soul; utterance of a boundless, godlike, unspeakable, implacable sorrow and protest against the world. But in Holywell Street, not long ago, we bought, for threepence, a book still mournfuler: the Pamphlet of one 'Marcus,' whom his poor Chartist editor and republisher calls the 'Demon Author.' . . . We have read Marcus; but his sorrow is not divine. We hoped he would turn out to have been in sport: ah no, it is grim earnest with him; grim as very death. Marcus is not a demon

[1] [Dante's name for Circle viii. of Hell (*Inf.* viii. 1)—there is no 'Lake of Malebolge,' nor mention of any lake in connection with it.]

author at all; he is a benefactor of the species in his kind. . . . A benefactor of the species, clearly recognisable as such: the saddest scientific mortal we have ever in this world fallen in with; sadder even than poetic Dante. His is a *no*-godlike sorrow; sadder than the godlike.

(*Critical and Miscellaneous Essays*, ed. 1872, vol. vi. Chap. x. pp. 184-5.)

1840. LECTURES ON HEROES.—THE HERO AS DIVINITY.

[Shakespeare, Dante, Goethe]

The robust homely vigour of the Norse heart attaches one much. . . . Is it not a trait of right honest strength, says Uhland, that the old Norse heart finds its friend in the Thunder-god? That it is not frightened away by his thunder; but finds that Summer-heat, the beautiful noble summer, must and will have thunder withal. The Norse heart *loves* this Thor and his hammer-bolt; sports with him. . . . There is a great broad humour in some of these things. . . . Huge untutored Brobdignag genius,—needing only to be tamed down; into Shakspeares, Dantes, Goethes!

(Ed. 1873, pp. 32-3.)

1840. LECTURES ON HEROES.—THE HERO AS POET.

[Dante and his Book]

In ancient and also in modern periods we find a few Poets who are accounted perfect; whom it were a kind of treason to find fault with. This is noteworthy; this is right; yet in strictness it is only an illusion. At bottom, clearly enough, there is no perfect Poet! A vein of poetry exists in the hearts of all men; no man is made altogether of Poetry. We are all poets when we *read* a poem well. The 'imagination that shudders at the Hell of Dante,' is not that the same faculty, weaker in degree, as Dante's own? . . . .

Here in these ages, such as they are, have we not two mere Poets, if not deified, yet we may say beatified? Shakspeare and Dante are Saints of Poetry; really, if we will think of it, *canonised* so that it is impiety to meddle with them. The unguided instinct of the world, working across all these perverse impediments, has arrived at such result. Dante and Shakspeare are a peculiar Two. They dwell apart, in a kind of royal solitude; none equal, none second to them: in the general feeling of the world, a certain transcendentalism, a glory as of complete perfection, invests these two. They *are* canonised, though no Pope or Cardinals took hand in doing it! Such in spite of every perverting influence, in the most unheroic times, is still our indestructible reverence for heroism.—We will look a little at these Two, the Poet Dante and the Poet Shakspeare. . . .

Many volumes have been written by way of commentary on Dante and his Book; yet, on the whole, with no great result. His Biography is, as it were, irrecoverably lost for us. An unimportant, wandering, sorrowstricken man, not much note was taken of him while he lived; and most of that has vanished, in the long space that now intervenes. It is five centuries since he ceased writing and living here. After all commentaries, the Book itself is mainly what we know of him. The Book;—and one might add that Portrait commonly attributed to Giotto, which, looking on it, you cannot help inclining to think genuine, whoever did it. To me it is a most touching face; perhaps of all faces that I know, the laurel wound round it;[1] the deathless sorrow and pain, the known most so. Lonely there, painted as on vacancy, with the simple victory which is also deathless;—significant of the whole history of Dante! I think it is the mournfulest face that ever was painted from reality; an altogether tragic, heart-affecting face. There is in it, as foundation of it, the softness, tenderness, gentle affection as of a child; but all this is as if congealed into sharp contradiction, into abnegation, isolation, proud hopeless pain. A soft ethereal soul looking-out so stern, implacable, grim-trenchant, as from imprisonment of thick-ribbed ice! Withal it is a silent pain too, a silent scornful one: the lip is curled in a kind of god-like disdain of the thing that is eating-out his heart,—as if it were withal a mean insignificant thing, as if he whom it had power to torture and strangle were greater than it. The face of one wholly in protest, and life-long unsurrendering battle, against the world. Affection all converted into indignation: an implacable indignation; slow, equable, silent, like that of a god! The eye too, it looks-out as in a kind of *surprise*, a kind of enquiry, Why the world was of such a sort? This is Dante: so he looks, this 'voice of ten silent centuries,' and sings us 'his mystic unfathomable song.'

The little that we know of Dante's Life corresponds well enough with this Portrait and this Book. He was born at Florence, in the upper class of society, in the year 1265. His education was the best then going; much school-divinity, Aristotelean logic, some Latin classics,—no inconsiderable insight into certain pro-

[1] [The portrait here referred to by Carlyle is, of course, not the so-called Giotto portrait, which was discovered in the Bargello at Florence on July 21, 1840, more than two months after the date of this lecture (May 12, 1840); but the portrait drawn by Tofanelli and engraved by Raphael Morghen (with the laurel wreath round the head) which was first published in 1795.]

vinçes of things: and Dante, with his earnest, intelligent nature, we need not doubt, learned better than most all that was learnable. He has a clear cultivated understanding, and of great subtlety; this best fruit of education he had contrived to realize from these scholastics. He knows accurately and well what lies close to him; but, in such a time, without printed books or free intercourse, he could not know well what was distant: the small clear light, most luminous for what is near, breaks itself into singular *chiaroscuro* striking on what is far off. This was Dante's learning from the schools. In life, he had gone through the usual destinies; been twice out campaigning as a soldier for the Florentine State; been on embassy; had in his thirty-fifth year, by natural gradation of talent and service, become one of the Chief Magistrates of Florence. He had met in boyhood a certain Beatrice Portinari, a beautiful little girl of his own age and rank, and grown-up thenceforth in partial sight of her, in some distant intercourse with her. All readers know his graceful affecting account of this; and then of their being parted; of her being wedded to another[1] and of her death soon after. She makes a great figure in Dante's poem; seems to have made a great figure in his life. Of all beings it might seem as if she, held apart from him, far apart at last in the dim Eternity, were the only one he had ever with his whole strength of affection loved. She died: Dante himself was wedded; but it seems not happily, far from happily. I fancy, the rigorous earnest man, with his keen excitabilities was not altogether easy to make happy.

We will not complain of Dante's miseries: had all gone right with him as he wished it, he might have been Prior, Podestà, or whatsoever they call it, of Florence, well accepted among neighbours, —and the world had wanted one of the most notable words ever spoken or sung. Florence would have had another prosperous Lord Mayor; and the ten dumb centuries continued voiceless, and ten other listening centuries (for there will be ten of them and more) had no *Divina Commedia* to hear! We will complain of nothing. A nobler destiny was appointed for this Dante; and he, struggling like a man led toward death and crucifixion, could not help fulfilling it. Give *him* the choice of his happiness! He knew not, more than we do, what was really happy, what was really miserable.

In Dante's Priorship, the Guelf-Ghibelline, Bianchi-Neri, or some other confused disturbances rose to such a height that Dante, whose party had seemed the stronger, was with his friends cast unexpectedly forth into banishment;[2] doomed thenceforth to a life of woe

[1] [Dante nowhere makes any reference to the marriage of Beatrice Portinari.]
[2] [Dante was not exiled during his Priorate, but two years later, in 1302.]

and wandering. His property was all confiscated and more; he had the fiercest feeling that it was entirely unjust, nefarious in the sight of God and man. He tried what was in him to get reinstated; tried even by warlike surprisal, with arms in his hand: but it would not do; bad only had become worse. There is a record, I believe, still extant in the Florence Archives, dooming this Dante, wheresoever caught to be burnt alive. Burnt alive; so it stands, they say: a very curious civic document. Another curious document, some considerable number of years later, is a Letter of Dante's to the Florentine Magistrates,[1] written in answer to a milder proposal of theirs, that he should return on condition of apologising and paying a fine. He answers, with fixed stern pride: 'If I cannot return without calling myself guilty, I will never return, *nunquam revertar*.'[2]

For Dante there was now no home in this world. He wandered from patron to patron, from place to place; proving, in his own bitter words, 'How hard is the path, *Come è duro calle*.'[3] The wretched are not cheerful company. Dante, poor and banished, with his proud earnest nature, with his moody humours, was not a man to conciliate men. Petrarch[4] reports of him that being at Can della Scala's court, and blamed one day for his gloom and taciturnity, he answered in no courtier-like way. Della Scala stood among his courtiers, with mimes and buffoons (*nebulones ac histriones*) making him heartily merry; when turning to Dante, he said: 'Is it not strange, now, that this poor fool should make himself so entertaining; while you, a wise man, sit there day after day, and have nothing to amuse us with at all?' Dante answered bitterly: 'No, not strange; your Highness is to recollect the Proverb, *Like to Like*;'—given the amuser, the amusee must also be given! Such a man, with his proud silent ways, with his sarcasms and sorrows, was not made to succeed at court. By degrees, it came to be evident to him that he had no longer any resting-place, or hope of benefit, on this earth. The earthly world had cast him forth, to wander, wander; no living heart to love him now; for his sore miseries there was no solace here.

The deeper naturally would the Eternal World impress itself on him; that awful reality over which, after all, this Time-world, with its Florences and banishments, only flutters as an unreal shadow. Florence thou shalt never see: but Hell and Purgatory and Heaven thou shalt surely see! What is Florence, Can della Scala, and the

[1] [Not to 'the Florentine Magistrates' but to a Florentine friend.]

[2] [Inaccurately quoted—Dante's words were 'nunquam Florentiam introibo' (*Epist.* ix. § 4).]

[3] [*Par.* xvii. 59.]

[4] [In the second book of his *Res Memorandae*.]

World and Life altogether? *Eternity:* thither of a truth, not elsewhither, art thou and all things bound! The great soul of Dante, homeless on earth, made its home more and more in that awful other world. Naturally his thoughts brooded on that, as on the one fact important for him. Bodied or bodiless, it is the one fact important for all men:—but to Dante, in that age, it was bodied in fixed certainty of scientific shape; he no more doubted of that *Malebolge* Pool, that it all lay there with its gloomy circles, with its *alti guai*,[1] and that he himself should see it, than we doubt that we should see Constantinople if we went thither. Dante's heart, long filled with this, brooding over it in speechless thought and awe, bursts forth at length into 'mystic unfathomable song;' and this his *Divine Comedy*, the most remarkable of all modern Books is the result.

It must have been a great solacement to Dante, and was, as we can see, a proud thought for him at times, that he, here in exile, could do this work; that no Florence, nor no man or men, could hinder him from doing it, or even much help him in doing it. He knew too, partly, that it was great; the greatest a man could do. 'If thou follow thy star, *se tu segui tua stella*'[2]—so could the Hero, in his forsakenness, in his extreme need, still say to himself: 'Follow thou thy star, thou shalt not fail of a glorious haven!'[3] The labour of writing, we find, and indeed could know otherwise, was great and painful for him; he says, this Book, 'which has made me lean for many years.'[4] Ah yes, it was won, all of it, with pain and sore toil,—not in sport, but in grim earnest. His Book, as indeed most good Books are, has been written, in many senses, with his heart's blood. It is his whole history, this Book. He died after finishing it; not yet very old, at the age of fifty-six;—broken-hearted rather, as is said. He lies buried in his death-city Ravenna: *Hic claudor Dantes patriis extorris ab oris.* The Florentines begged back his body, in a century after; the Ravenna people would not give it. 'Here am I Dante laid, shut-out from my native shores.'

I said, Dante's Poem was a Song: it is Tieck who calls it a 'mystic unfathomable Song;' and such is literally the character of it. Coleridge remarks very pertinently somewhere, that wherever you find a sentence musically worded, of true rhythm and melody in the words, there is something deep and good in the meaning too. For body and soul, word and idea, go strangely together here as everywhere. Song: we said before, it was the Heroic of Speech! All *old* Poems, Homer's and the rest, are authentically Songs. . . . I give Dante my highest praise when

[1] [*Inf.* iii. 22.] [2] [*Inf.* xv. 55.] [3] [*Inf.* xv. 55-6.] [4] [*Par.* xxv. 3.]

I say of his Divine Comedy that it is, in all senses, genuinely a Song. In the very sound of it there is a *canto fermo;* it proceeds as by a chant. The language, his simple *terza rima,* doubtless helped him in this. One reads along naturally with a sort of *lilt.* But I add, that it could not be otherwise; for the essence and material of the work are themselves rhythmic. Its depth, and rapt passion and sincerity, makes it musical;—go *deep* enough, there is music everywhere. A true inward symmetry, what one calls an architectural harmony, reigns in it, proportionates it all: architectural; which also partakes of the character of music. The three Kingdoms, *Inferno, Purgatorio, Paradiso,* look-out on one another like compartments of a great edifice; a great supernatural world-cathedral, piled-up there, stern, solemn, awful; Dante's World of Souls! It is, at bottom, the *sincerest* of all Poems; sincerity, here too, we find to be the measure of worth. It came deep out of the author's heart of hearts; and it goes deep, and through long generations, into ours. The people of Verona, when they saw him on the streets, used to say, '*Eccovi l' uom ch' è stato all' Inferno,* See, there is the man that was in Hell!' Ah yes, he had been in Hell;—in Hell enough, in long severe sorrow and struggle; as the like of him is pretty sure to have been. Commedias that come out *divine* are not accomplished otherwise. Thought, true labour of any kind, highest virtue itself, is it not the daughter of Pain? Born as out of the black whirlwind; true *effort,* in fact, as of a captive struggling to free himself: that is Thought. In all ways we are 'to become perfect through *suffering*' —But, as I say, no work known to me is so elaborated as this of Dante's. It has all been as if molten, in the hottest furnace of his Soul. It had made him 'lean' for many years. Not the general whole only; every compartment of it is worked-out, with intense earnestness, into truth, into clear visuality. Each answers to the other; each fits in its place, like a marble stone accurately hewn and polished. It is the soul of Dante, and in this the soul of the middle ages, rendered for ever rhythmically visible there. No light task; a right intense one; but a task which is *done.*

Perhaps one would say, intensity, with the much that depends on it, is the prevailing character of Dante's genius. Dante does not come before as a large Catholic mind; rather as a narrow, and even sectarian mind: it is partly the fruit of his age and position, but partly too of his own nature. His greatness has, in all senses, concentered itself into fiery emphasis and depth. He is world-great not because he is world-wide, but because he is world-deep. Through all objects he pierces as it were down into the heart of Being. I know nothing so intense as Dante. Consider, for example, to begin with the outermost development of his intensity, consider how he paints. He has a great power of vision; seizes the very type of a thing: presents that and nothing more. You remember that first view he gets of the Hall of Dite[1]: *red* pinnacle, redhot cone of iron glowing through the dim immensity of gloom;—so vivid, so distinct, visible at once and forever! It is as an emblem of the whole genius of Dante. There is a brevity, an abrupt precision in him: Tacitus is not briefer, more condensed; and then in Dante it seems a natural condensation, spontaneous to the man. One smiting word; and then there is silence, nothing more said. His silence is more eloquent than words. It is strange with what a sharp decisive grace he snatches the true likeness of a matter: cuts into the matter as with a pen of fire. Plutus, the blustering giant, collapses at Virgil's rebuke; it is 'as the sails sink, the mast being suddenly broken.'[2] Or that poor Brunetto Latini, with the *cotto aspetto*, 'face *baked*,'[3] parched brown and lean; and the 'fiery snow' that falls on them there, a 'fiery snow without wind,'[4] slow, deliberate, never-ending! Or the lids of those Tombs; square sarcophaguses, in that silent dim-burning Hall, each with its Soul in torment; the lids laid open there; they are to be shut at the Day of Judgment, through Eternity.[5] And how Farinata rises; and how Cavalcante falls—at hearing of his Son, and the past tense '*fue*'![6] The very movements in Dante have something brief; swift, decisive, almost military. It is of the inmost essence of his genius this sort of painting. The fiery, swift Italian nature of the man, so silent, passionate, with its quick abrupt movements, its silent 'pale rages,' speaks itself in these things. . . .

Dante's painting is not graphic only, brief, true, and of a vividness as of fire in dark night; taken on the wider scale, it is everywhere noble, and the outcome of a great soul. Francesca and her Lover,[7] what qualities in that! A thing woven as out of rainbows, on a ground of eternal black. A small flute-voice of infinite wail speaks there, into our very heart of hearts. A touch of womanhood in it too: *della bella persona, che mi fu tolta*;[8] and how, even in the Pit of woe, it is a solace that *he* will never part from her! Saddest tragedy in these *alti guai*. And the racking winds, in that *aer bruno*,[9] whirl them away again, to wail forever!—Strange to think: Dante was the friend of this poor Francesca's father; Francesca herself may have sat upon the Poet's knee, as a bright innocent little child. Infinite pity, yet also

[1] [Not the 'Hall,' but the City, of Dis—*Inf.* viii. 68 ff.]
[2] [*Inf.* vii. 13-4.]
[3] [*Inf.* xv. 26.]
[4] [*Inf.* xiv. 28-30.]
[5] [*Inf.* ix. 115 ff; x. 10-2.]
[6] [*Inf.* x. 32, 67-72—the word used by Dante was *ebbe* not *fue*.]
[7] [*Inf.* v. 97 ff.]
[8] [*Inf.* v. 101-2.]
[9] [*Inf.* ii. 1; but Carlyle means 'aer perso,' *Inf.* v. 89.]

infinite rigour of law: it is so Nature is made; it is so Dante discerned that she was made. What a paltry notion is that of his *Divine Comedy's* being a poor splenetic impotent terrestrial libel; putting those into Hell whom he could not be avenged-upon on earth! I suppose if ever pity, tender as a mother's, was in the heart of any man, it was in Dante's. But a man who does not know rigour cannot pity either. His very pity will be cowardly, egoistic,—sentimentality, or little better. I know not in the world an affection equal to that of Dante. It is a tenderness, a trembling, longing, pitying love: like the wail of Æolian harps, soft, soft; like a child's young heart;—and then that stern, sore-saddened heart! These longings of his towards his Beatrice; their meeting together in the *Paradiso;*[1] his gazing in her pure transfigured eyes, her that had been purified by death so long, separated from him so far:—one likens it to the song of angels; it is among the purest utterances of affection, perhaps the very purest, that ever came out of a human soul.

For the *intense* Dante is intense in all things; he has got into the essence of all. His intellectual insight as painter, on occasion too as reasoner, is but the result of all other sorts of intensity. Morally great, above all, we must call him; it is the beginning of all. His scorn, his grief are as transcendent as his love;—as indeed, what are they but the *inverse* or *converse* of his love? '*A Dio spiacenti ed a' nemici sui*, Hateful to God and to the enemies of God:'[2] lofty scorn, unappeasable silent reprobation and aversion; '*Non ragioniam di lor*, We will not speak of *them*, look only and pass.'[3] Or think of this; 'They have not the *hope* to die, *Non han speranza di morte.*'[4] One day, it had risen sternly benign on the scathed heart of Dante, that he, wretched, never-resting, worn as he was, would full surely *die*; 'that Destiny itself could not doom him not to die.' Such words are in this man. For rigour, earnestness and depth, he is not to be paralleled in the modern world; to seek his parallel we must go into the Hebrew Bible, and live with the antique Prophets there.

I do not agree with much modern criticism, in justly preferring the *Inferno* to the two other parts of the Divine *Commedia*. Such preference belongs, I imagine, to our general Byronism of taste, and is like to be a transient feeling. The *Purgatorio* and *Paradiso*, especially the former, one would almost say, is even more excellent than it. It is a noble thing that *Purgatorio*, 'Mountain of Purification;' an emblem of the noblest conception of that age. If Sin is so fatal, and Hell is and must be so rigorous, awful, yet

[1] [Not *Paradiso*, but *Purgatorio* xxx. 28 ff.; xxxii. 1 ff.]
[2] [*Inf.* iii. 63.] [3] [*Inf.* iii. 51.] [4] [*Inf.* iii. 46.]

in Repentance too is man purified; Repentance is the grand Christian art. It is beautiful how Dante works it out. The *tremolar dell' onde*,[1] that 'trembling' of the ocean-waves, under the first pure gleam of morning, dawning afar on the wandering Two, is as the type of an altered mood. Hope has now dawned; never-dying Hope, if in company still with heavy sorrow. The obscure sojourn of daemons and reprobate is underfoot; a soft breathing of penitence mounts higher and higher, to the Throne of Mercy itself. 'Pray for me,' the denizens of that Mount of Pain all say to him. 'Tell my Giovanna to pray for me, my daughter Giovanna; I think her mother loves me no more!'[2] They toil painfully up by that winding steep, 'bent-down like corbels of a building,'[3] some of them,—crushed-together so 'for the sin of pride;' yet nevertheless in years, in ages and æons, they shall have reached the top, which is Heaven's gate, and by Mercy shall have been admitted in. The joy too of all, when one has prevailed; the whole Mountain shakes with joy, and a psalm of praise rises, when one soul has perfected repentance and got its sin and misery left behind! I call all this a noble embodiment of a true noble thought.

But indeed the Three compartments mutually support one another, are indispensable to one another. The *Paradiso*, a kind of inarticulate music to me, is the redeeming side of the *Inferno*: the *Inferno* without it were untrue. All three make-up the true Unseen World, as figured in the Christianity of the Middle Ages; a thing forever memorable, forever true in the essence of it, to all men. It was perhaps delineated in no human soul with such depth of veracity as in this of Dante's; a man *sent* to sing it, to keep it long memorable. Very notable with what brief simplicity he passes out of the every-day reality, into the Invisible one; and in the second or third Stanza, we find ourselves in the World of Spirits; and dwell there, as among things palpable, indubitable! To Dante they *were* so; the real world, as it is called, and its facts, was but the threshold to an infinitely higher Fact of a World. At bottom, the one was as *preter*natural as the other. Has not each man a soul? He will not only be a spirit, but is one. To the earnest Dante it is all one visible Fact; he believes it, sees it; is the Poet of it in virtue of that. Sincerity, I say again, is the saving merit, now as always.

Dante's Hell, Purgatory, Paradise, are a symbol withal, an emblematic representation of his Belief about this Universe:—some Critic in a future age, like those Scandinavian ones the other day, who has ceased altogether to think as Dante did, may find this too

[1] [Not 'tremolar dell' onde,' but 'tremolar della marina,' *Purg*. i. 117.]
[2] [*Purg*. viii. 71, 73.]
[3] [*Purg*. x. 130-1.]

all an 'Allegory,' perhaps an idle Allegory! It is a sublime embodiment, or sublimest, of the soul of Christianity. It expresses, as in huge worldwide architectural emblems, how the Christian Dante felt Good and Evil to be the two polar elements of this Creation, on which it all turns; that these two differ not by *preferability* of one to the other, but by incompatibility absolute and infinite; that the one is excellent and high as light and Heaven, the other hideous, black as Gehenna and the Pit of Hell! Everlasting Justice, yet with Penitence, with everlasting Pity,—all Christianism, as Dante and the Middle Ages had it, is emblemed here. Emblemed: and yet with what entire truth of purpose; how unconscious of any embleming!—Hell, Purgatory, Paradise: these things were not fashioned as emblems; was there, in our Modern European Mind, any thought at all of their being emblems! Were they not indubitable awful facts; the whole heart of man taking them for practically true, all Nature everywhere confirming them? So is it always in these things. Men do not believe an Allegory. The future Critic, whatever his new thought may be, who considers this of Dante to have been all got-up as an Allegory, will commit one sore mistake! . . .

And so in this Dante, as we said, had ten silent centuries, in a very strange way, found a voice. The *Divina Commedia* is of Dante's writing; yet in truth *it* belongs to ten Christian centuries, only the finishing of it is Dante's. So always. The craftsman there, the smith with that metal of his, with these tools, with these cunning methods,—how little of all he does is properly *his* work! All past inventive men work there with him;—as indeed with all of us, in all things. Dante is the spokesman of the Middle Ages; the Thought they lived by stands here, in everlasting music. These sublime ideas of his, terrible and beautiful, are the fruit of the Christian Meditation of all the good men who had gone before him. Precious they; but also is not he precious? Much, had not he spoken, would have been dumb; not dead, yet living voiceless.

On the whole, is it not an utterance, this mystic song, at once of one of the greatest human souls, and of the highest thing that Europe had hitherto realised for itself? Christianism, as Dante sings it, is another than Paganism in the rude Norse mind; another than 'Bastard Christianism' half-articulately spoken in the Arab Desert seven-hundred years before!—The noblest *idea* made *real* hitherto among men, is sung, and emblemed-forth abidingly by one of the noblest men. In the one sense and in the other, are we not right glad to possess it? As I calculate, it may last yet for long thousands of years. For the thing that is uttered from the inmost parts of a man's soul, differs altogether from what is uttered by the outer part. The outer is of the day, under the empire of mode; the outer passes away, in swift endless changes; the inmost is the same, yesterday, today and forever. True souls, in all generations of the world, who look on this Dante, will find a brotherhood in him; the deep sincerity of his thoughts, his woes and hopes, will speak likewise to their sincerity; they will feel that this Dante too was a brother. Napoleon in Saint-Helena is charmed with the genial veracity of old Homer. The oldest Hebrew Prophet, under a vesture the most diverse from ours, does yet, because he speaks from the heart of man, speak to all men's hearts. It is the one sole secret of continuing long memorable. Dante, for depth of sincerity, is like an antique Prophet too; his words, like theirs, come from his very heart. One need not wonder if it were predicted that his Poem might be the most enduring thing our Europe has yet made; for nothing so endures as a truly spoken word. All cathedrals, pontificalities, brass and stone, and outer arrangement never so lasting, are brief in comparison to an unfathomable heart-song like this: one feels as if it might survive, still of importance to men, when these had all sunk into new irrecognisable combinations, and had ceased individually to be. Europe has made much; great cities, great empires, encyclopaedias, creeds, bodies of opinion and practice: but it has made little of the class of Dante's thought. Homer yet *is*, veritably present face to face with every open soul of us; and Greece, where is *it?* Desolate for thousands of years; away, vanished. . . . Greece was; Greece, except in the *words* it spoke, is not.

The uses of this Dante? We will not say much about his 'uses.' A human soul who has once got into that primal element of *song*, and sung-forth fitly somewhat therefrom, has worked in the *depths* of our existence; feeding through long times the life-*roots* of all excellent human things whatsoever,—in a way that 'utilities' will not succeed well in calculating! We will not estimate the Sun by the quantity of gas-light it saves us; Dante shall be invaluable, or of no value. One remark I may make: the contrast in this respect between the Hero-Poet and the Hero-Prophet. In a hundred years, Mahomet had his Arabians at Grenada and at Delhi; Dante's Italians seem to be yet very much where they were. Shall we say, then, Dante's effect on the world was small in comparison? Not so: his arena is far more restricted; but also it is far nobler, clearer;—perhaps not less but more important. Mahomet speaks to the great masses of men, in the coarse dialect adapted to such; a dialect filled with inconsistencies, crudities, follies: on the great masses alone can he act, and there with good and with evil strangely blended. Dante speaks to the noble, the pure and great, in all times and places. Neither does he grow obsolete, as the other does. Dante burns as a pure star, fixed there in the firmament, at which the great and high of all ages kindle themselves: he is the possession of all the chosen of the world for uncounted time. Dante, one calculates, may long survive Mahomet. . . .

As Dante, the Italian man, was sent into our world to embody musically the Religion of the Middle Ages, the Religion of our Modern Europe, its Inner Life; so Shakspeare, we may say, embodies for us the Outer Life of our Europe, as developed then, its chivalries, courtesies, humours, ambitions, what practical way of thinking, acting, looking at the world, men then had. As in Homer we may still construe Old Greece; so in Shakspeare and Dante, after thousands of years, what our modern Europe was, in Faith and in Practice, will still be legible. Dante has given us the Faith or soul; Shakspeare, in a not less noble way, has given us the Practice and body. . . . Two fit men: Dante, deep, fierce as the central fire of the world; Shakspeare, wide, placid, far-seeing, as the Sun, the upper light of the world. Italy produced the one world-voice; we English had the honour of producing the other.

. . . In some sense it may be said that this glorious Elizabethan Era with its Shakspeare, as the outcome and flowerage of all which preceded it, is itself attributable to the Catholicism of the Middle Ages. The Christian Faith, which was the theme of Dante's Song, had produced this Practical Life which Shakspeare was to sing. For Religion then, as it now and always is, was the soul of Practice; the primary vital fact in men's life.

(Ed. 1873, pp. 79-95.)

[Shakespeare greater than Dante]

I will not blame Dante for his misery: it is as battle without victory; but true battle,—the first, indispensable thing. Yet I call Shakspeare greater than Dante, in that he fought truly, and did conquer. Doubt it not, he had his own sorrows.

(*Ibid*. p. 100.)

[Shakespeare and Dante likely to outlive Mahomet]

Shakspeare did not feel, like Mahomet, because he saw into those internal Splendours, that he specially was the 'Prophet of God:' and was he not greater than Mahomet in that? Greater; and also, if we compute strictly, as we did in Dante's case, more successful. . . . Even in Arabia, as I compute, Mahomet will have exhausted himself and become obsolete, while this Shakspeare, this Dante may still be young.

(*Ibid*. pp. 103-4.)

[Dante the voice of Italy]

Truly, it is a great thing for a Nation that it get an articulate voice; that it produce a man who will speak-forth melodiously what the heart of it means! Italy, for example, poor Italy lies dismembered, scattered asunder, not appearing in any protocol or treaty as a unity at all; yet the noble Italy is actually *one*: Italy produced its Dante; Italy can speak! The Czar of all the Russias, he is strong, with so many bayonets, Cossacks and cannons; and does a great feat in keeping such a tract of Earth politically together; but he cannot yet speak. Something great in him, but it is a dumb greatness. He has had no voice of genius, to be heard of all men and times. He must learn to speak. He is a great dumb monster hitherto. His cannons and Cossacks will all have rusted into nonentity, while that Dante's voice is still audible. The Nation that has a Dante is bound together as no dumb Russia can be.

(Ed. 1873, pp. 105-6.)

1840. LECTURES ON HEROES.—THE HERO AS PRIEST.

[Luther and Dante contrasted]

As we have seen Great Men, in various situations, building-up Religions, heroic Forms of human existence in this world, Theories of Life worthy to be sung by Dante, Practices of Life by a Shakspeare,—we are now to see the reverse process. . . . The mild shining of the Poet's light has to give place to the fierce lightning of the Reformer: . . . The Poet indeed, with his mildness, what is he but the product and ultimate adjustment of Reform, or Prophecy, with its fierceness? No wild Saint Dominics and Thebaïd Eremites, there had been no melodious Dante. . . .

It is notable enough how a Theorem or spiritual Representation, so we may call it, which once took in the whole Universe and was completely satisfactory in all parts of it to the highly-discursive acute intellect of Dante, one of the greatest in the world,—had in the course of another century become dubitable to common intellects; become deniable; and is now, to every one of us, flatly incredible, obsolete as Odin's Theorem! To Dante, human Existence, and God's ways with men, were all well represented by those *Malebolges*, *Purgatorios*; to Luther not well. How was this? Why could not Dante's Catholicism continue; but Luther's Protestantism must needs follow? Alas, nothing will *continue*. . . .

No man whatever believes, or can believe, exactly what his grandfather believed: he enlarges somewhat, by fresh discovery, his view of the Universe, and consequently his Theorem of the Universe. . . . Dante's Mountain of Purgatory does *not* stand 'in the ocean of the other Hemisphere,' when Columbus has once sailed thither! Men find no such thing extant in the other Hemisphere. It is not there. It must cease to be believed to be there. So with all beliefs whatsoever in this world,—all Systems of Belief, and Systems of Practice that spring from these. . . . Dante's sublime Catholicism, incredible now in theory, and defaced still worse by faithless, doubting and dishonest practice, has to be torn asunder by a Luther; Shakspeare's noble Feudalism, as beautiful as it once looked and was, has to end in a French Revolution. . . .

Are not all true men that live, or that ever lived, soldiers of the same army, enlisted, under Heaven's captaincy, to do battle against the same enemy, the empire of Darkness and Wrong? Why should we misknow one another, fight not against the enemy but against ourselves, from mere difference of uniform? All uniforms shall be good, so they hold in them true valiant men. All fashions of arms, the Arab turban and swift scimetar, Thor's strong hammer smiting down *Jotuns*, shall be welcome. Luther's battle-voice, Dante's march-melody, all genuine things are with us, not against us. We are all under one Captain, soldiers of the same host. . . .

In prizing justly the indispensable blessings of the New, let us not be unjust to the Old. The Old *was* true, if it no longer is. In Dante's days it needed no sophistry, self-blinding or other dishonesty, to get itself reckoned true. It was good then; nay there is in the soul of it a deathless good.

(Ed. 1873, pp. 108-12, 126.)

1840. DEC. 9. LETTER TO RALPH WALDO EMERSON (from Chelsea).

[The sorrows of Goethe as deep as those of Dante]

You call Goethe *actual*, not *ideal;* there is truth in that too; and yet at bottom is not the whole truth rather this: The actual well-seen *is* the ideal? The *actual*, what really is and exists: the past, the present, the future no less, do all lie there! Ah yes! one day you will find that this sunny-looking, courtly Goethe held veiled in him a Prophetic sorrow deep as Dante's,—all the nobler to me and to you, that he *could* so hold it. I believe this; no man can *see* as he sees, that has not suffered and striven as man seldom did.

(*Correspondence of Carlyle and Emerson,* vol. i. p. 314.)

1843. PAST AND PRESENT.

[A workhouse a reminder of Dante's Hell]

'Passing by the Workhouse of St. Ives in Huntingdonshire, on a bright day last autumn,' says the picturesque Tourist, 'I saw sitting on wooden benches, in front of their Bastille and within their ring-wall and its railings, some half-hundred or more of these men. Tall robust figures, young mostly or of middle age; of honest countenance, many of them thoughtful and even intelligent-looking men. They sat there, near by one another; but in a kind of torpor, especially in a silence, which was very striking. In silence: for, alas, what word was to be said? An Earth all lying round, crying, Come and till me, come and reap me;—yet we here sit enchanted! In the eyes and brows of these men hung the gloomiest expression, not of anger, but of grief and shame and manifold inarticulate distress and weariness: they returned my glance with a glance that seemed to say, "Do not look at us. We sit enchanted here, we know not why. The Sun shines and the Earth calls; and, by the governing Powers and Impotences of this England, we are forbidden to obey. It is impossible they tell us!" There was something that reminded me of Dante's Hell in the look of all this; and I rode swiftly away.'

(Bk. i. Chap. i. p. 2, ed. 1873.)

['The Ugolino Hunger-tower']

At Stockport Assizes a Mother and a Father are arraigned and found guilty of poisoning three of their children, to defraud a 'burial society' of some £3 8s. due on the death of each child: they are arraigned, found guilty. . . . A human Mother and Father had said to themselves, What shall we do to escape starvation? We are deep sunk here, in our dark cellar; and help is far.—Yes, in the Ugolino Hunger-tower [1] stern things happen; best-loved little Gaddo fallen dead on his Father's knees! [2]

(*Ibid.* pp. 3-4.)

['Ugolino Hunger-cellars']

Two million shirtless or ill-shirted workers sit enchanted in Workhouse Bastilles, five million more (according to some) in Ugolino Hunger-cellars; [1] and for remedy, you say,—what say you?—'Raise *our* rents!'

(Bk. iii. Chap. vii. p. 147.)

['Follow thy star through chaos and the murk of Hell']

He who takes not counsel of the Unseen and Silent, from him will never come real visibility and speech. Thou must descend to the *Mothers*, to the *Manes*, and Hercules-like long suffer and labour there, wouldst thou emerge with victory into the sunlight. As in battle and the shock of war,—for is not this a battle?—thou too shalt fear no pain or death, shalt love no ease or life; the voice

[1] [*Inf.* xxxiii. 22-3.] [2] [*Inf.* xxxiii. 67-70.]

of festive Lubberlands, the noise of greedy Acheron shall alike lie silent under thy victorious feet. Thy work, like Dante's, shall 'make thee lean for many years.'[1] The world and its wages, its criticisms, counsels, helps, impediments, shall be as a waste ocean-flood; the chaos through which thou art to swim and sail. Not the waste waves, and their weedy gulf streams, shalt thou take for guidance: thy star alone,—'*Se tu segui tua stella!*'[2] Thy star alone, now clear beaming over Chaos, nay now by fits gone out, disastrously eclipsed: this only shalt thou strive to follow. O, it is a business, as I fancy, that of weltering your way through Chaos and the murk of Hell! Green-eyed dragons watching you, three-headed Cerberuses,—not without sympathy of *their* sort! '*Eccovi l' uom ch' è stato all' Inferno.*'[3]

(Book iii. Chap. xii. pp. 176-7.)

ANTONIO PANIZZI

(1797-1879)

[Antonio Panizzi was born at Brescello in the Duchy of Modena in 1797. He was educated at the University of Parma, where he graduated in law in 1818. In 1822 he was arrested on a charge of conspiracy against the government, but managed to escape, and eventually took refuge in England, where he was befriended by Ugo Foscolo and William Roscoe. After spending several years in Liverpool as a teacher of Italian, Panizzi was appointed in 1828 to the professorship of Italian at University College. London (Gabriele Rossetti being a rival candidate), through the good offices of Brougham, who in 1831, as Lord Chancellor, procured for him the post of Assistant Librarian at the British Museum. In 1837 he was promoted (over the head of H. F. Cary, the translator of Dante) to the keepership of printed books, and in 1856 he succeeded Sir Henry Ellis as Principal Librarian, which office he held until 1866, when he resigned on account of ill-health. His many years at the Museum were marked by the most important improvements in the organization of the library, and the development of the accommodation, the present reading-room—admittedly the most perfect of its kind—having been erected at his instigation and after his design. He was also instrumental in procuring the bequest (in 1846) of the magnificent library of Thomas Grenville. Panizzi, who was made a K.C.B. in 1869, died in London in 1879. His most important literary work was his *Orlando Innamorato di Boiardo: Orlando Furioso di Ariosto: With an Essay on the Romantic Narrative Poetry of the Italians; Memoirs, and Notes* (9 vols. 1830-4). He was a constant student of Dante, and superintended for Lord Vernon the splendid reprint of *Le Prime Quattro Edizioni della Divina Commedia* (1858). Panizzi was an occasional contributor to the 'Quarterlies,' one of his articles being a scathing criticism (in the *Foreign Review*, 1828) of Gabriele Rossetti's fantastic theory as to the *Divina Commedia*.[4]]

[1] [*Par.* xxv. 3.]
[2] [*Inf.* xv. 55.]
[3] [The exclamation of the women of Verona, on seeing Dante pass in the street—see Boccaccio's *Vita di Dante*, § 8.]
[4] [See above, p. 446.]

1827. Jan. WESTMINSTER REVIEW. NO. XIII. ART. VIII. LA COMMEDIA DI DANTE ALIGHIERI: ILLUSTRATA DA UGO FOSCOLO.

[The debt of Italy to Dante]

STRANGERS to Italy can hardly conceive how so fierce a contest can have been so long waged respecting Dante's doctrines as to the Italian tongue; doctrines which he has advanced in a little unfinished work, written in bad Latin, and entitled *De Vulgari Eloquio*, where he endeavours to establish what is the genuine Italian language: and after a train of cogent and profound reasoning, passing in review the different dialects of the Peninsula, discards them all, the Tuscan included, and decides, without hesitation, that the claim of the Florentines to the exclusive possession of the true dialect is an untenable and ridiculous pretension.[1] He adds, that the true Italian is that which is written and spoken by polished writers in every part of Italy, and is not restricted to any particular province. Since the discovery, in the sixteenth century,[2] of this workof Dante's, the Florentines, having failed in disproving the authenticity of the work, have strenuously resisted its authority. Thus this illustrious man, after having been condemned by the Florentines of old to be burnt alive, as a bad citizen, has been doomed afresh by their posterity to undergo, as it were, a similar punishment in his writings, for imputed ignorance of that language which he himself created. . . .

It is evident to all enlightened Italians, that it is of the first importance to their country to preserve her language. Living under governments where to be charged with having the feelings of an Italian is too often synonymous with condemnation, and the loss of all that renders life dear, and frequently of life itself, they also perceive that philological discussions may be productive of the happiest effects in keeping up the national spirit. Unable to speak the truth without disguise, yet feeling, that duty to themselves and to their country forbids them to preserve an injurious silence, they have discovered a way of involving their countrymen by the powerful spell of *national attachment*. This way presented itself to them in Dante's work *De Vulgari Eloquio*. The Italians to whom we have referred saw that the doctrines of Dante—that man to whom Italy owes everything, and who acknowledged but one language as the true Italian—were exactly those calculated to serve their design. Accordingly, on his authority they began, by showing that the Italian language is not, and ought not to be, either Tuscan,

[1] 'Post haec veniamus ad Tuscos qui propter *amentiam suam infroniti* titulum sibi Vulgaris illustris arrogare videntur.'—L. 1, C. 13.

[2] [It was first published, in an Italian translation, by Trissino at Vicenza in 1529; the Latin original was first published by Corbinelli at Paris in 1577.]

Roman, or Sienese; that the Italians should henceforth be only one nation; and that it was inadmissible to speak either of different or separate provinces. When this question began to be agitated three centuries ago, it was merely ridiculous and useless, not being directed to its proper object. . . . The doctrines of Dante were not then maintained in the spirit of their author, nor had Dante himself that magic power over a nation enervated by the dominion of Spain and the Council of Trent, which he possesses at this day, thanks to the ardour with which the study of his poem has been renewed. Now, the combat is carried on under the shelter of his name, that name so eminently Italian, and his doctrines are now propagated with various commentaries. This rekindles and increases the desire of studying the *Divina Commedia* itself, to which he owes his fame, and in which he introduces with such felicity the precepts laid down by him with equal force as a rhetorician, in his lesser work, *De Vulgari Eloquio.* But if these discussions had no other merit than that of extending the reading of the *Divina Commedia*, they would still be of incalculable advantage, since there is either no work capable of rousing Italy from her present state, and of making her again what she was, or, if there is, that work is the *Divina Commedia;* with this advantage, too that no human power can prevent its being reprinted, or can limit its study. . . .

Dante is now more than ever talked of in England; yet, without being identified with the author and his book, it is impossible to enter into what we have now said. All persons, however, would be judges, and, what is worse, some who evidently show that they have never read or heard more than a few passages from the poem, here and there. But it is not enough to be an Italian to feel and even to understand the *Divina Commedia;* and to enable the Italians to reap that advantage from it which we trust they will yet do, some assistance is required. From the moment that this poem was composed, the want of this was felt. . . . The volume of Ugo Foscolo, by its arranged facts and arguments, connected in succession, and supported by authorities, punctually quoted by volume, chapter, and page, endeavours to elucidate as much of the life of Dante as is necessary for understanding, or rather to prepare the reader for understanding the poem. . . . That which renders the work of Foscolo superior to all others, and entitles him to the gratitude of Italy, is his constant study to place the poem of Dante before the Italians under those points of view in which they ought to look at it, in order to reap more solid advantage from it than the mere study of verses and phrases. Besides this, the malignant and interested accusations of those whose delight it is, to keep the world in darkness, and who on that account hate the name of Dante, are unveiled without mercy, combated without respect, and destroyed beyond the power of reply. . . . Nothing will contribute more both to prove these truths and to exhibit the great soul of Dante, and the infinite obligations which Italy, and indeed the world, are under to him, than the knowledge of the wretched condition of the religion, science, and governments of Italy in his time. This interesting subject Foscolo proposes to elucidate.

(Vol. vii. pp. 153 ff.)

1828. FOREIGN REVIEW AND CONTINENTAL MISCELLANY. NO. III. ART. IX. LA DIVINA COMMEDIA DI DANTE ALIGHIERI CON COMENTO ANALITICO DI GABRIELE ROSSETTI.[1]

[Exposure of Rossetti's theory]

The modern Italian pretends to prove that what we have, till now, admired in Dante is nothing; that, instead of regarding him as the sublime poet, we ought to have looked upon him as an equivocator (after the manner of another Rabelais, or Lemuel Gulliver), who wrote always with a double meaning. Thus, when the Florentine says to Virgil, 'Thou art wise, and understandest me better than I do express myself' (Inf. ii. 34); he meant also to say, 'Thou art wise, and understandest me, *because* I do not speak reason,' (Rossetti, pp. 37-8), and such other perfect and sublime nonsense. . . . We have, attentively, read Signor Rossetti's Comments, and heard their praises in high-sounding words: but feeling convinced that these were uttered either by those who had taken the matter in trust from others, or by persons who knew as little of the Italian history as of Chinese politics, we have actually perused the commentator's lucubrations, with the purpose of bringing them under our impartial examination. . . . As we have the deepest veneration for the author of the 'Commedia,' and are unwilling that the creed propounded by this new expositor should lead the eyes of his worshippers astray from the true understanding of the attributes of this mighty poetical divinity, we have thought it our duty to expose Sig. Rossetti's fallacies. . . . The principal object of Sig. Rossetti's work is to explain the allegories of Dante's poem, and at every syllable he discovers some new and extraordinary meaning. He tortures grammar, and history, criticism, and poetry to prop up his system; he enlists on his behalf authority and no authority—even that of those penitential psalms, impudently ascribed to Dante by some shameless friar, and which all those who possess a knowledge of that poet must at once pronounce to be

[1] [An Italian translation of this article, together with Rossetti's reply and Panizzi's notes upon the latter, was printed by Panizzi at Florence in 1832 (*Osservazioni sul Comento Analitico della Divina Commedia pubblicato dal Sig. Gabriele Rossetti, tradotte dall' Inglese, con la Risposta del Sig. Rossetti corredata di note in replica*).]

impudent forgeries, from their frivolity, unharmoniousness, and vulgarity. He then asserts, without compassion or regard for any one, that the 'Divina Commedia' has been for five centuries an unknown world (mondo sconosciuto), which he alone, like another Columbus, has, under a wise Providence, been allowed to discover, and applauds himself so much that he reminds us of Lyca—

Fuit haud ignobilis Argis,
Qui se credebat miros audire tragaedos
In vacuo laetus sessor plausorque theatro.[1]

We are sorry to undeceive him. . . . We will now proceed to examine an entirely new allegory, which Rossetti supposes to exist in the ninth canto, on the discovery of which he prides himself, and with which he is more pleased than with any other.

Towards the end of the eighth canto of the Inferno, Dante perceives the city of *Dite*. A crowd of evil spirits are assembled near the gates, who invite Virgil to enter, leaving Dante behind. Virgil advances alone, and speaks privately to the demons, but not being able to come to an understanding with them, is obliged to return towards Dante. The demons enter the city and close the gates. Virgil counsels Dante to fear nothing. Then, in the ninth canto, a noise is heard, which, with inimitable beauty, Dante compares to the impetuous rushing of the wind.[2] He sees a figure approaching, whom he discovers to be a messenger from Heaven, who goes to the gates, which he opens with his rod without opposition, and, after reproving the demons, returns back without noticing either Dante or Virgil, who now enter the city. Rossetti styling this canto 'il vero mondo della novità,' gives us a whimsical explanation, quite after his own fashion. He says, that *Dite* is *Florence*, and the *messenger from Heaven* the Emperor Henry VII. of Luxembourg, through whose assistance Dante promised himself to return into his own country, in spite of his enemies. Among other consequences which the very acute commentator deduces from this interpretation—as he pretends that the most minute particulars in this canto correspond with historical fact—is the following: 'that this ninth canto was written after 1313,' that is to say, after the Emperor Henry's death, which took place on the 24th of August of that year. In order to have a clear view of the value and correctness of this discovery of Rossetti, it should be known, that in 1313, Henry VII. presented himself at the head of his army, before the gates of Florence, which were not voluntarily opened *to him*, and which he could not forcibly enter; that he was even obliged to raise the siege of Florence with disgrace, which place, to speak correctly, he was never able to put into a state of blockade, because so little

[1] [Horace, *Epist.* II. ii. 128-30.] [2] [*Inf.* ix. 64 ff.]

did the Florentines at that time fear the Germans, that they kept all the gates of the city open as usual, except that, near which the Emperor was encamped (Villani, l. xi. c. 45)[1]; that Dante never entered Florence again after his banishment, either through the Emperor's means, or otherwise.

Now, we ask every candid and impartial reader, if it be probable that Dante intended to describe an Emperor flying from Florence in disgrace, under the allegory of a heavenly messenger opening the gates of *Dite* (viz. Florence) without opposition? We ask how Dante could possibly represent himself a wanderer from Florence, until his death, under the allegory of his *unimpeded entrance* into the infernal city? What! would it be by describing Napoleon as landing victorious in England, or by proclaiming that he entered Cadiz without opposition or delay, that we should be said to sing his praises? or would not this be the bitterest irony, and an insult to his memory? Would Dante, in wishing to praise 'l' alto Arrigo,' whom he almost worshipped, have selected an allusion to an enterprise which ended in his defeat? We think we have said enough to prove how utterly the opinion of the perspicacious commentator is at variance with reason.

(Vol. ii. pp. 175 ff.)

1830. ESSAY ON THE ROMANTIC NARRATIVE POETRY OF THE ITALIANS.[2]

[Dante's knowledge of Greek]

The question as to Dante's knowledge of Greek has been much agitated. Pelli, and some minor writers, have eagerly contended that Dante was well acquainted with Greek, and Dionisi has gone so far as to assert that he taught it. Maffei, Tiraboschi, and last, not least, Foscolo, have denied this. To quote, as has been done, a pretended sonnet from Dante to Bosone Raffaelli in support of the affirmative, implies such a poor opinion of the reader's taste as to be unworthy of notice. It is true that Dante pronounced the words "Letè," "tragedìa," &c. very properly; it is true that he praises Homer; it is true that he knew the derivation of the word "Flegetonte;" yet his knowledge of the pronunciation and meaning of a few Greek words does not imply that he knew Greek thoroughly. He may even have been acquainted with a translation of Homer; for a version of the Odyssey, at least, was executed before that of Leonzio, procured by Boccaccio and Petrarca. In his poem he does not admit that anyone went to hell or paradise, and

[1] [Ed. 1823, l. ix. c. 47.]

[2] [Prefixed to Panizzi's edition of the *Orlando Innamorato* of Boiardo and the *Orlando Furioso* of Ariosto.]

returned, but Æneas, St. Paul, and himself (the knight who performed the journey by order of Charles Martel is out of the question) and consequently he excludes Ulysses. In the 28th canto of the Inferno he relates the travels of this gentleman, not according to the Odyssey, but according to the account of Pliny and Solinus. There is however an argument drawn from Homer's Iliad on the one hand and from Dante's Purgatory on the other, which has never been taken into consideration, and which yet almost induces a belief that on one occasion at least Dante knew the Iliad and imitated it. Still the question will be whether the Iliad was translated before Dante's time or not.

Any one conversant with Homer will remember that fanciful and highly poetic passage of the Iliad where Scamander addresses itself to the Simois threatening to drown Achilles with its waters, and bury him beneath its sands. According to Dante, Buonconte da Montefeltro, who was killed at the battle of Campaldino, but whose body was never found, was treated by the Archiano and Arno exactly in the way that the Scamander and Simois would have treated Achilles. The rivers Archiano and Arno were moved, not by themselves, but by a devil who was incensed by an angel's carrying away Buonconte's soul, on the possession of which he had relied. As he could not get the soul, he was resolved to do his best with the body. How far this may tend to elucidate the question as to Dante's knowledge of Greek, it is not here the place to determine. Certain it is, that the coincidence has not the air of being fortuitous, especially if we consider the admirable art with which Dante always imitates, but seldom or never copies: whence arises the difficulty of discovering the similarity between a passage in his poem and any of the writers with whom he vies.

(Vol. ii. pp. 153-5.)

[Dante's account of the fate of the souls of Guido and Buonconte da Montefeltro]

Dante, who wrote a Comedy which was never supposed to be a mock poem, records two instances of contests between angels, or saints and devils, to possess themselves of a favourite soul. In the twenty-seventh canto of the Inferno, St. Francis, it is said, came for the soul of Guido da Montefeltro, who late in life turned a Franciscan friar, and who, according to Dante, after he was a friar, at the instigation of Pope Boniface VIII who absolved him of the crime before it was committed, had given to that Pope the treacherous advice to promise much to his enemies to get them into his power, but then to break his word. A "black angel" thought he had as good a right to such a soul as St. Francis, and accordingly went to claim it also. The devil carried the point, arguing it in due form. He said that no man could be well absolved unless he repented; and contended, that since one cannot repent and sin at the same moment, it was evident that Guido could not have been absolved legally by the Pope. St. Francis is unable to answer this argument, and accordingly the devil carries Guido's soul to hell, where Dante happens to hear the story from the friar himself.[1]

A son of this same Guido, that is Buonconte da Montefeltro, was more lucky. He was killed at the battle of Certomondo,[2] but had time, before dying, to repent of his sins, which from Dante's relation, are insinuated as leaving a rather heavy balance against him. Not being a friar, it was not St. Francis, but an angel who came for his soul, as well as a fiend. The latter immediately discovered he had no chance, and although he complained of his loss, "only on account of a little tear shed by the old sinner in his last moments," he was obliged to submit, and was satisfied with causing the body to be lost, so that no one ever knew what became of it except Dante, who heard the tale from Buonconte in Purgatory.[3]

The lines respecting Guido have been ludicrously translated by Voltaire;[4] yet the two passages are not only in very good earnest, but are masterly directed against two opinions, which are held to this day by some of the followers of the church of Rome; by those who contend that the pope's power is not restrained. Guido is carried off by the devil, on the ground that the pope had not, and could not, have the power of absolving him; a power which many contend the pope has. Buonconte is carried to paradise by the angel, although he was excommunicated by the pope; which is an opinion quite at variance with that which the most hot-headed Catholics teach. Pulci was not the man to believe that either angels or devils were likely to come to fetch the souls of the damned or of the elect; and by ironically supposing it, he did not certainly wish to indulge a burlesque humour, but wanted to show the absurdity of it to his readers. It seems that both Dante and Pulci, by two different ways, had the same end in view; that of enlightening the people, and of exposing the cunning of those who lived upon their credulity, and who made an infamous traffic of absurdities.

(Vol. ii. pp. 213-5.)

[The doom of 'trimmers' in Dante's Hell]

Palmieri supposed that our souls were those angelic spirits, which, in the rebellion of the angels did not join either God or his enemies.

[1] [*Inf.* xxvii. 112 ff.]
[2] [Otherwise known as the battle of Campaldino.]
[3] [*Purg.* v. 103 ff.]
[4] [See vol. i. pp. 209-10.]

Dante, in a manner peculiarly his own, puts these wretches in the outskirts of hell, as unworthy alike of punishment and of mercy; and so despicable, that they cannot be received either into paradise or hell. It is a lofty conception, and the passage one of the most highly finished in a poem, which fully deserves the epithet which the judgment of five centuries has pronounced upon it (see *Inf.* iii. 37).

(Vol. ii. p. 219.)

1831. THE LANDSCAPE ANNUAL: THE TOURIST IN ITALY.

[Dante, Rimini and the episode of Paolo and Francesca [1]]

Rimini is interesting to the lovers of Italian literature, on account of its being connected with the tragical deaths of Francesca da Polenta and Paolo Malatesta, which form the subject of one of the finest episodes in Dante's poem (*Inferno*, c. v). . . .

Dante, although a Ghibelline, was well received at Ravenna by Guido da Polenta, whose hatred for the Malatestas found a kindred feeling in the breast of the poet, who never omits an occasion of branding them with infamy. Thus, he first speaks of the two Malatestas, il Vecchio and dall' Occhio, as 'two mastiffs eating Rimini' (*Inf.* xxvii. 46); and then he records the treachery of that felon, 'who sees but with one eye,' who murdered the two best persons of Fano (*Inf.* xxviii. 81). The poet's dislike for the Malatestas, who were Guelphs, and particularly for Malatestino dall' Occhio, is easily accounted for. Of this tyrant, a contemporary chronicler says, that he was 'bold, wise, and honest as ever man was. He had only one fault—he would neither see nor hear a Ghibelline; he persecuted them fiercely.' Dante, placed between his political principles and his gratitude for Guido, does not abuse him, but praises highly the Anastagi and the Traversari, and weeps over their misfortunes; which was an indirect, but bitter and decisive condemnation of Guido's conduct towards them.

The history of the Polentas and Malatestas, as well as that of the love of Francesca and Paolo, has been sadly confused, and turned into a mere romance, by Dante's commentators. There is but one old chronicler who incidentally mentions the tragical death of the two relations in the following few words: 'It happened that Zanne Sciancato found his lady with his brother Paolo and killed them both'? Their guilt is not even hinted at, and seems to be implicitly denied by Dante himself, who says that Zanciotto is destined to fall into hell's pit as a murderer of his relations. . . .

[1] [This account is assigned to Panizzi on the authority of I. C. Wright—see his note on *Inf.* v. 127 (ed. 1833, p. 347).]

Dante supposes that Paolo and Francesca fell in love on reading how Sir Lancelot's passion was returned by Genevre; a circumstance purely imaginary, as we may easily guess, but which has nevertheless been received as a fact by some good-natured annotators. . . . The dialogue between the party is interrupted, in the romance, at the moment at which the reading of Paolo and Francesca is supposed by the poet to be broken off; and the circumstance, which was so fatal to the two lovers, seems to have been the most celebrated of all the story long after the time of Dante. . . .

In a work like the present, we should consider it pedantry were we to enter into critical remarks on the beauty of the passage, and more particularly of the delicate manner in which it is interrupted by the poet. Wishing to confine ourselves to facts, . . . we shall here only add, that the line,

Soli eravam e senza alcun sospetto,[1]

seems to have been suggested to Dante by another romance, that of 'Sir Tristram,' which we know was very popular in his time, as we learn from the oldest of his commentators, his contemporary, who says, 'Everybody speaks of the death of Tristram and Iseutte.' When their mutual love was discovered for the first time, among other circumstances, it is remarked in the old romance; 'Ils sont tous deux seul a seul, qu'ilz n'ont nul destourbier, ne paour ni d'ung ni d' autre.'

(pp. 222 ff.)

HENRY NEELE

(1798-1828)

[Henry Neele, miscellaneous writer, the son of an engraver, was born in London in 1798. He was brought up to the law, and practised as a solicitor, but devoted much of his time to literature. He published two volumes of poems (1817, 1823), and delivered in 1827 a course of lectures on English poetry. In the same year he published the *Romance of English History*, and a collected edition of his poems. He died by his own hand in 1828. His literary remains, including tales and poems, and his *Lectures on English Poetry*, were published after his death, in 1829.]

1827. LECTURES ON ENGLISH POETRY.[2]

[Sackville's *Induction* and the *Inferno*]

THE *Mirror for Magistrates* was a work to which many of the most eminent Writers in Elizabeth's Reign contributed. . . . The most valuable portion of it is the Induction, by Lord Buckhurst.[3] The Poet supposes himself to be led, like Dante,

[1] [*Inf.* v. 129.]

[2] [Delivered at the Russell Institution, March-May, 1827, and published in *Lectures on English Poetry. . . . With Miscellaneous Tales and Poems; Being the Literary Remains of the late Henry Neele* (1829).]

[3] [See vol. i. pp. 49-50.]

to the Infernal Regions, under the conduct of Sorrow; where he meets with the Spirits of those persons, alike distinguished for their high station, and their misfortunes, whose narrations compose the Volume.

(*Lecture* ii. ed. 1830, p. 53.)

ENGLISH EDITION OF THE *DIVINA COMMEDIA*

1827. LA DIVINA COMMEDIA DI DANTE ALIGHIERI. CON NUOVI ARGOMENTI; ANNOTAZIONI DA' MIGLIORI COMENTATORI SCELTE ED ABBREVIATE; E COLL' ACCENTO DI PROSODIA. AI DILETTANTI E SCOLARI DELL' ITALIANA FAVELLA DEVOTAMENTE DEDICATA DA PIETRO CICCHETTI. LONDRA. 12MO.

[Printed by the Whittinghams at their Chiswick Press; published by C. S. Arnold. This is the first English-printed edition of the *Commedia* complete in one volume, and the sixth edition of the *Commedia* printed and published in England (previous editions appeared in 1808, 1819, 1819-20, and 1822-3). The editor claims that this volume, which consists of 610 pages, is the first single-volume edition of the *Commedia* in this small *format*—a claim which shows that his acquaintance with the bibliography of the subject was limited, since at least half-a-dozen single-volume editions in small *format* were published in Italy and France in Cent. xvi. This volume contains an engraving by J. Redaway, from a painting by H. P. Briggs, A.R.A. (c. 1791-1844), of Francesca and Paolo (*Inf.* v. 100-2.)][1]

ANONYMOUS

1828. January. QUARTERLY REVIEW. ART. III. THE REFORMATION IN ITALY.

[Dante as a theologian]

LONG before the era of the reformation, commonly so called, many of the sentiments of the reformers were cherished in several places to our certain knowledge, and, probably, in still more, where the tyranny of the time has left us in ignorance of them. Dante, undoubtedly, was not speaking at random, in his assertion, (and it is worthy of attention, if it were only for its very early date), that the burning sepulchres of his heretics were far more abundantly stocked with victims than was commonly supposed:—

'Qui son gli eresiarche
Co' lor seguaci d' ogni setta, *e molto*
Più, che non credi, son le tombe carche.'

Infern. ix.[2]

. . . Of Dante's hostility to the Church of Rome, we had re-

[1] [A brief notice of this edition of the *Commedia* appeared in the *Monthly Magazine* for March, 1827 (N. S., vol. iii., part i., pp. 316-17.)]

[2] [ll. 127-9.]

cently occasion to say something in our review of Mr. Todd's edition of Milton.[1] His feelings, however, towards it were perfectly distinct from those of the parties with whom we have been hitherto dealing. These latter denounced the *doctrines* of the church; the poet embraced its doctrines, but execrated their *abuse*. Signor Rossetti, indeed, in a most elaborate, learned, and ingenious commentary on the Inferno, recently published,[2] pronounces the Divina Commedia to have nothing to do with theology; that it is a purely political poem; that it attacks the pope as the head of the Guelphic party, without any reference to his spiritual character; that it is, in short, a covert enterprise of the Ghibellin against the Guelph; and that its language is a kind of freemason's phraseology, only to be understood by the initiated. . . . Now, supposing this scheme to be as sound as we are afraid it is visionary, we should think it a misfortune to be thoroughly versed in it. In our eyes, it would be the utter ruin of Dante as a poet, and sundry curious conundrums would be all that we should get in exchange for those noble bursts of inspiration which we had found in him, or thought we had found in him, in the days of our happier ignorance of these rabbinical expositions. Besides, to us it is an offensive idea, that the sublime scenes of an invisible world of souls, a hell, a purgatory, and a paradise, should, after all, be only parables relating to a factious squabble in Italy. This seems to us to be reversing the order of things grievously, and making the thing typified of ten-fold less consequence than the type. Who, for instance, would not rather believe that the city of Dis meant the city of Dis than the city of Florence? That the heretics it contained were really heretics than Guelphs? That the angel who descended to open the gates which were shut against Dante and Virgil, was actually a messenger of God, empowered with his wand to smite the portals, and make a way into that infernal town, than that it was the Emperour Henry, with his sceptre, demanding admission for the Ghibellins into Florence? . . .

For the reasons, therefore, which we have given, we shall continue to regard Dante more as the theologian than the politician, and proceed to say a word or two on the view he took of his church. Its doctrines, we repeat, he allowed, and only exclaimed against their perversion. For the accommodation of heretics in another world, he provides, like a good son of his intolerant mother, sepulchres glowing with fervent heat, and no suspicion seems to cross his mind that they were thus out of their proper element. A purgatory, he admits, and stations at its gate an

[1] [*Quarterly Review*, June, 1827—see above, pp. 471 ff.]

[2] [*La Divina Commedia, con comento analitico: Inferno.* 2 vols. Londra, 1826-7. (See above, pp. 446-7.)]

angel duly armed with his keys and commission from St. Peter: yet he tells us that the apostle had cautioned him against opening too freely, and admitting a herd of miscreants who would trample him to death (Purg. xi).[1] He believes it to be the duty of those who are alive, to pray for the souls that are therein, and he represents them, in their turn, making supplication for their friends on earth (Purg. xi); but he adds, in direct opposition to all excessive merchandise of souls, that purgatory did, in fact, receive very few—that its doors creaked on their hinges for want of use, and that mankind, in general, rushed headlong, and at once to the bottomless pit (Purg. x). Priestly absolution he does not dispute, yet he reckons it profitless without repentance; and a luckless friar, who had sinned at the pope's suggestion, and upon the faith of his promise that he would open heaven for him notwithstanding, finds himself, to his surprise, amongst the damned (Infern. xxvii). He condemns to a joyless abode, among the spirits in prison (as his church taught him) all who had died without baptism, however innocent their lives (Infern. iv). He constantly addresses the Virgin in language of the most chivalrous devotion, and sometimes with the most touching tenderness (Purg. xx). He kindles at the thought of a crusade, and bitterly reproaches the pope and cardinals with brooding over their gains; whilst Nazareth, 'where Gabriel spread his angel wings,' was left a prey to the infidels (Par. ix). He had no wish to interfere with the rights of the clergy as the ministers of God, and gratuitously selects as a subject for sculpture, the death of Uzzah, when he stretched forth an unconsecrated hand to bear up the ark (Purg. x). But the *union* of secular and ecclesiastical dominion he holds in abomination; this he would tear asunder; to this he imputes the spiritual downfall of the church (Purg. xxvi); and pouring out upon its consequent corruptions the fiercest vials of his wrath, he denounces it as the destroyer of his country (Purg. x), the beast (xvi), the harlot (xxxii). He peoples hell with its ministers, plaguing them with divers plagues; and they dash against each other huge stones in disorderly conflict; and they stand on their heads in burning jars; and are closed up in regions of thick-ribbed ice; and make their moan from the summits of pyramids of flame in which they are enveloped; and are crushed under excessive weights; and are torn by the forks of vindictive fiends, when they venture to peep out of the boiling pitch wherein is their everlasting portion.

Dante would have rejoiced to see his church efficient and prosperous. To its radical errors in faith he was not alive, for he was

[1] [*Purg*. ix. 127-9—an extraordinary misinterpretation—the Angel says that Peter told him to err rather in opening than in keeping the gate shut, provided the folk prostrate themselves at his feet (i.e. to ask pardon).]

a reader and admirer of Thomas Aquinas (Par. x et seq.), and was evidently better versed in the historical and picturesque parts of the scriptures, than in the doctrinal; but that there was something in it grievously wrong he was fully aware, and so was Petrarch who succeeded him.

(Vol. xxxvii. pp. 56 ff.)

ANONYMOUS

1828. Feb. LITERARY GAZETTE AND JOURNAL OF THE BELLES LETTRES. ROSSETTI'S DIVINA COMMEDIA DI DANTE ALIGHIERI CON COMENTO ANALITICO. VOL. II.

[Rossetti's discovery of 'the key to the hidden sense of the *Inferno*']

THE first volume of this interesting work was noticed in the *Literary Gazette* two years ago[1] . . . with praises and indications of its merits and importance. . . . The further Signor Rossetti proceeds, the more conclusive does the conviction become, that he has at last discovered the true key to the hidden sense of the *Inferno*, after the meaning of that extraordinary poem had lain five hundred years in darkness and mystery. . . . The second volume of Signor Rossetti's Exposition takes up the poem of Dante where it was broken off in Vol. i., namely at Canto xii., with which he pursues the same course as in his former enquiry, to the end of Canto xxxiv. The Notes and Reflections are equally ingenious and convincing; and no one can rise from the perusal of these pages without feeling that, if Dante himself could be recalled to life, he must sanction the opinions of his able Critic. We would say that Rossetti has perhaps, occasionally, found out beauties never intended by the writer; for it is far easier to supply a meaning than to create a thought or imagination: still, however, this will in no degree detract from the value of his work, which we consider to be one of the most important in the whole circle of the Italian tongue.

(No. 578, p. 104.)

ANONYMOUS

1828. October. QUARTERLY REVIEW. ART. III. HEXAGLOT GEORGICS.

[Influence of Dante in Spain]

IT was, probably, from the writings of Dante, in which the Mantuan bard makes so distinguished a figure, that the Castilian admiration of him first began. The Marquis of Santillane,[2] to whom the literature of Spain is so deeply indebted,

[1] [No. 468, Jan. 7, 1826 (see above, pp. 447 ff.).]

[2] [1398-1458.]

was an eminent lover of the Italian poet,[1] and the Marquis's friend Juan de Mena,[2] while he executed his translation of Homer, was not likely to leave untouched or unnoticed the rival work of the Roman bard.

(Vol. xxxviii. p. 372.)

LOUIS SIMOND

(1767-1831)

[Louis Simond, an anglicized Frenchman (born at Lyons in 1767, died at Geneva in 1831), published anonymously in 1815 a *Journal of a Tour and Residence in Great Britain* (1810-11); which was followed in 1822 by a *Journal of a Tour and Residence in Switzerland* (1817-19); and in 1828 by a *Tour in Italy and Sicily* (1817-18).]

1828. A TOUR IN ITALY AND SICILY.

[Romantic and classic poetry]

THE controversy about romantic and classic poetry, like that about gardening, seems after all to relate to a question of fact rather than of theory. . . . The romantic compared with the classic is not so much a different art of poetry, as it is poetry applied to different subjects; it might simply be denominated the modern style, and the other be called the ancient. . . . Something of the chivalrous and romantic taste is now reviving; not indeed as the classical taste was revived formerly, by the accidental discovery of ancient manuscripts, but by means of a closer observation of nature, of human feelings and human passions; in short, by the discovery of new powers in the human mind, as also of new powers in language. . . . Dante successfully united romantic sentiments with classic regularity.

(pp. 4, 6.)

[Michael Angelo and Dante]

In Michael Angelo's Last Judgment in the Sistine Chapel . . . a crowd of poor wretches are seen stepping reluctantly into a boat about to put off from the shore under the guidance of a single boatman, boisterous and rude, like Charon ferrying over the Styx, —a heathenish episode, scarcely becoming the place;—but the forehead of this boatman provided with a pair of horns, and his nether end with a tail, show him at once to be no heathen, but

[1] [On this subject see Mario Schiff, *La Bibliothèque du Marquis de Santillane* (1905), pp. 271-319].

[2] [1411-1456.]

an infernal being of more orthodox breed. . . . Michael Angelo I believe took many ideas from Dante; but a poet having no positive forms defined by lines to contend with, is much more at his ease in the region of fancy, where half the tale he has to tell, and all the awkward parts of it, may be left for the reader to supply as he will: what the poet eloquently suggests, the painter must heavily draw, at full length, horns and tails, winding-sheets, and skins of flayed saints.

(pp. 216-7.)

HENRY DIGBY BESTE

(1768-1836)

[Henry Digby Beste (or Best), was the son of Henry Best, Prebendary of Lincoln, where he was born in 1768. He was educated at Magdalen College, Oxford, of which he became Fellow in 1791. In the same year he was ordained and appointed to the curacy of St. Martin's, Lincoln. Eight years later he was received into the Roman Catholic Church. In 1818 he left England and resided for some years in France and Italy. He died at Brighton in 1836. Beste published in 1826 *Four Years in France*, and in 1828 *Italy as it is*, the two works (of which the former contains 'an account of the conversion of the author to the catholic faith') being narratives of his residence with his family in those countries.]

1828. ITALY AS IT IS; OR NARRATIVE OF AN ENGLISH FAMILY'S RESIDENCE FOR THREE YEARS IN THAT COUNTRY.

[Benvenuti's and Reynolds' pictures of Ugolino]

AT the annual exhibition at the Academia delle Belle Arti at Florence all eyes were attracted to the picture of Benvenuti,[1] representing Count Ugolino and his sons. . . . The figures were said to be too stiff; but it is the object of the painter to characterize the firmness and sternness of Ugolino, by the rigidity of his attitude. A friend observed to me, 'I do not wish Benvenuti to come off with flying colours,[2] like Sir Joshua Reynolds; but I do wish that the greater part of his colours had never been put on.'

(pp. 196-7.)

EGERTON MSS. AT THE BRITISH MUSEUM

1829. IN this year the British Museum acquired by bequest of Francis Henry Egerton, eighth Earl of Bridgewater (1756-1829) the collection of MSS. known as the Egerton MSS. which relate chiefly to the history and litera-

[1] [Pietro Benvenuti (1769-1844), of Arezzo, Director of the Florentine Academy.]
[2] [An allusion to the fugitive colours employed by Sir Joshua Reynolds in certain of his pictures.]

ture of France and Italy. Among them were three MSS. of the *Divina Commedia*—one of the fourteenth century (*Egerton* 943), and two of the fifteenth (*Egerton* 932, 2085).[1]

HIBBERT LIBRARY

1829. CATALOGUE OF THE LIBRARY OF GEORGE HIBBERT.

[The library of George Hibbert (1757-1837; West India Merchant; M.P. for Sleaford, 1806-12; F.R.S. 1811) was sold by Evans in March-June, 1829. The sale lasted 42 days and comprised nearly 9000 items. The collection contained eight editions of the *Divina Commedia*, the most important of which was the first Florentine (1481), with 15 of the Botticelli designs (sold for £40 19s.). Other rare editions were the Venice, 1477 (sold for £4 19s.); and the Venice, 1520 (sold for £11).]

JOHN WILSON

(1785-1854)

[John Wilson, famous as the 'Christopher North' of *Blackwood's Magazine*, son of a wealthy manufacturer, was born at Paisley in 1785. He was educated at Paisley Grammar School, and Glasgow University, whence in 1803 he went to Magdalen College, Oxford, where he graduated in 1807. He was called to the bar at Edinburgh in 1815, and two years later joined the staff of the newly founded *Blackwood's Magazine*, to which from 1822 to 1835 he contributed the celebrated *Noctes Ambrosianae*, besides many essays, included in his collected works. In 1820 Wilson was elected to the chair of moral philosophy at Edinburgh, which he filled until 1851. He died in Edinburgh in 1854. In one of the last of the *Noctes* the Ettrick Shepherd describes the impression made on him by Christopher North's reading aloud to him from the *Inferno*.]

1829. Sept. BLACKWOOD'S MAGAZINE. MRS. JAMESON'S LOVES OF THE POETS.[2]

[Poets' wives]

THE *Loves of the Poets* is a very ladylike theme;—for all truly great or good poets, from Homer to Hogg, have, in the only true sense of the word, been gentlemen. . . . The manners of all Poets are delightful—in the long run. . . . The morals of all Poets are good—in the long run. . . . Such being the endowments, the manners, and the morals of Poets, only think of them—in love! You must on no account whatever think of Shenstone, as silly as his sheep: . . . neither must you, on any account whatever, think of Hamilton of Bangour, the shabby-

[1] [For a description of these MSS., see Colomb de Batines, *Bibliografia Dantesca*, ii. 277; and Moore, *Textual Criticism of the Divina Commedia*, pp. 589-91, 597-8.]

[2] [Otherwise known as *The Romance of Biography*, published in 1829 (see above, pp. 452 ff.).]

genteel poetaster. . . . You must think of Petrarch, and Dante, and Ariosto, and Tasso, and poet-lovers of that calibre,

'Souls made of fire, and children of the sun.'

. . . Observe, we do not mean to assert that Poets must necessarily be unexceptionable husbands. Heaven, and earth, and hell—think of Dante with a Dowdy! Milton with a Mawsey! Shakespeare with a Slut! It might have so happened—and, if so, then, in all probability, the three would have been hanged, or otherwise executed for wife-murder.

(*Works*, ed. Ferrier, vol. v. pp. 277-9.)

[Dante and Beatrice]

When Dante won the heart of Beatrice Portinari, 'twas at a banquet given by her father, Folco di Portinari, when he was a boy, and she a girl—nine and eight years old. Won the heart? Yes—won the heart—

'Into his heart received her heart,
And gave her back his own.'

His face was not scarred with fire and brimstone then! His beard, in place of being singed and curled in the flames, was but an imperceptible down—and his hair as bright and curled as that of his bright little Beatrice. He was then almost fresh from heaven—

'And trailing clouds of glory did he come,
With tresses like an angel!'

No fit messenger was he then to go down to hell, and bring back tidings of the sinners below! But the time came, when he was the only mortal man, of all the millions, accomplished for such a mission. . . . On the death of Beatrice, Boccaccio, who knew Dante personally,[1] tells us that he was so changed by affliction that his best friends could scarcely recognise him. He scarcely ate or slept —he would not speak; he neglected his person, until he became 'una cosa selvatica a vedere,' a savage thing to the eye. . . .

The love, the sorrow, the despair, the prostration, and the resuscitation of Dante's spirit, are all most beautiful and most sublime. . . . While Beatrice was the sun of his life, he was sometimes happy in the light she shed over the world, without referring always in his happiness—nor need was—that light to the benign and gracious orb which was its ever-streaming fountain. When she was eclipsed—'total eclipse' it indeed was to him, and the skies were as the blind walls of a dungeon—we hear his troubled spirit crying—moaning—shrieking—almost yelling in the utter darkness. . . . He was then mad—perhaps he was mad long before

[1] [Boccaccio never saw Dante—he was only eight when Dante died at Ravenna.]

and long after; but then was a crisis—a paroxysm, in which life could not long have remained to mortal man. His after grief was gloomier than other men's despair—his subsequent sorrow sterner than other men's grief. Yet all the while how divine his tenderness, as the tenderness of a mourning and bereaved angel! His thoughts of his Beatrice do not lie too deep for tears! Dante weeps—often—long—we might almost say incessantly. But his are not showers of tears, which, by a law of nature, must relieve the heart, just as rain relieves the sky. Big drops plash down upon his page, like the first of a thunder-shower—but let them continue to drop at sullen intervals, for hours and hours, they seem still to be *the first*—the huge black mass of woe and despair is undiminished and unenlightened—

'Hung be the heavens with black,'

is still the cry of his agony, and at times he forgets that any other human beings ever had existence and lost it, save his own Beatrice Portinari. . . .

Dante's soul was gigantic; and there was the struggle in which he was overthrown—but overthrown but to rise again, as if he had drawn almost unnatural strength from the ideal dust of his Beatrice, to sing of that Hell and that Purgatory, all whose pains, except that of guilt—the greatest, it is true, of them all—he had gone through when she died, and to sing of that heaven which she even on earth had made him understand, and through whose regions her sainted spirit was afterwards the holy conductress. . . .

Dante, thy boyhood was blest beyond all bliss; and till the prime of manhood thou wert with thy Beatrice even on earth, in the heaven of heavens, cheaply purchased by despair and madness! Thy spirit sounded the depths of woe, but no plummet-line, even of all thy passions upon passions, could reach the bottom of that sea. When the blackness of night lay densest upon thee, arose before thine eyes thy own celestial Beatrice, and far and wide diffused a sacred and indestructible light over all thy stormy world. She disappeared, and thou didst follow her, even in the flesh, beyond the 'flaming bounds of space and time,' and beheld her among the highest angels. Therefore, man of many woes, and troubles, and disquietudes, and hates, and revenges! thy fierce spirit often slept in a profounder calm than ever steeps the stillest dreams of those who, by nature and fortune, love and enjoy on earth perpetual peace. The sleep of the eagle on the cliff-edge, above the roar of cataracts, and in the heart of the thunder-cloud, is hushed and deep as that of the halcyon on the smooth and sunny main!

But lo! the printer's devil! Please, sir, for a few minutes be seated.

(*Works*, ed. Ferrier, vol. v. pp. 290 ff.)

1831. Jan. NOCTES AMBROSIANAE. XXVII.

[The Ettrick Shepherd not a reader of Dante—Dante's married life]

North. Mr. Moore boldly avers,[1] that 'on the list of married poets who have been unhappy in their homes, are the four illustrious names of Dante, Milton, Shakespeare, and Dryden—to which we must now add, as a partner in their destiny, a name worthy of being placed beside the greatest of them—Lord Byron.'

Shepherd. I never read a word o' Dante's 'Comedy o' Hell,' sae I shall say nae mair anent it, than that the soobjeck seems better adapted for tragedy—and as for Dryden, I'm no sae familiar's I should be wi' 'Glorious John'—sae Byron may be equal, inferior, or superior to baith them twa.—But I hae read Shakspeer and Milton mony thousan' times, and, Mister Muir, ye had nae richt, sir, by your ipse-dixe, to place Byron by the side o' them twa, the greatest o' a' the children o' man—he maun sit, in a' his glory far doun aneath their feet.

North. He must. But Mr. Moore had no right to place Shakespeare and Milton on the list of miserable married men. Milton's character and conduct as a husband appear to have been noble and sublime. Of Shakespeare's married life we know nothing—or rather, less than nothing—a few dim and contradictory-seeming expressions, almost unintelligible, on the strength of which Mr. Moore has not scrupled to place him as a partner in destiny along with Byron, the most miserable of the miserable, and at last a profligate. The destiny of Dante lay not in his marriage, however unhappy it might have been,—and 'tis a sorry way of dealing with the truth to slur and slobber over all its principal features.

(*Works*, vol. iii. pp. 129-30.)

1831. April. NOCTES AMBROSIANAE. XXX.

[The Ghost of the Glasgow Gander and Dante]

North. I am not—either by nature or education—superstitious; yet I cannot help attaching some credit to the strange rumour——

Shepherd. What strange rumour? Let me hear't, sir; for there's naething I like sae weel 's a strange rumour.

North. Why, that the great Glasgow Gander has been seen since the last Noctes.

Shepherd. Whaur?

North. At divers times and in sundry places.

Shepherd. But no in the flesh, sir—no in the flesh.

Tickler. THE GHOST OF THE GANDER!!!

[1] [In his *Life of Byron*—see above, pp. 24-5.]

North.—

'Doom'd for a certain time to walk the night,
And, for the day, confined to fast in fires,
Till the foul crimes, done in his days of nature,
Are burnt and purged away.'[1]

Tickler.—

'But that it is forbid
To tell the secrets of his prison-house,
He could a tale unfold.'

North. That 'eternal blazon,' Tickler, must be reserved for another Noctes. A description of his Purgatory by the Ghost of the Glasgow Gander will eclipse Dante's.

(*Works*, vol. iii. pp. 263-4.)

1835. Jan. NOCTES AMBROSIANAE. XXXVIII.

[The Ettrick Shepherd on Christopher's reading of Dante]

North. No land on earth like Scotland for the landscape painter. Skies! I have lived for years in Italy—and—

Shepherd. And speak the language like a native, I'll answer for that—for I never understood Dante, till I heard you read up the greatest part o' *Hell* ae nicht in your ain study. Yon's fearsome. The terzza rima's an infernal measure—and you let the lines rin intil ane anither wi' the skill o' a Lucifer. When every noo and then you laid doun the volumm on your knees—mercy on us! a great big volumm wi' clasps just like the Bible—and receeted a screed that you had gotten by heart—I could hae thocht that you was Dante himsel—the great Florentine—for your vice keept tollin like a bell—as if some dark spirit within your breist were pu'in the rope—some demon o' which you was possessed; till a' at ance it grew saft and sweet in the soun' as the far-aff tinkling o' the siller bells on the bridle-reins o' the snaw-white palfrey o' the Queen o' the Fairies—as I hae heard them i' the Forest,—but that was lang, lang syne—

(*Works*, vol. iv. pp. 221-2.)

ANONYMOUS

1829. July. QUARTERLY REVIEW. ART. I. SOUTHEY'S COLLOQUIES ON THE PROGRESS AND PROSPECTS OF SOCIETY.

[The invectives of Dante and Petrarch against the corruptions of Rome]

IN a very curious and characteristic dialogue of Erasmus, two Franciscans, on being refused a night's lodging by the parson of the parish, who, as usual, had no great love for such society, are represented as taking refuge with the village publican.

[1] [*Hamlet*, Act I, Sc. v. ll. 10 ff.]

'What kind of pastor have you here,' quoth one of them to mine host of the Dog and Dish—'dumb, I warrant, and good for little?'—'What others find him, I know not, I find him a very worthy fellow; here he sits drinking all the day long; and for customers, no man brings me better: and now I think of it, I wonder he is not here.'—'He was not, however, over civil to us.'—'You have met with him, then?'—'We asked him for a night's lodging, but he bade us begone, as if we had been wolves, and recommended us to try you.'—'Ha, ha, now I understand; he is not here, because he is aware that you are before him.'—'Is he a dumb dog?'—'Dumb! tut; no man makes more noise in my taproom—nay, he is loud enough at church, too, though I never heard him *preach* there. But why waste my words; he has given you proof enough, I fancy, that he is not dumb.'—'Does he know his Bible?'—'Excellently well, he says, but his knowledge smacks of the confessional; he has it on condition of never letting it go further?'—'Probably he would not allow a man to preach for him?'—'Yes, I'll answer for it, *provided you don't preach at him, as a good many of your cloth have a trick of doing*.'

Many, indeed, did so; and in those fierce invectives which Dante and Petrarch so frequently launch at the corruptions of the church of Rome, they were, perhaps, only practising a lesson which they had learned from the friars.

(Vol. xli. pp. 11-2.)

ANONYMOUS

1829. FOREIGN REVIEW AND CONTINENTAL MISCELLANY. NO. V. ART. IX. ITALIAN COMEDY.

[The 'novelty' of the *Divina Commedia*]

THERE are three kinds of poetry—narrative, lyric, and dramatic. Now it requires but a slight acquaintance with Italian literature to know that the poets and master-spirits of the Peninsula not only, in those three branches, did not follow, in servile imitation, the example so gloriously afforded by their Latin and Greek predecessors, but that, by a noble spirit of emulation, they actually struck into paths of invention wholly unexplored, because unknown both to the one and the other. Trissino, and, with far greater success, Torquato Tasso, imitated Virgil and Homer, in the plan of a narrative or epic poem; but who, let us ask, gave to the mighty Dante the faintest idea of his marvellous performance wherein he so frequently vies with the bards of Maeonia and Mantua? Is not his a narrative poem entirely *sui generis*, whether we regard the singularity or novelty of argument, or its amplitude, and the wondrous vigour with which the design has been achieved? Homer invokes his Muse in order to sing the anger of Achilles, and the verses flow from his lips as though from the fountain of celestial inspiration; for the poet, neither directly nor indirectly, once appears. In the 'Divina Commedia,' Dante is his own prototype and hero. He it is, who wholly engrosses the reader's attention, and on and from whom all the figures of the immense gallery which he traverses reflect or draw, in alternation, the light which illumines their unearthly features. His name, indeed, is never pronounced, save once,[1] from necessity, in order to be reproached and blamed. For this, however, the reader's pardon is demanded, as though he considered himself an intruder.[2] But without Dante's presence the poem would be barren of interest. May not, therefore the 'Divina Commedia' boast, in the most unqualified terms, of novelty?

(Vol. iii. pp. 193-4.)

CHARLES HENRY HARTSHORNE

(1802-1865)

[Charles Henry Hartshorne, born in 1802, was the son of an iron-master of Broseley in Shropshire. He was educated at Shrewsbury School and St. John's College, Cambridge (M.A. 1828). In 1825 he went to Corfu with Lord Guilford, the owner of the famous Guilford collection of books and MSS., which was dispersed after his death. Hartshorne was ordained in 1827, and after holding various curacies and livings in the Midlands, he was presented in 1850 to the crown living of Holdenby in Northamptonshire, where he died in 1865. Among his publications were *The Book Rarities in the University of Cambridge* (1829), and *Ancient Metrical Tales* (1829), which is quoted by Scott in the introduction to *Ivanhoe.*]

1829. THE BOOK RARITIES IN THE UNIVERSITY OF CAMBRIDGE.

[In this work Hartshorne registers two rare editions of the *Divina Commedia*, viz. Florence (1481), with 18 engravings, in the Library of King's College (p. 185); and Bressa (1487), in the St. John's Library (p. 379).]

GERALD GRIFFIN

(1803-1840)

[Gerald Griffin, dramatist, novelist, and poet, was born in Limerick, where his father was a brewer, in 1803. He was educated at Limerick, and in 1823 he went to London in the hope of pursuing literature as his career, he having already commenced four tragedies, one of which, *Gisippus*, was eventually (1842) produced at

[1] [*Purg.* xxx. 55.] [2] [*Purg.* xxx. 62-3.]

Drury Lane by Macready. In 1827 he wrote a series of *Tales of the Munster Festival*, which was followed by a second series in 1829, and by various novels in the next few years. Griffin returned to Limerick in 1838, and shortly afterwards joined the Catholic Society of Christian Brothers, as a member of which he died at Cork in 1840. Griffin introduces a humorous reference to Dante in one of the second series of *Munster Tales*.]

1829. TALES OF THE MUNSTER FESTIVAL. SECOND SERIES.

[The lesson in Virgil at Mr. Lenigan's Academy]

ABOUT noon a sudden hush was produced by the appearance at the open door of a young man, dressed in rusty black, and with something clerical in his costume and demeanour. This was Mr. Lenigan's classical assistant; for to himself the volumes of ancient literature were a fountain sealed. Five or six stout young men, all of whom were intended for learned professions, were the only portion of Mr. Lenigan's scholars that aspired to those lofty sources of information. At the sound of the word 'Virgil!' from the lips of the assistant, the whole class started from their seats, and crowded round him, each brandishing a smoky volume of the great Augustan poet, who, could he have looked into this Irish academy, from that part of the infernal regions in which he had been placed by his pupil Dante, might have been tempted to exclaim, in the pathetic words of his own hero:

—'Sunt hic etiam sua praemia laudi,
Sunt lachrymae rerum et mentem mortalia tangunt.'

'Who's head?' was the first question proposed by the assistant, after he had thrown open the volume at that part marked as the day's lesson.

'Jim Naughtin, Sir.'

'Well, Naughtin, begin. Consther,[1] consther now, an' be quick.'

'At puer Ascanius mediis in vallibus acri
Gaudet equo; jamque hos cursu, jam praeterit illos:
Spumantemque dari——'

'Go on, Sir. Why don't you consther?'

'*At puer Ascanius*,' the person so addressed began, 'but the boy Ascanius; *mediis in vallibus*, in the middle of the valley; *Gaudet*, rejoices——'

'Exults, ara gal, exults is a betther word.'

'*Gaudet*, exults; *acri equo*, upon his bitther horse.'

'Oh, murther alive; his bitther horse, inagh? Erra, what would make a horse be bitther, Jim? Sure 'tis not of sour beer he's talking! Rejoicin' upon a bitther horse! Dear knows what a

[1] Construe.

show he was! what raison he had for it. *Acri equo*, upon his mettlesome steed; that's the consthruction.'

Jim proceeded:

'*Acri equo*, upon his mettlesome steed; *jamque*, and now; *praeterit*, he goes beyond——'

'Outsthrips, achree!'

'*Praeterit*, he outsthrips; *hos*, these; *jamque illos*, and now those; *cursu*, in his course; *que*, and; *optat*, he longs——'

'Very good, Jim; *longs* is a very good word there; I thought you were going to say *wishes*. Did any body tell you that?'

'Dickens a one, Sir!'

'That's a good boy. Well?'

'*Optat*, he longs; *spumantem aprum*, that a foaming boar; *dari*, shall be given; *votis*, to his desires; *aut fulvum leonem*, or that a tawny lion——'

'That's a good word again. *Tawny* is a good word; betther than *yellow*.'

'*Descendere*, shall descend; *monte*, from the mountain.'

'Now, boys, observe the beauty of the poet. There's great nature in the picture of the boy Ascanius. Just the same way as we see young Misther Keiley, of the Grove, at the fox-chase the other day, leadin' the whole of 'em right and left, *jamque hos, jamque illos*, an' now Misther Cleary, an' now Captain Davis, he outsthripped in his course. A beautiful picture, boys, there is in them four lines, of a fine high-blooded youth. Yes, people are always the same; times an' manners change, but the heart o' man is the same now as it was in the day of Augustus.'

THOMAS THORPE

(fl. 1830)

1829-30. SALE CATALOGUE OF MANUSCRIPTS FROM THE LIBRARIES OF THE EARL OF GUILFORD,[1] &c.

No. 237. Dante. Commentario sopra La Divina Commedia di Dante. 3 vols. 7l. 17s. 6d. *Large Folio.*[2]

(p. 25.)

[1] [The fifth Earl of Guilford (1766-1827), from whose collection Sir Thomas Phillipps purchased more than 1300 vols. of Italian MSS. (see below, pp. 621-2).]

[2] [This MS. reappears in the Catalogues of 1830 and 1832, priced £6 6s.]

1830. SALE CATALOGUE OF MANUSCRIPTS FROM MANY IMPORTANT ENGLISH AND CONTINENTAL COLLECTIONS.

No. 12614. Dante. Commentum Domini Petri de Andalgerii, sive Aldagerii, super tres Comaedias Dantes. 7l. 7s. *Folio.*[1]

(p 49.)

ANONYMOUS

1830. Feb. FOREIGN QUARTERLY REVIEW. ART. II. ROSSETTI'S INFERNO OF DANTE.[2]

[Dante's *Inferno*, and *De Vulgari Eloquentia*]

THOSE who can still recal the emotions excited in their minds when they first read the opening cantos of the 'Inferno,' may probably remember a mixed feeling of admiration and dissatisfaction, an unequal struggle between the judgment and the imagination. It is immediately discovered that the poem is founded on tenets of Christian theology, and that the hell and purgatory of the poet's creed are to be revealed; yet the guide appointed to conduct him through these awful scenes is a heathen bard, invested with no peculiar sanctity whatever—and fresh inconsistencies and objections crowd upon the mind as the plan of the poem gradually unfolds itself. The strength of the charm, and the whole power of the poetic delusion, would be annihilated, if so many grand and striking images, all pourtrayed by the hand of a master, did not follow each other in rapid succession. For none can enter the wild and gloomy forest, or share the poet's terror as he looks back aghast on the dark valley he has passed—none can read the dreadful import of the letters inscribed over the infernal gate—without feeling that the imagination is too deeply engaged ever to lose the impression. In a dream our thoughts may be haunted by a fearful spectre, while the reason is conscious of our situation, and while we know that it is the creation of fancy. By some strange and mysterious influence our terror is continued, although we desire to be awakened, and although we are sensible that the phantom is unreal. On first entering on the scene of Dante's Vision, the mind is agitated by a similar conflict of feelings, although our wishes flow in an opposite direction. We fear that the pleasing delusion cannot last, yet while our doubts continue the spell remains unbroken. We do not require historical consistency in all the events of a tale founded

[1] [This MS., of Cent. xiv. on paper, reappears in the Catalogue of 1832, priced £5 5s.]

[2] [*La Divina Commedia di Dante, con comento analitico di* Gabriele Rossetti. Vols. i-ii. *L'Inferno.* Londra, 1826 (see above, p. 446).]

expressly on a vision; on the contrary, we expect that probabilities will be violated—that there will be great confusion of images, and much that is marvellous and incomprehensible. The void and dark abyss, and the winged monster wheeling his downward flight with his trembling rider (*Inf.* c. 17), and other images, equally supernatural, are in perfect harmony with the design. But even in painting the fantastic fictions of sleep, it is possible that such incongruities may be admitted as are subversive of all truth and justice in the conception. . . . Of this nature is the perpetual confusion of things sacred and profane—the constant interweaving of two different systems of theology into the same composition. The Mantuan bard conducts our poet into the first circle, or hollow circular platform of hell, where they find the souls of thousands who lived virtuously, yet were doomed, for lack of Christian baptism, to desire the joys of heaven without hope, and be debarred for ever from sharing the bliss of Paradise; and in this number Virgil declares himself to be included. We afterwards behold Minos, presiding as infernal judge, visit the Stygian Lake and the City of Dis, and here discover heretics tortured in sepulchres burning with intense fire. We meet Cerberus, the Harpies, and the Cretan Minotaur; Cocytus and Phlegethon, and other fabled rivers of Erebus, are crossed. In the ninth circle we meet Nimrod, the builder of Babel, and by his side Ephialtes, Briareus, and other giants, who are declared to have made trial of their power against the supreme Jove, to have caused the gods to tremble (*Inf.* c. xxxi. 91); and after being thus surrounded by the mythological imagery of Greece and Rome, we arrive where, at the earth's centre, and farthest from the light of heaven, Satan, the parent of Sin, stands poised and surrounded by eternal ice. Milton has been reproached for having so frequently had recourse to the polytheism of the ancients for his illustrations in the Paradise Lost; but he has managed these allusions with such address, and has guarded so cautiously against their occupying too prominent a station in the picture, that they rarely detract from the unity and chastity of the design.

* * * *

Dante wrote a work, the 'De Vulgari Eloquio,' to encourage the cultivation of the genuine Italian language, which is full of very interesting and curious research, on the origin and history of the old Provençal dialects. Some of the introductory chapters, however, are characteristic of the extraordinary and ridiculous notions and style of writing then in vogue. He cannot lay down the position that speech is the exclusive prerogative of man, without immediately anticipating all the objections and cavils that a scholastic disputant would, beyond all question, have advanced against him in every university then flourishing in Europe He, therefore, proceeds with due caution, and gravely admits, that in the sacred scriptures the serpent which tempted Eve, as also Balaam's ass, are represented to have spoken, but that the devil in the first instance, and an angel in the latter, were the personages who really uttered the words: and as for the magpies in Ovid's Metamorphoses (for in those times, some pagan authority is ever coupled with the sacred) he says, Ovid merely intended them to speak figuratively.[1] He afterwards, in the same strain, enters into a disquisition on a subject which, no doubt, was favourite matter of argumentation in the schools of the thirteenth century, viz. what was the first language in the world? and whether did Adam or Eve first speak in Paradise? He grants that Eve's answer to the serpent is the first speech recorded in Genesis, but he argues, nevertheless, that Adam uttered the first word, and this word he says was 'El,' or 'God,' and then follow subtle arguments in the scholastic style in corroboration of this hypothesis. . . . When we say we can believe Dante to have been serious, and deliberately to have written the chapters alluded to, without the slightest consciousness of their inherent absurdity, it must not be imagined that we are in any way insensible tothe vast superiority of his genius above the standard of his own, or, indeed, of any other age, or that we do not fully appreciate the good sense and matchless eloquence of large portions of his prose works.

(Vol. v. pp. 420-2, 442-3.)

JOHN MACRAY

(fl. 1830)

1830. THE GOLDEN LYRE. SPECIMENS OF THE POETS OF ENGLAND, FRANCE, GERMANY, ITALY, AND SPAIN.

[The poets of Italy, represented by a single poem each, are Chiabriera, Dante, Della Casa, Filicaja, Monti, and Tasso. Dante is represented by the Sonnet: 'Negli occhi porta la mia Donna Amore,' from the *Vita Nuova* (§ 21, *Son.* xi). The book, which is dedicated to the Princess Mary Esterhazy, is printed throughout in gold.]

JOHN ABRAHAM HERAUD

(1799-1887)

[John Abraham Heraud, poet and dramatist, the son of a law stationer, was born in Holborn in 1799. He was privately educated, and intended for business, but in 1818 he began to write for the magazines, and he continued to follow literature

[1] De Vulg. Eloq. lib. i. cap. 2.

as a profession until he was in his eightieth year. Heraud, who was a friend of Coleridge, Southey, and Wordsworth in his earlier years, and later of the Carlyles, was assistant editor of *Fraser's Magazine*, 1830-33, and subsequently edited the *Monthly Magazine* (1839-42) and other magazines. He served as dramatic critic of the *Illustrated London News* for thirty years (1849-79), besides acting in the same capacity for the *Athenæum* (till 1868). In 1873 he was appointed a brother of the Charterhouse, where he died in 1887. Heraud's most ambitious efforts as a poet were two epic poems, *The Descent into Hell* (1830), and *The Judgment of the Flood* (1834). The former is written in *terza rima*, the suitability of which as an English metre he discusses in a prefatory *Analysis*. He subsequently (c. 1840) tried his hand at a translation of the *Inferno* in this metre, but his attempt, of which a specimen is printed below, was by no means a success.[1]]

1830. THE DESCENT INTO HELL.

[English writers in terza rima]

THE terza rima of Dante is not yet familiarized to the English reader. Hayley[2] translated some parts of the Divina Commedia into this measure, but his genius was too feeble to show its mighty capabilities: Milton rendered the second psalm into it, which it would seem Byron[3] forgot, when he looked upon his Prophecy of Dante as a metrical experiment. The measure was very judiciously chosen for one of the Psalms of David, being singularly fitted for lyrical expression, as exemplified by Dante himself in some of those fine apostrophes with which his vision is frequently embellished.

(*Analysis*, p. i.)

c. 1840. DELL' INFERNO OF DANTE ALIGHIERI, TRANSLATED INTO ENGLISH TERZA-RIMA.[4]

[Ulysses' speech to his companions]

'O Brothers,' cried I, 'who through toils and pains,
Into the west have thus in safety swirled,
Do not to that brief life, which yet remains,
Of pregnant sense, as yet a banner furled,
Deny the experience, to your labours due,
Following the sun, of the unpeopled world.
To live like brutes Heaven made not such as you
(Regard ye well your sacred origin;)
But knowledge, wisdom, virtue to pursue.'
With this short orison I made so keen
My comrades' wishes for more daring quest,
That after to withhold them hard had been.
Unto the morn our poop we turn, nor rest;

[1] [This translation has not been published—the MS. is in the possession of the editor of this work.]
[2] [See vol. i. pp. 359 ff.] [3] [See above, pp. 43-4.]
[4] [Unpublished.]

Wings of our oars we made for disard flight
And ever to the left sped further west.
Already of the other pole the night
Saw all the stars, our own depressed so low,
That scarce from the salt sea they challenge sight.
Four times rekindled, and, the moon below,
As many times extinguished were her beams,
Since we the perilous strait had entered now;
When from afar a mountain dimly gleams,
And far more loftily its summit shot
Than any we had seen, to us it seems.
High was our joy—but soon to change devote;
Now sprang a whirlwind from the new found strand,
And in the foremost part our vessel smote:
Thrice swung the bark round with the waters, and
The fourth time rose the poop above the main,
Sinking the prow—(such was His high command!)—
Then over us the sea was closed again.

(*Inferno* xxvi. 112-42.)

JAMES SMITH

(1775-1839)

[James Smith, best known as the joint author, with his younger brother Horace, of the *Rejected Addresses*, was the son of Robert Smith, solicitor to the Board of Ordnance, and was born in London in 1775. He was brought up in his father's office and succeeded him at the Board of Ordnance in 1812. *Rejected Addresses* was published in 1812, and in the next year he published, also in collaboration with his brother, a series of metrical imitations of Horace, under the title of *Horace in London*. In 1820-22 he wrote several comic sketches for Charles Mathews which met with great success. He died in London in 1839. In one of his comic poems James Smith perpetrates an atrocious pun on the name of the Count Ugolino celebrated by Dante.]

c. 1830. LINES ON SEEING A PICTURE OF UGOLINO.[1]

[An echo from Dante]

THIS Ugolino? Psha, says Will,
He's painted much too skinny.—
Prithee, replied his friend, be still,
You find fault like a ninny.

Were you imprison'd three long days,
With nought your teeth between-o',
When on the fourth you go your ways,
I'll warrant—*You-go-lean-o!*

(*Memoirs*, &c. vol. ii. p. 199.)

[1] [Published in 1840 in *Memoirs, Letters, and Comic Miscellanies in Prose and Verse, of the late James Smith.*]

HENRY STEBBING

(1799-1883)

[Henry Stebbing, a voluminous writer, who gained some reputation as poet, preacher, and historian, and was an associate of Coleridge, Scott, Moore, and Rogers, was born at Great Yarmouth in 1799. He was educated at St. John's College, Cambridge (M.A. 1827; D.D. 1839), and was ordained in 1822. In 1827 he went to London, where he soon became deeply engaged in literary work of various descriptions, including an active share in planning and starting the *Athenæum* (1828). In 1831 he published *Lives of the Italian Poets* (from Dante to Alfieri), of which a second edition appeared in the following year, and a third in 1860. The account of Dante, which includes metrical translations of three of the sonnets in the *Vita Nuova*, is based for the most part on the early Italian biographies, and on the works of Tiraboschi, Ginguené, and Pelli. Stebbing, who was appointed to the rectory of St. Mary Somerset in 1857, died in London in his eighty-fourth year in 1883.]

1831. LIVES OF THE ITALIAN POETS.

[Sonnets from the *Vita Nuova*]

'A ciascun' alma presa, e gentil core '[1]

TO every captive soul and gentle heart,
For whom I sing, what sorrows strange I prove!
I wish all grace, and may their master, Love,
Present delight and happy hopes impart.
Two thirds of night were spent, but brightly clear
The stars were shining, when surprised I saw
Love, whom to worship is my will and law;
Glad was his aspect, and he seemed to bear
My own heart in his hand, while on his arms,
Garmented in her many folded vest,
Madonna lay, with gentle sleep oppress'd;
But he awoke her filled with soft alarms,
And with that burning heart in humble guise
Did feed her, till in gloom the vision fled my eyes.

(*Life of Dante*, vol. i. p. 10.)

'Color d' amore, e di pietà sembianti '[2]

The form of pity and the hue of love,
Never before did beauteous lady's face,
From gentle looks and sighs deep sorrows move,
Take with such perfect and such wondrous grace
As thine, who late beheld me while I went,
With looks that only pity did bespeak;

[1] [*V.N.* § 3, *Son.* i.]

[2] [*V.N.* § 37, *Son.* xx.]

But now my thoughts, on thee too frequent bent,
Teach me to fear that with a heart so weak,
My eyes will ever seek thee, and intent
Rest fondly on thy pale and sadden'd brow—
Sad with that love of grief which in thee dwells;
Thus you their wish increase that tears should flow,
But with that wish my heart so anxious swells
That in thy presence, captive held, in vain
I seek by tears to mitigate its pain.

(*Life of Dante,* vol. i. 21-2.)

'L' amaro lagrimar, che voi faceste'[1]

The bitter tears, my eyes! which once ye shed
With such a fond and long unchanging woe,
In many a gentle heart deep wonder bred,
And bid soft pity in the bosom glow;
But, ah! I fear that ye could all forget
Would my heart join you in the felon wrong,
And let those memories fade which still belong
To her for whom ye were so often wet:
Vain wondering eyes! so do I fear your guide
That much I dread when you her form admire
To meet one gentle lady's pitying smile,
Oh ne'er forgetful be, till life expire,
Of one sweet mistress who untimely died:—
Thus spoke my heart, and speaking deeply sighed.

(*Ibid.* pp. 24-5.)

[The sublimity of Dante]

The distinguishing characteristic of Dante's poetry, though far from wanting in occasional passages of exquisite tenderness and beauty, is its sublimity, and hence by general consent the Inferno is placed at an almost immeasurable distance above the other two parts of the Commedia, which required a milder and more brilliant fancy. In respect to sublimity, Dante has but one superior, our own Milton. The scenes he depicts have the terrible distinctness of places beheld in a vivid dream; the language of his personages makes an equally powerful impression on the mind—it is short, pointed, and abrupt, and such as we might expect to hear from miserable beings dreading the fiery lash of pursuing demons, but retaining their sense of human sympathy. The same power appears in his comparisons as in the main subjects of the description. Over the images drawn from natural objects, or real occurrences,

[1] [*V.N.* § 38, *Son.* xxi.]

he flings the gloom, or the lurid light of his subterranean caverns, rendering at the same time the abodes of the condemned spirits the more terrible by the contrast of things still earthly and embodied. This sublimity, it is true, is far from being constantly sustained, and the verse not unfrequently falls off into a style as cold and harsh as it is obscure and unaffecting. But in the first place, it was not possible that he should be always alike elevated; and in the next, both the object of his poem, the learning which filled his mind, and the literary taste of the age, would lead him into most of the faults which disfigure the Commedia in the eye of a modern reader.

It may, however, be questioned whether the sublimity of Dante is ever of that high and moral species which, it may be said, affects the soul as well as the imagination, and diffuses over it that solemn tranquillity of thought which gives at the same time the highest moral as well as intellectual delight. The scenes and objects which he describes are clear and palpable; their very sublimity depends on their distinctness, and the emotions produced are akin to what they would be were the representation real; but it is not the most distinct view of a terrible object which excites the greatest terror; and deep and powerful, therefore, as is the impression made by Dante's images, it is inferior to that which is felt in the perusal of the Paradise Lost. Milton described scenes of physical torture and misery; we see the condemned writhing beneath the infliction; the fiery soul is palpable; the darkness visible; the raging of the hail and lightning 'shot after them in storm' is audible; but the sensible perception of these things is overpowered by the sublimer spiritual feeling which the moral grandeur of his sentiments never fails to inspire. Dante equalled Milton in the one respect, but not in the other, which gave to the English bard a diviner character than was ever attained by any other mortal poet.

(*Life of Dante,* vol. i. pp. 69-71.)

ANONYMOUS

1832. Jan. MONTHLY MAGAZINE (N.S.). LIVES OF THE ITALIAN POETS. BY REV. H. STEBBING.[1]

[Debt of English literature to the poets of Italy]

AMIDST the splendid ruins of the Grecian and Roman greatness, Italy, the nurse of learning and the arts, like the ark of the Israelites, still preserved the type of intellectual truth and beauty, and continued the links between the master-minds

[1] [See above, pp. 542 ff.]

and diviner spirits of the old classic ages, and the periods of civilization, discovery, and refinement, to which they roused mankind, down to the present day. The Muse of Italy was of the first to break into full and majestic song; her painters first pictured the works and the visions of heaven upon the wondering earth; her princely scholars raised the first institutions of learning,—science,—art;—models of all which we now possess; her philosophers made their discoveries before Bacon wrote; without her Dante, Petrarch, and Boccaccio, our Chaucer would not have been the same poet; without her novelists the mighty Shakespeare must elsewhere have sought his sources of magic power,—his Moor and his Juliet would not exist; Milton combined the majestic vigour and the splendid imagery both of Dante and Tasso; Dryden, Pope, and all the best and loftiest of our names turned from the classic stores which Italy preserved to us, to drink deeply after boyhood at the scarcely less inspiring fount of Italy's Helicon itself. But among the most gifted of her sons, whose genius spread light and civilization over the modern world, none assuredly hold a higher rank than her poets, standing in equally bold relief with the grand disciples of their sister art,—the Michael Angelos, the Raphaels, and the Titians of their respective times. . . .

(N.S. vol. xiii. p. 80.)

ANONYMOUS

1832. NOTIZIE INTORNO ALL' ORIGINE E ALLA STORIA DELLA LINGUA E DELLA LETTERATURA ITALIANA.

[Published in London by Rolandi. An account of Dante and of his principal works is given on pp. 43-7, with an extract from the episode of Paolo and Francesca (*Inf.* v. 97-142). In the same volume is printed Gabriele Rossetti's inaugural lecture as Professor of Italian at King's College, London (Nov. 1, 1831).]

MADAME D'ARBLAY

(1752-1840)

[Frances Burney, afterwards Madame D'Arblay, third child of Dr. Burney, was born in 1752 at King's Lynn, where her father was then organist. She was self-educated, and from the age of ten was constantly 'scribbling stories, farces, tragedies, and epic poems.' In 1778 she published anonymously her first novel *Evelina*, which was a great success, and brought her to the notice of the foremost literary personages of the day. Her second attempt, *Cecilia*, published in 1782, met with similar success. In 1786, through the influence of Mrs. Delaney, she was appointed second Keeper of the Robes to Queen Charlotte, an appointment which she held till 1790. In 1793 she married General D'Arblay, a French refugee in England. Three years later (1796) she published *Camilla*, by which she is said to have cleared 3000 guineas. General D'Arblay having returned to France in search of employment, his wife joined him in Paris in 1802, and remained abroad till 1812, when she came back to England. Her father died in 1814, in which year she published her last novel, *The Wanderer*. General D'Arblay died in 1818, and their only son in 1837. She herself died, at the age of 87, in Jan. 1840. Madame D'Arblay's last publication was the *Memoirs of Dr. Burney* (1832). In this work, which is written in what Macaulay describes as 'broken Johnsonese,' she records that Dr. Burney, on the death of his first wife in 1761, betook himself to the study of Dante, 'that hardest, but most sublime of Italian poets,' and completed a prose translation of the *Inferno*. The MS. of this translation was in existence when Madame D'Arblay wrote (in 1832), but was probably burnt by her, with the rest of Dr. Burney's papers, on the completion of the *Memoirs*. Madame D'Arblay herself possessed a copy of the *Divina Commedia* (the Venice edition, with the commentary of Landino, printed for Lucantonio Giunta in 1529), which afterwards came into the hands of Libri, at whose sale (4 Aug. 1859, No. 791) it fetched 36s.]

1832. MEMOIRS OF DOCTOR BURNEY.[1]

[Dr. Burney consoles himself with Dante after the death of his first wife[2]]

A TOTAL chasm ensues of all account of events belonging to the period of this irreparable earthly blast. Not a personal memorandum of the unhappy survivor is left; not a single document in his handwriting, except of verses to her idea, or to her memory; or of imitations, adapted to his loss, and to her excellences, from some selected sonnets of Petrarch, whom he considered to have loved, entombed, and bewailed another Esther in his Laura.

When this similitude, which soothed his spirit and flattered his feelings, had been studied and paralleled in every possible line of comparison, he had recourse to the works of Dante, which, ere long, beguiled from him some attention; because, through the difficulty of idiom, he had not, as of nearly all other favourite authors, lost all zest of the beauties of Dante in solitude, from having tasted the sweetness of his numbers with a pleasure exalted by participation: for, during the last two years that his Esther was spared to him, her increased maternal claims from a new baby;[3] and augmented domestic cares from a new residence, had checked the daily mutuality of their progress in the pursuit of improvement; and to Esther this great poet was scarcely known.

To Dante, therefore, he first delivered over what he could yet summon from his grief-worn faculties; and to initiate himself into the works, and nearly obsolete style, of that hardest, but most sublime of Italian poets, became the occupation to which, with the least repugnance, he was capable of recurring.

A sedulous, yet energetic, though prose translation of the Inferno,

1 ['Arranged from his own MSS., from Family Papers, and from Personal Recollections.' In three volumes.]

2 [Sept. 28, 1761.]

3 Charlotte.

remains among his posthumous relics, to demonstrate the sincere struggles with which, even amidst this overwhelming calamity, he strove to combat that most dangerously consuming of all canker worms upon life and virtue, utter inertness.

(Vol. i. pp. 150-1.)

ANONYMOUS

1832. July. EDINBURGH REVIEW. ART. X. ROSSETTI'S COMENTO ANALITICO ON THE DIVINA COMMEDIA.

[The extravagance of Rossetti's theory]

THE first volume of Signor Rossetti's Analytical Commentary on the *Divine Comedy*[1] appeared in the year 1826. It comprehended an emended edition of the first eleven cantos of the *Inferno*; a close and well-written paraphrase of the poem, according to its literal sense; together with historical notes and reflections, and an appendix, in which was contained the sketch of a new theory respecting the principal allegory of the poem. The boldness and originality of its views soon called down upon the author the critical fury of numerous 'Dottori in Dantismo:' for in proportion to the recognised obscurity of the Florentine Bard, is the pertinacity of his admirers in maintaining their own several interpretations of his mysteries. It must also be confessed, that this first essay was in no small degree obnoxious to their severity; from the self-confident manner in which much was assumed, which required, in fact, an extended proof; from not being entirely without historical inaccuracies; and from a somewhat ambitious style of self-recommendation, in the pompous announcement which it contained of discoveries both performed and intended. . . . Signor Rossetti published his second volume in the following year. In this he completed the *Inferno;* proceeded with his allegorical explanations; fortified them with multiplied proofs; and, extending his front like a bold yet skilful general, maintained that all the vulgar poets preceding and contemporaneous with Dante, were to be interpreted according to the same canons which he had laid down for the latter. Finally, he challenged the world to attack him in his new position. The gauntlet was speedily taken up. A shower of invectives, unequalled in merely literary controversy except among Italian combatants, was poured on the head of the daring author. His discoveries were denied, his researches and far-fetched explanations unmercifully ridiculed; he was accused as a libeller of the illustrious dead. . . . Finally, although he had as yet only endeavoured to show that the poem was dictated by a

[1] [See above p. 446.]

spirit hostile to the temporal power of Rome, he was accused of enmity to the religion which he professes. . . .

The volumes before us are composed in a very desultory style, and abound with repetitions. . . . Because much is clearly allegorical, Signor Rossetti will allow nothing to be merely literal; and when he arrives at a passage to which his ingenuity does not supply him with an immediate parallel, he solemnly promises that he will hereafter produce one for the satisfaction of his readers. . . . In no part of his labours is the disposition to over refinement evinced in a manner so unpleasant as in his triflings with the verbal equivoques, anagrams, acrostics, and similar specimens of perverted ingenuity, which are well known to exist in the verses of the early writers, and of Dante in particular. . . .

To say the truth, the elasticity of our author's system is such, that, in the hands of so bold and enterprising a discoverer as himself, it is difficult to say what may not be brought within the range of its comprehension. All that the reader can do with safety is, to follow his eccentric strides with a steadier pace, and to be careful not to reject conclusions deduced from proofs, because they are sometimes preferred in the same breath with the hypotheses of an ardent speculator.

(Vol. lv. pp. 531 ff.)

JOHN HOOKHAM FRERE

(1769-1846)

[John Hookham Frere, diplomatist and author, was born in London in 1769. He was educated at Eton and Caius College, Cambridge (M.A. 1795), of which he became Fellow. He was M.P. for West Looe in Cornwall, 1796-1802; Under-Secretary for Foreign Affairs, 1799; Envoy Extraordinary at Lisbon, 1800-2, and at Madrid, 1802-4; British Minister in Spain, 1808-9. After his recall from Spain in 1809 Frere retired from public life, and in 1818 went to live in Malta, where he died in 1846. As an author he is best known for his contributions to the *Anti-Jacobin*, founded by Canning and himself in 1797, and for his translations from Aristophanes (1839-40). Frere was a friend and benefactor of Gabriele Rossetti, who dedicated to him the first volume of his *Comento Analitico* on the *Divina Commedia*, and in whose extravagant theories as to Dante's writings he became a firm believer.]

1832. Dec. LETTER TO GEORGE FRERE (from Malta).

[Rossetti's books of Dante]

DO you see anything of Rossetti?[1] . . . I have sent presents of his books to some gentlemen in Italy. He is prohibited in the highest degree, and one of his old acquaintances knew nothing, or did not feel it safe to confess that he knew any-

[1] [Gabriele Rossetti, who had published a *Comento Analitico* on the *Inferno* (1826-7), the first volume of which was dedicated to Frere, and *Sullo Spirito Antipapale che produsse la Riforma* (1832).]

thing even of his Dante. In Malta I think the English are upon honour with respect to Catholicity, and therefore I have not communicated it.

(*Memoir of J. H. Frere*, by Sir Bartle Frere, p. 240.)

1833. June 29. LETTER TO GABRIELE ROSSETTI (from Malta).

[Rossetti's fears of persecution on account of his books on Dante]

Don't trouble yourself with the prospect of persecution and opposition. . . . If you were in Italy indeed, I have no doubt that the Duke of Modena would be willing to accommodate you with a Dungeon; which after you had consecrated it by making it for twenty years, the abode of persecuted Genius, would in future Ages be visited by sympathetic Tourists; and an Album would be kept there, in which they would each deposit their extempore effusions, composed beforehand at the Inn. . . . Or you might have a tomb like that of Dante at Ravenna, the resort of poetical and literary pilgrims—observe how magnificently I treat you! For my own part, I should not care to have a tomb where people should come to evacuate their bad verses—any other pollution would be more tolerable.

(*J. H. Frere and his Friends*, pp. 316-7.)

1836. April 6. LETTER TO GABRIELE ROSSETTI (from Malta).

[Rossetti's *Mistero dell' Amor Platonico*]

What, in the midst of many interruptions, I have been able to read hitherto of your work[1] (about 140 Pages) has filled me with alarm and astonishment; I feel convinced that those who read what I have been reading, those who draw any conclusion at all (or at least 99 out of 100 of them) will be led to this short inference, that all religions are a ike, all equally the result of human policy and contrivance, according to the words of the vulgar old infidel song—

'Religion's a politic trick
Devised to keep Blockheads in Awe.'

What I have read hitherto appears to be an illustrative comment upon this noble and elegant text.

Admire, my dear Rosetti,[2] the majestic energy and brevity of the English character and language, which comprises in a couple

[1] [His *Mistero dell' Amor Platonico* (issued in 5 vols. in 1840) of which Rossetti had sent the first printed sheets for Frere's approval. A presentation copy of the work from Rossetti to Frere, in which Frere has made many marginal notes, is preserved in the British Museum. For an account of the book itself, see above, pp. 446-7.]

[2] [*Sic.*]

of Lines the ennnciation of a proposition which your Petrarchs and Dantes are obliged to develop bit by bit in hundreds of Cantos and Cartloads of Commentaries.

(*J. H. Frere and his Friends*, pp. 327-8.)

FRANCES TROLLOPE

(1780-1863)

[Frances, daughter of William Milton, was born at Stapelton, near Bristol, in 1780. She married in 1809 Thomas Anthony Trollope, by whom she had six children, the fourth being the well-known novelist, Anthony Trollope. Mrs. Trollope was the authoress of many books, including novels and travels, the best known of which is probably the *Domestic Manners of the Americans*, published in 1832, after a four years' residence in America (1827-30). In 1855 she settled in Florence, where she died in 1863. Among her books of travel was a *Visit to Italy*, published in 1842, which contains many references to Dante, some of which are printed below.]

1832. DOMESTIC MANNERS OF THE AMERICANS.

[The mouth of the Mississippi compared to a 'Bolgia' of Dante]

THE first indication of our approach to land was the appearance of this mighty river pouring forth its muddy mass of waters, and mingling with the deep blue of the Mexican Gulf. The shores of this river are so utterly flat, that no object upon them is perceptible at sea. . . . I never beheld a scene so utterly desolate as this entrance of the Mississippi. Had Dante seen it, he might have drawn images of another Bolgia from its horrors.

(Vol. i. pp. 1-2.)

[Quotation (adapted) from Dante applied to America]

If we analyze an hour of enjoyment, we shall find that it is made up of agreeable sensations occasioned by a thousand delicate impressions on almost as many nerves; . . . where every sense brings home to consciousness its touch of pleasure or of pain, then every object that meets the senses is important as a vehicle of happiness or misery. But let no frames so tempered visit the United States; or if they do, let it be with no longer pausing than will store the memory with images, which, by force of contrast, shall sweeten the future.

'Guarda e passa (e poi) ragioniam di lor.'[1]

(Vol. i. p. 62.)

[American ignorance of Italian literature]

To speak of Chaucer, or even Spenser, as a modern, appears to Americans inexpressibly ridiculous; and all the rich and varied

[1] [*Inf.* iii. 51: 'Non ragioniam di lor, ma guarda e passa.']

eloquence of Italy, from Dante to Monti, is about as much known to them as the Welsh effusions of Urien and Modred, to us.

(Vol. ii. pp. 153-4.)

1842. A VISIT TO ITALY.

[Ugolino and the 'Torre della Fame']

Pisa.—Of course we failed not to seek and find, if not the Torre dell' Fame, at least the spot where it stood. The exact spot still is pointed out in the Piazza de' Cavalieri, but the ruinous remnant of its walls, notwithstanding all the interest attached to them, was removed a few years ago, to the lasting mortification of all poetical travellers, and a tidy-looking snug little dwelling has been erected in its stead. . . . I wonder whether one should sleep quietly in the room supported by the same spot of earth which umwhile sustained the floor on which groaned the wretched Ugolino and his sons? . . . If not a sleeping, there would be a waking-dream, that would paint, rather too distinctly for comfort, perhaps, the sound of the key as it turned in the lock of the *orribile torre* for the last time, and the fearful look with which the too well-punished traitor gazed in the faces of his innocent children!

E se non piangi, di che pianger suoli?[1]

I did not try the experiment, however, but passed on, after giving vent to a few of those groans, which the whole civilized world has been in the habit of emitting, during the last six hundred years, whenever accident has brought to memory the story of Ugolino . . . and that, for the most part, without any mixture of affectation whatever. Is there any other profane narrative existing on the earth, of which this can be said with equal truth? . . . There may be some *almost* as fine; but none so thoroughly appreciated, or so essentially popular.

(Vol. i. pp. 72-3.)

[Dante and Florence]

Florence.—Close under the houses which form the southern boundary to the Piazza del Duomo, there formerly stood a bench, on which, as tradition says, Dante used very frequently to sit. The spot is still marked by a stone, on which is inscribed the words 'Sasso di Dante.' Perhaps the glorious Campanile looks more beautiful from this spot than from any other. . . . So lovely is this noble erection, as seen from this Sassso di Dante, that I grieved to think he had never beheld it, as, unfortunately, it was not built till long after he had quitted Florence for ever. . . .

[1] [*Inf.* xxxiii. 42.]

Unconscious, however, of what might be, he appears to have been well pleased with what was. . . . Twice, it may be oftener, he alludes, in the 'Divina Commedia,' to the Baptistry which must have been in full view from his Sasso. In the Paradiso he names it as

Antico vostro Batisteo,[1]

and in the Inferno, he calls it, affectionately,

Mio bel San Giovanni,[2]

a phrase which makes one painfully feel that he loved the ungrateful city which sent him forth as an exile, not only better than she deserved from him, but well enough to increase the sufferings of banishment. Doubtless, Coriolanus thought, when he went over to the Volscians, that he had taken a deep revenge against ungrateful Rome. . . . But how it dwindles when set beside that of Dante against Florence, when he conferred an immortality of infamy on all who had disgraced her, and offended him! . . . Truly the arms of the spirit are stronger than those of the flesh.

(Vol. i. pp. 105-6.)

[Dante's monument in Santa Croce]

Florence: Santa Croce.—There sits Dante, with robes and head-gear, ay and features too, such as we have been used to see whenever the graver or the palette has attempted to portray him. The figure, and indeed the whole structure of the monument is colossal. And one man says it is heavy, and another that it is bulky, and another that it is tame. And one gentleman I heard remark at a dinner-table discussion, that 'Dante, as he is seated there, looks like an old witch.' Change but the sex, and the criticism will stand extremely well. Dante as he is seated there looks like a wizard whom one might fancy with his uplifted finger performing an incantation that should enchant the world. . . . And so, for my part I find great fitness in the simile, and nothing in the attitude to displease me. . . .

The inscription, at any rate, cannot, I think, be found fault with—

Onorate l' altissimo poeta.

On the pedestal we read

Dante Alighierio
Tusci
Honorarium Tumulum
A majoribus ter frustra decretum
Anno MDCCC XXIX
Feliciter excitarunt

(Vol. i. pp. 208-10.)

[1] [*Par.* xv. 134.] [2] [*Inf.* xix. 17.]

[The study of Dante in England]

Bagni di Lucca.—I see, and I grieve to see, that an intimate acquaintance with Italian literature is *not* on the increase among us. . . . I speak not of scholars . . . who read Italian as a sort of dialect of the Latin, and thus get at just as intimate an acquaintance with her poets, as their taste leads them to hunger and thirst for. . . . I speak chiefly of educated women . . . among these I suspect there is a less familiar acquaintance with Italian poetry than there was thirty years ago. Mr. Roscoe's books did much towards throwing light, and drawing eyes upon it; . . . so did the admirable publications of Mr. Mathias; but this influence seems to have in some degree passed away; and I believe it is now more easy to find intelligent women capable of giving a *catalogue raisonné*, nay a *critique coulante*, of the works of Victor Hugo, or Balsac than of Dante, Petrarch, Tasso, or Alfieri.

Going through life without a tolerably intimate knowledge of the *Divina Commedia*, by those who have the power of attaining to it, seems to me like the wilful abnegation of a great good for which it is impossible to atone to the mind by any other thing of the same nature. . . . Methinks there is in the very machinery of Dante's poem sufficient to excite the imagination, and to send it on a voyage of discovery through regions untrodden before, and through which no hand but his can guide it.

(Vol. i. pp. 334-5.)

CHARLES BUCKE

(1781-1846)

[Charles Bucke, dramatist and miscellaneous writer, was born at Worlington in Suffolk in 1781, and died in Islington in 1846. Among his numerous works was one *On the Life, Writings, and Genius of Akenside*, published in 1832, in which he remarks upon the severity of Dante's judgment of Brutus and Cassius.]

1832. ON THE LIFE, WRITINGS AND GENIUS OF AKENSIDE.

[Dante's condemnation of Brutus and Cassius]

DANTE seems to have regarded Brutus with particular indignation. He even represents him, with his friend Cassius, as standing in the inferior regions on each side of Judas Iscariot.

'Quell' anima lassù ch' ha maggior pena,
Disse 'l maestro, è Giuda Scariotto,
Che 'l capo ha dentro, e fuor le gambe mena.

Degli altri duo, ch' hanno 'l capo di sotto,
Quei che pende dal nero ceffo, è Bruto:
Vedi, come si storce, e non fa motto:
E l' altro è Cassio, che par sì membruto.'
Dell' Inferno, Cant. 34, 60.
(pp. 273-4.)

EDWARD CHENEY

(fl. 1830)

[Edward Cheney was an English gentlemen resident in Rome at the time of Sir Walter Scott's visit in 1832. Lockhart in his *Life of Scott* (vii. 362), after recording the arrival in Rome of Sir William Gell, says: 'Sir Walter was introduced there to another accomplished countryman, who exerted himself no less than did Sir William, to render his stay agreeable to him. This was Mr. Edward Cheney—whose family had long been on terms of very strict intimacy with the Maclean Clephanes of Torloisk, so that Sir Walter was ready to regard him at first sight as a friend.'—'The introduction of Mr. Cheney,' notes Sir William Gell, 'was productive of great pleasure to Sir Walter, as he possessed at that moment the Villa Muti, at Frescati, which had been for many years the favourite residence of the Cardinal of York, who was Bishop of Tusculum' (*ibid.* p. 363). Edward Cheney preserved memoranda of his conversations with Scott, which Lockhart printed in the *Life* (vii. 368-79). Among these are some most interesting remarks of Scott on the subject of Dante.[1]]

1832. May. MEMORANDA OF SIR WALTER SCOTT'S VISIT TO ROME.

[Scott and Dante]

SIR WALTER, though he spoke no foreign language with facility, read Spanish as well as Italian. He expressed the most unbounded admiration for Cervantes, and said that the 'novelas' of that author had first inspired him with the ambition of excelling in fiction, and that, until disabled by illness, he had been a constant reader of them. He added, that he had formerly made it a practice to read through the 'Orlando' of Boiardo, and the 'Orlando' of Ariosto, once every year.

Of Dante he knew little, confessing he found him too obscure and difficult. I was sitting next him at dinner, at Lady Coventry's, when this conversation took place. He added, with a smile, 'it is mortifying that Dante seemed to think nobody worth being sent to hell but his own Italians, whereas other people had every bit as great rogues in their families, whose misdeeds were suffered to pass with impunity.' I said that *he*, of all men, had least right to make this complaint, as his own ancestor, Michael Scott, was consigned to a very tremendous punishment in the twentieth canto of the Inferno. His attention was roused, and I quoted the passage—

[1] [See also above, pp. 278-9.]

'Quell' altro, che nei fianchi è così poco,
Michele Scotto fu, che veramente
Delle magiche frode seppe il gioco.'[1]

He seemed pleased, and alluded to the subject more than once in the course of the evening.

(*Lockhart's Life of Scott*, ed. 1833, vol. vii. pp. 370-1.)

THOMAS HOOD

(1799-1845)

[Thomas Hood, poet and humourist, son of a bookseller, was born in London in 1799. Being prevented by his delicate health from engaging in business, he turned his attention to literature, and became a contributor to the *London Magazine* (1821-3). He published his *Whims and Oddities* in 1826-7, and in 1829 became editor of the *Gem*, in which his *Eugene Aram's Dream* first appeared. In 1835, owing to pecuniary difficulties, he retired to the Continent, where he resided until 1840, when he returned to England. He edited the *New Monthly Magazine*, 1841-3, and in 1843 he contributed to *Punch* his famous *Song of the Shirt*. In 1844 he established *Hood's Magazine*, but his health broke down and he died in the following year. Hood had some slight acquaintance with Dante, whose *Inferno* he makes the subject of a jest.]

1832. TITLES FOR THE LIBRARY DOOR AT CHATSWORTH.

[Jest upon the *Inferno*]

On the Lung Arno in Consumption. By D. Cline.
Dante's Inferno: or Description of Van Demon's Land.

(*Memorials of Thos. Hood*, 1860, vol. i. p. 31.)

1841. MY TRACT.

[Dante, Boccaccio, and Rabelais, opponents of Popery]

In behalf of our literature I will boldly say that to our lay authors it is mainly owing that the country is not at this hour enthralled by Priestcraft, Superstition, and, if you please, Popery, which by the bye, has met with more efficient opponents in Dante, Boccaccio, and Rabelais (profane writers, madam), than in all the M'Neiles, M'Ghees, and Macaws, that have screamed within Exeter Hall.

(*Ibid.* vol. ii. p. 115.)

[1] [*Inf.* xx. 115-7—Scott's attention had been drawn to this passage five and twenty years before by Miss Seward during his visit to Lichfield; see Miss Seward's letter to Cary, May 10, 1807 (vol i. pp. 408-9).]

WILLIAM CLARKE

(fl. 1830)

1832. THE GEORGIAN ERA.

[Blake and Dante]

A FEW anecdotes of Blake—and his supernatural acquaintances are too singular to be omitted in our memoir. He boasted of a personal intimacy with Homer and Virgil, Dante[1] and Pindar. Moses occasionally looked in upon him; and Milton once intrusted him with a whole poem of his.

(Vol. iv. p. 115.)

CHARLES MACFARLANE

(d. 1858)

[Charles Macfarlane, miscellaneous writer, was a native of Scotland. He lived in Italy for eleven years, 1816-27, and thus acquired familiarity with the Italian language and literature, which qualified him to write on Italy in the *Romance of History* series (1832). He settled in London in 1829, and engaged in literary work, and eventually died in the Charterhouse in 1858. He was the author of a number of historical novels, biographical works, and books of travel, many of which were undertaken for Charles Knight. In his book on Italy Macfarlane makes frequent reference to Dante, and prefixes to many of the tales mottoes from the *Divina Commedia*, with which he was evidently familiar. He was also acquainted with the *Convivio*, from which he quotes and partially translates Dante's touching reference to his own exile.]

1832. THE ROMANCE OF HISTORY. ITALY.

[Dante in exile]

IN truth, I have been a ship without sail and without rudder, driven to various ports and shores by the cold blasts of disastrous fortune. And when on these wild voyages, how would my heart beat, when I heard, as at times I would, those who spoke of my native land!—of fair Italy, in which I was bred and nourished until I attained the age of manhood, and where, with due permission, I desire to repose my tired soul, and finish the time that is given me to live!'

The latter part of this speech is imitated from Dante's lament on his own exile, than which I know nothing more eloquent and touching.[2]

(*The Wandering King*, vol. i. pp. 71-2.)

[1] [See vol. i. pp. 455 ff.]

[2] [Macfarlane here quotes *Convivio* i. 3, ll. 20-43; iv. 27, ll. 96-100—for a translation of the former passage, see Toynbee's *Life of Dante* (ed. 1904), pp. 116-17.]

[Dante and the Italian language]

The valour of the warrior and the skill of the statesman interest us less than the passionate love of letters and the early refinement of Frederick II. and his favourite son Manfred. It was at that court that the literature of Italy may be said to have been cradled, and the foundations laid, of the rich and harmonious Italian language, which, somewhat more than a century after, reached at once the maturity of its strength and beauty in the hands of the immortal Dante Alighieri.

(*The Doomed King*, vol. ii. p. 221.)

[Dante's judgment on King Manfred]

A sceptical historian,[1] in relating the threat of Charles of Anjou to send Manfred to hell, would not decide on what was Manfred's doom in the other world; but Dante, (himself a Ghibelline,) who has eternized the infamy of his subjects,[2] has collocated the unfortunate gallant king in the purifying regions of Purgatory, where he makes him relate his own fate in verses of exquisite pathos.[3]

(*Ibid*. pp. 308-9.)

[Dante's debt to the times in which he lived]

'It is remarkable,' says Mr. Rogers, . . . 'that the noblest works of human genius have been produced in times of tumult, when every man was his own master, and all things were open to all. Homer, Dante, and Milton, appeared in such times, and we may add Virgil.'[4] This was certainly the case in Italy: during these troublous times, not only did Dante imbibe that spirit which was to render him immortal, but the energies of the Italians were roused to the very utmost in every little republic; and the seeds of enterprise, and emulation, and intellectual greatness, were seen on every hand.

(*Historical Summary of the Thirteenth Century*, vol. iii. pp. 2-3.)

LEITCH RITCHIE

(c. 1800-1865)

[Leitch Ritchie, novelist and miscellaneous writer, was born in Greenock about 1800. After serving as a merchant's clerk in Glasgow for a time, he went to

[1] Gibbon [Chap. lxii. 'Though I am ignorant of Mainfroy's doom in the other world, in this he lost his friends, his kingdom, and his life, in the bloody battle of Benevento' (ed. Bohn, vol. vii. p. 70).]

[2] [*Inf*. xxviii. 16-17.]

[3] [*Purg*. iii. 103 ff.]

[4] [See above, p. 77.]

London and adopted literature as a profession (1820). Among the numerous books produced by him were twelve volumes of *Heath's Picturesque Annual* (1832-45), for the purposes of which he travelled widely on the Continent, including Italy. He died at Greenwich in 1865.]

1832. TRAVELLING SKETCHES IN THE NORTH OF ITALY, THE TYROL, AND ON THE RHINE.[1]

['Sortes Danteanae']

DISAPPOINTED in her dependance on fortune and casualty, Lelia betook herself to the altars and gods of her people! Saints and martyrs were by turns invoked; vows were offered up, and pilgrimages and religious watchings performed. Then came dreams and prodigies into play, and omens, and auguries. *Sortes* were wrested from the pages of Dante, and warnings and commands translated from the mystic writings of the sky.

(*The Story of Lelia*, p. 107.)

BENJAMIN D'ISRAELI

(1804-1881)

[Benjamin D'Israeli, eldest son of Isaac D'Israeli, was born in London in 1804. He was articled to a firm of solicitors, and entered Lincoln's Inn in 1824. In the next year he published his first novel *Vivian Gray*. In 1837 he entered Parliament as member for Maidstone, and eventually sat for Buckinghamshire for twenty-nine years, from 1847 to 1876, in which year he was created Earl of Beaconsfield. He first took office as Chancellor of the Exchequer in 1852, and became Prime Minister in 1868. He was Prime Minister for the second time from 1874 to 1880, and died in 1881. In the *Revolutionary Epic* (1832) D'Israeli speaks of the *Divina Commedia* as a 'national epic,' and he several times introduces the *Inferno* in *Coningsby* (1844), but his acquaintance with Dante was evidently of the slightest.]

1832. THE REVOLUTIONARY EPICK.

[The *Divine Comedy* a national epic]

IT was on the plains of Troy that I first conceived the idea of this work. Wandering over that illustrious scene, surrounded by the tombs of heroes and by the confidence of poetic streams, my musing thoughts clustered round the memory of that immortal song, to which all creeds and countries alike respond, which has vanquished chance, and defies Time. Deeming myself, perchance too rashly, in that excited hour, a Poet, I cursed the

[1] [*Heath's Picturesque Annual for* 1832.]

destiny that had placed me in an age that boasted of being anti-poetical. And while my Fancy thus struggled with my Reason, it flashed across my mind, like the lightning which was then playing over Ida, that in those great poems which rise, the pyramids of poetic art, amid the falling and the fading splendour of less creations, the Poet hath ever embodied the spirit of his Time. Thus, the most heroic incident of an heroic age produced in the Iliad an Heroic Epick; thus the consolidation of the most superb of Empires, produced in the Aeneid a Political Epick; the revival of Learning, and the birth of vernacular Genius, presented us in the Divine Comedy with a National Epick; and the Reformation and its consequences called from the rapt lyre of Milton a Religious Epick.

And the spirit of my Time, shall it alone be uncelebrated? Standing upon Asia, and gazing upon Europe, with the broad Hellespont alone between us, and the shadow of Night descending on the mountains, these mighty continents appeared to me, as it were, the Rival Principles of Government, that at present contend for the mastery of the World. 'What!' I exclaimed, 'is the Revolution of France a less important event than the siege of Troy? Is Napoleon a less interesting character than Achilles? For me remains the Revolutionary Epick.'

(*Preface.*)

1844. CONINGSBY; OR THE NEW GENERATION.

[The Princess wishes life were 'more Dantesque']

Lord Eskdale looked round, and calling Sidonia, he presented his friend to the Princess.

'You are fond of music, Lord Eskdale tells me?' said Lucretia.

'When it is excellent,' said Sidonia.

'But that is so rare,' said the Princess.

'And precious as Paradise,' said Sidonia. 'As for indifferent music, 'tis purgatory; but when it is bad, for my part I feel myself——'

'Where?' said Lord Eskdale.

'In the last circle of the Inferno,' said Sidonia.

Lord Eskdale turned to Flora.

'And in what circle do you place us who are here?' the Princess inquired of Sidonia.

'One too polished for his verse,' replied her companion.

'You mean too insipid,' said the Princess. 'I wish that life were a little more Dantesque.'

(Book iv. Chap. 11.)

[The *Inferno* in the boudoir]

About half-an-hour after Mr. Rigby had entered the Princess Colonna's apartments it seemed that all the bells of Monmouth House were ringing at the same time. The sound even reached the Marquis in his luxurious recess; who immediately took a pinch of snuff, and ordered his valet to lock the door of the ante-chamber. The Princess Lucretia, too, heard the sounds; she was lying on a sofa, in her boudoir, reading the *Inferno*, and immediately mustered her garrison in the form of a French maid, and gave directions that no one should be admitted. Both the Marquess and his intended bride felt that a crisis was at hand, and resolved to participate in no scenes.

(Book v. Chap. 6.)

EDWARD FITZGERALD

(1809-1883)

[Edward Fitzgerald, third son of John Purcell, who in 1818 took the name of Fitzgerald, was born near Woodbridge in Suffolk in 1809. He was educated at Bury St. Edmunds' Grammar School, and Trinity College, Cambridge, where he graduated in 1830. At Cambridge he was a contemporary of Thackeray and of Alfred Tennyson and his two brothers, all of whom were life-long friends. Fitzgerald's life was passed for the most part in retirement in Suffolk, where he occupied himself with literature, chiefly translation. His now famous version (from the Persian) of the *Rubaiyat of Omar Khayyám*, which at first attracted little or no notice, was published anonymously in 1859. He died in 1883. Fitzgerald, as his friend E. B. Cowell, who used to read Dante with him, writes, 'was always a great admirer of the *Divine Comedy*.' Frequent references to Dante occur throughout his published letters, down to within a year of his death, but he seemed 'to feel the atmosphere of Dante's world somewhat oppressive and sombre as years grew on,'[1] and consequently gave up reading the *Commedia*. His favourite translation was Cary, of which he had a high opinion. A few lines from Dante were found inscribed in an old Common-place book of Fitzgerald's, written between 1831 and 1840. Cowell records that he had a great admiration for the later cantos of the *Paradiso*. He used to take Dante with him when he went sailing—in a letter to Cowell in 1863 he says, 'I am glad to find I relish Dante as much as ever: he atones with the Sea; as you know does the Odyssey—these are the Men!' (*Letters*, ii. 45).]

c. 1832. REMINISCENCES OF TENNYSON.

[The difference between Goethe and Dante]

A. T. was still afraid of blindness, which his brother Frederick said might accompany the perception of the inward Sublime as in Homer and Milton. The names of Dante and Michael Angelo in (the original form of) this poem[2] remind

[1] [See Cowell's letter, below, p. 697.]
[2] [*The Palace of Art*, first published in 1833 (see above, pp. 316-17).]

me that once looking with A. T. at two busts of Dante and Goethe in a shop window in Regent Street, I said, 'what is there wanting in Goethe which the other has?'—'The Divine!'

(*Memoir of Lord Tennyson*, by his Son, vol. i. pp. 120-1.)

1835. May 23. LETTER TO JOHN ALLEN [1] (from Manchester).

[Reading Dante, by aid of a dictionary]

I have not been reading very much—(as if you ever expected that I did!)—but I mean, not very much for me—some Dante, by the aid of a Dictionary; and some Milton—and some Wordsworth—

(*Letters of Edward Fitzgerald*, vol. i. p. 34.)

1835. July 2. LETTER TO ALFRED TENNYSON (from London).

[A small edition of the *Divina Commedia*]

When I was at Manchester, I bought a small *Dante* for myself: and, liking it well, the same for you: for I had never seen the edition before, and I daresay you have not. It is small, but very clearly printed: with little explanations at the foot of each page,[2] very welcome to me: the proper price was ten shillings, but I only gave three.

(*Memoir of Lord Tennyson*, vol. i. p. 156.)

1839. July 20. LETTER TO W. F. POLLOCK.[3]

[Dante and Alfieri perhaps to meet in Hell]

He was a very fine fellow, was Alfieri: they say his plays are very dull, and I think the Life becomes duller as he begins the Literary part of it. For he only began to *read* his own language at twenty-five; and his first plays were written first in French Prose and then drafted into Italian verse. What a process! Up to that time of his life he only rode horses over every country in Europe, and kept mistresses: his loves were very heroic and poetical: so perhaps he would have aided the cause of poetry more

[1] [Afterwards Archdeacon of Salop.]

[2] [Probably the edition in one volume, published in 1827 by C. S. Arnold (see above, p. 522).]

[3] [William Frederick (afterwards Sir W. F.) Pollock (1815-1888); he published a blank verse translation of the *Divina Commedia* in 1854.]

by leaving it to others to write about him. I wonder the French Playwrights haven't got hold of him: perhaps they have though. He was such a fellow for Liberty too: he calls Catherine the second, *codesta Clitennestra filosofessa*, which words have the whistling of the lash about them, I think. He would have been a capital Middle Age Italian: especially for Dante to put into hell. But perhaps he'll meet him there yet.

(*More Letters of Edward Fitzgerald*, p. 3.)

1841. Sept. 28. LETTER TO S. LAURENCE[1] (from Naseby).

[Giotto's portrait of Dante]

I wish you would ask at Molteno's or Colnaghi's for a new Lithographic print of a head of Dante, after a fresco by Giotto, lately discovered in some chapel at Florence.[2] It is the most wonderful head that ever was seen—Dante at about twenty-seven years old: rather younger. The Edgeworths had a print in Ireland: got by great interest in Florence before the legitimate publication: but they told me it was to be abroad in September. If you can get me a copy, pray do.

(*Letters of Edward Fitzgerald*, vol. i. pp. 90-1.)

1841. Oct. LETTER TO F. TENNYSON[3] (from Naseby).

[All Dante's poem in his face]

When you go to Florence, get to see a fresco portrait of Dante by Giotto: newly discovered in some chapel there. Edgeworth saw it, and has brought home a print which is (he says) a tolerable copy. It is a most awful head: Dante, when about twenty-five years old. The likeness to the common portraits of him when old is quite evident. All his great poem seems in it: like the flower in the bud. I read the last cantos of the Paradiso over and over again. I forget if you like him: but, if I understand you at all, you must.

(*Ibid.* vol. i. p. 93.)

1842. June 19. LETTER TO S. LAURENCE (from Boulge Hall).

[Print of Dante]

Keep the head of Raffaelle as long as you please. I am glad that one of the three pictures at all events is worth something. . . .

[1] [Samuel Laurence (1812-1884), the portrait-painter.]

[2] [The chapel of the Palazzo del Podestà, now known as the Bargello. For an account of the discovery of this portrait, see below, pp. 639 ff.]

[3] [Frederick Tennyson (1807-1898), elder brother of Alfred Tennyson.]

The head of Dante is, I suppose, the same as the one L. Hunt shewed us engraved in a book: a theatrical one, I thought.

(*Letters of Edward Fitzgerald*, vol. i. p. 117.)

1842. Aug. 29. LETTER TO JOHN ALLEN (from Bedford).

[Reading Dante]

I occasionally read sentences about the Virtues out of this collection of Stobaeus, and look into Sartor Resartus, which has fine things in it: and a little Dante and a little Shakespeare.

(*Ibid.* vol. i. p. 123.)

LADY CHARLOTTE SUSAN MARIA BURY

(1775-1861)

[Lady Charlotte Susan Maria Campbell, youngest daughter of the fifth Duke of Argyll, by Elizabeth Gunning, whose beauty she inherited, was born in London in 1775. When she was 16 Horace Walpole wrote of her to Miss Berry that 'everybody admires her person and understanding, but laments her want of education and control.' She married, firstly (1796) Colonel John Campbell; secondly (1818), Rev. Edward Bury. In 1809 she was appointed lady-in-waiting to the Princess of Wales, afterwards Queen Caroline, and she subsequently recorded some of her experiences in an anonymous *Diary illustrative of the Time of George IV.* which was published in 1838. Lady Charlotte, who died in London in 1861, was the authoress of numerous novels and poems, among the latter being one on *The Three Great Sanctuaries of Tuscany* (1833), which contains several references to Dante and mottoes from the *Divina Commedia*.]

1833. THE THREE GREAT SANCTUARIES OF TUSCANY, VALOMBROSA, CAMALDOLI, LAVERNA: A POEM, WITH HISTORICAL AND LEGENDARY NOTICES.

[Dante—Ghiberti]

HENCE the fierce strivings, hence the deep-drawn groans,
Hence the wild stories of this classic site.
That seem yet graven on its very stones—
The civil broils—the dreadful black and white![1]
Back on the mind, from dull, oblivious night,
Again recurs each long forgotten scene;
Again great Dante starts to life and light—
His eagle eye, his sad, wild poet's mien,
His glorious halo-ray, and wreath of deathless green.

* * * *

[1] The Negri and the Bianchi.

Allied to Dante's next in high degree
Ghiberti's works resplendent lustre shed
Around that precious spot, when gloriously
Still lives the genius of the mighty dead.
* * * *

(*Valle Ombrosa*, pp. 17, 18.)

[Landino's commentary on Dante]

Landino in his old age retired to a villa at Prato Vecchio, in the vicinity of Florence, which was bestowed on him by public decree, in reward for his critical labours on Dante.[1] . . . His notes in his editions of Virgil, Horace, and Dante, are much esteemed.

(*Historical and Legendary Notices of Camaldoli*,[2] pp. 48-9.)

[Giotto and Dante]

On the walls of the upper church of St. Francis at Assisi is painted the life of the Saint, by Giotto: the various incidents are forcibly told, but many of them are much faded in colour, and are passing rapidly into decay. Like all sublime works, they require intense and undivided thought to be duly appreciated: the same spirit dwells in them that dwells in Dante: that primeval conception of poetic inspiration, applicable alike to graphic or to lettered art, stamps them with a simplicity and vigour, only to be found in the early eras of genius, ere talent was weakened by diffusion, or originality intimidated by the cold dissection of criticism.

(*Historical and Legendary Notices of Laverna*,[3] pp. 108-9.)

[Dante and St. Francis]

A worshipper amidst these steeps and woods,
Here sainted Francis (so great Dante writes)[4]
Received symbolic wounds as precious goods
By heaven bestowed—and here he still requites
His sandelled brethren with supreme delights;
While, gifted thus by spell, they deem divine,
The stern Franciscans, yet observe his rites—
Strange dreams, but suited to so dear a shrine,
Where nature's wildest forms in savage gloom combine.

(*Laverna*, p. 116.)

[1] [First published at Florence in 1481.]
[2] [The poem on Camaldoli has a motto from *Inf.* ii. 7-9.]
[3] [The poem on Laverna has a motto from *Purg.* i. 1-6.]
[4] [Dante refers to St. Francis receiving the *Stigmata* at Laverna, *Par.* xi. 106-8.]

A. T. MALKIN

(fl. 1830)

1833. THE GALLERY OF PORTRAITS: WITH MEMOIRS.[1]

[Dante's minor works]

THE mass of Dante's writings, considering the unfavourable circumstances under which he laboured, is almost as wonderful as the extent of his attainments. The treatise 'De Monarchia,' which he composed on the arrival of Henry VII. in Italy, is one of the most ingenious productions that ever appeared, in refutation of the temporal pretensions of the Court of Rome. It was hailed with triumphant joy by the Ghibelines, and loaded with vituperation by the Guelfs. The succeeding emperor, Lewis of Bavaria, laid great stress on its arguments as supporting his claims against John XXII; and, on that account, the Pope had it burnt publicly by the Cardinal du Pujet, his legate in Lombardy, who would even have disinterred and burnt Dante's body, and scattered his ashes to the wind, if some influential citizens had not interposed. Another Latin work, 'De Vulgari Eloquentia,' treats of the origin, history, and use of the genuine Italian tongue. It is full of interesting and curious research, and is still classed among the most judicious and philosophical works that Italy possesses on the subject. He meant to have comprised it in four books, but unfortunately only lived to complete two.

Of his Italian productions, the earliest was, perhaps, the 'Vita Nuova,' a mixture of mysterious poetry and prose, in which he gives a detailed account of his love for Beatrice. It is pervaded by a spirit of soft melancholy extremely touching; and it contains several passages having all the distinctness and individuality of truth; but, on the other hand, it is interspersed with visions and dreams, and metaphysical conceits, from which it receives all the appearance of an allegorical invention. He also composed about thirty sonnets, and nearly as many 'Canzoni,' or songs, both on love and morality. The sonnets, though not destitute of grace and ingenuity, are not distinguished by any particular excellence. The songs display a vigour of style, a sublimity of thought, a depth of feeling, and a richness of imagery not known before: they betoken the poet and the philosopher. On fourteen of these, he attempted in his old age to write a minute commentary, to which he gave the title of 'Convito,' or Banquet, as being intended "to administer

[1] [Published by the Society for the Diffusion of Useful Knowledge—Reissued in 1838 as *Distinguished Men of Modern Times.*]

the food of wisdom to the ignorant;" but he could only extend it to three. Thus he produced the first specimen of severe Italian prose: and if he indulged rather too much in fanciful allegories and scholastic subtleties, these blemishes are amply counterbalanced by a store of erudition, an elevation of sentiment, and a matchless eloquence, which it is difficult not to admire.

(Ed. 1838, vol. i. pp. 9 ff.)

[The *Divina Commedia*]

These works,[1] omitting several others of inferior value, would have been more than sufficient to place Dante above all his contemporaries; yet they stand at an immeasurable distance from the "Divina Commedia," the great poem by which he has recommended his name to the veneration of the remotest posterity. The Divine Comedy is the narrative of a mysterious journey through hell, purgatory, and paradise, which he supposes himself to have performed in the year 1300, during the passion-week, having Virgil as his guide through the two regions of woe, and Beatrice through that of happiness. No creation of the human mind ever excelled this mighty vision in originality and vastness of design; nor did any one ever choose a more appropriate subject for the expression of all his thoughts and feelings. The mechanical construction of his spiritual world allowed him room for developing his geographical and astronomical knowledge: the punishments and rewards allotted to the characters introduced, gave him an excellent opportunity for a display of his theological and philosophical learning: the continual succession of innumerable spirits of different ages, nations, and conditions, enabled him to expatiate in the fields of ancient and modern history, and to expose thoroughly the degradation of Italian society in his own times; while the whole afforded him ample scope for a full exertion of his poetical endowments, and for the illustration of the moral lesson, which, whatever his real meaning may have been, is ostensibly the object of his poem. Neither were his powers of execution inferior to those of conception. Rising from the deepest abyss of torture and despair, through every degree of suffering and hope, up to the sublimest beatitude, he imparts the most vivid and intense dramatic interest to a wonderful variety of scenes which he brings before the reader. Awful, vehement, and terrific in hell, in proportion as he advances through purgatory and paradise, he contrives to modify his style in such a manner as to become more pleasing in his images, more easy in his expressions, more delicate in his sentiments, and more regular in his versification. His characters live and move; the objects which he depicts are

[1] [The minor works mentioned in the preceding paragraph.]

clear and palpable; his similes are generally new and just; his reflections evince throughout the highest tone of morality; his energetic language makes a deep and vigorous impression both on the reason and the imagination; and the graphic force with which, by a few bold strokes, he throws before the eye of his reader a perfect and living picture, is wholly unequalled.

It is true, however, that his constant solicitude for conciseness and effect led him, sometimes, into a harsh and barbarous phraseology, and into the most unrestrained innovations; but, considering the rudeness of his age, and the unformed state of his language, he seems hardly open to the censure of a candid critic on this account. On the other hand, it is impossible not to wonder how, in spite of such obstacles, he could so happily express all the wild conceptions of his fancy, the most abstract theories of philosophy, and the most profound mysteries of religion. The occasional obscurity and coldness of the Divine Comedy proceeds much less from defects of style, than from didactic disquisitions and historical allusions which become every day less intelligible and less interesting. To be understood and appreciated as a whole, and in its parts, it requires a store of antiquated knowledge which is now of little use. Even at the period of its publication, when its geography and astronomy were not yet exploded, its philosophy and theology still current, and many of its incidents and personages still fresh in the memory of thousands, it was considered rather as a treasure of moral wisdom, than as a book of amusement. The city of Florence, and several other towns of Italy, soon established professorships for the express purpose of explaining it to the public. Two sons of Dante wrote commentaries for its illustration: Boccaccio, Benvenuto da Imola, and many others, followed the example in rapid succession: and even a few years since Foscolo [1] and Rossetti [2] excited fresh curiosity and interest by the novelty of their views. Notwithstanding the learning and ingenuity of all its expositors, the hidden meaning of the 'Divina Commedia' is not yet perfectly made out, though Rossetti, in his 'Spirito Antipapale,' lately published,[3] seems to have shown, that, under the exterior of moral precepts, it contains a most bitter satire against the Court of Rome. But whether time shall remove these obscurities, or thicken the mist which hangs around this extraordinary production, it will be ever memorable as the mighty work which gave being and form to the beautiful language of Italy, impressed a new character on the poetry of modern Europe, and inspired the genius of Michael Angelo and of Milton.

(Ed. 1838, vol. i. pp. 11-3.)

[1] [See above, pp. 159 ff.] [2] [See above, pp. 445-6.]
[3] [It was published in the previous year.]

ICHABOD CHARLES WRIGHT

(1795-1871)

[Ichabod Charles Wright was born at Mapperley, in Nottinghamshire, in 1795. He was educated at Eton (1808-14), and Christ Church, Oxford, where he graduated in 1817. In 1819 he was elected to a Fellowship at Magdalen College, which he held until 1825, when he married and became joint-manager of the family bank at Nottingham. In 1833 he published *The Inferno of Dante, Translated*, with introduction and notes, the metre of the translation being a sort of bastard *terza rima*. This work, of which a second edition, with portions of the translation recast, and additional notes, was issued in the same year, was dedicated to Lord Brougham, as 'one of the most ardent admirers of Dante.'[1] The *Inferno* was followed by the *Purgatorio* (dedicated to William Howley, Archbishop of Canterbury) in 1836, and by the *Paradiso* (dedicated to his father-in-law, Lord Denman, Lord Chief Justice) in 1840. The three parts were published together in three volumes in 1845, and again in a single volume, with additional matter, in 1854. Wright's translation, the first since that of Cary, with which it challenged comparison, is an unequal performance, but at times it reaches a high level of excellence. It no doubt helped greatly to popularize the study of Dante in England. Wright, who died in 1871, published in 1859-64 a blank verse translation of the *Iliad*, of which Matthew Arnold said in his *Lectures on Translating Homer*, that 'it had no proper reason for existing.']

1833. THE INFERNO OF DANTE, TRANSLATED.[2]

[Dante a poet in spite of Rossetti's theories[3]]

IT has lately been attempted to prove, that several works, both prior and subsequent to the age of Dante, were entirely allegorical, and composed in a secret cypher, to avoid disclosure of the principles entertained in opposition to the Court of Rome;—that Dante was himself initiated in this supposed mysterious language, and believed he was devoting his genius exclusively to passing subjects and elaborate conceits. Were it, however, possible that he could have written a poem, abounding in sublime descriptions, and in passages of exquisite pathos, under the weight of such oppressive trammels—still, posterity will worship only the exalted Muse, which, guiding his unconscious pen, made him the instrument for rousing the noblest and most amiable sympathies of the human heart. Speculation on the various allusions embraced in so comprehensive a work may furnish an interesting employment to the curiosity of learned men; but we should never forget those sublimer qualities, which render the poet a fit companion for his immortal guide, and place the name of Dante in harmonious fellowship with that of Homer, of Shakspeare, and of Milton.

(*Introduction*, p. xviii.)

[1] [See above, pp. 432 ff.]

[2] [Reviewed in *Athenæum*, March, 1833; *Monthly Review*, March, 1833; *Quarterly Review*, July, 1833; *Edinburgh Review*, July, 1833 (see below, pp. 571-3, 574-8).]

[3] Rossetti, Comento and Sullo Spirito Antipapale [see above, pp. 445 ff.].

[Speech of Ulysses to his companions—his last voyage (*Inf.* xxvi. 112-42]

'Comrades,' I said, 'who now have reach'd the west,
And won your way through perils infinite,—
Short is the space ere all will be at rest;
Let each then rouse his drooping energies
That land without inhabitants to find—
Still unexplor'd, which to the westward lies.
Bear your illustrious origin in view;
For not to live like brutes were ye design'd,
But knowledge high and virtue to pursue!'
This brief oration, to my comrades made,
Avail'd so much their ardour to excite,
It could not afterwards have been allay'd.
When we had turn'd the poop to face the east,
We strain'd our oars to wing our foolish flight;
And thus proceeding gain'd upon the west.
The stars that o'er the other pole are spread
That night I saw, while ours was so deprest,
It rose not higher than the ocean's bed.
Five times the moon had shed her brightest ray,
As oft was robb'd of her transparent vest,
Since first we enter'd on our mighty way—
When, dim in distance, rear'd its brow on high
A mountain—which, now bursting on our view,
Appear'd the loftiest that e'er met mine eye.
Great was our joy—a joy soon turn'd to woe;
For, rushing from the land unknown and new,
A whirlwind sprang, and struck the vessel's prow:
Thrice did it drive the ship and waters round;
The poop ascended as the fourth wave rose;
The prow lay buried in the depth profound,
And o'er our heads Heaven bade the sea to close.

(pp. 242-3.)

1836. THE PURGATORIO OF DANTE, TRANSLATED.

[Invocation.—The confines of Purgatory (*Purg.* i. 1-27).]

O'er the smooth waters of a milder sea
The light bark of my genius hoists her sail,
Leaving behind the flood of misery;
For now that second kingdom claims my song,
Wherein is purified the spirit frail,
And fitted to rejoin the heavenly throng.
Wake into life the deaden'd notes again,
O ye most holy Nine! since yours' I am;
And let Calliope exalt the strain,

Following my verse with that extatic sound,
  Which, to the wretched Picae when it came,
  Dash'd all their hopes of pardon to the ground.
Sweet colours that with orient sapphire shone,
  Collected in the tranquil atmosphere,
  Far as the highest circle's purer zone,
Enjoyment to my weary eyes restored,
  Soon as I issued from that stagnant air
  Which o'er my sight and breast such sorrow pour'd.—
The beateous Star, to love and lovers dear,
  Was making all the orient laugh;—so bright,
  She veil'd the Pisces, who attended near.—
When to the other pole mine eyes I turn'd,
  And there beheld four planets on the right,
  By none save those in Paradise discern'd:
Heaven seem'd to view their lustre with delight.
  O northern region, how bereav'd art thou,
  These starry splendours banish'd from thy sight!

(pp. 3-4.)

1840. THE PARADISE OF DANTE, TRANSLATED.[1]

[St. Bernard's prayer to the Virgin on behalf of Dante (*Par.* xxxiii. 1-32).]

O Virgin Mother, daughter of thy Son!
  Humblest, yet most exalted of our race,
  Forecast of counsel in the Eternal One,—
Man's nature thou didst raise to such high station,
  That He who made it thought it no disgrace
  To vail His glory in his own creation.
Within thy womb renew'd its ancient power
  That love, beneath whose vivifying glow
  Put forth its buds in peace this blessed flower.
Here unto us a mid-day torch thou art
  Of Charity; and unto men below
  The living streams of Hope thou dost impart.
Lady, so great art thou, and such thy might,
  That whoso grace desires, and asks not thee,
  Desire indulges, ere equipped for flight.
Thy kindness succoureth not him alone
  Who asks thy aid; but oft spontaneously
  Runs in advance, and is, unask'd for, shown.
In thee dwells Mercy—Pity dwells in thee—
  In thee munificence—in thee abounds
  What'er of Goodness may in creature be.

[1] [Reviewed in *Dublin University Magazine*, Nov. 1840 (see below, p. 650).]

Now he, who from the nethermost abyss
  Of all the world, hath in their several rounds
  Beheld the spirits, or of woe or bliss,
A suppliant, asks thee, through the ministration
  Of heavenly grace, to lift his eyes above,
  That he may see the height of his salvation:
And I, who for that glorious sight did ne'er
  Burn with more ardour than for him I prove,
  Urge all my prayers; (and may they reach thine ear)
That by thy prayers thou would'st dispel each cloud
  Of the mortality that dims his brow;
  So may the Deity his face unshroud.

(pp. 321-2.)

ANONYMOUS

1833. March. ATHENÆUM. WRIGHT'S INFERNO OF DANTE TRANSLATED.[1]

[On translating Dante]

WE have looked with much interest, not unmixed with wonder, at the work before us; and this feeling was not a little increased by the circumstances under which it appeared. The intellectual habits of the day are not calculated to foster minds either capable of producing, or fitted to enjoy such productions. Dante, of all poets, is the most opposite to the conventional tastes of the nineteenth century. He lived, it is true, in an age of strong excitement, and so do we; he nourished and expressed the bitterest hate that could be generated in the strife of parties, and there is no want of such feeling in our day: he drew with a broad, strong pencil, gave huge and distinct forms to his groups, and made heaven and hell speak the language of earth; and all this is conformable with the wishes and appetite of our own time;—but the excitement of Dante's age was the fierceness of a giant in his youth; its politics were the direct calculations of power and freedom, its utilitarianism, the abstracts of poets and patriots. . . . Dante spoke with the voice of one having authority; and the moral obedience then accorded to the poet, directed him to employ the powers of his vast genius on themes which might influence the destinies of his race. But this reverence for the inspirations of poetry no longer exists; and great, consequently, as the

[1] [See above, pp. 568-9.]

appetite may be for whatever rouses and excites, it is not for what the poet may utter in his enthusiasm; that which, at one time, would have bowed the hearts of thousands, can now scarcely command the attention of a few solitary readers; because the poet has no longer the office of either a prophet or a teacher.

This was the first thing which made us look with surprise at the new translation of Dante; then came that derived from the nature of the task itself. It should be observed, in estimating the difficulties which a translator of Dante has to encounter, that there is one peculiar in his author—the perfect originality of his poetical diction and phraseology. He lived in the very dawn of Italian poetry, and was himself almost its father. There are, consequently, in his verses, none of the common-place, universal sentences of other writers—none of those phrases which have since become the property of poets in every country, and for which there are well known and acknowledged equivalents in every language. In Dante the metal is sculptured by the poet's own hand, and each line is sharp and distinct. The running into moulds was unknown in his day. It is evident from hence that the translator of Dante has none of those helps which the conventional language of poetry offers to others. He has to grapple with a stern and almost primitive phraseology; to exercise the highest powers he possesses in simple interpretation; and to be forcible by being literally exact. . . .

We have followed Mr. Wright through several passages line for line, and find him as exact as the most scrupulous admirers of the great Florentine could desire. . . . Mr. Wright has not only adhered closely to his original, but has preserved its grandeur and force. His verse is not less deserving of praise: we here and there meet with a few feeble lines; and he sometimes is on the point of sinking into a loose prosaic style; but this results almost necessarily from the great freedom he has indulged in, and to which we are indebted for the most valuable property of his version,—its combined variety and strength.

While giving this well-merited praise to Mr. Wright, we have not forgotten the admirable translation of Dante which has long taken its place among the most valued ornaments of our poetical literature. Mr. Cary's version has merits peculiar to itself, and it would not be less weak than ungrateful, to sacrifice one atom of our respect for that which is intrinsically excellent, because the same spirit of truth and beauty has manifested itself through another channel.

(Vol. 1833, pp. 177-8.)

ANONYMOUS

1833. March. MONTHLY REVIEW. ART. XI. THE INFERNO OF DANTE, TRANSLATED. BY ICHABOD CHARLES WRIGHT.

[The growing interest in Italian literature in England]

A NEW version in English of Dante's *Inferno* is we own an announcement full of interest for our minds. The performance has come upon us quite abruptly, and altogether unpreceded by those heraldic paragraphs of promise which usually usher in novelties of so much consequence as the translation of a poem of Dante. Italian poetry, particularly that of the illustrious poet just mentioned, has in recent times been rendered more familiar than at any former period of our history to British ears. The expatriation of Italians, distinguished for their genius and literature, and, in some instances for the union of these accomplishments with the happiest accidents of birth and fortune, has led to the introduction of a taste for their native language in some of the highest circles in England; and it is not to be wondered at that our publications should occasionally testify the influence which such a circumstance would naturally have over the current of our publications. We do not propose to enter minutely into an investigation of the merits of the present version. We shall content ourselves with presenting to the reader a few passages, selected on such a principle as will best enable him to understand the merits of Mr. Wright's performance. . . .

It will be seen from the extracts,[1] that the translator is, at all events, pretty faithful to his original, and that in no material instance is the meaning of Dante ever obscured. The measure adopted seems to us well suited to the nature of the subject, and the whole is executed in a very animated spirit, and with great ease and simplicity of expression, such as more nearly approximate its merits to those of the *Inferno* itself.

(Vol. i. pp. 428. ff.)

ANONYMOUS

1833. April. QUARTERLY REVIEW. ART. VIII. LORD JOHN RUSSELL ON THE CAUSES OF THE FRENCH REVOLUTION.

[Dante the exile]

IT is well observed by the author of Emile, that we compute the worshippers of Baal, but take no note of the thousands who have never bowed down before the brazen image. We have seen the real qualities of the French nobility and clergy tried

[1] ['While sadly I retraced'—'and pulses beat,' pp. 6-7; and 'Imagine then, if fancy thou possess'—'for all hath now been viewed,' pp. 318-20.]

by the severest and truest of all tests—adversity. We have seen them during the revolution dragged to the scaffold as victims, or thrust from their homes as beggars. They had to feel (in the words of another illustrious and heart broken exile)—

'Come sa di sale
Il pane altrui, e com' è duro calle
Lo scendere e 'l salir per l' altrui scale.'
Dante Paradiso, Canto 17.[1]

In all these trials, what high-minded patience, what unconquerable spirit was theirs! How heroically did they encounter an ignominious death,—how still more heroically did they bear a life of poverty and pain!

(Vol. xlix. p. 160.)

ANONYMOUS

1833. July. QUARTERLY REVIEW. ART. III. MERIVALE'S GREEK ANTHOLOGY.

[Dante's 'declaration to the frivolous']

ALL ages and all countries have exhibited, and continue to exhibit, conspicuous examples of the fashionable postponement of the beautiful to the pretty, of the majestic to the showy; and we cannot but think, that Pindar must have put the finishing stroke to many of his subtle and deeply-wrought odes, with a feeling akin to that contained in Dante's solemn declaration to the Frivolous:—

'Canzone, i' credo, che saranno radi
Color, che tua ragione intendan bene,
Tanto lor parli faticoso e forte!'[2]

(Vol. xlix. p. 377.)

ANONYMOUS

1833. July. QUARTERLY REVIEW. ART. V. WRIGHT'S INFERNO OF DANTE.

[Wright's version of the *Inferno* compared with that of Cary]

WE have, on various occasions, expressed our high opinion of the translation of the Divine Comedy executed in our own time by Mr. Cary. To say that it was on all points superior to every preceding English version of that extra-

[1] [ll. 58-60.]

[2] [*Canz.* vi. (*Conv.* ii.), ll. 53-5.]

ordinary poem, would have been little praise: they had all been execrable—it was really excellent. Mr. Cary understood his author as well perhaps as any Englishman did at the period of his labours—and he gave us a transcript, almost always clear, generally vigorous, and in many passages indicative of warm poetical feeling in the mind of the interpreter. We speak of the substance of Dante:—of his peculiar manner, as distinct—as unlike any other—in many respects as nobly original as that of Homer or of Shakespeare—the version, masterly as it was, certainly conveyed, as a whole, no approach to a likeness. The measure alone in which Cary wrote rendered this almost impossible. The sweeping, long-drawn-out harmony of good English blank verse could reflect no livelier impression of the compact, terse, if we may so call it *sculptural* precision of Dante's *terza rima*, than Pope's heroic couplets of Homer's hexameters; and when Cary, in the desire to come closer to Dante, flung away the guiding echo of his Milton, he produced an effect positively disagreeable. Tercets, without the grace of caesura, and the varieties of interlinked lines, in the absence of rhyme, are indeed unmelodious monsters. The attempt to introduce the *terza rima* itself as an English measure, often unsuccessfully hazarded in our earlier times, has been repeated, since Mr. Cary published his book, by a great master of versification; but although Lord Byron seems to have thought very highly of the execution of his Prophecy of Dante and his translation of an Episode in the Inferno,[1] the public taste has not in the main ratified his judgment. . . .

The most cursory perusal of Mr. Wright's *Inferno* will satisfy every one that, had there been no Cary, this work would have been a valuable addition to the English library. But with every disposition to encourage any gentleman in an elegant pursuit, it is our duty to ask, in how far, Cary's volumes being in every collection, it was worth Mr. Wright's while to undertake a new version of Dante? . . . Surely Dante could not be a judicious choice, unless the new translator felt himself qualified to surpass, to some very considerable extent, the effect of his predecessor's performance—to convey at once a more exact impression of his author's meaning, and a livelier one of his manner. If Mr. Wright has succeeded in rendering Dante more accurately than Mr. Cary had done *here and there*, only by availing himself of certain recent commentaries on the original, of which Mr. Cary might have been expected to make use in preparing a new edition of his work; if, with the exception of these detached passages, the later version is not a more faithful one—and if it does not, as a whole, wear an air

[1] [See above, pp. 38-40, 43-5.]

more Dantesque without being less English, than the former—we shall be compelled, not to treat disrespectfully a well-meant and industrious effort, but to express our regret that the time and talents devoted to it had not found some unpreoccupied field—and to urge the propriety of suspending a labour which, if completed, could at best conduct to a secondary place. We are bound to observe *in limine* that the version of Cary has been of infinite use to his successor; Mr. Wright has taken from him not a few *lines*, and in *innumerable* instances he has obviously and incontestably drawn his *words*, not directly from the Italian fountain-head, but from the previous English (and manly English that is) of his predecessor. Cary has been in the main the Dante of Mr. Wright; and he has departed from him nowhere, as far as we have been able to trace, to any good effect, unless when guided by Ugo Foscolo, or by Rossetti—of whose *Commentary*, indeed, he nor seldom inlays fragments into his text; a liberty which had better been omitted. No doubt, then, it is on his nearer approach to the air and manner of the Italian master, that the new interpreter rests his claim to supplant Cary; and when we opened his book, we certainly did not doubt that the gigantic task of rendering Dante in the *terza rima* had now at all events been accomplished. But a very brief examination dismissed this dream. Mr. Wright's measure is the Dantesque one to the eye, but not to the ear. It is printed exactly like the Italian verse—but the writer has not grappled with the difficulties, and he has missed the chief grace, of the *terza rima*:—he has few triple rhymes at all—and none in the right places; and the subtle link by which Dante binds every section of his measure into the succeeding one is thus wholly lost. The result, then, is not an English Inferno in the measure of Dante, instead of the measure of Milton; but only the sense of Cary twisted out of blank verse into a new and anomalous variety of English rhyme.

(Vol. xlix. pp. 449 ff.)

ANONYMOUS

1833. July. EDINBURGH REVIEW. ART. VII. WRIGHT'S TRANSLATION OF THE INFERNO OF DANTE.

[Difficulties of a translator of Dante]

IS it true that Dante in any age, past, present, or to come, could be the favourite poet of ordinary readers? No such thing. . . . Much—we should fear, most—of the 'Divine Comedy' must always have been extremely difficult; difficult from the allegories, one or more; from the crowd of historical and personal allusions; from transitive meanings, (more frequent, Foscolo says, even than in Virgil), and from the use of words (as Dante boasted, and Bembo afterwards complained) in a sense different from other poets. Difficulty is one of the elements of its power, in the concise construction and prophetical character, which form at once the energy and the obscurity of its style. There can be no mistake in saying, that such a work must, in the nature of things, be too abstruse, austere, and lofty for the majority of any nation. Mr. Wright's translation may be in the highest degree successful, without becoming popular. . . . A translator, who knows his place, will never expect to fare better than his original. It is almost impossible, for a variety of reasons, every one of which is all but conclusive, that he can fare as well.

* * * *

The 'Divine Comedy' was still a sealed volume in scholastic libraries, when the two Wartons, who had some life in them during one of the deadest periods of our literature, distinguished themselves by their endeavours to attract to it the attention of the English public. So little was it known, that Thomas Warton introduced an analysis of it in his History of English Poetry.[1] . . . Joseph Warton assigns the first place among the Italian poets to Dante, on account of his wonderful originality, and ranks the 'Inferno' second only to the 'Iliad.' Reynolds' picture of Ugolino[2] gave him the courage to declare that he recollected no passage in any writer so truly pathetic. A prose translation was, however, all he ventured upon.[3] . . . The wayward charms of Ariosto, and the more uniform, though not more studied elegance of Tasso, had found translators, almost from the first, in Harrington and Fairfax. Nothing but the immense difficulty of working on his granite to any purpose of use or ornament, can account for the distance at which, in the meantime, every one had been standing aloof from Dante. At last Boyd[4] and Hayley[5] laid hands upon the ark. They failed. Their boldness, however, broke the spell. Mr. Cary advanced next. If we are at all correct in our suspicion, that, notwithstanding the recommendation of Mr. Coleridge, he has been principally consulted as a help towards construing the original, the field is still open to Mr. Wright. Mr. Cary and Mr. Wright are both translators of very unusual merit. Their manner of dealing with their original is, however, very different. The present version may, we think, entitle Mr. Wright to hope, that, with due pains, he may yet secure to himself the English Dante as his own. Popularity is more than we can promise. . . .

[1] [See vol. i. pp. 283 ff.]
[2] [See vol. i. p. 343.]
[3] [See vol. i. pp. 301 ff.]
[4] [See vol. i. pp. 410 ff.]
[5] [See vol. i. pp. 359 ff.]

Mr. Wright's superiority over his predecessors is greatly founded upon the fact of his having endeavoured to transfer the precise versification of his author together with the thoughts. The similarity between Dante and Milton is admitted. Nevertheless, the selection of the blank verse, and an elaborate imitation of the style of Milton, in Mr. Cary's translation, have breathed over it a total estrangement of manner, which no ability or expedients can counteract. . . .

The motive of Mr. Cary in deviating from the *terza rima* of Dante into blank verse, is obvious. Mr. Wright has very luckily solved the problem of the English *terza rima*. In preserving the triplet, he has secured the entire effect of an analogous versification; while, by throwing off one of the rhymes (which nobody will miss) he has made it possible to reproduce the sense and freedom of his original within an equal compass. . . . A comparison of Lord Byron's 'cramp' version, as he truly calls it, of the 'Francesca di Rimini,'[1]—the single specimen he selected,—with the spirited version of the same story in the present volume, in a conclusive proof of the judiciousness of the point of compromise fixed upon by Mr. Wright. . . . In praising Mr. Wright, we must not be ungrateful to Mr. Cary. His version had great merit in important particulars—correctness, conciseness, and a certain gravity of manner. Still it never prevented us from speaking of the untranslateable Dante. There was in it both more and less than was consistent with being a satisfactory copy of its original. The present volume, by Mr. Wright, comprises only the first compartment of Dante's triple picture. The merit of the execution will unite all competent judges in cordially entreating him to proceed.[2]

(Vol. lvii. pp. 413 ff.)

HENRY ALFORD

(1810-1871)

[Henry Alford was born in London in 1810, and was educated at Trinity College, Cambridge, of which he became a Fellow in 1834. Among his Cambridge friends were Arthur Hallam and Alfred Tennyson. He was vicar of Wymeswold in Leicestershire (a College living) from 1835 to 1853, in which year he became minister of Quebec Chapel, Marylebone. In 1857 he was appointed to the deanery of Canterbury, which he held until his death in 1871. His great work, his edition of the Greek Testament, was published between 1849 and 1861. Alford was a student of Dante. In 1832 he writes to a friend (J. Allen) from Cambridge: 'Have you seen Hallam's pamphlet about the *Spirito Antipapale* of Rossetti[3]? If not, see it *quam primum*' (*Life*, p. 83); and in his *Journal* for the year 1833, written just after he had taken his degree, he speaks of a projected allegorical poem, after the mode of Spenser or Dante.]

[1] [See above, pp. 38-9.]

[2] [This is in amusing contrast with the advice of the Quarterly Reviewer to Mr. Wright 'to suspend' his labours (see above, p. 576).]

[3] [See above, pp. 422 ff.]

1833. Feb. 2. JOURNAL.

[Projected poem in the style of Spenser and Dante]

I HAVE been of late . . . sketching in my mind the plan of a long poem, which may be a bye-work of some years of labour or rest. . . . As to the vehicle in which it shall enter the minds of men, I have rather of late inclined to allegory; not that of modern times, but a mode of that of our sweet Spenser, and the great and holy Dante. Something approahing to the history of a blessed soul, including the various stages of its progress, and its nourishment and refreshment by the way.

(*Life, Journals, and Letters of Dean Alford*, p. 86.)

ANONYMOUS

1834. March. QUARTERLY REVIEW. ART. II. TRANSLATIONS OF PINDAR.

[Dante and Pindar]

WE have been partly led to the consideration of this subject by the appearance of an entire translation of Pindar by Mr. Cary.[1] . . . That the successful translator of Dante should become a successful translator of Pindar, though a fortune worthy of high congratulation, is not to us either unexpected or unaccountable. For, though it be true that Dante and Pindar were men of very diverse tempers, and the poetry of each exhibits traits of thought and feeling unknown to that of the other, there is, nevertheless, one characteristic by which, as poets, they are in common pre-eminently distinguished. We mean to say that Dante and Pindar are, in a strict sense of the word, the two most *picturesque* of the great poets of the world—that they display this power in so remarkably high a degree, that, in spite of all minor discrepancies, both of them must be ranked by the philosophic critic in the same class. In order to guard against mistake, we must add, that by *picturesqueness* we do not mean a frequency or prominence of *picturable matter*, such as may be found in every ode of Horace, and in almost every song in Metastasio; for this abundance of *matter for painting* is often conspicuous in the works of poets in whom *the power of painting* is signally deficient. We rather intend to mark the natural faculty—which is not acquireable by art—of producing by words a distinct image of outward form or compound action,

[1] [*Pindar in English Verse*, 1833.]

visible to the mind's eye, and so clearly visible, that the pencil cannot make its outline clearer. As for a single example, take the well-known passage:—

> Ella non ci diceva alcuna cosa,
> Ma lasciavane gir, solo guardando
> A guisa di leon quando si posa.
>
> *Purgatorio,* c. vi. v. 64.

. . . The sympathetic sense of the picturesque in poetry, and the power of preserving it in another language, which gave Mr. Cary so much advantage in translating Dante, have insured to him a proportionate success with Pindar. We do not say that his success, taken absolutely, is equal in this his later attempt; and it is not surprising that such should not be the case, the difficulties of adequately rendering Pindar being so much greater. Add to the mere talent a knack of translation which many possess, the generally pure and racy diction, and the strong sense of the picturesque which cannot be denied to Mr. Cary, and you have provided the main qualities of a good translator of Dante. The moral tone and manner of narrative of the Divine Comedy are very easily imitable, as may be inferred by the uniformity, in this one respect, of versions by Hayley, Cary, Byron, and Wright; but the difficulty of executing the terza rima in English is, we think, insurmountable. Perhaps Mr. Cary showed the soundest judgment in adopting the Miltonic measure—not as like, but as a satisfactory substitute for, the original. Certainly Mr. Wright's double triplets without the third rhyme, which so subtly links together the total rhythmic flow of the Italian, sound to our ears as little like the Dantescan[1] harmony as Cary's blank verse, and not so easy and noble. But, considerable as the difficulty of the terza rima is in the way of a translator of Dante, it is little in comparison with the task of rendering into English the various and complicated movements of Pindar's Odes. The great Florentine marches through the nether, middle, and upper worlds with an even step; learn his pace once, and you may keep up with him always. But it is not so with Pindar; the speed with which he sets out is often enough doubled or trebled before he gets to the end of his course; eagle of song as he was, and dared to call himself, he has all the movements of that imperial bird, now towering right upwards to heaven's gate, now precipitating himself to the earth—now floating with spread wings in the middle ether, and now couching with the setting sun on the gilded battlements of a temple. No poet is so slow—none so rapid. . . . The metre and rhythm of Dante in the Divine Comedy being so elaborately opposite to the prevailing movement

[1] [No instance of this word is given in the *New English Dictionary*.]

in Pindar—as the *incessus* of Jupiter might be to the *impetus* of his eagle—it is obvious that in the mechanism of the verse the translator of Pindar has to satisfy a very peculiar and very trying demand upon his skill. . . . To the sublimity resulting from the obscure and the dimly-seen, Pindar has no claim; his figures are distinguishable in member, joint, and limb; their robes are sun-bright, and the banners which they seem majestically to wave are bathed in the glory of high noon. Pindar was no David, no Aeschylus, no Milton; and, with Dante's power, he would have abhorred Dante's subject. But such as he was, he stood, and he stands, aloft and aloof—unsurpassable—inimitable—incomparable—the absolute Master of Lyric Song.

(Vol. li. pp. 20 ff.)

ANONYMOUS

1834. June. QUARTERLY REVIEW. ART. II. HISTORY OF THE HOUSE OF SWABIA AND THEIR TIMES.[1]

[The scriptural imagery of Dante]

THE first thing which strikes us in reading the controversy between Gregory IX and the Emperor Frederick II is the religious dialect in which the whole is couched. Those who have attempted to trace the scriptural expressions and imagery of Dante, have been scarcely aware that such had long been the language of the Christian world. These manifestos, indeed, were sent forth in Latin, but the Ghibelline party, as they were addressed to all orders, would take care that at least their substance should be made known in their popular dialects. . . . We do not distinctly recollect whether Signor Rosetti, in his ingenious though too refined and systematic attempts to elucidate the mysteries of Dante's great poem,[2] has included these manifestos of the emperor and the pope, as showing the tendency of the age to adapt the mystic allegories of the Revelations to the events and characters of the day. . . . There can be no doubt that these might contribute a curious chapter to a work not yet adequately executed, the 'Historia Reformationis ante Reformationem;' though, after all, perhaps they might chiefly command public attention now-a-days as throwing some light, however feeble, on the composition of the 'Divina Commedia.' How wonderful the privilege of true genius,—that state papers, which almost arrayed

[1] [Review of F. von Raumer's *Geschichte der Hohenstaufen und ihrer Zeit* (1825).]

[2] [See above, pp. 445 ff.]

Europe in hostile conflict, which spoke the contending sentiments of factions, that divided every county, every city, every household,—are chiefly interesting as illustrative of a single poem!

(Vol. li. pp. 332-3.)

[Dante and Pier delle Vigne]

Much obscurity still hangs over the fate of Peter de Vinea. According to the account of Matthew Paris, while Frederick II. lay ill, the confidential physician of Peter had prescribed for him, and prepared his medicine. The Emperor, who had received a private warning, said,—'My friend, I put my full trust in you. But take care, I entreat you, that poison is not administered to me instead of physic.' Peter answered, 'Sire, how often has my physician prepared for you wholesome medicine! why are you now afraid?' Frederick, with a darkening brow, said to the physician, 'Drink thou half of it, and give me the rest.' The physician conscious of his guilt pretended to stumble, and spilled the draught. A little remained in the cup, but that little caused death in some malefactors who were forced to drink it. . . . Peter, either conscious of the enormous guilt, or desperate because he had no means of proving his innocence, ran, as he was led to prison, his head against the wall, and died. M. von Raumer thinks, that this story may be true, yet that only the physician, not Peter de Vinea, might be guilty of the design to poison. He is not, however, inclined altogether to acquit the chancellor of tampering in the papal intrigues. It is fair, perhaps, at least it is a temptation we cannot resist, to quote the exculpation of Dante, whom the injured spirit intreats to rescue his memory from disgrace:—

'Conforti la memoria mia, che giace
Ancor del colpo, che invidia le diede.'[1]

(pp. 337-8.)

ANONYMOUS

1834. August. QUARTERLY REVIEW. ART. I. COLERIDGE'S POETICAL WORKS.

[Dante and Pindar]

MR. COLERIDGE does not belong to that grand division of poetry and poets which corresponds with painting and painters; of which Pindar and Dante are the chief;—those masters of the picturesque, who, by a felicity inborn, view

[1] [*Inf.* xiii. 77-8. In the next paragraph the reviewer quotes the preceding lines (ll. 58-75).]

and present everything in the completeness of actual objectivity—and who have a class derived from and congenial with them, presenting few pictures indeed, but always full of picturesque matter; of which secondary class Spenser and Southey may be mentioned as eminent instances. To neither of these does Mr. Coleridge belong: . . . but he, as a poet, clearly comes within the other division which answers to music and the musician, in which you have a magnificent image of words with the subjective associations of the poet curling, and twisting, and creeping round, and through, and above every part of it. This is the class to which Milton belongs.

(Vol. lii. p. 13.)

COUNTESS OF BLESSINGTON

(1789-1849)

[Marguerite Power, afterwards Countess of Blessington, was born near Clonmel, co. Tipperary, in 1789. At the age of fifteen she was married to an army captain, after whose death she married (1818) the first Earl of Blessington. She and her husband, who died in Paris in 1829, travelled in Italy during 1822-8, and she afterwards (in 1839) published a diary of their tour under the title of the *Idler in Italy*. In 1823 she met Lord Byron, and kept notes of her conversations with him, which she published in 1834 in *Journal of the Conversations of Lord Byron with the Countess of Blessington*. In 1831 Lady Blessington settled in London, where she lived until a few weeks before her death at Paris in 1849. Besides the *Idler in Italy*, the most successful of her books, which contains numerous references to Dante, she wrote several novels, and for many years she edited the *Book of Beauty* (1834-49) and the *Keepsake* (1841-9).]

1834. JOURNAL OF THE CONVERSATIONS OF LORD BYRON WITH THE COUNTESS OF BLESSINGTON.

[An extract from these *Conversations*, which took place at Genoa in 1823, is given under Byron (see above, p. 53).]

1839. THE IDLER IN ITALY.

[Appreciation of Dante in Italy]

FLORENCE. June 25, 1823. Saw the cathedral to-day. . . . One of the portraits in this cathedral possessed a peculiarly strong interest for me—I refer to that of Dante, the Shakspeare of Italy, by Orcagna.[1] This portrait, although but a posthumous one, cannot be viewed without strong feelings of interest; and these are increased by reflecting, that the same people who banished the original, were afterwards proud to possess this likeness of him. The ill-treatment experienced by poets from their country would form no bad subject for a work in the hands of

[1] [Not by Orcagna, but by Domenico di Michelino, a pupil of Fra Angelico. The picture was painted in 1466.]

D'Israeli. . . . How much of this ill-treatment, from the days of Dante down to those of Byron, might, if analysed, be attributed to the baleful passion of envy? . . . Dante is as enthusiastically talked of, and more universally read in his own country, than Shakspeare is with us. We have, it is true, many who read our divine bard with the zest which so inimitable a genius merits; but we have also still more who *talk of*, than who can appreciate his works; and these are precisely the persons who are the loudest in their injudicious praise. But in Italy, every one with any pretension to literary acquirements, reads Dante *con amore;* and are honest in their enthusiastic commendations of him.

(Vol. ii. pp. 131-3.)

[Associations of the Lanfranchi with Dante and Byron]

Pisa. December, 1823. The Lung' Arno is bordered by fine palaces, among which the Lanfranchi is conspicuous, not less interesting from the souvenirs of the middle ages attached to it, its founder being the leader of the Ghibelline party at Pisa, and the rival of Ugolino, whose terrible punishment Dante has immortalised, than from having been the residence of Byron.

(Vol. ii. p. 489.)

[Dante's tomb at Ravenna]

Ravenna. 1828. We suddenly came almost into personal contact with the bodies of three men hanging. . . . Never did I behold so fearful a sight! . . . Within view of the spot stood the tomb of Dante, whose 'Inferno' offers scarcely a more hideous picture than the one presented to our contemplation.

(Vol. iii. pp. 33-34.)

[Dante and Byron compared]

Ravenna. 1828. There is a sort of similarity in the fate of Dante and Byron that must have more than once occurred to the latter while here. Both were unhappy in their domestic lives, however different might have been the causes, and the characters of the ladies whom they wedded. Both exiles from their countries, and writhing under a sense of the injustice with which they had been treated, both sought and found that peace at Ravenna denied them at home.

(Vol. iii. p. 45.)

[Dante at Ravenna—Gemma Donati]

Ravenna. 1828. The noblesse of Ravenna remember, and are proud of the protection afforded by one of their princes, Guido Novello da Polenta, to Dante; and entertain a love of and taste for literature, not often to be found in a city so remote from what might be considered the more civilized parts of Italy. . . . The tomb of Dante arrests the attention of every traveller who visits Ravenna; and as we paused before it, I gave a sigh to the memory of that sublime poet, whose pages have charmed many an hour. Few great writers have left behind them a more noble character than that of Dante, whether regarded for the spirit of independence which so peculiarly characterized him,—a spirit that preserved him even when an exile and deprived of his fortune, from ever submitting to an indignity,—or for the ardent desire to render impartial justice to all parties, in a period of political excitement when few were capable of such conduct.[1] . . . Dante, like too many poets, was unhappy in his domestic life. His wife, Gemma Donati, was a woman of so violent a temper as to render her ill suited to be the partner of one whose poetical temperament peculiarly unfitted him for exercising the patience so indispensable to support it with equanimity. His early passion for Beatrice, and the homage rendered to her memory, not only in his first poems, but in his great one, was not calculated to ameliorate the temper of his wife; for though Beatrice was dead before Gemma Donati became the wife of Dante, a dead rival, if remembered with the fondness with which Beatrice was dwelt on by him, may excite as much jealousy in the mind of a wife, as could be awakened by a living one. Pride, too, that besetting sin in woman, might have increased the violence of temper in Gemma, which so much embittered the home of her husband. That another woman should be the subject of his lasting regret and most delicate eulogiums, regrets and eulogiums likely to be universally known, from the attractive medium of the fine poesy in which they were enshrined, was enough to ruffle the temper of even a more patient woman than Gemma, who might think that as a wife, and the mother of his six children, *she* had the best right to be immortalized by his muse. The circumstance, too, of having their only daughter named Beatrice, after the object of his youthful love, must have displeased Gemma; consequently while we condemn the ill-humour, which rendered the domestic circle of the great poet so miserable, we must not overlook the provocation, that may have produced it. How far may not Dante have been influenced in espousing the party of the Bianchi, by the circumstance that the Neri was the faction to which the Donati adhered? is a question I leave to casuists to decide on; yet motives not more noble have often been known to lead to similar results.

One of the inscriptions on the tomb of Dante is asserted to have

[1] [Here follows a sketch of Dante's life and political career, pp. 56-61.]

been written by the poet himself, during his last illness, and is as follows:—

'Jura monarchiae, superos, Phlegetonta, lacusque' &c.[1]

Another epitaph is,

'Exulem a Florentia excepit Ravenna,
vivum fruens, mortuum colens. Tumulum
pretiosum Musis, S.P.Q. Rav. jure ac aere
suo, tamquam thesaurum suum, munivit
instauravit, ornavit.'

This perpetuates a fact that Florence would gladly obliterate from her annals. Before a century had closed over the death of Dante, the republic of his native city, anxious to atone for the injustice rendered to him when living, wished to erect a monument to his memory, and during the fifteenth and sixteenth centuries, various applications were made to Ravenna to yield up the ashes of this great poet to Florence; but every effort was in vain, and the city which granted him an honourable asylum during his exile, still preserves his mortal remains. . . . With what different emotions are the limbs of those ennobled by genius, or merely illustrious by station, contemplated! . . . Who is it that pauses not with more reverential awe, before the last resting place of Italy's greatest poet, than before that of Theodoric, once the acknowledged master of Italy?

(Vol. iii. pp. 52, 55, 61-5.)

[Dante's *Quaestio de Aqua et Terra*]

Verona. 1828. Though nearly tired of inspecting churches, . . . I could not leave unseen that of St. Helena; in which Dante maintained a thesis in presence of a numerous audience, and on a subject wholly apart from those supposed to engross his thoughts, namely, on the two elements of land and water.[2] I pictured to myself the severe but intellectual countenance of *Il Padre Alighieri*, as surrounded by the learned Veronese of his day, he proved to them that he could do other things as well as write fine poetry.

(Vol. iii. p. 273.)

[Dante's simile from the Garisenda Tower at Bologna]

Bologna. 1828. The Garisenda Tower, not far from the Asinelli, inclines considerably from the perpendicular. This is said to have been caused by the sinking of the ground; but whether or not, for people maintain different opinions on the

[1] [For this epitaph, see under Fynes Moryson, vol i. p. 91.]

[2] This thesis was printed at Venice in 1518 [actually, 1508], and entitled 'De duobus Elementis Terrae et Aquae.'

subject, it must be looked on with unusual interest, as having furnished a simile to Dante,[1] who has beautifully used it.

(Vol. iii. p. 340.[2])

BIBLIOTHECA HEBERIANA

1834-36. BIBLIOTHECA HEBERIANA. CATALOGUE OF THE LIBRARY OF THE LATE RICHARD HEBER.

[Richard Heber, the famous book-collector, half-brother of Reginald Heber, Bishop of Calcutta, was born in Westminster in 1773. He was educated at Brasenose College, Oxford (M.A. 1797). In 1804, on the death of his father, he succeeded to large estates in Yorkshire and Shropshire. In 1821 he was elected M.P. for Oxford University, which he had unsuccessfully contested in 1806. He resigned his seat in 1826, and resided abroad until 1831, when he returned to England. He died at Pimlico in 1833. At his death Heber left eight houses full of books, 'all the rooms, chairs, tables, and passages overflowing with them,' four in England, and four on the Continent. The books in England, the sale of which lasted over three years (1834-6), fetched nearly £57,000. The collection was rich in copies of the works of Dante, of which there were upwards of 70. Among the most valuable items were six MSS. of the *Divina Commedia*, besides copies (in many cases several copies) of the Foligno (1472), Mantua (1472), Naples (1477), Venice (1477), Florence (1481), Venice (1484), Aldine (1502, 1515), Junta (1506), and Paganino (n.d.) printed editions; copies of the Spanish translation of Villegas (1515), and the French of Grangier (1597); and the first editions of the *Convivio* (1490), and *De Vulgari Eloquentia* (1529, 1577). Three of the items were of especial interest, viz. a MS. of the *Commedia* which had belonged to Charles James Fox (Part xi. No. 651);[3] Drummond of Hawthornden's copy, with his autograph, of the 1555 Giolito edition of the *Commedia* (Part viii. No. 619); and Milton's copy, with his autograph, dated 1629, of the third edition (1529) of the *Convivio*. This last item is described as follows in the Catalogue:—

Part iv. No. 1527. Dante L' Amoroso Convivio, 1529—Rime et Prose di Giovanni della Casa, 1563—Sonetti di Benedetto Varchi, 1555.

⁂ This volume belonged to Milton: At the commencement he has written the contents of the book, and on the first page of the Giovanni della Casa, is 'Jo. Milton, pre. 10d. 1629.' The corrections of the text and the marks at particular passages (many of which are imitated in his Poems) shew that he had read the Sonnets of Casa with great attention, and at the end in his own handwriting is 'Segue un altro sonnetto di M. Giovan. della Casa che si trova nell' editione di Venetia, 1623.']

JOSIAH CONDER

(1789-1855)

[Josiah Conder, bookseller and author, was born in London in 1789. His father was a bookseller, and he succeeded to the business in 1811, on his father's retirement. He was the author or editor of numerous works, comprising verses, essays, and religious tracts, besides the *Modern Traveller* in thirty volumes, (1825-9), and a book on Italy (1834). He died in London in 1855. In his *Italy*, which he wrote entirely at second-hand (as he never quitted England), and which contains some curious blunders, Conder several times quotes the *Divina Commedia*.]

[1] [*Inf.* xxxi. 136-8.]

[2] [This work contains sundry other references to Dante besides those given above.]

[3] [This MS. passed into the collection of Sir Thomas Phillipps at Middle Hill.]

1834. ITALY.

[Early MS. of Dante in the Trivulzian Library at Milan]

AMONG the few private libraries that will repay the visiter, is that of the *Casa Trivulzio*. . . . The library is singularly rich in MSS. and in rare and precious editions of the fifteenth century. Among the latter is a Petrarch, printed fifteen years after the death of the Poet.[1] Among the former is the oldest MS. Dante that is known to exist, with a date affixed.[2]

(Vol. i. p. 389.)

[Dante and the birthplace of Virgil]

About three miles from Mantua, on the banks of the Mincio, is the little village of Pietola, to which tradition assigns the honour of representing the birthplace of Virgil. . . . According to Donatus, the great Poet was born at Andes near Mantua; and, except that there seems no relation between the ancient and the modern name, there is no solid argument that can be urged in disproof of the long-established tradition which indentifies Andes with Pietola:—

E quell' ombra gentil per cui si noma
Pietola più che villa Mantovana.

Dante, Purg. xviii. [ll. 82-3].

(Vol. ii. pp. 56-7.)

[Dante and the imperial eagle]

The tombs of the Scaligers, once sovereign lords of Verona, which stand in a small enclosure in one of the public streets, form a highly picturesque object. They are six in number, each bearing the scaling ladder (*scala*) and eagle, the remarkable device of the family. The eagle was added to the more ancient device, by the first Scaliger, who obtained of the Pope[3] the title and office of Imperial Vicar, in addition to that of *capitano del popolo*. Dante, as a furious Ghibelline, calls the eagle a holy bird :—

del gran Lombardo
Che porta in su la scala il santo augello.[4]

(Vol. ii. pp. 82-3.)

[Dante's reference to the landslip near Roveredo]

The Adige (called by the Germans *Etsch*), the ancient *Athesis*, has its rise in the Tridentine Alps. . . . Flowing southward, it

[1] [That is, in 1389 (Petrarch having died in 1374), more than seventy years before the date of the first printed book (1460)!]

[2] [For a description of this MS., which is dated 1337, see Moore, *Textual Criticism of the Divina Commedia*, pp. 562-3.]

[3] [*Sic.*]

[4] [*Par.* xvii. 71-2.]

traverses the beautiful plain of Trent, and washes the walls of that ancient city. Between Roveredo, the next town, and Ala, the road passes through scenes extremely savage and dreary, occasioned by an *éboulement* from the *Monte Marco*, which has strewn the valley with enormous rocks and stones. The *Slavini di Marco*, as this scene of ruin is called, has been alluded to by Dante in the twelfth canto of his Inferno, in order to illustrate one of his infernal ramparts:—

> Qual' è quella ruina che nel fianco
> Di qua da Trento l' Adice percosse, &c.[1]

(Vol. ii. pp. 88-9.)

[The two leaning towers at Bologna]

The most remarkable, though by no means the most beautiful edifices in Bologna, are the two leaning watch-towers, called the *Torre degli Asinelli*, and the *Torre degli Garisendi*. The former is a slender tower, built at different periods, and rising to the height of nearly 400 feet. It leans over its base three feet two inches. . . . The tower of the Garisendi is only 130 or 140 feet high. It inclines six feet six inches to the south, and a foot and a half to the east. . . . They were both erected early in the twelfth century. The Garisendi tower, which was erected some years after the other, has furnished Dante with a noble simile. He compares the stooping statue[2] of the huge giant Antaeus to the effect of *La Carisenda*, seen from beneath.[3]

(Vol. ii. pp. 256-7.)

[Dante's tomb at Ravenna]

Ravenna contains another tomb, which, though not recommended by any architectural beauty, excites deeper interest as a memorial, than even the splendid mausoleum of the Imperial Goth.[4] . . . Exiled from his native city in 1313,[5] Dante travelled into the North of Italy, and resided for some time at Verona; but he finally took up his abode at Ravenna, where he died in 1321. He was buried in the cloisters of the Franciscan monastery. A handsome tomb was erected to his memory, in 1483, by Bernardo Bembo, father of the Cardinal of that name, and praetor or governor of Ravenna, for the Venetian Republic.

(Vol. ii. p. 297.)

[Dante's portrait in the Cathedral at Florence]

In the cathedral, among the illustrious dead, repose Brunelleschi and Giotto, the first who distinguished themselves respectively in

[1] [*Inf.* xii. 4-5.] [2] [*Sic.*] [3] [*Inf.* xxxi. 136-40.]
[4] [Theodoric.] [5] [*Sic*, read 1302.]

the architecture and painting of Modern Europe. Dante 'sleeps afar,' but his picture[1] is 'one of the idols of the cathedral.' . . . Although the 'mighty dust' of 'the all-Etruscan Three,' as Lord Byron styles Dante, Petrarch, and Boccaccio, repose on a foreign soil.—

> In Santa Croce's holy precincts lie
> Ashes which make it holier—[2]

the remains of, perhaps, the three greatest men to whom Florence has given birth: Machiavelli, Buonarotti, and Galileo.

(Vol. ii. pp. 327, 329.)

CAROLINE WARD

(fl. 1830)

[Miss Caroline Ward's English translation testifies to the great interest aroused by Gabriele Rossetti's remarkable book *Sullo Spirito Antipapale*, which had been published in London two years before. Some idea of the extravagant nature of Rossetti's theories as to the secret design of the *Divina Commedia* and other works of Dante may be gathered from the extracts given below. The English edition, as the translator announces (in the dedication to Cary), contains a considerable amount of matter which was omitted from the original. Incidentally Miss Ward furnishes some of the earliest English translations of many passages from Dante's prose works, besides occasional renderings (in prose) from several of the *Canzoni*.[3]]

1834. DISQUISITIONS ON THE ANTIPAPAL SPIRIT WHICH PRODUCED THE REFORMATION; ITS SECRET INFLUENCE ON THE LITERATURE OF EUROPE IN GENERAL, AND OF ITALY IN PARTICULAR. BY GABRIELE ROSSETTI. TRANSLATED FROM THE ITALIAN.[4]

[Conflicting interpretations of the *Divina Commedia*]

PERHAPS no classical work in any language has attracted the notice of so many speculative interpreters, as the poem of Alighieri. But do their opinions harmonize together? By no means; on the contrary, the Divine Comedy has been turned into a field of battle, on which commentators attack each other, some with mockery, some with abuse, and generally speaking, in terms of such violent invective, that it is hard to say whether the feelings they excite in the minds of those to whom they all offer themselves as exclusive and infallible guides, partake most of pity or amusement, anger or contempt. From what cause arise all these discrepancies? Have they not all been wandering far

[1] [By Domenico di Michelino, now over the north door.]
[2] [*Childe Harold*, Canto iv. 40 (see above, p. 34).]
[3] [A list of the passages translated is given in *A Chronological List of English Translations from Dante*, by Paget Toynbee, printed in *Report XXIV of the Cambridge (Mass.) Dante Society*, 1906.]
[4] [The original was published in London in 1832 (see above, p. 446).]

from the right path, while each thought himself in sole possession of it? That in spite of all their researches the poem has never, up to the present time, been thoroughly understood, is now the opinion of the most learned investigators of its secret pages; it is the sentence pronounced and confirmed by those who have long and deeply studied them. . . . We are quite at a loss to divine how it has happened, that after five centuries of assiduous research and repeated attempts, not one of those intelligent inquirers who have so deeply meditated on the subject of the Divine Comedy, has ever penetrated the secret of its allegory. They certainly could not be ignorant of the political opinions and religious doctrines of the time, for they were inscribed in thousands of volumes; neither have those doctrines been lost or forgotten, for they are inherited by the Protestants of the present day. They knew that Italy was then swarming with Patarini, who professed those opinions, and they knew that Dante's own friends were burned alive by the inquisition as Patarini.[1] They were aware that he was a proud and unfortunate Ghibelline, and (by his own avowal) that his poem was allegorical. It would appear that the interpretation of this dark work must have followed from all these guiding clues, but it has not done so, in spite of the many hints scattered by the author himself throughout all his works. As the secret sense of Petrarch's bucolic remained long unknown, and in a great measure remains so still; as the hidden meaning of Boccaccio's pastoral is still undiscovered: so has it been with Dante's Commedia; and we may venture to say, without presumption, that we were the first to extract its buried essence, in our analytical commentary.

(Vol. i. pp. 42, 56-7.)

[Examples of the artifices of Dante]

The instances are innumerable, in which Dante made his words bear a double meaning, to suit either friends or foes. When he wrote: '*Lo capo* reo, lo *mondo* torce dal dritto cammino,'[2] he left the explanation of the phrase *arbitrary*, the nominative and objective being both before the verb. The Guelphs read it: 'lo mondo torce lo capo reo:' taking *capo* in the physical sense of *head;* the Ghibellines on the other hand construed it: 'Lo capo reo (the wicked prince, the 'prince of this world,') torce lo mondo.' And thus the writer expressed his feelings in security. What, in our days, would be considered a vice in composition, was by him

[1] Cecco d' Ascoli, who in his Acerba speaks of Dante, and gives us to understand that he was in correspondence with him, was burnt as a Patarin, six years after the death of Alighieri.

[2] [*Purg.* viii. 131, misquoted.]

sought for and employed on all occasions; and he was so constant to this art, that even on his death-bed he did not forget it.[1] So far did he carry this, that sometimes when his abuse of the Pope is more severe than usual, he would almost persuade an ordinary reader, that he was his warm partizan and adherent. For instance in canto 2 of the Inferno, he refuses to follow Virgil any farther, asserting that Rome and the Empire were created and prepared by God, for the purpose of serving as the established seat of the Highest Peter; who is above all authority, even that of the Emperor; and that the victory of Eneas in Latium was gained to secure the establishment of the papal mantle. Now, how could he reconcile these opinions with his life and writings? In this manner: the sun, the emblem of Reason sinks: 'Now was the day departing,' and then he holds that Discourse; to signify that such opinions could only be entertained in the absence of reason. He concludes his speech thus:

'Se' savio, e intendi *me*, ch' io non ragiono:'

Here the *me* has a double meaning; it is the abbreviation of *meglio*, and the accusative of *io*; in the first sense it was intended for the Guelphs, 'Thou art wise, and canst understand *better* than I can speak;' in the second, it was meant for the Ghibellines, 'Thou art wise, and canst understand that I do not reason rightly.' On such minutiae sometimes depends the sense of a whole passage; and often too, while the literal subject is treated of at large, the allegorical or real one is contracted and veiled.

(Vol. i. pp. 134-6.)

[Rossetti's penetration of 'the jargon and allegories of the Divine Comedy']

Born and educated in the Catholic faith, I feel no sentiment but reverence for the religion I profess, and a decided inclination leading me to cultivate literature, I turned in preference to those authors who had written according to its holy precepts; the voice of ages proclaimed Dante to be no less profound as a theologian than matchless as a poet; deeply did I meditate on his works, and compare one with another: I investigated historical facts, I confronted his opinions with those of other authors; and as doubt swelled to suspicion, and suspicion became certainty, I cannot describe the feelings with which the full consciousness of his hypocrisy overwhelmed me. Still clinging to the hope that I might be mistaken. I studied the sectarian creeds of the time, and the history of different heresies; and then I returned to the perusal of

[1] [Rossetti is referring to the epitaph on Dante's tomb, said to have been composed by himself on his death-bed, in which it is possible to construe a couple of lines in two ways.]

his works; but the veil had fallen from my eyes, and reluctantly I was obliged to recognise him in his real character. But when I entered into an investigation of the mystic books of our own time, and found that the present secret associations are merely the continuation of those ancient ones, with the same rites: when comparing their language and mysteries, with the jargon and allegories of the Divine Comedy, I succeeded in understanding some of those guarded secrets, which until then I had difficulty in comprehending; when I saw that the study of Dante facilitated the apprehension of many modern productions of the same nature, and that by means of these, all that was obscure and doubtful in him disappeared; when in short, I saw such a connection between them, that one illustrated the other; certainty reached its very extremest limit, and I was compelled to acknowledge that the Eleusinian learned of those days had reason on their side, when they claimed Dante and his poem for their own.

(*Conclusion*, vol. ii. pp. 198-9.)

CHARLES LYELL

(1767-1849)

[Charles Lyell, father of the celebrated geologist of the same name, was born at Kinnordy, Forfarshire, in 1767. He was educated at St. Andrews, and at St. Peter's College, Cambridge (M.A. 1794), of which he became Fellow. From 1797 to 1825 he lived in the New Forest, where he devoted himself to botany, especially to the study of mosses, several species of which bear his name. In 1813 he was elected a Fellow of the Linnaean Society. In 1826 Lyell settled at Kinnordy, where he died in 1849. At Kinnordy he occupied himself chiefly with the study of Dante, in which his interest had been aroused by the publications of Gabriele Rossetti, whose *Disquisizioni sullo Spirito Antipapale* (1832) was dedicated to him, as was *La Beatrice di Dante* (1842). In 1835 Lyell published a translation of the *Canzoniere* of Dante, the first attempt of the kind in the English language, which was reissued in 1840. A corrected version, dedicated to H. F. Cary, which contained a great deal of additional matter, including a long essay on *The Antipapal Spirit of Dante Alighieri* (afterwards translated into Italian by Gaetano Polidori, and published in London in 1844), was issued in 1842. A third edition, further revised, and re-arranged, was published in two forms (to range with the similar issues of Cary's Dante) in 1845. In 1847 Lyell issued in Paris a reprint 'avec notes par C. L.,' of the Jesuit Père Hardouin's *Doutes proposés sur l'âge du Dante*. It appears from the preface to the first edition of his translation of the *Canzoniere* that Lyell also translated the prose portions of the *Vita Nuova* and of the *Convivio*, but these were never published and the MS. apparently has not been preserved. This is the first recorded English version of either of these works.[1]]

[1] [The earliest published English version of the *Vita Nuova* (by Joseph Garrow) appeared at Florence in 1846; the earliest of the *Convivio* (by E. P. Sayer), in London in 1887.]

1835. THE CANZONIERE OF DANTE ALIGHIERI, INCLUDING THE POEMS OF THE VITA NUOVA AND CONVITO; ITALIAN AND ENGLISH.[1]

[Origin of the work]

THE two remarkable works of Professor Rossetti, 'Il Comento Analitico della Divina Commedia,' and 'Lo Spirito Antipapale di Dante, &c.,' gave occasion to the following translations. The former of these, by the novelty of the view which it exhibits of the political scope of the great poem of Dante, the unexpected interpretation of many of its mysterious passages, and the deep research and ingenuity by which they are supported, produced a great sensation among Italian Scholars. Opinion was unanimous as to the talent displayed by the author, but much divided as to the foundation and solidity of some of his theories. The second work brought forward many powerful and curious illustrations in corroboration of the first, and converted many to the doctrines of the Professor. Doubts, however, were still expressed whether sufficient authority was adduced for the most singular of his speculations, the attributing a double sense to many common words and phrases, and for maintaining that it constituted a conventional language, or *gergo*, of which there is evidence in the works of all the Ghibelline writers of the era. To satisfy myself upon this point, and the better to put the question to the test, I amused myself with making an English version of the Vita Nuova and Convito, and of the lyrical poems of Dante, referred to by Signor Rossetti as affording the strongest proofs of a sectarian *gergo*. The poetical part of the performance (if it deserve the name) met with some commendation in manuscript, and I was flattered into a belief that by extending it, and giving a translation of the entire Canzoniere of Dante, accompanied with notes from the publications of Signor Rossetti,[2] I might make an acceptible contribution to literature, by drawing more attention to a very interesting controversy, and by supplying a supplement (however inferior) to the admirable work of Mr. Cary. The translation comprehends every poem attributed to Dante by Professor Arrivabene in the 'Amori e Rime di Dante' (Mantova, 1823).

(*Preface*, pp. vii-ix.)

[1] [Some copies of this edition, which was published by John Murray, have two leaves inserted between the half-title and title-page, containing two poems, each dated March 7 (his birthday), 1840. In the re-issue of this edition, by James Bohn, in 1840, these poems were not included. The first consists of the following lines—

Unless Love's labour, with unwearied pain,
Pull down and build the fabric o'er again,
Remove inversions, and weak paraphrase,
And expletives not found in Dante's lays,
Never can these Translations merit praise.

The second poem is an unrhymed sonnet addressed to a lady whose name is not given.]

[2] [The proposed notes were not included.]

The Burning Heart[1]

To every captive soul and gentle heart,
Into whose presence this my song may come,
Requesting their opinions on its theme,
Health in the name of Love, their sovereign lord.
A third part of the hours had almost past
Which deck the glowing firmament with stars,
When suddenly before me Love appeared,
Whose essence to remember makes me shudder.
Joyful Love seemed, and in his hand he held
My heart, and in his arms encircled lay
Madonna sleeping, in a mantle wrapt.
He then awoke her, and the burning heart
Presented humbly, which in fear she ate.
That done, Love wept and sorrowing went his way.

(*Poems of the Vita Nuova*, p. 3.)

Beatrice's Salutation[2]

So noble is Madonna's air, so kind,
So full of grace to all when she salutes,
That every tongue with awe is mute and trembles,
And every eye shrinks back from her regard.
Clothed in humility she hears her praise,
And passes on with calm benignity;
Appearing not a thing of earth, but come
From heaven, to show mankind a miracle.
So pleasing is her countenance, that he
Who gazes feels delight expand the heart,
Which must be proved or cannot be conceived.
And from her lip there seems to emanate
A spirit full of mildness and of love,
Which counselling the soul still says, O sigh.

(*Ibid.* p. 53.)

1842. THE POEMS OF THE VITA NUOVA AND CONVITO OF DANTE ALIGHIERI, ITALIAN AND ENGLISH.

[In this edition, which is dedicated to Cary, 'the unrivalled translator of the Vision of Dante,' the poems 'are presented in a corrected version, carefully revised, with a view to give the literal sense with more scrupulous fidelity; . . . a nearer approach to it has been made than in the version of 1835, principally through the kindness of Mr. Cary, whose valuable strictures have been attended to, and are

[1] [Sonnet i. in the *Vita Nuova*. Lyell's rendering of this and of the rest of the poems is considerably altered in the edition of 1842.]

[2] [Sonnet xv. in the *Vita Nuova*.]

acknowledged with pride as well as gratitude' (*Preface*). Besides the revised *Canzoniere* this volume contains a translation of Giovanni Villani's notice of Dante (pp. xi-xiii); an interesting letter from Seymour Kirkup concerning the Torrigiani mask of Dante[1] (pp. xvii-xix); remarks on the *Vita Nuova* and *Convito* (pp. xxi-xxxix); and a long essay *On the Antipapal Spirit of Dante* (pp. xli-cclxxxii), an Italian translation of which by Gaetano Polidori was published in London in 1844. In an Appendix (pp. 119-37) are sundry sonnets, several of them by Lyell, with references to Beatrice and Dante. This edition also contains one of the earliest, if not the earliest reproduction of the Giotto portrait of Dante, which had been discovered in Florence a year or two before.[2]]

JAMES MONTGOMERY

(1771-1854)

[James Montgomery, son of a labourer, who became a Moravian minister, and eventually died as a missionary in Barbados, was born at Irvine in Ayrshire in 1771. After serving for a time with a baker, in 1792 he became clerk and book-keeper to the *Sheffield Register*, of which he three years later became proprietor. In 1825 he sold the paper, but continued to reside in Sheffield until his death in 1854. Montgomery, who acquired a considerable reputation as a poet and hymn-writer, delivered lectures on poetry at the Royal Institution in 1830 and 1831, which were published in 1833. He also wrote lives of Dante, Ariosto, and Tasso for Lardner's *Cabinet Cyclopædia* (1835). The *Life of Dante* contains numerous translations in blank verse from the *Commedia*, and many others (including a version of the Ugolino episode) were published among his *Poetical Works* (1836).]

1835. LIFE OF DANTE ALIGHIERI.[3]

[Early appreciation of Dante in England]

DANTE, as he grew up to manhood, and for several years afterwards, continued successfully to pursue his studies in the universities of Padua, Bologna, and Paris. . . . On the authority of Giovanni da Serraville,[4] bishop of Fermo, it has been believed that he also visited Oxford, where, as elsewhere, his different exercises gained him,—according to the respective tastes of his admirers,—from some the praise of being a great philosopher, from others a great divine, and, from the rest, a great poet. Serraville,[4] at the request of cardinal Saluzzo and two English bishops (Nicholas Bubwith, of Bath, and Robert Halam, of Salisbury), whom he met at the council of Constance, translated Dante's 'Divina Commedia' into Latin prose; of which one manuscript copy only, with a commentary annexed, is known to be in existence, in the Vatican library.[5] The extraordinary interest

[1] [This letter is given below, pp. 643 ff.]

[2] [See below, pp. 639 ff.]

[3] [In Lardner's *Cabinet Cyclopædia*—published anonymously.]

[4] [Correctly, Serravalle.]

[5] [There is now also a copy in the British Museum, which was secured at the Wodhull sale in 1886, through the exertions of Dr. Edward Moore.]

which the two English prelates took in Dante's poem may be regarded as indirect, though of course very indecisive, evidence of his having been personally known at our famous university, and having been honourably remembered there. It is, however, certain that, soon after his decease, the 'Divina Commedia' was in high repute among the few in this country who, during the reigns of Edward III. and Richard II., in a chivalrous age, cultivated polite letters. This is apparent from the numerous imitations of passages in it by Chaucer, who was then attempting to do for England what his magnificent prototype had recently done for Italy.

(pp. 8-9.)

[The *Divina Commedia*]

Dante's poem is certainly neither the greatest nor the best in the world; but it is, perhaps, the most extraordinary one which resolute intellect ever planned, or persevering talents successfully executed. It stands alone; and must be read and judged according to rules and immunities adapted to its peculiar structure, plot, and purpose, formed upon principles affording scope to the exercise of the highest powers, with little regard to precedent. If these principles, then, have intrinsic excellence, and the work be found uniformly consistent with them, fulfilling to the utmost the aims of the author, the 'Divina Commedia' must be allowed to stand among the proudest trophies of original genius, challenging, encountering, and overcoming unparalleled difficulties. Though the fields of action, or rather of vision, are nominally Hell, Purgatory, and Paradise,—the Paradise, Purgatory, and Hell of Dante, with all their terrors, and splendours, and preternatural fictions, are but representations of scenes transacted on earth, and characters that lived antecedently or contemporaneously with himself. Though altogether *out* of the world, the whole is *of* the world. Men and women seem fixed in eternal torments, passing through purifying flames, or exalted to celestial beatitude; yet in all these situations they *are* what they *were;* and it is their former history, more than their present happiness, hope, or despair, which constitutes, through a hundred cantos, the interest, awakened and kept up by the successive exhibition of more than a thousand individual actors and sufferers. Of every one of these something terrible or touching is intimated or told, briefly at the utmost, but frequently by mere hints of narrative or gleams of allusion, which excite curiosity in the breast of the reader; who is surprised at the poet's forbearance, when, in the notes of commentators, he finds complex, strange, and fearful circumstances, on which a modern versifier or novelist would expend pages, treated here as ordinary events, on which it would be impertinent to dwell.

(pp. 51-2.)

1836. TRANSLATIONS FROM DANTE.[1]

The River of Life[2]

The greater part of the *Paradiso*,—while it exemplifies, almost beyond example, the power of human language to vary a few ideas and images in themselves so simple, pure, and hallowed, that they hardly can be altered from their established associations without being degraded,—shows also the utter impotence of any other terms than those which Scripture has employed, 'as in a glass darkly,'—and who can *there* add light?—to body forth what eye hath not seen, ear heard, neither hath entered into the heart of man to conceive. One elaborate specimen (however defective the translation may be) will elucidate this failure even in the noble original, which, like its ineffable theme, in this part is 'dark with excessive bright.' The poet here copies more directly than he is wont from the Sacred Oracles; or, as in the sublime simile of the rock, illustrates his subject with not unworthy natural objects; at the same time, with characteristic ingenuousness, he explains his own feelings on beholding 'things which it is not lawful for a man to utter.'

As sudden lightning dissipates the sight,
And leaves the eye unable to discern
The plainest objects,—living light so flash'd
Around me, and involved me in a veil
Of such effulgence, that I *ceased to see.*
'Thus Love, which soothes this heaven, all kindly fits
The torch to take his flame'![3]—These few brief words
Had scarcely reached mine ear, when I perceived
Power from on high diffuse such virtue through me,
And so rekindle vision, that no flame,
However pure, could 'scape mine eyes. I saw
Light, like a river clear as crystal, flowing
Between two banks, with wondrous spring adorn'd;
While from the current issued vivid sparks,
That fell among the flowers on either hand,
Glitter'd like rubies set in gold, and then,
As if intoxicate with sweetest odours,
Replunged themselves into the mystic flood,
Whence, as one disappear'd, another rose.
'The intense desire that warms and stirs thy thoughts
To understand what thou beholdest, yields
More joy to me, the more it urges thee;
But ere such noble thirst can be assuaged,

[1] [Published in *Collected Poems*, in 3 vols. 1836.]
[2] [*Par.* xxx. 46-96.]
[3] Beatrice addresses this remark to Dante.

Behoves thee first to drink of this clear fount.'
The sun that lights mine eyes [1] thus spake, and added :
—'Yon stream, those jewels flitting to and fro,
And all the joyance of these laughing flowers,
Are shadowy emblems of realities,
Not dark themselves, but the defect is thine,
Who hast not yet obtain'd due strength of vision.'
Ah! then, no infant, startled out of sleep,
Long past his time, springs to the mother's milk
More eagerly than o'er that stream I bow'd,
To make more perfect lustres of mine eyes,
Which, when the fringes of their lids had touch'd it,
Seem'd, from a line, collapsed into a round.
—As maskers, when they cast their visors off,
Appear new persons, stript of such disguise,
The sparks and flowers assumed sublimer forms,
And both the courts of heaven were open'd round me.

(Ed. 1854, p. 247.)

1838. March 8. EXTRACT FROM CONVERSATION.

[Light, music, society, rest, the chief constituents of Dante's 'Paradiso']

Scott [2] has some flippant, not to say irreverent remarks, on the opinion that good people make the bliss of heaven to consist chiefly in singing; an employment which, it seems, would not be welcome to *him*. The fact is, holy men, even the simplest of them, are very rarely guilty of excess in the notion thus attributed to them: indeed, why *should* they? since nearly all that the Scriptures authorise us to conclude of the state and the place of the happy departed, comes within the meaning of four words—light, music, society, and, especially, rest; and these, in some of their modifications, will be found to constitute nearly the entire subject of the 'Paradiso' of Dante.

(*Memoirs of the Life and Writings of James Montgomery*, ed. Holland and Everett, vol. v. p. 305.)

WILLIAM BROCKEDON

(1787-1854)

[William Brockedon, painter, author, and inventor, whose father was a watchmaker, was born at Totnes in 1787. After his father's death he carried on the watchmaking business for five years, during which he devoted his spare time to drawing.

[1] Beatrice.

[2] [Montgomery was reading the sixth volume of Lockhart's *Life of Scott*, published in 1837. The remarks he alludes to occur in Scott's *Diary* for Dec. 10, 1825 (*Life*, vol. vi. pp. 156-7).]

In 1809 he became a student at the Royal Academy, and from 1812 to 1837 he exhibited regularly both at the Academy and at the British Institution. In 1821 he was elected a member of the Academies of Rome and of Florence, to the latter of which in compliance with their rule he presented his portrait painted by himself. Brockedon made many journeys in the Alps, which he crossed nearly sixty times, the account of his travels being published in three volumes, illustrated by his own drawings, in 1827-9, and 1833. In 1835 he published a *Road Book from London to Naples*, illustrated by Prout, Stanfield, and himself; and in 1842-4 he produced a folio volume on *Italy, Classical, Historical, and Picturesque*, with numerous illustrations by himself and other well-known artists. At the same time Brockedon was busy with various useful inventions, which led to his election to the Royal Society in 1834. Four years before he had helped to found the Royal Geographical Society. He died in London in 1854. In his *Road Book* Brockedon draws attention to the recently executed paintings from Dante by German artists in the Villa Massimo at Rome.]

1835. ROAD BOOK FROM LONDON TO NAPLES.

[The Leaning Tower of Pisa]

THE Campanile, or Tower, declines so much out of the perpendicular, that it is known throughout the world as the Leaning Tower of Pisa. It is circular, with an elevation of one hundred and ninty feet to the rails of the upper gallery, which overhangs the base fifteen English feet. . . . Stairs lead up to the summit, whence the view of Pisa and the surrounding country is very fine. On the highest gallery is placed a bell, rung on all occasions of public alarm for safety: it is the same which tolled the signal of the revolution which led to the dreadful fate of Ugolino, immortalised by Dante.[1]

(p. 104.)

[MSS. of Dante at Florence]

The Laurentian Library contains objects of great interest. The celebrated Pandects of Justinian, which the Pisans are said to have brought from Amalfi, where they were discovered; a Virgil of the third century; and early copies of Dante and Boccaccio, nearly contemporary with their authors; &c.

(p. 119.)

[German paintings from Dante in Rome]

Among the recent paintings in Rome, the most distinguished are the productions of the German artists, whose works ought to be seen by every visitor there. Some fine examples are in the Villa Massimi, which has been painted in fresco with subjects drawn from the great poets of Italy: by Overbeck, from Tasso; by Schnorr, from Ariosto; and by Veite and Koch from Dante.[2]

(p. 160.)

[1] [*Inf.* xxxiii.]

[2] [Philip Veit (1793-1877) and Joseph Anton Koch (1768-1839) were employed in 1826-9 by the Marchese Camillo Massimo to decorate the Dante room in the Villa Massimo at Rome. The ceiling was painted with scenes from the *Paradiso* by Veit from designs of Peter Cornelius (1783-1867), while the walls were painted with scenes from the *Inferno* and *Purgatorio* by Koch (see Volkmann's *Iconografia Dantesca*).]

WILLIAM EWART GLADSTONE

(1809-1898)

[William Ewart Gladstone was the fourth son of John Gladstone, merchant of Liverpool, where he was born in 1809. He was educated at Eton (1821-7), and Christ Church, Oxford (1828-31), where in 1831 he took a double-first in classics and mathematics. In 1832 he spent six months in Italy and learnt Italian, and in the same year he was elected M.P. for Newark. Except for a brief interval in 1846-7 Gladstone sat continuously in the House of Commons from 1833 until his retirement in 1895. He first took office as Junior Lord of the Treasury in 1834, and was four times Prime Minister (1868-74, 1880-5, 1886, 1892-4). He died in March, 1898, and was buried in Westminster Abbey.

Gladstone's interest in Dante, in whom, it has been said, few, even of Italians, were so well versed as he, dates no doubt from his first visit to Italy in 1832. Dante's influence upon him may be best described in the words of his biographer:—'Mr. Gladstone's lifelong enthusiasm for Dante should on no account be left out. In him it was something very different from casual dilettantism or the accident of a scholar's taste. He was always alive to the grandeur of Goethe's words, *Im Ganzen, Guten, Wahren, resolut zu leben,* "In wholeness, goodness, truth, strenuously to live." But it was in Dante—active politician and thinker as well as poet—that he found this unity of thought and coherence of life, not only illuminated by a sublime imagination, but directly associated with theology, philosophy, politics, history, sentiment, duty. Here are all the elements and interests that lie about the roots of the life of a man, and of the general civilisation of the world. This ever memorable picture of the mind and heart of Europe in the great centuries of the Catholic age,—making heaven the home of the human soul, presenting the natural purposes of mankind in their universality of good and evil, exalted and mean, piteous and hateful, tragedy and farce, all commingled as a living whole,—was exactly fitted to the quality of a genius so rich and powerful as Mr. Gladstone's in the range of its spiritual intuitions and in its masculine grasp of all the complex truths of mortal nature. So true and real a book is it, he once said,—such a record of practical humanity and of the discipline of the soul amidst its wonderful poetical intensity and imaginative power. In him this meant no spurious revivalism, no flimsy and fantastic affectation. It was the real and energetic discovery in the vivid conception and commanding structure of Dante, of a light, a refuge, and an inspiration in the labours of the actual world. "You have been good enough," he once wrote to an Italian correspondent (1883), "to call that supreme poet, 'a solemn master' for me. These are not empty words. The reading of Dante is not merely a pleasure, a *tour de force*, or a lesson; it is a vigorous discipline for the heart, the intellect, the whole man. In the school of Dante I have learned a great part of that mental provision (however insignificant it may be) which has served me to make the journey of human life up to the term of nearly seventy-three years." He once asked of an accomplished woman possessing a scholar's breadth of reading, what poetry she most lived with. She named Dante for one, "But what of Dante?"—"The *Paradiso*," she replied.—"Ah, that is right," he exclaimed, "that's my test." In the *Paradiso* it was, that he saw in beams of crystal radiance the ideal of the unity of the religious mind, the love and admiration for the high unseen things of which the Christian church was to him the sovereign embodiment' (Morley's *Life of Gladstone*, vol. i. pp. 202-3).

As a young man Gladstone tried his hand at translating Dante in the triple rhyme of the original, specimens of which he subsequently published in a volume of translations by Lord Lyttelton and himself in 1861. He retained his interest in Dante to the end of his life, one of the cherished beliefs of his later years being that Dante visited England and Oxford. A somewhat curious remark, made in his 83rd year, is recorded by his biographer, viz. that 'Dante was too optimist to be placed on a level with Shakespeare, or even with Homer' (*Life*, vol. iii. p. 488).]

1835. TRANSLATION OF PURGATORIO XI. 1-21.

The Lord's Prayer

O FATHER ours, that dwellest in the sky,
Not circumscribed, but for Thy love intense
To Thy first Emanations there on high;
Let each and every creature that hath sense
Praise Thee, Thy name. Thy goodness, as 'tis fit
They render thanks for Thy warm effluence.
Thy kingdom come; Thy peace too come with it,
Which, if it come not by Thy gift divine,
Comes not to us by strength of human wit.
As of their wills the angel Powers to Thine,
Chanting Hosanna, render sacrifice;
So may we men our human wills resign.
Each day give daily manna from the skies,
Without the which, in this rough desert place
He backward slides who forward busiest hies.
And as we pardon each to each, efface
And blot away, benign, our heavier debt,
Nor hold our ill deserts before Thy face.
Our virtue, weak and easily beset,
Oh hazard not with the inveterate foe
That vexeth sore; but free us from his net.

(From *Translations by Lord Lyttelton and the Right Hon. W. E. Gladstone*, ed. 1861, p. 117.[1])

1835. TRANSLATION OF PARADISO, III. 70-87.

Speech of Piccarda

Love by his virtue, Brother, hath appeased
Our several wills: he causeth us to will
But what we have, all other longings eased.
Did we desire a region loftier still,
Such our desire were dissonant from His,
Who bade us each our several station fill:
A thing impossible in these spheres of bliss
If whoso dwelleth here, in Love alone
Must dwell, and if Love's nature well thou wis.
Within the will Divine to set our own
Is of the essence of this Being blest,
For that our wills to one with His be grown.

[1] [A second edition was published in 1863.]

So, as we stand throughout the realms of rest,
  From stage to stage, our pleasure is the King's,
  Whose will our will informs, by Him imprest.
In His Will is our peace. To this all things
  By Him created, or by nature made,
  As to a central Sea, self-motion brings.

(From *Translations by Lord Lyttelton and the Right Hon. W. E. Gladstone*, ed. 1861, p. 119.)

1835. DIARY.

[Tasso compared with Dante]

Tasso's *Jerusalem Delivered* beautiful in its kind, but how can its author be placed in the same category of genius as Dante?

(Morley's *Life of Gladstone*, vol. i. p. 132.)

1836. Nov. 11. DIARY.

[Reading the *Divina Commedia*]

Recommenced with great anticipations of delight the *Divina Commedia*.

(*Ibid*. p. 137.)

1837. TRANSLATION OF INFERNO XXXIII. 1-78.

Ugolino

The grim offender from his savage feast
  Lifted his mouth; and wiped it with the hair
  Of th' head unseemly mauled that he released;
Then thus began. "Am I anew to bear
  Desperate grief, that weighs my heart adown,
  Even as I think on what I shall declare?
Yet, if my words may, as a seed is sown,
  Bring shame to the foul traitor that I gnaw,
  In weeping I will speak. One all unknown
Thou com'st: unknown, by what decree or law
  Thus low thou didst descend: but Florentine
  I guess thy race, by what I heard, not saw.
Thou hast to learn, I was Count Ugoline:
  He, Roger, hight Archbishop. Now I tell
  The cause of this ill neighbourship of mine.
How by his evil thought's effect it fell,
  That I, in him confiding, was ensnared
  And put to death, thou, all men, know full well.

But what to boot I trow thou hast not heard,
  The manner of my death how horrible,
  Hear now; and judge, if ill by him I fared.
A narrow orifice within the cell
  (Which yet from me, they call the Famine jail,
  And wherein others, after me, must dwell,)
Had shewn me many moons both wax and fail
  Through its dim passage, when I slept the sleep
  That rent in twain the future's darksome veil.
A mighty lord, He seemed the plain to sweep,
  Chasing the wolf and cubs toward the hill
  Which Luccan towers from Pisan eyes doth keep.
With dogs high-bred and lean, of eager skill.
  By the Gualandi the Sismondi rides,
  And the Lanfranchi helps his train to fill.
Too short, too short the wasting strength abides
  Of sire or sons: I seemed to see the stroke,
  As the keen fangs dug through the weltering sides.
When I the first, ere break of morn, awoke
  I heard my sons moan faintly in their sleep
  That with me dwelt, and bread for life invoke.
Oh thou art hard, if careless yet thou keep,
  Learning the then sad presage of my thought!
  Oh weep for this, if aught can make thee weep.
The wonted hour for victuals to be brought
  Was near at hand: they were awake, and stirred;
  But each one, for his dream, was vexed with doubt.
Aye then, the doorway locked beneath I heard
  Of that infernal tower: I gazed upon
  The faces of my sons without a word.
I wept not; inwardly I turned to stone:
  They wept: and first my dearling Anselm said,
  'What ails thee, Father? such thy look is grown?'
I shed no tear for this: nor answered
  All that same day: nor till the night was gone:
  At last, another sun was overhead.
Then, as a scanty ray of light there shone
  Into the doleful dungeon, and I read
  In their four aspects what must be mine own,
I bit both hands for anguish, hard bestead:
  But they, misdeeming it was for distress
  Of hunger, in a moment rose, and said,
'Feed, Father dear, on us, so we the less
  Shall grieve: do thou, who didst our flesh bestow,
  Strip off these miserable limbs their dress.'

I held my peace; words had but fed their woe.
  Mute that day, mute the next, did we abide;
  Merciless earth, that didst not yawn below!
But when there came another morning tide
  Then Gaddo fell; and, by my feet reclined,
  'My Father, wherefore help'st me not?' he cried;
And lived no more. I, whom they left behind,
  I saw those three fall slowly, one by one,
  In the fifth day and sixth: and, now all blind,
I groped about me after every son:
  Two days I called upon their names, though dead;
  Then, grief was worsted, and the Famine won."
With savage glance awry, when he had said,
  He griped anew the wretched scull; his teeth
  Sharp as a mastiff's on that caitiff head.

(*Translations*, pp. 109-15).

1839. June 8. DIARY.

['Canons of living' from Dante]

I told her [1] what was my original destination and desire in life; in what sense and manner I remained in connection with politics. . . . I have given her (led by her questions) these passages for canons of our living:—

Le fronde, onde s' infronda tutto l' orto
  Dell' Ortolano eterno, am' io cotanto,
  Quanto da lui a lor di bene è porto.[2]

And Dante again—

  In la sua volontade è nostra pace:
  Ella è quel mare, al qual tutto si muove.[3]

(*Life*, vol. i. p. 223.)

1844. Jan. 21. LETTER TO MRS. GLADSTONE (from Carlton House Terrace).

['A rare gem' from the *Paradiso*]

There is a beautiful little sentence in the works of Charles Lamb concerning one who had been afflicted: 'he gave his heart to the Purifier, and his will to the Sovereign Will of the Universe.'[4] But there is a speech in the third canto of the *Paradiso* of Dante,

[1] [Miss Catherine Glynne, to whom he became engaged at this date.]
[2] [*Par.* xxvi. 64-6.]
[3] [*Par.* iii. 85-6.]
[4] [*Rosamund Gray*, chap. xi.]

spoken by a certain Piccarda, which is a rare gem. I will only quote this one line:—

In la sua volontade è nostra pace.[1]

The words are few and simple, and yet they appear to me to have an inexpressible majesty of truth about them, to be almost as if they were spoken from the very mouth of God. It so happened that (unless my memory much deceives me) I first read that speech on a morning early in the year 1836, which was one of trial. I was profoundly impressed and powerfully sustained, almost absorbed, by these words. They cannot be too deeply graven upon the heart.

(*Life*, vol. i. pp. 215-6.)

MARIE FRANÇOISE CATHERINE DOETTER CORBAUX

(1812-1883)

[M. F. C. D. Corbaux, commonly known as Fanny Corbaux, painter and biblical critic, was the daughter of an Englishman, a well-known statistician, who lived abroad. She studied art at the National Gallery and British Institution, and won several Society of Arts medals. In 1830 she was elected honorary member of the Society of British Artists, at whose gallery she exhibited in 1835 a subject from Dante. She subsequently joined the New Society of Painters in Water Colours, and was a constant exhibitor. She received a civil list pension in 1871, and died in 1883.]

1835. IN this year F. Corbaux exhibited at the Society of British Artists a picture with the following title:—

—"Nessun maggior dolore
Che ricordarsi del tempo felice
Nella miseria"—[2] *Dante*.

(*Catalogue of the Society of British Artists*, 1835, No. 86.)

EDWARD N. SHANNON

(fl. 1830)

[Edward Shannon appears to have been fond of mystifications. He published in 1836 a collection of poems (some of them purporting to be unacknowledged pieces by Byron), and a translation of the first ten cantos of the *Inferno*, under the name of Odoardo Volpi. In a 'Postscript to the Dante' he throws off his pseudonymity in the following paragraph, 'The reader will please to substitute the name of the translator, E. N. Shannon, in the title to these specimens, for the supposititious one of Odoardo Volpi.' Elsewhere, by way of advertisement apparently, he writes of himself as deceased, intimating that he was an Italian, and that Odoardo Volpi was his real name: 'Some time before his decease he completed translations of Dante and of Petrarca into our language, which he intended to have published under the assumed name of Edward Fox—that being the corresponding English of his own name. I have heard the former praised for its fidelity.' In the preface to his translation of the

[1] [*Par.* iii. 85.]

[2] [*Inf.* v. 121-3.]

Commedia, which is in the *terza rima* of the original (the first sustained attempt at an English translation from Dante in this metre), Shannon freely criticises the performances of his predecessors, especially Cary, to whom he devotes some thirty pages of detailed (and carping) criticism. He chiefly blames Cary for employing blank verse, while he takes great credit to himself for using rhyme, and further Dante's own metre, for his translation. Shannon appears to have been a good Italian scholar, some of the poems in his *Tales, Old and New* (1842), being written in Italian.]

1836. ARNALDO; GADDO; AND OTHER UNACKNOWLEDGED POEMS; BY LORD BYRON, AND SOME OF HIS CONTEMPORARIES; COLLECTED BY ODOARDO VOLPI.

Sonnet on Dante[1]

IT was his lot to bend, with humble brow,
Before the sordid throng;—to stretch his hand
For alms to strangers, driven from his land
With Freedom; glorious in her overthrow.
Nor did he deem it shame even thus to bow;
And only grieved that none could yet withstand
That impious crew who had infixed the brand
On Florence,—only blushed her shame to know.
Oh, how exceeding opulent was he,
In exile, worldly want, and solitude,
While came the sacred visions to their birth!
How lordly in that slave-abhorring mood!
How bondless in the thirst for liberty!
Could Dante's soul be poor, in fortune's dearth?

(p. 240.)

1836. THE COMEDY OF DANTE ALIGHIERI: TRANSLATED BY ODOARDO VOLPI.[2]

[Criticism of Cary and other translators of the *Commedia*]

English literature has been already, in some degree, enriched with one translation of the Comedy of Dante, and has also received the worthless addition of one or two loose and tumid paraphrases of the entire or of a portion of that first great poem of the middle age. Of these latter I shall scarcely say more: but it is requisite that I should enter into a minute examination of the plan and execution of the former; and, however invidious the task may appear, I trust that I shall be able to prove the defects of that version to be very great, notwithstanding the favourable reception which it has met with, at least from the reviewers.

[1][This sonnet was reprinted in *Tales, Old and New*, published in 1842 under Shannon's own name.]

[2][Published in Dublin—only the first ten cantos of the *Inferno* ever appeared.]

To me it appears to be an imperative duty of a translator to copy, as far as possible, not only the imagery of his prototype, but likewise to convey as clear an idea of the manner of his original, especially if that manner be remarkably appropriate to the subject treated. Now there never was an author whose manner was more peculiar to himself, or more fitting for his subject than that of Dante to his own; and I think every person of taste who is acquainted with the great poem of the Florentine, will readily acknowledge that the tertian rhyme in which it is written possesses a solemn harmony and grandeur of cadence which impart, as it were, an oracular dignity to the verse; and that this is, of course, the best form which the poet could possibly have selected in the composition of his sacred allegory. In this respect how has his copyist acquitted himself? He has chosen to translate the poem in question into blank verse; thereby relinquishing the task of accurately preserving one of the principal features in the style of that work. If he has, in some parts, preserved the pure gold of that costly shrine, it will be found that he has, in many places, defaced the imagery, in flinging away the gems which adorned it.

There is, besides, another quality in the poem of Dante which should, I think, have prevented his translator from making such a choice. It is, most truly, a Gothic poem; in other words, it is completely characteristic of the middle age in which it was produced, when all poems of all kinds were written in rhyme, and long before the invention of blank verse in modern languages. If an Italian was to render the poetry of Chaucer or of Spenser into *versi sciolti*, I imagine that his bad taste in doing so would be very evident to his English readers; and yet the different kinds of rhyme in which those poets have written, are much less fitly adapted to the subjects they have chosen, than is the tertian rhyme to the subject of Dante, whose poem bears the same relation to the classic remains as a Gothic Cathedral has to a Grecian temple. It was, probably, the great difficulty of this intricate species of rhyme which deterred Mr. Cary from endeavouring to bring the great Tuscan before us, clad in the dark but embroidered garments which he wore, rather than in a scanty and inappropriate imitation of the classic robes of antiquity; one, in fact not possessing the ample folds and graceful flow of the ancient, nor the rich adornments of the romantic garb. And I confess that, even after I had versified some cantos of the following translation, I was, from the same consideration, about to relinquish the task which I had undertaken, when I was urged by particular circumstances to proceed as I had commenced. In doing so, I have been really surprised to find the obstacles to my attempt disappear in a great degree.

The late Mr. Hayley[1] paraphrased the first three cantos of the Hell; and these are, perhaps, almost the only endurable things which he has written:—the list of proper names, however, in the fourth, fortunately frightened him, or we should probably have had a Dante *de sa façon*. A Mr. Boyd[2] also kindly offered to the English public a wordy paraphrase of that author, in a stanza of his own invention. There is, however, in his attempt so heavy a preponderance of Mr. Boyd that the bard of the Inferno sunk with him to a depth seemingly as great as that which he had described, and was again in the company of the damned: yet I doubt whether those attempts would not be as attractive, to most readers, as the far more accurate but rhymeless version of Mr. Cary. Indeed, I understand that this latter is, by many persons, considered to be inferior to its unwieldy rival, although it has had a much larger circulation. . . .

(*Preface*, pp. v. ff.)

Hell

Canto I

Midway upon the journey of our life,
  I found myself within a darksome wood;
  For the true way was lost, mid perils, rife.
And hard it were to tell how drear it stood,
  That savage mighty wild of shade embrowned
  Which still renews the fear that chilled my blood;
So bitter it is, death little more can wound.
  But now, to treat of good which me befell,
  I'll speak of other things that there I found.
How there I entered I can scarcely tell,
  So full of sleep was I, that time, alas!
  When the true way I left that guideth well.
But, when to a hill-foot arrived I was,
  There where it terminated that dim vale
  Which stung my heart with fear and sore amaze,
I looked on high, and saw its shoulders pale
  Clad with the radiance of that planet great
  Which leadeth others right, o'er hill and dale.
Then somewhat did that former dread abate
  Which had endured within my bosom's core,
  The livelong night of pain I past of late.
And, as a man escaped unto the shore
  From out the deep, with spent and panting breath,
  Turns to the perilous water, gazing sore;

[1] [See vol. i. pp. 359 ff.]

[2] [See vol. i. pp. 410 ff.]

Even so my mind that still fled, as from death,
  Turned backward to behold the passage dim
  Which living person never left beneath.
Afte. I had reposed each wearied limb,
  Still up the desert hill my way I went,
  My firmest foot being lowest, as I climb.
And lo! at the beginning of the bent,
  A swift and nimble Panther I descried
  Whose skin with many a spot was all besprent.
And from before my face she never hied.
  But rather hindered so my onward way,
  That, many times, to turn me back I tried,
It was the time of the beginning day,
  And the sun mounted up with every star
  That with him was, when fist the beauteous ray,
By love divine, was moved to shine afar.
  So by that gaily-spotted beast beguiled,
  And by the hour of time, and season fair,
I had a cause for hope, and inly smiled;
  But still not so that I could feel no dread
  At sight of a great Lion, raging wild,
Which came against me with uplifted head,
  And hunger mad, so that the air, before,
  Seemed all affrighted, as he onward sped.
And next a She-wolf that, with craving sore,
  Seemed heavy laden in her meagreness,
  And which gave many a one to want, of yore.
This creature cast on me such heaviness,
  With fear which issued from her hateful sight,
  That still my hope to gain the height grew less.
As one who seeketh gain, with all his might,
  And, when time comes to spoil his rich increase,
  Bewails in every thought, and saddens quite:
Such made me then that beast withouten peace,
  Coming by little and little against me, slow,
  And drove me back to where the sunbeams cease.

(*Inf.* i. 1-60, pp. 3 ff.)

1842. TALES, OLD AND NEW, WITH OTHER LESSER POEMS.

[Perfect originality not to be looked for in Dante and other great poets]

Where shall we look among the great ones for perfect originality? Is there even one unquestionably original?—Horace himself was *apparently* a close imitator of Alcaeus and of Pindar,—that is, he wrote like them, because they had evoked the kindred spirit within him, and not from any cold and painful study. Virgil was, in the same way, a civilized copyist of Homer,—and yet he is one of the front rank of the immortals. Whom did the blind old man imitate? Some elder rhapsodist without the smallest doubt,—only that we cannot name the gentleman, or rather the beggar. I trust that it is not requisite for me to point out the various imitative passages in Dante, Milton, Ariosto, Tasso, Spenser, and others of highest note.

(*Preface*, pp. viii-ix.)

[Lord Holland on translating Dante]

It was the practice in the seventeenth century, for authors, on coming before the world, to bring with them scores of recommendatory verses from the more noted of their fellows in the literary republic. Animated by a similar vanity, I cannot resist the opportunity of here presenting to the reader an extract of a letter, which I had the honour of receiving from the late revered and lamented Lord Holland,[1] in reply to one which I had addressed to him, relating to my translation of Dante. It is as follows:—'Your original poems show so much fertility of thought, and so playful and powerful an imagination, that you ought not to devote yourself to so long and laborious a task as the translation of Dante, which though it requires, no doubt, many of the other qualifications of a scholar and poet, does not afford an unfettered scope to those two particular faculties.'

(*Ibid.* p. xiii.)

T. BODDINGTON

(fl. 1830)

1836. IN this year T. Boddington exhibited at the Society of British Artists a picture with the following title:—

The Last Hour.
—'paia il giorno pianger che si more.'
Dante.[2]

(*Catalogue of the Society of British Artists*, 1836, No. 413.)

1837. In this year T. Boddington exhibited at the Royal Academy a picture with the following title:—

[1] [The third Baron Holland (see above, pp. 470-1).]
[2] [*Purg.* viii. 6.]

Terrace scene in the south.
'Era già l' ora che volge 'l disio
A' naviganti, e 'ntenerisce il cuore,
Lo dì ch' han detto ai dolci amici a dio.'
Dante Purg. Canto viii.[1]

(*Catalogue of the Exhibition of the Royal Academy*, 1837, No. 321.)

J. WALSH

(fl. 1830)

1836. IN this year J. Walsh exhibited at the Royal Academy a picture with the following title:—

Subject from the 'Inferno.'

(*Catalogue of the Exhibition of the Royal Academy*, 1836, No. 755.)

ANONYMOUS

[The anonymous author of *The Inquisitor—Letters addressed to Trelawney Tompkinson, Esq.* has not been identified. He was evidently a student of Dante, for Letters iii, v, vii, x, xiii, xvii, xix, are entirely taken up with a discussion of the *Divina Commedia*, together with an analysis of the *Inferno* (as far as the end of Canto vii), which is interspersed with translations (including the whole of Canto v) 'in stanzas of three blank lines,' and preceded by a dissertation (in Letter iii) 'On the Stile and Characteristics of Dante.' The translations have no poetical merit, the 'blank stanzas' being little better than prose chopped into lengths, sometimes of twelve, sometimes of ten, syllables.]

1836. THE INQUISITOR—LETTERS ADDRESSED TO TRELAWNEY TOMPKINSON, ESQ. LAND'S END, CORNWALL.

[On the style and characteristics of Dante]

I NOW come to the great Dante Alighieri—the sixth as he stiles himself among the ancient poets.[2] My admiration would claim for him a much higher rank among them; while among modern poets I am inclined to think he stands second to none. I am aware indeed of the sneers of Voltaire,[3] and that Warton[4] the learned author of the history of English poetry, has treated him with a very supercilious kind of indifference; but remembering that the land of his birth, and that too the land of Petrarch, Ariosto and Tasso, has stiled him the father of her language and

[1] [*Purg.* viii. 1-3.]
[2] [*Inf.* iv. 102.]
[3] [See vol. i. pp. 204 ff.]
[4] [See vol. i. pp. 283 ff.]

her poetry, that Florence established a professorship on purpose to lecture on his great poem, and that the celebrated Boccaccio was first appointed to fill that professor's chair—I think we may disregard both the sneers of the lively Frenchman, and the superciliousness of the laborious Englishman, when opposed to such a proof of his literary merits. . . .

* * * *

That Dante is a master of the terrible, I need hardly observe to you, unrivalled, and that he has occasionally soared to the height of the sublime, I need only remind you of his well-known inscription over the gate of hell, than which poetry never produced anything more highly wrought in its way, and of his magnificent description of the angel; in the eleventh canto, sent from heaven to open an entrance into the city of Dite to him and his guide. But I would also call your attention to another characteristic of our poet, not less undoubted, though perhaps less striking; viz. his tenderness and sensibility.

In referring you to these qualities displayed in the Commedia, the celebrated tale of Francesca di Rimini, will immediately occur to you, but I dwell not on this, because it forms an episode by itself—but beg you to remark throughout the *whole* of the Inferno, how repeatedly you will find Dante the sympathizing and compassionate spectator of the torments he awards against the sinners of every rank, nation, and grade, whom he cites before his tribunal without distinction of party and with equal impartiality, whether friend or foe—how often overwhelmed by his tears, and with his voice choked by sobs, he deputes the task of interrogating the spirits of the dead to his guide—of the tender nature of the connexion which subsists between himself and Virgil, showing the dutiful reverence of a son on the part of the one, and the affectionate care and watchfulness of a parent on the other. . . .

I go on to consider some few peculiarities of his stile and diction: and the first thing that strikes me is the economy of his words, contrasted with the prodigality of his imagination so fertile in ideas, and how disdaining all the trickeries of language, by the use of a few simple words he so often electrifies his reader. The force of the idea, which he may be said merely to sketch, he marks with so strong and clear an outline, that expressing much in a little, he sets the reader's mind to ruminate over the teeming image which he so concisely places before it.

I shall conclude with briefly adverting to the beauty, ingenuity and appropriateness of his similes and comparisons. You will observe how refreshingly they intervene to the mind of the reader, amidst all the horrors that Dante conjures up, by recalling him to images drawn from the most chearful and familiar objects of common life. Thus to illustrate the river of boiling pitch in which the usurers are immersed, he refers to the cauldrons of tar which stand boiling in the arsenal of Venice to caulk the leaky sides of the weather-beaten vessel. and takes the opportunity of presenting us with a picture of so bustling and animated a scene.[1] Again he compares them as they lift their heads above the surface to relieve their torments, to frogs peering with their muzzles above the water of a marshy pool.[2] and immediately afterwards to a troop of dolphins lifting their arched backs above the billows, and like faithful friends prognosticating to the mariner the approaching gale.[3] On another occasion, he likens the waving flames, each of which imprison the soul of an unhappy sinner, to swarms of fire flies in the dusk of evening, winging their glittering flight amidst vineyards and harvest fields.[4] . . .

Before we enter upon the Commedia, I must warn you that you are not to expect in such a poem the sustained march of the epic dignity and stateliness, or to grow out of humour with our author if he takes all advantage of the license afforded to him by the term by which he designates it.[5] You will in truth find him everything by turns, as the passion or humour of the moment is ascendant—terrible, sublime, tender, satirical, and even sportive, to the point of setting on his sinners at times to bandy abuse with each other.[6] But whatever latitude he may indulge himself in, whatever improprieties and inconsistencies may be charged against him, let this be recorded to his honour, and more it is than can be said for some writers of a more Christian age, and amongst them for Goëthe, the *Rousseau* of Germany, that never in a single instance has he played the pander to vice, or furnished from a polluted imagination the incentives to kindle into combustion the perhaps dormant passions of his readers. Dante, on the contrary, is ever the stern uncompromising enemy of vice in every form as well as the eloquent advocate of virtue and morality.

(*Letter* iii. pp. 37 ff.)

[*Inferno* v. 97-142. Francesca speaks :—]

On the sea-margin there doth sit my parent land,
Where the vex'd Po in Ocean seeks repose
And mingles with his tributary streams in peace.

Love of which gentle heart the ever ready scholar proves
Of this my charming lover's strong possession took,
Him from me torn in way that still my spirit grieves.

[1] [*Inf.* xxi. 7 ff.] [2] [*Inf.* xxii. 25 ff.] [3] [*Inf.* xxv. 19 ff.]
[4] [*Inf.* xxvi. 25 ff.] [5] [*Commedia.*]
[6] [*Inf.* xxx. 100 ff. (Sinon and Maestro Adamo).]

Love that ne'er one belov'd from debt of Love exempts,
With such transporting passion filled my soul for him,
That as thou seest not here abandon'd by him love I still.

To one, sad end, this fatal Love betray'd us both,
But waits the doom of Cain the spiller of our blood.
Such were the words that full of sorrow to our ear were borne.

When I had heard these ill-starr'd lovers' tale rehearsed
With head bent down upon the earth all mute I stood,
Until the poet wondering cried, what ponderest thou upon?

Soon as I words could find, ah me! I thus began,
That all these thousand tender and soft desires
Should but to this grievous pass this hapless pair betray!

Then turn'd I tow'rds them, and my speech I thus addressed;
O Frances, these thy Martyr's grievous pangs,
My heart so sadden that my eyes with tears o'erflow.

But tell me, in those sweet remember'd hours of lovers' sighs,
To which of ye, and how Love's secret was reveal'd
That of the doubtful passion full assurance to ye gave.

Alas! she answered, pang more bitter is there none,
And well thy sage instructor this doth ken,
Than steep'd in wretchedness past happiness to call to mind.

But if so great desire the fatal root thou hast to learn
From whence our growing love did first spring up,
Tho' mingling with my words flow tears together they shall flow.

One day we read together, 'twas to pass away the hour,
Of Launcelot, and how Love held him in its thralls,
Alone we were nor ought of evil were at hand suspect.

Our tears oft dimmed the page, and oft our kindling cheeks
Flush'd as enamor'd o'er the tale we hung.
But at one point alone it was that our sad fate was seal'd.

For of that smile so long'd for, when we came to read,
Which of so dear a lover answer'd to the kiss,
Then Paul, oh from me may he ne'er be sunder'd more,

All trembling with love with kisses cover'd o'er my mouth.
A pander was that book and he who wrote it unto us,
All of that day we opened not its leaves again.

Thus the one hapless spirit, while the other sobb'd the while
In mood so piteous, that compassion-struck I swoon'd
And tumbled unto earth as tumbles a dead corse.

(A translation of Canto v. of Dante's *Inferno* in stanzas of three blank lines, in *Letter* xiii. pp. 116 ff.)

CHARLES WEST COPE

(1811-1890)

[Charles West Cope, historical painter, was born in Leeds in 1811. He became a student at the Royal Academy in 1828, where he exhibited for the first time in 1833. From 1833 to 1835 he was in Italy, the greater part of his time being spent at Rome and Florence. In 1837 he exhibited at the Academy a picture of Paolo and Francesca, which was bought by the Art Union of London. Cope obtained a prize of £300 in the competition for the decoration of the Houses of Parliament in 1843, and in the following year he was one of the six painters commissioned to prepare decorations for the House of Lords. He was elected R.A. in 1848, and was Professor of Painting to the Royal Academy, 1867-1875. He retired in 1883, and died at Bournemouth in 1890.]

1837. IN this year Cope exhibited at the Royal Academy a picture with the following title:—

Paulo and Francisca.
'For our delight we read of Lancelot,
How him love thralled; . . .
Oftimes by that reading,
Our eyes were drawn together, and the hue
Fled from our altered cheek;
The book and writer both
Were love's purveyors.
Vide Cary's Dante Inferno.[1]

(*Catalogue of the Exhibition of the Royal Academy*, 1837, No. 39.)

THEODOR VON HOLST

(1810-1844)

[Theodor von Holst, historical painter, of Livonian descent, was born in London in 1810. At an early age he became a student at the Royal Academy, where he attracted the notice of Sir Thomas Lawrence, and of Fuseli. He first exhibited at the Academy in 1827, where in 1837 he exhibited a picture of Dante's Charon. He died in London in 1844.]

[1] [*Inf.* v. 127 ff.]

1837. IN this year Von Holst exhibited at the Royal Academy a picture with the following title:—

Charon—a study for a fresco.
'Guai a voi anime prave;
Non isperate mai veder lo cielo.
Io vegno per menarvi all' altra riva
Nelle tenebre eterne, in caldo, e in gelo.
* * * *
Ma quell' anime, ch' eran lasse e nude,
Cangiar' colore e dibattero i denti,
Ratto che inteser le parole crude.'
Dante Inf. chap. iii.[1]

(*Catalogue of the Exhibition of the Royal Academy*, 1837, No. 302.)

MUSGRAVE LEWTHWAITE WATSON

(1804-1847)

[Musgrave Lewthwaite Watson, sculptor, was born near Leeds in 1804. He was articled in 1821 to a solicitor in Carlisle, but on the death of his father in 1823 he adopted the profession of sculptor, and went to London. On the advice of Flaxman he entered the schools of the Royal Academy, and went to Italy to study. He exhibited at the Academy from 1829 to 1847, one of his exhibits being a group of Dante and Beatrice (1837). Among his works were statues of Lord Eldon and Lord Stowell, and of John Flaxman; he also executed the 'Battle of St. Vincent' bas-relief on the Nelson monument. Watson died in London in 1847.]

1837. IN this year Watson exhibited at the Royal Academy a marble group with the following title:—

Dante and Beatrice.
'In the tardiest sphere thus placed,
Here, mid these other blessed also blest.'
Paradise, Canto. iii.[2]

(*Catalogue of the Exhibition of the Royal Academy*, 1837, No. 1196.)

SIR FRANCIS PALGRAVE

(1788-1861)

[Francis Palgrave, historian, son of Meyer Cohen, a Jewish member of the Stock Exchange, was born in London in 1788. He was educated at home by an Italian, from whom he acquired great facility in the Italian language. In 1823 he married and became a Christian, at the same time changing his name from Cohen to Palgrave.

[1] [*Inf.* iii. 84-7, 100-2.]

[2] [*Par.* iii. 50-1 (Cary).]

He was brought up as a solicitor, but in 1827 was called to the bar. From 1827 to 1837 he edited many volumes for the Records Commission, and in 1838 he was appointed Deputy-Keeper of the Records, which office he held until his death in 1861. Palgrave was knighted in 1832, and was a Fellow of the Royal Society. His most important historical works were *The Rise and Progress of the English Commonwealth* (1832), and the *History of Normandy and England* (1851-64). He was also author of *The Merchant and the Friar*, dealing with 'truths and fictions of the Middle Ages' (1837), and of Murray's *Handbook for Travellers in Northern Italy* (1842). He was a frequent contributor to the *Edinburgh* and *Quarterly Reviews*, one of his most important articles in the latter being on *The Fine Arts in Florence* (1840). Palgrave was well read in Italian literature and was familiar with the works of Dante, as appears from his numerous quotations, especially in the *Handbook*, in the Preface to which he says 'Whenever an apposite historical or descriptive passage has occurred to us in Dante, we have inserted it.']

1837. TRUTHS AND FICTIONS OF THE MIDDLE AGES. THE MERCHANT AND THE FRIAR.

[Motto on title-page]

O VOI ch' avete gl' intelletti sani,
Mirate la dottrina che s' asconde
Sotto 'l velame degli versi strani.
[*Inf.* ix. 61-3.]

[The *Volgare illustre* of Florence]

Marco Polo speaks—I cannot discern any *Romance*, in the dialect of the English Landsman. You, Commons, are all *Tedeschi*, at the present day. The speech of the Flemings seems to me to differ from your English, scarcely so much as the *Volgare illustre* [1] of Florence, from our Venetian language.

(pp. 126-7.)

1840. Sept. QUARTERLY REVIEW. ART. I. THE FINE ARTS IN FLORENCE.

[The scanty demand for Dante in England]

By English readers, as a whole and on the whole, Italian literature is most strangely neglected. 'How does it happen,' said we to a respectable importer of foreign books, 'that your stock of Italian is so scanty, particularly since, in the Sardinian States, in Austrian Italy, and in Italian Switzerland, so many good new historical books, and cheap editions of standard works have been recently produced?'—'Why,' replied he, 'scanty as our stock is, we have more than we can sell: a few novels, Metastasio, Tasso, Ariosto, and a Dante now and then, is all that people ask for.'

(Vol. lxvi. pp. 316-7.)

[1] [Dante's phrase, which occurs frequently in the *De Vulgari Eloquentia*, e.g. i. 13, l. 3; 16, l. 58; etc.]

[Dante's comparison of Florence to a sick person]

With the revolution of 1250 began an era of pure self-government in Florence, varied by those vicissitudes of turbulence, faction, and despotism, which led her great poet to compare the republic to the sick man, who, unable to find repose upon his weary couch, seeks, by change of position, a temporary release from pain:—

'Fiorenza mia, ben puoi esser contenta,'[1] &c.

(pp. 319-20.)

[Dante's description of Florence in the olden time]

Florence appears to have continued increasing in prosperity under the government of the celebrated Countess Matilda; and in that early age she still retained, at least in the opinion of the poet, those virtues which abandoned her in the days of her prosperity. The passage in which Dante expatiates upon the simplicity of the 'good old days,'—days which recede from us like the rainbow if we attempt to approach them—is singularly pathetic, its beauty not being in the least diminished by the homely quaintness of the picture drawn by the exile, speaking in the person of Messer Cacciaguida, his venerated ancestor.

'Fiorenza dentro della cerchia antica,'[2] &c.

(pp. 329-30.)

[Dante's monument in Santa Croce at Florence]

So long as the remains of classical taste were consulted as the general models of grace and correctness, they imparted their merits to Italian art. But when, from being the type of beauty, the resemblance to the antique was prescribed as the only test of merit, invention became torpid: and historical sculpture in Italy, became in art what Latin prize poems are in literature, compositions too respectable to be contemned, but at which no creature who can help itself will ever give a second glance. Look but once at the monuments of Alfieri and of Dante in Santa Croce, and you will feel that Italian art is as empty as the cenotaph, and as dead as the bones and ashes in the sepulchre.

(p. 349.)

[1] [Palgrave quotes *Purg.* vi. 127-51, with Cary's translation. The same passage is quoted in the *Handbook to Northern Italy*, with Wright's translation.]

[2] [Palgrave quotes *Par.* xv. 98-129, and appends Merivale's 'excellent version' (see above, p. 197), with the suggestion that he should 'attempt the grateful labour of giving us a complete translation of the *Divina Commedia*.' This same passage is quoted in the *Handbook for Northern Italy*.]

1842. HANDBOOK FOR TRAVELLERS IN NORTHERN ITALY: STATES OF SARDINIA, LOMBARDY AND VENICE, PARMA AND PIACENZA, MODENA, LUCCA, MASSA-CARRARA, AND TUSCANY, AS FAR AS THE VAL D' ARNO.[1]

[Dante's villa near Verona—His granddaughters]

Verona to Mantua.—Towards the Adige, and on the north, is Gargagnano, where Dante is said to have composed his Purgatorio, and where he possessed some property, a villa which afterwards passed to the Serego family. . . . San Michele has some interest, as being the place where the three granddaughters of Dante, the children of his son Pietro, namely Aligeria, Gemma, and Lucia, took the veil.

(pp. 296-7.)

[The Arena at Padua—Dante and Giotto]

Padua.—The Arena passed to the Scrovigno family, in the person of Enrico Scrovigno, the son of Reginaldo, condemned by Dante for his usury and avarice in the following verses, in explanation of which it must be recollected that the *blue sow*, the *scrofa azzurra*, was the bearing of the family

'E un che d' una scrofa azzurra e grossa
Segnato avea lo suo sacchetto bianco
Mi disse: Che fai tu in questa fossa?'
Inferno, xvii. 64-6.

About 1303 Enrico built within the precinct of the Arena the chapel of Sta. Maria dell' Annunciata, commonly called Santa Maria dell' Arena. . . . At this period, Giotto, then young, was working at Padua, and Scrovigno called him in to raise this fabric. . . . The unity of design apparent in the chapel and in the paintings, no doubt resulted from both being designed by the same mind; and what adds to their interest, is, that Dante lodged with Giotto when the works were under his hand.

(p. 315.)

[Dante's reference to the Arsenal at Venice]

Venice.—The Arsenal attained its present dimensions, nearly 2 miles in circuit, between 1307 and 1320. Walls and towers, battlemented and crenulated, surround it. They are attributed to Andrea Pisano.[2] . . . At present, the business of the Arsenal is

[1] [This work contains numerous quotations from the *Divina Commedia* in connection with places mentioned by Dante. A few passages are given here which relate to Dante personally, or are of special interest otherwise.]

[2] [Vasari states that Andrea (c. 1270-1348) designed the Arsenal while Piero Gradenigo was Doge (1289-1311).]

just kept alive, affording a scanty memorial of the operations which so struck the fancy of Dante, as to furnish the subject for one of his most strange and striking similes.[1]

(pp. 336-8.)

[The 'Torre della Fame' at Pisa]

Pisa.—The Piazza de' Cavalieri was the centre of ancient Pisa, and in the days of the Republic was the Piazza degli Anziani, the Forum of the Pisans. . . . The Torre della Fame, formerly the tower of the Gualandi alle Sette Vie, was situated in this piazza, by the side of an archway, under which passes the street leading to the Duomo. No vestiges remain of this building, the scene of the sufferings of Count Ugolino, which Dante has immortalised. Its epithet is thus mentioned:—

'Breve pertugio dentro dalla muda,
La qual per me ha 'l titol *della fame*,
E 'n che conviene ancor ch' altri si chiuda,
M' avea mostrato per lo suo forame
Più lune già.

Inf. xxxiii. 22-5.

It was ruined in the 16th century, but some of the walls were apparent till a very recent period: they are now entirely incorporated in a modern house. It is wonderful that the Pisans should have allowed so interesting a relic to disappear.

(pp. 461-2.)

[Dante's portrait in the Duomo at Florence]

Florence.—Near the side entrance door of the Cathedral, on the north wall, is the portrait of Dante,[2] generally, but erroneously, attributed to Orcagna. The poet is represented in a long red robe, the countenance grave and beautiful, the head crowned with laurel: in features and costume it seems the pattern of the generally adopted idea of Dante, familiarised to us by Flaxman's designs. On the right hand are Hell, Purgatory, and Paradise, briefly symbolised in small groups; on the left is Florence as enclosed within its turreted circle of walls.

(p. 498.)

BIBLIOTHECA PHILLIPPICA

1837. CATALOGUS LIBRORUM MANUSCRIPTORUM IN BIBLIOTHECA D. THOMAE PHILLIPPS, BART. A.D. 1837.

[Sir Thomas Phillipps (1792-1872) was born at Manchester, and was educated at Rugby and University College, Oxford (M.A. 1820). He began to collect books and

[1] [Palgrave here quotes *Inf.* xxi. 7-18.]

[2] [By Domenico di Michelino.]

MSS. while quite a young man, and eventually his collection contained upwards of 40,000 MSS. He purchased more than 1300 volumes of Italian MSS. from the library of the fifth Earl of Guilford (1766-1827). After his death the whole of his collection, of a large portion of which he printed a catalogue at his private printing-press at Middle-Hill ('typis Medio-montanis'), passed to a married daughter, by whom a considerable number of the MSS. was sold twenty years later. Among Sir Thomas Phillipps' MSS. were four of the *Divina Commedia*, one of which (bought at the Heber sale) had previously belonged to Charles James Fox; a MS. of Boccaccio's *Vita di Dante*; and one of an unpublished commentary on the *Commedia* by Alberico da Rosciate.[1]]

WILLIAM WHEWELL

(1794-1866)

[William Whewell, for twenty-five years Master of Trinity College, Cambridge, was born in 1794 in Lancaster, where his father was a master-carpenter. He was educated at Lancaster, and at the Grammar School at Heversham, where he obtained an exhibition at Trinity College, Cambridge (1811), of which he became Fellow (1817), Tutor (1823), and subsequently Master (1841-66). Whewell, who died at Cambridge in 1866, was Professor of Mineralogy, 1828-32; and Knightsbridge Professor of Moral Philosophy, 1838-55. The most important of his many works was the *History of the Inductive Sciences* (3 vols., 1837) with the sequel, the *Philosophy of the Inductive Sciences* (2 vols., 1840). In the former is an interesting reference to Dante, in connection with 'the motions of up and down.']

1837. HISTORY OF THE INDUCTIVE SCIENCES, FROM THE EARLIEST TO THE PRESENT TIMES.

[Dante's account of his exit from Hell]

AS bearing upon the perplexity which attends the motions of *up* and *down*, when applied to the globular earth and the change of the direction of gravity which would occur in passing the centre, the readers of Dante will recollect the extraordinary manner in which the poet and his guide emerge from the bottom of the abyss; and the explanation which Virgil imparts to him of what he there sees. After they have crept through the aperture in which Lucifer is placed, the poet says,

Io levai gli occhi e credetti vedere
Lucifero com' io l' avea lasciato,
E vidili le gambe in su tenere. . . .

. . . .

Questi come è fitto
Sì sottosopra?

. . . .

Quando mi volsi, tu passasti il punto
Al qual si traggon d' ogni parte i pesi.
Inferno xxxiv. [ll, 88-90, 103-4, 110-11].[2]

[1] [See Batines, *Bibliografia Dantesca*, i. 582 ff., 610 ff.]
[2] [Cary's translation is appended.]

This is more philosophical than Milton's representation, in a more scientific age, of Uriel sliding to the earth on a sun-beam, and sliding back again when the sun had sunk below the horizon.[1]

(Vol. i. pp. 261-2.)

GIUSEPPE MAZZINI

(1805-1872)

[Giuseppe Mazzini was the son of a physician at Genoa, where he was born in 1805. He was educated as a lawyer and practised his profession for some years, but gradually came to devote his energies to literature and to politics. As one of the founders of the 'Young Italy' organization he came into conflict with the government, and in 1837 was obliged to take refuge in London, where he gained his livelihood by writing articles for various reviews, including the *Westminster Review*, the *British and Foreign Review*, and the *Foreign Quarterly Review*. During the revolutionary movements of 1848 he went back to Italy, served under Garibaldi, and defended Rome against the French, until compelled to surrender. Returning to London, he from that time continued to organise risings in Italy, and was several times condemned to death, but when at last Italian unity was accomplished under a monarchy, he refused to take the oath of allegiance. He died at Pisa in 1872, and was buried at Genoa. Mazzini was an enthusiastic admirer of Dante from early youth. His first published essay was on Dante's love of his country, and the articles he contributed to English reviews were many of them on subjects connected with Dante. He also edited Ugo Foscolo's *La Commedia di Dante Allighieri*, which was published in London in four volumes in 1842-3.]

1837. Oct. WESTMINSTER REVIEW. ON ITALIAN LITERATURE SINCE 1830.

[Manzoni's comparison of Monti to Dante]

THE stanza of Manzoni—

Salve o divino a cui largì natura
Il cor di Dante e del suo Duca il canto . . .

which compares Monti to Dante for his soul and to Virgil for his melody, savours more of bitter irony than of the conscientious verdict of one poet on another. Dante would not have flattered in turn the Pope and the Emperor, Austria and the Revolution. Dante would not have sacrificed his art to the outward senses; he would have worshipped her as an angel on whose wings he might elevate his soul to heaven, and bring thence instruction for his fellows. Dante is the founder of a school which has few, very few, representatives in the present day, but whose star will rise again in that hour when the people shall decree the Nationality of Italy.

(*Life and Writings of Mazzini*, vol. ii. pp. 166-7.)

[Foscolo's commentary on the *Divina Commedia*]

Foscolo was perhaps the first who undertook the study and the culture of Dante as of a profound patriot. I say *undertook*, for

[1] [*Par. Lost*, iv. 555-6, 589-92.]

Foscolo did not realise all that he was capable of. The miseries of a life of poverty, wandering, and excitement; the misfortunes of Italy and exile, were always obstacles. But he recognised in Dante more than the poet,—more than the creator of a language; he recognised in him the great citizen—the reformer—the poet of the religion, the prophet of the nationality, of Italy. Where others had amused themselves in dissecting and torturing words, he dived for ideas; where others had admired images, he sought for the feeling which had suggested them. He led criticism on the path of history, refuting all the groundless conjectures which had been heaped on the life and poems of Dante. He annihilated all the crowd of heartless commentators who, without a spark of patriotism, had dared to lay a hand on the work of a man all soul, all knowledge, all patriotism. He drove from the temple the money-changers and the Pharisees. His may not be a perfect commentary on Dante; but he rendered such a work possible.

(*Life and Writings of Mazzini*, vol. ii. pp. 172-3.)

1843. Oct. BRITISH AND FOREIGN REVIEW. ON THE GENIUS AND TENDENCY OF THE WRITINGS OF THOMAS CARLYLE.

[Dante on collective effort]

It matters little that *our* individual powers be of the smallest amount in relation to the object to be attained; it matters little that the result of *our* action be lost in a distance which is beyond our calculation: we know that the powers of millions of men, our brethren, will succeed to the work after us, in the same track,—we know that the object attained, be it when it may, will be the result of *all* our efforts combined. The object—an object to be pursued collectively, an ideal to be realised as far as possible here below by the association of all our faculties and all our powers—'operatio humanae universitatis,' as Dante says in a work little known, or misunderstood, in which five centuries ago, he laid down many of the principles upon which we are labouring at the present day—'ad quam ipsa universitas hominum in tantâ multitudine ordinatur, ad quam quidem operationem nec homo unus, nec domus una, nec vicinia, nec una civitas, nec regnum particulare, pertingere potest;[1]—this alone gives value and method to the life and acts of the individual.

(*Ibid.* vol. iv. p. 83.)

[Dante, and other great men of genius not unconscious of their powers]

Genius is not, generally speaking, unconscious of what it experiences, or of what it is capable. . . . Caesar, Christopher Columbus, were not unconscious: Dante, when, at the opening of the twenty-

[1] *De Monarchia* [Bk. i. Chap. iii. ll. 30-6].

fifth chapter of the *Paradiso*, he hurled at his enemies that sublime menace which commentators without heart and without head have mistaken for a cry of supplication,—Kepler, when he wrote, 'My book will await its reader: has not God waited six thousand years before he created a man to contemplate His works?'[1]—Shakspeare himself, when he wrote—

'And nothing stands . . .
And yet, to times in hope, my verse shall stand'[2]—

these men were not unconscious.

(*Life and Writings of Mazzini* vol. ii. pp. 85-6.)

1844. April. FOREIGN QUARTERLY REVIEW. ESSAY ON DANTE.

[Dante's minor works swamped by the *Commedia*]

Poor Dante! admiration has done him more harm since his death, than ever hatred during his life; it has mutilated the thought that lay below by attaching itself exclusively to its most brilliant surface; it has adored the flame and forgotten the heart; the poet has effaced the man, the inspired speaker, the thinker. Poetry is, however, only the power to symbolise, consecrated to the service of a great thought. As in the case of Milton, the splendour of the poem has thrown the minor works into the shade. The cupola has caused the lower part of the edifice to be forgotten. Lightly regarded even by his contemporaries themselves, they did not meet with a favourable medium, even when the press gave them a more extended circulation. The age of patriots was dead, that of thinkers had not yet arisen. In the midst of the torrent of pedantic, jesuitical, academical literature, which overflowed Italy, the *Divina Commedia* swam above all,—there was within it an eternal spirit of poetry, which no human efforts could destroy: the minor works were overwhelmed.

(*Foreign Quarterly Review*, vol. xxxiii. pp. 5-6.)

[The *Vita Nuova*]

The *Vita Nuova*, which Dante wrote most probably at the age of eight-and-twenty, and in which he relates both in prose and verse the emotions of his love for Beatrice, is an inimitable little book of gentleness, purity, delicacy, of sweet and sad thoughts,—loving as the note of the dove, ethereal as the perfume of flowers; and that pen, which in later years resembled a sword in the hands of Dante, here delineates their aspect, as Raphael might have done with his pencil. There are pages—those, for example, where is related the dream of the death of Beatrice—the prose of which is a finished model of language and style far beyond the best pages of

[1] *Harmonices Mundi*, libri quinque. [2] *Sonnets*, 60.

Boccaccio. There are sonnets in our opinion, far beyond the most admired of Petrarch's, almost untranslateable, so exquisite are they in their construction, and so purely Italian in their harmony. Shelley alone could have succeeded. At present we think that the task of translating the *Vita Nuova* can be confided only to the soul of a woman.

(*Foreign Quarterly Review*, vol. xxxiii. pp. 12-3.)

[How the author of the *Vita Nuova* came to write the *Inferno*]

Dante had too much greatness in his soul, and too much pride it may be, to make revenge a personal matter—he had nothing but contempt for his own enemies, and never, except in the case of Boniface VIII., whom it was necessary to punish in the name of religion and of Italy, did he place a single one of his enemies in the Inferno—not even his judge, Cante Gabrielli. The 'non ragioniam di lor ma guarda e passa,'[1] which in the beginning of his poem he applies to those who have been worthy neither of heaven nor hell, appears to have been his own rule towards his enemies. Strong in love and strong in hatred, it is never love of himself nor hatred of others. Life appeared to him with too few charms for him to attach much importance to anything personal; it was the love of right and hatred of wrong that animated him. . . . The point about which he concerned himself was not the length or shortness of life, not happiness or misery;—it was the end for which life was given. He felt all there was of divine and creative in action, he wrote as he would have acted, and the pen in his hand became, as we have said, like a sword—and it is in truth a sword that he places in the hand of Homer, the sovereign poet.[2] He wrestled, when it was against nothing else, with himself—against the wanderings of his understanding[3]—against the fire of the poet[4]—against the fury of his passions. The purification of heart by which he passed from the hell of struggle to the heaven of victory, to the calm of peace by the sacrifice of hope from his earthly life—'In violenta e disperata pace'—is admirably shown in this poem where so many things are shown. With a character such as we have sketched, haughty, disdainful, untameable—as the opinion of his contemporaries, even through imaginary anecdotes, tells us—looking upon himself as belonging to the small number of privileged beings endowed with high understanding, and worthy of the communion of the Holy Spirit—less calculated and intended to be governed by laws, than to control them—Dante evidently was one of those men who pass unscathed and erect through the most critical conjunctures

[1] [*Inf.* iii. 51.]
[2] [*Inf.* iv. 86 ff.]
[3] [*Inf.* xxvi. 21.]
[4] [*Purg.* xxxiii. 141.]

and never bow the knee except to the principle that works within. That power he adored with a trembling and religious fervour—*Deus fortior*;—he had experienced every frame of mind that passes, from the moment when a *thought* appears for the first time in the soul's horizon, down to that when it incarnates itself in the man, takes possession of all his faculties, and cries to him, 'Thou art mine.'

It was the *dust of the diamond*—the hidden, mysterious pain of Genius, so real, and yet, from its very nature, understood by so few—the torment of catching a glimpse of the ideal, the impossible to be realised in this life—the Titanic dreams of an Italy, at the head of the movement of humanity, an angel of light among the nations—contrasted with the reality of an Italy divided within herself, deprived of her temporal head, and betrayed by her spiritual head—coveted by all strangers, and too often prostituting herself to them—the strength to guide men towards good, and from circumstances and the sway of egotistical passions, no one to be guided—fightings within, between faith and doubt;—it was all these that changed the author of the *Vita Nuova* into the writer of the Inferno—the young angel of peace and gentle poetry, whose features Giotto has preserved to us, into the Dante with whom we are familiar, the Dante come back from hell.

(*Foreign Quarterly Review*, vol. xxxiii. pp. 28-9.)

THOMAS WADE

(1805-1875)

[Thomas Wade, poet and journalist, was born at Woodbridge, Suffolk, in 1805. At an early age he developed a poetical talent, and in 1825 he published the first of many volumes of poems and dramas. In 1845-6 he made a translation of the *Inferno* in the metre of the original, of which a specimen (*Inf.* xxxiv. 127-39) was printed by H. Buxton Forman (the owner of the MS.) in *Literary Anecdotes of the Nineteenth Century* (vol. i. p. 65). Wade, who for some time edited 'Bell's Weekly Messenger,' and the Jersey 'British Press,' died in Jersey in 1875.]

1837. THE CONTENTION OF LOVE AND DEATH.

[Death and Dante]

BE meek and dumb!
I tell thee that his hour is come:
And as for Sorrowers, what are they
But dust beneath my trampling way?
And, say, if Song were aught to me,
Think'st thou that I, whose strong decree
Swept Homer from Ionian air

When his allotted days were run,
And Dante from Italia's sun
When all his griefs accomplished were;
Down-looking Chaucer from his theme,
And Spenser from his Faery dream,
And Shakspeare from his own great world,
And Milton from his starr'd-throne, hurl'd,
Ere their fames were half-unfurl'd. . . .
Think'st thou that I, whose mission strong
Hath reach'd these mighty spirits of Song—
Or soon will reach—can pause for him?
Amid these suns a taper dim,
A mortal babe 'mid Seraphim!

(ll. 200 ff.)

J. H. HIPPISLEY

(fl. 1830)

1837. CHAPTERS ON EARLY ENGLISH LITERATURE.

[Historical value of the *Divina Commedia*]

IT has been justly observed that the 'Commedia' of Dante supplies a valuable commentary on the history of his times. To lovers of political history, the Italian poet is indeed full of interest, as exhibiting to view, and as placing before them in action, the most conspicuous characters of his age; but those who are studious rather of what concerns the moral and intellectual condition of mankind, will derive a yet more ample fund of instruction from the works of Chaucer. Dante paints individuals; Chaucer, if we combine his minor poems with his great work, an entire nation.

(*Introduction*, p. ix.)

[Dante, Chaucer, and the *Roman de la Rose*]

The translation of the 'Roman de la Rose,' which engaged Chaucer's youthful days, seems to have given a direction to his later compositions. Allegorical description, devotion to love, satire on women, and satire on the clergy, form at once the leading topics of the 'Rose,' and of Chaucer's original poetical works. As regards the prevalence of the form of the vision in poetry, the popularity of the French poem may be considered as amongst the leading causes of this general practice. Dante, who was born shortly after the composition of the earlier portion of the 'Rose,' is one of the first to follow in the track. In Italy, the 'Rose' continued a favourite work till the days of Petrarch, who professed to despise it.

(pp. 20-1.)

[The picturesqueness of Dante]

The term picturesque may, in poetry, be extended generally to the description of external nature, as opposed to that of moral qualities. The poet may be said to be picturesque, when his object is, not to unfold the heart of man, but merely to present an image or picture; and this, not merely when the imitation is of objects natural and real, but even when the poet is at once the creator of the original, and the portrayer of the resemblance. Dante is not less a picturesque poet, because the scene of his Commedia is removed from the visible world to one of his own creation. Amongst the modern names, Ariosto and Spenser, who both wander into all the extravagances of romantic fiction, are for ever picturesque poets.

(pp. 125-6.)

SYDNEY SMITH

(1771-1845)

[Sydney Smith was born at Woodford in Essex in 1771. He was educated at Winchester, and New College, Oxford, of which he became Fellow in 1791. He took orders in 1794. From 1798 till 1803 he resided with pupils in Edinburgh, where in March, 1802, he proposed to Jeffrey and Brougham to start the *Edinburgh Review*, of which he was the first editor. He remained a contributor for twenty-five years during which he wrote nearly eighty articles for the review. In 1803 he went to London, and soon became one of the Whig habitués of Holland House. In 1807 he published anonymously the *Plymley Letters* in defence of Catholic emancipation. From 1806 to 1829 he held the living of Foston in Yorkshire. In 1828 he was made a prebendary of Bristol by Lord Lyndhurst, and in 1831 Lord Grey appointed him Canon-residentiary of St. Paul's. He died in London in 1845. Sydney Smith is said to have taken to the study of Dante in his old age. Some remarks of his concerning the punishments of the *Inferno* have been preserved by his eldest daughter, the wife of Sir Henry Holland. It is recorded of him that once at a breakfast party at the house of Samuel Rogers, in a fit of exasperation at Macaulay's ceaseless flow of talk, he exclaimed, 'I wish I could write poetry like you, Rogers. I would write an *Inferno*, and I would put Macaulay amongst a number of disputants and gag him!' (*Life and Times of Sydney Smith*, by S. J. Reid, ed. 1884, p. 342).]

c. 1838. CONVERSATION OF SYDNEY SMITH, RECORDED BY HIS DAUGHTER, LADY HOLLAND.

[Inadequacy of Dante's tortures in the *Inferno*]

AT Mr. Romilly's[1] there arose a discussion on the Inferno of Dante, and the tortures he had invented. 'He may be a great poet,' said my father, 'but as to inventing tortures, I consider him a mere bungler,—no imagination, no knowledge of

[1] [John, afterwards (1865) first Baron Romilly.]

the human heart. If I had taken it in hand, I would show you what torture really was; for instance (turning, merrily, to his old friend Mrs. Marcet[1]), you should be doomed to listen, for a thousand years, to conversations betwen Caroline[2] and Emily,[3] where Caroline should always give wrong explanations in chemistry, and Emily in the end be unable to distinguish an acid from an alkali. You, Macaulay, let me consider?—oh, you should be dumb. False dates and facts of the reign of Queen Anne should for ever be shouted in your ears; all liberal and honest opinions should be ridiculed in your presence; and you should not be able to say a single word during that period in their defence.'—'And what would you condemn me to, Mr. Sydney?' said a young mother. 'Why, you should for ever see those three sweet little girls of yours on the point of falling downstairs, and never be able to save them. There, what tortures are there in Dante equal to these.'

(*Memoir of Rev. Sydney Smith* by his daughter, Lady Holland, vol. i. p. 268.)

A. D. LEMON

(fl. 1830)

1838. IN this year A. D. Lemon exhibited at the British Institution a picture with the following title:—

Paolo and Francesca.
'That day we read no more.'
Vide Dante, Inferno.[4]

(*Catalogue of the Exhibition of the British Institution*, 1838, No. 368.)

RICHARD WESTMACOTT

(1799-1872)

[Richard Westmacott, sculptor, eldest son of the sculptor of the same name, was born in London in 1799. He entered the school of the Royal Academy in 1818, and in 1820 he went to Italy to study, where he remained for six years. Westmacott exhibited at the Academy from 1827 to 1855, among his exhibits being a marble group of Paolo and Francesca (1838). He was elected R.A. in 1849; and was Professor of Sculpture at the Royal Academy, in succession to his father, from 1857 to 1867. He died in London in 1872.]

[1] [Mrs. Jane Marcet (1769-1858), writer of popular scientific text-books.]
[2] [Mrs. John Romilly.]
[3] [Sydney Smith's second daughter.]
[4] [*Inf.* v. 138 (Cary).]

1838. IN this year Westmacott exhibited at the Royal Academy a marble group with the following title:—

Paolo and Francesca, an alto-relievo in marble.[1]
'Que' duo che insieme vanno
E pajon sì al vento esser leggieri.

Nulla speranza li conforta mai
Non che di posa, ma di minor pene.'
Dante, Inferno, Canto 5.[2]

(*Catalogue of the Exhibition of the Royal Academy*, 1838. No. 1276.)

EDWIN GUEST

(1800-1880)

[Edwin Guest (born at King's Norton, Worcestershire, in 1800), was educated at Birmingham Grammar School, and Caius College, Cambridge, of which he was elected Fellow in 1824. He was called to the bar in 1828, and after practising for some years abandoned law for literature. His best-known work is *A History of English Rhythms*, published in 1838, which contains an incidental reference to Dante in connection with Arnaut Daniel, the inventor of the *Sestina*. Guest, who was largely instrumental in founding the Philological Society, was elected Master of Caius College in 1852, and held the office until shortly before his death in 1880.]

1838. A HISTORY OF ENGLISH RHYTHMS.

[Dante and the inventor of the 'sestine-stave']

THERE is a curious stave, which should be noticed, if it were only for the celebrity it once possessed throughout Europe —I mean the *Sestine-stave*, invented by Arnaut Daniel, the Troubadour eulogised by Dante[3] and Petrarch.[4] The stave consisted of six verses, which had no rhime, but the same final syllables were used in all the staves; and the order was so regulated, that each of the final syllables, in its turn, closed the stanza. Spenser has left us an example.

Ye wasteful woods bear witnesse of my woe,
Wherein my plaints did oftentimes resound:
Ye careless birds are privy to my cryes,
Which, in your songs, were wont to make a part:
Thou pleasant spring hast lull'd me oft asleep,
Whose streames my trickling tears did oft augment.

[1] [This group, which was executed for the Marquis of Lansdowne, is in the collection of the present Marquis at Bowood, Wiltshire.]
[2] [*Inf.* v. 74-5, 34-5.]
[3] [*Purg.* xxvi. 142; *V. E.* ii. 2, 6, 10, 13.]
[4] [In the *Trionfo d' Amore*, iv. 38-42.]

Resort of people doth my grief augment,
The walled towns do work me greater woe,
The forest wide is fitter to resound
The hollow echo of my careful cryes;
I hate the house, since thence my love did part,
Whose wailful want debars my eyes of sleep, &c.

Of course these changes would be exhausted with the sixth stave, and then came the Envoi of these verses, containing all the six syllables.

And you that feel no *woe*, when as the *sound*
Of these my nightly *cryes*, ye bear a*part*,
Let break your sounder *sleep*, and pity 'aug*ment*.

Celebrity was cheaply purchased, when an invention such as this could ensure it! [1]

(Vol. ii. pp. 372-3.)

RICHARD MONCKTON MILNES

(1809-1885)

[Richard Monckton Milnes, afterwards Lord Houghton, was born in London in 1809. In 1827 he went as a fellow-commoner to Trinity College, Cambridge (M.A. 1831), where he was intimate with Tennyson, Hallam, Thackeray, and other distinguished men of his time. After leaving Cambridge Milnes travelled for several years in Germany and Italy (1832-5). On his return to England he settled in London, and soon became a prominent figure in society. In 1837 he was elected M.P. for Pontefract, which he represented in six parliaments, until 1863, when he was created a peer as Baron Houghton. He died at Vichy in 1885. Milnes had strong literary tastes and was always ready to forward the interests of literature and of literary aspirants. He published numerous works, the best known of which, the *Life and Letters of Keats*, was first issued in 1848. In his *Poems of Many Years* (1838) he included a poem called the *Vision of Dante*, which is a blank verse rendering of an episode (related in prose by Dante) in the *Vita Nuova* (§ 23).]

1838. DANTE'S VISION. FROM THE 'VITA NUOVA.' [2]

[Dante's dream of the death of Beatrice]

WITH a deep sigh, I whispered to myself,
'It must be in Necessity, one day,
That the most gentle Beatrice shall die;'
And instantly such utter loss of sense
Came on me, that my eyes were closed,—my mind
Began to work, like one delirium-bound,
And its imaginations thus to frame.

[1] [Dante himself wrote several *sestine*, in imitation of Arnaut Daniel.]
[2] [An almost literal translation of *Vita Nuova*, § 23, ll. 16-83.]

In the first wande'ring of my phantasy,
Came certain female faces, with long hair
Dishevelled, telling me, 'Thou too shalt die.'
Then certain faces after these appeared,
Different,—terrible to gaze upon,—
Which same addrest me, saying, 'Thou art dead.'
Thus, from my phantasy's first wanderings,
I came at last to be—I knew not where,
And beheld ladies walking, with long hair
Dishevelled—walking marvellously sad;
I saw the sun grow dark, so that the stars
Appeared, and of such tint, that I could judge,
They were lamenting over some one dead,
And mighty earthquakes were about to be.
In such imaginations wondering,
And not without a sense of fear, I thought
Some friend came to me, saying, 'From this world
Thy admirable Ladie' has past away.'

Then I began to weep right piteously;
And not alone in phantasy I wept,
But with my eyes bathed in their own true tears.
While Heaven-ward I imagined that I gazed,
And seemed to see an Angel-multitude
Returning upwards, and before them spread
Was a small cloud of the most perfect white;
It seemed to me I heard those Angels sing
Gracefully sweet, and of the words they spoke,
I listened these,—'Osanna in excelsis'!
Other than these I did not seem to hear.
Then said to me the heart so full of love,
'Is the thing true,—lieth our Ladie dead?'
For this, it seemed, I went to see the form
In which had dwelt that noblest blessèd soul.
My wandering phantasy, become so strong,
Showed me that Ladie dead,—while ladies seemed
To cover up her head with a white veil:
Such gentle aspect bore her face, methought
It said, 'I look upon the Prince of Peace.'[1]
Thus thinking, such deep lowliness of spirit
Seized on me, that, to see my Ladie' again,
I called on Death to come and take me, saying,
'Come thou to me, who yearneth earnestly
For thee, and see I wear thy colour now.'

[1] [A mistranslation—the original is 'principio della pace,' 'the beginning of peace.']

And when I had beheld consummated
All mournful offices, which for the dead
Use sanctions, I returned, it seemed to me,
Into my room, and there lookt straight to heaven;
And such was the imaginative force,
That I began, loud wailing, to exclaim,
'Most beauteous Spirit! how blest is he who sees Thee!'

(*Poems of Many Years*, pp. 186-8.)

GEORGE BOWYER

(1811-1883)

[George Bowyer, writer on jurisprudence, eldest son of Sir George Bowyer, Bart., was born at Radley Park, near Abingdon, Berkshire, in 1811. He was called to the bar in 1839, and practised as an equity draughtsman and conveyancer. In 1850 he become a Roman Catholic, and two years later entered Parliament as member for Dundalk, for which he sat until 1868. He afterwards sat for Wexford County (1874-80). Bowyer succeeded to the baronetcy in 1860, and died in the Temple in 1883. His earliest publication was a *Dissertation on the Statutes of the Cities of Italy* (1838), accompanied by a translation of the pleading of Prospero Farinacio in defence of Beatrice Cenci, which contains references to Dante.]

1838. A DISSERTATION ON THE STATUTES OF THE CITIES OF ITALY; AND A TRANSLATION OF THE PLEADING OF PROSPERO FARINACIO IN DEFENCE OF BEATRICE CENCI.

[Many of the cities of Italy under a single ruler in Dante's day]

IN most of the Italian republics democracy, oligarchy, and tyranny succeeded each other alternately. In the fourteenth and fifteenth centuries the two latter preponderated greatly throughout Italy. The government of a single lord, usually a successful party leader or adventurer, was, however, very prevalent at a much earlier period, for Dante (Purg. l. 6) says,

Chè le città d' Italia tutte piene
Son di tiranni, e un Marcel diventa
Ogni villan che parteggiando viene.[1]

(*Dissertation*, p. 23.)

[Dante's reference to Averroes' commentary on Aristotle]

Bartolus of Sassoferrato was the first who commented copiously upon the text of the imperial law, and applied to jurisprudence the Aristotelic method and philosophy; but his writings are deeply imbued with the scholastic pedantry, and fanciful and innumerable

[1] [*Purg.* vi. 124-6.]

distinctions of the Arabian School of Aristotelians, who studied that author by means of the comment of Averroes, which at that time was of paramount authority, and is called by Dante *il gran comento* (Inferno, cant. iv. l. 144).

(*Defence of Beatrice Cenci*, p. 82 note.)

ANONYMOUS

1839. Oct. QUARTERLY REVIEW. ART. VI. MERIVALE'S POEMS.

[Merivale's translations from Dante]

MR. MERIVALE[1] has now for the first time given a series of specimens after the Latin and Italian poets . . . the version of the descent into Hell in the Aeneid—several canzonets and sonnets from Petrarch, Boccaccio, &c. and various episodes of Dante. Mr. Merivale modestly protests against any invidious comparison of these last with the corresponding pages in complete versions of the *Divina Commedia*; and it is true that there would be some unfairness in subjecting the authors of those laborious performances to such a scrutiny. We have here, no doubt, what of many experiments seemed to Mr. Merivale himself after the lapse of years, most successful. He intimates, too, that he had never designed a complete translation, but only handled parts of surpassing excellence, with the view of introducing them into a projected Life of Dante. The truth is, however, that, having very lately compared the versions of Cary and Wright pretty minutely, and quoted largely from both,[2] we should not on this occasion have thought it necessary to recur to Mr. Merivale's predecessors; nor shall we now say more than that in our opinion he has, as to the ground he does traverse, excelled them both. He, like Mr. Wright, adopts the *terza rima* of the original, but he does not follow the example of avoiding its chief difficulty, and consequently, as we think, its chief beauty. In short, his tercets have, like Dante's, the interlinking rhyme. We must give one of these exquisite episodes, and we take that of Paolo and Francesca, . . . partly because the subject has lately been rendered into the language of another art, in one of the most graceful and, we are scarcely afraid to add, *the most pathetic* of relievos. . . .[3] The episode has never before had so good an English dress.[4]

(Vol. lxiv. pp. 407 ff.)

[1] [See above, pp. 190 ff.]
[2] [See above, pp. 574-6.]
[3] We believe Mr. Westmacott's marble is now in the collection of Lord Lansdowne. [The group of 'Paolo and Francesca,' executed for the Marquis of Lansdowne, was exhibited at the Royal Academy in 1838. It is now at Bowood (see above, p. 631).]
[4] [Merivale's rendering of *Inf.* v. 25-142, is here quoted by the reviewer.]

CHARLES H. TIMPERLEY

(1794-c. 1846)

[Charles H. Timperley, printer and writer on typography, was born in Manchester, 1794. In 1810 he enlisted, and after being wounded at Waterloo, received his discharge. In 1821 he became a printer. In 1833 he published *Songs of the Press*, and in 1839 a *Dictionary of Printers and Printing*, which contains a brief account of Dante. He died in London about 1846.]

1839. A DICTIONARY OF PRINTERS AND PRINTING, WITH THE PROGRESS OF LITERATURE, ANCIENT AND MODERN.

[The biographical notice of Dante contained in this work (pp. 66-8), consists of a short sketch of Dante's political career, together with the anecdote of Dante and the buffoon (from the *Res Memorandae* of Petrarch) at the court of Can Grande at Verona.]

CARLO BEOLCHI

(fl. 1830)

1839. FIORI POETICI SCELTI ED ILLUSTRATI DA CARLO BEOLCHI, LL.D.

[This volume, which is dedicated to the Duchess of Roxburghe, was published in London by Rolandi. Pages 1-63 are devoted to Dante, viz. *Vita di Dante*, pp. 1-29; and *Poesie di Dante*, pp. 29-63. The latter are represented by three sonnets, viz. *Son.* xi. (*V. N.* § 21) 'Negli occhi porta la mia donna amore;' *Son.* xv. (*V. N.* § 26) 'Tanto gentile e tanto onesta pare;' and *Son.* xvi. (*V. N.* § 27) 'Vede perfettamente ogni salute;' by three canzoni, viz. *Canz.* i. (*V. N.* § 19) 'Donne ch' avete intelletto d' amore'; *Canz.* ii. (*V. N.* § 23) 'Donna pietosa e di novella etate;' and *Canz.* xviii. 'O patria degna di trïonfal fama;' and by the following selections from the *Divina Commedia*, viz. *Inf.* iii. 1-9; v. 70-142; xiii. 1-143; xxxiii. 1-90; *Purg.* iii. 79-84; viii. 1-6; *Par.* xxvii. 1-9, 16-66.]

ENGLISH EDITIONS OF THE *DIVINA COMMEDIA*

1839. LA DIVINA COMMEDIA DI DANTE ALIGHIERI. EDIMBURGO. 24MO.

[Published by A. & C. Black, edited by G. Rampini, forming part of a Biblioteca Classica Italiana. This is the seventh edition of the *Commedia* printed and published in England (previous editions appeared in 1808, 1819, 1819-20, 1822-3, and 1827. This edition, of which there is a copy in the Cornell University Collection, is not registered either in Colomb de Batines, or in the British Museum Catalogue.]

1840. LA DIVINA COMMEDIA DI DANTE ALIGHIERI. EDIMBURGO. 24MO.

[Published (according to De Batines) by Andrew Moffart (*sic*), and forming vol. iv. of 'Rampini's edition of Italian Classics, for the use of Schools.' This edition, of which there is no copy in the British Museum or in the Cornell Collection, is perhaps a reissue of the preceding.]

ANONYMOUS

1840. ITALY AND THE ITALIANS. BY FREDERIC VON RAUMER.[1]

[Dante in love three times]

VENICE. April 9. 1839. I was yesterday introduced at the Ateneo, a kind of Venetian Academy. Professor Paravia, from Turin, read an interesting and well written essay on Dante, and proved:—that Beatrice was not merely a creature of imagination, but a maiden with whose memory, particularly after her death, Dante associated much that was beautiful and allegorical. And why should she not appear to him as the picture and conception of all that was wise and good? The lecturer likewise proved that Dante, notwithstanding the severity of his character, and his imaginative fidelity, was in love at least three times in his life, and in support of this trio of all good things there appeared to be no lack of arguments. M. Paravia dwelt also on the difficulty of distinguishing Dante's genuine lyrics from the spurious ones that went under his name; but even the genuine ones, he maintained, would not place the poet more than on a level with many of the lyric writers of his own time. The *Commedia Divina* it was that first enabled Dante to step into a higher sphere, and to make it his own.

(Vol. i. p. 35.)

[Alfieri and Dante]

Florence. June 11. 1839. . . . Is Alfieri a native Italian plant, indigenous to the soil and climate? I am well aware that he was born in Italy and wrote Italian; but to me he appears to be an entirely foreign production, an exotic plant, which is tended and nursed, and is by no means thoroughly Italian, like Dante and Macchiavelli. . . . When I stated as a fact, that the other great poets of Italy were known and esteemed in Germany, that Goldoni was frequently represented, and even Gozzi found acceptance, but Alfieri nowhere excited admiration or even interest—this fact of course served for a proof of the continuance of northern barbarism, and — — — insisted that in six hundred years the world will discover that Alfieri is as great a poet as Dante. . . . There are distinguished writers whom it is extremely difficult for foreigners to understand, and out of courtesy one might class Alfieri among them. But how is it that among us the much more difficult Dante is understood?

(Vol. ii. pp. 10-2.)

[1] [Friedrich Ludwig Georg von Raumer (1781-1873), German historian; the above is an anonymous translation of his *Italien, Beiträge zur Kenntniss dieses Landes*, published in the same year.]

PHILIP BURY DUNCAN

(1772-1863)

[Philip Bury Duncan was born in 1772 at South Warnborough, Hampshire, where his father was rector. He was educated at Winchester, and at New College, Oxford, of which he became Fellow in 1792. He was called to the bar in 1796. In 1826 he was appointed Keeper of the Ashmolean Museum at Oxford, which office he held until 1855. He died near Bath in 1863, aged 91. Among his publications was a volume of *Essays and Miscellanea* (1840), containing an essay on the choice of subjects in painting, in which he remarks on the wealth of material furnished to artists by the *Divina Commedia* and other great poems.]

1840. ESSAYS AND MISCELLANEA.

[The *Divina Commedia* as a mine for artists]

ARTISTS of all kinds require to be warned against representing impossibilities and incongruities. . . . It may be, however, difficult in this case to draw an exact line between the admissible and the inadmissible. Some of Guido's and Domenichino's angels, and Michael Angelo's devils, and Fuseli's, and Richter's, and Martin's illustrations of Shakespeare and Milton, Flaxman's of Aeschylus, and Coch's[1] of Dante, are well calculated to fire the imagination, and to illustrate the pages of the most powerful of poets. . . .

Of dramatic poetry, Aeschylus, Sophocles, Euripides, have supplied many subjects; but no one of them, nor perhaps all united, as many as were drawn from our great poet to fill the Shakespeare gallery. As to heroic poetry, Homer, Virgil, Ovid, Dante, Ariosto, Tasso, Chaucer, and Milton, have all proved mines from which the painters have dug precious ore, on which to stamp their images of human life.

(*Choice of Subjects in Painting*, vol. i. pp. 7-8, 32.)

SEYMOUR STOCKER KIRKUP

(1788-1880)

[Seymour Stocker Kirkup was the son of a jeweller and diamond merchant in London, where he was born in 1788. He was admitted a student at the Royal Academy in 1809, and in 1811 he gained a medal. At this time he made the acquaintance of Blake, and of B. R. Haydon, with the latter of whom he corresponded for many years. In 1816 Kirkup went to Italy, and eventually settled in

[1] [Josef Anton Koch (1768-1839). Many of his illustrations of Dante are at present in Vienna; while a collection of 40 sepia drawings illustrating the *Inferno*, and one or two cantos of the *Purgatorio*, which were made originally for Dr. Nott (see above, p. 205), and eventually came into the possession of King John of Saxony, are preserved at Dresden.]

Florence. While living at Rome he was present in 1821 at the funeral of Keats, and in 1822 at that of Shelley. He was a devoted student of Dante, and was one of the few enthusiasts who accepted Gabriele Rossetti's fantastic scheme of Dantesque interpretation—a compliment which Rossetti returned by dedicating to him his *Mistero dell' Amor Platonico del Medio Evo* published in 1840.[1] Kirkup was largely instrumental in discovering the famous Giotto portrait of Dante in the chapel of the Palazzo del Podestà (now the Bargello) at Florence in July, 1840, and it is to his devotion that the world owes the preservation of a faithful copy of the original, before it was irretrievably ruined by the hand of the 'restorer.' Kirkup wrote two most interesting letters to Rossetti, describing the discovery, and sending him a drawing and a tracing of the portrait from which he made a facsimile.[2] The tracing Rossetti gave to his son, Dante Gabriel Rossetti, after whose death it was sold. The facsimile came into the possession of the fifth Lord Vernon, well-known for his devotion to the study of Dante, and by his permission it was reproduced in chromo-lithography by the Arundel Society. Kirkup, who also made some of the designs for the illustration of Lord Vernon's splendid edition of the *Inferno*, published in 3 vols. folio in 1858-65, was in 1861, on the restoration of the Italian kingdom, created for his services a Cavaliere di San Maurizio e Lazzaro, on the strength of which he subsequently styled himself, and was known by the title of, 'Barone.' In 1872 he went to reside at Leghorn, where he died in 1880, at the age of 92.]

1840. Sept. 12. LETTER TO GABRIELE ROSSETTI (from Florence).

[Discovery of Giotto's portrait of Dante]

I HAVE delayed writing in the hopes of sending you a sketch which will interest you, but I have hitherto been disappointed. We have made a discovery of an original portrait of Dante in fresco by Giotto! Although I was a *magna pars* in this undertaking, the Jacks in Office have not allowed me yet to make a copy. *Sono tanto gelosi*, most likely afraid I should publish it, and prevent some friends of their own reaping all the profit they hope from that speculation.

I was the person who first mentioned to Sig. Bezzi,[3] a Piedmontese and friend of Carlo Eastlake's,[4] the existence of the portrait under the whitewash of three centuries. We were joined by an American,[5] and we three undertook at our expense to employ a restorer[6] to uncover the walls of the old chapel in the palace of the Podestà in search of the portrait—mentioned by F. Villani, Filelfo, L. Aretino, Vasari, Cinelli, &c. Nothing but the constancy and talent of Sig. Bezzi could have overcome the numberless obstacles and refusals we met with. He wrote and spoke with the persuasions of an advocate, and persevered with the obstinacy and activity of an Englishman[7] (which I believe he now is). He alone

[1] [See above, pp. 446-7.]

[2] [See also a letter from Kirkup published in the *Spectator*, May 11, 1850, in which he gives further details. Extracts from this letter are printed below, p. 642 note.]

[3] [Giovanni Aubrey Bezzi.]

[4] [Charles (afterwards Sir Charles) Lock Eastlake.]

[5] [Richard Henry Wilde—see T. W. Koch, *Dante in America*, pp. 23-36.]

[6] [Marini, who afterwards retouched the face.]

[7] [Bezzi had spent many years as an exile in England.]

was the cause of success. We should have had no chance without him. At last, after uncovering enough of three walls to ascertain it was not there, the Government took the task into their own hands, on our terms, with the same restorer, and in the fifth wall they have succeeded. The number of walls is six, for the chapel has been divided in two—(magazines of wine, oil, bread, &c. for the prisoners).

The precise date of the painting is not known. The poet looks about 28—very handsome—*un Apollo colle fattezze di Dante.* The expression and character are worthy of the subject, and much beyond what I expected from Giotto. Raphael might own it with honour. Add to which it is not the mask of a corpse of 56—a ruin—but a fine, noble image of the Hero of Campaldino, the Lover of Beatrice. The costume very interesting—no beard or even a lock of hair. A white cap, over which a white capuccio, lined with dark red showing the edge turned back. A parchment book under his arm—perhaps the Vita Nuova. It is in a group of many others—one seems Charles II. of Naples. Brunetto Latini and Corso Donati are mentioned by the old authors.

(*Gabriele Rossetti: A versified Autobiography*; ed. by W. M. Rossetti, 1901, pp. 145-6.[1])

1841. Sept. 14. LETTER TO GABRIELE ROSSETTI (from Florence).

[Tracings of Giotto's portrait of Dante]

By the time you receive this, I hope that the portrait of Dante, for you, will be in London. The gentleman who has taken charge of it was in such haste to leave the country (from the consequences of a fatal duel) that I had not an opportunity for writing. You will receive, in fact, three portraits. They are as follows:—

No. 1. A drawing in chalk, on light-brown paper, of the face as large as the original. I had intended to write a memorandum on it, but in my hurry it was forgotten. Perhaps you would have the kindness to add it, if you think it worth while—viz.

'Drawn by S. K., and traced with talc, on the original fresco by Giotto; discovered in the Chapel of the Palazzo del Podestà, Florence, on the 21st July 1840, before it was retouched.'

No. 2. A small sketch in water-colours, giving the colours of the dress, and the heads supposed to be of Corso Donati and Brunetto Latini.

No. 3. A lithography by the painter and restorer Marini, who uncovered the painting. This is made on a tracing by himself.

[1] [The extracts from this letter and from those of Sept. 14, 1841, and Feb. 5, 1843, are reprinted by kind permission of Mr. W. M. Rossetti and of Messrs. Sands & Co.]

I thought it useful to send you these in order to give you a better idea of this very interesting discovery—Dante, under 30 years of age. With respect to No. 1, it is fixed with glue-water, and will not rub out with common usage. The only thing it is liable to is the cracking or bending of the paper, which sometimes in a face alters the expression.

Since I drew it, I have had the mortification to see the original retouched, and its beauty destroyed. You will perceive that the eye is wanting. A deep hole in the wall was found exactly on that spot, as if done on purpose. It was necessary to fill it that it might not extend further: not content, they ordered Sig. Marini to paint the eye on it, and he has daubed over the face in many parts, to the ruin of its expression and character. It is now 15 years older, a mean, pinched expression, and an effeminate character, compared to what it was. It is not quite so bad as the lithography I send you, but not far from it. When I saw what was done, I asked a young man, his assistant, if it was done with colours in tempera, and he assured me, with a boast, that it was in bon fresco. If so, Dante is gone for good. But I have still hopes that he spoke only of the eye, and many of my friends think it can only be accomplished on the old and hard painting by some distemper colour of glue, size, or egg; and, if so, a damp cloth fixed on it for half an hour will bring it all away without injuring the original fresco. I mean to take my time, and perhaps some day I may restore Dante to himself a second time. I had the principal part in the late discovery.

The lithography I send you is exceedingly unlike and incorrect, although a tracing. In shading and finishing he has totally lost and changed the outline, if he ever had it. It is vulgar, old, and effeminate—the contrary in every respect to the original. The Florentines of to-day cannot draw, nor even trace. Think of what such a hand would do, if allowed to paint over it! and that has been the case. It is a misfortune when the direction of the fine arts is in the hands of an ignorant man, chosen only for his *Nobility!*[1] Our Direttore with his cleaners has been the ruin of paintings in the Galleries, since I have been here, to the value of £60,000 or £80,000 sterling—and the money is the least part of the loss.

When I mentioned to you that my drawing was a secret, I only meant that, if known here that I obtained access to make a tracing by bribery, it would compromise those who assisted me. You are welcome to show it to whom you plesse, and *do whatever you wish with it.* But I recommend you not to give it away, for it is the *only* copy that has been made to my knowledge before the fresco

[1] [The Marchese Nerli.]

was retouched, except the miserable lithography which I send; and, if so bad a copy was produced by the help of tracing, and from the original in its pure state, nothing very good is to be expected in future. The eye in the said lithography was, of course, added by the copier. You will perceive by my drawing that the outline (the eyelash) remained, which was fortunate, as it gives the exact situation of the feature.[1]

(*Gabriele Rossetti: A versified Autobiography*; ed. by W. M. Rossetti, 1901, pp. 147-9)

1842. Jan. 4. LETTER TO BENJAMIN ROBERT HAYDON (from Florence).

[Dante 'three worlds of himself']

I am out of the world. I am very happy, perhaps more so than if I were in your volcano. I hear of nothing that makes me regret my present retirement. But I am not alone. Surrounded by the old masters, and the finest monuments in the land of Dante, Machiavelli, Buonarrotti, and Galileo, I am living with two dogs and a great collection of books. I now and then paint, a humble attempt, generally when I want some relique or MSS. beyond my purse. . . . My great resource and constant companion is Dante. He is a world of himself, or rather three worlds, and what worlds!

(*Correspondence of B. R. Haydon*, vol. ii. p. 177.)

[1] [About the same time Kirkup wrote an interesting account (in Italian) of the discovery of the portrait to G. B. Cavalcaselle, a translation of which was subsequently published in the *Spectator* for May 11, 1850. In this account (the translation of which was corrected by Cavalcaselle in the *Spectator* for July 13, 1850) Kirkup says:—'I went among the first to see the portrait. What a pity! the eye of the beautiful profile was wanting. There was a hole an inch deep or an inch and a half. Marini said it was a nail. It did precisely seem the damage of a nail drawn out; and so I suspect it was done instead of cutting off the nail. But I have no proofs of that. The hole remained for a year, nothwithstanding that I prayed that it might be filled up, because all who mounted upon the scaffold put their fingers into it, and I feared it would crumble more. Afterwards it was restored on the occasion of the congress of scientific philosophers, and I saw Marini, under the direction of the Minister of Public Works, who was by his side: he filled the hole, and made a new eye, too little, and badly drawn; and then he retouched the whole face and clothes, to the great damage of the expression as well as the character and costume. The likeness of the face is *changed*; and the three colours in which Dante is dressed, the same with those of Beatrice,* those of Young Italy, white, green, and red, are no longer there. The *green* is turned to chocolate colour; moreover the form of the cap is lost and confused. I desired to make a drawing to send it to my best friend Signor——†: it was denied to me by the Keepers, and I went to the gallery to speak to one of the inspectors to have permission. He answered me, that too many persons were jealous, and that it was not decided to whom it would be permitted to publish it. I asked no more. Perhaps if I had asked of a minister or director I should have been more fortunate, as they had on more than one occasion shown me politeness. But I obtained the means to be shut up in the prison for a morning; and not only did I make a drawing, but a tracing also, and with the two I then made a fac-simile sufficiently careful. Luckily it was before the rifacimento.']

*[In *Purg*. xxx. 31-3.] †[No doubt Gabriele Rossetti.]

1842. Feb. 27. LETTER TO CHARLES LYELL (from Florence).

[The Torrigiani bust of Dante]

Having met with a curious and unknown anecdote of a bust of Dante, I send you the following extract, which will interest you, as it probably relates to the one of which you have a cast.[1] It is from an inedited and autograph MS. in the Magliabecchian Library, No. ix., by Giovanni Cinelli,[2] a celebrated antiquarian and physician, who published *Le Bellezze di Firenze*, in 1677. The title of this MS. in four volumes is *La Toscana letterata ovvero Istoria degli Scrittori Fiorentini.* At page 325 begins the life of Dante. At page 340 he proceeds thus:—

'Fu con orrevolezza da cittadini di Ravenna, che cortesemente accolto l' avean, giusta suo merito, in morte con essequie e sepolcro onorato, al quale aggiunsero un bell' epitaffio di Giovanni del Virgilio, che nello stesso scolpito si legge. La sua testa fu poi dal sepolcro dal Arcivescovo di Ravenna fatta cavare e donata a Giambologna, scultore famosissimo, dalle cui mani, siccome tutte l' altre cose curiose di modelletti ed altre materie, in Pietro Tacca, suo scolare ed erede, passarono. Onde mostrando egli un giorno alla Duchessa Sforza, fra l' altre galanterie e singolarità, la testa di Dante, ella con imperioso tratto togliendola seco portar la volse, privando in un tempo medesimo il Tacca e la città di gioia sì cara, il che con sommo dolor di esso Pietro seguì, per quanto Lodovico Salvetti, suo scolare, e testimonio di questo fatto di vista, m' ha più volte raccontato.

Era questa testa per la parte anteriore di faccia, non molto grande, ma con grandissima dilicatezza d' ossi costrutta, e dalla fronte alla parte posteriore, occipite dimandato, ove la sutura lambdoidea ha suo termine, era molto lunga, a segno che non rotonda come l' altre, ma ovata era sua forma, riprova manifesta

[1] [Lyell, in a note on the frontispiece to the 1842 edition of his translation of the *Canzoniere* of Dante, to which is prefixed an engraved portrait of Dante, says: 'The drawing was made from a mask presented to me by Professor Rossetti, who received it from Florence as a cast from the bust of Dante in the Palazzo del Nero, which has descended by inheritance to the Marchese Torrigiani. There is a family tradition that the bust was formed from a cast taken after death from the head of Dante at Ravenna, 1321. It has been examined by eminent sculptors and painters, both Italian and English, who see so many traits of the expression natural to the features immediately after death, as to afford convincing proof of the probable truth of the above tradition. The bust is fixed in a square wooden frame, and suspended against the wall of a lower room in the palace. By favour of the Marchese Torrigiani an artist was permitted to make three drawings of the bust, a full face, profile, and three quarters' (p. xv). This bust is now in the Gallery of the Uffizi at Florence, to which it was presented by the Marchese in 1865, at the time of the celebration of the sixth centenary of Dante's birth. A photograph of it is given opposite page 168 of Toynbee's *Life of Dante* (ed. 1904.)]

[2] [Born at Florence in 1625, died in 1706.]

della memoria profonda di questo insigne Poeta, e per la di lei bellezze era bene spesso, come sceda, da' giovani del Tacca disegnata. La Duchessa però postala in una ciarpa di drappo verde, di propria mano la portò via, e Dio sa in quali mani e dove in oggi cosa sì pregiata e degna si trovi.'[1]

This Cinelli was the editor of the first edition of Leonardo Aretino's Life of Dante, printed in 1671.

The Marchese Torrigiani's bust of Dante is ascertained to be plaster coloured, and not terra-cotta as was supposed. The process of colouring may be the cause of the obliteration of the finer markings of the face observable in the mask from which your lithograph is taken, and of the smoother, fleshier, and more feminine appearance in the three drawings of Vito d' Ancona, which were made for you. The mask which you have is from the mould in my possession, which I procured from the Cavalier Bartolini, the chief sculptor here, as a cast from the Torrigiani terra-cotta. There is a third cast which belonged to Ricci the sculptor,[2] who made the Dante monument in Santa Croce. Ricci's heirs lent it to Fabris, who made use of it for the obverse of his medal of Dante. There are material, though slight, differences in all the three, and perhaps they are from different moulds; yet they all have the same peculiarities, which belong to nature and are not artistic. For instance, the eyes are neither closed nor open; the left eye is rather more closed than the right one. They are all three the same size, of life, with the same cap, the same lock of hair, all the same very natural wrinkles and veins, where not effaced, and they are all three fine heads, and much beyond any sculptor of those early times, and I think of any time, for they seem nature, only modified by accident, such as warping, shrinking, scraping, &c., perhaps retouching in some parts. May not Giovanni Bologna's be the original of all, cast on the real face, and removed from the monument at Ravenna when Cardinal Bembo put up the marble one?[3] In the beautiful fresco portrait of Dante, by Giotto, on the wall of the Capella del Podestà here, a treasure which has been recently recovered,[4] we see the same features

[1][A résumé in English of this passage is given in Toynbee's *Life of Dante*, pp. 166-7 (ed. 1904), from C. E. Norton's pamphlet *On the Original Portraits of Dante* (1865).]

[2][The mask possessed by Ricci, who utilized it for the purposes of his statue of Dante in Santa Croce, eventually also passed into the hands of Kirkup. One of the masks in the possession of Kirkup was presented by him to the Oxford Dante Society, in whose custody it now remains.]

[3][For a discussion as to the genuineness of the 'death-mask' of Dante, see Corrado Ricci, *L' Ultimo Refugio di Dante Alighieri*, pp. 278 ff. Ricci considers it to be derived from a head of Dante executed by the sculptor Tullio Lombardi, at Ravenna, at the beginning of Cent. xvi.]

[4][See Kirkup's letters to Gabriele Rossetti, above, pp. 639 ff.]

precisely as in the Torrigiani bust, but with the softer, happier expression of the age of about twenty-five.

(Printed in *The Poems of the Vita Nuova and Convito of Dante Alighieri. Translated by Charles Lyell*, 1842, pp. xvii-xix.)

1843. Feb. 5. LETTER TO GABRIELE ROSSETTI (from Florence).

[Giotto's portrait of Dante]

The three pomegranates in Giotto's fresco are so uncertain in their appearance, from injury and time, that I was doubtful about them, but a word from you decides the question in my mind. They are chipped and much obliterated; and, from their seeming a sort of double outline, and no shade or colour but the yellow drapery on which they are painted, I took them for an embroidery on the breast of the Barone.[1] Some remains of fingers and stalk, however, had led the Florentines to consider them as melograni, and they were puzzling their brains to find a meaning. . . .

Lord Vernon hopes you have received his book.[2] There is an outline in it from my tracing of Dante's head, and, though it is not very correct, it is the best yet done. . . .

(*Gabriele Rossetti: A versified Autobiography*; ed. by W. M. Rossetti, 1901, pp. 153-4.)

JOHN EDWARD TAYLOR

(1809-1866)

[John Edward Taylor, author of *Michael Angelo considered as a Philosophic Poet*—not to be confounded with John Edward Taylor (1791-1844), the founder of the *Manchester Guardian*, who belonged to a different family—was born at Norwich in 1809. His father, Edward Taylor (1784-1863), Gresham Professor of Music at Gresham College in London (1837-1863), was one of the seven children of John Taylor (1750-1826), the founder of the literary family of the Taylors of Norwich, of whom Sarah Austin was another. John Edward Taylor was educated at Bury St. Edmunds, and at the University of Geneva. From 1837 to 1851 he was a partner with his uncle, Richard Taylor (1781-1858), the naturalist, in his printing business in London. He died at Weybridge in 1866.[3] Taylor who was an excellent Italian and German scholar, translated several works from these languages, including the *Pentamerone* from the Neapolitan dialect, and some of Auerbach's tales, etc. In 1840 he published his work on *Michael Angelo considered as a Philosophic Poet*, from which it is evident that he was a close student of Dante. The book contains numerous quotations (in the original) from the *Vita Nuova* and *Convivio*, as well as from the *Commedia* and *Canzoniere*. It also contains translations (in unrhymed verse) of Michael Angelo's two sonnets on Dante, and of one of Dante's ballate.]

[1] [Corse Donati, whose protrait is supposed to be among those in the same group as Dante.]

[2] [His edition of *Inferno* i-vii. published at Florence in 1842. The head of Dante is engraved from Kirkup's drawing, by Lasinio.]

[3] [From information kindly supplied by his daughter, Lady Markby.]

1840. MICHAEL ANGELO CONSIDERED AS A PHILOSOPHIC POET. WITH TRANSLATIONS.

[Dante's friendship for Giotto and Casella]

IN the dawn of a new day of civilization, letters and the fine arts sprang twin-like to birth. Frederic the Second, Pier delle Vigne, and Guittone d' Arezzo, were the contemporaries of Guido da Siena and Cimabue; with Dante, Petrarca, and Boccaccio, appeared Giotto, Simon Memmi, and Gaddi. . . . It is an interesting fact, that an intimacy seems in most countries and ages to have subsisted between the greatest men who have adorned the sister arts. I may instance the friendship of Dante for Giotto and Casella, of Petrarca for Simon Memmi, of Shakspeare and Dowland, of Ben Jonson and Ferrabosco, of Milton and Lawes.

(Ed. 1852, pp. 1-2.)

[Parallel between Dante and Michael Angelo]

Never perhaps was there a more glorious parallel than that which might be drawn between Dante and Michael Angelo: the same mighty spirit guided the pen of the one and the pencil of the other. Michael Angelo was the Dante of Art, and Dante the Michael Angelo of Poetry. It would be easy to quote other parallels. What Dante was to Michael Angelo, Petrarca was to Raphael.

(p. 10.)

[Michael Angelo's admiration for Dante]

Michael Angelo was from an early age devoted to the study of the poetry of Dante and Petrarca: it is said that he knew by heart at one time nearly all the sonnets of the latter. Much however as he admired and imitated the imagery of Petrarca, the boldness of Dante's genius was more congenial to his own. . . . The wide difference between those great masters of the Italian language has been well defined by Foscolo [1] in his parallel of the two. But what is most admirable in the *Rime* of Michael Angelo is, that he so harmonizes the elegance of the one with the grandeur and solidity of the other, as to obliterate their discrepancies and to form a perfect unity of character. Out of differing elements he creates, rather than remodels, a style of poetry, and stamps it with originality; and his frequent imitation of passages both from Dante and Petrarca gives us more the impression of his perfect conversance with their productions, than of transcription and paraphrase. But in his poetry, as in his designs, Dante was the text-book of his thoughts, and innumerable instances in either

[1] [See above, pp. 167 ff.]

might be cited to illustrate this. In the 'Last Judgement' Dante has furnished the artist with many thoughts from the *Inferno* of the *Divina Commedia;* and one of the most interesting monuments of the genius of one artist illustrated by the kindred spirit of another, was the copy of Dante's great poem which Michael Angelo had enriched with marginal designs. This inestimable treasure perished, it is well known, in a shipwreck.

There is a similarity in the character of our artist to that of Dante, which I may here briefly notice. How gloriously is the sympathy of the two marked in the sonnets which he wrote on Dante![1] The mind of the latter was wonderfully fitted by nature to meet and to resist the injuries of the world, and the still greater trial of fortitude, the ingratitude of his own country. Strengthened for the task by the deep and severe studies of the schools, he felt himself superior to injury; his spirit recoiled within itself, and a philosophic equanimity, springing from the conscious dignity and purity of his own mind, never forsook him. We can hear him exclaim,

'Conscienza m' assicura,
La buona compagnia, che l' uom francheggia
Sotto l' osbergo del sentirsi pura.'[2]

And again, that noble exclamation he addresses to his old master, Messer Brunetto,

'Tanto vogl' io che vi sia manifesto,
Pur che mia conscienza non mi garra,
Ch' alla fortuna, come vuol, son presto.'[3]

(pp. 26-8.)

[Dante and his works]

The Revival of Letters forms the most interesting period in the history of philosophy. . . . This aera dates from the appearance of Dante, the most extraordinary philosophical poet of any age or country: the herald of a light which was to dawn upon Europe, not in his own but in an after age, he stood upon the limits of a region of darkness, and his mighty spirit stretched into the future, prescient of the issue of the conflict between truth and error in which he led the way. In him a devotion to scholastic study was wonderfully combined with a rich imaginative genius (of how individual a cast!) and a rare love of philosophy, hallowed by its association with a firm belief in the supreme sanctity and purity of Truth.

As I am obliged to limit my attention to a single feature of the poetry of this period, I select Dante as the representative of the

[1] See Mr. Southey's admirable version of these in Duppa's *Life of Michael Angelo*. [See above, p. 7.]

[2] [*Inf.* xxviii. 115-17.]

[3] [*Inf.* xv. 91-3.]

Italian mind, in which so many springs of imaginative thought and speculation met and mingled. . . .

The writings of Dante are so inseparably connected, in the order in which they were penned, that no one can unravel their mysteries without studying them consecutively. That most remarkable production the *Vita Nuova*, written in his twenty-eighth year, contains the first development of a genius, which had already conceived the marvellous structure of the *Divina Commedia*. In it is concealed the perfect germ of the tree of Paradise. There Beatrice first appears to Dante—'la gloriosa Donna della mia mente la quale fu chiamata da molti Beatrice, i quali non sapevano che si chiamare.' The poet there, in a mysterious and wondrous manner, opens to us her pure and lofty character, her divine offices; and he concludes with a remarkable and glorious passage, following the last sonnet. . . .[1]

The *Convito*, or *Amoroso Convivio*, of Dante consists of a comment upon three of his Canzoni (originally intended to have comprised fourteen), in which he explains their literal and allegorical meaning. . . . Dante treats of Philosophy as the highest object of man's pursuit: 'Philosophia è uno amoroso uso di sapientia, il quale massimamente è in Dio; però che in lui è somma sapientia e sommo amore.'[2] He commences by saying that 'all men naturally desire knowledge; the reason of which may be that everything is by Providence gifted with a natural inclination towards its own perfection; and as knowledge is the ultimate perfection of the soul, in which consists our highest felicity, we are all by a natural law subjected to a desire of it.' The love of truth and knowledge, which in its highest sense he terms Philosophy, is converted, after the manner of the amatory poetry of the age, into a mistress of his affection.[3]

(pp. 58 ff.)

[Dante on the love of beauty and love of knowledge]

The love of beauty and the love of knowledge, says St. Augustine, are the twin offspring of the same mind; the one beautiful in outward form, the other admirable for inward truth. Dante refers to these two characters in the following sonnet:—

Due donne in cima della mente mia,[4] &c.

(p. 70.)

[Dante and Michael Angelo both lovers of philosophy]

As Dante worshipped the Philosophy of Religion, Michael Angelo adored the Philosophy of Art; the 'donna Philosophia' of the poet

[1] [Taylor here quotes *V. N.* § 43, ll. 1-17.]
[2] [*Conv.* iii. 12, ll. 94-7.]
[3] [Taylor here quotes *Conv.* iv. 1, ll. 92-7; ii. 16, ll. 4-7, 20-3.]
[4] [Taylor here quotes *Son.* xxx.]

is under a different form, the 'donna Philocalia' of the artist: in the same spirit are they lovers, in the same figurative language do they immortalize their devotion.

(p. 82.[1])

From Dante[2]

Since that I ne'er can satisfy mine eyes
With gazing on Madonna's beauteous face,
  I'll fixedly regard her,
Till I grow blest but in beholding her;
And as an angel, clad in purity,
  Dwelling in heaven above,
Doth become blest in contemplating God;
So I, that am but human creature frail,
  In contemplating her
Who holds unshared possession of my heart,
E'en here on earth may taste beatitude;
Such is the influence her virtue sheds,
  Yet felt alone by him
Who in his love doth honour her he loves.

(p. 150.)

HARTLEY COLERIDGE

(1796-1849)

[Hartley Coleridge, eldest son of Samuel Taylor Coleridge, was born at Clevedon, Somersetshire, in 1796. He was brought up with the family of Robert Southey at Keswick, and educated principally at Ambleside School, whence he went to Merton College, Oxford. He graduated B.A. in 1819, and the same year was elected to a fellowship at Oriel, from which he was dismissed, after a year's probation (1820), for intemperance. He published a volume of poems in 1833; lives of Yorkshire and Lancashire worthies, 1833-6; and an edition of Massinger and Ford, 1840. He died at Grasmere in 1849, and was buried in the churchyard close to where Wordsworth was buried in the following year.]

1840. DRAMATIC WORKS OF MASSINGER AND FORD. WITH INTRODUCTION.

[The outline of the *terza rima* to be detected in Cary's Dante]

MR. COLLIER, in his 'History of Dramatic Poetry,' has given a short sample of the Countess of Pembroke's[3] blank verse, which is as heavy and monotonous as blank verse translation of rhyme generally is, from preserving the pattern

[1] [On pp. 89-101 Taylor illustrates the figurative and philosophical language of Michael Angelo's poems by numerous parallel passages from Dante.]

[2] [*Ball.* ix.: 'Poichè saziar non posso gli occhi miei.']

[3] [Mary, Countess of Pembroke (c. 1555-1621), 'Sidney's sister, Pembroke's mother'; she translated into blank verse from the French a tragedy ('Antonie') of Robert Garnier.]

and cadence of the original—a fault which even Cary, in his excellent 'Dante,' has not always avoided. Now and then you may detect the outline of the *terza rima*.

(p. xxvi note.)

ANONYMOUS

1840. Nov. DUBLIN UNIVERSITY MAGAZINE. WRIGHT'S PARADISE OF DANTE.

[Wright's translation not likely to add to the popularity of Dante in England]

WHILE we prefer Carey's[1] translation and the extracts from Dante by James Montgomery[2] to any other imitations of Dante, that we have seen, we cannot but feel that Mr. Wright has done good service both to the old Florentine and his English readers. He has, however, we think erred in the attempt to be too literal. . . . Some writers will not believe and cannot be taught, that a free translation may be more like the original not only in spirit, but may express the precise meaning, and exhibit the very style, more closely than one which is called *literal*. The plan of translating line for line, and almost word for word is one which while it imposes severe fetters on the translator is to the reader absolutely intolerable. No English imitation of the *Terza Rima*, in which Dante's great poem is written, has in the remotest degree been successful in producing the effect of the Italian measure, although Lord Byron and other great masters of versification have tested its capabilities. . . . The stanza in which Mr. Wright writes is not that of Dante, or of the English *Terza Rima*. Indeed we think its general effect better. . .

On the whole, while Mr. Wright's translation cannot have the effect of displacing Carey[1] from our shelves, nor can it be his wish that it should, it is a work which, at times, exhibits very great power, which is often true to the meaning of the original, where the Italian commentators are at fault, and which, if it adds little to the chance of Dante's becoming popular in England, fails only in that in which no man has yet succeeded, and in which success is perhaps impossible.

(Vol. xvi. pp. 590-1.)

CATHARINE TAYLOR

(fl. 1840)

[Catharine Taylor was sister of John Edward Taylor, author of *Michael Angelo considered as a Philosophic Poet*,[3] and niece of Sarah Austin, the well-known trans-

[1] [*Sic.*] [2] [See above, pp. 598-9.] [3] [See above, p. 645.]

lator of Ranke's *History of the Popes*. After a seventeen months' residence on the Continent Miss Taylor published *Letters from Italy to a Younger Sister*, in two volumes (1840-1). These letters, which were avowedly written for the benefit of 'young people,' contain numerous references to Dante, a few of which are given below.]

1840-1. LETTERS FROM ITALY TO A YOUNGER SISTER.

[Michael Angelo and Dante]

FLORENCE—The Church of Santa Croce, from the tombs it contains, has been called the Westminster Abbey of Italy. Here has Florence at length done justice to the memory of her Dante; nor is this a solitary though a striking instance of the fact, that posterity lavishes with jealous eagerness honours on those who have in life met only with persecution and injustice.

'Di Dante mal fur l' opre conosciute,
E 'l bel desio, da quel popolo ingrato,
Che solo ai giusti manca di salute.'[1]

In vain his fellow-citizens entreated that his ashes might be brought to Florence; the people of Ravenna, proud of having received the homeless stranger, and sheltered him in his last days, would not resign his dust. There is nothing more beautiful to my mind than the appreciation which one noble spirit has of the powers of another; and I cannot help remarking here, how true a worshipper Dante had in Buonarotti. . . .

When a petition was sent to Leo the Tenth, entreating him to raise a monument in Florence to the memory of Dante,[2] Michael Angelo signed it in these remarkable words: 'Io, Michele Angelo, scultore, il medesimo, a vostra Santità supplico, offerendomi al divin Poeta fare la sepultura sua condecente e in loco onorevole in questa città.' But the offer was not accepted, and it is only within the last century that Florence has raised this monument to her greatest poet. Canova was the artist,[3] and the work is worthy of him.

(Vol. i. pp. 73-4.)

[Dante's reference to the Veronica]

Rome—The San Sudario is a relic also shown at Easter. Tradition declares it to be a handkerchief which was presented to our Saviour while bearing his cross, by a woman named Veronica, and which, after he had wiped his face with it, retained the impression of his features. This saint, like many others, seems to have been a mere fiction of the Church; her name was probably derived . . . from

[1] [From Sonnet of Michael Angelo on Dante. Southey's translation (see above, p. 7) is appended.]

[2] [The petition, as a matter of fact, was that Leo X. should command the people of Ravenna to give up the ashes of Dante to the Florentines.]

[3] [Not Canova, but Stefano Ricci.]

vera icon (true image), and applied to the handkerchief. Dante alludes to this in a beautiful passage of the Divina Commedia.[1]

(Vol. i. pp. 191-2.)

ROBERT BROWNING

(1812-1889)

[Robert Browning, only son of a clerk in the Bank of England, was born at Camberwell in 1812. He was educated privately and at University College, London. He early determined to be a poet, and in 1833 published *Pauline*. In 1834 he paid his first visit to Italy. In 1845 he made the acquaintance of Elizabeth Barrett, whom he married in the following year. They lived in Italy (chiefly at Pisa, Florence and Rome), with the exception of short intervals in Paris and England, from 1846 to 1861, in which year Mrs. Browning died at Florence. Browning then settled in London, but frequently revisited Italy, where he died (at Venice) in 1889. He was buried in Westminster Abbey. Browning's chief early poems appeared as follows:—*Paracelsus*, 1835; *Strafford*, 1837; *Sordello*, 1840; *Bells and Pomegranates*, 1841-6 (among which were comprised *Dramatic Lyrics*, 1843). Though he was a constant reader of Dante—he speaks in a letter of having 'all of him in my head and heart'—the actual references to Dante in Browning's poems are few. The earliest occur in *Sordello*, which, of course, owes its genesis to Dante. The best known probably are the beautiful passages in *One Word More*, written in 1855, which fall outside the scope of this work. In a letter written to Elizabeth Barrett in 1845 Browning translates in blank verse a few lines from the *Purgatorio* (v. 52-7); and he wrote a touching passage from the *Convivio* (ii. 9, ll. 132-6) in her Testament shortly after her death.[2]]

1840. SORDELLO.

SORDELLO, thy forerunner, Florentine!
A herald-star I know thou didst absorb
Relentless into the consummate orb
That scared it from its right to roll along
A sempiternal path with dance and song
Fulfilling its allotted period,
Serenest of the progeny of God—
Who yet resigns it not! His darling stoops
With no quenched lights, desponds with no blank troops
Of disenfranchised brilliances, for, blent
Utterly with thee, its shy element
Like thine upburneth prosperous and clear,
Still, what if I approach the august sphere
Named now with only one name, disentwine
That under current soft and argentine
From its fierce mate in the majestic mass
Leavened as the sea whose fire was mixt with glass

[1] [*Par.* xxxi. 103-11, is here quoted.]

[2] [See O. Kuhns, *Dante and the English Poets from Chaucer to Tennyson*, pp. 218 ff.]

In John's transcendent vision,—launch once more
That lustre? Dante, pacer of the shore
Where glutted hell disgorgeth filthiest gloom,
Unbitten by its whirring sulphur-spume—
Or whence the grieved and obscure waters slope
Into a darkness quieted by hope;
Plucker of amaranths grown beneath God's eye
In gracious twilights where his chosen lie,
I would do this! If I should falter now!

(Book i.—*Poetical Works*, ed. 1872, vol. ii. pp. 15-16.)

Strange that three such confessions so should hap
To Palma, Dante spoke with in the clear
Amorous silence of the Swooning-sphere,—
Cunizza,[1] as he called her!

(Book vi.—*ibid.* pp. 183-4.)

The Chroniclers of Mantua tired their pen
Telling how *Sordello Prince Visconti* saved
Mantua, and elsewhere notably behaved—
Who thus, by fortune ordering events,
Passed with posterity, to all intents,
For just the god he never could become.
As Knight, Bard, Gallant, men were never dumb
In praise of him: while what he should have been,
Could be, and was not—the one step too mean
For him to take,—we suffer at this day
Because of: Ecelin had pushed away
Its chance ere Dante could arrive and take
That step Sordello spurned, for the world's sake:
He did much—but Sordello's chance was gone.

(Book vi.—*ibid.* pp. 214-15.)

1842. DRAMATIC LYRICS: UP AT A VILLA—DOWN IN THE CITY.

Ere you open your eyes in the city, the blessed church-bells begin:
No sooner the bells leave off than the diligence rattles in:
You get the pick of the news, and it costs you never a pin.
By and by there's the travelling doctor—gives pills, lets blood, draws teeth;
Or the Pulcinello-trumpet breaks up the market beneath.
At the post-office such a scene-picture—the new play, piping hot!
And a notice how, only this morning, three liberal thieves were shot.

[1] [*Par.* ix. 13 ff.]

Above it, behold the Archbishop's most fatherly of rebukes,
And beneath, with his crown and his lion, some little new law of
the Duke's!
Or a sonnet with flowery marge, to the Reverend Don So-and-so
Who is Dante, Boccaccio, Petrarca, Saint Jerome and Cicero,
'And moreover,' (the sonnet goes rhyming), 'the skirts of Saint
Paul has reached,
'Having preached us those six Lent-lectures more unctuous than
ever he preached.'
Noon strikes,—here sweeps the procession! our Lady borne smiling
and smart
With a pink gauze gown all spangles, and seven swords stuck in
her heart!
Bang-whang-whang goes the drum, *tootle-te-tootle* the fife;
No keeping one's haunches still: it's the greatest pleasure in life.

(*Stanza* ix. *Poetical Works,* ed. 1872, vol. iii. pp. 125-6.)

1842. DRAMATIC LYRICS: OLD PICTURES IN FLORENCE.

When the hour grows ripe, and a certain dotard
Is pitched, no parcel that needs invoicing,
To the worse side of the Mont St. Gothard,
We shall begin by way of rejoicing;
None of that shooting the sky (blank cartridge),
Nor a civic guard, all plumes and lacquer,
Hunting Radetzky's soul like a partridge
Over Morello with squib and cracker.

This time we'll shoot better game and bag 'em hot—
No mere display at the stone of Dante,[1]
But a kind of sober Witanagemot
(Ex: "Casa Guidi," *quod videas ante*)
Shall ponder, once Freedom restored to Florence,
How Art may return that departed with her.
Go, hated house, go each trace of the Loraine's,
And bring us the days of Orgagna hither!

(*Stanzas* xxxii-iii. *Poetical Works*, ed. 1872, vol. iii. p. 141.)

CONNOP THIRLWALL

(1797-1875)

[Connop Thirlwall, Bishop of St. David's, was born in London in 1797. He was educated at the Charterhouse (1810-13), and Trinity College, Cambridge, of which he was elected Scholar in 1816 and Fellow in 1818. He learnt French and Italian

[1] [The so-called 'Sasso di Dante' near the Duomo in Florence.]

while an undergraduate. In the winter of 1818-19 he resided at Rome, where he formed a close friendship with Bunsen, Secretary of the Prussian Legation. Me. Bunsen in a letter to her mother written from Rome at this time states that Thirlwall had evidently 'really and truly studied Dante's poetry,' and records his opinion that 'no person who had taken the trouble to understand the whole of the *Divina Commedia* would doubt about preferring the *Paradiso* to the two preceding parts.' (See above, p. 301.) In 1825 Thirlwall was called to the bar, but the law was distasteful to him, and in 1827 he returned to Cambridge and was ordained. From 1827 to 1834 he was engaged in College and University work as tutor, lecturer, and examiner. In 1834 he accepted the living of Kirby Underdale in Yorkshire, and in 1840 he was appointed to the Bishopric of St. David's, which he resigned in 1874. He died at Bath in the following year, and was buried in Westminster Abbey. His most important work, his *History of Greece*, was published in eight volumes in 1835-44.]

1841. Nov. 8. LETTER TO REV. F. MARTIN (from Abergwili[1]).

[Dante's solution of the difficulty caused by the supposed inequality of reward]

THE difficulty is solved by Dante in a beautiful passage. . . . The question is there raised (*Paradiso* III) 'Voi, che siete qui felici, desiderate voi più alto loco?' and the answer states,

Frate, la nostra volontà quieta
Virtù di *carità*, che fa volerne
Sol quel ch' avemo, e d' altro non ci asseta.
Se disiassimo esser più superne
Foran discordi gli nostri disiri
Dal voler di colui che qui ne cerne;
* * * *
È formale ad esto beato esse
Tenersi dentro alla divina voglia
* * * *
Sì che, come noi sem di soglia in soglia
Per questo regno, a tutto il regno piace,
Com' allo Re che 'n suo voler ne invoglia;
In la sua volontade è nostra pace.

The poet concludes:—

Chiaro mi fu allor, com' ogni dove
In cielo è Paradiso, e sì la grazia
Del sommo ben d' un modo non vi piove.[2]

(*Letters*, ed. 1881, pp. 173-4.)

WILLIAM SPALDING

(1809-1859)

[William Spalding was born in 1809 at Aberdeen, where he was educated at the Marischal College (M.A. 1827). In 1840 he was appointed professor of rhetoric and

[1] [Village near Carmarthen, where is the episcopal residence of the see of St. David's.]

[2] [*Par.* iii. 70-5, 79-80, 82-5, 88-90.]

belles-letters in the University of Edinburgh; this chair he exchanged in 1845 for that of logic and metaphysics at St. Andrews, which he held until his death in 1859. Spalding was a frequent contributor to the *Edinburgh Review*, chiefly on Shakespearean subjects. In early life he travelled in Italy, of which country he published a history in 1841 under the title of *Italy and the Italian Islands*. This work contains an account of Dante's life and writings, with an analysis of the *Divina Commedia*. His most important other work was a *History of English Literature* (1853).]

1841. ITALY AND THE ITALIAN ISLANDS. FROM THE EARLIEST AGES TO THE PRESENT TIME.

[Estimate of Dante's writings]

DANTE left compositions both in prose and verse, in Latin and Italian. His sonnets and Canzoni have a merit which is only eclipsed by that of his own great poem. The 'Vita Nuova' consists of those verses which he devoted to Beatrice, both before and after her death, and which he connects by a prose narrative, embellished with many flights of imagination, detailing the circumstances in which the rhymes were severally composed. His 'Convito' or Banquet, is a long mystical commentary on three of his Canzoni. Besides these works in the modern tongue, he wrote two in Latin. In the treatise 'De Monarchiâ,' addressing himself to Henry VII., he endeavours to prove the benefits of a universal empire, the right of the Romans to exercise it, and its immediate dependence on God, without recourse to the popes or other divine vicars. The unfinished essay 'De Vulgari Eloquentiâ,' relates the history of the new Italian language, and criticises some of the poems which had been already composed in it. The distrust which the writer entertained as to the capabilities of the spoken tongue is shown by the fact, that he began in Latin hexameters his great poem, the 'Divina Commedia,' which, as rewritten, became the highest model of the modern language.

This extraordinary work, which places Dante's name first among those of all Italian poets ancient or modern, and nearly first among all the poets of Christian Europe, describes in one hundred cantos, a vision of the three Catholic worlds of the dead,—Hell, Purgatory, and Heaven,—allotting, besides an introductory canto, thirty-three cantos to each. It is impossible to sketch its plan briefly, and at the same time to exhibit, with any fairness, the character of the genius which it displays; and we must recollect at the outset, that it is the colouring of particular scenes which gives to the poem its most obvious charm, and that the age in which it was conceived was one marked by partial knowledge, by unrefined taste in literature, by infancy in art, and by almost demoniacal passions, in the intercourse of life, both public and private. In politics,

Dante is at once a worshipper of freedom, and a Ghibelline or enemy of the popedom; in religion he is by turns a scholastic disputer, an adoring mystic, a stern reproacher of ecclesiastical vices. In better times he would have been a patriotic Florentine; but his wrongs, his hatreds, and his party attachments, master, at every struggle, his love for his country, of which indeed there remains little except a sickly longing for its soil, mixing strangely with a universal scorn of its inhabitants. The utterance which is incessantly given to these personal feelings, often at the expense of much that is sacred and good, is the most unpleasing feature in the composition; but the very same peculiarity contributes not a little to give it that air of reality which it so impressively wears. Its ruling poetical character is that of stern sublimity, abrupt, concentrated, never vague though often wild, sometimes melting into overflowing tenderness, and everywhere seen through a cloud of imagery, whose shapes are sketched with astonishing brevity, yet with unexcelled picturesqueness.[1]

(Vol. ii. pp. 194-6.)

A. BRUCE WHYTE

(fl. 1840)

[A. Bruce Whyte published two works:—*Histoire des Langues Romanes et de leur Littérature depuis leur Origine jusqu'au XIVe Siècle* (3 vols. 8vo, Paris, 1841); and *A Free Translation, in Verse, of the Inferno of Dante* (London, 1859), on the title-page of which he describes himself as Advocate. The *Histoire des Langues Romanes* was composed in English, with the intention of its being published in English, but the author, who had been for some years resident in France, found it difficult to get an English book printed in Paris; he therefore had his MS. translated into French and published the work in that language, with the exception of various poetical translations, which he was unwilling to sacrifice and which accordingly are printed in English. The majority of these occur in the chapters (xxxvi-xxxvii. vol. iii. pp. 229-337) devoted to Dante. Specimens of these, which consist for the most part of translations from the *Canzoniere* of Dante, are given below. Bruce Whyte held somewhat peculiar views with regard to Dante. He was convinced, for instance, that Dante knew Greek, and had read the *Iliad* in the original, and borrowed from Homer many of his most striking similes:—'Plusieurs des plus remarquables comparaisons dans la Divine Comédie sont littéralement traduites de l' Iliade!']

1841. HISTOIRE DES LANGUES ROMANES ET DE LEUR LITTÉRATURE DEPUIS LEUR ORIGINE JUSQU'AU XIVE SIÈCLE.

[Translation of *Inferno* xxiv. 1-15]

IN that cool season of the youthful year
When Phoebus laves his tresses in the urn
Of moist Aquarius; when dull night's career
Is shorten'd, and the hoar-frost of the morn

[1] [Here follows an analysis of the poem (occupying 10 pages) accompanied by extracts from Cary's translation.]

Like its pale sister looks, till from the sphere
The genial beams disperse it in their turn:
The villager, of fodder destitute,
Hies to the field; but when he views the plains
All white around, with disappointment mute
He homeward bends, and here and there complains,
Like desp'rate wretch, who errs irresolute.
Again he sallies forth; and hope's sweet strains
Ring in his ear, as he beholds a change
In nature's face: he merrily resumes his crook,
And leads his flock to their accustom'd range.

(Vol. iii. pp. 239-40)

[*Sonnet XII* from the *Vita Nuova*[1]]

O ye whose eyes, bent to the earth, display
Sad evidence of some o'erwhelming woe,
Whence comes it that your cheeks discolour'd show
Like stone[2] or marble, yet less pale than they?
Have ye beheld our lady's face bedew'd
With tears, by love or filial duty shed?
Say, for my heart forbodes some tidings dread.
Why wander ye in such dejected mood?
If ye came hither by compassion mov'd,
Tarry, in pity, for a while with me.
Tell me the worst! Speak, speak of my belov'd!
Your eyes in ill dissembled tears I see,
Your looks appear so haggard and so strange
That my heart trembles to behold the change.

(Vol. iii. p. 298.)

[Translation of *Canzone* vi. ll. 53-61 (*Convivio* ii.)]

In sooth, my song, there are but few, I wot,
Can comprehend the meaning of thy lays,
For tropical they be and hard to con.
If peradventure it should be thy lot
To meet with those who cannot thread the maze,
Be not discourag'd; bid them still read on.
Tell them, my child, they may at least admire
The beauty of the numbers and the fire.

(Vol. iii. pp. 302-3.)

1 [' Voi, che portate la sembianza umile,' *V. N.* § 22.]
2 [The translator appears to have read *pietra* instead of *pietà* in this line.]

ANTONIO CARLO NAPOLEONE GALLENGA

(1810-1895)

[Antonio Gallenga was born in 1810 at Parma, where he was educated at the University. Having conspired against the life of King Carlo Alberto, he was forced to leave Italy, and made his way to America, and eventually (1839) to England, under the name of Mariotti. In 1841 he printed a course of lectures on Italy (delivered in America in 1838) under the title of *Italy: General Views of its History and Literature*, which was afterwards (1846) reprinted as *Italy, Past and Present*. This work contains some interesting chapters on Dante, and on the debt of Italy to him. In 1846 Gallenga was naturalised, and in 1848 he was appointed Italian professor at University College, London, which chair he filled until 1859, when he went to Italy as correspondent of the *Times* with the French army. He was deputy in the Italian Parliament from 1859 to 1864. Gallenga was at various times correspondent for the *Times* in the United States (1863), Denmark, Spain, and Constantinople. He lived in London from 1866 to 1873, writing for the *Times*, his connection with which ceased in 1883. He died at Llandogo in Monmouthshire in 1895. Besides his *Italy*, the best known of his many books are probably his *Memoir of Fra Dolcino and his Times* (1853), and *Mariotti's Italian Grammar*, first published in 1858, and still held in esteem.]

1841. ITALY: GENERAL VIEWS OF ITS HISTORY AND LITERATURE.[1]

[Dante, the 'great father' of the Italian language]

THE Italian language languished for a long period of ages, a formless and lawless dialect, more and more spurned and neglected, as an impure bastard, by the scholars of the Middle Ages, in proportion as the revival of learning naturally led them back to the dead languages; but when the want of a literature of life called the living tongues into action, when the first examples of Romance poetry were set by the Provençal Troubadours, the Italian was found to have been silently matured by the secret working of the people, and, hiding its infancy amid the darkness of ages, it seemed to arise full-grown and armed, like Minerva, from the head of its great father, Dante.

(Ed. 1846, vol. i. p. 139.)

[The debt of Italian literature to Dante]

The elements of literature were at war in Italy at the close of the Middle Ages. There was, on the one hand, the unwieldy mass of scholastic erudition, on the other, the unsubstantial spirit of romantic poetry. The work of a genius was required to bring those elements together, to complete the work of creation—that genius was Dante.

(Vol. i. p. 165.)

[1] [Reissued in 1846, with the title *Italy, Past and Present*.]

[Dante and his commentators]

It was doomed that the warmest friends of Dante should prove no less fatal to his memory than his bitterest enemies. No sooner was his sacred poem rescued from oblivion than it fell into the hands of a swarm of commentators, who seized upon it like ravens crowding upon the body of a fallen warrior. Under pretence of rescuing the original text from the injuries of age and ignorance, of tearing asunder the veil of mysticism and allegory in which the poet, indulging the taste of his age, had mantled his eternal truths, they plunged the Divine Comedy into an ocean of doubt; they racked, they cramped, they stretched the sense, even of its most lucid poetical effusions, to shape it after their own narrow-minded conceits; they made of it a maze of enigma and mystery, a mosaic of quibbles and acrostics, a monster which timid minds cannot approach without awe and superstition. At length, in our days Ugo Foscolo,[1] a kindred genius, has turned his efforts to follow, in its soaring, the genius of Dante. His discourse on the text of the Divine Comedy written, as it was, when age and exile had fitted him rather for contemplative than creative pursuits, is still the work of a poet, and has rendered justice to the poet. It has cleared the fame of Dante from the stains of the calumnies of his opponents, and from the smoke of the incense of his worshippers. It has driven the Pharisees and money-lenders out of the temple. It has levelled to the ground all the wretched systems and hypotheses by which we had hitherto been introduced to the perusal of Dante. . . . The discourse of Ugo Foscolo is evidently tending to a literary scepticism, which ought to be recommended as most salutary to all admirers of Dante. The blind obstinacy by which commentators pretended to account for everything, has been too long the principal cause that nothing could be understood. The blank that time and adverse circumstances have brought upon our knowledge of the poet's mind cannot be filled up with vain gratuitous conjectures. The spirit of Dante must be studied in his verses, in his text, bare of all commentary. The Divine Comedy is to be read without any other aid than a previous knowledge of the spirit of the age in which the poet moved, and of which that work was a vast, vivid, all-embracing reflection.

(Vol. i. pp. 169-70, 171.)

[The *Divina Commedia*]

All the political passions of the roaming Ghibeline, all the tenderest ecstasies of the lover of Beatrice, all the deepest abstractions of the ripe scholar, all his age, all his heart, and all his mind,

[1] [See above, pp. 159 ff.]

found place in one work; but because such influences did not act at once with the same intensity, the different parts of the poem breathe a different spirit, according as the incidents of the poet's life gave one part of his feelings the ascendancy over the others.

The first part, the *Inferno*, is nearly all dedicated to politics; it was written during the first exasperation of exile, whilst the poet was striving to raise enemies against the enemies of his cause. Ghibeline rage and Ghibeline revenge engross all his time, and, with a progressive disdain, attacking Florence, Rome, and France —the Guelphs, the Neri, Charles of Valois, and Boniface VIII,— he restores the fame of a hundred Ghibelines, or, in the amazement of terror and pity, he conceals their crimes under the veil of a deep commiseration for their sufferings.

Hence, leaving behind the abyss of all sorrows, and breathing again the vital air, as he reaches the outskirts of the mountain of purgatory, he spreads over his rhymes a blessed calm, an ineffable abandonment. The shades he meets are breathing love and forgiveness; they are less anxious of hearing news from the living, and only send messages of joy: the heart lightens and brightens with the different strata of the atmosphere in the rising regions of the mountain. At length, on its summit, where he has placed the terrestrial paradise, Beatrice approaches. She is coming—all that human fancy ever created falls short of the pomp and glory by which she is announced. Her lover has seen her—all earthly remembrances have forsaken him; with his eyes riveted on her eyes, he wings his flight to the spheres, attracted by her immortal looks.

There, while soaring from star to star, Beatrice reads in the mind of her lover, as in a mirror, all the doubts with which he was troubled: she gives him the solution of all problems about the system of the universe, about the inmost secret of nature, about the most recondite mysteries of the Christian revelation; and, having thus explored the eternal light in all its emanations and reflections, Dante is allowed to turn his eyes towards the centre itself of all light, where dazzled, bewildered, and lost, he sinks, and abandons his subject, as if avowing that there is a limit even to the genius of Dante.

Thus, of the three parts into which the poem is divided, politics are almost exclusively the subject of the first, love is the soul of the second, the third is consecrated to knowledge.

(Vol. i. pp. 211-4.)

[Dante's gift to Italy]

The poem of Dante was to Italy what the spark of the sun was to the personified clay of Prometheus. Dante gave his country a language, and language is the soul of nations. Under his powerful will his age saw with surprise a popular dialect alternately assume the loftiest tones of the sublime and pathetic, clothe the noblest and elevate the humblest conceptions, and throw light and evidence on the most abstruse and recondite truths. The everyday words and phrases of the people appeared in those verses as a new discovery, and low-born vernacular idioms were handed down to posterity as the poets' creation. The Italian language seemed to recognise the hand of its maker. Never did it before or after, yield to any writer's impulse, never did it display more of nerve and energy, more of brevity, suppleness, and grace. As Italy was, perhaps, never more great and more free, so never since was her language nobler or mightier.

And yet the pen of Dante was a strong chisel, by a few bold strokes marking profound, indelible features, giving life to the marble wherever it touched, but abandoning the block unfinished, half-carved, half-polished, rude in its sublimity, grand in its disorder. The charge of purifying and refining, of taming and softening, the language of Dante, was left to the care of two kindred twin minds, which, although perhaps of a stamp by a great degree inferior, yet grown on the same soil and out of the same elements, born quite at the close of Dante's tempestuous course, were to take up the mantle at the moment it fell from the prophet's shoulders, and accomplish what remained unachieved of his mission—Petrarch and Boccaccio.

(Vol. i. pp. 218-9.)

THOMAS HENRY WHITE

(fl. 1840)

1841. FRAGMENTS OF ITALY AND THE RHINELAND.

[Dante and Florence]

FLORENCE.—Rome certainly did wonders towards the revival of my Classic tastes, but it is no less certain that this wild Baronial Town of Monastic Temples and Palace fortresses, breathing of Guelph and Ghibelline; with Hell, Purgatory, and Paradise, engraved upon her Streets by the diamond pen of Dante, bids fair to seduce me once more from any allegiance.

(p. 130.)

[The monument to Dante at Florence]

Florence.—To-day I have seen the Church of Santa Croce in which, as much as could die of Michael Angelo, Machiavelli, and

Galileo, render the aisles of this rude and unfinished temple illustrious, while all that Florence can display of her banished Dante frowns in most austere and therefore natural guise upon a recent monument [1] erected by—subscription! How feelingly does this remind us that we live no longer in the age of princely poets or princely patrons. Tardy justice done in a beggarly subscription! Florence need not stand so erect in this monument: had her citizens a grain of the spirit that such a Poet might well excite among them, each individual, at his own private cost, would have raised a statue to Dante, and Italy would have teemed with statues of Dante; but Guelph and Ghibelline are united now, and they can afford to—subscribe.

(pp. 155-6.)

[Florence the appropriate setting for the scenes of Dante and Boccaccio]

Florence.—O Florence, Florence, thou throne of Feudal Anarchy, thou cabinet of Baronial dismalities, how long will men call thee fair! I do not speak this in disparagement; to me wert thou fairer, thou wouldst not be so fair. I love thy huge, quaint, overbearing structures. Romantic in their massy gloom, they are the very home my Fancy would have built for the scenes of Dante and Boccaccio!

(p. 157.)

ANONYMOUS

1841. April. DUBLIN UNIVERSITY MAGAZINE.—POETS AND POETESSES.

[English translators of Dante: Boyd, Cary, Merivale, Montgomery, Wright.—Lamb's opinion of Boyd]

JOHN HERMAN MERIVALE'S 'Poems original and translated,' have been before greatly and justly praised in our Magazine; and our only object in now mentioning them is, to give our readers some extracts from the translation of Dante, which we had not read, when a few months ago we were reviewing Mr. Wright.[2] Could a word of encouragement from us give aid to the English public in obtaining from Mr. Merivale [3] a complete translation of Dante, we should feel we had done no light service to the literature of our country. As to anything of rivalry between such men as him and Carey,[4] and Montgomery,[5] it is altogether out of the question. We have read everything from Dante that we could find in English books, and no one of them in

[1] [The cenotaph, by Stefano Ricci, in Santa Croce, erected in 1829.]
[2] [See above, p. 650.]
[3] [See above, pp. 190 ff.]
[4] [*Sic.*]
[5] [See above, pp. 596 ff.]

the least degree interferes with the other. It would amaze us indeed to hear that Cary and Merivale,—each admirable in his way,—did not admire the other. The best thing we can do is, to send to the printer extracts from Carey, Wright, and Merivale; and give a passage in which all are excellent. We really do not know which is best.[1] We wish we had room for Boyd's translation of the passage. Boyd's book has the faults of style which are common to almost all the poetry of the period in which he wrote—[2] but he understood his author well, and is often right where later translators are in error. Charles Lamb thought Boyd the best translation of Dante.[3]

(Vol. xvii. p. 429.)

ANONYMOUS

1841. Oct. FOREIGN QUARTERLY REVIEW. ART. VIII. BRUCE WHYTE'S HISTOIRE DES LANGUES ROMANES.[4]

[The episode of Paolo and Francesca unequalled in any work, ancient or modern]

NO one ever gave to language such fearful power as Dante, or ever made its words shriek forth their fearful meaning. Whether in accents of horror and dread, or tenderest minstrelsy of love and passion, Dante Alighieri, with all the revolting character of the scholiast, with all the mysterious darkness of his style, with all the personages that it presents to us, whose interest is greatly gone, and would be wholly were they not married to his immortal verse,—Dante stands second to none of any age or time, though the greatest of modern romancers, who unconsciously often approached him closely, denies to him the highest niche in the temple of fame. We scarcely dare venture to glance at the fearful episode of Ugolino, unmatched in expressive terms, unequalled in description, or at that gush of tenderness from his soul in the Francesca da Rimini. Nothing equals that in any work, ancient or modern. The whirling forms of the eternally-united pair—their lone devotedness—their love in hell and pain—their wish to pray, yet conscious of its fruitless issue—the tale of their love—the unpremeditated result—the closing of Galeotto—the modest veiling of their fearful sin's fruition—

'Quel giorno più non vi leggemmo avante'—

the gushing sorrow of the other spirit, as the tale of their guilt and

[1] [Here follows the Italian text of *Par.* xv. 97-148, accompanied by the translations of Cary, Wright, and Merivale.]

[2] [See above, vol. i. pp. 410 ff.]

[3] [The writer does not say where this opinion of Lamb is recorded.]

[4] [See above, pp. 657 ff.]

sin is told—the overpowering crush upon the feelings of the iron-souled Florentine,

'Che cade come corpo morto cade,'

as the last 'parole di dolore' fell from Francesca. Never again will such a tale, and that in how brief a space, meet mortal ear. It is as though the fearful spirits of the lovers had, in their pained semblance, stood before the living and not the intellectual eye of Dante.

(Vol. xxviii. pp. 202-3.)

BIBLIOTHECA GRENVILLIANA

1842. BIBLIOTHECA GRENVILLIANA; OR BIBLIOGRAPHICAL NOTICES OF RARE AND CURIOUS BOOKS, FORMING PART OF THE LIBRARY OF THE RIGHT HON. THOMAS GRENVILLE.

[Thomas Grenville, book-collector, third son of George Grenville, was born in 1755, and was educated at Christ Church, Oxford. After serving for a time in the Army he entered Parliament, and sat successively for Buckinghamshire (1780-4), Aldborough (1790-6), and Buckingham (1796-1818). He was First Lord of the Admiralty (1806-7), in succession to Fox, in his brother, Lord Grenville's, administration, on the fall of which he withdrew from public life. He retired from Parliament in 1818, and from that time till his death in 1846 he devoted himself to the formation of his famous collection of books. At the instigation of Antonio Panizzi, Keeper of Printed Books, Grenville bequeathed his library, which consisted of 20,000 volumes, and was valued at £50,000, to the British Museum, where it now forms the Grenville Library. A Catalogue of the most valuable items, prepared by J. T. Payne and H. Foss, was published in 1842, to which a supplement was issued in 1848, after the collection had been placed in the British Museum. Among the printed books were many rare editions of the *Divina Commedia* (Part i. pp. 178-9, 831), including those of Foligno, 1472 (the *editio princeps*); Mantua, 1472; Venice, 1477; the very rare undated edition published at Naples by Francesco del Tuppo; Milan, 1478; and Florence, 1481 (a copy with the whole complement of nineteen plates—an item of excessive rarity); as well as the Aldine, 1502, on vellum; and the *editio princeps* of the *Convivio* (1490), and of the *Credo* (undated).]

CHARLES LOCK EASTLAKE

(1793-1865)

[Charles Lock Eastlake, President of the Royal Academy, was born at Plymouth in 1793. He was educated at Plympton Grammar School, and at the Charterhouse and studied art under B. R. Haydon. After visiting Italy and Greece he began to exhibit at the British Institution (1823), and the Royal Academy (1827). He was elected A.R.A. in 1827, and R.A. in 1829. From 1843 to 1847 he was Keeper of the National Gallery and was appointed Director in 1855. He was elected President of the Royal Academy in 1850, and held the office until his death at Pisa in 1865. In 1842 Eastlake edited an English translation (by Mrs. M. Hutton) of Franz Kugler's *Handbuch der Kunstgeschichte*, to which he contributed notes. Several of these contain references to Dante.]

1842. A HANDBOOK OF THE HISTORY OF PAINTING.

[The discovery of Giotto's portrait of Dante]

VASARI states that Giotto painted in the chapel of the Palazzo del Podestà the portraits of Dante, Brunetto Latini, Corso Donati, and others. He speaks of these works as the first successful attempts at portrait after the revival of art. The figures were plastered or whitewashed over, probably not long after they were done, during the triumph of the political enemies of Dante and his party. The hope of recovering these interesting works had long been entertained, and various unsuccessful attempts to that end had been made at different times; but it was reserved for the perseverance of Mr. Aubrey Bezzi, a zealous promoter of the interests of art and literature, to be at length instrumental in restoring these most valuable relics to light. The crust of plaster was removed, and the portraits discovered in good preservation, in July, 1840.

(p. 50, *note*.)

In alluding to the recent discovery of a fresco by Giotto, the editor has mentioned Mr. Aubrey Bezzi as having been chiefly instrumental in bringing so interesting a relic to light. That this would never have been accomplished but for the perseverance of Mr. Bezzi is acknowledged by all; but the editor believes it will be more agreeable to that gentleman to add that Mr. Seymour Kirkup and the Marchese Ferroni assisted him materially in his difficult undertaking.[1]

(*Preface*, p. x, *note*.)

[Orcagna compared with Dante]

Pisa—Campo Santo. The large pictures on the north wall belong to the middle of the fourteenth century, and are the work of a profound and imaginative artist. . . . The mind of this artist (generally known by the surname Orcagna or Orgagna) rises indeed above Giotto, whose steps he followed, and might be compared to the poet of the *Divina Commedia*, were it not that the very subordinate degree of his technical cultivation places him far below the perfection of Dante's *terza rima*.

(p. 70.)

CHARLES HINDLEY

(fl. 1840)

[Charles Hindley's *Plain and Direct Translation of the Inferno*, which comes to an end abruptly at Canto iv. 57, is the first sustained attempt at an English prose trans-

[1] [For Kirkup's own account, see above, pp. 639 ff.]

lation of any portion of the *Divina Commedia.*[1] It was not till seven years later that John Carlyle's prose translation of the *Inferno* was published (1849); and it was yet another three years before the whole of the *Commedia* was translated (by E. O'Donnell) into English prose (1852). In spite of Hindley's claim that his version is 'plain and direct,' he himself has to admit that 'in some instances the text is slightly paraphrased,' and that occasionally he has thought it necessary to improve on the original by supplying 'adjectival words to heighten the effect, which would otherwise be tame and unsuited.']

1842. A PLAIN AND DIRECT TRANSLATION OF THE INFERNO OF DANTE, INTENDED TO RENDER THE DESIGN, CHARACTER, AND INCIDENTS OF THE DIVINA COMMEDIA FAMILIAR TO ENGLISH READERS, WITH EXPLANATORY NOTES.

[Plea for a prose translation of the *Divina Commedia*]

TO the generality of readers the *Divina Commedia* of Dante may be considered a *sealed book;* many have heard of the poem, but few are able to say of what it consists, or how it is treated; this ignorance of a subject so interesting in itself may be ascribed to the absence of a popular and intelligible translation, suited to all readers.

To supply this deficiency is the object of this undertaking. . . .

It has been said the Divina Commedia is 'not translateable,' that is, poetically, which is so far true, for in proportion as the English version shall be poetically perfect, in that proportion will it be defective as a true representation of the original. A free unfettered prose translation is not open to that objection. . . .

When this translation was commenced, I had no expectation that English words could be found to approach sufficiently near to be admissible as a true representation of the text and at the same time agreeable to read, or even intelligible, but further trial and increased pains brought me to believe Dante might be so far faithfully rendered in plain and direct prose as not to be unacceptable to English readers, and especially those desirous of acquiring a correct knowledge of the design, character, and incidents of this extraordinary poem, but unable to obtain that gratification from the original Italian.

(*Preface*, pp. iii. ff.)

[*Inferno* i. 1-58]

In the midway of this our mortal life I found myself in a dark and gloomy forest, that from the direct path was turned aside.

Alas! how difficult would it be to describe the savage wildness of that dense and intricate wood, the remembrance of which fills me with so much horror,

[1] [Reviewed in *Spectator*, July, 1842 (see below, p. 669).]

That death itself could be little more painful; but to speak of the good I derived from it, I will relate what else I there encountered.

How I first entered it is not in my power to describe, so much were my senses absorbed at the time when all trace of the true path was lost.

But as soon as I had arrived at the foot of a mountain which terminated this dreary valley that had struck my heart with so much dismay,

I looked on high and beheld its broad shoulders gilt with the rays of that bright planet which lights all mortals and guides them through every way.

Then were for a while allayed the fears that had so agitated me during the whole night, and which I had passed in so much misery.

As those who just escaped the perils of the sea, with exhausted breath arrived at the shore, turn back their looks on the angry waves aghast:

So did my mind, still intent on flight, look back upon that dreadful pass, through which few or none escape with life.

After that I had reposed my weary frame, I resumed my journey up the deserted hill, one foot ever in advance of the other.

When lo! just at the commencement of the ascent, a panther, agile and swift, appeared, whose skin was covered with various coloured spots,

Which, constantly presenting itself before me, so impeded my progress, that often I turned myself round purposing to retreat.

The time was the commencement of the morning, when the sun was rising with those beautiful stars that were with him when the Divine love

Gave the first motion to the heavens, so that I had great cause for hope from all I saw around me; the gay skin of that beautiful beast,

The hour of the morning, and the sweet season, but yet not without fear from a lion's form which came in sight,

And appeared as advancing against me with crest erect and rabid with hunger, and so fierce his aspect that the very air might be alarmed at his presence,

Besides these, a she-wolf that from its meagreness seemed as if all desires were centred in itself, and that many had suffered grievously therefrom.

This last caused me so much disquiet from the dread its look inspired, that in despair I relinquished all expectation of gaining the eminence.

And thus it is with all those that are eager to acquire; a time arrives that brings loss with it, and then they abandon themselves to sorrow and bewailing;

Such was the effect of the presence of this beast, that stealing upon me step by step drove me back to where the sun never penetrates.

(pp. 3 ff.)

ANONYMOUS

1842. July 23. SPECTATOR. A PLAIN AND DIRECT TRANSLATION OF THE INFERNO OF DANTE. . . . BY CHARLES HINDLEY. PART I. CANTOS 1, 2, 3, 4.

[The 'solemn and primeval grandeur' of Dante]

THIS is one of the many guides to a most difficult writer; one of the least pretending, and one of the best. So far as we have read, it consists of a close prose translation split into paragraphs to correspond with the *terza rima* of the original, so as to be of easy reference; and it is illustrated by short notes, explaining the allegory. Besides the antiquated style of his age, and the Florentine words used by the poet, in cultivating a compression and directness of style which imparted greater force to his language than that of any other Italian writer, Dante necessarily increased at times the obscurity inseparable from his half-metaphysical half-political satirical dream. The chief faults of the work appear to be two, of an opposite kind—not a sufficiently literal adherence to the text; and too literal an interpretation of metaphorical passages. . . . Mr. Hindley justifies his departures from the text on the score of expression or euphony; but no amplification can increase the effect of Dante's stern simplicity, which partakes of the same solemn and primeval grandeur that dignifies the great works of early inspiration, divine or secular—as the Bible, the most ancient sculptures, the works of the first great painters in Italy herself, Dante's contemporaries. . . . With a caveat against the full adoption of all Mr. Hindley's interpretations, where doubt abounds, we take his translation to be a useful clue to a study which without some clue were hopeless to the beginner. . . .

(Vol. xv. p. 715.)

HENRY NELSON O'NEIL

(1817-1880)

[Henry Nelson O'Neil, historical painter, was born at St. Petersburg in 1817. He came to England in 1823, and in 1836 became a student at the Royal Academy; he subsequently studied in Italy. O'Neil was an exhibitor at the Academy from 1838 to

1866, one of his exhibits being a picture of Paolo and Francesca (1842), the motto of which he appears to have translated himself from the *Inferno*. He died in London in 1880.]

1842. IN this year O'Neil exhibited at the Royal Academy a picture with the following title:—

Paul and Francesca of Rimini.

'We read one day for pastime seated nigh
* * * *
But one point only wholly us o'erthrew
When we came to the long-wished-for smile of her
To be thus kissed by such devoted love.
He who from me can be divided ne'er,
Kissed my mouth trembling in the act all over.
Accursed was the book, and he who wrote:
That day no further leaf we did uncover.'[1]

Dante, Inferno, canto v.

(*Catalogue of the Exhibition of the Royal Academy,* 1842, No. 258.)

W. S. P. HENDERSON

(fl. 1840)

1842. IN this year W. S. P. Henderson exhibited at the Royal Academy a picture with the following title:—

The Sunny days of old.

'We read one day for pastime, seated nigh
Alone, quite unsuspicious;
And ofttimes by that reading
Our eyes were drawn together, and the hue
Fled from our altered cheek.
The book and writer both
Are love's purveyors'—

Dante.[2]

(*Catalogue of the Exhibition of the Royal Academy,* 1842, No. 523.)

ALEXANDER ANDREW KNOX

(1818-1891)

[Alexander Andrew Knox, journalist and police magistrate, was born in London in 1818. He was educated at Blundell's School, Tiverton, and Trinity College, Cambridge (M.A. 1847). In 1842 he travelled in Italy with Mrs. Shelley, widow of the

[1] [*Inf.* v. 127, 132-8.]

[2] [*Inf.* v. 127 ff. (Cary, altered).]

poet, and made the acquaintance of Trelawney, the friend of Shelley and Byron. Knox was called to the bar at Lincoln's Inn in 1844, and in 1846 joined the staff of 'The Times,' for which he continued to write until 1860, when he was appointed a metropolitan police magistrate. He died in London in 1891. In 1842 Knox published a volume of verse *Giotto and Francesca, and Other Poems.* The first poem contains a reference to Dante; among the miscellaneous poems are translations of Boccaccio's sonnet on the death of Petrarch (p. 140), and of one of Michael Angelo's sonnets on Dante (p. 142).]

1842. GIOTTO AND FRANCESCA, AND OTHER POEMS.

IT so befell, while musing on some scheme
  Might steer his bark to peaceful harbourage,
With ivory wand Sleep ushered in a dream:
  Two ladies bright, with tiny elfin page—
The sunshine of their angel smiles did seem
  To thaw the snow, and stay the tempest's rage,
Had choked the daisies, and primroses all,
That should on gentle soil hold festival;

And he, by dream-law, knew those ladies twain;
  Laura, and Beatricè,—Petrarch's star,
And her who captive held in flowery chain
  The grand old man[1] who raised Hell's portal bar:
As when God's cloud-bow is unstrung, again
  Melting they lost each hue particular,
And left a smile upon the yellow air,
To say, that something lovely had been there.

(*Stanzas* xxxi-xxxii. pp. 13-14.)

JOHN RUSKIN

(1819-1900)

[John Ruskin was the only child of a wine-merchant in London, where he was born in 1819. He was educated in London and at Christ Church, Oxford, where he marticulated in 1836. In 1843, the year after he took his degree, he published anonymously the first volume of *Modern Painters*, of which the second volume appeared in 1846, the third and fourth in 1856, and the fifth in 1860. Before *Modern Painters* was completed he published also his *Seven Lamps of Architecture* (1849), and *Stones of Venice* (1851-3). Between 1855 and 1870 Ruskin delivered lectures on art, economics, etc. in all parts of the country, some of which were afterwards published in various volumes. In 1870 he was appointed to the newly-founded Slade professorship of Art at Oxford, which he held until 1879, and again from 1883 to 1884. Ruskin died in 1900, at Brantwood, Coniston, which had been his residence since 1871. Ruskin's reverence for Dante was deep and abiding. It was during his visit to Italy in 1845 that he first read the *Divina Commedia*. Up to that time he says he had

[1] [Dante.]

never read a line of it, except the story of Ugolino.[1] 'From this time, for many years, perhaps no book, with the exception of the Bible, was his more constant companion than the *Divina Comedy*, either in the original or in Cary's well-known translation.'[2] In the *Stones of Venice*[3] Ruskin says, 'I think that the central man of all the world, as representing in perfect balance the imaginative, moral, and intellectual faculties, all at their highest, is Dante.' No references to Dante occur in the first volume of *Modern Painters.* They are numerous in the other volumes of that work (especially in vol. iii., which contains many translations from the *Commedia*), and in the *Stones of Venice*, as well as in his numberless later writings.[4] The solitary reference before 1844 occurs in a letter to Samuel Rogers, written from Venice in 1842, which certainly betrays a closer acquaintance with the *Inferno* than Ruskin confesses to in the passage quoted above.]

1842. June 23. LETTER TO SAMUEL ROGERS (from Venice).

[Hint for another scene of the *Inferno*]

ST. MARK'S PLACE and St. Mark's have held their own, and this is much to say, for both are grievously destroyed by inconsistent and painful associations—especially the great square, filled as it is with spiritless loungers, and a degenerate race of caterers for their amusement . . . and exhibitors, not of puppet shows, for Venice is now too lazy to enjoy Punch, but of dramatic spectacles composed of figures pricked out in paper, and turned in a procession round a candle. Among which sources of entertainment the Venetians lounge away their evenings all the summer long. . . . If Dante had seen these people, he would assuredly have added another scene to the *Inferno*—a Venetian corner, with a central tower of St. Mark's with red-hot stairs, up which the indolent Venetians would have been continually driven at full speed, and dropped from the parapet into a lagoon of hot café noir.

(*Rogers and his Contemporaries*, ed. Clayden, vol. ii. pp. 305-6.)

GEORGE PATTEN

(1801-1865)

[George Patten, portrait and historical painter, was born in 1801. He started as a miniature-painter, his father's profession, but in 1830 he took to oil-painting. In 1837 he visited Italy, and on his return to England he was elected A.R.A. In 1840 he went to Germany to paint a portrait of Prince Albert, to whom afterwards, when Prince Consort, he was appointed portrait-painter in ordinary. He exhibited many portraits and other pictures at the Royal Academy, among the latter being a picture of Dante and Virgil in the *Inferno* (1843). Patten died at Winchmore Hill in 1865.]

[1] [*Modern Painters*, ed. 1883, vol. ii. *Epilogue*—quoted by C. E. Norton, in Introduction to *Comments of John Ruskin on the Divina Commedia*, by G. P. Huntingdon, p. ix.]

[2] [C. E. Norton, *ubi supra*, p. x.]

[3] [Vol. iii. § 67.]

[4] [See G. P. Huntingdon, *op. cit.* p. v.]

1843. IN this year Patten exhibited at the Royal Academy a picture with the following title:—

Dante, accompanied by Virgil in his descent to the Inferno recognises his three countrymen, Rusticucci, Aldobrandi, and Guidoguerra.—*Divina Commedia, Inferno* Canto xvi.[1]

(*Catalogue of the Exhibition of the Royal Academy*, 1843, No. 67.)

FREDERICK RICHARD PICKERSGILL

(1820-1900)

[Frederick Richard Pickersgill, historical painter, nephew of Henry William Pickersgill, the well-known portrait-painter, was born in London in 1820. He studied at the Royal Academy schools, and exhibited his first picture at the Academy in 1839. In 1843 he exhibited at the Academy a pictute of 'Dante's Dream' from the *Purgatorio*. Pickersgill was elected A.R.A. in 1847, and R.A. in 1857, and in 1873 he was appointed Keeper of the Royal Academy, which office he held until 1887. He died at Yarmouth, Isle of Wight, in 1900.]

1843. IN this year Pickersgill exhibited at the Royal Academy a picture with the following title:—

Dante's dream.
"Thus she sang:
For my brow to weave
A garland, these fair hands unwearied ply.
To please me at the crystal mirror, here
I deck me."—*See the Purgatory of Dante*, Canto xxvii.[2]

(*Catalogue of the Exhibition of the Royal Academy*, 1843, No. 155.)

BIBLIOTHECA BODLEIANA

1843. CATALOGUS LIBRORUM IMPRESSORUM BIBLIOTHECAE BODLEIANAE IN ACADEMIA OXONIENSI.

[The Printed Editions of Dante's works in the Bodleian at this date comprised seven fifteenth-century editions of the *Commedia*, viz. Foligno, 1472 (*editio princeps*); Venice, 1477; Milan, 1477; Florence, 1481; Venice, 1484; Bressa, 1487; and Venice, 1497; and six of the sixteenth, including the Aldines of 1502 and 1515; besides the *editio princeps* of the *De Monarchia* (1559) and of the *Vita Nuova* (1576).]

[1] [*Inf*. xvi. 4 ff.—See Haydon's criticism of this picture in a letter to Seymour Kirkup, May 26, 1843 (vol. i. p. 667).]

[2] [*Purg*. xxvii. 99, 101-3 (Cary).—See Haydon's criticism of this picture in a letter to Seymour Kirkup, May 26, 1843 (vol. i. p. 667).]

WILLIAM DOWE

(fl. 1840)

1843. June. DUBLIN UNIVERSITY MAGAZINE.

The Death of Ugolino
Dante

[*Inferno* xxxiii. 37-75]

ERE dawn, awake upon my dungeon bed,
I heard my little children, in their sleep,
Murmuring and sobbing, and demanding bread:
Oh! thou art cruel if thou canst not weep
To ponder o'er my suffering in the dread
Foreboding of my heart; if thou canst keep
Thine own unmoved, what tale of passing woe
Can touch thy soul, or cause thy tears to flow?

They woke at last: and it was now the hour
That ever brought our wonted food; yet we
Doubted and feared; and moved the moments slower,
And still it came not; and I heard a key
Locking the portal of our prison-tower.
I gazed upon my children, and, on me,
They gazed again; and then my heart grew weak,
And I sat motionless; but could not speak.

I did not weep; my heart was turned to stone.
My children wept; and little Anselm cried:
'What ails thee, father?—for thy look is grown
So ghastly, fixed on something at thy side!'
Then did I feign to suffer loss; no moan
Passed from my lips, and nothing I replied
All that long day and the succeeding night,
Till o'er the world rose the slow morning's light.

When the first rays streamed from the outer air
Into the dungeon's dreary gloom, and I
Saw my own face in four pale faces there,
I gnawed my arms in utter agony!
My little ones, believing my despair
Demanded bread, rose, crying, 'Let us die
That thou mayest live; thou gavest us flesh and blood
Take them again, to be our father's food!'

Then I grew still, to make their sorrows less:
  And that day and the next in silence past:
Why yawned not Earth beneath our dire distress?
  And the fourth day arose; and then, at last,
Gaddo, my boy, lay pale and motionless
  Beside my feet, and sorrowfully cast
His glazing eyes on mine, and faintly cried,
'I'm dying, father, help me!' so he died.

And, as thou seest me, so did I behold
  Upon the fifth and sixth days, one by one,
My murdered children perish, stark and cold.
  And falling on them, when their life was gone,
Groaning their cherished names, did I enfold
  In my weak arms their faded bodies wan.
For six days more: then hunger came to close
All of my life that could survive my woes.

(Vol. xxi. pp. 657-8.)

JOSEPH BARCLAY PENTLAND

(1797-1873)

[Joseph Barclay Pentland, traveller, a native of Ireland, was born in 1797. He was educated at Armagh and at the University of Paris. In 1827 he was appointed secretary to the consulate-general in Peru, and in 1836 he became consul-general in the republic of Bolivia, which post he held until 1839. In 1826-7 he surveyed a large portion of the Bolivian Andes, in company with Woodbine Parish; and in 1838 he made a tour in the southern province of ancient Peru. From 1845 he made Rome his winter residence. His intimate acquaintance with the topography and antiquities of the city led to his being selected to act as guide to the Prince of Wales when he visited Rome in 1861. Pentland, who died in London in 1873, wrote the portion relating to Rome in Murray's *Handbook for Travellers in Central Italy*, published in 1843, and edited several other volumes in that series.]

1843. HANDBOOK FOR TRAVELLERS IN CENTRAL ITALY, INCLUDING THE PAPAL STATES, ROME, AND THE CITIES OF ETRURIA.[1]

[Michael Angelo inspired by Dante in his Last Judgment]

ROME. Vatican (Sistine Chapel).—The great fresco of the Last Judgment, sixty feet high and thirty broad, occupies the end wall immediately opposite the entrance. . . . On the left of the picture is represented the fall of the damned: the demons are seen coming out of the pit to seize them as they struggle to escape; their features express the utmost despair, contrasted with the wildest passions of rage, anguish, and defiance; Charon is

[1] [The portion relating to Rome was written by Pentland, the remainder was by Octavian Blewitt (see below, pp. 676-9).]

ferrying another group across the Styx, and is striking down the rebellious with his oar, in accordance with the description of Dante, from which Michael Angelo sought inspiration:

'Batte col remo qualunque s' adagia.'[1]

(pp. 389-90).

[MSS. and editions of Dante in the Biblioteca Barberini]

Rome. Palazzo Barberini.—In the Library there are twenty MSS. of Dante: one of these, a folio on vellum, is said to be the most richly illuminated of all the known copies of the *Divina Commedia*. . . . The rare Dante of Venice, 1477, is filled with notes by Bembo; and another edition of the great poet has some curious notes by Tasso.

(p. 439.)

[Illustrations of the *Divina Commedia* by Koch and Veit]

Rome. Villa Massimi.—This villa, formerly the Giustiniani, near the Lateran, is remarkable for its interesting frescoes illustrative of Dante, Ariosto, and Tasso, by modern German masters. The first room contains subjects from the *Divina Commedia* by Koch[2] and Ph. Veit.[3]

(p. 472.)

OCTAVIAN BLEWITT

(1810-1884)

[Octavian Blewitt, who was born in London in 1810, and educated at Plymouth Grammar School, entered the medical profession. He visited Madeira with a patient, and afterwards travelled extensively in Italy, Egypt, Greece, Turkey, and other countries. In 1839 he was elected Secretary of the Royal Literary Fund, which office he held until his death in London in 1884. Among his publications was Murray's *Handbook for Travellers in Central Italy* (1843), the Roman part of which was written by J. B. Pentland, and the volume in the same series for Southern Italy (1853). The former, which was originally published anonymously, contains many interesting references to Dante, a few of which are given below.]

1843. HANDBOOK FOR TRAVELLERS IN CENTRAL ITALY, INCLUDING THE PAPAL STATES, ROME, AND THE CITIES OF ETRURIA.[4]

[Dante's reference to the Carisenda Tower at Bologna]

BOLOGNA.—Near the Foro de' Mercanti, are the two celebrated leaning towers, called the Torre Asinelli and the Torre Garisenda, the most remarkable edifices in Bologna. . . . The Torre Garisenda, built by the brothers Filippo and

[1] [*Inf.* iii. 111.]

[2] [Joseph Anton Koch (1768-1839).]

[3] [Philip Veit (1793-1877). For an account of these frescoes by Koch and Veit, see Volkmann's *Iconografia Dantesca*.]

[4] [The portion relating to Rome was written by J. B. Pentland (see above, pp. 675-6).]

Oddo Garisenda, in 1110, is 130 feet high, according to the local authorities. Its inclination, measured from its axis, was, in 1792, 8 feet to the east, and 3 to the south; but the experiments of Professors Bacelli and Antolini, in 1813, showed an increase of an inch and half over the former observations. Alidosi and other writers have endeavoured to maintain that the inclination of the Garisenda is the effect of art; as if Italy did not present an abundance of such examples in situations where the ground is liable to gradual sinking and earthquakes are of common occurrence. The best answer to this absurd idea is the simple fact that the courses of brick and the holes to receive the timbers of the floors are horizontal, which they certainly would not have been if the tower had been built in its present inclined form. The Garisenda, however, has a higher interest than that derived from this question, since it supplied Dante with a noble simile, in which he compares the giant Antaeus stooping to seize him and his guide, to this tower, as it is seen from beneath when the clouds are flying over it.[1]

(pp. 62-3.)

[The tomb of Dante at Ravenna]

Ravenna.—Of all the monuments of Ravenna, there is none which excites so profound an interest as the tomb of Dante. In spite of the bad taste of the building in which it is placed, it is impossible to approach the last resting-place of the great poet without feeling that it is one of the first monuments of Italy. . . . The remains of the poet were originally interred in the church of San Francesco; but on the expulsion of his patron Guido da Polenta from Ravenna, they were with difficulty protected from the persecutions of the Florentines, and from the excommunication of the Pope. Cardinal Beltramo del Poggetto ordered his bones to be burnt with his tract on "Monarchy," and they narrowly escaped the profanation of a disinterment. After the lapse of a century and a half, Bernardo Bembo, Podestà of Ravenna for the republic of Venice in 1482, and father of the cardinal, did honour to his memory by erecting a mausoleum on the present site, from the designs of Pietro Lombardo. In 1692 this building was repaired and restored at the public expense by the cardinal legate, Domenico Corsi of Florence, and rebuilt in its present form in 1780, at the cost of Cardinal Gonzaga of Mantua, the legate of that period. It is a square building, internally decorated with stucco ornaments little worthy of such a sepulchre. On the ceiling of the cupola are four medallions, of Virgil, Brunetto Latini (the master of the poet), Can Grande della Scala, and Guido da Polenta, his patron.

[1] [Blewitt quotes *Inf.* xxxi. 136-41.]

On the walls are two Latin inscriptions, one in verse recording the foundation of Bembo, the other the dedication of Cardinal Gonzaga to the 'Poetae sui temporis primo restitutori.' The sarcophagus of Greek marble which contains the ashes of the poet,[1] bears his portrait, and is surmounted by a crown of laurel, with the motto *Virtuti et honori.* The inscription is said to have been written by himself. Below it, in a marble case, is a long Latin history of the tomb. . . .

The feelings with which this sepulchre was visited by three of the greatest names in modern literature deserve to be mentioned; Chateaubriand is said to have knelt bareheaded at the door before he entered; Byron deposited on the tomb a copy of his works; and Alfieri prostrated himself before it, and embodied his emotions in one of the finest sonnets in the Italian language:—

'O gran padre Alighier, se dal ciel miri
Me tuo discepol non indegno starmi,
Dal cor traendo profondi sospiri,
Prostrato innanzi a' tuoi funerei marmi.'

(pp. 88-9.)

[MS. of Dante at Ravenna]

Ravenna.—A MS. of Dante, on vellum, with beautiful miniatures of the fourteenth century, is preserved here, in the Bibliotheca Comunale: its version is little known.[2]

(p. 91.)

[Dante and the *Pineta* of Ravenna]

Ravenna.—The celebrated *Pineta* or Pine Forest, is approached not far beyond the Basilica of S. Apollinare in Classe, and the road to Rimini skirts it as far as Cervia. This venerable forest, the most ancient perhaps in Italy, extends along the shores of the Adriatic for a distance of twenty-five miles, from the Lamone north of Ravenna, to Cervia on the south, and covers a flat sandy tract, varying in breadth from one to three miles. . . . No forest in the world is more renowned in classical and poetical interest: it is celebrated by Dante, Boccaccio, Dryden, and Byron; it supplied Rome with timber for her fleets; and upon the masts which it produced the banner of Venice floated in the days of her supremacy One part of the forest still retains the name of the *Vicolo de' Poeti*, from a tradition that it is the spot where Dante loved to meditate:—

[1][As a matter of fact the tomb is a cenotaph; Dante's bones were laid elsewhere. For the story of their discovery in 1865 see Toynbee's *Life of Dante* (ed. 1904), pp. 139 ff.]

[2][It is described by Colomb de Batines, under No. 402, in his *Bibliografia Dantesca.*]

'Tal, qual di ramo in ramo si raccoglie,
Per la pineta in sul lito di Chiassi,
Quando Eolo Scirocco fuor discioglie.'
Purg. xxviii. 19-21.

(pp. 95-6.)

[The episode of Paolo and Francesca in the *Divina Commedia*]

Rimini.—The house of Francesca da Rimini is identified with that occupied by Count Cisterni, formerly the Palazzo Ruffi; or rather, it is supposed to have occupied the site of the existing building. There is, perhaps, no part of the Divina Commedia so full of touching pathos and tenderness as the tale of guilty love in which Francesca reveals to Dante the secret of her soul, and of her soul's master. Its interest is increased by the recollection that Francesca was the daughter of Guido da Polenta, Lord of Ravenna, who was the friend and generous protector of Dante in his old age. The delicacy with which she conveys in a single sentence the story of her crime, is surpassed only by the passage where the poet represents the bitter weeping of the condemned shades as so far overcoming his feelings that he faints with compassion for their misery.[1]

(p. 107.)

JOHN DAYMAN

(1802-1871)

[John Dayman, born in 1802, was admitted Scholar of Corpus Christi College, Oxford, in 1819; he graduated B.A. in 1823, M.A. in 1826, and was Fellow of the College from 1825 to 1831, when he accepted the College living of Skelton, in Cumberland, which he held until his death in 1871. Dayman published in 1843 a translation of the *Inferno* into *terza rima*, the first complete version of any one of the three parts of the *Divina Commedia* in the metre of the original.[2] In 1865 he published a version in the same metre of the whole of the *Commedia*,[3] the translation of the *Inferno* being revised and recast.]

1843. THE INFERNO OF DANTE ALIGHIERI, TRANSLATED IN THE TERZA RIMA OF THE ORIGINAL, WITH NOTES AND APPENDIX.

[Translator's apology]

IT was intended to have prefaced the translation of Dante's 'Inferno,' which is here offered to the public, by some remarks on metrical structure, as subservient to the principal object of the Poet. Such observations would not have been un-

[1] [Blewitt here quotes *Inf.* v. 127-42.]

[2] [Reviewed in *Spectator*, Aug. 1843; and *Athenæum*, March, 1844 (see below, pp. 681-2, 683-4).]

[3] [The fourth in *terza rima*, the other three being by C. B. Cayley (1851-3-4), J. W. Thomas (1859-62-6), and Mrs. Ramsay (1862-3).]

suited to this *first* attempt[1] (as far as I am aware) to present Dante to the English reader in the Terza Rima of his own choice; and to me they appeared almost necessary in self-justification, with a version so faithful and spirited, as I am told Mr. Cary's is, already in possession of the field. But as those arguments would have added greatly to the length of the prefatory notice, they have been withheld. . . .

By inspection of the Rimario appended to Lombardi's edition, it will be found that Dante has allowed himself, on more than one occasion, to use the same rhyme twice in the same Canto, and this license has been taken, though sparingly, in the following version.

In justice to myself, no less than others, I have rigidly abstained from making any acquaintance with the English translations which have preceded this; and hence the candid reader will refer whatever coincidences he may discover to our common original.[2]

The peculiarities of Dante's genius are too well known to make an excuse necessary here for the obscurity of occasional passages, which could hardly have been avoided, even by the unsatisfactory endeavour after a paraphrase, rather than a literal translation.

(*Preface*, pp. iii-v.)

[Bertrand de Born (*Inferno* xxviii. 112-42)]

I, remaining on the crowd to look
Beheld a thing, the which for very fear
To tell without more proof I might not brook,
If conscience, good companion, were not near
To reassure, who sets the spirit free
Within the hauberk of a breast sincere.
Certes I saw, and yet I seem to see,
A bust without the head go moving thus,
As moved the rest of that sad company:
And by its hairs the lopt head pendulous
It lantern-fashion with one hand sustained,
Which sighed, 'Ah! woe is me!' and glared on us.
So, as a lamp to light himself constrained,
There two in one, and one in two appears;
He knows how this might be, Who so ordained.

[1] [By no means the first; see, for instance, under Hayley, Bland, Leigh Hunt, Byron, Shelley, T. Roscoe, Gladstone, Shannon, and Merivale.]

[2] [In a copy of Dayman's 'Inferno,' which belonged to Ichabod Charles Wright, the Dante translator, the latter has inserted a number of MS. notes, such as 'my word,' 'my rhyme,' 'my line,' 'suspicious,' 'most suspicious.' showing that he did not believe Dayman's disclaimer, and evidently suggesting that Dayman had borrowed from his own translation. In a note on Dayman's preface he says: 'Pretends ignorance of my translation, though it had been published ten years,—reviewed in almost all the reviews—and quoted in numerous works.' He calls Dayman's translation, 'a burlesque upon Dante: rhyme without either sense or poetry, a mere verbal translation.']

Now fronting the bridge-foot, aloft he rears
  Arm, head and all, that nearer to our line
  His words more plainly might salute our ears;
Which were: 'See thou my troublous curse; 'tis thine
  Yet breathing 'mid the dead to make resort;
  See thou if any plague can match with mine.
And know me—so thou shalt my state report—
  Bertrand de Born, who did the Younger King
  With vile instilments banefully exhort.
'Twixt sire and son I caused rebellion spring;
  Not more Achitophel's malignant dart
  Did the lost Absalom 'gainst David sting.
Because I wrought so joined ones to part,
  Myself my brain must parted bear, alas!
  From its own source within this trunk, my heart
On me retaliation thus doth pass.'

(pp. 181-2.)

ANONYMOUS

1843. Aug. 19. SPECTATOR. DAYMAN'S DANTE.

[Dante's manner—Dayman compared with Cary]

OF all the Italian poets, Dante would seem susceptible of being most finely translated into English. His genius is not alien to that of our own clime. Though less laboriously straining after pomp of style than our own Milton—though possessing a majesty of which Bunyan, the author of what a stage-manager might term a 'coat-and-waistcoat' epic, was destitute—the real life-like aspect of his vision is not remote from the effect commonly ascribed to the homely English fabulist, and his exalted style exceeds in stern simplicity the lofty poet, while his subject is akin to that of both our popular writers. His manner is English: it is more direct, more concise, graver, than that of his countrymen in general; and though there are glimpses of passion, tender as well as fierce, his nature was less voluptuous and enjoying. He describes the reading, the tremours, the doom of Paolo and Francesca: Ariosto would have described their endearments. . . .

The real difficulty in handling Dante's text lies in the power and beauty of the idea, which a timid or feeble copyist may spoil. But the translator will find his greatest strength in the closest fidelity to his original. . . . A translation of Dante should as nearly as possible let the English reader know what Dante *is*—for that is what the English reader wishes to know—not what the poet might have been had he been our own countryman. In this respect, Mr. Dayman has gone rightly to work. He has endeavoured to keep as close to his author as two dissimilar vocabularies would admit. He has very properly imitated Dante's *terza rima*, for though the endless weaving of that verse is in itself tedious, and the multiplication of rhymes is more difficult in English than Italian, Dante did not write in blank verse, or any but *terza rima;* and metre is one characteristic of every poet's style. Mr. Dayman avails himself too of many licences, even to the literal translation of words not used in our language. This is not only fair, but useful, as bringing the translation closer to the text. . . . Altogether, Mr. Dayman gives the English reader a better idea of Dante, his matter, and manner, than any previous translator. . . . Upon the whole, if Cary's version is the more even composition as a piece of English writing, and less chargeable with incorrectnesses that additional pains might have removed from the other, Dayman conveys to the English reader a more spirited copy of the poet's images and a more vivid representation of his manner.

(Vol. xvi. pp. 786-8.)

ANONYMOUS

1843. Dec. ATHENÆUM. FOSCOLO'S COMMEDIA DI DANTE ALLIGHIERI.[1]

[Mazzini's edition of Foscolo's Dante]

THE history of this edition is briefly as follows.—Ugo Foscolo undertook to prepare, for Mr. Pickering, editions of the four great Italian Poets, but ill health and the perplexities of his later years, prevented the fulfilment of his intention. With Dante, however, the first of the Series, he had made such progress, that Mr. Rolandi purchased the MS. for £400, and the result is before us in a very handsome illustrated edition. The text is said to have been prepared with great care, and after a scrupulous examination of early manuscripts—and there is prefixed to the work an elaborate essay on its history, and a critical examination of the various biographers and commentators—and affixed to it a life of Dante drawn from his works, a bibliographical history of those works, and a very comprehensive Index.

(Vol. 1843, p. 1132.)

[1] [Published, under the editorship of G. Mazzini, in 4 vols. by Rolandi in 1842-3 (see above, p. 173).]

ANONYMOUS

1844. March. ATHENÆUM. DAYMAN'S INFERNO OF DANTE ALIGHIERI TRANSLATED INTO TERZA RIMA.

[English translations of the *Commedia*]

ONE great difficulty of Dante (perhaps his greatest), is the conciseness of his style; nothing tries a translator more than this. Only great authors write concisely, and they can do it with both energy and grace; in inferior hands, the concise style becomes hard and stiff. . . .

The subject and style of Dante form the medium of transition from the classic to the romantic, and as such unite both. What the translator has to do, is to present this peculiarity, and not by any artifice to seek to popularize it, or, in other words, to substitute something else. Whether or not he has reverence for his author, it is his duty, in this instance, to make as strict a transcript as can be rendered out of one language into another. Not amusement, so much as instruction, is sought by the knowledge of such a poet as Dante. The reader must be responsive to the sternness and severity of thought, which belongs to his author. He must seek to educate himself, by means of the book, into a capacity to understand the book. He must climb, step by step, the ladder of genius, which it presents to him; the first round whereof is in Hell, and the topmost in the highest Heaven. He must not expect to find such an ascent easy; but prepare himself for a journey of much toil and trouble; for it is, what it ought to be, difficult and full of peril. Let him learn too, that the diction of Dante presents to him none of the commonplaces of poetic phraseology, and that to translate him by means of those verbalisings which are hereditary among our native versifiers, were to palm a falsehood on the unwary reader, however delightful an English poem might thus be made out of the materials of the Italian one. A new Pope might doubtless do for Dante what the old one did for Homer; but Heaven forefend that any such presumptuous vicar of the wise and tuneful dead, should ever again secure a place on the English Parnassus. . . .

Dante has been, indeed, fortunate in his translators. To pass by the attempt of Hayley[1] to render him in his original *lilt*, which, though extremely feeble, was sufficiently elegant; the translations of Mr. Cary[2] and Mr. Wright[3] are such as have never fallen to the lot of any other modern poet. Fairfax's translation of Tasso is a fine paraphrase, like Chapman's Homer, and the late Mr. Wiffen's version of the same poet is not without its merit; but they take their stand upon different and lower ground than that assumed by

[1] [See vol. i. pp. 359 ff.] [2] [See vol. i. pp. 465 ff.] [3] [See above, pp. 568 ff.]

either Mr. Cary's or Mr. Wright's severally great performances. And now we have Mr. Dayman's work, which is a sincere, earnest, and laborious effort; sufficiently learned and accurate, with the addtional advantage of its being in the measure of the original, properly written, and with careful attention to the striking movement of the ternal line, in which consists, in fact, the musical beauty of Dante's verse.

(Vol. 1844, pp. 267-8.)

LORD JOHN RUSSELL

(1792-1878)

[Lord John Russell, third son of the sixth Duke of Bedford, was born in London in 1792. He was educated at Westminster (1803-4), and Edinburgh University (1809-12). He entered Parliament as member for Tavistock in 1813, and first took office as Paymaster-General in 1831 in Lord Grey's administration, in which capacity it fell to him to introduce the Reform Bill three times before it was passed in 1832. Lord John was Home Secretary (1835) and Colonial Secretary (1839) under Lord Melbourne, and in 1846 became Prime Minister. He resigned in 1852, and subsequently held office as Foreign Secretary under Lord Aberdeen (1852) and Lord Palmerston (1861). He was created Earl Russell in 1861, and was a second time Prime Minister from 1865 to 1866, when he finally retired from official life. He died at Pembroke Lodge, Richmond Park in 1878. Among Lord John Russell's many literary achievements was a translation (published in the *Literary Souvenir* for 1844) of the Francesca da Rimini episode, from the fifth canto of the *Inferno*, into heroic couplets,—an exploit which a writer in the *English Review* declared to be quite as venturesome in its way as taking command of the Channel Fleet at ten minutes notice (see below, pp. 686 ff.).]

1844. TRANSLATION OF THE 'FRANCESCA DA RIMINI,' FROM THE 'INFERNO' OF DANTE, CANTO V. 73-142.[1]

'I FAIN would speak to that unhappy pair
Who hand in hand so lightly float in air;'
In words like these to Maro I expressed
My wish; and thus he granted my request.
'Wait till the shades approach; then name the word
Of love, which rules them: straight you will be heard.'
Soon as I saw the constant ghosts were cast
Near to our station by the baleful blast,
Swift I conjured them: 'By your miseries past,
O speak!' And as two doves on wings outspread
Float to their darling nest, by fondness led,
So did these sorrowing spirits leave the throng
Where Dido broods o'er man's unpunished wrong,
Nor aught of woe concealed, nor aught refused,
Such magic power was in the words I used.

[1] [Published in the *Literary Souvenir* for 1844.]

'Oh, pitying stranger, that in this dread place
Canst feel for bloodstained hearts! Had we found grace
With the great Lord of all, we should not cease
To pray His mercy for your future peace,
For you shew mercy to our mortal sin.
But stay—while yet the tempest holds its din,
Speak what you list, ask what you seek to know,
And hear our griefs—'tis all we can bestow.
In lands where Po with ample torrent flows
To the broad sea, and finds at length repose,
We sprung. There love, by which each gentle breast
Is quickly fired, my Paolo's heart possessed,
For that fair form, torn from me in such chill
And cruel fashion as afflicts me still.
True love by love must ever be repaid:
I learned to please him so, that still his shade
Is seen, e'en here, to wander by my side.
For love we lived, for love together died.
But he by whose unnatural hand we bled
With Cain shall dwell.' These words the shadow said;
Thoughtful I listened,—when I heard th' offence
Borne by these gentle souls, in sad suspense
I bent my eyes: the silence Virgil broke,
And questioned of my thoughts: slowly I spoke.
'Alas!' I said, 'how soft and light a train
Of sweet desires led these to endless pain!'
Then, turning round, the lovers I addressed:
'Your griefs, Francesca, weigh upon my breast,
And fill my eyes with tears; vouchsafe to tell,
In love's spring season of fond sighs, what spell
First brought the bud of secret hope to flower,
And taught your hearts the presence of his power?'
'Alas!' she said, 'when only pangs remain,
The memory of past joy is sharpest pain,
And this your master knows: yet if desire,
So strong and eager, prompts you to enquire
Whence sprung our love, the story you shall hear,
Tho' every word be followed by a tear.
One day, intent to while away the time,
Alone, yet void of fear as free from crime,
We read of Lancelot's love. Oft from the book
We raised our eyes, and each commingling look
Led to a blush. The story we pursued
Till one short fatal passage all subdued.
For when we read, the lover crowned with bliss,

Her rapturous smile, and his more ardent kiss,
He, who is ever to my side attached,
He from my lips a kiss all trembling snatched.
No conscious slave th' impassioned message bore,
Save that frail book ; that day we read no more.'
As thus one shadow told the mournful tale,
The other did so feelingly bewail,
That pity checked my voice, my blood, my breath,
And sunk me to the ground as one in death.

(Reprinted in *English Review*, April, 1844, pp. 167-78.)

ANONYMOUS

1844. April. ENGLISH REVIEW. ART. V. LORD JOHN RUSSELL'S TRANSLATION OF THE 'FRANCESCA DA RIMINI,' FROM THE 'INFERNO' OF DANTE, CANTO V. 73-142.[1]

[Estimate of Dante—His English translators]

WE trust that no apology will be required from us for bestowing a somewhat detailed notice upon a translation of sixty-nine lines, made from an original of about the same number, when it is considered that the subject in question is one of the most celebrated passages in the stupendous work of Dante. In the interest, not only of literature but of religion, we are persuaded that the study of the works of that master-poet and rare Christian philosopher is of an importance not to be overrated. If we desire to escape from the sickly-scented atmosphere of a highly artificial civilization into larger and freer air; if we would adjust the notions of a particular place, time, and combination of circumstances, to the standard of what is universal and eternal; if we would know the whole scope of the destinies of man; if we would contemplate him in the most intense, sustained, and harmonious exercise of all his powers, and by seeing, learn, each in our degree and sphere, to imitate them; then, and for these reasons, without taking into view many others of a less comprehensive application, let his majestic verse share largely in our daily and our nightly toil. . . . Never was music so matchless wedded to thought so intense: never, in any merely human work, was truth so lofty and severe combined in such perfection with the boldest achievements of the imagination. The very difficulties of his style are, in our judgment, (like those of Thucydides) so nearly related to the character of his mind, and thereby to the matter of his work, that

[1] [In the *Literary Souvenir* for 1844—see above, pp. 684 ff.]

we cannot wish them away: and they give a character of discipline to the study of his poem which befits the nature and object of it, and in some degree affords a guarantee that those who read him shall likewise appreciate him.

We also believe that there never was a poet in whose case language and metre were more exclusively the handmaids of thought. To put the ideas of Dante into a tongue different from his own, is like dividing bone and marrow: and although that other tongue, when it is our own, may ill submit to the form of the *terza rima*, yet to use any other specific form of verse, is complicating the first act of violence by a second. Accordingly, Lord Byron has attempted the identical metre of Dante, in his version of the "Francesca."[1] Mr. Dayman has done the same in his translation;[2] and Mr. Cary has adopted the blank verse, which at least does not present any opposite character. How they, at least the two former, have reeled and staggered under their difficulties, their readers know. It is no reproach to any man to fail in translating Dante. Cary, we apprehend, is usually considered to hold a very high place among our English translators: but if he has laboured with vigour and effect in conveying the sense, has he not missed altogether that other aim of conveying the sound—of representing the body of the poem along with its soul? And does not the function of the translator essentially include both purposes? The truth seems to be, that none can match himself with such an original. One man after another may make the effort: but there stands Dante's work, like the Sphinx, not to be unriddled, and baffles and devours each of them in succession. Not that we deny the utility of their labours. Every, even the smallest, addition to our means of understanding this 'poeta sovrano,' increases the real treasures of literature.

We cannot but rejoice to see a distinguished and active politician, like Lord John Russell, allotting even mere fragments of his time for such studies as that of which the result is now before us. . . . The verses of Lord John Russell appear to us to be of an easy and flowing strain; as verses, they nowhere shock, if they do not powerfully please throughout; and in particular places, where he has been contented with a diction comparatively artless and unadorned, they do some considerable degree of justice to the original. We regret that we cannot go further: but we trust, that what we have to observe in a more qualified, or even in an opposite sense, will at least be free from gall. Of all authors, Dante most demands, we apprehend, a continuous study. It requires the greatest mental effort to reach his level; and the temperament of the reader, much

[1] [See above, pp. 38 ff.] [2] [See above, pp. 679 ff.]

more of the translator, cannot again and again be lowered and raised at will. The spirit, having attained its 'topmost bent,' should be kept as near it as possible. Mr. Sydney Smith[1] has told us that Lord John Russell would (amongst other things), with or without ten minutes' notice, assume the command of the Channel fleet; and it appears to us he has at ten minutes' notice sat down to translate Dante—an exploit, in its own way, quite as venturesome as the former. The translator of Dante must imbue and saturate himself with the spirit of Dante. Unless his intellectual being be in great part absorbed in that of his original, he must, we believe, fail in his task, whatever be his native powers.

[Here follows a detailed, and for the most part damaging, criticism of Lord John Russell's version, which is compared line for line with the original.]

If we have done Lord John Russell injustice, it has not been wilful. . . . But we are anxious to see a far higher conception of Dante spread abroad among our countrymen; and we are sure that if they are to advance in their moral health and intellectual vigour, he must advance in their estimation. For this end we desire, that everything which professes to represent him, should be strictly and minutely canvassed, lest he should be degraded by counterfeits and caricatures. And for *him*, no examination can be too severe and searching. He should be viewed both in the magnificence of his outline, and in the precision of his detail. He is like those ancient Egyptians, of whom it was said, that they wrought upon the scale of giants and with the nicety of jewellers: Dante has comprehended all creation in one vast picture; and portions of that picture, like the story of Francesca, are selected for admiring study, on account of their transcendent beauty: but let those portions again be resolved into their constituent parts, a new range of graces is unfolded in every line and almost every word, and we at length come to measure the extraordinary scope of his faculties, and acknowledge in him the jeweller as well as the giant. It is no slight matter, to transfer into a language other than his own, any one passage of his book. It is not an after-dinner relaxation. If we show that Lord John Russell has not adequately bent the bow of Ulysses, we have given an useful warning to weaker men. Dante was not made for annuals in silk covers. He is not to be the plaything of the butterflies of literature. It must be recollected that the translator of a poem becomes in no small degree a rival of him whom he translates; and they that grapple with this poet in such a capacity, will be apt to find that they have set their teeth upon a file. Let us not lightly match our dwarfish stature against his

[1] Second Letter to Archdeacon Singleton. p. 41.

majestic height. Let him tower unapproachable in his grandeur: let us contemplate him from the distance which befits inferiority combined with veneration.

(Vol. i. pp. 164-7, 179-180.)

GAETANO POLIDORI

(1764-1853)

1844. DELLO SPIRITO CATTOLICO DI DANTE ALIGHIERI. OPERA DI CARLO LYELL. TRADOTTA DALL' ORIGINALE INGLESE.

[This book, which was published in London by Molini, is a translation of the essay *On the Antipapal Spirit of Dante* inserted by Charles Lyell in the 1842 edition of his translation of the *Canzoniere* of Dante (see above, pp. 595-6). The translator, Gaetano Polidori, was born at Bientina, near Pisa, in 1764. He was destined for the law, but about 1786 he left Italy as secretary to Alfieri, with whom he resided at Colmar and Paris. On the outbreak of the French Revolution he came to London, where he made a reputation as a man of letters and teacher of Italian. Among his numerous works was a verse-translation into Italian of all the poems of Milton. Polidori, who died in London in 1853, married an English lady. His son, John William Polidori (d. 1821), was Lord Byron's travelling physician from April to September, 1816, and wrote the *Vampyre*, which for a time he fathered on Byron. Francesca Polidori, the second daughter, married (in 1826) Gabriele Rossetti, author of the *Comento Analitico della Divina Commedia*, and other well-known works on Dante (see above, pp. 445-7).]

GEORGE LILLIE CRAIK

(1798-1866)

[George Lillie Craik was the son of a schoolmaster of Kennoway, Fife, where he was born in 1798. He was educated at St. Andrews, and after engaging for a time in tuition and journalism, he went to London, where he devoted himself to literary work, chiefly in connection with the Society for the Diffusion of Useful Knowledge. In 1849 he was appointed Professor of English Literature and History at Queen's College, Belfast, where he remained until his death in 1866. Among his many works was *Sketches of the History of Literature and Learning in England*, in six volumes (1844-5, afterwards expanded into the *History of English Literature and the English Language*, 1861), which contains several references to Dante in connection with Chaucer and Spenser.]

1844. SKETCHES OF THE HISTORY OF LITERATURE AND LEARNING IN ENGLAND.

[The greatest poets (Homer, Dante, Chaucer, &c.) also the greatest men]

THE greatest poets have all been complete men, with the sense of beauty, indeed, strong and exquisite, and crowning all their other endowments, which is what makes them the greatest; but also with all other passions and powers correspondingly vigorous and active. Homer, Dante, Chaucer,

Spenser, Shakspeare, Milton, Goethe, were all of them individuals manifestly capable of achieving any degree of success in any other field as well as in poetry. They were not only poetically, but in all other respects, the most gifted intelligences of their times; men of the largest sense, of the most penetrating insight, of the most general research and information; nay, even in the most worldly arts and dexterities, able to cope with the ablest, whenever they chose to throw themselves into that game. They may not any of them have attained the highest degree of what is called worldly success; some of them may have even been crushed by the force of circumstances or evil days; Milton may have died in obscurity, Dante in exile; 'the vision and the faculty divine' may have been all the light that cheered, all the estate that sustained, the old age of Homer; but no one can suppose that in any of these cases it was the want of the requisite skill or talent that denied a different fortune.

(*Edmund Spenser*, vol. iii. p. 88.)

RICHARD HENRY HORNE

(1803-1884)

[Richard Henry (subsequently exchanged for Hengist) Horne, best known as the author of *Orion*, was born in London in 1803. He was educated at Sandhurst with a view to entering the East India Company's service, but receiving no appointment became a midshipman in the Mexican navy, in which capacity he served in the war against Spain. He began his literary career in 1828 by contributing a poem to the *Athenæum*, and he subsequently published numerous works, both prose and poetry. His most famous poem, *Orion*, an epic in ten books, appeared in 1843, and rapidly passed through eleven editions. Horne was a friend and correspondent of Miss Barrett (afterwards Mrs. Browning), with whom he collaborated in a collection of critical essays on distinguished contemporaries, which was published under the title of *A New Spirit of the Age* (as a continuation of Hazlitt's *Spirit of the Age*) in 1844. In this work is an interesting record of Landor's early opinion of Italian literature. Horne, who resided in Australia from 1852 to 1869 as commissioner of crown lands and magistrate, died at Margate in 1884.]

1844. A NEW SPIRIT OF THE AGE.

[Landor's unfavourable opinion of Italian literature altered on reading Dante]

AFTER leaving Trinity,[1] Mr. Landor passed some months in London, learning Italian. . . . He wrote verses in Italian at this period, which were not very good, yet not perhaps worse than Milton's. The poetry of Italy did not captivate his more severely classical taste at first; he says it seemed to him 'like the juice of grapes and melons left on yesterday's plate.' He had

[1] [Trinity College, Oxford, whence Landor was rusticated in 1794.]

just been reading Aeschylus, Sophocles, and Pindar. But his opinion was altered directly he read Dante, which he did not do till some years afterwards.[1]

(Vol. i. p. 159.)

THOMAS WRIGHT

(1810-1877)

[Thomas Wright, antiquary, was born at Tenbury, Shropshire, in 1810. He was educated at Ludlow Grammar School, and at Trinity College, Cambridge (B.A. 1834). While an undergraduate he compiled a *History and Topography of Essex*, which was published in 1836, in which year he left Cambridge to settle in London. In 1837 he was elected Fellow of the Society of Antiquaries, and the next thirty-five years of his busy life were spent in literary and antiquarian pursuits. His mind failed after 1872 and he died at Chelsea in 1877. Among Wright's numerous publications (of which 129 are registered in the British Museum Catalogue), was *St. Patrick's Purgatory; an Essay on the Legends of Purgatory, Hell, and Paradise, current during the Middle Ages* (published in 1844), which contains an interesting account of the *Vision of Alberic* and its relation to the *Divina Commedia*.]

1844. ST. PATRICK'S PURGATORY; AN ESSAY ON THE LEGENDS OF PURGATORY, HELL, AND PARADISE, CURRENT DURING THE MIDDLE AGES.

[The *Vision of Alberic* and the *Divina Commedia*]

THE poets of the thirteenth century, who had sung of purgatory and paradise, were, at the beginning of the fourteenth, thrown into the shade by the immortal *terza rima* of Dante. The 'Divina Commedia' of the poet of Florence has transmitted to modern ages the popular belief and knowledge of a period which has hitherto been very little understood by modern readers; who have therefore frequently set down to inventive imagination pictures and notions which were familiar to his contemporaries. Commentators have laboured to discover hidden meanings and allegorical descriptions, where an acquaintance with the popular science of the age of Dante would have shown nothing but literal description. I am satisfied that a diligent study of the literature of the thirteenth century is necessary for the explanation and appreciation of this celebrated poem. It is but recently that some writers have pointed out the class of legends to which the present essay is devoted as the real groundwork of Dante's imagery. It is supposed by these writers that Dante was more immediately influenced by a vision said to have been exhibited in Italy to a child named Alberic, at the beginning of the twelfth century.

Alberic, when he wrote his vision, was a monk of Monte Cassino.

[1] [For Landor's opinion of Dante, see above, pp. 84 ff.]

His father was a baron, lord of the castle de' Sette Fratelli, in the Campagna of Rome. In his tenth year, the child Alberic was seized with a languor, and lay nine days and nine nights in a trance, to all appearance dead. As soon as he had fallen into this condition, a white bird, like a dove, came and put its bill into his mouth, and seemed to lift him up, and then he saw St. Peter and two angels, who carried him to the lower regions. St. Peter told him that he would see the least torments first, and afterwards, successively, the more terrible punishments of the other world. They came first to a place filled with red-hot burning cinders and boiling vapour, in which little children were purged; those of one year old being subjected to this torment during seven days: those of two years, fourteen days; and so on, in proportion to their age. Then they entered a terrible valley, in which Alberic saw a great number of persons plunged to different depths, according to their different degrees of criminality, in frost, and cold, and ice, which consumed them like fire; these were adulterers, and people who had led impure lives. Then they approached a still more fearful valley, filled with trees, the branches of which were long spikes, on which hung women transfixed through their breasts, while venemous serpents were sucking them; these were women who had refused pity to orphans. Other women, who had been faithless to the marriage bed, were suspended by the hair over raging fires. Next he saw an iron ladder, three hundred and sixty cubits long, red hot, and under it a great boiler of melted oil, pitch and resin; married persons who had not been continent on sabbaths and holy days were compelled to mount this ladder, and ever as they were obliged to quit their hold by the heat, they dropped into the boiler below. Then they beheld vast fires in which were burnt the souls of tyrannical and cruel lords, and of women who had destroyed their offspring. Next was a great space full of fire like blood, in which homicides were thrown; and after this there stood an immense vessel filled with boiling brass, tin, lead, sulphur, and resin, in which were immersed during three years those who encouraged wicked priests. They next came to the mouth of the infernal pit, (*os infernalis baratri*,) a vast gulf, dark, and emitting an intolerable stench, and full of screaming and howling. By the pit was a serpent of infinite magnitude, bound by a great chain, the one end of which seemed to be fastened in the pit; before the mouth of this serpent stood a multitude of souls, which he sucked in like flies at each breath, and then, with the return of respiration, blew them out scorched to sparks; and this process continued till the souls were purged of their sins. The pit was so dark, that Alberic could not see what was going on in hell. After quitting this spot, Alberic was conducted first to a valley in which persons who had committed sacrilege were burnt in a sea of flames; then to a pit of fire in which simonists were punished; next to a place filled with flames, and with serpents and dragons, in which were tormented those who, having embraced the monastic profession, had quitted it and returned to a secular life; and afterwards to a great black lake of sulphureous water, full of serpents and scorpions, in which the souls of detractors and false witnesses were immersed to the chin, and their faces continually flogged with serpents by demons who hovered over them. On the borders of hell, Alberic saw two 'malignant spirits' in the form of a dog and a lion, which he was told blew out from their fiery mouths all the torments that were outside of hell, and at every breath the souls before them were wafted each into the peculiar punishment appropriated to him. The visitor was here left for a moment by his conductors; and the demons seized upon him, and would have thrown him into the fire, had not St. Peter suddenly arrived to rescue him. He was carried thence to a fair plain, where he saw thieves carrying heavy collars of iron, red hot, about their necks, hands, and feet. He saw here a great burning pitchy river, issuing from hell, and an iron bridge over it, which appeared very broad and easy for the virtuous to pass, but when sinners attempted it, it became as narrow as a thread, and they fell over into the river, and afterwards attempted it again, but were not allowed to pass until they had been sufficiently boiled to purge them of their sins. After this the apostle showed Alberic an extensive plain, three days' and three nights' journey in breadth, covered with thorns and brambles, in which souls were hunted and tormented by a demon mounted on a great and swift dragon, and their clothing and limbs torn to pieces by the thorns as they endeavoured to escape from him; by degrees they were purged of their sins, and became lighter, so that they could run faster, until at last they escaped into a very pleasant plain, filled with purified souls, where their torn members and garments were immediately restored; and here Alberic saw monks and martyrs, and good people, in great joy. He then proceeded through the habitations of the blessed. In the midst of a beautiful plain, covered with flowers, rose the mountain of paradise, with the tree at the top. After having conducted the visitor through the seven heavens, the last of which was held by Saturn, they brought him to a wall, and let him look over, but he was forbidden to tell what he had seen on the other side. They subsequently carried him through the different regions of the world, and showed him many extraordinary things, and, among the rest, some persons subjected to purgatorial punishments in different places on the earth.

There are, perhaps, more points of similitude between the poem of Dante and this Italian vision than in any of those which originated in the more western parts of Europe, although they all contain incidents more or less similar to some parts of the details of the 'Divina Commedia.' Dante evidently copies incidents from the vision of Owain. He is said also to have imitated an allegorical treatise written by his teacher, Brunetto Latini. . . .

In Dante the legends are adopted as a means of conveying political, moral, and theological doctrines; and, like Milton, the poet of Florence has softened down the harshness of Gothic imagery with the elegant pictures and sentiments of the classic poets of ancient times, which had then more influence in Italy than in the more western parts of Europe. He choose Virgil for his guide, as an intimation that he had ingrafted the descriptions of the western purgatory legends on the groundwork afforded him by the Mantuan poet.[1]

(pp. 117-22.)

THOMAS JOHN MAZZINGHI

(fl. 1840)

1844. A BRIEF NOTICE OF THE RECENT RESEARCHES RESPECTING DANTE ALIGHIERI.[2]

[The letter of Frate Ilario—the *De Vulgari Eloquentia*—Dante's letters]

WITH respect to recent researches, it should be noticed that the bibliographer, Stephen Audin,[3] has discovered the letter of the Frate Hilario,[4] whose authority has been matter of discussion in the literary world, transcribed by Boccaccio himself, and forming part of a miscellaneous volume (zibaldone) in the Laurentian library. All questions also respecting the authenticity of the treatise 'De Vulgari Eloquio,' and the good faith of Trissino, may be considered at an end since the recovery at Grenoble of the original Latin MS. of the 14th century, which whether in Dante's own writing has not been ascertained.[5] It was announced, we believe, for the first time, by Fraticelli.

[1] [Here follows an analysis of the *Divina Commedia* (pp. 122-8).]

[2] [Besides the matter indicated by its title, this work (in which the writer complains of the neglect in England of recent publications on Dante) contains a description of two MSS. of the *Commedia* in the British Museum (*Addit.* 10317; *Egerton* 943); a *canzone* attributed to Dante from a MS. in the British Museum; a chronology of the life and writings of Dante; and a genealogy of the Alighieri family (from Litta and Pelli).]

[3] [Stefano Audin de Rians.]

[4] [On this letter see Toynbee's *Life of Dante* (ed. 1904), p. 120 note.]

[5] [This MS., which was the basis of Corbinelli's edition of the Latin text (1577), is certainly not in Dante's hand—no scrap of writing in Dante's hand is known to exist; it was executed at the end of the fourteenth, or beginning of the fifteenth century. (See Toynbee's *Dante Studies and Researches*, p. 158.)]

In 1827, Professor Witte, of Breslau, published a small volume with the following title:—'Dantis Aligherii epistolae quae extant.'[1] It contained all the letters, or fragments of letters, seven in number, which the editor thought could be relied on as his, together with Witte's own notes and emendations. They were as follows:—

1. A letter to Can Grande respecting the Paradise.[2] Date, 1317.
2. One to a friend, a churchman apparently at Florence, rejecting humiliating conditions suggested with a view to a recal from banishment.[3] Date, Dec. 1316.
3. A letter to the Italian Princes, urging them to give Henry VII a favourable reception.[4] 1310.
4. One to Henry VII inciting him to leave Lombardy and march upon Tuscany, the hotbed of Guelfism.[5] April, 1311.
5. A missive to the Italian Cardinals, exhorting them to restore the Apostolic See to Rome.[6] April, 1314.
6. An original letter to Cino da Pistoja, answering a question of gallantry proposed by the latter.[7]
7. A letter to Guido da Polenta, written from Venice, where it would seem Dante had been sent ambassador. He affirms the inability of the senators to understand either the Latin or the Italian dialects; and accounts for their ignorance of the latter by their Greek or Dalmatian descent. This letter has been doubted by Witte and others.[8] Date, circ. 1313.

This publication of Witte arrested public attention. It was familiar to all scholars, from the testimony of Boccaccio, Bruni, and Filelfo, that Dante had written numerous letters in the Latin language; even the commencements of some had been preserved. Researches were made; and a few years since the same learned Professor announced in a German Review[9] the discovery of seven more letters, three of which he pronounced positively to be Dante's, whilst he thought himself justified in inferring the others to have been dictated by him, although bearing different signatures. These letters Witte was allowed to transcribe; but during his absence they were one day purloined from his table, and he was not allowed a second copy. From his account it would seem, that amongst the MSS. found on the taking of Heidelberg some centuries ago, and presented by Maximilian of Bavaria to Gregory XV in 1622, was a parchment volume in 4to numbered 1729, purporting to have been written in Perugia, in the summer of 1394, by Francesco da

[1] [Only twenty-five copies were printed.]
[2] [*Epist.* x.] [3] [*Epist.* ix.] [4] [*Epist.* v.]
[5] [*Epist.* vii.; this and the next two were printed by Witte for the first time.]
[6] [*Epist.* viii.] [7] [*Epist.* iv.]
[8] [Now commonly regarded as apocryphal.]
[9] [In *Blätter für literarische Unterhaltung.* 1838. Nr. 149-51; afterwards reprinted in Witte's *Dante-Forschungen*, i. 473-87.]

Monte Pulciano. It contained the ten eclogues of Petrarch, the well-known treatise by Dante 'De Monarchia,' and nine letters in Latin. Of these eight have never been printed: the ninth had been previously published by Witte,—it was the letter addressed by Dante to the Emperor Henry. Another of these epistles was the original Latin text of the one addressed to the Princes of Italy, which had been previously only known to scholars in an Italian translation. The remaining seven were hitherto wholly unknown; but in this ancient volume it is positively affirmed that three of them are the composition of Dante; and Professor Witte infers from the classification and tenor of the remaining four (which, however, bear other signatures) that they proceeded from the same pen.[1]

(pp. 33-5.)

[Alleged autograph of Dante]

M. Artaud has ascertained from M. Frederici of Padua, the error of Foscolo, who affirmed that there existed an autograph of Dante in that city. It appears that the family of Papafava possess a *copy* of an instrument, date 1306, 27 August, in which 'Dantino q. Alligerij de Florentia et nunc stat Padue,' is one of the witnesses to a loan of 1705 books,[2] contracted between parties therein mentioned. This copy is of the date 1335, and is authenticated by a notary. It is well proved that Dante, at the date of the instrument, was at Padua.

(p. 36.)

[Alleged visit of Dante to England]

The visit of Dante to England was supposed by Tiraboschi to stand merely upon the dictum of Giovanni di Serravalle, an early writer of the fourteenth[3] century, who affirms that the Poet had studied, 'Paduae, Bononiae, demum Oxoniis, et Parisiis;' but the fact rests, it appears, upon still earlier and more venerable authority—that of Boccaccio. See his Latin letter to Petrarch, which accompanied a copy of the Comedy, transcribed by Boccaccio himself: he imagines Dante led by Apollo—

[1] [Of the seven new letters published by Witte, four are commonly accepted as genuine, viz. *Epist.* i. (to the Cardinal Niccolò d' Ostia); *Epist.* ii. (to the Counts Oberto and Guido da Romena); *Epist.* iii. (to the Marquis Moroello Malaspina); and *Epist.* vi. (to the rebellious Florentines). The other three, addressed to the Empress Margaret of Brabant, wife of Henry VII, by the Countess Catharine of Battifolle, are not accepted as having been written by Dante. All these letters are printed in the editions of Torri and of Giuliani.]

[2] [Not 'books,' but 'lire'; Mazzinghi's mistake arose no doubt from his having got his information from a French source, in which the word was 'livres.'—For the document in question, see Bartoli, *Storia della Letteratura Italiana*, v. 181-3.]

[3] [Corr. 'fifteenth.'—The work in question was written in 1416-7.]

'per celsa nivosi
Cyrrheos, mediosque sinus, tacitosque recessus
Naturae, coelique vias, terraeque, marisque,
Aonios fontes, Parnassi culmen, et antra
Julia, Parisios dudum, extremosque Britannos.'

(p. 37.)

EDWARD BYLES COWELL

(1826-1903)

[Cowell, who was born at Ipswich in 1826, and married in 1847, went to Oxford (Magdalen Hall) in his twenty-fourth year at the instigation of his wife. In 1856 he was appointed Professor of History and Political Economy in the Presidency College, Calcutta; and, in 1858, Principal of the Government Sanskrit College, a post which he retained until 1864, when he was invalided home. In 1867 he was elected to the newly-founded Professorship of Sanskrit at Cambridge, and he held the chair for nearly 36 years, until his death (at Cambridge) in February, 1903. Among Cowell's early friends were Tennyson and Thackeray, who both visited him at Oxford, and Edward Fitzgerald, who was indebted to Cowell for his first acquaintance with Spanish literature and with the *Rubâiyât of Omar Khayyâm*. With Fitzgerald Cowell, who was a constant student of Dante throughout his life, used to read the *Divina Commedia*. In a private letter,[1] he says: 'Fitzgerald was always a great admirer of the *Divine Comedy*. I often read parts of it with him before I went to India in 1856, when I met him in Suffolk, or he came to stay with me in Oxford. I remember reading some of the later Cantos, of the *Paradise*, which he greatly admired. But after 1850 or so when I persuaded him to read Spanish, our attention was chiefly turned to Spanish when we met, until he caught his first enthusiasm for Persian. After I came home from India in 1864, we chiefly read *Don Quixote* when I spent part of every long vacation from Cambridge at Lowestoft. . . . But I do not remember our reading Dante at all, although from 1873 to 1877 I and some Cambridge friends read through the *Purgatory* and *Paradise*, meeting every Wednesday afternoon. I daresay I talked about these réunions to Fitzgerald at Lowestoft, but it did not rouse him to bring his Dante when I came. I half fancy he felt the atmosphere of Dante's world somewhat oppressive and sombre as years grew on. I certainly feel it so in my own experience. His favourite translation was Cary, but he used Longfellow as well.']

1844. April 1. LETTER TO GEORGE WILLIAM KITCHIN.[2]

[Dante's 'dark gnarled wood']

YOU talk of a beautiful shop were you saw Dante, Ariosto, &c., somewhere in the Strand. Next time you go there just ask about Bojardo and Pulci's *Morgante Maggiore*. . . . I intend reading Tacitus through next. I read in one of the Reviews that it is one of those dark pictures of mankind and this world that make our very hearts ache to read them. We seem to

[1] [To the editor of this work—printed in *Life and Letters of E. B. Cowell*, pp. 406-7.]

[2] [The present (1908) Dean of Durham, Cowell's schoolfellow at Ipswich Grammar School.]

find ourselves in a dark cloudy region in the midst of the dark gnarled wood of our life (as Dante says), where no ray of sunshine ever pierces the gloom, and dark shading ill seems to track us on every side.

(*Life and Letters of E. W. Cowell*, p. 12.)

ANONYMOUS

1844. August 24. ATHENÆUM. OBITUARY NOTICE OF THE REV. HENRY FRANCIS CARY.

[Cary's Dante one of the master-pieces of English literature]

THE death of the Rev. Henry Francis Cary must be regretted by every lover of earnest and severe scholarship; a kind of literary man now unfortunately too rare. Mr. Cary well deserved the place in Poet's Corner in Westminster Abbey, which on Wednesday last[1] was granted to his remains. His translation of Dante is one of the master-pieces in our language, and will ensure his name an abiding place in our literature, in connexion with that of the Florentine poet.

(Vol. 1844, pp. 777-8.)

[1] [August 21,—Cary died on August 14.]

APPENDIX

FRANCIS HARDY *

(1751-1812)

[Francis Hardy, Irish politician and man of letters, was born in 1751. He graduated B.A. at Dublin University in 1771, and was called to the bar in 1777. In 1782 he was elected M.P. for Mullingar, which he represented, 'in the three last Parliaments of Ireland' till 1800. After the Union he retired to the country, where he was closely associated with Grattan. In 1806 he was appointed a Commissioner of Appeals at Dublin. He died in 1812. Hardy, who was a good classical scholar, and was well acquainted with continental literature, co-operated with Lord Charlemont in the establishment of the Royal Irish Academy at Dublin in 1786, and was a contributor to its *Transactions*. In 1810 he published a *Life of Lord Charlemont* (second edition, 1812), which he undertook at the instance of R. L. Edgeworth. In this work he speaks of Lord Charlemont's unpublished *History of Italian Poetry* (a lengthy work which would fill 'two quarto volumes, or more'), which included translations of lengthy extracts from the *Divina Commedia*, if not a complete version of the poem (see vol. i. pp. 433, 436 *n*.). In an article on 'Dante and his Translators' in the *Dublin Magazine* for May, 1854 (vol. xliii. p. 560), Lord Charlemont is spoken of as 'one of the most accomplished men of his time, who was, probably, better acquainted with Italian literature than any other man of that day, and who seems to have possessed very great poetical talents;' and it is suggested that 'it would be a real service to literature' if Lord Charlemont's 'history of Italian poetry' and his 'version of Dante' could be published. Unfortunately this suggestion does not appear to have been acted on.]

1810. MEMOIRS OF THE POLITICAL AND PRIVATE LIFE OF JAMES CAULFIELD, EARL OF CHARLEMONT.

[Lord Charlemont's history of Italian poetry—Baretti's opinion of him as an Italian scholar]

LORD CHARLEMONT was well versed in the literature of ancient days; but Italian literature had long engaged his attention. He meditated a history of the poetry of that interesting country, from the time of Dante to that of Metastasio. . . . He has left a most pleasing, accurate, and critical account of the best poets of Italy, during the time I have mentioned. That Lord Charlemont was well qualified for the office of historian of Italian poetry, may, I think, be admitted from Baretti's dedication

* [This article should properly come before S. Rogers (above, p. 71).]

to him of the 'Account of the Manners and Customs of Italy.'—'Your knowledge of the manners and language of Italy is hardly less than my own, who am a native of that country; and your knowledge of its literature much more extensive.'

(Ed. 1812, vol. i. p. 306.)

[Lord Charlemont's opinion of Boyd's Dante—His own 'version of Dante']

It may be proper to mention, that in his history of Italian poetry, Lord Charlemont speaks in the warmest terms of Mr. Boyd's translation of Dante,[1] as 'one of the best poetical translations in our language, and which is only prevented from being a *real* translation, by the constant uniformity of its merit.' It first induced him to give a version of Dante, of which, as well as of all his translations, he speaks with the most engaging modesty and diffidence.[2]

(*Ibid.* vol. ii. p. 441.)

A. POZZESI *

(fl. 1820)

[The following work, apparently intended for English readers, was printed in London, and published by Messrs. Longman, in London, and by C. Duffield, at Bath; the author describes himself on the title-page as 'Professeur de Langue Italienne.' The work consists of a poetical vocabulary, in which are included various words and names used by Dante, besides brief notices of the chief Italian poets; followed by notes, in the course of which occur frequent illustrative quotations from the *Divina Commedia;* a compendious 'iconology;' and selections from the *Inferno*, Italian text with French translation, viz. 'Iscrizione posta al sommo della Porta Infernale' (*Inferno* iii. 1-11), translated by Chabanon;[3] 'Episodio di Francesca di Rimini' (*Inferno* v. 82-142), translated by the same; 'Episodio del Conte Ugolino' (*Inferno* xxxiii. 1-90), translated by the same;[4] and 'Trasmutamento inaudito di due Spiriti' (*Inferno* xxv. 46-114, 118-41), translated by Masse.[5]]

* [This article should properly come before Lady Morgan (above, p. 326).]

[1] [See vol. i. pp. 410 ff.]

[2] [The writer of the article on 'Dante and his Translators' in the *Dublin Magazine*, referred to above, remarks: 'From this passage it would appear that there exists a translation, probably of the entire of the *Commedia*, but certainly, of considerable parts of it, by Lord Charlemont. It also appears that it is constructed on principles of translation which exact entire fidelity to the author translated. Mr. Hardy has not stated what form of verse has been adopted; but as Lord Charlemont's translations from Petrarch and others imitate the very arrangements of rhyme which he finds, we have little doubt that in this case he adopted the *terza rima*.']

[3] [Michel Paul Gui de Chabanon (1730-1792). This and the following translations were printed by Chabanon in his *Vie du Dante* (Amsterdam, 1773). They were reprinted by Artaud de Montor in the notes to his translation of the *Inferno* (Paris, 1812), whence they were reprinted, without acknowledgment, by Pozzesi.]

[4] [The last fifteen lines of this translation are not by Chabanon, as Pozzesi states, but by Pierre Gassendi (see Artaud de Montor, *op. cit.* pp. 417, 420-3.)]

[5] [This translation was printed by Artaud de Montor (*op. cit.* pp. 358-61), whence it was borrowed, without acknowledgment, by Pozzesi. Étienne Masse, whom Artaud describes as 'un jeune auteur,' also translated the Paolo and Francesca, and Ugolino episodes (*op. cit.* pp. 261, 427-9).]

1821. VOCABULAIRE POÉTIQUE; OU, RECUEIL DE MOTS ET DE PHRASES CONSACRÉES LA PLUS GRANDE PARTIE À LA POÉSIE ITALIENNE, AVEC DES NOTES: SUIVI D'UN ABRÉGÉ D'ICONOLOGIE; ET D'UN CHOIX DES PLUS BEAUX MORCEAUX DE POÉSIE TIRÉS DE LA DIVINE COMÉDIE DU DANTE AVEC LA TRADUCTION FRANÇAISE.[1]

[Rivarol's estimate of Dante, 'the prince of poets']

LE but principal que les amateurs de la littérature Italienne se proposent dès qu'ils commencent à en étudier les élémens, est surement de pouvoir parvenir à comprendre nos classiques, mais surtout celui qui, en me servant des expressions de M. Rivarol,[2] a eu le courage de remonter du dernier gouffre des enfers jusqu'au sublime sanctuaire des cieux, et qui d'une manière étonnante, a pu embrasser la double hiérarchie des vices et des vertus, l'extrême misère et la suprême félicité, le temps et l'éternité; peindre à la fois l'ange et l'homme, l'auteur de tout mal, et le saint des saints. Il est bien facile de s'appercevoir que je parle du père de la Poésie Italienne, du prince des poètes, du Dante.

(*Preface*, p. iii.)

[Dante and his works—The *Commedia* an 'ocean of marvels']

Dante, Poeta Toscano. Egli è riguardato come il Padre della Lingua e della Poesia Italiana. La Divina Commedia di questo nostro immortale Poeta, può considerarsi come lo sforzo ultimo dell' ingegno umano pel sublime, per le immagini grandi e superbe, per i pensieri arditi e terribili, per la poesia forte e tutta energia; di modo che qualunque elogio far si potesse di questo vasto oceano di tutte le maraviglie, sarebbe sempre inferiore al vero suo merito. Le altre opere di Dante sono: la *Vita Nuova*, il *Convito*, dell' *Egloche*,[3] de' *Sonetti*, un' opera intitolata, *Allegoria sopra Virgilio*,[4] un trattato *de Monarchiâ* scritto in Latino, il trattato *de Vulgari Eloquentiâ*, e molte altre.

(From the *Vocabulaire Poétique.*)

[1] [A Londres: de l'imprimerie de S. et R. Bentley.]

[2] [Antoine, Comte de Rivarol (1753-1801). He published in 1783 a French prose translation of the *Inferno*, with an essay *De la vie et des poèmes du Dante*, from which the above quotation is taken (pp. xxii-iii).]

[3] [*Sic.*]

[4] [No such work of Dante's is known. Pozzesi took his list (including this item) from Rivarol (*op. cit.* p. xv).]

CHRONOLOGICAL LIST OF AUTHORS, ETC., WITH DATES OF WORKS QUOTED

CENTURY XIV

CENTURY XV

CENTURY XVI

CENTURY XVII

CENTURY XVII-XVIII

VOL. I

CENTURY XVIII

[1] [After Urry should come Jonathan Richardson, accidentally misplaced under 1719.]
[2] [Richardson should come after Urry (1714).]

VOL. I

[1] See also under 1807.

CENTURY XIX

VOLUME II

VOL. II

William Coxe (1747-1828):—Sketches of the Lives of Correggio and Parmegiano (1823) 367-368
Allan Cunningham (1784-1842):—Letter to Rev. H. F. Cary (1823) 368-369
Anonymous:—in *Quarterly Review* (1823) 369-370
Anonymous:—in *Monthly Review* (1823) 370-372
Henry Hart Milman (1791-1868):—Translations from Petrarch (1823) 372
Anonymous:—in *Retrospective Review* (1823, 1824) 373-374
Bibliotheca Regia (1824) 374
Anonymous:—Life of Joanna of Sicily (1824) 375-377
Richard Price (1790-1833):—Notes on Warton's *History of English Poetry* (1824) 377
Susan Edmonstone Ferrier (1782-1854):—The Inheritance (1824); Destiny (1831) 378-379
Thomas Medwin (1788-1869):—Conversations with Lord Byron (1824); Shelley Papers (1833); Angler in Wales (1834); Life of Shelley (1847) 380-390
André Vieusseux (fl. 1820):—Italy and the Italians (1824) . . 391
John Charles Tarver (1790-1851):—L'Enfer de Dante (1824) . 391
Lord Macaulay (1800-1859):—Criticisms on the Principal Italian Writers (1824); Essay on Milton (1825); Essay on Machiavelli (1827); Essay on Dryden (1828); Essay on History (1828); Essay on Hallam's *Constitutional History* (1828); Essay on Montgomery's *Poems* (1830); Essay on Moore's *Life of Byron* (1831); Letter to T. F. Ellis (1834); Letter to Margaret Macaulay (1834); Essay on Mackintosh's *History of the Revolution* (1835); Essay on Lord Bacon (1837); Journal in Italy (1838); Essays on Sir William Temple (1838); Essay on Ranke's *History of the Popes* (1840); Letter to Macvey Napier (1843); Essay on Addison (1843); Essay on Chatham (1844); Marginal Notes (18..) . 392-416
Arthur Henry Hallam (1811-1833):—Translation of Ugolino Episode into Greek (1824); Sonnet (1828); Letter to Alfred Tennyson (c. 1830); Letter to W. H. Brookfield (1831); Oration on the influence of Italian works of imagination, etc. (1831); Sonnet (1831); Essay on *Lyrical Poems* of Tennyson (1831); Remarks on Rossetti's *Spirito Antipapale* (1832) 416-424
Frances Anne Kemble (Mrs. Butler) (1809-1893):—Record of a Girlhood (c. 1824); Journal (1831, 1832); Letter from New York (1832); Letter to C. Greville (1843) 425-428
Robert Hall (1764-1831):—Remarks upon Dante (1825) . . . 428
Jane Baillie Welsh (Mrs. Carlyle) (1801-1866):—Letter to Thomas Carlyle (1825)'; Letter to Helen Welsh (1838); Letter to John Sterling (1842) 429
Anonymous:—in *Quarterly Review* (1825) 430
Anonymous:—in *Edinburgh Review* (1825) 431
Anonymous:—in *Retrospective Review* (1825) 432
Lord Brougham (1778-1868):—Inaugural Discourse at Glasgow (1825); Statesmen of the time of George III. (1843) . . . 432-435
George Crabb (1788-1851):—Universal Historical Dictionary (1825) 435
John Keble (1792-1866):—Sacred Poetry (1825); Works of Hooker (1836); De Poeticae Vi Medica (1837-41) 435-439
Edgar Taylor (1793-1839):—Lays of the Minnesingers (1825) . 439-441
George Procter (fl. 1820):—History of Italy (1825) 441-442
Emma Eleonora Kendrick (1788-1871):—Picture of Ugolino (1826) 442

INDEX

NOTE.—The *second reference* after the names (printed in small capitals) of authors represented in the book refers to the *Chronological Table* at the end of the second volume, where a full list is given of the works, etc., quoted of each author.

[1] Under this heading are entered books and articles the authorship of which the editor has not been able to ascertain. Articles, etc., which were published anonymously, but the authorship of which is known (as, for instance, in the case of Scott's contributions to the *Quarterly Review*, or Macaulay's to the *Edinburgh*), will be found under the names of the authors.

THE END

ABERDEEN: THE UNIVERSITY PRESS

Auden (T.), M.A., F.S.A. See Ancient Cities.

Aurelius (Marcus). WORDS OF THE ANCIENT WISE. Thoughts from Epictetus and Marcus Aurelius. Edited by W. H. D. ROUSE, M.A., Litt. D. *Fcap. 8vo.* 3*s.* 6*d. net.*

See also Standard Library.

Austen (Jane). See Standard Library, Little Library and Mitton (G. E.).

Aves (Ernest). CO-OPERATIVE INDUSTRY. *Crown 8vo.* 5*s. net.*

Bacon (Francis). See Standard Library and Little Library.

Baden-Powell (R. S. S.) THE MATABELE CAMPAIGN, 1896. With nearly 100 Illustrations. *Fourth Edition. Large Cr. 8vo.* 6*s.*

Bagot (Richard). THE LAKES OF NORTHERN ITALY. With 37 Illustrations and a Map. *Fcap. 8vo.* 5*s. net.*

Bailey (J. C.), M.A. See Cowper (W.).

Baker (W. G.), M.A. See Junior Examination Series.

Baker (Julian L.), F.I.C., F.C.S. See Books on Business.

Balfour (Graham). THE LIFE OF ROBERT LOUIS STEVENSON. With a Portrait. *Fourth Edition in one Volume. Cr. 8vo. Buckram,* 6*s.*

A Colonial Edition is also published.

Ballard (A.), B.A., LL.D. See Antiquary's Books.

Bally (S. E.). See Commercial Series.

Banks (Elizabeth L.). THE AUTOBIOGRAPHY OF A 'NEWSPAPER GIRL.' *Second Edition. Cr. 8vo.* 6*s.*

Barham (R. H.). See Little Library.

Baring (The Hon. Maurice). WITH THE RUSSIANS IN MANCHURIA. *Third Edition. Demy 8vo.* 7*s.* 6*d. net.*

A Colonial Edition is also published.

A YEAR IN RUSSIA. *Second Edition. Demy 8vo.* 10*s.* 6*d. net.*

A Colonial Edition is also published.

Baring-Gould (S.). THE LIFE OF NAPOLEON BONAPARTE. With nearly 200 Illustrations, including a Photogravure Frontispiece. *Second Edition. Wide Royal 8vo.* 10*s.* 6*d. net.*

A Colonial Edition is also published.

THE TRAGEDY OF THE CÆSARS: A STUDY OF THE CHARACTERS OF THE CÆSARS OF THE JULIAN AND CLAUDIAN HOUSES. With numerous Illustrations from Busts, Gems, Cameos, etc. *Sixth Edition. Royal 8vo.* 10*s.* 6*d. net.*

A BOOK OF FAIRY TALES. With numerous Illustrations by A. J. GASKIN. *Third Edition. Cr. 8vo. Buckram.* 6*s.*, also *Demy 8vo.* 6*d.*

OLD ENGLISH FAIRY TALES. With numerous Illustrations by F. D. BEDFORD. *Third Edition. Cr. 8vo. Buckram.* 6*s.*

THE VICAR OF MORWENSTOW. Revised Edition. With a Portrait. *Third Edition. Cr. 8vo.* 3*s.* 6*d.*

OLD COUNTRY LIFE. With 69 Illustrations. *Fifth Edition. Large Crown 8vo.* 6*s.*

A GARLAND OF COUNTRY SONG: English Folk Songs with their Traditional Melodies. Collected and arranged by S. BARING-GOULD and H. F. SHEPPARD. *Demy 4to.* 6*s.*

SONGS OF THE WEST: Folk Songs of Devon and Cornwall. Collected from the Mouths of the People. By S. BARING-GOULD, M.A., and H. FLEETWOOD SHEPPARD, M.A. New and Revised Edition, under the musical editorship of CECIL J. SHARP. *Large Imperial 8vo.* 5*s. net.*

A BOOK OF NURSERY SONGS AND RHYMES. Edited by S. BARING-GOULD. Illustrated. *Second and Cheaper Edition. Large Cr. 8vo.* 2*s.* 6*d. net.*

STRANGE SURVIVALS: SOME CHAPTERS IN THE HISTORY OF MAN. Illustrated. *Third Edition. Cr. 8vo.* 2*s.* 6*d. net.*

YORKSHIRE ODDITIES: INCIDENTS AND STRANGE EVENTS. *Fifth Edition. Cr. 8vo.* 2*s.* 6*d. net.*

THE BARING-GOULD SELECTION READER. Arranged by G. H. ROSE. Illustrated. *Crown 8vo.* 1*s.* 6*d.*

THE BARING-GOULD CONTINUOUS READER. Arranged by G. H. ROSE. Illustrated. *Crown 8vo.* 1*s.* 6*d.*

A BOOK OF CORNWALL. With 33 Illustrations. *Second Edition. Cr. 8vo.* 6*s.*

A BOOK OF DARTMOOR. With 60 Illustrations. *Second Edition. Cr. 8vo.* 6*s.*

A BOOK OF DEVON. With 35 Illustrations. *Second Edition. Cr. 8vo.* 6*s.*

A BOOK OF NORTH WALES. With 49 Illustrations. *Cr. 8vo.* 6*s.*

A BOOK OF SOUTH WALES. With 57 Illustrations. *Cr. 8vo.* 6*s.*

A BOOK OF BRITTANY. With 69 Illustrations. *Cr. 8vo.* 6*s.*

A BOOK OF THE RHINE: From Cleve to Mainz. With 8 Illustrations in Colour by TREVOR HADDEN, and 48 other Illustrations. *Second Edition. Cr. 8vo.* 6*s.*

A Colonial Edition is also published.

A BOOK OF THE RIVIERA. With 40 Illustrations. *Cr. 8vo.* 6*s.*

A Colonial Edition is also published.

A BOOK OF THE PYRENEES. With 25 Illustrations. *Cr. 8vo.* 6*s.*

A Colonial Edition is also published.

See also Little Guides.

Barker (Aldred F.). See Textbooks of Technology.

Barker (E.), M.A. (Late) Fellow of Merton College, Oxford. THE POLITICAL THOUGHT OF PLATO AND ARISTOTLE. *Demy 8vo.* 10*s.* 6*d. net.*

Barnes (W. E.), D.D. See Churchman's Bible.

Barnett (Mrs. P. A.). See Little Library.

Baron (R. R. N.), M.A. FRENCH PROSE COMPOSITION. *Third Edition. Cr 8vo.* 2*s.* 6*d. Key,* 3*s. net.*

See also Junior School Books.

Barron (H. M.), M.A., Wadham College, Oxford. TEXTS FOR SERMONS. With a Preface by Canon SCOTT HOLLAND. *Cr. 8vo.* 3s. 6d.

Bartholomew (J. G.), F.R.S.E. See C. G. Robertson.

Bastable (C. F.), LL.D. THE COMMERCE OF NATIONS. *Fourth Ed. Cr. 8vo.* 2s. 6d.

Bastian (H. Charlton), M.A., M.D., F.R.S. THE EVOLUTION OF LIFE. With Diagrams and many Photomicrographs. *Demy 8vo.* 7s. 6d. net.

Batson (Mrs. Stephen). A CONCISE HANDBOOK OF GARDEN FLOWERS. *Fcap. 8vo.* 3s. 6d.

THE SUMMER GARDEN OF PLEASURE. With 36 Illustrations in Colour by OSMUND PITTMAN. *Wide Demy 8vo.* 15s. net.

Batten (Loring W.), Ph.D., S.T.D. THE HEBREW PROPHET. *Cr. 8vo.* 3s. 6d. net.

Bayley (R. Child). THE COMPLETE PHOTOGRAPHER. With over 100 Illustrations. *Third Edition. With Note on Direct Colour Process. Demy 8vo.* 10s. 6d. net.

A Colonial Edition is also published.

Beard (W. S.). EASY EXERCISES IN ALGEBRA FOR BEGINNERS. *Cr. 8vo.* 1s. 6d. With Answers. 1s. 9d.

See also Junior Examination Series and Beginner's Books.

Beckford (Peter). THOUGHTS ON HUNTING. Edited by J. OTHO PAGET, and Illustrated by G. H. JALLAND. *Second Edition. Demy 8vo.* 6s.

Beckford (William). See Little Library.

Beeching (H. C.), M.A., Canon of Westminster. See Library of Devotion.

Beerbohm (Max). A BOOK OF CARICATURES. *Imperial 4to.* 21s. net.

Begbie (Harold). MASTER WORKERS. Illustrated. *Demy 8vo.* 7s. 6d. net.

Behmen (Jacob). DIALOGUES ON THE SUPERSENSUAL LIFE. Edited by BERNARD HOLLAND. *Fcap. 8vo.* 3s. 6d.

Bell (Mrs. Arthur G.). THE SKIRTS OF THE GREAT CITY. With 16 Illustrations in Colour by ARTHUR G. BELL, 17 other Illustrations, and a Map. *Second Edition. Cr. 8vo.* 6s.

Belloc (Hilaire), M.P. PARIS. With 7 Maps and a Frontispiece in Photogravure. *Second Edition, Revised. Cr. 8vo.* 6s.

HILLS AND THE SEA. *Second Edition. Crown 8vo.* 6s.

ON NOTHING AND KINDRED SUBJECTS. *Fcap. 8vo.* 5s.

A Colonial Edition is also published.

Bellot (H. H. L.), M.A. See Jones (L. A. A.).

Bennett (W. H.), M.A. A PRIMER OF THE BIBLE. With a concise Bibliography. *Fourth Edition. Cr. 8vo.* 2s. 6d.

Bennett (W. H.) and **Adeney (W. F.).** A BIBLICAL INTRODUCTION. *Fifth Edition. Cr. 8vo.* 7s. 6d.

Benson (Archbishop) GOD'S BOARD Communion Addresses. *Second Edition. Fcap. 8vo.* 3s. 6d. net.

Benson (A. C.), M.A. See Oxford Biographies.

Benson (R. M.). THE WAY OF HOLINESS: a Devotional Commentary on the 119th Psalm. *Cr. 8vo.* 5s.

Bernard (E. R.), M.A., Canon of Salisbury. THE ENGLISH SUNDAY: ITS ORIGINS AND ITS CLAIMS. *Fcap. 8vo.* 1s. 6d.

Bertouch (Baroness de). THE LIFE OF FATHER IGNATIUS. Illustrated. *Demy 8vo.* 10s. 6d. net.

Beruete (A. de). See Classics of Art.

Betham-Edwards (Miss). HOME LIFE IN FRANCE. With 20 Illustrations. *Fifth Edition. Crown 8vo.* 6s.

A Colonial Edition is also published.

Bethune-Baker (J. F.), M.A. See Handbooks of Theology.

Bidez (J.). See Byzantine Texts.

Biggs (C. R. D.), D.D. See Churchman's Bible.

Bindley (T. Herbert), B.D. THE OECUMENICAL DOCUMENTS OF THE FAITH. With Introductions and Notes. *Second Edition. Cr. 8vo.* 6s. net.

Binns (H. B.). THE LIFE OF WALT WHITMAN. Illustrated. *Demy 8vo.* 10s. 6d. net.

A Colonial Edition is also published.

Binyon (Mrs. Laurence). NINETEENTH CENTURY PROSE. Selected and arranged by. *Crown 8vo.* 6s.

Binyon (Laurence). THE DEATH OF ADAM AND OTHER POEMS. *Cr. 8vo.* 3s. 6d. net.

See also Blake (William).

Birch (Walter de Gray), LL.D., F.S.A. See Connoisseur's Library.

Birnstingl (Ethel). See Little Books on Art.

Blackmantle (Bernard). See I.P.L.

Blair (Robert). See I.P.L.

Blake (William). THE LETTERS OF WILLIAM BLAKE, TOGETHER WITH A LIFE BY FREDERICK TATHAM. Edited from the Original Manuscripts, with an Introduction and Notes, by ARCHIBALD G. B. RUSSELL. With 12 Illustrations. *Demy 8vo.* 7s. 6d. net.

ILLUSTRATIONS OF THE BOOK OF JOB. With General Introduction by LAURENCE BINYON. *Quarto.* 21s. net.

See also Blair (Robert), I.P.L., and Little Library.

Bloom (J. Harvey), M.A. SHAKESPEARE'S GARDEN. Illustrated. *Fcap. 8vo.* 3s. 6d.; *leather*, 4s. 6d. net.

See also Antiquary's Books

Blouet (Henri). See Beginner's Books.

Boardman (T. H.), M.A. See French (W.)

Bodley (J. E. C.), Author of 'France.' THE CORONATION OF EDWARD VII. *Demy 8vo.* 21s. net. By Command of the King.

Body (George), D.D. THE SOUL'S PILGRIMAGE: Devotional Readings from the Published and Unpublished writings of George Body, D.D. Selected and arranged by J. H. BURN, B.D., F.R.S.E. *Demy 16mo.* 2s. 6d.

Bona (Cardinal). See Library of Devotion.

Boon (F. C.), B.A. See Commercial Series.

Borrow (George). See Little Library.

Bos (J. Ritzema). AGRICULTURAL ZOOLOGY. Translated by J. R. AINSWORTH DAVIS, M.A. With 155 Illustrations. *Third Edition. Cr. 8vo.* 3s. 6d.

Botting (C. G.), B.A. EASY GREEK EXERCISES. *Cr. 8vo.* 2s.

See also Junior Examination Series.

Boulting (W.) TASSO AND HIS TIMES. With 24 Illustrations. *Demy 8vo.* 10s. 6d. *net.*

Boulton (E. S.), M.A. GEOMETRY ON MODERN LINES. *Cr. 8vo.* 2s.

Boulton (William B.). THOMAS GAINSBOROUGH. His Life and Work, Friends and Sitters. With 40 Illustrations. *Second Ed. Demy 8vo.* 7s. 6d. *net.*

SIR JOSHUA REYNOLDS, P.R.A. With 49 Illustrations. *Demy 8vo.* 7s. 6d. *net.*

Bowden (E. M.). THE IMITATION OF BUDDHA: Being Quotations from Buddhist Literature for each Day in the Year. *Fifth Edition. Cr. 16mo.* 2s. 6d.

Boyle (W.). CHRISTMAS AT THE ZOO. With Verses by W. BOYLE and 24 Coloured Pictures by H. B. NEILSON. *Super Royal 16mo.* 2s.

Brabant (F. G.), M.A. See Little Guides.

Bradley (A. G.). ROUND ABOUT WILTSHIRE. With 14 Illustrations, in Colour by T. C. GOTCH, 16 other Illustrations, and a Map. *Second Edition. Cr. 8vo.* 6s.

A Colonial Edition is also published.

THE ROMANCE OF NORTHUMBERLAND. With 16 Illustrations in Colour by FRANK SOUTHGATE, R.B.A., and 12 from Photographs. *Second Edition. Demy 8vo.* 7s. 6d *net.*

A Colonial Edition is also published.

Bradley (John W.). See Little Books on Art.

Braid (James), Open Champion, 1901, 1905 and 1906. ADVANCED GOLF. With 88 Photographs and Diagrams. *Fourth Edition. Demy 8vo.* 10s. 6d. *net.*

A Colonial Edition is also published.

Braid (James) and Others. GREAT GOLFERS IN THE MAKING. Edited by HENRY LEACH. With 24 Illustrations. *Second Edition. Demy 8vo.* 7s. 6d. *net.*

A Colonial Edition is also published.

Brailsford (H. N.). MACEDONIA: ITS RACES AND THEIR FUTURE. With Photographs and Maps. *Demy 8vo.* 12s. 6d. *net.*

Brodrick (Mary) and **Morton (A. Anderson).** A CONCISE DICTIONARY OF EGYPTIAN ARCHÆOLOGY. A Hand-Book for Students and Travellers. With 80 Illustrations and many Cartouches. *Cr. 8vo.* 3s. 6d.

Brooks (E. E.), B.Sc. (Lond), Leicester Municipal Technical School, and **James (W. H. N.),** A.R.C.S., A.M.I.E.E., Municipal School of Technology, Manchester. See Textbooks of Technology.

Brooks (E. W.). See Hamilton (F. J.)

Brown (P. H.), LL.D. SCOTLAND IN THE TIME OF QUEEN MARY. *Demy 8vo.* 7s. 6d. *net.*

Brown (S. E.), M.A., B.Sc., Senior Science Master at Uppingham. A PRACTICAL CHEMISTRY NOTE-BOOK FOR MATRICULATION AND ARMY CANDIDATES. Easy Experiments on the Commoner Substances. *Cr. 4to.* 1s. 6d. *net.*

Brown (J. Wood), M.A. THE BUILDERS OF FLORENCE. With 74 Illustrations by HERBERT RAILTON. *Demy 4to.* 18s. *net.*

Browne (Sir Thomas). See Standard Library.

Brownell (C. L.). THE HEART OF JAPAN. Illustrated. *Third Edition. Cr. 8vo.* 6s.; also *Demy 8vo.* 6d.

Browning (Robert). See Little Library.

Bryant (Walter W.), B.A., F.R.A.S., F.R. Met. Soc., of the Royal Observatory, Greenwich. A HISTORY OF ASTRONOMY. With 35 Illustrations. *Demy 8vo.* 7s. 6d. *net.*

Buckland (Francis T.). CURIOSITIES OF NATURAL HISTORY. Illustrated by H. B. NEILSON. *Cr. 8vo.* 3s. 6d.

Buckton (A. M.) THE BURDEN OF ENGELA. *Second Edition. Cr. 8vo.* 3s. 6d. *net.*

EAGER HEART: A Mystery Play. *Seventh Edition. Cr. 8vo.* 1s. *net.*

KINGS IN BABYLON: A Drama. *Cr. 8vo.* 1s. *net.*

SONGS OF JOY. *Cr. 8vo.* 1s. *net.*

Budge (E. A. Wallis). THE GODS OF THE EGYPTIANS. With over 100 Coloured Plates and many Illustrations. *Two Volumes. Royal 8vo.* £3, 3s. *net.*

Bull (Paul), Army Chaplain. GOD AND OUR SOLDIERS. *Second Edition. Cr. 8vo.* 6s.

A Colonial Edition is also published.

Bulley (Miss). See Dilke (Lady).

Bunyan (John). See Standard Library and Library of Devotion.

Burch (G. J.), M.A., F.R.S. A MANUAL OF ELECTRICAL SCIENCE. Illustrated. *Cr. 8vo.* 3s.

Burgess (Gelett). GOOPS AND HOW TO BE THEM. Illustrated. *Small 4to.* 6s.

Burke (Edmund). See Standard Library.

Burn (A. E.), D.D., Rector of Handsworth and Prebendary of Lichfield. See Handbooks of Theology.

Burn (J. H.), B.D., F.R.S.E. THE CHURCHMAN'S TREASURY OF SONG: Gathered from the Christian poetry of all ages. Edited by. *Fcap. 8vo.* 3s. 6d. *net.* See also Library of Devotion.

Burnand (Sir F. C.). RECORDS AND REMINISCENCES. With a Portrait by H. v. HERKOMER. *Cr. 8vo. Fourth and Cheaper Edition.* 6s.

A Colonial Edition is also published.

Burns (Robert), THE POEMS. Edited by ANDREW LANG and W. A. CRAIGIE. With Portrait. *Third Edition. Demy 8vo, gilt top.* 6s.

See also Standard Library.

Burnside (W. F.), M.A. OLD TESTAMENT HISTORY FOR USE IN SCHOOLS. *Third Edition. Cr. 8vo.* 3*s.* 6*d.*
Burton (Alfred). See I.P.L.
Bussell (F. W.), D.D. CHRISTIAN THEOLOGY AND SOCIAL PROGRESS (The Bampton Lectures of 1905). *Demy 8vo.* 10*s.* 6*d. net.*
Butler (Joseph), D.D. See Standard Library.
Caldecott (Alfred), D.D. See Handbooks of Theology.
Calderwood (D. S.), Headmaster of the Normal School, Edinburgh. TEST CARDS IN EUCLID AND ALGEBRA. In three packets of 40, with Answers. 1*s.* each. Or in three Books, price 2*d.*, 2*d.*, and 3*d.*
Canning (George). See Little Library.
Capey (E. F. H.). See Oxford Biographies.
Careless (John). See I.P.L.
Carlyle (Thomas). THE FRENCH REVOLUTION. Edited by C. R. L. FLETCHER, Fellow of Magdalen College, Oxford. *Three Volumes. Cr. 8vo.* 18*s.*
THE LIFE AND LETTERS OF OLIVER CROMWELL. With an Introduction by C. H. FIRTH, M.A., and Notes and Appendices by MRS. S. C. LOMAS. *Three Volumes. Demy 8vo.* 18*s. net.*
Carlyle (R. M. and A. J.), M.A. See Leaders of Religion.
Carmichael (Philip). ALL ABOUT PHILIPPINE. With 8 Illustrations. *Cr. 8vo.* 2*s.* 6*d.*
Carpenter (Margaret Boyd). THE CHILD IN ART. With 50 Illustrations. *Second Edition. Large Cr. 8vo.* 6*s.*
Cavanagh (Francis), M.D. (Edin.). THE CARE OF THE BODY. *Second Edition. Demy 8vo.* 7*s.* 6*d. net.*
Celano (Thomas of). THE LIVES OF ST. FRANCIS OF ASSISI. Translated into English by A. G. FERRERS HOWELL. With a Frontispiece. *Cr. 8vo.* 5*s. net.*
Channer (C. C.) and Roberts (M. E.). LACEMAKING IN THE MIDLANDS, PAST AND PRESENT. With 16 full-page Illustrations. *Cr. 8vo.* 2*s.* 6*d.*
Chapman (S. J.). See Books on Business.
Chatterton (Thomas). See Standard Library.
Chesterfield (Lord), THE LETTERS OF, TO HIS SON. Edited, with an Introduction by C. STRACHEY, with Notes by A. CALTHROP. *Two Volumes. Cr. 8vo.* 12*s.*
Chesterton (G. K.). CHARLES DICKENS. With two Portraits in Photogravure. *Fifth Edition. Cr. 8vo.* 6*s.*
Childe (Charles P.), B.A., F.R.C.S. THE CONTROL OF A SCOURGE: OR, HOW CANCER IS CURABLE. *Demy 8vo.* 7*s.* 6*d. net.*
Christian (F. W.). THE CAROLINE ISLANDS. With many Illustrations and Maps. *Demy 8vo.* 12*s.* 6*d. net.*
Cicero. See Classical Translations.
Clapham (J. H.), Professor of Economics in the University of Leeds. THE WOOLLEN AND WORSTED INDUSTRIES. With 21 Illustrations and Diagrams. *Cr. 8vo.* 6*s.*
Clarke (F. A.), M.A. See Leaders of Religion.
Clausen (George), A.R.A., R.W.S. SIX LECTURES ON PAINTING. With 19 Illustrations. *Third Edition. Large Post 8vo.* 3*s.* 6*d. net.*
AIMS AND IDEALS IN ART. Eight Lectures delivered to the Students of the Royal Academy of Arts. With 32 Illustrations. *Second Edition. Large Post 8vo.* 5*s. net.*
Cleather (A. L.). See Wagner (R).
Clinch (G.), F.G.S. See Antiquary's Books and Little Guides.
Clough (W. T.) and **Dunstan (A. E.).** See Junior School Books and Textbooks of Science.
Clouston (T. S.), M.D., C.C.D., F.R.S.E. THE HYGIENE OF MIND. With 10 Illustrations. *Fourth Edition. Demy 8vo.* 7*s.* 6*d. net.*
Coast (W. G.), B.A. EXAMINATION PAPERS IN VERGIL. *Cr. 8vo.* 2*s.*
Cobb (W. F.), M.A. THE BOOK OF PSALMS: with a Commentary. *Demy 8vo.* 10*s.* 6*d. net.*
Coleridge (S. T.). POEMS. Selected and Arranged by ARTHUR SYMONS. With a Photogravure Frontispiece. *Fcap. 8vo.* 2*s.* 6*d. net.*
Collingwood (W. G.), M.A. THE LIFE OF JOHN RUSKIN. With Portrait. *Sixth Edition. Cr. 8vo.* 2*s.* 6*d. net.*
Collins (W. E.), M.A. See Churchman's Library.
Combe (William). See I.P.L.
Conrad (Joseph). THE MIRROR OF THE SEA: Memories and Impressions. *Third Edition. Cr. 8vo.* 6*s.*
Cook (A. M.), M.A., and **Marchant (E. C.)**, M.A. PASSAGES FOR UNSEEN TRANSLATION. Selected from Latin and Greek Literature. *Fourth Ed. Cr. 8vo.* 3*s.* 6*d.*
LATIN PASSAGES FOR UNSEEN TRANSLATION. *Third Ed. Cr. 8vo.* 1*s.* 6*d.*
Cooke-Taylor (R. W.). THE FACTORY SYSTEM. *Cr. 8vo.* 2*s.* 6*d.*
Coolidge (W. A. B.), M.A. THE ALPS. With many Illustrations. *Demy 8vo.* 7*s.* 6*d net.*
A Colonial Edition is also published.
Corelli (Marie). THE PASSING OF THE GREAT QUEEN. *Second Edition. Fcap. 4to.* 1*s.*
A CHRISTMAS GREETING. *Cr. 4to.* 1*s.*
Corkran (Alice). See Little Books on Art.
Cotes (Everard). SIGNS AND PORTENTS IN THE FAR EAST. With 35 Illustrations. *Second Edition. Demy 8vo.* 7*s.* 6*d. net.*
A Colonial Edition is also published.
Cotes (Rosemary). DANTE'S GARDEN. With a Frontispiece. *Second Edition. Fcap. 8vo.* 2*s.* 6*d.*; *leather*, 3*s.* 6*d. net.*
BIBLE FLOWERS. With a Frontispiece and Plan. *Fcap. 8vo.* 2*s.* 6*d. net.*

Cowley (Abraham). See Little Library.

Cowper (William). THE POEMS. Edited with an Introduction and Notes by J. C. BAILEY, M.A. Illustrated, including two unpublished designs by WILLIAM BLAKE. *Demy 8vo.* 10*s.* 6*d. net.*

Cox (J. Charles). See Ancient Cities, Antiquary's Books, and Little Guides.

Cox (Harold), B.A., M.P. LAND NATIONALIZATION AND LAND TAXATION. *Second Edition revised. Cr. 8vo.* 3*s.* 6*d. net.*

Crabbe (George). See Little Library.

Craik (Mrs.). See Little Library.

Crane (C. P.), D.S.O. See Little Guides.

Crane (Walter), R.W.S. AN ARTIST'S REMINISCENCES. With 123 Illustrations by the Author and others from Photographs. *Second Edition. Demy 8vo.* 18*s. net.*

A Colonial Edition is also published.

INDIA IMPRESSIONS. With 84 Illustrations from Sketches by the Author. *Second Edition. Demy 8vo.* 7*s.* 6*d. net.*

A Colonial Edition is also published.

Crashaw (Richard). See Little Library.

Crawford (F. G.). See Danson (Mary C.).

Crofts (T. R. N.), M.A., Modern Language Master at Merchant Taylors' School. See Simplified French Texts.

Cross (J. A.), M.A. THE FAITH OF THE BIBLE. *Fcap. 8vo.* 2*s.* 6*d. net.*

Cruikshank (G.). THE LOVING BALLAD OF LORD BATEMAN. With 11 Plates. *Cr. 16mo.* 1*s.* 6*d. net.*

Crump (B.). See Wagner (R.).

Cunliffe (Sir F. H. E.), Fellow of All Souls' College, Oxford. THE HISTORY OF THE BOER WAR. With many Illustrations, Plans, and Portraits. *In 2 vols. Quarto.* 15*s. each.*

Cunynghame (H. H.), C.B. See Connoisseur's Library.

Cutts (E. L.), D.D. See Leaders of Religion.

Daniell (G. W.), M.A. See Leaders of Religion.

Dante (Alighieri). LA COMMEDIA DI DANTE. The Italian Text edited by PAGET TOYNBEE, M.A., D.Litt. *Cr. 8vo.* 6*s.*

THE DIVINE COMEDY. Translated by H. F. CARY. Edited with a Life of Dante and Introductory Notes by PAGET TOYNBEE, M.A., D.Litt. *Demy 8vo.* 6*d.*

THE PURGATORIO OF DANTE. Translated into Spenserian Prose by C. GORDON WRIGHT. With the Italian text. *Fcap. 8vo.* 2*s.* 6*d. net.*

See also Little Library, Toynbee (Paget), and Vernon (Hon. W. Warren).

Darley (George). See Little Library.

D'Arcy (R. F.), M.A. A NEW TRIGONOMETRY FOR BEGINNERS. With numerous diagrams. *Cr. 8vo.* 2*s.* 6*d.*

Davenport (Cyril). See Connoisseur's Library and Little Books on Art.

Davenport (James). THE WASHBOURNE FAMILY. With 15 Illustrations and a Map. *Royal 8vo.* 21*s. net.*

Davey (Richard). THE PAGEANT OF LONDON. With 40 Illustrations in Colour by JOHN FULLEYLOVE, R.I. *In Two Volumes. Demy 8vo.* 15*s. net.*

Davis (H. W. C.), M.A., Fellow and Tutor of Balliol College. ENGLAND UNDER THE NORMANS AND ANGEVINS: 1066-1272. With Maps and Illustrations. *Demy 8vo.* 10*s.* 6*d. net.*

Dawson (Nelson). See Connoisseur's Library.

Dawson (Mrs. Nelson). See Little Books on Art.

Deane (A. C.). See Little Library.

Deans (Storry R.). THE TRIALS OF FIVE QUEENS: KATHARINE OF ARAGON, ANNE BOLEYN, MARY QUEEN OF SCOTS, MARIE ANTOINETTE and CAROLINE OF BRUNSWICK. With 12 Illustrations. *Demy 8vo.* 10*s.* 6*d. net.*

A Colonial Edition is also published.

Dearmer (Mabel). A CHILD'S LIFE OF CHRIST. With 8 Illustrations in Colour by E. FORTESCUE-BRICKDALE. *Large Cr. 8vo.* 6*s.*

Delbos (Leon). THE METRIC SYSTEM. *Cr. 8vo.* 2*s.*

Demosthenes. AGAINST CONON AND CALLICLES. Edited by F. DARWIN SWIFT, M.A. *Second Edition. Fcap. 8vo.* 2*s.*

Dickens (Charles). See Little Library, I.P.L., and Chesterton (G. K.).

Dickinson (Emily). POEMS. *Cr. 8vo.* 4*s.* 6*d. net.*

Dickinson (G. L.), M.A., Fellow of King's College, Cambridge. THE GREEK VIEW OF LIFE. *Sixth Edition. Cr. 8vo.* 2*s.* 6*d.*

Dilke (Lady), Bulley (Miss), and Whitley (Miss). WOMEN'S WORK. *Cr. 8vo.* 2*s.* 6*d.*

Dillon (Edward), M.A. See Connoisseur's Library and Little Books on Art.

Ditchfield (P. H.), M.A., F.S.A. THE STORY OF OUR ENGLISH TOWNS. With an Introduction by AUGUSTUS JESSOPP, D.D. *Second Edition. Cr. 8vo.* 6*s.*

OLD ENGLISH CUSTOMS: Extant at the Present Time. *Cr. 8vo.* 6*s.*

ENGLISH VILLAGES. With 100 Illustrations. *Second Edition. Cr. 8vo.* 2*s.* 6*d. net.*

THE PARISH CLERK. With 31 Illustrations. *Third Edition. Demy 8vo.* 7*s.* 6*d. net.*

Dixon (W. M.), M.A. A PRIMER OF TENNYSON. *Second Edition. Cr. 8vo.* 2*s.* 6*d.*

ENGLISH POETRY FROM BLAKE TO BROWNING. *Second Edition. Cr. 8vo.* 2*s.* 6*d.*

Dobbs (W. J.), M.A. See Textbooks of Science.

Doney (May). SONGS OF THE REAL. *Cr. 8vo.* 3*s.* 6*d. net.*

Douglas (Hugh A.). VENICE ON FOOT. With the Itinerary of the Grand Canal. With 75 Illustrations and 11 Maps. *Fcap. 8vo.* 5*s. net.*

Douglas (James). THE MAN IN THE PULPIT. *Cr. 8vo.* *2s. 6d. net.*

Dowden (J.), D.D., Lord Bishop of Edinburgh. FURTHER STUDIES IN THE PRAYER BOOK. *Cr. 8vo.* *6s.*
See also Churchman's Library.

Drage (G.). See Books on Business.

Draper (F. W. M.). See Simplified French Texts.

Driver (S. R.), D.D., D.C.L., Regius Professor of Hebrew in the University of Oxford. SERMONS ON SUBJECTS CONNECTED WITH THE OLD TESTAMENT. *Cr. 8vo.* *6s.*
See also Westminster Commentaries.

Dry (Wakeling). See Little Guides.

Dryhurst (A. R.). See Little Books on Art.

Du Buisson (J. C.), M.A. See Churchman's Bible.

Duguid (Charles). See Books on Business.

Dumas (Alexandre). THE CRIMES OF THE BORGIAS AND OTHERS. With an Introduction by R. S. GARNETT. With 9 Illustrations. *Cr. 8vo.* *6s.*

THE CRIMES OF URBAIN GRANDIER AND OTHERS. With 8 Illustrations. *Cr. 8vo.* *6s.*

THE CRIMES OF THE MARQUISE DE BRINVILLIERS AND OTHERS. With 8 Illustrations. *Cr. 8vo.* *6s.*

THE CRIMES OF ALI PACHA AND OTHERS. With 8 Illustrations. *Cr. 8vo.* *6s.*
Colonial Editions are also published.

MY MEMOIRS. Translated by E. M. WALLER. With an Introduction by ANDREW LANG. With Frontispieces in Photogravure. In six Volumes. *Cr. 8vo.* *6s. each volume.*
A Colonial Edition is also published.
VOL. I. 1802-1821. VOL. III. 1826-1830.
VOL. II. 1822-1825. VOL. IV. 1830-1831.

Duncan (David), D.Sc., LL.D. THE LIFE AND LETTERS OF HERBERT SPENCER. With 15 Illustrations. *Demy 8vo.* *15s.*

Dunn (J. T)., D.Sc., **and Mundella (V. A.).** GENERAL ELEMENTARY SCIENCE. With 114 Illustrations. *Second Edition. Cr. 8vo.* *3s. 6d.*

Dunstan (A. E.), B.Sc. (Lond.), East Ham Technical College. See Textbooks of Science, and Junior School Books.

Durham (The Earl of). A REPORT ON CANADA. With an Introductory Note. *Demy 8vo.* *4s. 6d. net.*

Dutt (W. A.). THE NORFOLK BROADS. With coloured Illustrations by FRANK SOUTHGATE, R.B.A. *Second Edition. Cr. 8vo.* *6s.*

WILD LIFE IN EAST ANGLIA. With 16 Illustrations in colour by FRANK SOUTHGATE, R.B.A. *Second Edition. Demy 8vo.* *7s. 6d. net.*

SOME LITERARY ASSOCIATIONS OF EAST ANGLIA. With 16 Illustrations in Colour by W. DEXTER, R.B.A., and 16 other Illustrations. *Demy 8vo.* *10s. 6d. net.*
See also Little Guides.

Earle (John), Bishop of Salisbury. MICROCOSMOGRAPHIE, OR A PIECE OF THE WORLD DISCOVERED. *Post 16mo.* *2s. net.*

Edmonds (Major J. E.), R.E.; D.A.Q.-M.G. See Wood (W. Birkbeck).

Edwards (Clement), M.P. RAILWAY NATIONALIZATION. *Second Edition, Revised. Crown 8vo.* *2s. 6d. net.*

Edwards (W. Douglas). See Commercial Series.

Edwardes (Tickner). THE LORE OF THE HONEY BEE. With many Illustrations. *Cr. 8vo.* *6s.*

Egan (Pierce). See I.P.L.

Egerton (H. E.), M.A. A HISTORY OF BRITISH COLONIAL POLICY. A Cheaper Issue, with a supplementary chapter. *Second Ed., Revised. Demy 8vo.* *7s. 6d. net.*
A Colonial Edition is also published.

Ellaby (C. G.). See Little Guides.

Ellerton (F. G.). See Stone (S. J.).

Epictetus. See Aurelius (Marcus).

Erasmus. A Book called in Latin ENCHIRIDION MILITIS CHRISTIANI, and in English the Manual of the Christian Knight. *Fcap. 8vo.* *3s. 6d. net.*

Ewald (Carl). TWO LEGS, AND OTHER STORIES. Translated from the Danish by ALEXANDER TEIXEIRA DE MATTOS. Illustrated by AUGUSTA GUEST. *Large Cr. 8vo.* *6s.*

Fairbrother (W. H.), M.A. THE PHILOSOPHY OF T. H. GREEN. *Second Edition. Cr. 8vo.* *3s. 6d.*

Fea (Allan). SOME BEAUTIES OF THE SEVENTEENTH CENTURY. With 82 Illustrations. *Second Edition. Demy 8vo.* *12s. 6d. net.*

THE FLIGHT OF THE KING. With over 70 Sketches and Photographs by the Author. *New and revised Edition. Demy 8vo.* *7s. 6d. net.*
A Colonial Edition is also published.

SECRET CHAMBERS AND HIDING-PLACES. With 80 Illustrations. *New and revised Edition. Demy 8vo.* *7s. 6d. net.*
A Colonial Edition is also published.

Ferrier (Susan). See Little Library.

Fidler (T. Claxton), M.Inst. C.E. See Books on Business.

Fielding (Henry). See Standard Library.

Finn (S. W.), M.A. See Junior Examination Series.

Firth (J. B.). See Little Guides.

Firth (C. H.), M.A., Regius Professor of Modern History at Oxford. CROMWELL'S ARMY: A History of the English Soldier during the Civil Wars, the Commonwealth, and the Protectorate. *Cr. 8vo.* *6s.*

Firth (Edith E.). See Beginner's Books.

FitzGerald (Edward). THE RUBÁIYÁT OF OMAR KHAYYÁM. Printed from the Fifth and last Edition. With a Commentary by Mrs. STEPHEN BATSON, and a Biography of Omar by E. D. ROSS. *Cr. 8vo.* *6s.* See also Miniature Library.

FitzGerald (H. P.). A CONCISE HANDBOOK OF CLIMBERS, TWINERS, AND WALL SHRUBS. Illustrated. *Fcap. 8vo.* 3s. 6d. *net.*

Fitzpatrick (S. A. O.). See Ancient Cities.

Flecker (W. H.), M.A., D.C.L., Headmaster of the Dean Close School, Cheltenham. THE STUDENT'S PRAYER BOOK. THE TEXT OF MORNING AND EVENING PRAYER AND LITANY. With an Introduction and Notes. *Cr. 8vo.* 2s. 6d.

Fletcher (J. S.). A BOOK OF YORKSHIRE. With 16 Illustrations in Colour by WAL PAGET and FRANK SOUTHGATE, R.B.A., and 12 from Photographs. *Demy 8vo.* 7s. 6d. *net.*

A Colonial Edition is also published.

Flux (A. W.), M.A., William Dow Professor of Political Economy in M'Gill University, Montreal. ECONOMIC PRINCIPLES. *Demy 8vo.* 7s. 6d. *net.*

Foat (F. W. G.), D.Litt., M.A., Assistant Master at the City of London School. LONDON: A READER FOR YOUNG CITIZENS. With Plans and Illustrations. *Cr. 8vo.* 1s. 6d.

Ford (H. G.), M.A., Assistant Master at Bristol Grammar School. See Junior School Books.

Forel (A.). THE SENSES OF INSECTS. Translated by MACLEOD YEARSLEY. With 2 Illustrations. *Demy 8vo.* 10s. 6d. *net.*

Fortescue (Mrs. G.). See Little Books on Art.

Fraser (J. F.). ROUND THE WORLD ON A WHEEL. With 100 Illustrations. *Fifth Edition Cr. 8vo.* 6s.

A Colonial Edition is also published.

French (W.), M.A. See Textbooks of Science.

Freudenreich (Ed. von). DAIRY BACTERIOLOGY. A Short Manual for Students. Translated by J. R. AINSWORTH DAVIS, M.A. *Second Edition. Revised. Cr. 8vo.* 2s. 6d.

Fulford (H. W.), M.A. See Churchman's Bible.

Fuller (W. P.), M.A. See Simplified French Texts.

***Fyvie (John).** TRAGEDY QUEENS OF THE GEORGIAN ERA. With 16 Illustrations. *Second Ed. Demy 8vo.* 12s. 6d. *net.*

Gallaher (D.) and Stead (W. J.). THE COMPLETE RUGBY FOOTBALLER, ON THE NEW ZEALAND SYSTEM. With 35 Illustrations. *Second Ed. Demy 8vo.* 10s. 6d. *net.*

A Colonial Edition is also published.

Gallichan (W. M.). See Little Guides.

Gambado (Geoffrey, Esq.). See I.P.L.

Gaskell (Mrs.). See Little Library, Standard Library and Sixpenny Novels.

Gasquet, the Right Rev. Abbot, O.S.B. See Antiquary's Books.

George (H. B.), M.A., Fellow of New College, Oxford. BATTLES OF ENGLISH HISTORY. With numerous Plans. *Fourth Edition. Cr. 8vo.* 3s. 6d.

A HISTORICAL GEOGRAPHY OF THE BRITISH EMPIRE. *Third Edition. Cr. 8vo.* 3s. 6d.

Gibbins (H. de B.), Litt.D., M.A. INDUSTRY IN ENGLAND: HISTORICAL OUTLINES. With 5 Maps. *Fifth Edition. Demy 8vo.* 10s. 6d.

THE INDUSTRIAL HISTORY OF ENGLAND. With Maps and Plans. *Fifteenth Edition, Revised. Cr. 8vo.* 3s.

ENGLISH SOCIAL REFORMERS. *Second Edition. Cr. 8vo.* 2s. 6d.

See also Hadfield (R. A.), and Commercial Series.

Gibbon (Edward). MEMOIRS OF MY LIFE AND WRITINGS. Edited by G. BIRKBECK HILL, LL.D *Cr. 8vo.* 6s.

THE DECLINE AND FALL OF THE ROMAN EMPIRE. Edited, with Notes, Appendices, and Maps, by J. B. BURY, M.A., Litt.D., Regius Professor of Greek at Cambridge. *In Seven Volumes. Demy 8vo. Gilt top.* 8s. 6d. *each. Also, Crown 8vo.* 6s. *each.*

See also Standard Library.

Gibbs (Philip). THE ROMANCE OF GEORGE VILLIERS: FIRST DUKE OF BUCKINGHAM, AND SOME MEN AND WOMEN OF THE STUART COURT. With 20 Illustrations. *Second Edition. Demy 8vo.* 15s. *net.*

A Colonial Edition is also published.

Gibson (E. C. S.), D.D., Lord Bishop of Gloucester. See Westminster Commentaries, Handbooks of Theology, and Oxford Biographies.

Gilbert (A. R.). See Little Books on Art.

Gloag (M. R.) and Wyatt (Kate M.). A BOOK OF ENGLISH GARDENS. With 24 Illustrations in Colour. *Demy 8vo.* 10s. 6d. *net.*

Godfrey (Elizabeth). A BOOK OF REMEMBRANCE. Being Lyrical Selections for every day in the Year. Arranged by. *Fcap. 8vo.* 2s 6d. *net.*

ENGLISH CHILDREN IN THE OLDEN TIME. With 32 Illustrations. *Second Edition. Demy 8vo.* 7s. 6d. *net.*

Godley (A. D.), M.A., Fellow of Magdalen College, Oxford. LYRA FRIVOLA. *Fourth Edition. Fcap. 8vo.* 2s. 6d.

VERSES TO ORDER. *Second Edition. Fcap. 8vo.* 2s. 6d.

SECOND STRINGS. *Fcap. 8vo.* 2s. 6d.

Goldsmith (Oliver). THE VICAR OF WAKEFIELD. With 10 Plates in Photogravure by Tony Johannot. *Leather, Fcap. 32mo.* 2s. 6d. *net.*

See also I.P.L. and Standard Library.

Gomme (G. L.). See Antiquary's Books.

Goodrich-Freer (A.). IN A SYRIAN SADDLE. *Demy 8vo.* 7s. 6d. *net.*

A Colonial Edition is also published.

Gorst (Rt. Hon. Sir John). THE CHILDREN OF THE NATION. *Second Edition. Demy 8vo.* 7s. 6d. *net.*

Goudge (H. L.), M.A., Principal of Wells Theological College. See Westminster Commentaries.

Graham (P. Anderson). THE RURAL EXODUS. The Problem of the Village and the Town. *Cr. 8vo.* 2*s.* 6*d.*

Granger (F. S.), M.A., Litt.D. PSYCHOLOGY. *Third Edition. Cr. 8vo.* 2*s.* 6*d.*

THE SOUL OF A CHRISTIAN. *Cr. 8vo.* 6*s.*

Gray (E. M'Queen). GERMAN PASSAGES FOR UNSEEN TRANSLATION. *Cr. 8vo.* 2*s.* 6*d.*

Gray (P. L.), B.Sc. THE PRINCIPLES OF MAGNETISM AND ELECTRICITY. With 181 Diagrams. *Cr. 8vo.* 3*s.* 6*d.*

Green (G. Buckland), M.A., late Fellow of St. John's College, Oxon. NOTES ON GREEK AND LATIN SYNTAX. *Second Ed. revised. Crown 8vo.* 3*s.* 6*d.*

Greenidge (A. H. J.), M.A., D.Litt. A HISTORY OF ROME: From the Tribunate of Tiberius Gracchus to the end of the Jugurthine War, B.C. 133-104. *Demy 8vo.* 10*s.* 6*d. net.*

Greenwell (Dora). See Miniature Library.

Gregory (R. A.). THE VAULT OF HEAVEN. A Popular Introduction to Astronomy. Illustrated. *Cr. 8vo.* 2*s.* 6*d.*

Gregory (Miss E. C.). See Library of Devotion.

Grubb (H. C.). See Textbooks of Technology.

Hadfield (R. A.) and Gibbins (H. de B.). A SHORTER WORKING DAY. *Cr. 8vo.* 2*s.* 6*d.*

Hall (Mary). A WOMAN'S TREK FROM THE CAPE TO CAIRO. With 64 Illustrations and 2 Maps. *Second Edition. Demy 8vo.* 16*s. net.*

Hall (R. N.) and Neal (W. G.). THE ANCIENT RUINS OF RHODESIA. Illustrated. *Second Edition, revised. Demy 8vo.* 10*s.* 6*d. net.*
A Colonial Edition is also published.

Hall (R. N.). GREAT ZIMBABWE. With numerous Plans and Illustrations. *Second Edition. Demy 8vo.* 10*s.* 6*d. net.*

Hamel (Frank). FAMOUS FRENCH SALONS. With 20 Illustrations. *Demy 8vo.* 12*s.* 6*d. net.*
A Colonial Edition is also published.

Hamilton (F. J.), D.D. See Byzantine Texts.

Hannay (D.). A SHORT HISTORY OF THE ROYAL NAVY, 1200-1688. Illustrated. *Demy 8vo.* 7*s.* 6*d.*

Hannay (James O.), M.A. THE SPIRIT AND ORIGIN OF CHRISTIAN MONASTICISM. *Cr. 8vo.* 6*s.*

THE WISDOM OF THE DESERT. *Fcap. 8vo.* 3*s.* 6*d. net.*

Hardie (Martin). See Connoisseur's Library.

Hare (A. T.), M.A. THE CONSTRUCTION OF LARGE INDUCTION COILS. With numerous Diagrams. *Demy 8vo.* 6*s.*

Harvey (Alfred), M.B. See Ancient Cities and Antiquary's Books.

Hawthorne (Nathaniel). See Little Library.

Heath (Frank R.). See Little Guides.

Heath (Dudley). See Connoisseur's Library.

Hello (Ernest). STUDIES IN SAINTSHIP. *Fcap 8vo.* 3*s.* 6*d.*

Henderson (B. W.), Fellow of Exeter College, Oxford. THE LIFE AND PRINCIPATE OF THE EMPEROR NERO. Illustrated. *New and cheaper issue. Demy 8vo.* 7*s.* 6*d. net.*

AT INTERVALS. *Fcap 8vo.* 2*s.* 6*d. net.*

Henderson (M. Sturge). GEORGE MEREDITH: NOVELIST, POET, REFORMER. With a Portrait in Photogravure. *Second Edition. Crown 8vo.* 6*s.*

Henderson (T. F.). See Little Library and Oxford Biographies.

Henderson (T. F.), and Watt (Francis). SCOTLAND OF TO-DAY. With 20 Illustrations in colour and 24 other Illustrations. *Second Edition. Cr. 8vo.* 6*s.*
A Colonial Edition is also published.

Henley (W. E.). ENGLISH LYRICS: CHAUCER TO POE, 1340-1849. *Second Edition. Cr. 8vo.* 2*s.* 6*d. net.*

Henley (W. E.) and Whibley (C.) A BOOK OF ENGLISH PROSE, CHARACTER, AND INCIDENT, 1387-1649. *Cr. 8vo.* 2*s.* 6*d. net.*

Henson (H. H.), B.D., Canon of Westminster. LIGHT AND LEAVEN: HISTORICAL AND SOCIAL SERMONS. *Cr. 8vo.* 6*s.*

Herbert (George). See Library of Devotion.

Herbert of Cherbury (Lord). See Miniature Library.

Hewins (W. A. S.), B.A. ENGLISH TRADE AND FINANCE IN THE SEVENTEENTH CENTURY. *Cr. 8vo.* 2*s.* 6*d.*

Hewitt (Ethel M.) A GOLDEN DIAL. A Day Book of Prose and Verse. *Fcap. 8vo.* 2*s.* 6*d. net.*

Hey (H.), Inspector, Surrey Education Committee, and **Rose (G. H.),** City and Guilds Woodwork Teacher. THE MANUAL TRAINING CLASSROOM: WOODWORK. Book I. *4to.* 1*s.*

Heywood (W.). PALIO AND PONTE. A Book of Tuscan Games. Illustrated. *Royal 8vo.* 21*s. net.*
See also St. Francis of Assisi.

Hill (Clare). See Textbooks of Technology.

Hill (Henry), B.A., Headmaster of the Boy's High School, Worcester, Cape Colony. A SOUTH AFRICAN ARITHMETIC. *Cr. 8vo.* 3*s.* 6*d.*

Hind (C. Lewis). DAYS IN CORNWALL. With 16 Illustrations in Colour by WILLIAM PASCOE, and 20 other Illustrations and a Map. *Second Edition. Cr. 8vo.* 6*s.*

Hirst (F. W.) See Books on Business.

Hoare (J. Douglas). A HISTORY OF ARCTIC EXPLORATION. With 20 Illustrations & Maps. *Demy 8vo.* 7*s.* 6*d. net.*

Hobhouse (L. T.), late Fellow of C.C.C., Oxford. THE THEORY OF KNOWLEDGE. *Demy 8vo.* 10*s.* 6*d. net.*

Hobson (J. A.), M.A. INTERNATIONAL TRADE: A Study of Economic Principles. *Cr. 8vo.* 2*s.* 6*d. net.*

PROBLEMS OF POVERTY. An Inquiry into the Industrial Condition of the Poor. *Sixth Edition. Cr. 8vo.* 2*s.* 6*d.*

THE PROBLEM OF THE UNEMPLOYED. *Third Edition. Cr. 8vo.* 2s. 6d.

Hodgetts (E. A. Brayley). THE COURT OF RUSSIA IN THE NINETEENTH CENTURY. With 20 Illustrations. *Two Volumes. Demy 8vo.* 24s. *net.*
A Colonial Edition is also published.

Hodgkin (T.), D.C.L. See Leaders of Religion.

Hodgson (Mrs. W.) HOW TO IDENTIFY OLD CHINESE PORCELAIN. With 40 Illustrations. *Second Edition. Post 8vo.* 6s.

Hogg (Thomas Jefferson). SHELLEY AT OXFORD. With an Introduction by R. A. STREATFEILD. *Fcap. 8vo.* 2s. *net.*

Holden-Stone (G. de). See Books on Business.

Holdich (Sir T. H.), K.C.I.E. THE INDIAN BORDERLAND: being a Personal Record of Twenty Years. Illustrated. *Demy 8vo.* 10s. 6d. *net.*
A Colonial Edition is also published.

Holdsworth (W. S.), M.A. A HISTORY OF ENGLISH LAW. *In Two Volumes. Vol. I. Demy 8vo.* 10s. 6d. *net.*

Holland (H. Scott), Canon of St. Paul's. See Newman (J. H.).

Hollway-Calthrop (H. C.), late of Balliol College, Oxford; Bursar of Eton College. PETRARCH: HIS LIFE, WORK, AND TIMES. With 24 Illustrations. *Demy 8vo.* 12s. 6d. *net.*
A Colonial Edition is also published.

Holt (Emily). THE SECRET OF POPULARITY: How to Achieve Social Success. *Cr. 8vo.* 3s. 6d. *net.*
A Colonial Edition is also published.

Holyoake (G. J.). THE CO-OPERATIVE MOVEMENT OF TO-DAY. *Fourth Ed. Cr. 8vo.* 2s. 6d.

Hone (Nathaniel J.). See Antiquary's Books.

Hook (A.) HUMANITY AND ITS PROBLEMS. *Cr. 8vo.* 5s. *net.*

Hoppner. See Little Galleries.

Horace. See Classical Translations.

Horsburgh (E. L. S.), M.A. WATERLOO: With Plans. *Second Edition. Cr. 8vo.* 5s.
See also Oxford Biographies.

Horth (A. C.). See Textbooks of Technology.

Horton (R. F.), D.D. See Leaders of Religion.

Hosie (Alexander). MANCHURIA. With Illustrations and a Map. *Second Edition. Demy 8vo.* 7s. 6d. *net.*
A Colonial Edition is also published.

How (F. D.). SIX GREAT SCHOOLMASTERS. With Portraits and Illustrations. *Second Edition. Demy 8vo.* 7s. 6d.

Howell (A. G. Ferrers). FRANCISCAN DAYS. Being Selections for every day in the year from ancient Franciscan writings. *Cr. 8vo.* 3s. 6d. *net.*

Howell (G.). TRADE UNIONISM—NEW AND OLD. *Fourth Edition. Cr. 8vo.* 2s. 6d.

Huggins (Sir William), K.C.B., O.M., D.C.L., F.R.S. THE ROYAL SOCIETY. With 25 Illustrations. *Wide Royal 8vo.* 4s. 6d. *net.*

Hughes (C. E.). THE PRAISE OF SHAKESPEARE. An English Anthology. With a Preface by SIDNEY LEE. *Demy 8vo.* 3s. 6d. *net.*

Hughes (Thomas). TOM BROWN'S SCHOOLDAYS. With an Introduction and Notes by VERNON RENDALL. *Leather. Royal 32mo.* 2s. 6d. *net.*

Hutchinson (Horace G.) THE NEW FOREST. Illustrated in colour with 50 Pictures by WALTER TYNDALE and 4 by LUCY KEMP-WELCH. *Third Edition. Cr. 8vo.* 6s.

Hutton (A. W.), M.A. See Leaders of Religion and Library of Devotion.

Hutton (Edward). THE CITIES OF UMBRIA. With 20 Illustrations in Colour by A. PISA, and 12 other Illustrations. *Third Edition. Cr. 8vo.* 6s.
A Colonial Edition is also published.

THE CITIES OF SPAIN. With 24 Illustrations in Colour, by A. W. RIMINGTON, 20 other Illustrations and a Map. *Second Edition. Cr. 8vo.* 6s.
A Colonial Edition is also published.

FLORENCE AND THE CITIES OF NORTHERN TUSCANY, WITH GENOA. With 16 Illustrations in Colour by WILLIAM PARKINSON, and 16 other Illustrations. *Second Edition. Cr. 8vo.* 6s.
A Colonial Edition is also published.

ENGLISH LOVE POEMS. Edited with an Introduction. *Fcap. 8vo.* 3s. 6d. *net.*

Hutton (R. H.). See Leaders of Religion.

Hutton (W. H.), M.A. THE LIFE OF SIR THOMAS MORE. With Portraits after Drawings by HOLBEIN. *Second Ed. Cr. 8vo.* 5s.
See also Leaders of Religion.

Hyde (A. G.) GEORGE HERBERT AND HIS TIMES. With 32 Illustrations. *Demy 8vo.* 10s. 6d. *net.*

Hyett (F. A.). FLORENCE: HER HISTORY AND ART TO THE FALL OF THE REPUBLIC. *Demy 8vo.* 7s. 6d. *net.*

Ibsen (Henrik). BRAND. A Drama. Translated by WILLIAM WILSON. *Third Edition. Cr. 8vo.* 3s. 6d.

Inge (W. R.), M.A., Fellow and Tutor of Hertford College, Oxford. CHRISTIAN MYSTICISM. (The Bampton Lectures of 1899.) *Demy 8vo.* 12s. 6d. *net.*
See also Library of Devotion.

Ingham (B. P.). See Simplified French Texts.

Innes (A. D.), M.A. A HISTORY OF THE BRITISH IN INDIA. With Maps and Plans. *Cr. 8vo.* 6s.

ENGLAND UNDER THE TUDORS. With Maps. *Second Edition. Demy 8vo.* 10s. 6d. *net.*

Jackson (C. E.), B.A., Senior Physics Master, Bradford Grammar School. See Textbooks of Science.

Jackson (S.), M.A. See Commercial Series.

Jackson (F. Hamilton). See Little Guides.

Jacob (F.), M.A. See Junior Examination Series.

James (W. H. N.). See Brooks (E. E.).

Jeans (J. Stephen). TRUSTS, POOLS, AND CORNERS AS AFFECTING COMMERCE AND INDUSTRY. *Cr. 8vo.* 2s. 6d.
See also Books on Business.

Jebb (Camilla). A STAR OF THE SALONS: JULIE DE LESPINASSE. With 20 Illustrations. *Demy 8vo.* 10s. 6d. *net.*
A Colonial Edition is also published.

Jeffery (Reginald W.), M.A. THE THIRTEEN COLONIES OF NORTH AMERICA. With 8 Illustrations and a Map. *Demy 8vo.* 7s. 6d. *net.*
A Colonial Edition is also published.

Jeffreys (D. Gwyn). DOLLY'S THEATRICALS. *Super Royal 16mo.* 2s. 6d.

Jenks (E.), M.A., B.C.L. AN OUTLINE OF ENGLISH LOCAL GOVERNMENT. *Second Ed.* Revised by R. C. K. ENSOR, M.A. *Cr. 8vo.* 2s. 6d.

Jenner (Mrs. H.). See Little Books on Art.

Jennings (Oscar), M.D. EARLY WOODCUT INITIALS. *Demy 4to.* 21s. *net.*

Jessopp (Augustus), D.D. See Leaders of Religion.

Jevons (F. B.), M.A., Litt.D., Principal of Hatfield Hall, Durham. RELIGION IN EVOLUTION. *Cr. 8vo.* 3s. 6d. *net.*
See also Churchman's Library and Handbooks of Theology.

Johnson (Mrs. Barham). WILLIAM BODHAM DONNE AND HIS FRIENDS. Illustrated. *Demy 8vo.* 10s. 6d. *net.*

Johnston (Sir H. H.), K.C.B. BRITISH CENTRAL AFRICA. With nearly 200 Illustrations and Six Maps. *Third Edition. Cr. 4to.* 18s. *net.*
A Colonial Edition is also published.

Jones (H.). See Commercial Series.

Jones (H. F.). See Textbooks of Science.

Jones (L. A. Atherley), K.C., M.P., and **Bellot (Hugh H. L.),** M.A., D.C.L. THE MINER'S GUIDE TO THE COAL MINES REGULATION ACTS AND THE LAW OF EMPLOYERS AND WORKMEN. *Cr. 8vo.* 2s. 6d. *net.*
COMMERCE IN WAR. *Royal 8vo.* 21s. *net.*

Jones (R. Compton), M.A. POEMS OF THE INNER LIFE. Selected by. *Thirteenth Edition. Fcap. 8vo.* 2s. 6d. *net.*

Jonson (Ben). See Standard Library.

Juliana (Lady) of Norwich. REVELATIONS OF DIVINE LOVE. Ed. by GRACE WARRACK. *Second Ed. Cr. 8vo.* 3s. 6d.

Juvenal. See Classical Translations.

'Kappa.' LET YOUTH BUT KNOW: A Plea for Reason in Education. *Cr. 8vo.* 3s. 6d. *net.*

Kaufmann (M.), M.A. SOCIALISM AND MODERN THOUGHT. *Second Edition Revised and Enlarged. Cr. 8vo.* 2s. 6d. *net.*

Keating (J. F.), D.D. THE AGAPÉ AND THE EUCHARIST. *Cr. 8vo.* 3s. 6d.

Keats (John). THE POEMS. Edited with Introduction and Notes by E. de SELINCOURT, M.A. With a Frontispiece in Photogravure. *Second Edition Revised. Demy 8vo.* 7s. 6d. *net.*
REALMS OF GOLD. Selections from the Works of. *Fcap. 8vo.* 3s. 6d. *net.*
See also Little Library and Standard Library.

Keble (John). THE CHRISTIAN YEAR. With an Introduction and Notes by W. LOCK, D.D., Warden of Keble College. Illustrated by R. ANNING BELL. *Third Edition. Fcap. 8vo.* 3s. 6d.; *padded morocco,* 5s.
See also Library of Devotion.

Kelynack (T. N.), M.D., M.R.C.P. THE DRINK PROBLEM IN ITS MEDICO-SOCIOLOGICAL ASPECT. By fourteen Medical Authorities. Edited by. With 2 Diagrams. *Demy 8vo.* 7s. 6d. *net.*

Kempis (Thomas à). THE IMITATION OF CHRIST. With an Introduction by DEAN FARRAR. Illustrated by C. M. GERE. *Third Edition. Fcap. 8vo.* 3s. 6d.; *padded morocco.* 5s.
Also Translated by C. BIGG, D.D. *Cr. 8vo.* 3s. 6d.
See also Montmorency (J. E. G. de)., Library of Devotion, and Standard Library.

Kennedy (Bart.). THE GREEN SPHINX. *Cr. 8vo.* 3s. 6d. *net.*

Kennedy (James Houghton), D.D., Assistant Lecturer in Divinity in the University of Dublin. ST. PAUL'S SECOND AND THIRD EPISTLES TO THE CORINTHIANS. With Introduction, Dissertations and Notes. *Cr. 8vo.* 6s.

Kimmins (C. W.), M.A. THE CHEMISTRY OF LIFE AND HEALTH. Illustrated. *Cr. 8vo.* 2s. 6d.

Kinglake (A. W.). See Little Library.

Kipling (Rudyard). BARRACK-ROOM BALLADS. 83*rd Thousand. Twenty-fourth Edition. Cr. 8vo.* 6s. *Also Leather. Fcap. 8vo.* 5s.
A Colonial Edition is also published.
THE SEVEN SEAS. 70*th Thousand. Thirteenth Edition. Cr. 8vo.* 6s. *Also Leather. Fcap. 8vo.* 5s.
A Colonial Edition is also published.
THE FIVE NATIONS. 62*nd Thousand. Fourth Edition. Cr. 8vo.* 6s. *Also Leather. Fcap. 8vo.* 5s.
A Colonial Edition is also published.
DEPARTMENTAL DITTIES. *Sixteenth Edition. Cr. 8vo.* 6s. *Also Leather. Fcap. 8vo.* 5s.
A Colonial Edition is also published.

Knight (Albert E.). THE COMPLETE CRICKETER. With 50 Illustrations. *Demy 8vo.* 7s. 6d. *net.*
A Colonial Edition is also published.

Knight (H. J. C.), B.D. See Churchman's Bible.

Knowling (R. J.), M.A., Professor of New Testament Exegesis at King's College, London. See Westminster Commentaries.

Lamb (Charles and Mary), THE WORKS. Edited by E. V. LUCAS. Illustrated. *In Seven Volumes. Demy 8vo.* 7s. 6d. *each.*
See also Little Library and Lucas (E. V.).

Lambert (F. A. H.). See Little Guides.

Lambros (Professor S. P.). See Byzantine Texts.

Lane-Poole (Stanley). A HISTORY OF EGYPT IN THE MIDDLE AGES. Fully Illustrated. *Cr. 8vo.* 6*s*.

Langbridge (F.), M.A. BALLADS OF THE BRAVE: Poems of Chivalry, Enterprise, Courage, and Constancy. *Third Edition. Cr. 8vo.* 2*s.* 6*d*.

Law (William). See Library of Devotion and Standard Library.

Leach (Henry). THE DUKE OF DEVONSHIRE. A Biography. With 12 Illustrations. *Demy 8vo.* 12*s.* 6*d. net.*

THE SPIRIT OF THE LINKS. *Cr. 8vo.* 6*s*.

A Colonial Edition is also published.

See also Braid (James).

Le Braz (Anatole). THE LAND OF PARDONS. Translated by FRANCES M. GOSTLING. With 12 Illustrations in Colour by T. C. GOTCH, and 40 other Illustrations. *Second Edition. Crown 8vo.* 6*s*.

Lee (Captain L. Melville). A HISTORY OF POLICE IN ENGLAND. *Cr. 8vo.* 3*s.* 6*d. net.*

Lewes (V. B.), M.A. AIR AND WATER. Illustrated. *Cr. 8vo.* 2*s.* 6*d*.

Lewis (B. M. Gwyn). A CONCISE HANDBOOK OF GARDEN SHRUBS. With 20 Illustrations. *Fcap. 8vo.* 3*s.* 6*d. net.*

Lisle (Fortunéede). See Little Books on Art.

Littlehales (H.). See Antiquary's Books.

Lock (Walter), D.D., Warden of Keble College. ST. PAUL, THE MASTER-BUILDER. *Second Ed. Cr. 8vo.* 3*s.* 6*d*.

THE BIBLE AND CHRISTIAN LIFE. *Cr. 8vo.* 6*s*.

See also Keble (J.) and Leaders of Religion.

Locker (F.). See Little Library.

Lodge (Sir Oliver), F.R.S. THE SUBSTANCE OF FAITH ALLIED WITH SCIENCE: A Catechism for Parents and Teachers. *Ninth Ed. Cr. 8vo.* 2*s. net.*

Lofthouse (W. F.), M.A. ETHICS AND ATONEMENT. With a Frontispiece. *Demy 8vo.* 5*s. net.*

Longfellow (H. W.). See Little Library.

Lorimer (George Horace). LETTERS FROM A SELF-MADE MERCHANT TO HIS SON. *Sixteenth Edition. Cr. 8vo.* 3*s.* 6*d*.

A Colonial Edition is also published.

OLD GORGON GRAHAM. *Second Edition. Cr. 8vo.* 6*s*.

A Colonial Edition is also published.

Lover (Samuel). See I.P.L.

E. V. L. and C. L. G. ENGLAND DAY BY DAY: Or, The Englishman's Handbook to Efficiency. Illustrated by GEORGE MORROW. *Fourth Edition. Fcap. 4to.* 1*s. net.*

Lucas (E. V.). THE LIFE OF CHARLES LAMB. With 28 Illustrations. *Fourth and Revised Edition in One Volume. Demy 8vo.* 7*s.* 6*d. net.*

A Colonial Edition is also published.

A WANDERER IN HOLLAND. With 20 Illustrations in Colour by HERBERT MARSHALL, 34 Illustrations after old Dutch Masters, and a Map. *Eighth Edition. Cr. 8vo.* 6*s*.

A Colonial Edition is also published.

A WANDERER IN LONDON. With 16 Illustrations in Colour by NELSON DAWSON, 36 other Illustrations and a Map. *Sixth Edition. Cr. 8vo.* 6*s*.

A Colonial Edition is also published.

THE OPEN ROAD: a Little Book for Wayfarers. *Fourteenth Edition. Fcap. 8vo.* 5*s.*; *India Paper,* 7*s.* 6*d*.

THE FRIENDLY TOWN: a Little Book for the Urbane. *Fourth Edition. Fcap. 8vo.* 5*s.*; *India Paper,* 7*s.* 6*d*.

FIRESIDE AND SUNSHINE. *Third Edition. Fcap. 8vo.* 5*s*.

CHARACTER AND COMEDY. *Third Edition. Fcap. 8vo.* 5*s*.

THE GENTLEST ART. A Choice of Letters by Entertaining Hands. *Fourth Edition. Fcap. 8vo.* 5*s*.

A SWAN AND HER FRIENDS. With 24 Illustrations. *Demy 8vo.* 12*s.* 6*d. net.*

A Colonial Edition is also published.

Lucian. See Classical Translations.

Lyde (L. W.), M.A. See Commercial Series.

Lydon (Noel S.). See Junior School Books.

Lyttelton (Hon. Mrs. A.). WOMEN AND THEIR WORK. *Cr. 8vo.* 2*s.* 6*d*.

Macaulay (Lord). CRITICAL AND HISTORICAL ESSAYS. Edited by F. C. MONTAGUE, M.A. *Three Volumes. Cr. 8vo.* 18*s*.

M'Allen (J. E. B.), M.A. See Commercial Series.

MacCulloch (J. A.). See Churchman's Library.

MacCunn (Florence A.). MARY STUART. With 44 Illustrations, in cluding a Frontispiece in Photogravure. *New and Cheaper Edition. Large Cr. 8vo.* 6*s*.

See also Leaders of Religion.

McDermott (E. R.). See Books on Business.

M'Dowall (A. S.). See Oxford Biographies.

Mackay (A. M.), B.A. See Churchman's Library.

Mackenzie (W. Leslie), M.A., M.D., D.P.H., etc. THE HEALTH OF THE SCHOOL CHILD. *Cr. 8vo.* 2*s.* 6*d*.

Macklin (Herbert W.), M.A. See Antiquary's Books.

M'Neile (A. H.), B.D. See Westminster Commentaries.

'Mdlle Mori' (Author of). ST. CATHERINE OF SIENA AND HER TIMES. With 28 Illustrations. *Demy 8vo.* 7*s.* 6*d. net.*

Magnus (Laurie), M.A. A PRIMER OF WORDSWORTH. *Cr. 8vo.* 2*s.* 6*d*.

Mahaffy (J. P.), Litt.D. A HISTORY OF THE EGYPT OF THE PTOLEMIES. Fully Illustrated. *Cr. 8vo.* 6*s*.

Maitland (F. W.), M.A., LL.D. ROMAN CANON LAW IN THE CHURCH OF ENGLAND. *Royal 8vo.* 7*s.* 6*d*.

Major (H.), B.A., B.Sc. A HEALTH AND TEMPERANCE READER. *Cr. 8vo.* 1*s.* 6*d.*

Malden (H. E.), M.A. ENGLISH RECORDS. A Companion to the History of England. *Cr. 8vo.* 3*s.* 6*d.*

THE RIGHTS AND DUTIES OF A CITIZEN. *Seventh Edition. Cr. 8vo.* 1*s.* 6*d.*

See also School Histories.

Marchant (E. C.), M.A., Fellow of Peterhouse, Cambridge. A GREEK ANTHOLOGY *Second Edition. Cr. 8vo.* 3*s.* 6*d.*

See also Cook (A. M.).

Marks (Jeannette), M.A. ENGLISH PASTORAL DRAMA from the Restoration to the date of the publication of the 'Lyrical Ballads' (1660-1798). *Cr. 8vo.* 5*s. net.*

Marr (J. E.), F.R.S., Fellow of St John's College, Cambridge. THE SCIENTIFIC STUDY OF SCENERY. *Second Edition.* Illustrated. *Cr. 8vo.* 6*s.*

AGRICULTURAL GEOLOGY. Illustrated. *Cr. 8vo.* 6*s.*

Marriott (J. A. R.), M.A. THE LIFE AND TIMES OF LORD FALKLAND. With 23 Illustrations. *Second Edition. Demy 8vo.* 7*s.* 6*d. net.*

Marvell (Andrew). See Little Library.

Masefield (John). SEA LIFE IN NELSON'S TIME. Illustrated. *Cr. 8vo.* 3*s.* 6*d. net.*

A Colonial Edition is also published.

ON THE SPANISH MAIN: or, SOME ENGLISH FORAYS IN THE ISTHMUS OF DARIEN. With 22 Illustrations and a Map. *Demy 8vo.* 10*s.* 6*d. net.*

A Colonial Edition is also published.

A SAILOR'S GARLAND. Selected and Edited by. *Second Ed. Cr. 8vo.* 3*s.* 6*d. net.*

AN ENGLISH PROSE MISCELLANY. Selected and Edited by. *Cr. 8vo.* 6*s.*

Maskell (A.). See Connoisseur's Library.

Mason (A. J.), D.D. See Leaders of Religion.

Masterman (C. F. G.), M.A., M.P. TENNYSON AS A RELIGIOUS TEACHER. *Cr. 8vo.* 6*s.*

Matheson (E. F.). COUNSELS OF LIFE. *Fcap. 8vo.* 2*s.* 6*d. net.*

May (Phil). THE PHIL MAY ALBUM. *Second Edition. 4to.* 1*s. net.*

Meakin (Annette M. B.), Fellow of the Anthropological Institute. WOMAN IN TRANSITION. *Cr. 8vo.* 6*s.*

Mellows (Emma S.). A SHORT STORY OF ENGLISH LITERATURE. *Cr. 8vo.* 3*s.* 6*d.*

Methuen (A. M. S.), M.A. THE TRAGEDY OF SOUTH AFRICA. *Cr. 8vo.* 2*s. net. Also Cr. 8vo.* 3*d. net.*

ENGLAND'S RUIN: DISCUSSED IN SIXTEEN LETTERS TO THE RIGHT HON. JOSEPH CHAMBERLAIN, M.P. *Seventh Edition. Cr. 8vo.* 3*d. net.*

Miles (Eustace), M.A. LIFE AFTER LIFE: OR, THE THEORY OF REINCARNATION. *Cr. 8vo.* 2*s.* 6*d. net.*

THE POWER OF CONCENTRATION: HOW TO ACQUIRE IT. *Second Edition. Cr. 8vo.* 3*s.* 6*d. net.*

Millais (J. G.). THE LIFE AND LETTERS OF SIR JOHN EVERETT MILLAIS, President of the Royal Academy. With many Illustrations, of which 2 are in Photogravure. *New Edition. Demy 8vo.* 7*s.* 6*d. net.*

See also Little Galleries.

Millin (G. F.). PICTORIAL GARDENING. With 21 Illustrations. *Crown 8vo.* 3*s.* 6*d. net.*

Millis (C. T.), M.I.M.E. See Textbooks of Technology.

Milne (J. G.), M.A. A HISTORY OF EGYPT UNDER ROMAN RULE. Fully Illustrated. *Cr. 8vo.* 6*s.*

Milton (John). See Little Library and Standard Library.

A DAY BOOK OF MILTON. Edited by R. F. TOWNDROW. *Fcap. 8vo.* 2*s.* 6*d. net.*

Minchin (H. C.), M.A. See Peel (R.).

Mitchell (P. Chalmers), M.A. OUTLINES OF BIOLOGY. Illustrated. *Second Edition. Cr. 8vo.* 6*s.*

Mitton (G. E.). JANE AUSTEN AND HER TIMES. With 21 Illustrations. *Second and Cheaper Edition. Large Cr. 8vo.* 6*s.*

A Colonial Edition is also published.

Moffat (Mary M.). QUEEN LOUISA OF PRUSSIA. With 20 Illustrations. *Fourth Edition. Crown 8vo.* 6*s.*

A Colonial Edition is also published.

'Moil (A.).' See Books on Business.

Moir (D. M.). See Little Library.

Molinos (Dr. Michael de). See Library of Devotion.

Money (L. G. Chiozza), M.P. RICHES AND POVERTY. *Eighth Edition. Demy 8vo.* 5*s. net.* Also *Cr. 8vo.* 1*s. net.*

SOCIAL AND INDUSTRIAL PROBLEMS. *Demy 8vo.* 5*s. net.*

Montagu (Henry), Earl of Manchester. See Library of Devotion.

Montaigne. A DAY BOOK OF. Edited by C. F. POND. *Fcap. 8vo.* 2*s.* 6*d. net.*

Montgomery (H. B.) THE EMPIRE OF THE EAST. With a Frontispiece in Colour and 16 other Illustrations. *Second Edition. Demy 8vo.* 7*s.* 6*d. net.*

A Colonial Edition is also published.

Montmorency (J. E. G. de), B.A., LL.B. THOMAS A KEMPIS, HIS AGE AND BOOK. With 22 Illustrations. *Second Edition. Demy 8vo.* 7*s.* 6*d. net.*

Moore (H. E.). BACK TO THE LAND. *Cr. 8vo.* 2*s.* 6*d.*

Moorhouse (E. Hallam). NELSON'S LADY HAMILTON. With 51 Portraits. *Second Edition. Demy 8vo.* 7*s.* 6*d. net.*

A Colonial Edition is also published.

Moran (Clarence G.). See Books on Business.

More (Sir Thomas). See Standard Library.

Morfill (W. R.), Oriel College, Oxford. A HISTORY OF RUSSIA FROM PETER THE GREAT TO ALEXANDER II. With Maps and Plans. *Cr. 8vo.* 3*s.* 6*d.*

Morich (R. J.), late of Clifton College. See School Examination Series.

Morley (Margaret W.), Founded on. THE BEE PEOPLE. With 74 Illustrations. *Sq. Crown 8vo.* 2*s.* 6*d.*

LITTLE MITCHELL: THE STORY OF A MOUNTAIN SQUIRREL TOLD BY HIMSELF. With many Illustrations. *Sq. Cr. 8vo.* 2*s.* 6*d.*

Morris (J.). THE MAKERS OF JAPAN. With 24 Illustrations. *Demy 8vo.* 12*s.* 6*d. net.*

Morris (Joseph E.). See Little Guides.

Morton (A. Anderson). See Brodrick (M.).

Moule (H. C. G.), D.D., Lord Bishop of Durham. See Leaders of Religion.

Muir (M. M. Pattison), M.A. THE CHEMISTRY OF FIRE. Illustrated. *Cr. 8vo.* 2*s.* 6*d.*

Mundella (V. A.), M.A. See Dunn (J. T.).

Munro (R.), M.A., LL.D. See Antiquary's Books.

Myers (A. Wallis), THE COMPLETE LAWN TENNIS PLAYER. With many Illustrations. *Second Edition. Demy 8vo.* 10*s.* 6*d. net.*

Naval Officer (A). See I. P. L.

Neal (W. G.). See Hall (R. N.).

Newman (Ernest). HUGO WOLF. With 13 Illustrations. *Demy 8vo.* 7*s.* 6*d. net.*

Newman (George), M.D., D.P.H., F.R.S.E., INFANT MORTALITY, A SOCIAL PROBLEM. With 16 Diagrams. *Demy 8vo.* 7*s.* 6*d. net.*

Newman (J. H.) and others. See Library of Devotion.

Newsholme (Arthur), M.D., F.R.C.P. THE PREVENTION OF TUBERCULOSIS. *Demy 8vo.* 10*s.* 6*d. net.*

Nichols (Bowyer). See Little Library.

Nicklin (T.), M.A. EXAMINATION PAPERS IN THUCYDIDES. *Cr. 8vo.* 2*s.*

Nimrod. See I. P. L.

Norgate (G. Le Grys). THE LIFE OF SIR WALTER SCOTT. With 53 Illustrations by JENNY WYLIE. *Demy 8vo.* 7*s.* 6*d. net.*

Norregaard (B. W.). THE GREAT SIEGE: The Investment and Fall of Port Arthur. With Maps, Plans, and 25 Illustrations. *Demy 8vo.* 10*s.* 6*d. net.*

A Colonial Edition is also published.

Norway (A. H.). NAPLES. PAST AND PRESENT. With 25 Coloured Illustrations by MAURICE GREIFFENHAGEN. *Second Edition. Cr. 8vo.* 6*s.*

A Colonial Edition is also published.

Novalis. THE DISCIPLES AT SAÏS AND OTHER FRAGMENTS. Edited by Miss UNA BIRCH. *Fcap. 8vo.* 3*s.* 6*d. net.*

Officer (An). See I. P. L.

Oldfield (W. J.), M.A., Prebendary of Lincoln. A PRIMER OF RELIGION. BASED ON THE CATECHISM OF THE CHURCH OF ENGLAND. *Crown 8vo.* 2*s.* 6*d.*

Oldham (F. M.), B.A. See Textbooks of Science.

Oliphant (Mrs.). See Leaders of Religion.

Oliver, Thomas, M.D. DISEASES OF OCCUPATION. With Illustrations. *Second Edition. Demy 8vo.* 10*s.* 6*d. net.*

Oman (C. W. C.), M.A., Fellow of All Souls', Oxford. A HISTORY OF THE ART OF WAR IN THE MIDDLE AGES. Illustrated. *Demy 8vo.* 10*s.* 6*d. net.*

Ottley (R. L.), D.D. See Handbooks of Theology and Leaders of Religion.

Overton (J. H.). See Leaders of Religion.

Owen (Douglas). See Books on Business.

Oxford (M. N.), of Guy's Hospital. A HANDBOOK OF NURSING. *Fourth Edition. Cr. 8vo.* 3*s.* 6*d.*

Pakes (W. C. C.). THE SCIENCE OF HYGIENE. Illustrated. *Demy 8vo.* 15*s.*

Parker (Gilbert), M.P. A LOVER'S DIARY. *Fcap. 8vo.* 5*s.*

A volume of poems.

Parkes (A. K.). SMALL LESSONS ON GREAT TRUTHS. *Fcap. 8vo.* 1*s.* 6*d.*

Parkinson (John). PARADISI IN SOLE PARADISUS TERRESTRIS, OR A GARDEN OF ALL SORTS OF PLEASANT FLOWERS. *Folio.* £3, 3*s. net.*

Parmenter (John). HELIO-TROPES, OR NEW POSIES FOR SUNDIALS. Edited by PERCIVAL LANDON. *Quarto.* 3*s.* 6*d. net.*

Parmentier (Prof. Leon). See Bidez (J.).

Parsons (Mrs. C.). GARRICK AND HIS CIRCLE. With 36 Illustrations. *Second Edition. Demy 8vo.* 12*s.* 6*d. net.*

A Colonial Edition is also published.

Pascal. See Library of Devotion.

Paston (George). SOCIAL CARICATURE IN THE EIGHTEENTH CENTURY. With over 200 Illustrations. *Imperial Quarto.* £2, 12*s.* 6*d. net.*

LADY MARY WORTLEY MONTAGU AND HER TIMES With 24 Illustrations. *Second Edition. Demy 8vo.* 15*s. net.*

See also Little Books on Art and I.P.L.

Paterson (W. R.) (Benjamin Swift). LIFE'S QUESTIONINGS. *Cr. 8vo.* 3*s.* 6*d. net.*

Patterson (A. H.). NOTES OF AN EAST COAST NATURALIST. Illustrated in Colour by F. SOUTHGATE, R.B.A. *Second Edition. Cr. 8vo.* 6*s.*

NATURE IN EASTERN NORFOLK. With 12 Illustrations in Colour by FRANK SOUTHGATE, R.B.A. *Second Edition. Cr. 8vo.* 6*s.*

WILD LIFE ON A NORFOLK ESTUARY. With 40 Illustrations by the Author, and a Prefatory Note by Her Grace the DUCHESS OF BEDFORD. *Demy 8vo.* 10*s.* 6*d. net.*

Peacock (Netta). See Little Books on Art.

Patterson (J. B.). See Simplified French Texts.

Peake (C. M. A.), F.R.H.S. A CONCISE HANDBOOK OF GARDEN ANNUAL AND BIENNIAL PLANTS. With 24 Illustrations. *Fcap. 8vo.* 3*s.* 6*d. net.*

Peel (Robert), and **Minchin (H. C.)**, M.A. OXFORD. With 100 Illustrations in Colour. *Cr. 8vo.* 6*s.*
A Colonial Edition is also published.

Peel (Sidney), late Fellow of Trinity College, Oxford, and Secretary to the Royal Commission on the Licensing Laws. PRACTICAL LICENSING REFORM. *Second Edition. Cr. 8vo.* 1*s.* 6*d.*

Petrie (W. M. Flinders), D.C.L., LL.D., Professor of Egyptology at University College. A HISTORY OF EGYPT. Fully Illustrated. *In six volumes. Cr. 8vo.* 6*s. each.*

VOL. I. FROM THE EARLIEST KINGS TO XVITH DYNASTY. *Sixth Edition.*
VOL. II. THE XVIITH AND XVIIITH DYNASTIES. *Fourth Edition.*
VOL. III. XIXTH TO XXXTH DYNASTIES.
VOL. IV. THE EGYPT OF THE PTOLEMIES. J. P. MAHAFFY, Litt.D.
VOL. V. ROMAN EGYPT. J. G. MILNE, M.A.
VOL. VI. EGYPT IN THE MIDDLE AGES. STANLEY LANE-POOLE, M.A.

RELIGION AND CONSCIENCE IN ANCIENT EGYPT. Lectures delivered at University College, London. Illustrated. *Cr. 8vo.* 2*s.* 6*d.*

SYRIA AND EGYPT, FROM THE TELL EL AMARNA TABLETS. *Cr. 8vo.* 2*s.* 6*d.*

EGYPTIAN TALES. Translated from the Papyri. First Series, IVth to XIIth Dynasty. Edited by W. M. FLINDERS PETRIE. Illustrated by TRISTRAM ELLIS. *Second Edition. Cr. 8vo.* 3*s.* 6*d.*

EGYPTIAN TALES. Translated from the Papyri. Second Series. XVIIIth to XIXth Dynasty. Illustrated by TRISTRAM ELLIS. *Crown 8vo.* 3*s.* 6*d.*

EGYPTIAN DECORATIVE ART. A Course of Lectures delivered at the Royal Institution. Illustrated. *Cr. 8vo.* 3*s.* 6*d.*

Phillips (W. A.). See Oxford Biographies.

Phillpotts (Eden). MY DEVON YEAR. With 38 Illustrations by J. LEY PETHYBRIDGE. *Second and Cheaper Edition. Large Cr. 8vo.* 6*s.*

UP ALONG AND DOWN ALONG. Illustrated by CLAUDE SHEPPERSON. *Cr. 4to.* 5*s. net.*

Phythian (J. Ernest). TREES IN NATURE, MYTH, AND ART. With 24 Illustrations. *Crown 8vo.* 6*s.*

Plarr (Victor G.). See School Histories.

Plato. See Standard Library.

Plautus. THE CAPTIVI. Edited, with an Introduction, Textual Notes, and a Commentary, by W. M. LINDSAY, Fellow of Jesus College, Oxford. *Demy 8vo.* 10*s.* 6*d. net.*

Plowden-Wardlaw (J. T.), B.A., King's College, Cambridge. See School Examination Series.

Podmore (Frank). MODERN SPIRITUALISM. *Two Volumes. Demy 8vo.* 21*s. net.*

Pollard (Alice). See Little Books on Art.

Pollard (Eliza F.). See Little Books on Art.

Pollock (David), M.I.N.A. See Books on Business.

Potter (M. C.), M.A., F.L.S. AN ELEMENTARY TEXT-BOOK OF AGRICULTURAL BOTANY. Illustrated. *Second Edition. Cr. 8vo.* 4*s.* 6*d.*

Power (J. O'Connor). THE MAKING OF AN ORATOR. *Cr. 8vo.* 6*s.*

Prance (G.). See Wyon (R.).

Prescott (O. L.). ABOUT MUSIC, AND WHAT IT IS MADE OF. *Cr. 8vo.* 3*s.* 6*d. net.*

Price (Eleanor C.). A PRINCESS OF THE OLD WORLD. With 21 Illustrations. *Demy 8vo.* 12*s.* 6*d. net.*

Price (L. L.), M.A., Fellow of Oriel College, Oxon. A HISTORY OF ENGLISH POLITICAL ECONOMY FROM ADAM SMITH TO ARNOLD TOYNBEE. *Fifth Edition. Cr. 8vo.* 2*s.* 6*d.*

Primrose (Deborah). A MODERN BŒOTIA. *Cr. 8vo.* 6*s.*

Protheroe (Ernest). THE DOMINION OF MAN. GEOGRAPHY IN ITS HUMAN ASPECT. With 32 full-page Illustrations. *Second Edition. Cr. 8vo.* 2*s.*

Quevedo Villegas. See Miniature Library.

'Q' (A. T. Quiller Couch). THE GOLDEN POMP. A PROCESSION OF ENGLISH LYRICS FROM SURREY TO SHIRLEY. *Second and Cheaper Edition. Cr. 8vo.* 2*s.* 6*d. net.*

G. R. and E. S. MR. WOODHOUSE'S CORRESPONDENCE. *Cr. 8vo.* 6*s.*
A Colonial Edition is also published.

Rackham (R. B.), M.A. See Westminster Commentaries.

Ragg (Laura M.). THE WOMEN ARTISTS OF BOLOGNA. With 20 Illustrations. *Demy 8vo.* 7*s.* 6*d. net.*

Ragg (Lonsdale). B.D., Oxon. DANTE AND HIS ITALY. With 32 Illustrations. *Demy 8vo.* 12*s.* 6*d. net.*

Rahtz (F. J.), M.A., B.Sc., Lecturer in English at Merchant Venturers' Technical College, Bristol. HIGHER ENGLISH. *Third Edition. Cr. 8vo.* 3*s.* 6*d.*

Randolph (B. W.), D.D. See Library of Devotion.

Rannie (D. W.), M.A. A STUDENT'S HISTORY OF SCOTLAND. *Cr. 8vo.* 3*s.* 6*d.*

WORDSWORTH AND HIS CIRCLE. With 20 Illustrations. *Demy 8vo.* 12*s.* 6*d. net.*

Rashdall (Hastings), M.A., Fellow and Tutor of New College, Oxford. DOCTRINE AND DEVELOPMENT. *Cr. 8vo.* 6*s.*

Raven (J. J.), D.D., F.S.A. See Antiquary's Books.

Raven-Hill (L.). See Llewellyn (Owen).

Rawstorne (Lawrence, Esq.). See I.P.L.

Raymond (Walter). See School Histories.

***Rea (Lilian)**. MADAME DE LA FAYETTE. With many Illustrations. *Demy 8vo.* 10*s.* 6*d. net.*

Real Paddy (A). See I.P.L.

Reason (W.), M.A. UNIVERSITY AND SOCIAL SETTLEMENTS. Edited by. *Cr. 8vo.* 2*s.* 6*d.*

Redpath (H. A.), M.A., D.Litt. See Westminster Commentaries.

Rees (J. D.), C.I.E., M.P. THE REAL INDIA. *Second Edition. Demy 8vo.* 10*s.* 6*d. net.*
A Colonial Edition is also published.

***Reich (Emil)**, Doctor Juris. WOMAN THROUGH THE AGES. With 24 Illustrations. *Two Volumes. Demy 8vo.* 21*s. net.*
A Colonial Edition is also published.

Reynolds (Sir Joshua). See Little Galleries.

Rhoades (J. F.). See Simplified French Texts.

Rhodes (W. E.). See School Histories.

Rieu (H.), M.A. See Simplified French Texts.

Roberts (M. E.). See Channer (C. C.).

Robertson (A.), D.D., Lord Bishop of Exeter. REGNUM DEI. (The Bampton Lectures of 1901). *A New and Cheaper Edition. Demy 8vo.* 7*s.* 6*d. net.*

Robertson (C. Grant). M.A., Fellow of All Souls' College, Oxford. SELECT STATUTES, CASES, AND CONSTITUTIONAL DOCUMENTS, 1660-1832. *Demy 8vo.* 10*s.* 6*d. net.*

Robertson (C. Grant) and **Bartholomew (J. G.)**, F.R.S.E., F.R.G.S. A HISTORICAL AND MODERN ATLAS OF THE BRITISH EMPIRE. *Demy Quarto.* 4*s.* 6*d. net.*

Robertson (Sir G. S.), K.C.S.I. CHITRAL: THE STORY OF A MINOR SIEGE. *Third Edition.* Illustrated. *Cr. 8vo.* 2*s.* 6*d. net.*

Robinson (A. W.), M.A. See Churchman's Bible.

Robinson (Cecilia). THE MINISTRY OF DEACONESSES. With an Introduction by the late Archbishop of Canterbury. *Cr. 8vo.* 3*s.* 6*d.*

Robinson (F. S.). See Connoisseur's Library.

Rochefoucauld (La). See Little Library.

Rodwell (G.), B.A. NEW TESTAMENT GREEK. A Course for Beginners. With a Preface by WALTER LOCK, D.D., Warden of Keble College. *Fcap. 8vo.* 3*s.* 6*d.*

Roe (Fred). OLD OAK FURNITURE. With many Illustrations by the Author, including a frontispiece in colour. *Second Edition. Demy 8vo.* 10*s.* 6*d. net.*

Rogers (A. G. L.), M.A. See Books on Business.

Romney (George). See Little Galleries.

Roscoe (E. S.). See Little Guides.

Rose (Edward). THE ROSE READER. Illustrated. *Cr. 8vo.* 2*s.* 6*d. Also in 4 Parts. Parts I. and II.* 6*d. each; Part III.* 8*d.*; *Part IV.* 10*d.*

Rose (G. H.). See **Hey (H.)**, and **Baring-Gould (S).**

Rowntree (Joshua). THE IMPERIAL DRUG TRADE. A RE-STATEMENT OF THE OPIUM QUESTION. *Third Edition Revised. Cr. 8vo.* 2*s. net.*

Royde-Smith (N. G.). THE PILLOW BOOK: A GARNER OF MANY MOODS. Collected by. *Second Edition. Cr. 8vo.* 4*s.* 6*d. net.*

POETS OF OUR DAY. Selected, with an Introduction, by. *Fcap. 8vo.* 5*s.*

Rubie (A. E.), D.D. See Junior School Books.

Russell (Archibald G. B.). See Blake (William).

Russell (W. Clark). THE LIFE OF ADMIRAL LORD COLLINGWOOD. With Illustrations by F. BRANGWYN. *Fourth Edition. Cr. 8vo.* 6*s.*

Ryley (M. Beresford). QUEENS OF THE RENAISSANCE. With 24 Illustrations. *Demy 8vo.* 10*s.* 6*d. net.*

Sainsbury (Harrington), M.D., F.R.C.P. PRINCIPIA THERAPEUTICA. *Demy 8vo.* 7*s.* 6*d. net.*

St. Anselm. See Library of Devotion.

St. Augustine. See Library of Devotion.

St. Bernard. See Library of Devotion.

St. Cyres (Viscount). See Oxford Biographies.

St. Francis of Assisi. THE LITTLE FLOWERS OF THE GLORIOUS MESSER, AND OF HIS FRIARS. Done into English, with Notes by WILLIAM HEYWOOD. With 40 Illustrations from Italian Painters. *Demy 8vo.* 5*s. net.*
See also Wheldon (F. W.), Library of Devotion and Standard Library.

St. Francis de Sales. See Library of Devotion.

'Saki' (H. Munro). REGINALD. *Second Edition. Fcap. 8vo.* 2*s.* 6*d. net.*

Salmon (A. L.). See Little Guides.

Sathas (C.). See Byzantine Texts.

Schmitt (John). See Byzantine Texts.

Schofield (A. T.), M.D., Hon. Phys. Freidenham Hospital. FUNCTIONAL NERVE DISEASES. *Demy 8vo.* 7*s.* 6*d. net.*

Scott (A. M.). WINSTON SPENCER CHURCHILL. With Portraits and Illustrations. *Cr. 8vo.* 3*s.* 6*d.*

Scudamore (Cyril). See Little Guides.

Sélincourt (E. de.) See Keats (John).

Sells (V. P.), M.A. THE MECHANICS OF DAILY LIFE. Illustrated. *Cr. 8vo.* 2*s.* 6*d.*

Selous (Edmund). TOMMY SMITH'S ANIMALS. Illustrated by G. W. ORD. *Tenth Edition. Fcap. 8vo.* 2*s.* 6*d.*
School Edition, 1*s.* 6*d.*

TOMMY SMITH'S OTHER ANIMALS. Illustrated by AUGUSTA GUEST. *Fourth Edition. Fcap. 8vo.* 2*s* 6*d.*
School Edition, 1*s.* 6*d.*

Senter (George), B.Sc. (Lond.), Ph.D. See Textbooks of Science.

Shakespeare (William).

THE FOUR FOLIOS, 1623; 1632; 1664; 1685. Each £4, 4s. *net*, or a complete set, £12, 12s. *net.*
Folios 3 and 4 are ready.
Folio 2 is nearly ready.

THE POEMS OF WILLIAM SHAKESPEARE. With an Introduction and Notes by GEORGE WYNDHAM. *Demy 8vo. Buckram, gilt top*, 10*s.* 6*d.*
See also Arden Shakespeare, Standard Library and Little Quarto Shakespeare.

Sharp (A.). VICTORIAN POETS. *Cr. 8vo.* 2s. 6d.
Sharp (Cecil). See Baring-Gould (S.).
Sharp (Elizabeth). See Little Books on Art.
Shedlock (J. S.) THE PIANOFORTE SONATA. *Cr. 8vo.* 5s.
Shelley (Percy B.). See Standard Library.
Sheppard (H. F.), M.A. See Baring-Gould (S.).
Sherwell (Arthur), M.A. LIFE IN WEST LONDON. *Third Edition. Cr. 8vo.* 2s. 6d.
Shipley (Mary E.). AN ENGLISH CHURCH HISTORY FOR CHILDREN. With a Preface by the Bishop of Gibraltar. With Maps and Illustrations. Part I. *Cr. 8vo.* 2s. 6d. *net.*
Sichel (Walter). See Oxford Biographies.
Sidgwick (Mrs. Alfred). HOME LIFE IN GERMANY. With 16 Illustrations. *Second Edition. Demy 8vo.* 10s. 6d. *net.*
A Colonial Edition is also published.
Sime (John). See Little Books on Art.
Simonson (G. A.). FRANCESCO GUARDI. With 41 Plates. *Imperial 4to.* £2, 2s. *net.*
Sketchley (R. E. D.). See Little Books on Art.
Skipton (H. P. K.). See Little Books on Art.
Sladen (Douglas). SICILY: The New Winter Resort. With over 200 Illustrations. *Second Edition. Cr. 8vo.* 5s. *net.*
Small (Evan), M.A. THE EARTH. An Introduction to Physiography. Illustrated. *Cr. 8vo.* 2s. 6d.
Smallwood (M. G.). See Little Books on Art.
Smedley (F. E.). See I.P.L.
Smith (Adam). THE WEALTH OF NATIONS. Edited with an Introduction and numerous Notes by EDWIN CANNAN, M.A. *Two volumes. Demy 8vo.* 21s. *net.*
Smith (H. Clifford). See Connoisseur's Library.
Smith (Horace and James). See Little Library.
Smith (H. Bompas), M.A. A NEW JUNIOR ARITHMETIC. *Crown 8vo.* Without Answers, 2s. With Answers, 2s. 6d.
Smith (R. Mudie). THOUGHTS FOR THE DAY. Edited by. *Fcap. 8vo.* 3s. 6d. *net.*
Smith (Nowell C.). See Wordsworth (W).
Smith (John Thomas). A BOOK FOR A RAINY DAY: Or, Recollections of the Events of the Years 1766-1833. Edited by WILFRED WHITTEN. Illustrated. *Wide Demy 8vo.* 12s. 6d. *net.*
Snell (F. J.). A BOOK OF EXMOOR. Illustrated. *Cr. 8vo.* 6s.
Snowden (C. E.). A HANDY DIGEST OF BRITISH HISTORY. *Demy 8vo.* 4s. 6d.
Sophocles. See Classical Translations.
Sornet (L. A.), and **Acatos (M. J.)** See Junior School Books.
South (E. Wilton), M.A. See Junior School Books
Southey (R.). ENGLISH SEAMEN Edited by DAVID HANNAY.
Vol. I. (Howard, Clifford, Hawkins, Drake, Cavendish). *Second Edition. Cr. 8vo.* 6s.
Vol. II. (Richard Hawkins, Grenville, Essex, and Raleigh). *Cr. 8vo.* 6s.
See also Standard Library.
Spence (C. H.), M.A. See School Examination Series.
Spicer (A. Dykes), M.A. THE PAPER TRADE. A Descriptive and Historical Survey. With Diagrams and Plans. *Demy 8vo.* 12s. 6d. *net.*
Spooner (W. A.), M.A. See Leaders of Religion.
Spragge (W. Horton), M.A. See Junior School Books.
Staley (Edgcumbe). THE GUILDS OF FLORENCE. Illustrated. *Second Edition. Royal 8vo.* 16s. *net.*
Stanbridge (J. W.), B.D. See Library of Devotion.
'Stancliffe.' GOLF DO'S AND DONT'S *Second Edition. Fcap. 8vo.* 1s.
Stead (D. W.). See Gallaher (D.).
Stedman (A. M. M.), M.A.
INITIA LATINA: Easy Lessons on Elementary Accidence. *Eleventh Edition. Fcap. 8vo.* 1s.
FIRST LATIN LESSONS. *Eleventh Edition. Cr. 8vo.* 2s.
FIRST LATIN READER. With Notes adapted to the Shorter Latin Primer and Vocabulary. *Seventh Edition.* 18*mo.* 1s. 6d.
EASY SELECTIONS FROM CÆSAR. The Helvetian War. *Third Edition.* 18*mo.* 1s.
EASY SELECTIONS FROM LIVY. The Kings of Rome. *Second Edition.* 18*mo.* 1s. 6d.
EASY LATIN PASSAGES FOR UNSEEN TRANSLATION. *Twelfth Ed. Fcap. 8vo.* 1s. 6d.
EXEMPLA LATINA. First Exercises in Latin Accidence. With Vocabulary. *Fourth Edition. Cr. 8vo.* 1s.
EASY LATIN EXERCISES ON THE SYNTAX OF THE SHORTER AND REVISED LATIN PRIMER. With Vocabulary. *Twelfth and Cheaper Edition. Cr. 8vo.* 1s. 6d. KEY, 3s. *net.*
THE LATIN COMPOUND SENTENCE: Rules and Exercises. *Second Edition. Cr. 8vo.* 1s. 6d. With Vocabulary. 2s.
NOTANDA QUAEDAM: Miscellaneous Latin Exercises on Common Rules and Idioms. *Fifth Edition. Fcap. 8vo.* 1s. 6d. With Vocabulary. 2s. KEY, 2s. *net.*
LATIN VOCABULARIES FOR REPETITION: Arranged according to Subjects. *Fifteenth Edition. Fcap. 8vo.* 1s. 6d.
A VOCABULARY OF LATIN IDIOMS. 18*mo.* *Fourth Edition.* 1s.
STEPS TO GREEK. *Third Edition, revised.* 18*mo.* 1s.

A SHORTER GREEK PRIMER. *Second Edition. Cr. 8vo. 1s. 6d.*
EASY GREEK PASSAGES FOR UNSEEN TRANSLATION. *Fourth Edition, revised. Fcap. 8vo. 1s. 6d.*
GREEK VOCABULARIES FOR REPETITION. Arranged according to Subjects. *Fourth Edition. Fcap. 8vo. 1s 6d.*
GREEK TESTAMENT SELECTIONS. For the use of Schools. With Introduction, Notes, and Vocabulary. *Fourth Edition. Fcap. 8vo. 2s. 6d.*
STEPS TO FRENCH. *Eighth Edition. 18mo. 8d.*
FIRST FRENCH LESSONS. *Ninth Edition. Cr. 8vo. 1s.*
EASY FRENCH PASSAGES FOR UNSEEN TRANSLATION. *Sixth Edition. Fcap. 8vo. 1s. 6d.*
EASY FRENCH EXERCISES ON ELEMENTARY SYNTAX. With Vocabulary. *Fourth Edition. Cr. 8vo. 2s. 6d.* KEY. *3s. net.*
FRENCH VOCABULARIES FOR REPETITION: Arranged according to Subjects. *Thirteenth Edition. Fcap. 8vo. 1s.*
See also School Examination Series.

Steel (R. Elliott), M.A., F.C.S. THE WORLD OF SCIENCE. With 147 Illustrations. *Second Edition. Cr. 8vo. 2s. 6d.*
See also School Examination Series.

Stephenson (C.), of the Technical College, Bradford, and **Suddards (F.)** of the Yorkshire College, Leeds. A TEXTBOOK DEALING WITH ORNAMENTAL DESIGN FOR WOVEN FABRICS. With 66 full-page Plates and numerous Diagrams in the Text. *Third Edition. Demy 8vo. 7s. 6d.*

Stephenson (J.), M.A. THE CHIEF TRUTHS OF THE CHRISTIAN FAITH. *Cr. 8vo. 3s. 6d.*

Sterne (Laurence). See Little Library.

Steuart (Katherine). BY ALLAN WATER. *Second Edition. Cr. 8vo. 6s.*
RICHARD KENNOWAY AND HIS FRIENDS. A Sequel to 'By Allan Water.' *Demy 8vo. 7s. 6d. net.*

Stevenson (R. L.) THE LETTERS OF ROBERT LOUIS STEVENSON TO HIS FAMILY AND FRIENDS. Selected and Edited by SIDNEY COLVIN. *Third Edition. 2 vols. Cr. 8vo. 12s.*
LIBRARY EDITION. *2 vols. Demy 8vo. 25s. net.*
A Colonial Edition is also published.
VAILIMA LETTERS. With an Etched Portrait by WILLIAM STRANG. *Sixth Edition. Cr. 8vo. Buckram. 6s.*
A Colonial Edition is also published.
THE LIFE OF R. L. STEVENSON. See Balfour (G.).

Stevenson (M. I.). FROM SARANAC TO THE MARQUESAS. Being Letters written by Mrs. M. I. STEVENSON during 1887-8. *Cr. 8vo. 6s. net.*
A Colonial Edition is also published.
LETTERS FROM SAMOA, 1891-95. Edited and arranged by M. C. BALFOUR With many Illustrations. *Second Edition Cr. 8vo. 6s. net.*
A Colonial Edition is also published.

Stoddart (Anna M.). See Oxford Biographies.

Stokes (F. G.), B.A. HOURS WITH RABELAIS. From the translation of SIR T. URQUHART and P. A. MOTTEUX. With a Portrait in Photogravure. *Cr. 8vo. 3s. 6d. net.*

Stone (S. J.). POEMS AND HYMNS. With a Memoir by F. G. ELLERTON, M.A. With Portrait. *Cr. 8vo. 6s.*

Storr (Vernon F.), M.A., Canon of Winchester. DEVELOPMENT AND DIVINE PURPOSE *Cr. 8vo. 5s. net.*

Story (Alfred T.). AMERICAN SHRINES IN ENGLAND. With many Illustrations, including two in Colour by A. R. QUINTON. *Crown 8vo. 6s.*
See also Little Guides.

Straker (F.). See Books on Business.

Streane (A. W.), D.D. See Churchman's Bible.

Streatfeild (R. A.). MODERN MUSIC AND MUSICIANS. With 24 Illustrations. *Second Edition. Demy 8vo. 7s. 6d. net.*

Stroud (Henry), D.Sc., M.A. ELEMENTARY PRACTICAL PHYSICS. With 115 Diagrams. *Second Edit., revised. 4s. 6d.*

Sturch (F.), Staff Instructor to the Surrey County Council. MANUAL TRAINING DRAWING (WOODWORK). With Solutions to Examination Questions, Orthographic, Isometric and Oblique Projection. With 50 Plates and 140 Figures. *Foolscap. 5s. net.*

Suddards (F.). See Stephenson (C.).

Surtees (R. S.). See I.P.L.

Sutherland (William). OLD AGE PENSIONS IN THEORY AND PRACTICE, WITH SOME FOREIGN EXAMPLES. *Cr. 8vo. 3s. 6d. net.*

Symes (J. E.), M.A. THE FRENCH REVOLUTION. *Second Edition. Cr. 8vo. 2s. 6d.*

Sympson (E. Mansel), M.A., M.D. See Ancient Cities.

Tabor (Margaret E.). THE SAINTS IN ART. With 20 Illustrations. *Fcap. 8vo. 3s. 6d. net.*

Tacitus. AGRICOLA. Edited by R. F. DAVIS, M.A. *Fcap. 8vo. 2s.*
GERMANIA. By the same Editor. *Fcap. 8vo. 2s.*
See also Classical Translations.

Tallack (W.). HOWARD LETTERS AND MEMORIES. *Demy 8vo. 10s. 6d. net.*

Tatham (Frederick). See Blake (William).

Tauler (J.). See Library of Devotion.

Taylor (A. E.). THE ELEMENTS OF METAPHYSICS. *Demy 8vo. 10s. 6d. net.*

Taylor (F. G.), M.A. See Commercial Series.

Taylor (I. A.). See Oxford Biographies.

Taylor (John W.). THE COMING OF THE SAINTS. With 26 Illustrations. *Demy 8vo. 7s. 6d. net.*

Taylor (T. M.), M.A., Fellow of Gonville and Caius College, Cambridge. A CONSTITUTIONAL AND POLITICAL HISTORY OF ROME. To the Reign of Domitian. *Cr. 8vo.* *7s. 6d.*

Teasdale-Buckell (G. T.). THE COMPLETE SHOT. With 53 Illustrations. *Third Edition. Demy 8vo.* *12s. 6d. net.*
A Colonial Edition is also published.

Tennyson (Alfred, Lord). EARLY POEMS. Edited, with Notes and an Introduction, by J. CHURTON COLLINS, M.A. *Cr. 8vo.* *6s.*

IN MEMORIAM, MAUD, AND THE PRINCESS. Edited by J. CHURTON COLLINS, M.A. *Cr. 8vo.* *6s.*
See also Little Library.

Terry (C. S.). See Oxford Biographies.

Thackeray (W. M.). See Little Library.

Theobald (F. V.), M.A. INSECT LIFE. Illustrated. *Second Edition Revised. Cr. 8vo.* *2s. 6d.*

Thibaudeau (A. C.). BONAPARTE AND THE CONSULATE. Translated and Edited by G. K. FORTESQUE, LL.D. With 12 Illustrations. *Demy 8vo.* *10s. 6d. net.*

Thompson (A. H.). See Little Guides.

Thompson (A. P.). See Textbooks of Technology.

Tileston (Mary W.). DAILY STRENGTH FOR DAILY NEEDS. *Fifteenth Edition. Medium 16mo.* *2s. 6d. net.* Also an edition in superior binding, *6s.*

Tompkins (H. W.), F.R.H.S. See Little Books on Art and Little Guides.

Townley (Lady Susan). MY CHINESE NOTE-BOOK With 16 Illustrations and 2 Maps. *Third Ed. Demy 8vo.* *10s. 6d. net.*
A Colonial Edition is also published.

Toynbee (Paget), M.A., D.Litt. IN THE FOOTPRINTS OF DANTE. A Treasury of Verse and Prose from the works of Dante. *Small Cr. 8vo.* *4s. 6d. net.*
See also Oxford Biographies and Dante.

Trench (Herbert). DEIRDRE WEDDED AND OTHER POEMS. *Second and Revised Edition. Large Post 8vo.* *6s.*

NEW POEMS. *Second Edition. Large Post 8vo.* *6s.*

Trevelyan (G. M.), Fellow of Trinity College, Cambridge. ENGLAND UNDER THE STUARTS. With Maps and Plans. *Third Edition. Demy 8vo.* *10s. 6d. net.*

Troutbeck (G. E.). See Little Guides.

Tyler (E. A.), B.A., F.C.S. See Junior School Books.

Tyrrell-Gill (Frances). See Little Books on Art.

Vardon (Harry). THE COMPLETE GOLFER. With 63 Illustrations. *Ninth Edition. Demy 8vo.* *10s. 6d. net.*
A Colonial Edition is also published.

Vaughan (Henry). See Little Library.

Vaughan (Herbert M.), B.A. (Oxon.). THE LAST OF THE ROYAL STUARTS, HENRY STUART, CARDINAL, DUKE OF YORK. With 20 Illustrations. *Second Edition. Demy 8vo.* *10s. 6d. net.*

THE NAPLES RIVIERA. With 25 Illustrations in Colour by MAURICE GREIFFENHAGEN. *Second Edition. Cr. 8vo.* *6s.*

Vernon (Hon. W. Warren), M.A. READINGS ON THE INFERNO OF DANTE. With an Introduction by the Rev. Dr. MOORE. *In Two Volumes. Second Edition. Cr. 8vo.* *15s. net.*

READINGS ON THE PURGATORIO OF DANTE. With an Introduction by the late DEAN CHURCH. *In Two Volumes. Third Edition. Cr. 8vo.* *15s. net.*

Vincent (J. E.). THROUGH EAST ANGLIA IN A MOTOR CAR. With 16 Illustrations in Colour by FRANK SOUTHGATE, R.B.A., and a Map. *Cr. 8vo.* *6s.*

Voegelin (A.), M.A. See Junior Examination Series.

Waddell (Col. L. A.), LL.D., C.B. LHASA AND ITS MYSTERIES. With a Record of the Expedition of 1903-1904. With 155 Illustrations and Maps. *Third and Cheaper Edition. Medium 8vo.* *7s. 6d. net.*

Wade (G. W.), D.D. OLD TESTAMENT HISTORY. With Maps. *Fifth Edition. Cr. 8vo.* *6s.*

Wade (G. W.), D.D., **and Wade (J. H.)**, M.A. See Little Guides.

Wagner (Richard). RICHARD WAGNER'S MUSIC DRAMAS: Interpretations, embodying Wagner's own explanations. By ALICE LEIGHTON CLEATHER and BASIL CRUMP. *In Three Volumes. Fcap 8vo.* *2s. 6d. each.*
VOL. I.—THE RING OF THE NIBELUNG. *Third Edition.*
VOL. II.—PARSIFAL, LOHENGRIN, and THE HOLY GRAIL.
VOL. III.—TRISTAN AND ISOLDE.

Walkley (A. B.). DRAMA AND LIFE. *Cr. 8vo.* *6s.*

Wall (J. C.). See Antiquary's Books.

Wallace-Hadrill (F.), Second Master at Herne Bay College. REVISION NOTES ON ENGLISH HISTORY. *Cr. 8vo.* *1s.*

Walters (H. B.). See Little Books on Art and Classics of Art.

Walton (F. W.). See School Histories.

Walton (Izaak) and Cotton (Charles). See I.P.L.

Walton (Izaak). See Little Library.

Waterhouse (Elizabeth). WITH THE SIMPLE-HEARTED: Little Homilies to Women in Country Places. *Second Edition. Small Pott 8vo.* *2s. net.*
See also Little Library.

Watt (Francis). See Henderson (T. F.).

Weatherhead (T. C.), M.A. EXAMINATION PAPERS IN HORACE. *Cr. 8vo.* *2s.*
See also Junior Examination Series.

Webber (F. C.). See Textbooks of Technology.

Weir (Archibald), M.A. AN INTRODUCTION TO THE HISTORY OF MODERN EUROPE. *Cr. 8vo.* *6s.*

Wells (Sidney H.) See Textbooks of Science.

Wells (J.), M.A., Fellow and Tutor of Wadham College. OXFORD AND OXFORD LIFE. *Third Edition. Cr. 8vo.* 3s. 6d.
A SHORT HISTORY OF ROME. *Eighth Edition.* With 3 Maps. *Cr. 8vo.* 3s. 6d.
See also Little Guides.
Wesley (John). See Library of Devotion.
Wheldon (F. W.). A LITTLE BROTHER TO THE BIRDS. The life-story of St. Francis retold for children. With 15 Illustrations, 7 of which are by A. H. BUCKLAND. *Large Cr. 8vo.* 6s.
Whibley (C.). See Henley (W. E.).
Whibley (L.), M.A., Fellow of Pembroke College, Cambridge. GREEK OLIGARCHIES: THEIR ORGANISATION AND CHARACTER. *Cr. 8vo.* 6s.
Whitaker (G. H.), M.A. See Churchman's Bible.
White (Gilbert). See Standard Library.
Whitfield (E. E.), M.A. See Commercial Series.
Whitehead (A. W.). GASPARD DE COLIGNY, ADMIRAL OF FRANCE. With Illustrations and Plans. *Demy 8vo.* 12s. 6d. *net.*
Whiteley (R. Lloyd), F.I.C., Principal of the Municipal Science School, West Bromwich. AN ELEMENTARY TEXT-BOOK OF INORGANIC CHEMISTRY. *Cr. 8vo.* 2s. 6d.
Whitley (Miss). See Dilke (Lady).
Whitling (Miss L.), late Staff Teacher of the National Training School of Cookery. THE COMPLETE COOK. With 42 Illustrations. *Demy 8vo.* 7s. 6d. *net.*
A Colonial edition is also published.
Whitten (W.). See Smith (John Thomas).
Whyte (A. G.), B.Sc. See Books on Business.
Wilberforce (Wilfrid). See Little Books on Art.
Wilde (Oscar). DE PROFUNDIS. *Eleventh Edition. Cr. 8vo.* 5s. *net.*
A Colonial Edition is also published.
THE WORKS.
A Uniform Edition. Demy 8vo.
12s. 6d. *net each volume.*
THE DUCHESS OF PADUA: A Play.
POEMS.
INTENTIONS and THE SOUL OF MAN.
SALOMÉ, A FLORENTINE TRAGEDY, and VERA; or, THE NIHILISTS.
LADY WINDERMERE'S FAN: A Play about a Good Woman.
A WOMAN OF NO IMPORTANCE: A Play.
AN IDEAL HUSBAND: A Play.
THE IMPORTANCE OF BEING EARNEST: A Trivial Comedy for Serious People.
A HOUSE OF POMEGRANATES, THE HAPPY PRINCE, and OTHER TALES.
LORD ARTHUR SAVILE'S CRIME and OTHER PROSE PIECES.
DE PROFUNDIS.
Wilkins (W. H.), B.A. THE ALIEN INVASION. *Cr. 8vo.* 2s. 6d.
Williams (A.). PETROL PETER: or Pretty Stories and Funny Pictures. Illustrated in Colour by A. W. MILLS. *Demy 4to.* 3s. 6d. *net.*
Williamson (M. G.), M.A. See Ancient Cities.
Williamson (W.), B.A. See Junior Examination Series, Junior School Books, and Beginner's Books.
Wilmot-Buxton (E. M.). MAKERS OF EUROPE. Outlines of European History for the Middle Forms of Schools. With 12 Maps. *Ninth Edition. Cr. 8vo.* 3s. 6d.
THE ANCIENT WORLD. With Maps and Illustrations. *Cr. 8vo.* 3s. 6d.
A BOOK OF NOBLE WOMEN. With 16 Illustrations. *Cr. 8vo.* 3s. 6d.
A HISTORY OF GREAT BRITAIN: FROM THE COMING OF THE ANGLES TO THE YEAR 1870. With 20 Maps. *Cr. 8vo.* 3s. 6d.
See also Beginner's Books.
Wilson (Bishop.). See Library of Devotion.
Wilson (A. J.). See Books on Business.
Wilson (H. A.). See Books on Business.
Wilson (J. A.). See Simplified French Texts.
Wilton (Richard), M.A. LYRA PASTORALIS: Songs of Nature, Church, and Home. *Pott 8vo.* 2s. 6d.
Winbolt (S. E.), M.A. EXERCISES IN LATIN ACCIDENCE. *Cr. 8vo.* 1s. 6d.
LATIN HEXAMETER VERSE: An Aid to Composition. *Cr. 8vo.* 3s. 6d. KEY, 5s. *net.*
Windle (B. C. A.), D.Sc., F.R.S., F.S.A. See Antiquary's Books, Little Guides, Ancient Cities, and School Histories.
Winterbotham (Canon), M.A., B.Sc., LL.B. See Churchman's Library.
Wood (Sir Evelyn), F.-M., V.C., G.C.B., G.C.M.G. FROM MIDSHIPMAN TO FIELD-MARSHAL. With Illustrations, and 29 Maps. *Fifth and Cheaper Edition. Demy 8vo.* 7s. 6d. *net.*
A Colonial Edition is also published.
Wood (J. A. E.). See Textbooks of Technology.
Wood (J. Hickory). DAN LENO. Illustrated. *Third Edition. Cr. 8vo.* 6s.
A Colonial Edition is also published.
Wood (W. Birkbeck), M.A., late Scholar of Worcester College, Oxford, and **Edmonds (Major J. E.)**, R.E., D.A.Q.-M.G. A HISTORY OF THE CIVIL WAR IN THE UNITED STATES. With an Introduction by H. SPENSER WILKINSON. With 24 Maps and Plans. *Second Edition Demy 8vo.* 12s. 6d. *net.*
Wordsworth (Christopher), M.A. See Antiquary's Books.
Wordsworth (W.). THE POEMS OF With an Introduction and Notes by NOWELL C. SMITH, late Fellow of New College, Oxford. *In Three Volumes. Demy 8vo.* 15s. *net.*
POEMS BY WILLIAM WORDSWORTH. Selected with an Introduction by STOPFORD

A. BROOKE. With 40 Illustrations by E. H. NEW, including a Frontispiece in Photogravure. *Cr. 8vo. 7s. 6d. net.*
See also Little Library.

Wordsworth (W.) and **Coleridge (S. T.).** See Little Library.

Wright (Arthur), D.D., Fellow of Queen's College, Cambridge. See Churchman's Library.

Wright (C. Gordon). See Dante.

Wright (J. C.). TO-DAY. Thoughts on Life for every day. *Demy 16mo. 1s. 6d. net.*

Wright (Sophie). GERMAN VOCABULARIES FOR REPETITION. *Fcap. 8vo 1s. 6d.*

Wyatt (Kate M.). See Gloag (M. R.).

Wylde (A. B.). MODERN ABYSSINIA. With a Map and a Portrait. *Demy 8vo. 15s. net.*

Wyllie (M. A.). NORWAY AND ITS FJORDS. With 16 Illustrations, in Colour by W. L. WYLLIE, R.A., and 17 other Illustrations. *Crown 8vo. 6s.*
A Colonial Edition is also published.

Wyndham (George). See Shakespeare (William).

Wyon (R.) and **Prance (G.).** THE LAND OF THE BLACK MOUNTAIN. With 51 Illustrations. *Cr. 8vo. 2s. 6d. net.*

Yeats (W. B.). A BOOK OF IRISH VERSE. *Revised and Enlarged Edition. Cr. 8vo. 3s. 6d.*

Young (Filson). THE COMPLETE MOTORIST. With 138 Illustrations. *New Edition (Seventh), with many additions. Demy. 8vo. 12s. 6d. net.*
A Colonial Edition is also published.

THE JOY OF THE ROAD: An Appreciation of the Motor Car. With a Frontispiece in Photogravure. *Small Demy 8vo. 5s. net.*

Young (T. M.). THE AMERICAN COTTON INDUSTRY: A Study of Work and Workers. *Cr. 8vo. Cloth, 2s. 6d.; paper boards, 1s. 6d.*

Zimmern (Antonia). WHAT DO WE KNOW CONCERNING ELECTRICITY? *Fcap. 8vo. 1s. 6d. net.*

Ancient Cities

General Editor, B. C. A. WINDLE, D.Sc., F.R.S.

Cr. 8vo. 4s. 6d. net.

CHESTER. By B. C. A. Windle, D.Sc. F.R.S. Illustrated by E. H. New.

SHREWSBURY. By T. Auden, M.A., F.S.A. Illustrated by Katharine M. Roberts.

CANTERBURY. By J. C. Cox, LL.D., F.S.A. Illustrated by B. C. Boulter.

EDINBURGH. By M. G. Williamson, M.A. Illustrated by Herbert Railton.

LINCOLN. By E. Mansel Sympson, M.A., M.D. Illustrated by E. H. New.

BRISTOL. By Alfred Harvey, M.B. Illustrated by E. H. New.

DUBLIN. By S. A. O. Fitzpatrick. Illustrated by W. C. Green.

The Antiquary's Books

General Editor, J. CHARLES COX, LL.D., F.S.A.

Demy 8vo. 7s. 6d. net.

ENGLISH MONASTIC LIFE. By the Right Rev. Abbot Gasquet, O.S.B. Illustrated. *Third Edition.*

REMAINS OF THE PREHISTORIC AGE IN ENGLAND. By B. C. A. Windle, D.Sc., F.R.S. With numerous Illustrations and Plans.

OLD SERVICE BOOKS OF THE ENGLISH CHURCH. By Christopher Wordsworth, M.A., and Henry Littlehales. With Coloured and other Illustrations.

CELTIC ART IN PAGAN AND CHRISTIAN TIMES. By J. Romilly Allen, F.S.A. With numerous Illustrations and Plans.

ARCHÆOLOGY AND FALSE ANTIQUITIES. By R. Munro, LL.D. Illustrated.

SHRINES OF BRITISH SAINTS. By J. C. Wall. With numerous Illustrations and Plans.

THE ROYAL FORESTS OF ENGLAND. By J. C. Cox, LL.D., F.S.A. Illustrated.

THE MANOR AND MANORIAL RECORDS. By Nathaniel J. Hone. Illustrated.

ENGLISH SEALS. By J. Harvey Bloom. Illustrated.

THE BELLS OF ENGLAND. By Canon J. J. Raven, D.D., F.S.A. With Illustrations. *Second Edition.*

PARISH LIFE IN MEDIÆVAL ENGLAND. By the Right Rev. Abbott Gasquet, O.S.B. With many Illustrations. *Second Edition.*

THE DOMESDAY INQUEST. By Adolphus Ballard, B.A., LL.B. With 27 Illustrations.

THE BRASSES OF ENGLAND. By Herbert W. Macklin, M.A. With many Illustrations. *Second Edition.*

ENGLISH CHURCH FURNITURE. By J. C. Cox, LL.D., F.S.A., and A. Harvey, M.B. *Second Edition.*

FOLK-LORE AS AN HISTORICAL SCIENCE. By G. L. Gomme. With many Illustrations.

*ENGLISH COSTUME. By George Clinch, F.G.S. With many Illustrations.

The Arden Shakespeare

Demy 8vo. 2s. 6d. net each volume.

An edition of Shakespeare in single Plays. Edited with a full Introduction, Textual Notes, and a Commentary at the foot of the page.

HAMLET. Edited by Edward Dowden.
ROMEO AND JULIET. Edited by Edward Dowden.
KING LEAR. Edited by W. J. Craig.
JULIUS CAESAR. Edited by M. Macmillan.
THE TEMPEST. Edited by Moreton Luce.
OTHELLO. Edited by H. C. Hart.
TITUS ANDRONICUS. Edited by H. B. Baildon.
CYMBELINE. Edited by Edward Dowden.
THE MERRY WIVES OF WINDSOR. Edited by H. C. Hart.
A MIDSUMMER NIGHT'S DREAM. Edited by H. Cuningham.
KING HENRY V. Edited by H. A. Evans.
ALL'S WELL THAT ENDS WELL. Edited by W. O. Brigstocke.
THE TAMING OF THE SHREW. Edited by R. Warwick Bond.
TIMON OF ATHENS. Edited by K. Deighton.
MEASURE FOR MEASURE. Edited by H. C. Hart.
TWELFTH NIGHT. Edited by Moreton Luce.
THE MERCHANT OF VENICE. Edited by C. Knox Pooler.
TROILUS AND CRESSIDA. Edited by K. Deighton.
THE TWO GENTLEMEN OF VERONA. Edited by R. Warwick Bond.
ANTONY AND CLEOPATRA. Edited by R. H. Case.
LOVE'S LABOUR'S LOST. Edited by H. C. Hart.
PERICLES. Edited by K. Deighton.
KING RICHARD III. Edited by A. H. Thompson.
THE LIFE AND DEATH OF KING JOHN. Edited by Ivor B. John.
THE COMEDY OF ERRORS. Edited by Henry Cuningham.

The Beginner's Books

Edited by W. WILLIAMSON, B.A.

EASY FRENCH RHYMES. By Henri Blouet. *Second Edition.* Illustrated. *Fcap. 8vo.* 1*s.*

EASY STORIES FROM ENGLISH HISTORY. By E. M. Wilmot-Buxton. *Fourth Edition. Cr. 8vo.* 1*s.*

STORIES FROM ROMAN HISTORY. By E. M. Wilmot-Buxton *Cr. 8vo.* 1*s.* 6*d.*

A FIRST HISTORY OF GREECE. By E. E. Firth. *Cr. 8vo.* 1*s.* 6*d.*

EASY EXERCISES IN ARITHMETIC. Arranged by W. S. Beard. *Third Edition. Fcap. 8vo.* Without Answers, 1*s.* With Answers. 1*s.* 3*d.*

EASY DICTATION AND SPELLING. By W. Williamson, B.A. *Seventh Ed. Fcap. 8vo.* 1*s.*

AN EASY POETRY BOOK. Selected and arranged by W. Williamson, B.A. *Second Edition. Cr. 8vo.* 1*s.*

Books on Business

Cr. 8vo. 2s. 6d. net.

PORTS AND DOCKS. By Douglas Owen.
RAILWAYS. By E. R. McDermott.
THE STOCK EXCHANGE. By Chas. Duguid. *Second Edition.*
THE BUSINESS OF INSURANCE. By A. J. Wilson.
THE ELECTRICAL INDUSTRY: LIGHTING, TRACTION, AND POWER. By A. G. Whyte, B.Sc.
THE SHIPBUILDING INDUSTRY: Its History, Practice, Science, and Finance. By David Pollock, M.I.N.A.
THE MONEY MARKET. By F. Straker.
THE BUSINESS SIDE OF AGRICULTURE. By A. G. L. Rogers, M.A.
LAW IN BUSINESS. By H. A. Wilson.
THE BREWING INDUSTRY. By Julian L. Baker, F.I.C., F.C.S. Illustrated.
THE AUTOMOBILE INDUSTRY. By G. de Holden-Stone.
MINING AND MINING INVESTMENTS. By 'A. Moil.'
THE BUSINESS OF ADVERTISING. By Clarence G. Moran, Barrister-at-Law. Illustrated.
TRADE UNIONS. By G. Drage.
CIVIL ENGINEERING. By T. Claxton Fidler, M.Inst. C.E. Illustrated.
THE IRON TRADE OF GREAT BRITAIN. By J. Stephen Jeans. Illustrated.
MONOPOLIES, TRUSTS, AND KARTELLS. By F. W. Hirst.
THE COTTON INDUSTRY AND TRADE. By Prof. S. J. Chapman, Dean of the Faculty of Commerce in the University of Manchester. Illustrated.

Byzantine Texts

Edited by J. B. BURY, M.A., Litt.D.

THE SYRIAC CHRONICLE KNOWN AS THAT OF ZACHARIAH OF MITYLENE. Translated by F. J. Hamilton, D.D., and E. W. Brooks. *Demy 8vo.* 12*s.* 6*d. net.*

EVAGRIUS. Edited by L. Bidez and Léon Parmentier. *Demy 8vo.* 10*s.* 6*d. net.*

THE HISTORY OF PSELLUS. Edited by C. Sathas. *Demy 8vo.* 15*s. net.*

ECTHESIS CHRONICA AND CHRONICON ATHENARUM. Edited by Professor S. P. Lambros. *Demy 8vo.* 7*s.* 6*d. net.*

THE CHRONICLE OF MOREA. Edited by John Schmitt. *Demy 8vo.* 15*s. net.*

The Churchman's Bible

General Editor, J. H. BURN, B.D., F.R.S.E.

Fcap. 8vo. 1*s.* 6*d. net each.*

THE EPISTLE OF ST. PAUL THE APOSTLE TO THE GALATIANS. Explained by A. W. Robinson, M.A. *Second Edition.*

ECCLESIASTES. Explained by A. W. Streane, D.D.

THE EPISTLE OF ST. PAUL THE APOSTLE TO THE PHILIPPIANS. Explained by C. R. D. Biggs, D.D. *Second Edition.*

THE EPISTLE OF ST. JAMES. Explained by H. W. Fulford M.A.

ISAIAH. Explained by W. E. Barnes, D.D. *Two Volumes.* With Map. 2*s. net each.*

THE EPISTLE OF ST. PAUL THE APOSTLE TO THE EPHESIANS. Explained by G. H. Whitaker, M.A.

THE GOSPEL ACCORDING TO ST. MARK. Explained by J. C. Du Buisson, M.A. 2*s.* 6*d. net.*

THE EPISTLE OF PAUL THE APOSTLE TO THE COLOSSIANS AND PHILEMON. Explained by H. J. C. Knight. 2*s. net.*

The Churchman's Library

General Editor, J. H. BURN, B.D., F.R.S.E.

Crown 8vo. 3*s.* 6*d. each.*

THE BEGINNINGS OF ENGLISH CHRISTIANITY. By W. E. Collins, M.A. With Map.

THE KINGDOM OF HEAVEN HERE AND HEREAFTER. By Canon Winterbotham, M.A., B.Sc., LL.B.

THE WORKMANSHIP OF THE PRAYER BOOK: Its Literary and Liturgical Aspects. By J. Dowden, D.D. *Second Edition, Revised and Enlarged.*

EVOLUTION. By F. B. Jevons, M.A., Litt.D.

SOME NEW TESTAMENT PROBLEMS. By Arthur Wright, D.D. 6*s.*

THE CHURCHMAN'S INTRODUCTION TO THE OLD TESTAMENT. By A. M. Mackay, B.A. *Third Edition.*

COMPARATIVE THEOLOGY. By J. A. MacCulloch. 6*s.*

Classical Translations

Crown 8vo.

ÆSCHYLUS—The Oresteian Trilogy (Agamemnon, Choëphoroe, Eumenides). Translated by Lewis Campbell, LL.D. 5*s.*

CICERO—De Oratore I. Translated by E. N. P. Moor, M.A. *Second Edition.* 3*s.* 6*d.*

CICERO—The Speeches against Cataline and Antony and for Murena and Milo. Translated by H. E. D. Blakiston, M.A. 5*s.*

CICERO—De Natura Deorum. Translated by F. Brooks, M.A. 3*s.* 6*d.*

CICERO—De Officiis. Translated by G. B. Gardiner, M.A. 2*s.* 6*d*

HORACE—The Odes and Epodes. Translated by A. D. Godley, M.A. 2*s.*

LUCIAN—Six Dialogues Translated by S. T. Irwin, M.A. 3*s.* 6*d.*

SOPHOCLES—Ajax and Electra. Translated by E. D. Morshead, M.A. 2*s.* 6*d.*

TACITUS—Agricola and Germania. Translated by R. B. Townshend. 2*s.* 6*d.*

JUVENAL—Thirteen Satires. Translated by S. G. Owen, M.A. 2*s.* 6*d.*

Classics of Art

Edited by DR. J. H. W. LAING

THE ART OF THE GREEKS. By H. B. Walters. With 112 Plates and 18 Illustrations in the Text. *Wide Royal 8vo.* 12*s.* 6*d. net.*

VELAZQUEZ. By A. de Beruete. With 94 Plates. *Wide Royal 8vo.* 10*s.* 6*d. net.*

Commercial Series

Crown 8vo.

BRITISH COMMERCE AND COLONIES FROM ELIZABETH TO VICTORIA. By H. de B. Gibbins, Litt.D., M.A. *Third Edition.* 2s.

COMMERCIAL EXAMINATION PAPERS. By H. de B. Gibbins, Litt.D., M.A. 1s. 6d.

THE ECONOMICS OF COMMERCE. By H. de B. Gibbins, Litt.D., M.A. *Second Edition.* 1s. 6d.

A GERMAN COMMERCIAL READER. By S. E. Bally. With Vocabulary. 2s.

A COMMERCIAL GEOGRAPHY OF THE BRITISH EMPIRE. By L. W. Lyde, M.A. *Sixth Edition.* 2s.

A COMMERCIAL GEOGRAPHY OF FOREIGN NATIONS. By F. C. Boon, B.A. 2s.

A PRIMER OF BUSINESS. By S. Jackson, M.A. *Fourth Edition.* 1s. 6d.

A SHORT COMMERCIAL ARITHMETIC. By F. G. Taylor, M.A. *Fourth Edition.* 1s. 6d.

FRENCH COMMERCIAL CORRESPONDENCE. By S. E. Bally. With Vocabulary. *Third Edition.* 2s.

GERMAN COMMERCIAL CORRESPONDENCE. By S. E. Bally. With Vocabulary. *Second Edition.* 2s. 6d.

A FRENCH COMMERCIAL READER. By S. E. Bally. With Vocabulary. *Second Edition.* 2s.

PRECIS WRITING AND OFFICE CORRESPONDENCE. By E. E. Whitfield, M.A. *Second Edition.* 2s.

A ENTRANCE GUIDE TO PROFESSIONS AND BUSINESS. By H. Jones. 1s. 6d.

THE PRINCIPLES OF BOOK-KEEPING BY DOUBLE ENTRY. By J. E. B. M'Allen, M.A. 2s.

COMMERCIAL LAW. By W. Douglas Edwards. *Second Edition.* 2s.

The Connoisseur's Library

Wide Royal 8vo. 25s. *net.*

MEZZOTINTS. By Cyril Davenport. With 40 Plates in Photogravure.

PORCELAIN. By Edward Dillon. With 19 Plates in Colour, 20 in Collotype, and 5 in Photogravure.

MINIATURES. By Dudley Heath. With 9 Plates in Colour, 15 in Collotype, and 15 in Photogravure.

IVORIES. By A. Maskell. With 80 Plates in Collotype and Photogravure.

ENGLISH FURNITURE. By F. S. Robinson. With 160 Plates in Collotype and one in Photogravure. *Second Edition.*

ENGLISH COLOURED BOOKS. By Martin Hardie. With 28 Illustrations in Colour and Collotype.

EUROPEAN ENAMELS. By Henry H. Cunynghame, C.B. With 54 Plates in Collotype and Half-tone and 4 Plates in Colour.

GOLDSMITHS' AND SILVERSMITHS' WORK. By Nelson Dawson. With many Plates in Collotype and a Frontispiece in Photogravure. *Second Edition.*

GLASS. By Edward Dillon. With 37 Illustrations in Collotype and 12 in Colour.

SEALS. By Walter de Gray Birch. With 52 Illustrations in Collotype and a Frontispiece in Photogravure.

JEWELLERY. By H. Clifford Smith. With 50 Illustrations in Collotype, and 4 in Colour.

The Illustrated Pocket Library of Plain and Coloured Books

Fcap 8vo. 3s. 6d. *net each volume.*

COLOURED BOOKS

OLD COLOURED BOOKS. By George Paston. With 16 Coloured Plates. *Fcap. 8vo.* 2s. *net.*

THE LIFE AND DEATH OF JOHN MYTTON, ESQ. By Nimrod. With 18 Coloured Plates by Henry Alken and T. J. Rawlins. *Fourth Edition.*

THE LIFE OF A SPORTSMAN. By Nimrod. With 35 Coloured Plates by Henry Alken.

HANDLEY CROSS. By R. S. Surtees. With 17 Coloured Plates and 100 Woodcuts in the Text by John Leech. *Second Edition.*

MR. SPONGE'S SPORTING TOUR. By R. S. Surtees. With 13 Coloured Plates and 90 Woodcuts in the Text by John Leech.

JORROCKS' JAUNTS AND JOLLITIES. By R. S. Surtees. With 15 Coloured Plates by H. Alken. *Second Edition.*

ASK MAMMA. By R. S. Surtees. With 13 Coloured Plates and 70 Woodcuts in the Text by John Leech.

THE ANALYSIS OF THE HUNTING FIELD. By R. S. Surtees. With 7 Coloured Plates by Henry Alken, and 43 Illustrations on Wood.

THE TOUR OF DR. SYNTAX IN SEARCH OF THE PICTURESQUE. By William Combe. With 30 Coloured Plates by T. Rowlandson.

THE TOUR OF DOCTOR SYNTAX IN SEARCH OF CONSOLATION. By William Combe. With 24 Coloured Plates by T. Rowlandson.

THE THIRD TOUR OF DOCTOR SYNTAX IN SEARCH OF A WIFE. By William Combe. With 24 Coloured Plates by T. Rowlandson.

THE HISTORY OF JOHNNY QUAE GENUS: the Little Foundling of the late Dr. Syntax. By the Author of 'The Three Tours.' With 24 Coloured Plates by Rowlandson.

THE ENGLISH DANCE OF DEATH, from the Designs of T. Rowlandson, with Metrical Illustrations by the Author of 'Doctor Syntax.' *Two Volumes.*

This book contains 76 Coloured Plates.

[*Continued.*

ILLUSTRATED POCKET LIBRARY OF PLAIN AND COLOURED BOOKS—*continued.*

THE DANCE OF LIFE: A Poem. By the Author of 'Doctor Syntax.' Illustrated with 26 Coloured Engravings by T. Rowlandson.

LIFE IN LONDON: or, the Day and Night Scenes of Jerry Hawthorn, Esq., and his Elegant Friend, Corinthian Tom. By Pierce Egan. With 36 Coloured Plates by I. R. and G. Cruikshank. With numerous Designs on Wood.

REAL LIFE IN LONDON: or, the Rambles and Adventures of Bob Tallyho, Esq., and his Cousin, The Hon. Tom Dashall. By an Amateur (Pierce Egan). With 31 Coloured Plates by Alken and Rowlandson, etc. *Two Volumes.*

THE LIFE OF AN ACTOR. By Pierce Egan. With 27 Coloured Plates by Theodore Lane, and several Designs on Wood.

THE VICAR OF WAKEFIELD. By Oliver Goldsmith. With 24 Coloured Plates by T. Rowlandson.

THE MILITARY ADVENTURES OF JOHNNY NEWCOME. By an Officer. With 15 Coloured Plates by T. Rowlandson.

THE NATIONAL SPORTS OF GREAT BRITAIN. With Descriptions and 50 Coloured Plates by Henry Alken.

THE ADVENTURES OF A POST CAPTAIN. By A Naval Officer. With 24 Coloured Plates by Mr. Williams.

GAMONIA: or the Art of Preserving Game; and an Improved Method of making Plantations and Covers, explained and illustrated by Lawrence Rawstorne, Esq. With 15 Coloured Plates by T. Rawlins.

AN ACADEMY FOR GROWN HORSEMEN: Containing the completest Instructions for Walking, Trotting, Cantering, Galloping, Stumbling, and Tumbling. Illustrated with 27 Coloured Plates, and adorned with a Portrait of the Author. By Geoffrey Gambado, Esq.

REAL LIFE IN IRELAND, or, the Day and Night Scenes of Brian Boru, Esq., and his Elegant Friend, Sir Shawn O'Dogherty. By a Real Paddy. With 19 Coloured Plates by Heath, Marks, etc.

THE ADVENTURES OF JOHNNY NEWCOME IN THE NAVY. By Alfred Burton. With 16 Coloured Plates by T. Rowlandson.

THE OLD ENGLISH SQUIRE: A Poem. By John Careless, Esq. With 20 Coloured Plates after the style of T. Rowlandson.

THE ENGLISH SPY. By Bernard Blackmantle. An original Work, Characteristic, Satirical, Humorous, comprising scenes and sketches in every Rank of Society, being Portraits of the Illustrious, Eminent, Eccentric, and Notorious. With 72 Coloured Plates by R. CRUIKSHANK, and many Illustrations on wood. *Two Volumes.* 7*s. net.*

PLAIN BOOKS

THE GRAVE: A Poem. By Robert Blair. Illustrated by 12 Etchings executed by Louis Schiavonetti from the original Inventions of William Blake. With an Engraved Title Page and a Portrait of Blake by T. Phillips, R.A.

The illustrations are reproduced in photogravure.

ILLUSTRATIONS OF THE BOOK OF JOB. Invented and engraved by William Blake.

These famous Illustrations—21 in number—are reproduced in photogravure.

WINDSOR CASTLE. By W. Harrison Ainsworth. With 22 Plates and 87 Woodcuts in the Text by George Cruikshank.

THE TOWER OF LONDON. By W. Harrison Ainsworth. With 40 Plates and 58 Woodcuts in the Text by George Cruikshank.

FRANK FAIRLEGH. By F. E. Smedley. With 30 Plates by George Cruikshank.

HANDY ANDY. By Samuel Lover. With 24 Illustrations by the Author.

THE COMPLEAT ANGLER. By Izaak Walton and Charles Cotton. With 14 Plates and 77 Woodcuts in the Text.

THE PICKWICK PAPERS. By Charles Dickens. With the 43 Illustrations by Seymour and Phiz, the two Buss Plates, and the 32 Contemporary Onwhyn Plates.

Junior Examination Series

Edited by A. M. M. STEDMAN, M.A. *Fcap. 8vo.* 1*s.*

JUNIOR FRENCH EXAMINATION PAPERS. By F. Jacob, M.A. *Second Edition.*

JUNIOR ENGLISH EXAMINATION PAPERS. By W. Williamson, B.A.

JUNIOR ARITHMETIC EXAMINATION PAPERS. By W. S. Beard. *Fourth Edition.*

JUNIOR ALGEBRA EXAMINATION PAPERS. By S. W Finn, M.A.

JUNIOR GREEK EXAMINATION PAPERS. By T. C. Weatherhead, M.A. KEY, 3*s.* 6*d. net.*

JUNIOR LATIN EXAMINATION PAPERS. By C. G. Botting, B.A. *Fifth Edition.* KEY, 3*s.* 6*d. net.*

JUNIOR GENERAL INFORMATION EXAMINATION PAPERS. By W. S. Beard. KEY, 3*s.* 6*d. net.*

JUNIOR GEOGRAPHY EXAMINATION PAPERS. By W. G. Baker, M.A.

JUNIOR GERMAN EXAMINATION PAPERS. By A. Voegelin, M.A.

Methuen's Junior School-Books

Edited by O. D. INSKIP, LL.D., and W. WILLIAMSON, B.A.

A CLASS-BOOK OF DICTATION PASSAGES. By W. Williamson, B.A. *Fourteenth Edition. Cr. 8vo.* 1s. 6d.

THE GOSPEL ACCORDING TO ST. MATTHEW. Edited by E. Wilton South, M.A. With Three Maps. *Cr. 8vo.* 1s. 6d.

THE GOSPEL ACCORDING TO ST. MARK. Edited by A. E. Rubie, D.D. With Three Maps. *Cr. 8vo.* 1s. 6d.

A JUNIOR ENGLISH GRAMMAR. By W. Williamson, B.A. With numerous passages for parsing and analysis, and a chapter on Essay Writing. *Fourth Edition. Cr. 8vo.* 2s.

A JUNIOR CHEMISTRY. By E. A. Tyler, B.A., F.C.S. With 78 Illustrations. *Fourth Edition. Cr. 8vo.* 2s. 6d.

THE ACTS OF THE APOSTLES. Edited by A. E. Rubie, D.D. *Cr. 8vo.* 2s.

A JUNIOR FRENCH GRAMMAR. By L. A. Sornet and M. J. Acatos. *Second Edition. Cr. 8vo.* 2s.

ELEMENTARY EXPERIMENTAL SCIENCE. PHYSICS by W. T. Clough, A.R.C.S. CHEMISTRY by A. E. Dunstan, B.Sc. With 2 Plates and 154 Diagrams. *Sixth Edition. Cr. 8vo.* 2s. 6d.

A JUNIOR GEOMETRY. By Noel S. Lydon. With 276 Diagrams. *Sixth Edition. Cr. 8vo.* 2s.

ELEMENTARY EXPERIMENTAL CHEMISTRY. By A. E. Dunstan, B.Sc. With 4 Plates and 109 Diagrams. *Third Edition. Cr. 8vo.* 2s.

A JUNIOR FRENCH PROSE. By R. R. N. Baron, M.A. *Third Edition. Cr. 8vo.* 2s.

THE GOSPEL ACCORDING TO ST. LUKE. With an Introduction and Notes by William Williamson, B.A. With Three Maps. *Cr. 8vo.* 2s.

THE FIRST BOOK OF KINGS. Edited by A. E. RUBIE, D.D. With Maps. *Cr. 8vo.* 2s.

A JUNIOR GREEK HISTORY. By W. H. Spragge, M.A. With 4 Illustrations and 5 Maps. *Cr. 8vo.* 2s. 6d.

A SCHOOL LATIN GRAMMAR. By H. G. Ford, M.A. *Cr. 8vo.* 2s. 6d.

A JUNIOR LATIN PROSE. By H. N. Asman, M.A., B.D. *Cr. 8vo.* 2s. 6d.

Leaders of Religion

Edited by H. C. BEECHING, M.A., Canon of Westminster. *With Portraits. Cr. 8vo.* 2s. *net.*

CARDINAL NEWMAN. By R. H. Hutton.

JOHN WESLEY. By J. H. Overton, M.A.

BISHOP WILBERFORCE. By G. W. Daniell, M.A.

CARDINAL MANNING. By A. W. Hutton, M.A.

CHARLES SIMEON. By H. C. G. Moule, D.D.

JOHN KNOX. By F. MacCunn. *Second Edition.*

JOHN HOWE. By R. F. Horton, D.D.

THOMAS KEN. By F. A. Clarke, M.A.

GEORGE FOX, THE QUAKER. By T. Hodgkin, D.C.L. *Third Edition.*

JOHN KEBLE. By Walter Lock, D.D.

THOMAS CHALMERS. By Mrs. Oliphant.

LANCELOT ANDREWES. By R. L. Ottley, D.D. *Second Edition.*

AUGUSTINE OF CANTERBURY. By E. L. Cutts, D.D.

WILLIAM LAUD. By W. H. Hutton, M.A. *Third Edition.*

JOHN DONNE. By Augustus Jessopp, D.D.

THOMAS CRANMER. By A. J. Mason, D.D.

BISHOP LATIMER. By R. M. Carlyle and A. J. Carlyle, M.A.

BISHOP BUTLER. By W. A. Spooner, M.A.

The Library of Devotion

With Introductions and (where necessary) Notes.

Small Pott 8vo, cloth, 2s. ; *leather,* 2s. 6d. *net.*

THE CONFESSIONS OF ST. AUGUSTINE. Edited by C. Bigg, D.D. *Sixth Edition.*

THE IMITATION OF CHRIST : called also the Ecclesiastical Music. Edited by C. Bigg, D.D. *Fifth Edition.*

THE CHRISTIAN YEAR. Edited by Walter Lock, D.D. *Fourth Edition.*

LYRA INNOCENTIUM. Edited by Walter Lock, D.D. *Second Edition.*

THE TEMPLE. Edited by E. C. S. Gibson, D.D. *Second Edition.*

A BOOK OF DEVOTIONS. Edited by J. W. Stanbridge, B.D. *Second Edition.*

A SERIOUS CALL TO A DEVOUT AND HOLY LIFE. Edited by C. Bigg, D.D. *Fourth Ed.*

A GUIDE TO ETERNITY. Edited by J. W. Stanbridge, B.D.

THE INNER WAY. By J. Tauler. Edited by A. W. Hutton, M.A.

ON THE LOVE OF GOD. By St. Francis de Sales. Edited by W. J. Knox-Little, M.A.

THE PSALMS OF DAVID. Edited by B. W. Randolph, D.D.

LYRA APOSTOLICA. By Cardinal Newman and others. Edited by Canon Scott Holland, M.A., and Canon H. C. Beeching, M.A.

THE SONG OF SONGS. Edited by B. Blaxland, M.A.

THE THOUGHTS OF PASCAL. Edited by C. S. Jerram, M.A.

A MANUAL OF CONSOLATION FROM THE SAINTS AND FATHERS. Edited by J. H. Burn, B.D.

[*Continued.*

THE LIBRARY OF DEVOTION—*continued.*

THE DEVOTIONS OF ST. ANSELM. Edited by C. C. J. Webb, M.A.

GRACE ABOUNDING TO THE CHIEF OF SINNERS. By John Bunyan. Edited by S. C. Freer, M.A.

BISHOP WILSON'S SACRA PRIVATA. Edited by A. E. Burn, B.D.

LYRA SACRA: A Book of Sacred Verse. Edited by Canon H. C. Beeching, M.A. *Second Edition, revised.*

A DAY BOOK FROM THE SAINTS AND FATHERS. Edited by J. H. Burn, B.D.

A LITTLE BOOK OF HEAVENLY WISDOM. A Selection from the English Mystics. Edited by E. C. Gregory.

LIGHT, LIFE, and LOVE. A Selection from the German Mystics. Edited by W. R. Inge, M.A.

AN INTRODUCTION TO THE DEVOUT LIFE. By St. Francis de Sales. Translated and Edited by T. Barns, M.A.

THE LITTLE FLOWERS OF THE GLORIOUS MESSER ST. FRANCIS AND OF HIS FRIARS. Done into English by W. Heywood. With an Introduction by A. G. Ferrers Howell.

MANCHESTER AL MONDO: a Contemplation of Death and Immortality. By Henry Montagu, Earl of Manchester. With an Introduction by Elizabeth Waterhouse, Editor of 'A Little Book of Life and Death.'

THE SPIRITUAL GUIDE, which Disentangles the Soul and brings it by the Inward Way to the Fruition of Perfect Contemplation, and the Rich Treasure of Internal Peace. Written by Dr. Michael de Molinos, Priest. Translated from the Italian copy, printed at Venice, 1685. Edited with an Introduction by Kathleen Lyttelton. And a Note by Canon Scott Holland.

DEVOTIONS FOR EVERY DAY OF THE WEEK AND THE GREAT FESTIVALS. By John Wesley. Edited, with an Introduction by Canon C. Bodington.

PRECES PRIVATÆ. By Lancelot Andrewes, Bishop of Winchester. Selections from the Translation by Canon F. E. Brightman. Edited, with an Introduction, by A. E. Burn, D.D.

Little Books on Art

With many Illustrations. Demy 16mo. 2s. 6d. net.

Each volume consists of about 200 pages, and contains from 30 to 40 Illustrations, including a Frontispiece in Photogravure.

GREEK ART. H. B. Walters. *Fourth Edition.*
BOOKPLATES. E. Almack.
REYNOLDS. J. Sime. *Second Edition.*
ROMNEY. George Paston.
WATTS. R. E. D. Sketchley.
LEIGHTON. Alice Corkran.
VELASQUEZ. Wilfrid Wilberforce and A. R. Gilbert.
GREUZE AND BOUCHER. Eliza F. Pollard.
VANDYCK. M. G. Smallwood.
TURNER. Frances Tyrrell-Gill.
DÜRER. Jessie Allen.
HOLBEIN. Mrs. G. Fortescue.
BURNE-JONES. Fortunée de Lisle. *Third Edition.*
HOPPNER. H. P. K. Skipton.
REMBRANDT. Mrs. E. A. Sharp.
COROT. Alice Pollard and Ethel Birnstingl.
RAPHAEL. A. R. Dryhurst.
MILLET. Netta Peacock.
ILLUMINATED MSS. J. W. Bradley.
CHRIST IN ART. Mrs. Henry Jenner.
JEWELLERY. Cyril Davenport.
CLAUDE. E. Dillon.
THE ARTS OF JAPAN. E. Dillon.
ENAMELS. Mrs. Nelson Dawson.
MINIATURES. C. Davenport.
CONSTABLE. H. W. Tompkins.
OUR LADY IN ART. Mrs. H. L. Jenner.

The Little Galleries

Demy 16mo. 2s. 6d. net.

Each volume contains 20 plates in Photogravure, together with a short outline of the life and work of the master to whom the book is devoted.

A LITTLE GALLERY OF REYNOLDS.
A LITTLE GALLERY OF ROMNEY.
A LITTLE GALLERY OF HOPPNER.
A LITTLE GALLERY OF MILLAIS.
A LITTLE GALLERY OF ENGLISH POETS.

The Little Guides

With many Illustrations by E. H. NEW and other artists, and from photographs.

Small Pott 8vo, cloth, 2s. 6d. net.; leather, 3s. 6d. net.

The main features of these Guides are (1) a handy and charming form; (2) illustrations from photographs and by well-known artists; (3) good plans and maps; (4) an adequate but compact presentation of everything that is interesting in the natural features, history, archæology, and architecture of the town or district treated.

CAMBRIDGE AND ITS COLLEGES. By A. Hamilton Thompson. *Second Edition.*
OXFORD AND ITS COLLEGES. By J. Wells, M.A. *Eighth Edition.*
ST. PAUL'S CATHEDRAL. By George Clinch.
WESTMINSTER ABBEY. By G. E. Troutbeck. *Second Edition.*

THE ENGLISH LAKES. By F. G. Brabant, M.A.
THE MALVERN COUNTRY. By B. C. A. Windle, D.Sc., F.R.S.
SHAKESPEARE'S COUNTRY. By B. C. A. Windle, D.Sc., F.R.S. *Third Edition.*

NORTH WALES. By A. T. Story.
BUCKINGHAMSHIRE. By E. S. Roscoe.
CHESHIRE. By W. M. Gallichan.
CORNWALL. By A. L. Salmon.
DERBYSHIRE. By J. Charles Cox, LL.D., F.S.A.
DEVON. By S. Baring-Gould.
DORSET. By Frank R. Heath. *Second Ed.*
HAMPSHIRE. By J. C. Cox, LL.D., F.S.A.
HERTFORDSHIRE. By H. W. Tompkins, F.R.H.S.
THE ISLE OF WIGHT. By G. Clinch.
KENT. By G. Clinch.
KERRY. By C. P. Crane.
MIDDLESEX. By John B. Firth.
NORFOLK. By W. A. Dutt.
NORTHAMPTONSHIRE. By Wakeling Dry.
OXFORDSHIRE. By F. G. Brabant, M.A.
SOMERSET. By G. W. and J. H. Wade.
SUFFOLK. By W. A. Dutt.
SURREY. By F. A. H. Lambert.
SUSSEX. By F. G. Brabant, M.A. *Second Edition.*
THE EAST RIDING OF YORKSHIRE. By J. E. Morris.
THE NORTH RIDING OF YORKSHIRE. By J. E. Morris.

BRITTANY. By S. Baring-Gould.
NORMANDY. By C. Scudamore.
ROME By C. G. Ellaby.
SICILY. By F. Hamilton Jackson.

The Little Library

With Introductions, Notes, and Photogravure Frontispieces.

Small Pott 8vo. Each Volume, cloth, 1s. 6d. net; leather, 2s. 6d. net.

Anon. A LITTLE BOOK OF ENGLISH LYRICS.

Austen (Jane). PRIDE AND PREJUDICE. Edited by E. V. LUCAS. *Two Vols.*
NORTHANGER ABBEY. Edited by E. V. LUCAS.

Bacon (Francis). THE ESSAYS OF LORD BACON. Edited by EDWARD WRIGHT.

Barham (R. H.). THE INGOLDSBY LEGENDS. Edited by J. B. ATLAY. *Two Volumes.*

Barnett (Mrs. P. A.). A LITTLE BOOK OF ENGLISH PROSE. *Second Edition.*

Beckford (William). THE HISTORY OF THE CALIPH VATHEK. Edited by E. DENISON ROSS.

Blake (William). SELECTIONS FROM WILLIAM BLAKE. Edited by M. PERUGINI.

Borrow (George). LAVENGRO. Edited by F. HINDES GROOME. *Two Volumes.*
THE ROMANY RYE. Edited by JOHN SAMPSON.

Browning (Robert). SELECTIONS FROM THE EARLY POEMS OF ROBERT BROWNING. Edited by W. HALL GRIFFIN, M.A.

Canning (George). SELECTIONS FROM THE ANTI-JACOBIN: with GEORGE CANNING'S additional Poems. Edited by LLOYD SANDERS.

Cowley (Abraham). THE ESSAYS OF ABRAHAM COWLEY. Edited by H. C. MINCHIN.

Crabbe (George). SELECTIONS FROM GEORGE CRABBE. Edited by A. C. DEANE.

Craik (Mrs.). JOHN HALIFAX, GENTLEMAN. Edited by ANNIE MATHESON. *Two Volumes.*

Crashaw (Richard). THE ENGLISH POEMS OF RICHARD CRASHAW. Edited by EDWARD HUTTON.

Dante (Alighieri). THE INFERNO OF DANTE. Translated by H. F. CARY. Edited by PAGET TOYNBEE, M.A., D.Litt.
THE PURGATORIO OF DANTE. Translated by H. F. CARY. Edited by PAGET TOYNBEE, M.A., D.Litt.
THE PARADISO OF DANTE. Translated by H. F. CARY. Edited by PAGET TOYNBEE, M.A., D.Litt.

Darley (George). SELECTIONS FROM THE POEMS OF GEORGE DARLEY. Edited by R. A. STREATFEILD.

Deane (A. C.). A LITTLE BOOK OF LIGHT VERSE.

Dickens (Charles). CHRISTMAS BOOKS. *Two Volumes.*

Ferrier (Susan). MARRIAGE. Edited by A. GOODRICH-FREER and LORD IDDESLEIGH. *Two Volumes.*
THE INHERITANCE. *Two Volumes.*

Gaskell (Mrs.). CRANFORD. Edited by E. V. LUCAS. *Second Edition.*

Hawthorne (Nathaniel). THE SCARLET LETTER. Edited by PERCY DEARMER.

Henderson (T. F.). A LITTLE BOOK OF SCOTTISH VERSE.

Keats (John). POEMS. With an Introduction by L. BINYON, and Notes by J. MASEFIELD.

Kinglake (A. W.). EOTHEN. With an Introduction and Notes. *Second Edition.*

[*Continued.*

THE LITTLE LIBRARY—*continued.*

Lamb (Charles). ELIA, AND THE LAST ESSAYS OF ELIA. Edited by E. V. LUCAS.

Locker (F.). LONDON LYRICS Edited by A. D. GODLEY, M.A. A reprint of the First Edition.

Longfellow (H. W.). SELECTIONS FROM LONGFELLOW. Edited by L. M. FAITHFULL.

Marvell (Andrew). THE POEMS OF ANDREW MARVELL. Edited by E. WRIGHT.

Milton (John). THE MINOR POEMS OF JOHN MILTON. Edited by H. C. BEECHING, M.A., Canon of Westminster.

Moir (D. M.). MANSIE WAUCH. Edited by T. F. HENDERSON.

Nichols (J. B. B.). A LITTLE BOOK OF ENGLISH SONNETS.

Rochefoucauld (La). THE MAXIMS OF LA ROCHEFOUCAULD. Translated by Dean STANHOPE. Edited by G. H. POWELL.

Smith (Horace and James). REJECTED ADDRESSES. Edited by A. D. GODLEY, M.A.

Sterne (Laurence). A SENTIMENTAL JOURNEY. Edited by H. W. PAUL.

Tennyson (Alfred, Lord). THE EARLY POEMS OF ALFRED, LORD TENNYSON. Edited by J. CHURTON COLLINS, M.A.

IN MEMORIAM. Edited by Canon H. C. BEECHING, M.A.

THE PRINCESS. Edited by ELIZABETH WORDSWORTH.

MAUD. Edited by ELIZABETH WORDSWORTH.

Thackeray (W. M.). VANITY FAIR. Edited by S. GWYNN. *Three Volumes.*

PENDENNIS. Edited by S. GWYNN. *Three Volumes.*

ESMOND. Edited by S. GWYNN.

CHRISTMAS BOOKS. Edited by S. GWYNN.

Vaughan (Henry). THE POEMS OF HENRY VAUGHAN. Edited by EDWARD HUTTON.

Walton (Izaak). THE COMPLEAT ANGLER. Edited by J. BUCHAN.

Waterhouse (Elizabeth). A LITTLE BOOK OF LIFE AND DEATH. Edited by. *Eleventh Edition.*

Wordsworth (W.). SELECTIONS FROM WORDSWORTH. Edited by NOWELL C. SMITH.

Wordsworth (W.) and **Coleridge (S. T.).** LYRICAL BALLADS. Edited by GEORGE SAMPSON.

The Little Quarto Shakespeare

Edited by W. J. CRAIG. With Introductions and Notes

Pott 16*mo.* *In* 40 *Volumes.* *Leather, price* 1*s. net each volume.*

Mahogany Revolving Book Case. 10*s. net.*

Miniature Library

Reprints in miniature of a few interesting books which have qualities of humanity, devotion, or literary genius.

EUPHRANOR: A Dialogue on Youth. By Edward FitzGerald. From the edition published by W. Pickering in 1851. *Demy* 32*mo. Leather*, 2*s. net.*

POLONIUS: or Wise Saws and Modern Instances. By Edward FitzGerald. From the edition published by W. Pickering in 1852. *Demy* 32*mo. Leather*, 2*s. net.*

THE RUBÁIYÁT OF OMAR KHAYYÁM. By Edward FitzGerald. From the 1st edition of 1859, *Fourth Edition. Leather*, 1*s. net.*

THE LIFE OF EDWARD, LORD HERBERT OF CHERBURY. Written by himself. From the edition printed at Strawberry Hill in the year 1764. *Demy* 32*mo. Leather*, 2*s. net.*

THE VISIONS OF DOM FRANCISCO QUEVEDO VILLEGAS, Knight of the Order of St. James. Made English by R. L. From the edition printed for H. Herringman, 1668. *Leather.* 2*s. net.*

POEMS. By Dora Greenwell. From the edition of 1848. *Leather*, 2*s net*

Oxford Biographies

Fcap. 8*vo.* *Each volume, cloth*, 2*s.* 6*d. net*; *leather*, 3*s.* 6*d. net.*

DANTE ALIGHIERI. By Paget Toynbee, M.A., D.Litt. With 12 Illustrations. *Third Edition.*

GIROLAMO SAVONAROLA. By E. L. S. Horsburgh, M.A. With 12 Illustrations. *Second Edition.*

JOHN HOWARD. By E. C. S. Gibson, D.D., Bishop of Gloucester. With 12 Illustrations.

ALFRED TENNYSON. By A. C. BENSON, M.A. With 9 Illustrations. *Second Edition.*

SIR WALTER RALEIGH. By I. A. Taylor. With 12 Illustrations.

ERASMUS. By E. F. H. Capey. With 12 Illustrations.

THE YOUNG PRETENDER. By C. S. Terry. With 12 Illustrations.

ROBERT BURNS. By T. F. Henderson. With 12 Illustrations.

CHATHAM. By A. S. M'Dowall. With 12 Illustrations.

FRANCIS OF ASSISI. By Anna M. Stoddart. With 16 Illustrations.

CANNING. By W. Alison Phillips. With 12 Illustrations.

BEACONSFIELD. By Walter Sichel. With 12 Illustrations.

JOHANN WOLFGANG GOETHE. By H. G. Atkins. With 16 Illustrations.

FRANÇOIS FENELON. By Viscount St Cyres. With 12 Illustrations.

School Examination Series

Edited by A. M. M. STEDMAN, M.A. *Cr. 8vo. 2s. 6d.*

FRENCH EXAMINATION PAPERS. By A. M. M. Stedman, M.A. *Fourteenth Edition.*
KEY. *Sixth Edition. 6s. net.*

LATIN EXAMINATION PAPERS. By A. M. M. Stedman, M.A. *Fourteenth Edition.*
KEY. *Sixth Edition. 6s. net.*

GREEK EXAMINATION PAPERS. By A. M. M. Stedman, M.A. *Ninth Edition.*
KEY. *Fourth Edition. 6s. net.*

GERMAN EXAMINATION PAPERS. By R. J. Morich. *Seventh Edition.*
KEY. *Third Edition. 6s. net.*

HISTORY AND GEOGRAPHY EXAMINATION PAPERS. By C. H. Spence, M.A. *Third Edition.*

PHYSICS EXAMINATION PAPERS. By R. E. Steel, M.A., F.C.S.

GENERAL KNOWLEDGE EXAMINATION PAPERS. By A. M. M. Stedman, M.A. *Sixth Edition.*
KEY. *Fourth Edition. 7s. net.*

EXAMINATION PAPERS IN ENGLISH HISTORY. By J. Tait Plowden-Wardlaw, B.A.

School Histories

Illustrated. Crown 8vo. 1s. 6d.

A SCHOOL HISTORY OF WARWICKSHIRE. By B. C. A. Windle, D.Sc., F.R.S.

A SCHOOL HISTORY OF SOMERSET. By Walter Raymond. *Second Edition.*

A SCHOOL HISTORY OF LANCASHIRE. By W. E. Rhodes.

A SCHOOL HISTORY OF SURREY. By H. E. Malden, M.A.

A SCHOOL HISTORY OF MIDDLESEX. By V. Plarr and F. W. Walton.

Methuen's Simplified French Texts

Edited by T. R. N. CROFTS, M.A.

One Shilling each.

L'HISTOIRE D'UNE TULIPE. Adapted by T. R. N. Crofts, M.A. *Second Edition.*

ABDALLAH. Adapted by J. A. Wilson.

LE DOCTEUR MATHÉUS. Adapted by W. P. Fuller.

LA BOUILLIE AU MIEL. Adapted by P. B. Ingham.

JEAN VALJEAN. Adapted by F. W. M. Draper.

LA CHANSON DE ROLAND. Adapted by H. Rieu, M.A. *Second Edition.*

MÉMOIRES DE CADICHON. Adapted by J. F. Rhoades.

L'EQUIPAGE DE LA BELLE-NIVERNAISE. Adapted by T. R. N. Crofts.

L'HISTOIRE DE PIERRE ET CAMILLE. Adapted by J. B. Patterson.

Methuen's Standard Library

Cloth, 1s. net; double volumes, 1s. 6d. net. Paper, 6d. net; double volume, 1s. net.

THE MEDITATIONS OF MARCUS AURELIUS. Translated by R. Graves.

SENSE AND SENSIBILITY. Jane Austen.

ESSAYS AND COUNSELS and THE NEW ATLANTIS. Francis Bacon, Lord Verulam.

RELIGIO MEDICI and URN BURIAL. Sir Thomas Browne. The text collated by A. R. Waller.

THE PILGRIM'S PROGRESS. John Bunyan.

REFLECTIONS ON THE FRENCH REVOLUTION. Edmund Burke.

THE POEMS AND SONGS OF ROBERT BURNS. Double Volume.

THE ANALOGY OF RELIGION, NATURAL AND REVEALED. Joseph Butler.

MISCELLANEOUS POEMS. T. CHATTERTON.

TOM JONES. Henry Fielding. Treble Vol.

CRANFORD. Mrs. Gaskell.

THE HISTORY OF THE DECLINE AND FALL OF THE ROMAN EMPIRE. E. Gibbon. Text and Notes revised by J. B. Bury. Seven double volumes.

THE CASE IS ALTERED. EVERY MAN IN HIS HUMOUR. EVERY MAN OUT OF HIS HUMOUR. Ben Jonson.

THE POEMS AND PLAYS OF OLIVER GOLDSMITH.

CYNTHIA'S REVELS. POETASTER. Ben Jonson.

THE POEMS OF JOHN KEATS. Double volume. The Text has been collated by E. de Sélincourt.

ON THE IMITATION OF CHRIST. By Thomas à Kempis. Translation by C. Bigg.

A SERIOUS CALL TO A DEVOUT AND HOLY LIFE. W. Law.

PARADISE LOST. John Milton.

EIKONOKLASTES AND THE TENURE OF KINGS AND MAGISTRATES. John Milton.

UTOPIA AND POEMS. Sir Thomas More.

THE REPUBLIC OF PLATO. Translated by Sydenham and Taylor. Double Volume. Translation revised by W. H. D. Rouse.

THE LITTLE FLOWERS OF ST. FRANCIS. Translated by W. Heywood.

THE WORKS OF WILLIAM SHAKESPEARE. In 10 volumes.

PRINCIPAL POEMS, 1815-1818. Percy Bysshe Shelley. With an Introduction by C. D. Locock.

THE LIFE OF NELSON. Robert Southey.

THE NATURAL HISTORY AND ANTIQUITIES OF SELBORNE. Gilbert White.

Textbooks of Science

Edited by G. F. GOODCHILD, M.A., B.Sc., and G. R. MILLS, M.A.

Fully Illustrated.

PRACTICAL MECHANICS. S. H. Wells. *Fourth Edition. Cr. 8vo.* 3*s.* 6*d.*

PRACTICAL CHEMISTRY. Part I. W. French, M.A. *Cr. 8vo. Fourth Edition.* 1*s.* 6*d.*

PRACTICAL CHEMISTRY. Part II. W. French and T. H. Boardman. *Cr. 8vo.* 1*s.* 6*d.*

EXAMPLES IN PHYSICS. By C. E. Jackson, B.A. *Cr. 8vo.* 2*s.* 6*d.*

TECHNICAL ARITHMETIC AND GEOMETRY. By C. T. Millis, M.I.M.E. *Cr. 8vo.* 3*s.* 6*d.*

PLANT LIFE, Studies in Garden and School. By Horace F. Jones, F.C.S. With 320 Diagrams. *Cr. 8vo.* 3*s.* 6*d.*

THE COMPLETE SCHOOL CHEMISTRY. By F. M. Oldham, B.A. With 126 Illustrations. *Cr. 8vo.* 4*s.* 6*d.*

ELEMENTARY SCIENCE FOR PUPIL TEACHERS. PHYSICS SECTION. By W. T. Clough, A.R.C.S. (Lond.), F.C.S. CHEMISTRY SECTION. By A. E. Dunstan, B.Sc. (Lond.), F.C.S. With 2 Plates and 10 Diagrams. *Cr. 8vo.* 2*s.*

EXAMPLES IN ELEMENTARY MECHANICS, Practical, Graphical, and Theoretical. By W. J. Dobbs, M.A. With 51 Diagrams. *Cr. 8vo.* 5*s.*

OUTLINES OF PHYSICAL CHEMISTRY. By George Senter, B.Sc. (Lond.), Ph.D. With many Diagrams. *Cr. 8vo.* 3*s.* 6*d.*

AN ORGANIC CHEMISTRY FOR SCHOOLS AND TECHNICAL INSTITUTES. By A. E. Dunstan, B.Sc. (Lond.), F.C.S. With many Illustrations. *Cr. 8vo.* 2*s.* 6*d.*

FIRST YEAR PHYSICS. By C. E. Jackson, M.A. With 51 diagrams. *Cr. 8vo.* 1*s.* 6*d.*

Textbooks of Technology

Edited by G. F. GOODCHILD, M.A., B.Sc., and G. R. MILLS, M.A.

Fully Illustrated.

HOW TO MAKE A DRESS. By J. A. E. Wood. *Fourth Edition. Cr. 8vo.* 1*s.* 6*d.*

CARPENTRY AND JOINERY. By F. C. Webber. *Fifth Edition. Cr. 8vo.* 3*s.* 6*d.*

MILLINERY, THEORETICAL AND PRACTICAL. By Clare Hill. *Fourth Edition. Cr. 8vo.* 2*s.*

INSTRUCTION IN COOKERY. A. P. THOMSON. 2*s.* 6*d.*

AN INTRODUCTION TO THE STUDY OF TEXTILE DESIGN. By Aldred F. Barker. *Demy 8vo.* 7*s.* 6*d.*

BUILDERS' QUANTITIES. By H. C. Grubb. *Cr. 8vo.* 4*s.* 6*d.*

RÉPOUSSÉ METAL WORK. By A. C. Horth. *Cr. 8vo.* 2*s.* 6*d.*

ELECTRIC LIGHT AND POWER: An Introduction to the Study of Electrical Engineering. By E. E. Brooks, B.Sc. (Lond.), and W. H. N. James, A.R.C.S., A.I.E.E. *Cr. 8vo.* 4*s.* 6*d.*

ENGINEERING WORKSHOP PRACTICE. By C. C. Allen. *Cr 8vo.* 3*s.* 6*d.*

Handbooks of Theology

THE XXXIX. ARTICLES OF THE CHURCH OF ENGLAND. Edited by E. C. S. Gibson, D.D. *Sixth Edition. Demy 8vo.* 12*s.* 6*d.*

AN INTRODUCTION TO THE HISTORY OF RELIGION. By F. B. Jevons. M.A., Litt.D. *Fourth Edition. Demy 8vo.* 10*s.* 6*d.*

THE DOCTRINE OF THE INCARNATION. By R. L. Ottley, D.D. *Fourth Edition revised. Demy 8vo.* 12*s.* 6*d.*

AN INTRODUCTION TO THE HISTORY OF THE CREEDS. By A. E. Burn, D.D. *Demy 8vo.* 10*s.* 6*d.*

THE PHILOSOPHY OF RELIGION IN ENGLAND AND AMERICA. By Alfred Caldecott, D.D. *Demy 8vo.* 10*s.* 6*d.*

A HISTORY OF EARLY CHRISTIAN DOCTRINE. By J. F. Bethune-Baker, M.A. *Demy 8vo.* 10*s.* 6*d.*

The Westminster Commentaries

General Editor, WALTER LOCK, D.D., Warden of Keble College, Dean Ireland's Professor of Exegesis in the University of Oxford.

THE BOOK OF GENESIS. Edited with Introduction and Notes by S. R. Driver, D.D. *Sixth Edition Demy 8vo.* 10*s.* 6*d.*

THE BOOK OF JOB. Edited by E. C. S. Gibson, D.D. *Second Edition. Demy 8vo.* 6*s.*

THE ACTS OF THE APOSTLES. Edited by R. B. Rackham, M.A. *Demy 8vo. Third Edition.* 10*s.* 6*d.*

THE FIRST EPISTLE OF PAUL THE APOSTLE TO THE CORINTHIANS. Edited by H. L. Goudge, M.A. *Demy 8vo.* 6*s.*

THE EPISTLE OF ST. JAMES. Edited with Introduction and Notes by R. J. Knowling, D.D. *Demy 8vo.* 6*s.*

THE BOOK OF EZEKIEL. Edited H. A. Redpath, M.A., D.Litt. *Demy 8vo.* 10*s.* 6*d.*

A COMMENTARY ON EXODUS. By A. H. M'Neile, B.D. With a Map and 3 Plans. *Demy 8vo.* 10*s.* 6*d.*

PART II.—FICTION

Albanesi (E. Maria). SUSANNAH AND ONE OTHER. *Fourth Edition. Cr. 8vo.* 6s.
THE BLUNDER OF AN INNOCENT. *Second Edition. Cr. 8vo.* 6s.
CAPRICIOUS CAROLINE. *Second Edition. Cr. 8vo.* 6s.
LOVE AND LOUISA. *Second Edition. Cr. 8vo.* 6s. Also *Medium 8vo.* 6d.
PETER, A PARASITE. *Cr. 8vo.* 6s.
THE BROWN EYES OF MARY. *Third Edition. Cr. 8vo.* 6s.
I KNOW A MAIDEN. *Third Edition. Cr. 8vo.* 6s. Also *Medium 8vo.* 6d.
Austen (Jane). PRIDE AND PREJUDICE. *Medium 8vo.* 6d.
Bagot (Richard). A ROMAN MYSTERY. *Third Edition. Cr. 8vo.* 6s. Also *Medium 8vo.* 6d.
THE PASSPORT. *Fourth Edition. Cr. 8vo.* 6s.
TEMPTATION. *Fifth Edition. Cr. 8vo.* 6s.
LOVE'S PROXY. *A New Edition. Cr. 8vo.* 6s.
DONNA DIANA. *Second Edition. Cr. 8vo.* 6s.
CASTING OF NETS. *Twelfth Edition. Cr. 8vo.* 6s. Also *Medium 8vo.* 6d.
Balfour (Andrew). BY STROKE OF SWORD. *Medium 8vo.* 6d.
Baring-Gould (S.). ARMINELL. *Fifth Edition. Cr. 8vo.* 6s.
URITH. *Fifth Edition. Cr. 8vo.* 6s. Also *Medium 8vo.* 6d.
IN THE ROAR OF THE SEA. *Seventh Edition. Cr. 8vo.* 6s. Also *Medium 8vo.* 6d.
MARGERY OF QUETHER. *Third Edition. Cr. 8vo.* 6s.
THE QUEEN OF LOVE. *Fifth Edition. Cr. 8vo.* 6s. Also *Medium 8vo.* 6d.
JACQUETTA. *Third Edition. Cr. 8vo.* 6s.
KITTY ALONE. *Fifth Edition. Cr. 8vo.* 6s. Also *Medium 8vo.* 6d.
NOÉMI. Illustrated. *Fourth Edition. Cr. 8vo.* 6s. Also *Medium 8vo.* 6d.
THE BROOM-SQUIRE. Illustrated. *Fifth Edition. Cr. 8vo.* 6s. Also *Medium 8vo.* 6d.
DARTMOOR IDYLLS. *Cr. 8vo.* 6s.
THE PENNYCOMEQUICKS. *Third Edition. Cr. 8vo.* 6s.
GUAVAS THE TINNER. Illustrated. *Second Edition. Cr. 8vo.* 6s.
BLADYS OF THE STEWPONEY. Illustrated. *Second Edition. Cr. 8vo.* 6s.
PABO THE PRIEST. *Cr. 8vo.* 6s.
WINEFRED. Illustrated. *Second Edition. Cr. 8vo.* 6s. Also *Medium 8vo.* 6d.
ROYAL GEORGIE. Illustrated. *Cr. 8vo.* 6s.
CHRIS OF ALL SORTS. *Cr. 8vo.* 6s.
IN DEWISLAND. *Second Ed. Cr. 8vo.* 6s.
THE FROBISHERS. *Crown 8vo.* 6s. Also *Medium 8vo.* 6d.
DOMITIA. Illus. *Second Ed. Cr.* 8vo. 6s.
MRS. CURGENVEN OF CURGENVEN. *Crown 8vo.* 6s.
LITTLE TU'PENNY. *A New Edition. Medium 8vo.* 6d.
FURZE BLOOM. *Medium 8vo.* 6d.
Barnett (Edith A.). A WILDERNESS WINNER. *Second Edition. Cr. 8vo.* 6s.
Barr (James). LAUGHING THROUGH A WILDERNESS. *Cr. 8vo.* 6s.
Barr (Robert). IN THE MIDST OF ALARMS. *Third Edition. Cr. 8vo.* 6s. Also *Medium 8vo.* 6d.
THE COUNTESS TEKLA. *Fourth Edition. Cr. 8vo.* 6s. Also *Medium 8vo.* 6d.
THE MUTABLE MANY. *Third Edition. Cr. 8vo.* 6s. Also *Medium 8vo.* 6d.
THE TEMPESTUOUS PETTICOAT. Illustrated. *Third Edition. Cr. 8vo.* 6s.
THE STRONG ARM. *Second Edition. Cr. 8vo.* 6s.
JENNIE BAXTER JOURNALIST. *Medium 8vo.* 6d.
Begbie (Harold). THE CURIOUS AND DIVERTING ADVENTURES OF SIR JOHN SPARROW; or, THE PROGRESS OF AN OPEN MIND. With a Frontispiece. *Second Edition. Cr. 8vo.* 6s.
Belloc (Hilaire), M.P. EMMANUEL BURDEN, MERCHANT. With 36 Illustrations by G. K. CHESTERTON. *Second Ed. Cr. 8vo.* 6s.
Benson (E. F.) DODO: A DETAIL OF THE DAY. *Fifteenth Edition. Cr. 8vo.* 6s. Also *Medium 8vo.* 6d.
THE VINTAGE. *Medium 8vo.* 6d.
Benson (Margaret). SUBJECT TO VANITY. *Cr. 8vo.* 3s. 6d.
Birmingham (George A.). THE BAD TIMES. *Second Edition. Crown 8vo.* 6s.
Bowles (G. Stewart). A GUN-ROOM DITTY BOX. *Second Ed. Cr. 8vo.* 1s. 6d.
Bretherton (Ralph Harold). THE MILL. *Cr. 8vo.* 6s.
Brontë (Charlotte). SHIRLEY. *Medium 8vo.* 6d.
Burke (Barbara). BARBARA GOES TO OXFORD. With 16 Illustrations. *Third Edition. Cr. 8vo.* 6s.
Burton (J. Bloundelle). ACROSS THE SALT SEAS. *Medium 8vo.* 6d.
Caffyn (Mrs.) ('Iota'). ANNE MAULEVERER. *Medium 8vo.* 6d.
Campbell (Mrs. Vere). FERRIBY. *Second Edition. Cr. 8vo.* 6s.

Capes (Bernard). THE EXTRAORDINARY CONFESSIONS OF DIANA PLEASE. *Third Edition. Cr. 8vo.* 6s.
A JAY OF ITALY. *Fourth Ed. Cr. 8vo.* 6s.
LOAVES AND FISHES. *Second Edition. Cr. 8vo.* 6s.
A ROGUE'S TRAGEDY. *Second Edition. Cr. 8vo.* 6s.
THE GREAT SKENE MYSTERY. *Second Edition. Cr. 8vo.* 6s.
THE LAKE OF WINE. *Medium 8vo.* 6d.
Carey (Wymond). LOVE THE JUDGE. *Second Edition. Cr. 8vo.* 6s.
Castle (Agnes and Egerton). FLOWER O' THE ORANGE, and Other Tales. With a Frontispiece in Colour by A. H. Buckland. *Third Edition. Cr. 8vo.* 6s.
Charlton (Randal). MAVE. *Second Edition. Cr. 8vo.* 6s.
THE VIRGIN WIDOW. *Cr. 8vo.* 6s.
Chesney (Weatherby). THE TRAGEDY OF THE GREAT EMERALD *Cr. 8vo.* 6s.
THE MYSTERY OF A BUNGALOW. *Second Edition. Cr. 8vo.* 6s.
Clifford (Mrs. W. K.). THE GETTING WELL OF DOROTHY. Illustrated by GORDON BROWNE. *Second Edition. Cr. 8vo.* 3s. 6d.
A FLASH OF SUMMER. *Medium 8vo.* 6d.
MRS. KEITH'S CRIME. *Medium 8vo.* 6d.
Conrad (Joseph). THE SECRET AGENT: A Simple Tale. *Fourth Ed. Cr. 8vo.* 6s.
Corbett (Julian). A BUSINESS IN GREAT WATERS. *Medium 8vo.* 6d.
Corelli (Marie). A ROMANCE OF TWO WORLDS. *Twenty-Ninth Ed. Cr. 8vo.* 6s.
VENDETTA. *Twenty-Sixth Ed. Cr. 8vo.* 6s.
THELMA. *Thirty-Eighth Ed. Cr. 8vo.* 6s.
ARDATH: THE STORY OF A DEAD SELF. *Eighteenth Edition. Cr. 8vo.* 6s.
THE SOUL OF LILITH. *Fifteenth Edition. Cr. 8vo.* 6s.
WORMWOOD. *Sixteenth Ed. Cr. 8vo.* 6s.
BARABBAS: A DREAM OF THE WORLD'S TRAGEDY. *Forty-Third Edition. Cr. 8vo.* 6s.
THE SORROWS OF SATAN. *Fifty-Fourth Edition. Cr. 8vo.* 6s.
THE MASTER CHRISTIAN. *Eleventh Edition. 174th Thousand. Cr. 8vo.* 6s.
TEMPORAL POWER: A STUDY IN SUPREMACY. *150th Thousand. Cr. 8vo.* 6s
GOD'S GOOD MAN: A SIMPLE LOVE STORY. *Thirteenth Edition.* 150th Thousand. *Cr. 8vo.* 6s.
THE MIGHTY ATOM. *Twenty-seventh Edition. Cr. 8vo.* 6s.
BOY: a Sketch. *Tenth Edition. Cr. 8vo.* 6s.
CAMEOS. *Thirteenth Edition. Cr. 8vo.* 6s.
Cotes (Mrs. Everard). See Sara Jeannette Duncan.
Cotterell (Constance). THE VIRGIN AND THE SCALES. Illustrated. *Second Edition. Cr. 8vo.* 6s.
Crockett (S. R.). Author of 'The Raiders,' etc. LOCHINVAR. Illustrated. *Third Edition. Cr. 8vo.* 6s.
THE STANDARD BEARER. *Cr. 8vo.* 6s.
Croker (B. M.). THE OLD CANTONMENT. *Cr. 8vo.* 6s.
JOHANNA. *Second Edition. Cr. 8vo.* 6s. Also *Medium 8vo.* 6d.
THE HAPPY VALLEY. *Fourth Edition. Cr. 8vo.* 6s.
A NINE DAYS' WONDER. *Third Edition. Cr. 8vo.* 6s.
PEGGY OF THE BARTONS. *Seventh Ed. Cr. 8vo.* 6s. Also *Medium 8vo.* 6d.
ANGEL. *Fourth Edition. Cr. 8vo.* 6s. Also *Medium 8vo.* 6d.
A STATE SECRET. *Third Edition. Cr. 8vo.* 3s. 6d. Also *Medium 8vo.* 6d.
Crosbie (Mary). DISCIPLES. *Second Ed. Cr. 8vo.* 6s.
Cuthell (Edith E.). ONLY A GUARD-ROOM DOG. Illustrated by W. PARKINSON. *Crown 8vo.* 3s. 6d.
Dawson (Warrington). THE SCAR. *Second Edition. Cr. 8vo.* 6s.
THE SCOURGE *Cr. 8vo.* 6s.
Deakin (Dorothea). THE YOUNG COLUMBINE. With a Frontispiece by LEWIS BAUMER. *Cr. 8vo.* 6s.
Deane (Mary). THE OTHER PAWN. *Cr. 8vo.* 6s.
Doyle (A. Conan). ROUND THE RED LAMP. *Tenth Edition. Cr. 8vo.* 6s. Also *Medium 8vo.* 6d.
Dumas (Alexandre). See page 39.
Duncan (Sara Jeannette) (Mrs. Everard Cotes). THOSE DELIGHTFUL AMERICANS. *Medium 8vo.* 6d.
A VOYAGE OF CONSOLATION. Illustrated. *Third Edition. Cr. 8vo.* 6s. Also *Medium 8vo.* 6d.
Eliot (George). THE MILL ON THE FLOSS. *Medium 8vo.* 6d.
Erskine (Mrs. Steuart). THE MAGIC PLUMES. *Cr. 8vo.* 6s.
Fenn (G. Manville). SYD BELTON; or, The Boy who would not go to Sea. Illustrated by GORDON BROWNE. *Second Ed. Cr. 8vo.* 3s. 6d.
Findlater (J. H.). THE GREEN GRAVES OF BALGOWRIE. *Fifth Edition. Cr. 8vo.* 6s. Also *Medium 8vo.* 6d.
THE LADDER TO THE STARS. *Second Edition. Cr. 8vo.* 6s.
Findlater (Mary). A NARROW WAY. *Third Edition. Cr. 8vo..* 6s.
OVER THE HILLS. *Cr. 8vo.* 6s.
THE ROSE OF JOY. *Third Edition. Cr. 8vo.* 6s.
A BLIND BIRD'S NEST. With 8 Illustrations. *Second Edition. Cr. 8vo.* 6s.
Fitzpatrick (K.) THE WEANS AT ROWALLAN. Illustrated. *Second Edition. Cr. 8vo.* 6s.
Francis (M. E.). (Mrs. Francis Blundell). STEPPING WESTWARD. *Second Edition. Cr. 8vo.* 6s.
MARGERY O' THE MILL. *Third Edition. Cr. 8vo.* 6s.
Fraser (Mrs. Hugh). THE SLAKING OF THE SWORD. *Second Edition. Cr. 8vo.* 6s.

IN THE SHADOW OF THE LORD. *Third Edition. Crown* 8vo. 6s.

Fry (B. and C.B.). A MOTHER'S SON. *Fifth Edition. Cr.* 8vo. 6s.

Fuller-Maitland (Ella). BLANCHE ESMEAD. *Second Edition. Cr.* 8vo. 6s.

Gallon (Tom). RICKERBY'S FOLLY. *Medium* 8vo. 6d.

Gaskell (Mrs.). CRANFORD. *Medium* 8vo. 6d.

MARY BARTON. *Medium* 8vo. 6d.

NORTH AND SOUTH. *Medium* 8vo. 6d.

Gates (Eleanor). THE PLOW-WOMAN. *Cr.* 8vo. 6s.

Gerard (Dorothea). HOLY MATRIMONY. *Medium* 8vo. 6d.

MADE OF MONEY. *Cr.* 8vo. 6s.
Also *Medium* 8vo. 6d.

THE IMPROBABLE IDYL. *Third Edition. Cr.* 8vo. 6s.

THE BRIDGE OF LIFE. *Cr.* 8vo. 6s.

THE CONQUEST OF LONDON. *Medium* 8vo. 6d.

Gissing (George). THE TOWN TRAVELLER. *Second Edition. Cr.* 8vo. 6s.
Also *Medium* 8vo. 6d.

THE CROWN OF LIFE. *Cr.* 8vo. 6s.
Also *Medium* 8vo. 6d.

Glanville (Ernest). THE INCA'S TREASURE. Illustrated. *Cr.* 8vo. 3s. 6d.
Also *Medium* 8vo. 6d.

THE KLOOF BRIDE. Illustrated. *Cr.* 8vo. 3s. 6d. Also *Medium* 8vo. 6d.

Gleig (Charles). BUNTER'S CRUISE. Illustrated. *Cr.* 8vo. 3s. 6d.
Also *Medium* 8vo. 6d.

Grimm (The Brothers). GRIMM'S FAIRY TALES. Illustrated. *Medium* 8vo. 6d.

Hamilton (M.). THE FIRST CLAIM. *Second Edition. Cr.* 8vo. 6s.

Harraden (Beatrice). IN VARYING MOODS. *Fourteenth Edition. Cr.* 8vo. 6s.

THE SCHOLAR'S DAUGHTER. *Fourth Edition. Cr.* 8vo. 6s.

HILDA STRAFFORD and THE REMITTANCE MAN. *Twelfth Ed. Cr.* 8vo. 6s.

Harrod (F.) (Frances Forbes Robertson). THE TAMING OF THE BRUTE. *Cr.* 8vo. 6s.

Herbertson (Agnes G.). PATIENCE DEAN. *Cr.* 8vo. 6s.

Hichens (Robert). THE PROPHET OF BERKELEY SQUARE. *Second Edition. Cr.* 8vo. 6s.

TONGUES OF CONSCIENCE. *Third Edition. Cr.* 8vo. 6s.

FELIX. *Sixth Edition. Cr.* 8vo. 6s.

THE WOMAN WITH THE FAN. *Sixth Edition. Cr.* 8vo. 6s.

BYEWAYS. *Cr.* 8vo. 6s.

THE GARDEN OF ALLAH. *Seventeenth Edition. Cr.* 8vo. 6s.

THE BLACK SPANIEL. *Cr.* 8vo. 6s.

THE CALL OF THE BLOOD. *Seventh Edition. Cr.* 8vo. 6s.

Hope (Anthony). THE GOD IN THE CAR. *Tenth Edition. Cr.* 8vo. 6s.

A CHANGE OF AIR. *Sixth Ed. Cr.* 8vo. 6s.
Also *Medium* 8vo. 6d.

A MAN OF MARK. *Fifth Ed. Cr.* 8vo. 6s.
Also *Medium* 8vo. 6d.

THE CHRONICLES OF COUNT ANTONIO. *Sixth Edition. Cr.* 8vo. 6s.
Also *Medium* 8vo. 6d.

PHROSO. Illustrated by H. R. MILLAR. *Seventh Edition. Cr.* 8vo. 6s.
Also *Medium* 8vo. 6d.

SIMON DALE. Illustrated. *Eighth Edition. Cr.* 8vo. 6s.

THE KING'S MIRROR. *Fourth Edition. Cr.* 8vo. 6s.

QUISANTE. *Fourth Edition. Cr.* 8vo. 6s.

THE DOLLY DIALOGUES. *Cr.* 8vo. 6s.
Also *Medium* 8vo. 6d.

A SERVANT OF THE PUBLIC. Illustrated. *Fourth Edition. Cr.* 8vo. 6s.

TALES OF TWO PEOPLE. With a Frontispiece by A. H. BUCKLAND. *Third Ed. Cr.* 8vo. 6s.

Hope (Graham). THE LADY OF LYTE. *Second Edition. Cr.* 8vo. 6s.

Hornung (E. W.). DEAD MEN TELL NO TALES. *Medium* 8vo. 6d.

Housman (Clemence). THE LIFE OF SIR AGLOVALE DE GALIS. *Cr.* 8vo. 6s.

Hueffer (Ford Madox). AN ENGLISH GIRL: A ROMANCE. *Second Edition. Cr.* 8vo. 6s.

Hutten (Baroness von). THE HALO. *Fifth Edition. Cr.* 8vo. 6s.

Hyne (C. J. Cutcliffe). MR. HORROCKS, PURSER. *Fourth Edition. Cr.* 8vo. 6s.

PRINCE RUPERT, THE BUCCANEER. Illustrated. *Third Edition. Cr.* 8vo. 6s.

Ingraham (J. H.). THE THRONE OF DAVID. *Medium* 8vo. 6d.

Jacobs (W. W.). MANY CARGOES. *Thirtieth Edition. Cr.* 8vo. 3s. 6d.

SEA URCHINS. *Fifteenth Edition.. Cr.* 8vo. 3s. 6d.

A MASTER OF CRAFT. Illustrated by WILL OWEN. *Eighth Edition. Cr.* 8vo. 3s. 6d.

LIGHT FREIGHTS. Illustrated by WILL OWEN and Others. *Seventh Edition. Cr.* 8vo. 3s. 6d.

THE SKIPPER'S WOOING. *Ninth Edition. Cr.* 8vo. 3s. 6d.

AT SUNWICH PORT. Illustrated by WILL OWEN. *Ninth Edition. Cr.* 8vo. 3s. 6d.

DIALSTONE LANE. Illustrated by WILL OWEN. *Seventh Edition. Cr.* 8vo. 3s. 6d.

ODD CRAFT. Illustrated by WILL OWEN. *Seventh Edition. Cr.* 8vo. 3s. 6d.

THE LADY OF THE BARGE. *Eighth Edition. Cr.* 8vo. 3s. 6d.

James (Henry). THE SOFT SIDE. *Second Edition. Cr.* 8vo. 6s.

THE BETTER SORT. *Cr.* 8vo. 6s.

THE AMBASSADORS. *Second Edition. Cr.* 8vo. 6s.

THE GOLDEN BOWL. *Third Edition. Cr.* 8vo. 6s.

Keays (H. A. Mitchell). HE THAT EATETH BREAD WITH ME. *Cr.* 8vo. 6s.

Kester (Vaughan). THE FORTUNES OF THE LANDRAYS. Illustrated. *Cr. 8vo.* 6*s.*

Lawless (Hon. Emily). WITH ESSEX IN IRELAND. *Cr. 8vo.* 6*s.*

Le Queux (William). THE HUNCHBACK OF WESTMINSTER. *Third Ed. Cr. 8vo.* 6*s.*
Also *Medium 8vo.* 6*d.*

THE CROOKED WAY. *Second Edition. Cr. 8vo.* 6*s.*

THE CLOSED BOOK. *Third Ed. Cr. 8vo.* 6*s.*

THE VALLEY OF THE SHADOW. Illustrated. *Third Edition. Cr. 8vo.* 6*s.*

BEHIND THE THRONE. *Third Edition. Cr. 8vo.* 6*s.*

Levett-Yeats (S. K.). ORRAIN. *Second Edition. Cr. 8vo.* 6*s.*

THE TRAITOR'S WAY. *Medium 8vo.* 6*d.*

Linton (E. Lynn). THE TRUE HISTORY OF JOSHUA DAVIDSON. *Medium 8vo.* 6*d.*

London (Jack). WHITE FANG. With a Frontispiece by CHARLES RIVINGSTON BULL. *Sixth Edition. Cr. 8vo.* 6*s.*

Lucas (E. V.). LISTENER'S LURE: An Oblique Narration. *Fourth Edition. Cr. 8vo.* 6*s.*

Lyall (Edna). DERRICK VAUGHAN, NOVELIST. *42nd Thousand. Cr. 8vo.* 3*s.* 6*d.* Also *Medium 8vo.* 6*d.*

Maartens (Maarten). THE NEW RELIGION: A MODERN NOVEL. *Third Edition. Cr. 8vo.* 6*s.*

M'Carthy (Justin H.). THE LADY OF LOYALTY HOUSE. Illustrated. *Third Edition. Cr. 8vo.* 6*s.*

THE DRYAD. *Second Edition. Cr. 8vo.* 6*s.*

THE DUKE'S MOTTO. *Third Edition. Cr. 8vo.* 6*s.*

Macdonald (Ronald). A HUMAN TRINITY. *Second Edition Cr. 8vo.* 6*s.*

Macnaughtan (S.). THE FORTUNE OF CHRISTINA M'NAB. *Fourth Edition. Cr. 8vo.* 6*s.*

Malet (Lucas). COLONEL ENDERBY'S WIFE. *Fourth Edition. Cr. 8vo.* 6*s.*

A COUNSEL OF PERFECTION. *New Edition. Cr. 8vo.* 6*s.*
Also *Medium 8vo.* 6*d.*

THE WAGES OF SIN. *Fifteenth Edition. Cr. 8vo.* 6*s.*

THE CARISSIMA. *Fifth Ed. Cr. 8vo.* 6*s.*
Also *Medium 8vo.* 6*d.*

THE GATELESS BARRIER. *Fifth Edition. Cr. 8vo.* 6*s.*

THE HISTORY OF SIR RICHARD CALMADY. *Seventh Edition. Cr. 8vo.* 6*s.*

Mann (Mrs. M. E.). OLIVIA'S SUMMER. *Second Edition. Cr. 8vo.* 6*s.*

A LOST ESTATE. *A New Ed. Cr. 8vo.* 6*s.*
Also *Medium 8vo.* 6*d.*

THE PARISH OF HILBY. *A New Edition. Cr. 8vo.* 6*s.*

THE PARISH NURSE. *Fourth Edition. Cr. 8vo.* 6*s.*

GRAN'MA'S JANE. *Cr. 8vo.* 6*s.*

MRS. PETER HOWARD. *Cr. 8vo.* 6*s.*
Also *Medium 8vo.* 6*d.*

A WINTER'S TALE. *A New Edition. Cr. 8vo.* 6*s.*

ONE ANOTHER'S BURDENS. *A New Edition. Cr. 8vo.* 6*s.*
Also *Medium 8vo.* 6*d.*

ROSE AT HONEYPOT. *Third Ed. Cr. 8vo.* 6*s.*

THERE WAS ONCE A PRINCE. Illustrated by M. B. MANN. *Cr. 8vo.* 3*s.* 6*d.*

WHEN ARNOLD COMES HOME. Illustrated by M. B. MANN. *Cr. 8vo.* 3*s.* 6*d.*

THE EGLAMORE PORTRAITS. *Third Edition. Cr. 8vo.* 6*s.*

THE MEMORIES OF RONALD LOVE. *Cr. 8vo.* 6*s.*

THE SHEEP AND THE GOATS. *Third Edition. Cr. 8vo.* 6*s.*

A SHEAF OF CORN. *Second Edition. Cr. 8vo.* 6*s.*

THE CEDAR STAR. *Medium 8vo.* 6*d.*

Marchmont (A. W.). MISER HOADLEY'S SECRET. *Medium 8vo.* 6*d.*

A MOMENT'S ERROR. *Medium 8vo.* 6*d.*

Marriott (Charles). GENEVRA. *Second Edition. Cr. 8vo.* 6*s.*

Marryat (Captain). PETER SIMPLE *Medium 8vo.* 6*d.*

JACOB FAITHFUL. *Medium 8vo.* 6*d.*

Marsh (Richard). THE TWICKENHAM PEERAGE. *Second Edition. Cr. 8vo.* 6*s.*
Also *Medium 8vo.* 6*d.*

THE MARQUIS OF PUTNEY. *Second Edition. Cr. 8vo.* 6*s.*

IN THE SERVICE OF LOVE. *Third. Edition. Cr. 8vo.* 6*s.*

THE GIRL AND THE MIRACLE. *Third Edition. Cr. 8vo.* 6*s.*

THE COWARD BEHIND THE CURTAIN. *Cr. 8vo.* 6*s.*

A METAMORPHOSIS. *Medium 8vo.* 6*d.*

THE GODDESS. *Medium 8vo.* 6*d.*

THE JOSS. *Medium 8vo.* 6*d.*

Marshall (Archibald). MANY JUNES. *Second Edition. Cr. 8vo.* 6*s.*

Mason (A. E. W.). CLEMENTINA. Illustrated. *Second Edition. Cr. 8vo.* 6*s.*
Also *Medium 8vo.* 6*d.*

Mathers (Helen). HONEY. *Fourth Ed. Cr. 8vo.* 6*s.* Also *Medium 8vo.* 6*d.*

GRIFF OF GRIFFITHSCOURT. *Cr. 8vo.* 6*s.* Also *Medium 8vo.* 6*d.*

THE FERRYMAN *Second Edition. Cr. 8vo.* 6*s.*

TALLY-HO! *Fourth Edition. Cr. 8vo.* 6*s.*

SAM'S SWEETHEART. *Medium 8vo.* 6*d.*

Maxwell (W. B.). VIVIEN. *Ninth Edition. Cr. 8vo.* 6*s.*

THE RAGGED MESSENGER. *Third Edition. Cr. 8vo.* 6*s.*

FABULOUS FANCIES. *Cr. 8vo.* 6*s.*

THE GUARDED FLAME. *Seventh Edition. Cr. 8vo.* 6*s.*

ODD LENGTHS. *Second Ed. Cr. 8vo.* 6*s.*

THE COUNTESS OF MAYBURY: BETWEEN YOU AND I. Being the Intimate Conversations of the Right Hon. the Countess of Maybury. *Fourth Edition. Cr. 8vo.* 6*s.*

Meade (L. T.). DRIFT. *Second Edition. Cr. 8vo.* 6s. Also *Medium 8vo.* 6d.
RESURGAM. *Cr. 8vo.* 6s.
VICTORY. *Cr. 8vo.* 6s.
A GIRL OF THE PEOPLE. Illustrated by R. BARNET. *Second Ed. Cr. 8vo.* 3s. 6d.
HEPSY GIPSY. Illustrated by E. HOPKINS. *Crown 8vo.* 2s. 6d.
THE HONOURABLE MISS: A STORY OF AN OLD-FASHIONED TOWN. Illustrated by E. HOPKINS. *Second Edition. Crown 8vo.* 3s. 6d.

Melton (R.). CÆSAR'S WIFE. *Second Edition. Cr. 8vo.* 6s.

Meredith (Ellis). HEART OF MY HEART. *Cr. 8vo.* 6s.

Miller (Esther). LIVING LIES. *Third Edition. Cr. 8vo.* 6s.

Mitford (Bertram). THE SIGN OF THE SPIDER. Illustrated. *Sixth Edition. Cr. 8vo.* 3s. 6d. Also *Medium 8vo.* 6d.
IN THE WHIRL OF THE RISING. *Third Edition. Cr. 8vo.* 6s.
THE RED DERELICT. *Second Edition. Cr. 8vo.* 6s.

Molesworth (Mrs.). THE RED GRANGE. Illustrated by GORDON BROWNE. *Second Edition. Cr. 8vo.* 3s. 6d.

Montgomery (K. L.). COLONEL KATE. *Third Edition. Cr. 8vo.* 6s.

Montresor (F. F.). THE ALIEN. *Third Edition. Cr. 8vo.* 6s.
Also *Medium 8vo.* 6d.

Morrison (Arthur). TALES OF MEAN STREETS. *Seventh Edition. Cr. 8vo.* 6s.
A CHILD OF THE JAGO. *Fifth Edition. Cr. 8vo.* 6s.
CUNNING MURRELL. *Cr. 8vo.* 6s.
THE HOLE IN THE WALL. *Fourth Edition. Cr. 8vo.* 6s. Also *Medium 8vo.* 6d.
DIVERS VANITIES. *Cr. 8vo.* 6s.

Nesbit (E.). (Mrs. H. Bland). THE RED HOUSE. Illustrated. *Fourth Edition. Cr. 8vo.* 6s. Also *Medium 8vo.* 6d.

Norris (W. E.). HARRY AND URSULA: A STORY WITH TWO SIDES TO IT. *Second Edition. Cr. 8vo.* 6s.
HIS GRACE. *Medium 8vo.* 6d.
GILES INGILBY. *Medium 8vo.* 6d.
THE CREDIT OF THE COUNTY. *Medium 8vo.* 6d.
LORD LEONARD THE LUCKLESS. *Medium 8vo.* 6d.
MATTHEW AUSTIN. *Medium 8vo.* 6d.
CLARISSA FURIOSA. *Medium 8vo.* 6d.

Oliphant (Mrs.). THE LADY'S WALK. *Medium 8vo.* 6d.
SIR ROBERT'S FORTUNE. *Medium 8vo.* 6d.
THE PRODIGALS. *Medium 8vo.* 6d.
THE TWO MARYS. *Medium 8vo.* 6d.

Ollivant (Alfred). OWD BOB, THE GREY DOG OF KENMUIR. With a Frontispiece. *Eleventh Edition. Cr. 8vo.* 6s.

Oppenheim (E. Phillips). MASTER OF MEN. *Fourth Edition. Cr. 8vo.* 6s.
Also *Medium 8vo.* 6d.

Oxenham (John). A WEAVER OF WEBS. With 8 Illustrations by MAURICE GREIFFENHAGEN. *Second Edition. Cr. 8vo.* 6s.
THE GATE OF THE DESERT. With a Frontispiece in Photogravure by HAROLD COPPING. *Fifth Edition. Cr. 8vo.* 6s.
PROFIT AND LOSS. With a Frontispiece in photogravure by HAROLD COPPING. *Fourth Edition. Cr. 8vo.* 6s.
THE LONG ROAD. With a Frontispiece in Photogravure by HAROLD COPPING. *Fourth Edition. Cr. 8vo.* 6s.

Pain (Barry). LINDLEY KAYS. *Third Edition. Cr. 8vo.* 6s.

Parker (Gilbert). PIERRE AND HIS PEOPLE. *Sixth Edition. Cr. 8vo.* 6s.
MRS. FALCHION. *Fifth Edition. Cr. 8vo.* 6s.
THE TRANSLATION OF A SAVAGE. *Third Edition. Cr. 8vo.* 6s.
THE TRAIL OF THE SWORD. Illustrated. *Ninth Edition. Cr. 8vo.* 6s.
Also *Medium 8vo.* 6d.
WHEN VALMOND CAME TO PONTIAC: The Story of a Lost Napoleon. *Sixth Edition. Cr. 8vo.* 6s.
Also *Medium 8vo.* 6d.
AN ADVENTURER OF THE NORTH. The Last Adventures of 'Pretty Pierre.' *Fourth Edition. Cr. 8vo.* 6s.
THE SEATS OF THE MIGHTY. Illustrated. *Sixteenth Edition. Cr. 8vo.* 6s.
THE BATTLE OF THE STRONG: a Romance of Two Kingdoms. Illustrated. *Sixth Edition. Cr. 8vo.* 6s.
THE POMP OF THE LAVILETTES. *Third Edition. Cr. 8vo.* 3s. 6d.
Also *Medium 8vo.* 6d.

Pemberton (Max). THE FOOTSTEPS OF A THRONE. Illustrated. *Third Edition. Cr. 8vo.* 6s.
Also *Medium 8vo.* 6d.
I CROWN THEE KING. With Illustrations by Frank Dadd and A. Forrestier. *Cr. 8vo.* 6s.
Also *Medium 8vo.* 6d.

Phillpotts (Eden). LYING PROPHETS. *Third Edition. Cr. 8vo.* 6s.
CHILDREN OF THE MIST. *Fifth Edition. Cr. 8vo.* 6s.
Also *Medium 8vo.* 6d.
THE HUMAN BOY. With a Frontispiece. *Sixth Edition. Cr. 8vo.* 6s.
Also *Medium 8vo.* 6d.
SONS OF THE MORNING. *Second Edition. Cr. 8vo.* 6s.
THE RIVER. *Third Edition. Cr. 8vo.* 6s.
Also *Medium 8vo.* 6d.
THE AMERICAN PRISONER. *Fourth Edition. Cr. 8vo.* 6s.
THE SECRET WOMAN. *Fourth Edition. Cr. 8vo.* 6s.
KNOCK AT A VENTURE. With a Frontispiece. *Third Edition. Cr. 8vo.* 6s.
THE PORTREEVE. *Fourth Ed. Cr. 8vo.* 6s.
THE POACHER'S WIFE. *Second Edition Cr. 8vo.* 6s.
Also *Medium 8vo.* 6d.

THE STRIKING HOURS. *Second Edition. Crown 8vo.* 6s.
THE FOLK AFIELD. *Crown 8vo.* 6s.
Pickthall (Marmaduke). SAID THE FISHERMAN. *Seventh Ed. Cr. 8vo.* 6s.
BRENDLE. *Second Edition. Cr. 8vo.* 6s.
THE HOUSE OF ISLAM. *Third Edition. Cr. 8vo.* 6s.
'Q' (A. T. Quiller Couch). THE WHITE WOLF. *Second Edition. Cr. 8vo.* 6s.
Also *Medium 8vo.* 6d.
THE MAYOR OF TROY. *Fourth Edition. Cr. 8vo.* 6s.
MERRY-GARDEN AND OTHER STORIES. *Cr. 8vo.* 6s.
MAJOR VIGOUREUX. *Third Edition. Cr. 8vo.* 6s.
Rawson (Maud Stepney). THE ENCHANTED GARDEN. *Fourth Edition. Cr. 8vo.* 6s.
Rhys (Grace). THE WOOING OF SHEILA. *Second Edition. Cr. 8vo.* 6s.
Ridge (W. Pett). LOST PROPERTY. *Medium 8vo.* 6d.
ERB. *Second Edition. Cr. 8vo.* 6s.
A SON OF THE STATE. *Second Edition. Cr. 8vo.* 3s. 6d. Also *Medium 8vo.* 6d.
A BREAKER OF LAWS. *A New Edition. Cr. 8vo.* 3s. 6d.
MRS. GALER'S BUSINESS. Illustrated. *Second Edition. Cr. 8vo.* 6s.
THE WICKHAMSES. *Fourth Edition. Cr. 8vo.* 6s.
NAME OF GARLAND. *Third Edition. Cr. 8vo.* 6s.
GEORGE and THE GENERAL. *Medium 8vo.* 6d.
Ritchie (Mrs. David G.). MAN AND THE CASSOCK. *Second Edition. Crown 8vo.* 6s.
Roberts (C. G. D.). THE HEART OF THE ANCIENT WOOD. *Cr. 8vo.* 3s. 6d.
Robins (Elizabeth). THE CONVERT. *Third Edition. Cr. 8vo.* 6s.
Rosenkrantz (Baron Palle). THE MAGISTRATE'S OWN CASE. *Cr. 8vo.* 6s.
Russell (W. Clark). MY DANISH SWEETHEART. Illustrated. *Fifth Edition. Cr. 8vo.* 6s.
Also *Medium 8vo.* 6d.
HIS ISLAND PRINCESS. Illustrated. *Second Edition. Cr. 8vo.* 6s.
Also *Medium 8vo.* 6d.
ABANDONED. *Second Edition. Cr. 8vo.* 6s.
Also *Medium 8vo.* 6d.
MASTER ROCKAFELLAR'S VOYAGE. Illustrated by GORDON BROWNE. *Third Edition. Cr. 8vo.* 3s. 6d.
A MARRIAGE AT SEA. *Medium 8vo.* 6d.
Ryan (Marah Ellis). FOR THE SOUL OF RAFAEL. *Cr. 8vo.* 6s.
Sergeant (Adeline). THE MYSTERY OF THE MOAT. *Second Edition. Cr. 8vo.* 6s.
THE PASSION OF PAUL MARILLIER. *Crown 8vo.* 6s.
THE QUEST OF GEOFFREY DARRELL. *Cr. 8vo.* 6s.
THE COMING OF THE RANDOLPHS. *Cr. 8vo.* 6s.
THE PROGRESS OF RACHAEL. *Cr. 8vo.* 6s.
BARBARA'S MONEY. *Cr. 8vo.* 6s.
Also *Medium 8vo.* 6d.
THE MASTER OF BEECHWOOD. *Medium 8vo.* 6d.
THE YELLOW DIAMOND. *Second Ed. Cr. 8vo.* 6s. Also *Medium 8vo.* 6d.
THE LOVE THAT OVERCAME. *Medium 8vo.* 6d.
Shannon (W. F.). THE MESS DECK. *Cr. 8vo.* 3s. 6d.
Shelley (Bertha). ENDERBY. *Third Ed. Cr. 8vo.* 6s.
Sidgwick (Mrs. Alfred). THE KINSMAN. With 8 Illustrations by C. E. BROCK. *Third Edition. Cr. 8vo.* 6s.
Smith (Dorothy V. Horace). MISS MONA. *Cr. 8vo.* 3s. 6d.
Sonnichsen (Albert). DEEP-SEA VAGABONDS. *Cr. 8vo.* 6s.
Sunbury (George). THE HA'PENNY MILLIONAIRE. *Cr. 8vo.* 3s. 6d.
Surtees (R. S.). HANDLEY CROSS. Illustrated. *Medium 8vo.* 6d.
MR. SPONGE'S SPORTING TOUR. Illustrated. *Medium 8vo.* 6d.
ASK MAMMA. Illus. *Medium 8vo.* 6d.
Urquhart (M.), A TRAGEDY IN COMMONPLACE. *Second Ed. Cr. 8vo.* 6s.
Vorst (Marie Van). THE SENTIMENTAL ADVENTURES OF JIMMY BULSTRODE. *Cr. 8vo.* 6s.
Waineman (Paul). THE BAY OF LILACS: A Romance from Finland. *Second Edition. Cr. 8vo.* 6s.
THE SONG OF THE FOREST. *Cr. 8vo.* 6s.
Walford (Mrs. L. B.). MR. SMITH. *Medium 8vo.* 6d.
THE BABY'S GRANDMOTHER. *Medium 8vo.* 6d.
COUSINS. *Medium 8vo.* 6d.
Wallace (General Lew). BEN-HUR. *Medium 8vo.* 6d.
THE FAIR GOD. *Medium 8vo.* 6d.
Watson (H. B. Marriott). CAPTAIN FORTUNE. *Third Edition. Cr. 8vo.* 6s.
TWISTED EGLANTINE. With 8 Illustrations by FRANK CRAIG. *Third Edition. Cr. 8vo.* 6s.
THE HIGH TOBY: Being further Chapters in the Life and Fortunes of Dick Ryder, otherwise Galloping Dick, sometime Gentleman of the Road. With a Frontispiece by CLAUDE SHEPPERSON. *Third Edition. Cr. 8vo.* 6s.
A MIDSUMMER DAY'S DREAM. *Third Edition. Crown 8vo.* 6s.

THE PRIVATEERS. With 8 Illustrations by CYRUS CUNEO. *Second Edition. Cr. 8vo.* 6s.
A POPPY SHOW: BEING DIVERS AND DIVERSE TALES. *Cr. 8vo.* 6s.
THE ADVENTURERS. *Medium 8vo.* 6d.
Weekes (A. B.). THE PRISONERS OF WAR. *Medium 8vo.* 6d.
Wells (H. G.). THE SEA LADY. *Cr. 8vo.* 6s. Also *Medium 8vo.* 6d.
Weyman (Stanley). UNDER THE RED ROBE. With Illustrations by R. C. WOODVILLE. *Twenty-First Edition. Cr. 8vo.* 6s.
White (Percy). THE SYSTEM. *Third Edition. Cr. 8vo.* 6s.
A PASSIONATE PILGRIM. *Medium 8vo.* 6d.
Williams (Margery). THE BAR. *Cr. 8vo.* 6s.
Williamson (Mrs. C. N.). THE ADVENTURE OF PRINCESS SYLVIA. *Second Edition. Cr. 8vo.* 6s.
THE WOMAN WHO DARED. *Cr. 8vo.* 6s.
THE SEA COULD TELL. *Second Edition. Cr. 8vo.* 6s.
THE CASTLE OF THE SHADOWS. *Third Edition. Cr. 8vo.* 6s.
PAPA. *Cr. 8vo.* 6s.
Williamson (C. N. and A. M.). THE LIGHTNING CONDUCTOR: The Strange Adventures of a Motor Car. With 16 Illustrations. *Seventeenth Edition. Cr. 8vo.* 6s.
THE PRINCESS PASSES: A Romance of a Motor. With 16 Illustrations. *Ninth Edition. Cr. 8vo.* 6s.
MY FRIEND THE CHAUFFEUR. With 16 Illustrations. *Ninth Edit. Cr. 8vo.* 6s.
LADY BETTY ACROSS THE WATER. *Tenth Edition. Cr. 8vo.* 6s.
THE CAR OF DESTINY AND ITS ERRAND IN SPAIN. With 17 Illustrations. *Fourth Edition. Cr. 8vo.* 6s.
THE BOTOR CHAPERON. With a Frontispiece in Colour by A. H. BUCKLAND, 16 other Illustrations, and a Map. *Fifth Edition. Cr. 8vo.* 6s.
SCARLET RUNNER. With a Frontispiece in Colour by A. H. BUCKLAND, and 8 other Illustrations. *Third Ed. Cr. 8vo.* 6s.
Wyllarde (Dolf). THE PATHWAY OF THE PIONEER (Nous Autres). *Fourth Edition. Cr. 8vo.* 6s.
Yeldham (C. C.). DURHAM'S FARM. *Cr. 8vo.* 6s.

Books for Boys and Girls

Illustrated. Crown 8vo. 3s. 6d.

THE GETTING WELL OF DOROTHY. By Mrs. W. K. Clifford. *Second Edition.*

ONLY A GUARD-ROOM DOG. By Edith E. Cuthell.

MASTER ROCKAFELLAR'S VOYAGE. By W. Clark Russell. *Third Edition.*

SYD BELTON: Or, the Boy who would not go to Sea. By G. Manville Fenn. *Second Ed.*

THE RED GRANGE. By Mrs. Molesworth.
A GIRL OF THE PEOPLE. By L. T. Meade. *Second Edition.*
HEPSY GIPSY. By L. T. Meade. 2s. 6d.
THE HONOURABLE MISS. By L. T. Meade. *Second Edition.*
THERE WAS ONCE A PRINCE. By Mrs. M. E. Mann.
WHEN ARNOLD COMES HOME. By Mrs. M. E. Mann.

The Novels of Alexandre Dumas

Medium 8vo. Price 6d. Double Volumes, 1s.

COMPLETE LIST ON APPLICATION.

Methuen's Sixpenny Books

Medium 8vo.

Albanesi (E. Maria). LOVE AND LOUISA.
I KNOW A MAIDEN.
Austen (J.). PRIDE AND PREJUDICE.
Bagot (Richard). A ROMAN MYSTERY.
CASTING OF NETS.
Balfour (Andrew). BY STROKE OF SWORD.
Baring-Gould (S.). FURZE BLOOM.
CHEAP JACK ZITA.
KITTY ALONE.
URITH.
THE BROOM SQUIRE.
IN THE ROAR OF THE SEA.
NOÉMI.
A BOOK OF FAIRY TALES. Illustrated.
LITTLE TU'PENNY.
WINEFRED.
THE FROBISHERS.
THE QUEEN OF LOVE.
Barr (Robert). JENNIE BAXTER.
IN THE MIDST OF ALARMS.
THE COUNTESS TEKLA.
THE MUTABLE MANY.
Benson (E. F.). DODO.
THE VINTAGE.
Brontë (Charlotte). SHIRLEY.
Brownell (C. L.). THE HEART OF JAPAN.
Burton (J. Bloundelle). ACROSS THE SALT SEAS.
Caffyn (Mrs.). ANNE MAULEVERER.

Capes (Bernard). THE LAKE OF WINE.
Clifford (Mrs. W. K.). A FLASH OF SUMMER.
MRS. KEITH'S CRIME.
Corbett (Julian). A BUSINESS IN GREAT WATERS.
Croker (Mrs. B. M.). ANGEL.
A STATE SECRET.
PEGGY OF THE BARTONS.
JOHANNA.
Dante (Alighieri). THE DIVINE COMEDY (Cary).
Doyle (A. Conan). ROUND THE RED LAMP.
Duncan (Sara Jeannette). A VOYAGE OF CONSOLATION.
THOSE DELIGHTFUL AMERICANS.
Eliot (George). THE MILL ON THE FLOSS.
Findlater (Jane H.). THE GREEN GRAVES OF BALGOWRIE.
Gallon (Tom). RICKERBY'S FOLLY.
Gaskell (Mrs.). CRANFORD.
MARY BARTON.
NORTH AND SOUTH.
Gerard (Dorothea). HOLY MATRIMONY.
THE CONQUEST OF LONDON.
MADE OF MONEY.
Gissing (G). THE TOWN TRAVELLER.
THE CROWN OF LIFE.
Glanville (Ernest). THE INCA'S TREASURE.
THE KLOOF BRIDE.
Gleig (Charles). BUNTER'S CRUISE.
Grimm (The Brothers). GRIMM'S FAIRY TALES.
Hope (Anthony). A MAN OF MARK.
A CHANGE OF AIR.
THE CHRONICLES OF COUNT ANTONIO.
PHROSO.
THE DOLLY DIALOGUES.
Hornung (E. W.). DEAD MEN TELL NO TALES.
Ingraham (J. H.). THE THRONE OF DAVID.
Le Queux (W.). THE HUNCHBACK OF WESTMINSTER.
Levett-Yeats (S. K.). THE TRAITOR'S WAY.
Linton (E. Lynn). THE TRUE HISTORY OF JOSHUA DAVIDSON.
Lyall (Edna). DERRICK VAUGHAN.
Malet (Lucas). THE CARISSIMA.
A COUNSEL OF PERFECTION.
Mann (Mrs.). MRS. PETER HOWARD.
A LOST ESTATE.
THE CEDAR STAR.
ONE ANOTHER'S BURDENS.
Marchmont (A. W.). MISER HOADLEY'S SECRET.
A MOMENT'S ERROR.
Marryat (Captain). PETER SIMPLE.
JACOB FAITHFUL.
Marsh (Richard). A METAMORPHOSIS.
THE TWICKENHAM PEERAGE.
THE GODDESS.
THE JOSS.
Mason (A. E. W.). CLEMENTINA.
Mathers (Helen). HONEY.
GRIFF OF GRIFFITHSCOURT
SAM'S SWEETHEART.
Meade (Mrs. L. T.). DRIFT.
Mitford (Bertram). THE SIGN OF THE SPIDER.
Montresor (F. F.). THE ALIEN.
Morrison (Arthur). THE HOLE IN THE WALL.
Nesbit (E.) THE RED HOUSE.
Norris (W. E.). HIS GRACE.
GILES INGILBY.
THE CREDIT OF THE COUNTY.
LORD LEONARD THE LUCKLESS.
MATTHEW AUSTIN.
CLARISSA FURIOSA.
Oliphant (Mrs.). THE LADY'S WALK.
SIR ROBERT'S FORTUNE.
THE PRODIGALS.
THE TWO MARYS.
Oppenheim (E. P.). MASTER OF MEN.
Parker (Gilbert). THE POMP OF THE LAVILETTES.
WHEN VALMOND CAME TO PONTIAC.
THE TRAIL OF THE SWORD.
Pemberton (Max). THE FOOTSTEPS OF A THRONE.
I CROWN THEE KING.
Phillpotts (Eden). THE HUMAN BOY.
CHILDREN OF THE MIST.
THE POACHER'S WIFE.
THE RIVER.
'Q' (A. T. Quiller Couch). THE WHITE WOLF.
Ridge (W. Pett). A SON OF THE STATE.
LOST PROPERTY.
GEORGE and THE GENERAL.
Russell (W. Clark). ABANDONED.
A MARRIAGE AT SEA.
MY DANISH SWEETHEART.
HIS ISLAND PRINCESS.
Sergeant (Adeline). THE MASTER OF BEECHWOOD.
BARBARA'S MONEY.
THE YELLOW DIAMOND.
THE LOVE THAT OVERCAME.
Surtees (R. S.). HANDLEY CROSS.
MR. SPONGE'S SPORTING TOUR.
ASK MAMMA.
Walford (Mrs. L. B.). MR. SMITH.
COUSINS.
THE BABY'S GRANDMOTHER.
Wallace (General Lew). BEN-HUR.
THE FAIR GOD.
Watson (H. B. Marriott). THE ADVENTURERS.
Weekes (A. B.). PRISONERS OF WAR.
Wells (H. G.). THE SEA LADY.
White (Percy). A PASSIONATE PILGRIM.

A CATALOGUE OF BOOKS PUBLISHED BY METHUEN AND COMPANY: LONDON 36 ESSEX STREET W.C.

CONTENTS

OCTOBER 1908

A CATALOGUE OF

MESSRS. METHUEN'S PUBLICATIONS

In this Catalogue the order is according to authors. An asterisk denotes that the book is in the press.

Colonial Editions are published of all Messrs. METHUEN'S Novels issued at a price above 2*s.* 6*d.*, and similar editions are published of some works of General Literature. These are marked in the Catalogue. Colonial editions are only for circulation in the British Colonies and India.

All books marked net are not subject to discount, and cannot be bought at less than the published price. Books not marked net are subject to the discount which the bookseller allows.

Messrs. METHUEN'S books are kept in stock by all good booksellers. If there is any difficulty in seeing copies, Messrs. Methuen will be very glad to have early information, and specimen copies of any books will be sent on receipt of the published price *plus* postage for net books, and of the published price for ordinary books.

I.P.L. represents Illustrated Pocket Library.

PART I.—GENERAL LITERATURE

Abbott (J. H. M.). AN OUTLANDER IN ENGLAND: *Second Edition. Cr. 8vo. 6s.*
A Colonial Edition is also published.

Abraham (George D.) THE COMPLETE MOUNTAINEER. With 75 Illustrations. *Second Edition. Demy 8vo. 15s. net.*
A Colonial Edition is also published.

Acatos (M. J.). See Junior School Books.

Adams (Frank). JACK SPRAT. With 24 Coloured Pictures. *Super Royal 16mo. 2s.*

Adeney (W. F.), M.A. See Bennett (W. H.)

Ady (Cecilia M.). A HISTORY OF MILAN UNDER THE SFORZA. With 20 Illustratious and a Map. *Demy 8vo. 10s. 6d. net.*

Æschylus. See Classical Translations.

Æsop. See I.P.L.

Ainsworth (W. Harrison). See I.P.L.

Aldis (Janet). THE QUEEN OF LETTER WRITERS, MARQUISE DE SÉVIGNÉ, DAME DE BOURBILLY, 1626-96. With 18 Illustrations. *Second Edition. Demy 8vo. 12s. 6d. net.*
A Colonial Edition is also published.

Alexander (William), D.D., Archbishop of Armagh. THOUGHTS AND COUNSELS OF MANY YEARS. *Demy 16mo. 2s. 6d.*

Alken (Henry). See I.P.L.

Allen (Charles C.). See Textbooks of Technology.

Allen (L. Jessie). See Little Books on Art.

Allen (J. Romilly), F.S.A. See Antiquary's Books.

Almack (E.), F.S.A. See Little Books on Art.

Amherst (Lady). A SKETCH OF EGYPTIAN HISTORY FROM THE EARLIEST TIMES TO THE PRESENT DAY. With many Illustrations and Maps. *A New and Cheaper Issue. Demy 8vo. 7s. 6d. net.*

Anderson (F. M.). THE STORY OF THE BRITISH EMPIRE FOR CHILDREN. With 42 Illustrations. *Cr. 8vo. 2s.*

Anderson (J. G.), B.A., NOUVELLE GRAMMAIRE FRANÇAISE, A L'USAGE DES ÉCOLES ANGLAISES. *Crown 8vo. 2s.*
EXERCICES DE GRAMMAIRE FRANÇAISE. *Cr. 8vo. 1s. 6d.*

Andrewes (Bishop). PRECES PRIVATAE. Translated and edited, with Notes, by F. E. BRIGHTMAN, M.A., of Pusey House, Oxford. *Cr. 8vo. 6s.*
See also Library of Devotion.

'Anglo-Australian.' AFTER-GLOW MEMORIES. *Cr. 8vo. 6s.*

Anon. HEALTH, WEALTH, AND WISDOM. *Crown 8vo. 1s. net.*

Aristotle. THE ETHICS OF. Edited, with an Introduction and Notes by JOHN BURNET, M.A., *Cheaper issue. Demy 8vo. 10s. 6d. net.*

Asman (H. N.), M.A., B.D. See Junior School Books.

Atkins (H. G.). See Oxford Biographies.

Atkinson (C. M.). JEREMY BENTHAM. *Demy 8vo. 5s. net.*

***Atkinson (C. T.),** M.A., Fellow of Exeter College, Oxford, sometime Demy of Magdalen College. A HISTORY OF GERMANY, from 1713 to 1815. With many Maps. *Demy 8vo. 15s. net.*

Atkinson (T. D.). ENGLISH ARCHITECTURE. With 196 Illustrations. *Second Edition. Fcap. 8vo. 3s. 6d. net.*
A GLOSSARY OF TERMS USED IN ENGLISH ARCHITECTURE. With 265 Illustrations. *Second Edition. Fcap. 8vo. 3s. 6d. net.*